Planning Academic and Research Library Buildings

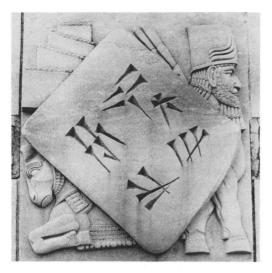

From a set of panels depicting the evolution of the book. Sculpted by Matchett Herring Coe, 1948, for front of the Fondren Library, Rice University.

Keyes D. Metcalf

Second edition by
Philip D. Leighton and David C. Weber

Planning Academic and Research Library Buildings

"First we design our buildings,
then our buildings design us."
Winston Churchill

American Library Association
Chicago and London 1986

Design adapted by Deborah Doering

Composed by Impressions, Inc., in Baskerville,
    Garamond and Optima on a Penta-driven
    Autologic APS μ5
    Phototypesetting system

Printed on 50-pound Glatfelter, a pH-neutral stock,
    by Malloy Lithographing, Inc.
    Bound in B-grade Joanna linen cloth by
    Zonne Bookbinders

Library of Congress Cataloging-in-Publication Data

Metcalf, Keyes DeWitt, 1889–
    Planning academic and research library buildings.

    Bibliography: p.
    Includes index.
    1. Library planning.   2. Library buildings.
3. Libraries, University and college.   4.Research
libraries.   5. Libraries—Space utilization.
I.Leighton, Philip D.   II. Weber, David C., 1924–
III. Title.
Z679.5.M49   1985   022'.317   85-11207
ISBN 0-8389-3320-3

To E. E. W., J. F. C., and E. G. M., who each in a different way made a major contribution toward the transformation of this volume from a dream to a reality.   1965

To K. D. M., the realist who shared his extraordinary knowledge, and to B. N. L. and N. M. W., who aided and abetted the second edition in ways both practical and poetic.   1985

Contents

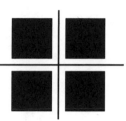

Preface

Several challenging tasks faced by colleges and universities require a comprehensive manual dealing with the problems involved in the planning and construction of academic library buildings:

1. Planning an academic or research library building is an important and complex undertaking.
2. The building design must be done exceptionally well since it can be altered later only with considerable difficulty and expense.
3. A building is a costly undertaking, and the raising of funds may be very difficult, particularly so for very large buildings.
4. The need for library space confronts every academic institution sooner or later, and often with great frequency.
5. The planning process all too often is the responsibility of persons who have little or no experience in this field.

The importance of library buildings is obvious, regardless of whether one is thinking of the institution's teaching and research program or its budget. A poor building can seriously handicap students; a good one can contribute to the intellectual health of the whole institution. Since buildings are expensive, a poor one is an enduring monument to wasted dollars. Moreover, a poorly planned and constructed building may force an institution year after year to spend much more on operation and maintenance than would be required by a better one.

Planning a library building is a complicated matter and a very time-consuming one. This book does not attempt to provide answers to all the problems that may arise, but it does try to identify the more important ones, break them down into the component parts, and indicate the factors that ought to be taken into account in arriving at solutions. Mistakes may be made after careful consideration of a problem, and indeed no building is perfect. Yet the most serious mistakes are likely to be those made when one does not realize that a problem exists. This volume, then, is intended to help provide a substitute for much of the understanding gained from firsthand experience.

Every college and university will sooner or later need to plan for a library addition, a major renovation, or an entirely new wing or separate building. Whether enrollments are being held steady, are decreasing, or are growing, the library will change because the collections will have a net increase in size, the types and quantity of materials in other than the book format will increase, and technological changes will prompt alterations if not major changes in a library building.

In the period since World War II well over a thousand new academic library buildings have been planned and constructed just in the United States. In the period 1961-65 alone, it is estimated that 504 were built at a cost of approximately $466,600,000, an average of over $93,000,000 a year. Despite the fact that college and university library building is proceeding at this rate, and regardless of the great increase in the number of publications about library building plans and the planning process, a large percentage of the new buildings are planned by architects, librarians, and other persons who have never before been responsible for designing a library building of any kind. That statement is as true in 1985 as it was in 1965. Architects have many opportunites to design residences and commercial buildings, but most have few commissions to design a hospital, computer center, prison, or academic library. Few chief librarians have more than one opportunity to work with architects on a new building. The number who do have several experiences and are available as building consultants is still small. Others who may be involved—college and university administrators, members of faculty committees, donors, and contractors—are even less likely to have had previous experience in this particular field.

Keyes Metcalf wrote the first edition of this book in the early 1960s. Sponsored by the Association of Research Libraries and the Association of College and Research Libraries, it was the product of Mr. Metcalf's sixty years of experience in planning library space and hundreds of building projects. This experience started in 1905–8 during the planning of a new building for the Oberlin College Library; the result proved to be one of the best college libraries constructed up to that time. His own work on space planning, at the New York Public Library and then at Harvard, contributed to his education. One exceptional product was the New England Deposit Library, a building designed as a book warehouse or auxiliary facility to be as simple, inexpensive, and functional as possible. A second was the Houghton Library for rare books and manuscripts, with a great deal of highly specialized space, and a third was the Lamont Library for undergraduates.

As Mr. Metcalf wrote in the first edition of this book: "Since Harvard had more than 80 special and departmental libraries, I had many occasions during my eighteen years as director to deal with alterations, additions, rehabilitation, and repair. Moreover, because the Lamont building was well received, invitations to serve as a consultant on building problems elsewhere began to come to me in increasing numbers. Indeed, since my retirement from Harvard in 1955, I have served as a building consultant to more than 250 libraries on six continents and have spent some fifteen months studying library problems in countries other than the United States." It was not realized in 1965 that Mr. Metcalf would thereafter serve as a consultant on at least another 250 projects.

The first edition of this work benefited by help from an advisory committee representing the two sponsoring library groups. The committee consisted of Professor Curtis Bradford, Verner W. Clapp, Ralph E. Ellsworth, Richard Harwell, William H. Jesse, Stephen A. McCarthy, Col. F. D. Rogers, Eileen Thornton, Frederick W. Wagman, and there were many others, including James F. Clapp and Edwin E. Williams, who made valued contributions. The present volume also benefited from an advisory committee as is noted in the Acknowledgments.

Clearly, the Metcalf product was a very specialized volume, a tour de force containing a good deal of his library philosophy. It will rest as a classic, the product of an extraordinary librarian who for over three quarters of a century worked in and for libraries. Keyes Metcalf's father was a prominent railroad engineer who retired in 1855. No doubt some of the organizational and analytic skills which Keyes later applied to building planning were inherited from this railroad engineer whose work from New England to Minnesota required precise measurement and exceptional planning.

The present authors are mindful that any revision of Metcalf's work is certain to lose some of the flavor of his creation. It is hoped that the many changes, deletions, and additions will serve the current need of architects, librarians, and others involved in the planning process without obscuring his wise guidance. The authors are grateful to Mr. Metcalf for his trust in putting the second edition of his product in their hands. It was a courageous act on his part.

Although this edition changes the organization of the material, it retains all of Mr. Metcalf's principles. It is intended for the same audience and to provide the same practical help which made the first volume universally acclaimed. Major additions have come in the treatment of branch libraries, building renovations, master planning, access for physically limited persons, and attention to the building problems in accommodating audio-visual and automated services and modern telecommunications. Most dimensional statements and plans are presented in both the metric and customary, or imperial, scales; and the metric are presented according to British architectural practice.

Although dimensional metric conversions have been made in most cases, it should be stressed that they are directly obtained from conversion of the customary foot/inch system. Actual practice in countries using equipment designed and constructed in the metric system will likely result in some variation of this data. In this case, the reader should use the text as a guide, and where accurate measurements are required, individual calculations based on actual conditions should be undertaken.

Acknowledgments

Our thanks go first of all to Keyes Metcalf, not only because he supported and encouraged our work from the very beginning and offered suggestions into 1983, but also because this second edition rests solidly on his classic produced twenty years ago. We are indebted to Keyes beyond words. Any weaknesses herein are, however, entirely the present authors'.

The Advisory Committee has assisted in critiquing individual chapters, advising on examples, supplying sample documentation, and in other ways contributing measurably to the soundness and utility of this volume. We appreciate the contributions and time of this distinguished group: Patricia Battin, Billie Bozone, William H. Busse, Roger Cairns, Evan I. Farber, Herman H. Fussler, James F. Govan, David Kaser, Nancy R. McAdams, Gerald B. McCabe, Jeanne E. MacLeamy, Phyllis Martin-Vegue, Gloria Novak, Richard H. Perrine, George J. Snowball, William H. Trogdon, Robert R. Walsh, and Walter C. Wilson. We are especially grateful to two who reviewed the entire text and contributed generously their extraordinary experience: Margaret Beckman, Executive Director for Information Technology of the University of Guelph, and Harry Faulkner-Brown, of Faulkner-Brown, Hendy, Watkinson and Stonor, Architects, Newcastle upon Tyne.

We are appreciative to these and others who helped along the way, notably our colleagues at Stanford, Shannon R. McEntee (for producing the text database), Jo Johnson (for executing the illustrations), Carol S. Nielsen (for the index), and not least of all our families who encouraged and supported the many months of work needed to see this project through.

Appreciation is also expressed to authors and publishers who gave permission to include statements or quotations in this volume. Gratitude is expressed to librarians and to libraries approving the use of excerpts from building program or planning documents, material used as illustrations, and texts of celebratory or dedication programs. Since a significant number of excerpts from the first edition have been retained, it is also appropriate to repeat Mr. Metcalf's appreciation to authors and publishers who gave permission. This edition rests so heavily on the original that it is essential to restate the appreciation for financial support received from the Council on Library Resources and sponsorship by the Association of Research Libraries and the Association of College and Research Libraries, a division of the American Library Association. Contributions to the original publication by James Ford Clapp, Jr., and Edwin E. Williams were exceptional.

Samuel M. Carrington, Jr., Rice University Librarian, helped obtain the photographs as the frontispiece as well as permission for their use.

The following permissions are gratefully acknowledged, for their materials assist substantially in describing, explaining, and illustrating the building planning process:

American Association for State and Local History
The American Institute of Architects
Arizona State University Library
The Association of Research Libraries
Asbury Theological Seminary Library
Brigham Young University Libraries
Butler University
David G. Cogan
Colby College
Columbia University Libraries
Cornell University Library
Dartmouth College
Educational Facilities Laboratories
Ralph E. Ellsworth
Gerald R. Ford Library
Godfrey Memorial Library, in memory of
    Mr. A. Fremont Rider
Harvard University Library
Harvard University Press
Interior Design
Lafayette College Skillman Library
Lake Forest College Donnelley Library
Louisiana State University Library
McLellan & Copenhagen, Inc.
Stephen A. McCarthy
National Center for Higher Education
    Management Systems
National Library of Medicine
New York Public Library

Princeton Theological Seminary Library
Princeton University Library
The Research Libraries Group, Inc.
San Jose State University Library
Shepley Bulfinch Richardson and Abbott
Simon Fraser University
Southern Illinois University at Carbondale
Stanford University Facilities and Services
Stanford University Libraries
Tufts University Library
University of California, Irvine
University of California, Los Angeles, Library
University of California Northern Regional
    Library Facility
University of California, Santa Cruz, Library
University of Chicago Libraries
University of Chicago Press
University of Delaware Libraries
University of Illinois Graduate School of Library Science
University of North Carolina, Chapel Hill, Library
University of Oklahoma Libraries
University of South Carolina Libraries
University of Southern California Hancock Library
University of Texas, Austin, Libraries
University of Toronto Library
University of Toronto Press
University of Wisconsin, Milwaukee, Library
Washington University Library
West Valley College Library
Western Illinois University Libraries

Introduction

Each library building is unique, just as is each academic and each research institution. A library building should reflect the needs of scholarship, the teaching program, the relative emphasis on different subjects, and the special character and style of the institution. Furthermore, the building reflects the individual philosophy and practice of library service at the time that the building is programmed and designed. It is conditioned by its particular site and neighboring buildings. Finally, each library reflects some of the architectural concepts and construction practices of its particular design team and era. These differences serve to fashion the interesting variety of physical settings in which scholarship and higher education are served.

The creation of a new, general library building is an expensive undertaking, one seldom achieved in the history of most institutions. The current generation of librarians and administrators will certainly wish to have the new construction reflect sound views on what is good for the institution, what arrangements should be emphasized, and which situations should be avoided. An addition to an older structure has its own kind of constraints, as does a major renovation project. Every entirely new building offers appreciably greater freedom of design.

The unique characteristics of each library building can be served by a book dealing with planning, design, and construction principles, which can be evaluated and selectively applied. (Selected applications are used as examples for clarification.) General principles are emphasized since local circumstances differ and the attitudes in architecture and librarianship as well as academic administration will change over the years to come.

This book is designed for practitioners in the field. It is intended to help those who are novices in planning library buildings, whether they be librarians, architects, or academic administrators. At the same time, the book is not intended as a primer, and it makes the assumption that those undertaking a major remodeling project, an addition, or a new facility have some understanding of the processes of analyzing an institution's mission and objectives, can determine the nature of space that should be provided, will be familiar with the appropriate local channels for obtaining academic and business support for the project, and have a rudimentary understanding of architecture, interior designing, construction and finance. To the extent that the reader seeks some detailed background in these aspects of a building project, the Bibliography may provide some assistance. The Glossary included in this volume is also designed to clarify terminology where uncertainty of usage in the United States or abroad may exist and where architects, librarians, and others may not know some terms common to others.

An overall goal of this volume is to assist those who will share responsibility for new library space. This book also attempts to show how a maximum of utility in library buildings can be achieved with the funds available, while at the same time assuring attractiveness and considerable flexibility for the years to come. Academic buildings are generally intended to last for a great many years. For a major building, a useful life of fifty years may be so short as to be a great disappointment to an institution; utility over a period of one hundred or more years is feasible and will be more common in the future. On the other hand, a warehouse or auxiliary facility may have a fairly short life span. Those involved in a project have the problem of how best to arrange the space and how best to use available funds. Is a handsome library building needed? Is the layout to emphasize the collections or reading spaces? May the building later be converted to some other use? Will an addition be required within the next half century? Is the library to be an educational symbol for the institution? These and many other questions must be answered, at least tacitly.

This volume obviously has limits, many by intent. Those persons responsible for building projects will have to rely heavily on standards, guides, and documents issued by the system headquarters of a college or university and by professional associations and governmental agencies with authority over various parts of the project, as well as on publications from the fields of architecture, interior design, engineering, academic finance, and other professionals who play some role in the total effort. These guides and documents may be brought in by administrative officers at one or another stage in the process. Some will be binding and others will be advisory. Again, each institution is unique and each library building project will be unique, and so the total array of documents pertinent to a particular project will need to be assembled. This is certainly the case where local, state, or federal governments bear major responsibility. Academic institutions in foreign countries will, of course, apply the local standards, guides, and planning documents.

While this volume is concerned with the planning of academic libraries, there are many similarities with the planning of research library buildings that are not part of academic institutions, such as those of historical societies, museums, county law libraries, governmental or special archives, commercial research and development firms, and state and national libraries that support professional studies. The principles of design for such libraries are similar as long as one has clear recognition of the particular purpose and goals of that individual organization, the requirements of its clientele, the standards and expectations of management in designing for that particular type of library, and the specific accommodations appropriate for the mix of book and non-book materials which form the collections of such a library.

Several points at which this volume may be useful for other types of libraries are here noted:

1. Much library planning involves an understanding of the special nature of an individual institution—its organization, objectives, dynamics, and the community it serves. Those responsible for planning any library building must realize that this is a matter of first importance.

2. Any building to be reasonably successful must have an architect to prepare the construction plans and specifications. The judgments involved in the selection of the architect are similar in whatever type of library is to be designed.

3. All libraries face financial problems involved in building planning. These may differ as much from one academic library to another as from an academic library building to some other type. The concerns are very similar regardless of the type of library.

4. The preparation of a program statement for a library building is generally, if not always, the most important single contribution by the institution's representatives. The accommodations and relationships for book storage, seating, furniture and specialized equipment, and aesthetics must be dealt with in any type of library. The general principles are the same, although details will, of course, differ.

5. Many of the physical considerations involving module size, structure, environmental control, durability, rearrangements and remodeling, and aspects of activation will have common applications in a vast majority of libraries.

What specifically does this volume try to achieve? In sixteen chapters it presents the planning, programming, design, construction and occupation processes from beginning to the end. These are arranged in the general chronological order in which most projects proceed, though there will be some variations from institution to institution, and several phases may overlap and a few may in special cases be omitted.

The Audience to Whom This Text Is Addressed

Before the library building is designed, a number of tasks discussed later should be carried out. The designated group of persons directly concerned should become acquainted with the basic issues involved in library building planning. This group may include a number of different individuals: the librarian and often several members of the library staff, representatives of the library committee of the faculty, the administration, and other persons whom the institution asks for help in the planning or whom it employs for a building project, and the architect selected for the task. Administrative officers, governing board representatives, and sometimes even a donor may be included. Faculty and students are commonly included since the building is designed primarily for their use and their needs must be kept foremost in mind. One or more consultants may be included at various times—a library building consultant, cost consultant, construction efficiency consultant, as well as those responsible for the engineering and mechanical aspects of the building.

In a large project well over a hundred individuals may play a significant role in decisions or approvals at one or another stage. Often few, if any, will have previously dealt with a library building project. Thus, it is hoped that this volume, from the chapters on the earliest administrative decisions on building alternatives to those on the activation of new space, will be of use to one or more of those involved. Clearly, not everyone will need to be familiar with everything in a volume of this scope, and therefore, it may be used more as a reference work or a handbook, than a volume to be read from cover to cover.

This volume is addressed to at least six different groups: presidents, governing boards and administrative officers; library building planning committees; librarians and their staffs; library schools, library school students, and other librarians interested in administration; the library building planning team; and architects, engineers, and consultants. Each group is interested primarily in different aspects of the planning of library buildings, although the objectives of all should be in harmony. Each group wants a good-looking, functional library that will attract intended users, will suitably house and safeguard the collections, will not cost too much to erect or for the library staff to operate, and will at the same time be economical of annual plant-operating maintenance costs. Each group will have particular interests in different factors, and a better building should result if each group has some understanding of the interests and concerns of the other groups.

The Effect of Growth and Change in Libraries

One condition of overriding importance in the planning of academic library buildings deserves emphasis. Libraries have particular pressures for continuing growth. Library buildings, therefore, must be able to accommodate change more readily than other types of academic buildings. Even assuming no growth in student enrollment, the library building is the one facility that may need expansion, primarily due to growth in the book and other collections. This is particularly true for a research institution.

If the library planning team can accurately forecast approximate rates of growth for a twenty-year period, and if the corresponding building plan can be financed, then it should be fifteen years before plans for further expansion may need to be undertaken. If a library could be planned for thirty years, then an institution may have twenty or even twenty-five years before it needs to again consider library expansion. This constant growth has continued for many decades. Nevertheless, in some cases, techniques are now available for ameliorating this inexorable demand for new library space on campus, and these will be dealt with in Chapters 1, 2 and 10.

Academic library collections tend to grow at the rate of four to five percent a year until they become what may be called "mature." This growth, which means doubling the collection size in perhaps sixteen or seventeen years, has been true in this country for at least two centuries. In due course, libraries become increasingly "mature," and the growth rate slackens to a rate of two to three percent a year—doubling in twenty-five to forty years instead of half that time. This slackening in the growth rate generally does not occur until the library is so large that even two percent is a serious increment. For example, at Harvard two percent now amounts to some 200,000 or more volumes a year, requiring some 14,000 square feet (about 1300 square meters) of floor space for additions to the book collection alone. Such growth must slow on a percentage basis, though perhaps not in the number of volumes added per year.

New technology such as microreproduction and electronic transference of information has so far seemed to have little effect on growth rates of library collections, although it has increased total resources.

The rates of collection space growth will necessarily have to slow down in the years ahead for obvious fiscal reasons. But the slowing process will be fairly gradual, conditioned by the development of different interinstitutional dependencies, auxiliary facilities, optical disk technology with electronic networks, and the various services that can be provided by multi-institutional programs, federal libraries, or consortia. Even with the above forces at play, libraries should expect space demands for collections to increase so that a new building should currently be planned, wherever possible, to house further growth should it be needed.

There also is bound to be considerable change in architectural and construction practice. One need only look back twenty to fifty years to see the contrasts in buildings designed and constructed by different generations. Just as there are today certain conditions of aesthetic taste, financing, construction techniques, sociological expectations, and management practices, so it is predictable that in another one or two decades many of these will again change. Academic institutions are very strongly affected by shifts in national and world economics and by birth rates. They are affected to some extent by governmental policies, for example, in accommodating the needs of the physically limited and disabled. The ability of both publicly and privately supported institutions to obtain major construction funds varies from decade to decade. The technological changes that derive from a shifting emphasis on audio or visual resources or on computer-processed information, and shifts in local and longline communications may all affect changes in optimal library building design.

It is then necessary to establish general planning principles and practices which have long-term applicability, although the specific examples provided in this volume will change with the passage of time. One of the great dangers in planning library buildings is that, in searching for planning formulas and rules, the planning team may make the mistake of adopting blindly what has been used by others. This tendency, perhaps, is the reason why, all too often, one may find a college library equipped with tables whose dimensions are entirely suitable for public libraries but which do not provide sufficient reading surface so that an undergraduate can use materials effectively, and thus all seats at a table may never be filled. Similar problems arise in other areas of planning. This volume tries to bring out points of this kind in the hope that they may help to prevent serious planning errors.

Keyes D. Metcalf wrote in the introduction to the first edition of this book:

The writer is a librarian, not an architect or an engineer, and it is only fair to admit that he was attracted to this phase of library work not because of any special interest or talent in architecture or engineering, but because he was looking for ways to stretch the library dollar so that more of it would be left over and made available for book acquisition and service. He will not attempt to tell the architect and engineer about their professions, but will try to explain to them the architectural and engineering features that help to make a building a functional library. . . .

The author has studied library building problems for many different types of libraries in many countries, in the belief that he would learn about possible solutions and would be enabled to broaden his background and outlook and obtain a better perspective. As a result, he hopes that this volume will be useful throughout the world. It is written from the American point of view, but it has tried to avoid a dogmatism that would limit its usefulness. No two libraries are alike, but they have much in common whatever their type, clientele, and nationality.

1

The Planning Process and Library Requirements

The functions of higher education are several: the sorting of untested human talent into useful career paths, advanced training in a wide variety of disciplines, provision of advanced professional contributions of new knowledge and social and aesthetic criticism, and the preparation of unformed minds for the changes and the challenges of a lifetime.

These translate into academic programs at the undergraduate, graduate, and professional levels. The programs are designed to convey principles, practices, methodology, and the content and evolution of information about nature, society, and human beings. They are intended to teach at an advanced level the ability of clear expression and a grasp of the scientific method and discipline, as well as an understanding of intellectual processes and values, and the capacity for judgment, discrimination, interpretation, synthesis, a tolerance for and understanding of new ideas

and concepts, and intellectual honesty. The research university and the independent research institution are deeply concerned with the advancement of knowledge.

A library plays a key role in these processes in community colleges, liberal arts colleges, technical colleges, universities, and other research organizations. The library is probably the major academic facility and resource complementing and supplementing the lectures, laboratories, critiques and counseling of the faculty.

1.1 Purposes of the Library Building

The library building serves the following ten purposes in furtherance of these academic objectives:

Protection of books and collections of other records from the elements, poor environment, and mishandling

1

Housing of books and other collections in a variety of accommodations for ease of access

Housing of the various catalogs and related bibliographic tools which enable the reader to find relevant materials in the local collections and supplementary holdings in other institutions

Accommodation of readers and other clientele who need immediate or frequent access to collections and services

Provision for staff who select, acquire, organize, care for, and service the collections, and who aid readers in their informational needs

Quarters for ancillary functions such as photocopy services, bibliographic instruction, audio-visual materials preparation, computer support facilities, etc.

Quarters for library administration and business offices, such functions as personnel, finance, fundraising, publications, graphics or signage, building operations, security, supplies, mail and delivery services, etc.

Study, research, and writing quarters for students, faculty, and visiting scholars

Space to publicize resources or services through exhibits, lectures, publications, etc.

Structure to serve as a memorial to an individual and symbolism of the institution's academic life in pursuit of scholarly achievement

Other functions may be added in particular institutions depending on the scope of the library program within the college or university. For example, a major media center may include classroom or language-laboratory facilities, or a learning-assistance center may be established to aid students in their writing or study habits. Quarters for a local historical society may be provided as an adjunct to a major archival collection. A preservation studio or laboratory is likely to be a necessary element in research libraries. Occasionally a student lounge or snack bar service is provided, although this is not an ideal facility in all libraries.

Not all the above functions need to be provided by any one academic library building. Although it is technically possible to house some of these functions in separate buildings, to do so may be awkward and more costly to operate. For example, the office of the head librarian could be in an adjacent building, as it is in a few institutions. So could the so-called technical services of acquiring and cataloging new materials, although such an arrangement would likely be less than desirable since it could create difficult communication, operational, and management problems. This possibility of dispersion is pointed out merely so that each of the functions will be individually considered and judgments made as to the relative importance of each function when designing the appropriate library for a particular institution.

1.2 Academic Objectives and the Library

The library must be an integral part of the academic institution. Thus, the academic goals of the institution constitute the framework within which the library should plan and function. Some institutions have carefully formulated goals and may have published sets of objectives, although regrettably most institutions have not done so in any formal fashion. Whatever the local circumstances, the academic goals of the institution should be determined and taken as the basis for setting the library mission, operations, goals, and objectives.

The varying nature of academic programs as well as the changing views of academic imperatives over the decades indicate the difficulty of sound library planning. Just in the past one hundred years, there have been major shifts in educational philosophy and goals. German universities were the first to emphasize research as a prime mission of the university, a development that led to the founding of Johns Hopkins University, with striking consequences for the future of American universities. Also, in the last third of the nineteenth century, the effects of the 1862 Morrill Act were a powerful partnership of American government and higher education in support of agricultural and technological development. The strong development of community or junior colleges as preparatory to upper-division collegiate programs, as well as providing terminal vocational studies, flourished only after the mid-twentieth century. More recently, there was the rude awakening in 1957 when Sputnik brought sharp increases in scientific and technological education. The enrollment boom of the 1950s and 1960s in the United States followed by the decline in the latter quarter of this century, provides its own influences. With more subtle consequences, there is a process of continuing reexamination, change, and fragmentation in many disciplines within the university. Knowledge in some fields is developing more rapidly than ever before. As economic and sociological conditions shape governmental policy, elicit foundation support, and induce faculty to conduct research programs in problem areas, so the need for library collections and services will grow correspondingly. At one time it may be biology or engineering where there is rapid change or growth in subject knowledge, publications, and library use. Later it may be in microbiology, plasmaphysics, or ecological studies. The point here is that all of the factors of growth and of new teaching or research endeavors need to be reflected to some degree in the library program and, ultimately, in the library building.

Reflect on the influence on the library of academic policies. A recent practice at Bard College, Sarah Lawrence, Washington and Lee, and the University of Denver has been to require a portion of faculty office hours to be scheduled in the library. Some of the more pronounced examples of academic philosophy affecting the library would be that at the University of Chicago, Stephens College in Missouri, Florida Atlantic University, Oral Roberts University, and the Open University in Great Britain, though similarly striking effects on the library building can be found in a large proportion of community colleges, state universities, and some of the finest privately supported colleges, such as Swarthmore, Bryn Mawr, Reed, and Occidental (fig. 1.1).

One can also consider changing attitudes toward smoking, the custom of wearing hats, and use of umbrellas and bicycles, each of which has some effect on library design. In a few libraries pillows now replace some library chairs. Headphones for wireless reception are in use. Around the corner, in every generation, are other changes.

The significance of a shift in institutional policy or governmental policy can be seen in the changes of just a decade or two. During the 1960s, American state universities were under pressure to admit all qualified applicants and the federal government provided some funds for assisting in the building of libraries. Federal assistance extended beyond construction to the acquisition of materials, the training of librarians, and research and development projects in the information sciences. Support soon shifted to bibliographic access, conservation, and networking.

Shifts in federal support, in the popularity of subjects, in enrollment, in educational philosophy, and in the particular academic goals emphasized by a president and his or her administration create moving targets at which a library must aim. However the institution is defined, and to whatever extent its special purposes are emphasized, the library must reflect the nature of the institution it serves and must strive to meet the academic goals that exist at the time of planning and for a good many years into the future. It behooves those responsible for designing the library to try to look twenty or thirty years into the future and to be as balanced in their view and to make their product as adaptable as possible.

1.3 The Stages of the Building Project

The particular steps taken in the building project will vary from institution to institution and the requirements within institutions may vary from administration to administration or even from project to project. There are certain broad similarities, however, between the creation of an academic library building and the design of any other complex and expensive product within a major organization. A logical progression flows from conception through design to execution. Following is a list of twenty stages which constitute the major steps in justification, design, and construction of a major library building. Many of these steps may be skipped or merged if the building is of modest size or is a small addition to an already existing structure. There will be many additional reviews and approvals beyond those indicated here. Thus in a large university it may be assumed that for every one of the steps beyond the seventh there may be one or several necessary approvals, perhaps including academic officers, almost always including business officers and representatives of plant operations as well as police and fire officers, city and county and perhaps state and federal officers, and there may also be approvals at the trustee or regent level, depending upon the scope of the initial approval at that level. Trustee approval may have been only for the building design schematics or may have extended through the contract documents but not to bidding. On the other hand, there may have been approval through construction so long as a spec-

FIGURE 1.1 Occidental College, Mary Norton Clapp Library. Note special rooms: Cumberland is an open browsing room for selected current light reading; Jeffers is a general classroom; Braun houses fine books; Bill Henry Room contains books and memorabilia of an outstanding newspaper correspondent. Both the Braun and Henry rooms are opened by special arrangement. Four other rooms on the third floor are used for U.S. and California document collections.

ified dollar figure for the construction of the project is not exceeded.

Furthermore, before, during, and perhaps even after the project there will be a parallel effort in fundraising. This process may have started well before the sixth stage listed below, but more often it does not start or certainly does not move into high gear until after the board of trustees has given program approval. The librarian, other university officers, and even the architect may be involved in the fundraising effort. There may be a series of checks and rechecks between the authorized cost of the project as reflected in the most up-to-date local construction cost esti-

mate and the progress of fundraising. This comparison may lead to an expansion in the project once in a while, for example, adding a specially furnished endowed room or a major art purchase. Much more often it will lead to some reduction in the size of the building project when fundraising falls short. In any event, the fundraising or governmental appropriations must be clear before the fourteenth stage is concluded.

The typical, but not necessarily complete, list of twenty stages in an academic or research library building project includes the following:

1. Definition and analysis of the problem, usually a statement written by the librarian, occasionally with help from a consultant

2. Considerations of options for avoiding, minimizing, or otherwise solving the problem in broad program terms (treated in parts of the first four chapters of this book).

3. Review of the academic plan of the institution to assure that the academic program matches and validates the library option which is being proposed

4. Preparation of the written library building proposal in terms of basic academic purpose, scope, and rationale for the specific size and costs to construct the building (treated in Chapter 3).

5. Consideration of the campus master plan by planning officers of the institution and perhaps a university architect in order to assure compatibility of the library proposal with respect to siting, traffic, utility trunk lines, and general physical mass (treated in Chapter 11).

6. Administrative review, negotiation, and approval, including the board of trustees or regents and, for a state-supported institution, the state government authorities. Such approval is a major hurdle in authorizing the project and may be granted for one or more stages of the project and within specified construction or project dollar limits.

7. Staff educational preparation for the project, including a study of published literature on academic library buildings and visits to selected libraries

8. Formation of the planning team within the institution (treated in Chapter 4). The team will include representatives of the library staff, faculty, and student body; certain academic and business officers in the institution; and such consultants to the institution as are deemed appropriate.

9. Preparation of the formal written building program. This document is a specification of the major requirements desired of the facility, including the site, and any major limitations (covered in Chapters 5 through 8). It must be agreed to by the library officers and principal academic and business officers. It sets the essential requirements that the architect is expected to meet in the construction plans and specifications.

10. Choice of architect and the consultants to the architect (also covered in Chapter 4). This choice may in large measure rest with the campus business office, the librarian, the president, the trustees or state government, and occasionally a donor. Selection of an interior designer should be considered at this time if this service is not provided by the architect.

11. Schematic designs prepared by the architect. These sometimes include site studies and a master plan phase, as well as actual building mass, floor size, and vertical and horizontal traffic patterns (covered in Chapter 12).

12. Design development plans which carry the schematics, when approved, into rather precise spatial plans including all walls and doors and provide the first mechanical and other non-architectural drawings (covered in Chapter 13).

13. Contract documents which constitute the final architectural working drawings with elevations and full drawings for structural, mechanical, plumbing, electrical, and landscaping details, as well as a volume of written business conditions and performance specifications on everything from hardware to the mechanical systems (treated in Chapter 14). A similar level of documentation will be required for interior design elements which may be part of this phase or treated as a separate phase.

14. Bidding process. Based on stage 13 contract documents, the process includes bid analysis, selection of general contractor and qualification of subcontractors, and signing of the base contract with the general contractor or the construction manager if there is to be no general contractor (covered in Chapter 15).

15. Construction stage. During this lengthy process, the architect and the librarian or other institutional representatives maintain weekly if not daily review of progress. Performance validations, document clarification, and consideration of and action on requests for changes or additions come up frequently and need programmatic as well as budgetary decisions (covered in Chapter 15). This stage may be begun with a ground-breaking or cornerstone ceremony (covered in Chapter 16).

16. Selection and purchase of furnishings. This stage should overlap construction and occasionally may even have started during the working drawing phase for items needing especially long lead times for acquisition. (A detailed treatment of furnishings is not included in this book.) It is useful to have the interior designer, if there is one in addition

to the architect, involved starting with stage 11.

17. Legal acceptance of the building and grounds by the institution from the contractor. This short activation stage frequently requires a good number of interactions among all the parties concerned (covered in Chapter 16).

18. Occupancy. Furnishings, equipment, furniture, and books are moved in (covered in Chapter 16).

19. Dedication. This event is occasionally omitted, particularly for a building addition, though it can be a particularly important stage for fundraising relations (covered in Chapter 16).

20. Warranty corrections. The last phase involves the completion of all deficiencies against the bid contract documents which are required of the contractor and subcontractors during the period of warranty that follows stage 17 (also treated in Chapter 16).

These stages vary from project to project; some are short and some lengthy, a number may overlap one another. There are also many reviews, approvals, and financial checks during or between many of the later design stages. The flow chart, figure 1.2, shows an elaboration of this progression.

Nearly all large academic institutions have an office for campus planning. It may be called the architects and engineers office, the facilities planning office, or the campus design and construction office. In statewide college and university systems there usually will also be an office in the system headquarters which reviews, approves, and sets some specifications and business conditions, and which is involved at certain times (fig. 1.3). At the other extreme, a small college or university may retain an architectural firm to provide that kind of consistency in planning and soundness in business management of each individual building project. Whatever the arrangements, this role is very important and should almost never be left to the librarian to perform. It is typically assigned to an office under the institutional business or financial vice-president because control over financial authorizations and preparation of and signatures on contracts constitute the official authorization for work by an architect, contractor, or other services which have been employed. The librarian is the prime academic officer who provides the business office with the program and guidance on functional requirements.

Representatives of both the library and the campus planning office sit in on most, if not all, project meetings between the architect and contractors. The planning office project manager is the official representative of the institution and thereby acts as the owner and is the architect's client. During construction the architect has an official role as mediator and facilitator, a role which during the design phase was filled by the project manager. On large jobs the architect usually represents the owner in meetings with the general contractor. The architect prepares and administers the contract, but the owner must approve and sign all changes. The librarian is advisor to, and client of, the project manager.

Effective communication and sympathetic understanding among these individuals is exceedingly important. It is up to all team members to assure that contracts are followed exactly, that timetables are met for completing documents and giving approvals, and that financial constraints are followed conscientiously. Occasionally things can go awry in such a lengthy and complex process, particularly when some of the individuals who were in on the first stages of the project may have left the project and have been replaced by others who are ill informed of earlier decisions. It then behooves the business officer or librarian or architect to bring to the attention of senior academic officers the need to get the project back on track if it has in fact run into difficulties.

The business decision process can be complex. A large university may have at one time as many as 250 renovation and construction projects in planning or construction, totaling well over $100,000,000. The financial responsibilities are very considerable. It is incumbent on the business office, which has responsibility for all building projects of the institution, to assure that the architect and librarian are informed of the institution's practices in this regard. Written decisions are important so as to validate what was agreed to orally. It should be customary for all offices directly involved to be sent copies of such decision documents so that all involved in the project are kept current on the stage of authorization and about the decisions under which the next stage is being undertaken.

1.4 Nature of Building Problems Needing Correction; or, Defining the Problem

This section treats the need to define the building problem before writing the program

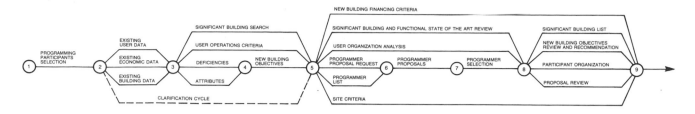

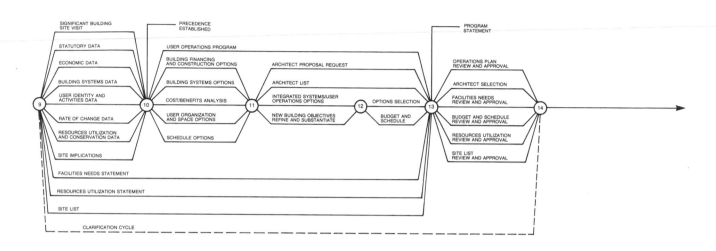

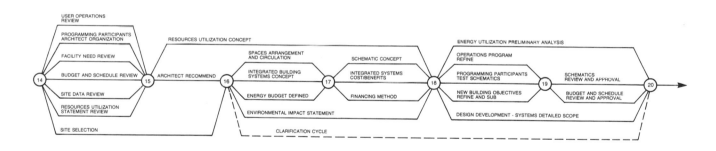

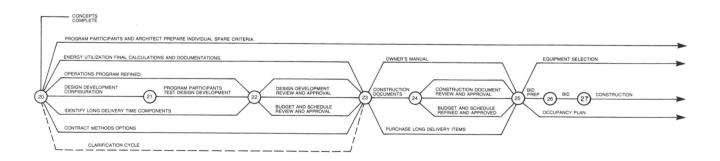

FIGURE 1.2 Project process (courtesy of McClellan & Copenhagen)

MAJOR PROJECT REVIEW PROCEDURES

REVIEW CHECKLIST

Reviewer columns:
1. Client
2. Provost
3. Plant Services
4. Medical Center Support Services (Facilities)
5. Purchasing
6. Police
7. Safety & Health
8. Marsh & McLennan
9. Univ. Comm. on Land & Bldg. Dev.
10. Arch. Advisory Council
11. President & Vice Presidents
12. Trustees
13. Santa Clara County Planning Dept.
14. Santa Clara County Bldg. Dept. & Fire Marshal
15. City of Palo Alto
16. Master Planner (Site, Landscape)
17. Fac. Engineer (M/E review)
18. FPCU — Coordinator Med. Ctr. Projects
19. FPCU — Principal Proj. Planner
20. FPCU — Dir. Planning
21. FPCU — Mgr. Constr. & Engineering
22. FPCU — Dir. Facilities & Properties
23. Controller
24. Anthropology Dept. (Prof. Gerow)

Phase	1	2	3	4	5	6	7	8	9	10	11	12	13	14	15	16	17	18	19	20	21	22	23	24
Programming: Academic Program	●	●							●		●	●												
Program Feasibility Study	●	●		●							●	●				●					●	●		
Site	●	●							●		●					●	●	●	●	●	●	●		●
Target Budget	●	●									●							●	●	●	●	●	●	
Space Program	●	●		●					●									●	●	●	●	●		
Schematic Design: Early Schematic Review	●	●	●	●	●	●	●		●	●						●		●	●	●	●			
Schematic Plans (& Outline Specifications)	●	●	●	●	●	●	●	●	●	●	●	●	●	●		●	●	●	●	●	●	●		
Plans Review Meeting	●	●	●	●	●		●										●	●	●	●	●			
Environmental Impact Statement	●	●											●		●			●						●
Formal Budget	●	●									●	●			●			●	●	●	●	●	●	
Design Development: Preliminary Plans (& Outline Specifications)	●	●	●	●	●		●									●	●	●	●	●	●			
Plans Review Meeting	●	●		●	●		●									●	●	●	●	●	●			
Construction Documents: Final Plans – 50%		●	●	●			●									●	●	●	●	●	●			
Final Plans – 100% (and Specifications)	●	●	●	●	●		●							●			●	●	●	●	●			
Plans Review Meeting	●	●	●	●	●		●										●	●	●	●	●			

FIGURE 1.3 Project review checklist (sample from a Stanford University project)

document, which is discussed in Chapters 5 through 8. The next section summarizes the options available for solving these problems. Taken together, these questions and their answers are of crucial importance. It is clear from looking at successful and unsuccessful academic library buildings that the basic success of the building is relatively assured if the staff have defined the needs of the institution adequately, explored the various options, decided on what is appropriate in its particular case, and can follow through with a well-executed construction.

The major problems with current library facilities usually are inadequate size, the limitations of the present site, the physical and mechanical quality of the building, or the lack of flexibility in the building.

Most typically, it is the space for books or for staff that runs out first in an academic library building. For a combination of reasons, inadequacy of staff quarters is a common occurrence. The librarian may feel subject to criticism if staff needs are pushed as hard as is space for books and reader needs. It may be that the institution finds it difficult to recognize that a major improvement in a library building quite often brings greatly increased use of the library. The potential readers had, in a psychological sense, been driven from the library when it was inadequate or environmentally disturbing; they now respond suddenly to greatly increased and improved library provisions. This change means more work for circulation and reference staff. It may result in more gifts to the library and more gifts of book funds. These developments, in turn, mean more material being acquired and needing cataloging and preparation for the shelves. The consequence is that staff space, which was felt to be reasonable during the planning stages, turns out to be too small under different circumstances than were projected.

The second and most important deficiency is typically a lack of shelves for books and other library materials. This is quite often the most convincing condition when an institution has to decide whether to embark on library construction or wait some number of years. For one thing, it is very obvious when the shelves are full and new materials are regrettably boxed, put on temporary shelves in corridors, or otherwise made difficult to find or impossible to access except by staff paging. The case becomes extreme when substantial parts of the collection must be shelved in auxiliary quarters outside the library building and when it may take a few hours or a day for the library staff to fetch a requested item. It is easier to determine the shelf space needed in future years than it is staff space; yet this does not mean that the calculations are much more accurate.

A shortage of space for readers is less likely to be compelling; even though in very real educational terms it is as important for the effective use of an academic library as is adequate book space or space for staff. It is more difficult to determine the consequences when students are forced to use classrooms as study halls or use their residence rooms for study. Quite clearly, many serious scholars will still use the library under the most adverse circumstances even if there is no place for them to sit down and study in a convenient and quiet location proximate to the books. Many take the path of least resistance and reduce library use; thus the teaching process suffers to an unquantifiable yet perhaps serious degree.

Other problem conditions can create unfunctional, unsatisfactory or unpleasant conditions. Lack of building flexibility can limit desired placement of library functions. Certain operations may take place under cramped conditions. Relationships among related functions may be distant or hard to explain to users. Utility capacities may be insufficient, and the atmospheric environment may be far below optimal conditions for the preservation of books or may be uncomfortable or unpleasant for staff and persons wishing to use the library.

The assessment of space needs and inadequacy of the current facility may be conducted in large measure or entirely by librarians. Such a study will ordinarily benefit by suggestion from faculty, students, and representatives of the physical plant and business offices, as well as from academic officers. The involvement of representatives of these other groups, and particularly the involvement of the faculty library committee, has the singular advantage of eliciting their support because their participation in the evaluation brings greater understanding of existing deficiencies. The relative inadequacy of current library facilities is a matter for each institution to determine by weighing all of the desired accommodations against what can realistically be afforded. The library, after all, must take its place among other institutional priorities whether it be for capital expenditures or other needs such as improvement in faculty salaries, scholarship aid, additional legal staff, or laboratory equipment.

As to the form in which the academic justification for a building is presented, each institution will have its own administrative style which suggests whether a lengthy statistical document will serve the purpose, one based more on subjective pedagogical consequences, a comparison with peer institutions, or a response limited to the academic plan and the goals set by the president for the decade ahead. Some buildings costing millions of dollars have received their blessing from chief administrative officers on the basis of a five- or ten-page statement of the problem; whereas others have required massive reports. The result can be the same, depending upon the management style, guidelines, and expectations in a particular institution.

One example may show how the nature of a building deficiency can be presented and at the same time show that this justification step in the total building project process is no more or less important today than it has been in the past or will be in the future.

Harvard University built Gore Hall in 1841 as its first separate building entirely devoted to the library. A two-story wing with the first modern tiered bookstack was added in 1877 and then another addition in 1907. After serving as the main library at Harvard for seventy-two years, it was razed in 1913 to make way for the Widener Library Building.

The director of libraries at Harvard had been disturbed for many years about the limitations of Gore Hall, just as his predecessor had found it a great limitation. In 1910, only three years after the second addition to Gore Hall was finished, the trustees of the university appointed an architectural committee to study the space needs of the library and to ascertain if there were stages of development which might temporarily alleviate the situation and promise at the same time some long-range relief. The committee conclusions of 1911 were as follows:

1. The Gore Hall site was appropriate.

2. As an alternative to a completely new building, one stack addition after another might be added to Gore until at some later time new "administrative offices" would replace Gore.

3. The initial stack addition would contain professorial study alcoves and seminar rooms as well as book space.

4. As units could be built, stacks would be added on three sides of a quadrangle with a court in the center.

5. Eventually Gore Hall would be removed and the main facade of the new building would form the third side of a quadrangle.

Furthermore, as their chief argument for razing Gore, the committee cited the librarian's statement concerning the inadequacy of the famous library building:

The present building is *unsafe,* and has been declared so by insurance experts; the electrical wiring has all been added since the construction, and it must remain a serious danger.

It is *unsuitable for its object.* The old stack . . . was modelled after an English Chapel. The whole construction is ill-suited to the working of a modern library, and no amount of tinkering can make it really good.

The building is *hopelessly overcrowded* in almost all respects, and every week makes the situation worse. The quarters of the staff are inadequate . . . the general reading room for the students is too small, it leaks when there is a heavy rain, it is often intolerably hot in summer, the ventilation is bad and must remain so with the present roof, and the room is frequently overcrowded . . . .

Finally, as to *the books themselves.* They have been shifted so often in order to gain space that at present practically every part of the library is equally overcrowded with shelves to their utmost capacity; books are put in double rows and are not infrequently left lying on top of one another, or actually on the floor. . . . and the moving of books is always a matter of inconvenience and expense. We have now almost fifty thousand volumes stored outside of the building, mostly in cellars, and yet everyday we have need of some of these works and are obliged to send for them.[1]

In addition to a written argument stating the nature of the building deficiency, one may also use photographs of conditions, statistical data to summarize the situation, statistical projections of needs over the next ten to twenty years, and comparisons with peer institutions. One may offer the faculty library committee or the president or provost a tour of the existing building and arrange a tour of one or two examples of good library buildings in comparable institutions.

[1] William Bentinck-Smith, *Building a Great Library: The Coolidge Years at Harvard* (Cambridge, Mass.: Harvard Univ. Library, 1976), pp. 51–52.

Sometimes the need is so evident and the timing is so right both administratively and financially that an affirmative decision comes easily. If the president or a major donor takes the initiative, it may come quickly. In other cases there may be delays for years while the situation steadily gets worse and, consequently, the argument for a major improvement becomes more convincing. It does no good to press for an immediate building addition or a new structure when the institution has other needs which are universally seen as of higher priority. Neither does it serve any purpose to wait until the library situation is near catastrophic, for any administration will need to be educated to the situation, to learn what options are available and feasible, and to determine how new library space can be financed.

1.5 General Considerations of Options and Span of Time for Which to Plan

Consideration of various imaginative, unconventional, "blue sky," and even far-fetched possibilities for solving the library building problem may be necessary. Some who are influential in the institution may believe that computers or microfilm will replace books in a few years. Others may feel that relying on other institutions for library support can serve to stabilize local library size, or that there are so many unused books that one can easily weed a volume for every one that is added. Some may assert that one can house the library in a number of different buildings on campus or have the library place its overflow in a former gymnasium or a former administration building. Depending on the receptivity of the university or college administration to nontraditional means of solving the library space problem, the library staff and the faculty library committee may need to give serious study to each one of these options. They may, in fact, find one or a variation thereof to be a reasonable short-term expedient or at least a way of moderating the amount of new space that is projected as needed. Chapter 2 treats alternatives to new construction.

Another question is the length of time for which the institution chooses to plan and build. Quite clearly funding possibilities provide a very real limit to the number of years. Other projects are awaiting their turn. There may be academic reasons for not planning

too far in advance. Yet there are reasons from the point of view of the library staff why a very short time span is undesirable. Some compromise needs to be found among these various forces. Since a major building project will take anywhere from three years to over ten, it is clearly undesirable to be limited to a program which will accommodate the size of library collection anticipated only five or eight years hence. Some institutions and indeed some states do not permit planning for space requirements which are projected more than four or five years ahead; however, this is undesirably short for the planning of an academic library building. If various additions are scheduled for the library building over quite a number of years, then the time frame for any one increment of new space can be shorter than if one is planning an entirely new building with no imminent expectation for incremental additions.

Even such large buildings as the Firestone Library at Princeton, the Sterling at Yale, or the Widener at Harvard were able to last little more than twenty or twenty-five years before some further space had to be found. Stanford's main library was built in 1919, and despite constrained acquisitions during the Great Depression and the Second World War, it was barely thirty years before space problems were so severe that two more stack levels were added within the existing structure. Later an adjacent undergraduate library was built, an extended basement was added beneath the main library, a major subject collection was moved out as a branch, and a significant auxiliary collection was established elsewhere to accommodate overflow of collections. These additions met the need for thirty more years until a major addition more than doubled its size.

Unless each college or university president wants to require his or her successor to finance one or more library buildings, it is a good rule of thumb to build so as to accommodate the collections and the people spaces that will be needed at least twenty years after occupying a new facility. Twenty-five years would be fifty percent better. If the institution can provide space close to that time frame, if it can provide a building which is flexible and of good quality, and if it can assure site space for one or two later satisfactory additions to such a building, then the institution will have been well served indeed. Financing is, of course, a major controlling factor. Every institution will have to find its own compromises between what is desirable and what can be achieved.

The choice among options is made more complex if the campus is already very crowded with buildings, if the quality of some buildings is marginal, and if the institution is in a dense urban area. If the academic planners have saved land which would enable the college or university to triple or quadruple its library over the next century, it will have done well. Some institutions have so many ad hoc building decisions, from one administration to the next, that a long-term rationale for library growth both centrally and in branches is difficult to achieve and maintain. In a dense urban setting major limitations are provided by the problems of buying land, converting land to different use, height and set-back restrictions, parking or open space requirements, utility line capacities, and occasionally historic site considerations. Again, each institution will need to study its own library problems and determine what options are available to it. As will be repeated below, the use of campus planners and architects for master planning will help greatly in such difficult circumstances.

Then there is the difference between a young and a mature institution. The latter will have built up research collections over the past century or more and the general deployment of laboratories and classrooms and the offices for academic disciplines will have taken some shape. The library pattern will probably have been formed as part of a master plan in past decades, and this will help in setting the future course for library space solutions, although at the same time it will act to inhibit some alternatives. Conversely, a very young institution may have a more fluid campus plan. As the young institution looks forward to a mature state, it cannot predict with certainty how the campus will grow—what enrollment patterns, percentage of majors by field, laboratories, or residential developments will occur. Therefore, the long-term prospects for library growth will be less clear than in an older institution. More attention will therefore need to be paid to assigning land for long-term requirements in order not to limit succeeding generations unduly. Consideration of branch library prospects in thirty to fifty years will be especially important. The University of California campuses at Irvine and Santa Cruz are examples of good planning—one a centralized scheme and the other a cluster arrangement.

Another kind of option may be required on a bifurcated campus. A few institutions, such as Rutgers and Minnesota, have been unable to accommodate their growth on a single campus and have therefore developed an adjacent or nearby satellite campus that may become even larger than the original. One must determine if the new campus will house sciences only or professional schools, what student housing is intended, what the long-term plans are for the physical plant, and how intercampus transportation will be handled. Library space planning in this instance poses a different challenge, and can seldom be done with the same degree of uncertainty as in a new institution. An option here is to start afresh on the new site. There will be some phasing advantages if the libraries on the old and new campuses can serve as safety valves when space pressures in one or the other become severe in future years.

Two other considerations need attention. One is that of shared facilities. The other has to do with the quality and grandeur of the desired structure.

There have been many examples of multifunctional buildings, where libraries have shared their facility with academic departments, audio-visual centers, computation centers, the president's office, classrooms, a student union and so forth. Since pre-biblical times the usual pattern was to have one or more rooms in a large building devoted to a library. This was true during the classical Egyptian civilization, in Greece, in medieval monasteries, and in all early colleges in the United States. (Recently there has been somewhat of a revival as expressed in the megastructure.) Sometimes this library "apartment" was a wing in a college building or rooms on one floor or in one portion of a building. Among the very first separate library buildings in North America were the University of South Carolina library (1840), followed by the Gore Hall Library at Harvard (1841), the Williams College library building (1845), Yale (1846), North Carolina (1851), and Amherst (1853).

Today there are many examples of shared facilities, although almost none among major colleges and universities where the main library is the minor or secondary building occupant. The campus may, on the other hand, include a megastructure with the library as one of the occupants, as at Simon Fraser University, Mission College in California, or the University of Wisconsin–Parkside. Typically the library is the primary occupant, with classrooms or other facilities, if any, occupying a small portion and having a separate entrance. This arrangement can be a mixed blessing. On the one hand, it provides expansion, or "surge," space. If the library is to be a very prominent building, as at Colby College and New York University, the president's office may rather appropriately share such a monumental or symbolic structure. If the president's office is located therein, it may bring more attention to and support for the library program. It can have certain advantages, as at Oklahoma State University when a handsome president's office with fireplace was later available to the library as the director's office. There are both academic and communication line advantages if a computer center or an audio-visual center is in the same or an adjacent building to the library. On the other hand, joint occupancy may present traffic and security problems; and the ultimate eviction of those who share the building, no matter how compatible they are in function, may be a very difficult matter indeed. Individual circumstances will dictate what is best.

Although the library should never be ugly, how important are its quality of construction and its architectural grace? The answers will not come easily. Time and costs, the desire of the institution, and the qualities of the design team become major factors. There are no one or two right answers. Considering that each answer makes a significant difference, especially in cost, the following are some of the questions to be asked. Should a minimum of funds be spent on structure, on the hard shell, on finishing surfaces, and on exterior appearance, or should an effort be made to build special quality into a building of such lasting importance and to have it harmonize in exterior design with that of other buildings in the vicinity? Should the architect aim to create a truly outstanding structure on the campus, one that will be remembered by alumni and may even be used in publications and other symbolic forms as signifying the entire institution? Need it be or should it be monumental in scale? Is there an imposing and suitable site? Should the construction of foundation and shell be of such high quality that the structure will still be sound after a

hundred years; or should its life be thought of in terms of a limited period, on the assumption that this library will be outdated and not worth preserving a century hence?

Institutional policies and trustee desires will give some of the answers. Questions such as the above can rarely be solved without understanding the future in academic and in business terms, and without deciding on campus priorities which in turn should be based on the objectives of the institution. Costs too often have more influence than one might wish in determining the answers. Financial realities of appropriations and gift fundraising can constrain as has been cited above. Even so, prudent management suggests careful consideration of the various options from alternative points of view. For example, for obvious management reasons tower libraries or monuments that are difficult to operate or expand must be guarded against.

1.6 The Ultimate Size of a Library

A word about library growth. Libraries do not necessarily have to grow if the student body and faculty size remain stable and if academic program elements which determine the size of the library staff can also remain static and the collection size is static or expands off site. However, library collections do grow, especially in research institutions, and therein lies the major problem in housing libraries. This is a fact which is so important that it bears emphasizing. Librarians and other academic officers responsible for libraries have never found a satisfactory way of preventing all growth in library collections or even of slowing up appreciably library space requirements. This is growth due to the nature of learning. Knowledge constantly expands. It is not always displacing prior knowledge, certainly not in the humanities and the arts and rather seldom even in the social sciences and much of the sciences. Thus a college can plan on a collection of rather limited growth for its undergraduate instructional purposes, and yet the faculty will need local access to additional publications in order to maintain their disciplinary skills. This need is true to an extent even in community colleges and technical colleges. It is obvious with respect to a university, particularly since graduate students will be undertaking very broad reading in their field of concentration and developing advanced papers or a thesis to be presented with documentation and defended as their doctoral dissertation. Major graduate programs therefore require collections that grow by many tens of thousands of volumes a year, carefully selected from current worldwide publications and the out-of-print book trade.

It is common knowledge that, in general, university library collections doubled about every fifteen or sixteen years during at least the first two-thirds of this century. Though this growth rate declines as the size of the library grows, and despite the increasingly heavy use of microtexts and the very considerable use of other nonbook forms of information, the book collections continue to grow in bulk. It seems clear that books will increase in number and continue in importance to academic institutions, will require a good deal of space in increasing amount, and will remain the basic format in libraries of academic institutions for at least the rest of this century. Keyes Metcalf in the first edition of this book made the following general prognostications, here slightly updated, with the full realization that they can be challenged, that details can be easily confuted, and that they should not be taken too specifically for any one institution. Each institution is and should be different from others.

1. The average strictly undergraduate library will continue to grow in the size and bulk of its collections and therefore its storage requirements; but its net increase, certainly by the time it approaches the half million mark, will be reduced to something like two percent a year because of greater reliance on other libraries for little-used material, use of microreproductions of one kind or another, and greatly increased application of digitized and optical disc storage technology. The increase in demand for seating will for the next twenty-five years go up at the rate of something like one percent a year, in addition to the increase in the number of students. This is to provide for increased intensity of use and for new equipment needed to access information. On that basis the recommended basic space per reader should be increased about one-fifth for prudent planning. Staff-area needs will go up at least as rapidly as the average of the other two and probably more.

2. The average university library will increase in its space needs for collections more rapidly than will a library for undergraduate use over the next twenty years. Until any particular collection reaches at least 2,500,000 volumes, that rate is likely to be not less than four percent per annum over that of the year before. The percentage of increase thereafter typically slows up. (Adverse economic conditions can, of course, depress this rate.) As was the case with the college library, an increase of one percent of its seating accommodation areas in addition to the percentage increase in the number of students will be required for uses such as bibliographic and computer-aided instruction, audio-visual services, online computer searches, and use of materials on optical discs. Increased staff needs will be at least as high as the increase in the collections and in reader accommodations. New machines will take as much space as is used for the staff that will be replaced by the machines.

3. The average large research library (that is, one with over 2,500,000 volumes), if it is already attempting to cover practically the whole field of knowledge, may increase no more rapidly than the undergraduate library group discussed under 1 above. The cost of space, the existence of national loan centers such as Boston Spa and the Center for Research Libraries, and the use of technology such as videodisc storage will slow up the growth rate for the very large research library.

These slightly updated predictions of 1965 still seem valid for the balance of this century and are made not as a guide for a specific library planning a renovation or a new building but as a basis for discussion. Each institution should consider its own special situation, its relations with neighboring institutions, the present size of its collections and their adequacy, its recent rate of growth, the prospects for changes in the composition and size of the student body, the quality and style of instruction, and particularly the present stage of institutional development and prospects for the years ahead.

Book collection growth rates in mature institutions will continue to slow up. But is there an ultimate size? Librarians and academic officers may well wonder if there will ever be an absolute end to the growth of academic libraries. Certainly it would be comforting to know that one might plan one last library building that would serve the college or university as long as any of its buildings will serve. Yet this is not feasible in the current nature of the academic world. Faculty and their students need to have immediate shelf access to nearly all of the materials required for their teaching and their immediate research. Even so, it is becoming increasingly necessary for them to purchase photocopies from a distance, rely on interlibrary borrowings, or visit other libraries that have specialized materials. With high-speed digital facsimile transmission, a much larger percentage of needed books and articles may be "borrowed" if the cost becomes comparable to the total costs of buying and shelving the original publication.

Another special solution is off-site storage. Many major university libraries have available to them an auxiliary facility into which they can place the less frequently used materials. Some (such as the Center for Research Libraries, the New England Deposit Library, and the northern and southern University of California facilities) are accommodations for many libraries. Some others (such as the University of London, Princeton, Yale, Michigan, and Texas) have specially designed auxiliary storage facilities on campus to handle the local overflow. It seems quite probable that this pattern will spread widely among universities and perhaps among colleges. Together with increased reliance on other institutions, this secondary-access collection may be the common future arrangement whereby faculty and graduate students continue to have access to larger and larger collections while the main or central library building(s) on campus tend toward a stable size. However, it should be realized that as the proportion grows of such collections that require greater staff effort, the staff space required will grow at a proportionately greater rate. Seating requirements in the future should remain proportionate to enrollment and the academic program. A trend toward stabilized size of collections could be accelerated if a national or regional center for serials and monographs is formed in the years ahead.

Regardless of governmental programs, of consortia, and of reliance on off-campus or back-campus auxiliary facilities, faculty and students still will need rather immediate access to the vast bulk of materials relevant to their current teaching and research. Time pressures in class require one- or two-day access to nearly all materials needed for class assignments. For research projects with a few weeks to complete, borrowing of 5 or even 10 percent of materials needed can be tolerated if 90 to 95 percent is readily at hand. If one looks at the Harvard University Library which exceeds ten million volumes, the addition of the Pusey Library in 1976 and the recent branch buildings for anthropology, art, education, music, and science indicate that the Harvard libraries do not yet have a static requirement for central space—even with the New England Deposit Library just across the Charles River. There have also been major recent additions at Colby, Michigan, Occidental, Princeton, Vassar, and Yale. Branch libraries on university campuses grow slowly in number; seldom are there consolidations. So it seems certain that university libraries as well as college libraries will grow at least for the immediate future in their requirements for book collections and campus space.

At least for now, the largest academic library structure is the 1973 University of Toronto Robarts Library of 16 floors, over 5,000,000 volume capacity, and a gross area of 1,036,000 sq ft (or about 96,250 sq m). Although some at Toronto feel it is too large, whether the next century will require larger academic library buildings is unknown. A cluster of facilities in the tradition of Oxford, Harvard, Michigan, and Stanford seems the common probability. Each institution can consider its local circumstances, relations with its neighbors, and current state or federal support; and an individual decision will then have to be made as to the nature of the library building that is needed.

1.7 Looking toward the Future

We live in a changing world. If the past can be taken as a guide, it is obvious that the requirements for a library building in 1990 or 2000 will be quite different from those in 1970 or 1950. Libraries planned more than eighty years ago are almost always so outmoded today as to be questionable assets. One very old university may serve as an example. Harvard University has no major library unit and only three research branches in buildings built previous to 1907. It is, however, quite reasonable to expect that well-built buildings with reasonable flexibility of internal space will serve academic institutions for a great many decades.

The cost of a new library building today is so great and represents such a large percentage of an institution's total capital investment that it is generally unwise to build deliberately for a few years only. Consequently, to last a great many decades, the building should within reason be as flexible as possible. Flexibility means adaptability to changing needs.

The characteristics of a flexible library building may be summed up as follows. As large a percentage of the floor space as possible should be usable interchangeably, with modest alteration for any of the primary functions of a library: reader accommodations, service to readers, space for staff activities, and housing for the collections. It follows that:

1. Floors must be capable of bearing live loads up to 150 pounds per square foot (7.182 kN/m²), which is the bookstack requirement in all areas of the building. If movable shelving is anticipated, floor loading requirements will be about 300 pounds per square foot (14.364 kN/m²). Certain other storage configurations may result in other loading requirements.

2. Floor heights must be adequate for any of these purposes, preferably not less than 8 ft 4 in. (2.540). Where a building is protected by a sprinkler system, the floor to ceiling height should be not less than 9 ft (2.743).

3. Atmospheric and other comfort conditions, such as ventilation and lighting, must be adaptable to any of these purposes with minimal change, but ceiling and floor treatments need not be identical throughout a building.

4. All library areas must be readily accessible; it is undesirable to have load-bearing interior walls in places where they might interfere with later traffic patterns.

5. Security and access will need careful consideration to permit reasonable flexibility.

6. The building module should be economical in handling shelving dimensions, as well as carrel, study, office, and reading area dimensions. Interior arrangements must not seriously interfere with satisfactory capacity for books, for readers, and for shelving.

It must be realized, of course, that in any library building, even if only one level, there must be supports to hold up the roof, and in most buildings interior columns are a necessity. With more than one level, vertical transportation, heating and ventilation shafts, and plumbing facilities are required and will limit complete flexibility.

Although flexibility is a very desirable condition, it does not mean that the use of the space should not be carefully planned for the original installation. In fact some buildings in recent decades have gone too far toward uniform interchangeable modular bays. Carried to an extreme, flexibility results in averaging requirements so that few spaces are completely satisfactory for their function because of flexibility compromises; and the building will look and act as if it were the result of a contractor erecting it as an investment speculation for any academic purpose. A very strong flexibility requirement will add to construction costs, and the only reasonable justification for such extra expense is that it can be expected to save money in the long run. Even here, though, if change cannot be anticipated, the principal effort should be limited to the more inflexible elements of a structural nature. Interior masonry or plastered walls, which are messy to remove, and permanent built-in installations of all kinds should be avoided as far as practicable. Heating and ventilation ducts, toilet facilities, and vertical transportation should be grouped in a core and provided in places where they are least likely to interfere with prospective changes in library functional-space assignments.

Even in a large building, the number of what are known as core areas that are permanently fixed in position should be limited; and, other things being equal, the fewer cores the better. A large building with up to 5,000 sq m (say, 50,000 or more sq ft) on each level can be planned with only one central core; and any stairwells, elevators, ducts, toilets, and other vertical shafts not within this core can be placed at the building's periphery where they will be as nonintrusive as possible. Some architects have gone so far as to place secondary stairs and other permanent features outside the main building structure as protrusions from it (see fig. 1.4) and have been able to fit them into the architectural arrangements without damaging the aesthetic appearance—even have made them important aesthetic features. Outside constructions can simplify interior traffic patterns and arrangements but should not be considered essential, because with many buildings they would not be suitable architecturally.

One important arrangement that may prolong the useful life of a library and prevent unnecessary expenditures later is to plan the building so that later additions can be made without undue expenses for alterations and rearrangements and without damaging it functionally or aesthetically. This can be accomplished only by providing for these additions in the basic plan adopted.

What changes in library needs can be anticipated? It seems obvious that the way to attack this problem is to consider what can be learned from the past and what can be deduced from studying the present.

Lessons from the Past. A study of the past makes it obvious that old library buildings are very different from those planned more recently. A brief summary should suffice. One hundred years ago thick exterior and interior bearing walls held up the buildings, which were planned with little thought of flexibility. No library had elevators, steel shelving (shelving was typically wood and cast iron), electric power or lighting, telephones, or air conditioning. Card catalogs were coming into use; the catalog in book form had been standard. There were no visible indexes. There were no typewriters or other copying machines, to say nothing of microfilm readers, computers, and audio-visual equipment.

Individual seating on a large scale was unknown. Compact storage, as we conceive it today, or even concentrated stack shelving had not been used. Except in libraries with a very limited clientele, there was, to all intents and purposes, no open access to the collections. It was not customary for readers to have accommodations close to the books, except in a few libraries where there were alcoves surrounded by books with a table in the center.

Of perhaps greater importance from the point of view of building, the largest collections in the United States in 1850 numbered about 100,000 volumes. By 1900 the number had grown to a million. Today there are many academic and research libraries of that size in the United States. The number of readers in academic libraries has increased at a somewhat similar rate, because of the growth of the number of students in institutions of higher learning, the increasing emphasis on individual work and wider reading, and a deemphasis of textbook instruction.

Several basic changes in the physical structure of libraries are the direct or indirect result of the different requirements. We no longer have to have light courts or great monumental reading areas reaching up to 50 ft (15.240) in height to provide ventilation

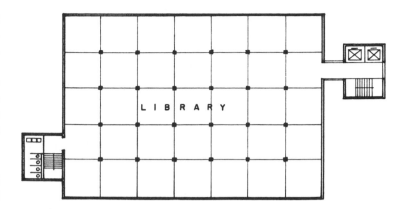

FIGURE 1.4 Secondary stairs outside main walls. This arrangement can simplify internal arrangements and traffic patterns, although access to collections from the first floor must be clear.

and natural light. This change alone has reduced cubage in areas open to the public by 50 percent or more. With good quality artificial light available at a reasonable cost, libraries can be open and comfortable on dark days and after sunset. Daylight can be, and it is to be hoped will continue to be, available in parts of the buildings for psychological purposes, if not for reading. Ceiling heights can now be determined by factors other than the need for natural light and ventilation.

These changes make it practicable and often desirable for the sake of reducing outside wall areas and costs and shortening and simplifying traffic lanes, to plan a squarish building without light wells instead of a relatively long, narrow, and irregular one. The choice, it must be admitted, may complicate the aesthetic problems.

What then have we learned from the past? Five things among others:

1. Changes in construction methods and in provision for comfort and convenience have come about, and more of them will undoubtedly be made in the future. As a result, a new building needs to be as flexible as possible although complete flexibility cannot be obtained.

2. The size of library collection has grown rapidly in the past and in most cases can be expected to continue to grow in the future. However space demands for shelving will abate somewhat in large libraries due to increasing use of compact shelving and auxiliary or warehouse facilities.

3. The demand made on academic libraries for seating accommodations has continued to

increase in this century. Because of re-entry students, continuing education programs, students from abroad, changes in methods of instruction, broadening of the curriculum, and dormitory and home conditions that are not conducive for study, space demands for reading accommodations will seemingly continue to increase.

4. The quality of accommodations has tended to rise, and more comfortable and convenient study conditions have been provided. These have included better temperature and humidity control, improved quality of lighting, safer exiting in case of fire or other emergency, a larger percentage of individual seating, semiprivate accommodation, and improved access for those who are physically limited. None of these improvements has as yet reached its limits.

5. The atmospheric conditions and controls now available have been found to be very useful for the preservation of books, and continued improvements in this respect will undoubtedly be made, particularly in energy conservation techniques. It might be said that any building built today without what is now regarded as satisfactory control of atmospheric conditions is already outmoded, and many would say that within a few years a non-air-conditioned academic library will be a thing of the past. Of course, energy concerns will result in innovative solutions to maintaining the environment (for example, the 1982 solar-heated library at San Jose State University, shown in fig. 1.5) which may differ dramatically from air conditioning as we know it today.

If past experience means anything, the planners of academic and research library buildings should be guided by the following:

1. Since physical changes of many kinds can be expected to take place as the years go by, the utmost reasonable flexibility is required.

2. Since long-term increase in space demands for collections and reader accommodations is almost inevitable, a building, to continue to be useful, must be so placed and planned that it can be readily enlarged at least once or twice.

3. Since accommodations will rise in quality, at least as far as the comfort of the occupant and the preservation of the collections are concerned, overeconomizing is unwise; if the financial situation dictates a certain economy, the plans should be laid so that later improvements will not be unduly expensive.

4. Since technology is advancing so rapidly, the building should be able to accommodate increased use of wired and cable devices and an increase in devices using electric and solar energy.

Deductions from the Present. A few conclusions can be deduced from the present that will help in planning academic libraries for the years ahead. These include the influence of governmental policy and of technological change. Only briefly referred to here, these particular program or design considerations will be dealt with in the appropriate places in following chapters.

Governmental policy controls an increasing number of the activities in any academic institution, whether it be publicly or privately supported. There are, of course, city, county, state, and national codes and standards for fire, earthquake, general safety, and general building construction. These by stages become increasingly stringent; seismic bracing in active earthquake areas in the United States and access convenience for physically limited persons have been very considerably increased in the past two decades. Professional standards may or may not be adopted or referred to in governmental codes, but they certainly often serve as having nearly the force of law and administrative regulation. There also are increasing guidelines by federal and state governments, such as requirements of the U.S. Office of Safety and Health Administration, regulations issued by the U.S. Department of Education for facilities for the physically handicapped, and energy guidelines or requirements from the U.S. Department of Energy. It seems likely that more will be developed to protect life and limb, maintain or improve the environment, economize on energy consumption, reduce pollution and waste, and otherwise assure safe buildings with minimal undesired consequences. All of this, of course, puts an extra burden on academic institutions and their architects and engineers, and most of these mandates result in some increased cost in building construction. Each institution must work within those codes and standards that currently apply locally.

Technological change has been very great in this century and particularly so in recent decades. Indeed, the situation is markedly more advanced than when the first edition of this book was published, for it was not until the 1960s that major library online computer

FIGURE 1.5 San Jose State University, Clark Library. Note that entire length of the south wall just above window height on the lower three floors is formed of solar collectors for building heat. These collectors are flat plate, diffuse radiation, double-glazed, water type with a total area of 3,000 sq. ft. Tiled entrance lobby roof projects on lower left (south) side.

systems were developed. It is now an accepted fact that most libraries rely heavily on computer-based systems which automate large parts of the library operation: the purchasing, cataloging, reference work, circulation, and business operations. Indeed, by the 1990s there will hardly be an area of library operation, no matter how small the library, where a computer typewriter terminal or cathode ray-tube screen display will not be in use.

Although building accommodations for computer applications are woven into later chapters, a few statements are appropriate here. The Educational Facilities Laboratories asked a conference of experts in 1967 to assess the impact of technology on the library building. The conclusion was that "library planners can proceed at this time with confidence that technological developments in the foreseeable future will not alter radically the way libraries are used. In planning library buildings today, we should start with the library as the institution we now know it to be.

Any departures in the future should be made from this firm base. To be sure, technology will modify library buildings. But the changes will involve trade-offs in space and demands for additional space, rather than less."[2]

One would today agree that "technology will modify library buildings." Indeed, there are greatly increased electronic requirements, though some developments since 1967 have lessened the anticipated physical consequences of new communications technology. Microcomputers take less space, use less power, and produce less heat than did computers ten years ago. Keyboards of terminals now make modest noise, and impact printers have been replaced with relatively quiet devices. Given major network services, local file management does not require a large-scale computer using one or two thousand square feet and needing a double floor and separate

[2] *The Impact of Technology on the Library Building* (New York: Educational Facilities Laboratories, 1967), pp. 19–20.

power and air-conditioning sources. Distributed processing typically depends on mini-computers with modest physical demands. In nearly all academic libraries terminals are ubiquitous, though building consequences are moderate except for a significant reallocation of space.

Other technological developments are also having considerable influence in the latter years of this century. Since the 1930s micro-reproductions of one form or another have grown to constitute very large collections, such that in some libraries there are nearly as many bibliographic items in microform as there are in book or codex form. It seems likely that the vigor of this recent publication program will continue (unless it is superseded by optical digital-disc technology). Microforms will not, however, replace the book to any large degree. This also does not mean that all large libraries should make provision for installation of a photographic laboratory. Such arrangements were fairly common in large libraries in the middle years of this century; however, all but the largest libraries now rely on commercial microfilming firms for filming to archival standards. Each institution will need to make a decision based on local circumstances in this regard.

Preservation of books requires much more stringent environmental control than was generally recognized as being necessary even twenty-five years ago. A reduction in temperature from 80 degrees to 70 degrees F in a bookstack will double the life expectancy of the books; or, on another scale, life expectancy is multiplied by a factor of about 4.5 with every temperature drop of 15 degrees C.[3] Temperature control becomes a very important consideration for an academic library that has invested huge amounts of money in acquiring and cataloging printed materials which future generations of students will continue to use. Fumigation chambers, paper casting machines, and freezers are now widely used; bulk deacidification chambers may soon be in common use if a suitable chemical process can be developed. The rapid technological developments for treatment of particular book problems are welcome, though cool storage for the general collections will remain the most economical con-

dition for helping prolong the useful life of the great mass of research collections.

The development of communication systems and devices, security systems, and information published in a wide variety of new formats create a great diversity in library management and put increasing demands on electronic and mechanical systems. Some machines produce heat and also require controlled temperature and humidity. Some machines are noisy and the walls of their rooms should be acoustically treated. In many cases these installations do not have to be immediately adjacent to the reading areas since the transportation of those materials is not a major problem. However, on the whole, it is desirable to be able to have such equipment as photocopy machines in convenient locations, provide ease of maintenance or replacement, and make arrangements so they are unobtrusive and inaudible to those who use the library. One should expect future applications of mechanically accessed high-density book storage, closed-circuit television equipment, local area ether networks, fiber optics data communication, microwave long-distance transmission and reception, videodisc installations, and other developments not yet thought of or available on the market. The technological developments will continue to affect the planning of academic and research library buildings.

This chapter concludes with some forward-looking comments on a university library by President Claude T. Bissell of the University of Toronto.

We must beware of a *1984* complex and, having starved our libraries in the past, of continuing to do so on the grounds that they will soon become obsolete. Technological change will mean that libraries will become even more central than they have been before, but they will also become more elaborate and more expensive; for they will need complex machinery, space in which to house the machinery, technicians to watch over them, and highly trained experts to use them.

From these general reflections I turn now to comments on the specific changes that will take place in the library with the technological revolution; I shall have in mind chiefly large libraries associated with the universities. One used to think of the large research library in the university as mainly a storage depot, a cultural warehouse. That concept was modified some decades ago by the introduction of the compact storage concept whereby books rarely used were transferred to central concentration points. The use of various

---

[3] *Strength and Other Characteristics of Papers 1800–1899* (Richmond, Va.: W. J. Barrow Research Laboratory, 1967) p. 34.

techniques of micro-reproduction further modified the idea of the library as a warehouse. One must not, however, indulge in science fiction fantasies of the abolition of the book; it is still the cheapest form in which to store knowledge, and will for most readers continue to be the *raison d'être* of the library. One must think too of the book as a physical object, in many cases as an *objet d'art,* which we will not readily abandon for an invisible world. Still the percentage of holdings in various forms of microtext will undoubtedly grow, and one can take some satisfaction in the prospect of space released from book storage for other purposes. . . .

The profile of the new research library in the university is that of an active scholarly headquarters with a close working relationship between professional supervisors and users. . . . Again, I may illustrate the new concept by referring to our plans at the University of Toronto. We plan a research library which, in a fundamental sense, is a series of private laboratories for the graduate student and faculty member, and where these are supplemented by small rooms for discussion and informal seminars. As the headquarters of the University, this library must not have an atmosphere of the puritan wake; it will be a place of activity, where the refinements of acoustics will release the human voice.

The best physical expression for this new type of research library has yet to be found. Thus far, changes in library structure have not been attuned to the new age. We have moved from the library conceived of as sarcophagus, a large elaborate tomb on which were inscribed the names of the illustrious dead, to the library as cathedral with an atmosphere of solemnity, grandeur, and mystery, to the library as combined head office and warehouse, with inevitable associations with that great archetype of modern architecture, the filing box. The new library must, to an extent, reflect the demands of the scientific age of which the marks are uniformity and repetition; but it must subordinate this to an expression of the unity of knowledge and the stubborn eccentricity of the human spirit. The library is a building that must be the chief symbol of the new university, the concentration centre of the systematic search for knowledge, which yet manages to cast a humorous and skeptical eye at man's pretensions to omniscience.[4]

[4] *The Strength of the University* (Toronto: Univ. of Toronto Pr., 1968), pp. 134–38.

2

The Alternatives to a
New Library Building

The price tag for a new library building in these days of high construction costs often comes to several times the library's annual budget, occasionally as much as twenty or more times the annual budget. This being the case, alternatives to new construction ought to be considered very seriously and may provide an excellent solution to the needs of the library. The judgment among alternatives must be based on three assessments. First is a projection of the future of the institution, its teaching and research programs. Second is the future nature of the library, its collections and its services. The third is an assessment of the present and future quality and adequacy of the existing library space.

One example is the University of Texas central library building, the condition of which in the 1970s constituted an especially clear case of need. The Tower, housing the main library on lower floors, was built in 1932 and is a campus landmark; but it had inherent traffic problems, some floors were inaccessible to the physically handicapped, and structurally permissible floor loads were uncertain. However, the worst problem was the worry about safety, for the structure was not fireproofed and all of the ductwork and most of the wiring were exposed. There were no heat or smoke detectors, no sprinklers, and no alarm bells; there were no fire hoses until the 1966 fire on the 22nd floor. Thus, despite faculty endorsement of the advantages of centralization of the library collection for interdisciplinary scholarship, the third assessment above clearly called for a completely new structure.

This example resulted in a decision which was appropriate at that university. For each library space problem solved by a complete new building there are several solved by additions, some conversions of adjacent nonlibrary space to library use, and many renovations or extensive remodelings.

This chapter is not intended to argue for or against any of the alternatives but merely to point out some of the questions that can be raised and answered so as to provide an institution with the best solution for its needs. This chapter will thus provide discussion of some ways in which there can be maximum use made of the library building, alternatives to new construction which may be used before needing to build an addition or a new building. Thus the chapter starts with some discussion of academic master planning and then deals with denser use of a library building, use of shared facilities, moderating conditions resulting from collection management, increased density of shelving derived from stack reformation, the use of remote or auxiliary shelving, the decentralization of library functions or collections, and interinstitutional or interlibrary dependences—all of these serving to postpone or moderate the demand for new space.

When a library building is first occupied, it should provide a suitable and relatively commodious home. Within a ten-year period it may be relatively cramped and some interior partitions will have been moved. In twenty or twenty-five years it will have become quite crowded and a number of changes will have been undertaken—unless there are severe economic conditions which restrain growth of collections or which otherwise reduce the institutional program and the library's support. By the time the library building is fifty years old, other types of problems occur due to the wearing out of roofs, plumbing, mechanical systems, electrical systems and interior surfaces, and there may be operational problems with doors and windows. New technologies may indicate new needs in terms of power, physical flexibility, or structural requirements. Short of some period of time like fifty years, major building components generally do not wear out. Yet they become inadequate for a variety of reasons: fashions, building standards, and operational needs change; remodeling and extensive maintenance work may be necessary.

Inadequate size is usually the most urgent consideration, and foremost is the pressure from growth of library collections. Collections strictly devoted to undergraduate purposes, and particularly to lower division students, can be maintained at a rather static size by weeding from time to time to maintain a collection deemed the most appropriate to support the curriculum. But the faculty and academic staff of any academic institution must be able to work in peripheral areas of their fields and to conduct research and publish: for these purposes older books may be of supreme importance. Older works may also be valuable for a different interpretation of a literary work or historical event, and thus the accumulation of carefully selected secondary materials can contribute measureably to the growth and understanding of an advanced student who is trying to become fully steeped in a discipline. New acquisitions for the most part do not, therefore, replace the books that are already on the shelves.

Except for such reduction as is the consequence of automation, the staff of a library must grow as the collection becomes larger and more complex, and it will grow to the extent that additional formats need to be supported and use increases. Increased use usually requires increased space for readers. Changes in teaching methods may result in larger demands on the library even in the days of online access to national databases. Although demographic fluctuation for a decade or two may reduce enrollment, hamper the finances of an institution, and affect the vigor of the library program, cyclical patterns will shift and again the library may need more space.

Beyond the more obvious possibilities described in Sections 2.2 and 2.3, the options can become complex and expensive. Careful use of an academic master plan should therefore be the guide to keep sights set on accepted long-term goals. Long-term cost considerations need also to be looked at in considerable detail. In this connection an early use of a library building consultant, a local or county building inspector, and the institution's insurance manager to advise on risk reduction and costs may result in some of the best insight and wisest advice when trying to sort out these alternatives and the consequences thereof. For a detailed description of factors that should be considered in analyzing various shelving options, Chapter 6 should also be consulted.

2.1 Academic Master Planning

Perceiving the shifts in the teaching program requires a very careful study of curriculum. It may be even more difficult to get a true grasp of the changing nature of research endeavors in an institution. Yet both have a direct effect upon the library program. Great changes in technological development, social and economic concerns, political conditions, and philosophical and moral attitudes also create major consequences for an academic institution and its library. It is therefore much more prevalent for libraries now than twenty years ago to have stated goals and objectives which reflect the changing demands on the library. Ideally, these program objectives constitute a library master plan for at least a five-year period of what is expected in its collection development, its processing programs, and its public services, and they will also outline broader goals for a decade or more ahead. There should be a complementary set of phased objectives for the physical plant needed to house the library. Library planning for an academic institution can only be as good as the planning for the entire institution, and the library should be recognized as a very important component of such institutional planning. Regardless of whether the institution as a whole has such a clearly documented academic master plan with a complementary physical master plan, the library needs to have such a program.

From twenty to fifty years ago, it was rather common for surveys to be conducted by outside experts whose recommendations proposed changes in the years immediately ahead. It was the experience, however, that the soundness of the recommendations, the understanding of them, and the effective implementation all depended on the extent to which the staff of the library and parent institution was involved and convinced.

Thus in more recent years, even with some guidance by outside consultants, key library staff have been deeply involved and frequently conduct the entire job of formulating long-term goals and setting down the phases for short-term objectives. This same rationale pertains when a library building program is written. A consultant may advise, question, and stimulate, but it is incumbent upon the local librarian to write the program since only that librarian fully understands the institution's academic objectives, the historical conditions within the institution, the style and standards desired by the current administration, and the particular library response that is justified in serving such an institutional need.

Colleges and universities are placing increased emphasis on planning as a defined function. Since 1945 planning departments have become common, sometimes divided into an academic planning office and a planning office for facilities. This latter office may be called the design and construction office or the engineers and architects office. By whatever name, the former office deals, for example, with the statistical conditions and trends of student matriculation, course enrollment, residence, and grading patterns. The latter office is commonly in the business side of the institution and deals with the financial and legal aspects of space planning on campus, choice of architects and planners, qualification of consultants and contractors, and facility project budget preparation and management. It assures that governmental standards as well as institutional standards are followed, that construction conforms to the bid documents, and that the process moves in a cost-effective and business-like fashion. This office seldom gets into the operational building-maintenance affairs after the construction warranty period.

Both the academic planning and the facilities planning offices are likely to have various master planning documents which can be useful for the library academic plan. In some institutions this planning procedure has become standardized and relies heavily on statistical formulation and the annual completion of special forms. There is some difference of opinion about whether this quantitative analysis assists or stultifies the academic planning process, though such analysis is fairly common in large publicly supported statewide systems of higher education. If used wisely, quantitative data can support the planning process. Each institution considering future library requirements will need to develop a planning process within the existing institutional framework.

In New Jersey, North Carolina, Florida, Michigan, Indiana, Illinois, Wisconsin, Colorado, and Washington, it is clear that state planning for higher education represents a major activity. Since the number of students and the annual operating budgets for state-supported systems in places like New York and California are huge, there are public requirements for careful accountability. Such plans and their justification present constraints and certainly demand extra lead time in resolving a physical problem on a particular campus.

California may be cited as one example. The University of California in the early 1970s committed itself to a system-wide approach to library planning which was based on the concept of a single university book collection rather than nine separate campus collections. Planning data were provided by a number of meticulous studies of collections overlap, lending from one campus to the other, and the amount of infrequently used materials. A master library planning document was prepared and reviewed on all campuses and by the statewide academic senate and president's office. The balancing of competing economic and academic forces led to a difficult conclusion, but one which was deemed on balance to be feasible and desirable. A first tangible result was a statewide serial listing to supplement the published book catalogs, then came the system online library catalog, followed in 1980 by construction of the Northern California Regional Library Facility as an auxiliary bookstack building in Richmond. The facility was intended to substitute at least in part for more campus library construction and was a direct product of academic master planning.

Some independent institutions have done excellent planning studies, Swarthmore College being notable. The libraries at Columbia and Harvard have at times prepared extensive planning documents. This is not to say, however, that a major tome is always necessary or justified. A good understanding among academic officers and the principal library administrators may constitute such a sound understanding of the institutional future that a formal academic master plan document may not be necessary. Yet even then the individuals involved in judging the alternatives to a new library building must thoroughly understand and agree on this institutional framework and direction for planning, and a summary of academic objectives and standards should be written into the library building program document so that planners and architects will have a consistent understanding of these matters.

2.2 More Exhaustive Building Use

This section provides an overview. The next considers shared use of a building and is followed by four sections on management of book-collection space needs.

Careful study of the existing building may show areas where some increased use of space can be achieved, at least postponing the date at which additional space will be essential. Care must be taken to assure that legal exit aisles are maintained, that floor loading capacities are not exceeded, and that access conditions for the physically limited are attained. When extra density of functions is achieved, one may face such problems as worsened acoustical conditions and air circulation, increased noise and consequent disruptions of staff operations, circuitous work flow, lessened aesthetics, and the loss of "sense of place," which can cause considerable morale problems. These need to be carefully considered in each case. Some increased use may be highly successful; some arrangements may entail alterations and rehabilitation which would cost more than can be justified.

Depending on whether the pressure is on reading quarters, staff work space, or book-shelving, space can be sought in desired locations. In some cases, however, a set of sequential moves may be needed. Questions such as the following may be asked. Is the main lobby large and could it therefore be partitioned so as to reduce its width or depth, maintain a reasonably gracious entrance, but provide new assignable floor area? Are corridors wide enough to accommodate a bank of carrels, housing for certain reference works, workstations for hourly employees, or other use? Can exhibition areas be given up temporarily to meet certain other functional requirements? Are there storage areas which can be dispensed with, or can bulk storage be moved to another campus building so as to return such library area for priority needs? Can office partitions be replaced by open office landscape furniture techniques so as to increase density and yet maintain a degree of visual privacy and reasonable acoustical isolation? Could a student lounge and a staff snack facility be combined or reduced in size? Can some parts of the technical processes be decentralized to one or more branches? Can all technical processes be relocated to a nearby building? Can books be shelved tightly in a closed collection or a collection shelved in a classification scheme not currently used so as to free empty shelves? Can some cross aisles in the bookstack be filled in with shelves without eliminating major traffic patterns? Can shelving be made taller? Can shelves be added along the walls? Can oversized books be shelved on spines or moved to a folio or portfolio section in order to add shelves in a section to handle more octavo volumes? Is the use of major reading rooms intense enough to justify devoting the entire room to reading, or could some part be partitioned off for work quarters or extra shelving for processing backlogs? Can shelves be moved closer together or can movable compact shelves be installed? (Refer to fig. 6.18.)

These and other questions can be raised in increasing the use of present space. While an excellent solution to a current problem may be found in better use of existing space, it is important, nonetheless, to consider the deleterious results of overcrowding which in turn may increase noise and reduce efficiency. Overcrowding of staff quarters in academic libraries is one of the most frequent space pressures, perhaps because the librarian at the time of construction was too modest in the assignment of staff space, failed to foresee the prospective needs, or at least did not convince the institutional administration that the staff size would need to grow as conditions change.

Remember that building codes may differ markedly since the building was constructed or last remodeled. If one plans alterations costing more than fifty percent of the replacement value of a particular building, one often has to bring the entire building up to current building codes. (All new work will naturally be required to meet code.) This means that fire exits, emergency lighting, handrails, electrical circuitry, ventilation, and dead end corridors may require correction. The best way to determine probable costs when considering substantial change is to have the structure carefully examined by a reliable building contractor who then provides an estimate of costs. Of course such an effort will only be effective once there is a fairly clear identification of the scope of work. A thorough review of current and potential building use, and answers to such questions as are posed above, will strengthen the hand of the librarian when going to an administrative office to request approval for remodeling a building addition or a new structure. The librarian ought to be able to demonstrate that all reasonable alternatives have been considered and to indicate why they would not provide the benefits needed over a suitable length of time. One must show that space now available is not being wasted and that continuing to operate in the present building bears certain demonstrable consequences.

2.3 Use of Shared Facilities

Nonlibrary functions within the library building have their advantages and disadvantages. One clear advantage is that the existence of other occupants in a shared facility provides the possibility of the library taking over more of the building as an alternative to building an addition or a new library building.

Some institutions are housed in a megastructure, such as Simon Fraser University, University of Wisconsin–Parkside, and Mission College in Santa Clara, California. Library expansion in such cases should be relatively easy if it was anticipated at the time of original design so that, for instance, classrooms rather than a "wet" laboratory (with piping for gas and liquids) are adjacent. Yet, even in much smaller buildings where the library is the dominant occupant, a great many other functions have been housed in the same building. These include the offices of the president, alumni secretary, classrooms, library school, audio-visual service not part of the library, student union or other food facility, university bookstore, student counseling service, university press stock, language laboratory, and campus computing facility. Even a college chapel! Classrooms have often been placed in a library with the idea that they would be removed later as the demands for space on the part of the library increased and a new separate classroom building could be made available.

Whatever the temporary occupant, this arrangement can provide the most satisfactory alternative to the task of designing and financing a new library building. With that prospect in mind, it is desirable to anticipate the greater eventual library use of the facility and therefore have it designed initially in a way so that column spaces, floor load capacity, ceiling heights, lighting, and utilities will work effectively and harmoniously once other parts of the building are available to the library. It does, however, require providing the other function a home elsewhere some day, and there are difficulties that need to be recognized in such mutual interim use of a building. These will be summarized here as if a new building were being planned, since the availability and cost of this option to take over more or all of the building may depend on the original plan.

The prime consideration is the main entrance, access, and control of exits. If book materials are to be inspected at the exit, it is desirable and almost obligatory to have a separate exit and entrance for other functions in the building. One need only consider traffic going to or from a large number of classrooms or the president's office to recognize how awkward would be a shared entrance and exit and how disturbing to library users if a sizable amount of extraneous traffic passes through or by library study quarters. Other occupants of the building should recognize that, if they must share the same entrance, they and their visitors must pass an inspection desk to see if library materials are charged out. When nonlibrary activities are assigned to a library, they should be given a separate entrance and exit. Keep in mind though that multiple building entrances can be very frustrating to the visitor if they lead to distinct functions that are not clearly defined.

Another problem that can be very serious is that the nonlibrary function may be difficult to remove at a suitable time, even when the library is in desperate need of space. If the institution's administrative staff is in the building and it is one of the most attractive buildings on the campus, this staff may not be motivated to ask for other space in spite of the fact that their remaining causes library problems. Even classrooms may be hard to remove once they are installed. The primacy of library need when the library requires the space may have been strengthened if all parties understand from the beginning the eventual assignment. The librarian must recognize institutional priorities and the difficulty of getting space with ideal timing. Thus the librarian must recognize building priorities and prove the library's case at a suitable time. It would be unreasonable for the librarian to expect to take over the nonlibrary portion when the library is only slightly pressed for space. Conversely, the library should not hold space that it does not need just for the sake of having it later when it will be desirable.

The Meyer Memorial Library at Stanford University is a case in point, having four extraneous occupants. The university chancellor has two rooms as an office on the top floor, and four language laboratories have quarters on the ground floor; all users have to go through the library exit control. In addition there are six small classrooms and an undergraduate learning assistance center (now the Center for Learning and Teaching) on the ground floor, each with its own en-

trance. Only the laboratories and classrooms were initial occupants, and after nearly twenty years the library needs are not yet more compelling than the others (fig. 2.1).

As for the physical aspects of shared space, the conversion of quarters taken over from another function may be relatively inexpensive because there are seldom major structural difficulties if the building was initially engineered to meet library requirements. For example, the floor loading and column spacing should be suitable for shelving. Lighting and ventilation will need some reconsideration, and it may be a problem to create continuity of feeling between the portion originally occupied and the section occupied at a later time. Finally, although no one location in a building that is predominately a library is best for a temporary occupant, it is well to consider one wing, a small portion of the first floor, lower-level space, and the top floor so long as separate stairs, elevator, and entrance can be arranged. Individual circumstances will lead to the best interim solution.

2.4 Collection Management

Control of the collection size may be a temporary palliative, but it needs serious consideration for two reasons. It can buy time for an institution to justify and raise funds for new space, and it also may show the administrative officers of the institution that sound use of present space has been achieved. Sound collection development policies are needed, as is wise professional judgment of which items to select and acquire. In a well-administered library, more rigorous selection may improve the quality of what is added, and it can save space.

Discarding or culling the collection may be a reasonable step, saving shelf space with only slightly more reliance on interlibrary borrowing. In many a library multiple copies must be obtained for current use but then may rest on the shelves without continuing purpose. Retention of multiple editions of encyclopedias and other large works may not be necessary. Little-used classes of books in a branch library may be appropriate in the main library. Despite the fact that it is expensive to alter catalog records as books are withdrawn or transferred from the collection, the space occupied by the average volume on the shelf is currently worth as much as ten dollars and more in some cases. Suffice it to say that a

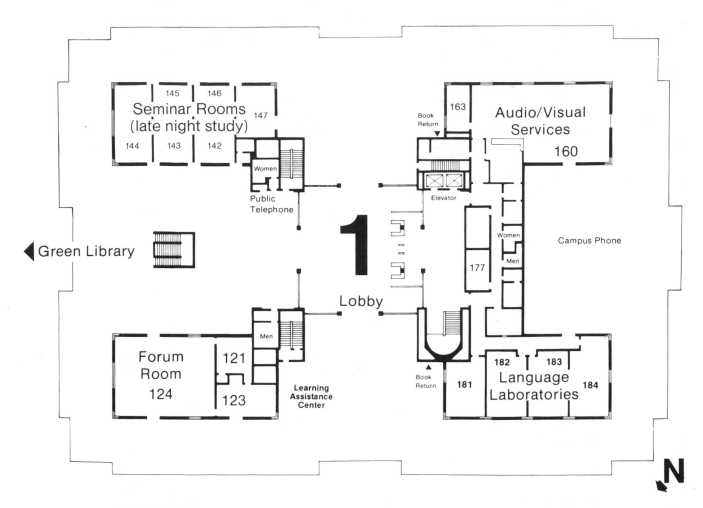

FIGURE 2.1 Stanford University, Meyer Memorial Library, first floor. This building houses principally undergraduate services. The bulk of the library accessible through the portals in the lobby is on the upper floors; two levels of basement stack are only accessible publicly through the Green Library (the main research library) to the left. Several of the nonlibrary functions are shown here on the ground floor. The southern exits from the audio-visual room and the corridor by the Language Laboratories are emergency only.

librarian ought to achieve judicious weeding in part because of the space consequences.

Library collections of materials in microform (whether it be roll or sheet) may constitute as many bibliographic items as a library has in book form. The replacement of newspapers and other materials on exceedingly bad paper is a common occurrence and as a byproduct saves the library from increasing space requirements. Some of this purchasing may be done for preservation purposes, particularly when the material is seldom used and is bulky. Most microtexts are purchased, however, because they contain the text of scarce publications, expensive sets, or manuscripts which cannot be obtained in any other way. Still, faculty, trustees, and administrative officers may regard conversion of parts of the collection to microtexts as a solution to a request for a new building. The goal of carrying the Library of Congress around in miniaturized form in a shoe box has at times been cited as preferable to a new library building. However, experience over the past sixty years has shown that this is illusory.

Materials in microformats and on optical or videodiscs can be space savers and are certainly increasing in number. Microtexts currently have a greater effect on library building design than the provision of computer terminals; yet they will seldom replace the book in any significant degree except in some colleges or science and technology libraries with severe space limitations. Journal runs, for example, can be replaced in microform with great space savings.

While many libraries find space advantages in microtexts and probably will increasingly in optical discs, one should keep in mind that there are some offsetting factors. The process of transferring printed materials to microfilm is costly. The cataloging of the item is every bit as expensive as it was in the original format. Environmental conditions appropriate to microfilm may be more difficult to obtain. Any browsing or quick reference is difficult. Ambulatory use of a microform is impossible, though many libraries make available fiche-to-fiche copiers and portable readers. Reader access is impeded where it has been necessary to rely on staff fetching of a particular item. Needing specialized reading quarters and arrangements for housing, microtexts are and will remain a very important supplement to printed collections of books and journals, but they are rarely a substantial replacement for library space needs. Optical and videodiscs may have a significant effect on library operations if their costs can be afforded; however, most of the disadvantages of microtexts also apply to videodiscs.

The handling of seldom-used materials is a different matter. Occasionally a relatively unused research collection may be offered as a gift or deposit by one library to another which does have an active academic program in that field. Placing seldom-used materials in auxiliary facilities, deposit libraries, or a shared facility like the Center for Research Libraries can be helpful for local space pressures. Judgment of what materials are little used and could be removed from the active collection is a matter of discretion. The published literature on weeding, relegation and collection management can help one work toward a suitable conclusion for any particular institution.

Temporary removal of certain sets, serial runs, archival materials, or subject classes to some other campus building may also provide breathing space for a few years while a building is being financed and constructed. One must remember the academic justification for parts of a collection and for the effect that weeding or relocating may have on the teaching and research program which cannot be quantified but which may nonetheless be harmful. This caution needs careful consideration.

2.5 Stack Reformation

The previous section dealt with management actions which give at least temporary relief and, in some instances, are an indication of desperation in storing collections. The physical alteration of the bookstack into a reformed pattern is another extreme action and one which is certain to be quite expensive. The means of reaching the highest stack density need careful analysis because of operational problems as well as the cost entailed. Compact shelving is given more extensive treatment in Section 6.3.

As was mentioned in Section 2.2, one may find certain empty walls in a bookstack where shelves can be added. If there is more than one main aisle, it may be possible to fill in all but one, so long as the building code requirements for exiting are still met. One may fit vertical extensions onto the stack columns so that more shelves can be hung near the ceiling, though stools will need to be conveniently located. In these instances, changes can often be made without a structural engineer or a building permit. Of course, the added weight, sprinkler clearance, lighting, air circulation, and other features may need review by experts.

In rare instances, usually where such an expansion was preplanned, a mezzanine or second tier can be installed in a bookstack. Still more ambitious would be narrowing range aisles to the minimum permitted by code or for wheelchair access, not less than 26 in. (660 mm). (California standards for handicapped access require a 32 in., or 313 mm, aisle. As a result floor space can increase 10 percent over what was previously normal spacing. If this is an unwanted limitation, a variance may be required.) Even though individuals in wheelchairs cannot normally reach the upper shelves, they are often able to pull themselves up by holding onto shelves. They may also need to go through the aisle to reach a carrel or to go from one part of the floor to another. Changing range aisles, of course, entails emptying at least the range that is being moved and probably replacing the carpet or patching the floor as well as relocating lights, unless they were running perpendicular to the range. In the case of the Yale Divinity Library, narrower aisles were achieved at the same time that the ranges were turned 90 degrees, a technique that may save on lighting changes. In these instances a structural engineer should advise on the safety of floor loading, and a building permit may be required. For adding a second tier, additional coordination of vertical communication will be necessary. Where the second tier is technically a mezzanine (i.e., it does not have direct emergency egress to enclosed fire stairs), it is limited in some codes to an area equal to one-third of the basic floor area.

It should be stressed that the more extensive of these reformations of the bookstack should be undertaken only after very careful analysis. They always cost a great deal for a modest amount of additional shelving. They increase the floor loading. They may detract from the good feel of architectural spaces. (At Wheaton College, Norton, Mass., a 1923 central atrium of classic beauty was filled with bookstacks in 1961, an expedient which was reversed only 19 years later.) The traffic patterns may be made much more difficult, not only for those in wheelchairs. The movement of book trucks in very narrow aisles may be impossible, requiring stack shelvers to hand-carry books from a main aisle down the entire length of the range aisle for reshelving. Two persons may not be able to pass in an aisle if it is as little as 22 in. (560 mm). An occasional oversized book will overhang the shelf and be hit by shoulders, hips and book trucks. The lighting, which adequately reached the bottom shelves, may become inadequate for narrow aisles even when properly positioned. Even ventilation would be slightly impaired. Operational considerations, public relations, architectural honesty, as well as results of a cost study should be weighed.

Movable compact shelving is a still more expensive alternative. It comes in various forms and the costs as well as advantages and disadvantages of each design and operational and safety aspects should be carefully studied. European libraries, such as Cambridge University and Newcastle upon Tyne, have used them for many years for public collections. More recently they have been used in many locations: for example, Rice University for rare books, the Law Library in the Library of Congress James Madison Building, and Stanford University for microtexts and a public collection of less heavily used medical works. The University of Illinois in 1984 occupied the sixth stack addition to its central library. On seven levels, this addition, with entirely movable compact shelving, is air conditioned and open for direct use by faculty and all advanced students.

Movable shelving seems to be widely accepted now so long as the cost of such installations is justified—where a building addition is not feasible or cannot be afforded for a good many years, where the site is ideal and conversion of adjacent space is not an option, where real estate values are high, and where existing physical conditions of column spacing and floor loading capacity permit it to be considered. In an older building being remodeled, the basement may be the only level that can structurally handle the weight. Since it has been demonstrated in Europe from the 1960s that compact shelving can be used by the public, there will be much more use of this shelving in academic libraries, though not for heavily used collections. Depending on pre-existing conditions or the arrangements in a normal stack, the increase in capacity may be anywhere from 50 percent to as much as 130 percent. Where this has long-term importance, movable compact shelving may be an excellent and cost-justifiable solution.

As early as 1878, an English librarian designed a bookcase attached by a hinge to another stationary bookcase. The user then had to swing open the outer case as if opening a cabinet door. At least one shelving manufacturer today produces a similar product. The movable case can have a single face accessible from the outside, or it can be a double case, so that when opened one can utilize the shelving on the back of the movable section as well as have access to the fixed section behind. These cases may have a floor wheel at the side of the movable case away from the hinge, and it will often have a handle to facilitate moving. The weight in a double-face hinged case filled with books is of course considerable, so much that it may be difficult for a slight individual to open the movable section. The installation of this type in the Center for Research Libraries, Chicago, has worked quite well since 1951.

Another type has movable sections which roll laterally on wheels or overhead tracks. Perhaps the earliest example of it was installed in the Bodleian Library at Oxford and dates from early in this century, although it was replaced when the 1946 building expansion was designed.

The most common movable compact shelving throughout the world is now the type where entire ranges of bookshelves move on tracks running perpendicular to the range. From Australia to Scandinavia, they are now widely used. The shelves are fixed on heavy carriages which move along tracks. The track in new buildings is mounted flush into the floor, whereas in installations in existing buildings it sits above it. On top of the carriage are standard bookshelf units with rigid structure. Movement may be by hand lever, a crank, or electrically driven by motor. Safety features are incorporated in all which are motorized, generally including at least a kickplate which automatically cuts off electricity if a book on the floor or someone's foot is in the way, torque limiting devices in the drive mechanism, and weight-sensitive flooring so that the case will not operate if any individual is standing on it (sensed by microswitches under the floor). In the 1980 Library of Congress Madison Building movable-shelving installation, there are louvered end panels and canopied tops to facilitate air circulation, three-phase 208-volt motors for great reliability, full solid-state controls, dual reset buttons, tracks set flush with the finished floor, and an additional safety arrangement using solenoid-activated brakes on the motor shaft which must be released before a shelf unit can be moved.

These movable compact units have some problems which are being reduced by manufacturers in Europe, North America, and Japan. Some shivering or other movement may result in an occasional volume dropping off the top shelf. A book that has inadvertently been shelved in front of another and may project out beyond the shelf can be crushed when the unit moves against the adjacent unit. An individual's hand can be hurt if, when not standing within the unit, one attempts manually to stop a moving electrically driven unit by putting a hand between two ranges. This latter risk can be reduced by the addition of a pressure-sensitive strip along the edge of the end panels which will stop the motors if touched, a safety feature offered by some manufacturers. Of course, anyone who stood on a bottom shelf to reach the top shelf would neither have the kickplate nor the floor weight device as protections. Slipping gears may become standard since the torque-limiting device will prevent serious injury. The technology is advancing.

These motorized units are gaining in popularity. In many cases it may be possible to demonstrate that the cost for added capacity is less than the cost for new space and more standard stack arrangements. Since it requires from ten seconds to twenty seconds to open aisles in an average installation, and only one person can use the block of ranges at a time, it is clear that movable compact systems are for collections that are seldom used or that are used by staff only. This limitation can be partially offset by creation of smaller blocks of movable shelving, each with its own open aisle. The spacing of stack columns, the need for earthquake bracing, electrical requirements, and the arrangement of lighting are details to be studied. Floor loading requirements of 250 pounds per sq ft (11.970 kN/m²) are required, although some materials such as phonograph records may require as much as 300 pounds per sq ft (14.364 kN/m²).

Other compact arrangements have been tried from time to time. A drawer-type unit mounted on shelves was available during the third quarter of this century and before. The tiered stack in the 1919 Main Library (now Cecil H. Green Library) at Stanford had such drawers which were removed in the 1970s because they were difficult to use. Labyrinthian mechanized bookstacks have also been designed where an operator at a keyboard instructs a mechanical picker which bin to retrieve. Rotterdam University in Holland and the Medical Library at Ohio State University have installed this type.

In considering compact shelving, it is essential to balance the consequences of operational conditions against the economic factors. Browsing is difficult in most of these systems and quite impossible in a few. This shelving may be very good for archive boxes but difficult for very large volumes. Some compact shelving requires fixed spacing of shelves, and, therefore, classified order of books may be difficult to maintain. Where the compact shelving will constitute housing for a separate auxiliary collection, the cost of changing catalog records and the extra staff to service such an installation needs to be considered. The possibility of further expansion into another unit of compact shelving also needs consideration.

As with other aspects of library planning, the total operational costs may be difficult to determine. There is not only the determination of book storage costs on a per volume basis when compared to land value and the cost per cubic foot of the building space, but also the difference in lighting costs, ventilation, staffing, and the effect on the library clientele. It may be found that the short-term savings from compact shelving are nonexistent, particularly when factors other than initial construction costs are considered. A cost study should be undertaken to aid in the decision, and local political or budgetary factors will often have an influence as well. For example, there may be an institutional budget for equipment while funding for a new facility may be impossible. Phasing of equipment additions to an existing space may be easier to achieve than phasing new space.

2.6 Decentralization of Resources

In planning library spaces any decision to decentralize the book collections must take into account the academic master plan for the campus and the direction in which interdisciplinary areas are moving. Parking facilities and on-campus transportation may be a factor. Other factors include campus geography, size and strength of departments, campus politics, fundraising opportunities, the need for large associated spaces such as studios or labs, and the bibliographic separability of a subject field without the need for extensive duplication of materials among library units. Decisions are made more complex by the fact that traditional disciplinary boundaries keep shifting. Fields change and today's discoveries become the historic base on which tomorrow's research efforts are built. This advancement occurs both in the traditional disciplines and in their interconnections, which themselves often emerge as new disciplines.

This section does not argue the merits of decentralization. Furthermore, the planning for branch library quarters will be dealt with elsewhere. This section merely addresses decentralization as a way of postponing the necessity for a major central-library addition or even an entirely new building. The Harvard University Library has, in fact, been moving toward increased decentralization for nearly 150 years. As late as 1887, 89 percent of the collections were in a central research library. Yet by 1927 there were as many volumes in branches as in the Widener building. Today hardly more than a third are in the central research collection, and even those are divided among the central cluster of library buildings known as the Widener, Houghton, Lamont, and Pusey buildings, together with those items stored across the river in the New England Deposit Library.

The controversy about the desirability of physical centralization versus decentralization continues on many campuses. Most large and long-established universities of high quality have many branch libraries. Several dozen and sometimes as many as a hundred may be distributed across the campus. The University of Tokyo has had as many as 312 different libraries. A few have achieved substantial centralization, among them being Johns Hopkins, Iowa State, Michigan State, Oklahoma State, Rice, Southern Illinois, Tulane, and the University of California campuses at San Diego and Santa Barbara. In some cases the main or central library is physically restricted by the site but may be of good quality, and so branch libraries are unavoidable.

Although there are very clear advantages in a physically unified and logically classified collection, most university libraries have been decentralized to some extent. This is also true in some colleges. Subjects that frequently have been given their own quarters are art, music, engineering, the sciences, and professional schools such as business, divinity, education, law, and medicine. Completely desirable or not, decentralization does commonly occur. Furthermore, one can look to old and respected universities such as Cambridge, Oxford, Harvard, and Yale to see that dozens of physical branches would seem to be inevitable in the course of time. What has happened in those universities is only a degree more developed than in those like Cornell, Michigan, Texas, Columbia, Berkeley, Ohio State, Illinois, and UCLA. Such physical decentralization can be a method for easing pressure on the central library building. Conversely, the creation of a new central facility, such as a central science library, may ease the pressure on a number of branches.

Multidisciplinary and interdisciplinary interests argue for a minimum of decentralization or at least for striving to keep decentralization limited to large units where possible. It would in theory be desirable for an early fragmentation to be a combined science branch. If it is properly located and of a size that justifies at least three or four staff members with at least ten or fifteen thousand volumes, the space may serve until there is justification to fragment again into a life sciences and a physical sciences library, and one of them is moved out to some other strategic location on campus. Those two might serve for another generation or more until further growth requires that the physical science library break into physics, chemistry, or the mathematical sciences, one of those staying in the original physical sciences branch and the other having a new location. Though such a planned decentralization is logical because of its deliberate progression, in practice the availability of remaining land and existing buildings, the clout of certain disciplines and their fundraising capacity, student course enrollment shifts, together with the general difficulty of adequate forecasting—all result in compromises from generation to generation from the ideal development plan. The logical planning of major branch units has at times been done well, as at Yale, University of California at Davis, Florida State, and Georgia.

The separation of major research collections is in distinction to the development of small departmental libraries which serve as "working" or convenience collections, sometimes being an adjunct of a seminar or laboratory, and duplicate in small numbers the core book collection held in the extensive research collections elsewhere in the library system. These departmental libraries are seldom spin-offs from the main library; they certainly are not satellites created because of central space problems. In contrast, a decision to separate from the central research collections an art library or an engineering library may be based either on academic reasons or space problems in the main library, or quite commonly on both factors when combined with financial feasibility. In more than a few institutions, a professional library or the main library has moved to new quarters and, with advanced planning, the released space can serve well as quarters for a branch library or for a book storage facility.

If the library can monitor the shelf capacity of each branch unit and its rate of growth, and thus predict the date when the shelves of each unit will be full to working capacity, it will help academic and space planners determine whether other campus buildings or newly planned quarters may be utilized to meet this need. In anticipating such physical fragmentation it is desirable for the library to keep in close touch with the academic and campus space planning offices. A meeting each year with the appropriate academic staff may elicit indication of what is anticipated in five or ten years for physical relocation of the social sciences or some of the physical sciences. It may reveal where new buildings are planned which may create the possibility of

adding a library to solve library problems elsewhere in the system or of relocating a branch library from inadequate space into better quarters. Planning officers who are aware of difficulties in various disciplines may put such facts together with problems faced by the library to create new space or remodeled quarters which can serve to solve both problems. In any event, the library needs to be aware of nonlibrary projects that are in the thinking stage so that its long-term plans fit in with campus programs.

Remote or Auxiliary Facilities. Storage should be considered when a library has many books that are used infrequently yet are judged to be worth keeping. Such books can be housed more inexpensively in a building on less valuable real estate, and perhaps in a remote structure especially designed for them, than if they are kept in expensive library buildings in the academic center. (California estimated the building cost at one quarter the cost of normal shelving for the same number of volumes.) Such auxiliary-facilities exist at the University of London, Queensland, Sydney, Western Australia, Michigan, and Iowa State; specially designed facilities have been used by Harvard, Cornell, Princeton, Texas, Yale, and the University of California to serve its northern campuses and other libraries in the northern half of the state. Most of these facilities are within a couple of miles, usually on the edge, of campus. However, the University of California building is in Richmond, six miles to the north of the Berkeley campus, and the University of London Repository is some twenty miles (33 km) west, in Egham. These auxiliary or storage facilities have a high density of book shelving, sometimes utilizing double-depth shelving, very narrow aisles, long ranges, and shelving by size divisions in order to approach maximum density. The type of material located there may be almost any which is seldom used, including archival material, manuscripts, superseded editions, foreign-language materials, newspapers, dissertations, old textbooks, etc. With use of online public catalogs and automated circulation systems, infrequently used materials can be charged out to storage, obviating the costs of changing card catalog records (fig. 2.2).
Cooperative storage with other libraries offers further administrative advantages through joint management and the possibil-

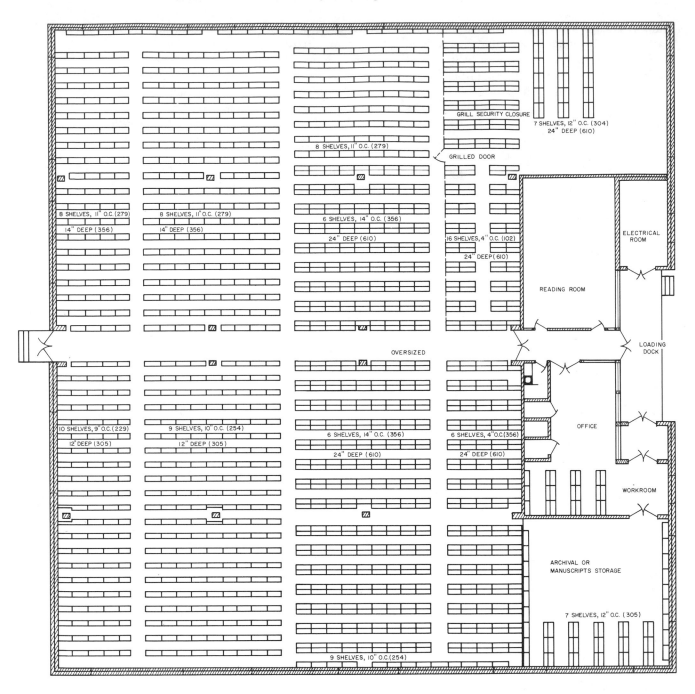

FIGURE 2.2 Princeton University, William Watson Smith Library of 1968. Materials in this "annex" on the Forrestal Campus are shelved by size in subject order, and they can be paged from the central libraries or used on site. Ceiling height is sufficient to add a second level in the future.

ity of shared transportation and elimination of some duplication among items placed there. Examples cooperatively owned are the New England Deposit Library and the Center for Research Libraries. The University of California northern facility is singly owned and managed but jointly used.

The future of campus auxiliary facilities seems assured. The size of college and university holdings and the cost of buildings create pressures toward this end. The future growth in the number of shared or cooperative storage libraries is less certain since the administrative advantages may be offset by the disadvantage of distance. Whatever option is judged best for a particular institution, these facilities provide relief, perhaps enough to obviate the need for a new library building. It would not be surprising if, just as the Harvard University Library found 50 years ago that 50 percent of its materials were not in the central library, the larger university libraries may have 50 percent of their collections in a secondary-access facility within a decade or so into the next century.

2.7 Increased Interdependence

Since the early 1930s and particularly since the 1960s, interinstitutional cooperatives and consortia have mushroomed in North America. A number of these focus on cooperative purchase arrangements that acquire an expensive item or a hard-to-find item which is shelved in one location for sharing among all in that cooperating group. The Farmington Plan was a prime example, followed by the National Program for Acquisitions and Cataloging, which concentrated scarce resources obtained in the national interest for housing in the Library of Congress. Regional and national programs which ease the local rate of acquisition are likely to be significant cost-beneficial ways of maintaining access to research resources without requiring frequent additions to library buildings.

Various models are still being developed and the exact shape of the future is uncertain. However, it can be asserted that increased interdependence among research libraries within a country or continent seems essential over the decades ahead, given the economics of higher education. The Center for Research Libraries has provided important service since 1949, backstopping all of its members with esoteric and scarce research resources as well as more common materials. Since 1975, the Research Libraries Group has approached the same problem on a distributed basis, whereby each of its members maintains selected subject collecting responsibilities to assure all members future access to and preservation of those resources, with a commitment to the partnership just as reliable as if those resources were in fact owned in great duplication, with one copy in each institution. The world has also looked to the British Library Lending Division in Boston Spa as an extraordinary achievement and a service concept which is discussed and may be followed in other countries; the BLLD already provides very considerable international service from its striking and specially designed 1972 building. Each of these approaches has its costs. They are not free alternatives to a new library building; nevertheless, they can offer effective remote access to seldom-used resources on a more economical basis than acquiring and storing them locally. They constitute but one of the options for mitigating the need for more library book collection space.

2.8 The Basis for a Judgment

Before embarking on a library building addition, a major renovation, or a new structure, any institution must give thorough consideration to building costs and the costs of administrative alternatives. Innovative solutions may obviate the need for construction, or at least postpone the day when new construction is needed, and may save an institution hundreds of thousands of dollars.

The best way to determine probable costs when considering the above possibilities is to have the existing structure carefully examined by a reliable builder and to obtain an estimate of costs for modernization and remodeling from the builder after consultation with an architect. Questions of floor loading capacities must, of course, be resolved by a structural engineer.

Let us take a hypothetical example. A library finds that the stack capacity of its building can be increased by 100,000 volumes if compact shelving is installed in an unused basement. This shelving would postpone the need for a new building for an additional ten years, but it would require the installation of a new stairway, sprinklers throughout the basement, and the removal of an unused coal bin. Old heating and water pipes would have to be torn out; a concrete floor should be given a new floor covering; new lights would have to be installed; and the ceiling would need refinishing and repainting. The cost of these alterations plus the new shelves might amount to as much as it would cost to build an addition to the library large enough to house the same number of volumes. An addition might be preferable.

However, other factors may need to be considered. From the point of view of financing, it may be easier to obtain funds for renovation than for a new construction, although this is not always true. Possibly only a small addition to the building is practicable at the present time and a larger one will be more feasible at some later date. A small addition now may use enough of the site so as to create very difficult design problems for a later larger addition. Yet, considering the rate of growth of the collection, the financial condition of the university or college, and indeed the national economic circumstances at that time, temporary expedients may be worthwhile if in fact not necessary. Renovation of existing space may be more easily phased to match a financing program.

On the other hand, providing for 100,000 volumes in the old basement may take care of only a fraction of the total needs for space that can be foreseen in the near future. A new building may be the only good solution, and, if so, renovation of the basement may be an expensive way of providing space that will become nearly useless as soon as the new building is constructed. If the new building will cost $1,500,000, each year that its construction is postponed might be regarded as saving the income on that sum. This income, at 10 percent, is $150,000, which means that renovation of the basement at the cost of $500,000 may be an economical course of action if it enables the library to postpone construction for more than four years. Prospective increases in building costs and trends in business cycles should not be forgotten.

The practical nature of fundraising at the time may be a crucial point, as are institutional priorities for financing new space. Finally, a good new building ought to enable a library to provide better services than are possible in an old one. It is difficult indeed to estimate how much this improvement is worth to the institution. All of these financial aspects need to be taken into account in making the decision.

Many a librarian may be sure, both before and after reading the above paragraphs, that only a new building or an addition can provide space of the kind and quantity needed. But the librarian's position will be stronger if, before asking for new construction, he or she has carefully investigated the alternatives, instead of waiting for others to do it. One ought to be prepared to demonstrate that the alternatives have been considered and that they will not be satisfactory, if that is the case. One ought to be able to show that the space now available is not being wasted and that the cost of continuing to live in the present building, including the cost of required rehabilitation work and the impaired efficiency in services, is greater than the cost of new construction. In the course of examining all the possibilities, the librarian may discover means of postponing such construction; if not, the examination ought to have provided convincing arguments for it.

3

Planning
Preliminaries

How much justification for new space is needed? Nearly every institution is pressed for space. If by chance it has enough total space, it will probably lack the right kind of space to serve as a library, laboratory, museum, or classroom. Space is a problem in both old and new institutions. The librarian must prove that the library need is greater than that of others and that giving the library additional space will be better educational policy for the institution than making any other arrangement. If the case is strong but not overwhelming, the library may have to wait until one or more other projects are achieved, or it may have to wait a few years until other conditions—a considerable increase in student enrollment, a substantial growth in the book collections, or new program requirements for which no space is at present available in the library—make the need more persuasive.

Undoubtedly there will be occasions when the library has great difficulty because of lack of immediate support. It will not, however, achieve any good purpose, and certainly not

engender support from the administrative officers of the institution, if the librarian presses unreasonably for space too early, asks for too much, or holds onto unneeded space for even a few years while someone else's need for it is urgent.

In the psychology of most institutions with a reasonable and stable administration, the librarian may, in fact, gain more support in the long run by being accommodating of others who have immediate pressing needs. In some instances the retiring president has been given a suite of rooms carved out of a library space, or a counseling or learning assistance center and an alumni office were added within the library. There is no point in the library being so bullish as to keep a secondary reading room which has one or two persons in it from time to time when nearby there is an administrative office of the institution with people in crowded conditions and very heavy traffic. After all, the library is not independent of the institution in which it operates and which it is designed to serve. The librarian needs to take a long-term view, as must institutional officers. True, the librarian must be the advocate for the library and press the case in timely and effective fashion, knowing that it may require several years to solve a library space problem when it does become urgent. Yet the library can lose out in larger terms if it does not recognize that it is but one member of a family of functions that make up the college or university.

One must keep in mind that the library takes its place in the long-range academic plan. That academic plan and its physical requirements form the touchstone. The library program and the decisions on major library policy issues must be based on the needs of the institution, a statement which also needs careful thought with respect to the independent research institution.

Comparative statistics can sometimes help people understand the circumstance. Comparisons of occupancy loads among various libraries of a university can be informative. Comparison with peer institutions is almost always of value, more so if one looks poor by comparison with the others and much less so if one is among the leaders. In the former case, data from other institutions and their libraries may show how much one needs to achieve to be similar in library space and presumably competitive academically. If one can use a dozen college libraries of institutions which are of about the same character, size, and program, one may analyze book space, reading space, staff quarters, and gross and net floor area. If one's own situation is in the lower half in terms of quantity, the story may be quite telling. For an institution in the upper portion, one asserts the concept of striving for excellence, looks at fewer peer institutions, and selects one where the comparison is striking, or one may need to address the local situation without reliance on such comparative data. In this case the complaints of students and faculty can be the most important evidence, as can traffic problems, lack of security, hazardous conditions which could lead to lawsuits, and the effect of library circumstances on the retention of faculty or the ability to attract graduate students. These and similar consequential matters may form the basis for the justification.

But a word of caution. Valid statistical comparisons are difficult; the argument can backfire if the data are not demonstrably sound. For example, stack capacity and current occupancy are not compared to any national standard. The determination of occupancy by readers can mean one condition if it is drawn over a twelve-month period and a different picture if only peak use is tabulated or if it is taken by only sampling in the middle part of the semester. There are varying ways of determining net floor area, so one must be careful in such definitions; the definitions of gross and net floor area are dealt with elsewhere in this volume. At this point it may suffice to say the obvious: comparative statistics must be drawn up on a comparable basis, and when well done, they can be more convincing than many pages of prose and passion.

3.1 Character and Nature of the Academic Institution

The initial step in a building project is that of securing the support of principal academic officers. This phase may require one or a few meetings with a dean, a provost, or the president of the institution. Or it may require a document to be prepared, reviewed, possibly revised, and approved by a faculty library committee, a library staff group, a committee on institutional program priorities, a committee on undergraduate or graduate studies, a committee on buildings and physical plant, a committee on traffic and parking, a committee on financial planning and priorities, a fundraising council, and the trustees. It is essential to have a clear grasp of the character and the nature of the institution before determining what should be the general library solution. Within the context of the particular nature of the institution, there will be certain major policy decisions needed with respect to the library itself. These constitute the fifth stage in a building project, as outlined in Chapter 1.

This treatment is divided into two aspects. The first is a set of seven characteristics of the institution which are likely to have the greatest influence on the library design. The second treats how to cope with a constantly changing set of conditions in the institution itself as well as in the library program and its administrative organization.

The first part provides brief comments on the seven most important institutional characteristics:

the kind and nature of the institution
the student mix in terms of educational preparation, economic background, age, the nature of commuting and residential patterns

the size and diversity of graduate programs
the number and fields of research institutes
the nature of developing or emerging academic programs
the physical setting of the campus and the nature of its physical development.

The Kind of Institution. Institutions have significant differences of purpose and character one from another if they are junior colleges, senior colleges, universities, or universities with a particularly heavy emphasis on research. Likewise, there are distinct differences if the institution focuses on the liberal arts or aims to concentrate on science and technology, religious training, legal or medical education, music theory and performance practice, or if it is a "service school" such as is supported by the federal government for preparing persons for a particular career in the federal service. There must be a clear understanding of the institution's stated mission, its specialized character, and its objectives for the next ten or so years.

The Student Mix. It is important to know the percentage of students who are enrolled in lower-division programs, upper-division programs, extension programs, professional preparation, and graduate programs in the pure or theoretical disciplines. It is also significant to understand the percentage who have had strong academic preparation before coming to the institution and the percentage who may come from underpriviledged parts of society and who may not have received good preparation for effectively utilizing libraries. Of less importance is the percentage from foreign countries, particularly those whose native language differs from that used in the institution. To a lesser extent the percentage who are over twenty-five or thirty years old may be indicative of somewhat different behavior and social needs which may affect library services. One also needs to know the probable trends in the total number of students that the institution anticipates in the next decade or two in each major program or subject. Each of these will be important in understanding the needs of students.

The Commuting and Residential Mix. It is similarly clear that there are differing library requirements if the institution is mostly serving a commuting population or a campus-residential population. The extent to which the on-campus residents are in sororities and fraternities in contrast to dormitories can be of significance, and institutions which have educational and cultural programs within the residence halls (such as theme houses devoted to Latin American studies or East European culture) also create different conditions for the library. To a lesser extent the commuting patterns can make a difference, as can the routes frequented as students enter and leave the campus.

Graduate Programs. As suggested above, it will be very important to determine the extent of the graduate and professional programs in the sciences, technology, humanities, social sciences, and other areas. Also it is important whether fields such as English, art, music, and drama focus on the literature and history of those disciplines or whether they are concerned with criticism and performance, such as would be the focus in studio programs, stage practice, and creative writing. Graduate programs are also affected more than are undergraduate programs by the proportion of students who are taking full-time studies and whether the part-time students are employed on campus or in occupations in the surrounding community.

Research Institutes. There is another dimension of considerable importance if the institution has created one or a number of institutes or centers. These programs generally are devoted to theoretical or applied research and provide little or no instruction. They include faculty among their senior staff together with research associates, post-doctoral fellows, and research assistants often on foundation or federal grants. These institutes are a way of drawing together faculty from a number of departments to concentrate on a particular social problem, technological challenge, industrial concern, or the like. Examples might be a center for environmental studies, a center for research on women, or an institute for research in international studies.

Factors to be considered are the distance of such institutes from libraries with related research collections, the existence of library collections in the institutes, the degree of permanency the institutes seem likely to have in the institution, the source of funding, and the nature of their programs.

Changing Academic Programs. Except in periods of economic depression and decreasing enrollments, institutions frequently add courses of instruction. Even in depressed circumstances, changes are made to address priority educational needs. These changes come about because of the dynamic nature of many academic disciplines and as a response to societal changes. Thus a traditional program in biology may give birth to a program in biophysics, another in the bio-psychology of youth development, and a third in human biology. Deans and presidents respond to or support these changes, often planning over five or more years in order to bring a program to maturity, or to achieve a combination or splintering, or to attract a young expert in the new field seen as gaining great importance in the decade ahead. Growth or reduction in continuing education programs also has its consequences. An understanding of these prospects is important in understanding the character and nature of the institution and its possible changes in the years ahead.

The Campus Physical Plant. The final important factor is the density of campus buildings and the degree of high-rise construction and important lines of sight. The means and paths for moving people on campus above ground level or on grade or underground are related aspects. The environment is significant—whether the location has severe cold, a great deal of ice and frost, a heavy rainy season, an exceedingly hot sun, or earthquakes, as well as what the prevailing breezes are, and the general frequency and nature of storms. The institution's central or distributed maintenance and caretaking also affects the need for a library supply room, maintenance staff quarters, tool shop, etc.

These and other issues are all important to a general understanding of the nature of the academic institution and thus of the character of library facilities which are appropriate for that institution. The seven cited areas would be quite obvious to those who have worked in the institution for several years and have been alert to its policies and operations. It is important for the architects and planners to understand them thoroughly. The more one understands about different institutions, even of the same kind, the more it will be evident how very different institutions are one from another. The difference in physical, ed-

ucational, cultural, and social environment between Harvard and Yale is great, or between any other two such as a Columbia, Chicago, Duke, and Rice. Even within state systems, one will find very marked differences, for example, among the campuses of the California State University and College System and certainly among the campuses of the University of California. Community colleges and junior colleges may also each have a distinct character.

What are the optimal responses when an institution is rapidly evolving or changing in character? Generally, one should: (1) plan to accommodate each of the existing academic programs which seem to be reasonably well entrenched; (2) probably try to avoid expensive and special accommodations for programs whose future and financial support are doubtful; and (3) try to plan for reasonable flexibility in all of the planned accommodations. Remember that the building is being planned for a great many years in the future and it must be responsive to those educational conditions just now emerging which will be important factors five and ten years from now or beyond. The librarian should ask senior academic officers for clarification when there seems to be uncertainty about future expectations or when there are contrary or competing statements.

What if there are rapid changes in the current library program? Since libraries are not static enterprises, there will be certain conditions quite different when the building is occupied than existed when the building was first being planned. Within a few years after occupancy, still other changes will come about, and changes will occur in the future. The library may be starting a considerable program in bibliographic instruction; a new government documents department may be intended; the loan department may be renamed the circulation division; the library may now have one associate director and later utilize three assistant directors.

Those planning the building should recognize that such changes are to be expected. One cannot plan extra space just on the chance that in five or ten years this or that new program will require extra staff. Yet, similarly, it would be unfortunate to plan without any foresight, leaving no options for responding to newly needed library space adjustments. There are no simple answers to this quandary. The obvious response is to build in at least a small amount of flexible contingency in those parts of the building where conditions are most likely to change. Flexibility in space allocations is an obvious need for the future—in carefully selected spaces in order to leave open some options. Generally speaking, one should try to project the probable requirements of the library as they will exist in the next ten to fifteen years and design the building program that will best meet those functions when the building is ready for occupancy and for a reasonable number of years thereafter.

One must try to freeze the library program in terms of areas, spaces, offices, and built-in furnishings—as it is envisioned at the time of building occupancy and immediately thereafter—and stay with that plan once it has been signed and given to the business officers and the architect. The librarian should not change program requirements in the course of building design unless there are very strong arguments to do so. Changes take extra time, they are certain to cost someone money, and they lead to uncertainty if not confusion in the entire planning process. Before the plans are finished, almost every architect will try to accept requested changes and may even recommend some when they are clearly advantageous. The desired changes must be brought up before the architects and engineers have detailed the space that is to be changed.

3.2 Major Policy Decisions before Detailed Planning Begins

Once the college or university administration understands that it has a library space problem and once the general academic approval to correct that problem has been received, it is time for serious planning to begin. Until such a general understanding has been arrived at by major administrative officers and perhaps by the board of trustees, it may be a waste of time for the librarian to do detailed planning. An academic need has to be understood and a high priority assigned to it. At that stage some effort at master planning to address the major issues will be needed. At least fifteen major policy decisions need then to be resolved before going further. Only if these have been decided by the institution should planning progress to the programming phase. Site considerations then become a crucial matter, as will be dealt with in Chapter 11.

Answers to the following policy questions may affect the whole enterprise. Advice on each numbered question is given here, or in other chapters in a few cases.

Can a building be avoided or delayed? This is treated in Chapter 2. Length of time for which to plan? This also is in Chapter 2. How will future growth be handled? This is treated in Chapter 9. What site is desired and logical? This is treated in Chapter 9.

1. Is the financing strategy clear and is there a fixed cost ceiling?

2. Should branches be centralized or decentralized?

3. Are faculty offices and classrooms to be included?

4. Will nonlibrary functions be included?

5. Will the library house a rapidly growing (research) collection or a more stable collection?

6. Are the bookstacks to be open or closed access, and is the book collection to be interspersed with the general accommodations for study and reading?

7. How will security and supervision be provided?

8. Is a divisional plan of service to be used?

9. What amount of seating is desired? Is smoking allowed?

10. Are automation and audio-visual services projected?

11. Is functionalism to take precedence over grandeur?

1. *Financing strategy.* The financing strategy provides such overriding constraints that it needs to be in the forefront of one's mind. No matter how persuasive the need, if the funds cannot be obtained, there will be no new construction. If the institution is embarking on a fundraising campaign of several years, the trustees may have made strategy decisions about how much effort to expend for scholarship aid, endowed faculty chairs, physical plant, or new programs. That approach sets a ceiling on the sum to be sought in the course of the campaign. If there are state or federal dollars involved, there may be automatic legislative limits set by virtue of a per capita assignment to an institution. If one prominent donor has an interest in the library, it certainly can have an effect on the goal on which the institution sets its sights. In any event there needs to be some guidance from financial officers about what the maximum and the strategy will be. Can the library be the most expensive project in that decade,

or the largest building the institution has undertaken? On the basis of experience, can individuals and foundations be counted on to provide certain percentages of the total cost and so many gifts in each range of donation for a project of this type? When and in what way is it best to launch the fundraising?

2. *Branches.* In universities and very large colleges where the present building is outgrown or where the campus is very extensive, collections may be decentralized, as is the case at the University of Texas (fig. 3.1). If this is done, there may be a central or main library for the institution and separate departmental teaching libraries. Or there may be a research library and a separate undergraduate library. It may be desirable to bring some or all branches into a proposed new main library in order to economize on staff and operating costs, reduce duplication among collections, and serve interdisciplinary needs in better fashion. As noted in Chapter 2, decentralization can take the form of providing separate quarters for the bulk of library collections in fields like music, art, or the sciences—fields where a relationship to laboratories, studios and performance quarters, or museums is an advantage. Decentralization can take the form of one central science library or the subject can be broken down into the life sciences, physical sciences, earth sciences or broken down further by discipline. The variations here are many and the impact on annual operating budgets can be great. Local campus circumstances must dictate whether a centralized library is best or whether a carefully planned program of decentralization is warranted.

Since library space is added by significant increments, it may be the strategy to centralize to a considerable extent when a main library or major branch can be provided, cope with the next twenty to fifty years by gradual decentralization, and then, in the next phase of library development, plan for some increase again in centralization. The academic consequences of doing this may be harmful, however, and it is far better to have a sound academic plan to guide the physical development rather than for the reverse to take place.

For the next decade or two it seems reasonable that undergraduate libraries will continue to be provided in at least some of the larger universities. Only in very few will separate library buildings be provided for rare books and manuscripts and for archives. There will be a greatly increasing number of institutions using auxiliary or storage facilities. Generally speaking one can predict a gradual increase in the number of substantial branch libraries on campuses of colleges and universities. If carefully defined and suitably coordinated, such branch libraries are seen to work effectively in old and large institutions, and there seems no reason to argue that they cannot sometimes be sound space-planning alternatives for smaller and newer institutions.

3. *Offices and classrooms.* These may be useful inclusions in the library building. Offices are, in a sense, library space because faculty offices and faculty library studies may be one and the same thing. A faculty office may have a telephone and be used for appointments with students; the faculty study in the library may be for professional writing and research. Either of these spaces may be used for preparation of class lectures, seminar problems, tests, etc. Many institutions combine these since it is difficult to justify an individual's having both a study and an office. The advantages of having faculty studies in the library are that they serve to improve the faculty's use and understanding of the library. A decision has to be made in each case.

Classrooms can be very useful though they take away from space that otherwise could be used completely for library purposes. Libraries with mature programs of bibliographic instruction will find them very useful for those librarians offering credit courses, workshops, or short seminars on the bibliography of a subject. Library tours may end up using a classroom for question periods or for slide or tape presentations and, if suitably equipped, instruction in computer searching for publications. Faculty members would find classrooms convenient in a library for seminars to which they may wish to bring books as examples and for discussion. When not assigned for class purposes, classrooms can also be used when library staff need meeting spaces for planning sessions, committee meetings, the library friends' club, or group interviews. They can also provide space for expansion when library growth requires. The particular needs of the institution must be weighed before a decision is made.

4. *Nonlibrary functions.* It is not unusual to use part of the library building for other than library purposes during the first years after

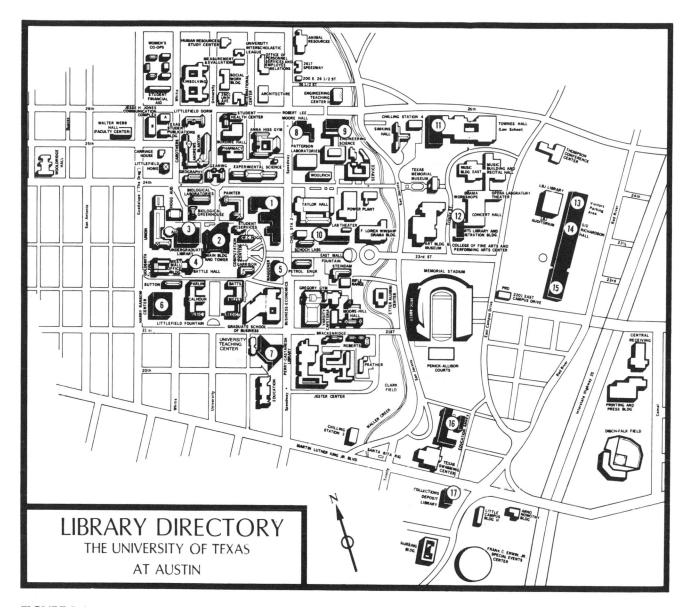

FIGURE 3.1 University of Texas, Austin, as a decentralized library system. (1) Chemistry (Mallet) Library; (2) Asian Collection; (3) Undergraduate Library; (4) Architecture Library; (5) Classics Library; (6) Harry Ranson Center; (7) Main (Perry-Castañeda) Library; (8) Physics-Mathematics-Astronomy (Kuehne) Library; (9) Engineering (McKinney) Library; (10) Geology (Walter) Library; (11) Law Library; (12) Fine Arts Library; (13) Public Affairs Library; (14) Texas Collection Library; (15) Benson Latin American Collection; (16) Film Library; and (17) Collections Deposit (Storage) Library. Note also the Lyndon Baines Johnson Library and Museum (near 13) which is on campus but not one of the university libraries.

its construction. For major spaces to be assigned to some other purpose, a separate entrance may be needed. The inclusion of such functions may help with the fundraising prospects. As was explained in Chapter 2, it would be important that any function regarded as a temporary occupant of the space not be so specially designed (as are audio-visual departments or wet laboratories) that they could not be relocated with a certain ease and the space readily converted to library purposes

at reasonable cost. If the space were so customized as to cost initially much more than average, it could constitute an economic argument not to remove the function later.

Including nonlibrary functions in the library is another major policy decision that each institution must decide given its local circumstances. However, the authors urge caution in combining the library with other functions because some problems are bound to arise. In many small institutions this combination has been forced on the librarian with very unsatisfactory results for the library services.

5. *Collection growth.* Depending on the function of the library unit, a decision has to be made about whether the collection is to be a growing research collection or whether the size is to be relatively static. In the latter case one need not worry as much about how the collection will be housed twenty or thirty years hence. For examples, small departmental teaching collections can be more or less static in size, and the undergraduate library in a university is generally regarded as providing the required reading, recommended reading, and a limited core collection of items most authoritative and relevant for the instructional program. Though such an undergraduate collection can be viewed as having limited growth, there is always some risk that a change of academic approach in the future may then require continued growth despite the limits of building designs.

Most library collections pose forecasting problems which are not relatively as simple as the above two examples. A decision will require balancing many factors, such as the extent of future reliance on microtexts, the potential for bringing some existing branch collections into the building, the intended growth of graduate programs, the long-term physical spread of academic programs and the concentration of buildings within a block or two of the library, and guesses about the nature of publishing in the years ahead. This decision is difficult for librarians and academic officers. Unless one or more forces will have a clear and dominant effect in the years ahead, the library may be wise to view the growth of the past ten to twenty years as a strong indication of the future growth rate.

6. *Open or closed stack access.* A related policy issue to the above is whether students, faculty, and others who are not on the staff of the library will be allowed stack access. Whereas there has always been a certain amount of access permitted to the main book collections by certain individuals such as the faculty, it was only after the middle of this century that in the United States and Canada most libraries permitted all students freely to use the books at the shelves. In the latter half of the nineteenth century, books were arranged on one tier after another of alcoves surrounding a great hall. Users of the library were admitted to these alcoves, sometimes

freely, sometimes under restriction, but under a certain amount of supervision. However, in the early years of this century, the accumulation of books was so great that there had to be large multitier stack rooms with parallel ranges close together so as to increase capacity. Stacks were then generally closed to the public although teaching staff were given access. Later, graduate students were admitted. The advent of departmental or branch libraries and the undergraduate library again facilitated direct access to the books. Once the undergraduates were well served, it then became somewhat more possible to open the entire research collection stack to their use since they might no longer flood the research collections and make that facility ineffective for the graduate students who had primary need for such large and broad collections in their fields.

Thus it has been in recent decades that seating is provided in the bookstacks for the convenience of advanced students. Charging out a book and reserving it in a carrel or study have become common. But will this evolution over the past century continue toward further open access, or will the disciplinary problems and book security difficulties alter the course of history and increase the number of closed bookshelves for some readers? Given the value of research collections and the prevalent ethical state, some substantial constraints on open access are predicted.

There is already a trend toward the transfer of more rare and expensive volumes in a department of special collections, including all eighteenth-century and even a good many rare early nineteenth-century volumes. To the extent that access to the general bookstack is restricted, the entrances and exits to it must be controlled. If the stack is to be completely open and the readers admitted anywhere, inspection is normally conducted at the exit to the building rather than from the stack. Yet if stack access is to be controlled, as in the ten-story bookstack with thirty-one stack doors in Harvard's Widener Library, there obviously cannot be staff at each exit. Thus Widener uses two staffed entrance/exits; the other doors are locked and some, by code, have "panic hardware" permitting egress in emergencies. Although this panic hardware requires breaking a piece of glass to operate the door release hardware, thus sounding an alarm, it has not been found sufficient to deter impatient people who choose to ignore approved operational processes. Escapes from these unstaffed exits are a problem in a research library since some people will use them knowing that rarely would the library staff be able to move quickly enough to find out who the individual was and determine whether library property was involved. Surveillance television cameras at unstaffed alarmed exits have been used with good results at the Perry-Castañeda Library at the University of Texas.

7. *Security.* Another major decision is whether control of book circulation is to be handled at the public exits of the building or at the exit from the bookstack and reading areas. There will also need to be a decision on whether everyone is permitted into the building or whether there are security clearances in order to sort out those who are authorized from those requiring permission. Decisions will also need to be made about whether electronic control systems will be used in some or all of these locations, both for automatic entrance checks as well as for screening books to assure they have been charged out for circulation. Each of these will affect the basic design in modest fashion but will have a considerable effect on staff facilities, traffic patterns, and the openness or compartmentation of spaces.

Many administrators of libraries, particularly smaller ones, branches, and those in rural areas, may feel that there is no need for exit controls of any kind either from the bookstacks or the building itself. If there is evidence that individuals at the institution will not take materials without authorization, one may forego controlled exits, except for rare books and similar materials which can be controlled at the point of use. Even so, the design should allow future controls if circumstances change.

The Lamont Library at Harvard was so planned that at least during quiet times of the day the attendant at the desk where books are regularly charged can also check any volume, whether owned by the library or not, that a student wants to take from the building. This procedure saves staff and in many cases saves a double check, one at the charging desk and one at the exit.

In large city libraries and in nearly all very large library buildings, exit controls are now commonplace. The very largest university library buildings, such as at Edinburgh, Toronto, Chicago, and Texas, all rely on staffed exit controls separate from other service points. Any new library should be planned so that exits can be controlled easily, either by electronic detection or staff, without adding unreasonably to the cost of the operation of the library. Narrow exit lanes will facilitate checking everyone who leaves the building. Turnstyles are sometimes used in order to assure a relatively slow flow of such traffic, but these may also require bypass exits in the event of fire or for handicapped persons. Still, many individuals object to turnstyles or to any personal inspection of their materials. Electronic circulation review systems are becoming increasingly common in all sizes and types of libraries; and, if they continue to prove effective, they could be the standard method of monitoring book security.

Most academic and research libraries have a considerable number of visitors from near and far. Particularly in urban areas there may well be an influx of high school students, students from other institutions, as well as the general public, some less ethical than others. In all cases entrance checks and exit controls present policy issues that require careful analysis and specification in the program statement.

8. *Divisional plan.* During the 1940s and 1950s large academic libraries often had separate reading rooms, reference services, and shelf areas for the humanities, the social sciences, and the sciences. This plan was implemented in greater or lesser degree in a large number of institutions; many have retained it and some other institutions have given it up.

A different divisional organization is to separate reference books, current periodicals, public documents, microtexts, rare books, and manuscripts. It is evident that when the collections are divided along subject lines or by format, the plan of the whole building is affected, particularly if the reading areas are to be divided or the components are to be placed on different floors. It is sometimes possible to adapt an old building to divisional organization if there are a number of large reading rooms, though it is generally easier to apply a divisional plan in connection with a new building.

Some of the difficulties arising from the divisional plan are here mentioned, not in order to criticize but simply to state the problem. The number of service locations directly affects the operational costs, especially if service for the full opening hours of the building is to be provided in each division. The larger the number of units, the more difficult it is to determine the long-term space requirements for each division. Estimating total library space requirements is difficult enough. Estimating the long-term space requirements of individual subject-related units becomes much more difficult. Staffing costs and staffing flexibility may present other difficulties.

On the other hand, no one can deny that having specialists select and service books in a particular subject field is advantageous. This feature is one of the attractions of branch libraries, which are another version of a divisional plan. The point to be made here is that if there is any thought that a divisional plan is to be adopted, it should be in the program for the new building; final decisions on the number, size, and relationships of the units should be made in advance of schematic drawings if complications are to be avoided.

9. *Seating and smoking.* Another basic decision concerns the amount and nature of seating to be provided. It may be as little as ten percent of the student body for a commuting institution and fully fifty percent for an institution with strong graduate and research programs. Furthermore, a decision is necessary on the proportion of the seats to be in the bookstacks, in the reference areas, and in other specified areas.

As individual readers enter a reading room, they will usually space themselves as far as possible from each other until the number in the room makes it necessary for them to choose a seat near somebody else. Some individuals will wish to sit together. Some like to be in very private spaces, almost as if they were closeting themselves, while others choose spaces as if they wanted to be in the center of traffic. In consequence, a wide variety of seating options is desirable. Other decisions are needed on how many seats are to be provided in relation to various book collections and services, as well as the types of seating to be provided.

The nature of seating arrangements is dealt with more thoroughly in Chapter 7. Here it is stressed that these decisions will be a major determinant of the character of the building. Whereas individual carrels have been provided for the past seventy years, they have become so popular that in new facilities since 1950 a majority of seating has been at individual carrels or partially sheltered individual tables. Since the 1970s there has been a perceived reversal of student habits with somewhat more individuals seeking lounge furniture or open tables. Trends seem to shift, and each institution will have to determine what is likely to be most functional, keeping in mind that a considerable variety is needed.

While individual seating accommodations properly arranged will tend to keep the library quieter and help reduce some disciplinary problems, they can cost somewhat more than tables accommodating several individuals and they also may require more space unless very carefully arranged. The disciplinary problems of carrels are of a different nature although they can be even more troublesome to control. Defacing of property and other undesirable social behavior are easier if one is hidden from sight. On the other hand, some libraries have found that carrels designed with the side panels, or shrouds, extending beyond the front table edge create few acoustic or disciplinary problems.

A serious question relates to smoking policies. Smoking, if permitted on an extensive basis, will affect nonsmokers, maintenance costs, air filtration and recirculation, and other issues, including insurance. The smoking issue is one which also has seen shifting trends from decade to decade and certainly from century to century. Until fairly recent decades smoking was prohibited altogether in almost all libraries. As smoking grew more popular in the middle part of this century, smoking was often permitted in some graduate departmental libraries although not in the main library. Special reading areas were sometimes set aside in all types of libraries. But four problems remain: the fire risk, the effect of smoking on ventilation, the dirt and damage which is bound to exist, and finally the discomfort for the reader who dislikes studying in a smoke-filled room.

In the first half of this century, about one-sixth of library fires resulted from smoking.[1] The fire hazard was particularly great in the old-fashioned tiered stack, but improvements in fireproofing and in fire-warning and suppression systems have very considerably minimized this problem.

Separate smoking areas or rooms in a building have been widely tried. Some libraries have found that when only one room was provided for smoking, the traffic back

[1] *Protecting the Library and Its Resources* (Chicago: ALA, 1963), p. 7.

and forth to that room caused a disturbance. Though smoking is very rarely permitted in general reading areas in Europe, one finds many examples in North America. Special lounges or conference and conversation rooms where smoking is permitted can be found at the University of Toronto Robarts Library, University of Northern Iowa, John Carroll University, University of Pittsburgh, the Science Library of the University of Georgia, Cazanovia College, and Wells College and in very nicely arranged rooms at the University of Minnesota Wilson Library. At Dalhousie University's Killam Library smoking is permitted in nine conference rooms, as well as in the current periodicals reading room and the reserved book reading room. Similarly, at the Brown University Rockefeller Library, smoking is permitted in two reserved-book rooms and in the exhibition lounge, though the ventilation system in this latter space is quite inadequate.

These separate rooms are quite suitable for conversation or group study, but they are a poor arrangement to handle smoking. Either the rooms are taken over by those who wish to smoke and do not serve the other function well, or the rooms may be a waste of space if not sufficiently used. If one must permit smoking in libraries, outside of private offices, a clearly designated and reasonably convenient part of the general reading areas should be so marked, with a sufficient number of heavy urns to minimize the reliance on ashtrays, the removal of which can make controlling the limits of such space difficult.

Smoking habits have changed. As a consequence, the proportion of seats where smoking is sanctioned would be much less now than even a decade ago. Students in some universities have demanded that there be no smoking in the libraries. It is an issue of balancing popular customs at the moment, with the need to protect the books, environment, and furnishings, and still provide library spaces where all individuals can use the materials without being disturbed by their neighbors. A librarian cannot alter human nature or be the dictator of personal habits; yet the librarian does have responsibility for protecting the materials and assuring a suitable environment for their use. On that basis the less smoking there is in the library public areas, the better it will be.

10. *Automation and audio-visual services.* If the building is to be connected to a major computation center located elsewhere, on campus or off, and if it will be linked to audio-visual source equipment located in some other building, then a minimum provision would be sufficient conduit capacity with distribution to all parts of the library building that in the future may need connection with these services. Or, a strategy of how to provide signal and power to various points in the building needs to be established—even if conduit is not provided to every possible point. Depending on the extent to which the institution plans to rely on such services, there may be one large trunk line or extensive feeder lines going to library reading areas or rooms, to some of the individual carrels, to faculty studies, and to a variety of library staff service areas.

However, if the institution plans to house within the library computer processors, data storage units, and other peripherals, and if it plans to include source equipment for a major audio-visual service, including language laboratory facilities or video capacity, these services will place demands on the entire building project. Thus a careful review of the probable educational goals of the institution and the probable methods of instruction is mandatory. The kinds and number of such special facilities must be determined reasonably precisely, and the probable extent of centralized or decentralized facilities within the building must be resolved. It must be determined whether such supporting space as a photographic laboratory and graphics design facilities are needed in support of the audio-visual services. As a substantial example, the Library of Congress Madison Memorial Building utilized a 3-duct system laid on 5-ft (1.524) centers in the slab of most floors above the basement. To handle power, telephone, and coaxial cable, these ducts are 3 in. deep and 6 or 12 in. wide (0.075×0.150 or 0.300). Such an installation can be a very costly element in a contemporary building.

In both automation and AV installations a very large number of technical as well as programmatic decisions need to be made. The basic intention of the institution, the scale of the facility, and the extent to which its services permeate the entire library service quarters are very important policy decisions. Use of a consultant may well be essential unless there is an in-house expert.

A major operational decision is whether the library will automate, whether there will be one or several in-house computers, and where they will be located. The computation facilities in the Johns Hopkins University Eisenhower Library and the use of media in learning center and library facilities at Oklahoma Christian University, Buffalo and Geneseo in the State University of New York (SUNY) system, Marywood College, and Grand Valley College in Michigan are examples. It is, however, too early to be sure whether, in the long run, major spaces in libraries will be routinely assigned to such services. At the present it appears that a campus computation center in the library will be very rare. However, remote job-entry stations may be common, and terminals to connect with local and off-campus information sources are ubiquitous. Furthermore, since a library building is the natural location for a computer to support many online library systems, microcomputers and minicomputers will frequently be located in libraries. These devices, combined with very high-density data and graphic image storage such as videodiscs, will increasingly handle all the library's internal operations and be linked to local area networks and to national utilities and telecommunication services. In some parts of the world, libraries are still facing such technical difficulties as sudden power drops when building elevators start and lack of spare parts or qualified service technicians. Building plans must be programmed with a realistic projection of what automation is desirable and feasible.

The provision of major audio facilities in libraries is increasing; they are almost universal in community or junior colleges and are becoming more so in senior colleges and universities. Programmed learning centers and language laboratories may be included, whereas a campus-wide TV studio and graphics facility is more likely to have its own building or be associated with the department or school of education or of communication.

11. *Grandeur versus functionalism.* A final major policy decision is the degree to which the library building should be massive and imposing. Some institutions have decided against making the library one of the most physically imposing buildings on campus. Examples are Arizona State, the University of Minnesota Wilson Library, Stanford University Green Library, or the University of California at Berkeley Moffett Undergraduate Library. Clearly, monumentality was not intended with respect to the undergraduate libraries at the University of Illinois and the University of British Columbia, both of which are mostly underground. Yet other institutions have wanted an imposing building, perhaps of striking architectural design to serve institutional purposes of publicity, recruiting, and symbolism. Examples of this sort would be tower libraries such as the University of Massachusetts, Hofstra University, California Institute of Technology, Notre Dame University, and the University of Glasgow. Those with striking architecture include Butler University, the University of California at San Diego, Clark University, and Northwestern University. In each case there are those who claim that in certain respects the imposing design hurts the long-term functionalism. An institution may opt for impressiveness like Yale's Sterling Library, quiet elegance as in Princeton's Firestone, the restrained symbolism of Dartmouth's Baker, or the charm of Scripps College.

Since this quality of symbolism, monumentality, or imposing character can greatly affect the architectural design and the cost, it becomes a very important policy decision that may involve the president and trustees more than any other of these major policy requirements. This particular issue is critical as it can easily increase the expense by 50 percent and it could as much as double the cost of the building. However, it should also be emphasized that an impressive site and beautiful building are entirely feasible at very near the cost of a utilitarian building. The central issues tend to relate to the design and the choice of materials.

3.3 Library Staff Preparation for the Project

Planning a new library building is expensive and complicated. It is exhilarating and may be one of the most pleasant, demanding, frustrating, and satisfying activities that a librarian can undertake. It should not be undertaken without proper preparation. Some of these activities need be done in conjunction with the design team, and these will be treated in Chapter 4. There are a number of things that need to occur before the architect is chosen and the program is written. Since these may be underestimated or overlooked by library staff, they are given prominence here as they may critically affect the smooth and effective completion of a building project.

Developing Staff Competence. The chief librarian or library director must understand a good deal about building design and operation in order to play an effective role in the planning process. This role is important even if the library is large enough to have a full-time or part-time planning officer or architectural building projects manager on its staff. Therefore, whether the institution is small or large, the head librarian or the associate or deputy librarian must have the ability to guide and participate in the project from the program point of view.

Whoever this individual is, it will be important for responsibility to be so vested that there can be a voice of authority and clear direction to the project month after month and year after year. If the director is to serve this function, it may well require at least 10 percent of that person's time over the entire number of years required from planning through occupancy. If, in fact, this individual is going to handle all interior planning and furniture selection, review of construction change orders, and participate in most meetings with architects, it can occupy from 50 to 100 percent of his or her time during substantial periods, depending upon the speed of the project and the care and effectiveness with which the project is executed. Indeed, for projects which are on the order of 300,000 to 600,000 sq ft (28,000 m² to 56,000 m²), it may require two or more individuals in the library, even if the institution has an effective architectural planning office which handles all business matters and resolves most of the problems with the architect and the contractor. This may appear to be an excessive use of the time of senior library officers at a time when many other things may be going on in the institution. That cannot be contested; yet it is also true that the process is a demanding one if the results are to be satisfactory. When a building project may cost up to ten times the library's annual operating budget, there clearly is reason for the chief librarian or the deputy librarian to give it the attention it requires. This point will be dealt with from a different aspect in the next chapter; however, the recognition of this time requirement must not be overlooked.

Releasing Staff Time. What has been said about the chief library officer can also be said in somewhat lesser degree about every department head and unit chief in all staff sec-

tions which will be housed in the new facility. Institutional officers will understand the attention to the project which is required of the head librarian; similarly the head librarian must recognize that unit heads will need to be informed of basic planning practices, involved in the programming effort, and deeply concerned about the exact details in their spaces and the possible effect of small deficiencies on their operating effectiveness.

Although it is almost never possible to provide departments and units with extra staff during a building project, the library administration can relieve those units of some tasks in order to compensate for the priority of attention that must be given to a building project. This time spent on the part of departments will be spasmodic which is, in a sense, a saving grace. It will not be as incessant as is the burden on the head librarian, who will have weekly if not daily issues needing to be resolved, week after week and month after month. It may be possible for the head librarian to reduce the frequency of certain administrative committee meetings during that time. Perhaps a departmental annual report can be written every two years instead of one year. Certain budget processes may be simplified during the course of building planning. Perhaps some salary savings can provide a bit of flexibility. However it is planned, the affected departments need to be involved and understand the basic criteria on which the design is based, and what the effects will be of space being planned for that particular department or unit.

A building project is usually a new experience for nearly all members of the staff involved. Furthermore, the pressures and nature of a building project vary so much from conventional library operations that alternative styles are required. In some instances the institution's architectural planning office may provide briefing sessions for some or all library staff that will be involved in the process. In other cases the head librarian, the deputy, or the planning associate may have the responsibility for the educational process which will help each unit to understand what is going on and to have confidence in the process. Occasional articles in a staff bulletin will be of help. Including oral reports in selected staff meetings can be useful. Posting in a staff room the planning schedules and sketches at various stages of plans development can help this educational process.

In order to have constructive and timely decisions, it is essential that the staff understand the processes and the rigorous and, sometimes, constraining nature of the planning procedures. A building is, after all, a way of expressing a philosophy of library service. A poor building can be exceedingly limiting and frustrating both to the staff and to its users. Conversely, a clear set of goals and objectives and a precisely drawn program expressing those components in terms of a physical structure can eventually result in a building which facilitates the operations in all library units and thus pleases staff, faculty, and students.

Study of the Published Literature. Since there are special problems involved in planning a library building, some knowledge of these problems is a reasonable prerequisite to the writing of the program, to say nothing of its importance in the actual planning by the architect. Reading selected literature on the subject can be useful. Although this literature is extensive, it is not well organized for the purpose. This volume is not intended to make further reading unnecessary, and it includes a selected, annotated bibliography which should be helpful. As a result of their reading, those responsible should be aware of much of the terminology, the range of problems, and the kind of basic information on which decisions should be based. The literature should help but the decisions must be determined by the local situation.

Who should become acquainted with the literature? Probably it ought to be kept in mind that "a little knowledge is a dangerous thing." If the study is too casual, and if the reader tends to consider everything as gospel truth, errors will occur. It is suggested that at least one senior librarian on the staff, including the head librarian if possible and certainly including the primary planning associate in the library, try to become acquainted with the more important materials in the bibliography, as well as more recent selected publications recommended by a planner or architect. It is further suggested that this volume be placed at the disposal of others involved in the program writing and that their attention be called to the parts of it that fall within their special fields of activity, as well as to other pertinent published material.

If the institution's president or provost expects to take an active part in the building project, the attention of this officer should be called to the literature, its technical content, and its possible usefulness. The same holds true for other officers of the institution who may be involved, such as the administrative vice-president, deans, the business manager, maintenance officers, the chair of the library building committee, and later the architect and the architectural and engineering consultants. Time spent in reading the literature and learning of problems in buildings elsewhere will save a good deal of grief.

Visiting Other Library Buildings. There is no better way to obtain insight into library building problems than to visit other libraries. Few persons have imagination enough to picture what these problems are without seeing examples of them, and a careful examination of the literature by itself is not sufficient. Ordinarily not more than six or eight libraries need be visited by any one person, and those selected should be examined carefully enough to make the enterprise worthwhile. On the other hand, interesting solutions to problems can be found in a great many libraries since each may offer unique arrangements. Thus it may be useful for all of the librarians on the staff to pool their experience from places they have worked or visited in the past to indicate what good and bad conditions they can remember and describe.

More on this topic of visits to other libraries is provided in Section 4.6, since some of this visiting should be done with the architect in order that each may learn from the other.

To give an example of what can be drawn from visiting other library buildings, the following list of design attributions was prepared in 1966 in connection with Stanford's undergraduate library, the J. Henry Meyer Memorial Library.

Alcove arrangement—Quincy House at Harvard *et al.*
Reference alcoves—Lamont at Harvard
Audio outlets on upper floors—Indiana University
Low-divided tables—University of Texas Undergraduate Library
Eye-height bookcases—Andover-Harvard Theological Library
Check-out desk—University of Michigan
Reserve card counter—Doe Library, University of California, Berkeley

"Character" of pavilions—Tower Library at
Dartmouth, Alumni Room at Bowdoin,
Morrison Room at Berkeley

Trash chute—John Carroll University, Cleveland

Desks around light well—Air Force Academy

Bulletin board arrangement—Colorado College

House phone provision—Countway Library
of Medicine, Harvard

Area signs—Santa Clara University

Bookshelf material and color—Washington
University, St. Louis

Lighting panels—Richard Blackwell's speech
at public meeting

Air conditioning—Washington University

Electronic pianos—Sinclair Library, University of Hawaii

Remote tape decks—University of California,
Los Angeles.

3.4 Cost Estimates and Fundraising

Before drafting the building program, it is essential to have some projection of the approximate size and probable cost of the project. Funding officers will need to determine whether these totals are acceptable to the institution. Chapter 9 gives considerable treatment of estimating construction and equipment costs, qualities, or features in the building which may have exceptional effects on the costs, the institutional policies for estimating costs, and any special factors which might affect building costs. It is also essential to have preliminary estimates on probable increases or reductions in the proposed library's services, energy, and other projected costs and to ascertain whether these are acceptable to the institution.

With the general idea of the size of the building derived from estimates of needs for bookshelving, reading space, and staff space, and with a sense of the difficulty of the site and the quality of the intended building, the institution's architectural planning office can put together a preliminary building budget. Construction costs for the anticipated type of structure can be provided by reputable contractors and, of course, must be projected ahead until the time when the building is under construction. Recent experience at the institution and in the same part of the state will serve as a guide. There will also need to be a budget for equipping and furnishing the building, landscaping around the site, moving in, and, sometimes, staff consultants and related planning expenses. Since conditions change and vary from one part of a large country to another, this volume can merely suggest that recent data from the institution's locale is necessary.

Library building costs have been tabulated from time to time in various forms and places. Those for individual libraries are often recorded in library publications. While these may be helpful, it should always be remembered that they may not include each of the six categories of expenditure discussed in Chapter 9 and are unlikely to be comparable with one another. One must remember the three basic cost factors: (1) time of construction and the economic climate when bids are accepted; (2) the size and location of the building and any soil or site problems; and (3) the type of architecture and the quality of materials to be used. In other words, it is difficult and seldom useful to compare costs of a proposed building with other libraries or other types of buildings unless it is done by architects or consultants who are able to delve deeply enough into the similarities and differences which affect cost in order to provide valid guidance for the current project.

The nature of the building concept has a powerful effect on the building cost and the ability to raise funds for its construction. Before Cornell, Texas, and Chicago built their large, impressive main libraries, the university library condition was so obviously unsatisfactory that it engendered a lot of on-campus support and support from those who had funds. A library space that has become desperate or truly shocking may be in the best position for effective fundraising. Sometimes a grand architectural design can be an asset for raising funds, though a finely crafted and demonstrably economical solution is also a type that garners support. Concerning impressive buildings, a donor problem was expressed to Mr. Metcalf by a well-known librarian in these words: "It is far easier to get money for a monumental or memorial style building than for one providing for the day-to-day needs which will make it live as a library. I doubt if this would be the case if the librarian or someone else who could speak with authority was prepared and able to explain the situation clearly and dispassionately to the institution's administration."

Before turning to fundraising for publicly and privately supported libraries, there are a few points to make about "selling the case" regardless of the type of institution. The financial strategy for raising funds needs to be based on the magnitude and type of library program that has been adopted. This program is shaped by the answers to consideration of alternatives to new construction which were treated in Chapter 2, together with decisions on the major policy issues outlined early in this chapter. Ordinarily an institution does not go far with planning until funds are in sight or it is believed that they will be readily available. There are cases, however, where schematic building plans should be drawn as part of the preparation for a campaign to obtain funds. The need for the new structure certainly must be made convincing in order that support from one or more sources can be solicited and can reasonably be expected to be forthcoming. A description of services which the building will provide is helpful. A brochure well written and carefully designed can be useful in explaining the needs and requirements of the institution. The use of such brochures is common in privately supported institutions. If the persuasive voice of someone who has real knowledge can be added at the critical and decisive moment, it may turn the tide. For instance, quoting a highly respected member of the faculty can provide real insight into the current situation and the correction that is needed. If the brochure is not printed, at least the required information should be readily available as institutional representatives work with governmental bodies, foundations, alumni supporters, and volunteer groups on the fundraising campaign. Following is a sample taken from a brochure issued by the Harvard University School of Medicine.

A NEW LIBRARY LONG OVERDUE

The need for a new library building may be quickly sketched by enumerating a few disturbing facts:

- The present Library has occupied the same space since 1938; the second floor location is a remodeling of an earlier amphitheatre lecture room, students' lounge, and classroom.
- Its reading space (12 tables, 100 chairs), adequate in 1938, remains the same; the number of readers has *quadrupled.*
- While its regular shelf space remains the same, the number of books, pamphlets and periodicals has *doubled.* (The excess has been accommodated by overcrowded shelves, improvised shelving in nooks and corners, and by piling books in almost inaccessible places. Now there is no more room for even these expedients.)

- Ten thousand volumes dispersed to departmental libraries are *not* available for student use on evenings or weekends.
- The Medical Library needs larger appropriations for purchases and for additional staff, but such sums literally could not be spent effectively at the present time. Where would they put more books? Where would they put more workers?
- The Library, designed in 1938 and fitted into existing space, contains no private study alcoves, no rooms for typing notes or dictating onto tape, no photo-duplicating laboratory, no seminar rooms for group discussions, no audio-visual room, no proper room for microfilm or microcard reading—in short, none of the special features of modern library planning that so enhance its effectiveness as a environment for creative thinking.

The inadequacy of the present library facilities has gone far beyond inconvenience; it is already close to the point where it is putting a ceiling on the School's programs of advanced teaching and research.

The architect will occasionally be brought into discussion with a major donor, and may make a presentation to the board of trustees, and prepare a written statement that can be used in fundraising documentation. The librarian is frequently involved as the expert witness to the present conditions and to what is needed by the institution and intended in the building project. The librarian may be involved in meetings as a representative of the institution with those who can appropriate or give funds, sometimes meeting with a volunteer committee, joining with the president to visit a major prospect, and always being ready to assist the principal officers of the institution with a tour of the existing facilities whenever requested. Guidance to fundraising is widely available, including the following: *Tested Ways to Successful Fund Raising,* by George A. Brakeley, Jr. (New York: AMACOM, 1980); *Fundraising; The Guide to Raising Money from Private Sources,* by Thomas E. Broce (Norman: University of Oklahoma Press, 1979); and *Designs for Fund-Raising: Principles, Patterns, Techniques,* by Harold J. Seymour (New York: McGraw-Hill, 1966).

This fundraising task is carried by the president, the vice-president for development, one or more members of the board of trustees, and perhaps a provost or chief academic officer. The librarian usually serves as staff to assist in the project, though in some private colleges and an occasional university the librarian has been asked to play a more prominent role. In any event, there can be nothing more important than assisting with the fundraising, for without funds there will be no building no matter how dire the need and how admirable the design.

Financing strategy may well include a variety of sources and several types of monies. The strategy will vary depending on the nature of the institution. The publicly supported college and university will rely primarily on state appropriations though other sources may be of great importance. Church-affiliated institutions may receive all or substantial construction funds from the church authority. Private professional schools may internally finance the construction. Bank loans or borrowing from endowment may be necessary. Most institutions use a mixture of funding sources. For instance, a medical center library in a university may have funding from the federal and state governments and perhaps the local city or county, as well as foundation grants, gifts from individuals, and maybe income from sale of real estate, endowment, and even from patient fees.

Funding sources may include public bonds, governmental appropriations, federal grants from programs specifically designed for academic library buildings, loans or gifts from private foundations, private individuals, and corporations, and very often a combination of these. The fundraising strategy may include an incentive program to provide funds when matched by individuals, perhaps one dollar from the principal source for one, two, or three dollars raised from other sources. In this decade both Harvard (for the Fogg Museum addition) and Yale (for the Seeley Mudd Library) have sold some of their collections to help cover building costs. In Yale's case it was the Brasher doubloon coin, sold for $650,000 in 1981 to help close a $1.5 million gap in funds for its $6.7 million social science and documents library.

In the financing of a publicly funded institution, most funds come from taxation. Federal legislation in the United States has from time to time made government support available, either by loan or outright gift, to public and private institutions for library building construction. State and municipal bodies have, on occasion, provided funds for this purpose. If the funds are to come from a government agency, institutional officers will develop the strategy. The question almost certain to arise in the case of a large building is whether it will be constructed at one time or in stages. This answer may be complex to respond to effectively, and the pros and cons need to be thoroughly analyzed. A building constructed in stages may be easier to finance, but planning is more difficult. One may not wish to build in stages; however, state policy for capital projects may require it.

If the funds come from a governmental body, a considerable hierarchy of offices must ordinarily be dealt with before an architect is chosen and the plans can be completed and approved. These actions are often quite political. The approvals may involve not only the chief administrative officers of the government concerned, the legislature, the finance and education departments, and the administrative officers of the institution but also one or more architects who are official representatives of the government involved, sometimes as many as four different ones. Threading one's way through the maze takes time and may be difficult. Capital requests can require five or more years of requests, justifications, and various approvals before being funded by state or other responsible governmental authorities. The institution's administrative officers and librarians should seek all the help they can get to prevent the project from bogging down.

Government participation, whether it be federal, state or municipal, also means acceptance by the institution of governmental rules, procedures and standards which may add something to the cost and with some of which the institution may not agree. Forms will need to be made out extensively, extra inspections will be required, and frequent reports given. The accounting process will be rigorous. However, state or county building requirements and standards will usually apply even if governmental funds are not involved.

If government funds are not available, private funds must be sought. In spite of the unprecedented large gifts to institutions of higher learning in recent years, funds are not ordinarily easy to come by for new library construction. Whereas monies for "bricks and mortar" were quite popular gifts four or five decades ago, more recent experience is that they are currently among the most difficult funds to raise. The particular methods used by institutions vary greatly, and some are more sophisticated than others. A few institutions can rely on a relatively steady flow of gift monies for buildings and other purposes.

Some have a particularly strong alumni network. Others must rely much more heavily on private foundations or local corporate resources.

A possible source of funds for a new building is one or more of the numerous private foundations which often support facility projects. Although foundations best known to academic and research libraries—Ford, Rockefeller, and Carnegie—are seldom prepared to make grants for new buildings, there are hundreds of other foundations, some of which will ordinarily be interested in the proposal of a new building. Some foundations do not, however, make grants to public institutions. Corporate donors also should not be forgotten, as a special interest may be developed for a specific area. For example, the newspaper reading room and stack might be of interest to a local newspaper publisher, or a science library could interest a major technically oriented firm. Local industries often will have an interest in supporting their neighboring educational institution, and a new library may well be a very attractive opportunity.

Many factors are involved. If the present library is named for a donor who is still alive, that individual may not be in a financial position to repeat a major gift or may even be opposed to a new building. If the donor is deceased, but family members, even into the second or third generation, are living and their whereabouts can be ascertained, the family should be informed of, or even consulted about, the institution's need for a new building. The courtesy will be appreciated and the possibility of hurt feelings lessened. Sometimes the family is able and willing to contribute to the renovation of the original building. Another prospective major donor may be interested in contributing a dormitory or classroom building but hesitate to give to a library which, judging from past experience, will outgrow its quarters. Thus a gift would not perpetuate a name in the same degree of prominence for more than a comparatively brief period.

The rapid growth of libraries brings another problem in its train. A new library tends to be one of the largest buildings on the campus, and consequently very expensive. Only a comparatively few individuals will have the capacity to make a gift of the whole amount required. Large gifts tend to come as bequests, and a bequest seldom provides for library construction because the donor does not know, when the will is drawn, what the institution's needs will be when the bequest becomes available. Such a bequest is more likely to be specified for a professorship, scholarships, book fund, or even a dormitory or athletic facility. Obviously, unrestricted bequests to the institution provide the desired flexibility.

It is rare that a building is named after a group of successive donors. There is one instance of a library building with two names, honored scholars rather than two donors. A donor may offer to pay for a percentage of the new library if the institution would wish to name it for that family or individual. In such cases the institution must decide whether a gift of one-quarter, one-third, or one-half makes the balance of the fundraising feasible and thus can justify putting the name of one person on the building.

Certainly if an institution agrees to name a building for a donor who gives less than the full amount, the donation should be accepted with the understanding that the names of others who contributed toward the total sum will also be recognized in some appropriate fashion. This recognition may be in the form of a tablet in the entrance or plaques in individual rooms. The possibilities here are many. This approach was used successfully at Princeton University, where up to a thousand individual gifts are recognized in the library in this way, and at Brandeis University Library, where it was adopted on a large scale. Donor recognition, important for the institution and for the individuals concerned, is treated in Chapter 15 as part of the dedication event.

For fundraising purposes, an arbitrary square foot or meter value may be put on space occupied by a room, carrel, alcove, courtyard, or other space. This value may properly be based on a pro rata percentage of the project cost, including nonassignable space, rather than the exact construction cost. These figures may be inflated somewhat for very desirable spaces and deflated for those that are less desirable from a donor's point of view. Examples are given in Section 9.1. Some institutions use professional fundraisers who have experience with effective methods of presentation and appeal.

A special college or university fundraising campaign among alumni and friends may include the library along with several other needs. Such a campaign usually extends over a number of years and must be well planned and scaled in order to have a reasonable degree of success. It should be recognized that in such campaigns, the dollars will not come designated in exactly the proportion required for the needs requested by the institution. Some gift opportunities will turn out to be more popular than others. Unrestricted gifts can be assigned to the less popular items. Twenty years ago a very large and successful fundraising campaign at Stanford University was concluded without the proposed undergraduate library's receiving the required major gift to lever the project. A year or two later two sisters made the gift that, together with about one-fifth of the needed funds by a grant from the U.S. Higher Educational Facilities Act of 1963, covered the entire cost of the project. Though this building had been delayed four years, funding for most large projects is not as simple.

There are a large number of amusing and sad stories about academic fundraising, some of them resulting in eventual success and some failure. Though it is by no means meant to be a typical case, the following statement from Saint Michael's College in Vermont is included to indicate some of the complexities, anxieties, and efforts that are involved in fundraising, nearly every instance of which has its unique set of episodes, and many are quite extraordinary tales.

The plan for financing of the construction was divided into three parts: A grant under Title I of the Higher Education Facilities Act, a loan from the same Act of 1963, Title III, and funds from the College Development Fund.

The grant in the amount of $300,000 had to be approved by the Vermont Commission on Higher Education Facilities which was established by the Governor of the State of Vermont. The State Commission will accept any application from any of the institutions, provided such applications are submitted on forms provided by the Commission. . . .

When the bids for the construction of the Library were opened June 9, 1966, it was revealed that the lowest bidder of six was $265,500 higher than had been anticipated.

The College set about trying to reduce the figure and arranging for the additional financing. We subtracted from the contract alternatives in the amount of $72,000. We adjusted the architect's fees according to the new contract and, on the advice of the New York Office of Housing and Home Finance Agency, we allowed only 2% instead of 5% construction contingency. We also found we could reduce the amount allocated for equipment cost in our original application by $20,000. Thus the original application for a loan of $595,500 was increased to $723,000 and the share of the College increased.

On October 16, 1968, Certificates of Project Costs were approved by the Office of Education. The eligible development costs were $1,349,895 (Title I) and $1,358,355 (Title III). This supported the Federal share of the grant of $300,000 under Title I and a loan of $718,000 under Title III of the Higher Education Facilities Act. Thus the financing was as follows:

Grant—Title I, Section 104	$300,000
Loan—Title III Section	718,000
St. Michael's funds	34,307
	Total: $1,363,307

The financial problems in the construction of the Jeremiah Kinsella Durick Library were like putting your last one dollar bill on the dice table and knowing that the sevens and the elevens had to keep coming up with each roll.

Special arrangements with the Office of Education in Washington were reached so that an escrow agreement establishing the account in a New York bank where funds that were to be approved by the Federal Government would be protected and the contract obligation of the College fulfilled. With this protection established, the contract was signed and ground broken. A short sixty days after the footings had been put in place, the Federal Government froze all construction funds and it was unknown, at this time, just when Washington might approve the additional funds for Education Construction.

As the first flowers of Spring, 'the Snowdrops,' showed their faces, the most welcome news came from Washington that our increase in the loan of $128,000 had been approved.[2]

It took over two-and-a-half years after bids were opened to resolve the financing. It is sometimes very very difficult, as many can attest, though seldom are the stories publicized.

[2] As quoted in Jerrold Orne, "Financing and the Cost of University Library Buildings," *Library Trends* 18: 152–52 (Oct. 1969).

4

The Planning Team, with Architect and Consultants

What is beauty? What is good design? What is great architecture? The answer is in the eyes and mind of each individual. It differs depending on one's background, sophistication, understanding of historical roots, and sensitivity to form, space, texture, color, and the harmonious interplay of all those elements. Architecture has been described by Sigfried Giedion as "the hope of escaping from transitory work and achieving a timeless rightness." Rarely if ever can one be sure about the greatness of contemporary architecture. An architect has achieved excellent but not great work if the creation is judged to be superb for a generation or two but the building cannot serve over a century.

There is something great and eternal about the Parthenon, the Alhambra, the Taj Mahal, the Lincoln Memorial, and Chartres Cathedral. There can be beauty and a sense of greatness in small creations as much as in the large, and libraries need be no exception.

Only an architectural achievement which is effective internally and externally can be considered superior. It must meet local needs. It commonly will use local idioms and indigenous materials. It usually is an expression of the social and cultural conditions of the period and locale. It must function well. It should be handsome at least, or have authenticity and grace.

A building is a composition of selected materials, given a shape and mass appropriate for its function, and carefully set in its surroundings as a compatible neighbor. Its form may provide interest and life; ornamentation may be added as embellishment. The architecture of the building is a molding of shape, lines, styles, and shadows, encompassing the requisite engineering fabric so that the building is structurally safe and operationally sound. The building should accept and work with existing land forms and characteristics. Architectural unity is achieved by honest form, not often by recreating former styles. Keep in mind that the physical environment is known to be a major influence on people's lives.

First impressions often govern the public image of great buildings. To an extent, the interior function is taken for granted, though that must meet as rigorous a test for success in operational terms as the exterior does in terms of its physical presence. However, the facade makes a statement and its image can be best remembered. An academic or research library, as much as any building, should express human dignity and assert the centrality of books for an informed civilization, the timelessness of materials therein which record human thoughts, successes, failures, theorems, and dreams.

The New York Public Library is not . . . one great confusion of ornamental episodes. Any one who looks even hurriedly at the New York Public Library can hardly fail to be aware of an order in the disposition of its parts. A central pavilion pierced with three deep arches anchors the building to the fine terrace upon which it stands; from this pavilion two peristyles march equal distances right and left and end in identical little temples; and the blithe ornament dances across the marble walls in rhythmical ecstasies. The intention of the architect was clearly so to relate all of these that taken together they would present a unity; and if we are persuaded of that unity, finding it complete and without adventitious parts or discordances, it may happen that we will find in such unity a mode of beauty.[1]

Opinions can of course change (see fig. 4.1).

Past centuries have produced a rich tradition of town and campus planning, architecture, and interior design. Every well-read individual can refer to dozens of outstanding architectural creations. The profession of architect is very long-standing and rich in tradition. Architects have produced some excellent libraries, some tasteful and some spectacular.

[1] Joseph Hudnut, *Architecture and the Spirit of Man* (Cambridge, Mass.: Harvard Univ. Pr., 1949), p. 5.

Remember how much tastes change and how much the circumstances in different parts of the country and of the world lead to unique solutions. Design idioms and interior decor preferences vary almost from decade to decade. While there may be a number of solutions appropriate for a particular locale and institution, the good ones provide functional excellence with a sense of propriety and beauty which is suitable for part of a country and for that individual institution. Furthermore, although the needs of institutions shift over time, good buildings can serve a very long time. While there are newer and larger library buildings at Oxford, Cambridge, and Harvard, buildings of previous centuries are still in use and are of historical interest and significant emotional value. The different approach to design in, for instance, Italy when compared with Sweden or Australia when compared with Japan or Scotland, results in distinctiveness—the best examples of each having considerable variety and, at the same time, basic architectural integrity.

Still, in any decade there are striking similarities among the best academic library buildings from one part of the world to another. The form of the library building is dependent to great degree on current principles of functional requirements, standards of taste, and the economics of building materials and the construction industry.

4.1 The Building Planning Team

The building planning team will create the aesthetics of its project just as it controls the operating practicalities for its occupants. The team is composed not only of librarian and architect working together, though they are the most important of the group, but rather of a group of individuals whose skills are all required and committed to creating an excellent library building. It is a team in the sense of teamwork, for, while each plays a particular role, the members will never all meet together at one time. It is made up of one or more committees, representatives of various offices in the institution, the architect and engineering associates, and probably one or more consultants for specialized aspects of the work. These people must cooperatively work toward the defined building goal over a great many months. Very few of them, maybe only three or four, will work full-time on the project.

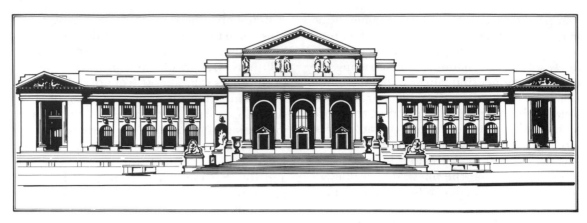

FIGURE 4.1 New York Public Library.

Since the team members have not worked together before and most of them have not worked on an academic or research library, or a building for this particular institution, the team should be formed with special care. The creation of this group and their relationships are the subject of this chapter.

Planning Committees. The following planning committees might be considered, though it would be unusual and probably needlessly complicated to use in any one institution all of those suggested in the following paragraphs. Indeed, there might be better continuity if fewer committees are used, though each committee may play a different role and be involved briefly at appropriate times. If several committees are formed, there may be a need to have a coordinating committee, or to treat all but one as subcommittees, or to define strictly and limit the responsibility of all but the principal planning committee.

A trustees' building committee may be desirable, particularly if the trustees expect to keep a tight rein on building design. Often trustees may find that they can control the situation satisfactorily by asking the president to represent them in the planning, but with the understanding that final policy decisions, especially those which involve financial matters and public relations, will be referred to them before action is taken. Sometimes one or more members of the board of trustees, having special interest, knowledge, and competence in the building planning field, can be asked to serve on a committee made up of representatives of the other interested groups.

A committee representing the institution's administrative officers is a second possibility. The president may want to be a member or even the chair, though often it is enough to be represented by an administrative assistant in whom there is confidence. Other members may include the treasurer, the business manager, the head of the building maintenance department, and the vice-president in charge of educational policy. To these might be added other officers, such as the provost and one or more deans.

Appointment of a faculty committee is certainly not out of place, to ensure that educational interests receive proper consideration. This committee might well include professors who are known to have special interest in the library, preferably those with some practical building knowledge and imagination. They should represent each of the major fields—science, social sciences, and the humanities—if the building covers all such fields.

A student committee can sometimes be useful in enlisting student interest and cooperation in the project. If there is a strong student council, it might be asked to appoint this committee. If not, the dean who deals most closely with the students should select its members.

A library staff committee should be considered. In a large institution such a committee can properly be appointed, often with the chief librarian as chair, but sometimes with a senior staff member in charge who has special knowledge of planning problems.

The librarian or a heavily involved representative should be a member of all of these committees as a coordinating officer, if nothing else. Often several of these committees may not be of much direct help. The problems involved may not be fully understood by the committee members. Decisions need to be made during school vacations and a rigorous schedule of sequential decisions must be met. However, it should be remembered that each group is deeply concerned with the results. Frequently, important help can come from one or all of the groups, and to include representatives of each in the planning process is a matter of first importance to the institution, if only to obtain the occasional helpful suggestion or point of view and to prevent unnecessary and destructive criticism of the building when it is finally erected.

If one or more of the committees are not appointed, the librarian or some other officer must have the responsibility of keeping in touch with all the groups concerned to make sure that their different points of view receive full consideration as planning proceeds.

The Question of Inside Library Help. Although a library staff committee may be used, as mentioned above, there are many patterns which can be appropriate in the particular institution. A staff committee may be suitable if no individual on the staff has very considerable building experience. If one or two have broad experience in building planning, the responsibility for coordinating and involving staff departments and units may be a natural expression of the existing organizational structure, and a special committee may not be needed. In such a case the group of department chiefs may meet regularly, and the building project would be a natural topic to include on their agenda. The same may be the case for the director's council or cabinet. Yet it must be realized that the building will demand its own time; therefore, there must be many extra group meetings devoted particularly to the building.

In the case of a departmental or branch library, the staff of that branch may in effect be a committee, or one or two representatives of that branch may work with one or two members of the central library administration as a committee. In this case, though, it must be made clear who has the final authority and who will be the speaker for the committee.

As an example, at Texas A and M University, one reference librarian with a degree in architecture worked almost full-time assisting the director of libraries with building construction matters. In many libraries there will be an individual who is good in planning and communicating, who is close to the chief li-

brarian, and who undertakes this major representation. At Stanford University, when the project was begun to enlarge and renovate the main library, a professionally trained building projects manager was appointed to the library director's office. This was a new position, reporting to the director of libraries, and it continued for more than ten years as the project effort moved along. Where an institution is faced with a large project or has quite a number of branch libraries and other planning and renovation tasks, it may be the best use of funds to have such a position. If in one year the project slows down while fundraising or authorizations are being obtained, the individual can usually be well used to plan furniture, review fire safety or earthquake hazards, check on compliance with standards for physically limited persons, or assess maintenance deficiencies in the library buildings.

Whatever pattern is chosen for the library, it is essential that clear lines of authority are established, communication is emphasized both up and down the organization, decision schedules are met, and the results are announced if they are ones which affect staff units. The process must flow along rapidly in pace with architects' and engineers' requirements. On the other hand, the library staff has a high professional stake in the results and has every reason to be involved to an appropriate extent week by week and month by month.

The Question of Outside Help. The problem of outside help is a complex one. Often the first question is whether or not an architectural firm or an individual architect should be employed to make a master plan for the development of the campus as a whole, including the selection of the site for the library.

A master plan is certainly desirable and too often is not available. But if the governing board approves the site chosen by the master planner, the architect, when selected, may for some good reason feel that a better site could be found and may properly recommend it. The librarian must also be given an opportunity to express an opinion on this important problem to the campus planning group and to the architect.

The institution may have a regular supervising architect whose approval is required for all new construction and who is involved before the library architect is chosen. The relationship between the two should be carefully defined in order to avoid misunderstanding. Instances could be cited where disagreements between supervising architect or campus planner and the library architect have caused serious difficulties.

Should one or more consultants from outside the institution be selected before or, perhaps, after choice of the architect? In general, with the exception of the library building consultant, such appointments should follow the selection of the architect, who should have an opportunity to express a preference. Indeed, sometimes the architect will select and appoint the consultants, and they will be working for and paid by the architect. Sometimes the institution will want help from a consultant in selecting the architect. As usual, circumstances alter cases.

Probably the most important consultant, so far as concerns problems considered in this volume, is one who has special knowledge and experience in library building planning and who is called in to advise and work with the architect. This may be a librarian with experience in building planning or an architect with experience in the library field. Whether one is appointed in advance or only after consultation with the architect will depend on local circumstances.

Sometimes the architectural firm selected has had little or no experience in library planning but understands that it will work with a library or architectural consultant. If the librarian has had some planning experience and the architect little or none with libraries, an architectural consultant with library planning experience should perhaps be appointed. If, on the other hand, the architect has had library planning experience and the librarian has had little or none, it may be better to appoint a librarian experienced in library building planning as a consultant. It sometimes happens, however, that both the architect and the librarian are inexperienced in library building planning. If the proposed library is large, running into millions of dollars, it may be worthwhile to have both an architectural and a library consultant. Yet if only one is needed, other things being equal, a library consultant will probably be more useful to keep the architect informed on special library functions and problems and to provide the librarian a fresh perspective on local issues. Fortunately, there are a substan-

tial number of architects who have planned a considerable number of library buildings and can serve as consultants to other architects, and a number of experienced library consultants are available.

Briefing and Coordination of Efforts. Whether or not all the individuals and committees mentioned above are asked to become acquainted with the literature, they should at least be briefed by the librarian or, perhaps better, by the president or senior officer on the basic financial and education problems that the institution faces in undertaking the planning of a new library building, and on the "ground rules" which are to be used in dealing with them. They should be told what is going on, and their help should be solicited. It is undoubtedly true that, when a large group is given an opportunity to comment, the floodgates may be opened to unnecessary comment; but this procedure should make everyone feel involved in the proceedings, and the suggestions or criticisms of all will have been aired. They should be less likely to criticize the results than if they had not participated. The publicity obtained may also help directly or indirectly in the fundraising, if that is needed.

Of course, if all these individuals and groups are involved, special care must be taken to see that their efforts are coordinated, that all understand what is and is not expected, and that their activities do not come into conflict with each other—something that could very readily happen. This matter of underlying importance is too often neglected by the institution's administrative officers.

By the time the administrative officers and others who are to have a part in the planning have become acquainted with the literature and have been briefed on planning problems to be faced, the advisory committees that are to be selected should be appointed, and agreement should be reached as to the relationships and responsibilities of each group.

Visiting Other Library Buildings. When should other academic library buildings be visited? Depending upon the degree of knowledge about academic library building planning, the principal members of the planning team may need one or several visits. As mentioned in Chapter 3, one or more of the library staff may need a visit to two or three institutions when considering their own space problems and what alternatives to pursue. Generally a visit to several academic libraries will be important once the architect has been chosen so that there can be a mutual exchange during site visits among the three or four or five individuals representing the library, the architectural firm, and perhaps an academic officer or a member of the faculty library committee. There may also be a visit when the design development work is completed and before the interior finishes and furnishings are settled. Thus, depending upon the project and the individuals involved, there may be as many as three or four trips, with each trip including one or more buildings.

What libraries should be selected? They should include very good examples, though one can learn almost as much from an unsuccessful solution of a library building problem as from a good one. One can learn from the good features and the failures found in even the best of buildings. As to what is a good or what is an unsuccessful solution, even the experts will often disagree among themselves and will emphasize different points. It is to be hoped that persons who study this volume and learn about the variety of possible solutions to particular planning problems will have fairly definite ideas about their basic objectives for the building being planned and will know what they want to look for.

Be sure to choose the libraries of several institutions that are similar in character to your own (that is, in the number of students, the size of the collections, rural or urban, and general outlook) because such institutions and larger ones are more likely to have dealt with problems that resemble yours. On the other hand, do not hesitate to go to smaller or larger libraries if they have something special to present, such as a similar site problem.

Among the things worth noting when one visits libraries are first impressions, general appearance, traffic patterns and spatial relationships, table sizes, dimensions of individual seating arrangements, the use of reading spaces by students, crowded areas, aisle widths and shelf depths, signage, coatrooms, arrangements for smoking, heating and ventilating installations, window treatment, background sound, lighting, ceiling heights, and the use of color and glass.

After an examination of the literature on library building planning, the prospective visitor might well put down a list of the things that should be noted in the program and of

which examples could be helpful before decisions are made.

What procedure should be followed when the libraries to be visited have been designated? One method is to have the librarian go first alone to one or two libraries and to suggest that the architect do likewise. Then a joint expedition is desirable, perhaps including a member of the faculty library committee and a representative of the institution's maintenance department. Probably not more than five should join in a visit. A larger number cannot easily keep together and see things that should be seen, and the librarian of the institution being visited is likely to be overwhelmed.

The library consultant, if one is to be employed, may be included in the visit, for such an expert is in a better position than others to point out both satisfactory solutions of problems and failures. It is a courtesy to make prior arrangements with all libraries to be visited.

Except in a very large library, half a day is ordinarily enough for one building. A large university building might require a full day but not usually. Be sure to reserve time after the visit to talk it over and prepare notes. Photographs of selected features can also be helpful. The notes and photographs should be organized so that they can be referred to and made available to others during the course of the project. If the librarian of the building visited will comment on its good and bad points, these remarks should be particularly helpful.

There is such a thing as getting too involved in details and seeing too many buildings. Yet visits can be very useful and enhance communication because of the common experience. They should be undertaken selectively even when the librarian and architect have worked on other academic library buildings.

4.2 Selection of the Architect

The architectural firm is commissioned under contract to the institution (known as the "client" or "owner") to design a building which will accommodate all the functional components, will operate effectively for years to come, and will be an aesthetically pleasing contribution to the community. The architect brings to the design team a background that calls on centuries of architectural practice. The training and skills in site placement, building styles, form and materials, three-dimensional space, mechanical needs and decoration are applied to provide a suitable environment for the library functions. From study or experience in design, the architect will be familiar with design theory and practice, technical problems and solutions, detail issues, and must relate mass and form and space to good effect.

The architectural firm may include a wide variety of specialists, particularly if it is a large firm with forty or more on the staff. The architect will supplement what talents exist in the firm by hiring one or more consultants. These may be engineering firms or other specialists as required by the particular nature of the project. (In contrast to the planning team, the design team is composed of the architects, engineers, and interior designers.) Yet the architect maintains overall responsibility for the performance of the building, its soundness of construction, its quality of materials, its cost, its basic safety for its users, and its attractiveness. In simple terms the librarian defines the functions and quantities in the building and their interrelationships; the architect is responsible for creating its shape and its appearance—a building with "firmness, commodity and delight."

Criteria for Selection. The selection of a well-qualified and talented architect is essential if a good library building is to come into being. The following fourteen characteristics are essential:

1. Must be professionally competent and licensed.

2. Must be able and prepared to interpret and understand the needs of the client.

3. Must have the imagination and creative ability to produce a unique and satisfactory design which is responsive to the program, site, economic conditions, and other factors which can influence the design. A library is to be the result, not a structure which speaks as a testimonial to the architect.

4. Must be a good listener with a clear mind and must also have the ability to explain clearly the architect's point of view, both orally and in writing when needed.

5. Must understand the client institution, its standards, its problems, and its educational objectives. The firm need not have designed a library, though commissions for academic institutions would provide a useful background.

6. Must realize that the client's functional needs are to be directly served by the architectural answers. If the client's wishes and needs do not coincide, the architect is free to try to persuade the client of that fact, but the primary task is to answer the client's needs functionally and aesthetically.

7. Must, of course, have good taste and a feeling for what is appropriate and must be prepared to plan a building so that the functional requirements of the inside are integrated and in harmony with the outside; must have a full understanding of the importance and weight of both function and appearance.

8. Must know the costs of constructing the building that is planned, and must not either underestimate costs so that extra time and costs are required to solve the problem or overestimate so much that the client does not obtain as good a building as it should from the available funds.

9. Must have readily available engineering competence, which is highly important in producing good plans today.

10. Must be prepared to get help, when needed, from an architectural, engineering, or library consultant. Must be willing to work effectively with an interior design firm, if one is used, regardless of whether the architectural firm has such a capacity. Must be talented in seeking solutions and gaining agreement.

11. Must have a staff proportionate to the task the firm is undertaking, so as to be able to design the project and produce the working drawings and specifications in reasonable time and not so busy that the commission is given poor attention or relegated to inexperienced staff.

12. Must have almost infinite patience; but if the client demands changes so late in the planning process that they cannot be carried through without extra cost, the architect must in due course say firmly that no more changes are possible.

13. Must always be ready to learn and must realize that genius alone is not enough.

14. Must be a person of integrity, prepared to admit that a distinguished building that is not functionally sound will not be satisfactory.

Beyond these characteristics other matters must be considered. The strictest of selection criteria for an architect is desirable for a building in the academic center of an institution or for a larger commission, whether it is for a new building or for the enlargement of an existing structure.

If a competent local architect can be found, certain advantages will undoubtedly result. The cost, other things being equal, may be less. Knowledge of building materials locally available, local building codes, construction firms, quality of specialized labor, and special community history and problems should be valuable. The client will not have to wait for days for a small but necessary consultation, something that can occur with a firm a great distance away. Architectural services will also be more readily available during construction when it is crucial for the architect to keep track of what is going on. For departmental or branch libraries and for remodeling projects, local firms are particularly good. Small firms may be entirely satisfactory and may offer distinct advantages deriving from extra personal attention. Of course, it is a way for an institution to test a young and promising firm or one that it has not used before.

On the other hand, there have been excellent experiences with architects located more than a few hours away. The Stanford campus plan by Frederick Law Olmsted and the Quadrangle architecture by Charles A. Coolidge in the firm of Shepley, Rutan and Coolidge were designed by skilled professionals three thousand miles away—in days before airplanes—and a hundred years later are considered superior and appropriate designs. An architect supplies contract administration of a job under construction as part of normal services. If an architect from a distance is selected, there must be a local representative during construction, in order to avoid complications.

It is re-emphasized that the architect must be astute and candid about construction costs. If the cost is underestimated, unfortunate compromises will generally have to be made; perhaps the soundness of the whole campus building program may be jeopardized. Too often the architect fails to face up to the real cost until so late that embarrassing situations result. It is suggested that an architect should not be selected until the institution has consulted some former clients on this and other points.

Dollars go a long way toward determining space both in terms of quality and quantity. To avoid unpleasant controversy which, combined with other complaints, may have deplorable consequences, it is suggested that the architect be told when receiving the commission that the institution wants as handsome a building as possible, but that there are definite limits to available funds; within these limits the requirements stated in the program must be provided for and the results must be functionally satisfactory. A maximum construction cost figure may be stated. One of the important considerations in the selection of an architect is a conviction that the selected firm can design an excellent building which can be built within an agreed-upon budget. The more difficult the problem, the greater the challenge to the architect, and the firm can properly be told that it was selected because it was believed capable of doing the job required. The architect should, however, be prepared to speak up promptly if asked to perform a miracle and produce something that cannot be built within the proposed budget.

Another question which deserves special consideration is whether the architect should be experienced in library building planning. This factor is much less important than skill, competence, imagination, willingness to listen, desire to find good solutions, and honesty in facing building costs. Ordinarily, of course, an experienced library architect should be selected for the major campus libraries. If the architect selected has not had experience in library building planning, and particularly if the librarian has never been through the process of planning a library and is not given a leading role on the planning team, it is of the utmost importance that consultants be called in. Given a strong and very able librarian, a skilled architect should produce a fine library on the first such commission.

The Selection Process. The institution may have a stipulated method for selecting an architectural firm. The institution should not be so wedded to a firm traditionally used that it must be given the library commission if it fails to meet the reasonable criteria. The librarian should play a major role in choosing the architect, perhaps as part of a small group representing the institution's business office or architects and engineers office. However, it is recognized that, especially in large state-supported systems, the choice may be made at systems headquarters or even in another state office.

The selection process may start with a list of fifteen to twenty firms compiled from various suggestions, some from the librarian and most probably from the architects and engineers office. It may include some firms which have previously been used with satisfaction by the institution and some which have not been used. The specific criteria for selection should be determined by the group. All firms which seem to meet the criteria should be asked to state their interest in the job and availability for interviewing, to describe their present workload, and to supply copies of their brochures and a list of professional experience. This procedure may enable the institution to narrow the number down to six or fewer firms that would be interviewed and for which references should be checked with previous clients. A visit to the architect's office is very useful before the institution comes to a final decision. One may consider who are the key individuals who would be assigned to the library project, what is their experience and where may they be weak, what kind of support staff they have for drafting or specialized talents, what is the office workload, what kind of personal relations exist, how business-like is the office, and how much time and effort is there in getting to and from the office. One can discuss the experience the firm had on previous academic jobs or on libraries, and try to evaluate whether it may be advantageous or even be disadvantageous.

The particular process of selection may have a great many variations. For example, one fine old New England college states the following process:

First, let me emphasize that we did not have a big formal AIA competition though I anticipate that many have construed it as such. We have followed a particular selection process of architects for the student union, science complex, the Theater, the recently completed dormitory and finally, the latest, the Library Addition and Renovation.

Very simply, the philosophy has been something like the following: If architects are invited to make presentations to whatever selection committee may be involved, they invariably discuss their successes in short projects with which the committee members are unfamiliar. This places us in an even more embarrassing position as frequently committee members are untrained in architecture or construction and therefore are unable to intelligently evaluate what they're hearing. In an effort to avoid this situation, we follow a different routine.

First, the Physical Plant Department recommends to the committee eight or so highly reputable architectural firms who are knowledgeable in the particular area. The committee after listening to the usual presentations will select three firms to continue. The three firms will each be paid $1,000 and asked to spend at least one day on the campus meeting with various groups or individuals to become somewhat familiar with the design problem. They are then asked to return after a few weeks to study the problem and to make a one-hour presentation to the selection committee (usually plus the Buildings and Grounds Trustee Committee). The presentation is expected to focus on the design problem at our college. Since they are discussing their approach and alternatives to a problem which is better known and understood by the members of the committee, they are better able to evaluate the capability of the architectural firms.

Following the presentations, the Trustee Buildings and Grounds Committee receives the recommendation of the Ad Hoc Committee and the Buildings and Grounds Committee takes the definitive action in making the final selection.

The acceptance by architects of this process has been uniformly positive. In all of the twelve to fifteen firms that were involved, there was only one who felt that they had been unfairly treated. In all honesty that firm did not make a sincere attempt to work with our requirements and the attempt at circumvention was poorly conceived. Obviously we do not award prizes nor do we widely publicize this procedure.

Sometimes a firm will propose a joint venture if it is small or lacks particular talent. The employment of joint venture architectural teams has had varying results, not all of which have been satisfactory. Such arrangements usually are a compromise in which a nationally prominent architect is brought in for the name and the hope of having a striking design. Pairing that firm with a local one is convenient for some practical tasks, is good public relations with respect to local employment, and may be necessary for political reasons since some states require selection of an architectural firm in the state on state-financed buildings. The working relationship between the two firms is of a critical nature and should be explored in depth. This is not to say that it is an impossible arrangement for obtaining a satisfactory building but only to point out that there are special problems which need to be explored. An absolutely clear understanding of divided responsibilities and of who makes what decisions is critical in order that a joint venture work to satisfaction.

A donor's selection of the architect is almost always suspect. Harvard's Widener Library was the result of the donor's choice of a favorite architect located in Philadelphia. The firm had done the Philadelphia Free Library building as well as work for Duke University. After architect Trumbauer visited Harvard, two draftsmen went to Cambridge for about a week and returned with a first plan to show the donor. Apparently the donor's commitment of funds was pending while the initial design was undertaken. Mrs. Widener made an offer of the funds for the building plans, and the proposal was accepted. The agreement between the university and the donor indicated that it would be "a library building in substantial accordance with plans and specifications which had been prepared by Horace Trumbauer." Many of the building problems of the Widener Memorial Library (fig. 4.2) derive from such an unsuitable method of selecting and working with the architect, and there are other much more recent examples.

In the last analysis, it is important that the institution and, particularly, that the librarian feel a suitable rapport with the principal architect and the project architect with whom work will go on in a close relationship. A mutual understanding can result in a satisfactory product; any sense that communication is not effective and that there is not a common understanding and confidence in one another is quite certain to result in an inferior product.

The importance of good architecture and the selection of a good architect cannot be overestimated. The architect's role is a major and demanding one. The American Institute of Architects (national headquarters at 1735 New York Avenue, N.W., Washington, D.C.) and its chapters and state organizations (as well as similar organizations in other countries) distribute pamphlets which should be useful in selecting an architect or architectural firm. The following titles indicate their scope: *The Role of the Architect, a Brief Outline; Facts about Your Architect and His Work; Architectural Services and Compensations.* Do not hesitate to write to Washington or the local AIA chapter for information.

4.3 Architectural Competitions

Early in the century architectural competitions were not unusual for a library, particularly in the case of large buildings. This method is still used occasionally in the United States and abroad in Argentina, Australia, Denmark, Federal Republic of Germany, Great Britain, Japan, and, in 1980, China, for the Peking (Beijing) National Science Library. Theoretically, it has several advantages. If a number of architects attack a specific building problem, results should be better than if one firm is chosen in advance and told to do the best it can. A competition calls attention to the building and provides publicity and extra excitement that may make fundraising easier. It may allay criticism after the building is built; people will feel that every effort has been made to obtain the best possible plan.

Often these arguments for an architectural competition are more theoretical than practical. It should generally be possible to select a competent architect and work closely enough so that a fine building will result without a competition, which in itself is bound to be expensive and take extra time.

Possible objections to a competition are that the winner may have presented a plan that is dramatic or sensational but unfortunately not particularly functional, and it is difficult to make changes after the winning design is announced. The architect may claim the competition was won because of certain features in the plan and may be unwilling to alter them. Competitions take extra time—sometimes six months or more. They are costly because of prize giving and other inevitable expenses. The winner's first prize is considered part of the regular fee if the building is constructed, but the other prizes and the expenses of the competition are all extras. Competitions are usually not judged by the client but by a group of judges, the majority of whom are architects and who may be more interested in architectural features than library function. Many of the better architects hesitate to compete because of the work involved and fear that their reputations will be damaged if they do not win.

There are two main kinds of architectural competition: (1) limited competitions, open only to a selected group of architects invited to participate, and (2) open competitions, to which one and all are invited. These may be local, national, or international in scope.

Attention is called to three library competitions, one in the United States and two abroad. The American one was for the Washington University Library (fig. 4.3). The original structures on the campus of that university were built largely to provide quarters for

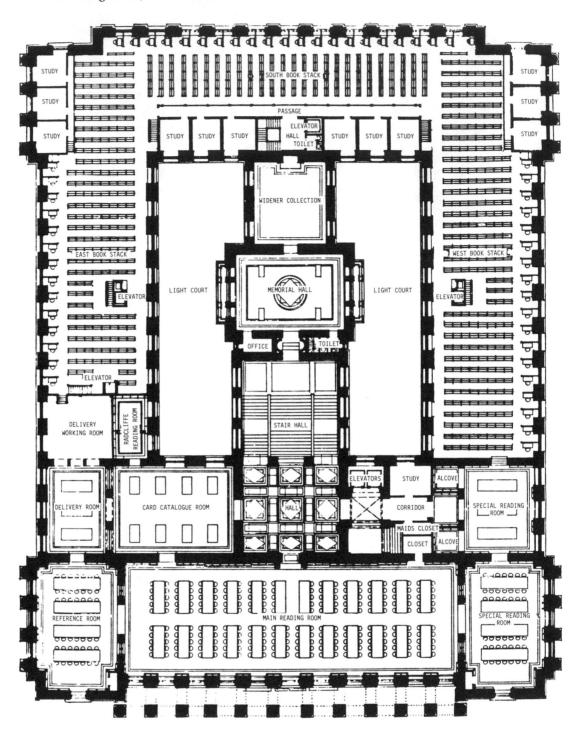

FIGURE 4.2 Harvard University, Widener Memorial Library second floor. The Widener stack has ten levels surrounding three sides of the building and two courts. The traffic pattern is simple, with only one range of stacks at right angles to the main aisle. Carrels (called stalls) are on the outside walls. Faculty studies are in the outside corners and on the wall facing the courts. The ranges are 50 in. (1.270) on centers with wide bases, so that the available aisle width is only 26 in. (0.660). The main aisle, which is 48 in. (1.219) wide, seems adequate for heavy traffic. The aisles by the carrels are only 38 in. (0.965), but, with open carrels on one side and stack aisles on the other, seem wide enough.

Problems with this fixed function arrangement include: (1) The main aisle is difficult to reach from the entrance; (2) the elevators are scattered and inadequate; (3) the stack aisles are quite narrow because of the wide (24 in., or 0.620) bases; (4) the distance from the entrance to the far end of the stack is over 400 ft (122); and (5) the main entrance is reached on the eighth of ten levels after going up five steps.

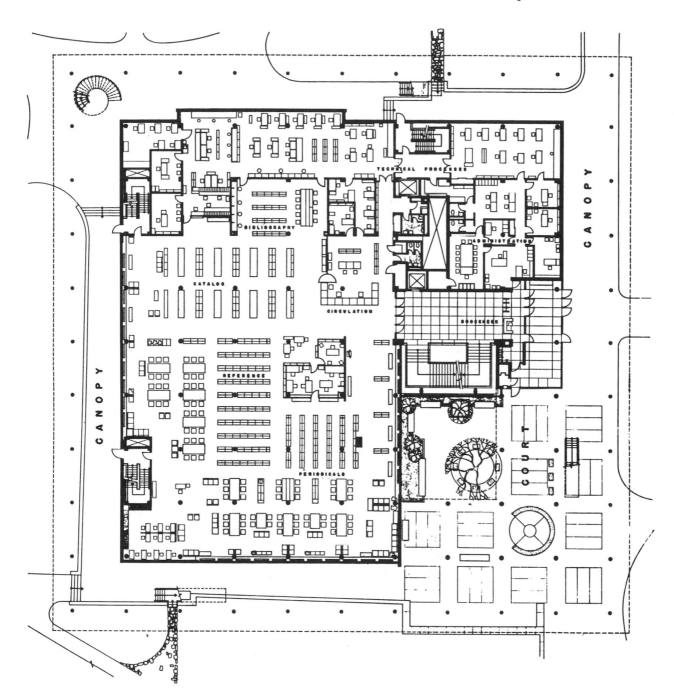

FIGURE 4.3 Washington University, John M. Olin Library entrance level. This level encloses 55 bays. Levels 1 and 2 below it enclose 84, level 4 encloses 60, and level 5 the equivalent of 67. The entrance level is very effective aesthetically; but the essential services there are unduly restricted, something which could have been avoided if the colonnade area were available for library use.

the St. Louis Exposition of 1904. Buildings added later followed the general architectural style of the exposition. Criticism was sure to arise if changes were made for new construction. There was a 1956 limited competition in which three local and three na-

tionally known architects were invited to participate, each being paid $2500 with the understanding that the winner would receive the commission and the fee would be 6½ percent of the total project cost. All the plans presented were for exciting buildings. The winner was a local architect, and the building is without doubt one of the better university libraries. More than one of the other plans submitted, while good from the architectural point of view, would have been disastrous functionally and perhaps financially.

Trinity College, Dublin, in 1960 and 1961 had a competition for an addition to supplement its great early eighteenth-century building, which is one of the finest libraries architecturally to be found anywhere in the world. It was believed that the publicity that would come from a competition would be useful in raising funds and that, while there was danger of serious criticism of any plan selected, this danger would be less if it could be selected from a large number. There were 218 submissions, and it is interesting to note that most of those that received prizes or honorable mention were, taken as a whole, functionally satisfactory. The winning design was built and is an exciting and distinguished piece of architectural sculpture. Yet it is extremely inflexible and is regarded by some as a functional disaster.

The third was for the Aalborg University Library, Denmark, serving four colleges which had been recently formed into the University Centre. In Denmark competitions for choosing an architect for government building projects are normal. Many young architects participate, and a majority of competitors are from Scandinavian countries. This 1974 open competition, sponsored by the Ministry of Education and Aalborg City Council, drew 37 proposals, which were judged by a board of architects and politicians. The competition was for a first-stage design, a layout proposal in principle for later stages, and design requirements for an integrated university center and housing development. Four prizes were awarded, five submittals were given honorable mention, and names of unplaced competitors were not revealed. A very satisfactory urban library resulted because of major involvement of library staff during the design effort.

As is usual, the Aalborg sponsors were not bound to use the first-prize winner but had the right to choose any receiving an award and to require modifications as they deemed best. It is not uncommon for the first prize to go to the outstanding design and the project to be awarded to the most economically viable proposal. The prizewinning Aalborg design group (architect, civil engineer, and landscape architect) was assigned the project, according to the principles of their competition submission but modified by specifications of the sponsors.

Architectural competitions should always be conducted under the direction of the local American Institute of Architects chapter or, in the case of international competitions, of the International Institute of Architects, which has its headquarters in Paris. There are accepted rules and regulations for these competitions, which are distributed by the various institutes.

4.4 Architectural Fees

The fees vary with the size and complexity of the project, from state to state, and also with the total cost of the project and the complexity of its architectural and mechanical character. A major part of the fees are those for architectural and engineering service. Consultant's fees, which are discussed below, should not be forgotten.

The architect's compensation is customarily based on a percentage of construction cost, although it may be a set fee plus office costs, a multiple of the technical payroll cost, a lump-sum agreement, or a per diem or hourly rate. Since these fees are related to the actual effort involved in buildings of different size and complexity, there is very little basis for negotiating except for a very small differential based on the complexity or simplicity of the building.

Usual services performed by the architect for the average building assignment include, in addition to the architectural concept and planning of the library, engineering services for structural, plumbing, heating, ventilation or air conditioning, and electrical work. This work may be performed within the architect's organization or by outside engineers employed by the architect. What are known as "usual" architectural services are ordinarily divided into three groups:

1. Preliminary services, which include: (a) conferences to determine the scope of the project, the problems to be solved and the general approach, and the preparation of schematic drawings; and (b) sketches, which include preliminary structural and mechanical design, preparation of preliminary or design development drawings of the approved solution together with outline specifications listing the materials to be used, and prelim-

inary estimates of cost. A "working" scale model may also be included.

2. Construction documents and specifications—also termed the "contract documents," which include preparation of the contractor's construction (working) drawings and specifications describing and illustrating in detail the work to be done, the workmanship, and the materials to be used; the preparation of structural, electrical, mechanical, and landscaping drawings and specifications; and assistance in preparing proposal and contract forms in securing bids and in awarding contracts.

3. Execution of work, which includes general administration of the construction work and necessary shop inspections; preparation as needed of additional large-scale and full-size detail drawings; checking of samples, subcontractors' shop drawings, and models or mock-ups submitted by contractors and subcontractors; issuance of orders for changes in the work required and approved by the owner; and checking of contractors' requisitions, issuance of certificates for payments, and final inspection of the work.

The architect's agreement with the client should make clear that the drawings and specifications, as instruments of service, are the property of the architect, whether the work for which they are made be executed or not, and are not to be used on other work except by agreement with the architect. However, in certain types of public work the authority involved sometimes stipulates that the original plans and specifications are the property of the public authority in question. This is also the case for many academic and research institutions. It should be added that no service, oral, written, or graphic, should be furnished by the architect without assurance of adequate compensation.

When the compensation for the usual services is a percentage of construction cost, it is commonly based on a percentage of the final construction cost, including fixed equipment and bookstacks, called the basic rate. Compensation for supplementary services is added to this. It used to be the case that basic minimum rates for institutional buildings, schools, banks, hotels, and theaters were recommended to be about 8.5 percent of construction cost for very small projects and as low as 5.5 percent for very large ones, plus 2.5 percent if they were renovation projects. These rates were designed to cover costs of

the architectural services with about 50 percent additional for profit. The particular character of any project would affect the amount. (Warehouses might be 1.5 percent lower, while laboratories and hospitals could be 1.5 percent higher.) While complete and adequate architectural services cannot reasonably be expected to be less under ordinary circumstances, long experience and outstanding reputation in a given field may entitle an architect to higher compensation.

The American Institute of Architects no longer recommends a schedule of rates because of anti-trust legislation. Rather, since 1975, the AIA has published *Compensation Guidelines*. A 1978 AIA leaflet, "Your Architect's Compensation, What It Covers and How It Is Derived," contains the following advice:

You have a choice of services. First, you and your architect meet to identify, from a schedule of designated services, the specific items required to carry out your project. The decisions may be recorded on a special form. At the same time, you and the architect assign responsibility for carrying out each item of service—either to the architect, to yourself and your staff, or to special consultants. . . .

The architect computes the cost of services. Once you and your architect have determined the general scope of services to your satisfaction and assigned responsibility for each item, the architect proceeds to compute the compensation. He or she does this by estimating the number of personnel hours and expenses needed to provide the services, and by adding amounts for overhead and reasonable profit and for expected reimbursable expenses. Normally the architect does this in-house, and only after summarizing the resulting figures by phase and for the entire project is there another meeting with you to review the amount of the proposed compensation and to complete and sign the owner-architect agreement. In addition to providing summaries, it may be appropriate under special circumstances for the architect to share details of the derived data. . . .

The architect sums up this personnel data and adds amounts for share of indirect expense or overhead (all items not directly chargeable to specific projects, as derived from office accounting records), and for other nonreimbursable direct expenses, outside services such as engineering and other consultation, and profit.

Profit is an important consideration. Profit is one main reason why the architect, like others who practice a profession or a trade, is in business. It is the tangible reward for professional and financial risk, and a return on investment. It is what is left of the total compensation after all expenses are deducted. The amount the architect includes for planned profit is derived in part from the nature of the project and the firm's financial goals, in part from taking into account certain expenses which the architect cannot include in compensation. Such "risk" items could include a rise in overhead costs after an overhead factor has been agreed upon, direct expenses not to be covered in compensation, and administrative costs tied to consultants' payments. . . .

Now you are ready to discuss compensation. Having taken into account all the factors in computing compensation, the architect is now ready to discuss with you the amount and the method of compensation for your project. As an aid, the architect may use the AIA's special project compensation summary form on which to record this cost information. The form contains space for proposed amounts of compensation by phase, a column that shows the same data cumulatively, a column for anticipated reimbursable expenses, and added space for revisions.

You are now at a most critical stage of the cost-based system, for it is here that you and your architect fix the actual amount of compensation. What yardstick can you, as the owner, use to see that the compensation being proposed is fair to both you and the architect?

Some owners budget what seems to them to be a realistic figure based on past experience. First-time owners rely on careful computation by the architect combined with open discussion. If, after all, your figure is still lower than the architect's proposal, a way must be found to reconcile the difference.

If you are still unable to agree, what happens? The best route to agreement in such cases is to pull out once more the schedule of designated services form and review the various items. Some costs may be brought down—for instance, by transferring responsibility for the service item from architect to owner. (Coordination, however, should remain with your architect.) An increase in the initial retainer will lower the architect's level of receivables and may induce him or her to modify the compensation amount. Sometimes, a second look at an item-of-service description will indicate a higher than average commitment of the architect's time, thereby justifying higher costs for that item.

Also, as you begin to discuss the type of construction contract, keep in mind that some kinds of contracts (such as a negotiated contract or one with several prime contractors) call for more from the architect by way of personnel hours than does a single contract, stipulated-sum arrangement. If you are a client with many projects, consider aggregating them in such a way that one architect could provide the needed services for several projects on a more cost-efficient basis.

Finally, you may wish to reduce the scope of services to bring the architect's proposed compensation into line with your budget. But be sure that the reduction in services will not hurt your project.

On occasion you and your prospective architect may run into the problem of ill-defined scope. If the early phases of your project fit that case, consider asking your architect to help you develop a scope of services; meanwhile you are billed on an hourly basis or other "cost-plus" arrangement. Then, as your program gains in precision, you can call for an accurate, cost-based proposal.[2]

This statement is provided to give some comprehension of the financial and other concerns involved in an architect's contract. Information about additional architectural services and payment practices is provided in Section 9.2 under Architectural and Other Fees.

4.5 Consultants

A major new building is a considerable undertaking. At the very least, the architect will employ structural, mechanical, and electrical or illuminating engineers. Very often a library building consultant will be used. Usually a landscape architect will be involved. Often an interior designer is included, and there may be other consultants involved from time to time, as cited in Section 4.5(5). Since a college or university does not have a full range of expertise and an architectural firm will not have all of these specialists even if it is a very large firm, the use of consultants is universal, although the number and choice of topics for consultancies will vary depending on the individual building project.

Finding qualified consultants is easy for some specialties because an architect can help greatly; other talents may be extremely specialized and a highly qualified consultant may be scarce in one or another part of the country. Yet with some inquiry of architects, of contractors, or of those who have planned buildings with similar problems, the names of individuals or firms will be obtained though they may be located quite far away. It is far better to select the distant specialist than a local amateur since use of the consultant is justified only when significant new talent is brought to the project.

In each case where a consultant is needed, sound selection criteria are called for. They can be, in some degree, similar to the criteria

[2] AIA Document 6N902. Copyright 1978 by the American Institute of Architects. All rights reserved.

for selecting an architect. In general terms one wants integrity and honesty, sound oral and written communication, highly professional and experienced talent, and an availability to the project and an interest in working on this particular building project. Consultants commonly work either on a percentage of cost or on an hourly or daily rate plus expenses. The fees will vary markedly, depending on the experience of the consultant and the scarcity of and demand for that expertise, but they should almost never be the primary basis for selecting a consultant. If a planning team needs to bring in a special expert, the need must be an important one, and a consultant who seems to be expensive may save the institution a great deal of expense.

As with selection of architects, a thorough interview and sometimes a visit by the consultant to the institution and a visit by institutional representatives to the consultant's office can be very helpful. Once the scope of the task is understood, the architect or the institutional representative should discuss the business aspects with the proposed consultant. A jointly signed document or contract is highly desirable even if it is merely a letter of understanding of the nature of the involvement, what is expected of the consultant, and what basis for payments is in the agreement.

In deciding where it is particularly important to have highly qualified expertise, one may look at significant errors or problems that have occurred during past building projects or are now plaguing the institution. Although there is no statistical frequency table that can guide, the following are frequent:

1. The whole project had to be postponed or given up because costs were underestimated. Cost overruns accumulated during construction.

2. The size of the building had to be reduced at the last minute. A costly change was required during construction to meet a local code.

3. The column spacing is so awkward that library reading or shelving capacity is lost and the columns fall awkwardly in passageways.

4. The lighting glares, reflects badly, or is very obtrusive in the peripheral field of vision.

5. Some types of seats are not used, or some writing surfaces or walls are covered with graffiti. The interior seems cold, unpleasant, or at least unattractive.

6. The ventilation or air-conditioning system is abominable for one reason or another. Vibrations cause disturbing sounds. The audio system components have not stood up for even three years of use.

7. Sunlight makes some areas very difficult to use because of heat gain; staff complain or readers will not use those areas.

8. The building was placed on the site in a way that makes it impossible or exceedingly awkward to build an addition.

9. Mezzanines are very awkward for housing part of the collection or using efficiently. A central well engenders anti-social behavior. Waste space exists through monumental stairways or halls.

10. The library sounds noisy. People are easily distracted by sounds coming from various activities in the building or from adjacent offices.

11. Floors or walls have not worn well, and show excessive wear.

12. Security and traffic problems abound. Main entrance door hardware is constantly loose, and the library is very difficult to find one's way around in without asking for help.

These and other problems can be found with unfortunate frequency in what are otherwise good, well-designed, and functional academic and research libraries recently built. The logical conclusion is that for various reasons, often very complex ones, the problem was not identified during the building project, a consultant may not have been employed who was expert in solving such problems, or the problem was a byproduct of some other forced change in the course of the project, which led to the architect and the client choosing the lesser of two evils. Though the above list is but a sampling, it may serve as a sober reminder that building a library is a complex undertaking and that use of consultants may be a requirement to eliminate or ameliorate what otherwise could be a very significant problem when the building is completed.

This section deals with a number of these consultants:

1. Library building consultant
2. Engineers
3. Landscape architect
4. Interior designer
5. Other consultants.

1. *Library building consultant.* In the past half century there have developed some individuals who had such extraordinary understand-

ing of library building planning that they were called upon frequently as consultants. Angus Snead Macdonald, Alfred Morton Githens, Joseph Wheeler, James Thayer Gerould, and John E. Burchard were pioneers. An experienced librarian-consultant, though rarely used in the United Kingdom, is more often used than not in some countries and certainly in North America. Even where the local librarian has considerable experience, a consultant has been found of distinct value.

Five questions should be answered in connection with library building consultants: Why have a consultant, how should a consultant be selected, at what stage in the planning should a consultant be selected, what should the consultant be paid, and what should the consultant do? Each of these questions will be addressed.

Why have a consultant? A consultant is ordinarily appointed because the institution realizes that without such a person it will have no one available, including the architect, who has had the desired experience in planning a library building. In spite of the large number of libraries that have been constructed since 1950, the typical librarian rarely has an opportunity to participate in the planning of more than one building during a career, and until recent years comparatively few architects had enough experience with library buildings to qualify as a specialist. The administration of an institution then may well believe that a consultant should be appointed in order to place at the disposal of its planning team the knowledge and experience that would not otherwise be available, or not available in sufficient degree.

Institutions sometimes have a local history or some influential persons holding rather extreme views which make a consultant particularly useful. There may be a trustee who wants what his or her grandfather wanted, and only a monumental or a gothic building will satisfy. There may be a dean who thinks that audio-visual support is more important than a library. There may be a professor who believes in excessive decentralization of library facilities or in seminar rooms for advanced classes in which basic collections of that special field are shelved. There may be a science professor who is convinced that no library is going to be needed in the future because of computer networks and other technological developments. There may be a librarian who is intimidated by videotext technology or cable television, or who has had bad experiences with major book thefts. There may be special problems, and the institution's representatives who have the overall responsibility for the building may very often believe that an outsider could provide a needed balance wheel. "A prophet is not without honor save in his own country."

But in most cases a consultant is wanted because of the realization that special knowledge is not locally available, that the cost of a library building is great—it sometimes doubles the institution's investment in its library, amounting to as much as twenty times the annual budget—and that mistakes would be extremely serious. Previously when libraries were planned, the librarian generally had comparatively little to say about the details; too often the architect went ahead without knowing library problems, and, being primarily interested in the aesthetic side of the matter, the result was not functional. This is an age of specialists, and it is not strange that library building consultants have been more in demand during the last few decades.

The chief reason for a library building consultant, then, is to make available special knowledge of the functional needs and requirements in a library building, and to make sure that an effective advocate will speak for these needs as planning proceeds.

How should a consultant be selected? Select a consultant with experience. Investigate and find out about the results of work done elsewhere. Keep in mind not only the consultant's knowledge of building planning but also his or her ability to influence persons and make them understand the basic problems involved. An expert in library building planning who cannot get ideas across to the architect, to the other members of the planning team, and to the institution's administration may be pretty useless, however much is known.

The consultant should have the ability to explain the reasons for a point of view and to persuade others of the importance of carrying out the suggestions. The consultant must not be overly dogmatic, should be fearless in expressing views, must avoid undue aggressiveness, and must understand the local situation.

There must be enough understanding of the architect and engineer to avoid unsuitable and impractical suggestions. One must realize that planning a library building involves not only functional but also very difficult and critically important architectural and engineering problems.

The desirability of picking the most appropriate consultant cannot be overemphasized. The person should be the right individual for the particular job at hand, perhaps suitable for one institution and not for another. The qualifications for a good librarian do not necessarily make a good library building consultant. Just because an individual is eminent in the library profession or a successful administrator of a large library does not mean competence in planning buildings. Neither should one be chosen just because of working in the same city or state, although close and convenient accessibility can be particularly helpful.

A successful public library building consultancy does not necessarily mean that the consultant can do the same on a college library or vice versa. Indeed, that would rarely be the case. Problems of college library building planning and university and research library building planning differ greatly from those of public libraries, and in details will differ considerably from each other. Pick a consultant who seems to have the knowledge, the experience, and the broad-gauge mind that will assure an understanding of your particular problem and help in the places where you need help. If you need someone to influence your governing board, library committee, or administrative officers, rather than to help with the details of the building planning, pick someone who, in your opinion, can be persuasive. A poor selection may be worse than none at all.

At what stage in the planning should a consultant be selected? If you are going to have a consultant, select one just as soon as possible. The person can be of use in deciding whether you should build a new building or add to an old one, can help to select the site, and can properly give advice on the selection of an architect. Normally the consultant should not recommend a specific firm, but can offer suggestions regarding the qualifications that should be met. If the consultant can be appointed early enough, before important decisions have been made which will be impossible or embarrassing or expensive to change, fundamental mistakes may be prevented. However, if one is not used at the beginning, problems may often develop which make the appointment imperative; better late than never.

Unfortunate developments sometimes arise, more often in a public, tax-supported institution than in a private one, where the governmental authority or the source of the building funds and the institution's administration, without consultation with the librarian or faculty library committee, decide on the amount of money to be made available for a new library, select the architect and the building site, fail to provide time for the preparation of a program or the employment of a library building consultant, and make basic irreversible decisions that almost inevitably bring about poor planning, an unsatisfactory library building, and a waste of funds. If the architect has had experience in library building planning, some of the hazards may be avoided; however, lacking such experience or a qualified consultant, the results can be and occasionally have been disastrous.

What should a consultant be paid? There is no accepted schedule of payments for library consultants. As yet library building consultants are not in an organized and accepted profession, and they may never be.

Three fairly definite methods are used in charging. One is on a percentage basis, the percentage varying according to what the consultant is expected to do. It may be scaled depending on the extent to which the consultant is involved in the procedure from beginning to end, as the architect is, being on call during the construction as well as during the preliminary planning and the working-drawings and specifications stage.

The second method is an agreement by which the work will be done for a definite sum, or at least an amount not exceeding that figure, with consideration given, as the plans develop, to the amount of time spent. Ralph Ellsworth has suggested one tenth of one percent of the total project cost may be budgeted for the consultant. He adds that it may not all be used, since it depends on how many days may be required.

The third method is for the consultant simply to say that charges will be so much a day, plus expenses. The per diem may range from $250 upwards, according to the experience and the prestige of the consultant and the job at hand. The consultant may set a rate which is equal to the full-time employment salary rate if he or she is relatively inexperienced or as much as twice the rate if very experienced. A small college branch library project costing $500,000 might need a consultant, but 0.1 percent of the total, or $500, might not be adequate budgeting for either the second or third method.

A consultant with a great deal of experience may feel that in a situation with complications of one kind or another the rate for an experienced person is not adequate and that a somewhat greater per diem is not unreasonable. A team of consultants, working together and contributing among them expert knowledge in various fields, may require altogether a larger percentage of the total cost though perhaps less per day per person, and so on. Some consultants, particularly those working with institutions in which they are personally interested for one reason or another, do a great deal without charge except for expenses.

In all cases the institution should not base its selection primarily on the cost but on the person whom it wants. The consultant should not try to bargain and charge as much as traffic will bear but should set a reasonable rate for the particular job and let the institution take it or leave it. Almost all consultants are in a sense volunteers. They usually have full-time jobs and serve as consultants to help other libraries, benefit other colleges or universities, and serve their professional goals. So they give of their spare time and deserve suitable recompense for this extra work.

What should the consultant do? The consultant should do everything within reason to plan the best possible building, making knowledge and experience available to those concerned, using best judgment about when to push and when perhaps to hold back temporarily or permanently, if it is believed that someone else's voice on a particular point at a particular time can be more valuable. One should defer to the specialist in a field for which one is not particularly qualified, although if a definite opinion is held based on good authority, one should state the case quietly and persuasively. One should avoid butting a head against a stone wall if there is a good way around it.

To be more specific, the consultant called on at the very beginning should as a first task go over the whole situation in general terms, so as to obtain a firm grasp of it. Then the consultant should try to learn enough about the institution, its history, its background, and its objectives, so that the framework of the

library's requirements becomes reasonably clear. These needs should then be translated into space requirements, with the realization, of course, that the results will be an approximation.

A consultant may have basic formulas for use in this way. Different formulas are required for different types of institutions. For a small academic library, for instance, something like the following might help: ten to twelve volumes can be shelved in one square foot of gross floor space, and in a larger library up to fifteen may be a safe figure. (This is a range of 107 to 160 per square meter.) Fifty square feet or a little more will accommodate a reader. This 50 sq ft (about 4.7 m²) will provide not only for reading-room space but for the staff to serve the readers, the processing work space, and the nonassignable space for the whole building as well. The two added together, that is, the space for books and for readers and services to readers, will give the gross square feet if no unusual special facilities are required, such as an auditorium, audio-visual areas, an exhibition room beyond normal lobby space, classrooms, more than a limited number of seminars or faculty studies, and special lounges. These are extras and must be added to the previous figure.

With a very rough total of space requirements available, the present building should be carefully investigated by the consultant. The questions should be answered about whether, with rearrangements within that building, the space required for a few years more can be provided or whether a wing could be added without leaving the building in an undesirable position aesthetically or functionally. The possibility and advisability of major alterations and an addition should always be seriously considered, so that no interested person can say that such alternatives were left out of consideration.

At this stage, of course, it is desirable to reach a decision about the time ahead for which plans are to be made, for not only the present but also the future requirements are of interest. Projected growth in book collections is the major determinant.

When a conclusion has been reached about the total space requirements, the problem of a site should be settled. Do not permit the decision on that point to be determined until you and the consultant know what is needed and can be sure that a satisfactory building of the size required can be placed on the plot selected. If the long view is to be taken, be sure that thought is given to the next stage when the new building will be outgrown.

It will now be time to consider in detail the written program for the architect and make sure it is complete. It should provide, if not the exact size of each area, an indication of the required size in terms of readers, staff, and collections to be housed and the desired spatial relationships among the different areas. The role and content of the program are discussed in Chapters 5 and 8.

The program is a matter of greatest importance. As often as practicable the program should be written locally by the librarian on the building committee or by someone on the scene who is skilled in a task of this sort. It is almost impossible for an outsider to obtain the required information in a short time. But the consultant can and generally should take a vital part in the program preparation, primarily by asking the questions that should be answered and by making sure that important points are not omitted. In other words, the consultant should be the guide and critic rather than the author. Sometimes a consultant may think that it could be better done personally, and perhaps that could be the case; but, on the whole, if the program is written by those who have to live with the results, it should be much more satisfactory. The building committee and the librarian, for instance, will understand the program better if they have written it or taken direct responsibility for it. They will then be able to explain it more successfully to the faculty and students or the governing boards and the public in general, than if it is written by the consultant.

Help in selecting the architect, either after or before the program has been completed, can be provided by the consultant. But, as has been already noted, this must be done carefully, preferably confining suggestions to the type and characteristics of the architect to be selected rather than recommending a particular firm.

The consultant, or the librarian for that matter, should ordinarily not prepare schematic drawings or preliminary sketches for the architect beyond those which indicate desired spatial relationships. It is important, however, for the consultant to see and discuss with the individuals concerned the drawings that the architect makes, particularly those that have to do with spatial relationships and

function, the adequacy of the space assignments proposed, and their capacity to fulfill the program requirements. There certainly should be involvement in detailed review of equipment layouts and traffic patterns, floor coverings, lighting, security, acoustic problems, ventilation, and so forth. Furniture design could well be included, particularly sizes, and, to a limited extent, color and finish. (See fig. 4.4.)

If the architects and one or more members of the planning team go to other libraries to learn how to solve planning problems, it is useful for the visits to be made under the sponsorship and direction of the consultant, who can suggest libraries to be visited and points to be kept in mind during the visits. If the consultant goes along, which is sometimes desirable, attention can be called to important features and causes, alternatives, and consequences can be discussed.

The consultant should be available by telephone and by letter as questions and problems arise, throughout the working-drawings stage and preferably during construction as well, even if appearance on the construction site is not necessary.

It should be noted that it is always dangerous to attempt to give advice without knowing fairly intimately the local situation, including the climate, the terrain, the campus and its master plan, if any, as well as the general spirit and atmosphere, philosophy, and objectives of the institution. It is difficult to get acquainted with these without being on the spot. Consulting in absentia, either here or abroad, is not effective.

A final question in connection with "What should the consultant do?" lies in how far this specialist/advisor should insist that the architect and the institution follow recommendations. For instance, should the consultant withdraw if major suggestions are not followed? Should the institution be asked to agree that it will not proceed without the written approval and the consent of its consultant? Since ultimatums almost never serve any constructive purpose—few persons are infallible, and circumstances alter cases—the authors believe that a "yes" answer to these questions is too drastic. If a prospective consultant believes that the answer to these questions is "yes," as some consultants have proposed, this should be specified and approved by both parties before the work is undertaken.

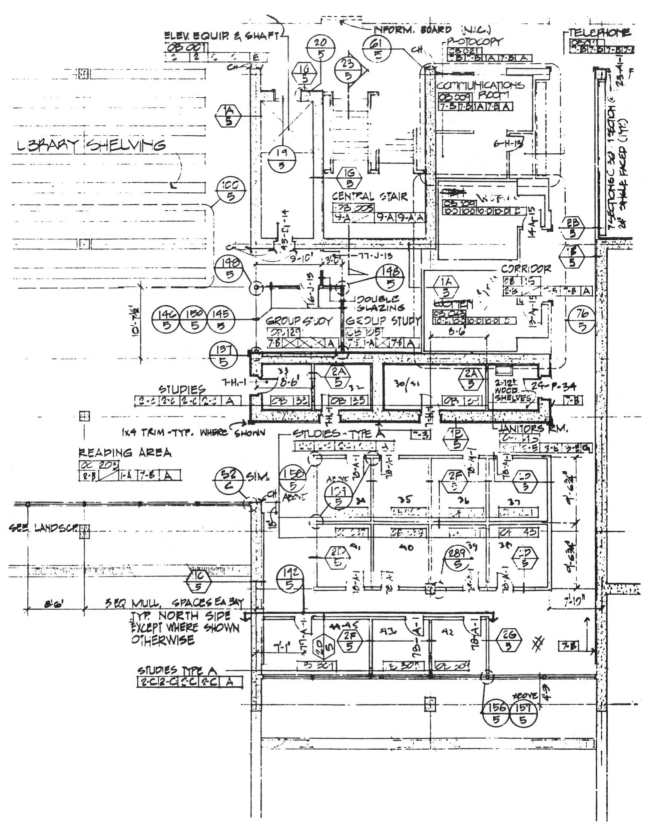

FIGURE 4.4 Architectural drawing. Much of the information on an architectural drawing is obtained by relationships to other drawings or the specifications as identified by a system of symbols and codes. To the inexperienced, understanding the drawing can be a frustration that can easily be circumvented with the help of a consultant. Such help is, of course, only a small part of the help that a consultant can provide for the librarian.

A consultant can, of course, always withdraw and refuse to be publicly associated with the project; however, Mr. Metcalf's experience with several hundred planning enterprises suggested to him that a procedure of this kind is seldom, if ever, necessary or justified. In the authors' experiences, architects as well as librarians and academic administrators tend to be very reasonable. They are all seeking the best possible results with the funds available. Although agreement cannot always be reached, compromises can be reached if people truly understand the case and communicate. The consultant is serving the institution. Only the institution will have to live with the result.

2. *Engineers.* An architect's contract ordinarily includes the foundation, structural, heating, air conditioning, plumbing, and electrical parts of the work. If the architect does not have in the firm those who can supply these services, as many competent architects do not, the architect will engage and pay for the consulting engineers. This arrangement is standard practice. Where unusual circumstances suggest, special engineering consultants may be needed. Such services as soil and foundation investigation, acoustical engineering, and lighting design are specific and common examples. Sometimes the institution may ask the architect to select the engineering consultant; and the institution may properly challenge a choice of consultant if it has had poor experiences with the firm. At other times it may ask the architect to work with one selected by the institution in order to ensure the desired results. If the initiative is taken by the institution, it must expect to pay for the additional cost but, whatever arrangements are made, the financial implications should be examined and agreements should be reached.

A great many library buildings have had unusual problems. Unstable soil may require caissons being carried down to bedrock. The building may need to be designed to "float" in the soil because of lack of suitable subsurface conditions. Simmons College and Tulane University libraries had such problems. The heating, ventilating, and air conditioning requirements in tropical climates, in very cold zones, or for portions of buildings housing unique materials may bring special problems. Library lighting and acoustical conditions are particularly critical in a building that must be conducive to serious and prolonged study. Each institution needs to decide whether these requirements are sufficient to justify the hiring of consultants who are particular specialists, beyond the architect's obligation to provide the solid and mechanically operating building meeting the basic needs of the institution.

Even though the institution ordinarily must leave it to the architectural firm to select its engineering consultants, the performance reputation of the chosen consultants can constitute one basis for judging among architectural firms. In any event, it is well to discuss with the architect the individual requirements in as much specificity as one might the functional layout or library furnishing requirements. Even very large U.S. architectural firms seldom have engineering consultants on their staff. If they do in their main office, branches in other cities will employ local engineering consultants who know the codes and local building conditions. The critical aspect here is how long and well the architect and the engineers have worked together, how competent are the engineers, and how effective they will be as part of the team. A building can be overdesigned structurally as much as it can be underdesigned, and coping with problems such as earthquake forces or subsurface water conditions can lead to designs which may be unnecessarily expensive, depending on the solution chosen. Agreement on the qualities needed by engineers chosen by the architectural firm thus becomes important in formation of the planning team.

3. *Landscape architect.* Few architectural firms in the United States have on their staff a landscape designer; however, most large firms in Canada do include such services. If the firm does not provide the service, it will know what firms in the area have good reputations and commonly will have a standing arrangement with one or more. The arrangement for this service is more flexible than it is for some other consultants. The college or university may have used a landscape firm to work on a master campus plan to include roads, pedestrian and bicycle paths, outdoor signage, and lighting. The institution sometimes asks the architect to work with a landscape firm with which it has had good experience in order to ensure continuity of campus treatment. The landscape drawings will be part of the bid documents. Coordination between the landscape firm and the

architect is particularly important on matters of drainage and access routes, and it may be very important in terms of wind or sun screening. Good landscaping can enhance a good exterior building design and can soften or mask mechanical necessities or an unattractive feature. Appropriate landscaping can be an important feature in almost every project (fig. 4.5).

4. *Interior designer.* The interior design commission may be performed by the architect or by an independent design firm selected by the architect or by the institution. Such a firm may be retained and paid by one or the other. In any event, all concerned should know whether the consultants are working for the architect or the institution and who is financing their effort.

Interior designing is certainly within the accepted province of the architect, since it involves the design and purchase of furniture and equipment and may include wall colors, carpets, signs, and exhibit cases. Sometimes it is taken out of the architect's hands and turned over to the purchasing agent of the institution, on the grounds that the architect's commission may run, for this particular type of work, up to ten percent of the total. However, if the furniture does not serve very effectively, the effects on library operation may be unfortunate. The library building consultant, on the other hand, has the functional arrangements as a primary responsibility and can rarely be counted on to give satisfactory advice in connection with the aesthetic side of the problem.

Since library furniture and equipment is a special field in itself, an interior designer (not an interior decorator) who specializes in library work is sometimes called in as a consultant. This expertise should be used more often. A poor interior design can be a disaster; and, indeed, some work by designers independent of the architect has led to dreadful experiences. Only if financial circumstances are severe should interior design work not be done by an interior design firm or the architectural firm with a competent staff expert (a member of the American Society of Interior Designers). In past years a furniture manufacturer may have done a layout as a marketing assistance. Occasionally the library building consultant may do it. Yet it will be far more satisfactory if a professional interior designer is given the commission. If an independent consultant is used, the firm

should, of course, work very closely indeed with the architect and with the library consultant, if there is one, to assure compatibility of product and avoid any conflict in interest. Quality interior design is essential in producing an outstanding project.

Choice of the interior designer can be approached with criteria similar to those used in choosing the architect and with a selective process of references and interviews, as with the architect. The cost of interior design services is treated in Section 9.2 under Architectural and Other Fees.

This volume does not try to deal extensively with the problem of furnishings and finishes. This is a matter with complexities of its own. At this point it can be indicated that the very early involvement of an interior designer with the architectural plan development can be a great benefit. The furnishings selected will need to be in harmony with the interior finishes. The interior designer may in fact have responsibility for the color of wall surfaces, the choice in some instances of applied wall surface material, and selection of carpet type and colors; may or may not be involved with built-in furnishings; always has responsibility for movable furnishings including their number, distribution, orientation, design, texture, color, and construction details, whether anchored or not; and may be involved with graphics or sign design as well as choice of art work. The scope of the individual contract needs to be carefully determined.

Effective working relations between the interior design firm and the architectural firm can and should be expected to work very well even if the architect had an interior design department which lost the commission. As in the choice of all other consultants, the resultant building is dependent on the quality of the individuals, their commitment to the project, their willingness to listen, study, and meet the objectives of the institution. An interior design firm will propose individual items of movable furnishings and will also prepare budget estimates on the equipment and develop written specifications for all furnishings. The firm may use entirely stock items from one or various manufacturers, may use companies which are not specialists in library furniture and do exceedingly well by this choice, and will occasionally design specialty items when a satisfactory design is not already on the market. The interior designer

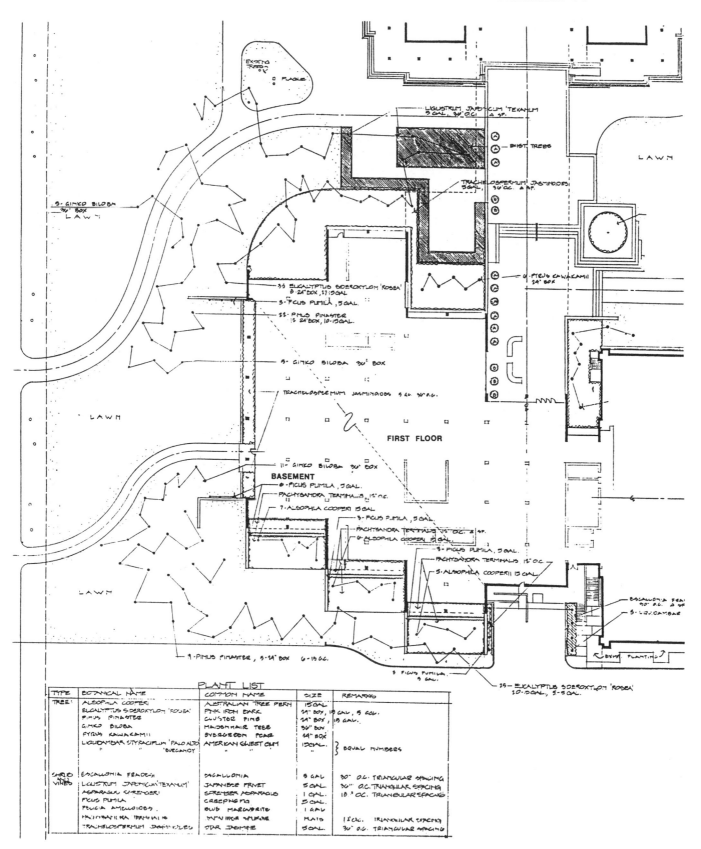

FIGURE 4.5 Landscape planting plan. While it is useful to look at the planting plan, it must be viewed in conjunction with the grading plan. In this illustration, the lawn to the left slopes down to the basement level. It was later discovered that because of the degree of slope, lawn tractors could not be used; hand mowing was required to maintain the lawn. This work forced eventual replacement of the lawn with ground cover.

may have access to types of furniture not otherwise readily available and should certainly be an expert at determining what—with reasonable cost and attractive design—is sturdy, comfortable, functional, and has a satisfactory finish.

A number of American interior designers and architects who have had considerable library building planning experience have designed satisfactory carrels, with special features to fit the decor of the building as a whole. Some of them have designed chairs as well. But unless they are experts in work of this kind or have expert help, the results have not always been sturdy and comfortable, even if they are aesthetically pleasing.

The choice of furnishings may come from ideas found in many sources. The institution may rely wholly or largely on the interior designer; it may also suggest features or small details which have been found suitable in other library buildings and which can be blended into the project design. As an example of such use of ideas from other institutions, the following lists items or arrangements in the Stanford University Green Library East Wing, the ideas for which came from one or more other institutions:

Reading areas—based on the Tower Room at Dartmouth, Alumni Room at Bowdoin, and the Morrison Room at U.C. Berkeley
Group study rooms—Northwestern and Chicago's Regenstein Library
Directors' suite and personnel office—Chicago's Regenstein
Reference staff offices—Minnesota's Wilson Library
Reference desk—Harvard's Widener
Compact shelving for microtexts—Rice University
Sound system—Washington University
Lighting—University of Denver
Stack lockers—Washington University and Chicago's Regenstein
Central service rooms on stack levels—Northwestern
Dissertation rooms for graduate students in the stack—Princeton
Administrative conference room—University of Utah
Faculty studies—Cornell and Harvard's Widener
Card catalog arrangement—UCLA
Card catalog split-level height—Harvard's Arnold Arboretum Library
New book display—Princeton's Firestone

Basement connection to an adjacent bookstack basement—Yale's connection between Sterling Library and the Cross Campus Library, and Harvard's connection between Widener and Lamont libraries.

Good ideas are to be found in many places; and there is every reason to copy, in concept if not in detail, so long as program need is met and harmony of design is achieved.

5. *Other consultants.* The possible need for other consultants should be considered. There is, of course, an expense in retaining a specialist in any field. Doing so may result in extra effort and possibly some slight delay in the project; on the other hand, it can save a college or university from some egregious errors.

There is no definitive list of what other consultants might be used. (While a major project may use many in different specialities, a few may be experts in specialty firms which are the chosen equipment suppliers, e.g., a lock company or security system firm. Yet it is obvious that in the latter case one may or may not have entirely objective advice, and there is usually no consultant fee since costs are covered in profit from the sale of equipment and installation.) The following list is an example of the type of consultants who have been used on major recent university library buildings in the United States:

acoustics
art work
audio systems
code conformity (building, fire, etc.)
computer facility design
construction management
cost estimation, or quantity surveying
design (sometimes shared by a master architect)
energy conservation
exhibition facilities
food service
hardware
security systems
signs or graphics
technological applications (including but not limited to automation)

While there is separate justification for each of these, and others can be considered, an explanation of one is provided as a sample. Acoustic problems can abound in libraries, though study and research clearly demand a nonintrusive environment. Compressors, ballasts, air mixing and distribution boxes, door hardware, and chair glides on a hard floor are among the sources which can be extremely disturbing. An acoustic consultant is useful for large buildings, not for audio systems, but to check the architectural and engineering design by examining the plans in terms of area functions, materials, and electrical and mechanical system details (fig. 4.6). This comment is not to urge the use of any or all consultants from this list. It merely points out some options which are worth consideration.

The process of selecting any of these consultants can follow a pattern similar to the choice of architects or interior designers. The choice should be based on reputation for integrity, ability, and professional competence. References can be checked even if the individual has not worked on a library before. The individual may be retained as a consultant to the architect, or as a consultant to the institution. For instance, cost estimation could be done for the institution as confirmation of the construction cost calculations provided as a standard obligation of the architect.

The key question is whether the design team needs extra special talent to solve an important problem area. The question should be openly raised and discussed, generally at an early stage in the design process. In general, there are three approaches if one has had bad experiences or seen problems others have had. Stay away from the problem altogether. Or ask the architect to specify, for example, highest quality heavy-duty fixtures. Or use a specialist consultant for guidance. The expense of the latter approach can make a good building an exceptional one.

4.6 Early Activities with Architect and Consultants

The matter of the relationship of the architect, the librarian, and the planning team is of primary importance from the time the architect is selected, during the planning process, and until the building is completed. If the architect was selected without the approval of the librarian, the whole planning process may have gotten off on the wrong foot. If, on the other hand, the architect knows that the librarian had an important part in the selection, the good rapport between the two may be a great help.

The first talk between them may be crucial, and every effort should be made by the institution's administration to see that a good start is made. If the president, in notifying the architectural firm of its selection, is able to, and does, say that the institution has great confidence in the librarian and hopes that the architect will work closely with the librarian and give due consideration to suggestions in regard to functional matters, the statement will help ensure a successful relationship. In one case in which the librarian recommended the architect who was selected, the president said to him, "Since you have recommended the architect, you should notify him of the selection." He did, and an important step toward the success of the building was taken.

A good atmosphere is created if the librarian has had a major part in the preparation of a good building program and the architect realizes this, and if the librarian appreciates and understands what his or her part in the planning process should be and understands that the architect is the designer to produce an aesthetically satisfactory and functional building. The librarian must, of course, be prepared to answer questions, and both parties should reach a mutual understanding of the part each is to play.

The architect must realize that the librarian's province is to provide readers' services conveniently, efficiently, and economically, and that the librarian or the library consultant is the expert for these matters on the planning team. The librarian should understand that the institution has placed the design responsibility in the hands of the architect who is equipped and trained to analyze and interpret functional needs spatially and to translate this interpretation into bricks and mortar.

If the librarian presents to the architect functional problems and requirements and if the architect then studies them seriously and solves them, each of these important members of the planning team is fulfilling a proper role. Sometimes the librarian has contributions to offer in the architect's province and vice versa; but only if a clear understanding of the ultimate responsibilities of each one is reached will a completely harmonious relationship exist. In many large architectural firms the principal architect or head of the firm is not the one who works directly with the librarian; this duty is turned over to one of the partners or associates who serves as the project architect. The architectural decisions mutually reached should, of course,

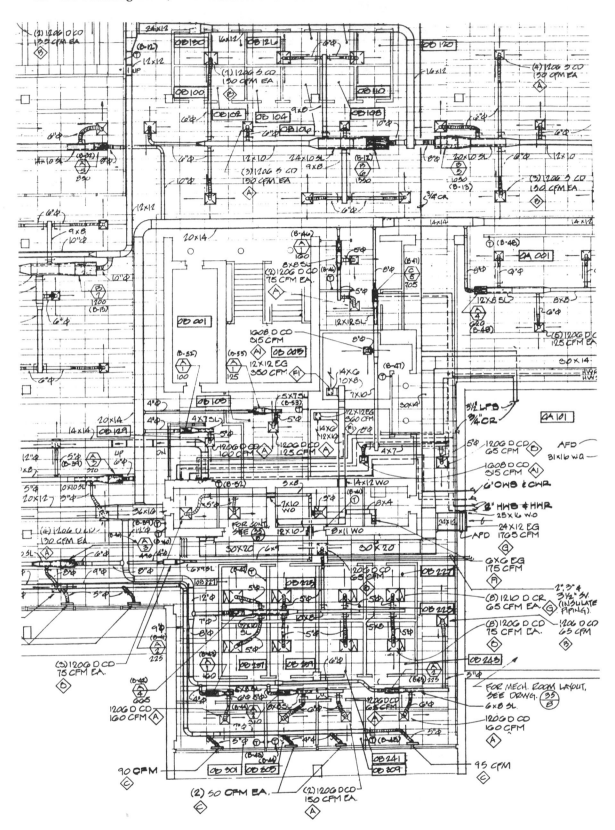

FIGURE 4.6 Mechanical system plan. An acoustic consultant would be interested in the potential sound transmission by ducts between offices and the speed of air delivery into a space and thus the sound it produces, both of which can be determined to a large extent from a plan like this. Other plans will show the isolation of mechanical equipment from the building structure, which is an equally important acoustic factor.

be reviewed by the principal architect before their submission to the institution for approval. The closest possible rapport is important.

All this can be summarized by saying that misunderstanding between the architect and the librarian must not be permitted. The same holds true for the other representatives of the institution. The administrative officers and the planning committee members, individually and as a group, must also understand the place of each person concerned in the planning process. They should never be played off one against another. In many institutions a first "kick off" meeting with architect, librarian, business officer, institutional planner, director of planning, plant services representative, principal consultants, and others is designed to clarify precisely the project scope, the role of each individual, the time schedule required, and the financial constraints.

Matters of Timing. The planning period should not be extended indefinitely. Neither should it be hurried too much; under pressure the best of architects and librarians will miss important factors. It is very rare for a satisfactory building to be planned and construction documents completed in less than a full year. Harvard's Lamont Library took more than a year and a half to plan, in spite of the fact that the librarian and the architect had already been considering possibilities and thinking about the building for six or seven years in advance. The same can be said for Stanford's Green Library addition. The planning process can be extended too far until all concerned become stale and unwittingly careless of important details. It is usually desirable to have a definite timetable worked out in advance, and both the architect and the institution should be expected to keep to schedule.

The timetable should include dates for completion and approval of each phase, when bids are called for, and the date when construction should begin. Do not try to push the preliminary phases too fast, particularly if for any reason frequent conferences between the two groups cannot be scheduled. The time required for preparing construction documents will depend largely on the size of the architect's staff and the other work on which it is engaged. Not less than six months is reasonable for a large building.

Taking bids and assigning the contract may require two months or more, and the construction for a building of 20,000 sq ft (say, 1860 m²) at least a year and for buildings over 100,000 sq ft (say, 9300 m²) as much as eighteen months or even two years or more, depending on geographical location and local labor conditions.

Try to plan so that the completion of the building will come at a time when it is possible to take advantage of it. A large college library should be finished in the spring or early enough in the summer so that occupancy can be carried out without too much pressure during the summer months, and allow for a shakedown period before the college opens in the autumn. A smaller college library or a university branch library might attempt to move in during the Christmas holidays or the Easter vacation, but if the winter climate is severe, this may be difficult or impossible. An addition to a main library can probably be occupied whenever it is finished; a completely new university library building can be very time-consuming to occupy no matter when. One must realize that delays are almost certain to occur, so little reliance can be given to timing the occupancy precisely.

Be sure that before any work is expected from the architect the contract with the architect is signed and agreement reached in regard to payments. The agreement should consider what will happen if for one reason or another, such as lack of funds or disagreement on the proposed plan, the building is never constructed.

At all times during the planning, the architect must keep in mind the total cost of the project, remembering that overall costs include equipment, fees, and landscaping, as well as the basic construction cost. The architect must not permit a misunderstanding with the library's representatives on the matter of cost, and vice versa.

After the program has been submitted to the architect and the firm has had an opportunity to study it carefully, the architect should be prepared to discuss with representatives of the institution all points that are not understood, aspects that need to be covered by more specific instruction, and program requirements that are judged to be too specific and on which the architect would like to propose changes. This is the time when most of the uncertainties should be resolved and definite decisions reached, if possible. The architect needs a clear understanding before preparing sketches for preliminary plans or setting drafters to work on details that might have to be changed because of previous failure to understand each other's wishes. Most difficulties come from a failure on someone's part to make a point clear and to explain the reason for wanting what is requested. If neither party has had experience in library building planning, it is easy to see why neither one understands the technical language to which the other is accustomed in one's own profession. Preconceived notions of what is right and essential easily become so deeply entrenched that they are hard to change. It is very important for the success of the enterprise that all members of the library planning team keep in close touch with each other and with the progress of the architect after the problem is tackled and the firm begins to prepare sketches indicating the proposed spatial relationships and space assignments.

Nothing more than the most preliminary plans can be made before the site is selected. As early as possible, but not too early, the module sizes (if the modular system is to be used) and the column sizes should be agreed upon. This cannot be done, however, until a decision has been reached on the size and number of floor levels and perhaps on whether a central utility and vertical communication core is to be used or whether these facilities are to be scattered. Make sure that in either case the core or cores do not interfere with present or prospective horizontal circulation patterns. Planning of the heating and ventilation system should not be delayed because it may take much more space than anticipated and reduce what is available for library purposes, thus complicating plans in other ways.

Before the construction documents are begun, the team members should all clearly understand whether the consultation will be frequent, regularly scheduled at certain stages of completion, or on a floor by floor and trade by trade basis. The institution should not abrogate its rights for further consideration at this time. Neither should it expect to interfere continually with progress. It is customary and good practice for the institution's chief business officer formally to sign off on schematics, and later on design development drawings, so there is legal understanding when one milestone is met and approved and work toward the next is officially authorized.

Authorization for the construction documents means that the basic plans are agreed upon, but there are still what may seem like minor matters where the librarian's opinion should be given consideration. These will include, for instance, the location of doors and the direction in which the doors swing. The placing of light switches is another example, as may be the selection of hardware and plumbing fixtures. As the construction documents are prepared, it may be found from time to time that an unexpected six-inch (0.150 m) difference in space available will require decisions regarding how the space is to be used or how to deal with the lack of it (fig. 4.7).

Meanwhile the furniture and equipment should not be neglected. Too often decisions on these matters are delayed, with the result that the design and selection process is hurried, and in too many cases the equipment is not available when the structure is ready for it. What part of the equipment will be in the general building contract? What are the architect's responsibilities for the furniture design and selection? Be sure that whoever has the responsibility understands the timetable so that construction will be completed and shipments can be made at a proper time that will not interfere with the building construc-

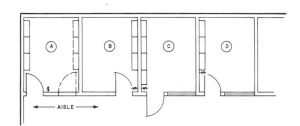

FIGURE 4.7 Door swings. Architectural drawings seldom show furnishings (shelving here), light switches (the "S" with a line through it), and door swings on the same drawing, but each can affect the other. Door A and B are so close to the wall with shelving that a fourth section cannot be added. Door B occupies important space in a small room. Door A placed to the right rather than the left (shown dotted) could provide a useful corner at the end of the aisle. Door C is typically best for handicapped access, especially for a small space, but care must be taken to avoid blocking the aisle. Door D, next to a glass panel, may require an awkward location for the light switch which, in turn, may limit the use of the shelving wall. Figs. 13.2 and 13.3 show other concerns about doors.

tion or involve furniture storage problems, and yet not delay the opening of the structure.

Study of Publications. Just as it has been stated that library staff should be prepared by reviewing selected publications on the planning of academic library buildings, so an early activity of the architect and consultants should also be such a review. This is desirable in order that the planning team have a good understanding of the terminology and process—and can understand the practices and attitudes of the other professions that go to make up the team. Librarians might look at some architectural and interiors magazines. The architects might look at some library periodicals, such as *Library Journal.*

However, the published literature is extensive and uneven in quality. Thus it may be that each individual can recommend key articles and a few most important chapters in books that the others should consider reviewing. This process can be useful throughout the course of the project. Some excellent works are cited in the appended bibliography, yet more recent publications may do a better job or deal with a more modern technology.

Visits on Site. It is well for several if not most of the planning team, when it is finally formed, to spend some time early on visiting and getting to know the architect's and consultant's key staff, just as they should visit the client's facilities and get to know key staff. Principal representatives of the library should be involved to some extent in conjunction with early meetings. No matter how brief the introductions, they can help early understanding and thus get the project off on a good footing.

Since buildings are three-dimensional spaces for human actions, it should be obvious that, as noted earlier, no publications no matter how carefully written can convey as much as seeing library buildings in use. Thus visits to key libraries are exceedingly important. If some college or university business officers question the value of that expense or time, they should be reminded that floor plans of their laboratories or libraries convey very little indeed of the actual physical appearance—the color and texture of materials, the shadows and glares, the human activity, the clutter and other visual and au-

ditory conditions. Reading may come first, but visits to a selected number of libraries of colleges or universities are exceedingly important. Since a library building involves huge amounts of money and a great deal of time for fundraising and for its design and construction, the expenses of site visits by three, four, or five principals in the team are an exceedingly modest investment for the potential of a very great payoff. Indeed the expenses of a cross-country trip are really nothing compared with the magnitude of the project and of the time and salaries of involved individuals who will use that time, even if they visit four or five sites all in the same state.

4.7 Level of Involvement

It is important for the college or university to realize the amount of time that will be required for a successful project. As has been mentioned earlier in this volume, the librarian or a principal associate to whom responsibility has been given should expect to spend anywhere from half-time to full-time on this project. The communication flow within the institution and indeed within the library staff is every bit as important as are the meetings with the architects and consultants. The involvement must be substantial and measure up to the magnitude of the task.

The design of meetings can be very important. Regular meetings with the architect will need to be called by some one individual in the institution, the agenda will need to be set and issued to all concerned, the objectives of the meetings will need to be clearly defined, and the results of the meetings will ordinarily need to be documented and distributed to all present and other concerned officials. Attention needs to be given to the size of the group. More than ten or a dozen can easily result in poor interaction, some being too timid to speak up or some wasting their time if they are needed on only one small aspect. Consider briefer meetings, scheduled well in advance, with fewer persons in attendance. The psychology of public meetings can result in bickering and attention to irrelevant matters if there is not a clarity to the purpose of the meetings. All too many building planning groups get off track, and poor feelings result. This can be the case for small projects just as much as for large projects, and it can be even more difficult with respect to branch libraries, where there are both library representatives and faculty departmental representatives and perhaps representatives from a dean's office. Though these may be small projects, there is frequently need for even more effort on communication and the conduct of meetings.

In general, the college university planning officer assigned to the project should arrange the meeting and preside. The meetings need to be conducted with some deftness so that there is a firm direction taken in the meeting while at the same time there are ample opportunities for the participants to express their points of view and contribute to the conclusions of the meeting. Sometimes a meeting may be deliberately staged as a brainstorming session. The interactive method of conducting such meetings, with a carefully prepared agenda, the use of a facilitator, a public record on flip charts, and a recorder, may be the best method. (A useful book is *How to Make Meetings Work; The New Interaction Method*, published by Playboy Press, Chicago, 1976.)

As has been indicated earlier in this chapter, there may be a great many consultants involved in the project. Each of these will be involved for varying amounts of time. A library building consultant may be involved for the entire process. Engineers and interior designers may be involved for very considerable periods of time. Others may be briefly involved, perhaps for only one or a few meetings. In each case the definition of the role to be played needs to be explicit for all concerned. Each consultant will need to be adequately briefed before being involved, especially before any sizable group meeting; the definition of services rendered must be precise, and the basis for concluding the consultancy must also be a matter of agreement.

A final word about involvement. The documentation of many decisions on building projects is exceedingly important. Dozens of people are involved in a small project, and there will be more than a hundred involved throughout a large project. The number of people involved means that the written record of decision meetings is essential. Minutes of important meetings must be prepared at once and distributed promptly. Major questions from one individual to another may deserve to be in writing and responses provided in writing. Any action which involves a policy matter, a financial commitment, a design cri-

terion, or an authorization must be in writing. Some interpretations or elaborations should be in writing. However, it should not be necessary to document the dozens and dozens of meetings which are held merely to review progress and check on the myriad of details that go into any large building.

Some institutional planning offices and some architectural offices have very formal documentation patterns. A specific numbering and lettering pattern may be followed. Forms may actually be used for certain kinds of documentation. This is not needed for many projects, or for smaller institutions or architectural firms. But in other cases formality has been found to be necessary, and it is well for the architectural firm and the institution to agree on a pattern of documentation at the very beginning of the architectural work.

Who Has the Last Word? It is obvious that sooner or later, and probably the earlier the better, some kind of an agreement should be reached about who makes the final decisions relating to architectural style, aesthetics, and function. Often five different individuals or groups may be directly involved:

1. The architect
2. The librarian
3. The donor, if there is one
4. The institution's administration represented by the president, or, through the president, the board of trustees
5. A special committee appointed by the administrative authorities to take the responsibility.

Which one of these individuals or groups should have the last word? Certainly, architecture is primarily the responsibility of the architect, but it is obvious that the administrative heads of the institution cannot avoid their share of responsibility and in the final analysis must approve decisions by the architect or others. The institution may, if it desires, delegate the authority and responsibility to a special committee made up of administrative officers, perhaps members of its own board, other officers of the institution, one or more consultants, or a faculty group. It may defer to the donor or leave the matter to the librarian.

Whatever is arranged, the architect should keep in touch with the librarian, or some other person assigned to the task of thoroughly acquainting the architect with the functional needs of the library, with the understanding that any disagreement which he or she cannot adjust should be referred to the administrative authorities.

The librarian is the library operations expert, and the functional aspect of the building should be regarded by the architect with as much seriousness as it is by the institution. Generally, the librarian or consultant is more familiar than the architect with the details of satisfying the functional aspects. The library representative and the architect can, if they cooperate, be of immeasurable assistance to each other.

The architect should be the one finally to recommend the methods of satisfying these functional necessities as well as the appropriate style and aesthetics. Having been selected on the basis of its competence and acquaintance with the problems involved, the firm is, or at any rate should be, the expert on the team for these matters. Its recommendation should be submitted to and approved by the responsible person or persons designated by the institution.

In too many cases deference to the principal donor has brought results which are not happy. This does not mean that the donor's wishes should not be given full consideration or that the donor should not be kept informed about the situation. Donors certainly are entitled to explanations if it proves impossible or undesirable to conform completely to their wishes. Unfortunately, not enough donors take the attitude that the late Thomas W. Lamont took in connection with Harvard's Lamont Library. The plans and model of the proposed building were placed before him, and he was asked to express his opinion. His reply was simply, "I like it, but if I didn't, I wouldn't say so. I want what the College decides that it needs."

The administrative authorities have a responsibility to the institution. It is to them ordinarily that complaints will come if the results are not satisfactory. With the shift in recent years from what is often called traditional architecture to a variety of contemporary and modern styles, some alumni of academic institutions have been upset by new buildings. They may be tempted to withdraw financial support. A few write letters to the alumni magazines and to newspapers, doing what they can to arouse antagonism in the hope that it will bring about changes. This statement makes no attempt to claim that architectural atrocities have not been perpetrated in library planning in recent decades, but it seems to be true that as one becomes more accustomed to new styles one is less likely to be offended by them.

It should be added that a great argument for modern or contemporary architecture, as some prefer to call it, has been that it can be simple, with good lines, functional, and relatively inexpensive to build and to keep in repair, and that it expresses future needs and hopes. But if the architect goes to extremes in an attempt to produce something different and the results are not functional, are more expensive, are not in keeping with the campus, and do not stand up physically, there is little excuse for the product.

From wide personal experience and from conversations with other librarians and library consultants, Mr. Metcalf had the distinct impression that there has been an unfortunate tendency in recent years (reversing the trend of the first decade after the Second World War) on the part of some of the more capable and better-known architects to attempt to attract attention by glamorous and exciting buildings which subordinate function to other features (fig. 4.8). They ignore the fact that most academic institutions must choose between a building which is primarily functional and quarters that will be more expensive, quickly outgrown, and be difficult to explain a generation hence when it will require an addition or even a replacement. Without question we need new architectural concepts and construction methods. We should not object to these just because they are new and different. There is no excuse for unattractive libraries; it is still true that form follows function in truly great architecture.

Sooner or later the institution must face the problem of the effect of architectural style on costs. Building a Gothic library today is so expensive as to make its desirability questionable. Anyone who has seen the previous main library in the University of Pittsburgh's Gothic Cathedral of Learning or the Sterling Library at Yale will understand this point and will also realize the functional problems that may arise from such a design today.

If the architect recommends a practically all-glass building that will require double windows and also sun protection of some kind on the inside or out or both, the net results in comfort and operating costs should be carefully considered. If irregular exteriors are

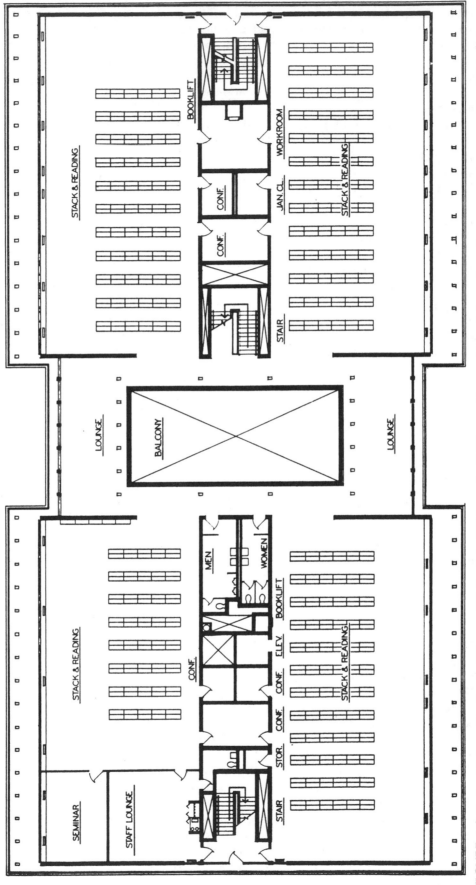

FIGURE 4.8 Butler University, Irwin Library. While this 1963 work of Minoru Yamasaki and Associates is an attractive example of his light, windowed style, with three levels of exterior repetitive vaulted-roof colonnade, its weaknesses include excessive windows (the entire east and west walls), constant maintenance problems from extreme narrowness and height of entrance doors, security problems due to safety doors on north and south sides, extremely limited and inflexible office and technical services areas, and a large light well limiting flexibility on the upper two floors.

planned with unduly large amounts of expensive outside wall areas which add to the construction costs, their desirability should be weighed. If the architect proposes a slanting roof with unusable attic space not required for the mechanical services and it adds a small percentage to the cost, its desirability should at least be questioned. These points are brought up to call attention to decisions to be made, not to object to any particular style of architecture. It may well be that the additional expenditures are worthwhile for symbolism or pride, but they should be incurred with open eyes.

Given the above, it is still obvious that the final responsibility for architectural style and aesthetic problems lies with the institution's administration. The institution can accept or reject final plans. It does not have to build the building as designed. It can even start again with a different architectural firm if it wishes and can justify to itself the extra time and costs.

The "last word" should never become an issue if the right architectural firm is selected. It will sincerely want to provide the institution with what is suitable. Cooperation and understanding of each other's problems by the two groups are prerequisites for the best results. Misunderstanding and an unwillingness to consider other points of view are the sources of most difficulties that arise. An architect should not be selected unless the institution is convinced that a good understanding will be achieved. A good architectural or library consultant can sometimes help to bring about a meeting of minds.

From the librarian's point of view, if the building planning can start from the inside, the result should be a better building functionally. For the architect to plan the building with the facade uppermost in mind, before knowing a good deal about the functional requirements, can be a serious mistake. While a few architects may be inclined to think that function is secondary and that planning from the inside out is impossible and illogical, the result is unlikely to be as useful a library as one that is planned with function uppermost in mind. Functional planning should be considered a challenge. Compromises may have to be made in connection with it, yet they

should be reached only after the persons directly involved have given full consideration to the consequences.

The Lamont Library building was planned almost completely from the inside out. The architect, when asked to comment on this statement, wrote as follows:

The architect's point of view on "planning from the inside out" should and I am sure does consider that a building is ideally a complete and homogeneous entity and has no inside that can be separated from the outside, any more than natural objects have bones or veins that can be separate from the skin. That the exterior of Lamont fits the inside is not a result of accident but of the disposition of the functional elements inside so that their expression on the outside results in some architectural unity.[3]

This principle would have held true for Lamont regardless of the style chosen. The basic disposition of the planned elements was decided long before any final decision was reached in regard to the style of the facades. The architect then made several studies and models, some more contemporary than others, which were presented for review at a meeting of the governing board. From these studies a final exterior design was selected and approved, but this step was not taken until some time after the major part of the inside planning was finished. The surest sign of a first-class architect is his or her ability to design a building which is functional and also distinguished architecturally.

In spite of Charles A. Cutter's too well-known statement to the contrary, architects and librarians should *not* be considered natural enemies. Very satisfactory and rewarding working relationships can be and usually are achieved. If the architects and the librarians really understand each other, there should be no conflict of opinion. The architects, realizing that they must take the first responsibility for form and beauty and rarely being authorities on the proper function of libraries, should leave that responsibility to the library experts.

---

[3] H. R. Shepley, statement prepared for use in the first edition.

5

General Programming

In nearly every significant building effort, the program is considered a major benchmark establishing the functional specifications for a new or renovated facility. Programs may take many forms ranging from an oral understanding to a complete set of documents setting down the expectation and design requirements of the institution. As is the case in many fields, each project justifies its own level of programming effort. For the purpose of this chapter, the program elements assume that the project is of considerable significance and that the program is a written document prepared to establish the scope of work for the architect and other consultants.

Earlier chapters, particularly Chapter 3, speak of elements that will ultimately shape the program. Certain of the more important elements are reviewed in this chapter. The following chapters address more specialized programmatic aspects of libraries, while appendices deal with formulas and equipment.

5.1 The Question of a Program

Before the task of preparing a program is undertaken, four points should be considered: What is the purpose of a program? Should there be one? Who should write it? Who should approve it?

What Is the Purpose of a Program? The purpose of the program document is for clarity in communication. It also serves as an educational text, an instrument for negotiation, and a formal administrative statement of understanding. This response deserves some elaboration:

1. The preparation of a program is the best way that has been found for the librarian, the library staff, and the institution's administration to determine the essential needs of the library and to make all concerned confront them.

2. The program provides the librarian with an opportunity to point out to the institution's administration and faculty the physical

and other requirements of the library and to obtain formal approval of the statement of requirements and methods to be used in dealing with them. This approval is a matter of first importance.

3. The program forms the basis of client expectation on which the architect can plan a satisfactory building. On occasion the architect's fee may be adjusted if there are program changes; thus it serves as a fee control mechanism.

Should There Be a Program? Before the Second World War, it was unusual for a librarian to prepare a program. On the Lamont Undergraduate Library, for example, Mr. Metcalf worked closely with the architect and developed a "program" as time went on and plans developed; a formal program was never prepared! Even so, a written program is strongly recommended and is now almost universally prepared. Without one the advantages will be lost that can and should come from the points above, the architect will be too free to explore all manner of topics without guidelines, and it will be difficult for the librarian and the institution to bring their influence and ideas to bear on those who design the library.

Who Should Write the Program? Ideally, the senior librarian responsible for the particular facility should write the program because of the level of understanding of the problems and requirements held by the individual in that position. In the case of a major branch library, such as engineering, art, or music, the chief librarian of that branch should be responsible for the content of the program or at least be directly and fully involved. There are competent librarians who are not equipped with sufficient background for the preparation of a program, although some of them could with time and effort acquire it. In some cases the librarian's time can be spent to better advantage in other ways. In any case, the librarian should be closely in touch with the preparation of the program, and the librarian should approve and support the program before it is passed to those who have to give final approval, and to the architect.

In a large library there will sometimes be a senior assistant to whom the main responsibility for the task can be assigned. In other cases there may be a building expert or non-library administrative officer to whom the task may be assigned by the president or trustees; but, if this is done, the person selected should work very closely with the librarian and the library staff to make sure that use is made of their special knowledge. The program writing in most cases should not be a one-person task. It should be a compilation of the best information that the institution can gather, and the individual primarily responsible for preparing it should not hesitate to call for help from others.

An experienced library consultant may be useful here, as at other stages in the planning process. Sometimes the consultant may be asked to write the program. An outside expert can help and be very useful, but it is nearly impossible for a consultant to know and understand the institution as well as the program writer ideally should. On the other hand, the consultant should be more familiar with the nature of what a program should contain and how it should be formatted. When the consultant is involved, interpretation and support of the program with other members of the design team may be stronger as well.

To whomever writes the program, engineering and technical help from the staff of the institution or from outside should be made available, because any statements dealing with engineering problems such as site limitations, construction, plumbing, heating, ventilating, and air conditioning should be examined and approved by someone who has more than a layperson's knowledge of what is involved.

Who Should Pass on the Program? If the architect is to pay proper attention to the completed program, it must be evident that it records more than the hastily prepared ideas of the librarian or an outside consultant. It must be considered an official document of the institution and its administration. Thus, for a major project, the program should be approved at least by the chief librarian, the library committee of the faculty, the administrative officers, including the president, and, finally, perhaps the governing board. Of course, smaller projects do not need the full weight of this formal process, but a broad base of approval and support is always important. After understanding the necessity of these formalities, the design team should also understand that the program is not a Bible that cannot be changed as planning proceeds and that mutually agreed-upon alterations are to be permitted and encouraged if they represent improvements that are cost beneficial or justified by their own merit. With care the entire design process should evolve toward the best possible solution within the constraint of time and money.

The architect will often wish to consider the program unchangeable in order to prevent the librarian, too late in the planning process, from altering the ground rules. There should be a definite understanding that up to an agreed-upon point in the planning process both sides are free to question the program and propose changes if they believe that a better building will result. Usually the conclusion of the schematic phase represents the last opportunity for change without potentially costly results. There should also be an understanding that the time must come when further changes cannot be made without an addition to the architect's fees, just as there should be an understanding that the plans submitted by the architect must be satisfactory to the institution and represent a building that can be built with the funds available.

5.2 Establishing Policy

A number of major policy decisions should be addressed before writing the facility program, some of which overlap with those outlined in Section 3.1 and elsewhere. Not all of these issues need be agreed upon at this stage, but those that are not must be resolved at an early date in the design process. These policy decisions, many of which will affect the whole enterprise, should answer at least the following questions:

1. How far into the future should the library needs of the institution be projected? See Section 5.2 under Future Needs of the Institution.

2. What provisions or options are anticipated for growth beyond the life expectation in the facility to be programmed? To what degree should short-term flexibility be considered? See Section 5.2 under Flexibility for Long-Term Growth and Short-Term Change.

3. Can or should a new building be avoided by undertaking alterations, additions, decentralization, reorganization or other means? Should any of these possibilities augment a new facility, either now or in the future? See Section 5.2 under Alternatives to New Space.

4. Where will the structure be placed? See Section 5.2 under Site Selection.

5. Will nonlibrary facilities be housed in the building temporarily or permanently? See Section 5.2 under Nonlibrary Facilities.

6. What percentage of the user population will be provided reading space? What will the nature of reading provision be? See Section 5.2 under Accommodations for Readers and Staff.

7. How much emphasis is to be placed on environmental control and energy conservation measures? What is the nature of the materials to be housed? What is the understanding about smoking in the library? These issues and others are covered in Section 5.3 dealing with the front matter.

8. What constraints are there to the external appearance due to its setting? See Chapter 11 Section 4, concerned with Library Site Determination.

Future Needs of the Institution. Assessing future needs, considered in Chapter 1, is difficult because of the dynamic character of a library. With few exceptions library collections are likely to continue to grow indefinitely. As new technologies evolve, service and access to these collections are in a constant state of change. Each time an increment of space is added to the library system, there is a considerable expense in adjusting to it. Leading up to construction of a new facility, the old building is constricted to intolerable levels due to excessive crowding. All these elements tend to indicate that ideally there should be a constant incremental growth of a facility, and lacking that capacity a facility should be planned for a considerable time period with sufficient internal flexibility to adapt to the evolution of new technologies.

On the other hand, if one calculates that the collections are growing at a rate of, say, 5 percent per year, each increment of five years will add about 25 percent to the project budget. With a building construction cost in the multimillion dollar range, it is easily seen that planning for five or twenty-five years will significantly alter the initial facility cost. Some would argue that the cost of money is nearly balanced by the cost of inflation, as it certainly has been in recent years. Thus the cost of a larger building now or later is nearly the same, and the management cost from construction, activation, and library operations should be less if done earlier. However, most institutions have limited resources and many projects worthy of funding. The decision of how far into the future one should plan must therefore reflect the institutional priorities and funding capability. While the authors suggest that fifteen to twenty years is an appropriate period for planning projections, factors far beyond the responsibility of the librarian must be considered. See Section 1.4 for discussion of rationale for an appropriate projection period.

Automation provides its own uncertainties in the late twentieth century. Information technologies are rapidly changing the ways in which information is accessed, managed, stored, and added. While one can look only so far ahead and be sure of precise needs, sometimes only two to three years, a building should and can accommodate changing uses. Planners will need to consider these projected needs under shifting circumstances. How will the library operate with only an on-line computer-based catalog? How will it provide for students who bring their own microcomputers to the library? Should all carrels be wet (that is, tied into power and signal wiring systems)? Are typing rooms to be superfluous? How extensive should be outlet taps into the local area network? How widely dispersed will be optical disk reading machines? How will libraries provide access to electronic journals and reference works? The ability to change and add electronic capabilities in nearly all parts of a library building seems a prime requirement in planning well into the future.

Flexibility for Long-Term Growth and Short-Term Change. What is flexibility? It means adaptability to changing needs. What characterizes a flexible library? Principally, it is the ability to assign to any part of the facility the collections, readers, service to readers, staff activities, or unrelated activities such as classrooms and offices. Section 1.7 outlines the major factors to be considered, and Section 5.3 under Module and Flexibility will deal more fully with some of the details that may affect flexibility.

One thing that a librarian can be sure of is that in nearly every case library space needs will increase as years go by. Possible exceptions include those facilities, such as an undergraduate library or certain branch libraries, where an institutional policy establishes a firm maximum collection and accommodation for staff and readers. However, the general rule is growth. Even if the number of students does not increase, the book, microtext, phonograph disc, and other collections will tend to grow. Of course, a college can, for one reason or another, absolutely limit the number of students and at the same time take the attitude that its growing collections can continually be weeded or selectively transferred to another facility such that the present central facility could house the library indefinitely. So far in history, no healthy institution has for long maintained an absolute limit on library collections, although with the growth of storage facilities and with the limitations of the central campus, this may change in the future. A few college librarians and more academic administrators have asserted that there is no need for the library ever to go beyond a certain figure. This figure may be 100,000, 250,000, 500,000 or even 1,000,000 volumes. The same situation holds in universities, but the figures for the maximum size of collections are much larger.

It is well to keep in mind three points: (1) the quality of the students tends to improve even when their number does not, their use of the library increases, and increased seating accommodation may become essential; (2) curriculum changes and a shift from textbook to other types of instruction are tending thus far in the computer age to increase demands for both seating space and larger collections; and (3) no one has as yet been able to find a fully satisfactory way of limiting the size of collections when the maximum agreed upon earlier is reached, though the future may witness major changes if high-speed digital facsimile transmission makes it easy and inexpensive to rapidly access little-used collections.

It is urged that, at the time a new building is planned, even if an agreement restricting the ultimate size of the collections has been reached, a way out be provided. It is very important to plan almost all new libraries so that they can be added to, unless it is admitted and agreed that nothing can be planned today to last more than a limited number of years and that at the end of twenty-five years or some other definite period, the building can be discarded as a library, if not for all purposes, and replaced.

Alternatives to New Space. As an alternative to costly construction is such an important issue, the entire content of Chapter 2 is devoted to this topic. At this point it is only necessary to suggest that in programming and in the early design phases of a new facility, as many options for future alternatives as possible should be maintained and developed. Of course, the flexibility of the structure has a significant effect on future options. However, the need for dealing with urgent space problems often will occur even before the new facility is completed. Aside from the alternatives Chapter 2 covers, one option to consider is partial occupancy of the new facility before the completion of construction; a word of caution—noise, dust, and other construction-related inconveniences may limit the usefulness of the occupied space. (See also Chapter 10 on remodeling and additions.)

While the effect on the program of an anticipated need for phased construction or partial occupancy should not be an overwhelming factor, except in renovations of existing space that will continue to house units of the library, it may be advisable to consider the practicality of such a possibility. Perhaps the most important aspects will be to ensure access to part of the building separate from that to the area still under construction. The provision of the necessary utilities, environmental control, security, etc., could create problems as well. Phased delivery of a building and its equipment will likely have a cost factor to be considered. For more discussion of partial activation or phased activation, please refer to Chapter 15.

Site Selection. While thought will undoubtedly be given to the site selection long before this stage is reached, in many cases there are options, or configurations of the site that may require review and consideration even into the early design phases. Chapter 9 is devoted to site considerations. However, aspects of site selection should be thought about during the early programming phase. Is the facility totally new? Should the institution adhere to the philosophy that the library should be at the heart of the campus? Or should the philosophy be that the library is better sited between the academic campus and major residential or parking facilities? Is the structure to stand alone, be attached to an existing facility, or join two or more facilities? Is there a desire to create a special configuration of buildings forming a court or quadrangle or giving direction to exterior space? Are there historical, environmental, local ordinance, or other factors to be considered? What is the influence of access and external traffic patterns? These and other questions are addressed in Chapter 11. It would be well to be familiar with these issues as the initial programming decisions are made.

Nonlibrary Facilities. As already noted, libraries tend to grow rapidly as suitable collections are gathered for use by large numbers of students. As a result it is usually desirable to construct a building considerably larger than will be necessary for the first five years or more; the additional space will inevitably be needed later. But any new institution that is growing rapidly will almost always have greater space demands than can be readily met. It has thus become fairly common to use part of the library building for other than library purposes during the first years after its construction. These other purposes may be of almost any kind. The space has often been used for the general administrative quarters of the institution. Classrooms have often been placed in a library building with the idea that they would be removed later as the demands for library space increased and a new separate classroom building could be made available. Separately administered audio-visual departments, computer centers, and similar functions have sometimes been assigned library space. Even entire campuses have been constructed in a single building with integrated plans for expansion involving multiple shifts of space assignment as the library grows (e.g., University of Wisconsin–Parkside).

Three points should be made in connection with the proposal for use of library space for other than library purposes. The first is that a multi-use facility which is intended to be fully occupied in future years by the library should be built to library standards for floor loading, module size, ceiling heights, etc., to ensure the flexibility to accommodate the eventual library expansion.

The second point is that if the library exits are to be controlled and if books and papers carried by the users of the library are to be checked at the exits, it is desirable and almost obligatory to have the capability of separate access to the library and nonlibrary areas, irrespective of hours of operation.

It should be noted that separate internal controlled-access points can generally be developed within a building with a single main entrance from the outside. It is sometimes irritating to the user to approach a building with two distinct entrances and no clear indication of which is the library. It is also irritating for the user of the other part of the building, who would like to enter directly into the library without going outdoors, to have to walk around the building only to return into the same structure again. However, if no other way can be devised than to have a positive separation of the functions outside the library control point, including separate security after hours, then it is strongly advised that nonlibrary activities assigned to library space be given a separate entrance and exit (fig. 5.1). Too often this is not the case, as is illustrated by ten classrooms in the Lamont Library at Harvard and four language laboratories in the Meyer Library at Stanford, where access in the building is through the entrance lobby and past a library control point. Such a configuration will necessitate checking the students who have attended classes and are leaving the building, just as though they had been using the library and library books. Closing the library must then include clearing the classroom space as well. Assignment of classroom activities must be restricted to library hours. In an era when concern about book theft and vandalism is at a high level, adding unrelated functions within the library confines is a poor security decision.

The third problem, equally serious, and one emphasized by many librarians, is that once extraneous services have been permitted into the library facility, it is almost impossible to eliminate them later, even when the library is in desperate need of space. The institution's administrative staff often find the library one of the most attractive buildings on campus. They hate to ask for other space, knowing the needs of other parts of the institution, and tend to maintain possession of their quarters in spite of the fact that they are no longer welcome. Classrooms are almost always in great demand, and the library will find it hard to reclaim the space once they are installed.

When an institution is pressed for space, and there is hope of obtaining additional space within the library facility or by new construction, the librarian must be able to prove that the library need is greater than that of others, and that giving the library additional space will be a better solution for the institution educationally than making any other arrangement. There will undoubtedly be occasions when the library will suffer, but it will not add to its prestige or popularity with administrative officers or with the institution as a whole if it holds space urgently needed for other purposes for the sake of having it available later when it is needed.

Accommodation for Readers and Staff. Planning for seating accommodation for readers involves four basic questions:

1. Who are the readers? Can and should they be divided into different groups with different types of accommodation for each? If so, can a formula be found and used for the number of places, space per place for each group, and from these figure the total net space required?

2. Should there be different rooms or areas for different subject fields, different forms of materials, or different types of use, and, if so, what fields, forms, and types should be considered?

3. Should different types of seating be used for different groups of readers or different reading areas?

4. After the decisions have been reached on these three points, how many seats should be provided for each group in each area and with each type of accommodation?

These questions are addressed in the various sections of programming. Section 5.3 deals with general aspects of 2, 3, and 4 while Section 6.2 deals with those specialized aspects associated with unique collections or fields. Layouts and arrangements are covered in Sections 10.6 and 11.3. Specifications are found in 12.3.

College and university libraries can expect to have demands for accommodation from five distinct groups of users—undergraduates, graduates, faculty members, visiting scholars, and others, including staff and the general public, although not every group will necessarily be represented in each library. These groups differ widely in library use; in order to estimate the number of seats that ought to be provided in a new library facility, one should estimate the needs of each group separately and then total them.

Undergraduates. In most institutions of higher learning, though not in all, undergraduates are more numerous than the other four groups combined. This statement does

BOWDOIN COLLEGE LIBRARY

FIGURE 5.1 Bowdoin College Library. For a first-time visitor, the two entrances could lead to confusion. When the library became overly crowded, an underground addition to the east (connecting with nearby stack floors of the former library) was chosen over conversion of the college administrative offices space.

not mean that their use of the library will be proportionate to their numbers compared with other groups or that the percentage will not change; use will depend upon the nature of the library being planned and the character of the institution and its objectives.

No definite formula can be proposed to determine the percentage of undergraduates the library should be prepared to seat at one time. Institutions and libraries differ widely in the amount of use expected at periods of peak demands, and future estimates are still more

difficult to make because of uncertainty about the effect of the new facility, changing academic programs, and the changing size of the user group. Change of admissions regulations, library lending policies, educational policies and emphasis, population trends, the job market, and other social and economic factors will all affect library use; the student body is constant neither in size nor in other characteristics. Finally, it is not easy to forecast how much a fine, new, comfortable, attractive, and adequate building will increase the demands for seating. Furthermore, the effect of other possible additions to the institution's building plant should not be forgotten. A new student union, study or library rooms in residential halls, small private study accommodation connected with dormitory suites, related branch libraries, or studies in academic departments—all will influence peak library loads. In spite of all these uncertainties, some estimate must be made before the program is finalized and plans for a new library are prepared if the institution expects to provide a building large enough, but not unnecessarily large, for a reasonably long period into the future.

It is suggested that the administrative officers of the institution should be responsible for a projection of student enrollment during the period for which the proposed building is designed to be adequate, and that they should also indicate whether plans for changes in admissions and educational policies will affect library use. In the past it was fairly certain, at least in the United States, that the numbers of students, and thus library use, would increase even without policy changes. However, the student population has recently decreased, and the next decade should see reduced student numbers until another increase begins. (Demographic studies have not, however, proved to be particularly accurate as predictors of enrollment, even in the short term, and should be used with caution.) Even so, when a well-planned, comfortable, and attractive building is provided, it can be predicted that there will be a dramatic increase in use, perhaps as much as doubling or tripling if the space provided makes the increase possible.

Other important factors may sooner or later bear on the number of required seats. Is the library service to undergraduates to be centralized in the proposed enlarged or new structure? If the university is a large one with departmental libraries, how much of the service to undergraduates will be provided outside the main building? Is it a residential institution with students living in the immediate neighborhood who can be expected to use the library heavily in the evening, or does the student body largely commute, leaving the campus as soon as possible after classes are over? Are there a large number of evening students? They are often very numerous in a city institution; however, if both day and evening students commute, it is unlikely that they

will use the facilities at the same time. Is the university in a city, where there are many attractions outside the campus? Or is it in comparative rural surroundings, where few outside activities attract the students, particularly during weekday evenings? Do most of the students live in dormitories on the campus? Do the dormitories provide an atmosphere conducive to study? Does the institution provide special reading rooms and library collections in the residential halls, as is done in the Yale colleges, the Harvard houses, and the larger dormitories in many public and private institutions? What are the library hours? Is the library open until midnight on weekday evenings or only until 9 or 10 o'clock? If it is in a residential institution with heavy evening use, do some students spend the early evening at the library, while others go to the movies first and then to the library from 10 to 12 o'clock, reducing the percentage who can be expected at any one time?

The following additional questions should also be considered by the program writer, although, like those that have been suggested above, there are no answers that can be translated into exact figures. Does the library expect to be able to take care of peak demands which tend to come just before and during the examination period or during the reading period, if there is one? These are the periods of heaviest library use. They may also be those when the students are most anxious to study and when dormitory rooms may be more suitable for that purpose than at other times. At these times students may, but not always, be willing and able to study at large tables in a reading room with chairs closer together than at other times in the academic year. However, it is a common experience that the student perceives the reading area to be full even if only half the chairs are taken at large tables with close placement. Is the institution prepared during peak loads to have the students use facilities outside the library, such as study halls, seminar rooms, and classrooms, on the basis that it cannot afford to increase the size of its library by as much as twenty percent for the convenience of its students during perhaps three or four weeks in the academic year?

Does the library encourage students to study using their own books in the library, on the basis that a more studious atmosphere will prevail there than elsewhere and that study with reference material immediately at hand tends to be especially advantageous?

Does the institution expect to assign seats in the library for honors students or graduate students? Whenever a seat is assigned to one student exclusively and use by others is prevented or discouraged, the total number of seats required is increased, because no student to whom a seat is assigned will use it during all hours of the day or even all the hours when the peak load is expected. Assignment of seats to undergraduates is not recommended. Very few institutions can afford a seating capacity large enough for this purpose.

All the foregoing questions suggest problems that ought to be considered, though they may do little to help the person drawing up the program to decide on the number of seats that should be available to undergraduate students. In 1968 Mr. Metcalf suggested that where institutions have students of the highest quality, and are in a small town or rural area, the library should be prepared to seat at least one-half of the undergraduate student body at one time. This recommendation echoed that of W. W. Bishop who recommended as early as 1920 that libraries be prepared to seat one-half of the entire student body at one time. At the other extreme, many state planning guides for libraries require seating for no more than 25 percent of the student population. Notable library consultants suggest that for a commuting campus, the library should be planned for 10 percent of the full-time equivalent student body. Clearly, interpretations of the type of questions outlined in this section will lead to a fairly broad spectrum of seating proportions for different institutions.

Some time ago at Harvard University, with an outstanding student group in a metropolitan area, the librarian estimated that three out of eight undergraduates should be provided study space in either the house libraries, departmental libraries, the research library, or undergraduate library. At Stanford University, assuming that about 75 percent of the undergraduate library and 25 percent of the research library seats are used by undergraduates, seating is provided for about 25 percent of the undergraduate user population plus what is used by undergraduates in various branch libraries. While there are times during the peak periods when students feel they cannot find a place, there have always been at least a few empty seats. Even so, a student may end up using a study space in

a building other than the one preferred. As it turns out, considerably more than 25 percent of the seats in the research library are being used by undergraduates at peak times.

At the University of Florida, Mr. Metcalf suggested that at the time of the peak load, up to 75 percent of the students could be expected to be studying at one time and that one-half of this 75 percent would, or at least could, properly use their own rooms for this purpose. This would leave 37½ percent to be cared for elsewhere. It was then suggested that one-fifth of this number, or 7½ percent, might well be cared for in reading or study rooms in the residential halls, and that, of the 30 percent remaining, one-third would find their study facilities in departmental libraries, leaving 20 percent to be cared for in the central building.

Manual four of the *Higher Education Facilities Planning and Management Manuals* prepared by Dahnke, Jones, Mason and Romney provides a general guide for each discipline and user group. Of course adjustments should be made for other factors, but the outlined approach is a useful way of considering seating requirements. See Appendix B.

Consideration of accommodation for students in undergraduate professional schools should not be forgotten. These may include law, medicine, divinity, education, public health, chemistry, pharmacy, nursing, veterinary medicine, architecture, engineering, home economics, agriculture, and physical education, among others. Library needs of these diverse fields are by no means identical and demands for seats will vary. Students of law and divinity are typically very heavy users; chemistry, education, and medicine less so; and the others much less, although local academic emphasis could change the order suggested.

Little has been said of departmental libraries for disciplines in the arts and sciences; i.e., the humanities, social sciences, physical sciences, and their subdivisions. Departmental libraries tend to multiply, and unless this tendency is kept under control, their cost to the institution may become very high. At Harvard University there are over one hundred libraries in all, and similar situations on a smaller scale can be found in many large universities. In too many institutions some of the departmental libraries have simply grown up, with the university library system more or less uninvolved in their existence, while others are definitely recognized as part of the university library.

A study of the circumstances should be made in each institution, and the foregoing statements can at best provide only some worthwhile guidelines that may help in solving the problem. No clear rules can be suggested for determination of needs, but most of the factors involved in the consideration of how many seats to provide have been outlined, and it should be emphasized that each institution must study its seating requirements carefully, with the years ahead in mind.

Graduate Students. Graduate students in arts and sciences, and those working for advanced degrees in professional schools, each represent somewhat different problems from undergraduates. Each graduate professional school is likely in a large institution to have its own special library. The percentage of students requiring seating accommodation at any one time in each of these libraries may be determined after consideration of the points dealt with earlier in this section, but with a separate calculation for each program. As suggested by the tables in Appendix B, the percentage of seats required will generally tend to be larger for graduates than for undergraduates, particularly in law schools where 50 percent, or in a few schools even more, may want to use the library at one time. The Association of American Law Schools recommends seating "with generous table or desk space" for 65 percent of the student body. City institutions with many part-time students will usually be an exception to this statement. In a medical school the percentage will typically be considerably smaller, as so much time is required in laboratory and clinical work, yet research and hospital staff must be considered. Similar factors are to be considered in engineering and technological institutions. Those working in the physical sciences resemble medical and engineering students; they spend much of their time in laboratories so that library demands are decreased because there are only 24 hours in the day, if for no other reason. Of course, the theoretical scientist is likely to be an exception, but it is seldom that this type of research accounts for more than a small fraction of the user group. Graduate students in arts and sciences, particularly in the humanities and social sciences, ordinarily require seats for a percentage of their number little, if any, less than those usually required in a law school.

Graduate students in the humanities and social sciences working for doctorates will make the largest demands on the library in the percentage of seats required. In these fields there is ordinarily a great difference between those doing the first and second year of their work toward the doctorate and those who are engaged in writing their dissertations. Many academics believe that any scholar writing a doctoral dissertation in the humanities or social sciences should have an assigned library seat, preferably at an individual table or in a carrel, with a bookshelf and security for personal papers, for the full period of this task. Security, in this case, must be more than low partitions; full height walls or a locker will be required. Let us say, then, that in the average institution there should be a seat in the library for every doctoral candidate actually working full-time on a dissertation in the humanities and social sciences; for others working for the Ph.D. but not yet engaged in writing the dissertation, one seat for every two full-time students should generally be sufficient; and for those working for the master's degree, a seat for 40 to 50 percent might be sufficient in many universities, depending on local conditions. As with previous seating figures given, circumstances in each institution will vary, and these estimates should be used as guides only. This subject is one on which an experienced library consultant may be helpful.

Faculty. The needs of faculty members differ from those of undergraduate and graduate students. Customs and study habits vary a great deal between institutions and among disciplines. If adequate library facilities for faculty members have been provided in the past, it is probable that many faculty members will prefer to do much of their research and preparation for lectures in the library. In other institutions, if facilities have not been satisfactory and particularly if faculty members have suitable offices in their departments or they typically live near the campus, many will have developed patterns of doing their research outside the library. The private study at home is, of course, favored as the likelihood of being disturbed is much less. However, as houses and apartments tend to become smaller, they become less suitable for study; and it should be noted that, for younger faculty members with children at home, the house may not be a satisfactory place to carry on research work. Also, a considerable percentage of faculty in many institutions are still working on their dissertations, and satisfactory quarters on campus for research are of great importance to them. In general, there is less demand proportionately for library faculty studies in colleges than in universities. Where the faculty member typically has a study at home and a departmental office, there may be some institutional concern about providing yet a third place where the faculty member can disappear to do reasearch. Some schools feel that in order to generate a cohesive academic atmosphere, the faculty should be encouraged to be in their offices, available for student consultation as much as possible. In such circumstances the introduction of library faculty studies may be viewed as undesirable. Clearly, the institution's policy in regard to the use of faculty offices is an important factor. Whether or not such use is a consideration, many faculty will request a quiet study in the library as well as an office elsewhere. Many universities have felt that they could provide library studies for senior members of the faculty only, although this group generally needs such accommodation less than their juniors.

While the number of faculty members may exceed ten percent of the number of students in a few institutions, they can probably be left out of calculations of seating capacity in the regular open reading areas of the library. This omission is not because they do not read, but because their heaviest library use tends to be in quarters specially assigned to them, when it is not in the reference room, the public catalog, or the current periodical room, where they are not likely to stay long or to add to congestion. Times of peak library usage by students are generally avoided by faculty.

While it has not been unusual in the past to provide special faculty reading rooms, their value is questionable. Faculty members doing research or preparing lectures prefer to be alone, rather than in a reading room, even if its use is restricted to their colleagues. The desirability of a small social area for use by faculty members and graduate students may be worth consideration. However, careful thought must be given to this concept because of the likelihood of demands for refreshments.

Another approach is to provide faculty studies or the type of cubicle or carrel provided by the library for graduate students. The dividing line between graduate students and faculty is not always clear; in the case of teaching fellows, the facilities ordinarily assigned to graduate students are usually considered adequate, but for the more senior professor these are seldom satisfactory. If quarters for the faculty in the library are intended as studies only, which the authors recommend, the number and size can be greatly reduced from what would be required if they also function as faculty offices. Most professors doing administrative work or who are frequently consulted by students do not like to do this work in their library studies, and would prefer an office in a departmental or other building. Office functions provided in a library will lead to demands for special consideration for access when the library is closed, and, of course, consideration of office support functions must be given. Included here would be secretarial space, phones, photocopy areas, supply storage, and the like.

Faculty members in the physical sciences are better satisfied if their studies or offices are in the buildings which are considered their headquarters. The same will be true for a certain percentage, varying in each institution, of those in the humanities and the social sciences. A number of libraries that have provided studies have had difficulties in assigning them, and frequently their level of use is less than anticipated, especially where suitable offices are provided. Yet, they do have a place in the library program. They may be assigned for limited periods only, and assignments renewed only when the need is clearly demonstrated. On the other hand, it should not be forgotten that much of the valuable research carried on in our academic institutions is greatly facilitated by faculty studies in libraries. In a few institutions, as many as ten percent of the faculty may have library studies; most have fewer in a central library building. Since local attitudes and concerns will affect the final decision, this problem could be placed before the library committee.

Visiting Scholars. Although visiting scholars will be a comparatively negligible factor in the great majority of institutions, they will be important in larger research libraries, and particularly those in large cities or on the way to and from "vacationland." Since faculty in all colleges and universities visit other libraries, as do graduate students, academic libraries should be hospitable to such visitors as a *quid pro quo.* In access to both general research collections and to rare book and manuscript reading rooms, reasonable needs of visiting scholars should be accommodated, and they must be considered seriously in building planning. Only local experience can serve as a basis for estimating the requirements. The basic requirement is often for a reading position at a table where library materials may be used for long hours or many days without interruption or disturbance.

At Harvard University for a large part of the year, both summer and winter, the central Widener Library could make good use of 25 studies for visiting scholars, in addition to 50 carrels. An equal number of both studies and carrels would be useful in its departmental libraries in addition to the Houghton rare-book and manuscript accommodation. At Stanford University half that number would suffice. It is suggested that accommodation suitable for graduate students will be satisfactory for visiting scholars using general research collections in most institutions, and that very few institutions will be able to justify space for a reading room dedicated to visiting scholars.

Others, Including the General Public. When a public institution considers it must provide open access to any visitor, as is the case at the University of California, Los Angeles, and Concordia University in Montreal, the effect of the public can be significant, perhaps limited only by the difficulty of parking and access. However, it is more often the case that visitors who are not scholars can be ignored in estimating seating requirements, yet they should not be forgotten because of the problems they may present. Their number is not necessarily negligible. In nearly all college or university libraries alumni of the institutions are welcome. High school and college students from local institutions can be expected to pour in unless they are actively discouraged from doing so. Here the decision of what to do with or about them is a matter of policy for the institution's administration after the librarian has set forth in detail the effect on the library. Certain aspects of public access may be established by law, such as is the case for government documents depository libraries in the United States. In Ontario, Canada, and many other areas, all libraries supported by public funding are legally required to be open to all residents. In most cases, however, the seating capacity provided for peak student loads will be sufficient accommodation for other visitors.

5.3 Front Matter

The principal reason for expending considerable effort to prepare a program statement is to record in one document the basic information necessary to establish the scope and character of the building project. The program will not answer all questions, and continued involvement will be required of the librarian and other members of the project team. As stated before, the program forms the basis for the development of a project budget as well as design fees for the various consultants. It also provides basic information that the architect should be cognizant of during the design period. While the detail of the program will vary with institutional circumstance and the size of the project, it is suggested that the following general topics be considered for inclusion in what is often called "front matter."

1. Goals of the library
2. Site concerns and access
3. General relationships of major functions
4. Aesthetic versus functional concerns
5. Module and flexibility
6. Security
7. Interior design concerns
8. Environmental control
9. Codes and standards

Much of this volume consists of discussion of the problems related to the concerns outlined above and discussed in the balance of this section. Marcus Vitruvius Pollio, the Roman architect and engineer, wrote in his *De Architectura Libri Decem*, at the time of the Emperor Augustus, of the three essentials in building which he called *firmitas, utilitas, venustas,* in that order. They can be translated as strength, function, beauty. The intent of the program front matter is to establish the basis for the interrelationship of these essentials in building as they are shaped by the design process. Clearly, all aspects cannot be resolved by a program document, for if they were, the design would no doubt be complete, the building constructed, and the library functioning smoothly in its new quarters. The purpose of the program is to identify the problems, not the solution. Nevertheless, direction should be established with the expectation that there will be change and compromise over the months, indeed, years to follow.

Goals of the Library. In most cases it should be assumed that the project architect has had little experience with libraries, particularly the libraries of the institution for which the program is being written. In a statement of library goals, it would thus be useful to outline briefly the current and recent past history of the library in its institutional setting. Important is the nature of the library as a teaching instrument, central research facility, a research branch, an undergraduate library, learning resources center, a storage library, a rare-books library, or other special library. Trends in growth of the collections, the student population, the characteristics of use, the impact of technology, and the impact of future facilities on these factors all warrant discussion. Then, with suitable caution, it may be useful to describe the librarian's view of this particular facility ten or twenty years in the future.

There will be facilities goals as well which should be discussed in succeeding paragraphs. For example, one will want to provide quarters that will, as far as possible, ensure the preservation of the collections. Suitable comfort for readers and staff is a likely goal. Convenience of access and operations, and effective, efficient utilization of space certainly are reasonable requirements. In some cases there will be need for phasing a project to permit partial activation before completion. This is particularly true in the event of a major addition to a building which is to be significantly remodeled as part of the same project. In order to facilitate the arrangement of a large library which is to be expanded into new contiguous space, part of the project may be a master plan that develops the direction of future renovations while limiting the main project effort to only the new addition. In this case the second phase, or the renovation of the existing building, may be treated as a separate project. Because of the timing and the different requirements between new and renovated construction, it may make considerable sense to keep the two phases distinct, including perhaps even separate contracts with the architect. Indeed, the two projects could even involve different architects, although this would no doubt be uncommon.

Renovation work within an existing building itself will likely require phasing. While the program does not need to spell out the exact phasing requirements, the fact that phasing will be required to provide for ongoing library operations should be established.

Site Concerns and Access. Chapter 11 covers the major aspects of siting and preparing a master plan. However, the program is an excellent instrument to establish guidelines for the site selection or, if the site is known, to describe significant factors that must be considered during the design of the building. The program, for example, should state the source of existing site data such as weather, soils tests, traffic patterns, surveys, utility locations, and the like. Should these vital pieces of information be missing, then it should be established that the architect is expected to develop or obtain all the necessary data or that the institution will undertake to gather this material.

Where the construction is to be connected with one or more existing structures, the needs should be detailed. The program may speak to the specific nature of the connection, covering such points as floor connections, sun or wind conditions to be preserved or avoided, and perhaps the character and function of the connecting element. If there are vistas of historical importance, they must be mentioned here as a feature to be preserved.

Policy or local sentiment, where it affects building design, should also be detailed. Does the institution maintain a certain architectural character? (Stanford University is sandstone and tile almost without exception.) Are there historical elements that must be preserved? (Concordia University had to preserve an older facade.) Does removal of a parking lot or a tree require the replacement of such items as part of the project in other locations? (The University of British Columbia was required to preserve trees within its undergraduate library.) Are there limitations of height? Is flooding or other natural disaster of special concern?

Where traffic data are known, they should be recorded. How many deliveries a day or week are made to the library? How large are the vehicles? Does special parking for staff, visitors, service personnel, or library vehicles need to be provided? What is the anticipated system of trash removal? Will there need to be a curbside book return? How many library visitors a day or week are anticipated? Will site lighting or remote signs be part of the project? Is bicycle parking for staff and users to be part of the project? If so, how much? Should there be benches, lighting, or other site features? Are there to be underground connections to other facilities? Is a part of the project to be art work—some of which might take the form of a sculpture or fountain? If there is need for irrigation systems, should automatic timers be included?

Many of the features of the site program may already be well established by the local environment or by institutional facility standards. Where this is the case, many of the proposed questions may not require elaborate discussion. However, where the institution wishes to achieve specific goals, those specifics must be established. As with the other building aspects, the front matter of the program is a good place to document the institutional requirements.

Clearly, the overall goal must be to develop a facility that works well with the site, particularly in response to the local architectural fabric, traffic patterns, environmental conditions, and the natural features of the site. Reference should be made to known documentation of site features, and any specific requirements that may be suggested by the questions above should be stated.

General Relationships of Major Functions. In a complete program there should always be a concise but careful statement of desired spatial relationships between the different services, as well as a description of how the library is to operate and will be administered. Supplementary information including perhaps a library organization chart and library phone book can be useful. A description with an illustration to outline both the flow of materials coming into the library through the technical processing offices and the flow of materials being used by patrons of the library is important in helping the architect to understand.

In preparing the statement on spatial relationships the librarian has the opportunity to reconsider the library's organization and operation. Just because work has been handled in a certain way in the past does not necessarily mean that old practices should be continued. This is the time to study the problems involved; it may be the ideal time to institute some improvements which an old building may have prevented. The convenience of faculty, students, and staff should be kept in mind and also the cost of services rendered. Relationships with any nonlibrary functions that are being programmed for the building should also be considered. The ar-

rangements decided upon may have a great effect on operating costs for security, for maintenance, for services, and for processing additions to the collections. Other things being equal, the fewer service desks and control points that have to be staffed for full hours, the better. The shorter the distances staff members have to travel vertically or horizontally at frequent intervals, the better also; but the building should not inconvenience readers or reduce the quality of service for the sake of staff convenience.

In arranging the relationships of spaces and functions in a diagrammatic way, the various uses made of the library by students and faculty must be kept in mind. They may include the following: reserve books for use in or outside the library; general recreational and collateral reading, the latter in connection with course work; preparation of reports of various kinds and research work; and use of current periodicals and newspapers, manuscripts, maps, microforms, audio-visual materials, computer data files, the reference collection, catalog, etc. Outside influences including nonlibrary functions within the same building, the location of parking, as well as residential, academic, and student activity centers on the campus, and important local topographical, architectural or environmental features should be noted when the site is established.

There are, of course, other uses of the library or outside factors that may influence spatial relationships. For all of them, the shorter the distances to be traveled by everyone concerned, the better. Even walking on the level through reading areas is likely to be disturbing, and traffic up and down stairs can be noisy. Visual and auditory distraction of readers should be avoided as far as possible. The use of terminals, photocopy machines, and toilet rooms should be considered in detail in planning their arrangement in relationship to areas where quiet is desirable.

The staff side of the picture is also important. Spatial relationships have a great deal to do with staff effectiveness. Salaries are often the largest single expenditure in libraries; if in a large library staff members have to walk considerable distances frequently or go up and down stairs often, the time consumed that could have been avoided by more careful planning is a distinct intrusion upon effective working time. Once or twice a day might not be serious; it is the total amount of travel that counts. Pushing one truck loaded with books each day from the mail room to the acquisition department is not serious, even if the distance involved is one hundred feet, but if the circulation desk is adjacent to the entrance and the service elevator or lifts are one hundred feet away and ten truckloads of books must go back and forth each day, the configuration may not be cost effective.

The relationship of staff functions to the user is yet another topic to be considered. Even with the introduction of automated catalogs with multiple access through remote terminals, it will probably be several decades before most large libraries convert all of their major card catalogs to machine-readable form accessible directly to users through user-friendly terminals. In the first edition of this book, Mr. Metcalf pointed out that few even advanced scholars enjoyed facing the 12 card catalog trays under "William Shakespeare" in the Widener Library at that time, or the 87 trays under the heading "United States," or the 14 trays listing the material on "Bible." Unless a reference librarian, equipped to handle the situation and available to assist is close at hand, undergraduates may give up in despair. Unless scholars can find a good reference and bibliographical collection, with an experienced and helpful librarian readily available when help is needed, they will be handicapped, if not baffled, in using the library. As the library grows larger in area and collections, these problems tend to increase in magnitude. The climax of it all is in the bookstack if it seems to lack logical arrangement.

Description of these relationships can take many forms, but one that is quite useful in terms of expressing and organizing one's thoughts is to develop a graphic vocabulary of circles and lines to express the various relationships. Rectangles are also often used (fig. 5.2), but circles avoid the temptation to start actually designing a building, an exercise best left to the architect. Circles may be sized to simulate the proportionate space represented by each function, but absolute accuracy is not necessary nor desirable at this stage. Critical relationships, where two functions essentially are to be juxtaposed, may be circles connected by a thick solid line; important but less critical connections can perhaps be represented by a thinner line. Frequent though even less important relationships could be shown by a dashed line. Other factors such

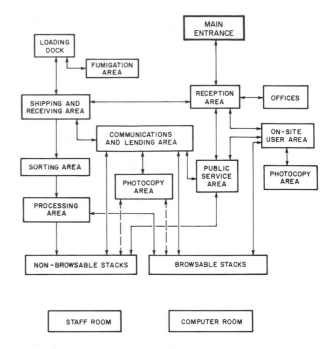

FIGURE 5.2 Organizational diagram for the University of California Northern Regional Library Facility. This is essentially a bubble diagram showing functional relationships of the various building components.

as security boundaries, noise, outside influences, etc., can be shown with either other simple graphic techniques or brief statements. Using tracing paper, one can quickly explore a number of possible relationships and discuss or ponder their merits until something close to expressing the needs of the specific institution is arrived at. When the architect starts work on the project, there will no doubt be a period of testing of the stated relationships which should be viewed as a positive contribution, for the architect may well discover factors that the librarian or other institutional representative missed.

The intent then in exploring spatial relationships is to develop a picture, either textually or graphically, of those functions that have close connections with the organization and service patterns of related functions. Discussion of the problem can well begin with the central or key services, that is, the circulation desk, the reference desk, the reference and bibliography collections, the periodical indexes, and the card and/or computer catalog—services to which the reader who does not know how to search for information will naturally turn to unlock the library information. These key services should be easy to find, and the user should be able to reach

each one quickly and easily, or to go from one to another without traversing great distances horizontally or vertically. Where there is a general reading area for the use of reserved books, privately owned books, or after hours study, it should be easy to find.

A common use pattern is represented by the reader who comes to find a book on a specific subject. To find the book, the reader must ascertain its location. The reader may first have to obtain a reference to it in the reference or bibliography collection, but later may have to go to the catalog to learn if the library owns it and, if so, to discover its shelf mark or call number and hence its location on the shelves. As already noted, help may be required, although the reader may go directly to the shelf location to get the item desired. When the book is found (if it is not already circulating), if the reader decides to take it out of the library instead of using it in the building, it must be charged out at a circulation desk or perhaps at a terminal supporting an automated circulation system. This can all be summed up by saying that if each of these staffed central services—excluding, of course, the main bookstack, remote charge out, reference and catalog terminals—can be near the entrance and readily found, a large part of the design battle is won.

Of equal importance are the requirements for the processing staff that selects, orders, receives, and catalogs books, serials, and the multitude of other library materials. Their work is closely involved with the reference and bibliography collections and the catalog. While need for access to the public catalog is reduced by the advent of computer-based cataloging, where there is a large card catalog that is unlikely to be retrospectively transformed to machine-readable format, or where the card catalog is being actively maintained, it is important to have the technical processing quarters as close as possible. Juxtaposing the processing area with the reference collection space is also desirable where practicable. Such an arrangement will reduce the need for duplication of expensive bibliographical collections and work will be simplified and speeded up. However, when the necessary bibliographic tools can be purchased in duplicate sets, and when the entire cataloging activity is done through computer terminals, the need for adjacent location is less essential.

For very large library systems, particularly where centralized processing is the accepted practice, consideration may be given to placing this activity in a separate building, perhaps related more to a delivery dock than to the operating library. Some including the authors may question the philosophy of such a division of functions since the collegial atmosphere of the library staff would be difficult to maintain. The notion of "them" and "us," which is often prevalent even when departments exist in the same building, is considerably greater where totally separate quarters are developed.

Answers to the following questions will bring out many of the problems involved in spatial relationships. Others will be based on local situations and details of organization, and the librarian will have to be alert for them as the program is prepared. In the following paragraphs, as elsewhere in this volume, questions are deliberately posed without answers because for each institution the answers will be unique. Also, the planners and program writer must subject their work to this type of questioning if they are to be confident in their responses to the questions of critics (and critiques) of the project.

1. What functions should be close to the entrance lobby? Functions that warrant consideration include a library privileges desk; the circulation desk and related staff quarters; a control portal; the entrance to the government documents, reference, bibliography, rare books, and current journals and newspapers areas; the reference and reserve book desks with their related space needs; the card catalog and other catalog devices; the library administration, personnel office, and development office where this is a library function; display area; a light reading or browsing area and access to the rest of the building via stairwells, elevators, etc. While it may be desirable to state the ideal arrangement of functions to be placed near the entrance lobby, some compromise is almost certain to occur. Priorities will need to be developed, and the list of functions near the entrance will need to be limited. In most cases functions such as reserve books, the administrative offices, or rare books can be somewhat more remotely located, provided the route to them can be clearly identified by the library visitor.

2. If space can be provided, should the quarters for the technical processing departments be on the level with some of the services listed in 1 above? Or can the space be

better used for some of the other reader services functions? If space cannot be found for all of the processing departments there, should they all be housed one floor above or below or elsewhere, or can they be divided, with accommodation for those functions most closely related to the reader service functions located on the main floor, and the others elsewhere? In many libraries up to one-half of the area used by these departments is for staff who have little to do with the public catalog. With the trend toward automated, computer-based systems, the need to be juxtaposed to the public catalog is diminishing. However, where a need for continued technical service staff access to the public catalog is anticipated, location on a different floor will result in some loss of staff efficiency.

3. What should the relationship be, as far as space assignments are concerned, between the shipping and receiving room and those areas that handle quantities of incoming or outgoing materials such as that generated by the acquisitions department, a gift and exchange department, bindery preparation, or serials processing? If they are on different levels, should they be sited one above the other close to the service elevator? It is suggested that in an academic library much less material is transported between these departments than between the central book return and discharge area and the stack areas; if the same elevator is used in both forms of materials traffic, the convenience of returning books to the stacks should be given priority. Usually the movement of materials to and from the shipping and receiving area can be batched so as to avoid conflict with other operations.

4. Should the administrative offices be on the same level as the major public services? There is a great difference of opinion here. Some librarians, especially in colleges and smaller branch libraries, want to be close to the operational reader service areas so as to be more readily available to the public. Some feel it is of first importance to be adjacent to the acquisition and catalog departments, and some prefer to be at a distance from all operations to make it easier to carry on administrative and sometimes scholarly work undisturbed by routine problems. In any case, it is desirable to provide accessibility without necessarily going through a control portal in most cases, although this is certainly not essential. Such an arrangement removes the need to provide access to the collections for visitors unaffiliated with the institution when they arrive to see the business manager, personnel officer, or the director. This question is probably of greatest concern in very large libraries.

A related question is whether the associate and assistant librarians should have offices adjacent to the chief librarian's office, in order to facilitate consultation, or close to the departments or the staff they supervise? For instance, if an assistant librarian is in charge of public services and the library's administrative suite is on the second floor, should the assistant librarian have an office next to the reference and circulation departments or on the second floor next to the chief librarian? Often this decision depends upon the current administrative style of the organization and perhaps even the individual administrators. What is done today may change a year from now. Because of this, it is suggested that the arrangements should be made with flexibility in mind. This solution is probably more important in the library administrative area where space is usually more fixed in size and configuration than in the larger operating departments.

5. If the library is to include an exhibition room or a rare-book room to which it wishes to attract visitors, especially friends of the library, should it be placed near the entrance so as to be readily accessible, or will space elsewhere in a quieter location be satisfactory? Should a basement level without windows be considered where special protection of books and manuscripts from sunlight would not be required, and where temperature, humidity control, and security might be easier to provide (but where flooding may prove a hazard), or would a top floor be preferable where, except for roof leaks, one might expect the hazard of water to be minimized? All too often, rare-book collections are soaked. Unfortunately, due to the frequency of deferred maintenance, rooftop mechanical rooms, sprinkler systems, and the like, placing these materials higher in a building does not remove the potential of water damage. In establishing the location for such a facility, one should keep in mind that many of the visitors may be elderly and thus elevator access is probably desirable. Also, this is often an area that attracts many visiting scholars and people with little or no need for general access to the main collections. Because of this, the rare-book room is often another candi-

date for placement outside the main portal control point. Size and local circumstances will greatly influence its location.

6. How important is it to place a large percentage of the seating accommodation on the entrance level, or, if that cannot be arranged, on levels up one or down one from the entrance to avoid unnecessarily heavy traffic on stairs or elevators? This arrangement should make for a quieter and less restless building where reader populations are large, though at the same time it increases the difficulty of combining accommodations for books and readers in close proximity. Of course, closed stacks dictate large, centrally placed reading areas while the concept of an open stack is, in part, to place the reader as near the collections as possible. The decision of how much centralized reading should be provided may be made easier if there is a separate undergraduate or course work (as opposed to research) area with many seats and comparatively few books, which might make it possible to house this aspect of the library's operations within one level of the entrance and make more distant levels or locations available to graduate students and faculty who require comparatively few seats but many volumes. Many factors such as the distribution of the collections, the nature of the user group, the size of the library, etc., need to be considered in reaching a conclusion on seating distribution.

These questions might be added to almost indefinitely, but it is hoped that the basic questions of most general interest have been suggested. Others will affect comparatively few libraries, and here, as elsewhere, decisions should generally be based on local conditions. Posing the questions and, in only a few instances, suggesting possible answers is not meant to dictate decisions but to clarify the problems.

Aesthetic versus Functional Concerns. While there may be some risk in establishing guidelines for aesthetic versus functional decisions, it is nevertheless useful to formulate a statement on the issues, with the recognition that the design team should be expected to test various options and possibilities. Obviously, the building should house the staff and collections adequately as well as provide sufficient accommodation for the readers. But these alone are not enough. Other problems must be dealt with in planning a new structure, and they can rarely be solved without deciding priorities, which in turn should be based on the objectives of the institution. It can readily be agreed that the library should not be ugly. But how important is its architectural style? Should a minimum of attention be given to the appearance, or should an effort be made to have it harmonize with other buildings in the vicinity; or should the architect aim to create an outstanding structure on the campus? Should special attention be paid to its interior design? Should the construction be of such high quality that the structure will be sound after a hundred years, or should its life be thought of in terms of a limited period, on the assumption that it will be outdated and not worth preserving thereafter? Costs too often have more influence than one might wish in determining the answers. There are codes and local ordinances that often dictate a certain level of quality or style. Other factors, some of which are discussed elsewhere in this section on the program front matter, will influence the aesthetic and functional quality.

No attempt will be made to write dogmatically on architectural style and aesthetics, important as these are in determining the success or failure of a library building. Architectural propriety and aesthetics are not exact sciences. However, they are basic, and they should not be completely subordinated to the functional aspects of the program; yet the beauty of a building should not conflict with its satisfactory operation. The ideal is to strike that delicate balance between the architectural requirements for aesthetics, the functional requirements as established in the program, and the resources to achieve both.

Traditionally library buildings have tended to be monumental in character. This distinction follows from the importance attributed to them, which has often resulted in libraries that are the central, most conspicuous, and largest buildings on the campus. The donor, wanting perhaps to perpetuate a family name, asks for an architectural gem, and incidentally a monument. The governing board may take advantage of an opportunity to build something quite special on a campus otherwise comprised of utilitarian buildings, and approves, at least in theory, a monumental structure. The library is probably used regularly by a larger percentage of the students and faculty than any other building, with the possible exception of a student union or the chapel in a church-affiliated institution. The architect naturally takes advantage of an unusual opportunity for a fine building. Because of the long-term inertia derived from the desire for monumentality, the impact of such a design should be clearly understood so that the decision appropriate to the institution can be reached. High ceilings, which historically have been associated with monumental structures, add cost that may limit the ability to provide a facility that meets the programmed operational needs. Tower libraries may add to the difficulty of managing the collections and thus may add to the ongoing operational cost, as well as make the collections more difficult to get to from the central service points. Future expansion of a monumental structure is often much more difficult to accomplish in an architecturally satisfactory way. Flexibility for alternative uses may be severely restricted. The cost for monumentality is generally high, and the advantage of such a structure should be carefully weighed against the disadvantages.

The librarian may go along with the architect in striving toward monumentality until it is found that the funds required are needed to provide useful floor area for library purposes; then a loud protest is generally heard. To avoid an acrimonious debate, the various points of view should be assembled and some agreement reached on what is most important for the institution as a whole. The direction of such an agreement should then be incorporated as part of the program statement.

Module and Flexibility. Basic to the design of any modern building is some form of a dimensional module. In libraries the standard dimensions of shelving, together with the needs for aisle space, readers, offices, work areas, structural and mechanical requirements, and possibly parking space, should be considered in establishing an appropriate building module. A carefully selected module will ensure a certain degree of flexibility or adaptability, particularly if anticipated future changes in the assignment of space can be accommodated. Other forms of adaptability include provisions for future expansion or deployment of functions or collections, the provision of utilities and environmental control that will permit a broad range of specific uses, and the planning of fixed elements so as to minimize the difficulty of future alterations.

Modules vary in scale from the small size of a specific building unit, such as a brick, to the dimension of a ceiling grid with lighting and mechanical systems included, to the shelving unit required to house a book, or to the structural column spacing. Other elements can be considered as the basis for a module, but at this stage of the project design only the concept of the desirability for a module should be established. In this case probably the most important factor for layouts and future flexibility will be the column spacing. Thus the modular system, as the term is used here, is a building supported by columns placed at regular intervals. All weight-bearing elements, including shear walls as required in earthquake areas, are assumed to be in a regular pattern as established by the module. To simplify the discussion, we will assume that fixed elements, such as the shear walls mentioned, will be carefully located so as to have a minimal effect on the concept that the columns act as the immovable framework within which all functions must be arranged.

A rectangle—usually, but not always, a square—defined by four adjacent columns, is known as a bay. The modular building then is made up of identical bays, any one of which may be furnished as part of a reading area, filled with ranges of shelving, divided by partitions into offices, or combinations of two or even three of these. No difficult structural alterations should be required when a bay that has been serving one of these purposes is assigned to another; furniture, shelving, and partitions, which may be dry and demountable or wet and more difficult to remove, can be shifted.

This flexibility is a major virtue of the modular system, and it appeals greatly to those who have attempted to adapt within one of the traditional structures characterized by massive interior walls and multitier stacks to changing needs, even when those fine older buildings do have some form of a module, which they usually do. There has been a revolution during the last thirty or more years, thanks in large part, as far as libraries are concerned, to the efforts of the late Angus Snead Macdonald, Ralph Ellsworth, and other forward-looking librarians, architects, and builders; the modular system is now prevalent, although not universally used. To sum up, a building consisting largely of space that can be used for almost any purpose without extensive or expensive alterations should in the long run save money and prevent complications which so often arise as space requirements change. The modular system or some adaption of it is now generally standard in libraries.

Like most innovations, however, the modular system is not a panacea; it has its faults and its pitfalls. The fundamental objection is that no one column spacing or bay size is ideal for all purposes; the module that is almost perfectly adapted to one function, such as book storage, will not be equally well suited to another. Mr. Metcalf once suggested that it might be desirable to construct one-third of a library in bays designed for book storage, one-third in a module well adapted to reading areas, and one-third in a reasonably satisfactory all-purpose size. This seemed a more promising procedure at the time it was proposed than it does today, when there is an increasing tendency to bring books and readers together in a single area. However, there are no doubt circumstances which make such a suggestion appropriate. A combination of different bay sizes was used in the Harvard's Lamont Library (see fig. 5.3) as a means of taking advantage of the useful features of the modular system and at the same time avoiding the handicap that it often brings in its train. The attempt to attain flexibility entails certain sacrifices, and some inflexible features, such as columns at regular intervals.

Furthermore, if the optimum module size for a new library is based on the present nature of the library's collection and its clientele, it must be recognized that many institutions change so rapidly that the size desirable today may be wasteful ten years hence. There may then be an 8 to 10 percent loss in space utilization, particularly if an addition is built without change in bay sizes. For instance, if a bay size suitable for an open-shelf undergraduate collection with stack ranges 4 ft 6 in. on centers is used for what becomes a large research collection where 4 ft 2 in. on centers may be adequate, some 8 percent of the stack area will be devoted to unnecessary aisle space. "On centers" is the distance between the center of the uprights in one range to the center of the uprights in the next parallel range. The term is also used in connection with table and carrel spacing, where it is the distance between the edge of one and the corresponding edge of the next one parallel to it. Column spacing is generally spoken of in a similar way.

Cases can also be cited in which the modular system has caused a librarian to suppose that since the building was assumed to be completely flexible, layouts did not need to be planned carefully in advance, so long as the total floor space was sufficient. The result has been a great deal of shifting that ought not to have been necessary; it is expensive, even with a modular system, to replace floor coverings, change lighting fixtures, rearrange air-handling ducts, relocate outlets, and move temporary partitions.

Totally modular buildings have sometimes resulted in serious acoustical problems because the movable partitions and bookcases on which they depend to divide up each floor have not proved adequate barriers to sound. Of course, a modular building need not have movable partitions, and even where movable partitions are used, there are often ways of reducing the acoustic problems.

In spite of the difficulties, the modular system is undoubtedly here to stay, and should be used with care in most new library construction. Its advantages can be summarized as follows:

1. It simplifies the task of estimating costs, with more accurate results.

2. It saves time on the site because materials are acquired in suitable sizes, and it largely reduces cutting, patching, and wasting materials.

3. It simplifies supervision and reduces construction error, as much of the work is routine.

4. It should improve the finished product because more of the work can be done under factory controls rather than field conditions.

5. It provides more flexible space adaptable for any purpose.

6. Where prefabrication is anticipated, standardization with a modular design is essential, and in most other cases it facilitates some of the planning processes.

By the time the program is being written, the administration should have decided whether it wishes to require the use of a module system. The program writer should hesitate to give definite instructions to the architect, unless there is some special reason for it. Usually, if the module system is to be used, the architect should propose the dimensions and say whether or not the bays should be square. The program, however, can properly outline the need to analyze the alternatives, with the involvement of the ar-

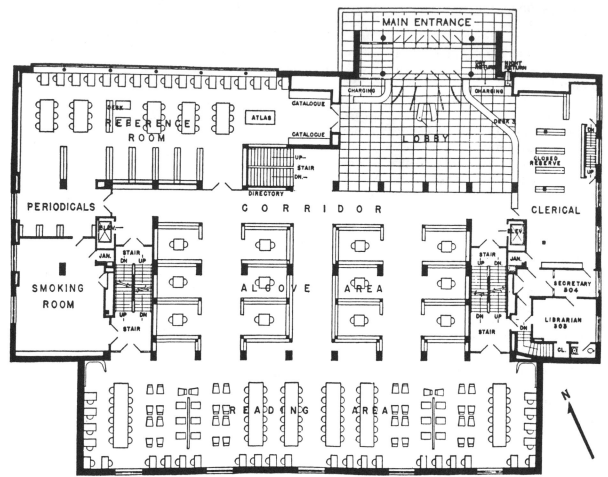

FIGURE 5.3 Lamont Library, third level, showing column spacing. The columns are irregularly spaced so as to make possible large reading areas and a lobby without obstructions, but the building is basically modular with columns 13 ft (3.962) on centers from east to west.

chitect and other consultants. Factors to be considered should also be detailed, including information on the anticipated dimensions of shelving units, a range of acceptable aisle spacing, the desire to include modular division for other functions such as offices, faculty studies, and the like, and the extent of flexibility desired. There may be zones of the building that are treated differently, especially if large areas are to be assigned to special functions or unique stack needs such as archival storage, map rooms, or movable shelving. The program writer is urged to find other specific requirements that should be established early in the project by reading Chapters 6 and 7 and Appendix B, where various modular considerations are discussed. In many cases it will be sufficient simply to state the requirement to establish a module suitable to the most frequent library spacing conditions and the structural and mechanical needs of the building.

Security. Security in libraries takes many forms, ranging from sophisticated intrusion alarms to concern about the use of windows. Planning for a secure facility will include aspects of layout and internal arrangements, where there may be several interior zones with varying degrees of security. Other aspects include the book control and charge-out system, exit alarms, book-detection systems, panic buttons, emergency phones, fire pull boxes, sprinkler systems, and radio systems. Factors such as the speed with which police or fire personnel respond to an alarm, the hours of operation, the exposure to vandalism, the value of the collections, and the philosophy of how the library should serve the user can all play a role in shaping security aspects of the facility. Because many of these factors change with time, provision for flexible response to security needs is of considerable importance.

In developing the program requirements for security, the following general aspects should be considered:

1. Outside the building, is planting to be maintained so as to minimize places to hide? Are lights to be provided? How do fire trucks or police vehicles approach the building? In most cases these site aspects can be developed as the design progresses, and usually a simple program statement of the need to incorporate security aspects into the design will be sufficient. Such details as a bike rack that permits locking bikes to a solid object might be a specific requirement. Another related requirement might be the absence of similar objects such as open fences, columns, or fixed furniture near the main entrance, to discourage securing bikes where they will influence traffic. External devices for fire annunciation may be required by the fire department, and some mention of these, unless they are covered in a published institutional standard, should be made.

2. The building envelope, or shell, warrants consideration. In some cases the use of glass is an invitation to vandalism to be avoided. However, the psychological cost of a windowless building is great, and the institution that feels it must have solid, window-free walls may be unfortunate. But local conditions may require such a design. Windows that can be opened represent an easy method of removing library materials without control. Reading porches near the ground level amount to another building entrance, and remember that students rise to challenges so that even a second floor porch is an invitation.

Where glass is desired but vandalism is great, glazing materials such as laminated glass or Lexan can add significantly to the security, but will also add significantly to the cost. Smaller windows are of course less expensive to replace if broken; one may have to wait a month or two for delivery of a large-sized replacement. To a large measure, energy concerns may dictate the amount of glass permitted. Local building codes may also help determine the maximum and minimum glazing.

Where the library is to be an addition to another building, roof hatches and rooftop mechanical systems will need to be carefully considered for required service access, which may also present security problems. Air intakes that are accessible to a pedestrian may

represent an invitation for a smoke or stink bomb. Remember that student pranks are traditional and that mass student protests and riots have occurred periodically in all countries throughout history.

Entrance doors often are double doors with panic hardware on the inside. Such doors always represent a security problem as, unless there is an astragal, they can easily be opened with the simplest of tools. With an astragal on double doors, there is nearly always a problem of banging or having the doors close out of sequence in such a way that one leaf is not fully closed. One good solution where double doors are considered desirable is to make the exit arrangements such that they are not a required exit. In this case most code authorities will permit a form of positive locking so that the doors cannot be opened without a key. A second solution is to have several single doors rather than double doors. Even with panic hardware single doors are far more secure than a double door.

Emergency exit doors that normally would be locked, which in most cases must always be free opening from the inside, should have a local buzzer or bell type of alarm. In a large library where there is a high probability that staff will not hear the local alarm, there should be a remote alarm and an annunciator panel to indicate the door that has been compromised. The remote alarm should probably be set up so that if a key is used to open the secured door, the alarm does not go off or the indication of alarm is simply a blinking light. The remote annunciator panel will need to be located in an area certain to be staffed during all hours of operation. After hours this alarm can be transmitted to a central communication or campus security office.

3. Internal arrangements, previously discussed in terms of functions, can also have considerable influence on security. Some libraries have established as a goal that all areas of the stack should be within sight of staffed positions. While this may be extreme, and even impossible in a large library, some aspects of this notion are probably beneficial. Major service points should be within sight of each other, and some reading accommodations should be provided in a supervised area. Usually this would be the reference, current periodicals, or reserved-book areas. Stack reading areas should probably be large enough to ensure their use by several readers at any given time, but not so large that they

become overwhelming seas of carrels or tables. Where the security of readers in the stacks is a great problem television monitors may be warranted. The librarians may prefer to schedule reshelving during the evening to increase security then or to finance a group of roving proctors, perhaps students, to frequent the more remote reading areas. Even though proctors are an expensive solution, many will argue that they are more socially acceptable and even more efficacious than television monitors. However, some libraries, including the Perry-Castañeda Library at the University of Texas, have found television to be effective when the monitors are located at the staffed exit-control portals in full public view. Planning on the basis of human security may prove expensive to change; building flexibility may be reduced.

Determination of whether the point of control will be at the building entrance, department entrance, or stack entrance is in part a security decision. At the University of Chicago Regenstein Library, provision for portal booths was made both at the stack entrance and off the lobby. The building opened with the control point at the stack entrance, but after a rash of arson attempts and vandalism, the control point was moved to the lobby. Flexibility to make such a change may be a prudent program requirement in many cases. If nothing else, conduit might be stubbed out to permit such a change with minimal utility and signal alterations.

Many libraries today either have or are planning to have a book detection system. Several different systems are on the market, and each will have slightly different facility requirements. The major distinction is a matter of permanent book targets or targets that can be shielded or disarmed as part of the charge-out process. In either case, a library book that is not properly processed, either by being passed around the detection device or by being deactivated, will set off an alarm, lock a gate, or both. *Library Technology Reports* has an excellent discussion of many of the systems available today. If there is any reasonable expectation that such a system may be required, conduit access to power should be provided. Of course, the nature of the exact system selected can have a significant impact on how it is set up. Representatives of the manufacturer can be helpful in regard to layouts and utility requirements. Most of this work can easily be done in later design stages,

but the basic requirement of provision for such a system should be established in the program.

Where a large library is being planned, there will probably be staffed areas that are not centrally located. In this case some remote service points can become very lonely and seem rather dangerous, especially if staffed by a timid soul. A panic button system may be one way of providing psychological or actual security for isolated staff. When pushed, the panic alarm should sound at a central location staffed during all hours of operation. It should not be so loud that the entire library will be disturbed. Then, according to policy, the police can be called, a staff member can call the panicked person to get a signal of the nature of the concern, or a staff member can visit the panicked individual. In the event that there is more than one panic button, an annunciator to determine the location of each activated panic button will be required. An alternative may be pagers carried by staff.

The local fire code will probably require fire alarm pull boxes at specific intervals within the building. These too, according to policy, can be used in a panic situation. Public phones at obvious or central locations throughout the building aid this form of security as well. However, experience with intercom systems or a house phone system indicates that they are seldom used, that maintenance of privately owned phone systems is usually difficult, and that eventually they fall to total disuse. Phones in the library generally ought to be those provided and maintained by the local telephone company, or at least by a reputable company with a demonstrated record of excellent service.

A public address system, if strictly limited to defined uses (such as closing and genuine emergencies), is a useful security device in a library. In a large facility care should be taken to keep phone lines and speaker lines electromagnetically isolated. Long runs of phone lines with a public address system may result in the broadcasting of phone conversations or the clicking of the phone equipment. At closing time a public address system is particularly useful for clearing the building of readers. The largest libraries must often rely on such a system combined with intrusion alarms, as the stack area may be so vast that clearing the building by a staff walk-through is virtually impossible. If a public address system is to be part of the building project, its operational location and the distribution of speakers should be generally addressed in the program. Staff areas and small public service units probably do not need to be covered separately, if other emergency signals can be heard in them. Where there are a number of enclosed studies, it may not be economical to include each of them within the system, and the speaker system will usually penetrate offices and other small rooms if the speakers are properly located. Major stack and associated reading areas are certainly candidates for such treatment.

The program or institutional standards should be quite specific in regard to documentation required for any systems, particularly electrical and mechanical systems. Without proper documentation of the various features, future maintenance and repairs will be difficult at best. An operations manual including maintenance instructions and detailed wiring diagrams should be required of the contractor and engineers by the contract documents.

Some institutions prefer not to program intrusion alarms too specifically. These generally are motion detectors and door contacts, although many other devices may be employed. Several varieties of motion detectors are in common use in libraries, including ultrasonic, radar, infrared, and light beam detectors. Each device has its weaknesses and strong points, and each situation will require special consideration. Requirements for a display area for rare books may include special laminated glass, vibration detectors in the cases, weight sensors at each display, and motion detectors within the space. In some cases television surveillance or a guard may be in order, as is the case at the Humanities Research Center at the University of Texas, where a Gutenberg Bible is on display. The field of intrusion alarms is changing rapidly with changing technology. Because of this, it is recommended that where such devices are deemed essential, a security consultant should be added to the design team. The program then should only state the security requirement for alarm systems in general terms, and the contract documents in regard to intrusion alarms should only detail conduit runs. The actual security devices should be contracted for separately, probably from the firm which will maintain them. This procedure is recommended because of the fairly large and often public distribution of the general contract documents. Where security is a serious concern, the documentation should be more limited. However, there should indeed be documentation just as there is for all the other building systems.

Another aspect of security is fire protection. As with pull boxes discussed earlier, other aspects of fire protection will be in part established by the local codes. Usually included in the code is a table of maximum floor areas for a given method of construction. Generally the floor area allowed is larger where there is a positive means of fire protection, such as a sprinkler system or a Halon fire suppression system. Another suppression system uses carbon dioxide, but in most cases it is not recommended due to the life safety aspects; in the event of a carbon dioxide release, occupants have only a few seconds to evacuate the building before they would succumb to suffocation. Most institutions will not be willing to risk the possible loss of life.

A Halon system is generally regarded as the best fire suppression system available today. However, it is very expensive. Few, if any, libraries will be able to afford a Halon system for more than a very limited space containing their most valuable materials. A rare-book vault may be a candidate for a Halon system. Halon, also referred to as Freon by some manufacturers, is a gas that, when present in the atmosphere, will not permit a fire to burn. But its most interesting characteristic is that an occupant of a space with a Halon system can survive a release of the gas without suffocating or other disabling effects. While it may not be an ideal atmosphere in which to breathe, it is at least not deadly like carbon dioxide.

The Halon gas is stored in pressurized tanks. A control valve is connected electrically with a product-of-combustion detector. Interconnections with duct louvers and magnetic door hold-open devices are also required so that when smoke is detected, the space is sealed, the gas is released, and a fire signal is sounded. Not only is the equipment sophisticated and costly, but the gas itself is expensive. Obviously, it must be replaced after each release. In a large space a system of space division might be considered so that in the event of a fire, the fire zone can be sealed off automatically and a Halon system sized for the smaller space division might suffice. Still, by current standards, a Halon system is not practical for the majority of library space simply because of its cost.

The only other fire suppressant system involves water. While many librarians are strongly against the use of a fire sprinkler system, the authors are convinced that the potential fire damage in a library without a sprinkler system substantially exceeds the potential water damage from sprinklers. However, we would be the first to admit that where there is water, some day there will probably be a flood. With modern techniques of freeze drying, flood damage can be limited. Fire damage, on the other hand, results in absolute loss. The likelihood of a fire is almost as certain over the years as an accidental flood caused by sprinklers, and the absence of spinklers by no means guarantees an absence of flooding.

Several things can be done to limit the flood effects of sprinkler systems. First, it should be understood that, unlike gas systems, when sprinkler heads go off, they do so individually as the heat of the fire melts a fusable link on the affected sprinkler head. Short of a roaring inferno, which is unlikely with an operational sprinkler system, few heads are ever likely to be set off simultaneously. When one sprinkler head goes off, a water flow switch activates the fire alarm which, in most cases, results in rapid response by the campus security service and the local fire department. Officials then can turn off the water as soon as it is determined there is no fire danger. Water detection devices placed at various locations about the floor, such as under bottom shelves, may serve to further reduce the risk of loss due to flooding. These devices may be as simple as a fixture containing a sponge that swells when wet to activate a microswitch. Floor drains, particularly in basement areas, often lead to sumps where a high-water alarm can be provided. None of these alarms will be effective unless they link to a remote annunciator at a communications center staffed to respond to alarms twenty-four hours a day.

Perhaps the most useful alarm system is the product-of-combustion, or smoke detection, system. In the event of a fire, the system devices, if properly distributed, will usually detect smoke and activate an alarm several minutes before the heat buildup is sufficient to set off the sprinkler. In many cases this means that the security service or fire department will be on the scene before the fire activates a sprinkler head.

There are several different kinds of sprinkler systems. The most common is the one that has been implied in the preceding discussion. It is always filled, or "charged," with water under pressure, and once a head is activated, the entire sprinkler zone must be turned off to replace the head and stop the water flow. There are special wedges that can be used to stop the flow of an individual head manually, but they probably are not very practical in most cases. Another system, which has been in use in the Bancroft Library at the University of California, Berkeley, and Western Illinois University at Macomb, is a preaction system which requires both the activation of a product-of-combustion detection system and a sprinkler head before water is present in the space. In this case the sprinkler feeder line is charged with compressed air. Water enters the system only when smoke is detected, and it is released only after the heat buildup melts a fusible link at a sprinkler head. Such a system can be further refined by adding sprinkler heads that turn themselves off when the temperature drops. In the past these heads had a tendency to leak and were usually not recommended for libraries, but it is the authors' understanding that more recently these heads have become fully reliable.

Other fire protection conditions are important too. Mechanical systems need to be designed to separate major areas in the event of a fire and to exhaust smoke while limiting the provision of fresh air in a fire zone. Compartmentalization can be an important concept in fire resistant construction; however, without additional fire protection devices, the risk of loss due to fire is only reduced to the size of the compartment. Finally, there is the possible reduction of combustible materials in libraries which will reduce fire risk. If it is decided not to install sprinklers, then the designer should question the use of such items as wood furniture or book trucks, carpets, combustible drapes, and combustible wall or ceiling surfaces. In a library oriented toward people, this decision may be difficult to face. *Managing the Library Fire Risk* by John Morris describes in considerable detail the risks and options for fire security. If the librarian is undecided about what the fire protection requirements should be, this book can be a great asset. The program document should state all expectations at least in terms of general security requirements. Local fire codes also specify the use of fire retardant materials, and may limit the use of materials such as polyurethane, which give off toxic fumes when smoldering.

Interior Design Concerns. Much of this book addresses interior design concerns from various points of view. Specific aspects that might be established in the program, aside from specific space requirements, include acoustic quality, durability of surfaces and furniture, the desire for mock-ups of especially important features such as lighting or carrel arrangements, who is to do room layouts, the general "feel" of the space desired by the institution, and whether an interior consultant will have defined contractual responsibilities. Perhaps the building goal is to provide comfort for the readers and staff. Reasonable comfort provides conditions that enable the occupant to be unaware of such matters as air quality, drafts, lighting, glare, visual and auditory distraction, chair and table configuration, and to use the library while being oblivious to the physical surroundings. Indeed, the physical surroundings ideally would promote and improve the quality of research or other work in the library.

The architectural and functional qualities of the library will be greatly influenced by the interior design, and obviously, the interior design will need to reflect these desired qualities. A building, even if handsome to look upon, will always be regarded unfavorably by users if it is not successful functionally, just as will one which is successful functionally but unattractive or so extreme in its architecture that it becomes outdated while still new. This does not mean that a good library building must be traditional in style; quite the contrary—the use of imagination and a contemporary outlook in the planning and design may make a significant contribution toward the success of the building; indeed, the building should reflect the period of its construction.

Architectural propriety, aesthetics, and the interior design for a new building are governed to some extent by the financial situation. Funding capacity will significantly influence space both in terms of quality and quantity. To avoid unpleasant controversy which, combined with other complaints, may have deplorable consequences, it is suggested that the architect be told when receiving the assignment that the institution wants as handsome a building as possible, inside and out,

but that there is a definite limit to available funds; within this limit the requirements stated in the program must be provided for and the results must be functionally satisfactory.

Several basic conditions are desirable in the interior arrangements of any library. The interior should be a comfortable place in which to study. It should be well ventilated, well lighted, and quiet, but not silent. A feeling of restlessness should be avoided, as should one of deadness. It should be so arranged that good library service can be provided easily, quickly, and inexpensively. It should have sufficient flexibility or adaptability to allow changing operations or other features as the library evolves. Finally, it should have a layout in which one's way around can be found with ease. These various factors may differ in importance in different parts of the building, according to the specific activity in each part.

In most cases the architect will develop furniture layouts as part of the schematic, or first design, phase. These layouts, however, are more to demonstrate the size of the space than to respond to specific program or operational needs. The process of detailing furniture arrangements usually is not done in the later design phases unless interior design is part of the contract. When an administration decides that it can do its own furnishing, someone on the staff will need to develop detailed furniture layouts to ensure appropriate built-in arrangements such as door locations and door swing, outlets, phone service, lighting, and the like. Even when the architect is not to do the interior design, the goals of the institution should be established, and the program represents an excellent starting point. However, interior arrangements and selection will be influenced by the architectural design, thus any statement is likely to be altered as the design progresses.

The desired "feel" of a space is at best difficult to establish in words. Words such as *inviting, stimulating, low key, quiet, durable, pleasant, easy to maintain, vandal resistant, student proof, conducive to research or reading,* and *comfortable* are common descriptions of the desired effect. Some librarians might prefer bold, bright colors, and others more subtle hues. An art librarian might wish an absence of color so as to provide a minimum of contrasting stimuli for the color found in the art books, prints, and other materials. Color is certainly one of the most important aesthetic features of any space. Libraries in the past were too often drab in their general effect. The walls, the bookstacks, floors, and furniture all tended to have an institutional aspect. This conventionality was completely unnecessary. Different colors on different walls of a room can give an effect of larger size. Bookstacks of different colors on different levels can add to attractiveness, to say nothing of making it easier for students who go to sleep to recognize where they are when they wake up. Bright colors, some argue, stimulate students and more study results. Others claim that such conditions are distracting and that quieter colors are more suitable in a library. A mixture of strong colors in some areas and quiet ones in others may provide an acceptable compromise. It is likely that the direction will not be clearly established in the program, but where there is a local or institutional philosophy, some statement should be made. The matter is for local decision, and that decision is not necessarily totally irrevocable. Repainting, after all, is possible.

Texture is another factor that influences aesthetics. Carpet adds both a softness and acoustic qualities. Other materials, largely because of their texture, can make a space feel richer. The use of brick, wood, fabric panels, exposed concrete in its many forms, acoustic ceiling materials, and smooth hard surfaces such as glass, chrome, painted gypsum board, or plaster all will shape the aesthetic quality of the building. Scale is still another aspect of aesthetics. It, together with proportion, can make a space feel too large or too small. Lighting can affect scale and highlight texture to alter the mood of a space. All of these factors can serve as relief during often tedious hours of reading. A view to the outside can often do much of the same.

It would not be proper to establish strict guidelines for these factors in the program. Elements such as color, texture, light, scale, and proportion will evolve as the design progresses. The program might state, however, that carpet, for example, is a desirable feature, that an exterior outlook for reading areas is desired, and that reading areas should not be so large as to be overwhelming or so small as to represent directional or security problems. Where typing or conversation is anticipated, acoustic separation of spaces may be a program requirement. The heating, ventilation, and air conditioning needs discussed later certainly represent a requirement. Durability and flexibility obviously are important.

The question of having built-in or freestanding furniture is important. Freestanding furniture usually results in greater flexibility to respond to change while built-in furniture usually has a quality of being more strongly related to the design and thus "belonging." Typing surfaces generally transmit less noise if they are freestanding. However, a small enclosed carrel or work station uses space more efficiently if the work surface is built in. In most cases the decision can wait for later stages in the design, but where the use of existing furniture is anticipated, it is important to establish this in the program. In this case thought should also be given to whether any or all of the existing furniture is to be refinished to more nearly match the new decor. There may be furniture especially associated with some aspect of the library that will need special consideration as part of the design. This is quite common for rare book rooms, though other areas may be involved as well. Some institutions may require that certain furnishings or even all furnishings must come from a specific source. The California State University system, for example, requires that its furniture be produced by the penal industries in the state. Other institutions may have selected a specific card catalog cabinet or other element that should be matched exactly.

Another important aspect, related to both space in general and interior design, is the design of the directional, informational, and emergency signs and graphics. Most building graphics should appear to be sympathetic with the building and its furniture, but not to blend in to the degree that they are not noticed. Perhaps the most important programmatic aspect of graphics is to establish the scope of the work and who is to undertake the design, text, and installation. Library signs, or graphics, represent a difficult problem. There is always more information to be conveyed to the user than there are appropriate graphic devices to use. Care must be taken to avoid graphic clutter. A graphics system that can easily be adapted to change, of reasonable cost, is usually a requirement. A directory that can only be changed at considerable expense will no doubt always be out of date. Names on rooms, diagrams of stack arrangements, campus maps showing branch libraries, and bins holding library handouts will all change. The ideal arrangement is to have a system that can be maintained by the library or, in the case of a small college, within the institution. Without this capability there almost certainly will be constant graphics problems.

Room numbering generally is not thought about until the end of the project. However, if nothing is said, the architect will establish room numbers in the contract documents which usually will not relate to the final room numbering scheme. This way of work almost always leads to confusion during the final stages of the project, when the phone company is looking for a room designated on the drawings as B16 but labeled on the door as 103. Movers and workers in other trades will have the same problem. It can be easily avoided if the architect is required by the program to establish a room numbering schedule compatible with the library and institution.

Other aspects of interior concern are found either in this section, the following section, or Chapter 6. While much of the interior design will and should evolve with the project, those aspects deemed important enough to be general requirements of the project should be established clearly in the program.

Environmental Control. Any building will create a controlled environment to some degree. However, without thoughtful specification the nature of the environment may discourage use by the facility or promote deterioration of the materials housed. Appendix F provides specific guidelines issued by two organizations.

In planning an environmentally functional building, two essential points must be considered. The balance of this Section discusses in greater detail the two issues with emphasis on the first, as this is a topic with which the designer may not be familiar.

1. The building should provide quarters that will as far as possible ensure the preservation of the collections. Proper atmospheric conditions—temperature, humidity control, filtered air, and the control of light—are important here. Optimum conditions can be very expensive, both in terms of their initial cost and in terms of their operating cost. It must be decided how much emphasis on such matters is warranted by the quality of the collections, the nature of local weather patterns, air pollution levels, and preservation goals of the library. The presence of rare and irreplaceable materials, particularly in a humid industrial region, should make the answer obvious.

2. Comfort of the readers and staff will need attention in any new facility. While we have all experienced difficult environmental conditions, and can usually continue to function, it is clear that the efficiency of either the staff or scholar will be improved as the environment approaches ideal conditions. Preservation and comfort, taken at their ideal levels, are not always compatible. Some level of compromise will probably be necessary.

It has become increasingly apparent in recent years that the vast majority of library materials are slowly being destroyed by abrasion and chemical reactions encouraged by light, air pollution, biological infestations, temperature, humidity, and acids in the papers commonly used by the publishing industry. In testimony on behalf of the National Conservation Advisory Council to the Department of Energy as reported in *History News*, May 1980, Peter Waters said: "Fluctuating temperatures and relative humidities . . . inevitably trigger chemical reactions in paper and binding materials, expressed in rapid acceleration of hydrolytic and oxidative energy. For example, at 68 degrees F. (20 degrees C.) and 50 percent relative humidity we can calculate that a particular paper may have a life expectancy of two hundred years. At 95 degrees F. (35 degrees C.) and 50 percent humidity, the life expectancy is reduced to about sixteen years. At 50 degrees F. (10 degrees C.) and 50 percent relative humidity, its life expectancy is increased to 1,260 years." From this it is easy to conclude that when it is the goal of the institution to maintain a collection of research materials for succeeding generations, then the designers of the facility must be concerned about maintaining temperatures at the lowest reasonable level.

The nature of paper produced over the last two hundred years of rising industrial technology has been increasingly subject to the impact of temperature and humidity. Most readers no doubt have observed the effect of leaving the daily newspaper out in the sun for a day or two. While much of the discoloration is caused by light, heat is also involved. If left in such conditions for a longer period, the paper will become so brittle that it will fragment when touched. The same is happening, although much more slowly, to the vast majority of the collections held in libraries. Microfilm, magnetic tapes, and other library materials are also subject to deterioration due to environmental conditions.

While lower temperatures result in longer book life, the limiting factor is usually related to people or to the cost of energy. In a library where books and people are closely associated, the temperature minimum should be that of a reasonable minimal comfort level for readers who must remain relatively inactive for hours at a time. Typically, the ideal temperature range for this condition is specified as 68 to 72 degrees F (20 to 22 degrees C). However, local customs of clothing and other factors can influence this range. At the lower end of the comfort range, drafts can result in a sense of coldness greater, or lower, than the actual temperature. A person sitting under an air register creating a draft will feel cold even though the temperature is accurately maintained at 70 degrees F or 21 degrees C. Conversely, a space with no perceptible air movement will feel stuffy when temperatures rise in the summer even though engineering calculations demonstrate sufficient air changes.

In a closed collection, such as a typical archive or collection of rare materials or perhaps a book-storage facility, the minimum temperature is more related to the concern for condensation when the materials are removed for use by a reader in a warmer room. Here, if one can be reasonably certain that the temperature in the reading room will not exceed 76 degrees F, or 24.5 degrees C, with a relative humidity of 50 percent, then the storage temperature could be as low as 57 degrees F, or 14 degrees C. Lower storage temperatures are of course possible, but special consideration for the removal of materials for use will be required.

The energy cost for creating an environment suitable for reasonable preservation of library materials is often significant, particularly where an older building is being used to house major collections. Much can be done to reduce this cost, including installing superior insulation, using structural mass to absorb heat (as in a cave), providing a good seal at windows, doors, and construction joints, and reducing the quantity of heat sources within the controlled space. The calculation of energy use for a given facility is complex; it is best left to a mechanical engineer. How-

ever, the program statement outlining environmental conditions relating to preservation should not be made without the realization that there will be associated cost. It is because of this that often a compromise will be reached during the design process. Clearly, the priorities and goals of the institution must be well established before such a compromise is reached.

The effect of high humidity is that it provides the water necessary for many chemical reactions as well as the growth of mold. Low humidity, on the other hand, tends to dry out binding glues, and paper or film becomes less supple or more brittle. Specific humidity ranges suggested for a large number of different materials, vary over the range of 30 percent to 65 percent relative humidity. Generally, 40 to 50 percent or 45 to 55 percent is regarded as ideal for libraries.

It has been stated by Paul Banks and others that fluctuations in temperature and humidity set up internal physical stresses in many materials in addition to increasing chemical activity. Fluctuations in humidity seem to be more serious than in temperature, but both are cause for concern. Certainly, the effects of extreme fluctuations in humidity can be easily observed. The boards used in the binding of books warp, and vellum, a form of leather used in a number of rare books, will badly distort. Because of these effects it is generally recommended that humidity be kept within a range of plus or minus 5 percent of the specific design level. In some cases, particularly for rare materials, the specified tolerance is lower. One expert recommends 50 percent relative humidity with a range of plus or minus 3 percent diurnally and plus or minus 6 percent seasonally. As with temperature, such a specification will add to both the construction and operating cost, but where preservation is a concern, it should justify the expense.

There may be other aspects of a new library facility that warrant special consideration for temperature and humidity. Obviously, if a facility is too hot or too cold, it will not be used as intended, and this can indeed be a costly error. Computer rooms and preservation vaults will require special consideration. An archive of sound recordings could be quickly ruined if it were to become too hot. The librarians may also wish to specify special devices to monitor the environmental conditions. In most cases portable recording hygrothermographs are probably more effective than if they are built in. However, thermometers and hygrometers can be mounted to walls near thermostats at various dispersed points for a reasonable cost. It should be kept in mind though that such devices may attract theft or vandalism. They may be more logical in a closed stack or controlled area than in an open stack.

Another preservation concern is air pollution. Nearly all impurities, both gaseous and particulate, are harmful to books. Where libraries are located in regions with typical urban air pollution, the gaseous pollutants are likely to be the more serious problem. Of particular concern are sulfur dioxide, nitrogen oxides, and ozone, although other pollutants can cause deterioration of library materials. One should not assume that a library in a rural area is free of pollutants, as there are indeed natural sources of air pollution. Particulate matter is perhaps a more superficial problem than the oxidizing and reducing gases. Still, all dust has sharp edges and, together with perspiration and skin oils, will cause disfiguring damage over time. Maintenance costs for dusting shelves and books are, of course, reduced with proper filtration of the air.

Clearly, some form of air filtration should be considered in most libraries for both preservation and maintenance. There is a considerable array of the types of filtration available, including fabric, cyclone, electrostatic, alkaline water sprays, and activated carbon. Because of the production of ozone, electrostatic precipitation should be avoided in libraries. It should be noted that the Library of Congress does not permit the use of oil or viscous impingement filters, due to the concern for the production of polluting aerosols. Except for "scrubbers," or the washing of air, dry filters are recommended. In specifying a level of filtering efficiency, it should be obvious that the more complete the filtering process, the higher the cost. This is due to restriction of air flow by filters, and as they become more efficient at filtration, they require larger fan systems which will consume more energy. The more efficient filter will require more frequent servicing or replacement as the particulate matter will accumulate more rapidly. As a guide the Library of Congress specifies a minimum filtration efficiency of 95 percent; at the Newberry Library in Chicago an efficiency of 90 to 98

percent was suggested. The main library at Stanford was designed with a filtration efficiency of 90 percent throughout, except for the rare-book area, which is 95 percent.

For reducing gases such as sulfur dioxide, the recommended system involves a water wash where the pH is kept at 8.5 to 9.0. As there are technical problems relating to corrosion and scaling in the system, it is suggested that expert advice be sought by the design team should such a system be desired. The Folger Shakespeare Library has used such a system for at least four decades, and the Library of Congress currently has specified this type of system.

For the removal of oxidants, activated carbon is used. Examples of this system can be found at the Beinecke Library at Yale University and the Winterthur Museum in Delaware. While these systems may be considered exotic and extravagant, there are libraries and librarians who are convinced that dust, ozone, oxides of nitrogen and sulphur dioxide are harmful to the collections and thus must be removed. To do so requires such exotic systems and the program should guide the consultants.

As already suggested, light can also cause accelerated deterioration of library materials. The degree of deterioration is related to the intensity, duration, and spectral characteristics of the light. Years ago the original manuscript of the United States Declaration of Independence was displayed where it was exposed to indirect sunlight. As a result it is nearly illegible today, thus serving as an excellent example of deterioration caused by light.

The preservation aspects of light are perhaps as important as the comfort aspects. While most light is converted to heat, library preservation experts suggest special concern for the effect of that critical fraction of light which is responsible for photocatalyzed degradation. The activation energy level of light from the ultraviolet end of the spectrum is considerably more damaging than the infrared end of the range. It is interesting to note that most fluorescent light tends to have a far greater component of ultraviolet than incandescent sources. In areas where this is a justified concern, fluorescent tubes with filtering lenses or tube-type filter shields can be specified to minimize the ultraviolet component. In determining the specifications for the various forms of ultraviolet control, maintenance routines should be reviewed. The special fluorescent tubes, for example, look like normal tubes even though they cost perhaps five times as much. The institution's maintenance department may simply not replace them with the original specification, or a natural mistake could be made and never detected. Some experts claim the tube-type filter shield has a limited life expectancy; however, if the lights are off most of the time, this should not be a serious factor. Their advantage is that they can be seen, and thus the responsible librarian should be able to easily determine the status of ultraviolet protection. Probably the best protection is through the use of special lenses that provide the appropriate ultraviolet filtration, but such a requirement may preclude a superior light fixture that does not have a lens to provide filtration. When preservation is a concern, the lighting consultant or electrical engineer should also determine the spectrum of other light sources such as the relatively new metal and quartz-halide fixtures. The arrangement of the collections should never allow direct sunlight to fall on shelved materials unless preservation is not a concern.

Deterioration resulting from exposure to light can easily be reduced to a minimum through various other means. While there is a distinct cost, individual range aisle switching in the stacks dramatically reduces the time of exposure for shelved materials. Such a system often can be justified on the basis of energy conservation. A low-voltage switching system or other device may be desirable in order to permit turning off or on all of the lights from one or more central points. One advantage of low voltage switching is that where electrical consumption is monitored in the interest of minimizing peak loads, it is a relatively simple matter to turn off all the range aisle lights as the power use approaches a predetermined level. Then, the library patron can simply return to the range end to turn on currently needed lights. With increasing public awareness of energy concerns, such a system may be considered an extravagance if one assumes strict patterns of turning lights off when they are no longer needed.

Another switching system that has been suggested by energy consultants utilizes timers for the range aisle lighting. Such a system is probably fine in a closed stack or warehouse facility, but it could lead to considerable frustration in an open stack area. With proper staff training even the use of timers in the closed-stack area may be considered an extravagance.

Reduction of light levels in reading areas and stacks is also becoming more common as institutions strive for energy economies. This change too is desirable from the preservation point of view. Reading positions can be developed with individually switched task lights permitting lower ambient light levels, although, because of the power requirements, some degree of flexibility may be lost. With glare-free lighting a level of 50 footcandles (say, 500 lux) is quite adequate for most library tasks. Even 35 footcandles (or about 350 lux), if maintained, works well in most cases.

The exact lighting level historically has been a very controversial subject. Lighting intensity, referred to as footcandles, lux, lumens, or lamberts (a lambert equals one lumen per square centimeter and 10.76 lux equals one footcandle, or one lumen, per square foot), should always be measured in terms of "maintained" intensity, that is, the amount available after several months of use, which usually can be estimated at approximately one-third less than in a new installation. The exact amount may vary from 25 to 40 percent, depending on the ballasts and fixtures used and how much the ceilings and surrounding surfaces darken as time goes on.

J. E. Woodwell, in "Data on Indoor Illuminations" (*Transactions of the Illuminating Engineering Society*, 1:246) wrote in 1906:

In the postal service, for reading addresses of mail in the endless variety of forms of pen, pencil and print with background of various color, a local illumination of from two to four foot-candles has been found by extended experiences to be required; two foot-candles is generally sufficient for desk illumination, though for work involving much detail three or even four foot-candles (30 to 40 lux) has not been found excessive.... In stores where dark goods are displayed or a brilliant effect is desired, five to ten foot-candles (50 to 100 lux) is not uncommon. The latter is also required for tracing, drafting, engraving and similar work.

In 1919, at the close of the First World War, the New York Public Library increased the lighting intensity in its newspaper room to 10 footcandles (100 lux) because its practice of mounting its newspapers with Japanese rice paper in the hope of preserving them made them more difficult to read. In 1925

Francis E. Cady and Henry B. Dates stated in a volume published by John Wiley & Sons, Inc., New York, entitled *Illuminating Engineering*, that "under some conditions" 5 to 10 footcandles (50 to 100 lux) should be used, and recommended 8 (80 lux). Three years later the figures were 8 for a minimum with 12 recommended (or about 80 lux minimum and 120 lux recommended).

Over the course of the succeeding years, recommended light levels continued to increase in the United States. As recently as 1970 the authors witnessed lighting in a library restroom that exceeded 180 footcandles (1936 lux)! Today, with the advent of energy concerns, the recommended lighting levels are generally returning to a reasonable level. While there are many variables and caveats which will need thoughtful design input from the architects and engineers, the 1981 edition of the *Illuminating Engineering Society Lighting Handbook* suggests 5 to 10 footcandles for inactive stacks and microform reading areas, 20 to 50 footcandles for active stacks, book repair and binding areas, cataloging, circulation desk, audio-visual reading areas, and map, picture or print rooms, and from 20 to 100 footcandles for reading areas depending on the nature of the detail, age of the readers, and other factors. The program should provide guidance on these conditions.

Design considerations for lighting is discussed in later chapters as the design process is developed. It should be noted here though that in addition to light levels, the quality of the light in terms of glare, color, shadows, contrast, or aesthetics is extremely important. Glare especially can render a work station nearly useless even though the measured light level is sufficient. Terminals with cathode-ray-tube screens (like television sets) are especially affected by glare. Their placement and lighting must be carefully considered in the design process.

The librarian may wish to specify a requirement for a mock-up of the proposed lighting. This can often be done at nominal expense, and it can be very instructive of the nature of the proposed lighting system. The design contract for any major building project should provide for such services as well as additional studies or alterations to the lighting design that result from viewing a mock-up configuration. If such services are not clearly established in the architect's or electrical engineer's contract, there will be subsequent fees for extra services. While this is not necessarily bad, all concerned should realize the budgetary implications.

Acoustics is one additional aspect that relates in some degree to the mechanical/electrical system and thus to environmental control. It is commonly thought that a library should be quiet, and in a general sense this is certainly true. However, a library can be too quiet. When this happens, every turning page or footstep can be heard by others. Sharp noises of any kind will become a distraction which, in the worst case, will render a library useless for more than a very few well spread-out users. Some college bookstores sell headphones merely to block out sounds in dormitories and libraries. To avoid this circumstance, some level of background or ambient sound is necessary and desirable. Probably the best form of background sound is the gentle whoosh of air entering the space through the duct system. A system that is exceptionally quiet should be avoided. Where it is anticipated that the mechanical system will be cycled or turned off for limited periods to conserve energy, an electronic white sound system should be considered.

White sound is not always received with enthusiasm; however, it does have a place in library design. A common problem with white sound is that the acoustic engineer will design a system that will cover all extraneous noise. Such a system generally does not sound good, and it is usually perceived to be too loud. It is suggested that the engineer be required to design a system that can be adjusted in various areas of the building. Such adjustment will permit a variety of acoustic perfume; for those who cannot stand it (which may be as much as 50 percent of the user group) the volume can be placed at a minimal level. For others, reading areas can be provided with somewhat higher levels. It is likely that no one will like a background level that covers all noise, thus the highest level probably will never be used. Such a system simply may not be appropriate in a music library.

A number of years ago the sound level was measured in about a dozen reading spaces in the Stanford University Libraries. The quietest was found to be about 30 decibels, which was so quiet it was distracting. The level that students regarded as best was about 45 decibels. Here quiet conversations, foot traffic, and other unwanted noise was nearly completely masked. The range of 40 to 45 decibels would seem to be a prudent goal for open reading areas. Of course, closed carrels, remote reading spots, and the general stacks can be less. And one would expect the lobby and the staff room might, on occasion, be higher. In any major library project involving significant reader space, an acoustics engineer should be consulted for both background sound and the control of sound which, except perhaps for duct insulation or carefully selected lighting ballasts, is generally more related to interior design concerns. When there is a row of offices sharing common walls, special considerations for acoustic isolation should be required if typing and conversations are likely.

Concern for such detail at this stage of the project may seem excessive, and in some cases no doubt is. However, if no mention is made of institutional requirements for such things as individual range aisle switching, strict temperature and humidity controls, filtration of ultraviolet light, or appropriate filtration of the air, adding such requirements later in the design process may be regarded as a program improvement with associated increases in design fees and estimated or actual construction cost. Where tight budget control is not a concern, the design team obviously would have the luxury of exploring each of these issues later in the design process. It is probably more common, though, that a statement of design requirements, or a program, must be established in concert with a fairly fixed project budget. Then any change in the scope of the project must go through an often difficult approval procedure, and trade-offs may be required. Clearly, time spent in formalizing specific requirements at the program stage can and will minimize financial and functional surprises later.

Codes and Standards. Buildings are still known to collapse because of faulty construction and faulty engineering techniques or materials, sometimes triggered by earthquakes, unprecedented floods, and hurricanes. Buildings often restrict access for handicapped persons in numerous ways. Electrical fires are frequently started as a result of poor construction quality, and the fire may spread rapidly through the structure for similar reasons. Energy consumption, especially in older buildings, is often excessive, resulting in the need for costly retrofitting of more efficient equipment or insulation. These

problems and many more are common where there is no control over construction requirements. Qualified architects and engineers should be able to avoid such problems; however, a building of any size is a very complex construction, and it is easy to miss details that can result in serious future problems.

Codes and standards represent essential minimal criteria for developing a sound project. However, even codes and standards will require thoughtful application. Combined with the code authority (often a city or county building inspector, fire marshall, or health and safety official), they represent some assurance but no guarantee that the end result will have lasting quality.

Codes generally have the force of the law. Standards may be legally enforced only in certain cases; for example, where there is federal funding, some standards take on the quality of a code. In other cases, standards represent minimal guidelines.

Local governing agencies will generally require that the project satisfy certain specific codes and standards. Typically these include the building, fire, electrical, elevator, handicapped access codes or standards, lighting standard, and zoning ordinance. An institution may also have its own facilities standards which detail procedural requirements, mechanical specifications, energy consumption goals, lighting standards, architectural limitations, or access requirements. In order to establish a clear understanding of the institutional requirements as well as those of the local government authorities, it is suggested that a tabulation of all the applicable codes and standards should be included in the program. A statement that all appropriate codes and standards are to be met may not be sufficient, particularly if the institution requires that certain standards are met that otherwise could be considered optional.

The front matter of the program should then contain as much information about the history, goals, operations, module, site, security, design criteria, and legal requirements of the project as practical. The amount of detail required depends on local circumstance, but it usually does not need to be a huge volume. It should in helpful, general terms clearly establish the scope of the project. The next section discusses the detailed space breakdown which completes the programmatic description of the project.

5.4 Detailed Space Breakdown

There are many ways to write a program, and the format selected by a given institution may vary substantially from the one suggested in this chapter. The intention of the information presented here is that it might be used as a guide. It is essential that the persons responsible for preparing the program should weave into the final product those elements that are unique to the given situation. Because of this, nearly any guide will have exceptions at some point.

As has been suggested before, the program is simply a tool to establish verbally the goals and scope of the facilities project. It establishes the basis for the design fees, project budget, and, ultimately, the entire project. However, it must be understood that it represents a snapshot which does not easily change. At the same time, the operations of the library and the academic program of the institution will indeed change. The front matter should establish sufficient flexibility in the proposed facility to permit minor changes as the project progresses. At some point, though, changes will add to the cost, thus the degree of accuracy that can be put into the program can easily affect the final cost.

The funding, design, and construction of a major project can take four or five years. Initial staffing, collections, and reader accommodation will need to be projected, together with anticipated growth for another ten to fifteen years. The detailed space breakdown should then represent anticipated space needs up to, and in some cases beyond, twenty years into the future.

In a major project it is useful to start the detailed space breakdown with a tabulation of space requirements by major departments. Generally, the space data are developed in terms of net space, which excludes the space required for the walls and column structure, mechanical rooms, duct shafts, stairs and other forms of circulation, janitor's closets, and other space that is not assignable to library functions. The gross area calculation will include all of these unassignable elements together with the stated net area requirements. The ratio of net to gross area is one measure of the efficiency of a building, but it should be cautioned that this ratio can be misleading. Smaller buildings typically will result in a net to gross ratio of about 60 to 70 percent while larger buildings will range from 70 to 75 or even 80 percent. A warehouse facility with limited corridors and minimal support space might have a ratio as high as 90 percent, provided stack cross aisles are included in the net space. Because of the variations in determining exactly what is included in the net or gross area, different planners will develop different figures for similar buildings. Thus the usefulness of this form of efficiency data is limited. Yet, once the net space is tabulated, the anticipated gross space requirement can be established by dividing the net space by the projected efficiency ratio expressed as a decimal. (For example, 50,000 net divided by .65 efficiency gives 76,923 gross.) This figure and current local construction costs for a given quality of structure then become the basis for the basic construction budget.

In a major library project the groups tabulated in the proposed synopsis of space requirements might include (in no particular order) the library administration, book selection, ordering or acquisitions, cataloging, government documents, circulation, reference, special collections or the rare-book area, the archives, the card catalog and national bibliographies, reading areas, studies, and the book collection stacks. Elements such as a preservation office, language lab, AV center, computer facility, classrooms, and the like should also be tabulated where they are part of the project.

Following the summary tabulation, the program might contain in outline form a tabulation of each discrete space, together with reference to the page on which the detailed space information can be found.

Finally, each space should be described clearly. The description should include a succinct statement about the function, location, furnishings, built-ins, and any special concerns about the space. Requirements for clocks, drapes, shelving, carpet, special environmental or mechanical features, unusual equipment, security systems, acoustic control, and the like, where they are unique to the function being detailed, should be established.

The following three chapters discuss the requirements of many of the spaces found in a library. The program writer may find it useful to read other programs which often are available at neighboring institutions or where similar projects are in process. Finally, Appendix A contains some program excerpts which may be useful.

6

Programming: Housing the Collection

In most libraries accommodations required for seating readers, providing service areas for them, and housing the service staff make the greatest demands on library space. The area required for housing the collections, including those shelved in reading areas and space for nonbook collections, runs a close second, and may even exceed it in a few libraries having very large research collections and limited clientele.

The shelving of collections is especially important, given the cost and effort to assemble good teaching and research materials. These constitute a major asset of the institution, and they must be housed for convenient access while being protected for future generations of students and teachers.

Although the cost of shelving in large quantity is in the range of $.50 to $.60 per volume in 1982 dollars, it is a small cost compared to the cost of the floor area, which can be as much as $10 to $12 per volume in terms

of total project cost. Of this total project cost the building shell, with its walls, floors, ceilings, lighting, and ventilation, is the greatest single project expense. To save even a small percentage in floor area used for shelving books, provided it does not negatively affect other program requirements, is worth considerable time and effort.

6.1 Bookstack Shelving

Bookstack shelving involves a language of its own, which may initially be almost unintelligible to architects who have not had experience in planning library buildings. The same is true for administrative officials, faculty library committee members, and even some librarians. Definitions of terms used in this section can be found in the Glossary.

In writing the program for shelving, it is important to be aware of shelving options and details of large stack design. Each of fifteen elements is discussed from a programming point of view in this chapter: the materials used, the option of multitier as opposed to single-tier stacks, stack types, stability, types of shelves, section lengths, shelf depths, aisle widths and range lengths, the height of shelving, stack lighting, color and finish, finished bases, panels and tops, stack accessories, and vertical communication. Additional information on many of these factors is given in the chapters on the design phases of the building project.

Materials Used. Standard library shelving today is generally built of steel. Wood is occasionally used, most commonly where special effects such as richness are desired, as it allows the designer greater flexibility to create a custom-built shelving unit. Where preservation of the library materials is a concern, the use of a sealant to prevent the emission of acidic vapors common to many woods should be a requirement. With few exceptions, shelving should be adjustable so staff can quickly alter the shelf spacing as collections grow or need to be shifted. In some cases wood shelving can be constructed at lower cost than standard library shelving, but it is generally less durable, may increase fire risk, and may be more difficult to brace properly in earthquake country. Other materials, such as plastic and glass, have been used in special cases, but they currently represent the exception rather than the standard.

The recommendation of materials to be used should be left to the designers in most cases. However, the end product must meet the criteria of budget limitations, flexibility, structural integrity, and durability as established by the librarian. Where it is likely that several choices of materials or manufacturers may exist, it is suggested that for any significant project, full-sized samples submitted for review and approval may be a prudent requirement. For wood shelving this would make sense only for a major installation, but jointing samples should be examined, and the construction closely specified.

Multitier or Single Tier. The structural configuration of shelving can be multitier, freestanding, or nonfreestanding. Multitier bookstacks represent a system of shelf uprights or columns and floor decks which is self-supporting. Each level of stack supports the level above, and sometimes also supports

a reading room on the top floor of the building, as in the New York Public Library, even the roof over the whole stack structure or the glass walls enclosing the stack tower, as in the Beinecke Library at Yale University. With the exception of various compact shelving systems, a multitier stack represents as concentrated shelving space as can be found.

A tiered stack installation, because of its structure, should be considered a very permanent component of the building, which cannot easily be moved or altered. The support structure can be based on a variety of modules related to the length of a section and the dimension between range centers. Generally, in countries using imperial measures, the sections are 3 ft (0.914) long, thus resulting in an upright every 3 ft in the direction parallel to the shelves and usually half as far again, or every 4½ ft (1.372), in the other direction. A section in metric countries is typically .9 or 1.0 meters, or about 3 ft or slightly over 39 in. Tiered stacks have been constructed with support uprights as much as 9 ft (2.743) apart in each direction, giving greater flexibility of use for the space between uprights. Spans of up to 6 ft (1.829) for main cross aisles are easily accommodated. Because the uprights are actually part of the shelving, they do not get in the way until there is need to open up an area for another use; then one must deal with a forest of columns. The floors above can be thin: cellular steel pan decks are 1⅝ in. or 3 in. (41 or 76 mm) and reinforced concrete decks are normally 3½ in. (89 mm) thick. The typical height of a single level of multitier stack is about 7 ft 6 in. (2.286). Where a fully sprinklered building is required, this may represent a problem as some fire codes require 18 in. (0.457) vertical clear space between the top of any combustible material (books) and the bottom of the sprinkler head. If this requirement is enforced, the useful shelving height would then be about 5 ft 6 in. (1.676), which represents fully a 25 percent reduction in shelving capacity. As an alternative some fire authorities may accept sprinklers in each range aisle.

While the tiered stack installation is part of the building structure and generally regarded as lacking flexibility, it is amazing what can be achieved by removing the shelving. During World War II the subbasement of the Littauer Center at Harvard, which was part of a multitier bookstack, was used as a radar teaching laboratory, and in it thousands of students received their training. In the Bancroft Library at the University of California, Berkeley, tiered stack space has been opened up for faculty studies and reading areas. The Government Documents Library at Stanford uses tiered stack space for a microform and reference reading area. In all these cases, the solutions work well even though they are clearly affected by the column system. The resulting space assignment is probably less efficient than it would be in modular buildings designed for freestanding stacks, but where there is no good alternative, multitier stack space can be used for other purposes. Still, it is obvious that a freestanding shelving solution offers greater flexibility.

Multitier stacks entail other problems. If wider shelves are needed, they can be used only by narrowing the range aisles, which often is not satisfactory, because the deeper the shelf, the wider the aisle should be. In earlier days multitier bookstacks were made with ventilation slots between each level, because forced ventilation and air conditioning were not available, and it was realized that books deteriorate more quickly in stagnant air. Pencils, call slips, and, all too often, books fell through these slots. Where they exist, they represent a serious fire hazard by virtue of providing a natural chimney. Several libraries have undertaken to correct this situation by sealing the floor to floor openings, but to be effective, open stairways and other penetrations must be isolated by a fire division. Such a reduction of air flow may also require the installation of a forced air ventilation system. Clearly, corrective action in this case is expensive, but it represents only a small fraction of the value of the collections that are being protected. Multitier stacks built today do not have ventilation slots. If the stairwells and elevator shafts are closed in, a tiered stack is hardly more of a fire hazard than other parts of the library building, although some would argue to the contrary, particularly where there is no fire supression system. Indeed, if a significant fire were to occur on a lower level of a tiered stack, there could be a risk of collapse due to the loss of strength in the unprotected steel columns. Furthermore, tiered stacks that have expanded metal grate-type catwalks, rather than solid floors, present a fire risk at least equal to the older tiered-stack system with ventilation slots.

A combination of multitier and single-tier stack is sometimes arranged. This plan was adopted in the Lamont Library, where every other level has a floor strong enough so that the uprights can support a metal pan floor above together with its single-tier bookstacks. The result is that a fixed stack on one level holds up a single-tier stack above it, thus giving flexibility in half the installation. A similar construction was used in the Engineering and Biology Libraries at Stanford. This type of construction can be used to advantage as a means of providing future expansion of the shelving capacity. In this case fixed elements such as elevators, stairs, and mechanical systems must be arranged to provide for the easy future installation of an additional level of stacks.

It is generally considered that the cost of a multitier stack is less per volume housed than that for single-tier stack. Multitier construction in a tower stack is undoubtedly cheaper than a long series of single-tier installations, but this would not necessarily be true with only two or three levels with a reading room above. The nature of tiered stack also suggests limited reading accommodations in the stack itself, which may be contrary to the philosophy of what the library should be. Of course, in closed stacks or largely storage facilities, this limitation is not a problem. In most cases there are ways of minimizing the effect of separate stack and reading facilities. If the decision to use multitier stacks is strictly based on economics, an engineer should calculate the savings in cost that might result from the reduction in the size of the building columns that would be made possible. Construction cost for floors and columns and ventilation arrangements must be considered in this connection. Where earthquakes are a possibility, the requirements for lateral bracing must not be overlooked. The program can easily require that such a study be made.

The other basic type of stack installation is the single-tier already mentioned. This is known among many librarians as freestanding, but many stacks which librarians think and speak of as freestanding are not so regarded by the manufacturers. The latter say that double-faced shelving units with 8 or 9 in. (203 or 229 mm) adjustable shelves over a 20 in. (508 mm) base, as well as 10 or 12 in. (254 or 305 mm) adjustable shelves over a 24 in. (610 mm) base, are freestanding. They otherwise insist the design is not freestanding and must be floor anchored or top tie strutted. Depending on the nature of a particular installation, they may insist on special rein-forcement to provide extra stability. In California, for instance, there should be no free-standing standard shelving. To meet California earthquake codes, all full height shelving requires the equivalent of a gusset at each upright with floor anchor bolts on each side. Top bracing may be added to take all deflection out of the uprights.

Many architects and librarians consider what they call a freestanding stack with a wider base as more flexible, more easily moved, and more satisfactory than a stack that is fastened to the floor or otherwise attached to the building structure. The authors are inclined to disagree with them on this point and recommend the nonfreestanding single-tier type in most concentrated book-stacks. Almost any bookstack, whether it is fastened to the floor or not, tends to damage the floor covering beneath it. If the stack is moved, it will generally if not always be found that the flooring will have to be replaced or at least patched, either because of the "punch" load from the uprights, which may amount to 900 pounds per square ft (43 kN/m²), the indentation made by the finished base, or the retention of color, because it has not been exposed to light.

There have been shelving units designed with a base that distributes the load which, installed with a neoprene gasket, are said to refute this statement. Even if this installation is found to be possible, the added cost of a special unit with a wider base should be kept in mind. If the flooring is installed around the stack and not under it, you are even worse off when stacks are moved. Some engineers will recommend that carpet should not be placed under stacks because of the extra "cush" which, particularly with an earth-quake, can result in less stability. In a building project the cost of fastening the stacks to the floor is almost negligible, and considerable although not complete flexibility is still provided. The authors are as yet unwilling to recommend any full-height bookstacks that are not fastened to the building structure in some manner, even when a broad base is used, and at least several manufacturers concur on this point. Without the fastening the stack can tip over, and one range falls against another until the whole group goes down like a house of cards. This has happened more than once. With a narrower base additional provision for stability may be desirable, which will be discussed later.

Stack Types. What type of shelf is to be used after the decision in regard to multitier or single tier has been made? There may be said to be three main types: industrial or commercial, case, and bracket.

1. *Industrial or commercial shelving.* Industrial shelving is used on a large scale in storage warehouses and elsewhere. (See fig. 6.1.) It is generally plain and unadorned enameled steel although some manufacturers have produced very attractive industrial shelving. The standard color is often gray or tan. Other colors can usually be obtained, sometimes at added cost. The shelves are adjustable only by the use of nuts and bolts or, in certain cases, special clips, but only with some difficulty. It is most suited to installations where subsequent adjustment, once installed, is not necessary. Because the bolts can be a hazard to bindings, they should be carefully detailed in the specifications. Usually each section is constructed as a discrete unit which is then fastened to adjoining sections to form a range. The exception to this is when a beaded or T-shaped post is specified for the front support. This post then serves to hold the shelving on

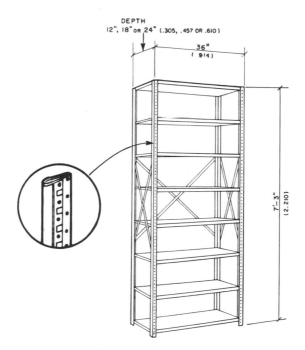

DEPTH
12", 18" OR 24" (.305, .457 OR .610)

36"
(914)

7'-3" (2.210)

FIGURE 6.1 Industrial or commercial shelving. Adjustable with nuts and bolts or special clips (see fig. 6.2); dimensions vary depending upon manufacturer. Inexpensive, it is often used for storage of little-used materials for which shifting is unlikely. Since the angle post and bolted fastenings can be hard on books and people, solid side panels and beaded post (inset) are superior for library storage.

both sides. Some form of beaded or T-shaped post is superior to the more common L-shaped post for library use as it interferes less with access to the shelf. The L-shaped post will reduce the effective width of the shelf by an inch (25 mm) or more on each side so that some 5 percent of the linear shelf space may be lost.

Because of the time and labor in adjusting shelves, commercial shelving is in nearly all cases considered unsuitable in a rapidly growing collection classified by subject. The initial cost may be no more than half as much as for other types of shelving, and it may provide excellent shelving for portfolios, boxed archival materials, boxed microforms, or phonograph discs. Where collections are housed by size groupings, industrial shelving is an excellent choice.

The shelving is available with solid sides (see fig. 6.2) and backs or the X-bracing as shown. Where there is a range of units, perhaps 50 percent of the sections will require a brace at the back. All of the side supports will require bracing of some kind, which generally means more bolts to be concerned about. Shelf dividers can be specified to create bins, but with this configuration fasteners must be looked at carefully. With bins, desirable for phonograph discs, the shelves really are not adjustable.

2. *Case shelving.* Another style of shelving is often used for legal folder and X-ray file storage. It has library application similar to the standard industrial shelving for archival storage and the storage of other materials where the quick and easy vertical adjustment of the shelves is not required. It is a more stylish, attractive product, and it is more easily assembled. Where sway bracing is not required, as is the case with the product of some manufacturers, one shelf may serve two faces of the shelving range. It is often used for systems on movable carriages, although it is somewhat more expensive than the clip-type standard industrial shelving. Until the 1960s case shelving was known as standard library shelving; bracket-type shelving has become the standard configuration today. Slotted-style case shelving has solid end panels separating sections which are the full depth of the range (see fig. 6.3), and the shelves are attached by sliding their ends into slots in these panels. They always have canopy tops. There usually are no backs, but backs can be installed and, when used, they add still more to the stability, which is already good. Slotted shelves are perhaps a little more difficult to adjust than bracket type.

The unit presents an attractive appearance and has been used in many rare-book rooms and in some reading rooms, instead of wood shelves. The percentage installed in concentrated bookstacks has been negligible in recent years because they employ more material and are thus somewhat more expensive

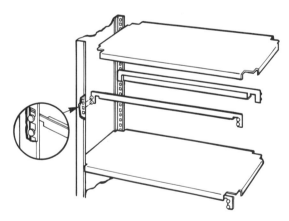

FIGURE 6.2 Industrial or commercial shelving. Even though the clip system permits somewhat easier adjustment than bolts, materials can still be hidden behind the front upright at the shelf ends. A filler can be used, but shelf capacity will be affected. With a 36 in. (914) shelf, loss of an inch (25.4 mm) at each end represents about 6 percent of the capacity. This type of shelving is best for materials that do not require support at the ends, such as boxed materials or elephant folios shelved on their sides.

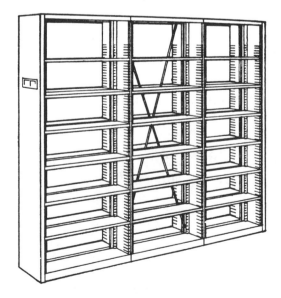

FIGURE 6.3 Slotted shelving. The sway brace shown in the center section is not necessary with a solid back panel or welded section corners.

than the other shelving types. There have also been occasional reports of bent metal at the support slots, but this is likely caused by vandalism rather than normal book loading. They are undoubtedly somewhat more stable in both directions and in most cases do not require all the extra bracing typically found with bracket shelving. In earthquake zones, though, the advice of a structural engineer should be sought in regard to bracing. Finally, they are somewhat less adaptable to configurations with different-sized shelves or stack carrels than the bracket-type shelving. Their strongest feature is their furniture-like quality of appearance.

The more common type of case shelving used today is an enclosure of steel open only in front. Each section has solid back and ends, canopy top and base shelf, which contribute to its cabinet-work appearance. Its appearance is similar to the slotted-type case shelving. Its shelves, fastened at either end to the closed upright panels, may be a little more difficult to adjust than the slotted type, but many people feel it is the most attractive type of steel shelving and employ it for special purposes (see fig. 6.4).

Case shelving has the advantage of being so constructed that glazed doors can be attached more readily than with other types of steel shelving (fig. 6.5). While this adds to the cost, where there are special concerns about dust control, security, or perhaps even added protection from dripping water, the addition of doors may have merit. Doors, when securely latched, would also help to keep the books on the shelves in an earthquake. However, if air circulation around the books is a concern, the doors may represent a negative feature although this should only be a problem where there are materials in the case exuding acidic vapors that might affect otherwise stable papers.

If fine wood shelving is not used in rare-book areas, the case or slotted type should be considered, giving special attention to finishes, and an effort should be made to avoid sharp corners or places where a book can be "knifed" when shelved. Solid backs are of prime importance in these areas to prevent loss and damage.

3. *Bracket shelving.* Central column, cantilevered, bracket shelving has been for a number of years by far the most frequently used type of library shelving; it offers the best available combination of satisfactory performance in storing a variety of library materials and reasonable cost. A great majority of librarians seem to prefer it.

It was first used early in the century. The installation in the Oberlin College Library in 1908 was the first seen by Mr. Metcalf. The bracketed shelf assembly is hung on the face

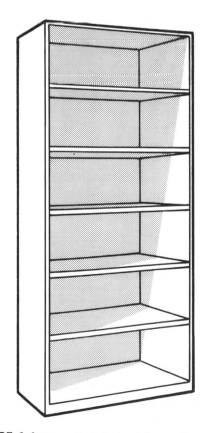

FIGURE 6.4 Case shelving without doors.

FIGURE 6.5 Case shelving with doors.

of the column uprights (see fig. 6.6). These uprights are formed in several shapes, the most common being a squared tube, a tube formed with two C shapes, and an H shape which also may be constructed from C forms. Some manufacturers construct frames that represent the support necessary for a single section. Others produce column uprights that share the load between two sections such that the sections must be thought of as "starters" and "adders." There are also column-like strips, sometimes called pilasters, that can be attached to a wall to support shelves. Where this is done, care must be taken to ensure that the wall is strong enough to support the weight of loaded shelving.

The columns have elongated holes arranged vertically on one inch (25 mm) centers to permit easy adjustment of the shelves which engage these holes. It is possible, if one is strong, to adjust the height of a shelf loaded with books, or even to move it to another section. Steel book trucks have been made with end supports so designed that bracket shelves can be hung on them and six shelves moved at a time from one section of a stack to another without handling a single book individually. It must be added that this is not easy to do and requires the services of a powerful individual.

There are two general varieties of bracket shelves, one of which has plate brackets that

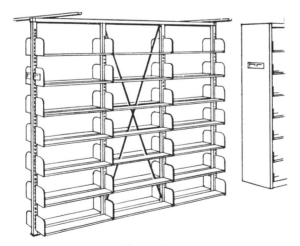

FIGURE 6.6 Bracket shelving. Open base, no end panel or canopy top, but with sway bracing and strut channels for top bracing. Range to right shows finished end panel, base, and canopy top. Note flat range-finder cardholders. A wider bottom shelf and other structural features may be added to make this shelving freestanding, but floor attachment is always recommended for full-height shelving.

grip the shelf at each end and rise above its surface, and the other has a bracket that is flush with the surface of the shelf. One is supported from above, the other typically from below, although there have been flush brackets that support the shelf from above. The flush bracket does not provide vertical support for books at the ends of the shelf; but where there is a need to house materials flat on the shelves, such as large folios or newspapers, the flush bracket works well. Both types of brackets can be removed from the shelves for storage unless rivets are used as fasteners.

Bracket shelves are also available with dividers which may be useful for technical reports, phonograph discs, and other materials that need frequent vertical support. Divider shelves have the back flange turned up, which can be a serious disadvantage in the general stack as it prevents "shelving through" for the occasional larger volume.

The decision to use bracket, case, or industrial shelving depends on judgments regarding appearance, utility, and cost. Case or slotted shelving, as already noted, is almost always somewhat more expensive. Bracket shelving is more flexible, but, as will be explained in the following discussion, it may require more bracing for stability. All types are available in both multitier and freestanding installations, although it should be noted that the previous discussion of multitier stack was based on bracket-type shelving. With the other types of shelving, the support for the multiple tiers will vary, and the ability to use portions of a tiered stack with the shelves removed may not be practical.

It might be said that practically every stack manufacturer offers shelving with special features, for which advantages are claimed in strength, ease of installation, adjustment, finish quality, durability, and safety. Competent engineers are at work trying to improve each line. Unquestionably, progress has been made. As with new lines in automobiles, cost should be kept in mind and weighed, and one should make sure that a change is a real improvement before reaching a decision to purchase.

Stability. This obviously is a matter of great importance. Many methods can be used to make the stack more stable where the stack is not part of the building (multitiered is in effect part of the building). Where stability is a critical issue, as in earthquake zones, the advice of a structural engineer should be sought on any significant installation. Many manufacturers have developed engineering calculations to demonstrate the earthquake resistance of their product with special bracing techniques. Where this engineering work does not exist, it can be established as a requirement in the program. However, it should be realized that for small installations or the reuse of existing shelving, a complete engineering analysis can be costly. While the authors cannot recommend an intuitive approach to structural bracing in such cases, it may in fact be the only practical approach. Where it is decided that stability bracing should be provided without an engineering analysis, it is advised that it should be as stout as practical.

Longitudinal bracing is generally approached in three ways within the shelving unit construction. First, there is the unit-constructed, welded frame where each section is a discrete structural unit. Manufacturers of this type of system claim to achieve adequate longitudinal range stability with their welded top and bottom horizontal spreaders between the column uprights. Special supplementary welding and/or additional cross members may be provided in extreme cases. The welded frame technique is not suitable as a retrofit for existing shelving.

The second and third techniques for adding longitudinal stability are common where starter and adder shelving is employed. The first of these represents one of the most common forms of providing additional stability and uses of what is known as sway bracing. Heavy cross rods forming an X (see fig. 6.7) connect the two sides of a single or double-faced section of shelving. The results are not attractive, and on many a shelf a book pushed back will run into the bracing, so that when sway bracing is used, the space between the shelves on one side of the range and those on the other is frequently unavailable for deep books. Bracket shelving in double-faced sections generally has 2 in. (51 mm) between the back of the shelf on one side and that on the other side; consequently, with a shelf 7 in. (178 mm) deep on each side, if there is no sway bracing in the way, it is possible to house a book 9 in. (229 mm) deep anywhere except where there is a similarly deep book on the other side. This is what was earlier referred to as "through shelving." Studies that have

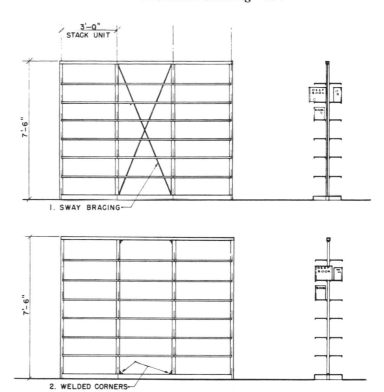

FIGURE 6.7 Sway bracing versus welded frames. The deep books shown at the right illustrate the difficulty with sway bracing. Full use of the space between the backs of opposing shelves may save up to 4 percent of the total stack area. The 7 ft 6 in. (2.286) height and 3 ft (.914) width are standard in the United States.

been made indicate that only 6 percent of the volumes in a college or university library are as much as 9 in. (229 mm) deep. Of course, sway braces are not used for every section. Some manufacturers recommend at least one sway brace in every five sections, and preferably a larger percentage than that; and one cannot be sure that the unusually deep books will not come in the sections where there is sway bracing.

Sway bracing costs something to install, although it is probably the cheapest method of adding extra stability. It has not been unknown for sway bracing to get out of order and come loose; it needs regular inspection and occasional tightening. Under severe longitudinal loading, the hooked ends of the rods have been known to rip out of the column uprights.

The last method of providing longitudinal stability is to install oversized spreader bars between the vertical columns. These may be installed at the top of each section and near the base. As with sway bracing, they limit the possibility of through shelving; however, some librarians prefer this limitation to that provided by the X-type brace, which is less predictable in terms of its location in relation to the collections. The bottom spreader bar can be at a height that would permit the shelving of large volumes flat on the full, double-faced depth of the base shelf. It is likely, though, that it will be too big to be concealed beneath the base shelf. Bracing of this type is probably required only in earthquake areas.

A variation of the oversized spreader bar is what at least one manufacturer has called "brace-built" construction, which utilizes a channel along the base of two sections in place of sway braces, spaced about as frequently. This helps to hold the uprights so that they cannot swing back and forth in the line of the range. A similar channel at the top in combination provides even greater insurance. This method might be called standard in most freestanding stacks where the stack column is a squared-O shape.

More than 90 percent of bookstack shelving installed in library public areas is of a closed-base style. A finished base, that is, an enclosed bottom shelf going down flush to the floor with its top 3 or 4 in. (say, 100 mm) above the floor, gives extra strength in both directions and also helps to protect the books. This shelving, of course, provides bracing for the full length and width of the range and also gives a more finished appearance. Since it closes the base, dust and stray books cannot get under it (see fig. 6.8). Where carpet is not desired under the shelving, the closed base provides a vertical surface to work to. A closed base is, of course, an added expense. Like

FIGURE 6.8 End panels, closed based, and canopy top. Note projecting range finder.

other features that have been described, it is not required for stability in a multitier stack although it may be desirable for other reasons.

Lateral bracing is increased by using a wider base bracket and shelf. Some manufacturers recommend a base shelf 20, 22, or in some cases 24 in. (508 to 610 mm) wide, even if the shelving above is 4 in. (102 mm) narrower from one face of the range to the other. Of course, this feature improves stability and, of course, it adds cost.

A second method for dealing with lateral forces, as already mentioned, is to bolt the base to the floor. Shot-in anchors are occasionally used, although some engineers will not accept these fasteners because of uncertainty about their pullout strength. Where flooring such as carpet is planned, the extra thickness results in a connection so that the lateral loading is cantilevered off the floor. The added dimension of the carpet, together with the spring-like quality of the carpet, may result in a decision to install the floor covering after the shelving.

A third method involves the installation of gusset plates or strap bracing from the base to the support columns. This form of bracing is becoming common in earthquake zones, but it is probably unnecessary in other areas. It too adds to the cost, and in some cases it blocks the installation of a shelf where the bracket is attached to the column. The gusset plate installed between two half columns, which is possible with some lines of shelving, is a better installation in this regard. It will add about $1/8$ in. (3 mm) to the length of the range for each gusset plate, a point that should be considered in determining the building column or bay dimensions. Where strap braces are used, the fasteners can also be a concern as they may have sharp edges that could damage books. Where such bracing is required, it is recommended that the librarian should see a sample before a final approval is given.

Manufacturers' bookstack components, usually thought of from the aesthetic point of view, can contribute to strengthening a shelving installation. A finished or canopy top (see fig. 6.8) provides extra stability in both directions. Still further lateral strengthening is provided by finished end panels. The end panels and canopy top, together with closed bases, result in what appears to be a more finished job, resembling a case in appearance.

They are often considered very desirable if not essential in reading rooms, although more than one librarian prefers bookstacks without finished end panels because more of the books can be seen and the installation gives a lighter, warmer appearance. And canopy tops limit the useful height of the top shelf. The cost of end panels and canopy tops is far from negligible and should be checked. The cost will depend on the length and width of the range as well as the design of the end panel. Ten to twenty percent of the total shelving cost is not unusual.

Finally, one of the most effective methods of laterally strengthening basic shelving installations is to use steel channels running from the channels at the top of one range to the adjacent ranges. These are called strut channels (see fig. 6.6 at upper left). Some think that they do not look good, and architects often object to them, but, if the bracing from one range to another is placed anywhere except immediately adjacent to the cross aisles, it will rarely be noticed. Standard channels provided by shelving manufacturers are comparatively inexpensive and, if extended to some part of the building structure and securely fastened, are an excellent method for bracing stacks against overturning. However, where earthquake codes are to be met, the strut channel and its connections will require structural analysis. One hesitates to recommend them in reading rooms, particularly if they can be looked down on from above, unless struts of a special design and arrangement are used. At the Milliken Library at the California Institute of Technology, struts were installed consisting of heavy square-tube structural steel with heavy steel mounting plates provided to bolt the system to the building structure. This installation was conceived and installed after a shelving collapse in an earthquake. A similar installation in a reading room could become a major design feature to overcome the concern about appearance, but of course it would be more expensive than the standard strut system.

The decision on bracing involves three major points: safety, cost, and appearance. In some cases the utility of the shelving installation may also be affected. As noted earlier, the authors are unwilling to recommend any freestanding stacks that are not firmly fastened to the floor; they want to be absolutely safe. Stacks should be stable enough so that they cannot sway in any direction. All the special devices just described will help. They will all cost money, adding up sometimes to more than 25 percent of the basic installation. The cost should not be a deterrent if it is necessary. It should be emphasized that the decisions here may change the practical or actual dimensions of the range spacing, thus influencing the ideal column spacing in the building.

The program should detail the type of shelving required to house the collections as well as the nature of the bracing desired. For various reasons the librarian may wish to specifically avoid certain kinds of bracing while favoring others. The final decision on exactly what the bracing is to consist of cannot be made at the program stage in most cases, but the degree of its need should be clearly established. The implication of various alternatives should be explored during the design phases.

Types of Shelves. Standard library shelving is usually constructed as a flat shelf with plate-type brackets. In the past there was common use of a bar shelf. Other shelves that are used for special installations include journal display, newspaper, and divider shelves. Commercial shelving also is available in several shelf configurations, as is cabinet or slotted shelving.

Bar shelving was popular because it was supposed to be stronger, and the slots between the bars were supposed to provide for ventilation that was desirable in humid climates (fig. 6.9). Today they are not so well thought of by most librarians. They tend to damage books. A heavy volume that has rested on a bar shelf for years will often show indentations on the binding from the bars. Small and thin volumes sometimes fall between the bars. With good mechanical ventilation the bars are not needed for air circulation. It is said that they have the advantage of letting the dust fall through. One may well ask, fall through to where? Why not let dust settle on a flat shelf where it will be easier to remove? Here it should be noted that the canopy top, which comes as part of the standard equipment of case-type shelving, is supposed to keep the dust from settling on the top shelf. Dust does not seem to be a serious problem in any case, and hardly needs be considered at all if the air is filtered by the ventilation system.

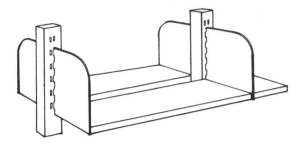

SOLID SHELVES

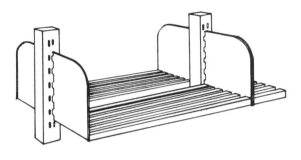

BAR SHELVES

FIGURE 6.9 Bar and solid, or flat, shelves. Bar shelves are no longer manufactured in the United States. They are not recommended as they tend to damage bindings, and the ventilation they provide is seldom necessary.

Flat shelves are generally considered to be strong enough for normal library loads. Where heavier loads are anticipated, as in a shelf designed to support the weight of tall piles of journals awaiting gift processing or large cartons with shipments to or from a bindery, additional strength can be provided by requiring heavier gauge steel or by adding a separate steel channel under the shelf at the front edge. (See the section toward the end of this chapter for shelf weight of journals and phonograph discs.) Where the width of the section is 4 ft (1.219) or more, special consideration of the shelf strength is recommended.

A variation of the flat shelf, produced by at least three manufacturers, has a single slot running nearly the length of the shelf which is designed to accept a specially designed book support. One would expect that this shelf should be stronger than the standard flat shelf because of the extra bends in the metal, but this is not necessarily the case. In fact, some would argue that it definitely is not stronger.

Special shelves for newspapers, microforms, and films in canisters are also available. There are sloping display shelves for journals, which are either fixed or hinged. The hinged display shelf permits access to back issues of the journal housed on a flat shelf, with inverted or flush brackets, which is hung under the display shelf. While rubber bumpers will help, this type of shelving tends to be noisy when used, and in terms of capacity there are serious limitations, as only about 15 titles per single-faced section can be displayed. The capacity can be increased to as many as 45 titles per section by storing them flat on flush bracket shelves, but, of course, the current issue is not clearly visible in this configuration.

A variation on the normally flat-base shelf is one that slopes down toward the middle of a double-faced section or back of one section. While it permits easier viewing of the book spine in the stacks, smaller volumes will have a tendency to slip out of view, and it is impossible to store the occasional oversized volume on the base shelf.

Most manufacturers also produce a shelf that can create a desk, carrel, or consultation surface in a standard stack section. Because these units are typically deeper than normal shelving, the aisle space may limit their utility in normal stack configurations. With such units it is essential that the shelving structure be well braced, or troublesome movement of the range will occur as weight is placed on the edge of the carrel unit. One manufacturer produces a unit with support legs at the front edge which would eliminate this concern. But, if the space for the seated reader is minimal, these legs will get in the way.

Section Lengths. Sections 36 in. (0.914) long are standard in the United States. This length is from the center of one upright to the center of the next and thus is considered a nominal or gross length. The net length is usually about 35½ in. (0.902), but this varies depending upon the type of shelving and the way the uprights are fabricated. Note that commercial or industrial shelving is often fabricated with the actual dimensions of the shelving being of full measure. The space required for the uprights in most commercial shelving, called growth, is about 1¼ in. (32 mm) for the first section and ½ in. (13 mm) for each additional section plus a nominal safety factor of ¾ in. (19 mm) per range. Uprights designed for tiered commercial shelving will often consume more space.

In countries using the metric system, sections are often 1 meter long, or slightly more than 39 in. Shelving that is no more than 30 in. (0.762) long, or even shorter, is often seen because it may fit into the space available. One should strive for no more than two or at most three different shelf lengths in any installation. The Boston Athenaeum has some 30 different shelf lengths in the same building, resulting in considerable inconvenience at the time of shifting the collections. In stacks designed for archival storage, sections 42 in. (1.067) long have been used to reduce the open shelf space where boxed materials are housed. Of course, different box dimensions would suggest other shelf lengths.

If a change in the length of the sections in a modular building is decided upon, bay sizes are involved. Since bays are ordinarily calculated on multiples of the section length, anything that affects their size can be a matter of considerable importance. However, longer than standard shelves should not be dismissed without further consideration. There have been installations of shelving 48 in. long (1.219) for which considerable reduction in cost is claimed. Since six sections 48 in. long have the same capacity as eight sections 36 in. long, the number of shelves is reduced by one-fourth and the number of uprights by two-ninths in a range 24 ft (7.315) long. The reduction may lead to a shelving cost savings of as much as 15 percent, even after allowing for the heavier-gauge steel required because of the longer span. The actual savings can be much less, depending upon the manufacturer. Experience demonstrates that 48 in. shelves of standard gauge and without reinforcement will on occasion bend. Before concluding that using the wider range is a true cost-saving technique, a careful study should be undertaken, but it may well be worth consideration. The Widener Library at Harvard has 40 in. (1.016) sections throughout its stacks. For a small library any shelf length that is not standard may be undesirable because it may mean special tooling if shelves are not in stock or if the manufacturing process must be altered. Special shelves may be even more of a problem at a later time if a few extra shelves are needed, however, most manufacturers can make custom lengths which, in quantities of 100 or more, are generally not much more expensive. For limited quantities, one manufacturer is currently making a two-piece adjustable shelf which, even though it is expensive, may permit limited shelf replacement or additions where unusual dimensions are encountered.

Long shelves suggest another problem on which more information is required before longer sections can be recommended, even if it can be proved that they cost less. This is the matter of inconvenience, if any, to the user. It seems that one can with ease scan back and forth over a 36 in. or even 40 in. (0.914 or 1.016) section, whereas eye motion and even rocking between the feet is more awkward over a wider section. Is the human body so put together that it can use to advantage a 4 ft (1.219) or longer shelf?

On the printed page, lines that are too long make reading difficult, and switching from one line to the next may lead to confusion and delay. In the United States catalog trays are arranged from top to bottom and then on to the next row to the right, to prevent one user from getting in the way of another more than necessary, while in some countries another method is used—the trays go from left to right on the top row and then down to the next one, and so on. Neither of these problems is completely comparable to that resulting from a long bookshelf, although there is some relationship between them.

It is certainly true that if shelves were 12 ft (3.658) long, users might unduly interfere with one another in a busy part of the stack. When one shifts to the next shelf, there may be confusion just as with a reader when lines of type are too long. But the basic problem with long shelves is: When a shelf is at eye level or immediately above or below, one can move along at least for the length of a 4 ft (1.219) shelf readily, but as one gets down lower in the section (or higher using a stool), it is quite a different proposition. When searching the bottom shelf and probably two shelves above it, even a young and agile person may find that hitching along will be difficult. When one gets along in the seventies and has bifocal glasses and a football knee, the situation may not be too happy. Such a person should not be considered a typical reader in an academic or any other library, and a 15 percent reduction in cost, if real, might make inconvenience to a few seem a very minor matter.

It should also be noted that as the collections reach capacity, longer shelves may permit a slightly denser housing of the collections. On the other hand, when a long row topples over, as books have a tendency to do, it will be just that much more difficult to straighten them up.

There probably is no completely satisfactory answer to the advantages and disadvantages of longer shelving. Anyone working on this aspect of the problem should keep in mind that the cost of the bookstack probably represents no more than 5 percent of the total building cost. A savings anticipated through the use of longer shelves can normally be equalled by lengthening the range by as little as one section or reducing the distance between range centers by between 1 or 2 in. (25 or 50 mm). Associated problems may result from adjusting accessories such as stack carrels, lockers, sloping periodical shelves, and the like.

Shelf Depths. The selection of shelf depth is fully as important as the length of shelves, if not more so. In this volume the dimension used will be the actual shelf depth unless noted otherwise. This is 1 in. (25 mm) less than what the stack manufacturers call "nominal" depth except in the case of commercial or industrial shelving and for shelves with backs where the actual and nominal depth of the shelf are the same. Bracket shelving, the variety most often used today, generally has a 2 in. (50 mm) space between the shelves on opposite sides of a double-faced range, so that the sum of the actual depths of the shelves plus 2 in. (50 mm), or the sum of nominal depths, represents the width of a range from front to back. Base shelves, which are usually continuous through the section, do not have this space, so that in this case, nominal and actual dimensions are essentially equal. Standard shelves are typically 7, 9, or 11 in. (178, 229, or 279 mm) actual or 8, 10, and 12 in. (203, 254, and 305 mm) nominal. Note that the metric equivalents, here converted from standards in the United States, are likely to be 200, 250, and 300 mm. In Canada, shelving of from 7 to 12 in., in 1 in. increments, is considered standard. Shelving for atlases, newspapers, books in the fine arts, reference materials, and other large-size volumes may require additional depth, and shelves varying from 11 in. to 17 in. (279 to 432 mm) deep are occasionally required or desirable. Shelves

as narrow as 4 in. (102 mm) are available for reels of microfilm, and divider-type shelving is typically 9, 11, and 13 in. (219, 279, and 330 mm) deep, although other sizes may be available.

It should be repeated that as bracket shelves have a 2 in. (50 mm) space vacant in the center of a range, a 7 in. (178 mm) shelf without a back stop, sway bracing, or other structural restriction can house a book 9 in. (229 mm) deep anywhere, unless the volume behind it is more than 7 in. (178 mm) deep. This arrangement will take care of about 94 percent of all books. An 8 in. (203 mm) "actual" shelf will take care of a 10 in. (254 mm) book in nearly all cases and will be adequate for 97 percent of all volumes in a general collection. At least four stack manufacturers currently provide an 8 in. (203 mm) actual, 9 in. (229 mm) nominal, shelf as a standard unit. Where there are no structural limitations, 8 in. (203 mm) actual shelves are perhaps best for most stacks, and no difficulty or undue cost is involved in fabricating them for any but very small orders. Collections having components such as sheet music or art books may require 9 or even 11 in. (229 or 279 mm) shelving.

The advantages of bracket shelves include the ability to use them with standard accessories and to use shelves of different depths on the same upright, something that is difficult to do with slotted, case, or commercial shelves without special arrangements or significant effort. The floor area occupied by bookstacks and their aisles is worth some six times the value of stacks themselves. Thus, where deeper shelves are used, there is an associated space cost that can be significant. This should be kept in mind when structural bracing devices force the use of the next larger shelf. However, there may be no reasonable alternative.

It has been noted that deeper bottom shelves are suggested by stack manufacturers for reasons of stability. They may claim that this shelf does not interfere as one goes up and down the stack aisles because it is at shoulder height that the full aisle width is necessary. While there is not full agreement among the authors on this issue, it can be stated that Mr. Metcalf opposed it. He was even more interested in the width for the wheels of book trucks. Any stack aisle that is 30 in. (0.782) across is wide enough for a person to get through safely without bumping into the shelves at either side. Others would argue that, with a wider base and less aisle space at the floor, for example 27 in. (0.686), the same is true. Metcalf commented that it is possible for most people to squat down in a 30 in. (0.782) wide aisle. The same is generally true for a 27 in. (0.686) aisle with a wider base shelf where the aisle dimension is measured at the base.

The primary reason for widening an aisle is to reduce the inconvenience when two persons pass in it, and except with very long ranges, this is probably of less importance than some of us have been led to believe. The wider base shelf serves as a bumper or protector for the occasional volume that is unusually deep and therefore sticks out slightly from the shelf. Metcalf argued that narrowing the ranges 6 in. (152 mm) from 24 to 18 in. (610 to 457 mm) by giving up the broad base increases the stack capacity about 12 percent by being able to reduce the range spacing, but without narrowing the aisles. Compared to a 27 in. (0.686) aisle and a 24 in. (0.610) base, the saving is still about 6 percent. Where deeper shelves are required because of the collections or for structural reasons, the savings are nominal.

On the other hand, if one is prepared to use ranges that are only 16 in. (406 mm) from front to back, which is not uncommon, the savings might be as great as 16 percent. Such a shelving configuration would require separate shelving for oversized volumes, but, in absolute terms of space efficiency, a case can be made for its use in many stack areas. Of course, there is no reduction in the number of running feet or meters of shelving that must be bought, but the narrower shelves should cost less per linear unit. However, as the shelves become narrower, more materials will need to be housed in special areas with deeper shelves. In an open stack this may result in the use of book dummies which take up shelf space. (The alternative is catalog records noting folio or portfolio volumes, and stack guides showing where these are separately shelved.) In fact, if only 94 percent of all books can be housed in a 16 in. (406 mm) deep range, then each single-faced shelf will average about one and a half dummies. At best this is an inconvenience, and it will add to the linear shelving required, perhaps offsetting the savings.

Another argument for the wide bottom shelf is that the larger books can conveniently be shelved there. With a 24 in. (610 mm) base

shelf and 9 in. (229 mm) actual shelves above, it is rare when there are more than two or three volumes on the base shelf; some argue that this is poor use of space and the extra deep shelf. Those subjects which are heavily skewed toward larger volumes, such as art and music, should probably have deeper shelving. In the arrangement described, there will still occasionally be need for book dummies, but they would be relatively infrequent. It could then be argued that the reader is best served with slightly deeper shelving, although Mr. Metcalf was absolutely right when he pointed out the facility cost associated with such service. Many librarians would agree that oversized books can properly be segregated and that to do so is less expensive and as convenient as keeping them more nearly within their specific subject sequence. As suggested earlier, there is by no means total agreement on this issue. To determine the course to be taken, each institution must weigh the advantages and disadvantages in view of the goals for the library and the physical nature of the particular collections.

To summarize, it is suggested that bookstacks should always be fastened to the floor and/or top tie strutted except for low shelving often found in reading rooms, that they be strengthened if necessary in other ways than by sway bracing, and that consideration be given to the alternatives of equipping the sections with shelves the same width top to bottom or of providing wider bases. As to depth of shelves, Mr. Metcalf suggested that most of them need be only 7 or 8 in. (178 or 203 mm) deep actual measurement, unless the bay size is such that columns will obstruct the aisles. While 7 in. (178 mm) shelves may be suitable for an academic library for the literature and a few other subject groups, 8 in. (203 mm) provides greater flexibility. Reference and engineering collections should be on 9 in. (229 mm) shelves, and music or art collections on 11 in. shelves. The greatest flexibility for a general stack area is probably provided by 8 or 9 in. (203 or 229 mm) shelves with, some would argue, a 24 in. (610 mm) total, front to front, base shelf. If the building module is to be uniform, it is recommended that it accommodate the deepest shelving anticipated for a large percentage of the collection.

As suggested, in reference sections the average book is larger and deeper. *The National Union Catalog*, for example, is just over 10 in.

(254 mm) deep. The volumes fit very nicely on 9 in. (229 mm) actual shelves. Very few reference books, except large atlases, are deeper than 10 in. (254 mm). Librarians who are acquainted with the 12 in. (305 mm) deep nominal reference shelves in the Cornell University Library and have seen books there pushed to the rear, making it difficult to see their labels or withdraw them, particularly those on the bottom shelves, can understand the disadvantage of shelves that are too deep. With poor stack management, problems can occur on narrower shelves too. It should be said that where shelves are not deep enough, volumes will protrude into the aisles and be damaged by passing bodies or book trucks, a phenomenon that can be essentially avoided with a deeper base.

Aisle Widths and Range Lengths. Before a final decision is made on shelf depths, aisle widths should be considered, as the two are closely connected in a modular building. Various factors are important, particularly the bay size available, the amount of use, and the extent of provision for wheelchair access. Whether access to the shelves is open or not makes a difference. The length of ranges and the cost of space are also important. Aisles 36 in. (0.914) wide are sometimes called standard for open-access stacks, but every inch that this can be reduced saves something like 2 percent of construction costs, not book-stack cost. A stack with a 1,500,000-volume capacity takes, to use a commonly accepted formula of 15 volumes per square foot, 100,000 sq ft (9,300 m²) of floor space. If the range depth can be reduced by 2 in. (50 mm), it should save 4 percent, or 4,000 sq ft (370 m²) of floor space, and if aisle width is also reduced by 2 in. (50 mm), the total savings will be in the order of 7 percent or 7,000 sq ft (650 m²), which at $100 each would be $700,000. This is not to say that the savings are necessarily desirable. In many circumstances it would not be worthwhile or very wise. Weigh your local situation and then decide.

To return to aisle widths: They should be wide enough so that the bottom shelves can be adequately lit (more of that later); so that the user can squat down and read labels on the bottom shelf and select and remove the desired volumes; and so that two persons can pass each other without too much difficulty. Ease of shelving the collections will be improved if the aisles are wide enough for a book truck, so the attendant can take a book from the truck and reshelve it. This problem can be partially solved by making the trucks narrower, but their capacity and stability is adversely affected thereby. Another alternative is to elect to reshelve returned books from a book truck parked in a wider cross aisle. This works best in a large collection where the number of items from a particular range being returned seldom exceeds a small armload. Major stack shifts, however, would remain a problem. The Sedgwick Library, University of British Columbia, shifts books from a large truck to a small square truck and then to the shelves, because of aisle width and distance from the main sorting area. For heavily used shelving areas there is much to be gained by being able to reshelve books directly from a truck.

The human limitation for being able to squat down depends a great deal on the size and agility of the person concerned. To what extent should elderly, stiff, rotund faculty members with bifocal glasses and poor eyesight be catered to? An occasional low stool can be a help, and adequate lighting is important. Again, the decision must be made locally. How heavily will the aisle be used and how long is it? Other things being equal, the larger the book collection, the less any one aisle is used. The length of aisles affects the amount of use and also affects the total stack capacity very considerably, as can be seen later. It is suggested that aisles in a reference room or in an undergraduate open-access stack, with no more than 100,000 volumes, should not be less than 3 ft (0.914) and ranges not more than 24 ft (7.315) and preferably only 18 ft (5.486) long. In a heavily used reference collection a 40 to 42 in. aisle (1.016 to 1.067) is better still. A strict reading of the needs for handicapped access suggests an aisle of 42 in. (1.067), which will easily allow a wheelchair and another person to pass and the person in a wheelchair to easily withdraw a book on lower shelves at the side of the chair. The minimum width a standard wheelchair can negotiate is 27 in. (0.685) although 28 in. (0.711) is preferred. Where the base shelf is the same size as upper shelves, a wheelchair will require more room for finger space. With minimal aisle space the occasional volume that sticks out will be a problem.

In a large collection with limited use, 33 or 34 in. (0.838 to 0.864) aisles are adequate;

32 in. (0.813) is not impossible. In a very large library with open access to relatively few readers, 30 in. (0.762) is not too unsatisfactory and as little as 27 in. (0.686) has been used with reasonable success; but the shelving is provided with a 24 in. (610 mm) base. Closed stacks and storage collections have been successfully arranged with 24 in. (610 mm) aisles, but this only works where the volume of transactions is small. With a 27 in. (0.686) aisle and a 24 in. (610 mm) base shelf or a 30 in. (0.762) aisle and 18 in. (457 mm) overall base, 48 to 51 in. (1.219 to 1.295) can be achieved for the center-to-center range spacing for large, little-used collections. And 51 to 54 in. (1.295 to 1.372) on centers can be considered standard, depending on the base size. The effect of this on column spacing is a matter of considerable importance and is discussed in detail in Chapter 5.

The desirability of short ranges in parts of the library with very heavy use is important, as has been mentioned, but a very large, comparatively little-used collection is a different proposition. In the past a 30 ft (9.144) length has generally been considered the outside limit for any library. However, the National Library of Medicine has ranges up to 36 ft (10.972) long, and the Cecil H. Green Library at Stanford has ranges up to 42 ft (12.802) long without a problem. The storage levels of the Lamont Library at Harvard have ranges as much as 51 ft (15.545) long, and the ranges have been quite satisfactory for the use to which they have been put. If the 51 ft (15.545) ranges had been divided by two cross aisles 3 ft (0.914) wide, or one cross aisle 6 ft (1.829) wide, the number of sections would have been reduced from 17 to 15 in each range. Seventeen is two-fifteenths, or over 13 percent greater than 15. If 13 percent is gained in capacity by narrowing ranges and stack aisles and this 13 percent is added to the 13 percent obtained by lengthening ranges, the result is a total increase of over 27 percent. However, it would be a mistake to narrow the aisles and lengthen the ranges in this way in an open-access, heavily used stack; this increased capacity would not be worth its costs in inconvenience. Give full consideration to the anticipated use.

The width of cross aisles is also an important factor. The difference in capacity with cross aisles 6 ft wide (1.829) instead of 4½ ft (1.372) is nearly 6 percent, with 21 ft (6.401) ranges. A 3 ft (0.914) instead of a 6 ft (1.829) aisle would add over 11 percent to the capacity. Again, use should be kept in mind; do not overeconomize. You will regret it.

Cross aisles can always be inserted in a long range, if finished bases and sway braces do not intervene, by simply removing the shelves. Relocation of the sway braces and removal of the finished base is usually possible, too, with added effort. The reverse is also possible if the uprights do not contain light switches, if they are notched so that shelves can be attached, and if the aisle is an exact multiple of a standard shelving unit or the space provided is sufficient for the frame of a unitized shelving section. Floor covering may be involved in any addition or removal of cross aisles.

Height of Shelving. Multitier stacks come with floor to floor levels of different heights. They have often been 7 ft 6 in. (2.286) on centers vertically, i.e., 7 ft 6 in. from one floor level to the level of the next floor. If 3 in. (76 mm) is lost in the floor thickness, each floor is 7 ft 3 in. (2.210) in the clear. Sometimes they have been only 7 ft (2.134). At least one multitier stack, that at the Pennsylvania State University, is less than 6 ft 8 in. (2.032) in the clear. Too often lights are so arranged that the top few inches of shelving are difficult to use because of the physical intrusion of the light fixture. This condition may be aggravated by a sprinkler system. In recent years the full 7 ft 6 in. (2.286) clear height has become more or less a standard, but if sprinklers are anticipated, it may not be sufficient. Some fire code authorities will insist that the sprinkler heads be 18 in. (457 mm) above the highest book. This would suggest that if 7 ft 6 in. (2.286) of shelving is desired, the clear height must be in excess of 9 ft (2.743). Local code authorities should be consulted in this event as it may be possible to seek a variance. The possible adverse effects of a variance in the event of a fire should be considered if this direction is to be taken.

The 7 ft 6 in. (2.286) total height for shelving is not so high that those using the stack cannot reach the top shelf. Most people can reach up to get a book off a shelf 6 ft 4 in. (1.930) from the floor, although it will be somewhat difficult for those who are only 5 ft (1.524) tall (see fig. 6.10). If the top shelf is higher than that, it is unreachable by so many persons without the assistance of a stool or ladder as to make its position inadvisable in most cases.

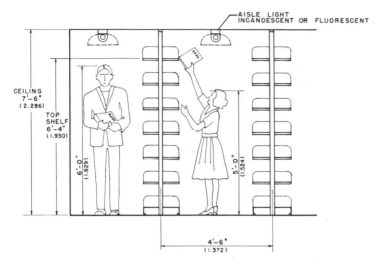

FIGURE 6.10 Tiered shelving of standard height. Top shelf of seven is 6 ft 4 in. (1.930) high. This is the lowest possible height with a 4 in. (102) base and shelves 12 in. (305) on centers. Anything higher would require a stool. Anything lower would decrease capacity by one-seventh or require reduced shelf to shelf spacing. The 12 in. (305) spacing should work for 90 percent of the general collections, while 11 in. (279) spacing will provide for only 79 percent. This arrangement will not apply to all collections; art, music, reference, and science collections often require six rather than seven shelves in a standard section.

Studies have shown that some 90 percent of all books are no more than 11 in. (279 mm) tall. A standard steel shelf (excluding commercial shelving) is not more than ¾ in. (19 mm) thick including the formed edges, and if shelves are placed 12 in. (305 mm) on centers, a book measuring 11 in. (279 mm) can slide in between. With seven shelves, counting the base, placed on 12 in. (305 mm) centers, and with the top one at 6 ft 4 in. (1.930) above the floor, giving a 14 in. (356 mm) margin there below a clear 7 ft 6 in. (2.286) ceiling, the top of the bottom shelf will be 4 in. (102 mm) above the floor, making possible a 3 or 4 in. (76 or 102 mm) base for the important protection of the books by a raised base shelf or kick plate from feet, water, book trucks, and brooms or vacuum cleaners. A canopy top will usually reduce the maximum clearance for the top shelf by at least 1 in. (25 mm). If the distance between shelves is reduced by 1 in. (25 mm), that is, to 10¼ in. (260 mm) in the clear, eight shelves including the base will still not be possible without raising the ceiling several inches.

Equal spacing on the shelves would require a clear height of a little over 91 in. (2.328). Unless the ceiling must be higher anyway, there is little to gain from it. The eighth shelf, if made possible by the higher ceiling, would be 6 ft 9 in. (2.057) above the floor and beyond reach of most persons shorter than 5 ft 4 in. (1.626). There will be some 21 percent of the volumes that will be too tall for this configuration. This is enough to make 11 in. (279 mm) shelf spacing for the general collections undesirable, although there may be some areas of the collection where, with careful adjustment of the shelves, an additional shelf could be added. With few exceptions, notably for phonograph discs or installations where there are sprinklers, 7 ft 6 in. (2.286) in the clear seems satisfactory for academic and research libraries. (In a stack that is not tiered, the floor to ceiling height must be somewhat greater if one is to install a shelving unit 7 ft 6 in. [2.286] high.)

A tiered stack that is much less than 7 ft 6 in. (2.286) clear height will be inconvenient, if not dangerous, for very tall persons. The Widener Library with 7 ft 2 in. (2.184) clear stack heights can use only six shelves, except in the literature sections. If it could use seven, capacity would be nearly one-sixth greater, and more than 300,000 additional volumes could be stored in it.

If a bookstack should be at least 7 ft 6 in. (2.286) high, should an upper limit beyond that be considered for ceiling height in non-tiered shelving arrangements? It depends on why the extra space is provided. The higher the ceiling, the greater the cost for a given floor area. As suggested earlier, the minimum ceiling height may be established at 9 ft (2.743) by the requirements of a sprinkler system. Where sprinklers are not a factor, a ceiling height of 8 ft 6 in. (2.591) would allow an eighth shelf which could be devoted to storage for less-used books. This addition would be comparatively inexpensive cubage, but it might also be confusing, as it would require a special ribbon arrangement for books on the eighth shelf. Location notation may be required in the catalog, which, if it must be added, is a cost to be considered. This type of storage is not recommended in most circumstances. However, if the entire collection is storage of less-used books, the extra shelf might serve to advantage. Even in an open stack, where space is at a premium and there is little alternative, the added eighth shelf on over-height frames can work provided there are sufficient stools or stepladders available, but the result is obviously an inconvenience. Providing the possibility of adding an eighth shelf at a future date may be viewed as a form of insurance against the day when the library runs out of shelf space. It should be noted that doing so will increase the floor loading and make lighting the lower shelves more difficult, both factors that should be anticipated in the initial design if eventual use of an eighth shelf on extended uprights is a possibility.

A bookstack area with 7 ft 6 in. (2.286) clear height is high enough for individual accommodation for readers in carrels anywhere in the stack, and, in fact, is adequate and satisfactory for small groups if care is taken to place them where each person can look out in some direction for a considerable distance. Larger groups may suggest a somewhat higher ceiling. In the Lamont Library there are two mezzanines 91 × 45 ft (27.736 × 13.716). Each provides seats for 75 readers who can apparently work in comfort with a 7 ft 9 in. (2.362) ceiling, but each one provides a view in at least one direction, although some of the seats are over 75 ft (22.860) from any window. At Princeton 8 ft 4 in. (2.540) ceilings on the stack levels permit adequate height for rooms largely given over to human occupancy which are as much as 25 × 36 ft (7.620 × 10.973) or even 25 × 54 ft (7.620 × 16.459) in size.

Manufacturers of library shelving provide standard heights of 3½, 5½, 6½, and 7½ ft (1.067, 1.676, 1.981, and 2.286). Commercial or industrial shelving is manufactured with slightly different standard heights of 6, 7, and 8 ft (1.829, 2.134, and 2.438). Some library stack manufacturers offer other heights, and in any significant shelving order a custom height is entirely feasible at reasonable cost. At least one manufacturer of commercial shelving provides heights of 39, 51, 63, 75, 87, 99, 111, and 123 in. (0.991, 1.295, 1.600, 1.905, 2.210, 2.515, 2.819, and 3.124), none of which is exactly equivalent to standard library shelving.

Special collections such as journals, newspapers, microforms, phonograph discs, oversized books, and film reels will require different shelving configurations. These are discussed in Section 6.6. A few of these collections can be efficiently accommodated on industrial shelving, and, as 8 ft (2.286) is a standard height for this type of shelving, it may be prudent to provide some space that will permit the use of 8 ft shelving. Of course, all of these collections can also be housed on various forms of bracket shelving, and the only reason to consider industrial shelving is the cost saving of the equipment.

Where a future installation of movable shelving is a possibility, provision for a track system and false floor may be desirable. With one system the clear height required, including lights, is 8 ft 6 in. (2.591). More on compact shelving later.

There is no precise upper limit for ceiling height in a stack area, except that extra height may look awkward and be wasteful, costs more, and that, where the lighting is ceiling mounted, it becomes less efficient as it becomes higher. Stanford's Branner Earth Sciences Library is a case in point, where the ceiling over the general collections is about 20 ft (6.096) above the floor. However, if the floor is designed for additional weight, extra ceiling height can be considered as a form of future expansion. Basement spaces in particular, where the floor loading is not such a problem, can be constructed to permit the future addition of a second tier of shelving. Where this is the plan, there might be advantages to installing the lights on bracing struts supported by the shelving itself. Planning stairs, elevators, and other services and utilities for this form of future expansion is important too.

Stack Lighting. The question of library lighting in its broader aspects is discussed in Chapter 13, which deals with the design development phase of a building project. In Chapter 5 it is discussed in the general terms that the front matter of the program might detail. Here the special lighting problems in relation to bookstacks are considered. With relatively narrow aisles lighting has always presented a problem, particularly for bottom shelves. Until well into this century in most academic and research libraries, efforts were made to provide enough natural light to find books. Four factors brought about a change.

1. Constantly growing collections and tremendous accumulations of volumes in many libraries made it virtually impossible to provide natural light for any large percentage of them.

2. Better-quality and less-expensive artificial light became available.

3. With higher standards of lighting possible, light fixtures inevitably and properly became regarded as necessities.

4. Hours of opening were lengthened, since they were made possible by artificial light.

As energy resources become scarcer, it is entirely possible that there will be a return to the use of some natural light for shelving areas to augment artificial light sources. The old techniques of skylights and glass flooring may become popular again. Because they may, it may be well to point out that natural light, in its full spectrum, is damaging to books. Furthermore, natural lighting systems are difficult, though not necessarily impossible, to turn off when not in use. The exposure to natural light day in and day out will eventually take its toll. Careful filtration may help, but of course, this will reduce the amount of light. Glass floors, while an interesting concept, have caused problems as well. There have been cases of the glass breaking, which would be a terrifying experience for anyone, and after years of use, its surface becomes so abraided with dirt that it is rendered nearly opaque. Glass also is notorious for producing static electricity which, while it is not lethal, is at best an irritation. New techniques to light stack areas with sunlight may be developed in the future, but librarians should be cautious and consider the preservation and practical aspects with great care.

Even with artificial light some bookstacks were built with glass floors and lighting so arranged that the bottom shelves could be illuminated more adequately by lights from the floor below. The problems of breakage, static electricity, and dirt remained. The bare incandescent bulbs that were first used were unpleasant, to say the least; frosted bulbs were developed and helped, but they were far from providing satisfactory light. Bulb wattage was increased from 15 to 40 watts or more, and bulbs were placed closer together, but users were not happy. Bulbs were sometimes protected with wire cages and hung from cords and could be carried to the spot where better lighting was needed, particularly in little-used areas, but this method was not satisfactory because it meant that one hand was unavailable for handling books. Special fixtures with reflecting surfaces were designed to keep the light from shining in the user's eyes and at the same time to direct it toward the books.

Finally, in the early 1940s fluorescent tubes housed flush with the ceiling or suspended close to it and protected by baffles or a form of plastic came into use and provided by far the best stack lighting up to then available. Early experience indicated that these tubes, however, had disadvantages of their own. If they were turned off and on too frequently, their life was shortened. They were more difficult to replace and more expensive than incandescent bulbs. Fortunately, they used approximately 40 percent as much current to give the same intensity of illumination. Because this illumination was spread out over the entire length of the aisle, they gave far better general light than was possible with incandescent bulbs with the most suitable fixtures. Fluorescent tubes seemed to be almost perfect for heavily used stacks, where they were required during all the time the library was open. Because of the lower cost for current, there was no need to consider installing individual range aisle switching or time locks that would automatically turn them off after ten or fifteen minutes, as was sometimes done with incandescent bulbs. In the past students and faculty, to say nothing of stack attendants, notoriously failed to turn off lights when they were through with them, although this attitude may be changing. With the possibility of continuous lighting, wiring and switches were simplified and became less expensive, proportionately.

Fluorescent lights still had four problems:

1. As noted above, if they were used for short periods only and were turned on and off frequently, they burned out quickly.

2. Since the light from them did not carry out from the ends very well, a nearly continuous row was required for good stack lighting.

3. A continuous row of regular, 40-watt 4 ft (1.219) tubes gave out more light than some librarians believed was necessary.

4. Regular wiring is fixed, and if the ranges were shifted to perhaps four instead of five ranges per bay, rewiring became necessary.

Because of these problems, it was reasoned that, if the ceiling height was increased to make other space on the same floor more usable for the concentration of readers or for other reasons, then the light fixtures could be placed at right angles to the aisles. By doing so, flexibility was increased in terms of shelving placement and adequate lighting could be provided by placing rows of lights as much as 6 ft (1.829) apart instead of the approximately 4 ft 6 in. (1.372) associated with range aisle spacing. Installation, maintenance, and energy costs were thus saved. Various ceiling patterns have been used which accomplish similar effects, including diagonal and square patterns.

The energy crisis of the 1970s, however, may have changed this approach dramatically. Normal 4-ft (1.219) fluorescent fixtures are now three to four times more efficient than incandescent fixtures in terms of lumens per watt. With regular ballasts, two 40-watt tubes draw about 92 watts. This can be improved further by using special energy-efficient ballasts and tubes so that essentially the same light output can be obtained from about 75 watts. The 4-ft (1.219) tube now lasts about 20,000 hours, compared to perhaps 1000 hours for a standard incandescent bulb, and up to 2500 hours for the long-life incandescent. While frequent cycles of on-off use will shorten its life, the modern fluorescent tube still has a significantly longer useful life than the incandescent bulb. The energy savings by turning the fixture off, even if only for a few minutes, now is considered greater than the cost of more frequent tube replacement. The payback period for the additional cost of individual range aisle switching resulting in energy savings is generally found to be favorable. Recent developments in light fixtures, particularly the use of specially treated aluminum reflectors and diffusers, has increased further the efficiency of fluorescent light. The comparative cost of the fluorescent tube has dropped to a point where it is considerably lower in terms of lumen hours than the incandescent bulb. Finally, even though the light levels may be greater than some regard as absolutely necessary, a row of single-tube fixtures running down the center of a range aisle is hard to improve upon. Because of this, it is recommended that for general stack lighting, serious consideration should be given to individual range aisle lighting with local switching.

As noted above, library users have historically demonstrated poor habits in terms of turning lights off. The authors consider that with the growing awareness of the need to conserve energy, this is becoming less of a problem. Stack attendants can be trained to turn off lights when they are found on and not in use. Devices that may be considered include timer light switches and low-voltage switching systems that permit turning off all of the lights from time to time, after which

individuals can turn them back on as they are needed. Both possibilities are discussed in Section 5.3 under Environmental Control.

Light fixtures can be mounted at the ceiling, suspended from the ceiling, or mounted on the ranges themselves. Two configurations are shown in figure 6.11. In a stack with a high ceiling, such as a warehouse, it is suggested that lights mounted on struts between the ranges would be most efficient. Mercury vapor or other high-intensity lighting sources are not much more efficient, and because of the placement that they require, the lower shelves will be difficult to adequately light. Of course, any form of general illumination must be all on when the stack is in use. General illumination only makes sense where energy costs are of concern in heavily used shelving areas such as, for example, a reference room. Even then, be aware of the problems of ultraviolet light that may occur with both fluorescent and mercury vapor light sources.

It should be remembered that the narrower the ranges, the more difficult it is to light the bottom shelves properly. There may be good light on the floor, but the backs of the books are at right angles and receive little light, perhaps as little as 1½ or 2 footcandles (21.5 lx), particularly if aisles are narrow. This may seem completely inadequate, but actually it is as good for stack lighting as any library had early in this century, if not better, and few people use bottom shelves for long consecutive periods.

A comparison test of seven lighting systems was undertaken in 1977 by a California lighting manufacturer. The light fixtures included the Parabolume, or reflective lens, a fixture with a refractive grid, and an extruded-aluminum fixture manufactured by the particular company. While the cost comparisons and other features were carefully outlined, one point of special interest is that in no case was the light level on the bottom shelf less than 7.7 footcandles (82.851 lx), and in most cases it exceeded 10 footcandles (107 lx). This was in a 36 in. (0.914) stack aisle (excessive in many cases) with the light fixtures mounted 8 ft (2.438) above the floor.

In an attempt to improve lighting on bottom shelves, they are sometimes tipped upward so the light will strike the back of the books at a better angle. As mentioned earlier, such shelves are generally not recommended since they reduce flexibility, may be costly in

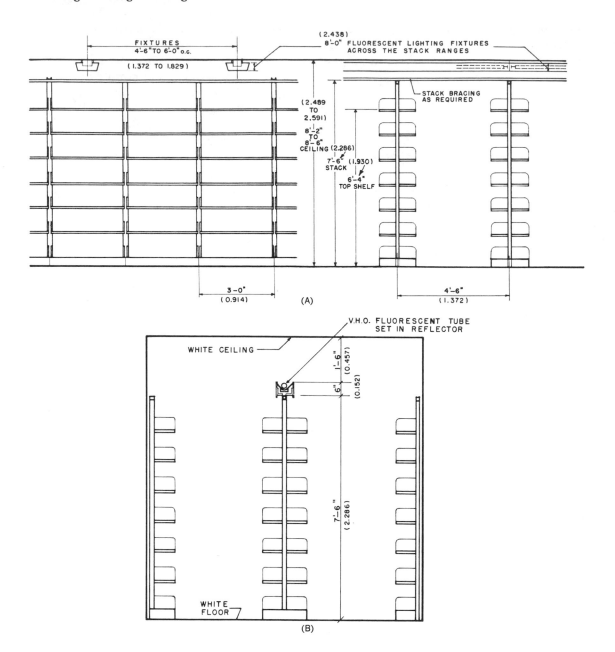

FIGURE 6.11 (A) **Lighting at right angles to ranges. Provides good lighting for the lower shelves and permits a future shift in range spacing, but all of the lights must be on when the stacks are in use. The clear ceiling height must be at least 8 ft 2 in. (2.489) and preferably 8 ft 6 in. (2.591) to prevent heat damage of books on the top shelves. (B) Fluorescent light on the top of a stack range. This is not as efficient as a direct down-light fixture in the aisle between the ranges, but it is an alternative. A white ceiling and a very light floor are required with the tube set in a specially designed reflector. Individual range aisle switching could be accommodated, although two rows of light fixtures would need to be on for the use of any range aisle. The switching would thus be somewhat more complex than for an overhead aisle fixture.**

space, as well as in construction, and have the added disadvantage of tending to let the book slide or be shoved to the back of the shelf where the book loses the advantage of the better angle and looks bad. A light-colored floor will help even more, reflecting light to the backs of the books. However, with improved lighting fixtures, this may not be a critical point, depending on the arrangement of the fixtures.

If the stack area has a clear height of 9 ft 6 in. (2.896), what is known as the Lam fixture placed on the channel or canopy top over a range can be used and can provide completely indirect light. However, where individual range aisle switching is desired as an energy conservation measure, this system will not be as effective as the more common overhead light fixture. Some of the light will be absorbed by the ceiling, resulting in lower light levels than would otherwise be possible with the same wattage. Except where a special effect is desired, this is probably not a very practical system. Dust accumulation on the reflecting surfaces of the Lam fixture is another problem.

Color and Finish. Shelves used to be almost exclusively black or khaki-colored. With standard shelving some installations had the divisions between sections and the end panels painted white; so that while they would show the dirt, they could be washed and would also brighten up the whole area. It was finally realized that the cost of using other colors would not be large and that the use of color would make shelving less monotonous and perhaps more attractive. A dozen or so colors are typically available, although these will vary with each manufacturer. A different one can be used for each stack level if desired, and contrasting colors for book return shelves or other special shelving can be selected.

Color can also be used to introduce variety to satisfy the notion that some people like intense colors while others prefer quieter tones. Lighter colors are said to be helpful for improving the light level, although the effectiveness is very limited with filled shelves. Dark colors tend to show books better, as they compete less for the attention of the eye. In a stack with shelving of a light or bright color, the shelving itself becomes a prominent visual element. While the light levels with dark shelving may be slightly lower, the reduced distraction of color contrast may make the spines easier to read. Except for paperbacks, books tend to be fairly dark.

Of equal or greater importance, at least from the functional point of view, is the finish. The paint or enamel must be hard enough so that it will not chip or wear easily. If it does, the underlying steel may rust, with distressing results. With increasing environmental concerns in the painting process, the paint product may change dramatically over the next decade. At least one manufacturer recently was using a dry powder painting process which was then fused to the metal with

heat. One result of this process was that custom colors were very difficult to achieve. Most manufacturers now paint by means of an electrostatic process which normally applies one coat of paint. Before the application of paint, the shelving is cleaned and etched for proper paint adherence. The *Library Technology Reports* on library shelving include testing of paint finishes which may be useful in making a selection of a shelving product. The architect's specifications should ordinarily require some form of finish test before acceptance of the product. Furthermore, since stack installations have often not been satisfactory because of poor paint quality, recent installations elsewhere should be checked.

Finished Bases, End Panels, and Tops. These components were discussed under stability. Should they be used and should panels and tops be 16, 18, or up to 24 in. (406, 457, or 610 mm) deep to match the base as sometimes recommended in order to provide greater stability? Each library must decide for itself what depth of shelving it prefers to have, but the following factors should be kept in mind. Bases, end panels, and tops present a more finished-looking result and all are stabilizing factors. There is no place under the bases for dust and dirt or stray books to collect. Just as the cost of shelving goes up nearly 10 percent with every 2 in. (51 mm) added to its depth, the reduction in tops would have a somewhat similar affect on costs. Yet the cost of space is much more important than the cost of shelving. Where cost is a concern, one might equip only those areas where the finished appearance is of greatest importance. Consideration can be given to uniform color for all bookstack components except end panels where color may be varied, perhaps by floor, alternating ranges, or type of collection, or to indicate where main cross aisles are located or where carrels or folio shelving can be found. Finished end panels tend to add 10 percent to the shelving cost, the exact figure varying with the panel and the length of the ranges. The same figure applies to canopy tops except that the range length is not a key factor.

Stack Accessories. Almost all bookstacks require accessories such as range label holders and book supports. Other features that may be regarded as accessories include pullout reference shelves, shelf label holders, stack mounted carrels, work shelf or counter, shelf dividers (used only on shelves designed for dividers), newspaper racks, divider film reel shelves, filmstrip trays, solid back panels, and lockers. Each of these should be considered. They cost money but will cost more later if they are ordered separately or in small quantities.

Range label holders can be flat against range ends, stand out at right angles, or be wedge shaped, so as to be in view as one walks down the cross aisles. If they project into the aisle space, they should be very high; 6 ft 6 in. (about 2 m) is enough so that tall people should not bump their heads or shoulders on them. Either variety should be large enough to contain the required information without the print or type being so small as to be difficult to read. The projecting type should be of a size to hold classification information that can be read 10 to 12 ft away. This is particularly important with all open-access stacks. Standard-sized range label holders typically designed for a 3 × 5 in. (76 × 127 mm) card do not give enough space for all the information that some libraries wish to place on them. While larger label holders are usually not carried by the library shelving companies, it is possible to achieve the size desired with a custom design. In this case the label holders may or may not be part of the shelving contract; they may perhaps be part of a graphics contract.

Label holders are desirable at both ends of a range, and one for each side of a double-face range can be useful. Some libraries require both the projecting and flat label holder. In this configuration the projecting label holder contains the book classification number start and conclusion for the range while the flat label holder is used for a verbal description enumerating the subject contents of the range and perhaps for more general information such as "Return books to the red shelf" or "Turn off the lights when not in use," and the location of folio or portfolio volumes. Range numbers are also useful, particularly for maintenance purposes. Occasionally, directional information may be placed in these label holders. While the flat type of label holder is more difficult to install when finished end panels are not used, installation is certainly possible. (See fig. 6.12.)

Shelf label holders are particularly useful where unbound journals or newspapers are stored flat on a shelf. They typically contain

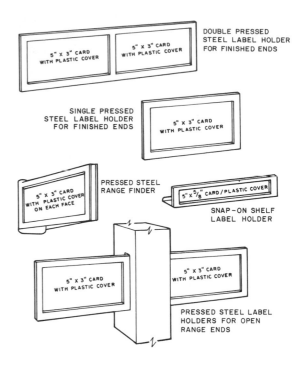

FIGURE 6.12 Shelving accessories. Common range aisle and shelf label holders for 3 × 5 in. (76.2 × 127 mm) cards or ⅝ × 5 in. (15.9 × 127 mm) labels. The plastic covers are optional.

the title of the serial housed in a specific location. In the general stacks shelf label holders are not useful except in rare circumstances. They are used occasionally in reference collections, particularly where a great proportion of the shelving may be along walls, making it somewhat difficult to introduce range end label holders. Shelf label holders should be easily installed but not easily moved once installed. The quantities required will obviously depend upon their intended use. In an area of unbound journals housed flat, 3½ label holders per standard shelf is generally adequate. In a newspaper area 2 per shelf is sufficient.

Book supports should stay put where they are wanted, yet at the same time be easily shifted. They should be so made that they will support books of various heights and will not present front edges which may knife a book when it is shelved. (See fig. 6.13.)

Wire book supports are suspended from the shelf above by sliding in the channels at the front and back of the shelf. It is important that the wire is strong and spring-like enough to prevent bending. If the supports bend too easily, they are next to useless. Properly constructed, they represent a good, economical

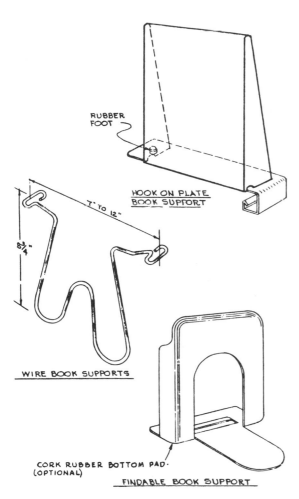

RUBBER FOOT

HOOK ON PLATE BOOK SUPPORT

7" TO 12"

8¾"

WIRE BOOK SUPPORTS

CORK RUBBER BOTTOM PAD· (OPTIONAL)

FINDABLE BOOK SUPPORT

FIGURE 6.13 Book supports. Three types of book supports are shown. The wire support attaches to the shelf above, the hook-on-plate support attaches to the shelf below, and the findable book support is suitable for any shelf. For large volumes the hook-on support is improved with an extended and turned-down back tab. Note that the rubber plug, cork, or other friction base is designed to inhibit the support slipping along a metal shelf due to the weight of leaning books. Bricks covered with acid-free paper or buckram or fixed supports constructed of wood have sometimes been used in place of these standard book supports.

book support which many librarians prefer. Unless there is a canopy top that will carry a wire book support, the top shelf will require another type of support. They can be lost between books, and standard 6 in. (152 mm) wire supports are almost useless where tall and short books are intershelved since the latter will frequently slip out to the right. Some manufacturers have available an optional 9 in. (229 mm) high wire support especially useful in such cases.

The hook-on-plate support is designed to hook over the front edge of the shelving. Because these supports are slightly more difficult to adjust and occasionally have a tendency to scrape the paint, they are not too popular. They are formed with a front flap which adds to stability and prevents them from being lost between books. They can be made in several heights. An improved design, recommended for large, heavy books, is at least 9 in. (229 mm) tall, with front and back flaps, and has a tab that drops down behind the back edge of the shelf, but this may be a custom design which will add to the cost. This type of book support, with the added tab, works well for art libraries where the volumes tend to be large and the tab gives greater stability for their support. An advantage of both the plate- and wire-type supports is that they do not work on normal home shelving. Because of this, they tend to stay in the library.

Perhaps the most common book support is the findable plate type which will work on any shelf. This support should always have the front flap or folded edges, for otherwise it can easily be lost between two books or inside a volume. A cork or rubber pad can be added to the bottom of the support to improve its grip on the shelf surface, though this is not as certain a support as the hook-on-plate type.

All of the book supports are available in different sizes. The findable type is usually 6 or 9 in. (152 or 229 mm) high; the larger one is probably more satisfactory in most cases. It is recommended that a sample be required before final approval. Due to the fact that full shelves of bound journals do not need book supports, five book supports to a single-faced section is usually an adequate quantity, but one per shelf is no doubt the typical specification—perhaps to make up for previous deficiencies or to replace those bent or stolen.

A few libraries have preferred to use bricks or concrete blocks covered with heavy brown paper or, better still, with buckram for book supports. The Houghton Library at Harvard has done this but has used decorative glass bricks in its exhibition cases. A disadvantage of a brick or block is that it will reduce the total available shelf length, and 5 to 10 percent of the stack capacity can be lost. The use of such blocks is only recommended in small installations of very special materials.

Pullout reference shelves are mounted under a standard shelf, usually at counter height.

(See fig. 6.14.) They have been used where space is at a premium; however, in metal shelving they tend to produce noise, and the useful surface, which is no wider than the standard shelf, is quite narrow. They also reduce the aisle space when in use, and wire book supports cannot be used on the shelf below. Pullout reference shelves have been effective at Rice University, Fondren Library in a bibliography room with wooden shelving and aisles 51 in. (1295 mm) wide. Most librarians prefer to find other methods of providing a reference counter or ignore the need. Chance will usually provide a partially empty shelf nearby.

Stack-mounted carrels are available in several forms. In ranges with sufficient spacing, they can represent an economical seating arrangement. They have been used effectively at the end of dead-end ranges (along a wall) where the shelves on the facing section are removed to provide space for a chair. They are usually 24 in. (610 mm) deep and limited typically to the standard shelf width, although other widths are possible. By placing them in a row, an index table configuration can be created out of standard shelving units. However, unless the shelving is well braced, it will seem to be unreasonably flexible, much more so than a regular index table. This type of unit can be useful in a technical processing area for some of the large sets of bibliographies and book catalogs. The work shelf or counter is essentially a variation of the carrel.

Divider-type shelving, discussed earlier, is particularly useful for collections of fairly thin materials that tend to flop over. (See fig. 6.15.) The dividers do add some risk of knifing materials. Because the back of the shelf must

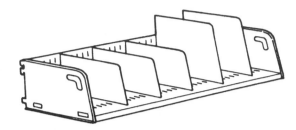

FIGURE 6.15 Divider-type shelf. This type of shelf is often used for phonograph records, music scores, technical reports, and other thin materials requiring additional support. The dividers can knife materials if carelessly shelved.

turn up to support the divider, the two inches of space between the back edges of the shelving in a double-face range is lost. Divider-type shelves are not recommended for books, but variations of them may be suitable for phonograph discs, journals, technical reports, and the like. Shelving designed for the storage of film reels is another type of divider shelving.

Newspaper racks hold a current issue on a stick placed in a rack. (See fig. 6.16.) This type of newspaper storage is also available in furniture-like holders. The rack provides easy access to the newspapers housed, but replacing the stick and newspaper in any but the front position on the rack is often difficult, as the pages tend to curl out. Architects frequently use what they call a "plan rack" which is similar. The type that holds one end of the stick is easier to manage. Many librarians prefer to simply place the current issue of a newspaper flat on a shelf, which seems to work well in most cases. Probably the greatest advantage of placing the newspaper on a stick is that it is less likely to get out of order, and, of course, it is more difficult to fold it up and walk off with it.

Filmstrip trays also duplicate storage that is available as a furniture item. Essentially, a filmstrip tray is a sloping shelf with dividers going from end to end which permit storage of filmstrips in canisters.

Solid-back panels represent an expensive way to add bracing to shelving, and, like sway bracing, they prevent flexibility for shelving through. They can only be recommended where there is a desire to create separation from one side of a range to the other, perhaps behind stack carrels or in a range that serves as a wall for security or complete visual separation.

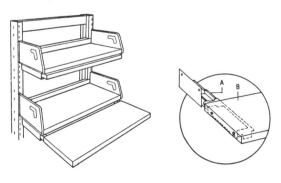

FIGURE 6.14 Sliding reference shelf. The side mechanism (A) is suspended under a standard shelf allowing the reference shelf (B) to be pushed out of the way when not in use. The shelf tends to be noisy and often is left in the pulled-out position.

Shelf-hung lockers work well in stack areas near reading areas. They should be considered in lieu of assigned carrels with lockers. Any lockers in a library represent a management problem, in that they provide places for library materials to disappear without a charge-out record. They also tend to encourage the storage of nonlibrary items, such as food, which can become a problem. Many libraries feel that by providing lockers that can be seen into, either through a grate or a glazed panel in the door, the need for routine inspection is reduced. In any case, the keying should be set up with a master key to facilitate routine checks for library books that are not charged out, and the published policy should establish the fact that the library maintains the right of inspection. The lockers work well with combination locks with a master key which are designed to permit changing the combination when the locker assignment is changed. Experience with coin operated lockers has been mixed. In at least one case an enterprising student bought all the keys at the beginning of a school term and then sold them to fellow students at a tidy profit! Normal key locks result in a constant process of replacing keys and re-keying the locks, which can be an irritation. Key locks are common though not recommended.

Consideration should also be given to the location of the lockers, as they tend to be noisy. Placing them a range or two away from an open reading area tends to help in this regard. The typical size of a shelf locker is 36 in. wide, 12 in. deep, and 18 in. high (914 × 305 × 457 mm) with two compartments in each unit. Where ranges are designed for minimal aisles and shelf size, their depth may be a problem. Also, a separate locker facility may be desired with dimensions sufficient to house a portable typewriter or perhaps a briefcase, as the shelf locker is too small for these items. Alternatives to shelf lockers, as suggested, include lockers at the carrels, separate banks of lockers, or small book trucks that are designed to serve as rolling lockers. There is no magic formula for the quantity of lockers needed, although it is clear that a library planned for extended research probably would have greater demand for lockers than one planned mostly for course-related support. An undergraduate library might have sufficient locker capacity if lockers number about 10 percent of the seating count, while a main research library might find that

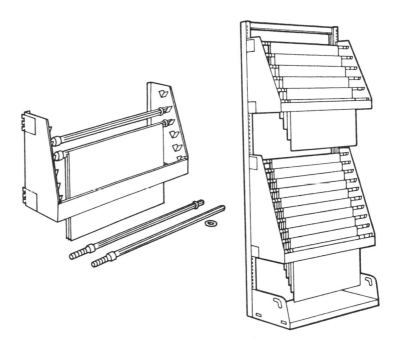

FIGURE 6.16 Newspaper rack. This type of rack requires feeding the newspapers down through a narrow slot. A rack that holds the sticks (shown on the left) by one end is easier to use; but unless the sticks are sturdily built, breakage may be more of a problem.

50 percent or more would be an appropriate number. Where lockers are primarily for library-related purposes, they should be located inside the library exit control, since books kept within the library do not need to be checked by the exit attendant and since readers find repeated access to a locker more convenient than when it is outside the control. However, where lockers serve the nonlibrary storage needs of commuters, the percentage may be greater, and the lockers are best treated as unrelated to book collection use and should generally be located outside the library exit control.

Vertical Communications. Vertical communications in a bookstack may include stairs, booklifts, elevators, ramps, pneumatic tubes, and endless-belt conveyors. Slides and chutes may be employed for the return of books to lower levels, and various forms of electronic devices have been used for the paging of books.

Stairs take space, and sometimes confuse the user if they go around several corners and terminate on different levels in different orientations. They should be not too wide or too narrow, and if possible neither too steep or too gentle. (See fig. 6.17 for stack stair

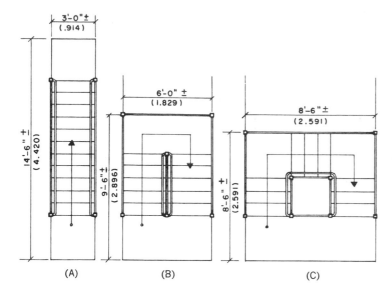

FIGURE 6.17 Stack stairs. (A) Straight-run minimum stair; (B) stair with one turn and intermediate landing, which has the advantage of the same relative position and orientation on each floor; (C) stair with two turns and intermediate landings. All three examples are for tiered stacks; normal floor to floor height will require more space, as would an enclosure for fire separation. In this example stair B requires 31 percent more space than A, and stair C is over 65 percent larger than A.

types.) They ought not add to fire risks by making a chimney, and they should not be so hidden by shelving as to be difficult to find. Usually the stairs required for emergency egress plus a main public stair are sufficient for vertical communications in terms of stairs. However, where emergency stairs are used, special attention to stack security will be required. Signs that read "Exit" will need to have "Emergency Only" added, and graphics indicating the route to the circulation desk or lobby may be required. The actual emergency exit door, while it must always open freely from the inside in most code jurisdictions, should have at least a local alarm. Provisions for the possible addition of remote alarms and even television surveillance at a future date may be prudent, even if they are not intended as part of the initial operation.

Booklifts must sometimes be installed because of the lack of funds for elevators, but unless there is an attendant at both ends, the booklift may be a snare and a delusion. Librarians will not be saved from climbing the stairs, and unless the lift is designed to receive a loaded book truck, the books will be subjected to unnecessary handling at each end of the line. Some code authorities will not permit a lift of sufficient capacity for a book truck, reasoning that such a capacity would permit the use of the lift for people. They will then require all of the safety features found in an elevator, and the supposed economy of the lift would be lost. If a book truck lift is desired, it is suggested that the local code authorities be consulted before a final commitment is made.

An elevator, even if it is just large enough for a fairly thin attendant and a book truck, will save weary hours of labor and wear and tear on books. It will also provide stack access for a person limited to a wheelchair or crutches or a senior faculty member with heart problems. Its use can be restricted by having it operated only by key. In order to facilitate a wheelchair, the standards for handicapped access suggest a minimum cab size of 4 ft 3 in. × 5 ft 8 in. clear (1.295 × 1.727), which is somewhat larger than the thin attendant and book truck would require.

Some recent library facilities, such as the Engineering Library in the Bechtel Center at the University of California, Berkeley, have introduced a system of ramps to provide for vertical movement of both books and handicapped persons. Considering that a ramp for wheelchairs should not be steeper than one in twelve and that ramps with less slope are often recommended, the space required is considerable. Excluding landings, a ramp required to negotiate 8 ft (2.438) vertically will need to be 96 ft (29.260) long. At least one standard requires a landing for every 2 ft 6 in. (0.762) rise which, in our example, would result in three landings plus top and bottom landings. Based on the same standard, this requirement adds 5 ft (1.524) per landing, for a total length of 121 ft (36.880). With a minimum width of 3 ft (0.914) clear, the required ramp thus would consume at least 363 sq ft (33.72 m²). Steeper ramps can be found in libraries; yet with a fully loaded book truck, they can be extremely dangerous. The cost for a system of ramps of any extent could easily equal or exceed the cost of an elevator. However, ramps do not break down, and elevators should not be used as emergency exits. It is speculated that libraries of the future will have more ramps, particularly for handicapped access.

Pneumatic tubes to carry call slips from the circulation desk to stack stations have been used for many years. They tend to be noisy and, if call slips are in the form of punched cards that should be kept flat, they involve other complications. At the University of California, Los Angeles, a pneumatic tube was installed to move books between the two main library collections a block apart. In this case there were problems initially with the abrupt changes in speed which seemed to be causing damage to some materials. It is possible to use pocket radio pagers, computer terminals, TelAutograph, or Teletype in place of pneumatic tubes for the paging of books. However, hard copy transfer of the required information results in less error than a spoken or copied message. Unless there is significant demand for paged books or other use of the equipment, such systems typically become white elephants. In most open-stack libraries their need does not justify their existence for book paging, and other means of transferring this information can be found. The major exception is in interlibrary loan links over some distance, which may be best facilitated by Teletype, facsimile machine, or computer linkage.

Endless-belt conveyors have been in use in libraries at least since early in the century for both vertical and horizontal transmission of books. They tend to be noisy. Too often they get out of order, generally because they are too complicated, having been made to turn too many corners, run on different planes, and receive and drop books at many stations. The more satisfactory installations have usually been the simplest, although at least one example (at California State University, Long Beach) is quite complex and reportedly successful. Of course, they are now used on a large scale in industry, and manufacturers know much more about their problems than in earlier years. Such a system probably should be at least considered in a library with a proportionately large user population where circulation rates are exceedingly high. Other aspects of vertical communications are discussed in the chapters on the facility design, particularly Section 12.4.

6.2 Space Requirements for Books

This section deals with space requirements for book collections in terms of stack sections and floor area. It will not attempt to discuss book storage in reading areas, storage of non-book materials, or compact storage. All of

these aspects are discussed in subsequent sections. This section is concerned only with books, pamphlets bound as books, and bound periodicals stored in standard bookstacks.

As suggested in previous chapters, libraries traditionally have run out of storage space for books before they were scheduled to do so. Crowded conditions and ineffective services have resulted. It has been difficult to obtain funds for new space, even if the old building proved to be expandable. Space for staff and readers frequently becomes inadequate first, but, although books cannot talk and complain, lack of space for them is more evident visually and often receives greater attention. Additional seating accommodation is needed for a limited number of hours only during the year, and, if students cannot find seats in the library, they may go to their rooms or decide to do something else rather than read or study. The librarian works on the principle that space can always be found for one more staff member and hesitates to complain. But the books, although not vocal, suffer physically; their suffering is easy to demonstrate, as is the resulting poor service.

The shortage of stack space too often may be the result of an overestimation of its capacity at the time of construction. The fault may lie with a too optimistic librarian, or with an architect who has tried to crowd more capacity than is practicable into the limited space that can be provided from the available funds, or with those responsible who may have failed to realize that, with subject arrangement, shelves become uncomfortably crowded by the time 80 percent of the total space is occupied and become almost unusable when 90 percent is used. But other factors may be to blame.

Collections historically have grown more rapidly than anticipated, geometrically, or exponentially, rather than arithmetically. While this is not true in all cases, the exceptions tend to be those collections where strict policy requires essentially the removal of a volume for every book added, a factor which may become more common as more remote storage facilities are developed and institutional budgets are restricted. Even so, it seems to be difficult to understand in advance that faculty and students will not be content in most cases with a fixed collection of, for example, one million volumes any more than they were earlier with half that many, and that they will continually and inevitably demand more.

There is often disagreement in regard to how many volumes can be stored in a given amount of space, and the optimists who tend to overestimate the number usually prevail. In order to decide how much space will be needed for books in the bookstack of a new building, eight basic questions should be considered.

1. *What is a volume?* This question must be answered in order to determine how many are to be provided for or how much space a given number will require. There is considerable room for judgment in defining a volume. Some libraries call anything with over 50, or perhaps 100, pages a volume and, if it has fewer pages, a pamphlet. Some would count 6 pamphlets as a volume, while others call anything that is cataloged as a separate item a volume. Some insist that a volume must have hard covers. If space requirements are to be estimated with any degree of accuracy on the basis of the number of volumes to be shelved, then a volume must be defined.

Methods of counting library holdings are far from uniform. This is not the place to attempt to summarize the lengthy debates between those who advocate counting bibliographical units and those who prefer to count physical volumes, but it should be emphasized that the rules used and the interpretations of them vary greatly in different institutions, with confusing results. Moreover, most library collections contain numerous unbound and unprocessed items that have not been counted and may be forgotten but that must be housed, preferably on regular library shelving. Space requirements may be affected by an unusually large proportion of oversized volumes in such fields as music and fine arts, or by collections of unbound newspapers, or by a policy of binding periodicals into unusually thick volumes.

One definition, outlined by the Higher Education General Information Survey (HEGIS) in 1971, for a volume is "a physical unit of any printed, typewritten, handwritten, mimeographed, or processed work contained in one binding or portfolio, hardbound or paperbound, which has been classified, cataloged, and/or made ready for use." Since HEGIS is currently the national reporting vehicle in the United States for college and university library collections, this definition may be useful. A more detailed breakdown of types of material may be desirable for accurate space planning. Do not forget materials that have not been fully processed for use but that may be housed in the stacks.

2. *How tall and, even more important, how thick is an average physical volume?* This is as complicated as the preceding question and depends in part on the answer to that question. A figure must be determined in order to use the number of volumes as a basis for capacity estimates. Height and depth, as well as thickness, are involved, at least indirectly. The height and depth parts of the problem were carefully studied in the 1930s and 1940s by Henry B. Van Hoesen and Norman L. Kilpatrick (table 6.1) and by Fremont Rider (table 6.2).

Thickness depends partly on the subject (see table 6.3); partly on binding policy, particularly for periodicals and pamphlets (some libraries never bind a periodical in volumes more than 2 in. or 51 mm thick); and partly, as already noted, on the policy adopted for defining a volume. The proposed thickness of a typical volume may vary from country to country, century to century, or even decade to decade. The thickness of paper at different periods has its effect. Collections that have survived a flood will tend to require more shelf space, due to the warping and deformation of the papers and bindings. Other variables can modify the space required for a volume in any specific instance.

There was probably a larger percentage of quarto and folio volumes in the eighteenth century than there is today. Fine arts volumes tend to be taller, if not thicker, than others, while music volumes are likely to be taller and thinner than the norm. If volumes are over 11 in. and under 13 in. (279 and 330 mm) high, six shelves at the most will be possible in a standard-height 7 ft 6 in. (2.286) section.

TABLE 6.1 Measurement of Book Heights

| Group | Size | | No. of vols. | Percentage of the whole | Cumulative percent |
	mm	in.			
I	up to 190	7½ or less	88,582	25.0+	25.0
II	230	9	101,924	29.0+	54.0
III	250	9⅞	86,262	25.0−	79.0
IV	280	11	38,315	11.0−	90.0
V	298	11¾	14,777	4.0+	94.0
VI	330	13	10,348	3.0−	97.0
VII	400	15¾	7,268	2.0	99.0
VIII	450	17¾	2,377	0.6	99.6
IX	over 450	over 17¾	119	0.04	100.0

Computations based on measurement of 350,000 volumes at Brown University Library.

TABLE 6.2 Measurement of Book Heights

Metric Depth × height	Imperial Depth × height	Percentage	Cumulative percentage
130 × 200 mm	5 × 8 in. (or less)	25%	25
150 × 230 mm	6 × 9 in.	29	54
180 × 255 mm	7 × 10 in.	25	79
200 × 280 mm	8 × 11 in.	11	90
230 × 305 mm	9 × 12 in.	4	94
255 × 330 mm	10 × 13 in.	3	97
over 255 × 330 mm	over 10 × 13 in	3	100

TABLE 6.3 Space Requirements for Various Classifications of Books When Shelves Are Filled Solidly

Kind of book	Vol./ft of shelf	Vol./ single-faced section
Circulation (nonfiction)	8	168
Fiction	8	168
Economics	8	168
General literature	7	147
History	7	147
Technical and scientific	6	126
Medical	5	105
Law	4	84
Public documents	5	105
Bound periodicals	5	105
Art (not including large folios)	7	147

If they are over 13 and under 16 in. (330 and 406 mm), only five shelves can be used. If over 16 inches and under 20 (406 and 508 mm), four can be used, but extra-deep shelves will be required, and it is desirable to shelve books of this size on their sides to prevent unnecessary wear and tear. The effect of tall volumes on capacity is great.

It is obvious that total capacity per section is a matter of great importance in determining space requirements. A formula of 6 volumes per linear foot (or about 20 volumes per meter), including modest space for growth, has been suggested as a basis for comparing shelving arrangements. If a means of inserting one additional volume, or even one-half volume per linear foot of shelf (about 3, or 1½ volumes per meter) beyond the six (20 per meter) provided by the formula were possible, the capacity would be increased by as much as 16⅔ percent, which would provide space for an additional 167,000 volumes in a 1,000,000-volume stack. The construction cost for the floor area required for that many volumes may amount today to as much as $1,000,000. However, arbitrary adjustment of the figures used to calculate the

shelving capacity in order to reduce construction costs must not be permitted without a clear understanding of the implications.

Table 6.2 represents Rider's interpretation of Van Hoesen and Kilpatrick's compilation to include depth as well as height of books. Rider's figures for depth of books are used as a basis in the discussion of shelf depths throughout this volume.

Table 6.3 is adapted from one in common use by stack manufacturers. It was used by Wheeler and Githens, who suggested that 125 volumes per single-faced section should be considered practical working capacity.

3. *Is there a satisfactory formula for capacity that can be used?* No. Many different formulas have been used to determine space requirements. They vary widely. The "cubook," which was proposed some fifty years ago by Robert W. Henderson of the New York Public Library,[1] has been used; it was used in planning the National Library of Medicine. This formula provides for 100 "cu" or "average" size books per standard single-faced stack section; it goes one step farther and assumes that a section of this kind occupies 10 sq ft (0.929 m²) of floor space. This gives 10 volumes per sq ft (108 volumes per m²) of floor space in a bookstack. At the other extreme some architects, under pressure to provide more stack capacity than their clients can afford or from lack of experience, have used estimates of as much as 175 volumes per single-faced section and 20 volumes per sq ft (215 per m²) even when subject classification was to be used. Collections arranged by size and stored by an accession number or its equivalent might fit into these estimates, as will be shown in Section 6.3. The authors have seen a full section of Far Eastern materials with 295 volumes by count! But this is by no means universal. In between these extremes, a typical formula suggested by the

---

[1] *Library Journal* 59: 865–68 (Nov. 15, 1934) and 61: 52–54 (Jan. 15, 1936).

University of California and the *Higher Education Facilities Planning and Management Manuals* (May 1971) proposes that a standard single-faced section will require 8.7 sq ft (0.808 m²) and house 125 volumes. This works out to a little over 14 volumes per sq ft, which is certainly possible in many cases but not all. For example, in a music library with shelving deep enough to house phonograph discs and provision for full access by handicapped persons, the floor space required will be nearly 11 sq ft (1.022 m²) per single-faced section. But, depending upon how volumes are counted, a music library may have as many as 120 "volumes" per standard shelf. Assuming 6 shelves per section, this works out to about 65 "volumes" per sq ft (or over 700 per m²). A similar calculation for a reference collection, assuming 18 volumes per standard shelf, 6 shelves per section, and 11 sq ft (1.022 m²) per section, which is not especially generous for a well-used reference area, would suggest a capacity of less than 10 volumes per sq ft (or 105 volumes per m²). Formulas for capacity are dangerous, and none of them is completely satisfactory.

4. *Are the books to be shelved primarily by subject, with perhaps a limited amount of segregation by size for oversized volumes, or primarily by size?* Shelving by size is discussed in some detail and its effect on capacity is indicated in Section 6.3, dealing with compact storage. This section deals with the first alternative—shelving primarily by subject, which might be said to be essential in an open-access academic library.

5. *How much space is occupied by the present book collections?* This question should be answered to give a firm basis on which to make further computations. It is always safer to measure the collections in terms of the number of standard sections that they would fill if each shelf were filled to capacity. This is not as difficult as it might seem, particularly if the shelves are well filled at present and the timing is one selected to represent a date when a minimum of library materials are in circulation. It need not be done with a tape measure; careful eye estimates of empty space which amount to a full shelf is almost always sufficient. The chief task is to count up the vacant spaces, in terms of sections, and subtract the number from the total now available. The remainder will be the desired figure. Do not forget to include all the library's collections, not just the regularly classified

ones; small and uncommon caches may deserve to be measured more exactly. It will be suggested later in more detail that if 50 percent is added to this figure, the result will be the number of sections that the present collections would fill comfortably and leave room for modest growth. Doubling the shelving filled to absolute capacity will normally provide a good growth figure, accommodating the collections for about 20 years in many cases. But, as with other formulas, this factor needs consideration and adjustment to reflect the nature of the specific library.

6. *At what rate are the collections expected to grow in the years immediately ahead?* Any formula used for this purpose must be based on (a) the nature of the collections, (b) the present rate of growth, and (c) changes in that rate which can properly be expected. The third is a particularly difficult problem.

In this era of rapidly advancing technology, will developments in videodisc storage or electronic transmission of information enable libraries to slow their rates of growth? This basic question has been asked for decades, and with few exceptions (most notably certain college and undergraduate libraries) the answer appears to remain negative in spite of the fact that libraries will continue to benefit greatly from the new technologies. Microforms, for example, have preserved for posterity large collections of newspapers that were published on disintegrating paper stock and took a great amount of space. They have also enabled libraries to acquire large collections of other materials. The videodisc holds promise of even greater space savings where the represented materials, if they could have been or had been obtained in original format, would occupy many sections of bookstacks.

Nonetheless, to date, the growth of regular stack collections in libraries has continued unabated in most cases, and there is little indication that the rate will dramatically diminish as the result of miniaturization or increased interlibrary cooperation coupled with improved communication systems and devices in research libraries. The authors would be pleased to be proved wrong on this point, but history and our conservative natures tell us that the book as we know it will continue to proliferate in numbers for at least several decades, if not indefinitely, and that libraries will continue to buy and house books.

All libraries do not grow at the same rate, and they will not continue to grow at the present rate. In the past relatively young institutions frequently grew at a rate of 10 percent or more per year. Today in the United States the more typical rapid growth rate is about 4.5 percent per year, and the average growth rate for the 101 libraries that are tabulated in the Association of Research Libraries statistics for 1980–81 is 3.2 percent each year. Of course, a new institution is likely to have a much higher growth rate for the first decade or more, and the large, mature library is probably going to have a growth rate in the 2 to 2.5 percent range. The growth rate from 1976 to 1981 declined in absolute numbers by about 3 percent per year. While this may in part be a result of improved technologies, the recent history of inflationary cost increases for both materials and processing and static or diminished budgets for books has typically forced reductions in collection growth. Even Harvard University, where the growth rate is only 2 percent, is adding over 200,000 volumes a year. It is suggested that, in most cases, the best data for projection are found in the individual library's statistical history. The current growth rate should at least be projected as a compounded percent annually over the anticipated life of the programmed space, unless known factors would suggest otherwise. For a very young library this type of projection would be too high; it may be more accurate to project a growth rate in terms of absolute volumes per year in this case, with some adjustment for anticipated budget changes.

Other factors may also affect the rate of a library's growth. Increase in the size of the student body has a relatively slight effect on a large university library, but it may be a factor of considerable importance for a small college. By the same token, declining enrollment may imply a reduced growth rate. One standard suggests that 50,000 carefully chosen volumes are required to support the instructional program of even a very small college and may be adequate for as many as 600 students; for each 200 beyond that number, at least 10,000 volumes should be added. It must be emphasized that these are minimum figures and that strong institutions will demand considerably larger and richer collections.

Broadening the curriculum ordinarily calls for extensive additions to the library. So does the development of honors courses for undergraduates. These facts are closely related to the adoption of more selective admission requirements and improvement in the quality of the student body. Moreover, a new, attractive building, with the improved services it makes possible, is sure to stimulate a significant increase in library use, which in turn will result in pressure for an increase in the size of the collections. It is also not uncommon for a new facility to generate more gifts to the library which will swell the collections at a pace somewhat more rapid than the historical statistics may suggest.

When a university undertakes advanced instruction and research in a new field, its library almost certainly will be called upon to add thousands of volumes which would not otherwise be required. Meanwhile, the breadth of collecting demanded by the older fields of research continues to increase; it is no longer sufficient to buy books and periodicals from the United States and Western Europe. Nations from all parts of the world are becoming increasingly important sources of library materials as their scholarly programs multiply.

In this connection attention should be called to the fact that good research material in a library helps an institution to attract a better faculty, and, in turn, a good research faculty tends to insist that a library improve and enlarge its collections. Clearly, there must be a sound understanding of the academic and program goals of the institution as a whole in order to shape a reasonable projection of the growth of the library. Equally clear is the fact that any projection is a guess and that it will in almost all cases be somewhat off, which suggests that options and contingencies must be part of the planning process.

Estimating growth, then, is something that must be done for each library individually in the light of its present situation and its institution's plans for development. No formula can be proposed, and, if any general advice is in order, it is that estimates nearly always prove to be too low rather than too high.

7. How full does the library propose to fill its shelves before the situation is considered intolerable? Librarians will not agree on the answer; some will say, "When the shelves average over 80 percent full," because when that stage is reached, a great deal of shifting is required whenever large sets or a considerable number of single volumes in a limited subject field are acquired. It is suggested as a basis for discussion here that 86 percent be considered complete working capacity; this would leave 5 in. (127 mm) vacant on the average on each 36 in. (914 mm) shelf (actually about 35.5 in. or 902 mm in clear measure). New space should be available, not just planned for, by the time that figure is reached, or the growth rate should decline to zero, which in most cases is simply not practical. Staying within a reasonable working capacity is particularly a problem for branch libraries. Certainly the cost of labor required for shifting, plus the resulting inevitable wear and tear on the books, will be so great once the working capacity is reached that it will be uneconomical to permit further congestion. If any figure other than 86 percent is adopted, similar computations to those presented below but with the different base should be made.

If the library shelves are 75 percent full and the collections are growing at the rate of 3.5 percent a year compounded annually, the available capacity (86 percent) will be reached in almost exactly four years. Four years is none too long a time in which to obtain funds and to plan and build a new library or an addition, unless building funds and detailed plans are available on demand. In too many cases a considerably longer period will be required. A period of 10 years from the first proposal to the activation date is not unusual. This calculation gives some idea of a desirable timetable, but if it cannot be carried out on schedule, shelves are bound to become overcrowded, books will be damaged, and costs for shifting will mount up rapidly. It may be necessary to place in some outside temporary storage, or even permanent storage, volumes selected by subject or by the amount of use they are expected to receive. (See Chapter 2, Alternatives to a New Library Building.) These may be difficult to select; changing their records will be expensive in some cases; and the change will certainly cause inconvenience.

Table B.12 (in Appendix B) shows the length of time required to fill shelves to their working capacity at different rates of growth. It should be noted that in a storage library where the books are added to the shelves by an accession number or its equivalent (fixed location), the working capacity can be essentially 100 percent. However it must be cautioned that this leaves no room for error; additional space should be available well before 100 percent is reached lest the materials be piled on the floor. Even here, 86 percent may

be a prudent planning target although 90 to 95 percent is probably more easily justified.

8. *How long should the new building be expected to be adequate before it is replaced, enlarged, or an alternative space arrangement is activated?* This topic is discussed in Chapter 5. Because it is an important issue, additional comments will be made here. The question of the time span for planning a new facility must be answered in accordance with the institution's general building and planning policies; one may suggest only that it is unwise and generally impossible to attempt to plan for long years ahead just as it is usually unwise to plan for very short periods. If a new building includes satisfactory provision for the construction of an annex or annexes when they are needed, it should not be necessary to construct extensive and expensive stack areas a great many years before they will be used. Some tax-supported institutions have been unfortunate enough to be subject to governmental regulations, made because of pressure for funds from many directions, that forbid new construction that will be sufficient for more than five years. This is undoubtedly a penny-wise and pound-foolish policy if a long-term view is taken. It should also be remembered that in such cases, if space requirements are based on the date when planning begins, and some years must elapse before the new quarters are ready for occupancy, the library will be beyond suitable capacity when the move finally takes place.

To summarize: What can be done in estimating bookstack space requirements? Here is one possible approach in terms of a specific library, assuming that the eight questions have been answered as follows:

1. A volume is any physical unit of material that is to be shelved in the bookstacks being planned.

2. The height and thickness of volumes is such that the number now at hand fills completely the 2,000 single sections noted under 5 below.

3. No formula for a definite number of volumes in a section is selected, as the figures used in 5 below are considered more accurate. (It is desirable, however, to compare the 2,000 single-faced sections with the count of volumes that are believed to be in the library.)

4. The books are to be shelved primarily by subject.

5. The present book collections would occupy 2,000 standard-sized single-faced sections, 3 ft (0.914) wide and 7½ ft (2.286) high, if the shelves were completely filled to what might be called absolute capacity.

6. The collection is expected to increase in size by 3.5 percent each year compounded annually.

7. The stack is to be considered full to working capacity when the shelves on the average are 86 percent full, leaving approximately 5 in. (127 mm) unused space on each shelf, and additional space should be available not later than at that time.

8. It is hoped that the new building or additional stack area will be adequate for fifteen years from the date on which the estimate in 5 above was made.

Given these answers, the required stack capacity in the new building could be calculated as follows:

Two thousand single-faced sections, increasing at the rate of 3.5 percent a year compounded annually, will fill completely 3350 sections at the end of that time. Since the new stack is to be considered full to working capacity when the shelves on the average are 86 percent full, the number of sections required for the new construction will be 3900.

But another extremely important factor suggested under 7 above should be repeated here. When the shelves are 75 percent full (using the proposed rate of growth), which will be about four years before working capacity is reached, the next campaign for more space should begin. With a faster growth rate, the time to start planning will be reflected by a smaller percentage of absolute capacity, i.e., if the growth rate were 5 percent compounded annually, the time to start planning new capacity would be when the shelves are about 70 percent full, which again would provide about four years. For a 10 percent growth rate, the time for planning is when the shelves are about 60 percent full. That will be only eleven years from the present, seven years from activation of the currently planned facility, if the space requirements are based on the space occupied by the collections at this time and the facility can be actually programmed, designed, funded, constructed, and activated in a four-year time frame. Planning for only fifteen years beyond the present need is probably an altogether too conservative approach. The dilemma of those institutions restricted to five-year planning projections can

easily be seen from this sketch. Space for twenty to twenty-five years from the present is undoubtedly more desirable.

Tables in Appendix B will give an indication of the desirable schedules for planning new space when different rates of growth are used.

Space Requirements. So far the discussion has dealt only with the number of standard sections required. The number of these sections does not determine the floor area required because, as it was seen in Section 6.1, variations are possible in distances between range centers, which are affected in turn by shelf depths and aisle widths. Variations are also possible in the length of ranges between cross aisles and in the width of cross aisles. The space required for vertical communications, such as elevators, lifts, stairs, ramps, supporting columns, air ducts, and other services, should not be forgotten although these elements are normally not counted as part of the net space. The "density of reader population" or the use factor is of importance here as has been noted; aisles in a relatively small stack used by many scholars need to be wider and shorter than those in a very large stack to which proportionately few persons are admitted. The requirements for handicapped access may also have a significant affect on the overall space need.

The generous "cubook" formula, already referred to, suggests 100 volumes and 10 sq ft (.93 m²) per single-faced section. A much more compact arrangement is practicable if access to the stack is severely restricted, as it is at the New York Public Library and the Library of Congress. If ranges are only 4 ft (1.219) on centers and 30 ft (9.144) long, and 125 volumes to a section are estimated, 15 volumes per sq ft, or even 17, are easily possible (160 or 180 volumes per m²) although access in a wheelchair may be difficult, if not impossible. This is generally regarded as quite dense storage for normal stack arrangements. The trend, at least in the United States and Canada, is for increasing use of stacks by undergraduate students, and the average college or university can expect its stack population to increase rather than to decrease. The educational value of stack access is a major consideration, as is the provision of satisfactory seating accommodation and good service. Each is expensive, but is almost always worth the cost.

It is tentatively suggested, therefore, in order to provide a basis for estimates, that 10 volumes per sq ft (108 volumes per m²) of floor space be used for small undergraduate collections with completely open access. Not more than 12 volumes per sq ft (129 per m²) should be used for larger undergraduate collections of up to 100,000 volumes. Thirteen (140 per m²) is safe for considerably larger collections, and 15 (160) might be used for universities with great research collections and open access for graduate students and faculty only. Handicapped access will generally imply a reduction of these figures depending on the specific circumstances, particularly for the denser capacities. Where handicapped access is not a problem, using shelf spacing to maximize capacity can result in up to 20 volumes per sq ft (215 per m²) in a great research library with very limited stack access, narrow stack aisles, long ranges, and a minimal base shelf. The chapters on design, particularly Chapter 12, as well as Appendix B should be consulted for layouts.

Estimating the space requirements for a library's book collections is but one of the problems that must be faced when a new building is programmed. If a completely satisfactory formula could be provided for such estimates, the task would be greatly simplified, but experience suggests rather that the first rule should be *Beware of formulas.* Libraries differ, and there is no satisfactory substitute for consideration of the individual case by an expert librarian, library consultant, or architect. The figures that have been given here, if not accepted blindly, should be useful in making preliminary estimates of space for book collections, and they give at least some indication of the problems involved.

Finally, remember when in doubt another basic rule in library planning: *A healthy library tends to outgrow its bookstack space and its building sooner than expected.*

6.3 Methods of Increasing Capacity

Chapter 2 discusses the possibility of increasing stack capacity by a number of methods as an alternative to new space planning. As many of these techniques may be desirable as part of a proposed facility, either upon activation or as a future option, the physical aspects will be further discussed here, particularly in terms of a program statement.

As detailed in the preceding section, it is not easy to define precisely what a volume is

or to determine the average thickness of the volumes in a library. Here, in order to simplify matters, two formulas will be taken as a base; these are arbitrary and debatable and by no means satisfactory for all institutions, but they will make it possible to compare book capacities resulting from different shelving arrangements. For a discussion on book sizes, Section 6.2 should be consulted.

The first of these formulas is that *six volumes equals the average comfortable capacity per linear foot of shelving (or 20 volumes per meter) if the collections are classified and space is provided throughout for growth.* This formula is commonly accepted and is conservative for a college, university, or research library; it can properly be used as a basis for this discussion. It means that a standard section 3 ft (0.914) wide, 7½ ft (2.286) high, with seven shelves including the base where possible, can hold 125 volumes. The figures will vary, of course, from library to library and subject to subject within the same library; bound volumes of periodicals, for example, ordinarily take more space than monographs. Seven shelves of quarto or folio volumes cannot be provided in a section, but six volumes per linear foot (20 per m) is a figure conservative enough to make up for the extra space occupied by the 5 to 10 percent of the ordinary collection that is oversized and still provide a reasonable amount of space for growth. Newspapers in their original form should be dealt with as a separate or distinct group as should other nonbook materials.

The second arbitrary formula that will be used here provides that *15 volumes can be housed per sq ft (160 per m²) of stack floor space.* This matter was also discussed in the preceding section, and more is said in the chapters on design, particularly Chapter 12. It should be noted that this is a fairly dense capacity for an open-access stack; 12 or 13 volumes per sq ft (130 or 140 per m²) may be a more satisfactory figure to use in an open-shelf college library, and some planners are currently using 10 volumes per sq ft to provide for handicapped access.

Three basic methods can be used to increase the storage capacity within a fixed floor area. Each has its advantages and disadvantages. The total cost of housing any given number of volumes may be reduced under some circumstances, if not all, by any of the three, and savings in space and cost may be even greater if a combination of two methods is used or even all three. The most significant problem is whether or not their disadvantages overshadow the anticipated savings resulting from their use.

The three basic methods can be characterized as: (1) methods of shelving more books in the existing or standard library sections; (2) methods of devoting a larger percentage of the available floor space to standard shelving; and (3) methods of increasing the capacity of a given floor space by using special kinds of shelving.

The first two methods have been in use for many years throughout the world. The third, with minor exceptions, has been developed during the last quarter of a century under the pressure of high building construction costs.

1. *Methods of shelving more books in the existing or standard sections.* There are five options, all of which will increase the weight of the collections; it may be prudent to consult a structural engineer, particularly about an existing stack where the more condensed storage procedures are being planned.

a. *Less space may be left for growth in the estimate used.* This practice has been used from the earliest times. It may take either of two quite different forms.

Under the first, books are arranged in fixed location, chronologically by date of receipt, and shelves are filled to capacity one after another as the collection grows. This has been the traditional plan in many large libraries in other countries and often, too, in small ones where closed stacks are common. It facilitates the use of each linear unit of shelving to full capacity; once shelved, a volume need never be shifted. Many library remote storage facilities use essentially this technique. The arbitrary figure of six volumes per linear foot (20 per m) proposed for this discussion will fill a stack to something like three-quarters of the absolute capacity of the shelving. Under this system, consequently, if the formula's 125 volumes per standard section is correct, then the chronological arrangement should accommodate 168 volumes in the same section. Still, some factor for growth for the entire collection should be added in; it is suggested that reasonable capacity might occur when 95 percent of the shelves are full. This leaves little room for timing errors, and a smaller percentage may be prudent. All things being equal, assuming a very accurate analysis of the average book size, 95 percent of

the absolute capacity will represent a contingency of about one year in most cases depending, of course, on the growth rate. The chronological plan should not be used with a subject arrangement.

The second alternative is simply to decide that, though fixed locations are not to be adopted, a larger percentage of each shelf may be filled without too great difficulty. If seven volumes instead of six are shelved per linear foot (23 rather than 20 per m), the working capacity will be only seven-eighths of complete capacity, yet the estimated capacity will have been increased to 147 volumes per section. There will still be room for a 14 percent increase in the bulk of the total collection before the absolute capacity is reached. However, as pointed out before, experience has shown that whenever shelves of classified books are filled on the average to 80 percent or more of the absolute capacity, library service begins to suffer. Constant shifting of books is required because of unequal growth that is difficult, if not impossible, to predict; individual shelves and sections overflow; and space has to be found for expansion of entire subject classifications that are growing more rapidly than the collections as a whole. Bindings will be damaged by moving and pulling books from shelves filled too full.

It should be added that institutions all too rarely provide additional shelf space as soon as it is needed; often they delay until books have to be piled horizontally on top of other books, on window ledges, or shelved on their fore-edges in order to add an additional shelf, a procedure which inevitably damages the books and impairs service. For this reason the authors strongly recommend that, in estimating stack capacity, a more conservative figure (125 volumes in our example) per section be used. Also, as a rule of thumb, the library should begin planning for additional space or alternative measures as soon as the library stack is filled to two-thirds or, at the most, three-fourths of complete capacity, depending on the growth rate and anticipated planning time as shown earlier.

If a fixed location arrangement is adopted, the only way to use the stacks is through consultation of the catalog; all the advantages of classified collections in relation to the shelving arrangement must be forgone. Unless the location number appears on the spine of the book, misshelved volumes may never be found. While the reader may still be permitted open access and allowed to determine the arbitrary location of the desired items, the reader's activities would simply be that of a stack attendant, and an untrained one at that; the disadvantages of open access would result without any of the manifold advantages it normally offers. Having a carrel or study near the specific collections of interest would no longer make sense. The possibility of a serendipitous discovery of an important or useful volume is all but lost; the only means of browsing a subject collection is the shelflist or catalog, which usually is less than satisfactory. Many readers will be interested in several books at once on the same or related subjects. Since these books normally were not acquired at the same time, the attendant or reader in a fixed-location stack may have to go to widely separated areas for them, taking more time than would be required under a subject-classification system. This is one of the reasons for slow service in many libraries that do not shelve their books by subject.

To be weighed against these considerations, the great advantage of the fixed location arrangement is its saving in space. Use of this shelving alternative may be most easily justified in a large, seldom-used storage collection, particularly one housed at a remote location and accessed by staff rather than readers. If a building for 1,000,000 volumes is taken as an example, the space required for books in chronological order of accession with a planned contingency of 5 percent would require about 78 percent of the space a classified plan would need with a moderate provision for growth. This change alone might save more than $1,500,000 in construction for a 1,000,000-volume capacity. Even so, in the United States and Canada at least, scholars and librarians are, for the most part, convinced that open access and subject arrangements are of vital importance and that the cost is not unreasonable.

Do not overestimate stack capacity. This has been done altogether too often by architects and librarians.

b. *Books may be shelved by size.* If books are shelved by size and the system divides them into five or more groups—e.g., books less than 7 in. (180 mm) high, those between 7 and 8 in. (180 to 200 mm), 8 and 9 in. (200 to 230 mm), 9 and 11 in. (230 to 280 mm), and those over 11 in. (280 mm), it should be possible to place on the average 8 or 9 shelves per standard section. If the average is 8½, compared with 7 shelves on the average for regular shelving, the shelving available has been increased by approximately 20 percent (Fremont Rider has calculated the figure at approximately 25 percent), which would bring the average capacity per section up to 150 volumes. If combined with the chronological arrangement described above, the figure will rise further to 200, a total increase of 60 percent.

This technique has been used at the storage facility at Princeton University for a number of years with support of the faculty (materials are stored in subject order). Other facilities combining shelving by size and by chronological order include the New England Deposit Library, the University of California storage facility pre-1983, the Center for Research Libraries, and many reference and research libraries of the United Kingdom, countries on the Continent, and elsewhere. It often comes as a shock to an American librarian to discover the prevalence of shelving by size abroad; foreigners are often equally surprised to find that great American libraries shelve their books by subject. A decision one way or the other, particularly if chronological shelving is involved, usually will have significant influence on the thinking for seating arrangements and open- versus closed-stack access.

c. *Fore-edge or spine shelving.* A third means of increasing the capacity of a given area is to shelve books on their fore-edge or spine as well as by size. The sequence number is marked on the top edge. Where conservation of the library materials is a concern, this technique cannot be recommended, as the weight of the text block will eventually cause severe damage to the binding. However, it is a stopgap measure when other alternatives are not appropriate. It has been adopted for infrequently used materials at Yale University and elsewhere. A variation is to pile books flat one on top of another, top edge showing; yet selecting and reshelving results in some physical damage to bindings and makes misshelving easy. A method of saving still more space has been suggested in which books are not only placed on their fore-edges, but their margins are sometimes cut down with a power-driven paper knife and boxed in inexpensive cardboard containers. Any good conservation officer should strongly object to this technique!

It is estimated that fore-edge or spine shelving, if used in conjunction with arrangement by size, will increase by at least 50 percent the capacity per section made possible by the chronological plan. It may bring capacity up to at least 250 volumes per section, an increase of 100 percent over the subject-arrangement plan, and provide for 30 volumes per square foot of floor space instead of 15 (or 320 as opposed to 160 volumes per m²). The procedure has all the disadvantages that have been noted above plus the issue of injured bindings. When normally shelved books are packed tightly, some stack attendants may squeeze in an extra shelf by turning only extra tall volumes down to enable closer shelf placement. If this is done as a temporary expedient, the spines should be down, as this placement is less damaging to bindings than if books are shelved on the fore-edge.

Where more than an occasional volume is shelved on the spine, shelf reading is difficult, as is finding an item, although inserting between or in the volumes cards which exhibit the call number of the individual item or call number groups can help. Cards with call number groups are used at the University of Texas, Austin, storage facility with minimal difficulty for seldom-used materials. To double the capacity by shelving books chronologically, by size, and on their fore-edge or spine may save over $3,000,000 in the construction of a 1,000,000-volume bookstack if construction costs are approximately $100 per sq ft (or $1,076 per m²).

d. *Shelving two or three deep.* Books can be shelved two deep, that is, one row behind the other, on shelves 12 in. (305 mm) deep, or three deep on 18 in. (457 mm) shelves. Many libraries, because of lack of space, have occasionally resorted to the two-deep plan, temporarily at least. The inconvenience is extremely serious. When President Eliot of Harvard University proposed cooperative storage for the Boston area, which came into being forty years later as the New England Deposit Library, he suggested that the "dead books" be shelved three deep, which is even worse—two or perhaps four times as unsatisfactory as two deep. The procedure will, however, increase capacity materially. Two-deep shelving, where books are on 12 in. (305 mm) shelves, with no change in aisle width, could bring the total up to as much as 400 volumes per section or 50 per sq ft (540 per m²), assuming the arrangement is also chronological and by size. If the three-deep plan

were adopted and the distance between range centers were increased from 4 ft 6 in. to 5 ft 6 in. (1.372 to 1.676), as would be desirable if not necessary, capacity would rise to 600 volumes per section and, in spite of the reduced number of ranges, more than 60 volumes could be housed per sq ft (or 650 volumes per m²). If long term use of this configuration is anticipated, a wider aisle permitting direct removal of the contents of a shelf to a book truck may be desirable.

A variation of this scheme is to shelve boxed materials with the box sized to permit double or triple rows of books. This might aid access, but the increased aisle width to permit handling the boxes would still be desirable. The new Northern Regional Library Facility of the University of California, opened in 1982, was designed for double-depth shelving—the hidden row for seldom-used archival boxes and the front row for monographs, perhaps shelved by size in continuous ribbons, as a set of 5 or 6 exceedingly long horizontal layers of books each of a specific height.

e. *Higher sections.* There is one further method of increasing capacity without abandoning standard shelving; it is to increase the height of the shelf sections. It can be done, of course, only if the ceiling height is sufficient, there are no code limitations related to sprinklers, and the shelving can be properly braced. If, as in many bookstacks, there are no sprinklers, no particular concerns about bracing, and an 8 ft 6 in. (2.590) ceiling (which is lower than the ceilings in most areas of modern libraries that are used for both book storage and readers), the capacity theoretically will be increased by more than 14 percent. This move does not call for giving up a classified arrangement with open access, but it places the top shelf out of reach of all but the tallest readers unless footstools are used. In warehouse buildings, where shelves are closed to the public, the disadvantage is much slighter. The rare-book stack in the University Research Library of the University of California, Los Angeles, and the collections housed in the Monterey Boatworks building in the Hopkins Marine Station at Pacific Grove, California, are but two examples of extra-height shelving that work fairly well.

Five methods have been described by which, without making a basic change in standard stack installations, the capacity of a given area can be increased. As has been noted, various combinations of these methods are possible; the total number of plans that might be adopted is therefore considerably greater than five. Any such method offers the potential for saving construction and facilities maintenance costs although stack maintenance costs may increase. All of them will increase the possible floor-loading which must be considered both in existing facilities and when programming a new facility where some form of compact storage is anticipated. Each institution must carefully consider its service methods and requirements before deciding to adopt one or more of these procedures. No one of the five is recommended for an open-access library although some would clearly be more difficult than others. Their use in a closed-access stack for any but little-used collections is decidedly questionable. These methods should be compared with procedures that will be described below.

2. *Methods of devoting a larger percentage of the available floor space to regular shelving.* There are three options:

a. *Shallower shelves.* If the depth of shelves is decreased without changing aisle widths, the center to center spacing could be reduced, making it possible to install more ranges in a given floor area, thereby increasing the capacity. This issue is discussed in Section 6.1, but it is of sufficient importance to warrant further discussion here. A large percentage of the shelving installed in college, university, and research libraries is 20 in. (508 mm) from front to back, often with bases or bottom shelves and, when used, end panels 24 in. (610 mm) wide. The justification for this width is to increase the flexibility to house the occasional deeper volume within its subject sequence and to provide greater stability.

The argument for narrower shelves suggests that about 94 percent of all general collections in college and research libraries measures not more than 9 in. (230 mm) from fore-edge to spine. If one accepts the fact that the remaining 6 percent of the collections might be housed in separate, deeper shelves, then shelving that is actually 7 in. (178 mm) deep, together with the 2 in. (51 mm) space between shelves, should be sufficient for most volumes. This proposal results in a range 16 in. (406 mm) deep rather than 20 in. (508 mm) or more, as is common. Provided there is no sway bracing, and provided two 9 in. (230 mm) books do not occur exactly opposite each other, this scheme no doubt works.

It would require the user to check at least two locations to find an item if it is not at the first place checked. Occasionally two 9 in. (230 mm) books will occur back to back and each must project into the aisle by one inch. If dummies are used (a wood block indicating that the volume with the specified call number is located elsewhere), the anticipated space savings would be slightly reduced. Assuming no dummies, bracing, or back-to-back volumes, the space savings for the proposed 94 percent of the collections would be 8 percent. It is possible and perhaps even more acceptable from the service point of view to use narrower shelves in conjunction with size arrangements. Further, it should be noted that newly purchased shallow shelves should cost less than deep ones. Finally, some small percent (usually less than 3 percent and often less than 1 percent) of volumes will require special shelving in any event. It is thus suggested that in planning a new stack facility, or considering new arrangements for an existing facility, narrower shelves of 7 in. actual or 8 in. nominal (178 or 203 mm) dimension should be considered. Of course, in an existing facility a change to narrower shelves would be a costly alteration perhaps limited by the structural module, lighting, and other features, which will relegate this approach to new facilities in most cases.

b. *Narrower aisles.* The standard width of aisles in academic libraries varies from 30 to 36 in. (0.762 to 0.914) or 42 in. (1.066) where handicapped access codes are fully applied; in housing infrequently used books, particularly in closed-access stacks, the width may well be reduced considerably provided wheelchair access is not required. This topic also was discussed in Section 6.1, but bears additional brief comment. Combined with shallower shelving, ranges have been installed on as little as 40 in. (1.016) centers instead of 54 in. (1.372) which, excluding the effect of bracing, dummies, and back-to-back larger volumes, increases the capacity for about 94 percent of the general collections by 35 percent. On this basis, without resorting to any of the other procedures that have been considered, the capacity per square foot will become approximately 20 volumes instead of 15 (or 215 as opposed to 160 volumes per m²). It should be noted that narrow aisles increase the difficulty of lighting the bottom shelves adequately, and that stack management as well as user service may be affected.

In Dublin the Trinity College Library uses a colonnade under its famous Long Room as a stack area, with ranges 40 in. (1.016) on centers; the arrangement is by size, with the result that some 30 volumes are housed per sq ft (320 volmes per m²). In the New England Deposit Library, with shelving 44 in. (1.118) on centers, and aisles 26 in. (0.660) wide, capacity has been increased by 23 percent over standard shelving, in addition to the gains resulting from arrangement by size. Much of the Newberry Library and the south wing of the Cecil H. Green Library at Stanford have ranges 48 in. (1.219) on centers. Widener has a heavily used stack with ranges 50 in. (1.270) on centers.

The authors suggest that aisle widths be carefully considered with present and prospective use in mind. They are not easily changed. For a heavily used stack open to a large undergraduate group, 36 in. (0.914) is recommended; 32 to 34 in. (0.812 to 0.864) is adequate for a collection of 500,000 volumes and over if the use is not heavily concentrated; and 30 in. (0.762) is enough for a limited-access collection of over 1,000,000 volumes. These dimensions can be reduced by two to three inches (51 to 76 mm) if the measure is at the base and the bottom shelf is two inches (51 mm) wider nominally than those above it. Handicapped access, however, may suggest a minimum of 32 in. (0.813) clear aisle space or more depending upon the local code, although many wheelchairs can negotiate aisles as narrow as 27 in. (0.686) where the base shelf is larger than the standard shelf. In a storage stack for less-used books, 26 in. (0.660) will do, but less than 24 in. (0.610) should not be tolerated. Before deciding on aisle widths, the planner should consider range lengths; other things being equal, the narrower the aisle, the shorter the range should be. Both factors are part of the same problem.

With shallow shelving and narrow stack aisles, special provision should be made for deeper shelving for the limited number of oversized volumes. This can sometimes be done by placing them along end, elevator, and stair walls which are adjacent to wide aisles. In this case one should be careful not to so disguise major vertical communication elements in such a way that they are made difficult to find. Another option is to set aside bays where one less range than elsewhere is installed.

c. *Lengthening ranges and reducing the width of cross aisles.* Some people have asserted that no range in an open-access stack should be more than five sections or 15 ft (4.572) long. This may be valid for an undergraduate collection, though it could well be disputed. Indeed, short ranges interrupted by cross aisles only complicate shelving arrangements, particularly in a large stack area. If the ranges are clearly labeled and if floor plans are readily accessible, with broad subjects or class marks clearly indicated on them, long ranges may be more satisfactory than short ones, because they may simplify traffic patterns and a comprehension of collection deployment. Ranges that extend 33 ft (10.058) before a cross aisle is reached will provide 10 percent more shelving in the same floor area than two 15 ft (4.572) ranges separated by a 3 ft (0.914) cross aisle. A range 36 ft (10.973) long will provide 20 percent more shelving than two shorter ranges with a 6 ft (1.829) cross aisle between.

On the other hand, long ranges add some degree of difficulty for reshelving returned books or shifting a collection, especially where the aisle is too narrow for removing books from a book truck. These concerns should be weighed and answered on the basis of local conditions and with present and prospective use in mind, but it is obvious that shallower shelving, narrower aisles, and longer ranges can increase the capacity of a given area materially.

Additional discussion of this topic may be found in Section 6.1.

3. *Methods of increasing the capacity of a given floor area by using special kinds of shelving.* As outlined in Chapter 2, several special kinds of shelving can be used with the normal subject arrangement of books or with one or more of the other procedures suggested above. Not all combinations are practical. Books cannot be shelved two or three deep on some of the special shelving described below; in effect, these special shelving devices are a means of achieving the savings in space that two and three deep shelving provides without most of the disadvantages that are entailed if books are crowded two and three deep on regular shelves. The height of ranges of special shelving should not be increased beyond the standard height because the shelving generally does not lend itself to use with the aid of footstools. In spite of this statement, higher than standard ranges have

been used with special shelving at the University of Wisconsin Library and elsewhere. Four general methods are discussed.

a. *Hinged shelving.* Hinged shelving was first used at the Center for Research Libraries where it made possible an increase in capacity for a given floor area of up to 75 percent over the standard 125 volumes per section. To this possibility can be added the savings that result from shelving by size if that procedure is also adopted. This hinged shelving is a custom installation designed by that great innovator Angus Snead Macdonald. His proposal was accepted before the design had been completely perfected, and the shelving is not as satisfactory as it might have been if a rush order could have been avoided. This shelving consists of double-faced sections hung on each side of standard sections; each range, therefore, has what amounts to three-deep shelving on both sides. Since the hinged sections are nearly 3 ft (0.914) long and are deep enough to accommodate books on both sides, the aisles had to be nearly 40 in. (1.016) wide; they thereby lost part of the gain, but provided considerably larger capacity than would be available with ranges no more than 40 in. (1.016) on centers.

A variation of this concept consists of swing units occupying a little less than half the length of a regular section. These units are hung at both ends of each section; they swing out into the stack aisles and expose to view the regular shelves that are behind them when they are closed. The swing units have been offered in either single- or double-faced shelving. The latter, like the installation at the Center for Research Libraries, makes it possible to shelve books three deep on both sides of each range and provides access to books on the inside rows without individual handling of the books on the outer row. Since these units are only half as long as those designed by Mr. Macdonald, the aisles need not be widened, and there is less weight to contend with in the movable portion. As pointed out in Chapter 2, hinged shelving often has wheels which roll over the floor to assist in carrying the weight. Because of this, carpet may not be appropriate in installations of this type.

b. *Drawer-type shelving.* Drawer-type shelving when first introduced by the Hamilton Company of Two Rivers, Wisconsin, was called Compo. Similar units called Store-Mor Drawers were also made by the now defunct W. R. Ames Company of Milpitas, California. The drawers ranged in length from 3 ft (0.914) to 6 ft (1.829) with the longer drawers designed to be pulled out from either side of a very deep range. Drawer storage makes it desirable or, in many cases, necessary to increase the width of stack aisles, which reduces to some extent the savings of space. Further, drawers that are placed above the height of a normal counter are exceedingly difficult to use unless they are designed like shelves, as most are. The box-type drawer is put to best use when the books are stored on their fore-edge, which in the long run will result in damage to the bindings. The authors would be reluctant to recommend any drawer of the box type for storage for normal book collections, although there are no doubt cases when box drawer storage is justified. The shelf-type drawer is far superior for most library installations.

c. *Movable shelving.* There are currently two general types of movable shelving which are fairly available. Several other systems have also been designed to move entire sections or even ranges on tracks or suspension systems to provide access to the collections. The first type started as Compactus shelving designed by Hans Ingold in Zurich, Switzerland, in the early 1900s. Shelving of this type is now available from a number of manufacturers worldwide. It consists of carriages upon which standard or special shelving is placed. The carriages ride on tracks set into or on top of the floor; in the latter case, the surface of the floor is slightly raised to accommodate the tracks. The system provides shelving ranges that can be pushed tightly together so that a given group of ranges (within one bay) will have a single aisle. The space utilization—depending on the aisle width, the range length, and the number of movable ranges—will usually increase capacity 100 percent, and sometimes much more, over standard static shelving in the same amount of space (see fig. 6.18).

Movable carriages can be braced either by special guides that grip the rails or overhead fixed beams with rollers on the shelving units, or by use of an overhead pantograph or collapsing beam system which can serve to carry wires and lights as well. Some manufacturers may recommend a combination of bracing techniques in certain areas of the country that are vulnerable to earthquakes. Where energy conservation is a concern, the pantograph lighting system offers the same advantage as

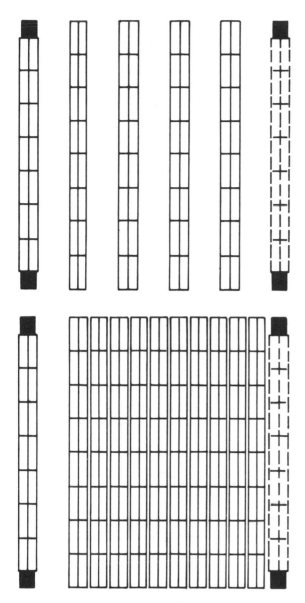

FIGURE 6.18 Standard versus compact movable shelving. The entire range is moved to relocate the aisle. In this example, the standard configuration has 39 double-faced sections compared to 87 sections in the same space for the compact shelving, for an increased capacity of 123 percent. Note in the lower illustration that only the 7 double-faced sections running between two columns are not movable.

range aisle lighting; without it or an alternative, an entire bay must be illuminated for the use of a single aisle. At least one manufacturer provides lighting that is supported by one carriage/shelving unit, which is a much simpler installation.

With a module of ranges, perhaps eight or more, it is recommended that motorized carriages be specified where heavy use is expected, even though manually or mechanically (no motor) assisted carriages are available

for ranges up to 10 to 12 sections long. The problem is that even with a mechanical leverage system and steel wheels with excellent bearings riding on steel tracks, the force required to overcome the inertia of loaded ranges of books is significant. To overcome this force with a fairly long range will require up to 15 revolutions of a crank to create an aisle, a tiresome effort if use is heavy. Also, safety is a factor and should be considered when utilizing mechanical leverage systems, especially in public areas where misuse can occur. The safety risk results from the lack of automatic safety features; the manual force of the operator determines the speed of the carriages and thus the force required to stop them. In a manual system, it is easy to move a single range, and two or three at a time are possible, but if the aisle needs to be relocated ten or so ranges away, a considerable amount of cranking or pushing is required. Princeton's Fine Hall shelving facility has mechanically assisted ranges over 30 ft long, and it is easy to move three at a time; six at a time can be moved although the effort is considerable. With motors the ranges can be 60 ft (18.288) or even longer. The aisle can be formed where desired by simply pushing a button.

There have in the past been injuries resulting from movable-shelving systems just as there have been injuries from nearly any mechanical system. However, safety features that have been developed for electrically operated movable-shelving systems, if employed, will make it nearly impossible to incur a serious injury in normal operation. A completely passive safety system should be employed in any electrically operated movable-shelving system so that it does not require any conscious effort by the operator to ensure proper safety. A key feature of the passive system is incorporated in the flooring (safety floor) that fills in the space between the tracks and consists of panels which, when depressed, activate a micro switch which turns off the system. Other devices that detect the presence of a user in the aisle are offered by some manufacturers to take the place of a safety floor. A "safety sweep" can be added at the bottom edge of the carriage which will stop the system if a stool or book is left on the floor. A second pressure-sensitive strip is sometimes installed at a higher (waist high) level to stop the system, but it may affect the adjustability of the shelf involved and at waist height the strip is less passive than the floor system. The shelving would in effect already be pressing against you unless you knew that the safety strip was there and consciously pressed it. Vertical safety strips can be installed at the end panels to reduce the chance of the system closing on an arm or the fingers of an operator standing outside the range aisle. Systems of lights can be employed to indicate when the system is in use. Most manufacturers offer a torque-limiting feature on the drive mechanism which would prevent serious injury even if all of the other systems fail. It should be noted that the safety floor or alternative presence sensing systems are the only systems with automatic reset. When the system is turned off by any other safety device (for example, the range closes on a book left on the floor), the attendant will need to operate the system mechanically or use a special safety over-ride circuit in order to open up the aisle enough to enter it and remove the book from the floor. Without the special over-ride circuit, the attendant must go to the master control panel, which is often in another space, to reactivate the system. This inconvenience can be reduced by provision of reset buttons at the shelving units. To ensure proper use of the reset buttons and the over-ride circuit, keyed operation may be desirable. As can be assumed from the comment above, in the event of power failure, most motorized systems can be operated manually, although it is not particularly convenient or easy to do so with long ranges.

When this type of system is installed in an existing space, the tracks and safety floor will add 2 to 3 in. (51 to 76 mm) to the overall height of the shelving. A ramp at the edge of this flooring is installed to permit wheelchair or book truck access. In a new building, the floor slab can be depressed to provide for a completed floor installation that is level. The carriage itself will add about 5 in. (127 mm) to the height. The minimum depth of the carriage, front to back, is 18½ in. (470 mm) including bumpers, which suggests a minimum shelf size of 9 in. nominal dimension. The carriage can be up to 48 in. (1.219) deep or more, which is useful for microform cabinets, newspapers, or oversized book storage. Standard shelving, commercial or industrial shelving, case shelving, or even file cabinets may then be mounted on top of the carriage. With standard shelving, the overall height installed in an existing space will be a little over 8 ft (2.438). To this must be added another 6 in. (152 mm) where a pantograph,

or beam bracing, or lighting system is installed. A pantograph system for wire management only may add about 4 in. (102 mm) to the height.

A typical installation places the ranges perpendicular to a wall and within a column bay. The power requirements and wiring for the controls is then done through a duct way on the wall. Generally, fire code authorities will view the system as furniture and allow ranges of any length. Other local authorities may view the units as built in, thus the range aisle length may be limited to that allowed for a dead-end corridor or, in the United States, 20 ft (6.096). In this case the planner may wish to arrange modules of movable shelving with one cross aisle in the middle of 40 ft (12.192) or with cross aisles at each end with an overhead wire management system.

One of the additional advantages of the movable-carriage system, beyond the potential space savings, is that it offers the possibility of superior protection for the collections when an aisle is closed, as it amounts to a closed cabinet. The safety floor can be integrated with the building security systems, and the electrical aspects can be locked off if provision is made for a key-operated master switch. Also, the safety floor can automatically operate the building overhead lighting for the module when a person enters an aisle, thus saving energy and maintenance expense.

The use of a movable-carriage system will essentially limit access to a given block or collection to one person at a time. It once was thought that these systems would be suitable only for paged materials or collections that have relatively limited use. However, motorized systems have been used in public areas, including along a public corridor, with no undue difficulty, although the authors would have concern about such a system with heavy user access or in a facility where immature students might regard it as a toy. These concerns reinforce the need for electrically controlled systems which employ passive safety devices.

A variation of the movable-carriage system, the second type of movable shelving, provides rows of mobile units in what would otherwise be aisle space. In this installation individual sections are moved manually, longitudinally along the length of the range to provide access to sections that otherwise would be hidden. The movement somewhat resembles methods used in solving Chinese puzzles. The shelving capacity gained is somewhat less than that gained by hinged shelving described earlier or by the movable-shelving system described above, as, except for the innermost unit, one section in a range must be left vacant. (See fig. 6.19.) As with the manual movable-carriage system, where a number of sections must be moved to create access to a hidden unit, a fair amount of pushing will be required. Where access to inner shelving is required, only one person at a time can use the system.

The technology exists to manufacture two additional types of movable shelving, which might be called the "carrousel" and the "monorail." The carrousel provides perhaps 100 ft (30.480) or more of shelving which traverses an oval-shaped track. The shelving can be programmed to stop at specific locations at an attendant station. Also, the format can be designed to operate in a vertical or horizontal configuration. Monorail shelving consists of an overhead track that carries shelving modules. The configuration can provide very dense storage in a large area. Individual shelving modules can be switched to a spur track for access. Like the carrousel, the monorail has specific units that can be programmed to arrive at an attendant's station. Both of these systems at this time would be custom installations, and they probably would prove to be expensive to install and maintain. Other systems are likely to be found more suitable for library storage.

Finally, there is a warehouse type of system called the "flow rack," in which containers are housed in racks 15 to 50 ft (4.572 to 15.240) long which are stacked from 20 to 40 ft (6.096 to 12.192) high. The containers are circulated on these racks and are retrieved, using photosensors and bar codes, to an attendant's station. While such a system is quite costly, there may be cases when land values, construction costs, and utility costs warrant its consideration for its exceptionally dense capacity. The more exotic systems may prove to be nothing more than interesting mechanical means to unimproved ends; careful analysis including cost projections over a ten-year period for these compared with proven systems would seem to be necessary.

d. *Movable access.* Warehouse storage techniques, used for many years, suggest that an alternative to other methods of compact storage is to provide shelving that is 15 or 18 ft (4.572 or 5.486) high or higher together with

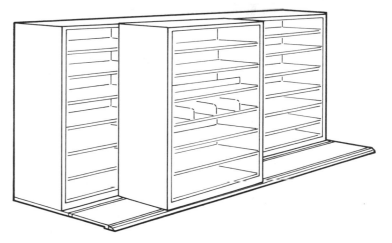

FIGURE 6.19 Longitudinal compact shelving. Here the section is moved from side to side to provide access to other hidden sections. In this illustration there could be two movable sections. While less efficient of space than the movable range, sections of this type may be appropriate in some cases.

a mechanical means of accessing the collections. Two such systems, the order picker and the Randtriever, have been used and are currently available. Both systems are quite costly; their justification probably would require unusual circumstances. Each would only be suitable in a closed-storage collection where shelving in the most compact format, that is, by size and in chronological order, is appropriate.

The Randtriever is often thought of as an automated book-retrieval system which may be tied into an automated circulation system. Library materials are stored in bins on shelves, the contents and location of each being recorded in a computer file. Each range aisle is equipped with a "master column," which moves the length of the aisle, and an "extractor-discharger," which moves vertically up and down the column. By computer control, the bin containing a desired item is removed from the shelf and placed on a conveyor, which in turn transports the bin to a centralized work station. There the attendant retrieves or refiles, as required, the items requested by the user. The bin is then returned to the shelf by a similar reverse process.

Arguments supporting the use of this system include:

Books can be housed in as little as one-third the cubic space required for standard shelving.

Stairs, elevators, and booklifts are not required for stack access.

The space need not be finished for human occupancy; savings may be realized in finishes, lighting, air conditioning, and ongoing energy costs.

Where collections are to be paged anyway, there may be significant staff savings.

Other advantages no doubt can be discovered, but these must be weighed against the significant cost of the system, the access implications, and what happens when this complex device fails to function.

The order picker is essentially a variation of the Randtriever system designed for warehouse use principally for parts or other products. While the Randtriever was specifically designed for library storage needs, the order-picker system can be adapted to book storage. This system houses the materials in tote boxes in racks which are 24 ft (7.315) high and 42 in. (1.067) deep with 15 shelf levels. The tote boxes are fetched by an order-picker vehicle which resembles an electrically powered forklift with a platform that carries an attendant to the desired location. The controls for the lift are on the platform. Movement up or down, forward or backwards permits direct access to any location in the storage rack. A variation of this system involves a computer-controlled lift which can automatically fetch a specific tote box and deliver it to an attendant's station.

With any of the compact storage techniques, the weight of the system must be considered. With movable-carriage systems a floor load in the range of 300 lbs. per sq ft (14.364 kN/m²) should be provided for. Somewhat lower floor loadings are possible with the other systems. Also, all of the movable-shelving systems are costly, but local analysis may demonstrate that their cost is less than that of additional space with standard shelving. It is clear that they can add significantly to the capacity of a given space.

Against the advantages of special types of shelving, the following drawbacks must be assessed:

1. Books are not as readily available to the reader as they would be on standard shelving, although in most cases they can be publicly accessed. Most of the systems are not appropriate for heavily used collections. Browsability is always impaired and in several of these systems it is impossible.

2. As ranges roll, sections swing out, or drawers pull out, there is danger of books falling and becoming damaged. The extent of this danger depends on the design, and is probably greater with hinged and movable-carriage shelving than with the other systems. Even with the safety devices on a motorized-carriage system, the carriage will not stop instantly; there is risk of some damage to an item left on the floor.

3. All types of special shelving have moving parts and, unless it is as well made as the old Packard or Rolls Royce engine, anything with moving parts may sooner or later fail. Design and quality of construction are vital considerations. The motors, hinges, rollers, and other parts, if well made, should be capable of standing heavy use for many years. When they do fail, means of repair or replacement should be convenient and expeditious.

4. As already mentioned, the cost per linear unit of shelf is much greater for any of these types of shelving than for standard ranges; this is inevitable in view of the moving parts and the heavier construction required. The cost may cancel out a large number, but not necessarily all, of the advantages resulting from increasing the capacity, particularly when added to the other disadvantages.

Summary. Two major questions need to be answered before one reaches a decision on whether or not to use any method of compact shelving.

1. Is the resulting inconvenience great enough to outweigh the saving in space that will be achieved? Capacity can be increased by any of the number of possibilities discussed, or a combination of them. They all have their disadvantages. It is suggested that anyone considering one of the alternatives consult libraries that have had experience with it, although a few of the techniques are either so unusual or so disruptive of operations that examples may not be easily found. Included here are the more elaborate mechanical systems where the best advice may come from warehouse facilities rather than libraries. Double and triple shelving is usually used as a last resort for, one hopes, limited periods of time; examples of this technique may be difficult to find.

2. What is the actual monetary saving that can be anticipated from adoption of any specific plan? Local conditions including land value, construction cost, salaries, anticipated

service, utility costs, as well as political or budgetary constraints must be considered. Local codes, potential for earthquakes or floods, conservation concerns, access for handicapped persons, and the nature of the materials being stored all play a role. Are there other alternatives such as microfilming, recording on a videodisc, or weeding for discard?

Many mistakes have been made in the name of economy. There are libraries that could have used one or more of the methods of compact storage to advantage, but have failed to do so. Others have used one or more of these methods with unfortunate results.

It is not easy to estimate costs accurately, and it is difficult indeed to weigh costs against convenience. What, for instance, is the dollar value of open access and collections classified by subject? Still, it is likely that over the next decade or two, there will be a far greater interest in library storage facilities with some form of compact shelving. Studies, such as one commissioned by the University of California in 1979, will be more common. In this study factors of land value, construction, equipment installation, maintenance, and staff costs were analyzed for some eighteen different compact storage systems. While local conditions play an important role, it is interesting to note that the result of this study recommended the use of an order-picker system. The final decision, however, was double-depth regular shelving. Indeed, each institution must reach its own conclusion on the basis of the economics and technology of the time. This volume can provide no one with the answer; it can only indicate the questions that ought to be asked.

Microreproductions and Videodisc Technology. As implied above, compact shelving should not be dismissed without pointing out that microreproduction of one kind or another is used much more extensively than all forms of special types of shelving put together. The advent of the videodisc is but another more sophisticated step in this direction. This is not the place for a definitive discussion of this important development, except to say:

1. It represents greater space savings by far than any of the methods described in this section.

2. The inconveniences in connection with its use and the dislike that some scholars have

for reading at a terminal or machine must be kept in mind.

3. To replace material already in a library with microfilm or videodisc storage may cost more than the savings in space are worth, unless it is reproduced in a fairly large edition.

4. Reading machines and video terminals are expensive, not very portable, and involve a good deal of extra reading area.

5. The use of microreproduction, in one form or another, will undoubtedly continue to increase rapidly in the years ahead, but not rapidly enough to reduce present requirements for storage areas for collections. In most cases, this type of technology will serve to supplement rather than replace the book as we know it. While growth rates will be affected, collections will continue to grow for the indefinite future.

6.4 Shelving in Reading Areas

Chapter 7, in dealing with the housing of readers, outlines some two dozen different types of reading areas, many of which require book shelving on a larger or smaller scale in nonstandard sizes and with different spacing. Some of them require storage for nonbook materials which will be considered under Section 6.6 below. Shelving in reading areas, speaking in general terms, tends to differ from regular bookstack shelving in four ways.

1. An effort may often be made to make this shelving aesthetically more pleasing than stack shelving, as it is in constant view of library users and therefore more conspicuous. This may make it desirable to use shelving of a more attractive or stimulating color than that in the main stack area; or to install case shelving instead of the bracket type if for one reason or another that is preferred; or to use special end panels or even shelves constructed of wood and finished as fine furniture. If the latter costs more than can be afforded (it may double the cost, particularly if oak, walnut, or a special design is used), the addition of finished-wood end panels can dress up an otherwise utilitarian shelving system. Finished bases or base supports of special design are in many cases found desirable, as are canopy tops. Each of these will add cost to the shelving, but it distinctly adds to the general appearance of the space.

2. If floor cases or shelving are used, the spacing between them is usually and probably

should be wider than that required in a bookstack. Books ordinarily placed in a reading room are there because they are heavily used; with heavy use wider aisles are advisable, the width depending upon the amount of use. A width of 3½ ft (1.067) might be considered a minimum, and from there on up to 6 ft (1.829) is not unusual, depending on local circumstances and the length of the ranges. If wall cases are used with adjacent tables for users, it is obvious that chairs should not be placed so as to back into the aisle in front of the shelving unless additional space is provided. Furthermore, the aisle should be wide enough so that the reader can consult books on the bottom shelf without obstructing the aisle. This probably means a width of at least 4 ft (1.219). At least 5 ft (1.524) is indicated if a chair on the shelving side of the table is used. Although these dimensions can be squeezed a bit, reduction will result in an increase of inconvenience and disruptions under heavy use.

3. The height of the shelving presents another problem. Wall shelving or shelving dividing a large space can go up to the standard height of 7 ft 6 in. (2.286), although it may well be held down a few inches if reference books, which tend to be large and heavy, are to be stored. Six shelves 13 in. (330 mm) on centers, instead of the more common 12 in. (305 mm) recommended for most stack shelving, may be desirable, and with a 4 in. (102 mm) finished base, the top shelf will be 69 in. (1.753) above the floor. That distance will be considerably easier for a short person to reach than 76 in. (1.930) up, as proposed in the bookstack for a seventh and top shelf. This is not intended to suggest that the shelves may be fixed; it is still of great importance to have adjustable shelving. The six shelves and a 2 in. (51 mm) molding or canopy at the top will result in a total height of 84 in. (2.134). With a reading area 10 ft (3.048) in height or higher, at least 36 in. (0.914) above the cases will remain that can, if desired, be used for pictures or prints. Still, the full standard-height shelving unit will offer a little greater flexibility to accommodate the occasional collection that is slightly higher than the average volume. Many architects and librarians will prefer to have wall shelving in a reading area built into the wall because of the pleasing appearance. (See fig. 6.20.) Some librarians feel that wall shelving in a reading area is often undesirable because readers

going back and forth to consult the heavily used volumes make the whole room more restless and noisy, even with good acoustic protection. On the other hand, a library reading room without books in sight suggests a study hall atmosphere.

When freestanding shelving or cases are used, height is a more complicated problem. If the room is high and spacious in appearance, freestanding shelving of the same height as the wall cases may be indicated. If the shelving is reduced to approximately 6 ft (1.829) in height, only five shelves instead of six will be available, but a more open feeling can be obtained. This is treading on the territory of the architect and the interior designer and is mentioned simply because it is a question that must be decided sooner or later; there is a distinct space implication that should be reflected in the program. To go down to four shelves will place the finished top at about 4 ft 10 in. (1.473), which would make it possible for a person of average height to look over the top and, in turn, would mean that heads will be bobbing up and down as people walk through aisles, which may not be unpleasant at a reasonable distance but may be disconcerting in an adjacent aisle. The fifth shelf avoids this and increases capacity, other things being equal, by 25 percent.

A height of three shelves will, if carefully controlled, bring the finished top to a level where it can be used as a 43 in. (1.092) consultation counter, with definite advantages. In a large reference collection, alternating high and low shelves in either adjacent sections or ranges can serve to assist the use of those typically larger and heavier volumes, particularly where only a short consultation is required. Use of this configuration of shelving will, however, result in readers standing at those counter-high sections obstructing access to some volumes by other persons; it may not be an appropriate approach in a busy area.

4. A final question deals with the depth of the shelves. As already noted, reference books tend to be thick, heavy, and tall. They also tend to be deep, and, as a result, many reference shelves have been specified a full 12 in. (305 mm) deep with, some would argue, unfortunate results. The number of books over 10 in. (254 mm) deep is extremely small, except for atlases and a limited number of books in fine arts and a few other disciplines; and the disadvantages resulting from shelves too deep, particularly lower shelves, may be

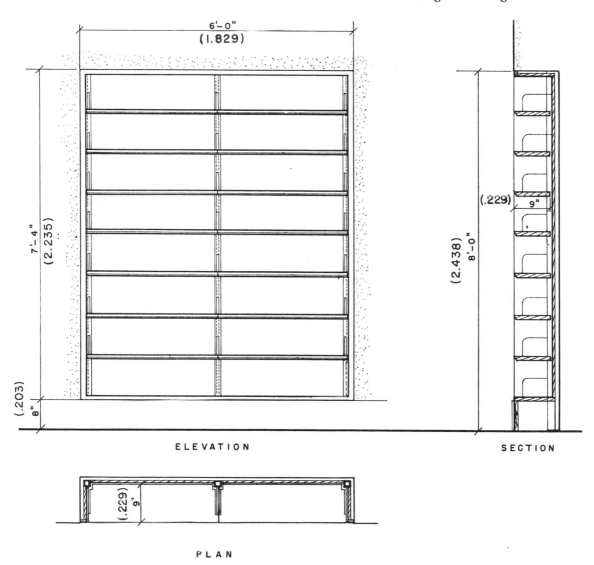

ELEVATION   SECTION

PLAN

FIGURE 6.20 Built-in shelving. Shown as used at Harvard University's Littauer Library.

so great that shelves of a 10 in. (254 mm) nominal dimension in metal bracket shelves or 11 in. (279 mm) in solid-backed wood cases should be considered. When a 12 in. (305 mm) bottom shelf is used and a 7 or even 8 in. (178 or 203 mm) deep volume is shelved on it, the volume will sooner or later be pushed back and be very difficult to find and remove. The same will happen, of course, to a lesser degree on 10 in. (254 mm) shelves. One means of obviating this problem where a whole shelf of smaller volumes occurs is to place a length of wood as a block at the back of the shelf. If this is very common, one must ask about the value of providing deep shelves and then blocking the back; however, the deeper shelves do, of course, provide flexibility to accommodate deeper volumes when collection shifts occur. If a substantial portion of the collection is larger than normal, the

advantage of having a single standard shelf dimension in the reading areas has merit. A program of shelf reading and collection maintenance should reduce the likelihood of "losing" volumes. If, as is true of regular stack shelving, the bottom or the two bottom shelves are tilted up toward the aisle, theoretically the backs of the books will be more easily seen, but the problem just discussed will be aggravated, and the bindings of heavy volumes will eventually suffer.

The block at the back of a shelf works well where the top shelf for reference or bibliographic volumes has to be set at 76 in. (1.930) or higher. In such a case the block can be of a dimension to require books such as the U.S. *National Union Catalog* and large-library published catalogs to overhang the top shelf by an inch, thereby letting one push up the volume to enable grasping between thumb and fingers, since short people could not reach to the top of the spine. Of course a narrower top shelf can also create such a useful overhang.

A word of caution in connection with the last three points made about aisle widths, height, and depth of shelves should be given. Any change from the standards used for stack shelving—that is, wider aisles, deeper shelving, and reduced height—reduces the volume capacity per unit of floor space. To this might be added the fact that obviously reference volumes occupy more linear units of shelf. Fortunately, on the other hand, while reference collections are ordinarily classified and shelved by subject, it is customary and probably desirable to fill shelves fuller than those in the stacks, removing old and outdated material when new books are received. (Reference librarians are hesitant to relegate older volumes to the stack and readily find grounds to avoid discarding from the reference collection, just as librarians tend to find reasons for not weeding for discard or transferring books from the main stack collection to storage until there is no alternative.) It is suggested that 100 volumes per standard height reference section with six shelves 3 ft (0.914) long be considered full capacity, instead of the 125 figure used in regular bookstacks; that this figure be reduced to no more than 85 volumes for five shelves, to 65 to 70 for four shelves, and to 50 for three shelves. When it comes to square footage (or square meterage) capacity, it is suggested that, with double-faced, freestanding, standard-height shelving units, if the ranges are 15 ft (4.572) long with 3 ft (0.914) of cross aisles charged against the shelving, and if the ranges are 6 ft (1.829) on centers, no more than eight volumes per sq ft (86 volumes per m²), instead of 15 (160) in a regular bookstack, or 12 (130) in an open-stack undergraduate library, be considered capacity. Where the use of lower shelving is anticipated, this figure must be adjusted downward or a contingency factor should be added.

6.5 Shelving for Miniature and Oversized Volumes

Miniature Volumes. Fortunately, miniature volumes are so few in number as to prevent their being a serious problem, but this warning seems desirable. When a volume is much, if any, under 6 in. (say 150 mm), it should not be shelved on regular stack shelving because of the potential for its being inadvertently pushed behind larger books and lost for long stretches of time, its slipping out from wire bookends, and, due to the very uneven support of much larger adjacent volumes, its causing warped bindings. Miniature books are also prone to be removed from the collection without authorization because of the ease with which they can be slipped into a pocket and the temptation they seem to present to the light-fingered. Special housing should be provided for them in a secure area. Some librarians prefer to use boxes that will hold a group of volumes of approximately the same size. One method is to use three different sized boxes, each 10 in. (254 mm) long—one for those under 6 but over 5 in. (150 to 130 mm) in the largest dimension, one for those between 5 and 4 in. (130 to 100 mm), and a third for those with neither dimension over 4 in. (100 mm). Alternatively they can be kept in accession number order, perhaps loosely laid in piles in boxes, each holding 20 or 25 volumes, or in numbered envelopes rather closely filed. These boxes can be placed on standard shelving but should, in general, never be in areas of open access.

Oversized Volumes. Section 6.2 states that 90 percent of the general collection volumes in research and academic libraries are no more than 11 in. (280 mm) high and that with standard shelving of 7 ft 6 in. (2.286) in height, seven shelves can be used for volumes up to that size. With the same height six shelves, 14 in. (356 mm) on centers, leaving room for books up to 13 in. (330 mm) can be provided for; this will care for 7 of the remaining 10 percent, leaving only 3 percent more than 13 in. (330 mm). It should be noted that if minimal shelf depth for the main stacks is provided, the shelving for oversized volumes may need to accommodate more than 3 percent of the collection because of the depth limitation. The 11 to 13 in. (280 to 330 mm) volumes may well be segregated and placed on deeper shelves spaced 14 in. (360 mm) on centers vertically.

Do not overestimate the proportion of volumes over 13 in. (330 mm) high. The 3 percent proportion was determined over forty years ago in a rather mature university library collection. Folios and elephant folios may have been published more often fifty or a hundred years ago. They were expensive scholarly works issued in relatively few copies, and so libraries today can seldom if ever find them on the market. Further, undergraduate collections will have very few if any. Branch libraries in the fields of art, anthropology, classics, and philology may have more than others. Unless a research library has a good base of oversized volumes, only 1 or 2 percent may be sufficient, depending on the fields of graduate study. By far the best basis for determination is to count the current exact holdings and project growth. Conservatism is recommended.

It is desirable to segregate oversized volumes on shelves where they can be laid on their sides, which will reduce damage from warping and save the heavy text block from pulling out of the binding. Even where the base shelf in the general stacks is intended for this purpose, there will be need for some concentrated storage of larger volumes. Shelving these volumes will require extra shelf depth, at least 12 and preferably 14 in. (305 and 356 mm) or more so as to prevent books from protruding into the aisles and being damaged. With a little ingenuity a place for this special shelving can be found. At the end of a bookstack, there may be a wider aisle where the extra depth will not be troublesome. Close to a large table and to the elevator would be advantageous. Generally, other locations will suggest themselves as the design effort progresses. It is further suggested that when bracket-type shelving uprights are used, the deep shelves be of the cantilever or flush-bracket type, so shelf ends will not interfere and space will be gained. A very few ranges of this kind will provide for the extra large volumes in most libraries, except for the newspapers, which will be dealt with later. Elephant folios, such as the Audubon *Birds of America,* or tremendous volumes, such as the set that Napoleon sponsored about Egypt, may require special treatment or custom-built housing. Industrial or commercial shelving is often used for these giant volumes. It should be noted that shelving for those very heavy volumes should not exceed shoulder height; 5 ft 4 in. (1.626) should probably be considered a maximum height for the safety of the user. Ideally, only one or two volumes would be placed on each shelf. This is one of the penalties resulting from riches of that kind; a sort of super graduated tax.

Newspapers. Most American libraries, and those in other countries for that matter, do not preserve and bind large quantities of recent newspapers because of (1) their bulk and awkwardness in handling or photocopying, (2) the cost of binding, (3) the space they would occupy and its cost, (4) the paper on which nearly all newspapers are printed is so poor that they often fragment in a generation or so and leave the library empty-handed, and, finally, (5) the availability on microfilm of most large city newspapers of importance worldwide and, in the future, in videodisc format at a cost exceeding little if any that of binding.

But there is still a large collection of newspapers in bound and unbound form in libraries throughout the world, and the storage problem is great enough in many cases to make special newspaper shelving desirable so as to increase the storage capacity for a given floor area for this material. It should be added at this point that at least a few newspapers are still issued on reasonably permanent paper and are kept by libraries because of the great demand for them. Libraries also tend to keep runs of small local papers, including the student newspaper, where conversion to microformat may be costly or generally not justified.

Bound or unbound newspaper volumes will last longer if they are shelved flat. Most papers today are no more than 25 × 16 in. (635 × 406 mm) when bound, and many are in tabloid form, considerably smaller than that. Shelves 16 in. (406 mm) deep in actual measurement are sufficient for most. If these shelves are cantilevered out from the uprights at the end of each section, four (or more, in the case of tabloids) vertical rows lying on their sides will go in three sections each 3 ft (0.914) wide, and if ranges are placed half again as far apart as standard shelving and are made from 32 up to 36 in. (0.812 to 0.914) from front to back, they will increase the capacity by nearly 80 percent over that obtained when papers are shelved on standard stacks going through from the front to the back of a range. (See fig. 6.21 and 6.22.) The same can be said about housing significant collections of other oversized volumes, although the natural tendency is to place one volume per shelf until pressure for space leads to several being stacked. Note that the brackets supporting the shelves, even though flush with the top surface of the shelf, do project down in such a way that there may be some risk of damage to the top volume in a stack

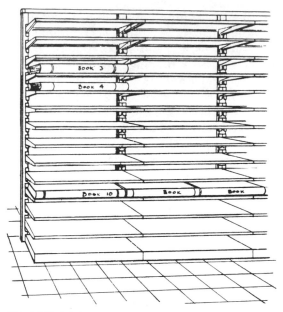

FIGURE 6.21 Newspaper shelving. When the length of a set of books is less than that of the shelf, books may overlap the shelf and thereby increase its total capacity. This is an instance when shelf labels may be useful.

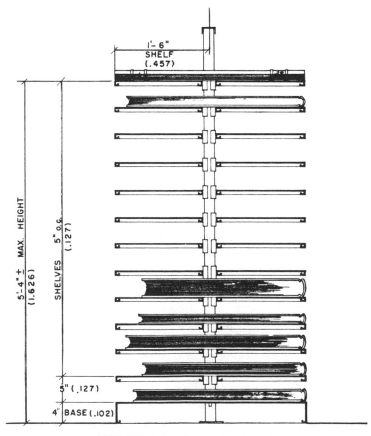

FIGURE 6.22 Elephant folios on newspaper shelving. Note that a label holder is useful for the extra tall volume on the top shelf in the illustration since the spine cannot be read.

of several if it is carelessly pushed back and if it straddles two shelves. This type of shelving configuration may suggest the use of shelf label holders described in Section 6.1, particularly where unbound volumes are housed.

A library may provide special shelving of the kind just noted if it expects to try to keep permanently any large number of bound newspapers. For heavy bound volumes or portfolios, special shelves with a set of built-in rollers can be used but are very expensive. On the other hand, if a library expects to hold its newspapers unbound and discard them in a few months, special shelving is not worthwhile, and those that are kept can be placed on regular shelving, going through from front to back of a double-faced range. As noted earlier, hanging file folders are available which can be adapted to conventional shelving for this storage purpose.

There are still a few older newspapers in existence, and, indeed, a limited number still being published, which are 36 in. (0.914) long and more than 18 in. (457 mm) deep. They can be shelved through on the extra deep type of shelving described above, with their length at right angles to the range. As with giant books, because of the weight of these volumes, they should not be stored above about 5 ft 4 in. (1.626).

Atlases. Atlases represent another common type of oversized volume. Publication of them will not decrease, and the use of many of them is frequent. Those kept in a reference collection are generally stored in specially designed atlas cases, which are made available by library-equipment supply houses or built locally to special order. (See fig. 6.23 and 6.24.) These units typically have rollers or trays which reduce the need to slide the volume over a shelf surface. They also typically have a sloped top for brief consultation of an individual volume, but as is the case with the storage of all large books, it is best to have a good-sized table nearby for more extended reading of the material. Since superseded atlases still have scholarly usefulness, the collection will grow, and all but the most heavily used may be housed in a map room. A map room, if there is one, may store atlases on shelves similar to those discussed above for newspapers or oversized books. Heavy atlases, wherever possible, should be stored horizontally.

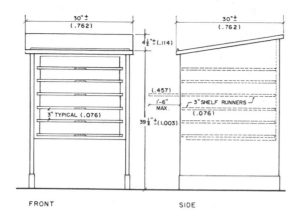

FRONT   SIDE

FIGURE 6.23 Atlas case, front and side elevations. Shelves are constructed to pull out for ease of use.

Unabridged Dictionaries. Unabridged dictionaries can be used to advantage on a slanting top, standing-height consultation table. (See fig. 6.25.) The programmer will need to identify the frequency and general location for these units to ensure that they are included in planning for the furniture. Where a number of small reading areas are planned in an open stack, it may also be convenient to provide for briefly consulted and heavily used subject dictionaries on a nearby shelf juxtaposed to the subject reading area. Larger reading areas and the general reference area, or a central location on each stack level, may be the most appropriate location for a special dictionary stand. These stands are appropriate for any briefly consulted and heavily used

tome; a counter may be best if several stands are needed, as for large manufacturing or computer science reference manuals.

6.6 Nonbook Materials That Require Special Equipment for Storage

Practically all libraries have collections of material for which special storage facilities, differing from those for books, may be desirable. They are discussed below under various headings.

Current Periodicals. Current periodicals present a special shelving problem. The basic decision to be made is whether to provide what is known as display shelving, so arranged that the cover of the magazine can be seen and readily identified, or, in order to save space, regular library shelving, on which the periodical is placed flat or in pamphlet boxes. The decision may be to display selected titles, which are the more popular issues, and house the bulk of the collection in the more compact shelving. Some libraries display only the current week's receipts and house all the back files and other titles on standard or flush bracket shelves.

Journal cover display shelving, described in Section 6.1 and illustrated in figure 6.26, is expensive and it takes considerably more space than other forms of journal storage. Furthermore, those with movable shelves (type 1 in the illustration) tend to be noisy,

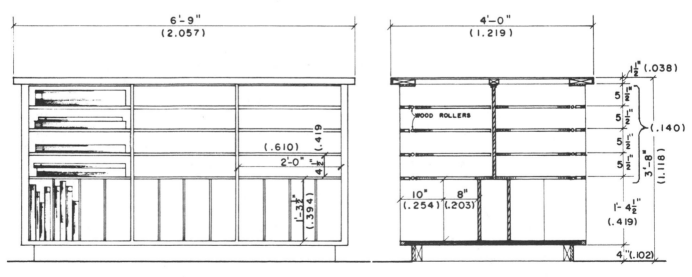

ELEVATION   SECTION

FIGURE 6.24 Custom-built atlas case, designed for the Lamont Library at Harvard.

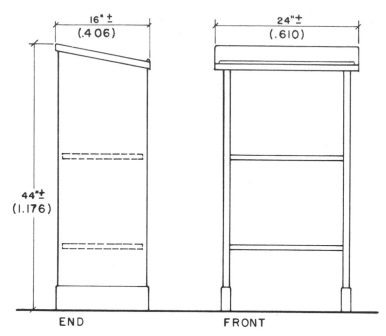

END   FRONT

FIGURE 6.25 Dictionary stand, front and side elevations. Note slanted top to aid use.

especially where sound-deadening devices are not provided. Six journal display shelves per standard section is generally considered the maximum; with 3½ titles per shelf, the capacity is 21 titles per single-faced section. At 10 sq ft (0.929 m²) per section, which is probably too little for most journal display shelving in heavily used areas, this results in 2 titles per sq ft (or 23 per m²). Even so, many librarians feel that the advantage of service to the reader justifies this type of storage. Other things being equal, journal display shelving is to be preferred, but in a library with many hundreds or thousands of current periodicals, it may be impossible or at least undesirable to use it, except perhaps in limited quantity, because of the space it requires if not because of its cost.

The generally preferred configuration for housing journals on standard shelving is to place the issues flat on shelves, often with the back of the issue parallel to the shelves (but certainly not always), and to have the shelves fairly close together, perhaps no more than 5 in. (127 mm) apart vertically on centers. Flush bracket or cantilever shelving works best for this arrangement. Labels should, of course, be attached to the shelves, to make it easier to find the desired title (a practice which is often true of the journal display shelving as well). Typically, a section of shelving of this type will hold 14 shelves, if not

limited by the height of the end bracket; assuming an average of 3½ titles per shelf, a single-faced section has capacity for 49 titles. For the sake of comparison, if we assume 10 sq ft (0.929 m²) per section, the capacity is increased by 233 percent over the display shelving.

A third storage technique is to house the journals in pamphlet boxes placed upright on standard bracket shelves. Only seven shelves per standard section can be used. Assuming that 4 in. (102 mm) wide pamphlet boxes are typically used, eight titles per shelf are possible, with a total capacity of 56 per section. It should be noted that narrower pamphlet boxes will suffice for many titles. Given a fixed floor area, this represents an increase of 267 percent over the journal cover display system. However, journals housed upright in boxes do tend to curl; many librarians feel that the damage that results is not worth the more economic use of space. Furthermore, where display shelving is not used for a particular title, it is generally more difficult for the reader to see if the most recent issue has been placed on the shelf.

A variation of the pamphlet box system involves the use of specially designed hanging files that fit into shelving units. The advantage of the hanging file is that its width is essentially adjustable to the thickness of a given title, but the materials still tend to curl. Newspapers are sometimes housed in this type of unit as well. At Rice University Library, for example, the current issues of sixteen frequently used newspapers are shelved in hanging files. Each newspaper has a separate file for each day of the present month, and below that another file labeled for each day of the past month. This permits the reader easily to locate any issue and simplifies the reshelving.

Slotted, divider-type shelving is another alternative similar to the pamphlet box. The advantage of slotted shelving is that the dividers can be placed much closer together (1 in. or 25 mm), thereby adding support and increasing capacity.

The key factor, which should not be forgotten, is the amount of use that can be expected in relation to the number of titles in the collection. Current periodical areas are among the most heavily used spaces of the library. Aisle width should be larger, particularly for a small collection with large proportionate use. It is suggested that for display shelving or even more compact standard

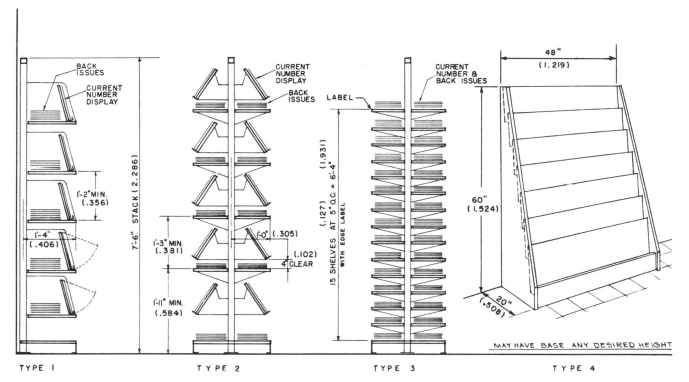

FIGURE 6.26 Shelving for current periodicals. Type 1: slanting shelving hinged at the top with storage space for unbound back numbers behind. Type 2: slanting shelving with visible storage space for unbound back numbers below. Type 3: flat shelving with current and unbound back numbers shelved flat; capacity is tripled, but advantage of display is lost. Type 4: display shelving with no space for back numbers; plastic dividers can greatly improve visibility of covers.

shelving in a heavily used periodical area, 10 sq ft (0.929 m²) per single-faced section be considered an absolute minimum; in many cases as much as 15 sq ft (1.394 m²) may be appropriate. Larger collections, where the proportionate use is less, can be housed in shelving arranged with the same spacing as the general stacks, except where absolute minimal stack spacing has been employed. The result will usually be an area requirement of between 8 and 9 sq ft (0.743 to 0.836 m²) for a single-faced section.

In any case, in a large library, current periodicals should be housed separately from the main collections and provided with their own reading area. Many large libraries accept the compromise suggested at the beginning of this section and use display shelves for a few hundred of the more popular titles or, in some cases, the current week's receipts, and standard or flush-bracket shelving for the back files and less-used issues. This has the disadvantage of resulting in two alphabets or, in the case of temporary display of recent receipts, double handling. Nevertheless, faculty and students soon get used to it, and some

prefer it. If there is an attendant to step in when help is needed, the problem will not be too serious.

A variation of this compromise is to display the popular, most-used titles on display racks, and the remainder of the collection on standard shelving behind a staffed service counter. Loss and mutilation are prompting this in many academic libraries. Unless the service counter serves other functions, this solution is expensive. However, if students have to sign up for the material taken to a nearby area, loss and confused shelving can be largely avoided and at least part of the extra cost cancelled. It may result in less use of closed-shelf titles, since it severely discourages browsing, which is of great educational value with current periodicals.

Since loss and vandalism with current periodicals are continuing problems, duplicates of certain titles on the display racks are often kept behind the scenes for binding and permanent preservation. (Shelving duplicates should not be forgotten when writing the program.) Another decision that could significantly alter the program is whether or not the runs of bound journals are to be placed in their subject classification in the general stacks, placed in the same area as the unbound collection, or replaced with microforms in lieu of binding. In planning the current periodical area, keep in mind that many journals of the future may be viewed on a screen rather than in hard copy. This is one area where flexibility is important.

Manuscripts and Archives. For manuscripts and archives, acid-free boxes of several specific sizes will be found desirable, as it is rarely wise to bind the loose sheets into volumes, and more protection is ordinarily needed than tying them up with brown paper and string and placing them on standard shelves. At least two types of boxes are frequently used; the larger records storage box often serves for the shipment or transfer of materials which are then kept in this container until the materials are sorted and processed and placed in smaller manuscript boxes.

While acid-free boxes are available in a variety of dimensions, one major source produces records storage boxes that are 10½ in. (267 mm) high with a lid that slips over the top that is about 16½ × 13¼ in. (419 × 337 mm). There are handholds on each end, and the box is ideally placed on the shelf with one handhold facing out for easy removal. With standard shelving these boxes can be through shelved, but in this arrangement only two boxes per double-faced shelf are possible, or seven boxes per single-faced section. If we assume that each section requires 9 sq ft (0.836 m²), it works out to about .8 boxes per sq ft (or about 9 boxes per m²). If 15 in. (381 mm) nominal shelving is provided, the two boxes can be placed on a single shelf although they will protrude somewhat into the aisle. Considering that the materials are protected by the boxes, this should not present a serious problem, provided the aisle width will accommodate the loss of space. If we assume that ranges are set up for 15 in. (381 mm) shelves and require 11 sq ft per single-faced section (1.022 m²), the capacity is increased by nearly 60 percent. By increasing the length of the shelves to 42 in. (1.068), a standard size with many manufacturers, three boxes can easily be housed on a 15 in. (381 mm) shelf. Adding a proportionate floor area for the added length, we find that the capacity is again increased to over 1.6 boxes per sq ft (over 17 per m²) for a gain of about 100 percent over through shelving in standard sections.

As the size of the boxes seldom changes, this may be an ideal area in which to use commercial or industrial shelving. It should be remembered, however, that the space economies suggested will be somewhat reduced if the building module does not readily adapt to the spacing requirements of larger, wider shelving. It should also be remembered that even though archival storage is usually in a closed stack, because of the size of and security for the records storage boxes, the aisles will need to be somewhat wider than those required for closed-access book storage. It is suggested that the minimum aisle width for this type of storage should be 30 in. (0.762) clear of obstructions; a wider aisle would make handling of the boxes safer. Often a rolling stepladder, which must be able to enter the aisles, is desirable for boxes stored on shelves above head height.

Smaller manuscript boxes may also be obtained in a variety of sizes; one common variety is 10½ in. (267 mm) high, 12 in. (305 mm) long, and 5 in. (127 mm) wide for letter-sized papers, and 15 in. (381 mm) long for legal-sized papers. As with records storage boxes, manuscript boxes can be shelved through on standard shelving where it is not desirable to have the boxes project into the aisles. In this case, because of the space required by the shelf columns, only six boxes per double-faced shelf are possible. Using the same space requirement assumptions outlined in the previous paragraph, this results in about 2.3 boxes per sq ft (25 per m²). Using 15 in. (381 mm) deep shelves, assuming 7 boxes per shelf, and increasing the required floor area proportionately, results in a capacity of nearly 4.5 boxes per sq ft (48 per m²) for an increase of over 90 percent. The capacity on shelves 42 in. (1.067) wide and 15 in. (381 mm) deep should be similar. Again, industrial or commercial shelving is well suited for this type of storage. Additional capacity can, of course, be achieved through the use of a mechanical compact-shelving system.

Estimates of the amount of shelving that should be provided for manuscripts and archival storage will be difficult to determine because the growth of these collections is generally more uncertain than that of books. Because of this, the partition or caging separating this shelving area from the general shelving areas in the building should allow for future adjustment of the archival stack space while maintaining security for the collections. A common technique to accomplish this is through the use of heavy wire-mesh caging fastened directly to the shelving columns in panels that project to the ceiling. If done correctly, these panels can be relocated at modest expense in the event the archive and manuscript collections grow at a faster rate than projected. Use of this technique will, of course, mean that the environmental conditions of the adjacent stack areas will be similar. For security of collections, caging should be very snug to the floor and quite close at walls and ceiling. The means of fastening the cage panels should also be carefully reviewed, and emergency egress requirements must be provided for in each stack area.

Pamphlets. Pamphlets are acquired on a large scale by some research libraries but to a smaller extent in most libraries. They may be kept in one of four ways:

1. In vertical filing cases, preferably near the reference or service desk, with their use restricted. Material in these files is generally kept for limited periods only and then discarded. Pamphlets kept in this way often get hard use and tend to deteriorate.

2. In inexpensive pamphlet binders, preferably acid-free, classified and shelved by subject in the bookstack. In an engineering library where there may be a large collection of technical reports, divider-type shelving is sometimes used to provide physical support.

3. Bound in pamphlet volumes by broad subject or author and shelved in the bookstacks.

4. In pamphlet boxes similar to those used for manuscripts, except they are typically open topped and small enough to fit on a standard shelf, classified by subject, and kept in a separate pamphlet-box file or scattered in subject locations in the stacks. The pamphlet box file is an alternative for large collections of technical reports which offers more shelving flexibility than the divider-type shelf, principally because divider shelving has serious drawbacks for book storage resulting from the upturned flange at the back of the shelf. Also, the dividers on divider-type shelves tend to be hidden by the shelved materials; eventually they may cause damage to the materials due to knifing.

Microreproductions. Microreproductions, in this discussion, includes six types: strip microfilm, reel microfilm, microcards, microprints, microfiche, and optical disks. There are advantages in making special provision for each, although some of the forms will be collected in small quantities.

There are probably more systems designed to store microforms than there are systems to store books. The major survey by Deborah A. Raikes, contained in the July/August 1979 issue of *Library Technology Reports,* tabulates over 900 devices for housing roll film or microfiche, ranging in cost from $.08 for a kraft paper mailer that holds 30 fiche to $275,000 for an automatic search and retrieval system that can house 150,000 fiche. Most libraries will find either extreme to be undesirable for storage of their collections, even though each has a place. The example is meant only to illustrate the breadth of possibilities.

Microfilm in 16 or 35 mm format represents the largest bulk of microproduction in the United States, if not abroad. Storage techniques are basically the same for both film sizes; for the sake of comparison of several storage techniques, the housing of 35 mm microfilm will be discussed here. Reels of film are generally stored in cardboard boxes, preferably acid-free, which are 4 in. (102 mm) square and a little under 2 in. (51 mm) thick. Shelving manufacturers frequently offer a special shallow shelf with a turned-up back which can be placed in standard shelving uprights. If one assumes a capacity of 20 reels per shelf, and 14 shelves per section placed 5 in. (127 mm) apart, the capacity results in about 31 reels per sq ft (330 per m²) of floor space if stack spacing is arranged for 9 sq ft (0.836 m²) per section.

A common method of increasing capacity involves storage of several boxed reels in a larger box, which is then placed on standard shelving. One such box, and there are a number of varieties, is 4⅛ × 4⅛ × 10¼ (105 × 105 × 260 mm) and holds six reels of microfilm. These boxes can easily be stacked two high on a standard 10 in. (254 mm) nominal shelf. Some libraries prefer not to stack them, but they are light enough to allow easy shelving or removal even when stacked. A three-high stack is awkward though. Stacked two high, a standard 3 ft (0.914) shelf will hold 16 boxes. With seven shelves per section, the capacity is 672 reels which, given equal shelf spacing, represents an increase of 140 percent over the shallow shelf solution. Deeper boxes are available which, given the flexibility to adjust aisle widths, will increase the capacity further. However, the larger boxes will be more difficult to manage if stacked; individual shelves for each row of boxes are recommended.

A third common storage technique involves the use of cabinets. Again, there is a wide variety of sizes available; one example is 23¾ in. wide and 28½ in. deep (603 × 724 mm). In its maximum capacity configuration, it contains eleven drawers in the basic unit with an additional five drawers of over-file storage. The total height in this case is 90½ in. (2.299), which is virtually the same as that for standard shelving. Clearly, cases of this height should be braced in a way similar to shelving in order to minimize the risk of their tipping over. Because of the space required by the drawers, the aisle space must be quite generous. If one assumes that the floor space required for a single cabinet is 2½ times the area of the cabinet, a factor that may vary depending upon the layout, then the area required for each cabinet is approximately 12 sq ft (1.115 m²). One unit of this type will hold, according to the manufacturer, 1330 reels of film, which works out to 111 reels per sq ft (1195 per m²), for a 258 percent increase over shallow shelving. It should be noted, however, that the cabinet is expensive; the example given is about $1600. Similar capacity in standard shelving with boxes would cost in the order of $700, exclusive of the cost of floor space. Assuming a construction cost of $100 per sq ft (0.093 m²), the cabinet solution is about $300 more for a capacity of 1300 reels. While this analysis may serve as an example of one way to look at the problem, it is not intended to demonstrate the best solution for a given situation. Many feel that cases offer greater accessibility than boxed materials on shelves; therefore, in some libraries a handful of frequently used titles may be in cases while the rest are on shelves. There certainly will be circumstances when the dimensions of the case will be more appropriate for a given space than shelving. Finally, the case has a more finished appearance than shelving, and it can be locked. A special purchasing agreement may significantly alter the results of the cost analysis.

The carrousel-type unit (consisting of a framework of slots for roll film which forms a circular or square column mounted on a lazy Susan–type base) offers yet another general type of storage. Most carrousels are designed for 16 mm film, but for comparison a unit that will house 35 mm film is discussed. The example is 17⅜ in. (0.441) square and 62¾ in. (1.594) high. The clear circular space required for its rotation is little over 24½ in. (0.622) in diameter. This particular unit holds up to 360 rolls of film. If one were to arrange rows of these units in a configuration similar to shelving, with two rows back to back, and an aisle space of 30 in. (0.762), the equivalent floor space required, compared to 9 sq ft (0.836 m²) or a standard single-faced section, is 10 sq ft (0.929 m²) per unit. This arrangement results in a capacity of 36 rolls of microfilm per sq ft (390 per m²) which is only slightly more efficient than shallow shelving. The great advantage of this type of unit is that it places within easy reach and easy access a maximum number of microfilm units, which is of particular benefit where a single reader station or perhaps a pair of reader stations are juxtaposed to the storage unit. Clearly, this easy access would be of special importance to a business function that relies heavily on microfilm records, though it probably makes sense for very few uses in a library. Plausible applications might be for a heavily used collection of, for example, the *New York Times*, or *Chemical Abstracts*, or the local library's supplementary catalog kept on microfilm reels. For general storage there are more efficient systems.

Warning should be given here that no library should store in its building nitrate microfilm in any form because of its explosive qualities, and that all films acquired should be examined to make sure that they are made of acetate or another nonflammable base. It should also be remembered that acetate film will dry out and become brittle and that it can be easily torn or damaged if subjected to low humidity. High humidity also results in damage which can be irreversible. Environmental control for a microform collection is particularly important.

Microfiche in libraries may represent, next to books, the largest bibliographic collection in sheer numbers, and this collection may be growing more rapidly than the microfilm reel collection. While small collections of fiche are frequently available for public access, large collections are generally housed in ways that encourage or require access through a library staff member. This is due to their small size and ease of misplacement. Publicly accessible collections may be housed in binders, table-top stands, flip files, drawers in cabinets, or small boxes. Their use seldom affects the facility space requirements, except that counter space or a special consultation carrel may be appropriate. Few libraries now house fiche (or, for that matter, roll films) along with books in their subject classification on standard shelves, though the University of Guelph and Earlham College find this advantageous. In large collections it is almost universally the practice to centralize the collections within the main library and in major branch libraries, for control and because of the equipment needed to use the materials.

One typical system for the bulk storage of microfiche involves the use of boxes which may be placed on standard shelves or housed in a special cabinet or rack. An example for 4 × 6 in. fiche is a file box with a follower block that is 5 in. high, 6½ in. wide, and 12 in. deep (127, 165, and 305 mm). This particular box holds some 500 fiche in protective envelopes. A standard shelf 12 in. (305 mm) deep nominally would hold five boxes, and with the shelves placed 7 in. (178 mm) on center, 12 shelves could comfortably be placed in a section resulting in a capacity of 35,000 fiche. Assuming 10 sq ft (0.929 m²) per section, this obviously results in 3500 fiche per sq ft (37,700 per m²). It should be noted, however, that a box this size filled with fiche will be fairly heavy and that, if dropped, it will require a considerable job of refiling. Also, in order to withdraw a single item, the box must be moved to a table or consultation counter which, in a heavily used collection, may suggest either a fair amount of additional staff time or additional space devoted to consultation areas. This situation may suggest the use of pullout reference shelves (see Section 6.1).

Another common system for housing microfiche involves the use of a cabinet similar to that used for roll film but with a different drawer configuration. Over-file storage is not available for fiche, although other forms of storage can be devised in this otherwise wasted space. As with other equipment, there is a considerable variety to choose from. One example is a ten-drawer cabinet that is 57½ in. high, 21¼ in. wide, and 28½ in. deep (1460 × 540 × 724 mm), which holds up to 36,500 4 × 6 in. fiche in protective envelopes. Use of the same assumption proposed for roll film cabinets suggests that about 10½ sq ft (0.976 m²) per cabinet should be allowed, which results in a capacity nearly equal to the shelved boxes. Of course, other examples will result in different conclusions; the illustration is meant only to demonstrate a way of viewing the alternatives. Cost will be a factor; cabinets tend to be quite expensive, but systems of boxes are not necessarily cheap. Local analysis is suggested.

Other storage devices include safes (which might be considered for master negatives), fiche carrousels, tabletop flip stands, binders, and various other devices, most of which serve specialized needs. Where a microfiche catalog is anticipated, the programmer should detail the particular needs; the floor area requirements, however, are more likely to relate to the furnishings than to the storage devices. Filmstrips, which are not particularly common, at least in microform collections in the United States, are sometimes stored in filing cases wide enough to hold a strip 35 mm, or about 1½ in. high, and up to 8 in. (203 mm) long. Filmstrips may be stored on sloping tray shelves, which hold 98 canisters of film, or in special cabinets. When a library has a collection of this type, the facility requirements may reflect the existing means of storage unless improvements are specified.

Microcards are designed to be stored in standard catalog trays for 3 × 5 in. (76 × 127 mm) cards. Cabinets similar to the fiche cabinets discussed above are available. While these cases are expensive, they are standard and house enough cards so that the cost is a comparatively minor factor. The chief problem with cards, which is similar for fiche, is that if available to the reader, and withdrawn for use, they are easily misplaced. Providing space of 2½ times the footprint of the cabinet should suffice for most collections, although this often will be minimal.

Microprint cards or sheets, which are 6 × 9 in. (152 × 229 mm) in size, can be placed in filing drawers designed for that size card. They often come from the publishers in boxes designed for the purpose, and those boxes can be, and ordinarily are, stored like books on regular library shelving.

Optical disk technology is emerging as a useful library high-density storage medium. (The Glossary distinguishes between the two types of optical disks.) One means of access has the disks self-contained within a machine similar to a juke box. Another maintains the disks in arrangements similar to those of phonograph records, which are discussed below, and kept in a staff control and service area.

Because of the capability of placing huge quantities of information on a single disk, the library storage requirements are not likely to be significant for some time into the future, though reader access stations will require space. Developments in this and other new information technology will require attention for their influence on library collections, services, and building accommodations.

All of the storage techniques discussed, including cabinets, can be adapted to compact storage, such as the carriage type of movable shelving. The increase in capacity would be similar to that found for books, as discussed in the previous section. The problem for all this material is projecting how much space one should provide for future growth. The growth of microform collections is likely to be at a greater proportionate rate than that of book collections. Local statistics of growth rates are probably the best guide. It is suggested that space should be provided for at least double the amount of that currently occupied, and that the shelving area be so arranged that allocation of space to microforms can be substantially increased in the future or the capability of changing to more compact storage techniques at a future date can be provided.

Phonograph Records and Tape Recordings.
Phonograph records for music, drama, poetry, language instruction, or archives of recorded sound require specialized storage devices, often made up of standard shelving units with divider-type shelves, although there are distinct problems that the programmer should be aware of where there are collections of significant quantity. First, phonograph records are heavy! A 3 ft (0.914) shelf of bound journals may weigh about 105 lbs. (48 kg), while a shelf full of 12 in. (305 mm) LPs will weigh about 145 lbs (66 kg) and 12 in. (305 mm) 78s will weigh 200 lbs (91 kg). Normal shelves are often designed for a maximum load of about 120 lbs (about 55 kg), thus stronger than usual shelves must be provided.

The second problem is that phonograph discs need support to prevent warpage. This is why divider-type shelving is common; however, normal shelf dividers become hidden as the shelf is filled, thereby representing a risk of knifing the materials as they are reshelved. Custom shelving designed with dividers that extend to the front edge of the shelving and have some width so that they can be seen will provide a superior means of supporting the discs. If commercial/industrial shelving is used, the method of attaching the dividers must avoid exposed bolt, rivet, or screw heads on the shelf surface in order to minimize damage to the housed materials.

The third problem is that a 12 in. (305 mm) disc in its protective jacket is actually more than 12 in. (305 mm) in dimension. This means that where one wishes to avoid having the materials project into an aisle, the next larger shelf size will be required. This is usually 15 in. (381 mm) nominal depth in standard shelf units; 13 in. (330 mm) would be preferable but it is not a standard shelf size for most manufacturers. As with oversized book storage, the size of shelf chosen will affect the space required for ranges.

Finally, phonograph discs, and tapes, too, for that matter, are dramatically damaged, if not destroyed, by extreme heat. Temperature control is essential. Many older discs are extremely fragile, as well. In earthquake country, in addition to the normal shelf bracing, consideration should be given to some means of keeping the materials on the shelf during a tremor, particularly if the collection has significant historical value, as might be the case in an archive. This consideration may suggest case shelving with latching doors, although other devices may be designed.

Phonograph disc space requirements can be projected in ways similar to those of books, using the existing collection as a base. The area requirements for individual units of shelving would also be similar to book shelving, although the greater depth requirement should be kept in mind. Custom shelving may be the best solution where maximum capacity for a given area is desired, but for the purposes of the program, standard shelving requirements should suffice for all but the largest of collections.

Open reel tapes are typically stored in their boxes on standard library shelving. Cassettes can be housed in card catalog cabinets or in cabinetry similar to the microform cabinets discussed earlier. There has been some controversy about the effect of storing magnetic tapes on steel shelving or in steel cabinets due to a possible magnetic field which could alter the stored information. Where this is viewed as a valid concern, wood shelving or cabinetry should be specified. The authors decline to make a recommendation here except to note that a lot of magnetic tape is stored in or on steel shelving. However, magnetic storage devices (i.e., tapes) should not be housed near motors or transformers.

Few libraries will find a need to house collections of magnetic computer tapes or other computer information storage devices, except for local word-processing systems or in-house mini- or microcomputer administrative processing. Publications that contain a supplementary floppy disk may be of sufficient quantity in the future to require special furniture. Currently, floppy disks are very limited in number; tabletop equipment can easily accommodate the need. If left in the books, magnetic devices such as the components of some book security systems could be a problem. When more information is needed for the program, it is suggested that local vendors or the institution's computation center can provide the information. This is a highly technical matter, and constant developments in miniaturization and packaging are altering and often easing the specifications for housing and performance.

Slides, Photographs, Prints. Slides, photographs, and prints are generally stored in filing cases selected for the purpose. The important decision relates to the suitable size of the filing drawer and the total capacity to be provided. The objects cannot be housed above shoulder height without requiring use of a stool or ladder. As with other filing cases, a factor of 2½ times the floor area covered by the case itself should generally be sufficient for programming, provided space needs for sorting tables, viewing machines, and the like are separately provided. Floor weight should be no problem in a normal installation. If the librarian has no special knowledge of the problem, it may be advantageous to consult with dealers and libraries with special collections in the field that have recently installed equipment.

Maps and Broadsides. Sheet maps, architectural drawings, plans, large aerial photographs, and broadsides are generally placed for protection in large acid-free folders and stored flat in drawers in cases designed for the purpose. These drawers may be as little as 1 in. (25 mm) deep, on the basis of a limited number of folders per drawer, which will be easier to handle, particularly the upper drawers. A commonly available case made of steel is fabricated in units of five drawers; the cases

are typically set up with two or three units plus a base, which permits use of the top surface for sorting or viewing the maps. Cases have been put together that are 6 ft (1.829) high or higher, but sheets and folders stored at this height may be damaged when they are removed from or replaced in the cases. When a drawer is so high, one's vision is cut off unless a stool is used when filing. Weight can become a significant factor when these cases are assembled to greater heights. Deeper drawers, each containing more folders, have a much larger capacity; however, a 1 in. (25 mm) stack of large sheets is very heavy, and getting materials in and out becomes more difficult as the individual stack of sheets grows. It is suggested that 1 in. (25 mm) of materials per drawer, which would be about 100 sheets including folders, should be considered capacity and that fifteen drawers in height should be a reasonable limit.[2]

Some companies design drawers in which folders are shelved vertically, as in a correspondence filing case. Architectural plans racks are similar, but in general these are not as satisfactory as flat drawers, certainly not for any sizable collection.

Roll maps present a different problem. Libraries often must store quantities of them for private study or use in classrooms. They can sometimes be fitted into frames that hold them in place vertically and might be said to resemble racks for garden tools or umbrellas. They can also be stored horizontally on brackets, but to prevent sagging, they may have to be frequently rotated. Tubes or honeycomb-type bins are also possibilities for convenient horizontal housing, though the vast variety of sizes constitutes a minor problem; if the storage unit is designed for the largest map, space will be wasted. The authors have frequently seen rolled maps simply stashed in a closet. While they are out of sight, access to items hidden in the back is difficult. An umbrella rack can work for smaller rolled maps, and in some cases a means of hanging larger rolled maps from a ceiling-mounted frame may be possible. The recommended solution is left to the devices of the map librarian; it is a detail that should be brought out in the program and can greatly influence ease of use, as well as required floor area, for the map collection.

[2] See C. E. LeGear, *Maps: Their Care, Repair and Preservation in Libraries*, rev. ed. (Washington, D.C.: Library of Congress, 1956).

The shelving equipment for reading areas and nonbook materials is ordinarily not large enough in quantity to affect module sizes seriously, and therefore it is not discussed in detail in Section 5.3. However, bound newspaper collections, institutional archives, reference collections, and even the microform collection can be so large that the module size will be of importance where shelving methods vary from standard shelving dimensions. It is suggested that if two ranges of deeper shelving take the place of three ranges for regular books, the stack module selected will work out to advantage. This may provide an aisle a little wider than absolutely necessary, but it avoids involvement with supporting columns. The lighting configuration must, of course, be considered.

7

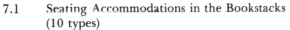

Programming:
Accommodations
for Readers and Collections

No suggested approach can serve for all given situations; each library program must be created with full recognition of all the local factors and influences. If nothing else, this chapter should expose the program writer to questions that must be considered in dealing with reader accommodations. While Section 5.2 dealt with accommodations for readers in terms of who and how many, this chapter addresses the specific needs of readers in the bookstacks, in general reading areas, and in reading areas in various subject fields, and reader requirements in terms of different types of use or materials.

Many different types of accommodations are available to the present-day reader. In many of the older academic libraries, all seating was in one or more large rooms, where books, except for those shelved around the walls, were brought to those who requested them. This concept still has merit where closed collections are planned. As libraries grew larger and readers increased in numbers, additional reading rooms came into use for current periodicals, for instance, or for other limited purposes such as public documents, reserve books, rare books, and manuscripts. As time went on, divisional reading rooms for groups of disciplines—the humanities, social sciences, and physical sciences—and for more limited subjects—such as fine arts and music—came into use, particularly in larger libraries. In the meantime, an increasing number of libraries in the United States and elsewhere began to open their bookstacks to many if not all readers. In due course, accommodations were provided in carrels adjacent to the books, and finally, over the last twenty years or so, individual table seating has been made available with certain exceptions throughout the library. Each arrangement and each room or area has its purposes and its advantages and disadvantages.

The sociology of seating arrangements is enlightened by several researchers who have shown what are regarded as good and poor arrangements. Some results will be summarized. People prefer sitting across from one another, but not directly. Chairs side by side are acceptable to most people; 15 in. (381 mm) between chairs is the most satisfactory distance, 9 in. (229 mm) is close, and 3 in. (76 mm) is quite unpleasant. Most people, but not all, prefer a semi-isolated space, giving at least a sense of privacy. Yet many prefer to feel they are part of their group (they study in comfort because their chums are there also; they are not losing out on a rap session or game), and so complete isolation is for some quite unwelcome. Extraverts will wish more group inclusion and will sit closer together than intraverts. A person whose surroundings, or personal space, is encroached upon by another will move the chair away a bit, may set up psychological protection with notebook and papers, and ultimately will seek a more protected seat the next time. Unless they are good friends, most people do not relish the feeling that someone is staring at them; they may feel awkward and perhaps self-conscious when reading and taking notes. This is so even in a college library where the reader will know a much higher percentage of library users than in large institutions. More or less taking over a room or area is a way for a group of friends to gain psychological encouragement and guard against undue invasion of personal space, not merely to be

with friends who can explain a study problem or with whom one may gossip about classmates.

These factors affect seating arrangements. Yet they are of varying importance. Furthermore, seating preferences are conditioned by other options in study places—sound and light factors, density of overall seating and occupancy, the degree of familiarity the readers have with each other, cultural mores and traditions, the variance in personalities (from the campus clown to the Phi Beta Kappa prospect), and even the difficulty and nature of the reading matter. Variation in seating options is thus needed. Varying degrees of privacy are useful. Planners should realize that studying can be hard. Until the inflatable study environment is invented, decisions on types and arrangements of seating will have to be made and lived with.

The architect should be informed in the program that the special reading areas requested must be arranged as far as possible so that they will not require additional staff members for supervision or, for that matter, for service. A service desk is hard to defend unless the attendant can be expected to be kept reasonably busy. Also, remember that many of the areas can be separated from others by shelving instead of full-height partitions. In using shelving to divide space, it should be realized that such a technique may not be suitable in busy, crowded libraries unless sufficient space is provided to access the collections without undue disruption for the reader. Shelving used to divide space needs to be carefully plotted to maintain a logical sequence of the collections. This shelving should sometimes have solid-back panels or a divider partition down the center of a double-faced range to shut out vision. Back panels can be provided by most shelving manufacturers or constructed of Masonite to form a simple, inexpensive divider. Sometimes, for acoustical purposes, glass can be placed above the top of a case running up to the ceiling; however, a single sheet of glass will transmit a fair amount of sound. Laminated glass is better and double glazing is best for good acoustical separation, but these add to the cost. Where there is a suspended ceiling, sound often passes freely over the partition, too. Often a number of stack ranges running parallel to the reading area will provide an adequate visual and acoustic barrier.

The desirability of providing multiple reading areas depends to some extent on supervision policies, which are discussed in the next chapter. The different types of rooms and reading areas in common use in academic and research libraries will be discussed in this section.

7.1 Seating Accommodations in the Bookstacks

As the years go by, a larger and larger precentage of library seating accommodation is being placed in stack areas. In the United States and Canada it is common that more than half of the total seating is in the stacks, including open and closed carrels, alcoves, "oases" (as seating clusters located amidst bookstacks may be called), studies for advanced students and faculty members, and so on. Ten types of seating arrangements are possible. They will be discussed also in the chapters on the design phases as well as in Appendix B.

1. *Standard library reading room tables.* Until about 1950 practically all seating accommodations in libraries were at reading room tables, generally in fairly large reading rooms. One of these tables accommodated from four up to perhaps twelve or even more readers. In a few libraries these tables were 4 ft (1.219) across with one chair on each side every 3 ft (0.914). This arrangement was considered quite satisfactory. But in many college and university reading rooms, in order to increase the seating capacity, tables were 3½ or even no more than 3 ft (1.067 or 0.914) wide, and in a few cases even less. Too often, in order to increase capacity still further, only 2½ or even no more than 2 ft (0.762 or 0.610) on the side was assigned for each reader. This resulted in such crowded conditions that it was almost impossible to fill all the seats, and the total use might have been greater if more space had been allowed for each reader. To make matters worse, the tables were crowded together, sometimes with several long tables in the same line without a cross aisle in between, and with an aisle no more than 3½ or 4 ft (1.067 or 1.219) between two parallel rows. The arrangement was very unsatisfactory. Even with ideal arrangements, students will tend to view a table with every other seat occupied as being in full use, the exception being the week preceding final examinations. With minimal space arrangements, serious study with full occupancy is virtually impossible. Students usually would rather sit on the floor than be forced into such minimal accommodations.

When tables for multiple seating are provided in academic reading rooms, as they should be, it is recommended that they be 4 ft (1.219) across. If task lighting is provided in a fixed position at the center of the table, a width of 5 ft (1.524) or even more in some cases may be appropriate, particularly where the table will be used to read large volumes. At least 3 ft (0.914) should be assigned along the side for each reader, and readers should never be placed at the ends of the tables. There should be at least a 5 ft (1.524) aisle between two parallel tables, although a 4½ ft (1.372) aisle is possible if the tables are only 6 ft (1.829) long. A 6 ft aisle is preferable if the tables are continuous for as much as 15 to 18 ft (4.572 to 5.486).

The authors tend to prefer four-person tables of 4 × 6 or 4 × 7 ft (1.219 × 1.829 or 1.219 × 2.134) because of the flexibility they provide. These tables can be arranged in a line when the space required by cross aisles is considered a luxury, or they can be placed as individual units. Such a table will provide sufficient space for the occasional student to spread out a large project. Futhermore, with tables of this size, the "full look" will be kept to a minimum. The structure of any multiple seat furniture must be stout enough to avoid what might be called "writers wiggle." If arm chairs are provided, the arms should easily clear the under-edge of the table. Keep in mind also the need to provide a few tables that may be slightly higher for use by a person in a wheelchair.

Architects often recommend round tables, but they result in accommodation of unsuitable shape and reduced flexibility, and so should be discouraged, except possibly in rooms for the use of current periodicals. Occasionally one may be used for what might be called "aesthetic relief." On the average, they will be used less than other tables with the same number of chairs. Tables provided for outdoor reading areas are often round. Care must be taken with exterior tables to provide a surface on which one can take notes; an open wire fabric or grille is not suitable for an outdoor reading area. Many of the disadvantages of round tables also apply to square tables for four persons.

2. *Reading-room tables with dividing partitions.* As a cross between a carrel and an open table, the divided table is provided, with low

partitions in front and often at the sides of each reading position. (See fig. 7.1.) Some librarians refer to this type of accommodation as a mock-carrel. At least a degree of privacy is obtained in that the reader's "turf" is clearly defined. If the divider is 8 in. (203 mm) high, a reader with head down to read a paper flat on the table will see little or no nearby distracting motion. With somewhat higher dividers it is possible to provide task lighting hung from the partition in front, but this form of lighting tends to result in unpleasant reflective glare. With the higher partitions the student in effect faces a blank wall; where the side partitions are also high, one cannot see out without leaning back in the chair, and then the next-door neighbor is uncomfortably close. In the case of tables for only four, or with low partitions, this problem is largely avoided. As used at the J. Henry Meyer Memorial Library, Stanford University (fig. 7.2), and the University of Texas, Austin, Undergraduate Library, the mock-carrel serves those students who prefer to be able to see around while at the same time feeling a need for a well-defined spot. The table with high dividers, on the other hand, serves the same function as a line of carrels placed side by side, but with a great deal less flexibility for future arrangements. As with open tables, it is essential that the structure be stout to avoid movement as a vigorous writer works. The minimum dimensions of the divided work surface should be similar to those provided in carrels.

3. *Slanting-top tables.* The only difference between these tables and those that have been described above is that their tops slant downward toward the reader; the slant makes it easier to read a volume that lies on the table and also helps to prevent the glare that too

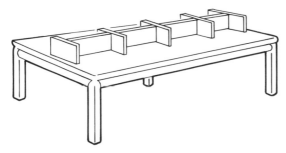

FIGURE 7.1 Divided reading table, or index table. Extending the table top dividers to the table edge would make what is sometimes called a "mock-carrel." See fig. 7.16 for a more common index table configuration.

often reflects from the table into the eyes of the reader. (See fig. 7.3.) Index tables are often a variation of this type of table, with a double-faced set of one or two shelves running down the center. Another variation is a table designed for the reading of exceptionally large volumes, such as might be found in the art library or a newspaper reading room, whose reading surface is of increased size. If the slant is too great, the book tends to slide down into the reader's lap, unless there is a molding or stop of some kind to prevent it. Where such a very low molding is specified, it must be of a durable design, as some readers will tend to pick at it and, in many cases, ultimately mutilate it. A limited number of tables of this kind can be useful, as at least some readers prefer to work with their books slanting slightly toward them. In the original furnishings for the Lamont Library at Harvard, about 3 percent of the seating accommodations were of this type.

4. *Tables in reading alcoves.* Tables resembling those described above may be placed in alcoves with books and shelving on at least two sides, a third side often being an outside wall with a window and the fourth opening into a larger reading or stack area (see fig. 12.10). A nest of four individual tables or carrels in a pinwheel arrangement can sometimes be used to advantage with an alcove if it has inside measurements of at least 11 ft (3.353) and preferably 12 ft (3.658). Additional space is required where the individual tables or carrels are larger than the 2 × 3 ft (0.610 × 0.924) tables illustrated, as may well be the case in graduate research libraries and even certain undergraduate libraries.

The above arrangement has the advantage of placing the readers close to books. Alcoves adjacent to large monumental reading rooms were common in the nineteenth century and a few very early twentieth-century buildings, with a central hall going up to the roof and one or more levels of balcony or gallery alcoves on mezzanines along the sides. While the passageways between the reader and the bookshelves were generally narrow, the number of readers wanting to consult the books in any one alcove was small enough so that their movement was not too disturbing. If the alcove has the proper dimensions, this is an economical arrangement for book storage and reader accommodations as far as floor area is concerned.

One problem in connection with alcoves, at least in the eyes of some librarians, is that

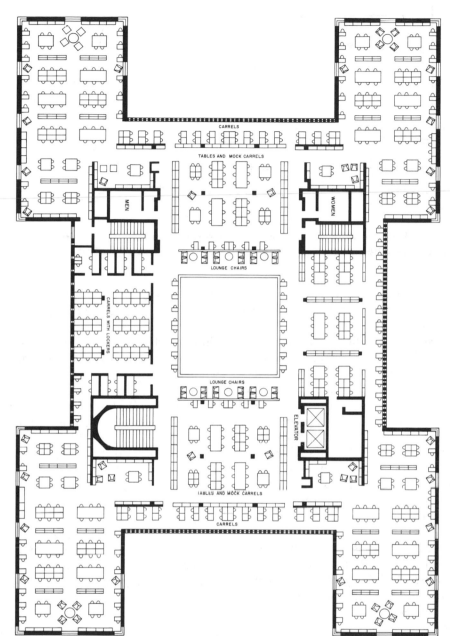

FIGURE 7.2 J. Henry Meyer Memorial Library, Stanford University. In approximately 23,000 sq ft (2140 m²), the mixture of seating includes 230 at carrels (33%), 76 at lounge chairs (11%), 150 at mock-carrels (22%), 214 at tables (31%), and 22 in small studies (3%). Subtracting the area provided for shelving (about 415 sections), the seating works out to about 27 sq ft (2.5 m²) per reader, including circulation space on the floor.

they have occasionally been arranged in what amounts to a maze. Such an arrangement makes management of the collections somewhat more difficult, and the reader seeking a seat may feel some degree of frustration in wandering from alcove to alcove looking for a suitable spot. On the other hand, many students like to discover a place that may not be so obvious; they like the maze character as it may be found at, for example, Northwestern. While there is no doubt disagreement on this

issue, it has been argued by many, including Mr. Metcalf, that it is exceedingly important to develop the simplest possible circulation patterns throughout a library, particularly in main corridors, bookstacks, and reading areas. This point of view has much merit, even though there may indeed be valid circumstances that lead the design toward a maze-like solution. It should also be remembered that emergency egress and certain aspects of security are facilitated by clear and

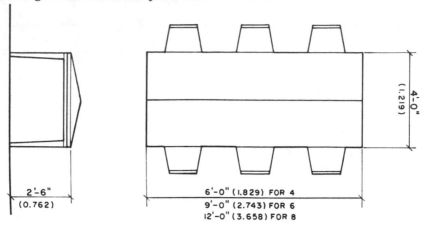

6'-0" (1.829) FOR 4
9'-0" (2.743) FOR 6
12'-0" (3.658) FOR 8

FIGURE 7.3 Slanting-top table. Avoid too steep a slant, which will necessitate a molding that may damage books when pages are turned and may be picked at and mutilated.

direct circulation patterns. Graphics in the form of directories, floor plans, and directional signs are always a poor substitute for an obviously simple and direct arrangement. Finally, some librarians feel that alcoves introduce an undesirable level of inflexibility, particularly in a general reading room. The means of creating the alcoves can play an important role here. Also, depending upon how the carrels or tables are constructed, the pinwheel arrangement may be inflexible, susceptible to rearrangement by users, or there may be added cost in order to ensure flexibility and discourage creative arrangements.

5. *Individual tables or carrels in a reading room or stack area.* Individual tables or carrels have been used in the past where they were placed with an aisle on each side so that each table was at least 2 ft (0.610) from an adjacent one. (See fig. 7.4.) Tables so placed take somewhat more space than other arrangements, particularly if adequate aisles are provided. However, if individual tables are against a wall and at right angles to it, with an aisle on one side only—one that is required under any circumstances—floor area can be saved. Over the last twenty-five years the use of individual tables of the open-carrel type in reading rooms or stack areas increased to 50 to 75 percent or more of the seating capacity in an academic library. However, there are those students who prefer tables for four or more readers or other accommodations; it would likely be an error on the part of the planner if individual tables or carrels represent over 65 to 75 percent of the accommodations. People vary greatly in their preferences.

Individual tables or carrels present five problems. How large should they be? How

can they best be separated from their neighbors? How can lighting be provided to minimize shadows and reflective, as well as peripheral, glare? How much gross space do they take? What happens to the overall cost figures when they are used?

Some librarians feel that an undergraduate student, working with one or two books only or with one book and a notebook, can manage in a pinch with a table 30 in. (0.762) wide by 22 in. (0.559) deep if the tables are not placed side by side. This size is exeedingly small; the authors do not recommend the use of tables this size except in very unusual circumstances. The preferred dimensions are 36 in. (0.914) by at least 22 in. (0.559). Individual carrels as large as 42 × 24 in. (1.067 × 0.610) have been used in undergraduate libraries. Even though students no doubt like them, many librarians would consider their size luxurious. For a student working on a major paper or a thesis, though, it is none too large. In fact, at Stanford's Cecil H. Green Library carrels with a working surface of at least 8 sq ft (0.743 m²) were specified for the open reading areas. These are well used and liked by the students although they probably represent the upper end of the scale of carrel size, with the exception perhaps of carrels provided in rare-book, newspaper, microtext, and art reading areas, which may be in the order of as much as 10 sq ft (0.929 m²) depending upon their design and use. When it is affordable, many faculty and advanced students would undoubtedly be pleased and benefited by as much as 4 × 2½ ft (1.219 × 0.762) or 10 sq ft (0.929 m²) of reading surface. (For writing a major paper, the dining room table at home is often commandeered.)

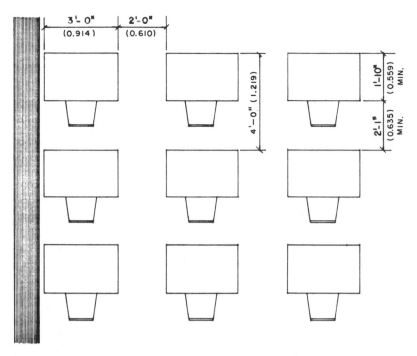

FIGURE 7.4 Individual tables in reading rooms. These are exceedingly small tables for anything but reading. The arrangement is not recommended because of poor space utilization and because of the confusion and disturbance arising when one goes to or from a seat.

In the Lamont and many other libraries, individual tables or carrels are placed frequently at right angles to the walls of the reading areas. In Lamont they are 4 ft 4 in. (1.321) on centers and attached to the walls to prevent their being moved. (One of the problems that often results from small tables is that they are easily moved and an untidy appearance can result. This problem is reduced where there are electrical connections which limit the possibility of creative arrangement or where the units are sufficiently heavy so as to discourage movement.) Similar individual tables can be placed on both sides of screens and at right angles to them in a reading area. Then, with a partition the same height in front and back but with an open aisle on the fourth side, practically individual accommodations are obtained and, again, no undue amount of space is used. Figure 7.5 illustrates that partitions at least 4 ft 4 in. (1.321) high are required to prevent all visual distraction. Arrangements of this kind have been used on a large scale in a number of libraries. Central libraries of the University of Wisconsin and Brigham Young University in Provo, Utah, provide good examples.

Double carrels with readers facing in opposite directions are another means of providing almost individual accommodations.

Carrels of this kind can be found at the Douglass College Library at Rutgers University in New Brunswick, New Jersey, and at the Uris Undergraduate Library at Cornell. If they are staggered, they give more seclusion and take very little more space. Various arrangements for double- and triple-staggered carrels are possible and are described in Chapter 12.

Individual seating can also be provided in almost any bookstack by omitting two ranges of shelving and replacing them with one double row of carrels, with a screen running between the double rows. (See figs. 13.12–13.14.) If ranges are 4 ft 6 in. (1.372) on centers, the tables or carrels can be 3 ft (0.914) wide, and there is still space for a 3 ft (0.914) aisle on each side before coming to a bookcase. If the ranges are only 4 ft 3 in. (1.295) on centers, the tables and aisles must be reduced to 34 in. (0.864). Both configurations provide minimal reader space, but they are probably adequate as supplementary seating or seating in an essentially undergraduate library. While it is true that readers will occasionally come down these stack aisles to obtain books, the number of persons using any one aisle should not be great enough to cause much difficulty. There are many seats of this kind in the Louisiana State University Library in Baton Rouge and a still greater num-

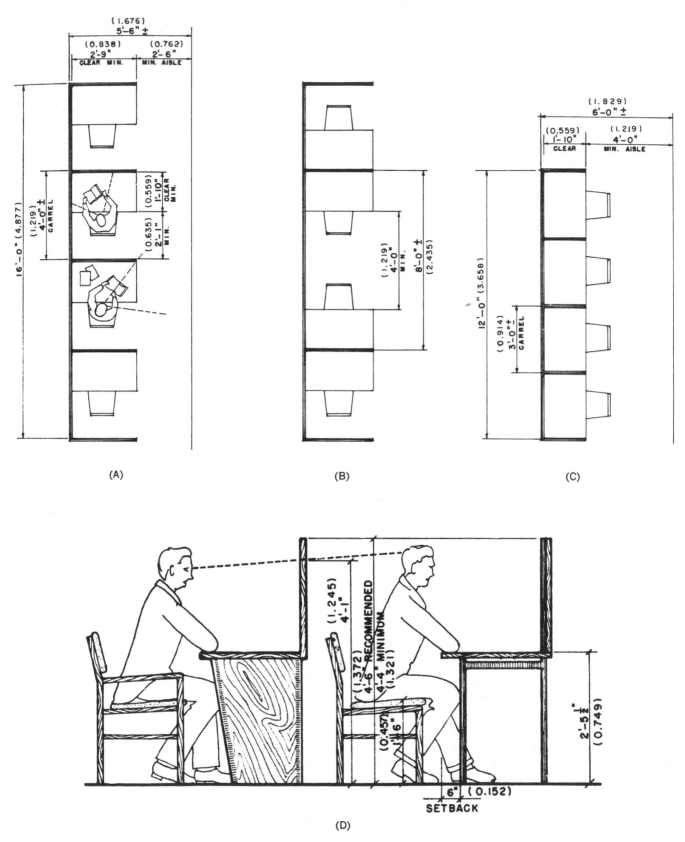

FIGURE 7.5 Open carrels along a wall or a partition at least 52 in. (1.321 m) high. (A) Carrels along a wall facing the same way (recommended). (B) Carrels along a wall in pairs. In both examples the space for the chair is very constricted, requiring the setback of 6 in. (0.152 mm) shown in D. (C) Carrels facing a wall (not recommended). (D) Carrel elevation to show desirable height of partitions to prevent visual distraction.

ber in the Louisiana State University Library in New Orleans. (See fig. 7.6.) These double rows of carrels can also be placed in reading areas between parallel rows of standard reading tables.

Another arrangement is to place individual seating on the periphery of a bookstack, preferably adjacent to the outside aisle or even at the end of a blind aisle along an inside or outside wall. If tables are next to a window, so much the better, although glare may sometimes be a problem. Either the window should not go to the floor or some form of a modesty panel should be provided. Long rows of tables or carrels, with a window for each, can

be found in Cornell's Olin Library as well as the libraries at the University of Utah and the University of California at Los Angeles.

Individual carrels placed at the end of blind aisles can be arranged within the range spacing. If the ranges are as close as 48 in. (1.219) on centers, the chair must be fairly small and without arms in order for a reader to get into it easily, and the table leg next to the aisle and the reader should be set in at least 6 in. (152 mm) toward the back of the table. (See fig. 7.7.) This usually means that the tables must be fastened to the wall or floor to keep them steady. With carrels on 51 to 54 in. (1.295 to 1.372) centers, there is adequate

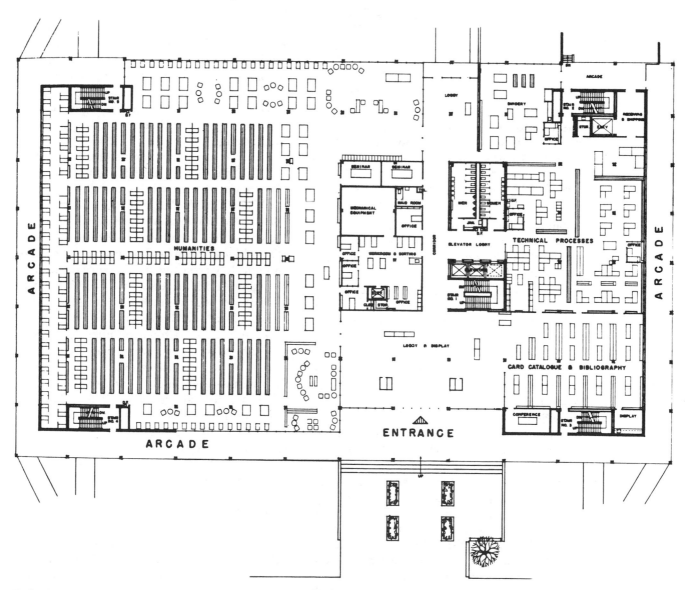

FIGURE 7.6 Louisiana State University Library, Baton Rouge. An example of the use of double rows of carrels. A lot of space is devoted to circulation in the arcade and entrance lobby, perhaps at the expense of constricted space in other areas.

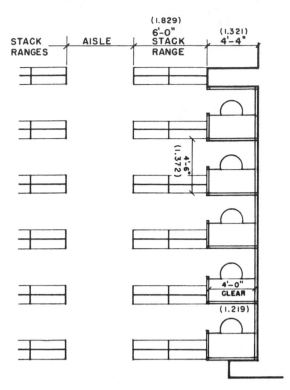

FIGURE 7.7 Carrels at range ends. Carrels like these, without doors but in an area with acoustically treated walls and ceilings, have been used successfully for typing. They also provide an excellent sense of privacy, although the spacing as shown is minimal.

room for an armchair, particularly if the carrel is not more than 23 in. (584 mm) in depth; 21 or 22 in. (533 or 559 mm) is possible but hardly desirable.

Nonrectangular carrels and tables in the form of an L or a modified L represent another approach. Generally, they will result in somewhat greater space requirements, but with careful design, they can create a very pleasing atmosphere with a sense of reduced formality that is common with the previously discussed examples. Where task lighting is provided under a shelf, this type of carrel can be arranged so that the light comes across the book at an angle, which reduces the reflective glare that is always a problem with this kind of fixture. One example (patented by Marquis Associates of San Francisco) may be found in the Cecil H. Green Library at Stanford and the California Polytechnic Library at San Luis Obispo. This particular form can also be used to incorporate a high intensity kiosk-type ambient light fixture in the center of a pinwheel arrangement, although other arrangements can be developed similar to the standard rectangular carrel. (See fig.

7.8.) It should be noted that L-shaped carrels tend to be right or left handed, thus a mixture of the two possible orientations is recommended. Another variation of this general pattern may be found along a wall at the Lilly Library, Earlham College in Richmond, Indiana.

With careful planning, individual accommodations of freestanding tables or carrels can be provided in approximately the same floor area as that occupied by regular seating accommodations, with similar table area assigned to each seat in a large reading area. The nonrectangular carrels require some additional space, though it should not be substantial. The furniture cost will be higher, though, as it simply costs more to construct four individual tables or carrels, each with its own structural support, than it does to construct a single four-person table. While all seating should not be at individual carrels, the advantages of carrels are significant, and in most cases the added costs are justified. Carrel and individual table arrangements are discussed again in Chapter 12 on the schematic design.

6. *A tablet armchair.* Chairs of this kind (see fig. 7.9) have been used for many years in classrooms. Thomas Jefferson designed one for his own study, apparently finding it more convenient for certain types of work than a table and regular chair. There is no reason why tablet armchairs should not be used, although they typically are not very decorative and they tend to result in a confused and irregular traffic pattern. Until 1983 in the Music Library at Stanford, where space was severely restricted for a number of years, a few tablet armchairs were placed in range aisles. While this use is extreme, it does illustrate possible supplemental seating where there are few alternatives. The College of Agriculture Library of the University of the Philippines in Los Banos placed tablet armchairs on three walls of a large reading area as close together as they could stand, just over 2 ft (0.610) on centers, and the report from the librarian was that they have been heavily used. Of course, this may be because of limited accommodations at other seating. Even so, there may be a place for tablet armchairs in a library, and some lounge chairs have an arm wide enough to serve somewhat the same function.

7. *Lounge or semi-lounge chairs without a table or a tablet arm.* Lounge chairs in a library al-

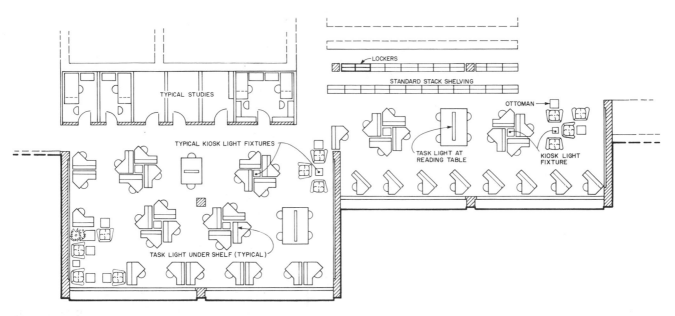

FIGURE 7.8 Cecil H. Green Library reading area. An example of a variety of seating accommodation. Note that the arrangement of lounge chairs is designed to discourage conversation. The lockers are slightly removed from the reading area to help control the noise they often produce, and the collections are located well away from the windows.

FIGURE 7.9 Tablet armchair used in place of chair and table. A tablet which slides on and off the arm is used with an attractive chair for a multipurpose meeting room in Stanford's Meyer Memorial Library. A much larger arm, such as Thomas Jefferson designed, would be more suitable but would take more space, be less stable, and might not be aesthetically pleasing.

most always stir up a controversy. (See fig. 7.10.) Some librarians feel that they are often too large, particularly in browsing areas, and therefore take too much space, are unnecessarily expensive, and encourage the occupant

to slumber and to stretch out and obstruct the aisles. Students like to arrange lounge chairs to create nests or, in effect, a bed. One chair is often used as a footrest for a second chair, a situation that can largely be avoided by providing proper footstools or, in problem areas, securing the chairs to the floor. On the other hand, many feel that a chair with a padded back, padded seat, and perhaps padded arms, if properly designed, may be more comfortable than a regular library chair, and it should require no more space than a chair with an associated table or carrel. (Padded arms will ordinarily wear out before the rest of the chair.) A number of lounge chairs can be used to advantage in current periodical rooms and in other areas. Almost always a certain percentage of readers, if not taking notes, prefer to sit in a somewhat larger and more comfortable chair. A great many of these chairs have been used in libraries, not only in the current periodical area, but in browsing areas and even in the stacks. Public multi-seat furniture (couches or love seats) should not be used at all in reading areas.

If 8 to 10 percent of the total number of seating accommodations are of this kind, the number should be quite adequate in most academic libraries. Lounge chairs usually can be purchased for little more and sometimes less than a chair and an individual table, or

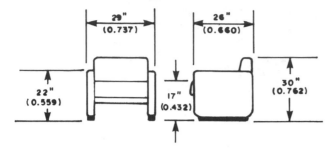

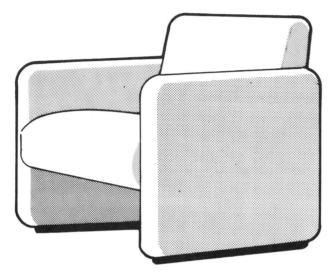

FIGURE 7.10 Lounge chair. **While some would argue that such a chair is unduly expensive, uses an unneccessarily large amount of floor space, and encourages slumber, they are popular in libraries and they do add comfort and variety in seating. Use of footrests is recommended with this type of chair.**

even a chair and a section of a larger table. They are sometimes used to break up the monotony of a long row of tables or carrels. They can be used successfully in pairs, or even in clusters of three or four, if they face at least slightly away from parallel or are provided with small side tables, preferably 12 to 24 in. (305 to 610 mm) wide to give a place to rest books and at the same time to separate two readers, thus reducing the likelihood of conversation. Single units of two or three chairs with associated tables are possible, but they reduce flexibility for future arrangements. If footstools aren't provided, small, unattached tables will tend to be used for this purpose.

8. *Enclosed carrels or dissertation rooms.* In some cases carrels are completely closed in by walls of some kind; if so, they must be larger in size than would otherwise be necessary in order to prevent claustrophobia.

Where they are not properly designed with adequate light, ventilation, and size, they have seldom proved satisfactory. However, where there is a desire to provide full enclosure so that the user can lock the cubicle, leaving papers and books spread out and secure, then closed carrels make sense even if some must be located within the interior of the library. Location of enclosed carrels would be ideal along an exterior wall, each carrel with a window; but as a number of functions would ideally have a similar outlook, some compromise is usually necessary. For ventilation the carrel walls may be designed to come short of the ceiling, but this can cause a problem if there is sufficient space for an intruder to climb over the wall, as there initially was in Stanford's Green Library East Wing. The door can be fitted with a louver or undercut an inch or two (25 to 50 mm) to further aid ventilation. The dissertation rooms at Stanford are 5 × 6 ft (1.524 × 1.829), with the work surface being the full width of the cubicle and 30 in. (762 mm) deep. Each cubicle is provided with a two-drawer file, the equivalent of one single-faced section of shelving mounted on the inner wall, and a door fitted with a panel of glass. Typing in such a cubicle is a problem acoustically. In this case certain blocks of dissertation rooms might be assigned for those who insist upon typing. Clearly, these should not be near open reading areas, but where they can be well isolated acoustically, such as where a double row of cubicles displaces three ranges of shelving in a large stack area. Similar units may be found in the Firestone Library at Princeton; they are well used at both institutions. As with all seating arrangements, care should be taken to provide for handicapped access. It will affect the door as well as the height of the work surface of enclosed carrels. The doors on the Princeton cubicles are sliding, which, if they are wide enough, would work well for this purpose. Four-person cubicles have also been used with good results at Princeton (see fig. 7.11).

9. *Studies of various sizes, ordinarily for one or two persons.* These are often referred to as faculty studies. (See figs. 7.12 and 7.13.) Most academic institutions feel that they should provide individual studies only for faculty members. Independent research libraries often provide some for selected long-term fellows or visiting scholars with special needs. The studies may be essentially like the dis-

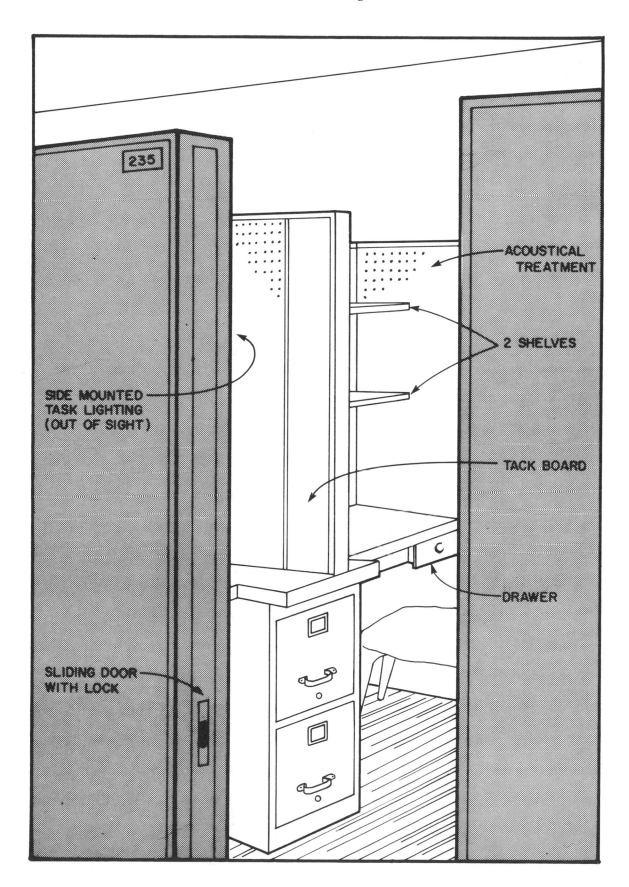

FIGURE 7.11 A four-person cubicle with two seats to the right of the door. This configuration is similar in plan to the typing room (fig. 7.7).

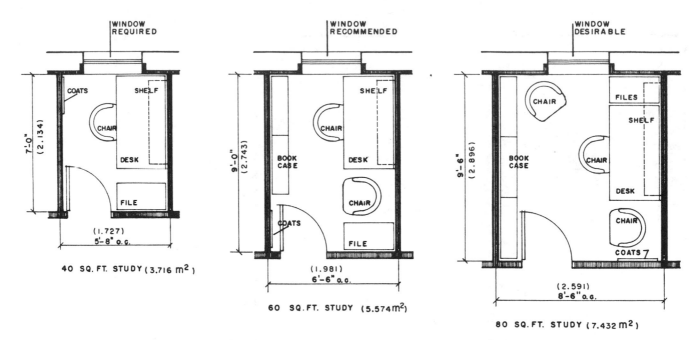

FIGURE 7.12 Faculty studies of different sizes. The study at the left is the minimum size for a completely enclosed room, and a window is required. The one in the center is adequate if there is a window, but it might be complained about without one. The size of the right-hand study is generous; while a window is desirable, it can be omitted if a clerestory window opening into a lighted bookstack or other area is provided.

sertation rooms described above, or they may be a good deal larger, with added shelving, a coatrack, a side chair or a lounge chair, increased file space, and a typing stand. A reasonable minimum size can be 65 sq ft (6.039 m²) to 70 sq ft (6.503 m²); studies with a window can be smaller. They should be provided with full-height walls for acoustic privacy and, like the dissertation room, have glass either in the door or next to it. The reason for glass is simply to aid the closing procedure (a light left on in a study can readily be seen), while giving the occupant of the study a slight sense of greater space with the door closed.

Even though very satisfying philosophical arguments can be made in support of faculty studies, their real need is sometimes more political than actual. This is not to suggest that a library should have no faculty studies; Harvard's Widener and Stanford's Green each has over one hundred. Rather it is intended to remind the planner that many of these spaces will not be heavily used, particularly where faculty have individual offices; yet studies are always in demand, at least in terms of assignment. Visiting scholars also need consideration; faculty visit and use research libraries other than their home library, and the reciprocity of accommodation should be recognized in reasonable number

and quality. Along with the planning for the facility, a very careful assignment policy should be established, ideally with faculty support. This policy should include a means of reassignment to other persons or uses in the event a study is not used. It should also be realized that the addition of significant numbers of closed spaces like studies or dissertation rooms will measurably increase the collection management function, as each space represents a niche which can house library materials which are not properly charged out, which, in turn, means that another reader will not be able to find them. Clearly, faculty studies and dissertation rooms need careful planning.

10. *Other seating.* There is one or more miscellaneous seating type for every standard library seating accommodation described. Swarthmore's library has a reading pit, which is a depressed floor area with steps serving as casual seating accommodation. The Penrose Library at the University of Denver once had a furniture form which was just the reverse. It formed a stepped mound which, being covered with carpet, provided a popular seating area. Carpet itself can be thought of as providing potential seating; in fact some students rather like sitting on the floor in the stack right where they find the item they wish to

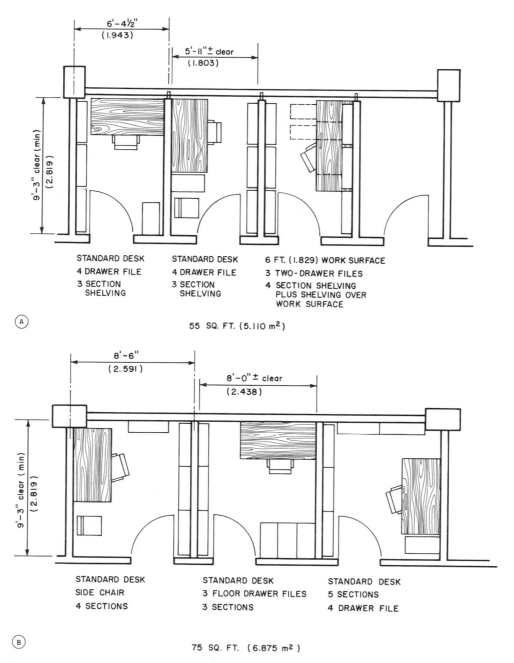

A

55 SQ. FT. (5.110 m²)

STANDARD DESK
4 DRAWER FILE
3 SECTION SHELVING

STANDARD DESK
4 DRAWER FILE
3 SECTION SHELVING

6 FT. (1.829) WORK SURFACE
3 TWO-DRAWER FILES
4 SECTION SHELVING PLUS SHELVING OVER WORK SURFACE

B

75 SQ. FT. (6.875 m²)

STANDARD DESK
SIDE CHAIR
4 SECTIONS

STANDARD DESK
3 FLOOR DRAWER FILES
3 SECTIONS

STANDARD DESK
5 SECTIONS
4 DRAWER FILE

FIGURE 7.13 Alternative layouts of faculty studies. The smaller studies (top) are on a window wall while the larger studies (bottom) are in an interior space. Both examples are based upon a building bay module of 25 ft 6 in (7.772 m).

read. The Hillis Library at Radcliffe provides cushions for students to spread about on the floor at peak hours. Double-deck carrels have been suggested, and the authors have seen one carrel designed to hang off the edge of a balcony (Law Library at the University of Michigan, Ann Arbor). The point is that the librarian should be open to suggestions from the designer even though a great deal of thought will have been put into the program detailing the exact needs of the library. As long as there are active imaginations, there will be new and unique solutions to the problem of seating. The librarian should review unusual solutions in the context of cost, functionalism, and flexibility. There is still merit in providing what has worked well historically.

7.2 Reference Rooms or Areas and Bibliographical Collections

As suggested in Section 5.3, dealing with relationships of various functions, reference service and related book collections are preferably placed on the entrance level where space is at a premium, close to the main entrance lobby and the card catalog, and not far from the professional staff of the processing department. If the reference space is larger than necessary, it is likely to be used by persons simply looking for a place to read, as well as by those wanting reference information. Experience shows that the number of persons actually using reference books at any one time is comparatively small, even in very large libraries.

In many of our older university libraries, large reference reading rooms seating hundreds of readers can be found, although many of them are being converted to other functions as the main library is replaced with a new facility more suited to the philosophy of open-stack access. In a number of cases, the old monumental reference room now serves as a rare-book reading room, an undergraduate library reading area, or, in at least one case, a map room. These reading rooms were originally designed to be filled with large reading tables and to have walls lined with bookcases. One reason for making these rooms so large was to provide sufficient wall shelving for the reference collection. Wall space is not a significant factor in figuring book capacity, particularly where there are windows coming down to the floor. It was not uncommon for freestanding shelving to be added between the tables to make up for the limitations of the wall surfaces, and as shelving is added, it is never difficult for a wide-awake reference staff to fill all the shelving available with reference books and then look for more. These rooms have had the disadvantage of making it necessary for the user of the reference books to travel long distances to find the material wanted, and as a result, the rooms almost always give an impression of restlessness and tend to be noisy. Lighting them usually is a problem, at least after dark; in many cases general lighting from the ceiling and skylights or windows has been supplemented by lighting over the bookcases and by table lamps or, in current jargon, task lighting. While reference works continue to be published, developments in electronics already suggest that information access by computer terminals may lead to a reduction in the size of large reference book collections early in the next century.

But to go back to the optimum size of a reference area: Even in a great academic library, it is unlikely that more than 50 readers will use the reference collection at one time for reference purposes, and it is suggested that, unless a good reason can be found for a larger number, fewer than 100 seats are adequate for reference space in an academic library, except in cases where it is expected to be used for other purposes as well. Obviously a room seating no more than 50 persons, with 30 or even 35 sq ft (2.787 or 3.252 m²) per person allowed, will not have enough wall space for the shelving required by a large reference collection. The valuable periphery of the room might therefore be used for individual seating, with seats along at least two or three of the walls, and the books might be concentrated in double-faced floor cases, either in the center of the room or at one end or side. (See fig. 7.14.) If books are at one end or side, and if the space is high enough, a mezzanine over the reference collection may make comparatively inexpensive additional floor area available and also absorb under it some of the inevitable noise. However, the problems of access and collection management need to be considered; for example, will elevator access be required? There are other techniques to deal with noise, and with the addition of a mezzanine, particularly one supported by the shelving below, a certain amount of flexibility will be lost.

Careful study should be given to the spacing of the bookcases. If they are kept down in length to 15 ft (4.572), for instance, and if there is a good cross aisle at each end, there seems to be no reason why reference collection shelving should be more than 6 ft (1.829) on centers even if the shelving is made extra deep, except perhaps as the building module may dictate. Since reference books on the average are larger in size than others, it is quite customary to provide shelves for them up to 12 in. (305 mm) in depth, and usually only six shelves per standard section. But this would still leave an aisle 4 ft (1.219) wide, which is enough to enable two persons to pass readily on the occasions when two readers are working in the same aisle at the same time. As noted in Chapter 6, some libraries have found 12 in. (305 mm) deep shelving to be a nuisance because books may be pushed back and may become hard to get, particularly on lower shelves. If the aisles are dead-end, the length of the ranges should not exceed 9 to 12 ft (2.743 to 3.658).

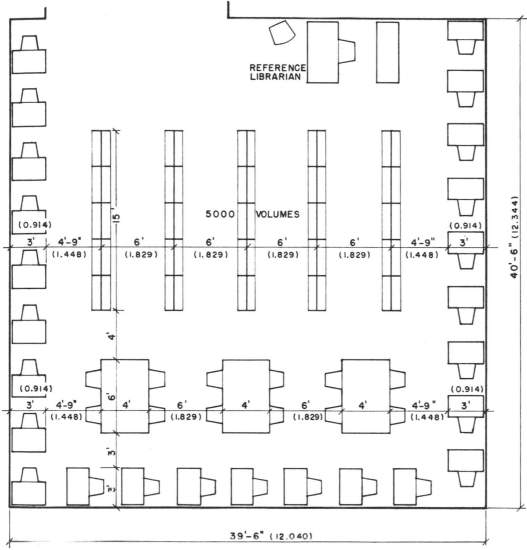

FIGURE 7.14 Reference area for 5000 volumes and 37 readers. This area of 1600 sq ft (about 150 m²) provides approximately 30 sq ft (2.79 m²) for each reader and 10 volumes per sq ft (108 volumes per sq m), if figured at 100 volumes per section for the collection. This can be considered as minimal spacing; it does not include elements often found in a reference room such as index tables, an atlas case, a computer terminal, or a card catalog, all of which will add to the space requirement.

Many of the reference books are quite heavy. Because of this, it is desirable to have the reference shelving and the associated reading positions closely juxtaposed. One technique that has been used with success is to alternate full-height and counter-height ranges to provide a convenient consultation surface for those volumes the reader may not wish to carry very far. Such a configuration also serves to visually open up the space, although there is a modest reduction in the absolute capacity. The low ranges may, however, be considered as a form of flexibility, as they could be replaced with full-height ranges at a future date as a need for additional capacity becomes convincing.

Other devices have been used to provide what amounts to a consultation surface, including ranges where each shelf up to counter height is essentially 24 in. (610 mm) deep, with 10 or 12 in. (254 to 305 mm) shelving above. Another method is to provide pullout reference shelves at counter height. In both of these approaches, the depth of the usable surface is hardly adequate, and the pullout shelves tend to be noisy unless the shelving is wood. There are probably better solutions; the authors prefer the close placement of tables or the use of high/low shelving in most cases, except where index tables are appropriate, as discussed later.

There is less reason to provide for any large amount of growth in a reference collection than elsewhere, as older volumes can frequently be shifted to the stack when new ones are acquired. In the future, with the development of more intensive computer or perhaps optical disk reference sources, the need for large reference collections may further diminish. Even so, it is still prudent to provide for a reference collection in book format, perhaps even with some modest growth potential. It is generally feasible to estimate 100 volumes to a single-faced section, with six shelves each 3 ft (0.914) wide. Counter-height units would, of course, hold no more than half this amount.

The size of the reference collection is indeed a controversial matter. Mr. Metcalf suggested that a well-selected collection of 10,000 volumes, particularly if the bookstacks are open access, should be sufficient for most central reference collections in large libraries if the bibliographical material discussed below is provided for elsewhere. This size is probably too restrictive for many general university libraries. On the other end of the scale, several major libraries have reference collections of 30,000–50,000 volumes or more, although this number includes the bibliographies, indexes, and published library catalogs. Many would argue that today a reference collection of 25,000 volumes, including bibliographies and indexes, would be about the right size for most large libraries, 10,000 for colleges, and under 1000 for branches. The decision about the size of collection to provide clearly must be a local one.

Seating in a reference area where open-access stacks are provided should not encourage long-term research, particularly if only 50 to 100 seats or less are provided, as suggested earlier. The authors prefer a mix of seating in the reference area with perhaps 50 percent at tables, 45 percent at carrels, and no more than 5 percent if any in lounge chairs. The carrels probably should not be provided with a shelf, as this would suggest long-term use. A photocopy service should be convenient for both staff and patrons. And provision for considerable future access to video terminals should be made. Tables and carrels that are joined together need to be sturdy enough to prevent wiggling when a person is writing. While 30 sq ft (2.787 m²) per reader is generally sufficient, larger carrels designed for terminals will likely require more space, perhaps as much as 45 to 50 sq ft (4.181 to 4.645 m²). For handicapped persons perhaps 5 percent of the tables and carrels should be high enough for the arms of a wheelchair to fit under. A few rooms off the reference room may be desired to provide for such activities as a seminar on bibliographic access, a program of reading to the blind, special equipment for the partially sighted, or simply typing or composing at a microcomputer, although the last can be provided for elsewhere in the building.

The requirements for the reference desk should not be overlooked. Generally, the reference desk should be visible from the entry area, close to the card or computer-access catalog, and convenient to the staff area. Ideally, it should be placed to facilitate directing a patron to the desired materials and to provide some degree of control over the reference collections and seating areas. Depending on the distance among reference desk, catalog area, and front lobby, an information desk may also be needed. Details should be thought out and described—such as a ready reference collection, computer terminals, phones, a counter or sit-down desk, number of staff to be accommodated, provision for handouts, a place for a diagram illustrating the distribution of the collections, other graphic needs, provision of a seat or several seats for patrons, drawers for special catalogs and normal desk supplies, and the like. While some of this detail can be established in the design phase, as much information as possible should be provided in the program. More comment is provided in Chapter 8.

Remember that the necessary conversation by telephone and between library users and reference librarians can be disturbing. This should be kept in mind in selecting the room arrangement and particularly the location of the reference desk. The reference room should probably be considered for carpeted floors, acoustical ceilings, and perhaps the introduction of background sound, either air conditioning or electronic white sound.

While figure 7.14 demonstrates a configuration for a minimum reference area allocating 30 sq ft (2.787 m²) per reader and 10 volumes per sq ft (108 per m²), it should be noted that this illustration is not intended as an objection to larger or more monumental reference space but to demonstrate an approach to a minimal reference room. Note that the carrels are a smaller size; many research libraries would prefer larger carrels. Also, there is no provision for video terminals or microtext readers, which would likely require larger units together with space for operating documentation. Furthermore, the space happens to be column-free, and without a catalog, dictionary stand, or atlas case (assuming the unit behind the reference desk is the ready-reference collection). It assumes that the bibliographies and indexes are separately housed and that the associated staff office or offices are located nearby. Clearly the illustration does suggest the basis for a formula which provides a point of departure for discussion by the librarian and the facilities programming committee. Figure 7.15 il-lustrates an actual reference space in a research library where approximately 34 sq ft (3 m²) are provided for each reader, and 5.37 volumes per sq ft are allowed. While neither illustration is ideal, each demonstrates different points of view.

The situation for bibliographies is very similar to that for the reference collections, but the number of bibliography volumes to be shelved can probably be cut to perhaps one-half that allowed for reference in most libraries. This general advice will become even more sound as bibliographical information is made more readily available in computer or perhaps optical disk format. For both reference and bibliography, about half of the

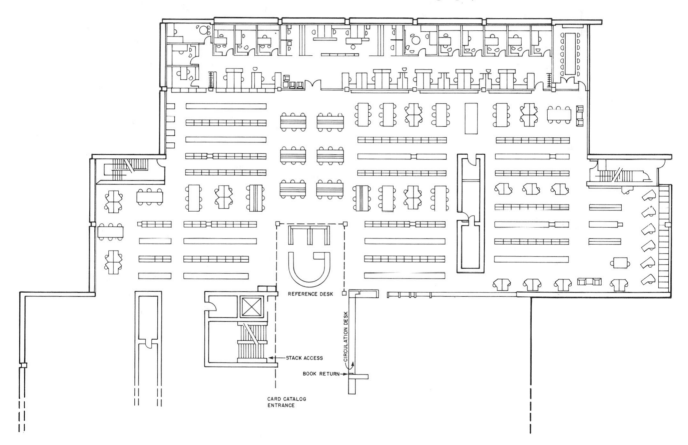

FIGURE 7.15 Reference room of the Cecil H. Green Library at Stanford provides approximately 7450 sq ft (692 m²) for a capacity of 40,000 volumes on a combination of full-height and counter-height shelving (the counter type are shown here without section divisions). This works out to 5.37 volumes per sq ft (57.8 volumes per sq m). The 163 seats (including the eight index tables as seating) occupy about 5550 sq ft (516 m²), or 34 sq ft (3.159 m²) per reader. The service counter and the ready-reference collection behind the counter are not included in this calculation. In this example space utilization efficiency was not the primary goal.

Note the structural elements (heavy walls) required in this design to meet the applicable earthquake code. One such element severely hampers the reference collection traffic flow and visibility. Also note the eight index or bibliography tables and the atlas case. The reference counter has two terminals, and an information desk near the card catalog entrance has one terminal. The card catalog area (see fig. 13.5) has provision for eight terminals with chairs.

seats may be individual, with the others at tables which provide more rather than less than 6 sq ft (0.557 m²) of table surface per reader. In all cases where there are multiple seating positions at a table, joined carrels, or other specialized seating, the specification must ensure that the furniture is sufficiently sturdy to avoid "writer's wiggle," a phenomenon which, if it occurs, will make multiple use of the equipment nearly impossible. Special equipment (index tables, for example) for at least part of the bibliography collection, such as the *Cumulative Book Index*, the *United States Catalog*, the *Library of Congress Catalog*, the *National Union Catalog*, and the catalogs of other great libraries and periodical indexes, if they are kept in this area, might well be provided. (See fig. 7.16.) The special tables or shelving in place of standard shelving may require several hundred additional square feet (20, 30, or more sq m) of space in a large library. It should be remembered that a large part of the consultation of bibliographical books by readers and library staff is frequently carried on at stand-up consultation counters which can be provided as described earlier. Where a counter is provided, it may well be equipped with high stools which can be pushed under it.

If the reference and bibliography collections are located as they generally should be, adjacent to each other, near the public card catalog and entrance lobby, they are likely because of the type of use as well as their location to have a restless atmosphere, and noise will be almost inevitable. While steps can be taken to reduce the problems of noise as suggested earlier, the noise should discourage the general reader seeking a place to study. It should be remembered that un-

dergraduates, when looking for a place to study, will sit almost anywhere an attractive empty space is perceived. The use of seating accommodations in a bibliography area sometimes has to be restricted or eliminated altogether to prevent their use for general reading; low stools without backs are suggested at index tables or other specialized equipment, particularly where a seated reader partially blocks access by others to the shelved materials.

If the bibliography area can be adjacent or close to the quarters of the acquisitions and catalog departments as well as the curators or book selectors, it should be possible to avoid a good deal of duplication of expensive bibliographical and reference material. Of course, where this material is replaced with electronic information storage and distribution devices, the need for close proximity of the technical processing functions is reduced or even eliminated. Even though this technology will surely provide future alternatives for the functional organization of the library, it is still prudent to provide for systems as they are known and understood today, but flexibility for adjustments in space assignment and space use must be a basic part of any new facility. This is discussed in Chapter 5 in some detail.

7.3 Current Periodicals and Newspapers

To encourage the use of current periodicals there may well be nearby seating for some 3 to 5 percent of the total readers, or in some cases (e.g., physical science branch libraries) even more. Much of this capacity may be in lounge chairs (perhaps 60 to 70 percent), ideally with footrests, such as hassocks or ottomans. Without footrests, students will turn the chairs to create the desired comfort, which results in undue wear on a fairly expensive piece of furniture. It is not unreasonable to expect one reader out of 20 to 30 in the library to be using current periodicals, but this figure will, of course, vary in different institutions or even different libraries within an institution. A science or engineering library, for example, is certain to have higher use of the current periodical area than a central research library for the humanities. The periodicals area should be near the entrance if that is possible, and if use of current periodicals is not sufficient to fill all the seats, they are likely to be occupied by readers using their own material.

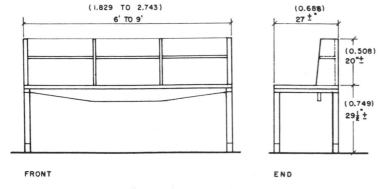

FIGURE 7.16 Index table for selected bibliographies, indexes, abstracting services, and directories.

There is, of course, the problem of deciding how periodicals are to be shelved, and how many of them can be provided in a given space, which is discussed in Section 6.6. Because of the ease of vandalism, the periodical area probably will require supervision, and in many cases special provision for controlled access to some, if not all, of the collections will be desired. This may involve controlled access to the reading area, storage of periodicals in shelving behind a service desk as reserved materials, or housing the collections in a separate closed stack and either paging the materials or providing for controlled access and special charge-out procedures for the reader. In any case, this is an issue to be decided and fully explained in writing the program.

Special provision should be made for periodical indexes if they are to be kept in this area instead of in the reference or bibliography area. If they are in book format in the latter area, they should be as close as possible to the periodical shelving. Libraries use large index tables, or bib tables, for these indexes as well as for selected abstracts, bibliographies, catalogs, and directories. These tables may be up to 12 ft (3.658) long and about 5 ft (1.524) wide—this is a critical dimension—with two double-faced shelves down the middle; the reading area is sometimes flat and sometimes gently sloping on each side. The tables must be very sturdy, of course, because of the weight of the materials and their heavy use, and they should have a stool for each 3 ft (0.914) of table. They are excellent for short use of the most heavily used indexes or reference sources. (See fig. 7.16.)

A photocopy service should be convenient to the periodicals. Even though little space may be required, provision should be made for the file of holdings, which often is in the form of a microfiche serials record, visible index, or a card file. In the future this service will no doubt require a computer terminal.

Smaller libraries find it possible and advisable to combine in one area the reference, bibliography, and current periodical collections. Some libraries prefer to have the bound back files of their periodicals served by the same staff that cares for the current numbers; they are therefore shelved close at hand, on the same level (often a difficult arrangement), or perhaps on the level directly above or below, with a stairway making convenient connection between the two. This arrangement can be particularly desirable for the heavily used titles recorded in the standard periodical indexes. Because of the additional weight of the bound volume, more table or carrel seating should be provided in proportion to lounge seating. But remember, in arranging for the seating accommodations for periodical reading, that peace and quiet and comfort are desirable, and that the readers' purpose is quite different from that of students who are consulting standard reference works.

Many libraries subscribe to only a few newspapers and keep only the current issues of most of them, sometimes discarding the others after a week or a month. They may be kept in the current periodical area, although, of course, a different type of equipment is required. Because of their size, newspapers are not easy to read. If placed on a regular library table, they tend to interfere with readers on each side and perhaps even across the table as well. A small individual table is hardly wide enough for comfortable perusal of a newspaper. If taking notes is required, further complications ensue. Some individuals find it convenient to read a newspaper seated in a not too large easy chair, although newspapers mounted on a stick may make this difficult. Others may prefer to read at a stand-up counter, an oversized carrel, or a large table. The various possibilities should be considered and a decision reached, so that the architect can plan the space satisfactorily. A few of each reading option may be best, though room aesthetics should be given consideration. It is obvious that the area required for each reader is larger in a newspaper room than elsewhere; an area of 40 sq ft (3.716 m²) per reader should be adequate in most cases. The total number of readers will rarely be large.

In a state university library, if local papers from throughout the state are made available, a considerable amount of space may be required for newspaper reading, and sometimes a special room may be provided. A journalism departmental library may also have special requirements. It should always be remembered that additional rooms present complications, particularly if they have walls and doors, and that small rooms may tend to be more difficult to keep quiet and orderly than large ones. At any rate, if a library is to have current newspapers in their original form, some provision for them and for those who use them is required.

Back files of newspapers are generally provided today on microfilm. The future may find back files housed on optical disks. For either of these, some form of reading machine is required, with special seating accommodations which are discussed under Section 7.9. If the seats can be close to the storage place for microfilm and other reproductions, and also close to a service desk, so much the better. Of course, the future use of a video terminal will not require that the collections be nearby, but occasional reader need for assistance may suggest a close service desk, at least until technological literacy has developed among library users.

Many university research libraries are still plagued by back files of newspapers, generally but not always bound. Those issued before the wood-pulp age (which began gradually about 1870 and was almost universal by 1880) are still treasured and should ordinarily be kept or transferred to the special collections department or to a library which is ready to preserve them. Heavy use will wear them out more rapidly than books, because the strain on the paper increases geometrically as the sheet size increases. These newspapers should be given special care and should be microfilmed if heavily used. Microfilm copies are even more strongly recommended for wood-pulp newspapers, because the life of the original is limited at best and because the cost of binding and storage space is often greater than the cost of the film. Methods of microfilm storage and shelving for bound newspapers are discussed in Chapter 6.

7.4 New Books, Light Reading, and Browsing Rooms

New books are often withheld from circulation for a week after they are placed on view, but arrangements can be made to reserve them for future borrowing. The light reading collection is generally a circulating collection with a fairly limited circulation period of perhaps one week; in some libraries the books are referred to as the "7-day books." It is not recommended or proposed that a special room be provided, even in a very large library, for new books or a light reading collection. Rather it is customary to place the collection in a prominent position, often adjacent to or even in the entrance lobby, in order to call them to the attention to those interested, to make them easily available, and to give the library user a collection to browse while waiting for a search, or a paged item, or a friend. The books should be placed within the exit-controlled area, or the loss rate will be high. Libraries may want to provide a small amount of seating nearby, perhaps of the lounge type. Footstools may be useful. Where there is an annunciation panel to tell a patron of a completed service transaction, it is well to have it within view of this seating area. A location near the circulation desk is often suitable, particularly in a closed-stack library, and the inviting view of a small collection together with a few comfortable chairs can be developed as a real asset in an area that otherwise is all business.

Popular in college and university libraries for many years, browsing rooms are essentially another means of providing for the kind of seating suggested above. Perhaps the earliest browsing room was the Farnsworth Room at Harvard, located from 1915 through 1948 in the Widener Library and later moved to the Lamont Library. The movement for browsing rooms spread rapidly, and they were established throughout the country, often in a room with handsome fittings and more spacious accommodations than most others in the library, with a collection of standard volumes (perhaps classics as well as the "7-day," or public library–type, books mentioned earlier) intended to encourage general reading. They might be thought of as an example of an idealistic personal library. It was soon found that browsing rooms which had funds available for the acquisition of new and popular books were most used. As public libraries have found, new books are, on the average, used more than older ones. Smoking, often prohibited elsewhere, was generally permitted, which naturally made the rooms popular, although views on this point have probably changed in many libraries. The Linonian and Brothers Room at Yale and the Morrison Room at the University of California, Berkeley, have been glamorous examples.

With the opening of the main collections to student access in many libraries, the whole bookstack has been made available for browsing, and many buildings have been planned without a separate browsing room. Other libraries, such as at Stanford and Princeton, have followed the example suggested above and placed in or near the entrance lobby a small collection of perhaps 200 to 400 volumes of attractive and popular books available to those interested, almost without effort on their part. The Yale College Libraries and the Harvard House Libraries perform similar functions with 3000 to 10,000 volumes. Undergraduate libraries also in part meet this need.

While a browsing room or area is entirely appropriate and useful, it is probably no longer essential. Obviously it costs money for books, yet the space it requires may be used to good advantage if it serves general education purposes, relieves the pressure on other rooms, adds to the total use of the library, or provides for future flexibility in a critical area. Without a specific area for this type of reading, lounge chairs can, of course, be added to general reading areas throughout the library, which has been done with reasonable success at Stanford. If supervision is supplied by checking at the building exits, the extra operational expense is nominal or nonexistent. The philosophical need for a specific area for this function will need to be determined locally. The authors have no formula to suggest for the ideal size or seating capacity, though it should be small and comfortable enough to be inviting, homey, and offer a relief from academic pressures.

7.5 Reserved-Book Rooms and Study Halls

Practically all libraries in institutions of higher learning have found it necessary to segregate most if not all materials which are required reading for courses. These materials are "reserved" for short loan periods to maximize access, and staff generally service the material. Since this type of service originated in the 1870s at Harvard, the reserved-book system has spread and increased in scope, in spite of widespread discontent with its results. Some institutions have found it possible to place all reserved books on open shelves and to rely on the students not to misuse them and to sign for them if they are taken out of the library overnight or over the weekend. Others have decided that it is better and less troublesome to put them on restricted shelves, where students have to sign for them either after helping themselves in a suitably restricted area behind the desk or by asking for the book by call slip. Many libraries divide their collections into "open reserve," for what they sometimes speak of as collateral or recommended reading, and

"closed reserve," for assigned or required reading or for books used by large classes where there are multiple copies but still not enough of them to go around during the peak period of demand. Libraries vary greatly in their use of reserved-book areas and may over time shift at least in degree from open to closed and closed to open arrangements. They also vary in the percentage of material in each group. It is suggested that plans be made so that either system can be put into effect. Few if any large institutions have been able to avoid closed reserves for long periods.

If there are to be closed reserves, a special area must be provided for shelving them. At most institutions the reserved books that have to be restricted at any one time can be kept to a comparatively small number. A college may have a maximum of 4000–5000 books and photocopies, but in a few universities more than 6000 are required at one time on closed reserve. The quantity depends on pedagogical methods, the number of undergraduate students, the number of courses in the current semester, and library practices—such as the proportion on open shelves or a decision to keep all except one copy of each title on closed reserve year around to save labor. Since these volumes can be shelved tightly together or, in the case of multiple copies, perhaps turned on their sides and stacked, it should be possible to shelve up to 175 volumes in a standard single-faced section of closed-access shelves, so that 15 double-faced sections may be adequate for 5000 volumes. A smaller quantity of shelving will be required in most institutions except where other types of reserved materials—such as headphones, current issues of current journals, typewriters, and the like—are maintained in this controlled area. In branch libraries one shelf for each two courses may suffice.

If insufficient space is provided, the results may be serious; this is one area where it may be prudent to include flexibility either by adding a contingency factor to the amount of capacity needed or by placing the shelving in such an area that by shifting a cage-like partition, adjustments can be made in the quantity of shelving available. There is a persistent tendency on the part of many faculty members to increase the number of reserve books as if they taught better or justified their course thereby. These books should be removed from the restricted shelves promptly when they are no longer in active use. If students can select their books at the shelves, wide aisles are desirable, but if the library attendant pages the books after a call slip is submitted, standard-width aisles are in most cases possible.

A problem that often arises is whether these books are to be used only in a special reserved-book room and taken out of it only overnight or over the weekend or whether, after being signed for, they may be used anywhere within the library building or even elsewhere for a limited period. The latter system has many advantages and is generally preferable, as it makes it unnecessary to provide a special reserved-book reading room, and readers are free to select the type of space and seating accommodations which they prefer. Furthermore, the potential savings of staff time resulting from the possibility of combining the main circulation desk with the reserve book function could be significant. Such a savings would be difficult to achieve with a separate room. However, it has the disadvantage of making it easier for students to hide books for their own use or for that of a friend at a later time. This is another decision that must be made locally.

If the books are to be used within a special reserved-book room and withdrawn from it only during limited hours, the room should, in most institutions, be the largest reading area in the building. It is sometimes said that well over 50 percent of all the use of library books in most undergraduate college libraries is of reserved books. Sometimes the reserved-book room is provided with its own entrance and can be kept open after the rest of the library is closed for the night. Careful consideration should be given to planning a library to make this possible now or later, though students should generally be able to plan well enough to get through required study in regular library hours. This, of course, may be less true where the economy forces budget restrictions leading to dramatically reduced library hours. Do not forget to provide for photocopy service and a quick-access catalog to the books on reserve. Restrooms should be available, particularly during the late evening or night hours.

Students' rooms in dormitories or other living areas are often unsuitable for serious study. As a result, if the institution's library is adequate in size, attractive, comfortable, convenient, and quiet, it will be heavily used by students reading their own books and papers or materials such as course reserves previously charged out of the library. In many libraries this may represent half the total use of the library. To the authors this use seems entirely proper and suitable. It has two major advantages. A studious atmosphere is provided, and dictionaries, encyclopedias, and other useful reference and general books are close at hand.

The cost of providing the space in the library is often less, and rarely greater, than making it available elsewhere in an institution, since the space required does not need to be individually assigned, but is available for use by anyone whenever it is wanted. It has the additional advantage that every time a student occupies a library chair there will be that much less congestion in the crowded dormitory rooms, and, in theory at least, those rooms should become more suitable places for study by others. One of the most serious problems in an academic institution stems from the limited number of hours when its physical facilities are used to their full capacity. Library reading areas available to any student for long hours should tend to reduce space requirements elsewhere in the institution. One reading area seat for every four students, occupying from 25 to 35 sq ft (2.323 to 3.252 m²), goes farther toward providing suitable study facilities than an equal area added to dormitory accommodations, because the space there has to be provided for each individual rather than every fourth one.

Most students and faculty members find that with a little planning they can complete the work that needs to be done in the library during the fairly long hours maintained by their libraries. A significant exception is in a library that supports laboratory research, where the research project may be scheduled on a 24-hour basis; this is a special problem of security in scientific and sometimes engineering branch libraries. Another exception are those students in residential institutions who are convinced that they study better in the middle of the night than before a 10 or 11 o'clock library closing hour, and are constantly advocating longer library hours. As suggested earlier, it may be claimed that the dormitory rooms are not suitable for study because of noise and visiting until perhaps 1 o'clock in the morning, and by that time, if there is one roommate who wants to sleep, the situation is no better unless a private study for each student is provided. Four possible solutions of this problem are suggested.

1. Library hours of operation may be extended, at least from Monday through Thursday evenings until 11 o'clock and perhaps to midnight or even later, particularly before and during examination periods. Where there is a separate undergraduate library, its hours are often longer than those for the main research facility. Many academic libraries are open until midnight, but some students seem to be almost as unhappy as ever. The library is faced with the cost of staff service for longer hours and of the utilities required to light and air condition the building, as well as with security and safety issues.

2. Study halls may be provided in the dormitories, perhaps in the dining hall, and can be kept reasonably quiet with the aid of proctors. A special study hall represents just that much more space which is used for very short hours—one more factor in the inefficient use of academic space which has been prevalent but is becoming more difficult to defend.

3. Dormitory rooms may be enlarged by providing individual study accommodations for each occupant or by providing a larger percentage of single rooms. However, to do either of these for every student will, as noted earlier, cost far more than adding more library seating accommodations for use during regular library hours, and will fail to provide the studious library atmosphere or reference books and other printed material that may be wanted. With the current popularity of loud music, the intrusion of one's neighbors is nearly impossible to avoid. On the other hand, some institutions have borrowed funds for dormitory construction and are paying the interest and amortization on the resulting mortgage from the rental rate. The library normally does not have this funding advantage; thus there is a temptation to build more elaborate residential halls and restrict the number of library seating accommodations, though this is a questionable procedure.

4. A section of the library can be separated from the rest of the building and have its own entrance open after regular closing hours. A number of academic libraries have tried this solution and keep one room open for long hours or even for all twenty-four. This is the practice in the Firestone Library at Princeton, Bennington College, the universities of Denver and Vermont, and elsewhere. At Bennington no library books, except perhaps a dictionary, are available, and there is no attendant of any kind. At Stanford the Meyer Library closes at midnight (or 1:00 A.M. before and during exam week), yet outside-accessed seminar rooms are available all night for study use. It would, of course, be possible and comparatively inexpensive in a large institution to keep a single attendant on duty to give a bare minimum of supervision and make it practicable to supply those who use the room with the library books which they are most likely to want, that is, reserved books and reference material—particularly dictionaries and encyclopedias. This modest level of staffing would obviously improve the utility of the room while reducing the likelihood of vandalism.

It is important to remember that if an all-night room is to be provided, it should have its own entrance, arranged so that it can be cut off from the rest of the building at night when the remainder of the library is closed, but with the outside entrance closed in the daytime so that the room can be used without an extra control point during regular hours of operation. This problem has been well solved in Chicago's Regenstein, Indiana, Hofstra, Earlham College, and Georgetown University. The aesthetics of such rooms usually leave a great deal to be desired, and vandalism can be a problem.

7.6 Special Collections—Rare Books, Manuscripts, and Archives

A reading room for rare books should be arranged to assure staff clearance of those who are exiting. The number of readers at any one time tends to be very small. In most institutions the books should not be on open-access shelves, with the possible exception of certain reference books. If housed in the reading room, the rarities should be in locked cases or shelved in a closed area behind the service desk. The size of rare-book collections varies tremendously from one institution to another. Some institutions have comparatively few rare books and seem to be not particularly interested in them. On the other hand, some comparatively small private institutions have received, as gifts from generous friends and alumni, large collections of rare books. The size of the institution may therefore have little to do with the size of the collection, though the older institutions tend to have larger collections.

Five problems of importance come up in connection with planning a rare-book room.

1. How many readers and how much space per reader should be provided for? As mentioned, the use of rare-book rooms is comparatively small, and perhaps the most important aspect is that the reading area should not be so large that it is difficult to supervise. In the Houghton Library at Harvard, where a considerable proportion of the rare books belonging to the university are housed, there is a reading room approximately 30 × 55 ft (9.144 × 16.764), which can seat up to 35 readers. Including the service desk, this works out to about 47 sq ft (4.366 m²) per reader. Within the room microfilm reading machines and "noiseless" typewriters (which today would likely be an electric typewriter with an acoustic hood or perhaps a microcomputer) are provided for use by readers. When it was designed, the planners felt that it was as large a room as could be supervised from a desk at the center of one of the long sides of the room. The desk is on a raised platform, to provide the attendant with a better view of the readers. This room, particularly in the summer, is frequently filled to capacity, but it must be remembered that the Houghton Library has one of the great rare-book collections in the world and one that has always emphasized usefulness to scholarly research rather than the acquisition of rarities for their own sake.

The Chicago Regenstein quarters for special collections seat 24 in one reading room plus a small typing and microtext-reading room, three private studies, and three small seminar rooms. Indiana's Lilly Library seats 28, with a small adjoining room for typing and microtext use. Yale's Beinecke seats 60 plus a similar number in special purpose rooms. The University of Illinois can seat 83 and has a microtext reading room as well. The Spencer Library of the University of Kansas has 67 individual studies plus separate reading rooms for rare books, manuscripts, maps, university archives, and regional collections, for a total of 109 seats. Still, only a few libraries will have to provide seating for 30 for use of special collections and rare books, unless a practice of class projects for advanced students is instituted.

Reading positions in a rare-book reading room generally should be at open tables arranged for maximum supervision from staff areas. It is common to provide fairly generous individual tables, often with task lighting, typewriters, and a few large table lecterns for holding large books. A few larger tables are desirable, as some rare books are exceedingly huge. Many rare book librarians prefer not to have lounge chair seating because of the implied casual use of valuable and often fragile materials. However, two or three such chairs may add atmosphere and provide a spot for brief talk with a donor or professor within the room itself. Space should not be forgotten for specialized equipment that is locally useful. It is suggested that at least 35 and preferably 40 or even 45 sq ft (3.252, 3.716, or 4.181 m²) per reader be provided.

2. How much shelving is required? This is difficult to determine. One should probably admit from the start that few rare-book collections can hope to be shelved indefinitely within the reading area assigned to rare books; they will have to be provided for in secured but otherwise regular bookstacks, preferably as close as possible to the rare-book reading area. Of course, provision for housing elephant folios may be required. The shelving area can sometimes be on the same floor, sometimes directly above or below, preferably with ready access for the staff between the two by stairs or elevator, or both.

Numerous factors will influence the growth of rare-book collections in the future. Increasing efforts at preservation of brittle papers may argue for special housing and handling of many books even though they may not be literally as rare. However, as the years pass, these and other older out-of-print books will increase in value and eventually be considered rare. It should also be remembered that the practice of giving rare books to academic libraries is something that often is cultivated, as it generally should be, and that first-class accommodations for rare books help to attract gifts. Because of these factors, rare-book collections will generally tend to grow more rapidly than other parts of an academic library.

The Department of Special Collections in Chicago's Regenstein Library has 1758 standard double-faced sections with some special shelving; it moved into its new quarters with 100,000 volumes and 3,000,000 manuscript pieces, and had initial room for 250,000 volumes. The Houghton has a 225,000-volume capacity; there is that much again both under Lamont and in Pusey. The Spencer Library at Kansas began with a 670,000-volume capacity, the Lilly at Indiana with 300,000, and Yale's Beinecke with 800,000. Many other universities have 50,000- to 100,000-volume collections, and quite a number of colleges have several thousand and are growing rapidly.

3. How should the space be arranged? Some libraries have found that having the rare-book area divided into a considerable number of separate rooms has made it easier for them to attract gifts of rare books from donors who want to have their names and their collections perpetuated. However, separate rooms can lead to reduced long-term flexibility and potentially to a more difficult problem of supervision. Another technique is to provide alcoves that can be named, but again supervision must be carefully considered. A third possibility is the provision of specially designed and secured cases to house named collections, with a donor designation to perpetuate the name of the donor in a dignified way. There, except perhaps in fairly small institutions, the planner must be careful to avoid combining exhibit and reading functions. Where collection cases are provided in a reading area, they should be supplemented with a separate exhibit area which can be open to the general public.

All of these possibilities require special design, and if the material is to be shown as the donor undoubtedly wants it to be, supervision and control may be greatly complicated. Experience in some institutions that have faced the problem on a large scale has been that donors, when the problems are properly presented to them, come to realize that if what they are interested in is to have their collections used and their names remembered favorably, the collections should be shelved as far as possible with other similar material on the same subject. Perhaps each item could be identified by a bookplate and also listed in a catalog of the collection. Nothing is so sure as the ultimate stagnation and, to all intents and purposes, death of a collection that must be kept in a room by itself, without an attendant to make it readily available and funds for enlarging it and keeping it up to date. Even when a collection is donated with a supporting endowment, in an inflationary age an endowment fund tends to decrease in purchasing power over time. Such support should not in most cases be sufficient to justify a separate collection.

Even so, quite a number of universities have special rooms that they do not consider white elephants. They may be tourist attractions, encouragements to friends or donors, or locations for seminars or receptions, and their educational, or at least inspirational, value should not be ignored. Examples can be found at Harvard, Indiana, Stanford's Hoover Institution, Texas, and elsewhere.

Mr. Metcalf speaks of the summer of 1908 when he had charge of moving the Oberlin College Library into a new building, and was finally bold enough to ask the librarian why he placed in his new office an unimpressive old mahogany bookcase filled with a miscellaneous collection of books. He replied, "In my early years here I accepted this collection as a gift with the condition that it would always be kept together in this bookcase. The library was poor in those days and welcomed almost anything that came to it as a gift. I have been glad to have it ever since, not because of the case or its contents, but because it reminds me day by day that gifts of this kind with strings attached are undesirable and should never be accepted. With it here before me there is no danger of my making a similar mistake again."

4. What about the importance of providing the optimum atmospheric conditions for the preservation of the material? It has become general knowledge that books deteriorate, even if they are not heavily used, particularly if they are printed on poor paper, as many of them are. One way to prolong the life and usefulness of any volume—and this is of special importance for rare books and other materials difficult or impossible to replace—is to provide an even temperature of 70 degrees F (21 degrees C) or less and a relative humidity of 50 percent, together with excellent air filtration, control of light, fire and flood control, and control of pests. These points are discussed in greater detail in Section 5.3 under Environmental Control and, to some degree, 13.2. See also Appendix D.

5. What degree of security is appropriate for the collections and their quarters? Local circumstances will play a large role in determining the nature of the security necessary. The program should spell out the requirements. Questions that should be answered include: Is there need for a vault or strong room? Should there be intrusion alarms, and if so, where? Should there be door contacts and other forms of perimeter protection of various areas? What about other kinds of alarms such as high or low humidity alarms,

smoke detectors, water alarms, panic buttons for the staff, special alarms in display cases, etc.? How should the various alarms be controlled—by clocks, keys, touch pads—or should they always be active? Should there be special keying? special doors to lock off areas? special glass? Many of these issues are discussed in Section 5.3 under Interior Design Concepts. Do not forget to think through how the alarms will be responded to and where their signal should be seen or heard.

"Special collections" in the sense of scarce associated items of greater or lesser rarity and value often come from gifts of friends whose collector's instincts brought them together or who acquired them in order to present them. In some instances they are purchased by the institution and are so highly regarded that they are kept together as a unit. They present the same problems as rare books. Their use will sooner or later be hampered if they are shelved out of regular subject order. To make their full research value available, they must be kept up to date by additional acquisitions, and there must be a knowledgeable attendant to service them. Their housing, if they are separate and growing units, will present problems sooner or later. Do not be overly tempted by what may seem to be generous offers and be prepared to explain in detail the problems involved.

Manuscripts and original typescripts present very much the same problem as rare books and special collections. Not much provision needs to be made for seating accommodations, but special close supervision of the material is desirable as it stands on the shelves and as it is used. It can often be provided in the rare-book room. Suitable atmospheric conditions are also important.

Storage presents a special problem because manuscripts come in all shapes and sizes, and special attention needs to be paid to accommodations for their shelving, discussed in Section 6.6. The ideal shelving configuration may differ somewhat from that for books.

Archives fall into the same general category as rare books and manuscripts. Many of them are manuscript or typescript in form. If they represent primarily the archives of the institution to which the library belongs, one of the great problems is collecting them and preventing their loss through neglect in the departments where they originated. At the time of change in an institution's administration or when professors transfer to another

institution, go off to Washington, to war, or elsewhere, departmental and other records tend to disappear. The administrative officers of an institution hesitate to allow what they consider confidential records to be removed from their own supervision, and want to hold them in their own quarters. One hazard after another may come up.

The bulk of archival material in a great university is frightening. In the eighteen years while Mr. Metcalf was in office at Harvard, material with bulk as great as that occupied by 350,000 average-size volumes was collected. A program for discarding as well as collecting is essential, but every institution should make provision somewhere for its archival material and for the proper supervision of its use. Perhaps the most intensive use of archival and manuscript material for colleges and universities is for doctoral and master's dissertations. As with manuscripts, special problems of literary rights are involved, and control and supervision must be provided.

Accommodations for readers of rare books, manuscripts, and archives are often and quite properly combined in one room in order to reduce overhead expenses. The same area per reader is appropriate for each group. It is often desirable to make this group of functions directly accessible to the general public without going through building entrance or exit controls, although this is not necessary. Finally, exhibit space is essential to the functioning of these special collections. It should be publicly available (some portion of it at least with superior environmental control), easily accessible when mounting an exhibit, and free of any reflection on glass. Some if not all cases should be of sufficient height for quarto volumes and sufficient depth for a good-sized folio. See extended comments in the next chapter. Visits to special collections quarters and discussion with experts are advised in designing for special collections.

7.7 Public Documents

Many universities provide special accommodations for the storage and use of public documents because they are unable to catalog them, or do not want the trouble and expense of cataloging them. At the same time, since documents are difficult to use, a trained staff to service them is often required and a special reading area for documents may be desirable.

For a U.S. depository library the documents collection must be accessible to the general public. In this case access to the collections should ideally be kept separate from the general building controls to maintain control over the more restrictively accessed collections.

If a library attempts to collect public documents on a large scale, their bulk increases rapidly, and a good deal of shelving may need to be assigned for them. The growth rate for documents can vary dramatically with a change in the political world. Small liberal arts colleges in the U.S. tend to acquire an unduly large collection of documents, partly at least because they cost little. The reading space required, on the other hand, is ordinarily not extensive, particularly if documents used for assigned or collatoral reading are placed on restricted reserved-book shelves during the period when they are in demand.

Special provision of some kind must be made for documents in most cases, however, unless they are cataloged in full. This is true even with U.S. documents that can be arranged by the Superintendent of Documents number. The more limited number of documents from other countries or from state and municipal governments is often more difficult to use without help from trained library staff. United Nations documents present problems of their own, whether in their original form or in microproduction. It should be noted that public documents are being distributed in microformat in even greater proportions, which suggests the need for microform readers as well as open seating. Seating for a documents area is much like seating in the general reference area, because use of these collections is fairly short term. A mixture of seating similar to the reference area—at carrels, probably without shelves, and open tables seating no more than four but with sufficient surface to unfold a large map—is probably appropriate. In smaller institutions documents are serviced by the reference staff. Each institution must determine the best service and staffing arrangements.

If the use of public documents is largely limited to a special reading area, its relationship to the storage area for the material may be very important. If the collection is large, it will probably have to be in the main bookstack; if the use is restricted or more accessible than the general collections, it may have to be in a position of the stack that can be cut off from the rest of the shelving area.

This is particularly important where the documents department has a separate entrance and control point, as the documents staff will not want to be responsible for checking out the general collections. Document collections often include unbound material, and housekeeping will be difficult. Since trained librarians are often required to assist the patron in finding an item, the reading, reference, and staff areas must be close to the stacks. Ideally, a significant portion of the collection should be housed on the same floor.

The floor area required for each document reader is similar to that required for general reading, or about 30 sq ft (2.787 m²), except that provisions for microform reading should be somewhat larger, with a minimum of 40 sq ft (3.716 m²) per reader provided. The number to be provided for depends almost altogether on the service patterns adopted. With the current shift of the U.S. Government Printing Office to microforms, the need for a microform storage and reading area associated with the document collections is becoming more common. The user requirements for microforms are discussed below.

7.8 Maps

The use of a map collection in an academic or research library is ordinarily not large, although it may be important. Since map storage requires special equipment and maps are often difficult to use, a separate map area is frequently provided, though sometimes it is in one part of the reference space or room. In an undergraduate or small college library, a map and atlas case in a reference area, together with a few nearby tables, may suffice; separate rooms and large collections of sheet maps may well be an unnecessary luxury. Atlas cases may be locally designed and constructed, or purchased from a library-equipment firm. In addition to material that can be so housed, many institutions possess collections of the United States Geological Survey topographical maps. Others have large collections of historical maps in either flat sheets or rolls, the latter being used from time to time in classrooms. A considerable number of American institutions acquired the Army War Maps after the Second World War, and these alone take a great deal of expensive equipment and space for housing. A careful estimate should be made of the prospective growth of the map collection (see Section 6.6) and the amount of use that is to be expected. Since the transportation of sheet maps is difficult, there should be facilities for use as near as possible to their storage location. In selecting a suitable location for a map room or area, remember that service by staff members will probably be needed. Map filing cases may be very heavy and can present a serious floor load problem. It is a mistake to overcrowd in space assignments, as shifts to provide more space at a later time may be difficult and expensive to arrange. Thirty-five, and preferably up to 50, sq ft (3.252 to 4.645 m²) per reader is suggested, including perhaps a light table which will probably require at least 50 sq ft. Unless there will be class projects, the number of readers provided for need not be large, and the total space for them should be generally less than that for map storage. Large tables may have a slot just inside the front edge or a special sheet rolling device, as may be found on an architect's drafting table, so a person can bring the far portion of a sheet closer without leaning on and creasing it.

7.9 Microtexts

Practically all college and university libraries today have accumulated microreproductions on a fairly large scale, and these collections of microfilm, microfiche, microprint, and microcards are continuing to grow, especially microfilm and microfiche. Each of these requires special equipment for housing, as well as for use. While the optical disk will no doubt eventually supplement the microform collections, it is still reasonable to assume that these collections will continue to grow in use and bulk for years to come. However, it may be prudent to plan sufficient flexibility into the housing and reader facilities so that future adjustments in use and space assignments can readily be made as other technologies are implemented. All of this suggests location on other than the entrance or first floor of the building. The amount of use and the size of the collection of microreproductions do not depend primarily on the size of the library's other collections. Indeed, even though a large library may have a considerable number of microforms, their use in such a library is often far less proportionately than in smaller libraries because large libraries have already acquired originals of much of the material that so far has been put onto microfilm.

It is not essential to provide a darkened room, except perhaps occasionally when readers must use poor copies of difficult manuscripts. A darkened room will enhance the ability to see the projected image, but almost any convenient space without an excess of light is satisfactory. It should be obvious that, as with video display terminals, a reading machine should not be placed so that the sun or a bright light of any kind will shine on the reading surface. Positions of reading machines with vertical or nearly vertical screens must be arranged to avoid reflecting more distant bright light sources; for example, the screen should not face an exterior window. While some libraries have distributed their microform collections and reading machines throughout the book collections in their appropriate subject classification, some librarians would argue that it is essential to centralize the machines in one location in the main library building and in research branches where an attendant is available to assist the patron, replace light bulbs, and ensure that proper maintenance procedures are undertaken. Also, it may be argued that the small size of the reproductions makes them easy to misplace or lose, and that some supervision is desirable. All this, in most cases, means that the microtext reading area should be near, and if possible immediately adjacent to, a desk where a staff member is regularly on duty.

Few libraries have really provided adequate facilities for reading machines, particularly in view of the fact that many machines are large, heavy, and not easily moved. An additional consideration is the need to provide for both right- and left-handed readers, who will tend to use surfaces on opposite sides of the machine for taking notes or comparing a microform text with that of a book. Since the bulk and weight of a reading machine generally limits its position being shifted by the reader, reading comfort must be supplied by the chair, which should permit the reader to shift position. Booth or carrel arrangements with surfaces at least 30 in. (0.762) deep and up to 5 ft (1.524) wide will provide good flexibility. Narrower carrels can effectively be used with pullout boards or L-shaped extensions. Be sure to provide for the left-handed reader both note-taking space and a low-intensity rheostat-adjustable lamp on the left as well as the right. If accommodation cannot be provided for both types of readers, then one in ten should be set up for the left-handed. A minimum of 40 sq ft (3.716 m²) per reader is suggested. Do not forget the reader-printer or photocopy requirements. Storage for microforms is discussed in Section 6.6, and future growth must be estimated.

7.10 Music, Audio-visual, and Learning Resources

Many libraries provide special accommodations for one or several media, at least in their music collections. There are a variety of reasons for this. Music material, particularly music scores and sheet music, tends to be outsized and requires special equipment. Phonograph discs and tapes used in connection with music courses can be an important part of the program of the music department, and their special storage and use should be provided for somewhere in the institution. For other departments motion picture film may be exceedingly important, or a program in oral history or recorded lectures will result in accumulations of tape cassettes and playback equipment. Some institutions have collections of video tapes, slides, and other related sources which may not be produced in-house, but which require organization and storage. Recorded poetry, dramatic readings, and recordings for modern-language instruction are common uses of this type of medium.

It is often thought that a collection of audio-visual materials can better be supervised in a library than elsewhere. The difficulty with material of this kind is that it is costly, fragile, easily mishandled or lost, generally not well cataloged, and not easily browsable. Furthermore, a certain amount of service staff and supervision is desirable, and this may require another service point unless service points can be combined. It is even possible that accommodations for a language laboratory will be desired separate from those provided for the balance of the audio-visual material. If the library is planned to have audio-visual production facilities, which a few institutions have, then a significant added programmatic need is established.

Questions outlined in the *Higher Education Facilities Planning and Management Manuals* that should be answered include the following:

1. Is a central audio-visual production and service facility desired as part of the library?

Is the service of a size and nature that it can be combined with the course reserve function?

2. Are instructional facilities (lecture halls, classrooms, language laboratories, film-making, television and radio studios, and the like) to be included in the central facility?

3. What is the market area for audio-visual services? campus? multi-campus? local or regional industry? statewide? national?

4. To what extent will the audio-visual service engage in the production of instructional materials and of radio and television programs?

5. Based upon the answers to the preceding questions, how many and what kinds of professional and technical staff are required to operate the services and production operations? What are the clerical staff support requirements? What amounts of film, tape, slides, and other materials need to be stored, maintained, and retrieved? What type and amounts of storage are required for equipment such as television monitors, recorders, and projectors? Will equipment be repaired and maintained in-house? Will graphic arts services be supplied? Will the facilities be used for training in communication arts and education? Will faculty offices be required?[1]

Clearly, the concept of a centralized audio-visual facility in the library can mushroom into a substantial program element, some of which goes well beyond the functions normally associated with a library. Although many librarians are skeptical about having a full-scale audio-visual service and production center within the library context, growth and development of programmed learning techniques including computer-aided instruction will continue to have a significant influence on the nature of college and university facilities in the future. Major media or learning resources centers exist in libraries of junior colleges and sometimes in colleges or state universities. These quarters may occupy as much as a third of a junior college facility. One good plan is shown in figure 7.17. The local administrative organization and functional variety required by the academic curriculum will dictate the program inclusions.

[1] Harold L. Dahnke, Dennis P. Jones, Thomas R. Mason, and Leonard Romney, *Academic Support Facilities,* Higher Education Facilities Planning and Management Manual no. 4 (Boulder, Colo.: Western Interstate Commission for Higher Education, 1971), pp. 64ff.

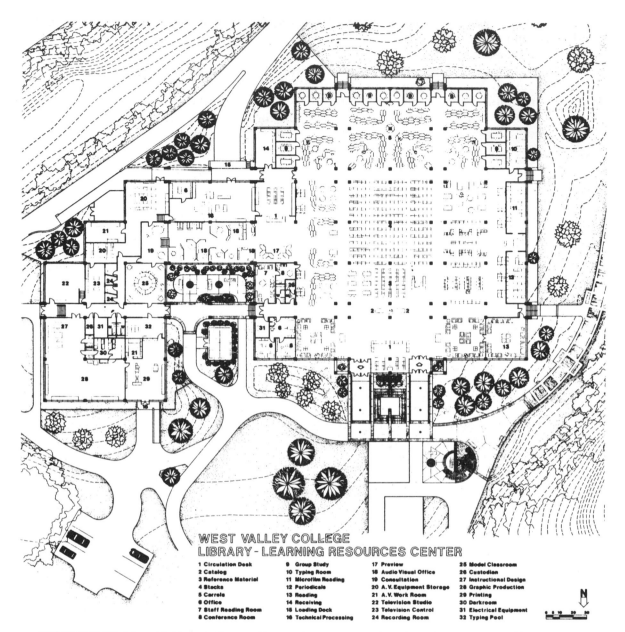

WEST VALLEY COLLEGE
LIBRARY - LEARNING RESOURCES CENTER

1 Circulation Desk	9 Group Study	17 Preview	25 Model Classroom
2 Catalog	10 Typing Room	18 Audio Visual Office	26 Custodian
3 Reference Material	11 Microfilm Reading	19 Consultation	27 Instructional Design
4 Stacks	12 Periodicals	20 A.V. Equipment Storage	28 Graphic Production
5 Carrels	13 Reading	21 A.V. Work Room	29 Printing
6 Office	14 Receiving	22 Television Studio	30 Darkroom
7 Staff Reading Room	15 Loading Dock	23 Television Control	31 Electrical Equipment
8 Conference Room	16 Technical Processing	24 Recording Room	32 Typing Pool

FIGURE 7.17 West Valley College Library is an example of a community college or junior college. Note the unusual arrangement and proportion of carrels. In this type of library, seating tends to take more space than the collections. The relationship of the library (1 through 16) to the media center (17 through 30) should also be noted.

The variation among institutions in terms of the types and amounts of audio-visual facilities and the organization of these facilities covers an enormous range, the upper limits of which go far beyond the scope of this book. Although no serious objection can be made to housing these facilities in a library, they can be provided for elsewhere; in their most inclusive form they are not an essential feature in all academic libraries. If a library being planned is seriously limited in area, it is suggested that the floor area for shelving media

materials and providing audio-visual services (not production) be restricted to easily foreseeable needs, and if its requirements expand later, that some or all of the material then be transferred to other quarters.

The number of readers to provide for will be a difficult decision where there is no history of audio-visual service. It is suggested that the number of seats provided for the general reference collection may be an appropriate quantity for the audio-visual area, although this suggestion should be taken with care as individual institutions will have significantly different emphases on the use of this type of material. In most cases there should be provision for some modest degree of maintenance for the equipment, including a separate room to store minor components, test and repair equipment, and house machines needing work. Provisions for the storage of portable projectors, screens, television monitors, and the like is probably appropriate, too.

Reader stations for audio-visual quarters may take the form of tables or carrels especially designed to accept terminals, rear screen projectors, tape decks, record players, and the like. A centralized facility for playback of audio-visual materials has been used in a number of institutions, and such a facility continues to have merit for certain types of material, including recorded lectures, or a language laboratory-type function. In this case the reader accommodations need not exceed those provided for a normal carrel, or 25 sq ft (2.323 m²) per position.

Students of music, poetry, and perhaps even languages will need to play the material at their own pace, often backing up and repeating a passage. While this can be done in a centralized playback facility, it may be found to be less expensive and more appropriate to provide individual playback devices over which the student has direct control. This concept should not be applied to archival materials which need special care in handling. In addition to the playback equipment where independent playback is provided, there should be sufficient space to refer to a related text or music score and to take notes. From 35 to 40 sq ft (3.252 to 3.716 m²) should be provided per position, ideally in an area that has some supervision and where sound isolation is not a problem.

Provision for small groups can be accommodated in separate rooms or by the use of a centralized playback facility which can transmit the signal to multiple listening or viewing positions. As one example, Stanford's Meyer Library has an audio room with 50 positions, each of which can access central programs or sources independently controlled. In addition, 262 seats, or 17 percent of the library proper, can receive programs from several of 34 audio room central sources. There are also two soundproof listening rooms for nine persons, not requiring earphone use, and four language laboratories;

and the music library is two buildings away. Each institution will decide the best pattern for its academic programs.

As all audio-visual equipment is attractive to those with light fingers, security of the area and equipment must be carefully established. It should not be forgotten that this equipment all produces heat, and that the materials being used are all dramatically damaged if exposed to extreme temperatures. This will be one area where special attention to the current and future mechanical and electrical systems will be required. For example, underfloor electrical ducts or grids may be needed. Headphones, portable playback devices, tapes, or records can be charged out in a fashion similar to that established for closed-reserve books, with shelving for these items provided behind a service desk. Shelving for these materials is discussed in Section 6.6.

The program statement for a music library may contain several unique elements not found in other libraries beyond those already discussed. For example, some music faculty will be absolutely opposed to any form of what Mr. Metcalf refers to as acoustic perfume or white sound. If open-air listening is required, acoustic isolation is a must. Earphone listening, while it is not the ideal for the scholar, does save space and expense, and listening stations can be easily distributed through the library. There is some acoustic leakage with headphones, thus reading areas should be somewhat separated from listening areas. Open-air listening might be limited to a seminar room where a piano or electronic keyboard may be desirable. The music library will sometimes have its own technical processing staff, even where the library system has centralized processing. Compared to those in other libraries, the secured stacks, reserves, or noncirculating collections are often larger than is normally the case in proportion to the open collections, the exception being a rare-book library where none of the collections circulate. Because of this, use of the collection is more staff intensive than many other collections.

7.11 Fine Arts, Pictures, and Prints

A considerable portion of the collections for fine arts and related fields consists of large volumes with pictures and prints, outsized in shape and difficult to deal with, as well as mounted photographs and slides. Each of these requires special equipment for service and for storage. In this fairly distinct and well-defined discipline, faculty tend to want a departmental library, as they do in music. Many of the advantages of such an arrangement can be made available in a special room in the main library, and this practice is sometimes adopted, more frequently in a college than in a large university library. The decision, as with audio-visual materials, may well depend on the size of the institution, the number of majors and graduate students in the department and the vigor of the department, the size of the collection, and the geography of the campus.

Reader positions will usually consist of little more than oversized carrels and open tables, although occasionally a slide projector may be required. Seating accommodations for each reader should amount to at least 35 sq ft (3.252 m²); special tables have been designed to facilitate the use of large folios. Some designers may insist that the colors and quality of light in this area are more important than in most in order to be able to properly view the art collection. In the art library at Stanford University, for example, the only colors allowed are white, black, or gray, to avoid influencing the color perception of the human eye. Of all branch libraries the art library is the most likely to have very rare and expensive volumes, and, therefore, it will need caged or otherwise secure shelving for part of the collection; the proportion of quarto and folio shelving will need to be great.

7.12 Divisional Libraries within the Main Library

In many institutions, particularly in large universities, there is a constant and perhaps inevitable struggle between advocates of a centralized library and those who demand a large number of departmental collections, perhaps one for each discipline. Some universities have sought to compromise by establishing broad divisional collections in the central library instead of a larger number of departmental libraries. This has worked out fairly well in some of the large and middle-sized institutions. This plan and the need for a decision in connection with it are discussed in Chapters 3 and 5, and the question should be resolved before getting into the building planning process. If the division library plan is adopted, it may completely change seating

arrangements throughout the library and affect provisions for catalogs, reference books, periodicals, shelving, graphics, and perhaps staff areas. It should not dramatically affect floor area requirements for each seating accommodation, except as any subdivision results in the provision for unit peak loads, resulting in an increase in total requirements. There is, in effect, some repercussion resulting from a form of duplication of services, which will vary significantly depending upon the scope and scale of the unique division.

7.13 Typing, Smoking, Group Study, Conference, and Seminar Rooms

Accommodations for typing have become popular, if not necessary, with the increased use of portable typewriters by students. Some institutions provide larger typewriters for use by students as a free service or with coin-operated machines. In the future microcomputers will likely replace the typewriter to a large extent. Provision of publicly accessible computers or terminals may be treated much like typewriters, or because they are quieter, they may be distributed throughout the library. Computers tend to generate conversation, and the keyboard does click, so microcomputers should probably not be placed in an open reading room where computers are not in general use.

There are four quite different but possible arrangements.

1. In a regular reading room. In general this is not recommended, but in a rare-book reading room, where supervision of the library materials in use is deemed essential, it may be required. The Bancroft Library at the University of California, Berkeley, provides typewriters with noise shields, which are fully effective in controlling unwanted sound. Without some form of noise control, typing in an open reading area is likely to be intolerable. The microcomputer will help in this regard.

2. Typing rooms where from two to a dozen or more students using typewriters or computers are seated. Possible arrangement of one of these rooms is shown in figure 7.18. Such a room concentrates and segregates the noise, but necessitates acoustically treated walls and seclusion. If the room provides for too many users at once, it will be a bit of a zoo at certain times of the year. Tables or carrels separate from the walls and each other

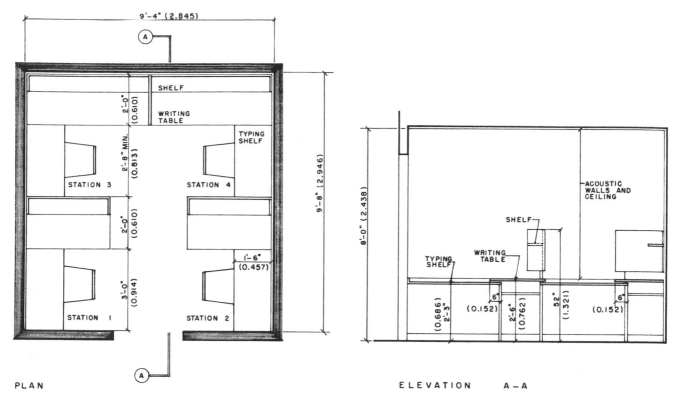

FIGURE 7.18 Minimum typing room for four. Replacement of the typing shelf by an articulated computer stand with an adjustable keyboard surface would adapt this plan for a microcomputer room, although the unit would be about 30 in. (0.762 mm) deep rather than the 18 in. (0.457 mm) shown here.

will help to reduce the transmission of sound. Some positions for personal typewriters or computers should be provided even when the library provides typewriters.

3. Regular carrels in the bookstacks. This solution is often possible if the use of typewriters or portable personal computers is confined to one side of one stack level or to a specific stack area, and if only those who expect to use typewriters are assigned to this particular area. In a typical tiered stack, the pounding of a typewriter is likely to be transmitted through the structure, and this approach may not work well. At the University of California, Los Angeles, main research library, individual typing stations are provided in the center of a large stack area so that the books themselves absorb most of the typing noise. This arrangement has worked well there, and it would be well suited for microcomputer use, assuming power is available.

4. Special acoustically protected individual typing cubicles or carrels. Various arrangements are possible. In addition to quiet floors and acoustically treated ceilings in these cu-

bicles, acoustic material of one kind or another is often placed on the walls. The carrels do not require doors if they are placed at the dead-end of a stack aisle, as they are in the Wellesley College Library with complete success. (See fig. 7.7.) They can be held down in size and still be acceptable, although at least a few should provide for use by a person in a wheelchair.

If the use of typewriters and portable personal computers is permitted in a library, it may be convenient and desirable to have lockers where they can be stored, unless their use is in locked cubicles. Lockers of this kind are available with either combination or key locks, each with a master key. In some institutions they are rented for a nominal fee.

Smoking in the library is a problem, as was dealt with in Section 3.1. This is particularly true with the increased use of carpet in reading areas widely distributed throughout the bookstacks. There has always been a demand for smoking accommodations, and if they are not provided, students and faculty have been inclined to break the rules, the former smoking in corridors and toilets if not in reading rooms, and the latter in their studies, thinking they would be undetected. Some institutions permit smoking only in private offices or areas specifically set aside for smokers; others have no specific rules. Some regions are populated with greater numbers of smokers; other regions have accepted the norm that smoking is not acceptable in public areas. A number of states have passed laws to protect the rights of nonsmokers to breath clean air.

There are three obvious objections to smoking: the fire hazard for paper products and furniture as well as buildings, the dirt which inevitably results, and the increasing recognition that smoking is a health hazard even for the nonsmoker. Even where there is no actual fire, damage to table tops, upholstery, and floor coverings is almost inevitable.

Where there are no legal restrictions or institutional rules governing smoking, the library planner should keep in mind the problems associated with the habit. A growing number of people dislike studying in a room filled with smoke, and yet there are still those who find it difficult to study for any considerable period of time without smoking. Because of them, it is not uncommon for a library to permit smoking in specified areas, which experience tells us will reduce illicit smoking. The University of Minnesota Wilson Library has excellent smoking rooms by the stack on most floors. On the other hand, in the University of Michigan Undergraduate Library, smoking is permitted throughout the building (and the ceilings show one result). In the J. Henry Meyer Memorial Library at Stanford, smoking within the building, except for private offices, is not permitted by edict from the board of trustees; however, smoking is allowed on four fourth-floor rooftop decks.

It is suggested that, when college rules and regulations permit smoking in academic buildings, the whole problem is simplified if certain areas in the library, preferably one on each floor, are set aside for this purpose. When provided, these smoking areas or rooms should not have a fire detection system activated by smoke; where fire detection is necessary, a rate-of-heat-rise system is the only practical approach in areas where there may be heavy smoking, even though this form of fire detection is less effective. If the building

is airconditioned or there is forced ventilation, special care should be given to the ventilation in smoking areas. No extra floor area per reader is required in smoking areas.

Many students are gregarious by nature and, at least on occasion, they like to study with others. They may sit in twos or in larger groups of up to eight to discuss their assignments together or work on a joint project. This is especially the case in the scientific and engineering fields, and technical schools in particular have found it desirable to have in the libraries small rooms where students can talk over their work without disturbing others. If such rooms are provided, there is far less excuse for whispering in the reading areas. It is suggested that every library should have one or in some cases a considerable number of these rooms; if possible, at least one or more on each floor. They should seat not less than four and generally not more than six. Seating for four is probably ideal as larger groups tend to be rare outside an organized seminar.

The rooms can be as small as $11 \times 8\frac{1}{2}$ ft (3.353×2.591) for six students, although this is minimum spacing; a few extra inches would help. Slightly more space will be required if handicapped access is facilitated. Rooms should be equipped with one table, four to six chairs according to size, and a chalkboard. The table need be no more than 3 ft (0.914) deep instead of the 4 ft (1.219) recommended for regular reading room tables. The minimum spacing of $2\frac{1}{2}$ ft (0.762) on each side can be tolerated, although 3 ft (0.914) is more comfortable and should make it easier for a person in a wheelchair. The door or a panel next to the door should contain a large section of glass to permit easy supervision and ease in determining if the room is available. The walls that adjoin other similar rooms or reading areas of any kind should be acoustically treated, including double glazing where there is glass and continuing the walls through the ceiling to the underside of the floor above. If the door opens into a part of the bookstacks where no seats for readers are close at hand, the need for special acoustical protection will be reduced.

Most college and university libraries built before the Second World War contained a considerable number of what were called, perhaps incorrectly, seminar rooms. This practice was taken from German university libraries. Specialized collections were kept in these rooms, and were made available to faculty and students, and small advanced classes and discussion groups met in them. Oberlin, a liberal arts college, made provision for some 15 seminar rooms as early as 1908, not unusual at that time. One difficulty with this arrangement comes from the fact that, if the rooms house books, the books are not available while the seminars are in progress, and the rooms are likely to contain more and more books because of the inevitably increasing pressure for shelf space. To avoid this dilemma, a limited number of small rooms without shelving, in which seminars can meet, may be placed adjacent to other rooms or areas filled with collections on limited subjects gathered together for use by advanced students. In this way collections can be made available to others when the seminars are in progress.

A slight variation of the seminar room with its specialized collections, which might be called a subject reading room, has been used at Princeton, for example. In this case a room or well-defined area is set up with reading accommodations and a collection relating to a specific topic. It is intended as a research or reading area rather than a seminar or teaching room, although a seminar could take place there, and provision may be made for a staff attendant to add control to the room and to assist readers when they have bibliographic or research questions. The staff member may be a graduate student assistant, and the staffed hours may be quite limited. In some cases use of the room is open to any student, while in others it may be limited to those majoring in the specific field. Philosophically, one can argue that such a facility promotes collegial interaction, but this sentiment is probably best limited to fundraising efforts, which may be quite attractive with both seminar rooms and subject reading areas, as a true realization of collegial interaction would probably turn the room into a lounge or club rather than an area intended for research or teaching. Nevertheless, there is probably merit in the concept of encouraging students of similar interests to work together in a specially provided area or room.

When either the seminar room or subject reading area plan is carried out, it may involve unnecessary duplication of little-used materials, and, in libraries with open-access stacks, it is much less defensible than in libraries with closed access. If the rooms are not exclusively assigned to any one discipline, it should be possible to schedule classes in them for so many hours a week that they will not be an extravagance to the institution, even if they seem to be for the library. So much the better if they are placed immediately adjacent to the bookstacks or, in limited quantity, near special materials such as the reference room, public documents, or rare books so that books from the main collections are readily available.

If, as suggested above, these rooms do not have books, they are simply small classrooms, and while it may be useful to have a number of small rooms for this purpose in a library, they do take space, the construction cost of which must be figured at or higher than $100 a sq ft (or about $1100 per m²). Unless used a considerable number of hours each week, they tend to be a luxury. There are many fewer seminar rooms being provided in American libraries built since the Second World War than are found in those planned earlier. They can, however, represent "expansion joints" that can be used for other library purposes later, particularly if their walls can be easily removed. Acoustically they should be treated in the same manner as group study rooms, which may make the walls slightly more costly to alter. However, rooms such as these can be used for special projects, or they can often be made into several smaller rooms for group study or faculty assignment, which may sometimes seem desirable. They can be planned with these possibilities in mind.

Summary

There are three major questions to be dealt with in deciding upon the type of seating accommodations.

1. What do the readers want? One can be sure that not all readers want the same thing and that a variety of reading accommodations is desirable. The problem comes in determining the number or percentage of each, and all ten types of seating should be considered.

Studies done in the past indicated that over three-quarters of all students prefer individual accommodations, although this finding is likely to vary, depending on local customs as well as the exact nature of the accommodations. Individual seating can, of course, be provided in dormitory rooms in a residential institution, but, as noted before, it is usually more expensive to provide satisfactorily for every student in a dormitory than for, let us say, every third or fourth student in the library. One thing that is certain is the strong tendency toward a large percentage of individual seating in libraries, often with as much as 75 percent of all the seats individual in character. There should be a quantity of seating at tables too.

Two examples from Stanford University can provide a comparison. The student seating percentages were determined by judgment, the undergraduate Meyer Library before it opened in November 1966 and the Green Library East Wing before it opened in January 1980. Note in table 7.1 that the Meyer clientele is about 75 percent undergraduates and 15 percent graduate students, while Green's clientele is about 50 percent graduate students and 15 percent undergraduates.

Experience in Meyer during the 1970s was that rarely were more than half the seats used at one time and that the proportion of flat tables was too high. Experience in Green suggests that the proportions are reasonable; the level of use often approaches 100 percent.

It seems that the *quality* of the individual position may be just as important as the basic type. That is, the degree of comfort, the size, the degree of privacy, the bookish surroundings, the natural and artificial light, amenities such as a locally controlled light or a footstool—these give a sense of prestige space and will draw students. Except during the "forced feeding" of pre-exam days, a library is, after all, competing as a drawing card against the student union, dorm room, local pub, and other options. The "bloom" wore off Meyer

after a very few generations of students, as is the experience in many other libraries. Its recent efforts at refurnishing have been welcomed by students. Green, as the new kid on the block, became immediately popular. The maintenance of the attractiveness in any new library is not easy to achieve and yet is a factor in its effectiveness as an educational institution.

2. How much space do the different types of seating accommodations take? This is a matter of considerable importance, both financially and in terms of how the reading positions are to be used. On the one hand, with a total project cost in the range of $150 per sq ft (or about $1600 per m²), the difference between 25 sq ft (2.323 m²) and 35 sq ft (3.252 m²) for each reader station represents a potential savings or cost of $1500 per reader. On the other hand, insufficient space for the reader simply will not be properly used. As already suggested, the space requirement for readers will vary depending upon the nature of use, with the recommended range running from 25 sq ft (2.323 m²) per reader in typical undergraduate libraries, to 30 to 35 sq ft (2.787 to 3.252 m²) for use by a master's candidate, to perhaps 50 sq ft (4.645 m²) per reader in a law library or where a student is expected to write a thesis. Faculty studies are typically larger, being often as much as 75 sq ft (6.968 m²) or more. More space should also be allowed per reader in special areas, such as typing rooms and areas for using portable personal computers, microforms, newspapers, archives, and rare books.

The determination of the space requirement, as already outlined in this chapter, includes consideration of three points: (1) the

TABLE 7.1 Seating Comparisons

Type of seating	Meyer Library		Green East Wing	
	No. of seats	Percentage	No. of seats	Percentage
1. Flat tables for 2 or more	468	30	126	12
2. Tables with low dividers	208	13	0	—
3. Slanting-top tables	0	—	0	—
4. Individual tables or carrels	565	36	424	41
5. Lounge chairs	163	11	68	7
6. Enclosed carrels	0	—	107	10
7. Group study rooms (type 1)	0	—	64	6
8. Reference collection (mostly types 1 & 4)	60	4	164	16
9. Current periodicals (mostly types 1 & 5)	40	3	44	4
10. New books and light reading (type 5)	12	1	6	1
11. Study hall (type 1)	32	2	0	—
12. Microtexts (type 4)	4	—	29	3
Total	1552		1032	

desirable amount of working surface at a carrel or table; (2) the aisle space required for access to the seat; and (3) the extra space for psychological "air space," for comfort and for special equipment, particularly in a closed carrel or study. The range of space recommended above should normally be sufficient to provide for these three points. Excluded from these space recommendations is the space required for readers in other parts of the library, such as lobbies, public service areas, public catalog rooms, rest rooms, corridors, stairwells, elevators, and nonassignable and architectural space in general, to say nothing of exhibition and seminar rooms and areas used for what might be called nonlibrary purposes.

3. What level of detail should be programmed? Aside from the number of readers to be accommodated, the area to be provided for each reader, and the mix of seating accommodations, there are other features of reading positions that are very important. Lounge chairs should be arranged to either promote or discourage conversation, depending upon the circumstance. There may be need to provide for the capability of supporting media access, electronic information systems at wet carrels or studies, or perhaps a number of public-access terminals. With concern about energy conservation, task lighting has become once again a popular feature, although it has problems, particularly glare. A mock-up of reading positions with their lighting configuration is probably desirable in all but the smallest library project. Special consideration for the needs of the handicapped should be detailed; even though physically limited persons will almost never constitute as much as 5 percent of clientele, between 5 and 10 percent of the reading positions spread among the library areas and functions should provide for full access by handicapped persons. Outlets for personal equipment such as portable computers should be provided.

The materials used to fabricate the reading positions should be durable and refinishable where damage is likely to result. Anything that can be picked at should be avoided, which includes exposed screws or raised caps over fasteners. The chairs should be exceptionally strong but comfortable enough to allow a person to sit for several hours at a time. While armchairs are generally preferred, a quantity of armless chairs should also be provided for those who like to curl one leg under them, a position that many find comfortable and which is often impossible in an armchair. Where carpet is used, sled-base chairs are preferred, as they tend to be easier on the carpet. In this case, glides attached to the base of the sled defeat the intent of the design. Because of power or signal outlets, some furniture may need to be bolted to the floor or otherwise restricted in placement, such as by a short-chain tether. Colors of the reading surface should not represent dramatic differences from the colors encountered in printed texts; too dark and too light both tend to be distracting to the eye.

In adding to or remodeling an existing building, the disposition of the existing furniture should be established. If it is to be kept, is the new furniture to be sympathetic to it or can the existing furniture be used in isolated areas? Most designers would, of course, prefer the freedom of using all new furniture. Without that freedom, it is usually desirable to incorporate the use of existing furniture, perhaps refinished, in as compatible fashion as possible. The question of who is to undertake the inventory of existing furniture should be addressed. It is suggested that the persons responsible for the interior design should at least share in this effort, even if they do not undertake the full responsibility.

Details such as these will affect both the design fees and the final cost, but to avoid false expectations, they should be spelled out. All that may influence the design should be in the building program; the rest can be included in the specifications document or in furniture specifications. As with other aspects of the program, attention to detail will increase the likelihood of a satisfactory product. Further, it conveys to the architect a good understanding of actual operational conditions and of the institutional expectations with respect to design detailing. Yet the advice of the design team should not be discouraged. The program presents the facility goals of the library which, with a suitable degree of communication and understanding between designer and client, can be refined as more is learned of the project as it proceeds through the design phases.

8

Programming: Space for Staff and General Purposes

Adequate accommodations for the library staff are essential for effective service. In academic institutions the space required does not loom large in proportion to space for readers and books. However, with few exceptions, it seems fair to say that accommodations for the library staff tend to become inadequate before those for books or for readers. This situation may be due to modesty or timidity on the part of the librarians or to a failure to realize how much the staff may have to grow in order to process new material and provide public service. Some would argue that the advent of automation is reducing the need for staff accommodations, particularly in the technical processing areas, and in some cases this is no doubt true. However, library staff quarters all too often are congested, and activities such as gift pro-

cessing, indexing projects, administrative studies, cooperative programs, conservation, bibliographic instruction, or interlibrary loan seem to grow to overfill the space. The resultant crowding hinders, even if it does not prevent, effective work.

It is true that an overly generous supply of work space at a circulation desk has been known to encourage poor housekeeping and that an unnecessarily large amount of storage area for books in process may slow up cataloging by relieving pressure to push books through, but good administration should prevent both difficulties. In any event, where there is limited flexibility for future reallocation of space to provide for staff, either as the result of a natural pattern of growth or as the result of one or more special projects, then some surge space or a slight excess of staff space in terms of absolute need is generally prudent, even where it is anticipated that staff space needs will shrink as a result of automation. While the authors would be pleased to be wrong, it is likely that over the long term, automation will not dramatically reduce staff, although the increase in staff numbers may be less dramatic in the future. With microcomputers, printers, disk drives, monitors, etc., the space required for an automated work station will be somewhat larger than that for its manual predecessor. It is suggested, for example, that at least 20 sq ft (1.858 m²) should be added to a secretary's work station where use of a microcomputer or word-processing terminal is involved in addition to typewriting and other space needs.

Space is needed for four major staff groups—administrative personnel, public service staff, processing staff, and maintenance staff—as well as for rest rooms and lounges. The program writer is urged to review the discussion on general relationships of major functions found in Section 5.3.

8.1 Administrative Personnel

The size of the administrative staff depends, of course, very largely upon the size of the total library operation. The chief librarian should have adequate quarters for office work and also for meeting with members of the staff and public. The space assigned to the chief librarian will depend on the work required and on whether or not the office is to serve as a conference room. The office may require as little as 125 to 150 sq ft (11.613 to 13.935 m²) in a small library or as much as 400 sq ft (37.161 m²) or even more in a very large library if small group meetings will be held there. An office of 240 to 260 sq ft (22.297 to 24.155 m²) is not uncommon. For political reasons the size of this office is often affected by the size of offices provided for deans and other academic officers in the institution.

For all offices the program should outline the nature of the furnishings. This is, of course, a local decision. Is there to be a seating group in lounge chairs or at a small table? Are bookshelves required? files? sink? coat closet? What kind of work surfaces are desired? Is there any special furniture or art work that belongs in this office? Are there to be drapes or blinds at the windows? Is there to be, either now or in the future, access to

an electronic information system or computer terminal? In a branch or other small library, does this office require a secured file or space for keys and personnel records? Does the shelving of a sampling of rare books require special security or environmental consideration? Should there be extra outlets for such things as a clock, dictation equipment, a fan, radio, calculator, terminal, desk or side lamps, and the like? In general, each work station should be provided with at least four outlets, which is double that normally provided. If the office is to be used as a conference room, is there need for an easel? projection screen? tackboard? chalkboard? Should these be worked into the design of the space so that they are hidden when not in use?

If the chief librarian's office is not to be used for conferences of various kinds, a room for that purpose elsewhere in the administration suite is desirable. It may also serve as a board room or for meetings of the faculty library committee, for staff conferences, and for other small groups. The size, of course, will depend upon the maximum typical meeting size; 25 sq ft (2.323 m²) per seat is usually adequate. A small college library may require sufficient space for a group of 8 to 10 persons, while a large library may find accommodation for double this number or even more is appropriate. In addition to the items mentioned above, should there be space for folding or stacking chairs? a tea and coffee service area? a sink or small refrigerator? phone? Should the table be sectional? Should this room have access separate from that of the administration suite? As this room may be occupied at near capacity for long periods of time, excellent ventilation is required. If projectors will be used for slides, films, or other media, the ability to dim the lighting will be desired.

In larger libraries there will be one or more associate or assistant librarians. For flexibility it is suggested that where several offices are provided for this group, they should all be the same size, although they may not be furnished the same. An assistant librarian for collection development, for example, will need relatively more shelving, while a business manager may need secure storage for keys or financial files. These offices ordinarily will be smaller than the chief librarian's office, typically within the range of 125 to 250 sq ft (11.613 to 23.226 m²), with 160 to 180 sq ft (14.864 to 16.723 m²) being common. As with the librarian's office, the size of the assistant or associate librarian's offices may be influenced by the size of faculty offices provided by the institution. Unlike many faculty members, however, these administrative officers often have a number of departments or managers reporting to them, and it is convenient and desirable to be able to meet with most if not all of their immediate staff at a small table within their office. The urge to personalize these offices beyond a certain degree of uniformity should be resisted, because personnel changes are inevitable. For example, the desks should probably all be similar, although there may be several options in each office for desk placement. Shelving and other built-in features should also be of the same quality and otherwise similar, with the exceptions noted above. Personalization, of course, can easily be provided for in art work and other items of a less permanent nature.

Secretarial space is normally required in all but the very smallest libraries. The secretary's office may also serve as a waiting area. If there are a number of administrative officers—that is, associate or assistant librarians, more than one secretary quite likely will be required. A space of 125 sq ft (11.613 m²) is suitable for each secretary, with additional space provided for a reception area and perhaps a microcomputer, as noted earlier. The secretary usually needs a very large desk for paper work, typewriter and/or word processor, small file, and side chair. Space for filing cabinets and supply cupboards is essential; in a larger office, it may be desirable to have a fairly large separate file room, perhaps with a sink, an office coffee service, supply storage, a photocopy machine, a table for sorting, a computer printer, umbrella stand, and a coat closet. Space needs should be worked out based on local circumstances.

Accommodation for a business manager or administrative assistant librarian must also be provided in a large library. As already suggested, this office should probably be the same size as that of the associate or assistant librarian's because it can be expected that the business officer will have numerous visitors. Business support staff, including accountants, perhaps a building manager, security officer, and a procurement officer, will require an open office landscape system or fully partitioned office space as well, which should be near the administration suite, if not part of it. At least 100 sq ft and preferably 125 sq ft (9.290 to 11.613 m²) per support staff member should be provided, in addition to space for a flat file of library plans, a safe, and perhaps a coin-counting room, which will need careful acoustic isolation as well as reasonable security. The business manager may be responsible for a word-processing service, which also needs acoustic isolation.

Many libraries have other functions that are closely associated with the administration. There may be one or several assistants to the senior administration who typically are junior librarians doing special tasks of all kinds. Ideally, they should have individual spaces of 125 sq ft (11.613 m²), and the nature of some projects will require at least some extra space with a large table. There may be a graphics technician who will probably need more studio space. A larger library may have, for example, a space planner, public relations officer, publications editor, systems officer and staff, research office, and library intern or visiting fellow working with the librarian as part of a training experience. There may be a development officer responsible for donor-related matters, grant applications, and coordination of a "friends" group. The extent to which such professional staff need private offices is a local matter. The size requirements will vary. A system of movable panels creating low-partitioned "landscaped" offices is initially cheaper and provides flexibility, but the authors favor full partitions in most cases for administrative offices since privacy of conversation and sound control are much improved thereby. Remember that serious planning discussions, hard private thought, job applicant interviews, performance discussion sessions, and occasional emotional meetings all deserve complete privacy.

A personnel office, perhaps with a separate entrance to encourage interaction with the library staff, is common in larger libraries. This office will probably need larger and more secure file space than most offices. There is always a quantity of handouts describing staff benefits, educational programs, and the like which will need special housing. A library with a large number of student employees will require space for reviewing job requisitions as well as filling out forms. A large tackboard for displaying a variety of notices for staff and potential staff will be required. The offices of the personnel managers will need careful acoustic isolation, because of the need to conduct confidential business, although they need not be larger than the 125 sq ft (11.613 m) provided for other support staff and managers. The space needs for files and a reception area should be calculated in addition to that for the staff positions.

In each group, if there is a person who is equivalent to a department chief, he or she should be provided with an extra 25 to 50 sq ft (2.323 to 4.645 m²) for guests and small group meetings. Clerical staff in the administrative support areas can be accommodated in 100 sq ft (9.290 m²) per staff position unless they are using a microcomputer, which will require an additional 20 sq ft (1.858 m²). To this should be added 10 sq ft (0.929 m²) for each file cabinet plus similar space for general storage and supply cabinets or shelving units in a closet.

While it need not be next to, or even on the same floor as, the administrative suite, another administrative support function (sometimes part of the technical processing or business function) is the library mail and supply room. The mail room, often referred to as shipping and receiving, is where outgoing books and other library materials are wrapped, letters and packages are franked, incoming mail is sorted, and incoming supplies and equipment are received and inventoried. In a large library there will need to be a fairly significant area devoted to the sorting of incoming mail, particularly serials. An extra-deep counter, perhaps 3 ft (0.914) from front to back and 10 or 12 ft (3.048 to 3.658) long, with a portion at one end provided with a solid edge rail, serves well. This counter should be about 36 in. (0.914) high. Mailbags are easily emptied on to the counter, and the serials may be sorted toward the end with the edge rail. Mail other than serials (which are assumed to be destined for the serials check-in division) may be sorted on to open shelves or boxes on racks which should be placed nearby. If this area is to also serve as the site for unwrapping incoming materials, then provision for extra-large trash containers should be made.

The letter mail, or first class mail, generally is delivered separately from the other mail, and may be sorted in another area at a 39 in. (0.991) high counter, which need not be deeper than 30 in. (0.762) from front to back. A lower counter here will cause back problems. It is a convenience if first-class mail can

be sorted directly into post office–type bins, which have locking access doors, in a staff corridor. Ideally, the bins should be large enough to hold easily the largest commonly used envelope flat on its side. The access doors may be provided with a slot which permits staff to do minor sorting of their own, but if this is specified, ensure that the slot is wide enough for the widest envelope. Even though the door will certainly be wide enough, a slot cut into the door may be limited in size due to the lock mechanism or structural requirements, a factor that may suggest that the bins should be 2 or 3 in. (51 or 76 mm) wider than the largest envelope. Some departments, for example the public documents department, may require either a larger bin or several bins due to their heavy mail receipts. It is suggested that the bins should all be of the same size, but that there should be considerably more bins than addressees by perhaps 50 percent. Labeling the bin doors in alphabetical order will aid staff in their sorting procedures. In addition to the bins, there should be a pass-through window to accommodate large items and mail slots for outgoing mail, perhaps designated for branch libraries, campus mail, the national postal system, and foreign mail.

Most mail rooms will have a franking machine, which can simply be placed on an extension of the first-class sorting counter. Provision should also be made for a large stapler, paper rolls, paper-tape machines, and generous storage for wrapping supplies, including boxes, mailing bags, stuffing material, and the like. An open area of floor space should be available for the receipt and processing of large shipments of equipment, furniture, supplies, or books returning from a bindery. Storage of first-aid and emergency supplies for coping with the early hours of a flood or other disaster may also be in the mail room. At least 250 sq ft (23.226 m²) per mail room staff member should be provided; 300 sq ft (27.871 m²) is preferred. If there is a supervisor, an office of 120 sq ft (11.148 m²) should suffice. In a small library, of course, this operation can be scaled down dramatically.

The supply room should house the major supplies used in the everyday operations of the library. A small branch library may get by with a supply cabinet or closet, but a major library will need a substantial supply room. Local circumstance will suggest the amount of storage space needed, which generally can be fitted with commercial or industrial shelving, perhaps with one or two sections of bins for small items. If the room cannot be secured, then the storage of small items should be in a locked cabinet, as certain of these supplies will tend to disappear too rapidly otherwise. A dutch door opening into a staff corridor works well for serving the supply room. Some open floor area should be provided for the bulk storage of materials such as pamphlet boxes or photocopy paper on pallets. A book truck or two will be handy for stocking the shelves, and there should be a work station for a clerk. It is suggested that 10 sq ft (0.929 m²) per single-faced shelving or bin section plus at least 250 sq ft (23.226 m²) for the supply clerk should be sufficient.

Surplus equipment, including an occasionally used lectern, spare exhibit case, Christmas decorations, surplus typewriters, extra desks, old catalog cabinets, extra carpet, damaged chairs, and similar items, almost always is a problem in a library, and at today's cost of construction, it probably should remain a problem to a large degree. Even so, some space should be allocated for such items. If it is not in the supply room, it may be what architects sometimes call "sloip" (space left over in planning). It is almost certain that any space provided for such storage will be used, and it is suggested that the programmer should require a modest amount of general storage space that can be located nearly anywhere in the library, although elevator access is a convenience. Many library planners have erred in not providing adequately for this need. Without sufficient storage space, mechanical rooms, attics, hidden corridors, and underfloor crawl spaces usually fill the purpose, much to the displeasure of the fire marshal and maintenance personnel who from time to time will require the removal of stored materials. Storage in these areas is often against the law, and thus it is not recommended.

The loading dock itself should not be forgotten. Deliveries from all types of vehicles can be anticipated, including giant trucks, vans, private cars, and from a branch library by a book truck. It is suggested that provision be made in all but the smallest libraries for a dock area, ideally with a device that accommodates trucks with beds of different heights. For best results the loading dock should have a height of 48 in. (1.219), thereby accommodating most delivery trucks but not vans,

for which a lower height is preferable. There should also be a lift or ramp to the ground to facilitate the movement of book trucks or hand dollies. The dock area should have some degree of protection from rain. A rain canopy or overhang high enough to avoid collision with the tops of the delivery trucks can provide protection from rain and snow. In cold climates the dock area is often actually inside the building, which of course adds significantly to the cost. The library van or delivery cart may be garaged here in some cases. At some point, and it can just as well be in the program, the library will need to establish the size of delivery truck that can be accommodated. Where there is a campus receiving point, large trucks can make deliveries, but transfer of the items to the library will need to be made, at added cost. Ideally, the length of the dock should permit the receiving of at least two trucks at the same time, other space permitting. The needs here clearly require local discussion.

Provision for the removal of trash from the library is often a requirement for the area near the loading dock. This may involve a large trash receptacle which should be arranged so that smaller containers can easily be dumped into it. A fumigation room, chamber, or blast freezer may be another feature ideally located near the loading dock so that materials that are infested need not be brought inside the library proper until it is safe to do so.

8.2 Public Service Staff

The public service staff as treated here includes those responsible for reference and circulation work, supervision of the public stack, paging of the collections, interlibrary loan, and sometimes a staffed photocopy service. Most of this work is done from one or more desks or service counters which take space themselves, to say nothing of the area required by those working at each desk and those who are served by it.

In a large library private offices will be needed for the heads of the various public service departments or divisions, including circulation, reference, public documents, the rare-book room, and perhaps interlibrary loan, newspapers and periodicals, microtexts, and the archives. A space of 125 to 150 sq ft (11.613 to 13.935 m²) for each department head should suffice, with the rare-book librarian sometimes being an exception if the library intends to impress potential donors. Curators, reference librarians, and assistant heads often feel a need for an office as well, particularly as they may need to confer with visitors on a frequent basis. These offices can be somewhat smaller, but anything less than 100 sq ft (9.290 m²) is likely to be inadequate.

For the other members of the staff, the space required will depend largely upon the amount of equipment, but a rough estimate of 100 sq ft (9.290 m²) per person on duty at one time is not extravagant. Indeed, unless the sharing of a desk is planned, which is not recommended except perhaps for student assistants, this allocation of space will be exceedingly difficult. A safer factor is 100 sq ft for each regular staff member, including those who are not full time. This allowance does not include space for book-sorting rooms, the ready-reference collection behind a desk, reserves or "hold" shelves behind a desk, or conference rooms or space for the public in front of the desk. It should be emphasized that demands for service, and incidentally for a larger service staff, tend to increase year by year and certainly in the early years after remodeling or occupancy of a new wing or new building.

Typical subjects that the programmer should address include the following:

The specific needs of each office

At least four outlets?
Shelving?
One side chair or several?
Any work space beyond a normal desk?
Typing stand or typing return on the desk?
Special concern for acoustic isolation?
Provision for a terminal? printer? phone? book trucks?
Any special concern about location beyond the obvious library organizational requirements?
Sun control?
Carpet?
Tackboard, chalkboard?
Any unusual lighting requirements?

In the circulation department

Privileges desk or area—
Should it be visually closed during periods when the library is open?
Should it be accessible outside the portal control?

Is there special provision for a cash register for fines and fees?
What kind of patron files are there?
Number of staff? Specific staff requirements?
Should there be a public place for handouts?
Should there be a display space for library regulations, a campus map, or other information?
Does this area serve a dual function?
Will there be a terminal here?
Is this where lockers, studies, or carrels are assigned?
Is there need for a secure key cabinet?

At the loan desk—
Is the circulation system manual? If so, is it going to be automated at a future date?
Is there to be some form of numerical annunciator to advise users when their book is found or question answered? If yes, how many numbers? Where should the numbers be seen? In any remote locations such as the reference room or other reading areas?
Will there be typing, discharging, or other activities at the loan desk?
Is there to be a public address system?
Is there need for one or more book returns? If so, is there a requirement for special features? What is the maximum size of book it should accommodate? What quantity must be accommodated in the receptacle?
Is there shelving nearby for reserved materials? For equipment to be signed out? For hold or will-call books being paged from the stacks or auxiliary collections? If so, how much shelving is required?
Will the sorting of books being returned to the shelves be done here?
Are overdue notices prepared here?
How many service points should there be? How long is the anticipated queue?
Is there need for special traffic control similar to that found in banks?
Should there be a bell or other signal to summon an assistant?

Behind the loan desk—
Is the circulation department responsible for closing the library? Should there be a control or annunciator panel for various security alarms and lighting systems?

Should the outside book-return deliver books to this area or to a sort room? Where are the books discharged? Is there need to store extra books in bins?

Are there to be staff lockers? If so, how many? What size? What kind of lock is preferred?

Should there be a coatrack?

How many staff? terminals? file tubs?

Is there need for a conference room?

Are other functions such as bindery preparations, minor repairs of damaged books, or the attachment of identification marks, spine labels, bar coding, or book pockets to be provided for here?

Is there need for a sink?

What is the maximum number of book trucks likely to be parked in the area? How many book trucks should be provided as part of the project?

Is some form of office partition system required? What are the requirements for the work stations?

Building or stack entrance portal control—

Is this to be part of the circulation desk function or a separate booth?

What should be within the controlled area?

How will staff enter the controlled area?

Are there to be separate "in" and "out" controls? Will identification be required for those entering the library?

What kind of control system is in use or anticipated?

Should there be options for the location of the point of control or the method of control?

Is the control point to include other functions such as building security, charging out books, holding items for patrons, providing general information, or other filler tasks?

If the control point is in a lobby, should there be special consideration for extra lighting or protection from drafts? Should there be a heater?

Might there be a computer terminal? phone? intercom? Is there to be more than one control point?

Stack sorting rooms or areas—

Are staff work stations needed?

Is the stack supervisor responsible for stack security? Should there be a door alarm annunciator panel here? Is there need for a secure key cabinet?

How much shelving is needed?

What is the maximum number of book trucks anticipated in this area? How many book trucks are to be provided in the project?

Are there to be lockers for staff? coatracks?

Is there need for a tackboard or chalkboard?

How is the information required to page a book handled? hand carried? telephone? terminal? vacuum tube? radio?

In the reference, interlibrary loan, current journals, newspapers, maps, and microform areas

At the reference desk—

Is this to be a desk, counter, or both?

Are special features required in the desk or counter such as:

Provision for handouts?

A phone placed off the top surface?

Terminals? Intercom?

Catalog trays?

A glass-covered display in the counter surface for a campus map, building plan, or arrangement of the collections in the reference room?

Typing?

Is there a ready-reference collection? If so, how much shelving is required? Are a few of the volumes oversized?

What special considerations should be made in regard to the location of the desk besides the obvious? In sight of circulation or documents? Are the reference collections controlled? If so, how?

How many service points are there to be?

Should there be chairs for the patrons?

Is this where a lengthy computer search would occur? Is space needed for the librarian to map out a search strategy with the patron?

Are there to be card catalog cabinets for the reference collection nearby? If so, how many?

Reference staff area—

Is this area to be accessible to the library user? If so, during all hours of operation?

How many staff members are to be provided for, both professional and assistants? Are the librarians to have offices?

What are the specific requirements for shelving, terminals, book trucks, office landscape systems, and the like?

Is there to be a conference or bibliographic instruction room? Will a computer training room be needed?

Is a staff photocopy machine required?

Are curators and their support staff to be housed here?

Would a separate terminal room with a small desk and two chairs be useful for conducting interviews with patrons and online database searching?

Interlibrary loan—

Is there need for terminals or for a closet to house a noisy Teletype machine?

Are there likely to be cash transactions?

Are photocopies made here?

Is there need for a service counter? book trucks? terminals? special files?

Are incoming books held here or elsewhere for the patron?

How many staff members are there? What are their specific requirements?

Current journals and newspapers—

Does bindery preparation occur here? journal check-in?

Are materials to be paged? Is there need for an annunciator? intercom? book trucks?

Is there to be a desk or counter? Will it have a place to return journals?

How many staff members are to be provided for? What are their specific needs?

Is there to be a photocopy machine nearby?

How is the serials record or file handled?

Can a patron charge out a journal?

Is there a "morgue"?

Does the library provide any form of clipping service?

Is there need for any special display?

What provision is needed for current or future computer and videodisc technology in the staff area?

Newspapers are dirty; is a sink required in this area?

Map room—

Are there special requirements for the processing of maps in a staff area such as a light table, large sorting bins, or an extra large table?

Is there to be a service desk or counter? If so, should it have an extra-large surface for viewing maps?

How are the maps controlled? Are they charged out? Is there a special place to return maps?

Is a card catalog nearby? If so, how many cabinets or drawers?

How many staff members are there? What are their specific requirements?

Is there need for storage of special supplies such as acid-free map folders?

Is encapsulation of brittle maps done here?

Microtext areas—

Is there to be a service desk or counter?

How are the microforms controlled? Are they charged out? Are they paged from a closed stack? Is an annunciator panel or intercom needed? Are the microforms and readers distributed throughout the general collections?

Is there special equipment for cleaning films, making microform or full-size copies, or maintaining the microform readers?

Is there a card catalog nearby? If so, how large is it? Is a terminal nearby? A reference collection?

Is the production of microforms done here?

Is there need for the storage of portable readers which may be signed out?

How should the microforms be returned after use? Is a return chute needed?

Is there need for a bell or other device to summon an assistant?

Will this be the area that maintains the central optical disk equipment?

What is the need for the special storage of supplies?

How many staff are to be provided for? What are their specific needs?

Service desks and counters include three basic types, and some details will be provided here, though many of the specific details are developed during contract document preparation, as covered in Section 13.6. These types are:

1. Circulation or charging desks from which books are borrowed for use within or outside the library and to which they are later returned. They are also called delivery desks.

2. Reference desks, sometimes called information or inquiry desks, from which readers are helped in the use of library collections.

3. Control desks for reading areas or entrances and exits. A library privileges desk might be considered in this category.

These service desks can properly be of many shapes and sizes. In small branches one desk or short counter serves for authorizing library use; handling general circulation, course reserves, and current periodicals; providing reference and quick information; receiving interlibrary loan requests; conducting computer searches; perhaps servicing a clipping or pamphlet file; and offering research advisory conferences. In college libraries these functions are divided between two or three locations, and in very large libraries there may reasonably be separate service points for each function. Treatment in this volume assumes the separate service locations; all the same functions and theory of layout pertain and need consideration in small libraries.

The reference assistance function may include brief directional guidance, simple informational help, in-depth reference work, computer-aided bibliographical searches (sometimes of a very time-consuming nature), and extensive term paper or dissertation advisory conferences. In a classroom or on tour, groups may be given course assignment lectures or explanations or more extensive forms of group bibliographic instruction. Leaving aside the latter, the reference or information desk will be serviced at times by one staff member, sometimes in large libraries by as many as three or four, and at times it will be closed. Consequently, the counter or desk needs space for the maximum staff, and yet must be convenient when one person is alone to handle in-person queries, take notes, hand out leaflets, answer telephone questions, search on the terminal, and check the desk collection of ready-reference volumes. The desk needs to be inviting, uncluttered, easy to find, near reference staff offices, and not so monumental as to be intimidating. This is not a simple design task. The size and design will, of course, be determined largely by the way the space is to be used and the amount of use it will have. Each type will be discussed in turn.

1. *Circulation desks.* The six basic essentials for a circulation desk or counter are:

a. Enough length for the staff to provide good service at the time of peak load and to work comfortably together. The area should accommodate a few simultaneous transactions, perhaps in each of several functions such as borrowing, asking for a recall, paying a fine.

b. A place where the reader may charge books and return them after use. It should have room for each individual to rest an armload of books or a purse while transacting business.

If the desk is a busy one, the book-return area should be separated from the charge-out area to prevent unnecessary crossing of traffic lines. In some cases several return points may be needed, with perhaps one for general circulation books, another for reserve books, and possibly a third for some other category such as returned headphones, microfiche, journals, and the like. The returned materials can be placed on top of the desk, or handed to staff, or placed in a book drop, or sent down a chute to a secure area. The space should be large enough so that confusion will not result, but not so large that the books will be ignored until they pile up, become unsightly, and give the impression of poor housekeeping. A large pile of returned books within sight of the public will result in their challenging the accuracy of the library's records, particularly when the book has not been discharged and could easily be picked up by another reader. This accusation will be difficult to deal with; it suggests that, in most libraries with a high volume of transactions, a fairly secure book-return chute is a preferred solution and, in smaller libraries, a protected drop to a depressable bin is desirable. In some cases, the concern for conservation will suggest that all materials be returned to an attendant in order to avoid the possibility of damage from a book-return drop.

Some libraries have a return-book slot below the surface or in the top of the desk through which books can be slid into a waiting box on wheels which can be removed when full. Another technique is to have a slot over the counter at about shoulder height with a slide down to a sorting surface. Return slots, slides, and boxes should be carefully designed to prevent damage to the books by rapid movement, too great a fall, and one volume's knifing another. Another return-book slide or box can be placed next to a slot in an outside wall for use after library hours, but as it may be an invitation to vandalism, special precautions should be considered, including perhaps placing this unit in a separate room for fire protection. Boxes, with false bottoms over a heavy spring, sometimes referred to as depressable book bins, are available from library-equipment houses; however, they often provide no convenient means of access to the space under the false bottom. Eventually a slim pamphlet will be lost to this space, a situation that can easily be remedied by the provision of an opening in one side of sufficient size to permit the retrieval of lost items.

The Lamont Library formerly had a book-return bin equipped with an electric eye. When the eye sensed a book, a motor started and dropped the false bottom just far enough so that the next volume would not fall too far, but would not jam into the preceding ones. Another novel return is found at the Delft Technological Institute in Holland, where a spiral slide delivers books to a discharge room in a lower floor. The University of Minnesota has a similar system with a straight chute which, perhaps because of its slope, continues to cause damage to the books in spite of repeated efforts to solve the problem. Systems of rollers to accomplish the same thing have been used in a number of libraries, but these often are noisy and, in some cases, tend to catch small pamphlets. When the return slot is designed to coordinate with a depressable book bin, care should be taken to ensure that the slot is high enough to feed above the edge of the bin. The design of the slot also should not encourage the surreptitious removal of books by a library patron.

c. A place adjacent to, or in, the circulation desk for the storage of books returned from use. This may require a considerable open space for trucks onto which returned material is sorted, or a bank of shelves to handle maximum loads in the same process. This feature can largely be eliminated, of course, if the returned materials are delivered directly to a separate discharging and sorting area. Sort and reshelving operations in a very large library may also require designated areas or shelving on each major stack level.

d. A place in the desk or adjacent to it for the equipment in constant use and for circulation records. The nature of this requirement will depend upon the specifics of the circulation system, but where it is currently manual, thought should be given to the possible future needs of an automated system. This may involve little more than the provision of a sectionalized counter that can easily be altered at a future date to accept the necessary terminals or other equipment, plus the provision of access to power and signal services. Specific requirements will need to be developed with representatives of the system's manufacturer, though electricity is certain to be required.

e. Working space adjacent or conveniently close to the desk for staff members record work and, in a large library, for an office for a circulation librarian and possibly an assis-

tant or two. Where there are to be impact printers or Teletype machines, a separate space with acoustic isolation should be provided, although special space for computer equipment is generally (but not always) no longer a requirement other than to ensure that there is sufficient accommodation for terminals and their associated equipment. When a library expects to have a minicomputer, a separate large office-sized space (say, 200 sq ft or 18.581 m²) should suffice. Raised floors and special air conditioning are seldom required for a library computer, although it is urged that the planner review specific requirements with a representative of the computer company. Where the current records system is manual, a future addition of an automated system will more than likely save space. This clearly is an area where thought should be given to the future growth of power and signal services.

f. If the desk is to serve reserved books, adequate shelving for them and extra staff work space should be provided as close by as possible. This is covered in Section 7.7.

Library-supply houses have available stock units of various sizes and designs for circulation desks which can be combined to suit the customer. They are expensive, but are usually well made and designed by experts who understand library needs. Among other things they may include space sunk in the surface to house circulation-card file trays or a typewriter, as well as cubbyholes, drawers, shelves, book returns, locked cabinets, and so forth. It is often possible to have a desk specially designed to the librarian's specifications and custom-built by the library-equipment house. Sometimes a local cabinetmaker can build one to specifications at a lower price. Desks represent less of a problem than catalog cases, and a good cabinetmaker should be able to build a suitable desk successfully. However, the librarian should keep in mind that for desks with specialized and unique designs, future adjustments or alterations often are more difficult.

Special care should be taken in the design. A toe hole at the bottom, both in front of the desk and behind it, will make its use more comfortable for the readers and staff members who work at the desk while standing. A staff member who is expected to sit at least part of the time should be provided with a kneehole at least 2 ft (0.610) wide at the proper spot, and if the desk is counter height, a built-in footrest should be provided, although it may be wise to make it adjustable.

Five other points in the design of the desk should be considered: the length, the shape, the width, the height, and the built-in flexibility. As already noted, the length should not be so great as to discourage good housekeeping or to make it necessary for the staff member to walk greater distances than necessary, but it should be long enough. Some desks, particularly in large university libraries, have been too long. The desk can be curved to present a greater length to the reader than to the staff. A curved desk costs more than a straight one of the same length; file drawers placed side by side can only be used one at a time; and the staff, being on the shorter side of the curve, may not have the space within the desk that is required. On the other hand, with only one or two staff on duty at a time, the curved desk may be useful and in some cases have an advantage aesthetically. If the desk is more than one bay long and in the column line of a modular library, the column in it may prove inconvenient by cutting off the view between readers and staff. Many desks turn one or two corners of 45 or 90 degrees, making them the shape of an L or two or three sides of an octagon, or may be curved to form part of a circle or a flat bottom U. A turned corner or a column in the center of the desk may make a desirable division between charging and return, or the side of the desk beyond the corner may make possible, by careful planning, a satisfactory, easily controlled, narrow lane leading to the bookstack or other restricted areas.

A desk made up of modules of, say, 3 ft or 1 m offer the flexibility of reshaping the desk area and thus encouraging rather than inhibiting beneficial re-arrangement. Power and signal (phone, computer, public address system, or annunciator control panel, for example) may limit the extent of real flexibility. Having a top that is equally modulized is important in this regard. Such modular construction will add slightly to the cost, as each module side or upright support must be duplicated, where they can be shared in the normal construction. It may also be desirable to require finished sides so that each module could stand alone or become an end of the counter in the future.

The width of the top of the desk can be a controversial matter. If it is too far through from front to back, the staff member and reader are too far apart, and passing books back and forth may seem awkward. A few desks are as much as 3 ft (0.914) wide, which may be desirable in a map room, and many are 2 ft 6 in. (0.762) or more. The wider they are, the greater the storage space on top and below, although if the shelves are too deep, the shelved books are likely to be piled up like cordwood two or more deep, and be difficult to remove. A width of 22 to 24 in. (0.559 to 0.610) is generally enough, although if a terminal or two is to be incorporated within this desk, the depth requirement of the equipment, which may be as much as 24 to 30 in. (0.610 to 0.762) can be a controlling factor, depending on the design of the desk. A cash register may be fairly deep, too.

The standard height for desks or counters—once as low as 33 or 36 in. (0.838 to 0.914), which today is considered too low—has been for the last 25 years 39 in. (0.991), and 40 to 42 in. (1.016 to 1.067) is not uncommon. The latter is a good height, particularly where the typical height of the user is average or above. In countries where the average height of readers is less than that in the United States, 39 in. (0.991) may be enough. But keep in mind that if the staff member behind the desk is to sit during a large part of the time, a high stool will be necessary for comfort, and the sitting height of the high stool should bring the attendant's eye level to approximately that of the reader for the sake of the comfort of each. The stool, if it is to be used for long hours, should have a back, and a footrest should be built into the knee space of the counter so that the seated posture can simulate that of a person seated in a normal chair.

One other warning about circulation desks, or any desk, for that matter, where the reader may have to stand for a few minutes or more. They are often paneled for the sake of appearance. Panels are expensive and apt to be damaged and hard to repair. One solution is the use of half rounds on the front of the desk (see fig. 8.1), where the damaged portion can easily be removed and replaced by a new one. Projection of the top beyond the paneled surface an inch or so can also help to protect it from damage caused by belt buckles, rings, purses, and the like. Of course, a more durable material could be substituted to solve the problem.

2. *Reference, information, inquiry, and reader's advisory desks.* These are all the desks

where information about the library and its use and its collections is provided by staff, where readers are assisted, and where such reference work as is provided has its public service headquarters. Very large libraries may have an inquiry desk in an entrance lobby to enable the reader who is overwhelmed by the magnitude of the building to get started in the right direction. At any reference or inquiry desk immediately adjacent to the entrance or elsewhere, there should be a limited number of what might be called quick or ready-reference works, which will enable a good many readers to find the answer to their questions without going farther into the library. This is also a suitable place for the display and perhaps the distribution by sale or otherwise of library publications of one kind or another.

A regular reference desk will ordinarily have in or adjacent to it a number of quick-reference books, which require some restrictions in their use in order to keep them from disappearing. This desk should, of course, be placed close to the main reference and bibliography collections and also to the public catalog, which may be used by reference librarians as much as the reference books. Access to a computer-based catalog, provided it is relatively complete, will reduce or even eliminate the need to be close to the catalog, except for the possible need of staff assistance for the catalog user. Ideally, the desk should be clearly visible to the patron from the entrance lobby as well. Again, the question of size comes up, as with the circulation desk. Ordinarily it does not need to be as long as the circulation desk. Many librarians like to have a regular office desk, 30 in. (0.762) or a little less in height, with a chair adjacent for the reader to sit down and talk over problems with the librarian. This arrangement can be very satisfactory, particularly if what has come to be known as a reader's advisory service is given, but it can also result in serious abuse. The average librarian can serve satisfactorily twice as many readers if the reader is standing. On the other hand, both persons will find it undesirable for the reader to stand while the librarian is sitting down, a factor which in part leads some to feel that this configuration may inhibit certain readers from asking questions.

On this account it is suggested in most cases, particularly in large libraries, that a reference desk should be a counter rather than a

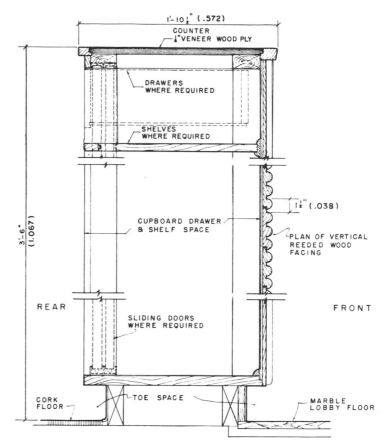

FIGURE 8.1 Charging desk designed for Lamont Library uses half rounds instead of panels. Note top projecting beyond vertical surface and toe space on each side, both important features. This circulation counter is higher and narrower than many, but it has proved adequate.

desk, and that it be at least 42 in. (1.067) high with seating as described earlier. Even a short librarian with a stool adjusted to proper height can sit comfortably with eye level approximately that of the reader, everyone concerned will be happier, and more business will be transacted. Sometimes the librarian will want two or more desks, one at counter height and the balance for extended business at sit-down height. With the introduction of automated bibliographic services with their terminals, the sit-down desk makes sense. In fact, the height may be as low as 27 or 28 in. (0.686 or 0.711) to facilitate ease of typing on a terminal keyboard, or a separate typing-height surface may be provided.

If it is the policy of the library to have the attendants do a great deal of reference work for the readers, the staff must, of course, be larger than would otherwise be the case. Office space, or at least desk space, in addition to and behind the reference counter should generally be provided where the librarian can work on difficult problems, answer reference letters, and consult with inquirers who can then sit down and be dealt with on a basis different from that at what might be called the "front" desk. This is a matter for local decision, but it does have a good deal to do with the area required for the reference staff and incidentally with the cost of the service. Almost any large library should provide one and sometimes a number of offices for reference workers, and a very large library may use 1,000 sq ft (92.903 m²) or more for this purpose.

3. *Control desks.* Control desks to maintain discipline or to prevent unauthorized removal of books are not a recent innovation. In earlier days in academic libraries, each reading room had a control desk or at least a desk from which supervision was provided and from which, if need be, both circulation and reference service might be given. Over the last twenty-five years reading-area supervision has been pretty well given up, and in many libraries the only real control point is at the entrance, or perhaps it is better to say the exit lobby or lobbies. There specially designed desks should be available. Again, as with circulation desks, the problem of the preferable length, depth, and height comes up. If the traffic load is so great that more than one person has to be assigned to the control task at one time, it may be better to have two or even up to four or five separate desks in a very large library rather than one long desk with a number of attendants working at it. There will be less chance for confusion. The introduction of electronic book security systems, which are becoming increasingly common, greatly speeds up the checkout process and, where such a system is to be used, the number of control portal positions can properly be reduced.

If there is more than one control desk in the same lobby, lanes, defined either by cords or dividing lines of one kind or another, can lead past the desks to the exit door or doors. These aisles should be sufficiently wide to accommodate a wheelchair, or there should be an alternate route for wheelchairs. Where electronic book-detection systems are specified, there may be a need for a gate or turnstile, both of which have their problems, but they do provide regulated traffic control, at least for the honest. (Note that turnstiles are

forbidden by fire laws in some states.) While some would argue that such devices should be avoided because they are perceived as offensive, many students welcome them since they are impersonal checks when compared with staff checks of bags and cases. Because of the belief that the collections are thereby under better supervision, the casual removal of library materials is reduced, thus the desired books are more likely to be found.

The desk itself typically is counter height, perhaps with a raised floor so that the attendant may be seated in a normal chair. This aids the inspection of briefcases, backpacks, and the like. A further feature that aids inspection of containers is to provide a lower section of the counter where the top of a shopping bag or other container can be viewed at table height. Other features at the control portal may include storage for first-aid equipment, a panic alert button, television monitors if part of the library security system, a phone or intercom, supplementary task lighting, a heater, and perhaps an inset in the countertop covered with glass for schedules, campus maps, or other information.

The other public service areas, including music, art, and branch libraries in general as well as a learning assistance center or a central photocopy facility, should prompt similar questions and design issues to be addressed by the programmer. Many of the topics are discussed in other parts of this book; the balance will require local consideration.

8.3 Processing Staff

Areas frequently considered as library technical processing and so treated here include those involved with order and acquisition work of various kinds, the handling of gifts and exchanges, descriptive and subject cataloging, classification, work with serials and documents, preparation for the shelves and for bindery, conservation or preservation work, often automation or systems personnel, and the typing and clerical staffs that go with these activities. Processing staff in some libraries include shipping and receiving, which was dealt with earlier. In a major branch or small library all of these functions are generally carried out with a few people, often in a single room, while a large library system may have decentralized processing and a number of separate work areas divided by function.

As noted earlier, in Section 5.3 the general relationships of major functions in the library are discussed. Because the technical processing areas are staff intensive, their functional relationships to each other and to the receiving area, public catalog, and perhaps the major bibliographies usually housed in the vicinity of the reference collection are a very important matter deserving careful attention. It is almost certain that compromise from the ideal arrangement for any single group will be required. Many of the linkages will change with the increased use of automation; indeed, with full retrospective conversion of card catalog data to computer files, the time may come when much of the technical processing area could be located in a separate building. For most libraries that time has not yet arrived, and, in any case, it should not be a goal of the planner to isolate these activities unless there are substantial reasons to do so.

Placing the shipping room close to and on the same level as the acquisition, serials, and other departments with large receipts or shipments is a convenience. If other considerations make it preferable to place the shipping room on another floor, a service elevator should be at hand; but do not upset more important relationships to accomplish this proximity. Remember that the cost of using an elevator and pushing a book truck 200 ft (60.960) is much less than the cost of professional staff time that could be lost because of poor spatial relationships between the major bibliographic tools and their working quarters. Even with the advent of automation, cataloging in most academic and research libraries is not yet a production line, as it may be in a large public library with many branches. The topography of the building site will often be a deciding factor in shipping room location.

Order and acquisition work in small institutions may be carried out primarily by the chief librarian with perhaps some secretarial or clerical help. In large institutions it may be divided into as many as five groups: selection, ordering, checking in acquisitions, billing, and gift and exchange works. At least 100 and preferably 125 sq ft (9.290 to 11.613 m²) for each person expected to be employed as regular staff members should be provided, with an extra 25 to 50 sq ft (2.323 to 4.645 m²) for the person in charge. If unwrapping occurs here, provision for one or more extra large trash containers plus a large worktable will also be required. A separate room for dust control may be desirable for the unwrapping function. Or this function may occur in the shipping room. Shelving for recent purchase receipts, for books received on approval, and for the processing of the gift and exchange materials will be needed, too. Security in this area is often a problem because until the books receive ownership marks, they represent attractive items for the light-fingered. Rare books usually receive special treatment in this regard, either with a decentralized processing unit in the rare-book area or with special secure cabinets in the main processing area. Files for vendors, order forms, invoices, and the like will need to be provided for, as well as space for terminals which, in many cases, will take the place of these files. A terminal will require from 50 to 75 sq ft (4.645 to 6.968 m²). Books received on approval may be reviewed by various faculty and staff in an area which should be convenient but supervised to avoid theft. An area or arrangement that allows book sales in the gift department without extra trucking is often welcome.

A catalog department may include professional members for subject-heading work, classification, and descriptive cataloging, and also clerical assistants, filers, and typists. Members of this department are often responsible for preparing material for the shelves, work that is carried on chiefly by clerical workers but requires space for equipment and storage of material in process. Since preparation-for-the-shelves work and typing tend to be noisy, a separate acoustically treated area will be useful. The catalog department also will have various files, including an authority file, a shelflist, and sometimes a duplicate of portions of the main catalog. Card stock may be a large supply needing space. Again, much of this file space will eventually be replaced with computers and terminals, but in many facilities they will continue to exist in hard-copy format for years to come. Certain of the more heavily used bibliographic sources may be shelved in this area, typically on shelves fitted with consultation counters, although the staff would, no doubt, prefer index tables which consume considerably more space. Carpet for the entire technical service area is not amiss, considering the high level of work required and the need for quiet.

The preparation work for the bindery is also largely clerical in character. It may be in a separate department, or part of the public service or acquisitions department, or the serials section; and as the amount of material in process tends to vary at different times of the year, storage space is essential. Sometimes a preservation or conservation office is affiliated with this department. (Figure 8.2 shows a conservation lab.) There may be special equipment such as paper cutters, joggers, book presses, drying racks, a fume hood, sink, glue pots, irons, dry-mount machines, paper creasers, and the like, which will require unique space and power service. The location of outlets for hand tools and other equipment becomes crucial where extension cords are to be avoided. Worktables with accessible outlets above the work surface may be desired. Glare-free lighting is perhaps a bit more important here, particularly if sophisticated repair work is being done. Spine labels, book pockets or circulation slips, bookplates, targets for book security systems, pamphlet bindings, binding tapes, and other miscellaneous supplies will need to be stored here in cabinets and on shelves. A nearby sink is almost essential. As fixatives and glues often are malodorous, excellent ventilation will be required.

Conservation of the collections will sometimes involve treating infested materials, drying those items that sadly are soaked from time to time, or in the future applying techniques of mass deacidification. Any of these activities may involve the use of a blast freezer or vacuum chamber, special chemicals, water, and special ventilation. If it is anticipated that this activity will occur in-house, it is suggested that a space of at least 200 sq ft (18.581 m²) might be set aside for a future blast freezer or chamber, even if one is not to be provided as part of the project. (See fig. 8.3.) If full-time ventilation with direct 100 percent exhaust to the outside is provided for this space, it can be used as a staging area for those materials arriving from hot, humid climates where infestation may be suspected. The room should have fairly easy access from an exterior delivery point so that potentially infested materials need not expose unduly the balance of the library collections. Doors will, of course need to be wide and high enough for the delivery of a chamber, if it is not to be built in. Utility requirements should be discussed with a chamber manufacturer to

ensure that reasonable future requirements may be met. The exhaust may have to be carried up to the roof level if toxic material is to be used. In some facilities this function is adjacent to or actually part of the receiving room.

The question of providing a full-service bindery in a library must be decided before programming. With the exception perhaps of fairly simple binding procedures and, in some cases, fine binding, the equipment required to be competitive in a large-scale binding operation is indeed substantial; thus at least in North America it is quite likely that there is little economic justification for such equipment within the individual library. Even so, in some countries a bindery is still fairly common, perhaps because large-scale commercial binderies are not as readily available, and advantages result from keeping material to be bound always under the library roof where it can be obtained without delay in cases of emergency. As suggested by the facilities that need to be considered in the bindery preparation area, most libraries expect to do a certain amount of mending, repair, and simple binding within their own walls; larger ones, when possible, will do well to employ a hand binder or conservator to repair books in great demand and those so valuable that one hesitates to let them leave the building. If any provision for binding and repair work beyond the preparation for binding is to be made, space must be assigned, and the floor area required cannot be determined until the extent of the work to be undertaken has been decided. Floor loads must not be forgotten because heavy equipment may be involved.

Over the last quarter century many large libraries have provided separate quarters and staff for the handling of serials, including in some cases ordering, checking receipts, preparing for the bindery, and perhaps the service to the public of this important category of material. Shelf and table space for materials and equipment are essential. Special shelving with bins or cubicles for the sorting of journals may be required, together with various cabinets for the necessary records that must be maintained. The processing of thousands of titles means tens of thousands of pieces to handle—very space consuming. The trend for at least twenty-five years has been for serial acquisitions to represent a larger and larger percentage of the library budget, if not the total accumulation of new mate-

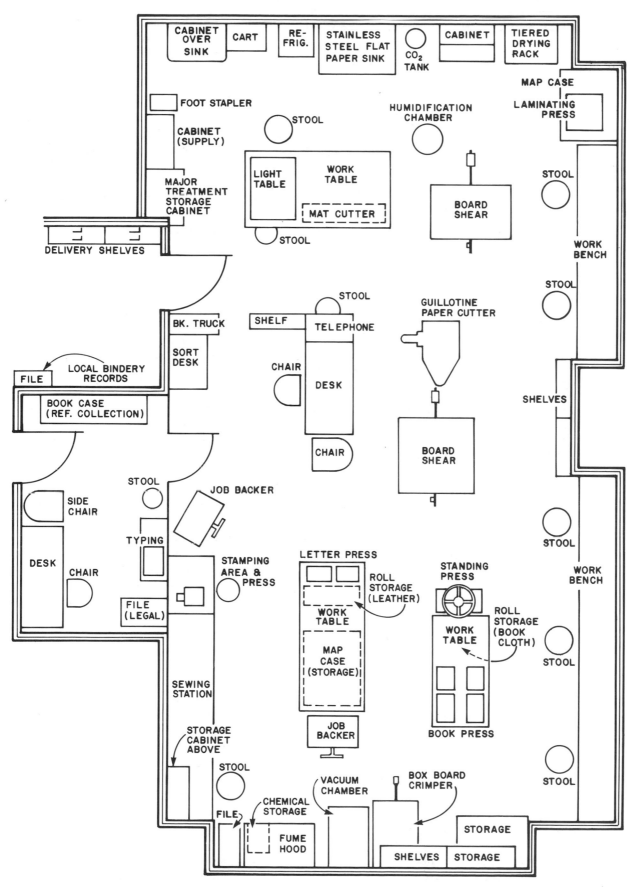

FIGURE 8.2 Southern Illinois University at Carbondale, Morris Library. Floor plan of conservation lab.

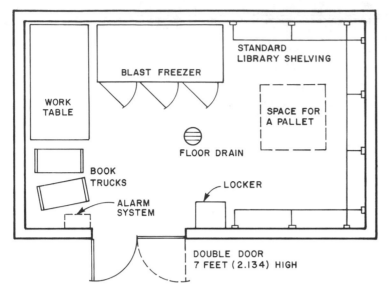

FIGURE 8.3 Fumigation room. Current technology suggests the use of a blast freezer for fumigation purposes. A room for this purpose should have ample power, excellent ventilation (preferably with negative pressure), and clear access. Flexibility for the future may be improved by providing access to water and a drain. The space illustrated would be approximately 11 ×18 ft (3.353 × 5.486). The alarm system is intended to be used to monitor the blast freezer in operation.

rials. While it seems unlikely that there will be a reversal in this trend in the near future, some would argue that the development of the optical disk will in due course reduce the bulk of the materials. The same was speculated for microforms, which really did not significantly reduce the flow of book materials in most cases, but rather supplemented the hard-copy materials that the library was able to obtain. Even so, provision for equipment in the processing area to permit the checking and processing of materials in their miniaturized format will be necessary.

Technology is having its greatest influence, in terms of staff work patterns, in the technical processing areas. Because of this a degree of flexibility, discussed in Chapter 5, should be a requirement. This suggests large, open work areas where the allocation of space to different functions can be easily adjusted; however, staff nearly always resist an open office pool with exposed rows of desks. If nothing is done to break up the open areas, the processing staff are likely to use the books themselves to create partitions and their own sense of place. To avoid this, the planner should arrange to separate workstations with

shelving, movable panels, and other equipment, while striving to provide a cheerful, uncluttered work area. This is no simple task, as the concepts of semiprivacy and pleasant outlook tend to fight against each other.

For all these groups that can be lumped under the heading "processing," 100 sq ft (9.290 m²) per person as an absolute minimum can properly be provided for work desk, equipment, shelves for material in process, and a book truck, plus another 25 sq ft (2.323 m²) for the section head of each section with as many as five to ten persons. In a research library 125 rather than 100 should be the absolute minimum. If 150 sq ft (13.935 m²), instead of 100 or 125 sq ft, can be made available, there will be that much more margin if the staff increases in size more rapidly than anticipated, if special projects are funded, or if there are unanticipated receipts or backlogs. To these figures should be added the space required for significant other elements, particularly large worktables for sorting receipts or repairing books, shelving for bibliographic tools, and space for terminals, photocopy machines, or other specialized equipment. Space for staff lockers and coatracks, where they are appropriate, should not be forgotten. With all elements included, the space required will be in the order of 175 sq ft (16.258 m²) per staff member. The implementation of automation tends to increase the space per staff member rather than reduce it; any savings due to automation will only accrue from reduced staff, and caution is advised where such a staff reduction is proposed as a space-saving measure. It is possible, of course, to crowd the staff more closely together, but undue congestion prevents or at least hampers effective work while flexibility for future adjustments is all but lost.

Movable office partition systems can save space by using more economically vertical space and wall-mounted equipment. However, caution is urged in this regard. Crowding staff to the maximum degree should be a last resort, not a planned-for condition in the program for a new facility. The cost of landscaped maximum space use will include some or all of the following: loss of flexibility, frequent acoustic problems, a more maze-like layout of the quarters, more difficult air circulation, and difficult lighting conditions. This is not to say that landscaped panel systems are bad, but rather to urge that they should be used to supplement more traditional office arrangements in terms of the program statement.

For any processing staff of five to ten or more, at least one office should always be available where the unit manager can talk without interruption with a subordinate. This requirement refers to the department as a whole, but not necessarily to individual sections. In a large processing area a conference room usually will be heavily used. Also, mini-conference rooms for perhaps four people may serve as quiet areas for supervisory consultations, training sessions, committee work, etc.

Most academic libraries make use of part-time student assistants on a fairly large scale in both public service and processing departments. They may require locker space for wraps and at least a desk drawer in addition to work space. The total amount of floor area that should be allotted to them is difficult to determine, and the decision should be based on local conditions. It is suggested that not less than 50 sq ft (4.645 m²) should suffice for each assistant who can be expected to be on duty at one time.

Most larger libraries will have a systems office, particularly those libraries moving to local integrated systems, even turnkey systems. There may be a requirement for a computer room, a training and demonstration room, and space for several staff members. The space requirements for the staff should be similar to the rest of technical processing except for any need envisioned as a training room or area. The training room can be thought of as a conference room (25 sq ft, or 2.323 m², per occupant) fitted with the appropriate computer terminals and perhaps display monitors, microcomputers, and other equipment. If each occupant is to be provided with a microcomputer or terminal, then up to 50 sq ft (4.645 m²) per occupant is needed. As noted elsewhere, the computer room can, in most cases, be a space like any other, perhaps with slightly better security and with air conditioning at least equal to other spaces. Access to data signal ducts and/or conduit is important. The size will be determined by the actual equipment; but unless it is supporting a significant user group beyond the normal automation needs of the library, it is likely to be modest in size, say, 200 to 500 sq ft (18.581 to 46.452 m²). Many minicomputers are no larger than a desk, and thus the larger size suggested would be excessive in most cases.

Some computer experts recommend "clean" power for small computers, but with improved filters, even this requirement is diminishing.

8.4 Maintenance Staff

It should not be forgotten that almost any library requires janitorial personnel who must have their own quarters. They will need a place which they can use as a base and where they can keep brooms, mops, vacuum cleaners, and other equipment as well as supplies such as toilet paper, soap, and towels. A janitor's closet with running water and a mop sink for cleaning the equipment is a requisite on each floor. Adequate supply and equipment rooms for material required for staff and public use are of great importance and in the long run will be an economy. A space of 100 to 125 sq ft (9.290 to 11.613 m²) for each full-time member of the maintenance staff or the equivalent should be enough to cover all these items.

Another maintenance need is for space to store the inevitable ladders, replacement light bulbs, touch-up paint, extra ceiling tiles, broken chairs waiting for repair, tools, carpet remnants, and the like associated with the physical maintenance of the building and its equipment. It must be acknowledged that in any large library building, particularly a central library with many functions, there will frequently be maintenance projects, with skilled laborers bringing in tools and supplies for the job. Michael McCahill has written of the University of Toronto Robarts Library: If you must have a very large library, "remember in your planning that the library will never be free of construction workers. From the moment it opened, one part or another of the Robarts Library has always been under construction, or reconstruction, or alteration, or renovation. . . .Technological change, changes in priority at university or higher levels of authority, will ensure that no matter how well you plan, your building will become a permanent construction site."[1]

For this space requirement, an area might be set aside of up to 500 sq ft (46.452 m²) in a large library as a combination shop and service storage area. If repair work is anticipated

[1] Michael McCahill, "The Impact of the '80s on Academic Library Design" (Paper delivered at a workshop of the International Federation of Library Associations and Institutions, Toronto, 1982), pp. 5–6.

there, the room should not be fitted with a fire detection system based upon the products of combustion, as the first use of a power saw will set it off. Where fire detection is desired, a rate-of-heat-rise device will be required. The room should be provided with a workbench, and lockers for tools and flammable materials. Ideally, such a room will be well isolated in terms of dust control and acoustics from the rest of the building.

8.5 Staff Rest Rooms and Lounge

The staff should, if possible, be provided with rest rooms, lounge space, and a kitchenette, complete with a large refrigerator or two depending on the size of staff and meal customs. Freestanding refrigerators and stoves are preferable to built-ins. A microwave oven is particularly important if there are no suitable lunch facilities in the neighborhood. There should be a quiet room with a cot or two to be used as an emergency room by the library as a whole, adequate toilet facilities for both sexes, preferably separate from those for the public (the numbers required are generally spelled out in the building codes), and, unless the staff is quite small, a place to eat one's lunch and to lounge during the lunch hour as well as normal breaks, if these are the custom. The lounge may also be used for staff lectures, receptions, retirement parties, and the like. Ten to 15 sq ft (0.929 to 1.394 m²) per staff member would seem to be adequate for these combined facilities, if they are available to the library staff and janitorial crew only.

It is generally unwise to allow the public to use these facilities, and few libraries feel that it is necessary to provide public lunchrooms; they cannot be said to serve a legitimate function of the library, and where they are provided, they usually represent a major maintenance headache. Libraries with public food-vending areas usually find that food travels to all parts of the building. The main libraries at both the University of Chicago and Northwestern University have had to hire special staff to monitor the snack bar exits to see that no food goes out of the area. It should be remembered that any kitchen facility must be carefully controlled to make sure that vermin of one kind or another are not attracted and that noise and food odors do not spread to other areas.

The greatest problem in connection with staff accommodations is to know how many

to prepare for in the years ahead. With modern modular buildings it is, fortunately, easier to provide for the shifting required by future growth, either within the present building or in an addition, than it was in buildings with fixed interior bearing walls; but, as already stated, staff quarters almost invariably become inadequate before those for books or readers.

8.6 Card Catalog

The card catalog is crucial to the function of any but the fully automated or the smallest libraries. Even small branch libraries generally have card catalogs. A few libraries have other forms of catalogs, including book catalogs (which are expensive to keep up to date), microform catalogs, and computer catalogs accessed through terminals, or a combination of these. At the current rate of computerization, academic libraries will still be using card catalogs through the end of this century, although most will not be growing.

Information in regard to the card catalog area and its arrangement should be made available to the architect after being considered and approved by the librarian. It should cover nine points, as follows:

1. An estimate of the largest number of cards to be housed during the life of the building, and a definite statement of the number on hand when it is first occupied. A commitment on the part of the library to close the catalog at a future date (i.e., to stop adding cards for new acquisitions) when all subsequent entries will be in another format is an important planning decision here. Some thought about how the selective transfer of books to an auxiliary facility in the future will be recorded may be useful too. Will those items transferred be withdrawn from the card catalog? Will there be a separate file that must be searched? Will slipcovers or jackets be added to the cards representing the transferred materials? If it is to be the latter, the added cabinet space for the slipcovers must be considered as, in effect, adding cards. Do not forget the shelflist if it is to be in the catalog area.

The estimated number of cards, excluding slipcovers, will depend upon the number and character of cataloged titles the library expects to include in card format at the end of the period for which the space is planned, and the library's policy in regard to cataloging. For some libraries, 2½ cards per volume or 4 per title will be sufficient, while for others the figure may be somewhat larger. Music libraries may have 6 or more cards per title on the average. Remember in the estimates the difference between volumes and titles and remember that if bound volumes of periodicals are included, as well as multivolume monographs, the number of titles in some libraries may be little if any more than half the number of volumes. In recent years some libraries have found that computer production of cards tends to generate more cards per title than was the case in the past. The number of cards per title is also affected by the number of entries for editors, compilers, and joint authors; the cross-references that are made; the extent to which title cards are included; the amount of analytical work carried on; the length of entries, which may result in more than one card for a title; and, most important of all, the number of subject cards used. If the number of volumes or titles now in the library is known with a fair degree of accuracy and the number of cards now in the catalog can be estimated, and if no change in cataloging or acquisition policy is expected in the years ahead, a fairly accurate estimate can be made of the number of cards that should be provided for during the period for which the library is being constructed.

The next problem deals with the number of cards that can be suitably housed in an inch of filing space. This, of course, depends on the thickness of the cards; those used early in the century were much thicker than the new cards that are standard today. Also it must be remembered that cards tend to become thicker as the result of use. Seventy-five years ago 80 cards to an inch (3.15 per mm) was a good basis for estimate. New cards may run to as high as 110 to 120 to an inch (4.33 to 4.72 per mm) when filed closely together. It is probably safer to figure on no more than 100 to an inch (3.94 per mm) of net usable filing space in making provision for a catalog. In order to give space for consultation and also to allow for irregular growth, and thus reduce the cost of shifting, net filing space should be estimated at approximately 70 percent of the total inside measurements of the drawers between the front and back blocks.

2. An estimate of the largest number of readers and staff expected to use the catalog at any one time now and later. It is very likely that virtually every academic library will eventually have catalog records housed in a format other than the card catalog. This other format, probably involving a computer and terminal, will easily support distribution of the catalog to many points within or even outside the library building which, as the number of records increases in this format, will dramatically reduce the number of people in the card catalog area. Where full retrospective conversion of the card catalog to computer format is undertaken, the need for a specialized area for the catalog is largely eliminated; however, it is unlikely that many libraries will be able to take this step for years to come. It is most likely, however, that current occupancy of the card catalog area is at or near a peak now, barring dramatic changes in the academic program or student enrollment. The advent of computer-based catalogs actually increases the total space needed for catalog access until the day of the completely automated and decentralized catalog.

Aside from the obvious need for floor area that will be required to accommodate the staff and readers, there is also the factor of how the cases themselves should be arranged. As the number of persons at the catalog increases, so in effect does the number of access points, which implies that the physical catalog should be more spread out. Taken in the extreme, if you have 90 drawers of catalog cards and one catalog user, then one cabinet, 15 trays high and six wide would suffice. With 20 users of that same catalog, you would probably want the trays arranged one high and spread out 90 wide. Still there would be problems of access for those wanting to use the same tray—suggesting perhaps the use of more but smaller trays. It should be remembered that in a closed-stack library the use of the card catalog will generally be greater than in an open stack, as the catalog in the closed-stack arrangement essentially represents the only way a reader can find a book.

3. The overall height permissible for the cases. This is not only related to aesthetics; there is an important relationship to the anticipated growth and nature of use. How many trays in height can the catalog be without making it too inconvenient for users to reach the top or bottom trays? without causing them to interfere with one another? A large percentage of cases provided by library-equipment houses are ten drawers high. This height is certainly suitable in some libraries. Unless

the card catalog is closed, it will continue to grow as the collections grow, and sooner or later space for it may be at a premium. There is no reason why adults without physical limitations cannot reach considerably higher than is required for ten trays. Twelve is not all that unusual today, and is in fact a standard in most academic libraries; the top drawer is no more than 68 in. (1.727) above the floor. Some years ago in the Smith College library, where space for card cases was at a premium, cases 15 trays high with a very low base were installed; the results were reported to be satisfactory. Many academic libraries are now using cases 13 to 16 trays high. Cabinets of this size will be a problem for some; low trays are often as difficult to access as very high trays, and the labels may be difficult to read at the extremes. Further, if a person is standing at a cabinet of this size, access to perhaps 60 trays will be effectively blocked for others, although this should not be a serious problem if use is light and "bread boards" or pullout consultation counters are not provided.

Several possibilities are available. If the librarian is convinced that there will never be a shortage of storage space and if the anticipated use of the catalog is not excessive, it is suggested that cases 10 or 12 trays high be used. Twelve will give 20 percent greater capacity than 10. If the librarian is worried about the future, the cabinets might be sectioned in 5-tray units (or 4-tray units) so that at a later date they can be stacked in a higher arrangement to provide room for additional capacity. The base normally would require replacement or alteration in this scheme. Another alternative would be to identify space for future cabinets. Perhaps it is reasonable to assume that sometime before the programmed capacity is reached, the catalog will be closed.

4. The width of the cases and the number of rows of trays that is required to fit the width. The standard in the United States is six trays, with an overall width of about 40 in. (1.016). They can be built five trays wide, or just over 33 in. (0.838), which can easily fit between stack uprights in tiered or free-standing stack. A case five trays wide and 12 to 14 high is in itself a bit too narrow to be aesthetically pleasing, but as part of a series it avoids this handicap. The smaller width may be used to advantage to fill out a column bay where a row of 40 in. (1.016) cabinets might leave wasted space.

It should be mentioned that in the past (and it can still be done if wanted) tremendously large cases—12, 13, 14 trays high and as much as 14 ft (4.267) long, with a similar row backing up to them, all in one great unit, housing altogether over 500 trays—were not unusual in large libraries. They are unwieldy, of course, inflexible, and almost immovable, as well as expensive. Too frequently they have become white elephants. They are not recommended.

5. The overall depth of the cases. There have been three depths of catalog case made in the past: 15, 17, and 19 in. (381, 431, and 483 mm) to which about an inch (25 mm) should be added for the drawer handles. The 15 in. (381 mm) drawer is generally not recommended because of its lack of efficient use of space; the 19 in. (483 mm) drawer tends to be fairly heavy when full. Today, the 17 in. (431 mm) drawer is more or less the standard, and it is recommended in most instances. In any event, two depths should not be mixed, for if this is done, the shorter drawers will frequently be dropped. Using 100 cards per inch (3.94 per mm) and a 70 percent working capacity, the 17 in. (431 mm) case will normally hold 1000 cards per drawer, while the 19 in. (483 mm) case has a capacity of 1150 per drawer. Filling them fuller makes them difficult to use and easy to drop because of the added weight. Removing a full tray from the top of a 15-tray high cabinet can be a bit of a surprise, particularly with the longer drawers. The decision to use this capacity at such a height is a matter for local discussion.

6. The question of reference shelves and consultation tables. Where there is heavy use of the card catalog, many libraries have acquired comparatively low cases which permit readers to use the tops for consulting cards. If the cabinets are sectionalized so that they can be stacked in the future, this may serve to advantage. As the use of the catalog eventually shifts to other formats, the space required for the hard-copy catalog may be reduced to provide space for terminals or microfiche readers which will likely have heavier use. Another technique is to develop a pattern of high and low cabinets which can serve much the same function. A third possibility is to provide pullout boards or reference shelves, which are often placed halfway up in the catalog case, so that the reader standing at the catalog can conveniently use the trays from the lower or upper part of the

case without moving away from it. Finally, there is the possibility of providing a separate consultation counter or table which offers the advantage of getting the reader away from the catalog cabinet so that others may have access to it. Consultation tables should, of course, be placed conveniently close to the catalog. They may be a shelf fastened between two cases or they may stand independently between two parallel rows of cases. They are often designed with pockets for charge cards and scratch paper, and a few may be found with phones or phone jacks (to aid the reference librarian in responding to a bibliographic question) or the capacity for a terminal or fiche reader to supplement the card catalog. In most university main libraries the consultation counter seems to be the ideal approach, but the other methods have their place, especially in branch libraries. If both consultation counters and pullout reference shelves are provided, the reference shelves are likely to be used by all except those who wish to sit at a stool or take notes.

The distance between the consultation table and the catalog case is important. If the catalog is heavily used and tables are too close, it will be difficult for the users to pass each other. If they are too far away, the filers and readers will complain that they have to carry the trays too great a distance and will demand a sliding shelf in the case or will rest the tray they are consulting on another that is pulled out part way. Either plan will obstruct the passageway, and the latter procedure tends to damage the guide cards. An aisle of 3 ft 6 in. (1.067) is minimum; 4 ft (1.219) is better; and 5 ft (1.524) is excessive in most cases.

Two other problems arise in connection with consultation tables. How high should they be and how wide? The decision must be a compromise. The users will differ in height. A height of 42 in. (1.067), or at least 40 in. (1.016), is suggested, rather than the earlier 39 in. (0.991) standard. The amount of use is a factor in deciding the width, which depends on whether the use is heavy enough so that a number of readers can be expected to be working on each side at the same time. If this is the case, the table can be 3 ft (0.914) across, but that is very unusual. Generally, 24 in. (0.610) is adequate, and often 18 to 20 in. (0.457 to 0.508) is considered sufficient, depending on the length of trays and the pressure for space. A desire to incorporate other features such as the possibility of terminals

or fiche readers, within this piece of equipment will of course affect the thinking on width and height, at least within the area where the additional features would occur. In this case the decision must be made about whether they would add a seated or standing user position. A seated position for either a fiche reader or terminal will obviously require chair space and a lower surface. A height of 28 to 29 in. (0.711 to 0.737) for using a reader or terminal is normally acceptable.

Special requirements for trash receptacles or the storage of stools for catalog cabinets of extra height may be part of the design of the consultation counter. When the counter has an enclosed base, cabinets or niches for these occasionally overlooked items may be desirable.

7. Suggestions about the preferred arrangement of the cases and the aisle space required between them. In many libraries catalog cases have been placed along a wall, sometimes recessed in it. The latter may give a very satisfactory appearance, but it more or less arbitrarily limits future adjustments of the physical arrangement of the cabinets, either for growth or consolidation, and it may also mean that the cases must be custom-built, which usually makes them more expensive. In a few instances the catalog has been used as part of or all of a wall between the public catalog room and the catalogers' quarters, with the drawers so designed that they can be pulled out from either side. This has certain advantages, but it may have disconcerting results when a tray is pulled away just as one starts to reach for it; it may even be dangerous if one's finger is caught in the handle. Special hardware is required on the staff side to prevent a reader's pushing a tray completely through the case.

When cabinets are placed as freestanding units within the space, which is a more flexible arrangement, they are generally placed in double-faced rows parallel to each other at suitable distances apart and so spaced that it is possible to go around either end of each row to reach the next one. As catalogs become larger, it may be desirable and perhaps necessary to fill in one of the ends, making an alcove closed on three sides. This may add to the capacity of the area by as much as 50 percent, but it must be remembered that if corners are tight together, there is danger of bruised knuckles when a tray from the row next to the corner is pulled out. A 4 to 6 in. (102 to 152 mm) break, preferably covered with a filler, is desirable on each side of the corner. A double row of alcoves with a corridor in between, perhaps 6 ft (1.829) wide, may give the largest possible capacity in a given area. A number of possible layouts are illustrated in Chapter 12.

8. Describe any perceived need for a bibliographic display. The techniques used by libraries to aid new students in learning the means by which the holdings of the library may be accessed range from handouts, which may require little more than a bin or series of bins at some convenient location, to a staffed information desk which may be part of the reference area or operated as a totally separate function. In between are posted instructions or a detailed display showing the various components of information that may be found in the card catalog, or for that matter any catalog, and how this information can be used to find the material needed for research. There may be tabulations of what may or may not be found in the catalog—for example, manuscripts, maps, some microtext analytics, or prints—together with directions giving alternative places to search for materials. The anticipated needs of the library being programmed will require discussion and detailing.

9. An estimate of the total area required to house the catalog and those who are using it. As the previous eight elements imply, this is a variable issue. The factors of tray depth, cabinet height, number of users, consultation counters versus pullout consultation shelves, number of drawers, etc., all play a role in determining the floor area required for the catalog. In libraries with small collections serving large numbers of readers, the problem is generally to provide space for the user rather than for the catalog. In a great research library with a comparatively small clientele, the opposite holds. The area required can be calculated after all the previous factors have been considered. It will likely fall in the range of from 1000 to 4000 cards per sq ft (about 11,000 to 43,000 cards per m²). It is suggested that the layouts illustrated in Chapter 12 be studied before the programmer specifies the floor area requirement for the catalog.

Sheaf catalogs, which are in loose-leaf binders, are used in many other countries but rarely in the United States. They have the advantage of taking less space and can be used with regular library shelving, but their adoption in any large way in the United States seems most unlikely. It is much more probable that libraries will go to online computer terminals or computer-output microfiche to supplement or in some cases replace catalogs. When microfiche or computer terminals are used, a considerable number of access points should be made available. Even if less space is required to store the catalog, the space for those using it will not be reduced, and there will be little difficulty in making use of the areas assigned for the public card catalog that the alternative format replaces.

8.7 Exhibit Area

Exhibition or display cases may be freestanding or built in; they may be fairly simple, resembling little more than a glass box on a table, or they may be quite complex, with built-in lighting, air conditioning, humidity control, alarms, and special devices for the display of books. The area itself may be a room, a lobby to the special collections area, or the building entrance hall, or it may be spread along a corridor. As an example, in 1971 the New-York Historical Society furnished a small room with a mixture of built-in exhibition cases and grille-fronted shelves displaying highlighted collections—an effective use of a small space. In establishing the requirements for the display of library materials, several factors will need to be considered.

1. *Size.* The nature of the materials being displayed and the method of display are of course critical to the size of the case. If the case is to be principally used for maps or broadsides, it probably should be vertical, perhaps as much as 4 ft high by 5 or 6 ft wide (1.219 by 1.524 or 1.829). Remember that for short people or for those using bifocal glasses a case that extends above 6 ft (1.829) will be a problem. This flat broadside type of format clearly would not require a case of great depth, but if at a future date there may be a need to display books, a depth that permits the installation of shelves would be welcome. For that a depth of about 15 in. (381 mm) is generally adequate.

For the display of rare books, the ideal case is flat or slightly sloped. The size of the case may be determined from the overall space required for the largest volume likely to be placed on display plus sufficient space for a card containing a brief written description of this item. A case of about 3 ft by 5 ft (0.914 by 1.524) is generally adequate, but other dimensions may be equally satisfactory. The depth of the case should be sufficient to permit placing items on low stands; 8 to 10 in. (203 to 254 mm) will probably be minimal for this, and a greater depth will be desired by many librarians. In fact, most research libraries, especially independent research libraries, have museum objects of great interest, as is the Bancroft Library's Plate of Brass once ascribed to Sir Francis Drake. Some objects may require even deeper cases for effective display. The dioramas in Harvard's Widener Library sit in very large, deep cases. The size of built-in display cases will often be influenced by the building module or the space available, which should not present a problem if the specific requirements of the materials to be exhibited are provided for. Extra space is nearly always welcome, up to a point, and it will allow spreading out the materials so that viewing them is more pleasant.

2. *Lighting.* Perhaps the most difficult design problem for the exhibition of library materials is the proper lighting. Ideal lighting conditions occur only when the sole function of the area containing the display cases is dedicated to exhibitions and the designer has complete control of the lighting conditions. However, in libraries these conditions are rare, if not unheard of. Even where there is a special exhibit area, the lighting conditions are often influenced by juxtaposed areas or exterior windows. As a result, lighting is almost always a compromise.

There are four key problems in display case lighting: heat, intensity, color, and glare. To a certain extent, these factors are interrelated. The ideal condition is one in which the space is dimly lit, to a degree that might be thought of as dark, so that the displayed materials can easily be seen with a minimum of light within the case. As the ambient light level is increased, the light on the displayed materials must be increased as well to maintain clear visibility. With increased light there is reason to have greater concern about its effect on the materials. Certainly the ultraviolet spectrum should be minimized, either by filtration or through the use of a light source that produces minimal amounts of this damaging light component. Heat is also a

concern as the intensity increases, suggesting in some circumstances that the light source should be outside the case or that the case should be well ventilated or air conditioned.

With light sources outside the case, glare is almost always a problem. Careful attention to the angle of the light in relation to the eyes of the viewer can greatly reduce the problem of glare, but it is rarely avoided altogether. The use of black grillwork rather than glass will solve the glare problem, but then the books may be exposed to damage by a schoolchild with a long pencil (depending on the depth of the case) and, of course, the grill reduces the clear vision of the displayed materials. Even so, the use of a black grill can be very effective for shelving lining the walls of a rare-book reading room, for example, and reasonable security can be maintained.

Shadows are another problem with display case lighting, particularly with vertical cases. Vertical light sources, often filtered fluorescent or cold cathode bulbs, may be placed within the case at the sides and toward the front. With this system of lighting, shadows will still occur, though they can be greatly minimized depending on the depth and width of the case as well as arrangment of the display. Glass shelves are also used to reduce shadows, and they are essential where the light source is in the top of the case. While there are distinct aesthetic considerations, a light fixture suspended about 2 to 3 ft (610 to 914 mm) in front of the case at a level of the top of the case can provide a very good light, and glare, heat, and shadows can be minimized.

3. *Security.* Often the most valuable items the library owns will be placed on display, which generally means that security is a concern. There is no such thing as absolute security, and an item on display is probably at greater risk than one in a vault. The need for security will of course vary with the item. A Gutenberg Bible on permanent display may have a case especially designed with bulletproof glass, an alarm mechanism within the case, and a television monitor or guard to maintain constant observation of the case while the exhibit area is open. After hours the entire case may drop into a vault, or the display area itself may be constructed like a vault with various alarms and safety features. This precaution is of course extreme.

In between the Gutenberg Bible and the latest acquisition of books hot off the press are many volumes that, while of significant value, are not million dollar items. The degree of security to be provided for these materials is of course for local discussion. However, the following might be considered:

a. Place the display cases in an area that will have a staffed position, such as an information desk, within the same space. In lieu of this, consider hidden television cameras or, depending upon the desired psychology of the situation, provide obvious television cameras with blinking lights.

b. The display area should permit closure when the staff supervising the area are off duty. This may mean that, for example, the display area is open for viewing only during the hours maintained by the rare-book department.

c. Provide intrusion detection devices in the display area, to be activated after hours.

d. Provide a silent panic alarm for the supervising staff that alerts staff at another location in the library and perhaps the local police.

e. Use laminated safety glass in the cases. Tempered safety glass may be considered in combination with lamination, but used alone, it adds little to the security of the materials over the use of normal plate glass. Lexan is an excellent material, but its optical quality is difficult to maintain.

f. Have alarms in the case that detect both the motion of an item being moved or removed and the sound of breaking glass. These alarms should be active at all times, except during the period that the display is being installed.

g. Consider having a number of smaller cases rather than one large one, to make accessibility to a large quantity of materials more difficult.

h. Avoid case designs that encourage tampering or vandalism. For instance, where security is a concern, one should avoid external hinge pins, light wooden doorframes, gaps in the doors, the use of a grillwork closure, or light movable cases near the exterior door.

i. If a particularly valuable item is to be displayed, consider the possibility of removing it after hours to a more secure location. In this regard, it is well to consider the route that must be traveled from the display area to the vault or more secure area.

j. The display of exceedingly valuable items should be reviewed with the institution's insurance and security representatives.

4. *Environmental control.* Mechanically controlling the environment within the case is a difficult engineering problem, particularly the control of humidity. Part of the difficulty derives from the fact that the volume of a display case is significantly smaller than the volume of architectural spaces that are normally air conditioned. A common method of increasing humidity involves the introduction of steam into the air supply, but the jets typically used are of such a size that a slight release of steam will dramatically increase the humidity in the case. In a large space the volume of air acts as a buffer, yet in a display case what normally would be a minor adjustment becomes a major change in the environment. Most designers feel that the use of steam is too risky for display cases, and thus they choose an evaporative humidifying system. The removal of humidity, done by a process of refrigeration, may be basically similar to that used for a larger space. Heating, cooling, and filtration of the air may also be similar; however, the engineer will need to take special care of the control mechanism.

For cases without air conditioning, there are two schools of thought. The first suggests that the case should be well ventilated, so that the environmental conditions within the case are essentially similar to those within the larger display area. When there are light fixtures within the case, a means of removing the heat from them must be found in order to avoid undue exposure of the materials to high temperatures. More than a few small holes at top and bottom of the case will be required. The second school of thought argues that a constant, average environment is maintained when the case is sealed and provided with a tray, out of sight, in which silica gel can be placed to control the humidity. This type of case of course requires external illumination, which, ideally, is not too intense. In a flat case the bottom can be constructed from a fabric-wrapped sheet of perforated metal under which alarm devices and a tray for silica gel may be placed. The fabric should of course be acid-free. In a sealed case any wood used should be well sealed to avoid acid migration. In fact, everything placed in a case that is sealed should be as free of acids as possible. Vertical cases can be constructed in a similar fashion with a tray for silica gel in the base or behind a false back.

5. *Design details.* In terms of the general arrangement, the sequence of cases should be

clear so a viewer can grasp the start and direction of the exhibition. And one of the obvious concerns that must be addressed is the means of access to the case and the ease of preparing the display. Vertical cases may be constructed with sliding or swing-open doors. Both types can provide poor or excellent results. If the case is to be sealed, the swing-open doors are probably easier to detail in an airtight fashion. They also offer the advantage of full access to the case, and normally the lock mechanism is easier to install unobtrusively. The doors can be in frames, or they can be like storefront doors of solid glass, which offer the least obstruction to viewing the contents. An astragal will be required on double doors when an airtight seal is desired or where there is concern of vandalism with a long pencil or similar object, but the astragal can be designed of a clear material which, although it can be seen, is not terribly objectionable. It should be kept in mind, though, that solid glass doors are expensive and that they are usually constructed with tempered glass, which can be shattered with relative ease.

Sliding doors also may be framed or made of solid glass. Unless there is considerable care taken in the design of the case, the locking mechanism frequently ends up being a strap lock that hangs directly on the glass. While this type of lock works well, it is not attractive. Where appearance is a concern, locks at the top or bottom of the case, perhaps concealed from view, should be carefully detailed; experience tells us that it may not be enough to simply specify that this is the type of lock to be provided.

Flat cases may be actually flat or slightly sloping, as noted earlier. A major reason for sloping the case is to try to avoid reflective glare while providing a better angle of view of the displayed materials. Both designs can be quite satisfactory. Access to a flat case may be by tilting up or removing the entire top or by opening up one side, or by creating what amounts to a drawer. Each has its problems. The top of the tilt-up case is typically quite heavy, and care must be taken to ensure the safety of the attendant dressing the case by having prop rods on both ends. This type of access is probably the easiest for preparing the case, and the inside glass of the case is easily cleaned. The case with the side opening is the most difficult to dress, but the opening mechanism is probably the simplest and least expensive. The drawer case is easy to dress, provided the drawer opens fully, but the inside of the case may be difficult to clean. Often the drawer can be removed to make cleaning somewhat easier. Keep in mind that the weight of the drawer itself plus that of the items being placed on it may make it necessary to bolt the cases to the floor, which in some small measure adds to the security but reduces the flexibility of arranging the cases. Flat cases are a little more difficult to ventilate, particularly if there is a small frame around the glass. On the other hand, they are probably easier to seal than vertical cases.

There is a considerable range of possibilities in regard to the devices or furniture used to hold and display books and other materials, details which will be left to the designer. The librarian, however, should be concerned about how to mount manuscripts or broadsides without damaging them. Any tackable surface should be acid-free and sharp edges should be avoided.

Finally, when the case is to be naturally ventilated, the slots and holes should be generous, especially when there are enclosed light sources, and a means of ensuring thorough ventilation, with openings both at the top and bottom of the case, should be provided. Too often the means of ventilation is inadequate or left out.

8.8 Other Space Uses

Two other types of space use should be kept in mind:

1. *Space for other functions.* Several types of public facilities sometimes included in libraries are not ordinarily used for seating accommodation of readers, for book storage, or for staff quarters. These include space used for auditoriums, a learning assistance center, quarters for the local historical society or friends-of-the-library group, a journal editorial office, a college museum, a special faculty reading room, a visiting scholars room, photographic laboratories, and perhaps some other areas used for what are generally not direct library activities but which may be related strongly to the library. Remember the occasional need for reception space for a few hundred who may attend an exhibition opening, a staff retirement party, or a memorial or dedicatory event.

If it is intended that an active hand-operated printing press will be established within the library to demonstrate the art of fine printing, it is recommended that a local expert be consulted in order to develop an appropriate program. The library may wish to have on display a fine antique press, but if it is to be used, consideration must be given for the support equipment, such as supply cabinet, storage for flammable solvents and inks, a composing stone, cases for the type fonts, and the like. The operation of the press can be messy; the floor should readily resist ink stains if its appearance is important. If the press is to be used for instructional purposes, sufficient space will be required for observers and students.

Unrelated activities, such as academic offices, headquarters for other departments of the institution, and classrooms, may be included as well. In a rapidly growing library, in order to provide adequate space for a reasonably long period ahead, it is often desirable and even necessary to house nonlibrary activities at first. These activities should be selected from among those that will not interfere with library service and that will be easy to dispose of when the space they occupy is needed for library purposes. For treatment of shared facilities, see Section 2.5.

2. *Architectural space* (more properly called nonassignable space). This space is the difference between gross and net floor areas. The net is the space used for the various program requirements of the library; the architectural space consists primarily of areas or volumes occupied by walls, structural elements, duct and utility shafts, stairwells and vestibules, corridors, rest rooms, elevators, mechanical rooms, and the like. This is space required to enclose, support, and service the net usable areas. It is the architect's responsibility to see that the amount of unassignable space does not become disproportionate to that of the assigned net. A ratio of the net space divided by the gross space, expressed as a percentage, is said to represent the assignable efficiency of a building. This ratio typically will range from 65 percent to 75 percent and higher, depending on the size

and nature of the facility. Larger facilities usually tend to have a higher efficiency, but other factors are often involved. For example, a one-room storage warehouse may be, by the definition, nearly 95 percent efficient, while the efficiency of a bookmobile is probably no more than 50 percent (if one could consider such a machine an architectural space).

Conclusion

Four chapters have been devoted to the issues that should be addressed in a program; clearly the formulation of the program is exceedingly important to the success of the facility project. While many of the issues have been discussed in detail that goes well beyond the program, it is well for the author of the program to have a clear understanding of the broader aspects of the specific issues. Samples of program documentation are provided in Appendix A.

On the other hand, these four chapters should not be regarded as exhaustive. Specific issues, such as the construction of the catalog cabinet, the protection of exposed wall or column corners, the specification of a book truck, points about the concern of vandalism, and others, will be discussed in the chapters on design and design development. In many cases it will be appropriate to cover issues such as these in the program; a review of the design chapters may be well worth the time of the programmer. Experience, visitations, discussions with a library committee, not to mention the rest of this volume plus other publications on planning and academic libraries, may well provide other desirable elements that should be in the program.

The program writer should not lose sight of the fact that the program can be no more than a snapshot of a continually changing environment of facility need. Many aspects of the building should evolve through the design process, with the program serving only as a point of departure.

9

Budgeting and
Expense Control

In dealing with the financial aspects of the library facility project, librarians should keep in mind the often held sentiment that the library profession puts little emphasis on economy; the pressure comes from the presidents and deans of the institution when they make up their annual budget. Presidents need somehow to be convinced that college and university librarians are not out to see how much money they can spend, but rather how the work of teaching, research, and service to which the institutions are committed can be put forward. Architects should keep in mind that academic institutions and their librarians are interested in and appreciate the importance of handsome and attractive surroundings, yet they are always under pressure to acquire more books and expand li-

brary service. These points suggest that clear justification is required from the very beginning of the library project. There certainly should be no fundamental conflict between the institution's administration, the librarians, and the architect if they have good will, a true sense of educational values, an understanding of library priorities, and a desire to make sound financial judgments in planning a new library.

9.1 Provision of Funds Required

Although discussions of funding a project may be found in Chapter 3, it is of such importance that it warrants extended discussion here. Ordinarily an institution does not go far with planning until funds are in sight, or until it is believed that they will be readily available. The actual realization of funding, however, particularly on a large project, may require a fairly well-developed program and perhaps even the completion of schematic drawings in order that the scope of the project may be clearly understood. To reach this level of planning, some initial funding will be required, and before the initial funding, preliminary planning by the library and other administrative offices will have been completed.

Projects normally start with a statement of need which, except perhaps for the very smallest projects, will take the form of a written document, which must receive the support of the institution's administration, if not the trustees. The document should contain at least a description of services which the proposed facility will provide, justification of the need, including comments on the alternatives considered, and a first estimate of the space required. There is nearly always a continuing give-and-take between the scope of the project and the funding realities which start at the earliest phase of most projects. The statement of need can serve to establish priorities and to a rough degree the scope of the project and an assessment of the level of funding that may be required.

Once the project is given administrative encouragement, the statement of need is translated into an outline program statement (if it is not already part of the statement of need), including a breakdown of floor area requirements which can be used to establish a rough order of magnitude for the project cost. This is easily determined by applying a cost per unit area as determined from buildings recently constructed under similar circumstances. Local experience of the added costs that typically make up the total project cost (more on this later), including a factor for inflation, can then be applied to establish an initial idea of the funding need. At this point decisions will be required to formulate adjustments in the program scope or funding forecast so that the two conform.

One of the questions that frequently must be addressed is whether the facility will be built at one time or in stages. This decision is a matter of considerable importance. The latter plan if adopted makes planning more difficult, but it may have funding advantages.

In many cases the next step involves partial funding, to permit the design process to proceed at least through the first design phase, the product of which may be used as part of the preparation for a campaign to establish funds. The need for the new structure must be persuasive in order that support from one or more sources can be solicited and can reasonably be expected to be forthcoming. For small projects the statement of need is often sufficient to establish funding, but a large project usually requires much more information.

If the funds are to come from a government, various requests, justifications, and studies are generally needed; often special requirements are imposed on the project which can add to the cost. Ordinarily the president of the institution, with the authorization of the governing board, originates the request to the governmental authorities, although the library and other administrative offices may prepare the actual application and supporting documents. If the question of priority arises between the library and other needs of the institution, the decision will probably be made by the governing board; but the librarians should be prepared to present the case clearly and succinctly. Answers to the policy decisions discussed in Chapter 3 should be clearly detailed, and the justifications of need should be well established.

Often in fundraising an arbitrary value is put on the space occupied by a stack section, carrel, table, dissertation room, faculty study, or reading area. This value may properly be based on the project cost, including nonassignable space, rather than the cost of the equipment or the construction cost of specific rooms; that is, the cost of unsalable areas of the building, such as toilets, stairs, mechanical rooms, and corridors, can be prorated among the salable areas. For example, assuming that 40 percent of the project cost applies to areas that are not attractive as gift packages and project cost of $150 per sq ft (or about $1600 per sq m), a tabulation of potential gifts may be as follows:

Double stack section @ 10 sq ft	$ 2,500
Open carrel @ 35 sq ft	9,000
Dissertation room @ 50 sq ft	12,500
Faculty study @ 80 sq ft	20,000
Seminar room @ 200 sq ft	50,000
Reading area @ 900 sq ft	225,000[1]

---

[1] These figures are determined by simple algebraic formula: Gift Value equals $150 times the Area of Gift divided by .60. Clearly the cost and percentage will need to be established for each unique project.

Of course, the funding strategy of a given institution may well shape the thinking for such a list of gift opportunities. A few major gifts, for example, may reduce the value of individual gift packages, while an expected decline in giving may argue for increasing their value. Furthermore, while $225,000 may seem reasonable for a reading area of considerable prominence, $20,000 may be excessive for a faculty study hidden in the basement stacks. It may be appropriate to introduce other factors in establishing such a list, thereby increasing somewhat some gift opportunities and decreasing others. Employing professional fundraisers who know different methods of presentation and appeal may be useful.

The desirability of obtaining an endowment for a new building, as well as the funds for its construction, should not be forgotten. After Mr. Lamont's gift of $1,500,000 for Harvard's Lamont Undergraduate Library, the Alumni Fund Council agreed to accept responsibility for raising the endowment for the operating costs of the library. Another $1,500,000 was secured for the purpose, thereby relieving the university of a large part of the additional operating expenditures resulting from the new building. While times have changed, the point is still valid. The Regenstein Library at the University of Chicago is a more recent endowed library building. The question of endowment can be a matter of long-term importance.

9.2 Costs Involved in Construction

The costs involved in new construction may be divided in a number of ways. One division into six groups is as follows:

1. The basic structure itself including finishes and fixed equipment

2. Electrical and mechanical installations including elevators, fire protection, and plumbing systems. (The ventilation system is by far the most costly in this category.)

3. Furniture and movable equipment which may or may not include shelving, carpet, and sun control (drapes or blinds). If these items are not included here, they frequently are found in the first category.

4. Site development, including utility connections and landscape work

5. Architectural and other fees of consultants

6. Administrative costs, including the cost of activation, insurance, plan check fees,

phone installation, final cleaning costs, and perhaps an increment for the first year of plant operation and maintenance plus any institutional surcharge or local taxes applied to new projects.

Each of these costs may be affected by the geographical location of the building, and most of them by the economic climate prevailing when bids are taken and the contract is let. Is it a high-cost area? What are the local wage rates for the various construction trades? Are the demands great for new construction at the time in the particular locality? Construction costs may be low in parts of the country, such as the rural southeast, and as much as 50 percent higher in a place such as New York City, Hawaii, or Alaska. The architectural style selected and the quality of construction can have a great effect, as these may represent a considerable percentage of the total cost. The result of factors such as these is that any rule-of-thumb cost per unit area applied to the program or various design stages can represent only an educated guess. When budgets are prepared, suitable contingency monies should be built in.

On a large project it is not uncommon to have an estimate prepared by the architect at each phase of the project. When there is great concern for the best accuracy possible, a confirming estimate might be prepared by a separate estimating firm or construction consultant, for which of course there will be a fee. To track a large project and readily be able to compare estimates, a more detailed breakdown of the costs, sometimes called a "project cost model," is a useful tool. The elements in the cost model may include sixteen or more items:

1. Site preparation, including perhaps demolition, grading, and the relocation of utilities

2. Special foundations, including underpinning and basement excavations

3. Substructure, typically the structure required up to the first floor

4. Superstructure

5. Exterior walls, including windows and perhaps exterior sun-control devices

6. Roofing systems, including roof insulation, decks, flashing, gutters, waterproof membranes under floors in bathrooms or basements and, where they occur, custom shower stalls

7. Interior construction, including partitions, paneling, and sometimes carpet

8. Conveying and vertical transportation, including stairs, lifts, and elevators

9. Fixed equipment, such as toilet partitions and accessories, shelving, cabinets, chalkboards, and built-in equipment

10. Plumbing and fire protection, including rest room fixtures, roof and court drains, standpipes, sprinkler systems, and carbon dioxide or Halon gas systems for restricted areas such as rare-book stacks

11. Heating, ventilating, and air conditioning, commonly referred to as HVAC

12. Electrical systems, which include power, lighting, signal systems, and alarms as well as conduit for future systems. The HVAC controls are usually under the previous section.

13. Miscellaneous, which could include special protection for an adjacent structure, work in a joining building necessary for the addition, and trash disposal, which may be substantial on a renovation or building addition project

14. Site development or landscape work, including irrigation systems, area drains, plantings, paths, site furniture and lighting, and separate parking areas for bicycles and motor vehicles

15. Utility connections which may not be within the defined building site

16. General and special conditions applied to those portions of the work under the general contractor. This includes the cost to the contractor for bonds, insurance, and any other special costs incurred by the contractual conditions.

A final item might well be the contractor's overhead and profit. As this is usually a straight percentage of the total of the elements in the contract, it can be omitted from the cost model for comparative analysis, but it should not be forgotten in the total budget. A factor for inflation and contingencies can also be included and will be a straight percentage applied to the factors above. It is suggested that when the cost model is used, it should tabulate the total cost for each category together with the cost per standard unit of area and the percentage of the total cost represented by each category. With this information changes in cost or disagreement between estimators can easily be identified and, when necessary, corrective action can be taken. The tabulation should have appropriate subtotals, particularly for those items which are not part of the general contract and thus to which the general and special

conditions would not apply. Once the format for the cost model is established, each estimator should be required to prepare their estimates to fit the cost model in order to assure reasonable comparison.

In each of the estimates following a design phase, the architect and confirming estimator will clearly need to prepare costs based on an actual quantity survey, rather then on a cubic or square unit of area approximation. The latter is appropriate for the initial budgetary review, and it should be based on the program, including a factor for unassigned space. Quantity surveys are usually required under architectural agreements for government projects, and they are essential when careful control of the budget is required. In the early design phases the architect will need to establish criteria for assumptions that are not yet fully developed in the plans so that a reasonable cost factor can be applied to cover those missing elements that are certain to emerge in later phases. Estimating is at best an informed forecast; while it is far from an exact science, the detailed estimate tends to be more accurate.

In some cases it may be desirable to tabulate other cost breakdowns. For example, in a project that involves insurance, such as reconstruction of a building after a fire, it may be necessary to separate those elements which are not covered by the insurance policy. Consultation with the institution's risk management officer and perhaps an insurance adjuster will be necessary. Another example may be where there is need to tabulate the cost of energy-saving features in order to analyze their appropriateness or to seek separate funding or tax advantage. Or, major computer-area costs may be aggregated if separate funding is available and exact cost accounting is desired. Such tabulations, while they may be required, can probably be best treated separately from the cost model.

In the creation of a project budget, the cost model represents only the basic construction cost. Figure 9.1 outlines an example of a project budget. It is not suitable for all institutions, but it can serve as an illustration. At the heading of the budget is some general information, including an entry for the Engineering News Record (ENR) Cost Index which is available for various regions in the United States. This index is useful for comparing the costs on your project with costs of a similar project completed within the last

STANFORD UNIVERSITY
FACILITIES PROJECT MANAGEMENT OFFICE
PROJECT COST AND TIME SUMMARY

Project Name_____ Proj. No. _____

Phase_____ Date _____ ENR Cost Index _____ at _____

Sq. ft. net assignable _____ Sq. ft. gross _____ % net/gross_____

1. Construction   % $/Sq. Ft.

   a. Basic Construction (Architect's Scope)

      1. Building Systems $_____   _____   _____

      2. Equipment (in Contract) $_____   _____   _____

                        Subtotal $_____   _____   _____

      3. Site Work $_____

                        Subtotal $_____   _____   _____

      4. Cost Rise (to:) $_____

                        Subtotal $_____   _____   _____

      5. Design/Construction $_____
        Contingencies (%)

              BASIC CONSTRUCTION TOTAL $_____   _____   _____

   h. Other Construction $_____

                 CONSTRUCTION BUDGET $_____   _____   _____

2. Equipment & Furnishings (Not In Contract) $_____   _____   _____

3. Professional Services $_____   _____   _____

4. Administrative Costs $_____

5. Activation $_____

                        Subtotal $_____   _____   _____

6. General Plant Improvements Pro Rata
   (% x Constr. Budget) $_____

7. Replacement Parking (___ spaces @ $_____ per space) $_____

8. Other: $_____

             TOTAL BEFORE FINANCING $_____   _____   _____

9. Construction Financing Allowance $_____

           TOTAL PROJECT BUDGET $_____   _____   _____

Prepared by:_____ Date: _____

Reviewed by:_____ Date: _____

Approved by:_____ Date: _____

Rev. 5/83

FIGURE 9.1 Example of the project budget. Such a form is frequently attached to numerous other pages elaborating each of the cost components.

few years. However, comparing current costs with costs more than five years ago is fairly difficult; it may be risky to rely on comparisons spanning many years as a means of measuring recent economies. The Engineering News Record Cost Index is also useful as a guide to future costs, but again, cost comparison is risky business in a changing economy, and it should be approached with care.

The first construction cost entries are expressed in terms of current costs. These figures may be the basis for the architect's fees which are discussed later. Some architects wish to include the design/construction contingency in their fee calculations; to do so is appropriate only if the initial estimate of construction cost upon which the fees are established did not include such a contingency. This contingency is intended to cover the cost of minor changes in the design and changes required because of unknown field conditions. At the earlier phases of a project, it should be as much as 12 to 15 percent. As the project progresses, it typically is reduced to 7 to 10 percent at the beginning of construction. Much less than 7 percent at this point is generally regarded as risky unless there are other clearly established mechanisms to deal with construction surprises.

The practice in the United Kingdom with respect to contingencies is to include from the time of first estimate a percentage of not less than 3 percent as a design reserve, the figure varying depending on the complexity of the problem. This reserve is generally reduced to nil by the time the job goes to bid. An additional 3 percent maximum is a contingency for unforeseen site problems.

Since the contractor will include a factor for cost rise in the bid, it is appropriate to project the cost rise to the midpoint of construction for large projects that will take one or several years to construct. For smaller projects a cost rise projected to the anticipated start of construction may be adequate. Probably the best guide to establishing the cost-rise factor involves taking an educated guess after consultation with various cost indexes, a contractor or two, and perhaps an architect or construction consultant. In some countries with adverse economic conditions, this factor can be major, 50 percent or even more. It should be applied to the preceding subtotal.

"Other construction" generally applies to construction which is properly charged to the project yet is not part of the architect's scope of work. Examples might include a replacement parking lot, if the project site takes an existing parking lot, or it might include temporary quarters to house functions during a remodeling project. This item also should include separate contracts for pre-purchased items (for example, the institution may purchase a major piece of equipment or structural component at a favorable price and assign it to the contractor once the contract is let) and the cost for utility connections that are outside the basic contract. Care must be taken to consider the need to include factors for contingency or cost rise on this line item.

"Equipment and furnishings" generally includes all the facility-related elements that are to be purchased outside the construction contract. This figure commonly ranges from 6 to 20 percent of construction cost, depending on factors such as the amount of audio-visual equipment. Movable furniture, discussed later, is usually budgeted here. Interior plants, art work, building graphics, security alarm systems, pencil sharpeners, coat hooks, waste baskets, carpet protectors, and the like would normally be budgeted here. On some projects chalkboards, tackboards, shelving, carpet, interior sun-control devices, and other elements may be in this budget category. In establishing the budget figure, do not forget mock-ups, shipping, tax, storage and installation costs as well as the cost of inflation.

"Professional services" of course includes the architect's fees. Other fees would include an acoustics consultant, soils testing, survey work, library consultant, interior design, construction consultant, and cost consultants. If there is to be an exercise of "value engineering," or a review of the energy effectiveness of the design, the fees for this work should be budgeted here as well.

Budgeting for administrative costs will, to a certain degree, be shaped by the policy of the particular institution. If the facility project management offices charge their time to the project, then this can be a significant budget element. In fact, if all internal administrative costs are charged to the project, it could total as much as the architect's fee. Included here may be other costs for insurance, plan check fees, and perhaps the cost of travel to other similar facilities during the design stages of the project. The cost for printing extra sets of the various documents prepared during the course of the project should be included here as well. If a special model or rendered drawings of the project are required, their cost should be here unless budgeted under professional services.

"Activation" of a new facility normally includes the installation of phones, moving expense for books, staff desks and equipment, and a thorough cleaning of the building. Institutional policy may require a factor for the first year's plant operation and maintenance cost unless it is covered in the physical plant annual operations budget. It may be prudent to budget for the services of an activation coordinator which, on a large project, could require a full-time staff position for a year or more to plan the activation strategy and supervise the installation of furniture and the actual move into the new facility.

A project contingency is sometimes included which may be as much as 10 to 15 percent of the preceding subtotal at the early stages of the project. The sum budgeted as a contingency can generally be reduced as the project nears completion. It is intended as a reserve for possible scope changes and it typically cannot be spent without going through a special approval process. If institution policy permits, and if there is an unexpended balance at the end of the project, it would be prudent to authorize some maximum figure such as one-tenth of one percent of construction cost for changes after the building is occupied. There is almost always some condition that was not anticipated, perhaps a missing door, an increase needed in the security control system, some additional carpeting, extra signs, or a few plants.

"General plant improvements" in this example is a self-imposed tax used to pay for improvements in the central steam and chilled water plants, utility distribution systems, campus streets, and the like. Clearly the use of this line item will vary from institution to institution. At Stanford University this item amounts to 7 percent of the basic construction cost on interior remodeling projects in excess of $175,000, and a similar pro rata charge is applied to any new structure regardless of cost. It should be noted that this budget structure (and there are other similar cases) suggests a cost advantage by removing as much as reasonably possible from the basic construction and placing it in the equipment and furnishings category or another appropriate line item. The prudent project manager must be aware of the budget structure in order to decide the wisest management of the project.

The entry for "other," while seldom used, might be the appropriate category to charge the professional services incurred by an earlier design that may have been shelved pending funding and later scrapped because it was found to be too expensive. The decision to include such an expense in the current project must come from the institution's financial administrators, which is the case for the construction financing allowance as well. This latter item assumes that gifts or other receipts intended to pay for the construction will not be in hand before the start of construction and that interest may have to be paid on borrowed money.

From this discussion it can be inferred that the creation of a project budget is fairly complex and that there are a number of different ways to put it together, each having somewhat different end results. Because of this, it often is not very useful to compare total project costs between different institutions without a complete understanding of how the total project cost was arrived at and what it includes. The example shown here probably includes more expense items than many, particularly the items for general plant improvements, construction financing, and perhaps administrative costs and "others." Returning to the six categories suggested at the beginning of this section, the following discussion elaborates on each of them in greater detail. Taken together, they form the basis for creating the total project budget, perhaps in the format suggested earlier.

The Basic Structure. The largest single factor in the cost of a new building is the structure itself, which typically would include categories 2 through 7 and part of 8 in the cost model. Factors in other areas of the cost model may, of course, have an effect on the structural costs. In general in the United States, the structure will be less expensive in the South than in the North; on the average, southern labor rates are lower, and heating requirements tend to be lower, although cost of air-conditioning equipment may be greater, as may be the cost of transporting to the site material fabricated at a distance. It must be remembered that the midsummer temperature is little if any hotter in the South than in many other parts of the United States. But cooling equipment, if available, will be used there for longer periods of time, and so the charges for energy and maintenance may be greater, and the cost of components, which include energy-saving factors such as insulation or double glazing, may be higher where ambient temperatures require long periods of heating or cooling. In earthquake country there is added cost in the basic structure required to provide suitable seismic-resistance strength. Living standards in the area, as well as the mechanical or structural details, are important factors, both in terms of initial construction cost and of the ongoing costs of plant operations and maintenance.

In general, costs are reduced by distance from large cities, where the labor rates tend to be higher; but it is sometimes found that, because there is a shortage of local labor, the workers must be imported from a nearby city day by day or for the duration of the construction period and that city rates prevail and sometimes "portal-to-portal" charges are involved. Some rural areas, therefore, may be more expensive than urban.

If plans are submitted for bids at a time of great or prospective labor and/or materials shortage, quotations are likely to be high. An uncertain economic environment can be an equally troubling influence on the final bid. If the work must be rushed for one reason or another and overtime or weekend work is expected, the effect must be considered. In some places where there is a labor shortage, unions may insist on overtime with its increased costs. An important factor in determining costs may be the need of the bidding contractors for work to hold a labor force together in slack periods. Under some circumstances they are ready to submit bids which produce a comparatively small profit or none at all. In a few cases institutions are able to take advantage of the fact that a contractor is available who for one reason or another is prepared to make little or no profit on the job—because of a philanthropic interest as an alumnus, because of religious affiliation, or because of an interest in obtaining other work at the institution. It should be realized, however, that such a reduction in price is difficult to establish as a gift for tax purposes, and it should also be realized that a contractor who for any reason bids too low and is in danger of losing money, may skimp and require special supervision if quality work is to be expected. Beware also of the inexperienced or inadequately financed contractor who may not be able to produce and so may involve the institution in a complicated, expensive, and embarrassing situation. These problems apply to both the general contractor and subcontractors, which may suggest the institution should prequalify or reserve the right to reject any bidder, which is commonly the case.

The clarity and completeness of the plans and specifications will have a considerable influence on bids. On the one hand, an unethical contractor may submit a bid on exactly what is shown in the contract documents with minimal or no profit, expecting to make ample profit on the change orders required to complete the project. Negligence and fraud are always a possibility. On the other hand, if the bidders cannot be absolutely sure of just what will be expected of them, they may quite properly add a significant contingency to their bids or make their own interpretation of the details—a proceeding which is generally inadvisable. Both approaches result in extra costs, and the final budget cost may be 5 percent or more higher than it would have been with better-prepared working drawings and specifications.

The effect of soil conditions on the cost of excavations and foundations must not be forgotten. The excavation of basement space was expensive for the Cornell University Olin Library, placed where rock was close to the surface, and on that account its extent was limited. To avoid budgetary surprises from circumstances such as these, it is essential that soil tests and a site survey be completed in the early phases of the design effort, perhaps even before the first feasibility study is completed. The cost for this kind of survey is always in addition to normal architectural services, and normally it is contracted for by the institution directly with a soils engineer or survey firm. In completing the site survey it is important to identify accurately existing utilities as well as building elevations where two buildings are to be joined. While this may be obvious advice, all too often the recorded information is inaccurate or incomplete, which ultimately will add to the total cost.

When rebuilding on previously used land, as occurs frequently in urban areas, old foundations unless excavated can cause serious problems, even forcing the relocation of new footings at some expense. This happened during construction of the Tompkins-McCaw Library of Virginia Commonwealth University in 1971. Poorly placed footings for an adjacent building can cause similar problems when the new building abuts the older one. Furthermore, in known rock areas, ample test borings should be made and checked carefully, since occasional large cracks in subterranean rocks cause false impressions when a test drill encounters soil. This was the experience during the 1966 construction of the University of Arkansas library. Estimated excavation costs rise rapidly when unexpected rock is encountered.

Several factors then result in different costs under different conditions—location, time, and the contractor's need for work or interest in getting a particular job at the time when the contract is bid, a factor referred to as the bid climate. While each of these is important and should be kept in mind, the primary considerations are what the drawings and specifications require. Those providing the funds want to know what will be the final total expenditures. They will be interested also in estimates of the cost of unit area or cubage, which may be compared with other recently constructed facilities, and in the number of readers to be served and the number of volumes housed in relation to the cost. More than on any other factors, the answers will depend on the quality of construction, the type of architecture selected, and the use made of the space.

It has already been indicated that construction costs vary widely in different locations. They may be 15 percent higher or more in Washington, D.C., Boston, or San Francisco than in southern Virginia or central Maine. In 1982 construction cost in San Francisco was some 44 percent higher than in Birmingham. In any location stone exterior walls for a Gothic building will cost perhaps 75 percent more than brick in regions where brick is common or 100 percent more than concrete. Of course the walls may involve only 10 percent of the total construction cost. Likewise, air conditioning may add to the total as much as 10 percent over the cost of a ventilation system or 15 percent over a heating system alone because of space used by ducts and the price of the mechanical equipment. Lighting installations, though they may vary widely in cost, represent only a comparatively small percentage of the total. The floor covering costs may vary tremendously. The same holds true for furniture. However, decisions to reduce the total costs in these areas are difficult or the options limited by other factors. If proper care is used, you get what you pay for, and you must decide what is worthwhile under your particular circumstances. One can pay for beauty, for utility, for comfort, for spaciousness, and for long life. One can pay for monumentality that gives little in the way of function or capacity for books and readers but that may be desirable for other reasons. The institution should select what it wants and be aware of what it can afford, always remembering that in the long run, floor area is the primary factor of costs. If one can increase the functional capacity 25 percent by careful planning without interfering with function or creating a congested effect, one should do it. The cost of the time spent in careful planning will be well rewarded in the final cost of the facility.

Construction costs can be examined from another point of view and divided into nine categories, which will be discussed.

1. *The basic costs of the building.* Do everything possible to get the most for the money expended. Engage a good architect and construction consultant, and obtain a satisfactory bid from a good contractor, preferably as a result of competitive bids, who will carry out the work efficiently and without wasted motion. Consider carefully the materials selected and the construction methods used. Reach considered and clear decisions and do not wait until the last minute to reach them. Hastily reached decisions are apt to be retracted or modified and can have a serious effect on construction costs. Change orders, even where the cost is reduced, seldom are equal to the cost that would be incurred through a competitive bid. In general, changes made after the construction contract is signed are expensive; they should be kept to a minimum although it is seldom possible to avoid them altogether.

2. *The cost of flexibility.* While it is prudent to provide flexibility in the design or construction of a new building, the degree of flexibility must be balanced against the cost. There is no such thing as absolute flexibility, and maximum flexibility is expensive. Zones of greater flexibility may be properly established. For example, the capacity to install movable or compact shelving may be limited to the basement, or the capacity to install sophisticated electronic systems may be intentionally provided only in reading and staff areas. A required ability to put an electrical outlet any place in the building may suggest a ducted floor system, which is expensive, or an open trough above a suspended ceiling, or it may suggest that a future outlet will be installed by drilling a hole through the floor and installing conduit in the ceiling space below, which, though resulting in a greater cost later, may be an appropriate compromise. Keep in mind that virtually every partition, even those thought of as easily moved, will require patching and changes in electrical services, if not mechanical and other services, when the space is changed in the future. The flexibility provided by so-called movable partitions may not be worth the added initial cost. Open office movable panel systems are costly too; yet, of the flexible means of dividing space, these systems probably offer the greatest options for flexibility but often at the

expense of acoustic privacy. As in the other areas of cost consideration, there must be a clear understanding of the alternatives with which cogent decisions can be made.

3. *The costs resulting from monumentality.* There may sometimes be a place for monumentality. The question is, is the institution ready to pay for it if the architect proposes it? The world would be poorer if it had no monuments, but much if not most aesthetic satisfaction comes from beauty and distinction not from monumental spaciousness that adds little else. The 1932 Doheny Library of the University of Southern California is brick, limestone, and marble in a northern Italian Romanesque style, with the main hall 38 ft (11.582) high and the main reading room 131 ft (39.929) long. The Doe Library at Berkeley has one space 45½ ft (13.868) high. Both buildings are functionally difficult. The Low Library at Columbia University has been termed the perfect example of the victory of architect over librarian. Particularly if funds are scarce, monumentality may be seriously questioned, unless its value for the overall objectives of the building is clearly shown.

4. *Costs arising from nonfunctional but aesthetic architecture.* This is a difficult problem and the returns, while still a matter of choice, may be so clear and evident that they are often more defensible and desirable than those for monumentality. One may ponder the question "Is true beauty ever nonfunctional?" The costs should be known and understood and weighed against what could be accomplished by using the funds in another way. If one has to choose between marble walls and space for the storage of 50,000 more volumes or air-conditioning, a decision must be made. Those responsible should listen to the architect's proposal, be sure that they understand what is involved, and then act as they balance the pros and cons. If an extra $100,000 for architectural distinction will result in students using the library more or provide stimulation and foster a love for the finer things of life, it may be more important than the space for additional books which are not yet at hand. This line of thinking may well be applied to other aspects of the project, including furnishings, lighting, and those elements that make up the total environment of the library. The answers are not easily found, but the decisions should not go by default.

5. *Costs for additional comfort.* These expenditures can go for comfortable chairs, for instance; quieter rooms, through the use of acoustic materials that will enable one to forget about the surroundings; lighting as satisfactory as possible; or better air conditioning, heating, and ventilation. All these help one to forget about physical surroundings which too often interfere with concentration. Some may say that students studied just as much and as well by candlelight or kerosene lamps, and with hard, uncomfortable chairs. Temperature and humidity in all libraries until the last half century were certainly secondary in design emphasis to a place to sit. Nevertheless, with the technical capacities and knowledge of psychology we now have, there is general agreement that comfort obtained at reasonable cost is worthwhile. Furthermore, control of the temperature and humidity will make use of the library more comfortable as well as add to the expected life of the books. Again, the suggestion is to weigh the costs and know what you are spending your money for if you have to decide between, not two evils, but two goods.

6. *Costs for utility and function.* Utility and convenience, as it might be called, are a lot more tangible than comfort. Anything within reasonable limits that will provide arrangements so that books can be found more easily seems unquestionably worthwhile. Convenient methods of transportation for books from one floor to another save time for the staff and therefore operating costs for the institution. Individual tables which encourage study may be included in this category as well as an underground tunnel to an adjacent building which will help solve the space problem and aid operations of a branch located therein.

7. *Costs for sturdiness, long life, and lower plant operations and maintenance.* These costs are often not fully considered, and they prompt two sharply conflicting points of view. One may say that if by spending $100,000 more on construction the annual upkeep and maintenance cost will be reduced by $3000 or more, the expenditure will be desirable; and that if at the end of twenty-five years the building is physically as good as it is now, so much the better. The other philosophy is that within twenty-five years the building will be outmoded and no longer functional because of changing educational methods and demands; and that the common business practice of counting on a depreciating asset and inevitable obsolescence should be followed.

When potential savings in maintenance or operational costs can be identified and quantified, it is often useful to analyze these savings in relation to the projected initial cost, using present value formulas. To do this, a number of assumptions must be made, including the rate of inflation, interest rates, the life expectancy, and the anticipated annual savings, all of which can be little more than educated guesses. The technique however does provide interesting data in terms of an annual rate of return or a comparison of future savings in relation to current expense. The analysis, while complex, is greatly facilitated with the modern business calculator. A good book on business economics will explain the procedures in detail.

Some would argue that academic institutions should reject the prevailing business philosophy on construction, which may well be the case where design flexibility and remodeling can prolong life value. However, in those areas where savings in future cost can be established without affecting the academic program, the business philosophy may be appropriate. Clearly, the definition of the academic or operational program must be well established in order to avoid losing important elements of it for economic reasons without realizing it.

At Harvard the first of the philosophies mentioned above has been the accepted norm. In addition, it typically has set up a maintenance reserve against each building with the funds always available for repair and emergency, and there is no limit to a building's length of life. Massachusetts Hall may be taken as an example. That 265-year-old structure is as good as ever and indeed, as a result of modernization, far better. It is not the function of this volume to tell the reader which is the preferable philosophy but to point out the problem and suggest that each administration make its own conscious decision.

8. *Costs resulting from wasted effort and space.* These costs are perhaps easier to see by hindsight than foresight. The item is the opposite of, but closely related to, the final point below. If lack of planning provides a module size that reduces the capacity for books by 10 percent, little or nothing can be done about it after the building has been built. If poor planning necessitates extensive rearrangement and alterations within a few years, it entails money lost. Sometimes the waste and unfortunate expenditures result from ignorance with no one really to blame. For instance, a floor covering proves to be of poor quality because of a change of formula or materials available to the manufacturer. Perhaps research simply had not gone far enough.

Mr. Metcalf identified one of his major blunders as a recommendation he made for cork tile in the sub-subbasement of the Lamont Library, which is 36 ft (10.973) below the entrance level and well underground. While he knew that it was not customary to lay cork in such a place, he also knew that it had been used successfully in the Houghton Library, almost as far beneath the ground and only a few yards away, and his technical adviser did not discourage him. It proved to be a bad gamble, with resulting large expenditures for replacement. The best planning efforts will usually result in several similar stories, even if they are not of the same scale.

9. *Costs of special planning which may save on the costs mentioned above.* To give proper consideration to each category will take time and will cost money that should be well worth the effort. A few thousand dollars worth of time and study is a bargain if it results in a module size that saves $10,000. The same amount used in preparing the layouts for seating accommodations is money well spent if it makes available 50 more seats without reducing aisle widths or table space per reader or causing a feeling of congestion. This list could be lengthened almost indefinitely, but the desired results will not be forthcoming without the availability of knowledge, experience, time, and patience. It is hoped that the information presented in this volume will help.

If these nine points are kept in mind and if there is a reasonable meeting of minds between the architect and the administration in regard to the needs of the latter, misunderstanding or complications need not arise. Each of the expense categories may involve disagreements, unless the problems have been talked out thoroughly. While the architect should, of course, be in a position to advocate changes in the administration's point of view, the latter's needs should in the long run prevail once the problem is clearly understood.

Electrical and Mechanical Installations. These installations would include categories 10, 11, 12, and part of 8 in the cost model suggested earlier in this section. Together they may range from 20 to as much as 35 percent of the total cost. The chief factors are lighting, plumbing, heating, air conditioning or ventilating, mechanical transportation, information technology communication, security, and control systems. In each case there is a question of the initial cost of installation as well as costs for maintenance, replacement, and operation.

Increased lighting intensity will in many cases mean a higher original cost and greater cost for the replacement of tubes or bulbs; in addition, the increased cost of energy may be even greater over time than that of the other factors. A 10-footcandle (107.6 lx) difference may gain nothing, yet 30 or 40 will. On the other hand, individual range aisle switching and task lighting is not inexpensive, yet the energy savings may be substantial. Furthermore, light originating in high ceilings is in general much more wasteful than a source closer to the working level, though the need for aesthetic ambient light is acknowledged. Certainly no one wants to build a building with unsatisfactory lighting.

Even in the Deep South heating of some kind is necessary; this is true in most parts of the world outside the tropics, although in the past many libraries in Australia, New Zealand, South Africa, India, and even the British Isles had little in the way of satisfactory provision for heating. With an increasing concern for preserving library materials, air conditioning has become common in the United States even in the relatively cool and dry climates found along parts of the West Coast. It may add 10 percent or even more to the total cost of the building, although it may make possible certain savings through making practicable lower ceilings, more fixed windows (with improved security), less exterior wall, and more regular shapes. Moreover, even if the need for human comfort does not convince one of the necessity for cooling, its usefulness in significantly prolonging the life of the book, manuscript, microform, and other collections should at least be considered. This issue is discussed in greater detail in Chapter 5.

Plumbing is another expensive item, particularly where the library is fitted with a fire suppression system. While there is considerable controversy over the use of such a system, the authors feel that in most cases the risk and cost is well worth the protective ben-

efit of it. One way to reduce the risk of loss by fire while reducing the risk of water is to divide the library into relatively small fireproof compartments which minimize loss potential or may be small enough to avoid the requirement for sprinklers. In secure private stacks, such as those that house manuscripts and archives, a carbon dioxide or Halon gas system may be used, thus eliminating water hazard. Of the two gaseous systems, Halon is to be preferred because of the considerable risk to human life with a carbon dioxide system. (Yale's Beinecke Library below ground stack is compartmentalized and carbon dioxide protected.) Of course compartmentalization will add to the structural costs, and it may be contrary to the intended function of the library.

The costs for rest rooms and drains may be reduced if the building is planned so that the pipes are limited in number and shortened by being largely stacked vertically. Consideration can be given to not providing hot water in rest rooms, though this saving is not recommended, and it may not be permitted by some codes.

Mechanical transportation by means of elevators, booklifts, conveyors, escalators, and pneumatic tubes is another large item included in the mechanical group. Very large libraries may require a number of elevators. Unless they are automatic, as they generally are today, elevators are expensive to operate because of labor costs, but automatic elevators are apt to require more maintenance unless they are little used. In this connection it should be noted that air conditioning or heating and ventilating systems, as well as vertical transportation, are usually operated by automatic equipment of considerable complexity, which in turn means that specially trained personnel need to be readily available either through a maintenance contract or through the institution's plant maintenance group. To be fully effective, dumbwaiter-type booklifts involve staff members at both ends. There are automatic booklifts, but these often are problematic and tend to be noisy. Endless belt conveyors tend to present similar difficulties unless they are kept to the simplest possible terms. Escalators are in use in a few libraries, such as at the University of Connecticut, although they are expensive to construct and operate, and they use a great deal of space. They are justified only where there is a large flow of people; and even then an elevator will be required for handicapped access. Pneumatic tubes are not without their difficulties; frequently simpler means of transporting materials and information result in a more satisfactory solution. A great many library buildings which had booklifts, conveyers, and intercoms ceased using them after a few years.

Signal transmission includes phones, intercom systems, public address systems, security alarms, fire-detection systems, audio and television distribution, and all forms of electronic or computer related information systems. This area where there is frequently the greatest concern for flexibility, as suggested earlier, will need careful planning in order to avoid excessive capacity which will never be used.

Each of these items is complicated and may involve a not negligible percentage of the total cost of the building. A fuller discussion of these problems will be found as follows: in Section 13.2 on lighting; Section 13.2 on heating and ventilation; Section 13.2 on plumbing; Section 12.4 on vertical transportation; and Sections 13.2 and 13.4 on signal transmission and computer installations.

Furniture, Movable Equipment, and Bookstacks. Movable equipment and furniture are normally not considered as part of the basic construction cost, and thus they are budgeted and tracked separately. Bookstacks may be treated as built-in equipment in the basic contract, or they can be contracted for separately and handled as furniture. Where there is coordination of electrical, structural, or other work in the installation of the bookstacks, it is recommended that they should be made part of the basic construction contract so the contractor can coordinate the various trades and assume the responsibility for the completed facility.

The cost of movable equipment is no minor matter; it may represent up to 15 percent of the project cost of the new facility and may exceed that considerably if bookstacks, carpet, and sun control are included.

Other important and expensive equipment includes special shelving (often of wood), tables and carrels with chairs for readers (generally the largest single item after the bookstack), service desks (when they are not built-in for the circulation department, reference area, the exit control desk, and so on), office equipment, index tables, and catalog cases. The last of these is very expensive. Carpet in some cases is included in the furnishings budget as it is often specified by the interior designer; it can be contracted for outside the general construction contract, generally at a savings to the project due to the avoidance of the general contractor's overhead and profit. Movable furnishings and carpet in 1982 could cost as much as $10 per gross sq ft (or about $108 per gross sq m) although this can vary dramatically. Stacks would be added to this cost, and they could add up to $100 or more per sq ft (over $1000 per m²) for motorized compact shelving, if used.

Art works can make a house a home. They are generally included in the budget for furnishings, though sometimes they are part of the base construction where they can be treated as an "allowance." Occasionally they are handled separately from the building project and treated in the category for special gifts. Choices can include paintings, sculpture, murals, graphic prints, photographs, banners, and even plants. While allowing one-tenth of one percent of the budget for art may be reasonable, especially if a sculptural fountain or large specimen of a rare tree is desired, selecting at least some items from existing library or museum collections can keep costs down. An interesting example is the Trinity University Library stair wall mural, *Man's Evolving Images, Printing and Writing*, a collage measuring 15 ft by 80 ft (4.572 by 24.384), which took over six years for research and execution.

Certain equipment may be treated separately for various reasons and may not be part of the basic facility budget. This type of equipment often includes microform readers, photocopy machines, special equipment for the blind or partially sighted, typewriters, audio equipment (unless it is built in), television equipment, computer terminals, and perhaps security equipment. This last item is occasionally treated separately in order to limit the publication of specifications for security reasons. The balance of the equipment may be thought of as capital equipment, properly financed through the annual operating budget or through other special programs. It seldom fits the definition of movable furniture or facility-related equipment. On the other hand, if it is useful and persuasive for building fundraising to make a sizable and appealing component package of audio-visual equipment or computers, then inclusion is appropriate.

The following general comments on equipment costs may be made. They tend to require a larger percentage of the total cost in a low-wage area; unless equipment can be locally designed and fabricated, it may be more expensive there than in otherwise high-cost areas. A library in India might be taken as an example because steel shelving and other items have in the past had to be imported.

The larger the amount of equipment of any kind that is purchased, the lower the cost per piece should be. In many small libraries the number of chairs, tables, catalog trays, and other items required in each group is so small that they will probably be too expensive to justify custom design. This means that the library must depend on standard equipment houses, a procedure with real advantages. The quality and design, while not always aesthetically pleasing to those belonging to the avant-garde, will be sound and sturdy. You can generally count on the equipment's long life, but you can expect that the cost will be fairly high, partly because of the large overhead costs of the companies. Fortunately, there is generally enough competition among companies to maintain costs at a reasonable level.

Basic decisions—such as whether to use custom-designed furniture or standard library equipment or what materials, particularly metal or wood, carpet or vinyl tile floors, or marble or plastic laminate countertops—will influence the ultimate cost of the furnishings. As already suggested, the definition of what is to be included in this budget item will have its effect as well. There may be trade-offs between what is included in the basic construction and what is included in equipment costs—especially with respect to carpet, stack shelving, standard modular counters rather than built-in units, wall hangings as opposed to stained glass for art works, task lighting as opposed to overhead lighting, furniture-type partitions in place of built-in walls, individual clocks in lieu of a master clock system, or, to take an extreme, portable fans with windows that open instead of a ventilation system. While the general contractor's overhead and profit may be saved by treating the furnishings separately, the responsibility for error can become clouded and the institution assumes additional labor when these elements are separately contracted. Furthermore, as this part of the project generally comes late on the project schedule, unwise as this practice is, the funds may be viewed as a form of

contingency for the basic construction effort; as a result expectations for the furnishings are necessarily reduced. Care should be taken to avoid a first-class structure housing second- or third-class furnishings. Probably the furnishings create a stronger impression on the reader than any other aspect of the facility, all other things being equal. They should fit the facility in a complementary manner and satisfy the programmatic need just as completely as the basic structure. Even so, it remains a fact that this area is often looked upon as a resource for budget savings. Such savings in the long term may be shortsighted, and any decisions to make budget cuts here should be carefully considered.

It should be kept in mind that union rules may not permit the installation of movable equipment during construction. Carrels that are attached to walls or floors and bookstacks, even if called freestanding, can sometimes be considered part of the building, thus avoiding complications. If they are considered part of the building, they may become part of the general contract, or a separate contract can be arranged. The difference between the two procedures may be important. By making movable equipment part of the general contract, the institution can often avoid trouble because the primary responsibility for the complete installation is that of the general contractor. On the other hand, by placing them under a separate contract, the institution can make its own purchases and, unless it is under governmental regulations forbidding this procedure, can select the manufacturer and weigh the quality and functional requirements against cost, rather than depend on the contractor's purchase of a specified quality. (No matter how carefully described, quality is open to varied interpretations when manufactured items such as bookstacks are to be acquired.) This problem can sometimes be solved by specifying a single manufacturer, but the cost advantage of competition is lost. It should also be remembered that a separate contract might lead to union trouble if either the general contractor or the manufacturer is nonunion, just as there are always likely to be difficulties when responsibilities are divided and two prime contractors are working in the same building at once. In any case, if the institution decides to enter into separate contracts, this decision should be stated in the specifications or in the agreement with the general contractor, because coordination of two or more contracts may impose certain hardships and entail added work and cost for the contractor and perhaps for the architect and the institution.

Sometimes the advantages of both plans can be realized by carrying the equipment in the general contract documents as an allowance. This means that the contractor is required to include in the contract bid an amount previously determined, a specified sum to be set aside for the purchase of the equipment or material desired, and that the final selection of the manufacturer or supplier and the cost will remain in the control of the architect or the institution. When a final decision has been reached, the contractor assumes the contractual obligations negotiated by the institution; and the total contract amount is adjusted up or down, in accordance with the difference between the final cost of the equipment or material and the specified sum previously set aside as an allowance.

Allowances are frequently carried for such items as bookstacks, hardware, elevators, special built-in equipment, art works, and landscape planting. They are sometimes, but less frequently, used to purchase movable equipment such as furniture and drapes.

Allowances are generally not permitted in public work for municipal, state, or federal governments, which usually require that the lowest responsible bidder be awarded a contract. Governments often consider allowances as a means of avoiding the competitive method of selecting a manufacturer; the open-bidding procedure is a safeguard against political favoritism in the selection of a successful bidder. Separate contracts are generally permitted, however, and the federal agencies will often accept allowances, provided the final award is made to the lowest responsible bidder.

Site Preparations: Utilities and Landscaping. In many institutions today the energy sources for heating and cooling (steam, hot water and chilled water) will be generated in the institution's central heating plant rather than in the library. Of course heating or cooling coils, fans, ducts, filters, and controls must still be provided in the library. Funding of the central plant may be part of the project in the form of a pro rata tax on the construction cost or as a direct cost of any expansion required by the new facility. A new library can make expansion of the central plant necessary or even require the construction of a new one. Wherever the building is located, it must receive water, electric power, phone and other signal systems, storm and sanitary sewers, steam if provided from outside, and sometimes chilled water for air conditioning. If the distance is great or if there are special problems in connection with the new installations, these costs may be considerable. The means of funding the utilities can dramatically alter the total library budget.

Construction of any kind is bound to require more or less extensive landscaping. The total cost ordinarily is not large in proportion to that of the building as a whole. In some cases the institution may do the landscaping with special funds allocated for this purpose and with its own grounds-maintenance force, but ordinarily the cost is assigned to the building budget. Depending upon how these elements are treated, they may be included in the cost model as discussed earlier.

Architectural and Other Fees. A major part of the fees are those for architectural and engineering services, although fees for consultants and other professional services should not be forgotten. There are three common approaches to establishing the fees: (1) as a fixed lump sum, (2) as a percentage of the construction cost, and (3) as an hourly charge plus a factor for overhead and profit. A combination of these fee structures is common when, for example, the basic work established in a contract with the architect is performed for a percentage of the construction cost as established by the first cost estimate, and any extra services outside of the scope of the contract are paid for on a cost plus overhead and profit, which may total 2½ times the wage rate of the personnel working on the project. Some years ago guides were published recommending compensation levels for architectural services, but to avoid accusation of price fixing, they are not generally used in the United States. Such a guide, however, may be useful for the client or the academic institution to have a feeling for the level of expense that may be expected for the design effort. It should be cautioned that the rates differ from state to state and even from firm to firm and that they vary with the project construction cost and with the complexity of its architectural and mechanical character. Typically the architect's fee will fall between

6 and 10 percent of this construction cost for a significant new building. A renovation project can run as high as 12 to 15 percent, and even higher if the project is small or exceedingly difficult.

When the compensation for the usual services, as described in Section 4.4, is a percentage of construction cost, it may by agreement be based on an early estimate of the construction cost. In this case, any increase in the scope of work can rightfully be claimed by the architect to require additional fees. A common method of avoiding this problem is to make the fee based on a percentage of the final construction cost including fixed equipment and bookstacks, called the basic rate. Even better is to agree on a flat fee for services regardless of final cost, thereby eliminating an incentive for the architect to "gold plate" (the greater the cost, the more the fee). Compensation for supplementary services is added to the fee. Interior design work may, for example, be based on a percentage of the movable furniture and equipment budget (more on this later). Other services may be cost plus overhead and profit or a flat, lump-sum fee.

A building of a simple architectural character may involve complex mechanical services and a variety of technical problems. The extent of these complications and the study required in their solution will be considered by the architect in selecting the appropriate rate. While a few architects may still use a schedule similar to the one issued through 1952 by the Massachusetts State Association of Architects (see page 37 in the first edition of this book), it is no longer promulgated by the American Institute of Architects, thus it could only be used for a rough idea about the fees that can be expected. Even when it was common to use such a chart, there was some considerable variation among firms. Section 4.4 provides further information on the determination of fees for architectural services.

When payments for architectural services are based on a percentage of construction cost, the total fee for such services is initially based on a reasonable construction cost projection, refined later as determined from construction cost estimates based on the completed drawings and specifications, and, if bids have been received, then adjusted to the lowest bona fide bid or bids. Payments ordinarily become due as follows:

1. Ten percent of the estimated fee is due as a retainer for services to be rendered in connection with initial conferences and schematic studies at the time the architect is engaged. In some cases no retainer is paid, but the first invoice from the architect covering these services may be 10 percent of the estimated fee.

2. An additional 15 percent of the estimated fee is due at the completion of the design development phase. On a large project there may be monthly invoices based on the percentage of the work completed, or based on a schedule of costs incurred by the architect.

3. The total of 50 percent of the estimated fee, in monthly payments, based on the percentage of the work completed and with this 50 percent entirely paid by the conclusion of contract documents.

4. Of the remaining 25 percent, proportionate payments are due from time to time during the execution of the work, and in proportion to the amount of service rendered by the architect, until the aggregate of all payments equals 98 percent of the amount of the final fee computed on the basis of the actual total cost of the work, including all change orders. The final installment of this portion of the fee becomes due when the work is substantially completed.

5. The final 2 percent of the fee is due upon receipt of a record set of drawings, usually called "as-builts," together with any operations manuals or other documentation or staff training as required by the institution. No portion of any compensation should be withheld or reduced on account of penalties, liquidated damages, or other sums withheld from payments to the general contractor.

One large university has followed a standard architect's payment schedule: 15 to 20 percent at completion of schematics, another 15 percent at completion of design development, 45 percent at end of construction documents, 18 percent at end of construction, and then the final 2 percent as above. The payments are billed monthly by the architect during all stages.

Reimbursements for incidental expenses and extra compensation for supplementary services become due when the expenses are incurred or the extra work is performed. These are generally considered to include expenses incurred for transportation and living, long-distance telephone calls, reproductions of drawings and specifications in excess of five copies, and other disbursements on the architect's account approved by the institution. Much of this portion of the expense can be covered by the basic architectural agreement, but it may be expected that if this is done, the basic fees may be somewhat higher.

When the institution or the nature of the project requires them, the architect offers certain additional services, such as those below, for which increased fees may be expected in proportion to the value of the services rendered.

1. Site development, including unusual or complex engineering design for underground and overhead utilities, grading, streets, walks, planting, water supply, and sewage disposal.

2. General surveys of existing conditions to aid in establishing the building program.

3. Detailed surveys and preparation of measured drawings of existing structures preparatory to alterations.

4. Special analysis or design in connection with exceptional foundation conditions or with unusual structural or mechanical problems.

5. Study of special or complex acoustical or electronic problems.

6. Research reports, cost and income analyses, expert testimony, preparation of special drawings or developed scale models. The most costly extra services are generally those for programming, interior design, signage programs, and redesign of elements which have previously been approved.

Some would argue that many of these elements should be identified and made part of the architectural agreement, but a higher fee than would normally be expected may result.

This long statement on the architect's fees is provided to give the librarian or other nondesign professional some comprehension of the financial and other problems involved in an architect's contract. It should not be considered definitive in scale or scope.

As already suggested, there may be other professional fees. For example, it may be appropriate to budget for the services of a library consultant. In this case there is no accepted schedule of payments for library consultants although, as is the case with architects, there are three fairly definite methods used in establishing the charges. One is on a percentage basis, the percentage varying according to what the consultant is expected to do. Is the consultant to follow the procedures through from beginning to end, as the

architect does, being on call during the construction as well as during preliminary planning and the working drawings and specifications stage, or will the assignment be completed when the working drawings are authorized? The answer of course makes a difference in the percentage.

The second method is an agreement that the work will be done for a definite sum, or at least an amount not exceeding that figure, with consideration given as the plans develop to the amount of time spent. In 1960 Ralph Ellsworth very modestly suggested that one-tenth of one percent of the estimated building cost may be budgeted for the consultant. This is probably still a reasonable measure today, provided that the size of the project, experience of the consultant, and the degree of use of a consultant are accounted for.

The third method is for the consultant simply to say that the charges will be so much a day plus expenses. The per diem may vary from $250 up, according to the experience and, you might say, the prestige of the consultant and the job at hand. A small college library or a branch library costing $1,000,000 might need a consultant, but one-tenth of 1 percent of the total or $1000 may not be adequate, even if a few days were involved, especially when one adds the expense of transportation, food and lodging for the consultant.

A consultant with a great deal of experience may feel that, in a situation where there are likely to be complications of one kind or another, $250 a day is not adequate and that $300 or more is not unreasonable. A team of consultants, working together and contributing among them expert knowledge in various fields, may require altogether a larger percentage of the total cost but perhaps less per day per person, and so on. This work is not sufficiently well organized or set in its ways at present so that a definite scale for any of these methods can or should be proposed. Some consultants, particularly those working with institutions in which they are personally interested for one reason or another, do a great deal without charge except for expenses.

The authors make two definite suggestions in connection with charges. The institution should not base its selection primarily on the cost but on the person whom it wants. The consultant should not try to bargain and charge as much as traffic will bear but should set the rate for a particular job and let the institution take it or leave it.

Interior design often suggests yet another consultant for which funds must be budgeted. While interior design is certainly within the accepted province of an architect, it generally is not part of the basic services of the architect. Often this aspect of the work is taken out of the architect's hands and, unfortunately, turned over to the purchasing agent of the institution to save the architect's commission, which may run, for this particular type of work, up to 10 percent of the total furniture budget. If the furniture does not fit the structure, however, the effects may be unfortunate. The library building consultant has primary responsibility for the functional arrangements and can rarely, if ever, be counted on to give satisfactory advice in connection with the aesthetic side of the problem. Since library furniture and equipment is a special field in itself, it is sometimes thought best to contract for the services of an interior designer who specializes in library work, although a good designer who has never done a library often will produce superior results. While the fee scale for interior design services is difficult to state, it is certainly unwise to propose a definite formula. In the first edition of this volume, Mr. Metcalf included a statement prepared by one of the foremost interior planning consultants and designers specializing in library work. It is still valid, and is included here.

This work may entail critique of architect's preliminaries to equipment layouts, color schemes, furniture selection, the writing of detailed construction specifications, including "conditions [now "instructions"] to bidders," aid in assessing alternate proposals— this is most important—and final inspection of the installation. There are several different methods of charging.

One is a percentage of the overall cost of furnishing and equipment; normally this is ten per cent, although the size of the project can affect this. Another is a percentage of the overall building and furnishing budget, with one per cent being a common base. Again, the one per cent figure can be unfair. On one project recently the budget was approximately two million, yet a survey of the program made it clear that a twenty thousand dollar fee was considerably too high.

Of the two methods stated above, the percentage of overall budget has the advantage of immediately clarifying the approximate amount the fee will come to, since this budget is normally a known factor. On the other hand, a percentage of furniture cost alone can be greatly altered as the job proceeds: 1. The original furnishing budget might prove to be entirely unrealistic and require revision.

2. The cost of the building itself might force a drastic cut in final furniture allowances—not a happy thought, but it does happen. In such an event, I have found a reverse ratio occurring: my fee is thereby cut, but my required time and energy to cope with a greatly reduced budget is expanded.

3. Steel stacks are sometimes included in the furnishing budget, sometimes in that of the architectural work. Since the cost of stacks is high, this matter must be clarified before arriving at a fair percentage fee.

4. In some instances a library will require a time-consuming survey of existing furniture to determine what might be re-used in non-public areas. This, too, must be determined since the use of existing furniture reduces expenditure and thus the fee.

In brief, I have had some clients question a percentage of furniture costs by saying: "But we must have some idea what we will actually pay you." (In one case which I won't mention by name, I contracted with a Board on a percentage of furniture basis, and only after my contract was signed did they inform me of anticipated reductions, additional surveys and studies that were necessary, and planned use of considerable existing furniture. That job was a source of loss as well as bitterness, I must admit.)

A third method of charging is of course a flat fee, in which a study of the program is made and a definite dollars-and-cents amount is quoted.

Rather than complicate matters I usually work out a fee arrangement to include travel, with a stipulated number of trips this is to include. Six seems to be an average in my case.

There are two additional points which might require comment: sometimes it is necessary or advantageous for one reason or another to place the interior designer's contract under the architect's. Often when this is done it is because the Authority refuses to hire such a consultant—who perhaps is wanted by the librarian—but is agreeable to extending that of the architect to include interior matters. The second point has to do with consolidating consultants into a single contract—that of the library buildings consultant and the interior planner. I have started doing this in some cases. Under this method I will accept an entire contract to cover the entire scope of consultation with the agreement that I will in turn retain a competent library consultant, paid from my fee, to round the "Team." This is done because some Boards resist the hiring of one consultant after another, becoming confused by the multiple advisory "needs" requested.

Finally, there may be special consultants for acoustics, signs, special systems, energy design auditing, soils testing, and site survey work. As with the consultants already discussed, each of these will have a practical fee structure. Probably the best method of establishing the budget for services such as these is to rely on the experience of the institution on other projects. Furthermore, discussions with the various consultants may provide the necessary budget information, short of asking for a complete proposal, which of course would be the basis of a contract. While the proportionate project costs for these consultants may be small, their value is often very great indeed.

Administrative Costs. There are other expenditures which, while often representing a comparatively small percentage of the total, may have to be provided for. Most larger institutions maintain an office for facilities project management which is staffed with architects and various engineers. Some project management offices may include experts in contracts or purchasing agreements, urban or campus planners, plant accountants, construction administrators, and construction inspectors or coordinators. The intent and function of this office is to assist the "client" in obtaining the best possible building for the least cost and to ensure that institutional standards, program requirements, and contractual obligations are met within budget and on schedule. When these services are charged against the project, the expenses can be substantial, and in some cases they may be as much as the architect's fee, although these are exceptions and would be likely only on small projects.

Administrative costs may include the expense of writing and publishing the program, preparing a master plan, selecting an architect and other consultants, preparing a budget and schedule, writing contracts of all types, coordinating design reviews with the various offices that must be involved, coordinating information gathering for the trustees or others who may need to make key decisions, and, in general, managing the project from start to finish including day-to-day inspection during construction. There may be a similar and somewhat parallel effort within the library administration which may be charged to the project as well. In some institutions the costs of raising funds might appear in this category.

It is imperative that the owner have on duty during all phases of construction an independent, qualified inspector whose responsibility it is to avoid errors, oversights, or omissions. The employment of an independent construction inspector may be necessary as part of administrative costs, unless it is covered by regulating government agencies or by the institution itself. The larger the project the more important this becomes. Large institutions will always have inspectors on staff.

The institution may require that a significant project be insured to cover institutional liabilities beyond those covered by the contractor's insurance as spelled out in the general conditions. Some institutions are self-insured, which means that the budgeted sum for insurance is transferred to an insurance reserve account. While the proportionate cost of insurance and, for that matter, many of the other budgeted elements is small, it is an expense that, if required, must be accounted for. It should not be overlooked.

Other costs that may appear under the title of administrative costs include county or city plan check fees, architectural review board fees, printer's costs, travel costs, and the like. The cost for an environmental impact report may appear here or within the professional services of the architect. Several thousand dollars may be required to print extra sets of the plans and specifications for bidders and internal reviews. Most architectural contracts specify a limited number of prints beyond which copies must be financed separately. Building permits are generally the responsiblity of the construction contractor, although many code jurisdictions have a separate review process referred to as the "plan check" for which fees similar to the permit fees may be charged. There may be special fees for required code review by local health departments, the fire marshall, and other state, county, or city offices.

The total of these six groups plus the other costs discussed earlier (see the sample budget) represent the project cost, as contrasted with the construction cost. The latter is usually the major part and, therefore, the one which should be determined with the greater accuracy; yet all of them should be estimated as closely as possible. The project cost must at best be a very carefully informed forecast; estimating is an art, not an exact science. Unless a satisfactory estimate can be made, the institution may find when the bids are opened that the cost is greater than anticipated and consequently that it is impossible to go ahead with the building or that its size or quality must be reduced. The latter happens all too frequently, and the results can sometimes be disastrous.

Estimating Procedures. Estimating procedures, mentioned earlier, are of such importance that they warrant further discussion here. A good estimating procedure in a library project might include the following:

1. A first order of magnitude estimate can be prepared based on the facility program, usually expressed in terms of net floor area. An efficiency factor can be applied to project an estimated gross floor area for the project. For a large project it is suggested that multiplying the net area by a factor of 1.43, which represents 70 percent efficiency, is reasonable. Smaller projects might be more appropriately multiplied by a factor of 1.50, while a warehouse storage facility might be best projected with a factor of 1.33, which represent efficiencies of 67 and 75 percent. For major new academic library space 75 percent efficiency is frequently achieved, and 80 to 90 percent is possible. The unit area construction estimate is then based on buildings similar as far as size, complexity, layout, and location are concerned together with an appropriate adjustment for inflation, which can be obtained from, for example, the Engineering News Record Cost Index. With the sample project budget outlined earlier, the estimated construction cost is usually about two-thirds of the total project cost, although this is little more than a rough rule of thumb and will vary greatly depending upon contingencies, cost rise, fees, and costs of special conditions.

2. At the time of completing the schematic phase, the architect should prepare an outline specification which establishes basic assumptions about all building systems which have not yet been detailed. With this information the architect should prepare a cost estimate which with a large project should be confirmed by a separate estimate prepared by a professional estimator or a responsible general contractor who is paid for this work. Even if the contractor bids on the job, it can be valid; for if the contractor bids, it is competitive. The contractor has gained advance time to know the plans and determine the best means of construction; the institution can invite helpful advice from the contractor about

where design details or particular specifications may inadvertently push costs up due to current construction methods or materials known to the contractor and perhaps not to the architect. This estimate should result from an actual quantity survey which should conform to a cost model such as that outlined earlier.

3. This process should be repeated at the end of the design development phase and when the working drawings or contract documents are essentially complete. Adjustments, as appropriate, can be instituted at any of these phases, although major changes late in the project will result in delay and perhaps additional architectural fees, depending on the details of the design contract.

In all of these estimates, the total project cost should be projected with as much detail as practicable, including factors for cost rise and contingency. It is believed that if this estimating is done conscientiously by competent persons, a project will rarely be unable to proceed because of the need for additional funds. It is wise in all cases, however, to have plans so prepared that some part of the building or finish or equipment may be omitted if estimates run somewhat higher than anticipated. Having an option is highly prudent and strongly advised. Similarly, one can have "add alternates" in anticipation that the bid may be lower than expected. Alternates are frequently included in the bidding (in limited numbers, e.g., three to six) which will indicate accurately the monetary value of constructing or finishing some specified part or parts of the proposed building, and these can be added or dropped from the contract, as will be detailed in Chapter 14. It should be added that renovation projects may well have more than a handful of alternates, due to the unknown conditions and therefore the wide range of bids that are sometimes received. A very large, complex library renovation has been known to have as alternates: 2 for plumbing, 2 for HVAC, 6 electrical, and 11 general contracting, the last of which included storm sash, a refrigeration room, and cabinetwork in several rooms for special collections and photographic services.

In any case, a careful and accurate estimate must be made at some time, based on a quantity survey rather than on unit area costs, in order to ensure the institution as far as possible against finding that the construction cost is greater than anticipated and that it is difficult or impossible to go ahead with the project.

To attempt to give here any precise construction cost figures is extremely dangerous, because it is practically impossible to avoid misunderstanding and misinterpretation. Wishful thinking too often leads those involved to believe that costs can just as well be less than should be expected. But beyond this human failing are three cogent and concrete reasons for misunderstanding.

1. Anything that is true and accurate today may not and probably will not be true tomorrow. Whether we like it or not, we are living in an inflationary age; ever since 1935 costs have tended to go up several percentage points almost every year, and for some of these years the cost increase has been 1 percent or more each month. There is a good likelihood that this pattern will continue and, in some countries, it may be a truly staggering figure. Any cost figures mentioned in this book are only illustrative and might well be doubled geometrically each decade in the future.

2. Costs vary considerably from place to place because of materials cost, local labor conditions, and building codes, to say nothing of building practices.

3. Each institution decides for itself, with the aid of course of the architect, what type of construction, architecture, and materials it is prepared to use; these have a great influence on costs. A rare-book library, planned as an architectural gem to attract gifts, may properly cost much more per unit area than a remote book-storage facility or a one-story library structure for a poor, struggling rural college that will have few if any irreplaceable volumes in its collection and may be able to use non-fire-resistant construction without building-code restrictions.

It has been suggested that a calculated cost per reader and volume housed satisfactorily may be a more meaningful measure of facility costs, but even it has factors which will lead to misunderstanding. In addition to those mentioned, the program will have a significant effect on such a cost figure. For example, a large library system with centralized technical processing will have quite a different cost per reader and volume in a branch library than would an institution with decentralized processing. The word *satisfactorily* must come under scrutiny as well. A building that has accommodations for 200 readers but

can seat comfortably only 150 is not recommended any more than one which claims to be able to house 200,000 volumes when it will actually be uncomfortably full with 150,000, because its stack capacity has been exaggerated by overestimating the number of volumes that can be shelved in a standard section. Self-deception about items like these seldom helps anyone.

After all these warnings and qualifications, what can be expected in the way of costs per square foot of floor space or for each reader accommodated and 1000 volumes shelved?

One definite thing can be said. Costs have been going up. Since 1965 the average Engineering News Record Cost Index has increased over 250 percent; current prices are about four times what they were when the first edition of this volume was published. At that time it was stated that a total project expenditure of approximately $2000 for each reader housed plus another $2000 for each 1000 volumes of estimated book capacity was to be expected. In 1985 the figure would be about $8000 for each category. Remember though that this is average and that the figure can be influenced by many factors. The cost per reader would include not only reading area space but also that required for the staff that services the readers, the nonassignable architectural space, and the space for special facilities such as auditoriums, exhibition rooms, and audio-visual areas, which vary greatly from library to library. The cost per reader or for 1000 volumes could range from about $6000 in 1985 for a very plain building in a low-cost area with strictly limited special facilities, inexpensive construction, and careful planning to $10,000 or more in 1985 for a building in a high-cost area with different objectives. These figures represent the total project cost, including a reasonable number of special accommodations for faculty studies, a few seminar rooms, a map room, and a rare-book room in the larger buildings, and possibly a small auditorium and facilities for audio-visual work. Please remember that these are indications only.

Other warnings seem necessary. A library with a small book collection to which a large student body has completely free access should not shelve as many volumes in a given area as a research library with many books in open stacks. The percentage of nonassignable, or architectural, space is generally larger in the small library. This is one reason why the estimating factor of net to gross varies, as indicated above. Adding special facilities to a small library seems to increase more rapidly the percentage of space not useful for housing readers and books than it does in a large library. Small libraries on one or two floors generally cost more for a unit of area than a larger building. These are but a few of the complications that must be kept in mind. A good library consultant can often be useful at this stage in explaining pitfalls that may be encountered and possible ways of avoiding them.

One final word on estimating costs. Wishful thinking is a natural tendency for many persons. Too often many costs are underestimated even by professionals, either because of a desire to encompass the total program within a predetermined budget or because of an unwillingness to face facts. On the other hand, to overestimate and not use all available funds sometimes results in leaving out a much needed security system, air conditioning, or such an essential facility as a service elevator and in providing a booklift instead. As suggested above, this situation can be largely avoided by including a few bid alternates as part of the final design. Every effort should be made to strike a happy medium in estimating. The architect should realize that good estimating will raise the client's ability to properly plan for funding the project. A librarian who is even indirectly involved in underestimating may lose face with the institutional administration and find it even more difficult to obtain additional sums later for other library purposes.

Library building costs have been tabulated from time to time. Those for individual libraries are often recorded in library periodicals. While these may be helpful, it should be remembered that they may not include each of the six categories of expenditure discussed in this chapter and on that account are too often not comparable to each other. Do not forget the three basic cost factors: (1) time of construction and the economic climate when bids are submitted; (2) the geographic location of the building and the site problems; and (3) the type of architecture and the quality of materials used. In other words, it is difficult and seldom useful to compare apples with pears!

9.3 Special Factors That Affect Building Costs

With one exception this section will refer to but not discuss in detail special factors which affect building costs. Most of these factors are discussed elsewhere. It will however list a limited number of them with just enough comment to explain their importance. They all cost money, and under some conditions they can be avoided or omitted. The point to be emphasized is that an institution should understand what it is spending its always inadequate funds for and should choose intelligently if any choice is available.

Any cost estimate in this book should be considered to be for illustrative purposes only. The estimates are at best rough, and in all cases costs should be obtained locally. The authors do not oppose the use of funds for the elements discussed below; any of them may be desirable, and under some circumstances essential.

The first point has to do with the construction methods and materials used. The higher the quality of each, other things being equal, the better the results and the greater the construction cost. On the average, outside-wall costs may amount to about 10 percent of the construction as a whole, but there can be tremendous variations, according to the type of wall used, not all of which directly affect the prospective length of life or operational and maintenance costs of the building. For example, in California, a reinforced brick wall is more than twice the expense of a tilt-up concrete wall or a wall constructed of concrete masonry units. In other areas of the country, where brick is a common material, its cost may well be competitive with concrete. A precast wall-panel system with a granite finish may be nearly four times the cost of a simple concrete wall. Of course the insulation and interior finish, typically required of all exterior walls, will tend to reduce the proportionate difference of cost, but these cost variations should be realized as decisions are made in regard to the materials and techniques of construction.

There is another cost factor for exterior walls based primarily on the ratio of the length of the exterior wall to the inside area. Curved walls and walls with many corners are somewhat more expensive than straight walls. A square building might be said to make the most efficient use of the exterior wall per square foot of floor space enclosed, although it will be about 12 percent longer than a curved wall. For each corner that is turned, a distance of approximately 2 ft. (610 mm) should be added to the length of the wall used to calculate its cost in order to record comparable relative costs. The shape of the building will therefore affect the total cost of construction.

To use a specific example, a wall for a building with 20,000 sq ft (1858 m²) if square, would be just under 141½ ft (43.129) long on each of the four sides (fig. 9.2). Adding the four corners, the total outside measurement would be some 574 ft (174.555) long. A rectangular building measuring 200 × 100 ft (60.960 × 30.480) would have the same

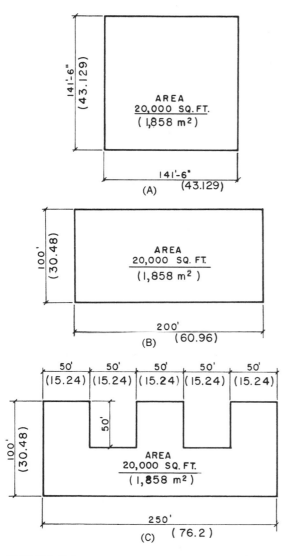

FIGURE 9.2 The effect of irregular walls on costs. A, B, and C each have an area of 20,000 sq ft (1858 m²). If the cost of the outside wall for A is estimated at 10 percent of the total for the construction, that for B will be increased by 6 percent of 10 percent, or ⁶⁄₁₀ of 1 percent. The cost of C over B will be 50 percent of 10 percent, or 5 percent of the total. That of C over A will be 60 percent of 10 percent, or 6 percent of the total.

20,000 sq ft (1858 m²) of floor area, but its walls, adjusted for the corners, would be 603 ft (183.794) long, for an increase of about 6 percent. If the wall cost for the square building is 10 percent of the construction cost, then the increase in cost for the rectangular building is about three-fifths of 1 percent.

If the building were E-shaped, with overall dimensions of 100 × 250 ft (30.480 × 76.200) and with two partially enclosed courts each 50 × 50 ft (15.240 × 15.240), the area would be the same; but with 12 corners the adjusted length of the outside wall is 924 lineal ft (281.635), or just over 60 percent greater than that required for a square building. All other elements being equal, this shape would add 6 percent to the construction cost. At $100 per sq ft these calculations suggest an added cost of some $12,000 per floor for the rectangular building and $120,000 per floor for the E-shape. For a building 5 or 10 stories high this added cost can result in a very considerable sum. It should not be forgotten however that changes in the type of wall construction might make an equal or greater difference; that is, the cost of a fine stone building, even if square, might be greater than that of the E-shaped building faced with brick or with one of the other less expensive methods of wall construction.

This statement is not presented in order to argue that the building should be square in order to save $12,000 per floor or that it should not be E-shaped to save $120,000. The point to be made is simply that, as this example illustrates, costs mount up. A square building provides more square footage in contents than buildings of other shapes, other things being equal. On the other hand, in an E-shaped building, no space is more than 25 ft (7.620) from an exterior wall, assuming each leg is only 50 ft (15.240) wide. This fact may serve to advantage in moderate climates for natural lighting and ventilation. However, in climates with temperature extremes, the heat gain and loss through the longer exterior wall will result in increased energy consumption. The E-shape will also increase somewhat the cost of floor and roof construction. The same cost factor applies to a building with straight vertical walls instead of overhangs or setbacks. A simple shape in plan and elevation will always cost less than a more complicated one. Those responsible must decide, given all the factors, which they prefer to select.

Interior light wells, which used to be common in large libraries for ventilation and light, go back to the days when electrically monitored mechanical environmental control was in its infancy. Such courts are often proposed today, not so much for light and ventilation as for aesthetic, or what might be called humanistic purposes, affording a spatial relief to the library as a structure and an intimate attractive outlook for the reader. This consideration may be of special importance in an unattractive urban environment even though the wells reduce the available floor area, increase expensive wall areas, and interfere with traffic patterns. When an old library with courts is relighted and air-conditioned, there is a natural temptation, if more space is needed, to fill in the courts, as doing so provides assignable space where it is greatly appreciated and seems a natural development. It has been done in a number of libraries, including the Library of Congress and the Vassar College Library, but it turns out that filling in the space is typically more expensive for a unit of net floor area gained than a new wing would be. The excuse for filling in courts is that the location may make the added space worth the difference because there may be no other land available, the space in the heart of the existing building may be more valuable and usable, or the balance of the building may be enhanced by improved internal circulation and juxtaposition of functions.

The following paragraphs discuss more briefly other items to be watched out for and show where money can be saved. This does not necessarily mean that it should be, but the possible savings should be carefully weighed and decisions reached about which procedure is better to choose.

An inexpensive flooring material may cost in excess of $.50 a sq ft less throughout the whole building than another that might be chosen. If the building has 100,000 sq ft (9290 m²), the difference could be $50,000 or more. It should be remembered, however, that the less expensive flooring may be unsatisfactory from the acoustic point of view. It may also be unsatisfactory because of the cost of maintenance, because it lacks static control properties needed in computer areas, or because it will wear out and have to be replaced in a comparatively few years. The cost of replacement at more frequent intervals may exceed the cost savings of the original installation. The use of present value analysis, discussed earlier, may be appropriate here, although it cannot be used to analyze the value of acoustic benefits.

When it comes to other acoustical material, the question may be a little more difficult to decide. A cheaper variety may last just as long and require no more upkeep; but the question is whether it satisfactorily performs its other functions and is fireproof and looks acceptable.

The cost of monumental stairs may be in the stair construction itself; however, a more important consideration is likely to be the amount of floor area involved, which might be used for other purposes. Since the area is the same for every floor reached by those stairs, an unnecessary 20 sq ft (1.86 m²) stair area in a five-story building means the loss of space to house, for example, 1500 volumes.

The cost of an entrance lobby with 2000 sq ft of space where 1000 would be sufficient (185.80 m² rather than 92.90 m²) would be an additional $100,000 if figured at the rate of $100 per sq ft. On the other hand, if the lobby houses the check-out, entrance control, circulation, and reserved-book desks, for instance, and it is too small to handle the peak loads without congestion, the insufficient space is a serious fault and often one that cannot be corrected later. The lobby should be large enough to provide a satisfactory distribution point from which emanate the circulation traffic patterns for the building as a whole.

Complete air conditioning can be expected to add as much as 15 percent to the net construction cost, even if one takes into consideration the savings in cubage that it may make possible by reducing ceiling heights. Even so, it probably is of vital importance in connection with the preservation of books and in making the library an inviting place for students and faculty.

Each additional elevator or booklift has a price attached. While one can build the shaft and leave out the equipment for years, it is cheaper to install one at the time of construction than later. Remember that a shortage of service elevators may be very expensive in staff time.

The cost of shelving can be reduced up to 30 percent by stripping it of finished bases, end panels, and canopy tops, and by limiting shelf depths to a minimum, but in many cases economies of this kind are not desirable. The cost of the floor area occupied by the equipment is, however, much more important than the cost of the equipment itself. The fact that less expensive shelving is possible does not mean that industrial or commercial shelving should be used in regular bookstacks; it is far more difficult to adjust and its appearance generally is much less satisfactory. In most cases, the decision can be based on utility and appearance rather than on cost.

The above discussion relates to only one of at least five aspects of the whole story. The second one deals with the utilization of the space. If only 60 percent of the total gross area is what is known as assignable, or net usable, space, one has no more use from a 100,000 sq ft (9,290 m²) building than from one with 80,000 sq ft (7,432 m²) where 75 percent is net usable. In this case, the differences in construction costs alone could come to $2,000,000 or more, which is probably greater than any possible difference in costs between the various types of outside walls, floor coverings, shelving, etc. A rough estimate would place the maximum difference between the best interior and exterior finishes and the most economical but feasible ones at only 15 percent; much more than that is often expended on what could be an unnecessarily low percent of net to gross floor area.

The extra floor area is one of the items that it helps to plan carefully with costs in mind. The amount of floor area may be considerable if used for a monumental stair, a circular stair, an entrance lobby or corridor larger than required to take care of peak loads (unless it is used also for exhibition purposes, making a separate exhibition room unnecessary), extra cross aisles in the stacks, unnecessary walls, and other assignments of space which perhaps are not functionally essential or aesthetically justified.

A third important factor is the use of the floor area available for library purposes. For example, if reading areas are so arranged that one reader can be housed in 25 sq ft (2.32 m²) of floor space instead of 30 (2.79 m²), and 1000 readers are to be seated in the building, the difference of 5,000 sq ft (464.50 m²) could, at current cost, result in a savings of $500,000 or more. If allowing only 25 sq ft (2.32 m²) per reader results in unsatisfactory accommodations and many seats will not be filled because they are inconvenient or perceived to be occupied or pre-empted by other readers, it makes no sense to crowd them in. How-

ever, if one is convinced that by careful planning, readers can be seated just as satisfactorily as in the larger amount of space, one should make the change. Do not be overly influenced by wishful thinking. It is not uncommon to find a well-arranged seating area with minimal spacing to be never more than 50 percent occupied, while a similar seating area with perhaps larger carrels and fewer chairs at the tables may have 100 percent use in what may be regarded a more extravagant assignment of space. Absolute frugality is not recommended here, but careful planning is very much desired. An increase or decrease in the size of a reading area without changing the number of seating accommodations does not affect proportionately the other facilities of the building; they will still require the same amount of furniture and equipment, the same number of doors, janitor's closets, stairs, toilets, and similar added costs, which prorate themselves over the total area of the building.

The same thinking holds true for book storage. If, by careful planning and without causing any inconvenience, 15 volumes can be stored per sq ft instead of 12 (or 160 versus 130 volumes per sq m), and 900,000 volumes are to be provided for, the difference will be 15,000 sq ft (about 1,400 m²), which of course could result in a substantial cost savings. Again, watch out for wishful thinking!

Sometimes space can be utilized to better advantage by using it for different purposes at different times, that is, making it multipurpose space. For instance, a small auditorium if properly designed can be used for a reading area during the examination period when pressure for reading space will be at its peak. Collapsible tables can be stored in a very small area and be made available quickly, but it should be cautioned that these do not make ideal reading tables; this approach should only be used where there are no better alternatives. Main corridors can serve as satisfactory exhibit areas or can house open-access reserved books if they are made a little wider, but the degree of control over these materials may be compromised. Excessive restrictions of space in any regard may significantly reduce long-term flexibility, and thus it should only be undertaken with careful thought and planning.

A fourth cost factor deals with cubic space rather than floor area and relates to the height of rooms. This issue is discussed elsewhere, but it should be noted here that if, in order to place reading areas, book storage, and staff anywhere in a building, greater total height is required, it will cost money. If the bookstacks are all on certain floors with low ceilings and all the areas requiring higher ceilings are on other floors, height and money will be saved. This does not mean that a building should be planned inconveniently for use by readers and staff in order to save cubage, but the difference in cost should be kept in mind in making the decisions. At the least, all floors do not have to have the same height as the entrance level, which for psychological reasons may at times be somewhat higher than absolutely necessary.

A closely related factor is that if the services to readers are concentrated in one part of a building and heavy book and other storage in another, floors with a lower load-bearing capacity can be used for the former group, thereby saving a considerable sum of money in a large building. On the whole, however, it is better to make all space available for any library purpose, in order to obtain more complete flexibility. Those who have tried to economize by limiting the structural capacity of the building to the currently planned need have too often lived to regret it.

The effect on costs of the column spacing that is selected should not be forgotten. Generally, the closer the column spacing, the cheaper the floor construction. The columns themselves are expensive though, and a building 110 ft (33.500) square with 27 ft (8.230) bays will have just over one-half as many columns (assuming interior columns and an exterior bearing wall) as one of the same size with bays 18 ft (5.486) square. It is not easy to pick the most economical size of bay. As shown elsewhere, the column spacing can have a great effect on the capacity of the building for housing readers and books, particularly the latter. The economic factors to be reckoned with here are thus (1) the maximum use of the resulting net space (a library factor) and (2) the cost of the columns and footings versus the cost of the floor slabs and beam spans (a structural factor).

Closely related to the column-spacing problem is that of the coordination of sizes of building materials and equipment on a basic standard module of 4 in. (102mm), which is common in construction work. It can result in considerable savings in field-labor costs by making it possible to use materials produced on a production line in a factory without alteration.

It is suggested then that these five different factors in construction and equipment costs should be kept in mind:

1. Those that deal with the construction itself which are affected by the type and cost of materials used, the amount of outside wall that it takes to enclose the desired area, and the size selected for column spacing.

2. The percentage of architectural, or nonassignable, space that cannot be used for library purposes; this space includes that occupied by walls, columns, ducts, and pipes, as well as by lobbies, corridors, stairs, elevators and lifts, mechanical rooms, and rest rooms.

3. The utilization of the space that is available for library purposes.

4. Ceiling heights.

5. Load-bearing capacity throughout the building.

Each member of the building team should be on the lookout for other factors that should be weighed and discussed so that all concerned will know and understand just what is involved.

Renovation projects are often more difficult to estimate than are those for new structures. Additional problems may be faced—for example, when a wall is penetrated, a ceiling exposed, or a utility run traced, or when logistical or access issues arise in a building which is partially occupied by staff and users. Project contingencies therefore need to be slightly higher, often one or two percent higher. Large renovation projects range widely in cost per unit of floor area, generally comparing with the lower half of the typical range of floor area costs for new library construction. It will naturally vary greatly, depending on the amount of structural work, new utilities, waterproofing, furniture to be replaced, and a host of other factors. When a project combines an addition with renovation of the existing structure, the economy of renovation can be somewhat assured through the protection given the contractor's bid by the contract's covering the completely new work on the addition as well as the renovation. Note however that some contractors specialize in renovation, and renovation work may best be handled by a different contractor. Contract bid add and deduct alternates are especially important for renovation projects.

9.4 Financial Implications of New Construction

Too many institutions become involved in planning new library quarters without considering all the financial implications of the undertaking. Sections 9.1, 9.2, and 9.3 have dealt with the obvious considerations: funds must be provided for the project; an estimate of construction and equipment costs must be made; and ways should be considered by which construction costs can be reduced.

There are two other groups of expenditures which may result from a new building and which, in the long view, are often as great or greater than those already discussed and as difficult to finance. The first of these depends directly on how well the building has been planned as a structure. The second results from the increased use of and demands on the library, which are apparently the inevitable and indeed exceedingly desirable results of an attractive, convenient, and comfortable building. Too often, unfortunately, sufficient attention is paid to neither.

Financial Effects of the Planning Itself. A building can be well planned from most functional points of view, but become overnight a white elephant. Some librarians, brought up in the days when every library room was supposed to be supervised from the time it was opened until closing, may minimize the fact that savings can be obtained by limiting the number of service points that need to be staffed during all hours of opening. They have assumed that full-time staff members must be kept at the circulation desk, the periodical room, the rare-book room, and in a large library at a number of other areas assigned for special subjects, such as public documents, fine arts, music, microforms, audio-visual facilities, and perhaps divisional reading rooms for humanities, social sciences, and sciences. Each desk requiring full hours of service results in an addition to the payroll that may approach or equal the salary of a full professor. This is more likely to be the case today with the very long hours of opening which prevail in the average academic library than it was several decades ago when many libraries closed during the lunch and dinner hours and at 9 or 10 o'clock on weekday evenings. The many forms of budget-reduction programs that have been common over the last decade have resulted in shorter hours in some libraries, yet 90 to 100 or more hours a week is not unusual. The Meyer Memorial (undergraduate) Library at Stanford, for example, is open 106 hours a week during the academic term.

Careful planning should hold the number of service points to the minimum that will permit the desired type of service to be given. This is not an attack on the divisional plan, if the institution is convinced that it is worth the cost. It does not mean that students can serve themselves completely or that there is no such thing as a disciplinary problem today. It suggests that a considerable amount can be saved if the new library or addition or the remodeled space can be planned so as to minimize service points that require staffing.

A challenge to the librarian in planning a building is the anticipation of student ethics and social behavior for decades to come: will there be respect for the honor code or further disdain for public property, greater or lesser marking of library books and graffiti on desks and walls, the desire for more privacy or a trend toward group study, rebelliousness or conformity to rules? These trends seem to ebb and flow over the generations. Also, as secondary schools have gone through cyclical periods of one philosophy or another, so undergraduate education has varied in methodology and expectations: e.g., mass courses in Western civilization or undergraduate seminars, a January project period between semesters, or heavier reading assignments during quarters. The extent of necessary supervision has changed over recent decades. As scarce scholarly books become dearer, should the library segregate an ever larger proportion in a supervised rare-book room, close the bookstacks to all except faculty and graduate students, use closed-circuit television or student proctors or staff employees for supervision? Will texts be used much more widely and the competition of students in the stacks be reduced? Will the "wired campus" prompt much heavier dorm use and less use of the library, or will computerizing the library study accommodations result in much greater use? It is necessary to monitor the trends, manage wisely and economically at the present, and prepare for emerging future needs.

If today one service desk instead of two will suffice, so much the better. For instance, when the reference load is comparatively light, perhaps all types of guidance and service can be provided from one desk instead of two, or from two instead of four. Seating may be so arranged that reading rooms do not require supervision; individual seating, which is used so much today, is a great help in this connection. A building exit check may suffice and may be electronic, without staff at a desk.

Microforms and current periodicals can possibly be served from a desk used for other purposes, at least evenings and weekends. A building plan that requires service staff to travel unnecessarily long distances naturally increases the size of the staff that is needed. Going up and down stairs frequently is a matter of particular importance; it takes time, which is always costly. Where an automated catalog is not planned, efforts should always be made to house members of the processing staff close to the card catalog, without upsetting other features of the plan that might be even more important. If a library is not a large and very busy one, and the reference, reserved-book, and circulation desks can be fairly close together, one or two assistants may be able to serve all three during meal hours and other slack times of day.

Although it may be that none of these economies would be wise in a particular library, they should be kept in mind in planning; the most critical service desk and other important relationships should be thought out, and the desired relations detailed in the program document.

The second type of expenditure that may be curtailed by proper planning comes in connection with maintenance, operations, and repair costs. Since utility charges are so high, special attention needs to be given to this aspect. At some institutions all plans for HVAC and lighting must be approved by energy consultants before design documents are approved. A study of energy costs is also important as part of any renovation project, and some colleges and universities have funded special projects just to address what are considered excessive energy costs in certain parts of a library building, such as bookstacks, corridors, lobbies, and exterior lighting. Effort to assure operating and maintenance economy of HVAC and lighting systems will have long-term financial benefits.

There are many detailed arrangements which can contribute to operating savings. Many of them are mentioned elsewhere in this volume; they are only briefly noted here.

1. Items that may reduce building maintenance and operations cost:
    a. Janitor's closets with water connections and sufficient storage space for cleaning equipment and supplies on each level; placement should allow them to be used without entering reading areas.
    b. Furniture that can be cleaned under and around easily; lighting fixtures that can be easily cleaned.
    c. Windows that can be cleaned without the use of exotic equipment.
    d. Floors that can be kept in order easily without constant buffing and waxing.
    e. Window shades, blinds, and draperies that do not constantly require repair or replacement or staff attention for opening or closing.
    f. Maintenance operations planned so that as large a share as possible of the cleaning can be done during daytime or evening, rather than during night hours when wages may be higher and supervision less satisfactory.
    g. The avoidance of too much glass, inadequate insulation, and unsatisfactory protection from the sun through lack of shades, blinds, draperies, awnings, overhangs, tinted or mirror glass each of which affects heating, ventilating, and air-conditioning costs.
    h. Lighting that avoids unnecessarily high intensities, inefficient light sources, and too few light switches, (which make it difficult to cut off light when it is not needed).
    i. Mechanical installations that are not so complex that an engineer must be on duty all the time, and mechanical rooms that are so well planned and lit that access for routine maintenance procedures is not excessively difficult.
    j. A proper number of telephones, since too many add to current operating expenses and too few frustrate staff and use more time.
    k. Fire extinguisher tanks in wall receptacles rather than on brackets protruding from walls.
2. Items that affect repair and replacement costs:
    a. Furniture that will not withstand wear, such as chairs, tables, and catalog trays with joints that weaken or with finish so poor that it must constantly be renewed.
    b. Poorly designed rest rooms; they should be as vandal resistant as possible.
    c. Exposed, unprotected corners in corridors or columns which may be damaged if hit by a loaded book truck. They should be specially treated with hard edges at least three feet up from the floor.

d. Vulnerable surfaces. Walls near pay phones and of elevators, lobbies, rest rooms, and perhaps certain major corridors as well as the vertical faces of all service desks or counters should be extra durable or easily refinished.

e. Lighting installations that make it difficult and expensive to change tubes, ballasts, and bulbs.

f. Inadequate heating and ventilation installations which make necessary constant repairs, to say nothing of opening and closing windows.

g. Leaking roofs, skylights, and windows and inadequate gutters, downspouts, and exterior surface drains.

h. Floor or floor coverings that require frequent replacement, expensive repairs, or refinishing.

i. A graphics system that requires difficult or expensive processes to accommodate change.

j. Dark shelves or light-colored handrails or countertops that show dirt easily.

The cost of servicing the building and keeping it in good condition may be double in one library what it is in another with the same area.

One theoretical estimate of the cost for monitoring a building (exclusive of energy and custodial service) suggests a figure of 1.5 percent of the construction cost. Custodial costs currently range from $.50 to $1.00 per net sq ft ($4.65 to $9.30 per m²) per year. At Stanford the current cost is $.65 per net sq ft ($6.04 per m²). In a building of 100,000 sq ft (9.290 m²) which might cost $10,000,000 to construct, the custodial and physical maintenance could cost some $215,000 per year. Clearly, a savings of as little as 10 percent over the years could be substantial.

Better planning and quality of construction, although it may increase the original cost considerably, may reduce the total capital expenditures if the long-term view is taken. Remember that if a 100,000 sq ft (9.290 m²) building has no more useful space than a 75,000 sq ft (6.910 m²) building, it is better to choose the latter and to improve the quality of the construction and reduce the maintenance cost.

In connection with this consideration of maintenance and repair expenditures, it is strongly recommended that whenever possible an additional sum of money amounting to 20 percent of the cost of the building be set aside as endowment to be invested, and the income be used to maintain and repair the structure. If a single donor can be persuaded to add endowment to the basic donation, so much the better. For older buildings a certain percentage of annual operating cost for heat, light, and power could be budgeted as a building repair fund, and it could properly vary according to the age and nature of the building.

Results of Increased Use. A fine new building almost inevitably increases the demands made on the facilities, to such an extent that the staff must be increased. When the Lamont Library for undergraduates at Harvard was made available, it was heavily used from the start, though the reduction in use of the old building, Widener, was negligible, and use of Widener is now greater than ever. When the new library at Louisiana State University in Baton Rouge was occupied, the use of the library by students more than doubled immediately. Similar experiences have been observed at Cornell, Michigan, Stanford, Northwestern, and elsewhere. Remember that this may and probably will happen in your institution, and be prepared for the additional demands and for the cost of the additional service that is required.

Forecasting increased use is a matter of judgment. One method would be to collect use data for very good libraries in a selection of peer institutions. The local institution can expect a greatly improved library to result in use that may be near the mean and at least within the range of use in its peers, and a rough percentage increase can be estimated. Another method would be to look for a comparable institution which had a recent roughly comparable improvement in its library facility and find out how the use increased in each of the first few years after occupying the new space. One can then adjust this growth pattern somewhat to reflect any different characteristics between the two situations. No matter what method is used, change should be expected and some estimate of the consequences to staff anticipated.

At Stanford University, in anticipation of the opening of the much enlarged and improved Cecil H. Green Library, designed as the main research library, there was concern that the nearby J. Henry Meyer (undergraduate) Library would fall into disuse. It turned out that this was not the case, as the Meyer Library continues to be well used. It has its devotees, social attractions, and reserved book collections. However, the new Green Library has attracted many more users, at times being virtually 100 percent occupied, while the undergraduate library has never been more than 42 percent full. To reduce the adverse influence on graduate research by undergraduates needlessly moving into Green, there was a costly effort to make improvements to the Meyer Library so that its reader accommodations would be perceived as being equal to the newer Green Library. Where an adverse reaction can be predicted, an expense of this kind of effort may well be warranted.

One might go further and add that as the library use increases there is also inevitably a demand for a larger collection, which again adds to the costs. The authors refuse to admit that this is a vicious circle, although some harassed treasurers and trustees might be inclined to refer to it in that way! It does mean however that every effort should be made to plan a new building, not only so that it will be functional but also so that its maintenance and service costs will be held to a reasonable figure. Above all else, the library and its use will change; flexibility to cope with this change is essential.

10

Building Additions and Renovations

The better-designed academic and research library buildings of post–World War II can often continue to serve effectively, which was not the case for many of post–World War I. For at least the rest of this century, this condition will prompt many more renovations of and additions to existing library space than separate new library buildings. Other reasons for the preponderance of renovations and additions are less space on campus for new structures, a greater emphasis than fifty years ago on sharing collections instead of larger independent collections, the tight economic conditions forecast for at least the next ten years, and greater appreciation for older structures even if not of quality.

This chapter examines some of the special conditions encountered during a building addition project and some of the problems when renovation is part of that project. The chapter addresses both additions and renovations because the former often involves the latter, or at least raises questions about renovations. Furthermore, the remodeled structure with or without the enlarged building is the unified expression of a new space need. To put it another way, the eventual building expresses the whole of a projected program need which may be attained by substantial renovation with no addition or with an addition and no remodeling. Both renovating and adding on create several significant planning, design, and construction problems which do not exist in work on a separate new structure.

There is even more variety in building addition projects when compared to construction of new and separate structures. This comes about because of the variety of preexisting conditions which must be accommodated when working with an existing structure, whether or not that structure is currently occupied and in use. When a building project is concerned with a new structure, one that is separate from other structures, it is simpler than if the project is a building addition and the original structure is to undergo substantial renovation as part of the same project. Providing for future flexibility is an especially important point in any addition, just as much as in a new separate structure.

The academic justification for a building addition or major remodeling is essentially similar to that for a new and separate structure. However, it will need to take one of several possible courses in the presentation. First, it can assume that the existing building will be retained; the program would then explicitly deal with the functional use of that structure as part of the total program document. Second, it can start with the assumption that the program will be written without any reference to the current structure. The design team would thus be presented with a program pure of any bias about the current structure, and the architect would be free to resolve the question of whether all or some of the present structure should be used to meet part of the program. Third, the program can be written merely to state in very broad terms the academic needs and functions to be covered and to provide the basis for an engineering and architectural study of feasibility. This latter course may be very wise when there are serious doubts about the structural and mechanical conditions of the existing building, when its quality may be marginal, and when its site is less than the ideal. Otherwise it is usually best to use the second option; the solution to the problem will then be applicable to existing conditions yet not be restrained by them.

Whatever the nature of the program document, a similar thought process must take place in analyzing the library for its academic purposes, but it is complicated by the existence of a structure which one way or the other must be taken into account. College or university officers as well as the librarian and the

chosen architect will need to decide exactly what steps to take when dealing with an existing structure. In most cases at least cursory architectural and engineering review of the present structure would be advisable. For any building which is to have an addition twice as large as the original structure, such a review would be very wise indeed. An original structure more than forty years old will have been designed and built under conditions which differ substantially from today's code requirements or standards, and so an engineering and architectural review is essential. Even a twenty-year-old building could require substantial improvements to make it structurally and functionally sound.

10.1 Basic Questions before Deciding on a Building Addition

On what basis can an institution decide to settle on an addition to an existing structure rather than a replacement of that structure? Furthermore, if there is to be an addition, should it be with no renovation or considerable or extensive renovation of the original structure? These crucial questions may take months or even a year of thorough study to decide. Seven basic questions need answering before making this decision.

1. *Is the location of the existing structure a good one?* Consideration must be given to campus plans for building changes and functional use over several decades to come. If the library is in an ideal location, then there is a strong argument to work with the existing structure or to consider a replacement on the same general site. Architects should remember that the surest thing about a general academic library is that its space needs are almost certain to grow over time. In due course and long before the building is worn out or outmoded, new space will be required, and the need for a new wing or additional areas provided in some other way will be a matter of future importance. Thus, two prerequisites to an addition must be kept in mind: the amount of space on the site and a building design without serious aesthetic, construction or functional complications.

2. *Is the original structure sound?* All buildings sooner or later need renovation or extensive refurbishing, such as repainting, new flooring, or new light fixtures. Over some decades the ventilation system may become difficult to maintain, electrical and telecom-

munications capacities may be exceeded, heating pipes may become corroded, foundations may crack and roofs wear out, window sashes may develop problems, and safety requirements may be more exacting than when the structure was built. A special study may be needed to determine whether the building can handle digital, video, and audio data transmission through existing conduits or cable trays. Whether the existing structure was designed for a library or not, a special engineering study of floor loads may be essential since book collections are far heavier than almost any other academic activity except certain scientific or engineering equipment. Microtexts housed efficiently will weigh twice as much as books, and phonograph discs are even heavier.

As one example, the Harvard Yard includes Boylston Hall, an 1857 structure of handsome stonework and with a mansard roof. It has been remodeled four times, most recently in 1960. At that time the Harvard Yenching Library moved out, and a small modern language branch library was assigned part of the first floor and a new mezzanine. Insertion of a new complete floor between the second and third levels was also possible. Reconstruction was $800,000 for new space of 14,000 sq ft (1300 m²) and extensively renovated old space—some $500,000 less than was estimated to construct a new building on the site.

A decision on the feasibility for renovation may relate to a judgment about the value of the existing facility. In this context, it may help to realize that the exterior envelope and structural skeleton typically represent about 33 to 40 percent of the total value; interior construction represents 20 to 25 percent; and the mechanical and electrical systems 35 to 40 percent. Unless all systems and structure are in need of replacement, a potential for cost savings is often realized even though renovation work is generally more expensive than new work when the same components are compared.[1]

Renovating a building of rather mediocre quality may be sending good money after bad. One will not wish to dress up a poor building with superficial improvements. A thorough engineering evaluation to assess the structural, code, energy, access, programmatic, and

other aspects of the existing structure may be a very wise expenditure of time and money.

3. *Is flexibility in the original structure acceptable and can the existing floor heights work satisfactorily with an addition?* In adding on to a small original building with fixed interior walls, there will always be significant problems. It is thus necessary to weigh the amount of limitation that is caused by those fixed elements. Consideration can be given to breaking out an occasional wall if there is enough head room to put in a new beam, and almost always one can break through to install a passageway or a new door unless a mechanical or plumbing shaft is within that wall. As a general rule, limited flexibility is easier to accept if the original structure was of fairly good size and, particularly, if the addition is to be much larger than the original structure. In this case, the original structure may be used for certain administrative offices, for small functionally discrete sections or units of the library that can be separated from larger units, such as a learning resources center or instructional services, or for such specialized collections as rare books, manuscripts, oral history archives, or maps where the size of the spaces may be suitable and the feeling of the older space or its nostalgic character may be suited to the housing of cherished rarities.

Floor heights of the original structure are an important aspect of flexibility. Modern developments in lighting, heating, and ventilation have changed the required distances from floor to floor, and great distances in old construction are often inconsistent with today's requirements. To match the heights used in the original construction might result in increasing the cost of an addition so much that little would be left of a savings that otherwise might result from the use of an old building. Always remember that height greater than is necessary or desirable functionally and aesthetically costs money, both initially and in annual operation, and should be questioned. Fitting two levels of bookstack into a high reading room may of course gain assignable footage. If floor heights between the existing structure and the addition do not match exactly, that may be entirely satisfactory although steps or a ramp will be required on one or more levels to go from the old to the new. Wheelchair movement may be a problem. Considerable difference in floor height between one or more levels may require a very long ramp or several ramps, with

[1] Harvey H. Kaiser, *Crumbling Academe* (Washington, D.C.: Association of Governing Boards of Universities and Colleges, 1984), p. 23.

resultant inconvenience, accidents, and extra effort in transporting books back and forth.

4. *Is the original structure of sentimental importance or controlled by a state or federal historic building regulation?* Since a library is frequently a central building on campus, may be prominently situated, and have an imposing facade, graduates and friends of the college or university may feel very strongly about retaining the building and perhaps maintaining it as a central library. As one case in point, the University of Tulsa in 1928 adopted a campus development program that firmly established the library as the central campus building. That structure of 1930 was very pleasant space with a very large park in front of it. In 1965 the University added an addition on the back with some renovation of the original structure. Within ten years it became necessary to plan another addition, and in this case, given the location of the library and the importance of its facade, a very large underground addition in front toward the park was added. An addition of 66,000 sq ft (6.130 m²) was made to the existing 61,000 sq ft (5.670 m²). The symbolic or sentimental importance of an existing structure should not be underestimated.

5. *Are the costs of the alternatives a trade-off over a ten- or twenty-year period?* Although costs are not the only determinant of whether to add on or build anew, the financial conditions may well weigh very heavily indeed. The costs of the new structure can rather easily be estimated, and a thorough analysis should result in rather accurate estimates for dealing with the existing structure.

In figuring the expense of remodeling, the institution will need to decide whether it wishes to attach a new structure to a building which will have nothing done to modernize it. Alternatively, there will need to be a decision about the extent of renovation, which can vary greatly. In the simplest condition there may be some repainting, some new carpeting, perhaps replacing some weakened furniture, and providing new signs. The remodeling can be carried further, to replace chairs with ones of a new style, replace unfunctional shelving, provide new light fixtures, even add a contemporary entrance door. Or it can be carried even further, to alter some partitions, improve or replace mechanical systems and lights, deal with acoustical problems, correct fire hazards, add air conditioning, and improve the condition of the exterior shell of the building.

After fifty years or so of snow, ice, rain, wind, and very hot weather, the building shell must often be repaired in order to not let faults increase and costs of repair compound. Roofs of slate, copper, tile, and built-up tar and gravel will all deteriorate. Brick and stone walls need to be scrubbed down and repointed. The beloved ivy holds moisture to rot windowsills, crawls into crevices and forces gaps, gets behind downspouts and gutters, and causes hidden havoc. Ground settling can crack foundations, and lack of suitable groundwater drainage can undermine exterior walkways just as roots can cause upheaval. How far to go in such projects needs careful study. One should consider the nature of problems one will be leaving for one's successor. How wisely did one's predecessor plan and what problems were left? One should try to do at least as well for those who will follow.

Decisions of this sort require a determination of whether this is the best time in the history of the institution to bring the old structure up to date, whether fundraising for remodeling costs is feasible, and whether the resultant building will have the old and the new parts work well together. This last point is of great importance and is dealt with later in this chapter.

6. *Is there another institutional facility need that can be best met by the use of an existing library facility?* While many older libraries have significant features such as tiered stacks and monumental reading rooms which would not be easily adapted to an academic department or other functions, it may be practical to consider reassignment of portions of an existing library to capitalize on the potential opportunity to create a better library facility. Even when tiered stacks are a problem, they might serve as a practical auxiliary storage site should the new library site be separated by some distance. More recent libraries generally can be readily adapted to other functions, a possibility which may be particularly attractive where the existing library really does not provide for adequate future expansion.

7. *Is fundraising possible just for the addition or for renovations as well?* Just as the estimate of costs for various options must be in hand, so it is necessary to estimate the capacity to raise the funds for the addition, or for modest or substantial renovations in the existing structure, and to compare the fundraising capacity if the present structure were to be re-

placed altogether. If the institution does not have experience at funding major renovation projects or with tearing down an original structure, inquiring about the experience of similar or neighboring institutions may provide insight into the nature of the problems and prospects for success. These financial matters, of course, are critical for the success of the project even though they are but one of the seven basic questions in deciding whether to plan an addition or a replacement to the building.

The institution needs to give particularly careful attention to how to assign names in recognition of donors for an addition or renovated space. It has been common experience that raising funds for a separate structure is difficult enough, even though there is a possibility of putting the major donor's name on the building and giving important rooms within the building the name of other significant contributors. However, if the building addition is small, if it is merely a bookstack wing, if it is all underground, or if much of the money goes into renovating an old structure, there will be increased difficulties in attracting large donors. It takes a very understanding and devoted friend of an institution to be willing to contribute to providing rather utilitarian space, or space that is rather invisible, or certainly to renovation of space which already bears another's name. In a few instances families have continued a tradition of supporting an institution or its library. Most institutions are nevertheless likely to find the fundraising for a modest addition to be easier than for a whole new and separate structure, and for considerable renovations to be more difficult.

Although not as fundamental as the above, there are at least seven other questions which need to be answered before plans are made for an addition.

8. *When the present building was planned, was an addition contemplated? If so, were drawings for it prepared? Are they available and still suitable?* Many architects fortunately have realized that an addition would eventually be needed and have proceeded accordingly by at least schematically establishing the possible character of a future addition.

The plan of the main library building of the University of Illinois may be regarded as an example in this connection. Repeated additions have been made, and still more are practicable; there is room at the rear for al-most indefinite expansion of stack and reading areas. The limitations of the Illinois plan are that additional cubicles in the stack are available only in places where there is no outside light, new space for readers and stacks may not be in a satisfactory proportion in each addition, and, finally, it is not easy to provide for new staff housing.

9. *Is it possible when adding to a library building to obtain an easy and satisfactory circulation pattern with direct access to the new part of the structure?* It was not unusual during the past century and, alas, even later to plan a library in which it was impossible on any level, even the main one, to go from one end of the building to the other without ascending or descending a few stairs along the way. American technology has not yet devised a satisfactory and inexpensive method of taking a loaded book truck up and down short flights of stairs. Additional elevators may help, but they are expensive, particularly if they must be capable of making frequent stops a few feet apart.

The Cornell University Uris Library, dating back to the 1890s, is a good example of what ought not to be done. Shifting books from one part of the building to another was seriously complicated by the numerous short flights of stairs, many of them without elevator connections. There is also the danger that the users of the building will fall on unexpected stairs. In the Widener building at Harvard, where there were two steps and then a landing just before the main stairway to the reading room began, someone fell on the average of every week for thirty years. The two steps were finally replaced by an unattractive ramp, which has now saved countless sprains and breaks to say nothing of bruises. It is recommended that short flights of stairs, primarily for architectural purposes, be avoided wherever possible in library buildings.

The University of Florida Library at Gainesville, which was built in 1929 and has already had two additions, is an example of a building that is still in good physical condition but is hard to enlarge because difficult circulation patterns would result and would require the sacrifice of valuable space. Moreover, sufficient additional space to provide for a considerable period ahead is not available on the site in any direction. Libraries with excellent circulation after a major addition are the University of Northern Iowa and Brigham Young University. However, circulation is poor at the University of California at Santa Barbara and exceedingly bad at Walla Walla College and at U.C. Davis.

10. *Is it possible to accommodate greatly expanded needs for electrical power and signal runs?* Libraries in the last third of this century need far more wiring and cabling than before. There are not only requirements for telephone lines, vacuum cleaners, microform readers, copying machines, and a variety of traditional pieces of equipment, but also for computer terminals, word processing machines, personal computers, videotext display facilities, optical disk playback machines and technological devices still to come. Older buildings can create significant problems for pulling coaxial cable for hard-wiring local area networks: e.g., penetrating walls that may be two or even three feet thick, surfaces that may be marble, and locating room in underground conduits. Without suspended ceilings it may be nearly impossible to guard against unsightly installations. All such conditions will push the cost up significantly.

11. *How large an addition will be required?* It is one thing to add a small stack or small wing for reading areas, increasing the size of an old building by 20 to 25 percent. It is quite a different matter to build an addition that is larger than the original building, something that is more often required these days. The small addition, if it will provide satisfactory space and will not crowd other buildings or encounter other complications, is often desirable. The Waterloo Lutheran University in Ontario solved it by adding two floors on top of the library. A large addition is likely to be more cost efficient though it tends to perpetuate any unfortunate features of the old building. Eventually the additions become so massive that the scale used in the original exterior treatment may be wrong aesthetically. Facing that circumstance, the University of South Carolina in 1976 added 260,000 sq ft (24,154 m²) to the 1959 Undergraduate Library of 30,000 sq ft (2787 m²), forming the Thomas Cooper Library, with four of the new seven levels being underground.

12. *Are there serious aesthetic obstacles to an addition?* Following the style of an older structure may be prohibitively expensive, but building a contemporary wing on a collegiate Gothic, Classical, or Georgian building may be very difficult. Even if it is done to the satisfaction of many persons with good taste, it may arouse violent alumni criticism. It has been done successfully—the 1958 addition at Wellesley is an example and Duke University's library addition is another—but there have been many failures. Remember that though architectural form may follow function, human needs go beyond function and beyond mere style. The architectural form, its style, its presence, its symbolism can be powerful influences. For a library to be used and appreciated by students, for it to be worth some of the cost of an education, for it to be conducive to serious study, it should be human space, creating an inviting and pleasant environment for intellectual effort, not merely function well from the staff point of view. There are libraries which indeed function well yet lack much student use because they are aesthetically cold or unpleasant.

13. *Is there a very strong commitment to retain the Georgian style or another predominant style?* If so, special consideration should be given to retaining the same firm that designed the original structure, if it is still in business. Some institutions have a long-standing relation with an individual or a firm. If the firm has within the past decade continued to do well-regarded work for the institution, that also might argue that the commission should be given to that firm. However, most institutions feel that a major building, even a major addition, is a project for which various architectural firms should be considered. There is no necessity of using the same architectural firm unless the college or university has previously made such a commitment. In any event, one wants to be certain that the principal designer and the project architect are competent and that their time is available for the project.

14. *How long can the proposed addition, plus the present building, be expected to provide adequate space, and what can be done at the end of this period?* Some librarians have found that poorly planned and hastily constructed additions have exhausted the possibilities for later expansion. Will still another addition then be practicable, or will this one be the last? Are the institution and the space needs of its library growing so rapidly that a much larger building will be needed within twenty years? If so, it may well be uneconomical to enlarge now instead of starting over. In a privately endowed, liberal arts college, an addition may be desirable, even if the existing building is fifty years old, so long as the col-

lege does not expect to increase its student body to any considerable extent. This is especially so if its library collections are mature enough to be growing not more than three percent a year. Tremendous physical expansion of its library must be expected by a tax-supported state university if it now has 5,000 students but plans to have 15,000, if its maturing collections are growing at the rate of ten percent a year, and if it expects to support advanced research in an increasing number of fields. Money may well be saved in this case by replacing a mediocre building that is only twenty years old or even less. Each institution has its own problems that must be examined before an intelligent decision can be reached.

Since building additions are common, and becoming more so, an institution ought to ask the architect to provide a site utilization study which will show how one or more further additions could be accommodated if and when they are needed. Important issues for the architect to keep in mind are the following:

The location for connections should be anticipated. This issue is dealt with later in this chapter, Section 10.3.

The traffic lanes to, around, and inside the building should be planned so that they can work with one or more additions. This consideration is particularly important inside the buildings so that it does not end up like a maze. As successful as it is, Stanford University's Green Library offers a challenge to students needing to find collections in the original West Wing building or in the collection space beneath the Meyer Library. The route from the Widener Library Reference Room to the Widener-level collections under the Lamont building also is quite a circuitous hike.

Utility cores, stairs, and elevator placement are critical, both in terms of horizontal layouts as well as vertical. The horizontal will, of course, more deeply affect the potential addition, but the mechanical space is especially important and needs consideration as much as the architectural arrangements. The Sacramento State University Library has stairwells which project outside the initial structure and should make for a particularly easy accommodation to an addition.

Knock-out walls may be useful if one can project exactly where the addition will connect. If so, floor to ceiling window walls may be placed in that location so that ma-

sonry does not have to be removed and so that sentimental or financial objections will not be raised against a wide and fully effective connection.

Consideration of areas to be placed next to the potential addition are important. Consideration needs to be given to which rooms or functions will need expansion so that they might be placed next to the junction. This is particularly the case for mechanical space in order that heating or ventilating equipment can be added without the problems incurred by an additional and separate equipment room.

Remodeling is more common than it was fifty or a hundred years ago. The reasons for recent college library remodeling have included: reducing noise and future energy costs, increasing handicapped access and comfort of users, preventing loss of book materials, and enhancing the building attractiveness. Data from a study by Michael S. Freeman also reveal that 63 percent of American college library buildings built in 1967 received interior relocations or adjustments by 1981, and over one-third had three or more such changes.[2] The nature of these changes were, in decreasing order of frequency: audio-visual services, microforms, current and bound periodicals, government documents, maps, reference department, special collections, acquisitions, staff lounge, public card catalog, interlibrary loan, and serial processing.

Since there are so many variations in the handling of additions, it is particularly desirable to visit and study several and see whether some of them have conditions similar to those faced at one's own institution.

10.2 Historical Lessons and Trends

The study of building additions and renovations is especially rewarding. Looking at library building projects of the past forty years, one can find quite a number of examples where an existing building was given up and a completely new structure provided at a site a great many yards or even some blocks away. Examples include Bowdoin College, Indiana University, the University of Minnesota, UCLA, the University of Glas-

---

[2] "College Library Buidings in Transition: A Study of 36 Libraries Built in 1967–68," *College and Research Libraries* 43: 478–80 (Nov. 1982).

gow, and the University of Toronto. Also in recent decades there have been a much larger number of additions, sometimes a second or third addition. Some representative examples are Occidental College, Vassar, Wellesley, Trinity College in Dublin, Fresno State University, the University of North Wales, Georgia Tech, Duke, Vanderbilt, Brigham Young University, Birmingham, Newcastle upon Tyne, Harvard, Yale, Princeton, Illinois, Colorado, Michigan, Pennsylvania, Stanford, Northwestern, and again UCLA. These examples are merely indicative of the frequency of additions. Given the financial conditions of colleges and universities, it seems probable that over the next several decades there will continue to be a heavy emphasis on additions. Particularly, since buildings constructed over the past forty years have far greater flexibility than those built earlier in this century, retaining the original structure is far more reasonable.

Some conclusions can be drawn from the recent history of library construction. First, there will be a great many more examples of additions than of completely new and separate buildings, at least in terms of central facilities. Second, there will be much more use of underground space, partly as buildings in the central part of a campus become more crowded and one needs to retain planted area and open space for air and pleasantness. Third, additions will sometimes be larger than the original and can work very well. Fourth, the older structure may be used for such functions as mentioned above, including an undergraduate collection, one or more branch libraries, special collections, audiovisual services, administrative and processing offices, and sometimes in part for nonlibrary functions. Fifth, the old building will very seldom be razed. One of the last notable libraries razed was Gore Hall at Harvard very early in this century. Sixth, there will be an increase in the number of library storage facilities located away from the campus center.

Although each campus situation is a special set of circumstances, one university library may be taken as an example. This is meant merely to suggest some of the prevailing effect of timing, university priorities, fundraising, philosophy of library service, and traffic patterns. Stanford's Main Library was a 1919 structure with fixed functions, meaning that the tiered bookstack, light courts, monumental reading room, and monumental main stairs together with a relatively fixed pattern of corridors considerably limited moving many functions. There had been no modification to the building when a distinguished consultant was brought from Chicago to California in March of 1948 to survey the space problems. The report included the following:

Functions and concepts of functions are fluid and change with time, while a physical structure is more static in character. Thus a building that structurally closely matches its functions at the time of its erection, may fail more quickly than a building which originally was a poorer "fit" in relation to function. . . . The Main Library at Stanford is one which gives the impression of having been very carefully fitted to its functions at the time of construction, but in which very little consideration was given to the possibility of future changes in needs. . . . The monumental features, together with the light courts, not only take a high proportion of the available cubage, but interfere most seriously with the internal communication in the building. There are areas of the building, particularly on the mezzanine and top floors, which would be extremely useful if they were more accessible.

The four major light wells, the 30 ft (9.144) ceiling in the main reading rooms and the monumental stairway, and the domed ceiling delivery hall on the second floor presented formidable problems. The recommendation included removing the monumental stairway, building new stairs in the larger two light wells, bridging over monumental space on the second and at least some of the third floor, adding forced-air ventilation, and providing an underground passageway to the Hoover Institution library tower next door.

It is interesting to note that the university solved its central library problems with a feeling of considerable satisfaction even though none of the above recommendations were followed. Financial limitations and university priorities played a major role. In the late 1950s, the upper two unfinished main library stack levels were completed. In the mid-1960s a new basement floor was constructed beneath about three-quarters of the building since the footings were not deep enough for more. Also in the mid-1960s an undergraduate library was opened some yards away, with a two-level basement to handle the overflow of the main library book collections. In the 1960s, the Hoover Institution tower received a major building addition and in the late 1970s a second major building addition. Finally, in 1980–81 a first large addition to the main library was provided, which connected with the undergraduate library basement, and a considerable renovation was then accomplished in the original 1919 structure.

Thus, over thirty years passed while the problems were solved piecemeal, decade by decade. Very little money was expended in altering the original structure until its major renovation, and the renovation was largely an expense for the air conditioning and security of quarters for rare books, manuscripts, archives, and rare government documents. Indeed, the monumental spaces were deliberately retained and became considerable assets. It is, of course, unknown what might have been the course of history if other options had been followed. The building development was based on acceptance of the site, the assessment that the quality of the original structure was good, and a tolerance of the degree of flexibility provided by the original structure, combined with financial considerations which were major determinants. It required diligent work over a great many years to solve a complex space problem that seemed never to go away; nevertheless, the operating condition at any time was reasonable, and future options were left open in nearly all instances. This history is recounted only to underscore the necessity of very careful thought, the usefulness of engineering and architectural studies, and the strong effect of financing on a library building project.

10.3 Special Planning Issues

An addition can be an economical and entirely satisfactory solution from the standpoint of the library. There are, however, a number of issues which need additional consideration or a different approach from that of a new separate building. The following will be of special concern to one faced with such a project.

1. *Site issues.* Site studies are exceedingly important in considering any addition. When considering an addition, or before attempting extensive and expensive renovation of an existing structure, one should make sure that the site permits a later addition that will still be satisfactory functionally and aesthetically when space gives out, as it probably will if past experience is a guide. As noted before, there are, in fact, more and more libraries with two or more additions. Particularly im-

portant in site studies are the traffic patterns, both internal and external. If the original building has an imposing entrance, as is very often the case when compared with more recent buildings, the addition may need to be to one side or the other or in back of the original building. In the case of Harvard's Pusey Library and in the 1979 addition to the University of Tulsa McFarlin Library, the additions are in front and underground. However, the University of Alberta Rutherford Library and the University of Kentucky King Library have additions in front and neither is underground.

If the library is near the center of campus, one must realize that doubling the ground area of the library will require outside traffic to go that much farther in bypassing the building. Eventually that can become quite a trek. The Harvard central complex of library buildings solved the problem by having walkways around each of the three principal structures and over the top of the fourth. The Hoover Institution's three buildings permit walking over the top of connecting basements; however, the combination of stairs and a ramp makes for an exceedingly awkward situation whenever one wishes to go north and south through that building location.

Vistas favored by the board of trustees and alumni as well as campus planners, can control the site, as can trees. In the case of Vassar College, the Lockwood addition took an awkward L-shaped configuration because of a 150-year-old Norway maple tree to the north of the original structure and a line of trees serving as a buffer between the library and a major avenue to the west. Underground utility lines can also block some sites because of relocation costs. As examples, the desired connection between the Stanford University Green Library and Art Library was not made because of a utility corridor, one which also would frustrate any underground connection between the Hoover Institution and the Green Library. The Braun Music Center at Stanford constitutes a building addition to a music auditorium, with an exceptionally frustrating site due to underground utilities and to a student and faculty pedestrian route which cuts right through the middle of the site and which university planners concluded was sacrosanct. The design which evolved is an awkward and somewhat expensive result.

2. *Mass and nature of the connection.* Architectural studies need to be done with great

care for the height and visual mass of the addition when seen next to the original structure. The older architectural styles, such as Gothic, Renaissance, Classical, and to a lesser extent Georgian (particularly if it has a pitched roof), are often too costly to duplicate. An addition can depart radically from the style of the original building, but the design has to be accomplished with consummate taste.

It is well to remember that close buildings of sharply contrasting styles are not necessarily bad. If each building seems to respect the other, the eye may well enjoy the difference, the variety. The Seagrams Building and its adjacent St. Patrick's Cathedral provide a striking New York City example. The Beinecke Library at Yale sits nicely amidst Gothic structures. Some, however, seem to jar or crowd, like the 1962 Carpenter Art Center by Le Corbusier at Harvard, crowded and discordant between the Fogg Art Museum and the Faculty Club. Indeed, the architect was shocked when he saw it for the first time.

In some cases the Gothic or other distinctive architectural style has had to be matched. Additions to Princeton's Firestone Library were done in conformity, as was the addition to the Andover-Harvard Theological Library, also at great cost and in an awkward site. In other cases, such as Vassar College or Stanford's Green Library, the architect developed a contemporary idiom using a glass connecting link or section which helps soften the juxtaposition by a visually distinct separation between the old and new even though they are functionally linked. Placing the new structure well away from the facade of the original building can help. In the case of the Vassar addition, the study of mass and site resulted in the contemporary and the earlier Tudor-Gothic stating their own stylistic identity yet being compatible since the architect used a similar scale, continuation of horizontal window and roof lines, comparability of columns to the turrets on the earlier structure, and a narrow, glazed connecting space between old and new. The limestone exterior also matched the stone trim on the earlier building.

Studies of mass at the University of Michigan led to an eight-floor addition connected to the General Library, towering fully four stories above the earlier structure. In this case the original stack building of 1898 had been wrapped in the early 1920s by additional

space. The possibility of wrapping a third building around the second was considered in the middle of the century, but the Undergraduate Library was built instead. Still later the General Library eventually had to have another addition, even though the Undergraduate Library, a special storage library, and numerous branches had postponed the day of reckoning. The new Hatcher addition in the 1970s is but the first unit of what could be several units, and there still is the question of whether the pre–World War I portion may be eventually replaced. Studies of massing also had to reckon with the requirement to provide for pedestrian traffic along and through the complex, to avoid impinging on part of the president's residence property, and to maintain an underground tunnel housing the existing heating and utility loop system.

Given an understanding of the site limitations and the ability to mass the required addition, the next consideration is the nature of the connection between the old and the new. Should it be that all levels are connected? Will there need to be ramps to go from one level to another on certain upper floors if the first floor and the basement can be kept at the elevation? Can the connection be broad throughout the depth or width of the building or will it have to be a passageway only? Generally, all floors should connect and at least the main floor be level. A very broad connection between the two is usually desirable to achieve maximum flexibility.

The site may have a great deal to do with the nature of the connection, and the configuration and degree of ornate exterior of the original structure will also have a bearing. Those libraries with a full-width connection of old and new include the universities of Durham, Reading, North Alabama, Northern Iowa, Pennsylvania, and the University of California at Los Angeles, Santa Barbara, and Santa Cruz. Some examples of buildings that have a moderate connection are Brigham Young, Duke, Occidental, Stanford, and Tulsa, where the site, traffic, and the nature of spaces in the existing buildings constitute a restraint. Some others with very narrow connections are East Carolina University, Georgia Institute of Technology, Harvard's Houghton with Lamont and Pusey, Michigan, Northwestern, as well as Vassar. In these cases there were even more rigid site conditions which led to the corridor-like connections even though, from a point of view of internal library operations, the configuration is very undesirable.

To see a bad example of two building additions, one need only study the University of California at Davis. The current connections are substantial, but the room division, passageways, and unharmonious floor levels create a severe problem. The nature of the connection between the old and new requires special study for the two parts to work well together to provide required flexibility over decades to come. It can be one of the more difficult parts of a building addition project.

3. *Functional distribution between old and new.* From the comments above it can be seen that there can be considerable variations in deciding which functions go into the new structure and which remain in the original, whether it is remodeled or not. This determination must be based on consideration of floor area requirements in the building program and the degree of flexibility in accommodating them. One useful approach is to work from both ends: thus, if the addition is large and flexible, determine those functions which require the largest space, have the greatest growth potential, and should, therefore, be in a large addition; at the same time determine those functions that are small, can be operationally separated from other functions, and for which the prospect for growth is minimal, and put those in the older structure. If the old structure cannot receive much renovation and is in mediocre condition, consider which reader services or staff processes can be accommodated and operate well in such quarters.

Librarians should seldom leave that basic layout entirely to the architect. The librarians who worked at writing the building program should have the best feel for what future growth may be required, what interaction among functions is common, and what operational and political conditions may affect placement in the old or new. It is well to work up a number of variations of functional deployment and to test each of the possibilities against a set of basic criteria. One tries not to have a formal entrance and a banal rear. Such anomalies have been created and certainly they create a degree of dissatisfaction for the entire institution.

At the time that the layout is being considered, there may be further discussion of whether a branch should be brought into the enlarged structure or whether one or more functions could be moved out to a different building altogether. These and other questions raised in Chapter 2 and Section 3.1 need resolution. Futhermore, university and college officers should understand that fitting a library into a completely new building is one thing but requiring that the library fit into an old and inflexible and awkwardly shaped structure is quite another. In the latter case it is hoped that officials will be understanding if the match is not perfect and if the floor area requirements do not work out to ideal efficiency. Almost always in dealing with an old original structure, there is much less efficiency in assigning floor area than in a more modern and flexible building.

Another point. There may be fundraising advantages in giving one function a more prominent location. Experience shows that named areas in the old wing, if it is being nicely renovated, may be as attractive for fundraising as are areas in the new wing. This is especially the case if the old wing has some areas of special character, has discrete rooms in contrast to open unpartitioned modular regions, and has some sentiment attached to either the room or the function going into that room. Cornell's Uris Undergraduate Library is an example. A room that was uniquely paneled and will now house, for example, the college archive may be appealing to a prospective donor. If the rooms are already named, double names, such as the Rockefeller-Smith Room, may be possible. In most cases, however, the funding advantages should not be the dominant reason for functional assignments.

4. *Code problems.* The requirements in different states and countries for meeting building codes vary. Frequently after a notorious hotel, restaurant, or dormitory fire or severe earthquake damage, local codes are reviewed and made more stringent. The result is that over decades, codes are more demanding. At the least, variance from current codes may become more difficult to achieve for a given project. Whenever a building is to have a substantial renovation or an addition, there is a question in regard to the requirement to bring the original building up to code. This requirement is generally not made for a very small renovation job. Whenever the work to be done is equal to one half the value of the original building, authorities will usually require that the old building be brought fully up to the current code. Of course, all new work must meet current codes.

There is some leeway at times for negotiation with local authorities. For example, if existing basement areas have inadequate exiting capacities, the requirement may be waived if the institution agrees to install a sprinkler system throughout the entire building. Likewise, there may be an authorized variance given on exiting from quarters that house rare books or manuscripts, particularly if the code has a museum or bank type of category which can be broadly defined to encompass the enclosed storage quarters for rarities—where only staff are permitted access to the shelf areas. A strict interpretation of California code would require all stack aisles to be wider than wheelchairs and no stack higher than could be reached from such chairs. Those who apply the building codes may be more or less strict in their interpretation. This review and authorization sometimes seems motivated by ego or political purpose. A knowledgeable officer of the institution, the local construction chief or fire department captain, or a skilled architect may be able to negotiate reasonable terms for conditions which otherwise might prevent any renovation or addition whatsoever to the building if a very strict interpretation were applied.

Particular attention needs to be given to access and exiting routes, fire protection, and seismic conditions. Problems may be found in almost any building which is several decades old. The width of corridors and stairs may be inadequate by current standards, particularly if the seating in the library has been increased by adding spaces in nooks and crannies. Any use of wide corridors for shelving, seating, or offices may make the route too narrow to be legal. Corridors or stack aisles which exceed 20 ft (6.096) in length and which dead-end, frequently found in older fixed-function buildings, may be illegal. The seismic bracing in elevator shafts may be less than currently required. Entrance requirements for fire department staff will also have to be reviewed, and the location of sprinkler systems and standpipes may need to be extended. In many cases the new and old buildings may be treated differently by code and may require a legal fire separation between the two.

This list could go on at considerable length. The point is that institutions should be alert to the possible problems. In any estimate of the cost of renovation, an architect and engineer as well as a representative of the local fire department should review the building in order that cost estimates can include those changes which may be mandated.

5. *Engineering improvements to consider.* Since the new addition will look fresh, clean, and contemporary and will have modern hardware and fixtures, consideration needs to be given to the extent to which the old and the new should be brought to more nearly equal quality. If the original structure is not to be retained after the next ten or twenty years, it will, of course, be wise to spend as little for cosmetic improvements as one can. In those cases where the building is regarded as a long-term investment, study should be made and costs determined for such improvements as fire protection and safety, water protection, heating, ventilation and air conditioning, lighting, underpinnings, floor alignment, earthquake seismic protection, and waterproof joints. One could, of course, add to this list. It would be well to list all of the present deficiencies—those things that do not operate well, where there have been leaks, cracks, or breaks, where appearance is shabby, where discoloration is evident, where severe storms or wind conditions have periodically caused problems—as well as those which are more superficial but will provide an obvious difference when a new building is sparkling and the old building is dreary.

Priorities can be assigned once the possible improvements have been defined and costs estimated. First priority attention might very well be given to those elements of very fundamental importance. For example, the integrity of the foundation and the waterproof condition of the roof as well as seismic bracing will be most basic. Second, attention might well be given to fire smoke-detection devices, sprinklers, hose cabinets, extinguishers, and annunciation systems. Third, water protection for the book collections is of obvious importance. One can go on down the list considering the value of various potential expenditures. One can even consider adding air conditioning in an old building if it does not already exist, for it is universally recognized that the cooling of the air and the maintenance of stable temperature and humidity night and day as well as summer and winter is the best way of preserving book collections, particularly if they include difficult-to-replace books or manuscripts and archives. It is, of course, more expensive to install air conditioning in an old building than in a new construction, and sometimes it is practically impossible, yet it may be one of the best investments.

When one gets to the question of replacing lighting systems, it is not only a question of aesthetics, but also one of operating costs. Fluorescent tubes provide up to three times as much intensity with less heat from the same amount of wattage as it takes for incandescent lighting. Conduit may not have to be changed for the conversion from incandescent to fluorescent lighting for satisfactory light levels even though the building may have been previously underlighted.

A review of the existing structure by an engineer and architect will bring out the range of possibilities to supplement those identified by the library staff. The cost judgments will have to be made about putting a lot of money into the older structure, and many officials in the institution will have what may be competing priorities among the various options. Each institution will need to make these trade-offs for itself.

6. *Design issues within the original structure.* Besides the usual architectural and engineering issues which are mentioned above and treated elsewhere in this volume, there are some special issues that should be considered whenever a building addition is projected. One question may be whether one or two floors could be added in the original structure in order to gain more assignable floor area. Depending upon the ceiling heights, structural requirements, and the feasibility of adequate ventilation if additional floors were inserted, the cost could be well worth it. Even if new forced-air ventilation has to be added, the additional area may be in such important places in the building and be so helpful in providing flexibility and growth in key functions that it may be a wise expenditure. There must be structural studies to see if the footings and load-bearing elements carry through the building and would tolerate extra loads. Disruption due to noise, fumes, and dust may be a factor. Of course, there is the aesthetic question whether it is desirable to lose some or all of the higher volume spaces that cannot be afforded in most modern library buildings. Another issue would be floor alignment. Ramps may need to be strategically placed in the original structure so that one can move book trucks from one to another level without having to go up two, three, or more steps.

Another consideration is filling in light wells, courts, or an atrium. This may be relatively easy space to claim so long as it does not present ventilation or structural problems. Some atriums were put in primarily to bring natural light into interior space. If that was the original justification, then filling it in may be space well gained; whereas, if it was designed for ventilation purposes, it may require adding a mechanical duct distribution system to compensate for the loss of exterior exposure. Another type of study might be of lobbies, corridors, and arcades. These may be claimed for assignable space if exit requirements permit. Power outlets and improved lighting may account for much of the cost of added space. Another question is about basement or attic spaces and whether there is problem with ground water, drains, and other utilities or heat buildup in the attic.

These and other issues have been treated more extensively in the second chapter, on alternatives to new construction. They certainly need consideration when planning an addition. Many libraries built before World War II have presented opportunities for improved use and may still offer possibilities. As in so many instances, local circumstances will dictate what are the best choices. As an example, architectural studies of Stanford's Green Library have repeatedly advised against adding a floor in two very high reading room spaces. Floor connections in the upper part of the original building have therefore not been resolved and probably never could be justified in cost. The lowest part of two large light wells was filled in, resulting in useful gain of shelving space. It was decided not to fill in more for ventilation and aesthetic reasons and because that area was not where the press for space existed. The major front lobby of the old structure was reduced in size so that over half of its floor area was made useful for staff quarters. Basement space was also gained. Examples can be found in many other institutions, and architectural advice is of great importance in judging these design issues.

7. *Design issues of branch libraries.* Major subject libraries may have their own physically separate building (for example, law, medicine, business, and sometimes the unified science library) in which the problems of design, expansion, and renovation are fundamentally similar to a central research library in a college or university. This section deals with

those departmental or branch libraries which share quarters with the department. Such libraries sometimes have one entire floor, part of one or more floors, or a several-story wing of a building; the alternatives are many. For such branch libraries the expansion is less often into a new addition than it is into an adjacent section of the building they are in. Such an addition of space brings special problems. Even though the options may be very few, some of the issues which should be considered will be enumerated. It would be well for such an expansion to be regarded as a very serious matter even though it may seem like a small amount of floor area and cost compared to those for a new building. Remember that for the one or several academic departments which regard that branch as their "main library" for teaching or research purposes, it is an exceedingly important matter—just as important as the main library may be to those in the humanities.

If the expansion of the branch library was anticipated and provided for at the time it was originally designed, which is sometimes the case, the growth may be accommodated with some ease. Offices or large flat-floored lecture halls or dry laboratories may provide feasible room for expansion. Wet laboratories are more difficult. Museum space may be so open and have such a high ceiling that expansion is a bit difficult. Subject or disciplinary libraries that often have the greatest rate of growth are those such as art, biology, geology, law, music, and others that have a strong historical base which requires cumulative collections rather than the much more prevalent weeding that takes place in the engineering and physical sciences.

Need an architect be used for such an addition of space? Not always, especially if the expansion was anticipated, if the addition is modest, and if an institutional planner is available to take care of such important details as location of light switches, installation of security devices, etc. In general, one should use an architect if the job entails extensive spatial studies, new walls and surfaces, structural review, and mechanical equipment and lighting. One may rely merely on an engineer if the project almost exclusively deals with the installation of air conditioning or plumbing or fire protection systems. Qualified experts are needed, and the staff in the university planning office or in the office of the university or college architect may be quite

sufficient for such a task. Remember that a very large library building may well have enough flexibility so that the results of a planner's oversight and omission may be a few mistakes in any one area, whereas in a branch library an oversight can rarely be afforded, since the flexibility within a branch is less and the competition for extra space within the total building may be severe.

If there are several options for expansion, then consideration should be given to whether horizontal or vertical access is preferred. Generally, the first floor for major public service areas and staff quarters, with a commodious basement for bookshelving and associated reading spaces, may be ideal. This arrangement is based on the fact that future expansion in a basement may be much easier than on the first or second floor. A second preference might be for the first floor alone or for having the entire library in a basement. Where water hazards are extreme, the second floor would be far preferable to any basement space whatsoever. Least convenient may be a top floor of a building. However, there are advantages and disadvantages to these locations. Long-term growth possibilities may often be the controlling factor. One should remember that if access is exceedingly convenient, the library may well become a student lounge or social center for that part of campus. The restlessness of a student who is passing time between classes can be extremely disturbing. If the library is too hidden, that also is unfortunate.

Points to consider in the nature of expansion should include the following. How easy is access to the branch found? How direct a route would there be evenings and weekends if the rest of the building is closed? How can books be most conveniently brought from a central library receipt and processing center or bindery to the branch? How can the heavy traffic to and from classes be kept away from open windows or the front door of the library so that such conditions are not noisy and visually disturbing? Is safety a consideration in the expansion? How safe from human harassment will the library be for readers or staff, including routes away from the library during evening hours or at closing, especially if that part of the building is rather lonely? Can the addition provide expansion for book and reading spaces so that the flow of the collection classification can be natural and the spaces contiguous?

Up to a point, a horizontal expansion is usually the best. It eliminates the elevator issue, at least until further expansion is considered. Such an expansion should not cross a public corridor unless that corridor can be taken over or the corridor can terminate at the library entrance. However, an elevator can be within the library and access to it from other parts of the building can be controlled by a library key, although careful analysis will be required to ensure that security of the branch is not compromised. Last but not least, try to consider what will happen to the branch library in ten or twenty years when the question of adding space once again must be faced.

Another point needs consideration. A branch library project is complicated by the special nature of the planning team. Campus politics can be compounded in such a project, and all involved should make particular efforts to work as an effective team. In addition to those who may be involved in a main library project, there will usually be one or more representatives of the academic department which "owns" the building, probably the departmental library committee, and perhaps a representative of the appropriate dean's office. Few of them will be as knowledgeable about libraries as those who deal with the main library. Few in the department will believe they are less than experts. Almost certainly none will have library building experience. Few if any will take the time to learn and study library planning. Departmental "turf" becomes an issue if, for example, favored offices are considered as part of the expansion. The departmental regard for the branch librarian and feelings of quasi-independence from the main library administration also affect the weight given to various opinions. There is one real advantage, however. In contrast to a project for a new departmental building where the library is a minor consideration in the arguments, all participants in an expansion project for the branch library are primarily focusing on how best to resolve the library space needs.

10.4 Construction Problems

In any library building project which includes remodeling or major additions, a great deal will go smoothly. However, just as certainly, a few things are bound to go wrong. These are not exactly predictable, although one or more environmental conditions will surely go awry for any number of reasons. One should expect some problems from reduced security, dust, noise, temperature and ventilation extremes, and possibly water problems and fire.

Even with very conscientious contractors, security, dust, and noise problems are certain to occur. The contract documents can help minimize difficulties by careful specification of conditions. However, one must not draw the specifications so tight that the contractors will bid high accordingly. It may, for example, be better to tolerate a bit of dust and expect to have to clean thousands of books after the construction is finished—and budget accordingly—than to have the contractor take extreme precautions to control dust at the origin. It is possible for water sprinkling to be done periodically during excavation work. One can also require polyethylene sheeting to be put up over openings and to tape all edges in order to be dustproof, and yet dust can be carried out one window and in the next, sheeting can become damaged, and some work requires going between the old and the new structures. Special keys may need to be issued for access to various areas within the existing facility, and special precautions will likely be required to ensure that the building is secured at the end of the day. While most contractors are honest, they are human; and they do sometimes forget to lock doors or supervise an entry while they are bringing materials in. Smoking in work areas may also be a problem. With work scheduled within an existing building, it is prudent to plan on having some library staff time devoted to supervising these areas of concern. Even when the contract documents indicate the possibility of litigation, construction specifications generally do relatively little to control problems without constant institutional supervision.

This is also true of noise, since there is no way that pavement breakers, jackhammers, powder-activated fasteners (also known as shot-in fasteners), compactors, and hammers will not create noise that can be transmitted through the air or through the structure itself. Although limiting hours for certain jobs with particularly bad noise can be required, the convenience of library staff and readers can come at great financial penalty to the project if the contractor is not enabled to do the job in an efficient way. It can, in fact, cost two-and-a-half times the normal charge for work that is done outside normal hours. However, special consideration for exam periods is reasonable and can be specified. It is important to alert staff and readers to disruptive work as far in advance as possible—certainly days or a week or more in advance rather than just a day. Reporting what may be called a "rolling schedule" can be useful, based upon a total project schedule updated weekly to describe what is to follow the next week and the week thereafter.

Sharp variations in temperature and ventilation may occur, depending on the nature of the construction. Here again, good advance notice to staff and readers can lead to some acceptance of the discomfort. Most people will be able to find alternative reading spaces or put up with the temporary environmental problems as they look forward to much better conditions in the near future. Realizing that mechanical engineering is often more art than science, one needs to be prepared for what may be months or several years of HVAC trouble from almost any new system. Balancing the controls should start early and often requires at least a year under various climatic conditions before good adjustment is achieved.

It is fortunate that problems due to water and fire are somewhat less common than are the preceding. Yet it seems that more problems of water and fire are caused during construction or renovation than at other times. The danger goes up sharply whenever workmen are altering water lines, welding, using temporary electrical connections, and using water for some aspects of the construction job.

Although their construction activities should be insured under builder's risk coverage by the contractor, specific instructions on the degree of protection to be provided may, in fact, be limiting in such a way that the institution becomes partially liable in the event of a fire loss. Because of this, careful consideration must be given to what is specified. In other instances, where the institution keeps the responsibility for builder's risk insurance, it is quite appropriate to specify the exact protection that is required. For example, this specification can require a contractor to provide one ten-pound ABC fire extinguisher for every 3,000 sq ft (278.70 m²) under construction; welding safety procedures can require a second person present with at least one fire extinguisher in hand;

and all welding can be done before noon in order to ensure an absence of lingering hot spots after the day's work ends.

As one example, work on Stanford's Green Library addition brought two instances of severe water problems. In one case holes were cut in an adjacent basement wall for connecting pipes between the old and new buildings; and, by chance, an old pipe in the ground outside the actual construction area gave way (probably caused by galvanic corrosion when a copper, a steel, and a cement-lined cast-iron pipe were laid too close to one another without a sand bed to give some protection from corrosion due to adverse soil conditions) and water accumulated in a trench which fed to the open core holes. Obviously, the holes should not have been left open even for one night; yet such oversight occurs and accidents happen. In a second case the contractor was worried about fire and activated the sprinkler line system before the waterflow alarm was hooked up to a campus monitoring center. A sprinkler head under a new skylight was by accident rated at 160 degrees F (61 degrees C) instead of 220 degrees F (104 degrees C). As a result the sprinkler blew on a hot summer weekend, and it was Monday morning before staff found that wood paneling and some uninstalled carpeting had been flooded. Once again, there needs to be eternal vigilance and monitoring of remodeling projects as well as additions.

Other difficulties may surprise one. Security of the old building can be breached as exterior door keys are handed around. Entire rolls of carpet have been known to disappear, not to mention books. Interruption in utility service to the existing occupied building can be anticipated when an addition is under construction, and this can, of course, affect several buildings in the vicinity. When excavations occur, there may be disturbance to existing utility lines. Older materials may have become fragile; for example, a fiberglass material called Techite was once thought to be sound and reasonably priced, but a much sturdier material, such as Transite, which is a cement and asbestos substance, or an even different material without asbestos, may now be specified. Telephone, electricity, drinking water, sprinklers, and plumbing lines may all inadvertently break down with service interrupted for hours or several days.

The best advice is that any construction costing as little as $300,000 today may require a full-time and full-scope inspector, not an occasional technical inspection by one who oversees several projects. One can also try to anticipate as much as possible—know a dependable source of emergency pumps, provide cover for books and selected equipment, have staff on hand when testing occurs, train key library staff so they may take immediate action if called upon, and anticipate that significant problems will come evenings and weekends when workmen are not present to see the consequences of some condition they have left.

These problems are not unique to a job of remodeling or adding on to an existing building. However, the impact on staff and those who need to use the library makes the events upsetting. It is good advice to prequalify contractors for remodeling jobs.

Finally, no library staff should remain in the construction area if at all possible. This advice is easy to give but in many cases is impossible to follow. The presence of staff during construction will compound difficulties several fold. It is always best to build the addition, move in and free areas in the older space to be remodeled, and then make the final deployment. Really major reconstruction requires it; in modest renovation it is desirable, though circumstances will alter what is best practice. In any instance where construction is going on under the same roof as an operating library, one must make special effort to communicate frequently and explicitly in clear language with construction management as well as with library staff and library users. This point needs emphasis, as any library staff can attest if they have gone through a major remodeling or addition.

10.5 Making Old and New Work Well Together

The environmental psychology of working in and using both old and new space is important. Serious attention needs to be given to the effect on staff and on library readers of spaces that are contiguous. Though architects will pay attention to this, the library staff who will live their working hours in the building should also give consideration to this condition. It is by no means automatic for the old space to work well or feel comfortable next to the new, or in some cases the reverse.

In some instances there have been staff who feel they have been left in second-class areas.

Their morale may drop. There may be many more complaints about workloads, backlogs, the visual appearance of the area, and the lack of fresh paint or new carpeting or modern lighting. Some conditions which were accepted before the new addition may now be the cause of persistent complaints. It is true that staff newly hired after the addition may feel less put upon because they are tempted to take it as a given; however, older staff may well convince them that their area has been neglected.

This psychology is natural and should be expected. It is, in fact, desirable for the building to feel as if its parts work well together. Some attention to detail, to wall color, carpeting, art work, and signage can help. Such relatively inexpensive improvements, which are sometimes called "cosmetic," can help a great deal. It may be possible to go further in improving an old facility by modernizing an elevator, rest rooms, the principal entrance from new to the old, and selected furniture.

A good example of achieving harmony is the 1970 addition to the American Antiquarian Society. The original classic structure of 1910 had additions in 1924 and 1950, but the 1970 work added more space and excellently related the four parts. Only the original bookstack looks its age, and nearly all staff quarters feel as if they were part of the new construction.

When building construction budgets are under financial pressure, it may be quite easy to postpone treatment of the old wing since so much emphasis is being placed on the new wing. Realistic budget expectations for improvements in the next few years may lead to some phasing in of the improvements, but all too often the problem is merely ignored. Do not concentrate just on the rare-book department or a faculty reading lounge; consider technical processing staff and other "behind the scenes" areas and try to preserve the warmth and comfort of older spaces, while blending those qualities with the freshness of newer spaces. No responsible person would wish to discard sound furniture or otherwise dress up old space merely to be able to say that it has been redone. Thus change merely for the sake of change is seldom warranted. However, attention to how the new space and the old space feel next to each other and some attention to the psychology of those who will use the old and the new is an important part of any addition and renovation project. As has been said, although form may follow function, human needs go beyond function and beyond mere style. No specific advice can be given because the local conditions will be unique; but the point is made that this concern needs conscious attention in order that the effect of the total space available can be regarded as satisfactory.

10.6 Conversions

Another aspect of building renovation is that of converting a building or part thereof into library space. In most large universities that date back a century, there will be a number of small branches and maybe a few larger branches which are now in space that was not originally designed for library purposes. Given the cost of construction, the scarcity of good building sites on older campuses, and greater attention to preserving well designed or historic buildings, it seems probable that more conversions will take place in future decades. These are not likely to be for very large units although, even there, some conversion of adjacent space may help solve, at least temporarily, the space problems in a large or central library facility.

As an example from the 1980s one can cite Stanford. None of the professional schools has a library in converted quarters. Yet, of the departmental branch libraries, conversions provided the current quarters for chemistry, communication, philosophy, mathematics, marine sciences, and the food research institute. Space had been converted from warehouses, an office loft, wet laboratories, a student snack facility, and general teaching spaces. In some instances the building was quite completely gutted before the library and other quarters were built; in other instances nothing structural was changed and the costs were kept down to those for removing laboratory plumbing, a new door between the old and the new sections of the library, and some superficial improvements in appearance.

Such conversions can be very tasteful in treatment of small spaces, as in the Ticknor Modern Language Library in Boylston Hall at Harvard, or of extensive projects such as the Harvard-Yenching Library, which included addition of a modern stack structure and very extensive remodeling for reading room and staff quarters in the original build-

ing. In Berkeley the University of California used a former Ford assembly plant as its storage library for lesser-used materials for some two decades before a larger new structure was designed. At Oxford University there was a conversion of All Saints Church into the library for Lincoln College. Strathclyde University converted a publisher's warehouse into a 107,640 sq ft (10,000 m²) unified library on four floors. Indeed, the first home of the British Library Lending Division was a wartime factory.

Laws may govern the changes possible in historic buildings. Even where they do not exist, good architectural practice will urge saving and reusing well-designed spaces and limiting the nature of external changes that may be made. City ordinances may lead to scrutiny by governmental agencies whenever a significant change of use is contemplated. Different countries as well as different states and cities deal with the issue in somewhat varying ways, though a prime motive is the desire for sensitive treatment of those buildings, courtyards, and vistas which have aesthetic and cultural values, qualities that may be as important as the monetary value of the structure itself.

The possibility of a conversion raises some of the same issues that come up in any remodeling. There may be a requirement to bring the existing space up to current building codes in order to protect personal safety and health. The architects and planning team will need to have firm principles to apply in making such a conversion so that the original building does not constitute an unreasonable constraint on the library program—making the foot fit the shoe instead of the shoe fitting the foot. There will need to be a decision whether the conversion is temporary, and thus the effort much more modest than a complete change. One must remember that a conversion is not necessarily a cheaper alternative to a new building, though some administrators may jump to such a conclusion. When the Stanford Quadrangle buildings have been rebuilt they have almost always cost more than a new structure; however, an additional floor was fitted within the older structure in most cases. The historic, visual, and aesthetic factors made conversion worth the expense. One must remember that evaluation of design and functional effectiveness is made more difficult in any conversion because of the number of constraints imposed.

These may be constraints of siting, perhaps orientation, floor-to-floor height, probably the base size, the fenestration most certainly, vertical shafts to a considerable extent, and limitations on future flexibility depending on the extent of interior bearing walls and other similar elements.

The facade may be the last part that an architect can change. Even then, new glass doors, new signs, and lighting can create a new effect. If the site is larger than that of the original building, an addition or at least an underground extension can increase the assignable floor area. Underground extension of the Fogg Art Museum at Harvard provided the library needed growth space, as did the underground addition for the Avery Architectural Library at Columbia University. If the site has no spare land, then a connection to an adjacent building may permit easy growth, such as the tunnel between the Houghton and Lamont buildings at Harvard. The underground Pusey Library later provided further Houghton expansion. Vertical expansion may be all but impossible because of weight. Carrying new columns through an old building in order to support additional superstructure is usually exceedingly expensive, even though it may occasionally be justified in one portion where the floor loads require or perhaps for only the lower floor. Remember that, without taking mechanical HVAC space in the building being converted, a basement connection to an adjacent building may provide the solution to a major problem.

Although every remodeling project will differ from others, one excellent example at Brown University will be briefly described. Listed in the National Register of Historic Places as part of the College Hill Historic District, the John Hay Library dates from 1910; since 1971 it has been devoted to archives and special collections. A decade of study and fundraising was required before the antiquated building was turned into proper quarters to protect rare materials for scholars. A 1977 program documented requirements to bring the structure into code compliance, including replacement of plumbing and sewer lines, addition of air conditioning and humidity and security equipment, and control of ultraviolet light. After work by a planning consultant, a study concluded that equivalent new library space would cost more than renovating John Hay and that renovating it for other purposes would be more costly than as a library. With funds from the federal government, foundations, and alumni, Brown then retained an architectural firm to prepare plans—including phases of work so that the library could function during the renovation.

Although John Hay already had a new roof, the white marble exterior walls had suffered from industrial pollution. On advice of a stone consultant, the marble was not cleaned or sealed for fear of trapping moisture; however, the mortar joints were raked and repointed. New light-filtering, sealed windows were installed in new mahogany frames, the glass a three-layer sandwich with a vacuum between two layers. Many fluorescent lights were replaced with incandescent fixtures and those fluorescent fixtures which were retained were equipped with ultraviolet filters. A major cost was the new air conditioning, with temperatures controlled within two degrees of 68 degrees F (20 degrees C) and relative humidity within 2 percent of 50 percent with 90 percent recycled air and particulate filtration. Humidity heads and reheat coils were widely distributed to assure constant environment in stacks, exhibition cases, and reading rooms. (Areas not used for storage or exhibition were given only standard air conditioning.) To meet fire protection codes, all electrical wiring was replaced, new corridors and fire stairs were equipped with dry-pipe sprinklers, and a 47-zone products-of-combustion smoke-detection system was installed with city and university alerts. It was possible for Brown to receive a code variance from the fire marshal so no sprinklers in collection areas were required. (Halon had been rejected due to the cost of purchasing and maintaining the extinguishing system.) Finally, a combination 87-zone security alert system was installed, including ultrasonic and infrared devices, window and door contacts, and vibration sensors, as well as sealing all stack windows. From the above one can begin to see the range of technical issues involved, each one deserving careful professional resolution for concerns of cost, durability, aesthetics, legality, and operational convenience and dependability.

Conclusion

Projects which entail an addition and remodeling can be particularly difficult. There are usually unique and often awkward conditions with which the architect and engineers must deal. There will be uncertainties, and surprises will turn up during construction. The budgeting is a more complicated matter, and the fundraising will be more difficult than for a completely new building costing the same as an addition and renovation. One should merely be alert to these aspects of such a project. This type of project is becoming increasingly common. It certainly constitutes a significant challenge to the planning team.

During the effort one should make sure that available space is used to advantage without crowding seating, staff, or bookstacks, discouraging readers or handicapping the staff. There have been too many cases where, to gain space, additions of that kind have been made to the long-term disadvantage of staff and readers. It is unfortunate that in the past many a building was planned as a complete architectural unit by an architect who did not want to have his or her "gem" modified or damaged aesthetically by future generations. Although this basis for the design may have been inadvertent on the part of the architect, it was most unwise and caused problems for administrators in following decades.

This last point calls for further comment. More than one architect has said that a commission would be refused if the instructions from the institution included a requirement that the building be planned in such a way that additions would be readily practicable without impairing it functionally. It would be rash to propose a universal rule that no library building should be planned without a suitable addition or two in mind. However, the presidents and governing boards of colleges and universities ought to realize that most academic and research libraries, unless they are much more mature than most of those in this country, still grow at a rate that doubles their space requirements every twenty years or less—every ten years in some cases. Unless the institution is prepared to provide completely new housing for its library at frequent intervals, it ought to arrange for expansion at a later time. The economic conditions in higher education will make it all the more important that building additions and extensive remodeling of existing quarters must be accommodated in the coming decades. A wise planning team will always leave options open for its successors.

11

Master Planning and Siting

11.1 The Campus as City

Each institution has a unique physical character. A college or a university may be part of a city; some institutions are more integrated into the city than others. If set apart from a city, the institution takes on many of the characteristics of a city, though it is more homogeneous. In all instances, the interaction of town or city and state or province with the educational institution has been and always will be substantial, even if the institution is in unincorporated territory. A rural setting will in due course become suburban and probably urban as the activities of the institution draw supporting services and related occupations. Employees of a college have families, and homes will be built. Food, clothing stores, automotive stores, and recreational facilities are needed, and eventually inns or motels for visitors to campus will be necessary. So even the rural settings of Hampshire College, Washington State University, the University of California at Davis,

and the University of Connecticut are affected by these entrepreneurial enterprises.

A campus is, therefore, substantially involved with urban planning concerns and pressures. They may involve zoning studies, environmental impact statements, spheres-of-influence studies, and hearings as well as pressures from various groups for or against open space or any of dozens of other causes. Furthermore, the campus uses the same design elements and the same architectural options and engenders the same human reactions to space, color, and form as those in other communities over hundreds of years of trial and error. (Dober and Turner, cited in the Bibliography, provide useful treatments of campus planning issues.)

To understand planning, one should know some design concepts, which each campus applies in different ways. For some, Gothic architecture was best suited for conveying a sense of age and permanence. For others, Colonial seemed more indigenous and nostalgic. Romanesque was elsewhere favored. "This

301

desire that college architecture be 'venerable' and 'substantial,' be laden with 'associations,' and testify to an 'old and honored' institution, became common in the mid- and late-nineteenth century."[1] Thus a special image, or "feel," may be created by an institution, developing its own local fabric as an expression of the academic needs and philosophies of successive generations. Some images are, of course, more distinctive than others. Some plans succeed fairly well, others brilliantly; most do well in some respects and fall short in others.

Eight qualities in the design vocabulary will be mentioned as suggestive of the many elements which affect campus planning. Those chosen are accretion, balance, linkage, open space, sculptural form, spine, surprise, and thigmotropism. The idiom of the planner may be as abstruse as the acronyms of the information scientist!

"Accretion" is the incremental physical growth, the additions of wings, the occupation of new acreage. Each growth should be so placed, in balance or contrast, to maintain spatial harmony and coherence. Consider how Harvard, Illinois and Princeton libraries were enlarged.

"Balance" may mean symmetry, such as the two towers on Notre Dame de Paris, or relations of mass, such as the Low Library and Butler Library at Columbia University, or the rhythmic repetitions of form, shape, and definition which relate one space to another.

"Linkage" may be expressed as traffic requirements for bicycles, goods, pedestrians, vehicles, and wastes. Yet it may connote a positioning of paths and building lines to provide desirable relationships, or the contemporary use of classical architectural vocabulary, such as a frieze. Continuities in a college are of special importance, the arcades in the Stanford University Quadrangle serving that purpose.

"Open space" emphasizes the advantages of nature, whether it be playing fields, a picnic grove, an outdoor bench for reading, or a bower for post-class lecture discussion. The green before Dartmouth College's Baker Library is a noted example.

"Sculptural form" denotes the softness or relief from rigid shapes that comes from a rounded arch, a dome, a knoll and careful

[1] Paul Venable Turner, *Campus; An American Planning Tradition* (Cambridge, Mass.: MIT Pr., 1984), p. 117.

landscaping. The texture of the facade of library buildings can help provide this treatment.

"Spine" refers to the "main street," be it an internal linear arrangement within a megastructure or an external path giving alignment to clustered rows of buildings.

"Surprise" refers to the interest that humans experience in an unexpected building form or vista, which may be a spire, an outdoor sculpture, a high void inside a building, a changing shadow, or the glimpse of a lake between distant buildings. The two, differing, towers of Chartres Cathedral can be an example. A university attempt is the central library of the University of California, San Diego.

"Thigmotropism" is the extent to which people find comfort or pleasure in walls, nooks, cubbyholes, carrels, courtyards. For many the object seems to provide a psychological security blanket, an environment conducive to serious study in a library.

The planner uses a catalog of concepts which have historic validity and which convey from expert to expert a precise and useful design meaning. The artistry and skill of the individual designer comes into play; taste can be educated but it cannot often be created where none existed before. So the planner is expected to create functional and pleasant spaces with a feeling of comfort, awe, surprise, strength, and liveliness. No one building may achieve all that; however, the academic institution as a whole should strive to satisfy those human yearnings. The campus plan and its architecture should inspire and educate while young people are still in their formative years, often living away from home, sometimes fearful of being on their own, under pressure, and trying to live mature lives while hardly beyond adolescence. Campus planning needs to fulfill a significant social need.

11.2 Planning Concepts and Influences

The history of community planning has many lessons for colleges and universities. When campus planning permits great latitude in library site selection, and particularly when the campus is new or relatively young, experiences in community planning can provide instructive lessons. Without providing a detailed discussion of this topic, five concepts will be treated.

Privacy and Protection. From the earliest times, students have needed both privacy and protection. The life of the student and the life of the church required quiet and privacy (thigmotropic space) for study and contemplation. Campus walls and gates used to be common due to the "town and gown" exuberances of a student's night on the town or the town boys' distaste for the student. Oxford University's private residential halls and colleges, founded in 1264 and later, provide a protective environment; the interconnecting quadrangles, containing farms, gardens, or greens, look inward. Yet it was not until the seventeenth century that many comforts of nobility were available to the middle classes, including privacy—privacy in sleep, prayer, and family needs, and the home was less and less the place of one's business. Since so many colleges were founded for the study of theology, it is no wonder monastic designs had an effect. Considerations of privacy for study and reflection and protection from vandalism and assault exist today, though the campus is no longer a walled city. Even so, many institutions are strongly influenced by the high cost of land or even the limited availability of sites; their buildings are often closely placed and they take on the character of cities. Where buildings are closely placed, it is now considered undesirable to have one window directly face another closer than 75 feet (22.860m) away, and paths are often laid out so that there are not nearby hiding places.

The Square. Town squares used for markets, proclamations, plays, hangings, and parades had existed for centuries. Park-like squares in residential neighborhoods became common in the seventeenth century. The campus makes good use of such plazas, courtyards, and greens. The Dartmouth College Green and the Harvard Yard are sentimental places, with the libraries dominating. Where no such formal area exists, as at Berkeley, students will find its counterpart by Sather Gate at the head of Telegraph Avenue. As the Boston Common can serve pageantry and provides its varied diversions, so serve Columbia University's common acreage in front of Alma Mater and Stanford University's White Memorial Plaza.

In the latter case, during the 1950s this ill-defined area replaced, by students' choice, the formal central Quadrangle faced by the Memorial Church and a square of classrooms.

The preferred Plaza was the rallying ground in the late 1960s for masses of demonstrating students. The street vendors are more appropriate in the current setting, protecting the academically oriented Inner Quad, and indeed the nearby Library Quad, from distracting sounds. However, beside the Plaza are the Music Library and the Department of Music which had to have double-glazed windows as protection against the cacophony of amplified street oratory and music!

Clearly, one of the major concerns about placing a library on "the square" is noise and disruption. Where a campus has multiple squares, it may be desirable to site the library on a secondary square, to remove it from what could be the negative influence of some activities. Such a secondary square can be designed to discourage loud musical concerts, speeches, and other activities that can disrupt library activities. For example, through the use of plantings, benches, walks, steps, and other landscape elements, small groupings of people may be encouraged rather than the large gatherings that can occur in a main square. The introduction of a fountain which produces pleasant noise can further reduce disruptive activities. Bicycle parking, where bicycles are common, should also be part of the design of the square.

Axis and Connections. Students have only a few years to adjust to the campus. Its symbolism in those years can be profound and replete with idealism and memories. The church, the library, and the stadium can have great importance; and those buildings are important for what goes on, as well as for what they represent. The human actions and statements are the interest; the buildings merely represent those actions of the past, or the high points of one's college years.

The frequent view of the church or the library reminds one of the intellectual and spiritual purpose of higher education. So the physical setting becomes important, such as the central axis which can provide a view from many places of the symbolic structure, the frequent glimpse of which is a reminder of our purpose. Paris provides sights from the Louvre to the Arc de Triomphe, or Sacré-Coeur to Notre Dame. The design of Pierre L'Enfant links the U.S. Capitol, the White House, and Lincoln Memorial, showing that ground level connections can be as significant in planning as are those of higher structures.

Campus planning or site planning for the library in terms of axis and connections is generally not terribly controversial as far as the operation of the library is concerned. It can be important to a prospective donor. It can clarify exterior circulation patterns, and it may suggest axial views which might be an asset worth developing as the design of the library proceeds. But perhaps the greatest concern for the librarian is the notion that designing around an axis may imply a rigid symmetry which can lead to problems later when it is necessary to add to the building. Care should be taken where the site may be too prominent or precious.

Clusters and Superblocks. The grouping of academic buildings or student residences can follow several options. The alignment around a square or on either side of a street offers easy orientation, though it may be visually monotonous. Buildings massed around courts or cul-de-sacs can eliminate through traffic. The access may be only for pedestrians with service access from the periphery. The approach may be formalized by a gate and fences. Experience with residential development shows that cul-de-sacs should not extend downhill, due to surface drainage and utility waste-flow problems as well as to the feeling at the end of the circle. The same applies to the library site.

Clusters form an alternative used for both academic and residential purposes as well as a large module for planned campus accretion. Clustered buildings provide proximity and visual interest, offer great variety for massing, engender social relations, and save open space; yet they may make orientation and access more difficult.

Although the Harvard Yard has become a superblock, with internal access only by essential service vehicles through a single gate, the planned development of insular neighborhoods dates from the Radburn, New Jersey, plan early in this century. By having the buildings face inward instead of fronting the street, privacy and quiet are increased; the center block can be park-like. Letchworth and Welwyn Garden City (just north of London) and Baldwin Hills Village (now Village Green, in Los Angeles) provide historic examples of "precinct planning" where roads and paths are connected yet provide useful functional separation. The application of the superblock plan is particularly useful in campus planning, including the library component.

Where the main body of the campus is in effect a superblock with limited vehicular access, care must be taken in considering the needs of the library. Recognizing use patterns during class hours, access to the library should be influenced by the location of significant groupings of classrooms, lecture halls, laboratories, and other teaching facilities. At other times the library orientation should recognize relations to the living quarters or external transportation, including, most notably in this country, the automobile.

Renovation and Symbolism. Some of the meaning of campus life, or urban life, comes from the juxtaposition of old and new. This visible association of episodes of institutional development is enriching to the sensitive eye and mind. Furthermore, the reuse of good old structures for new purposes can provide the new functions with a charming patina. Thus it is that Ghirardelli Square in San Francisco and Society Hill and environs in Philadelphia are admired.

True, there have been massive renewal projects which have been extremely disruptive of families and social conditions. Though campus development is sometimes an important component of an urban renewal plan, most commonly the campus deals with one building at a time. One building may be judged too wasteful of space to retain and the construction of another too poor, while others may have qualities which argue for retention and renewal.

Cities now do better jobs of selecting good older structures for renewal, some of them merely for sentimental or symbolic reasons. The campus can do likewise. Even in the 1970s one aged and wasteful academic building in the treasured Harvard Yard was demolished to provide a new student residential site. In other cases, such as the Stanford Quadrangle, renewal within the original shell was the architectural choice, and the use of old wrought iron stair balustrades in Stanford's History Corner of the Quad is an instance of the tasteful detail that can provide special pleasures.

Terrain and Climate. A planner using the concepts mentioned above, as well as others, will be influenced by natural conditions. Each piece of land is composed of a set of interrelated factors—some above ground (atmosphere, wind, precipitation), some on the ground (drainage, plant and animal life), and some below (soil characteristics, seasonal water table, bedrock). Each condition in some degree affects the land use, or at least the economics of overcoming limiting conditions. While the Simplon Tunnel and Verrazano Narrows Bridge are costly solutions to natural conditions, most city and campus land uses are more accommodating to the terrain and climate. As Rome and San Francisco worked with their hills, so does Simon Fraser University (fig. 11.1) blanket and dominate its elevation. As Venice has water and soil problems, so Simmons College, the University of Bremen, and Tulane University have had to cope with adverse soil and water table. Earthquakes test library structures, as was experienced in 1906 at Stanford University, 1963 at Rhode Island College, 1971 at UCLA, and 1978 at the University of California campus at Santa Barbara.

Climate is also a constant influence on plans, partly for site density and partly to protect against occasional storm conditions (e.g., hurricane areas by the shore, tornado stresses, spring tide, or tsunami). Prevailing winds, snow depths, humidity, solar angle, even the length of daylight—from Arizona to Alaska or even Quebec to coastal Maine—may be striking.

Soil conditions may change markedly over just a few feet of terrain. Careful studies are needed to detect problems, the greatest deriving from a high water table, evidence of subsidence or floods, silt or water-bearing sand, mud or muck, clay or adobe, or filled and uncompacted land. Such sites may tremendously increase normal foundation costs, while rocky sites will cost only slightly more than normal, depending on the nature of the rock and the necessity of blasting for a basement, utility lines, or surface drainage.

Tulane University's Tilton Library is a case in point. The foundation, on muck soil only two feet above sea level, supports four floors with the footings sufficient for four more levels, since there is said to be no land for horizontal expansion. A building hazard in any such hurricane region is glass to windward, especially on the top floor, which may bear the brunt of high winds over lower adjacent buildings, and on the ground level, where branches and outdoor furniture or bicycles may be blown, hitting and damaging the building.

To conclude, the above concepts and factors have much more effect on campus planning than is often imagined. The design precepts that have succeeded in urban development over the past four millennia will in all probability have a similarity of success today. Nevertheless, the subtleties can escape even very good planners and designers. The Stanford Meyer Memorial Library of 1966 uses Greek temple elements: a classical columnal style mounted on an historic three-step platform base. The roof to column proportions, however, fail in comparison to the Greek. To many it seems that the lesson was not adequately learned!

11.3 Long-Term Campus Planning

Site selection is related to master planning, either for the library specifically or for the institution as a whole. It might be supposed that the logical order of procedure would be to decide that a new library is needed, then to decide the sort of building it ought to be and the architectural style to be used, and finally to decide where it should be placed. The situation is practically never so simple as this. The availability of a satisfactory site is one of the factors that affect the decision whether or not to build.

One can hardly determine how much space is necessary for an adequate site unless one has studied the objectives of the library and projected its space needs and its future growth. One can hardly judge whether or not a particular location will be reasonably convenient for those who use the library unless one can predict the extent and direction of future physical growth of the institution served by the library. If the institution is in its infancy and there is ample room, it may be wise to select the library site first and to plan the future building program for the whole college or university around it. More often, however, the problem is one of fitting a large building or addition into an existing pattern that may have made no provision for it.

It should be emphasized also that one cannot design a satisfactory building and then look about for a vacant space that is large and convenient enough for its placement. Instead, many features of a good building are determined by its site. In order to compare the advantages of two sites, one must compare the two somewhat different buildings that could be erected on them.

The problems that have been suggested above indicate that the selection of a library

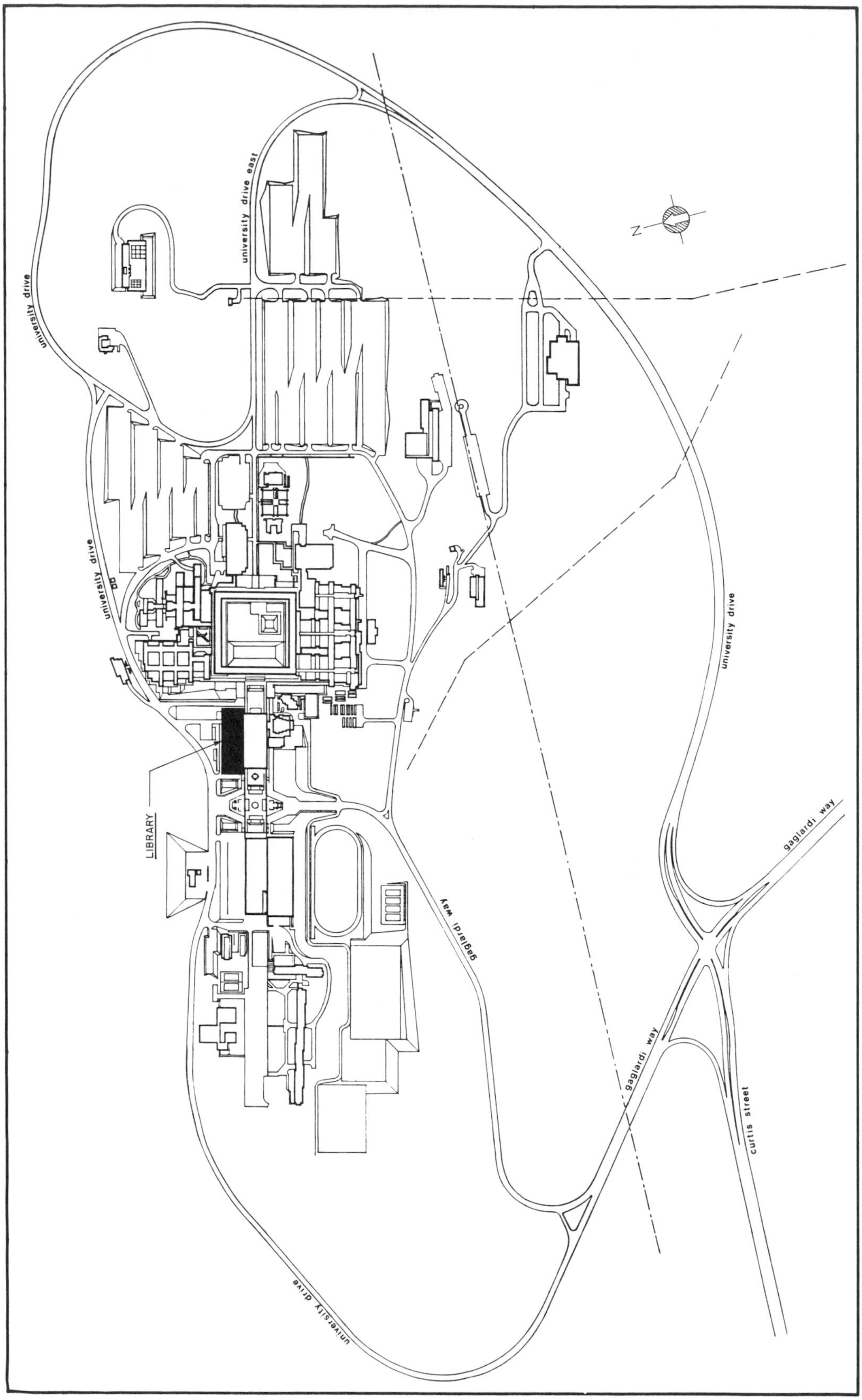

FIGURE 11.1 Simon Fraser campus plan. The library, designated "04," is on a hillside that slopes upward toward the major academic center, shown as "02" to the right of the library.

site is so important for an institution as a whole that it should be preceded in many instances, if not most, by the preparation of a master plan for physical development of the campus. Master planning of this sort is a problem for the institution as a whole, not just for the library. Even neighboring communities or the host city will be a major influence on the master plan. This master plan should consider among other things the following:

1. The objectives of the institution.

2. The estimated prospective size of the student body and faculty, including separate figures for graduate and undergraduate students and professional schools, if there are or are to be any.

3. Intellectual affinities among disciplines, which may suggest physical clusterings of academic departments and library sites.

4. The size of the physical plant that will be required in the next twenty-five years and, if possible, longer. Therefore density studies are needed.

5. The parking facilities required for faculty, staff, and students, and means of transportation used by commuters.

6. The general landscaping and servicing plan for the campus.

7. Policy decisions in regard to the type and architectural style of the buildings to be erected.

Without a master plan for development of the institution's physical plant, the difficulties of selecting a satisfactory site for a new library will be greatly increased. It should be noted that certain architects and landscape architects make a specialty of preparing master plans for the development of colleges and universities. Furthermore, if a master plan exists or if the governing board has approved a building site, the selected architect may for some good reason feel that a better site could be found and may properly recommend it. If such a suggestion is made, the institution should give it serious consideration, and the librarian should certainly be given an opportunity to study the suggestion and express an opinion to the campus planning group, to the architect, and to the regular supervising architect of the campus, if one exists, since that architect's approval may be required for all new construction.

The Process. Master planning involves a skillful blending of analysis, quantification, and synthesis. As is mentioned above, the analysis includes data on the nature, size, and trends of each component of the institution. This covers students, subdivided by undergraduate, graduate, and special (such as postdoctoral) and by major field, teaching faculty and research staff similarly broken down; business, maintenance, and administrative staff; and numbers, types, peak loads, and timing for campus visitors: parents, entertainment audience, delivery and service personnel, construction and other contractual staff, visitors for academic purposes (public lectures or library use) or official purposes (accreditation, governmental review, foreign delegations, etc.). The analysis also requires that the current philosophy of education processes and trends be thoroughly understood—including developments in intellectual or departmental affinities, the nature of sponsored research, the attitude toward housing students on campus and using student residences as a setting for informal teaching, the extent and type or extra-curricular activities, such as club sports or dormitory theatricals.

The quantification process is a numeric and topographical formulation of the analysis data. It results in tables of campus population and of land and buildings, even noise levels, as well as plans detailing land use, building sites, roads and paths, hydrants, outdoor lighting, and underground conditions. It may include contingent and conjectural data for projections ten or twenty years ahead. The result may constitute several volumes of organized planning data and dozens of land maps, aerial photos, survey sheets, zonal and building plans, and so forth. It may well include a physical model of the entire campus.

The synthesis process is iterative and to a considerable extent, subjective. It takes the data and the trends, the philosophies underlying the institution, the external forces of a social, political, and economic nature, and blends them into an assessment of current suitability and a forecast of changes needed in the years ahead. As the intellectual modeling process alters one factor (for example, a plan for increased adult education, less intercollegiate athletics, or more micro-laboratory–based courses), the quantified data of needs are revised and tested against constraints. The revised synthesis results in a new model or master plan.

As an example of this iterative process, a "Facilities Plan" is annually submitted to

Stanford's trustees to report renovations and new construction over the past two years, estimate and seek approval of such work for the year ahead, list projects seriously considered for the following two years, and present funding strategies and a report on current debt financing. Some projects are described as growing from university objectives, some are stimulated by donor interests, others reflect governmental priorities, and many are "the result of the march of time and the demands of progress." Stanford's facilities goals are:

1. To provide adequate facilities for teaching and scholarship ("For some this may mean a solitary study with access to library collections; for others, extensive laboratories; and for both, adequate classrooms and other instructional support services, e.g. audio-visual aids and computer facilities.")
2. To provide most effective use of existing buildings (code problems, obsolescence, etc.)
3. To support peer grouping
4. To support interaction among disciplines
5. To preserve the essential physical qualities of the campus.

The overriding constraint is financing. The process of facility development is presented in Figure 11.2, and one representative table (fig. 11.3) summarizes 131 projects, of which the first two had significant branch library components and several others supported the library.

Major Considerations. As the planning process advances and shapes the library options, there are five factors which bear heavily on the viability of the master plan, which in turn expresses the physical goals toward which the institution and its library need to move to satisfy the scholarly goals.

1. *The financial capacity* is paramount, as can be seen in the Stanford example above. No matter what the source, and no matter how persuasive the other influences, available funds will unyieldingly constrain the capacity.

2. *Academic factors* should in the course of time hold sway. Interesting examples can be drawn from the statements of guiding phi-

losophies which gave shape to six new English universities.[2]

Bath (est. 1966): The interaction of academic, social, and residential life underlies all the plans. Since only a minority of the students can be housed there, the twelve schools are the focus for social life, with each "entrance" providing a nucleus of common rooms, coffee bars and meeting placcs. In turn this entrance leads to a "central pedestrian parade," the linear center of the university beside which will develop clubs, societies, student union, sports center, theater, shops, restaurants, and bars.

Bradford (est. 1966): This undeniably urban technological university has firm links to industry. Thus a structure must present few barriers to the mixing of disciplines. "Individual buildings are out—installments of a continuous structure are in!" Yet the library is a separate central structure.

Essex (est. 1965): On 200 acres (80.940 ha) in an eighteenth-century park, the university is expected to be large. The scheme, therefore, aims at concentration of people so one should not walk more than five minutes on the ground. To make a continuous teaching building, the structure has "the beginnings of a snake with rather square bends in it." The library is at the arts and administration end.

Kent (est. 1965): Its stated goal is not merely to train but to educate, to get away from the "9–5" university, from the limited collegiate commitment. Thus the teaching and residential functions are mixed in college buildings. The large structures of the colleges are spaced on a ridge, the campus being half in the city of Canterbury. Near the colleges are the library and a considerable site on which to develop "the ganglion of sciences."

Sussex (est. 1961): Three and a half miles (5.632 km) from Brighton is a site rich in trees and lovely landscape. The architect believed the architecture should be low and the trees should break the skyline. Growth will be handled by adding courtyard to courtyard. The architect has said, "I feel strongly that a rigid axial plan will fall by

[2] Statements adapted from *University Planning and Design: A Symposium*, ed. by Michael Brawne. Architectural Association Paper no. 3 (London: Lund Humphries, 1967).

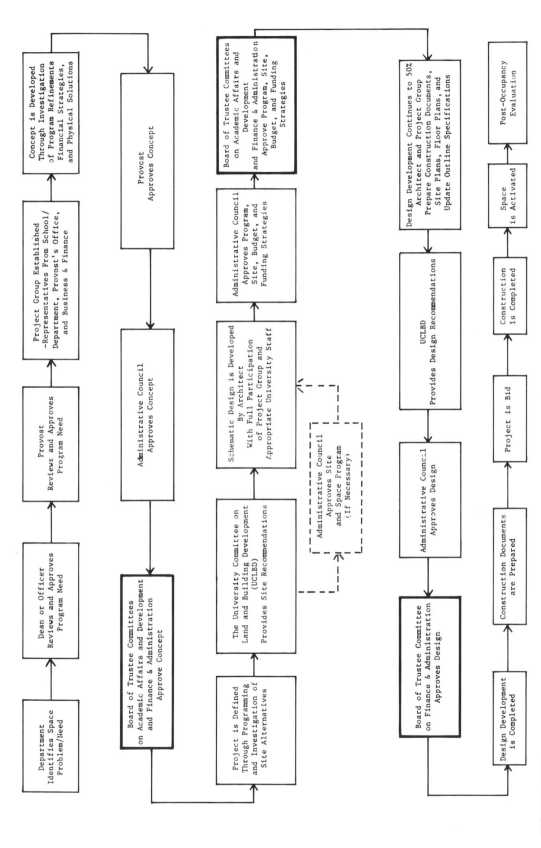

FIGURE 11.2 Stanford University project development and approval process. This chart applies to projects with a total cost exceeding $500,000. University Committee on Land and Building Development, a standing committee appointed by the university president, has faculty, staff, and student representation. It reviews virtually all projects that affect the looks and operation of the general campus; in many respects it functions like an architectural review board.

Facilities Projects Approved As Of FY 1980-81
And In Construction During FY 1981-82
(In $000's)

Project Title	Project Budget	Facilities Reserve	Unrestricted Other	University Designated	Funding Plan Gifts In-Hand	Gifts Pledges	Gifts Projected	Debt	Other
ACADEMIC - EXCLUDING MEDICAL SCHOOL									
1. Building 120 Reconstruction	$11,121	$ 3,321	$	$	$ 2,620	$	$ 680	$ 4,500	$
2. Braun Music Center	$ 7,416	$ 1,716	$	$	$ 742	$ 4,200	$ 758	$	$
3. McCullough Building, Fume Hoods	$ 2,252	$ 2,252	$	$	$	$		$	$
4. Memorial Church New Organ/Structural	$ 1,632	$ 413	$	$	$ 1,219	$		$	$ 288
5. 36 Projects Under $500,000	$ 3,652	$ 1,673	$ 987	$ 234	$ 436	$	$ 34	$	$
	$26,073	$ 9,375	$ 987	$ 234	$ 5,017	$ 4,200	$ 1,472	$ 4,500	$ 288
ACADEMIC - MEDICAL SCHOOL									
6. Cardiovascular Research Building	$14,000	$	$	$	$ 9,000	$ 5,000	$	$	$
7. 16 Projects Under $500,000	$ 2,538	$	$ 2,142	$ 396	$	$	$	$	$
	$16,538	$	$ 2,142	$ 396	$ 9,000	$ 5,000	$	$	$
AUXILIARY - ATHLETICS									
8. 1 Project Under $500,000	$ 35	$	$	$	$ 35		$	$	$
AUXILIARY - FACULTY PRACTICE PROGRAM									
9. 2 Projects Under $500,000	$ 416	$	$ 300	$ 116	$		$	$	$
AUXILIARY - STUDENT RESIDENCES									
10. New Student Housing	$36,223	$	$	$	$	$	$	$36,223	$
11. Storey House Reconstruction	$ 1,852	$	$	$	$	$	$	$ 800	$ 1,052
12. 7 Projects Under $500,000	$ 629	$	$	$ 629	$	$	$	$	$
	$38,704	$	$	$ 629	$	$	$	$37,023	$ 1,052
ENERGY/MAINTENANCE RETROFITS									
13. Housing Energy Conservation	$ 1,251	$	$	$ 60	$	$	$	$ 1,191	$
14. 3 Projects Under $500,000	$ 50	$	$ 50	$	$	$	$	$	$
	$ 1,301	$	$ 50	$ 60	$	$	$	$ 1,191	$
OTHER									
15. 1 Project Under $500,000	$ 300	$	$ 300	$	$		$	$	$
GENERAL PLANT IMPROVEMENT									
16. Chilled Water, Medical Center Loop	$ 1,550	$	$	$	$	$	$	$ 1,550	$
17. 56 Projects Under $500,000	$ 6,569	$	$	$ 2,779	$	$	$	$ 3,790	$
	$ 8,119	$	$	$ 2,779	$	$	$	$ 5,340	$
TOTAL	$91,486	$ 9,375	$ 3,779	$ 4,214	$14,052	$ 9,200	$ 1,472	$48,054	$ 1,340

FIGURE 11.3 A university list of projects. This table is abbreviated to list only individual projects that exceed $500,000. The number of projects in process at the time of this list is 131. (Libraries are included in the first two projects listed.) This quantity is not unusual for a major university.

the wayside." The architectural unity comes from the internal rhythm of materials and arched forms, a sensitive use of site, a consistent feeling of enclosure, and an attempt to leave a lasting visual memory.

Warwick (est. 1965): The site is 420 acres (169.96 ha) in open country over two miles (3.219 km) from Coventry. Over 15,000 students could be accommodated, a maximum of two-thirds to be given lodgings. The plan is compact to achieve economies in roads and services and to preserve open spaces for sports and general amenities beyond buildings aligned on each side of a central spine. The library is at the center, with other general use buildings (assembly hall, chapel, senior common room, shops, arts center, and coffee house) important in establishing the community of the university.

One can find here different planning approaches, in part coping with what has been described as the different student subcultures, such as those fostered on American college campuses: the collegiate (the club or frat type), the academic (the library and lab denizen) the vocational (often the commuter), and the nonconformist (independent and aggressive, perhaps acting out emotional problems or fixated on what is held to be solutions to societal problems).

3. *Utility and other non-academic factors* at times can dominate some of the planning. Rather like the economic influence, it should be subordinate to the academic. However, there are times when some service function in the college or university will have some substantial influence on the exact site.

An example would be utility lines which usually follow trunk routes on campus and streets in a city. A good separation is necessary between incompatible systems. Relocating utilities can be extremely expensive, and closing a street does not solve the below-ground problems. Having the library bridge the utilities may finesse the problem, as was done at Brooklyn College and the University of Pennsylvania.

The University of Michigan Hatcher Library site was rigidly controlled by utility lines underground, pedestrian traffic right through the plot, as well as a political constraint. The librarian, planner, and architect should try either to dodge such factors or to use them to advantage.

On most campuses the surface drainage is a critical issue. Studies of rain and meltwater

will cover flow accumulations of the entire site as well as adjacent sites and capacities of ditches, swales, ponds and storm drains. The historic experience with a particular site may be a warning to stay away or build high, as Hawaiians are well aware.

Parking in an urban center was a key factor in planning the Ruhr University of Bochum, an institution of 25,000 students which opened in 1965. The library and a broad open forum behind it are located above a large parking garage. A few large urban public libraries have below-ground patron parking. When one remembers that nearby parking is impossible at Columbia, Berkeley, and Harvard, such a utilitarian service requirement can at times be a boon, especially for visiting scholars and others making brief use of the library. One wonders about the campus parking solutions of the future—parking structures, underground parking, or remote parkings with shuttle transportation?

An intriguing problem existed at Lyndon State College in Vermont. With buildings sitting on two slight hills beside a meandering stream, the campus was bisected by a county road and overhead power utilities. This division was overcome in the early 1970s when the road was rerouted, utilities were put underground, and a library was built between the hills. The roof of the structure is a pedestrian causeway, capable of supporting a future additional floor of the two-level library. The stream was piped beneath the library, creating three ponds great for winter skating and key elements in the unified campus master plan.

4. *Aesthetic factors* frequently dominate the siting. The prominence of a building like the Baker Library at Dartmouth controls planning within its visual domain. There is no question that the 42-story University of Pittsburgh Cathedral of Learning created an aesthetic impression, as did the new University of Glasgow Library with its intent to dominate the skyline.

The first decade of this century saw the beginning of highly professional city planning, in part for the purpose of enhancing living and working conditions. In 1909 the first British Housing and Town Planning Act was passed and the Chicago Burnham Plan was published. In 1916 New York City passed the first zoning law regulating land use and the height and coverage of buildings. Such laws are now almost universal and, together with the national control of historic buildings and districts, serve to restrain the worst excesses.

These governmental controls exist for good reason, yet resolution of conflicts can take years. The problems faced by Concordia University in Montreal in planning a new library serve as an example. First, zoning bylaws for the library site restricted height to four floors whereas eight were desired. Second, an existing building on the site had a rare glazed terra-cotta facing, which the Save Montreal Architectural Protection Society wished preserved. Third, immediately across the road from the site was a building on the list of historic buildings, and design of buildings within 150 ft (45.720) is subject to provincial approval.

In California, to discourage urban sprawl, local commissions since 1971 have responsibility for shaping orderly environmental development in their sphere of influence, including social and economic interdependence and interaction with the area which surrounds it. Thus even if a private college is in another jurisdiction, such as unincorporated land, its plans for housing, roads, utilities, etc., are subject to review since the environmental evaluation covers substantial air emissions, changes in drainage patterns, increased noise, new light or glare, increased density of humans, additional traffic and traffic hazards, substantial use of energy, need for new utilities, impact on quality of existing recreational opportunities, and any proposal which obstructs a scenic vista. A community can set high aesthetic environmental expectations, and an institution can need support from its neighbors.

Trees may take on significance. Certain mature specimens may be untouchable for a particular shade pattern, a prominant vista with an appealing silhouette, or historic or sentimental meaning. Many a campus has altered a building site to spare such a tree, sometimes at great expense.

5. *Politics* can all too often influence in major degree the siting of a building. Within a city it is natural that real political issues control a site. Urban renewal priorities can reflect political influence or civic conscience. (How many Martin Luther King or John F. Kennedy libraries are there?) The civic political ramifications of choosing a campus site for the Kennedy library— first at Harvard and then at the University of Massachusetts

in Boston—or the state and campus rumpus over the Richard M. Nixon library are only the best-known cases.

On most campuses there is what one distinguished university librarian has accurately called:

an inordinate amount of local political machinations which often have nothing to do with a rational and logical approach to library space planning. I could cite several examples where planning documents have been prepared and never considered or implemented because of political and financial problems peculiar to venerable private institutions.

Our efforts to consolidate the eight departmental science libraries is a good example. That effort was initially thwarted by the contribution of $2,000,000 by a foundation to complete a floor in the Life Sciences building, a floor which the foundation stipulated had to include a Biology library in space far too small by any rational standards. We were able to fit into the space by including in the plans a substantial sum for conversion of backfiles to microfiche. We then lost the proposed space for a consolidated science library to the School of Engineering which won the political battle for space for the new Department of Computing. The third event in this historic struggle is the University's commitment to the Chemistry Department to assist in raising funds for a new Chemistry building on the condition that it contain a joint Chemistry/Physics Library.

Such factors can, regrettably, override the most logical master planning and the best library arguments.

11.4 Library Site Determination

Although the choice of site is irrevocable only when construction begins, the choice should not be changed once design is started since, if it is, added cost will result. The most limited choice is usually for expansion of a branch library within a building, described in Chapter 10. The project with somewhat more options is a building addition, also treated in Chapter 10. The greatest leeway is for a new building, especially on a new or young campus, the focus of this section. One should recognize that site selection gets rapidly more complex when the campus is full of existing buildings. Solutions to the problem may even include acquisition of noncampus property or demolition of outmoded structures as the only options. Although it is an extreme case, consider the site of the New York State Library, which was assigned within the Cultural Education Center building all of floors 6 through 8 and parts of 10, 11, and the basement, which houses a three-tier stack!

Five major factors should be taken into account in evaluating a site for a library. (This section assumes ownership of the land. If this is not the case, cost of acquisition may be a primary factor.) First, is the location suitable and is its size adequate? Second, what is its relation to neighboring buildings and to the whole population distribution and traffic flow of the institution? Third, what orientation is possible for a library building erected on it? Fourth, are there advantages or disadvantages in the slope of the land or other natural features? Finally, what complications will arise from the nature of the ground beneath the building?

It may be, of course, that only one site will be available that is large enough and in an acceptable location. Even so, the other factors should be examined to determine how they will affect the proposed building. How, in other words, can it be designed to make the most of favorable circumstances and to overcome the difficulties presented by this site?

Size. A new building ought, if possible, to provide for present collections, staff, and readers, plus anticipated growth and, preferably, for later additions. There may be cases where for one reason or another it is impossible to build a new library large enough to meet foreseeable needs. In some cases to build for more than five to eight years would be irresponsible. The principle of incremental growth can wisely be applied in particular growth conditions, for instance, auxiliary shelving facilities. The State of California planning authorities, because of the tremendous demands for additional space in the tax-supported institutions of higher learning in that state, have in certain instances ruled that new buildings should be large enough for five years only, after which a second stage of construction should be proposed. The size of an addition to an old building or of the first stage of a new building is determined more by the size of the capital appropriations that the administration is able to obtain from the state's fiscal authorities than by precisely determined prospective needs during a specified number of years ahead. This question of total space needs is dealt with elsewhere, but two points should be emphasized here.

1. The long-term financing strategy needs consideration. If a new library or an addition to an old one is inadequate for space requirements for the next twenty to twenty-five years, obvious disadvantages will result. It may be more difficult to obtain funds for new space if the recent additional space has proved to be inadequate more quickly than many expected. If the present or about-to-be-built structure is named for the donor or in honor of a benefactor of the institution, an early necessity to obtain replacement space might cause great dissatisfaction and make future money raising a problem. The financing of a large addition may be, but is not always, more difficult than of the original structure.

2. The site selected, wherever it is, should be large enough for additions that will extend the useful life of the building until it is outmoded functionally or in other ways. Even when the desirable floor area has been determined for a building and its prospective additions, there is, alas, no definite formula that will translate it into the minimum dimensions for the site. A building on a campus with typically separate buildings does not look good if it fills a plot too full. Spacing of buildings is an aesthetic problem and is affected by what has been done already on a campus or is planned for the future. Another point is that fire equipment vehicles must be able to approach all exposed sides of a building. Proper landscaping can often help to make space go farther than might be expected, and its possible usefulness in this connection should not be neglected.

The size of the plot also depends on the height of the building, which involves functional as well as aesthetic considerations. The number of floors that will be satisfactory from the functional standpoint cannot be determined without taking account of the total floor area, the type of library, its collections, and use. As explained in Section 12.3 under Problems Relating to Height, a library requiring 10,000 sq ft (929 m^2) or less, will usually be more satisfactory functionally if it is all on one floor, and very large buildings may have as much as 50,000 sq ft (4645 m^2) on one floor.

Sometimes a site will prove to be large enough for a building and its additions only if expansion takes the form of additional floors. This solution is expensive and inconvenient, but, even so, it may be preferable to any other alternative. At Louisiana State

University in Baton Rouge and also at the New Orleans campus, the libraries have a central location in the heart of the campus, and fill the available plot almost completely. This situation was realized and accepted when the buildings were planned, and the architects provided for structures to which can be added two more floors when they are needed.

The total height of a building above ground is determined by four factors: the percentage of the building that is below ground level, the number of levels above ground and their floor to ceiling height, the height of the spaces between finished ceilings and finished floors above, and the type of roof used. If a large part of a building can go below the main entrance level, as at the Princeton University Firestone Library and the Green Library East Wing at Stanford (which in some ways resemble icebergs, with the major portion of their floor areas in the basement floors), the total apparent height can be correspondingly reduced. It should be noted that the percentage of space required for stairs and elevators generally, although not necessarily, increases with each level that is added. Also, three levels with 8 ft (2.438) ceiling heights require no more height than two with 12 ft (3.658) ceilings, except for the thickness of one additional floor. In buildings with as many as five floors above ground, the space between the ceiling in one room to the floor level above is an important factor in the total height. If each one, for instance, is 5 ft (1.524) thick instead of 2 ft (0.610), the five would take 5 × 5, or 25 ft (7.620), instead of 5 × 2, or 10 ft (3.048), making a difference of 15 ft (4.572) or almost enough space to provide two additional stack levels. While this section comments on exterior mass and site issues, detailed treatment is under schematic development in Section 12.3.

Central or Eccentric Location? The library has often been called the heart of the university; it is visited frequently by nearly everyone in the institution and, if a good library, will be used at least as much as any other building on the campus. Obviously, its location ought to be convenient. Does this mean near the dormitories, the classroom buildings, the laboratories, the student union, or the athletic field?

No one answer is correct for all institutions. If most students commute to the campus, it may be best to place the main library near the transportation center, enabling the student to return books on the way to classes and borrow others when leaving for home. The location of lockers for commuting students may also be an important consideration.

A location near the classroom center is usually preferable to one near the dormitory center; to lengthen the walk to the library between classes by two minutes is more disadvantageous than to lengthen by five minutes the time required to reach the library in the evenings from dormitories. If there are dormitories on opposite sides of the campus, as was once the case in many coeducational institutions, a location near classroom buildings may be approximately equidistant from the dormitories. If a choice must be made, such as for a college which may have only one library, it is preferable to place the general library near classrooms for the humanities and social sciences rather than near those for the sciences, since the former disciplines usually generate heavier use than do the sciences.

In the larger institutions, the location of a general library in relation to various buildings housing academic disciplines raises questions of intellectual affinities. On a particular campus, for instance, do the departments of classics and art have strong connections, perhaps shared faculty, considerable use of museum objects, and course assignments requiring heavy library use? Are the language departments offering service courses with heavy reliance on a language laboratory? If the answers are affirmative, the affinities argue that the main library be at least as convenient to art and classics as to language departments. The academic patterns on each particular campus must be studied to sort out these intellectual determinants. The same approach can be followed in placing branch libraries. Yet one should recognize that, especially in the laboratory disciplines, faculty will opt for an in-building branch rather than a multi-disciplinary branch over fifty meters from their laboratory and office. Except where tight economy is controlling, this 50-meter rule may be a major determinant on branch library composition and site selection.

Convenience implies a central location, but it is possible for a site to be too central. Some campuses will have a large unoccupied space in the central square, and this might at first glance seem to be an ideal site for a new main library. In fact, however, there are usually serious drawbacks. (See figs. 11.4 and 11.5.)

First, because the space is so centrally located and conspicuous, the donor and, less frequently, the officers of the college and even the architect may be tempted to decide that it is the place for the single most imposing building on the campus. To be sure, it is possible for a good library to be impressive, but it is less likely to be a good functional library if it is planned primarily for grandeur. The successful combination is rare. Moreover, a monumental building usually costs much more than one that is primarily functional. If funds available for library construction are limited, it may be impossible to pay for the space that is needed if this space has to be housed in a building that is to be the showpiece of the campus.

Second, if a library is in the center of the campus, with students approaching it from all directions, there will be inevitable demands for public entrances on all sides. The University of Connecticut 1978 library is a case in point. One objection to multiple entrances is that each entrance, with the lobby attached to it and the corridors leading from it to the circulation desk and other central services, takes valuable space. If, for example, an extra entrance requires a vestibule of only 100 sq ft (9.29 m²), plus a small inside lobby of 500 sq ft (46.45 m²), plus a corridor (otherwise unnecessary) 100 ft (30.480) long and 10 ft (3.048) wide, there is a total of 1,600 sq ft (148.64 m²) that adds nothing to the building's seating or shelf capacity, may interfere seriously with its functional properties, and costs perhaps $150,000. This is some 5 percent of the total in a $3,000,000 building, but it would provide space for shelving 25,000 volumes or, used as endowment, might bring in an income of $15,000 per year for books or services. The extra entrance will involve costs for staff or for electronic exit monitoring. It will be hard to resist the demand for one or more additional entrances and exits if the building is too centrally located; students and professors do not like to walk around a building and then have to return part of the way as soon as they enter.

Third, and the most serious objection of all to a location at the center of the campus, is that it increases the difficulties of making an addition to the building that will be aesthetically and functionally satisfactory. Often, indeed, it makes an appropriate addition al-

most impossible. A centrally placed building tends to be symmetrical, and an addition usually threatens to destroy this symmetry. If it is also monumental, the cost of an addition will be greatly increased. It should be emphasized once more that most library buildings, if they continue to serve the purpose for which they were designed, have to be enlarged sooner or later, and ought to be planned with this in mind, even with underground expansion if in no other fashion.

A final and not unimportant objection to a too central location is that it may occupy space that is very precious particularly in an urban area, and should be used for an attractive lawn and planting. This objection can lead to underground libraries which, if skillfully done, can be very effective and tasteful—witness structures at British Columbia (Sedgwick), Columbia (for the Avery Architectural Library), Harvard (Pusey), Hendrix College, Illinois (Undergraduate), Oregon (Science Library), and Yale (Cross Campus).

What is wanted, then, is a convenient location for the main library, but not one so central that it calls for an unreasonably expensive, monumental, and unfunctional structure. Figures 11.6 and 11.7 illustrate some of the points that have been made.

Orientation. No single orientation is ideal for all seasons, climates, and other conditions. Orientation is nevertheless a factor to be considered, particularly in areas where extremes of heat or cold, strong winds, or intense sunlight may be expected. Near the tropics the sun shines in east and west windows more than in south. As one goes farther north, the southern sun becomes more and more of a problem; the situation is reversed, of course, south of the equator. While architectural design can handle such problems, they can be significantly ameliorated by a site which permits a beneficial orientation of the building. Comments in this section are applicable for the North Temperate Zone, and they must be interpreted in other geographical locations.

The extent to which the sun penetrates into rooms at the hottest time of day is a matter of some importance in most areas. The problem is minimized if it is usually cloudy. In a country where central heating is not customary, the winter sun may be a useful source of heat. More commonly, however, when direct sunlight streams into a building it creates glare

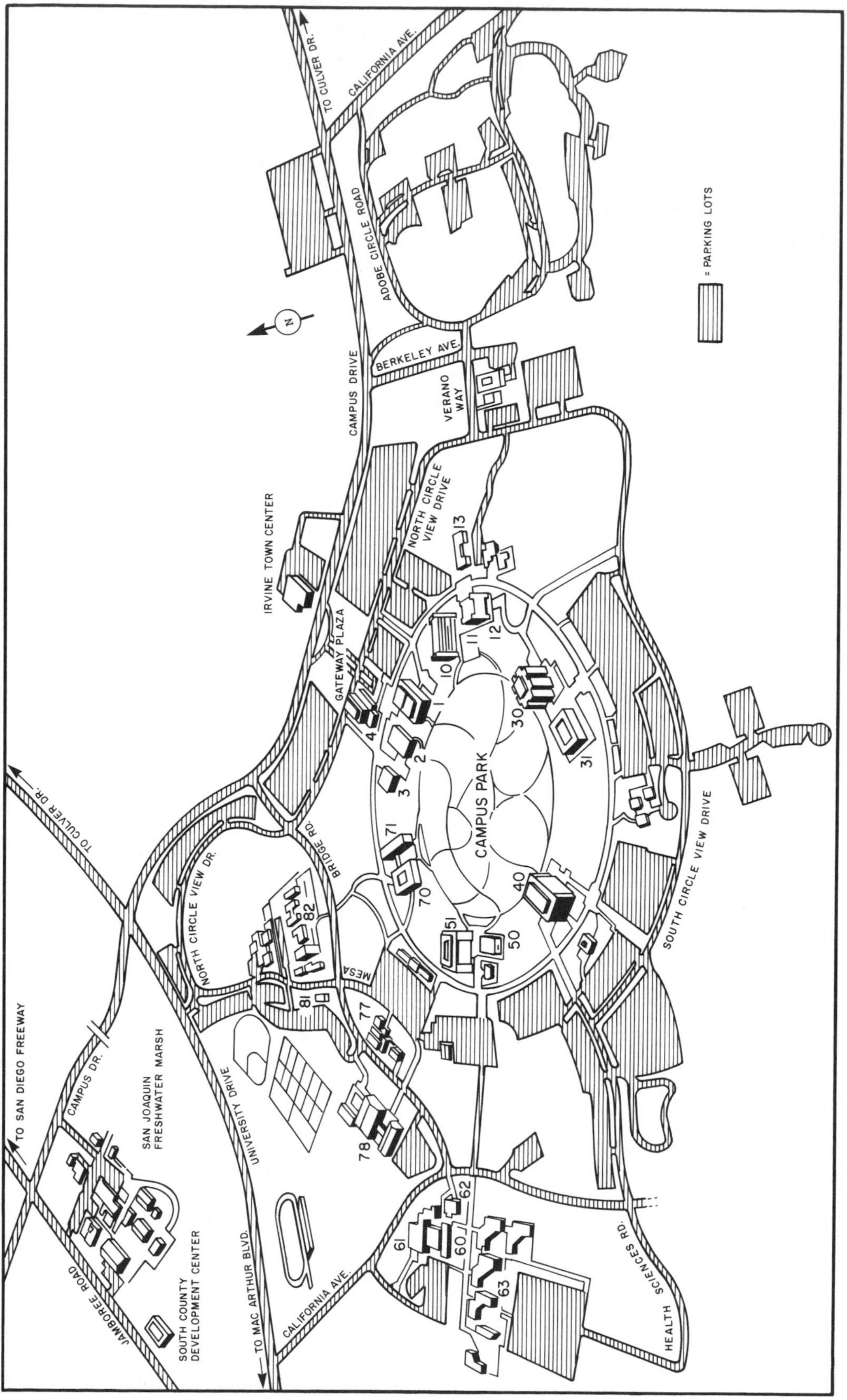

FIGURE 11.4 University of California, Irvine. Selected identification includes: (1) main library; (2–3) student services; (4) administration; (10–13) social sciences; (30) engineering; (31) computer sciences; (40) physical sciences with a branch library; (50–51) biological sciences and branch library; (60–63) medical sciences with branch library; (70–71) humanities; (77) central plant; (78) physical education; and (80–81) fine arts. Note that the library is juxtaposed between a major parking area and the academic campus.

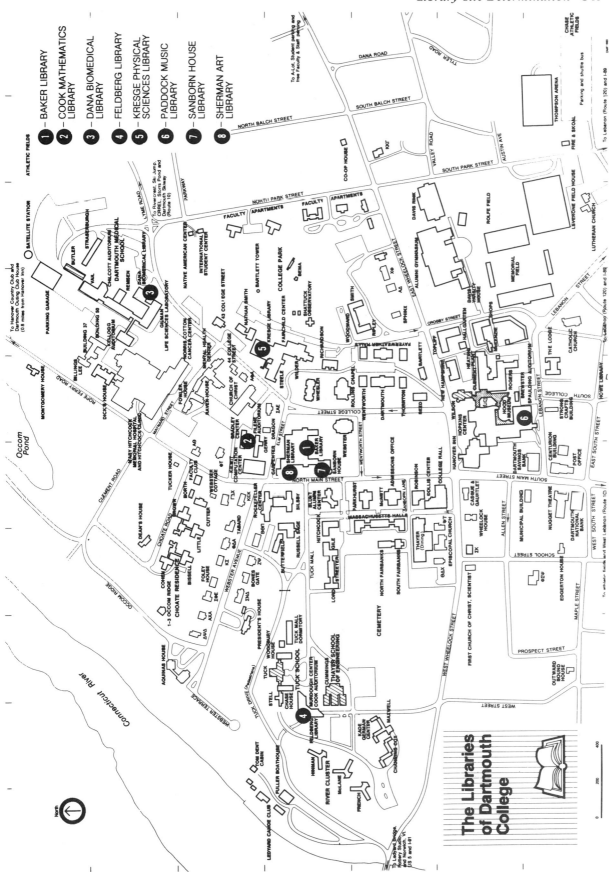

FIGURE 11.5 Dartmouth College. In many respects the main library (Baker) is at the heart of the campus.

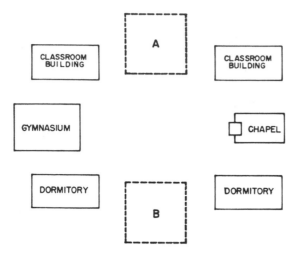

FIGURE 11.6 Library site selection. (A) Suitable site for library because of nearness to classroom buildings, but limited in expansion possibilities. (B) Possible site for library, but one closer to classroom buildings is preferable, other things being equal.

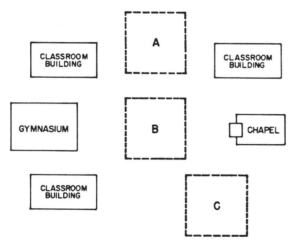

FIGURE 11.7 Library site selection. (A) Site too small and limited possibilities for an addition. (B) Site difficult if not impossible to expand and would encourage demand for entrances on all sides, which would reduce assignable areas on the critical entrance level. A shipping entrance would present problems. Its central location would increase the temptation to erect a monumental structure. (C) Apparently the most desirable location for the library since expansion possibilities are substantial and problems presented by B are lacking.

and overheating and is bad for the books; the need for air conditioning will add to costs. An architect should be able to provide drawings showing the penetration of the sun into a room at any latitude during any month of the year for any proposed orientation of a building.

The amount of direct sunlight, as well as heat and cold, that enters a room depends also on the height of windows, the percentage of wall space that they occupy, and the depth of the room from windows to inner walls. Double windows and certain special kinds of glass may do much to counteract unfavorable conditions, but they are expensive and, if broken, are sometimes difficult to replace. Prevailing winds and extremes of heat and cold should also be taken into account.

In most parts of the United States the western sun is the most difficult to control. The eastern sun generally presents much less of a problem because it is rarely as hot, and the sun is ordinarily higher above the horizon and penetrates a room a shorter distance by the time the library is open in the morning or is heavily used. The southern sun becomes more of a problem as distance north from the equator increases. Sunlight rarely causes trouble in northern windows in this hemisphere, as it occurs only in early mornings and late afternoons in midsummer. The sunshine and its glare can be kept out during these periods by relatively inexpensive landscaping because the sun is low in the sky.

Outside screens of concrete, tile, brick, wood, or metal have been developed to reduce the problems resulting from excess sunlight. Solar energy collectors can be designed to serve in the same fashion. These screens may be placed a few feet beyond the outside wall and protect windows from direct sunlight except, possibly, for a few minutes at the end of the day on a western exposure. Examples of such screens can be found in the undergraduate library of the University of South Carolina, the University of Southern Florida in Tampa, and the Oregon State University. In place of screens, awnings or wide shelves projecting horizontally from the building above windows, or metal vertical venetian blinds outside the building can be used. Inside the windows venetian blinds (vertical or horizontal), curtains, or drapes will help. The inside and outside installations sometimes tend to interfere with the circulation of air in an unexpected fashion if there is no air conditioning. Each is an expense, often a good deal to construct or install and replace when required. An engineer should be asked to supply estimates for the specific locality.

Considering the negative aspects of the sun, it follows that a rectangular building with long north and south sides and short east and west sides is to be preferred if practicable in other respects. A building placed at a 45-degree angle to the major coordinates may be found to suffer even more. However, with an increased interest in energy conservation and the general desire to utilize the energy of the sun for heating loads, it may be found that orientation earlier thought to be a problem is now an asset. Numerous technologies may be employed to capture the sun's heat, and not all of them are contingent upon the orientation of the building. The building orientation only becomes critical where solar collectors are made part of the exterior wall, in which case the collector wall must obviously face the most intense sun, especially in the winter when the heating demand will be at its peak.

If the north side of a building is the best area for reading, it will be preferable, other things being equal, to have the main entrance on the south, leaving the entire north side free for reading space. Furthermore, if the stronger winds and storms usually come from the north and west, an entrance on the south or east is preferable and may require a smaller entrance vestibule than would otherwise be needed.

It should be kept in mind that direct sunlight with its ultraviolet rays, and indeed even indirect light, is harmful to book bindings and paper. Book ranges should not extend to a wall where the sun can come through windows between them; if ranges extend to any wall, they should do so only on the north. As far as possible the ranges should be at right angles to walls that have windows; if they parallel such walls, the full force of the sun will strike the volumes in the first range.

The ideal orientation may be impracticable in many cases because of other considerations. A convenient location may be more important than an ideal orientation; but orientation is a factor to be considered, and its effects on building costs and energy consumption should not be overlooked. If other factors dictate a particularly undesirable orientation, special attention should be given to avoiding the complications that would arise from large areas of unprotected glass and to the corrective measures that should be taken.

The Slope of the Land. If a campus is not flat, the extent to which the ground slopes and the direction of the incline may warrant consideration. In the following comments it must be remembered that the overriding consideration should be ease of access for readers, staff, those who are physically limited, and service vehicles. However, other concerns being equal, the use of the land slope may help solve a number of other problems.

A flat site for the library is not always ideal; it has distinct disadvantages. If the main entrance is to be at ground level or only one step up, it will probably be difficult, but not impossible, to have windows in the basement. This point may not be of too great importance, but even with the best of air conditioning and lighting, some persons are inclined to think that reading and staff accommodations without any outside light are substandard. This is particularly likely to be true if the rooms also have low ceilings, as they often do in basements. A basement is not essential, and may be impractical because of ground and soil conditions; but a basement can usually provide a large amount of useful library space comparatively inexpensively. With central heating and air-conditioning plants for whole campuses, basement space may not be needed for mechanical rooms, and as much floor area may be assigned to readers, staff, or books in the basement as on any other floor—more, usually, than on the main floor, where a large entrance lobby is almost always required. If the basement has windows, this space may be highly attractive, and it has the great advantage of being only a short flight of steps from the entrance level. It may also make possible an additional separate entrance and, if so, can house facilities that are open at times when the rest of the building is closed.

It should be noted that a short flight of steps leading to the entrance on the main floor may make it possible to have a basement with windows all around; however, a building without such steps, entered directly from the grade level, has a much more inviting entrance and facilitates access by physically limited persons. Areaway windows can sometimes provide nearly as much light as those completely above ground, but they entail problems of landscaping and drainage. If the first floor is approximately 30 in. (762 mm) above ground level on a flat site, a loading platform at the rear is automatically available. Although not essential, it is a convenience when sending or receiving crates, furniture, large mail sacks, binding shipments, large supply orders, or other material on pallets.

One further observation on flat sites may be made. If soil conditions permit, modern earth-moving machinery can change ground levels a few feet at small expense, and with adequate landscaping the results may be excellent. It may thus be possible to have a front entrance at ground level and with a loading platform at the rear.

A considerable slope may be a distinct advantage or disadvantage, depending on its relationship to the main entrance. At a given site there is usually one side where the main entrance ought obviously to be, a point at which traffic to the library naturally converges. If there is a fairly steep downward slope from this entrance to the rear of the building, as at the University of California, San Diego, it should be possible to have windows in the basement, possibly on as many as three sides and even part or all of the fourth. Indeed, if the slope is sharp enough, there may also be windows in a subbasement or, as it is sometimes called, the minus-2 level. At Princeton and the University of Cincinnati libraries, even the minus-3 levels have windows on one or more sides. A slope of this kind offers the further possible advantage of reducing the height of the building above the entrance level on the most prominent facade. One may enter a building with three to five floors at or near the middle of its levels; this may make it possible to dispense with a public elevator if there is a service elevator for the transfer of books and for persons who cannot climb stairs.

In order to get a minus-1 level with windows, some libraries have an entrance set back from the top of a hill and approached by a bridge, as at the Carleton College Library in Northfield, Minnesota, Douglass College in New Brunswick, New Jersey, and Trinity University in San Antonio. Construction of a short ramp up to the front entrance can serve the same purpose. At the Grinnell College Library there is a ramp and then a bridge to the entrance; the result is that, though the campus is relatively flat, windows can be provided wherever wanted in the basement.

On the other hand, if there is a sharp upward slope toward the rear of a building, the back of the first floor may have to be sunk into the ground; windows may not be possible on one or more of its sides and there will be none at all in the basement. This may be a disadvantage if natural lighting is desired and may also involve difficult drainage problems.

If the ground falls off to one side of an entrance and rises on the other side, the slope may facilitate basement fenestration on one side but make it impossible to provide windows on the other side of the main floor. It may complicate the landscaping and make architectural planning of the building more difficult. There are successes such as the UCLA Research Library, Emory University, and the Moffitt Library at U.C. Berkeley. It is necessary, however, to consider whether it could seriously complicate plans for a subsequent addition.

In general, then, a site is to be avoided if the ground slopes upward from the entrance or if it slopes from one side of the entrance to the other. A flat site is to be preferred to one that slopes objectionably; but it is better yet if the ground slopes from the entrance downward toward the back of the building. No one of these factors is of overriding importance. Nevertheless, they may prove to be the deciding considerations in site selection.

Soil and Ground Conditions. A site for a library should never be selected without some knowledge of ground conditions. When information on this subject is not available, at least one or two and in some cases a considerably larger number of test borings should be made. The tests may cost hundreds of dollars for each hole, but they will be well worth the total of several thousand dollars if they prevent great unanticipated expenses for excavation and foundations—misfortunes that have been much too common in library building. The cost for a boring report will vary dramatically depending upon the depth and difficulty of the soil. Local advice is the best source of information. One university library had spent more than $60,000 on its plans before it was determined that foundations alone would cost approximately $500,000 extra because of ground conditions.

Since this volume is not an engineering treatise, it should suffice to give a brief summary of the points that ought to be considered.

If the foundation runs into ledge or boulders over ½ cubic yard (0.3823 m³) in size, there may be substantial additional costs for removing this material. The extra costs which would result from placing a building in this type of soil should be carefully estimated by a qualified professional estimator or a contractor familiar with this kind of work. On the other hand, it should be kept in mind that solid rock makes a fine foundation for a library; books are heavy, and stack areas in particular need a firm foundation. In an excavation for one library, shale was reached before the foundation was excavated to the proper depth, but practically all of it was friable enough to be handled by a power shovel, and as it was removed, an excellent foundation of harder rock was exposed for the footings.

If loose, fine sand, soft clay, silt, or peaty materials are encountered, piles or caissons may have to be driven down great distances in order to provide an adequate foundation. Along the Charles River in Cambridge and in the Back Bay section of Boston, Massachusetts (areas that once were tidal swamps) it may be necessary to go 200 ft (60.960) or more below the surface to reach a solid bottom, and the cost of driving piles or sinking caissons to this depth is great. Under certain conditions it is possible to pour a concrete mat on which the building will "float." The Charles Hayden Library of the Massachusetts Institute of Technology is built in this way. But adoption of this method dictated the construction of the building around a large court in order to spread the weight, and this resulted in a disadvantageous traffic pattern. The Yale University Library is built over quicksand on which a concrete slab was poured; however, conditions were such that it was possible to build a tower stack, despite the great weight of such a structure.

There are problems in connection with floating a building on a concrete slab or mat. It may sink quite a number of inches. This may not be too serious in itself, though if the sinking is greater on one side than another, it may be a serious matter! Also, if an addition is to be constructed later, the problem may occur again.

In many sections of the country there are numerous springs, subsurface groundwater flow, or other water conditions to complicate the construction of foundations. It is possible to excavate for a foundation, keep the water pumped out, and waterproof the building either outside or in; but these undertakings are expensive, and unless the construction is of highest quality, difficulties will arise sooner or later. During flash floods the water table around the Widener Library at Harvard occasionally rises above the subbasement floor; twice during nearly fifty years, water has come up through the concrete slab in small sections of the floor.

The Louisiana State University Library in Baton Rouge is built on Mississippi River delta land that can carry only a limited weight per unit area of surface. It was necessary to reduce the pressure on the bearing strata by removing the overburden. This made it necessary to include a basement in the building, and consequently a drainage problem was involved. The basement and the drainage difficulties could have been avoided if the site had not been so small that it was necessary to plan for what will ultimately become a five-level building.

A summary of ground and soil concerns includes bearing capacity of the soil, site drainage, frost and water table levels, and seismic activities potential. Poor conditions can always be overcome, but doing so can have very significant cost implications.

A specific example illustrating some of the considerations involved in the selection of a site may be provided by the Lamont Library at Harvard. This site was selected from four possibilities after some weeks of discussion and the preparation of rough sketches of a suitable building in each location. Its position in the southeast corner of the Harvard Yard was chosen because:

1. It was the only remaining available site in the Yard large enough for a building of the desired size. Its location in the Yard close to the two other central library buildings, Widener and Houghton, to which it could be connected by tunnel, was an important factor.

2. It was so placed that the freshmen passed its front entrance six times a day going to and from their meals in the Freshmen Union. It was near a main walk between the houses where the upperclassmen lived and the classrooms, and closer to the latter.

3. It had a long east-west axis, giving the desirable long north and south exposures for the reading areas.

4. The ground slope was such that two levels with windows below the main entrance, which was only one short step up, were possible, with two more without windows below them. It was possible to have above the entrance level a mezzanine, a full second floor, and a penthouse with a good deal of useful

space in it, and still have the latter closer to the ground than the main reading room in Widener.

5. Policy decisions by the university administration, limiting the number of undergraduate students, and by the library authorities, limiting the size of the undergraduate book collection, indicated that provision did not have to be made for a future extension.

One other chance condition may provide a concern about the site and especially about the time required for excavation. Colleges and universities may occupy sites with important archeological artifacts or fossils which can come to light during excavation, if they were not in fact previously known. As an example of the planning consequences, the following is from the Facilities Planning Manual of Stanford University.

Stanford lands contain archeological sites which are known to have yielded evidence of historic or prehistoric human occupation. These sites should be avoided in planning and construction activities. If they can *not* be avoided, they must be monitored scrupulously, with sufficient archeological surveying to ensure the protection of artifacts suspected or found.

Current practice is for the Project Manager to determine from appropriate University sources whether the proposed site of a new facility or project of any kind involves *any* work which may be significant from an archeological viewpoint. If so, an archeological consultant will be engaged to study the site, and perhaps to monitor the excavation. Should any artifacts be found on site, the Office of Design and Construction is obligated to halt construction until their presence can be verified and the items removed. If construction on or near any known archeological site is anticipated, California environmental regulations may require full-time monitoring during excavation or re-siting of the facility or bar the work completely. Interruptions to contractor's construction resulting in monetary loss will be handled by an appropriate change order.

To recapitulate, the site should be large enough to provide for the building and for projected additions, and it should be in as convenient a location as possible. This does not mean that it ought to be in the exact center of the campus; but a general library ought to be readily accessible from classroom buildings, particularly those for the humanities and social sciences. The orientation, ideally, should be on a long axis running directly east and west, with the entrance on the south.

A site that slopes downward from the entrance to the rear may be advantageous. Costs of construction may be greatly increased if ground conditions are unsatisfactory. Parking and delivery problems should not be forgotten. Since a site will rarely be found that is ideal in every respect, careful assessment of the advantages and disadvantages of each possible site is called for before a decision is made.

11.5 The Review Process and Refinement

As can be surmised from some of the above, the process of site selection is one of the most significant decisions in the planning of a building. It is a principal influence on success or weakness of the library building. Even when the architect and librarian may be left alone to decide on the interior arrangement, many individuals are involved in exterior appearance and in site selection. Boards of trustees should always be involved, as should the president and the chief librarian.

This stage of a building project may also have the greatest duration, except for funding, and can have a changing cast of participants if it extends over ten years, which is sometimes the case. The master campus plan may have designated precincts or zones for sciences, for humanities, for open space, etc. Thus the library site (or sites) on older campuses has been a matter for preliminary discussion or tentative decision long before the institution is ready to make a final precise determination for a library building or building addition. Over the years various deans or officers may have eyed desirable plots, the sizable piece of land adjacent to the existing library or a poor building nicely located which has been discussed for possible razing. The librarian or other officers must guard against inappropriate assignments of land. The librarian may need to muster all the supportive help possible—individuals, committees, officials, and even trustees—to protect what in the long run may be the best library site. This may often occur even when a new facility is not an immediate prospect but is anticipated years in the future.

As the final site selection process takes its course, it may require quick actions. As implied above, a tree or utility or a dean's academic goal may suddenly alter or reduce the site. The librarian may never hear some of the arguments—maybe a trustee's private talk with the president argued some change—and in the last days before the trustees are to make a final determination, the unseen maneuver may surface. The University of Alberta is a case in point where the site for the library addition was usurped for another purpose. Most campus decisions about site involve compromises. The skills of the librarian, help by the faculty library committee, and counsel by a consultant should assure a wise outcome.

Beyond that, once the building program records the selected site, the architect has the final say. The architect may have good reason to suggest some change or minor shift. The whole nature of the building, its height, exterior configuration, orientation—the refinement goes on as a steady process which is part of the architect's discipline. Once schematic plans are produced, debated, and accepted, the refinement of site has ceased. The structure begins to assume its final design form.

12

Schematic Considerations

By the time the first phase of the design process is reached, a great deal of work will have been completed by the institution in terms of the academic and facilities program, selection of the architect, funding strategy, and often the site selection. This chapter will address those concerns that typically are part of the schematic phase.

It should be realized that there can be considerable overlap of the various phases; much of the information discussed in the chapters on programming, budgeting and expense control, additions and renovations, and siting and master planning (Chapters 5 through 11) may in many projects be developed as part of the schematic phase. By the same token, concerns that are discussed in later chapters, particularly in regard to the details of mechanical systems, room numbering, furniture selection, color selection, and the like may

well receive careful consideration in the schematic phase, although final decisions and detailed specifications for these elements generally are not developed until later in the design process. It is suggested that the uninitiated reader who is responsible for some aspect of the schematic phase should have a firm understanding of the programming considerations as well as the later phases of the design effort.

In this and other chapters, the word *room* is used when *area* can often be substituted. It was formerly routine to have rooms with doors, for acoustic, heating, and security reasons. Heating and ventilation practices have changed, and most security is now commonly at the building exits. Thus more open spaces are favored. "Rooms" appear more often as "areas" with greater or lesser demarcation by use of shelving, carpet color, furniture, or subtle architectural treatment. The concept of rooms as areas should therefore be kept in mind.

12.1 The Scope of the Schematic Design Phase

The schematic design phase is the portion of the design process that translates the written facilities program into a graphic representation of an architectural concept. It provides a tentative, feasible design solution involving site usage and building spaces, rooms, and relationships, both horizontal and vertical, to meet the program. It leaves for the design development phase the changes, alterations, refinements, and details to reach a final plan.

The schematic phase should be a period of intense communication between the architect and the other members of the design team. Written information will include the facilities program, soils test reports, a site survey (including utility locations, adjacent buildings, and other significant features), and in many cases a copy of the institutional facility standards. Supplementary information may include existing building plans, existing furniture and equipment inventories (although this often comes later), an academic program statement, library statistical reports, an organization chart and staff list, and perhaps a booklet describing the history and nature of the institution. Most if not all of this documentation should be given to the architect at or before the first meeting.

Following the initial transmittal of what may be a considerable volume of written material, there generally is a "getting-to-know-you" period during which site visits to other similar libraries, with the project architect responsible for design and the chief librarian as essential participants. The establishment of a solid rapport during this early period of the design effort is essential. A mutual vocabulary will develop so that both the librarian and architect will understand what is meant when words such as *circulation, section, range, scale, mass, space,* and *volume* are used. Each profession is likely to have a completely different understanding of what these and other concepts are, thus clear communication must be established at the start.

Site visits that involve overnight travel should not be discouraged. The discussion that often develops in the less formal atmosphere during the evening can be exceedingly useful. Such topics as the philosophy of architecture and librarianship, the discussion of architectural or library arrangements that were observed during the day, or even a discussion of other projects in which the participants are currently involved can lead to a fuller understanding of the desires for and scope of the project at hand. The importance of these early meetings cannot be overstated. They establish the communication linkage that will be necessary during the balance of the project to ensure that the end product fully meets the goals of the library and the institution.

The first design efforts of the architect will generally involve working with the facilities program to develop space or function relationships. This study of relationships will be directly related to the site requirements as well as to any larger master planning effort that may be required as part of the project. Early studies will be fairly crude with rough floor areas blocked out for each major function so that the form and mass of the proposed building can be studied. Meetings during this phase of the design may include the chief academic officer or provost, a member of the development office (fundraising), the university architect, the project manager, and one or more members of the library administration. The issues of siting, height, number of floors, and the general outline of the building will be fairly well established during this period, although they may be adjusted later as more details are added.

The question of aesthetics will be apparent nearly from the start, and there is always a give and take between the client and the architect. It is often said that the design of a building, good or bad, is 50 percent the client's and 50 percent the architect's. It is often difficult to draw the line in making decisions that affect the aesthetics, but it is suggested that issues in this area should generally be left to the design professionals and a representative of the institution, provided that the anticipated funding level and the academic or operational program are not adversely affected. Few librarians, if any, are qualified to decide on aesthetic issues. Unfortunately, it is often the experience that others, directly or indirectly involved in planning, who are no better equipped in this respect than the librarians have decided opinions on these matters and do not hesitate to express them. The struggle to deal with these opinions too often results in more confusion, complaints, and emotional unhappiness than almost any other phase of planning library buildings.

A statement by Nikolaus Pevsner, the British author and critic, is pertinent: "Architectural quality is of course aesthetic quality but it is not aesthetic quality alone. The work of architecture is the product of function and art. If it fails in either, it fails in quality."[1] At the convention of the American Institute of Architects in May 1963, Pevsner said that the great ages of architecture have depended "as much on knowledgeable clients as on the flowering of architectural genius," and added that today "clients tend to be too timid." They "take the architect's vision with rather less checking of the fulfillment of the brief than they ought to do."

On the other hand, Donald Canty, editor of the *AIA Journal*, wrote:

For every architect who follows his "vision" to the disadvantage of the building's function, there are others who are pushed by the client into doing things which they know are mistakes.

The client must strike a rather delicate balance. On the one hand, he cannot let himself be "controlled" on this point where the building becomes no longer his, but solely the architect's. On the other hand, presuming that he has chosen an architect of some talent, he should not hamstring that talent to the point where he is no longer getting his money's worth in terms of design quality. . . .

Most architects stand . . . somewhere in the midst of a diamond. The four corners of the diamond are esthetics (what the building should look and feel like), technology (how it can be built and its interior environment controlled), economics (the limitations of the budget), and function (what the building is to do). Each corner exerts a magnetic force on the architect, and his outlook largely depends on the degree of his response to the tugs of one over the others.

There is nothing in the rules to say that the client can't do a little tugging too, providing he knows what he is about.[2]

The role of various members of the design team is further discussed in Chapter 4.

12.2 In Response to the Site

It is argued, and properly so, that if the building planning can start from the inside,

the result should be a better building functionally. It can be a serious mistake for the architect to plan the building with the facade uppermost in the design priorities before knowing something about the functional requirements. Nevertheless, unless the library is intended to form the basis for a new campus situated on a flat site with little or no environmental influence, there will be factors from outside the building envelope that should affect the interior arrangements. These site factors should be identified and utilized in the development of the functional facility. It should be noted, however, that it is not suggested that a perfect building envelope should be designed, and then the functional aspects squeezed in. Rather it should be a balanced process with cogent recognitions of both the functional internal factors and the external influences as the design process proceeds. Compromises may have to be made between dealing with external and internal factors, but they should be reached only after the persons directly involved have given full consideration to the consequences.

The orientation of the building will nearly always be determined by the site, including existing nearby buildings, rather than internal requirements. For example, vehicle access will likely be limited to only one or a few points on the parameter of the building. Seldom is vehicle access appropriate to more than one side of the building. If the building is a major addition, will an existing delivery point suffice, or will a new one be constructed to serve both the old building and the new addition? From what distances and approaches should the entrance be seen? Major foot-traffic routes may well suggest the best location for an entrance, but care must always be taken to avoid the temptation for multiple entrances unless they can be arranged to feed into one control point. Through traffic for a building located in the middle of a major pedestrian route can be a problem too, particularly in climates where considerable energy is required to maintain the environment.

The location of other related facilities may be important in determining the entrance location. Is there another library next door? Are there negative influences such as a busy street, a railroad track, or a prevailing wind that could influence the entry location? Is there a bus route or subway system that will serve the library? Are bikes a problem, and will there need to be some allocation of the

---

[1] Nikolaus Pevsner, "News: Quote . . . Unquote," *Architectural Forum* 120:13 (Jan. 1964).

[2] Donald Canty, "What It Takes to Be a Client: 3. How to Turn a Problem into a Set of Plans," *Architectural Forum* 119:94–95 (Dec. 1963).

site for bike parking? Will there be provision for returning books from an automobile? These factors and others must be considered in simply dealing with the entrance location.

The location of major utilities often will influence the shape of a building. This can present a very serious limitation, as was indicated in the previous chapter. Few would welcome the expense of relocation of utility corridors, although this has been done. The machine room, transformer vault, phone room, and other supporting services may well be located near the utility services.

The topography and soils condition of the site can influence the building configuration in a number of ways. There may be practical height limitations or basement depth limitations due to local soils and the water table. The height of the building and its mass may also be influenced by nearby buildings or even local codes and ordinances. Natural features such as a flood plain, a rock outcropping, forest, or views may influence the shape of the building. Colors, scale, and materials often are suggested by the local architectural fabric.

These factors and others are discussed in detail in Chapter 11. It should be clear, however, that the arrangement of internal functions must reflect such essential elements as where traffic will be, how books are returned, how the building will relate to other buildings, where library materials are delivered, and the like. This arrangement can be achieved in the early design phases as the design team reviews and critiques various options and possibilities presented by the architect. Of course, the architect should be well aware of the assets and limitations of the site before any design effort is started.

Soil Mechanics and Foundation Problems. A firm foundation is essential for any building. Because of the weight of books, if nothing else, libraries place a heavier load on their foundations than many other structures. These loads must be carried with a reasonable margin of safety. To oversimplify, the static, or "dead," load is the weight of the structure itself and fixed elements; "live" load is the weight added to the structure by its contents. In libraries the latter consist primarily of the furniture and equipment, the book collections, and persons using them. There is no need here to discuss what are known as repeated loads, impact loads, and

a number of other kinds, including those that come from wind, earthquakes, and weight of snow on the roof. These are of importance to the architect and engineer and must be provided for in the structure, but are outside the field of this volume.

Except for bookstacks, map cases, and a few other pieces of heavy equipment, it is fair to say that, in general, 60 pounds per sq ft (2.929 kN/m²) for reading areas is considered sufficient as far as live load is concerned. But l00 pounds (4.882 kN/m²) should ordinarily be provided for corridors, l50 (7.324 kN/m²) is standard for stack rooms, and up to 175 (8.544 kN/m²) may be required for rather dense book-storage areas and map cases. As much as 200 pounds (9.765 kN/m²) may be required for garages with heavy trucks, and 250 pounds per sq ft (12.206 kN/m²) for vaults. And 300 pounds per sq ft (14.647 kN/m²) is recommended for areas where compact movable shelving is anticipated, although some may argue that this is excessive. The floor loading at the University of Edinburgh was designed for 11.200 kN/m² (230 lb/ft²), which should be adequate for many compact shelving systems provided they do not house phonograph records or other exceedingly heavy collections.

Today it has become customary, and on the whole wisely so, to construct all library floors strong enough to carry a live load of up to 150 pounds per sq ft (7.324 kN/m²). Such strength will make it safe to install bookstacks anywhere, to change internal arrangements freely, and to place practically any equipment wherever it is wanted. For instance, in many older libraries, which were not so constructed, it has often been found unsafe to place bookstacks in reading areas. This limitation has complicated matters when additions were being planned or changes were made in space assignments.

In some cases it may be argued that the added cost for a structure sufficient to house compact shelving adds about 10 percent to the construction cost while doubling the potential storage capacity. On this basis it may make sense to require that extensive portions of the building be of sufficient capacity to house movable compact shelving.

Buildings are supported by columns or bearing walls or a combination of the two. Bearing outside walls do not present a problem, except that they may be very much in the way if an addition is made to an old building, because they may restrict connections between the old and new anywhere except where there has been a door, window, or other opening. This should be kept in mind if an addition is anticipated later in a building now being planned, or if plans are now being made for an addition to an old building. Internal bearing walls present more of a problem, as they complicate any alteration of shifts within a structure. If a flexible building is desired, they should be avoided, except perhaps around fixed features, such as stairwells, elevators, and toilet rooms. Of course, they often are a fact of life where the structure must be designed to resist earthquakes, but with careful planning they can be designed with minimum negative effect. Remember that interior bearing walls are not the same as nonbearing wet walls. The latter are inflexible only in that they are difficult and messy to remove, but removal of a bearing wall requires a structural change in what might be called the building's skeleton.

Adequate footings under both columns and bearing walls must be provided so that no part of the building will sink. Chapter 11, on site selection, discusses this problem. Sometimes deep piles are required and may prove to be very expensive. If the piles are of wood, they must not be allowed to dry out, or they will rapidly deteriorate. Sometimes it is desirable to sink caissons because of soft soil conditions. Sometimes the whole building must be supported by or floated on a concrete slab, to spread the weight and avoid the possible shifting of the soil beneath if there is quicksand or slippery clay. Sometimes soil must be removed to a considerable depth to lessen the ground load before the new building is constructed. Sometimes the problem is expensive excavation of solid rock by blasting, which can be difficult and annoying, if not dangerous.

Always be sure that soil conditions are known before a site is irrevocably selected. If a later addition is anticipated, remember that it should be arranged without interfering with the footings in the original structure. This can sometimes be managed through cantilevering out beyond supporting columns or load-bearing walls in the new part of the structure. If the addition or the old structure is floated on a concrete slab, very careful calculation will be necessary to avoid having the addition sink too far or not far enough, and so leave a step up or down between the two. Do not forget the danger that a floating

building or one with unstable foundations may tip slightly to one side or the other, as happened to the Leaning Tower of Pisa.

Steel or Masonry Framing. Except in a few quite small libraries, construction above the foundations, whether supported by columns or bearing walls, is ordinarily of masonry, concrete, or steel. In some locations local sand for use in concrete may be unsuitable and present a problem, as in certain parts of upstate New York. Careful estimates of the comparative costs of concrete and steel should be made. The latter may amount to considerably more than the former, but if it makes possible smaller columns, particularly in the bookstack, the saving in space may make up for the additional cost.

It is important for the architect to keep up to date with innovations in construction which are developing rapidly throughout the world. A new type of steel beam may be introduced which is claimed to be cheaper and stronger than beams used in the past. Can it be used to advantage in your building? Will prestressed or precast concrete make possible the effects desired and still save funds for other purposes? Will lift-slab construction be useful or are there advantages from the long spans that can be provided by prestressed beams? Some of these techniques may be functional but not particularly satisfactory aesthetically.

It is not easy, perhaps not possible, for anyone but an expert in the particular branch of the construction field to decide on the suitability of new methods or units for incorporation in a building. A great danger in the use of new materials and methods is their lack of time testing. This can sometimes be provided only by experiments which require considerable technical equipment and involve considerable expense. Unfortunately, changes in the quality of products, both new and old, occur frequently with what may be unfortunate results. Examples of this kind will be found in the discussion on flooring later in this section. Sometimes new materials and new methods are difficult to make use of because of labor restrictions of one kind or another.

Roofs. Roofs may be flat or they may be sloped, or pitched, as the inclination is sometimes called. A sloped roof has the advantage of letting water run off and consequently is easier to keep waterproofed. Heavy snow will tend to slide off, but the live load from wind will be increased. It may also provide inexpensive mechanical space in the attic, if that is desired. But the greater its slope, the larger its area and cost.

A flat roof is always difficult to make watertight. It must be custom-built and seamless. Roof drainage systems are important, especially with flat roofs. Some codes require the provision of a back-up or overflow drain, which may be overlooked. The overflow drain that was designed for the Cecil H. Green Library at Stanford emerges below the roof from a soffit. When activated, it drains over a window area leaving water marks which are only removed during the rare window washings. This detail could have been picked up during the working drawing phase, but it was overlooked.

A flat roof will be walked upon at one time or another, and if access to mechanical equipment is through the roof, walking on it will be frequent. This may suggest special treatment for the access route which will increase the life expectancy of the roof. If it is necessary to use the roof to service equipment, guard rails may also be required by code.

12.3 Early Structural Concepts

The most important structural concept that must be settled early in the design process is the module. Under the modular system, as the term is used here, a building is supported by columns placed at regular intervals. With the exception of shear walls in earthquake country and in a few cases exterior walls, nothing within the building is weight-bearing except the columns. Columns in this case include the shelving uprights in a tiered stack. It follows in theory that nothing within the building is fixed and immovable except the columns, though in fact it is generally impracticable if not impossible to shift the location of stairways, elevators, air ducts, plumbing, and utility risers.

Programmatic aspects of the module are discussed in Chapter 5, the details of shelving dimensions and aisle widths are covered in Chapter 6, and reader requirements will be found in Chapter 7.

If the modular system is to be used, what should be the column spacing? No one has been able to find an ideal size for all libraries or, indeed, for all parts of even one library, and it is doubtful if anyone ever will. Spacing depends on the library and the use to which it is to be put. If the library is to be primarily for undergraduates, with a very large seating capacity and a small book collection that can be shelved chiefly in the reading areas, spacing is quite a different problem from that which exists in the library that is primarily for advanced research work, with a tremendous stock of books and comparatively few accommodations for readers. Therefore, if a primarily undergraduate college becomes a research institution, what was once a suitable module size will then no longer be entirely satisfactory.

An examination of the module sizes selected in recently constructed libraries shows a tremendous variation from as low as 13 ft (3.962) in the short dimension to as high as 33 ft (10.058) or more in the other. On top floors in those instances where only the roof needs to be supported, a much wider space, of course, is practicable. This was the case in the Rutgers University Library main reading room, where there are spans of 83 ft (25.298). Recent developments in trusses and concrete have made available very large spans, which are not unduly expensive under some circumstances. In the Illinois Institute of Technology Library in Chicago, much of the weight of the building is hung from tremendous steel roof beams which make possible bays of over 2,000 sq ft (185.80 m²) and an area without columns on the first floor of some 20,000 sq ft (1858 m²).

The Lafayette College Library with the aid of special construction methods was able to provide spaces as large as 45 × 99 ft (13.716 × 30.176) separated by smaller areas. Larger module sizes may be possible, but there are trade-offs. Structural codes are becoming more conservative with the passage of time; and with the higher than normal library loading of 125-50 lbs. per sq ft (6.000 kN/m² to 7.182 kN/m²), longer spans will require greater structural depth, which increases the volume and height of the building, all other things being equal. Of course, as the columns must carry more weight, they themselves become more significant elements.

If the modules are square, with standard construction, they may vary in each direction from 16 ft 6 in. to 27 ft (5.029 to 8.230) where 3-ft (914 mm) shelving is used, or in a limited number of cases, even more than that. Almost every imaginable combination between 18 and 27 ft (5.486 and 8.230) in one or both directions can be found. Some dimensions selected seem to have been accidents rather than the result of deliberate decisions. Some were chosen for reasons which are now obscure and may have been based primarily on the fact that the architects, because they wanted the building to be so many feet long by so many feet deep, adopted a module size to fit those dimensions. The size in more than one library has been determined by the size in adjacent buildings, since this may affect facade designs.

Dimensions of the module need not be determined by the total length and breadth of the building; it is possible to cantilever out beyond the outside columns up to at least one-third of the distance between columns and thus increase the overall building size up to two-thirds of a bay by the cantilever in both directions. This creates no serious engineering problems, but aesthetic involvements should not be forgotten, and careful planning is required to make sure that all the cantilevered space will be useful. (See fig. 12.1.) Perhaps because of the difficulty of deciding on the optimum module size, some architects and librarians have reached the conclusion that almost any size can be adapted to library use and have selected one arbitrarily, failing to realize that the one chosen may reduce bookstack or reading accommodations by perhaps as much as 10 percent or in some cases even more. If this loss is only 3 percent in a $4,000,000 building, the $120,000 involved could be used to better advantage, and if, for instance, it took even 10 percent of this saving to figure out a better size, it would be money well spent.

The balance of this section will deal with the problems involved and attempt to state as clearly as possible the points on which the decision should be based. No attempt will be made, however, to find a solution for all libraries or even for any one of them; a choice must be made for each library with its specific requirements in mind.

Selection of the Module for Bookstack Areas. In a majority of cases in university and research libraries, as distinct from college libraries, bay sizes and column spacing have been determined by bookstack needs. Perhaps the commonest module used in libraries has been 22 ft 6 in. × 22 ft 6 in. (6.858 × 6.858), with columns preferably no more than 14 in. (356 mm) in diameter or square. This

allows five stack ranges in a bay if they are placed 4 ft 6 in. (1.372) apart and room for seven 3 ft (914 mm) sections in each range between columns. Of course, if the standard stack section is 3 ft 3.37 in. (1.000) in length, the bay size would be more like 24 ft 3.34 in. (7.400), which would give a range spacing of about 4 ft 10 in. (1.480) on centers that would be considered wasteful in some libraries.

Similar logic suggests that a bay size that would accommodate eight sections between columns up to 21 in. (533 mm) square would require a bay spacing of 26 ft (7.925) while a similar bay with 14 in. (356 mm) columns requires only 25 ft 6 in. (7.772). Here the range spacing would be 4 ft 4 in. or 4 ft 3 in. (1.321 or 1.295), depending on the column size. This is good spacing for a middle-sized university with a collection of over 500,000 volumes and a relatively small number of students, not more than 5,000 for instance, or for a larger university with access to the stack limited to faculty and graduate students. If the shelves are 3 ft 3.37 in. (1.000) in length and the space required for the column and range ends is limited to 1 ft 7.69 in. (½ m), the bay size for a similar number of sections would obviously be 27 ft 11 in. (8.500) which is sufficient to handle six ranges at 4 ft 8 in. (1.420) on center, or seven ranges at about 4 ft (1.210) on center. The latter would only be suitable in a closed stack or a storage facility with light use. It can be seen that as the section length increases from 3 ft to 1 m, the aisle space also increases, all other things being equal, which may suggest somewhat different modules in terms of the numbers of standard sections held between columns for the two measuring systems given similar anticipated use.

The decision in regard to bay sizes for bookstacks might seem to be easier and simpler to make than for reading areas, because, in general, one part of the bookstack differs from another less than one reading area from another. Taken as a whole, however, it is the most complicated of the module-size problems, because of the possibility, and often the desirability, of different depths of shelving and widths of aisle in different parts of the stack. If these variations do not exist, multitier fixed stacks, discussed in Chapter 6, might well be preferable. The ten following points should be kept in mind, and it is desirable to delay the final decision until the

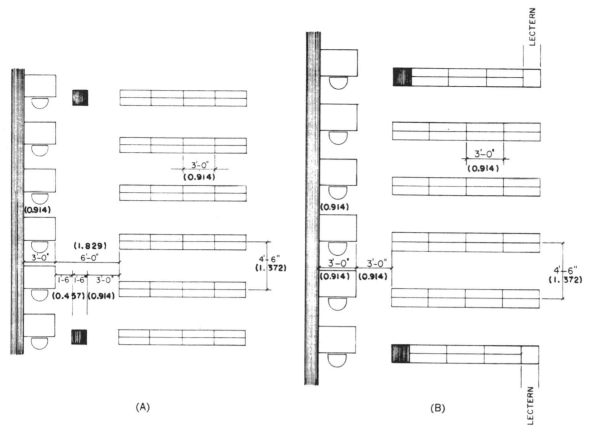

(A)   (B)

FIGURE 12.1 Cantilevered construction in a bookstack. (A) A cantilevered construction providing 4½ ft (1.372) beyond the outside columns. This is not wide enough for even a minimal carrel and aisle. (B) The cantilever provides 6 ft (1.829) in the clear beyond the columns, which is sufficient for a minimal carrel and aisle, with the shelving reaching to the outside line of the column. This arrangement saves floor area amounting to from 1½ to 3 times the length of the area. Note the use of lecterns in the column ranges at the right.

effect of each on the whole has been considered. This does not mean that the architect must wait for the best solution of all ten to be reached before work is started. The process of making rough sketches will be started early in the design to show the possible effect of the decisions made later on the different points and on other areas of the building. It is hoped that this section will help both the architect and the librarian decide what they would like to do. Here, as elsewhere, compromises will inevitably have to be made.

The ten points are:

1. The size and shape of the supporting columns
2. Arrangements for housing ventilating, mechanical, and wiring services
3. The length of the stack section
4. The length of the stack ranges between cross aisles
5. The design of the shelving upright or columns, and providing for error in the layout

6. The depth of shelves and ranges, and width of the stack aisles between ranges
7. The width of the main and cross aisles
8. The direction in which the stacks run, now or later
9. The clear ceiling heights
10. The type of lighting

These will be discussed in the order listed above, and several of them will be dealt with in other connections elsewhere in this volume. It should be repeated with emphasis that a decision on each of them may affect one or more of the others. They are interrelated. Column spacing should be decided with all ten problems in mind.

1. *Column sizes.* The size of the columns in a library building depends on: (a) technical requirements based on the loads to be carried; (b) the type of construction; (c) whether they enclose heating and ventilation services; and (d) their shape.

Older library buildings were supported not by columns but by load-bearing walls, both external and internal, except for the concentrated book-storage area in multitier stacks, where the section uprights supported all the stack levels above, and sometimes, in addition, the top floor, which was used for other than book-storage purposes, as in the Widener at Harvard and the New York Public Library central building. The section uprights may support the roof also if stacks go up to it. Multitier stacks are still used and, in most but not all cases, will be somewhat less expensive than freestanding stacks. The latter are recommended, however, because of the flexibility they provide.

It should be noted that the size of the columns is of importance anywhere in a library, because the larger they are the more they tend to get into the way of activities, services, and equipment. The effect on seating arrangements and other facilities will be dealt with in Section 12.6. It is obvious that the columns in a bookstack should always come in the line of the stack ranges, not in between where they would partly or completely block the aisles. It is also evident that if the column is thicker through than the book range, it will partially block an aisle and get into the way of the readers, staff, and book trucks passing through the aisles. This means that the first requirement, if it can be managed, is to keep the columns no wider than the ranges in the direction at right angles to the ranges. (See fig. 12.2.) Range widths will be discussed under 6 below, which deals with shelf depths.

a. *Weight-bearing requirements.* The heavier the weight to be carried by the columns, other

things being equal, the larger the column must be. The weight to be carried includes the dead load (the floors themselves) and the live load (the equipment, books, and persons which the floors may be called upon to support). In earthquake country the lateral loads caused by the horizontal movement of the ground are sometimes partially carried by the columns as well, although a specially designed wall, called a shear wall, usually does most of the work of handling this type of load. The vertical weight and the amount of lateral force which must be resisted, of course, depend largely on the size of the bay. Books and standard bookstacks are heavy. Maps and map cases may be even heavier. Compact storage of any kind, which is discussed in Chapter 6, increases the load. Certain machinery is in the same category, but heavy equipment can often be placed on the lowest level, where it may not present a problem. The architect and engineers should understand the weight requirements and provide for them. Building codes always require a safety margin. If construction provides for 125 to 150 pounds live load per square foot (6.00 kN/m² to 7.182 kN/m²) throughout all parts of the library, the floors will hold anything required of them with few exceptions (most notably compact storage). If bay sizes get much beyond 25 to 27 ft (7.620 to 8.230) in each direction, the column dimensions and floor thickness may have to be increased and the cost of construction tends to rise correspondingly. If flexibility is desired—and in most cases it should be—it is suggested that the whole building, with the possible exception of cantilevered space, be designed for 150-pound (7.192 kN/m²) live loads. The extra cost will rarely be as much as one percent of the total cost of the finished building and its equipment.

As suggested earlier, consideration should also be given to even higher load capacity if the use of movable compact shelving systems in the future is a possibility. The cost to increase the full load capacity to 250–300 lbs per sq ft (11.978–14.384 kN/m²) should be less than 10 percent of the construction cost, and the storage capacity is doubled.

b. *Type of column construction.* Columns are generally of reinforced concrete or of steel covered with concrete or vermiculite for fire protection. Occasionally heavy timber or pipe columns may be used in a structure although they are rare in institutional buildings. Building codes generally forbid the use of steel

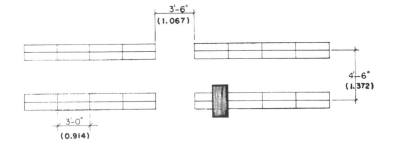

FIGURE 12.2 Columns wider than range. Columns in a bookstack should always be in line with the ranges and not so large as to project into a stack or a cross aisle as they do here. They present a fixed obstacle in a traffic artery and sooner or later will inevitably be bumped into. They also often necessitate a stack section of irregular length.

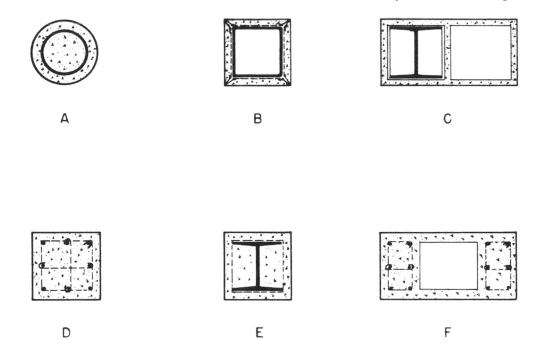

D   E   F

FIGURE 12.3 Types of column construction. (A) Lally column; (B) hollow steel column protected by concrete with services in center; (C) divided column with left-hand section of reinforced concrete or steel protected by concrete, and right-hand section enclosing a duct for services protected by reinforced concrete; (D) reinforced concrete column; (E) steel column protected by concrete; (F) column similar to D with duct in center.

alone unless protected by concrete, because fire in the building might cause the steel to buckle. It may be impossible to hold a reinforced-concrete column to the desired size of 14 in. (356 mm) in diameter or square if a large bay size is selected or if there is a multistory stack. Four variables determine the minimum size of the column: the construction of the column, the size of the bay, the height of the columns, and the total forces that must be resisted by the column. One or more may have to be changed to suit the situation. A reinforced-concrete column takes more space than a steel column protected by concrete but almost always costs less. The larger the bay or taller the column, the stronger and the larger the columns must be, other things being equal. The more floors in the building, the heavier the total load will be on the columns on the lower levels. But remember that a larger column may get in the way and decrease capacity and should be avoided if possible.

c. *Location of services.* Another factor closely related to column sizes deals with whether or not they are to include heating and ventilating ducts. Angus Snead MacDonald recommended that these services be placed in the center of hollow steel columns, thereby taking little or no space that could be used for other purposes and making the services available in each bay or even in each corner of each bay. Most building codes forbid this use of columns because of the fire hazard it would present. Types of column construction and arrangements for services in them are shown in Figure 12.3.

Types C and F in figure 12.3 require more space than do A, B, D, and E and will necessitate more than 14 in. (356 mm) in at least one direction. D may also if the number of levels is more than four. In a range that includes two 14-in. (356 mm) columns, the two take the place of one 3-ft (914 mm) section. In many cases 32 in. (813 mm) overall the long way should be sufficient for C and F, although at least one library has columns which include ducts and have a long dimension of almost 6 ft (1.829). If 15 in. (381 mm) or, better still, 14 in. (356 mm) proves impossible, 32 to 34 in. (813 to 864 mm) is a convenient length in the direction of the book ranges, because the column then takes the place of one 3-ft (914 mm) stack section, and irregular-length shelf sections are avoided.

It is best to use 14 and 32 in. (356 mm and 813 mm) columns instead of 18 and 36 in. (457 mm and 914 mm) because they leave a margin of 2 full in. (51 mm) on each side to provide for irregularities which occasionally appear in column sizes and for the end upright and a finished end panel of the bookstacks if one is used. It should be noted, however, that 14 in. (356 mm) is not critical; 16 or 18—even 20 in.—(406 mm or 457 mm, even 508 mm) is suitable where 10 in. (254 mm) shelving is used. But these larger dimensions will affect column spacing, and they may require odd-sized shelving which, after all, is a workable though slightly less convenient solution.

It should be remembered that if ducts are largely vertical, whether in the columns or elsewhere, they take only a comparatively small amount of square footage; whereas if they are horizontal, they require deeper spaces between a ceiling and the floor above which, in some libraries, have been up to 5 ft. (1.524) in thickness overall. These very thick spaces enable the engineer to run the ducts any place desired without careful planning, but they take a tremendous amount of expensive cubage and, in addition, may make a multistory building considerably taller than is necessary. This result will be good or bad architecturally as the case may be. Of course, where the new facility is an addition, a key factor will be the floor levels necessary to tie into the existing structure with a minimum number of ramps. The best method of dealing with ducts may therefore be determined without much further thought.

d. *The shape of the column.* Should the columns be square (or perhaps round) so that the ranges can be turned in either direction? Or should they be rectangular, longer in the direction of the ranges so that they can be large enough to carry the required weight (and, if desired, the ventilation services) and yet not interfere with the aisles? The question of range direction will be discussed under 9 below. The columns, with occasional exceptions, should be square or round if the ranges are to run in different directions in different parts of the bookstack now or later, because, as already shown in Figure 12.2, they should be no wider than the ranges.

A rectangular column occupying the space of a standard section of shelves has the advantages, however, of making the ranges, whether they contain columns or not, end at the same line without the use of odd-length sections and of permitting cross aisles at the end of any section instead of only after two 14 in. (356 mm) columns are included in a range. (Since it takes two 14 in. (356 mm) columns to occupy the space of one section, there must be two of them in each range if the measurements are to come out even.)

One other comment about the shape of columns is pertinent. Often a circular column is cheaper than a rectangular one, and in some places it will look better. In a bookstack either one will leave spaces which are difficult to

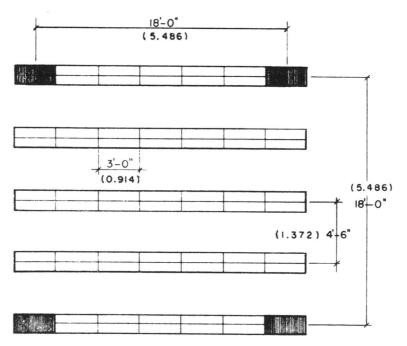

FIGURE 12.4 Effect of long rectangular columns on bay sizes. The capacity is reduced by two sections instead of one in each bay. The ranges all come out even. The dimensions between column centers should be a multiple of the shelving length, not the shelving length plus half a section (in this case, a multiple of 3 ft, not 3 ft plus 1½ ft).

keep clean unless fillers are used to cover the gaps. In reading areas furniture frequently does not fit curves. Yet the corners of rectangular columns are particularly vulnerable to bumping and disfiguration. In this connection it should be stated that any column covered by plaster, whether it be round, square, or rectangular, is impracticable in an exposed position, adjacent to a traffic artery of any kind, unless it is protected in some way. It can be covered with plastic cloth, sheet rubber, or even metal protecting surfaces, preferably noncorrosive, up to the height of a book truck, if not higher. A wide base, which may protect it from most collisions, may be a hazard in other ways.

The problem of column sizes might be summed up by saying that they can be square, rectangular, or round. A square or round column will not get in the way of stack ranges if it is no greater in dimension than the depth of the ranges and will result in greater flexibility than an elongated rectangular one. Each such rectangular column will probably take the space of a double-faced stack section in each bay, whereas a square or a round one may well occupy only one-half that amount of floor space and may thereby make available one more single-faced section of shelving in many bays. If rectangular columns that are not square are used, the direction of the stack ranges cannot be changed later without inconvenience and loss of space. The bay sizes also are affected because in this case, as shown in Figure 12.4, they should be multiples of a standard stack section, not of a standard section plus a half section.

It is sometimes possible to reduce the size of most of a column by making it expand near the ceiling. This will not cause trouble except in a bookstack with shelving going all the way to the ceiling. It is not completely impossible to have columns that project into aisles, particularly if the stack is little used by the public and if the aisles beside them are wide enough to permit passing; but, as will be shown in 6 below, every inch (25 mm) added to a stack aisle reduces stack capacity by approximately 2 percent. The additional cost of a steel column protected by concrete (beyond the cost of reinforced concrete) may be less than the value of the space lost by widening stack shelving, so that the columns will not project into the aisles, or by widening the aisles, to make the projecting columns less dangerous to the users and the equipment.

A further statement relating to column sizes and their effect on column spacing is presented after the other factors which determine module sizes have been discussed.

2. *Arrangement for housing services.* This has been discussed under 1c above, and no further comment is required here.

3. *The length of the stack section.* In many parts of the world, the standard section will be 3 ft, or 914 mm, nominally on centers; in other areas shelving of 1 m (about 3¼ ft) on centers may be the standard. The actual length of the shelf will be about ¾ in. (19 mm) less than the center-to-center measure although this dimension loss will vary from 2 in. (51 mm) to as little as ½ in. (13 mm) depending on the manufacturer and the type of shelving. This dimension is a key factor if it is anticipated that there will be a mix of existing and new shelves, as the shelves themselves may not be interchangeable between manufacturers. It should also be noted that the difference between a 2 in. and a ½ in. space loss for a 3 ft nominal shelf can represent over a 4 percent difference in shelving capacity, which is not insignificant. As discussed in Chapter 6, other shelf lengths are possible. With a column size selected to be about 2 in. (50 mm) less than one-half of the standard section, two columns take the space of one section, and with the clear space between the columns being a multiple of the standard section plus "growth" space discussed in 5 below, there will be practically no waste space. The ranges will come out even with those where there are no columns as shown in Figures 12.5 and 12.7.

There is one difficulty with this proposal, however. The main cross aisles tend to be limited to a few widths, and no one of them may be just right. This problem will be discussed under 7 below.

All of these problems can be simplified if the library is ready to accept odd-length sections when they are required by the column spacing. A 14 in. (356 mm) column may require an 18 in. (457 mm) shelf section to fill out the range. (See figs. 12.8 and 12.9.) There is nothing impossible about this arrangement; however, an 18 in. (457 mm) section may cost about as much as a 36 in. (914 mm) one, and it complicates planning for shifts of books. It is sometimes advisable to fill out the range, which is 18 in. (457 mm) or less too short because only one square or round column is in it, by hanging a lectern from the end of the last stack section and thus providing a convenient stand-up reading accommodation for persons examining books at the

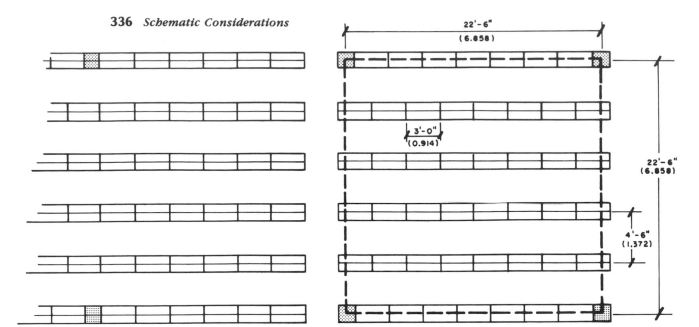

FIGURE 12.5 Column spacing 22 ft 6 in. × 22 ft 6 in. (6.858 × 6.858) with 15 in. (0.381) columns and with standard shelving provides 74 single-faced stack sections (within dashed lines) and 4 ft 6 in. (1.372) between range centers. Cross aisles, as here illustrated, are not included in this capacity figure. This arrangement gives 506¼ sq ft (47.032 m²) per bay, or 6⅘ sq ft (0.635 m²) per section. If 110 sq ft (10.219 m²) are added for cross aisles, a single-faced section will occupy 8⅓ sq ft (0.774 m²) which may be considered as standard for this configuration. The columns in one bay occupy altogether the space of one single-faced section, or 1⅓ percent of the shelving without columns.

nearby shelves. This should generally be done in the column ranges only, as a lectern is rarely worthwhile at the end of more than one range in a bay. But the important point to note here is that, if possible, the distance between columns should be an exact multiple of the shelf section length plus extra space for stack uprights.

4. *The length of the ranges.* There are several problems in connection with range lengths. The first is a question of what length ranges can be permitted without undue inconvenience to the reader and staff. This matter is discussed in Chapter 6. It is sufficient here to say that: (a) range lengths should vary with circumstances; (b) ranges longer than those that have been considered standard are possible, particularly in large installations where the use is light; (c) long ranges may increase total stack capacity up to 10 percent or more; and (d) other things being equal, the longer the range or the heavier the use, the wider the stack aisle should be.

A second problem, which deals with column sizes, was discussed under 1 above, where it was stated that if column size in the direction of the range is 14 in. (356 mm) and the range, before a cross aisle is reached, includes two columns, it will not interfere with the cross aisle.

The third problem is that if the module size is based on the distance between columns and hence is a multiple of the standard section, the width of cross aisles will also normally be a similar multiple, that is 3, 6, or 9 ft for 3 ft (914 mm) shelving, or 1, 2 or 3 m for shelving 1.00 m long. This is dealt with in 7 below.

5. *The design of the shelving upright or column, and providing for error in the layout.* Though this has been discussed earlier, it is of such importance as to warrant further mention. Certain manufacturers construct standard library shelving units with a structural frame which is the exact measure of the shelving module. With this type of construction, the exact length of a range should be an exact multiple of the shelving unit, and the clear space provided between the columns needs to be only slightly more than this exact dimension. However, if there is any gap between adjoining sections, such as might occur where gusset plates are installed between the sections, there will be "growth" in the length of the range. For a range of eight sections, this could easily amount to an inch (25 mm) or more, a factor which, if not provided for, can result in considerable frustration when it is time to install the shelving.

Growth is also a factor with commercial or industrial shelving, discussed in Chapter 6 in detail. With this shelving, the growth factor is considerably larger. Even where shelving units are made up of "starters" and "adders", as is the case with much standard library shelving, the projection of the shelf uprights at the ends of the range must be accounted for. In this case 2 in. (50 mm) is not an uncommon dimension that must be added to the multiple of standard units.

Finally, construction techniques are seldom exact, and where a standard manufactured product must fit between structural members, it is only prudent to allow a small dimension for error. For standard library shelving, it is suggested that the clear space between columns ideally should be 4 in. (102 mm) greater than the multiple of standard shelving units, and that for commercial or industrial shelving, this dimensional requirement may well be greater, depending upon the range length.

6. *The depth of shelving and width of stack aisles.* On first thought one might fail to see why the bay sizes are affected by the shelf depth or, for that matter, the stack-aisle width. But they are, and affected greatly. This is because if space is to be used to advantage, the distance between columns should be an exact multiple of the distance from the center of one range to the center of the next, and this distance should be determined by two things: the optimum depth from front to back of each range and the optimum width of the aisles. Figure 12.6 shows the results when this rule is not followed. Many stack layouts have been unsatisfactory and uneconomical because this necessity has not been kept in mind in deciding on the column spacing. The question of range depth is considered in Chapter 6.

Aisle widths are also discussed in Chapter 6. It is noted there that in libraries with comparatively small collections but with large numbers of students and faculty using open-access shelves, 3 ft (914 mm) wide stack aisles are indicated, and ranges 4 ft 6 in. (1.372) on centers might be called standard. Any distance up to 5 or even 6 ft (1.524 or 1.829) may be desirable in locations where reference books or other very heavily used collections are stored. Note that if range aisles are to be finished with pre-cut carpet squares, it may be desirable to choose an aisle width between

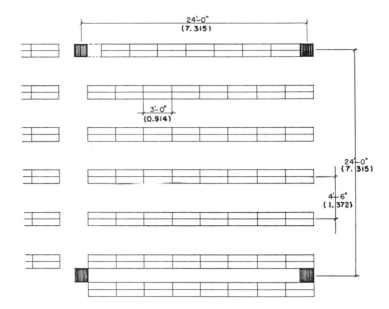

FIGURE 12.6 Columns and range spacing fail to gear together. A 24 ft (7.315) square bay with ranges 4½ ft (1.372) on centers shows the disastrous results of improper spacing. Ranges with this bay will need to be 4 ft or 4 ft 9 in. (1.219 or 1.463) on centers, but there is still trouble in the direction of the ranges, unless the columns are a long rectangle and occupy the space of a full section.

base plates which is an exact multiple of dimensions for squares on the market.

In a stack designed around 3 ft (914 mm) standard sections and ranges 4 ft 3 in. (1.295) on centers (with a range 16 or 18 in., 406 mm or 457 mm) deep and with a 35 or 33 in. (889 or 838 mm) stack-aisle width, the bay sizes can be 25 ft 6 in. (7.772), with six ranges installed in each bay and in the other direction eight standard sections between columns. (See fig. 12.7.) A bay of this size has a further advantage. If more compact storage is required later, seven ranges can be placed in a bay instead of six, giving 3 ft 7⅜ in. (1.108) from center to center, which is fairly comfortable and certainly possible in the case of little-used material with closed access. On the other hand, with this same bay, it is possible to use only five ranges 5 ft. 1 in. (1.550) on centers, a useful arrangement in a heavily used section or for oversize books on deeper than standard shelves. In the case of reference books in a reading room or of a newspaper stack, four ranges can be installed, giving 6 ft 4 in. (1.930) on centers with this column spacing.

A smaller size bay which fits many stack situations with 3 ft (914 mm) sections and one

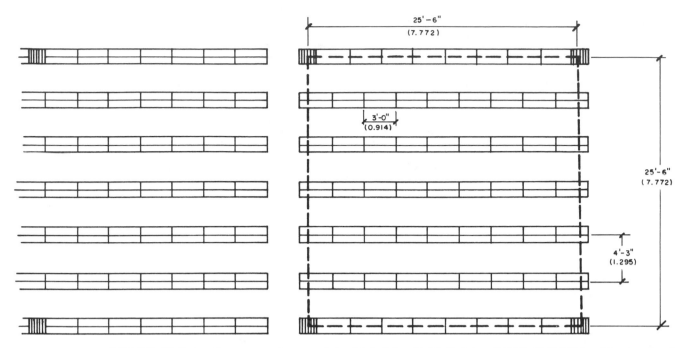

FIGURE 12.7 A column spacing module 25 ft 6 in. × 25 ft 6 in. (7.772 × 7.772) with standard shelving provides for 101 single-faced stack sections, exclusive of cross aisles (i.e., within dashed line), with 4 ft 3 in. (1.295) range centers. The result works out to 6⅖ sq ft (0.598 m²) per section. If 130 sq ft (12.077 m²) are added to each bay for cross aisles, stairs, and an elevator, each single-faced section will require approximately 7¾ sq ft (0.720 m²). If the columns could be replaced with shelving, the shelving quantity would increase by 1 percent. The net increase in capacity over the bay shown in figure 12.5 is over 6 percent per a fixed unit of area.

that, as already indicated, has probably been used more than any other in libraries constructed in recent years is 22 ft 6 in. (6.858) in each direction. (See fig. 12.5.) This is the next possible square bay that is smaller than 25 ft 6 in. (7.772) and is a multiple of 3 ft plus 1½ ft. It gives approximately 6 percent less capacity per square foot because the ranges will be 4 ft 6 in. (1.372) on centers, instead of 4 ft 3 in. (1.295). It will make possible an increase from five to six ranges, which will be 3 ft 9 in. (1.143) on centers, if at a later time more compact storage is desired, or a decrease to four ranges 5 ft 7 in. (1.702) on centers for reference books or in other heavily used sections. Other possible bay sizes will be considered later in this chapter.

It should be repeated here that unless the range spacing is changed correspondingly, an increase of 1 in. (25 mm) in range depth decreases the aisle width a similar amount or decreases the stack capacity provided one assumes that the ranges would be placed on closer centers if the shelving was narrower. In this case the difference of 1 in. results in a potential savings of 2 percent in the construction cost for the stack area. However, it

may not be desirable to save the 2 percent and have crowded conditions.

7. *The width of the main and subsidiary cross aisles.* Here a problem arises in a modular stack that can be avoided in a multitier stack. In a multitier stack it is possible to arrange for aisles of any width desired, so long as those above and below use the same layout. They can be found from as narrow as 2 ft 6 in. (762 mm) or even less for a subsidiary or side cross aisle up to 6 or even 7 ft (1.829 or 2.134) for the main central aisle. But in a modular stack, if the plan is based on 3-ft stack sections and a multiple of 3 ft between columns, these aisles apparently must be 3, 6, or 9 ft (0.914, 1.829 or 2.743) wide. It seems obvious that 3 ft (0.914) minus the extra inches occupied by the adjacent uprights, while wide enough for a subsidiary aisle, will not be satisfactory for the main aisle of a heavily used stack. Six feet (1.829) may be wider than necessary, although in a very large, heavily used stack it may be ideal. Each needless 6 in. (152 mm) in aisle width will decrease capacity of the adjacent bays. In other words, a 4 ft 6 in. (1.372) cross aisle in place of a 6 ft (1.829) one will, if the ranges are 30 ft (9.144) long,

increase capacity by 2½ percent. A 3 ft (914 mm) aisle would save another 2½ percent, but as already noted, it is not wide enough for a main cross aisle, although it will do very well for a secondary one which is comparatively little used. A width of 1½ standard sections is entirely adequate, but ordinarily will not work out if the distance between columns is a multiple of a standard section. There are two possible remedies to this situation.

a. Make the distance between columns in the direction of the ranges multiples of standard sections plus a half section in every other bay, and place the cross aisles in those bays as shown in Figure 12.8, but make no change in the column spacing in the other direction. Doing so does away with the advantageous square bay and flexibility suffers.

b. Use a lectern to fill out any column range that includes only one column. This will permit a section and one-half wide main aisle, as shown in Figure 12.9.

8. *The direction in which stacks run.* If the column spacing is so designed that the stacks must always run in one direction, a certain amount of flexibility is lost. Is this serious? It may well be, particularly when portions of the stack are used for reading areas, and shelving meeting at right angles would be useful. If the bay is square, there is no reason why all the shelving in any bay should not be turned at will at right angles to that in other bays, except that it may affect both the natural and artificial lighting and will probably necessitate replacement of the floor covering that is used. (See 9 below in connection with the lighting arrangements.) Also, in earthquake country, as well as elsewhere, there may be overhead bracing that may be more difficult to change. The architect and the librarian must decide whether the extra flexibility, made available by a square bay with its other advantages in economy, is worthwhile.

A stack with shelving all running in the same direction tends to make the traffic patterns somewhat simpler. Many librarians therefore prefer to have all main-stack shelving run in the same direction and find that, if a comparatively small amount of shelving

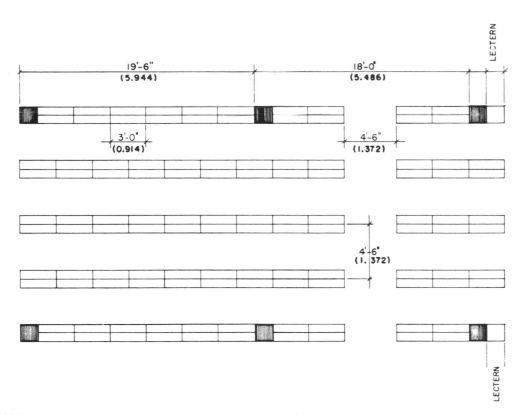

FIGURE 12.8 Cross-aisle width controlled by increasing column spacing. This figure shows that if the distance between columns is changed or staggered in the direction of the ranges, with every other row of columns ½ section farther apart or closer together than in the next bay, main aisles equal to 1½ sections become possible instead of an aisle equal to one or two sections, but the bays will not be square.

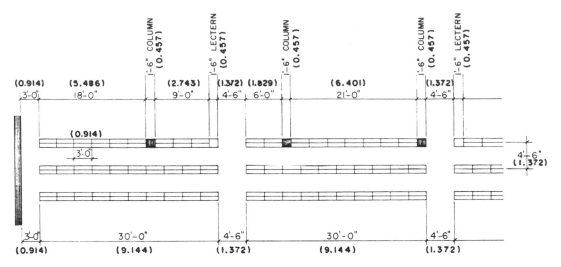

FIGURE 12.9 Use of a lectern to fill out a column range. While 1 ft 6 in. (0.457) is reserved for columns here, the column itself should not be more than 15 in. (0.381) in order to provide space for stack uprights, shelving growth, and a margin for irregularities.

is wanted in other areas with a different orientation, it can well have different range spacing and that at worst the book capacity lost is negligible.

It should be noted that a stack range parallel and adjacent to an outside wall is undesirable if that wall has windows and is so oriented that the sun will shine on the books. This problem can be solved by changing the direction of stack ranges on that side of the building. But such a change may turn out to be a complicated affair, because it also changes the direction of the cross aisles and the traffic lanes. A row of carrels along the window wall and then an aisle may help to solve the problem without changing the range direction.

9. Ceiling height. The clear height of a stack level between the finished floor and the finished ceiling is a bay-size problem only indirectly, but it may be a matter of importance in connection with cubic footage in the building. The lowest ceiling that will permit seven shelves 12 in. (305 mm) apart on centers is just under 7 ft 6 in. (2.286). (See Chapter 6 for a full discussion.) But any space for shelving above 7 ft 6 in. (2.286) in the clear is useless, except for semidead storage, because the top shelf will be 6 ft 4 in. (1.930) above the floor, and only a very tall person can reach it. Of course, where the code requires a full sprinkler system for the library, there may also be a code requirement for at least 18 in. (460 mm) clear vertical space between the sprinkler head and the storage of combustible materials.

It should be noted that a number of recently constructed libraries have stack rooms 8 ft 4 in. or 8 ft 6 in. (2.540 or 2.590) in clear height, with room for inserting an extra shelf for storage or for shelving books in an auxiliary collection or in a superseded classification. Portable one-step stools would need to be within a short distance. This arrangement will, of course, increase the gross capacity by nearly 15 percent, but it may be confusing to the reader if it is in an open-access stack. The extra height can also be useful for two purposes other than increasing book capacity. The first is discussed in the next paragraph. The second is that the additional height makes the space convertible for multiple-seating accommodations with pleasant room proportions.

10. Lighting. The effect of lighting in the determination of the size of a stack bay relates to ceiling heights and also to the number of fixtures to a bay and their spacing. In a modern bookstack there must be artificial light available in every stack aisle. Normally, the lighting is installed down the center of each aisle in lines parallel to the ranges. If this practice is followed and at a later time capacity is increased by providing an additional range in each bay, the wiring and fixtures must be changed. Or, if it is decided to turn the shelves at right angles for one reason or another, the lighting must also be changed if the ceiling height is only 7 ft 6 in. (2.286). If the clear height of the ceiling is 8 ft 4 in. or 8 ft 6 in. (2.540 or 2.590) or more and fluorescent lighting in long strips is used, it can be placed at right angles to the ranges, and the shelves will still be illuminated even if the range spacing changes. The library at John Carroll University in Cleveland and the Wellesley College Library are examples of this arrangement. However, such an arrangement removes the possibility of range aisle switching which has become important as an energy conservation measure.

The points above indicate the large number of variables. The cost significance of small dimensions becomes clear when multiplied in conditions of a large bookstack installation. The Yale University Seeley G. Mudd Library of 1982 provides one example of attention to detail resulting in very high density in a traditional stack. In this instance octavos are on eight shelves per section with 23 in. (584 mm) aisles, sixteen sections per range, and quartos on six shelves per section and a 25 in. (635 mm) aisle. The octavo shelves are 7 in. (178 mm) nominal depth; the quartos are 9 in. (229 mm). Under these arrangements studies showed that squatting to use bottom shelves and using a one-step stool for top shelves were reasonable though the limits of convenience were strained. The Mudd Library basement provides higher ceilings so that octavos can in most places be nine shelves high, with 11 in. (280 mm) clear between the shelves. Because the sprinkler placement is less than the fire code requires, the stack has been classed "limited access."

This discussion of the ten points that affect module sizes in a bookstack has brought out the principal problems involved, indicated the interrelationships, and shown that final decision on column spacing should be made after consideration of all factors. No one column spacing is suitable for all library stacks. As can be seen in the discussion that follows, there are other factors to be considered.

The Module Size and Other Accommodations. Space for purposes other than concentrated book storage is dealt with throughout this volume, but only rarely is such space seriously affected by column spacing. There may be some inconvenience if the areas required are larger in both directions than the bay size selected, as columns will be required in those areas instead of around the periphery. Likewise, bay sizes should be taken into account if there are numerous identical small units, such as enclosed carrels, dissertation rooms, faculty studies or offices, that ought to fit evenly into the module if space is not to be wasted.

If the wrong bay size is selected, the areas so large that they may be affected by columns might include the following:

1. Large reading areas for any use, such as for reference collections, current periodicals, reserve books, public documents, divisional reading, maps, large special-subject rooms, and night-study areas
2. Public areas around service desks and the card catalog room
3. The processing room or rooms
4. Classrooms and auditoriums; audio-visual rooms and library-school areas
5. Nonassignable space for lobbies, mechanical areas, and stairwells.

Small areas that might cause difficulty because two or more of them should fit in between columns should not be forgotten. Faculty studies are a case in point.

Spacing problems in most of these areas can be disposed of without difficulty. As will be noted elsewhere, in open-stack libraries the tendency is away from large reading rooms; but with the tremendous seating capacity still required in a large library, some may still be unavoidable. This will be particularly true in a closed-stack library such as the independent research library or many university libraries found in Europe and elsewhere. A reading room 18 ft (5.486) the short way (this is generally the smallest bay recommended) can be extended to 72 ft (21.946) in length through four bays without seeming to be completely out of proportion. With the larger bays, 22½, 25½, and 27 ft (6.858, 7.772 and 8.230), rooms 90, 102, and 108 ft (27.432, 31.090, and 32.918) in length, respectively, can be available without columns. If the room is next to the outside wall and additional width is wanted without a row of columns down the center, it can be obtained by cantilevering out beyond the last row of columns for 6 to 9 ft (say, 1.800 to 2.700) and widening the room in that way. Of course, the result will be a row of columns down one side of the room unless unusual structural tricks are contemplated (see below). On the other side, space for an aisle required under any circumstances can be included, making a room up to 30 ft (9.144) wide the narrow way with an 18 ft (5.486) column spacing and perhaps 42

(12.802) or more feet wide with a 27 ft (8.230) column spacing.

There are at least five other methods of providing larger areas unbroken by columns.

1. Place the room on the top floor with no weight but the roof, supported by special trusses, overhead. Interior columns can then be left out, as was done in the very large reference room at the Rutgers University Library.

2. Make the room high enough so that heavier beams can be used in the ceiling. As noted below under Problems Relating to Height, which discusses mezzanines, this decision will not necessarily require high rooms elsewhere on the same floor.

3. Make the column spacing narrower in one direction and so make possible a wider spacing in the other, as in the three large reading areas in the Lamont Library which has 13 by 33 ft (3.962 × 10.058) column spacing.

4. Hang the upper part of the building from heavy roof beams, as was done at the Illinois Institute of Technology Library in Chicago.

5. Use one of the precast-concrete methods which permit larger spans.

If a small bay size is used in a reading area and columns protrude into it, they may interfere with seating arrangements, particularly if long tables are used. Table sizes are discussed in Section 12.6, but remember that if tables are 4 ft wide and 12 ft long (1.219 × 3.658) or more, there should be an aisle at least 5 ft (1.524) wide between and parallel to them, in order to give comfortable access. It is important too that aisles adjacent to tables and at right angles to them should not be obstructed by columns. Ingenuity in preparing layouts ordinarily can overcome most difficulties without undue loss of valuable floor space.

In two public areas complications may arise. One of these is at a large service desk. Many university libraries and some colleges have circulation desks longer than the distance between columns. The size may be inconvenient if the column comes just in front of or behind the desk, as vision may be obstructed. A column dividing a desk into two is rarely satisfactory. Four comments may be useful:

1. If possible, place the desk far enough in front of or behind the column line so that neither staff nor readers are bothered by it. A desk should have free space behind and in front of it without column interference.

2. Try to plan the service so that the space between the columns will be long enough for any desk required. Many desks, if the staff is effective and makes use of good housekeeping procedures, do not need as much space as is provided between columns in a 22½ ft (6.858) or larger bay. This should be even more evident as automated circulation systems are installed provided they reduce the transaction time at the service point.

3. Plan a curved or L-shaped desk, which will be in one bay, not in two, but will thus provide the required extra length.

4. If no one of these methods is possible and work is so heavy that a longer desk is necessary, break the desk-work assignment into two, and use one part for the return of books and the other for charging, each in a different bay. If the desks are adjacent, one person may be able to service both during quiet hours.

The card catalog room is another public space that may cause trouble. There an 18 ft (5.486) column spacing may complicate matters. But again, a little ingenuity will generally make suitable any bay size that is likely to be adopted, although the results may not be completely satisfactory. The space lost is rarely large enough to warrant changing spacing for the whole building.

In a very large library it may be desirable to have an entrance lobby so large that a column will fall into it, but this ordinarily should not create a problem. The same is true in large staff areas such as the catalog department.

Finally, stairwells should be considered. With the low ceiling heights now in use and with reasonably large bays, stairwells should not create a problem, unless they are monumental. But the complications that may arise should not be neglected.

Turning now to certain small areas, we should give some attention to: walled-in areas for offices, studies, and enclosed carrels; reading alcoves combining shelving and reader accommodations; and individual seating, both for staff and readers. Reading alcoves present the most difficulty, but again, a little ingenuity should solve the problems. (See fig. 12.10.)

With any of the bay sizes recommended, such as 18, 22½, or 27 ft (5.486, 6.848 or 8.230, although these dimensions may vary with metric shelving), the chief librarian's office can be fitted in easily without column

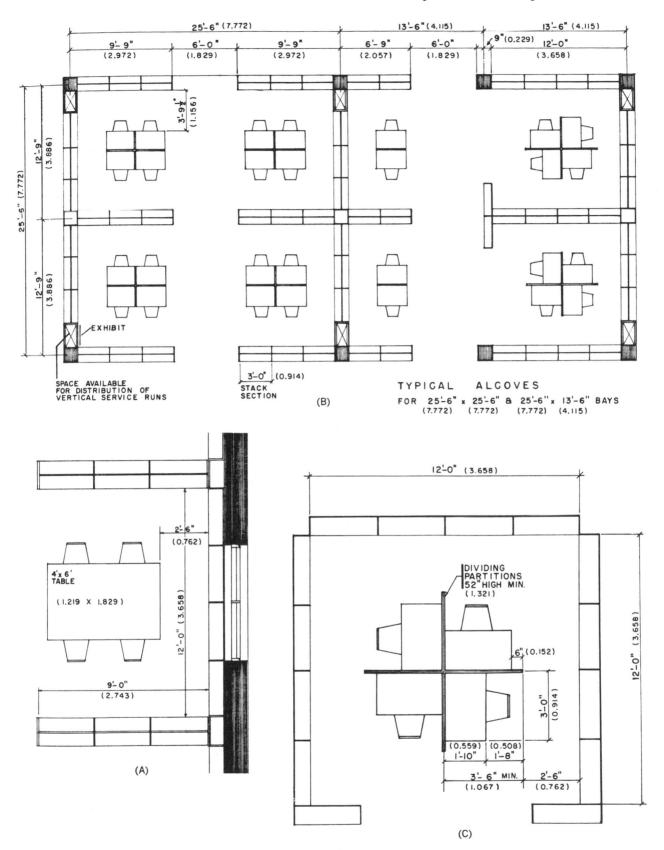

FIGURE 12.10 Tables in book alcoves: (A) standard table with no partitions; (B) tables for two to four persons, with partitions fitted in different column spacing and with exhibit space replacing a short section; (C) nest of tables in pinwheel formation with partitions to give additional privacy.

troubles. Two small offices can be placed in any of these sizes. They do not need to be square; for instance, a 9 × 12 (2.743 × 3.658) office has just about as much space as one 10 ft 5 in. × 10 ft 5 in. (3.175 × 3.175 m). But another problem arises. If these areas are adjacent to outside walls and the walls have windows, sizes must to a greater or lesser extent conform with the fenestration pattern. Remember that window space for offices is at a premium, and in most cases an office or study or closed carrel should use as little outside wall space as possible and reach back into the building far enough to provide the desired floor area.

If the column, particularly one on an outside wall, juts into a room, it may complicate matters for an office or study, and even more for a carrel, because the column size is a greater percentage of the area under consideration.

An 18 ft (5.486) bay will take care of one large office, two small ones, two adequate studies or three small ones, three good-sized closed carrels, or four open ones.

A 22½ ft (6.858) bay will provide outside wall space for two fine small offices or large studies, three adequate studies, four good closed carrels, or five open ones.

A 25½ ft (7.772) bay will provide for two fine offices, three minimum ones, three good or four small studies, five closed carrels, or six open ones.

The extra 1½ ft (457 mm) provided by a 27 ft (8.230) bay will not provide any more offices, studies, or carrels than a 25½ ft (7.772).

Appendix B lists in tabular form recommended sizes for offices, studies, and carrels, both open and closed, and for reading alcoves.

Problems Relating to Height. At least six general factors influence the height of a building, which will in turn affect the structural system and arrangements considered in the early design phases of the project. These six factors are:

1. Is the building project an addition that must relate to an existing facility?
2. How much clear height from floor to ceiling is desirable functionally and aesthetically in a library?
3. How thick should the floors be (from ceiling to floor level above)?
4. Are mezzanines desirable?
5. What considerations should one keep in mind in determining the preferable size and number of floor levels?
6. Does vertical transportation affect height problems?

Each of these factors will be discussed in order, and the compounding effect of most of these factors should be recognized.

1. *Is the building project an addition that must relate to an existing facility?* The question of additions is discussed generally in Chapter 10. It should be noted that the floor-to-floor height in an older building, particularly one that depends upon natural ventilation for air circulation, often will be significantly higher than required for a modern building. Matching the height of an original building, where the dimensions are inconsistent with modern construction techniques, might result in increasing the cost of an addition so much that little would be left of the savings that otherwise might result from the use of an old building. Always remember that height greater than is necessary or desirable functionally and aesthetically costs money and should be questioned. On the other hand, the floor heights in old multitier stack constructions are often so low that a modern free-standing stack with thicker floors and more flexibility cannot be installed in the same vertical space. If floor heights do not match, the few steps up or down that must be added to allow passage from the old to the new areas become difficult for the persons involved to manuever, and inconvenience and accidents may result. Furthermore, the transportation of books may present serious problems.

Systems of elevators that stop at half or partial levels can be considered, but their design is complex and their use awkward. Ramps may offer a better solution, yet they require a considerable amount of space. A typical ramp will be at a slope of 1 in 12; it takes little calculation to realize how quickly a large space may become devoted to such devices. A compromise may be considered where the main and second floors are designed to align with the existing structure while remaining floors are accommodated with a combination of ramps, stairs, and elevators.

2. *How much clear height from floor to ceiling is desirable functionally and aesthetically in a library?* Questions relating to the clear height of library areas are complex. It may be functionally desirable to use one level for many different purposes or for a single purpose,

such as reading accommodations, as well as for rooms that differ in size. A height that is functional and economical may not be aesthetically satisfactory. The height selected affects construction costs. Plans that make a library building satisfactory from the operational point of view are likely to call for areas on the same floor level which aesthetically as well as functionally differ widely in optimum height requirements. An added complication arises from the fact that library needs may change as time goes on. Every effort should be made to provide a building in which practically all the space can be used to advantage for book storage, or for reader accommodations, or for staff. Ideally, it should have heights throughout that are usable for all of these purposes, without involving expensive building alterations when shifts are made from one function to another.

The problem of flexible space has always been difficult. Early in the century when one feature of a library was a monumental reading room, that room was at least 22½ ft (6.858) high in the clear, or enough for three multitier stack levels. One of the first requisites in a reading room was natural light. To provide it in an area 35 to 40 ft (10.668 to 12.192) or more across required a room something like two-thirds as high as it was wide, with large windows going practically to the ceiling. Skylights were also often thought to be necessary, and the main reading room was therefore sometimes placed on an upper floor. Its height went a long way toward providing more or less satisfactory ventilation, at least at standing and sitting height, since hot and polluted air tends to rise without the aid of forced ventilation, which was not generally available. As already indicated, a height of 22½ ft (6.858) or more made it possible to place in other parts of the same floor three levels of a multitier stack and thus avoid short flights of stairs.

As much as fifty years ago, with better artificial light and forced ventilation available, it was found that a 22½ ft (6.858) ceiling height could be cut to 15 ft (4.572). This was done successfully in a large reading room at the University of Virginia Library in Charlottesville and was a surprise to many who had come to believe that the need for greater height went back primarily to a sense of proportion and not just light and ventilation.

Long before that, many libraries had experimented with a two and a half stack-level height with fairly large reading rooms, as was done at Oberlin College and elsewhere early in the century. Access from other parts of the building to the in-between stack levels was sometimes provided by ramps so steep that it was almost impossible, and certainly dangerous, to push a book truck over them.

But as time went on and building costs increased, as architects and interior designers learned how to effect changes in impressions of height, and as lower ceilings become customary in private homes, apartments, and office buildings, even lower heights were experimented with for reading areas of various sizes. More recently the cost of heating, cooling, and lighting a large space with expansive windows and perhaps a skylight have further argued for lower ceilings. Of course, skylights have their own special problems of heat, glare, leaks, and sunlight damage to the library materials.

The reading room on the fifth level of the Lamont Library is 131 × 31½ ft (40.000 × 9.600) in dimension. Since nothing but the roof is overhead, it was possible, without floor-level complications, to place the ceiling at any height which appeared aesthetically suitable. Requested to make the ceiling as low as he thought would be aesthetically desirable, the architect decided that 9½ ft (2.896) in the clear would be satisfactory if the room was partially divided into three equal areas, each nearly 44 × 32 ft (13.411 × 9.754), by open slatted screens that were some 7 ft (2.134) high and 15 ft (4.572) long. This room has generally been regarded as a success, and while there are certain positions in it from which, when one looks down the full length, the ceiling seems rather low, little or no criticism has been heard.

At about the same time, the Firestone Library at Princeton was being planned, and it had been decided that a large part of its total area was to consist of three levels below the entrance floor to be used primarily for a bookstack. It was important to keep down the height of these levels if they were to have outside light. This was accomplished and made easier by the downward slope of the ground to the rear of the building and the construction of a waterless moat. The desirable height was complicated by the requirement of providing, on the same levels, seminar and reading areas of at least two bays, making them 25 × 36 ft (7.620 × 10.973) in size. A mock-up was erected with an adjustable ceiling which could be cranked up and down. "Guinea pigs," including professors, administrators, students, and architects, as well as librarians, were assembled and were asked to complain when the ceiling was lowered too far for comfort and appearance. The conclusion was reached that 8 ft 4 in. (2.540) in the clear would be adequate for a reading and general-purpose areas as large as 25 × 36 ft (7.620 × 10.973). The decision made at Princeton has been accepted generally throughout the United States, and a minimum of 8 ft 4 in. (2.540) has been considered standard for small reading areas, if for other reasons no greater height seems desirable or necessary.

The University of Michigan Undergraduate Library and the library at Louisiana State University are buildings which have very large reading areas with ceilings approximately 9 ft (2.743) in the clear. The planners have found that this height is satisfactory with the use of divider screens, recessed lighting, light-colored ceilings, and, when desired, space broken up by bookcases. It is suggested that librarians and architects perplexed by this problem visit libraries with low reading-area ceilings and talk with librarians and students about the results.

The above applies to the theoretical minimum satisfactory heights of fairly sizable areas for multiple human occupancy. But many libraries in recent years have found that it is desirable to scatter small groups of readers among bookstacks in what are sometimes called "oases" or in alcoves or by other methods that are discussed in Chapter 7 and in Section 12.6 below. Here ceilings of even less than 8 ft 4 in. (2.540) have been found to be possible and satisfactory. One mezzanine in the Lamont Library, which measures 91 × 45 ft (27.737 × 13.716), proved adequate for shelving 30,000 volumes and for seating 75 readers at individual tables and tables for four. It has a ceiling height of 8 ft (2.438). Another mezzanine of the same size has a ceiling height of 7 ft 9 in. (2.362). The latter height has proved adequate and satisfactory in a large mezzanine in the Georgia Institute of Technology Library. In the Iowa State University Library in Iowa City even larger areas have an 8 ft (2.438) ceiling. A height lower than 7 ft 9 in. (2.362) has been widely used for many years for individual seating in carrels and faculty studies adjacent to bookstacks.

The ceiling height of the Widener stack area at Harvard is just over 7 ft 2 in. (2.184) in the clear, and some 400 open carrels—they are called "stalls," which is perhaps a better name for them—are in use, with little if any complication on account of the lack of height. A number of carrels are placed among the Amherst College bookstacks, but any fixture suspended from the 6 ft 9 in. (2.057) ceiling will become a problem for basketball players. This is true of 7 ft 2 in. (2.184) ceilings as well. Lower ceilings can be found, but they are not recommended. Indeed, they would not be allowed by many current codes.

From the point of view of the comfort of the reader, aesthetics, and proportion, the above seems to indicate that a large reading room need not be more than 9 ft 6 in. (2.896), although this would be a minimum height if high-intensity kiosk-type lighting fixtures are proposed to provide ambient light. With lighting in the ceiling and air conditioning, a 9 ft (2.743) height is possible if the room is broken up by bookcases or in other ways. A room 25 × 36 ft (7.620 × 10.973), which is large enough for up to 36 readers and 75 to 100 persons sitting in a conference is not unpleasant with an 8 ft 4 in. (2.540) ceiling if ventilation and lighting are adequate. With a smaller concentration of readers, 8 ft (2.438) or even 7 ft 9 in. (2.362) is enough for individual seating. To go below that to the figures that have been used in some libraries is to go below the height needed for economical book storage. It is suggested that the minimum height, except perhaps for storage spaces and doorways, should not be less than the height of standard shelving plus an inch or two (25 mm or 50 mm). In this regard, music libraries or archives, which may use commercial or industrial type shelving to advantage, may need somewhat higher ceilings. Shelf heights are discussed in detail in Chapter 6.

What is the maximum desirable height for bookstacks? First, remember that any additional height increases cost without materially adding to capacity. The following figures cannot be considered as definitive because conditions will vary, but it might be helpful to estimate that a 6 in. (152 mm) increase over a 7 ft 6 in. (2.286) height, while increasing cubage by nearly 7 percent, will probably increase the square footage cost by less than 1½ percent. So small an increase in height will not change the cost figures for equipment, ceilings, floors, doors, and furniture, or for lighting, although the last would be affected if there were any considerable increase in height. The extra cubage, of course, adds to the cost of both exterior and interior walls, of stairs, and of heating and ventilating although it may also be helpful by facilitating the horizontal distribution of sprinkler lines and ventilation ducts where they are suspended below the ceiling.

The question then is whether or not the additional height is worth what it will cost. If 8 ft 6 in. (2.590) in the clear increases square-foot costs of the building by less than 3 percent, 9 ft (2.743) by 4 percent, 10 ft (3.048) by something like 6 or 7 percent, and so forth, the answer will depend upon what the extra height contributes aesthetically, or in capacity, comfort, and flexibility. As far as books are concerned, nothing is gained in capacity unless an eighth shelf is installed; it will be beyond the reach of most readers and is not generally recommended. When it comes to flexibility, there are certain advantages resulting from the additional height. As has already been seen, a very few inches over 7 ft 6 in. (2.286) makes it possible to use space for multiple occupancy by readers. How much is this flexibility worth? The room should certainly be high enough for the convenience and comfort of those who use the stack. Additional height is not required unless it is needed for code requirements, light, and air, or unless the rooms are so large as to make a low ceiling seem oppressive.

The aesthetic problem is hard to deal with objectively and specifically. It involves a sense of proportion. The architects' advice will be helpful.

What about height in areas used by the staff? Staff members are likely to be in the library longer hours than readers and should have more, rather than less, comfort, but in general the same rules apply to both. In the 1960s the Pennsylvania State University Library located processing staff on one of the stack levels where an additional 10 in. (254 mm) beyond its standard of 6 ft 8 in. (2.032) is provided. This is a multitier stack with the uprights every 9 ft (2.743) in each direction, instead of the commoner 3 ft × 4 ft 6 in. (0.914 × 1.372). Of necessity staff worked there for some years without serious complaint, but the arrangement is not recommended. With good light and ventilation, a ceiling height of 7 ft 6 in. (2.286) will do in small areas if divided up by shelving and catalog cases.

The greatest problem in connection with height comes when large reading areas are required on the same floor level with extensive book-storage areas. If the reading room is large enough to require a 10 ft (3.048) ceiling, and the ceiling adds 7 percent to the square-footage cost of the stack portion (or, let us say in order to be specific, $7 a square foot), it may increase the cost of the construction of 10,000 sq ft (929 m²) of stack space by $70,000. This figure will, of course, vary according to local construction costs. The dilemma can sometimes be avoided to a large extent by deciding to keep large reading areas off levels with large book-storage areas, or by using mezzanine stacks where a greater height is required for the readers. The alternatives will be discussed later in this section.

One other point in connection with ceiling heights. If they are under 7 ft (2.134), tall persons going down staircases placed one above the other may bump their heads on the steps above. But as heights increase, stairwells take more floor space.

Advantage can sometimes be taken of different requirements for different uses on the same floor. Ventilation ducts can sometimes run under the ceiling in a bookstack and leave greater heights in adjacent reading areas.

3. How thick should the floors be from ceiling to floor level above? The answer will depend on bay and module sizes which were discussed in Section 12.3; on the weight to be carried and the type of construction, which is dealt with in Chapter 13; on what mechanical services a floor is to contain between the finished ceiling below and the finished floor above; and, last but not least, on the ingenuity of the mechanical and structural engineers and the care with which they work. These last two points are discussed briefly here.

Other things being equal, the larger the bay size, the heavier the floor beams or flat slabs required, and the greater the thickness of the floors. If the plans provide for floors everywhere in the building on which bookstacks can be placed, something that should be required in most libraries, any bay size over 27 ft (8.230) square will tend to require more steel and extra thickness, which in turn takes additional cubage. Library floors that will hold bookstacks anywhere have been made with flat-slab construction no more than 8 in. (203 mm) thick and with bays 18 ft (5.486) square. With reinforced concrete slabs, the floors need be no more than 12 or

13 in. (305 mm or 330 mm) thick and with bays up to 27 ft (8.230) square if they do not have to provide space for ducts and pipes. These thicknesses are structural and do not include the finished floor or ceiling. It should be noted that additional thickness will likely be required in earthquake country to resist lateral forces.

Space required for the utility services varies greatly. Plumbing and wiring require little in the way of additional thickness for floors. Air ducts for heating, ventilation, and air conditioning involve much more, although heating pipes for steam and hot water without ventilation take little space. Complications always arise when air ducts have to cross each other. If the ventilation engineer is careless or lacks ingenuity, a floor thickness of up to 5 ft (1.524) may be required to include the structural floor itself, space for ducts, for plumbing, and also for recessing the lighting fixtures into the ceiling, something that is often desirable. It seems absurd, however, to use floors 5 ft (1.524) thick, and then reduce clear ceiling heights to as little perhaps as 8 ft (2.438). Too large a proportion goes into space, most of which is not used. Vertical runs and distribution of the ventilation take more floor space but often reduce total costs, if one takes into account the additional height in the underfloor space required by horizontal runs for ventilation ducts. Clearly, this subject requires careful analysis by the architect and engineers.

4. *Are mezzanines desirable?* The answer to this question involves aesthetics, function, and cost. The excessively high ceilings of the past are no longer required functionally, and yet one should hesitate to plan a large library building today with no room in it higher than strictly functional needs demand. A mezzanine over part of a level (typically no more than 33 percent to qualify for the code definition of a mezzanine) might make up for all or a large share of the extra cost of providing an area which would give the desired effect of greater spaciousness. As long as the added level is classified in the building code as a mezzanine, most codes will allow emergency exiting via the main floor.

If the formula suggested earlier is assumed to be correct for comparative purposes, a floor 17 ft (5.182) high may cost some 20 percent more than one of a minimum height. If 75 percent of this floor has a mezzanine over it and only 25 percent of it is full height, the construction would add something like 5 percent to the construction cost of the floor as a whole. It should be noted, however, that many codes would regard a mezzanine of this size as a separate floor; exiting and other requirements thus are somewhat different than for a mezzanine as defined by the code. If the floor is not a mezzanine, there must be at least two protected routes of egress directly from that floor. If it is a mezzanine, egress may be via the floor below. Even so, in our example, if the floor described is one of five in a building and the others have low ceilings, the increase in average construction cost of the whole building is cut to only 1 percent. In order to obtain one spacious room, this addition might well be worthwhile, depending on the local code requirements. The cost comparisons are at best approximations and will differ, of course, in different places under different conditions; the architect should be asked to check them.

Let us see now what would happen if, instead of using a mezzanine over part of the floor, the whole floor were made 12 ft (3.658) high in the clear, one-fourth of it for a large reading area and the remainder for service placed in the earlier plan on or under the mezzanine. The increase in the cost of the whole area—using the same formula for cost approximation for increased height as before—would be about 10 percent, or 5 percent more than with the mezzanine arrangement. (The cost of the furniture and equipment on the mezzanines must not be forgotten.) These percentages are simply rough estimates to illustrate the problem, but they indicate that if a mezzanine covers the major portion of a floor level and a clear height of 12 ft (3.658) or more is wanted for aesthetic reasons in at least one large reading area, it is not a luxury to go up to 16 or 17 ft (4.876 or 5.182) for the part without a mezzanine, if the area concerned is not too large. Angus Snead Macdonald once said that a mezzanine, to be practicable from the cost point of view, must occupy at least 60 percent of the floor area. The code implications mentioned above must not be forgotten. The general principles underlying these observations are confirmed by talks with architects and contractors.

While the chief value of a mezzanine suggested above is to make it possible and reasonably economical to have a room two stack levels or higher on part of a floor, another advantage is to provide for the possibility of future expansion by adding a mezzanine at a later date. Where this is done, provisions for structural support must be made in the initial construction, and provisions should be made then for ventilation, book lifts, elevators, stairs, and utilities. It should be noted that, when the mezzanine is added, even though the structure is designed for the additional weight, doubling of the load will cause some deflection which can cause cracks in plaster ceilings or doors that stick on the floor below. Even so, such a plan can provide excellent expansion possibilities, particularly in a branch library where adding space in the future may be particularly difficult due to the disposition of the library in the host department.

Another point to be considered in the planning of a mezzanine is that noise is a problem if the spaces created are open to each other. It is especially a problem where the mezzanine creates a natural theater, a situation which should be avoided in a library. A central, open light well can create similar problems, as was the case in the Meyer Library at Stanford University before the well was glazed in.

5. *What considerations should be kept in mind when determining the preferable size and number of floor levels?* The site chosen may have much to do with this, as was seen in Chapter 11. The question often cannot be answered properly until the architect has undertaken some study of the program requirements in relation to the site. Even so, some discussion would seem to be in order.

No set formula can be recommended for size and number of levels. Until the advent of mechanical systems and improved lighting techniques, the dimensions and shape of library buildings were determined to a considerable extent by lighting and ventilating requirements. Often the extreme limit in the depth of a building was placed at 80 ft (24.384) so that no part of it would be more than 40 ft (12.192) from windows. Skylights over the center, with a great hall below and galleries on the outside, made somewhat deeper buildings possible. The situation has now changed basically. Artificial light and ventilation can be relied on, and windows can be reduced to a minimum if desired.

Some persons with considerable knowledge of the problems involved have suggested that a library of up to 10,000 sq ft (929 m²) should be kept on one floor if possible, and there should not be three levels unless 20,000 sq ft (1858 m²) is exceeded. However, a library with 50,000 sq ft (4645 m²) on a single floor can work perfectly well if properly arranged. Where there are three levels, there is advantage in making the entry level the middle of the three so that few persons will regularly have to go up or down more than one floor at a time. Total areas of the exterior walls and roof will have considerable effect on costs, both in terms of construction and ongoing operating costs. In general, the nearer the building is to a square and the fewer the floor levels, the less the wall cost; the more levels, the less the roof cost.

How many levels high can a library building have from the points of view of function and cost? Four factors should be taken into consideration.

a. In general, the larger the square footage on each floor, the smaller the percentage of the total gross square footage that is required for stairwells, elevators, and book lifts, and the smaller the proportion of outside wall to total square footage.

b. If all parts of the building used regularly by readers are no more than two flights of stairs above or below the entrance, passenger elevator service can be minimized and funds saved for other purposes. A site on a hillside with windows on one or more basement levels is advantageous in this connection.

c. If the librarian expects to provide service and supervision on each level, the number of levels should be held to a minimum in order to reduce the number of posts to be covered by the staff.

d. It is important in many if not most libraries to have the entrance level—whether it is called the main, first, or ground floor—large enough to house the central services of the library. These include the main information and circulation desks, the reference and bibliographical collections and services, the public catalog, and in many libraries the current periodicals and the closed reserved-book collections. It is also desirable that as many reader seats as possible be placed on this floor, or be easily accessible, particularly in a library with closed stacks. While it is not essential, there may still be an advantage to providing quarters for the members of the processing staff who are directly responsible for the various services and for the public catalog. In a small research or academic library these services may require more than one-half of the total net floor area. Even in a library with 100,000 volumes and seating 300 readers, this figure should probably not be reduced to under one-third. But in a university or research library with large book collections which occupy up to one-half of the total floor area, and particularly where there is a considerable percentage of the seating scattered in one way or another through the stacks, additional floors are not so serious, although the effect on the elevator problem should not be forgotten.

Tower stacks, such as those at the University of Massachusetts and California Institute of Technology, have not been found satisfactory. The ones at Yale's Sterling Library and Columbia's Butler Library are large enough in area so that they are less troublesome. Harvard's Widener Library has a large enough area per floor so that its ten stack floor levels are not a serious inconvenience, although a user who is concerned with material in widely different fields may find that a tiresome amount of walking and stair climbing is involved. Some would suggest that stack floors as large as the A level in Princeton's Firestone Library (fig. 12.11) and the National Library of Medicine (fig. 12.12) are too large for convenient use, because the traffic patterns tend to become too complicated. However, the lowest level of Stanford's Green Library is quite convenient to use though it extends 643 ft (195.830) from north to south and has 75,000 sq ft (6970 m²).

If the total required floor area in a library is as large as 80,000 sq ft (say, 7430 m²), three or four or even five floors can properly be considered. Even if extra elevator service is required, the increased number of floors will not be unduly expensive and inconvenient. The value of the available ground space and the desirability of limited ground coverage must also be considered. Skyscrapers are the only economical form for construction on Wall Street. The aesthetic effect should also be considered in relation to local conditions.

The total floor area that can satisfactorily be included in a library building before it becomes so unwieldy as to be avoided is a problem that, with the rapid increase in the collections and the number of seating accommodations called for, will have to be faced in our larger libraries in the years directly ahead. However, the reader quickly learns the library layout (at Northwestern, for example),

and the size should not be too serious a problem. Several library buildings in the 500,000 sq ft (46,440 m²) range exist, and while they may require some getting used to, they are manageable.

6. *Does vertical transportation and mechanical equipment affect height problems?* Usually not, except that there is less money for usable space if an unnecessary amount is expended for transportation. Only rarely does an elevator machinery room need to be on the roof, and able engineers can solve that problem in nearly all cases in order not to require a rooftop eyesore. Mechanical space can be a more difficult problem, especially if an air conditioning cooling tower must go on the roof. If a machine room requires head room higher than the library requires, and if soil conditions prevent a lowered mechanical room in the basement, the building height will probably be increased. Mechanical needs can usually be provided in an area with low head room or in a building extension under landscaping.

The preceding comments in relation to building height and module illustrate the problems involved. Their solutions may differ in a closed-access research collection, such as the American Antiquarian Society, the Huntington Library, or the New York Public Library, from those for an open-access academic library. The early structural concepts should respond to the facility program, the site, the selected module, the economies of various structural systems at the time, the distribution of the mechanical systems, the number of floors, and other factors. It is clear that the selection and application of a structural system must be carefully planned, for, once decided upon, it is usually difficult to change at a later date.

12.4 Internal Configuration of Major Elements

Chapter 5 and, to a lesser degree, the other chapters on programming discuss in some detail the interrelationships of various functions of the library. One of the essential characteristics of a functional building is the accessibility of all parts with a minimum of disturbance. If planning is to produce satisfactory traffic patterns, it must take into account the problems of supervision and control of the building and its exits, facilities for communication and vertical transportation,

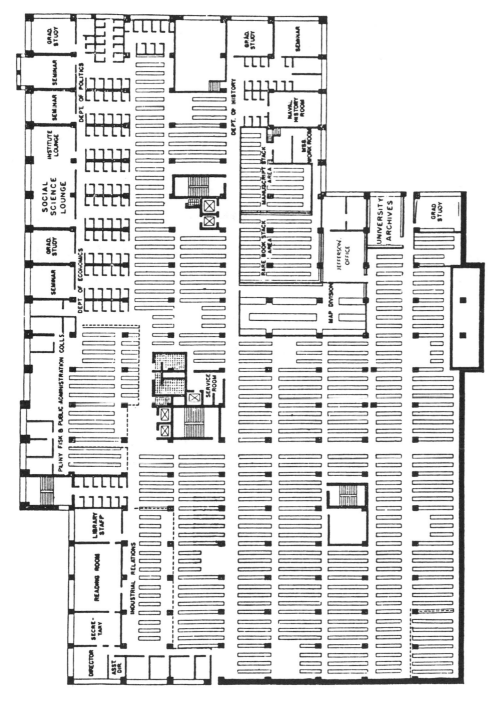

FIGURE 12.11 Princeton University Firestone Library, A floor. Note the very large stack area, which has tremendous book capacity but a more complicated circulation pattern than that in figure 12.12. Only two of the nine main aisles run from one end of the area to the other. However, students probably enjoy the possibility of a unique hideaway. (The B and C levels were expanded underground in 1970.)

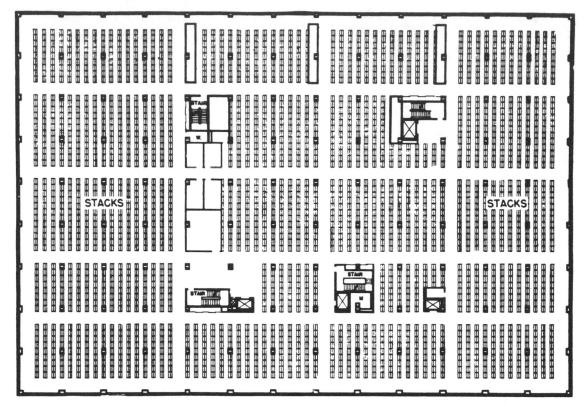

FIGURE 12.12 National Library of Medicine, B level. A very large stack area with a simple circulation pattern. No one of the four cores intrudes on a main aisle. Each of the eleven main aisles goes through from one side of the building to the other.

the location of various fixed elements, and means of minimizing noise and other distractions. Clearly the relationships of the many functional areas are involved as well.

Supervision and Control. Most librarians would rather help than supervise those who use their buildings; they have no desire to act as police officers and are eager to make controls as inconspicuous as possible if they cannot be eliminated. Fortunately, less supervision is required now than was thought necessary earlier in this century when closed-access libraries were the accepted standard. Today students, both graduates and undergraduates, seem to be more serious than their predecessors and most come to the library for study rather than for social purposes. There will always be exceptions, and, in some cases, the design of the library can regrettably promote unwanted social activities. Most libraries in the United States and Canada now admit students to the stacks, where close supervision is impossible; consequently, it is hard to justify intensive supervision of reading rooms. At least three out of four students

prefer individual seating; and seating of this kind, which is being provided generously, discourages conversation in reading areas and hence reduces the need for supervision. Improved acoustics, better traffic patterns, better designed carrels, and improved seating layouts help to reduce noise, confusion, and create an atmosphere conducive to orderly behavior. Finally, there is a realization that the most economical, and in many ways the most satisfactory, location for control is at the building's exit or exits.

It should be emphasized that no one advocates supervision anywhere in a library if it can be eliminated without serious consequences. Unfortunately, students seem to be tempted to appropriate library materials for themselves; the problem is particularly serious in the case of reserved books. Attendants at the exits cannot effectively search those who leave the building; books can be concealed in clothing, particularly during the winter; and electronic systems can be circumvented. If it is known that repeated unauthorized borrowing is a serious offense punishable by dismissal or suspension, inspection at the exits can be more effective than the traditional method of reading-room supervision. Given the advent of the electronic book-detection systems, most new buildings provide either for control at the exits or for no control at all.

Control at the exits is no safeguard against theft of rare books by professional thieves; the only satisfactory procedure is to keep very valuable materials in closed stacks, make them available only to persons who have signed for them, supervise their use, and check them in immediately on their return, before the reader leaves, in order to make sure that they have not been mutilated. Exit controls can be expected, however, to prevent unauthorized borrowing by forgetful or impatient professors and students, and to deter deliberate theft. If individuals must conceal a book or mutilate its binding to get it past the controls, they can hardly pretend that it has been taken thoughtlessly rather than deliberately.

It may be suggested also that, though controls may not seem necessary at the time a building is planned, conditions do change. The building should be planned, therefore, so that staffed exit controls, with or without an electronic book detection system, can be provided at some later date without expensive alterations and without harming the appearance of the lobbies.

Various methods of exit control are possible. Turnstiles were used for some years in the Widener Library at Harvard, and have been used at the New York Public Library for a long period. It should be noted that persons entering a building may also be required to pass through turnstiles, as they are at Princeton's Firestone Library. Either electric eyes or turnstiles can be used to count those who enter, though neither can be relied upon for a completely accurate count. Also, as a typical turnstile provides about 16 in. (406 mm) for passage, an alternative means of passage must be provided for some who are handicapped. Generally though, turnstiles provide a fairly positive means of traffic control which is certainly more effective than an attendant or merely relying on signs.

Velour-covered ropes or railings on stanchions of some kind can be used to channel readers through a narrow lane past a desk. At the Lamont Library as many as four exit lanes can be opened at one time in the main entrance (see fig. 12.13), but only half of these have proved to be necessary in order to handle the traffic without forcing students to line up. In this regard, it may be prudent to provide for excess capacity, for it would be very difficult to add it later if it is found to be needed, and the cost initially is small in relation to the total project.

A third method, which has been used in the Widener Library since the unattractive turnstiles were removed, is to leave a passage more than 4 ft (1.220) wide with a counter on the right-hand side behind which an attendant sits on a high stool (see fig. 12.14). This arrangement has proved to be reasonably satisfactory at Widener, which is used most by professors and graduate students. In an undergraduate library, where there is very heavy traffic just before each class period begins, and in Widener at times of peak loads, narrow passages would be preferable if not as pleasant. Furthermore, an electronic book detection system would serve to advantage.

There are several types of electronic detection systems suitable for use in libraries, and each will have its own set of facility requirements. It is suggested that the library staff should review the literature, perhaps visit several different installations, and select a specific system for which the control area should be designed. In determining the ideal facility arrangements, it is essential to consult an expert engineering representative of the firm selected, as sales representatives frequently are not aware of some of the details of an ideal installation. Besides the obvious requirements for power, the more subtle requirements of spacing and layout may be derived from such a consultation. Failure to follow this procedure can result in considerable frustration resulting from false alarms, ineffective detection, or inadequate response to an alarm when it occurs. It should always be recognized that any system can be circumvented by the intentional thief. Rare books and perhaps current journals, reserves, and other attractive or heavily used materials often will require more intense supervision.

Control counters may also serve as information desks where the stranger can obtain directions, which are often needed in any large library. Counters are preferable to desks, because it is not convenient for readers to show books on a low surface; and height of 39 in. (990 mm) is suggested because some persons feel that this is high enough to lift a heavy briefcase. A portion of the control booth or counter may be constructed with a

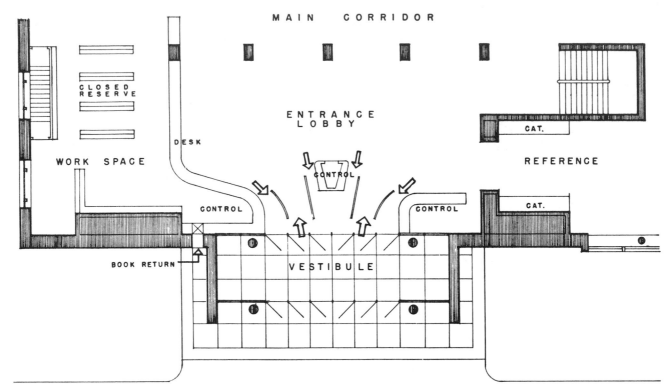

FIGURE 12.13. Harvard University, Lamont Library, main exit control. There are six doors between the vestibule and lobby. Door handles are on the vestibule side of only the second and fifth, counting from left to right. On the inside these doors are labeled "No Exit." Door 1 is always in use when the building is open. Doors 3, 4, and 6 can be used whenever necessary, as each has a control station available, but when not in use, they are blocked by bars.

lower, table-height surface, so that the attendant can easily inspect shopping bags or backpacks. For use when not standing, the attendant should be provided with a high stool having a back and footrest or a platform in the kneehole of the counter. A slightly raised floor can aid the inspection process, and with a raised floor, a standard secretarial chair should be adequate. The booth should be provided with a phone. Other features may include a panic alert button, first aid supplies, and a covered display area in the counter for a campus map, library diagrams, or other information that may aid the visitor. It should be possible for the attendant to reach the outside door quickly if necessary.

A long control desk at the exit can in some cases serve also as the main circulation desk and even as the desk for service of books on closed reserve, as at Lamont. If this is possible, there are advantages. The noise and confusion that circulation services always create is confined to the entrance lobby; the number of staff members who must be on duty during quiet periods is reduced, a fact which may be an important financial consideration; and the reader may avoid having

books checked twice, once when they are charged out and again upon leaving the building. On the other hand, staff may not juggle effectively the task of exit checking with circulation service. The former is likely to suffer. Electronic exit review can help solve this quandary.

Nothing has been said thus far of how many entrances and exits may be needed. Most libraries, of course, must have a separate shipping and receiving entrance, which may be available for use by members of the staff. Each public entrance and exit is expensive; attendants must be paid and floor space must be provided in the building plans. Moreover, the whole traffic and security problem within the building can be simplified if there is a single entrance and exit. In a large library, however, traffic is often so heavy and distances so great that a second controlled entrance and exit is essential. Fire laws may require it; if they do not, emergency exits with crash locks or panic hardware and an alarm system with a loud local alarm and perhaps a remote signal should be available.

Control of an additional exit may require payment of two or three salaries in a library

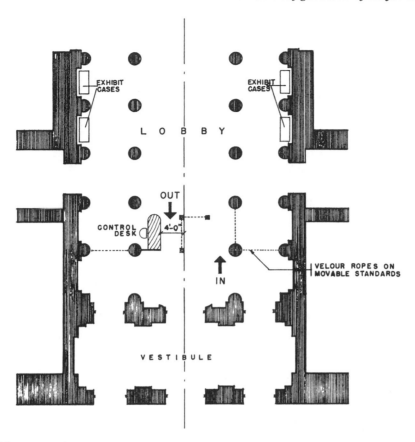

FIGURE 12.14 Harvard University, Widener Library, main exit control. Incoming traffic automatically keeps to the right. Persons leaving the building automatically keep to the right past the control desk. This arrangement can easily be adapted for any of the several book-detection systems, although the remote location will always require a staffed position. Being near a service point can be an advantage in this regard.

that is open for 75 to 100 or more hours a week; moreover, a secondary exit will normally be used considerably less than the main one and may not be a suitable place for circulation or reserved-book services; there may be a problem in keeping the attendant profitably occupied. In the Lamont Library at Harvard a portion of the reserved-book collection was once kept behind the desk at the now-closed secondary entrance (see fig. 12.15), which is on a different floor level from the main entrance. In the Widener Library, the second entrance is also on a different level from the front door and controls a secondary entrance to the bookstack, which is a great convenience in a ten-level stack (see fig. 12.16). Fire regulations require that two exits be provided in both Widener and Lamont at all times they are open.

Elsewhere, however, there are equally large buildings operating under regulations that call for one regular exit, supplemented by emergency exits guarded by electrical or mechanical alarms which operate automatically if the door is opened. This type of exit control is fairly effective if it is very obvious that use of the exit will sound an alarm. A clearly visable sign stating "Emergency exit only—Exit sounds alarm" will help. A crash lock can be broken, of course, and a thief or errant student can escape even though there is an effective alarm system. Where a serious problem is expected, the alarm system can be augmented with television surveillance, such as that at the Perry-Castañeda Library at the University of Texas, Austin. Proliferation of entrances should be discouraged in almost all instances.

A discussion of problems of control and supervision would be incomplete if it did not mention the difficulties that sometimes occur when there are outdoor reading terraces. These can be attractive, and some architects delight in them, but their disadvantages ought not to be overlooked. Unless they are carefully designed so that external access is at least difficult, books can be dropped from them to

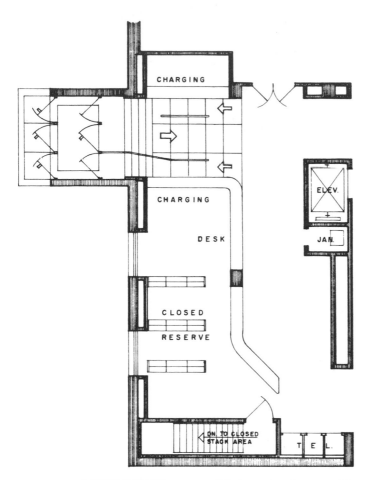

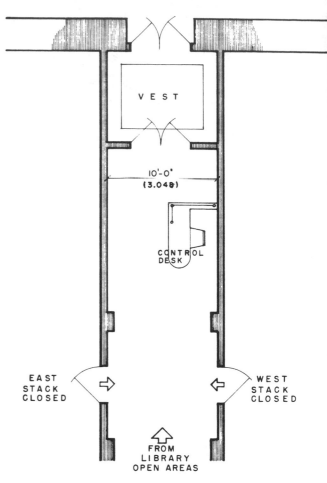

FIGURE 12.15 Harvard University, Lamont Library, secondary exit control (no longer in use). At this entrance, only the middle door is provided with a handle on the outside. The reader goes down five steps immediately after entering which almost automatically restricts the use of this entrance.

FIGURE 12.16 Harvard University, Widener Library, secondary exit control at ground level. Checking counter is on the right as one leaves. Secondary stack entrances a few feet from the door are controlled by pushbutton from the desk; thus stacks are available only on request to the holders of permits. Because this type of entrance must be staffed, it may not be justified in times of operating budget restraint.

a waiting confederate or to the ground if a secluded spot is available. Dust and air pollution may make them unsatisfactory places for reading and, in most sections of this country, the number of dry and warm days when they can be used is discouragingly small. Operable windows create similar problems.

Entrances and exits are where traffic patterns begin and end; the decisions made regarding them also affect the security of the library's collections and its operating costs. It is important, therefore, that entrance lobbies be designed with a view to installation of control desks in the future if not at once, with space for channeling past a desk those who are leaving, and with the capacity to handle rush-hour traffic.

Facilities for Vertical Transportation and Communication. Unless a library is very small

or on a single level, mechanical and/or electronic devices for communication will probably be needed when books and people move from one floor to another and where service points, collections, and staff areas are widely distributed. These considerations will need initial work during schematics, though detailing them will be part of later design phases. A discussion of communication and vertical transportation must consider stairs, ramps, escalators, book lifts, elevators, conveyor belts, and pneumatic tubes. (Other communication devices are dealt with in Section 3.2. The needs of telephones, public-address systems, TelAutograph, Teletype, television, and computer terminals may affect the schematic planning and are important in the specifications document, but they are commonly detailed in design development or construction documents.) The uses of these varied devices will be discussed as a means of helping the librarian to decide what is needed and of indicating something of library requirements to architects and engineers.

The desirable number of stairways will depend, of course, on the amount of traffic, the size of floor levels, and, to some extent, the total floor area of the building. Local building regulations and fire codes may also impose specific requirements. They often state that no place in a building shall be more than a limited distance—sometimes 100 ft (30.000)—from a stairway providing direct access to an exit from the building. The codes often permit only one open stairway; that is, only one outside a fireproof enclosure with closed doors at each level. They may permit the open stairway on only one level; if it is open on the first floor, it must be enclosed at the second or the basement level. They may also determine the stair widths according to a formula or formulas based on occupancy (discussed later) of the floor or floors that are served.

Some buildings do not come under code restrictions, either because there is no applicable state law or local regulation or because the institution is exempt for one reason or another; sometimes a limited exemption can be obtained if sprinkler systems are installed. Fire risks are discussed in Chapters 5 and 13. No building should be planned without checking the codes and regulations to which it must conform.

The location of both main and subsidiary stairways is important; indeed, it is usually a primary factor in determining floor layouts. Stairways should be convenient for use, and reasonably conspicuous if students are to find them readily and use them instead of looking for mechanical transportation; on the other hand, they should not be allowed to obstruct the major traffic arteries on each floor. Architects may recommend that open stairways, often monumental ones, rise from the main floor as an architectural and aesthetic feature. A monumental stairway in a small library may be out of proportion, but it can be attractive and also functional in a large building.

Stairways are often placed in one or more building cores, together with elevator shafts, shear walls, duct shafts, toilets, and other vertical services, leaving the remainder of the building as flexible and adaptable as possible. Such a core will extend in a stack from the basement through the top floor. This plan also reduces the extent of the interior walls that will be required. Another possibility is to place the main stairway immediately adjacent to the main entrance and next to an outside wall, leaving the rest of the building unobstructed by a permanent installation. As has been noted, however, the fire laws and also the amount of use usually necessitate at least one secondary stairway, and large buildings require more than one; in some cases a stairway in each corner may be desirable in addition to the central stairway.

Decisions on the steepness of stairs involve questions of design, comfort, and the use of space. If a stairway ascends too gradually, space will be wasted and many persons will find it awkward to climb. If stairs are too steep, many persons will find them difficult to ascend or descend. In general, the most acceptable height for risers is no more than 7½ in. (190 mm), and risers of less than 6 or 6½ in. (152 mm or 165 mm) should be avoided. Treads may vary from 10½ to 12 in. (266 mm to 304 mm). Bookstack stairs may be steeper, particularly if the number of levels is limited. The following simple formulas are often used:

1. The product of the riser and the tread should be between 70 and 77 in. sq (or about .045 m² to .050 m²).

2. The riser plus the tread should be from 17 to 17½ in. (432 mm to 444 mm).

3. The sum of the tread plus twice the riser should be between 20 and 25 in. (508 mm to 635 mm), preferably between 24 and 25 in. (610 mm and 635 mm).

Decisions on stair widths depend primarily on the occupancy of the building or the traffic expected at times of peak load. Indeed, many decisions in library planning must be based on anticipated peak loads which often are established by the code or negotiated with code authorities. For main stairs in academic institutions, these peaks normally occur when classes change. However, the minimum width of the stairs and exit routes will be established for emergencies such as fire; at such times traffic can be expected to move in a single direction making the full width available, and alternate routes of egress may be used. The Uniform Building Code, for example, specifies a minimum width for an exit route or stair of 44 in. (1.118) including the handrails for an occupancy of 50 or more people. Where the occupancy is less than 50, a stair 36 in. (914 mm) wide is permitted. The handrails may project into the required space no more than 3½ in. (89 mm) from each side. The total width of all exits from a given floor must provide at least 12 in. (304 mm) for each 50 people served on that floor. For the first adjacent floor that must exit through the same passage, 6 in. (152 mm) for each 50 people is added, and for each subsequent floor 3 in. (76 mm) is added for each group of 50 occupants. The maximum width of a stair between handrails is 88 in. (2.234) in this particular code.

The handrail must be placed from 30 to 34 in. (762 mm to 864 mm) above the nosing of the tread. There must be a landing for every 12 ft (3.658) of vertical rise. Where a landing requires a guardrail, it must be 42 in. (1.066) high, and the space below the rail must be protected so that a 9 in. (228 mm) sphere cannot be passed through. This also applies to stair-tread rails where there is an exposed edge.

Numerous other details are typically specified in the code, including dimensions of the handrail and construction of the stair. It should be remembered that local authorities may apply different code requirements, and, of course, these will be controlling.

Concerning handrails, where a code does not specify diameter or configuration, it is wise to make them of modest diameter (a golf ball is better than a tennis ball) and configuration so that a falling person can immediately get a good grip from the top. Be sure they extend smoothly around turns, are of material so hard that cracks or splintering will not occur and so constituted that it will not get uncomfortably hot if it stands in a baking sun, are free of sharp edges, are very firmly anchored, and start and end in a way that clothing can never get caught. Architects must not make them major design features, even if the stair is monumental, for they quickly can lose their utility if over-scaled.

The occupancy is generally established by a formula which, in a large library, can result in an unrealistic number. However, if the building is being designed for sufficient flexibility for future use—for example, as an office building—this factor should be considered in establishing the occupancy.

Occupancy levels in some cases can be negotiated, but care must be taken to be realistic in evaluating maximum potential occupancy loads if the proscribed formula is not used, as it is often difficult to add stairs at a future date. A recent code specifies that for assembly areas such as an auditorium one should calculate 7 sq ft (0.65 m²) for each occupant; for conference rooms it is one occupant for each 15 sq ft (1.39 m²); classrooms and lounges are one for 20 sq ft (1.86 m²); library reading rooms are one for 50 sq ft (4.65 m²); offices are one for 100 sq ft (9.29 m²); and warehouses, which may be regarded as stack areas, require providing for one occupant for each 300 sq ft (27.87 m²). While this information may be used to estimate the occupant load, the local governing codes should be used to establish the final design.

If a stairway is to be a fire exit, it must lead as directly as possible to an outside door, and this door must always be made to open without a key from the inside during periods when the building is open to the public. All library stairways should have handrailings. A railing that goes a short distance beyond the bottom step will help those who are handicapped, but it must be so installed that it is not a hazard for persons rounding the corner to go up the stairs.

Clearly, the code requirements apply primarily to the emergency exiting requirements of the building, and a main central stair often does not serve this purpose. The width of the main stair becomes a design question. In most libraries a width of 5 ft (1.524) is a typical minimum for a main stair; 8 ft (2.438) might be considered generous. Some code authorities might require an intermediate handrail if the stair exceeds 88 in. (2.234) in width, although it can often be argued that if this stair is not a required exit, the intermediate rail is not required. Monumental stairs 15 or 20 ft (4.572 or 6.096) wide sometimes do not have an intermediate handrail, although this type of stair is not encouraged.

Architects sometimes propose circular stairs because of their aesthetic advantages, but they are to be avoided in most cases. If the narrow edge of the circular stair tread is wide enough to be reasonably safe, considerable space must be left in the center; legal requirements often set a minimum diameter for the well. The total floor area required by an adequate circular stairwell is considerably greater than that needed for a direct stairway or for one going around one, two, or even three corners. This is particularly apparent if it is realized that the space immediately outside the circle is ordinarily useless for library purposes because of its shape. If a circular stairway is to be installed in spite of these disadvantages, it should be designed, in countries where pedestrians normally keep to the right, so that the person going downstairs on the right uses the wide end instead of the narrow end of the tread; this will reduce to some extent the dangers presented by any nonrectangular stair tread. Of course, where pedestrians keep to the left, a stairway rising counterclockwise is indicated. It appears that in too few instances this principle has been taken into account. (See figs. 12.17 and 12.18 for circular and rectangular stairs.)

When stairs turn a corner at a landing, particularly if they are heavily used, try to arrange the landing width on the down side a full stair tread wider, as shown in fig. 12.18.

Apropos of stairways and safety, one further warning may be offered: always avoid a flight of only two steps; a single step is even worse. In some places it is illegal to create a hazard in this way, but the infraction cannot be excused whether it is an offense against the law or only against common sense. If a library is afflicted with such stairs, they should be properly marked and lighted. In some cases it may be possible to replace them with ramps. Another danger is the underside of stairs, which should be protected or blocked to prevent one from walking below the rising stair and butting one's head, a condition which is all too prevalent in circular stairs.

Obviously, it should be possible to move books by truck throughout a library building with a minimum of trouble, yet architects of earlier days sometimes placed short flights of steps at a variety of points in a building. The old library at Cornell, now completely rehabilitated as the Uris Undergraduate Library, was an example of this style.

Steep ramps are to be avoided if book trucks must traverse them, and any slope greater than 5 percent will be difficult for a person on crutches. A 5 percent incline entails 80 ft of ramp for only 4 ft in altitude (20 m of ramp for 1 m of altitude); a 10 percent gradient takes only half this space for the same rise, and 10 percent should be the limit even for short ramps. A typical code maximum slope is 1 in 12, or about 8 percent. A nonskid surface is essential on all ramps, and handrails

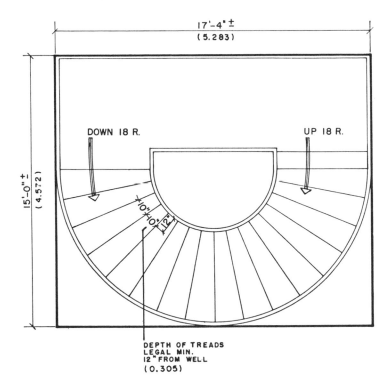

AREA USED: 17'-4" x 15'-0" = 260 SQ. FT.
(5.283 X 4.572 = 24.154 SQ. m)

FIGURE 12.17 Circular stairway. The total area required for circular stairs exceeds that for rectangular stairs with landings. The space around the stairway on each floor is less usable because of its shape. It is more expensive to construct, particularly if enclosed by walls. It is dangerous because of the varying depth of each tread. If circular stairs are used, persons going downstairs should go counterclockwise, as shown in the drawing, so that when walking to the right, they are on the wider part of the treads. (Persons should go down clockwise in countries where people walk to the left and drive cars on the left.)

should be provided. If a change in level is required at the approach to a staff elevator, a ramp is preferable to stairs, but the change in level should be avoided altogether if possible. A ramp may be the lesser evil when an addition is made to an old library and it is impossible to make floor levels match.

Escalators, which can handle a large volume of traffic and use relatively little power, can be useful in some cases. They function continually without requiring an operator. It is doubtful, however, that any library, even a very large one, can afford to install them between as many as four levels, and it is generally out of the question to go beyond three. For heavy traffic between only two levels, they

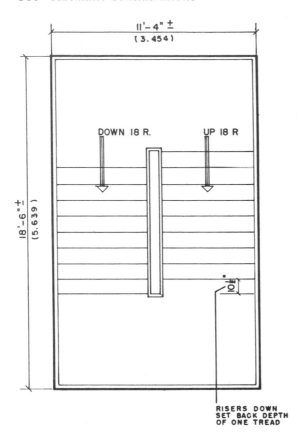

AREA USED: 18'-6"x 11'-4" = 210 SQ. FT
(5.639 X 3.454 = 19.50 SQ. m)

FIGURE 12.18 Normal stairway. It takes less space, is safer, but in some ways is less attractive aesthetically than a circular stairway. Rails on both sides are often required by code.

may be both useful and economical, as in the University of Connecticut Library and in the Columbia Law School Library where every reader must go up one high-ceiling level to reach the library from the floor below. However, at the University of Minnesota, the escalator was removed in the late 1970s at considerable cost because it monopolized some of the most desirable space on the main floor and the lower level entrance-exit had been closed except in the winter. Energy costs were thereby significantly reduced. In the University of Miami Library in Coral Gables, escalators go from the first to the third floor, with three lifts in all, as two are used between the first and second floors. These escalators go up only, although they can be reversed at closing time. Service in both directions at the same time would cost twice as much and would require twice as much space. It was estimated at Coral Gables that, though only of medium

width, these escalators have a greater capacity than four elevators, and cost less for space, installation, and operation; it is exceedingly doubtful that four elevators would have been necessary to handle the traffic in question. Because of their expense, escalators can only be justified where there are exceptionally heavy flows of traffic.

The location of escalators calls for careful consideration, and each end should be located where it will not obstruct traffic. Particular care is necessary if more than two levels are involved. It is also essential that escalators be very carefully installed; they must be tailor-made for the building if they are not to be unduly noisy. Special fire-protection devices may also be required.

Book lifts, sometimes called dumb waiters, vary widely in size; some are only large enough to hold a folio volume; others will take a loaded book truck. A few book lifts survive that must be operated manually by pulling a rope, but electric power and pushbutton controls now prevail. One disadvantage of any book lift is that, if no staff member is stationed at the level to which the lift is sent, the person who loads the lift must climb up or down stairs to unload it; even in a large library, where an attendant is stationed at each level, confusion may result if the attendant is temporarily absent. Also, if the lift is too small to handle a truck, its use almost inevitably involves at least one or two extra handlings of each book transported. It is recommended that, as a minimum, all lifts be able to accommodate a large book truck and an attendant member of staff, which, of course, means that the recommended lift is what we would call an elevator in this country. Many book lifts in libraries are rarely used; however, in a branch library, with no elevator conveniently located in or next to the library, a book truck lift is usually essential.

Wear and tear in handling books is an important consideration; staff, particularly when working under pressure, are inclined to throw books into a lift. For many years at the New York Public Library, thousands of books, sometimes 5000 a day, were transported between the stacks and the main reading room by book lift, and the resultant damage to bindings was serious. Yet if a full-fledged elevator is beyond the library's means, a book lift, particularly if large enough to carry a truck, is better than nothing. If the lift is to carry a book truck, it must, of course, open at the floor level, not at counter height. In this type of installation, building codes may require fire-resistant shafts, and insurance rates may be affected.

Elevators are clearly preferable to book lifts in every respect but one: they are more expensive. The cost, in a small library, may represent a substantial fraction of the total expenditure for construction. It will be affected by several factors. Is the elevator propelled by cables or water or oil-driven pistons? What is the size of the cab? What is the maximum weight to be carried? What is the total length of the rise? What speed is stipulated? How complex are the controls required to provide service without an operator? Is there to be an accurate leveling device?

Electrically powered elevators using cables are always used in high buildings, and often in others. Elevators propelled by water or oil-driven pistons are sometimes used in lower buildings, and they are considerably less expensive to install. They are recommended where economies force this choice, and, in fact, they have in recent years been used in most new libraries in the United Kingdom.

The machinery for electrically operated cable elevators is usually located in a penthouse rather than in the basement; this saves in costs of installation and operation, reduces wear and tear on the machinery, and helps to minimize noise enough to obviate special acoustic treatment. Where there is a desire to reduce the height of the penthouse for architectural reasons, the machinery can be placed in the basement. If the basement machine room is near reading or staff areas, it will need heavy internal sound absorbent treatment, including an excellent door gasket. When heavy loads are to be handled and speed is not important, what is known as two-to-one roping is used instead of one-to-one.

The number of passenger-elevator cabs that will be needed depends on the volume of traffic and the waiting period that will be tolerated, the capacity of the cabs, and their speed. Traffic customarily is measured by the number of persons to be transported in a five-minute peak-load period, and certain standard formulas can be used. These take into account the time required for a full-speed round trip without stops, plus time for accelerating and slowing down at each stop, time for leveling at each stop, time for opening and closing gates and doors, time for passengers to move in and out, lost time resulting from false stops, standing time at top and bottom floors, and reaction time of the operator if there is one. The wider the doors, the more rapidly passengers can move in and out; doors that open at the center of the wide side of the cab speed up operation to a considerable extent.

Nearly all new elevators are automatic, and, if wages are to be saved by eliminating operators, automatic elevators must be installed. These are of three principal types. The simplest responds to the first button pushed and does not "remember" any other calls. The selective-collective type answers only calls in the direction in which the car is moving. Finally, a fully automatic system can be adjusted to operate in a variety of ways designed to suit traffic demands of different levels and of different times of day. For instance, it can automatically proceed to a "home" floor when not in use. The more complicated the controls, the more the elevator costs. Small libraries are rarely justified in installing anything but the simplest type. Safety devices, however, should always be used to prevent the car from moving when doors are open. Automatic leveling devices appropriate for heavy loads are also necessary, particularly for the movement of book trucks. Car speed should be increased in high buildings.

Two elevators in one bank will carry more traffic without undue delay than three widely separated ones, and three together in a large building will probably be as satisfactory as five or six that are widely separated. In the Widener Library, where there are four automatic elevators averaging something like 125 ft (37.850) from each other, a passenger often has to wait five minutes or more for a car; three elevators in a single bank would have given better service, though passengers on the average would have had to walk greater distances to reach them.

A major question in locating elevators is whether or not to place them in a part of the building not open to the general public or to restrict their use in other ways. Traffic may be unduly heavy if they are used unnecessarily by undergraduates going up or down only one or two floors. Use can be restricted by having elevator doors and call buttons operate only by key, and distributing keys only to members of the staff and to physically handicapped readers. Another possibility is to locate elevators behind desks where an attendant is always on duty. Control has been facilitated in several new buildings where the bank of elevators is at the rear of the circulation desk lobby or in the central core of the building. The location of stairways leading to restricted levels in similar space is an advantage. Control may be needed for two purposes—to restrict stack access to professors, librarians, and graduate students, and to relieve the load on elevators which are expensive to operate and maintain.

The gravity of the problem will be recognized by anyone who has waited fifteen minutes for an elevator in the University of Pittsburgh's Cathedral of Learning, as well as by anyone who has helped to plan an 18-story library building in which six elevators for passengers and one for freight, including space for them and for their lobbies, would cost at least $1,000,000 today. It should be added that when an automatic elevator is pushed too hard by heavy traffic, its electrical control system is likely to break down, and repair is costly.

One means of reducing the load on elevators is to confine the library's most heavily used facilities to the entrance level and the levels immediately above and below, which readers can be expected or required to reach by stairways. If this can be done, it will be much easier to provide satisfactory elevator service for the professors and graduate students who use the library intensively and who will use the further reaches of the building but do not rush in and out in such large numbers between classes.

If the reader is inclined to think that questions of cab size and elevator speed or number of cars and their location are minor matters, consider the fact that a single elevator in a five-level building may cost at least $100,000 in addition to the cost of the space occupied by its shaft and by the lobby in front of it. This is an investment large enough to warrant careful consideration.

Finally, the details of interior surfaces, phone, bells, braille indications of floor levels, and signs need consideration, though consideration of these aspects will often be left for a later design phase. Examples of concerns about these features include the observation that the phone should be low enough so that a person who has collapsed on the floor can reach it; the interior surfaces should be exceptionally durable or easily repaired; graffiti should be discouraged by avoiding surfaces inviting defacement both inside the

elevator and in the vicinity of the elevator lobby; and, in terms of the signs, while the elevator user should know the desired floor before the elevator is entered, decisions are needed about the information to be displayed inside the elevator.

Conveyors should be considered if there is a fairly continuous flow of books or other library materials through a multitier building; they may provide a more satisfactory solution to book transportation problems than either book lifts or a second service elevator. An endless-belt conveyor is similar mechanically to an escalator, but it goes straight up and down. Like elevators, conveyors should be enclosed in fire-resistant shafts. Carrier prongs are attached, usually at approximately 9 ft (2.743) intervals, to the chains that go up and down. Books can be placed on the prongs as they go past. It is more desirable to provide light trays in which the books can be placed to guard against books falling down the shafts. The books or trays laden with books can be placed on the conveyor at any level; they then go to the level that has been indicated by pushing a button when they were loaded. If this level is below their starting point, they first go to the top, swing around, and then come down.

It should be noted that the simplest conveyor installations have proved to be the most satisfactory; those that pick up material at any level but deposit it at only one—e.g., the reading-room level—are the least likely to get out of order. Two conveyors of this sort have been in operation at the New York Public Library for nearly sixty years with very few difficulties. More complicated installations are to be found at Yale and in the original Library of Congress building where, because the stack is not directly above, below, or adjacent to the charging desk or reading room, the conveyors have to travel horizontally for a considerable distance. The California State University at Long Beach Library has a complex system of conveyors and sorting areas used to facilitate the return of large quantities of books to the shelves. A central location for conveyors is highly desirable, of course; installation by a stairwell is advantageous because it may facilitate access for servicing and repair. Precautions should be taken to make conveyors as quiet as possible; many have caused trouble by creaking and groaning or banging when making a delivery.

An example of conveyor advantages and problems exists at the Robarts Library, University of Toronto. In this huge building there are two vertical conveyors serving all 16 floors. One, used by library pages in filling requests, is connected on each of the stack floors, 9 to 13, to horizontal conveyors that encircle the stacks. The other is for internal mail, returning empty totes and books for reshelving, but it can also be used for paged books if the first is shut down. All floors have short horizontal runs off the second conveyor. At each entrance to the conveyors, the opening is guarded by a photoelectric cell; if the beam is broken by an overloaded tote, the conveyor automatically shuts down, and can only be restarted by the building engineer after the blockage has been cleared. Both conveyors accept two containers 6 by 12 in. (152 by 305 mm)—a tote tray 4 in. deep and a tote box 10 in. (or 102 and 254 mm deep) deep. These are made of molded fiberglass, and both sizes can be nested for easy storage. To load, totes are placed on a slide, manually or automatically depending on location, addressed to a specific floor at a single control panel. The slide moves forward into the conveyor shaft, and the tote is lifted by the next pair of arms ascending on the continuous chain. To unload at the previously designated floor, the slide moves forward into the shaft on the descending side and catches the tote, moves back out of the shaft, and ejects the tote onto the horizontal run.

As reported in 1983, the system has had problems:

1. During the first year or so there was a good deal of misuse of the system by library staff unfamiliar with conveyors. This caused some damage, and far too many shutdowns. It is essential that a system be used by staff who have been thoroughly trained.

2. The horizontal ring conveyors on the five stack floors are no longer used. If the Robarts had been designated as an open stack library during the planning stage, the horizontal conveyors would probably not have been built. Most patrons prefer to go up to the stacks and find books for themselves, so the horizontal conveyors were never much used. Then, after a few years of operation they began to get rather noisy, which led to complaints from people studying in the stacks, so use of them was discontinued.

3. The vertical continuous chain conveyors are in operation for 94.5 hours a week, and have been subject to considerable wear and tear; more than was anticipated. In the ten years that Robarts has been open, there have been several extended shutdowns for major maintenance and repair. And despite the continued existence of the company that made and installed the conveyors, some replacement parts have proved difficult to get. The design is now rather out of date; if it were being installed today, the loading and unloading mechanisms would be quite different.

Despite the shortcomings, it is difficult to imagine how the Robarts Library could function effectively without the conveyor system.[3]

Pneumatic tubes have been used for many years to transfer call slips from circulation desks to attendants in the stacks. Propulsion is by compressed air or vacuum, and slips can be delivered much more rapidly than by elevator or conveyor. For very large closed-stack libraries, use of a rapid message system and conveyor for book delivery can be very efficient.

Much larger pneumatic tubes have been used for transporting books over considerable distances when vertical or horizontal endless-belt conveyors did not seem practicable. The connection between the older two buildings of the Library of Congress is an example. Another is the pneumatic connection between the undergraduate and main research libraries at the University of California, Los Angeles, where the containers used are approximately a foot (305 mm) in diameter and 18 in. (457 mm) in length. Unfortunately, they can stop at their destination with an abrupt jar, and books are likely to be damaged unless they have been tightly strapped in place. Moreover, to strap books tightly does them no good. Careful adjustment or improved controls are necessary to any such installation.

Other forms of communication should be considered, either for their own merits or as supplemental to those already discussed. These, of course, include computers for electronic mail, telephones, TelAutograph, Teletype, and television. Their detailed requirements will be discussed in Chapter 13 as their use, other than possibly reducing the need for the mechanical systems discussed here, will have less of an impact on the schematic phase of the design effort. Their potential advantages should be considered, however, as the design team thinks through the various possibilities of spatial relationships, and the

[3] Correspondence from library administrator, University of Toronto, 1983.

internal configuration of the major elements. One caution: many library buildings have installed elaborate intercoms or book conveyors as part of initial construction and ceased using them in a very few years. Though it is obviously more expensive to add them at a later time, one should consider carefully whether inclusion of such devices is justified.

Spatial Relationships. Section 5.3 discusses spatial relationships from a programmatic point of view. Appendix A gives examples in the section on Program Divisions covering spatial relationships. The schematic design effort will test the program statement and, to a significant extent, establish the basic relationships of major components of the library. Because of the importance of this aspect of the design, it is discussed further here.

Ease and convenience of use is a matter of prime importance. This is certainly true of a college library, where some of the students may never have used anything but a small public or high school library and are quite awed by what may seem to them to be a tremendous collection of 100,000 volumes, particularly if they are given stack access. Convenience is even more important in a great university library where the necessarily large and complex areas for reading, public service, and book storage may seem maze-like in character. A large public building of any kind with many rooms may be difficult to find one's way about in; but an academic or research library, with 1,000,000 volumes and 30 linear miles (48.280 km) of shelves and with reading accommodations for 1500 persons, can well present a formidable problem to even an experienced scholar, particularly during the first few visits to the library. On the other hand, a large library is often highly regarded by students once they master the system, as they can find a "sense of place" or their own niche which is convenient for their studies.

Taking the major relationships outlined in the program, the architect must piece together a plan that works within the context of the module, the size of a given floor, and external influences. This is an effort that should command the involvement of the librarian and others in the decision process, as some degree of compromise is almost certain to develop. It is during this stage of the design that key elements such as the stair and elevator cores, shear wall locations, and rest rooms must be located. Care must be taken to ensure that no element precludes needed flexibility in another element. As has been suggested several times elsewhere in this volume, it is certain that the library operations will change with the passage of time.

As the layout of the library emerges and compromises are made, it should be remembered that vertical movement is normally more difficult and time-consuming than horizontal movement, and stairs are not preferred. Elevators are expensive and may cause delays. As a result, there has been a strong and desirable tendency in recent years to plan the "central services" on the entrance level of the library. Space on that level is properly considered the most valuable area in the building. Entrance lobbies are important and must be fairly large in a busy academic library, because of the movement of users in large groups between classes. Therefore, less space on the entrance floor can be left for books, readers, and services than on the other floors, and choices must be made.

One solution is to restrict the use of this floor largely to the central or key services, including perhaps the technical processing staff, even if this means that less reading space and less shelving for main collections are available than would have been preferred on this level. In order to overcome the difficulty at least in part, the Olin Library at Cornell University has a first floor much larger than the size of the levels above, which has made it possible to put all these services, as well as several special collections, on the main floor (see fig. 12.19). In spite of this, its processing department space is already congested, a fact that is all too common in library design, though the condition may be moderated by increased automation. But the particular points to be made are that these central services should be placed as close to each other as possible and that their relationships to each other are a matter of importance. The whole area should be planned carefully to leave available as much space as possible for reading accommodations and heavily used parts of the collection, but the areas assigned for lobby space and the central services should not be reduced to an extent that will cause congestion in these areas. Library staff should carefully study the probable traffic patterns in and around the lobby and advise the architect on the effectiveness of the scheme. The lobby should be especially attractive and

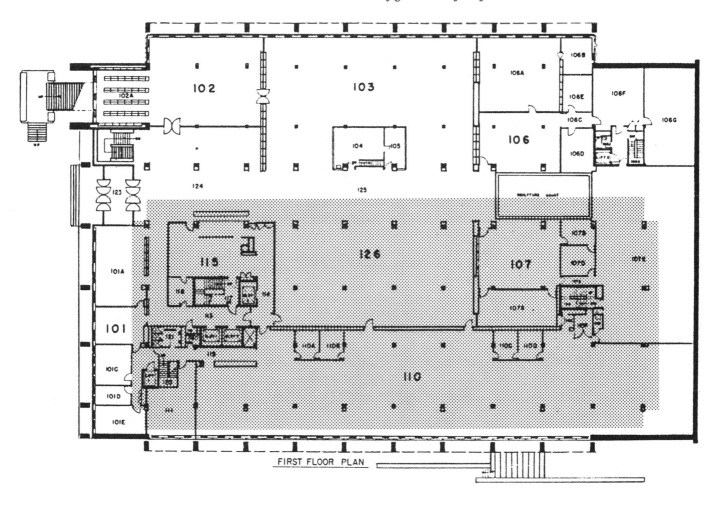

FIRST FLOOR PLAN

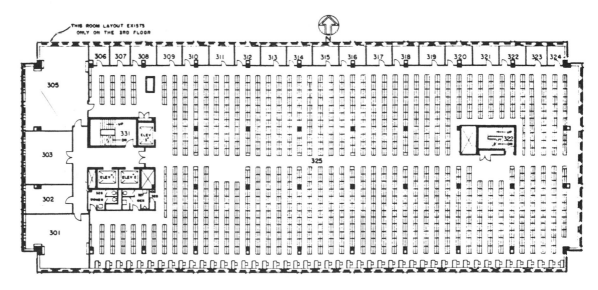

TYPICAL FLOOR PLAN
3RD, 4TH, 5TH, & 6TH FLOOR

FIGURE 12.19 Cornell University, Olin Library, entrance level and a typical upper floor. The shaded area on the entrance level indicates the location and outline of the upper floors. The first floor is larger than those above it in order to house the central services and three important special collections. Key to significant functions: 102—current periodicals; 103—reference: 110—technical services; 115—circulation; 126—catalog and biliography; 101, 106, 107—special collections; 301 to 305—seminar and study rooms; 306 to 324—faculty studies; 325—stacks.

give a feeling of spaciousness which can carry through the whole building, but an extravagant amount of space should not be assigned to it for monumental rather than functional purposes. There is no room here for space that will not be heavily used.

In a number of new libraries, a great deal of space that would otherwise have been available on entrance levels has been sacrificed by having a setback of the outside wall on one, two, or even four sides for the sake of an architectural effect. Such a setback can be very attractive. In certain circumstances there may be special reasons which make it desirable in spite of the obvious disadvantages. A good example of this situation would be a library designed for an urban university where, because of the limited ground space available, a skyscraper building may be a necessity. In this case, it may be determined that even if it used all the possible area the site afforded, it could not have an entrance lobby and what might be called the main distribution points (exit control, elevators, stairwells, and escalators to the basement and the second floor, which may be desirable to relieve the load on the elevators) in addition to the central services. Such a circumstance may suggest transfer of all or most central services to the second floor, where these services could have the whole level and would require less space because the undergraduate use of course reserves, which does not require these services, could be funneled off to a lower level.

One spatial-relationship problem, which is too often neglected, is shelving for the main bookstack collections. It has already been noted that a large bookstack—there are some today and there will be many more in the years to come—with 500,000 volumes shelved on one level may become a maze. Equally serious is the problem of a logical arrangement of the books on the shelves. This problem has become more complicated with the great efforts made in recent years to house readers and books in juxtaposition. Anything that tends to break up a logical arrangement of the books should be avoided if at all possible. The situation is complicated by fixed areas for stairs, elevators, toilets, special rooms of any kind and by reading "oases" or irregularities of any kind in walls or aisles; but careful study and planning can generally prevent many of the difficulties even in a very large library.

The very large A stack level at Princeton, with nine main aisles (see fig. 12.11) at right angles to the ranges and with several elevators and stairwells, many special rooms, carrels, and oases, illustrates the problem. The B level at the National Library of Medicine in Bethesda, Maryland, which was planned by the same competent architectural firm, represents a simpler pattern (see fig. 12.12), and the still simpler pattern at Cornell's Olin Library (see fig. 12.20) shows what can be done.

The plans of the Widener stack (fig. 4.2), the Widener level in the Lamont building at Harvard (fig. 12.21), the main stack at Columbia's Butler Library (fig. 12.22), and the New York Public Library main stack (fig. 12.23), show other simple layouts. That of the first phase and second phases for the University of California at Los Angeles (see fig. 12.24) shows in the heavy black lines the problems created by special building requirements (shear walls) to prevent earthquake damage and the great effort made to prevent complications which could easily have arisen. However, even with an addition, the building works well.

It should be stressed that these plans probably do not reflect ideal solutions for any proposed library. Indeed, the academic program and goals of the library staff may suggest quite different solutions. While complexity for its own sake may not be desirable, not all librarians are opposed to more complex arrangements. There are even some who find the three short towers of the Northwestern University main research library an agreeable solution, although many would argue this point because of the radial shelving and inflexible layout.

In summary, this section has briefly dealt with a variety of traffic problems, the solution of which plays a large part in the planning of a successful library building. Among them, directly or indirectly, these traffic issues affect all the basic elements of planning. A successful library must have its public service, its reading accommodations, and its housing for collections and staff conveniently related to each other, to the supervision and control arrangement, and to the vertical transportation. Nothing in the design should be "frozen" until each of those three primary traffic aspects and their relations to one another have been given adequate thought and study. Audible and visual distraction must be minimized so that a quiet, comfortable place for study and work will be provided. Unless these requisites are fulfilled, aesthetically pleasing exteriors and interiors and the other important features of a library will not make up for

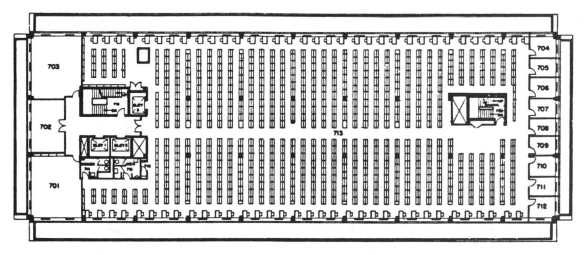

FIGURE 12.20 Cornell University, Olin Library, floor 7. Note the clear circulation pattern with the main stairs and elevators at the main entrance end of the building (see fig. 12.19). Note also the fairly wide center aisle and the narrower side aisles with open carrels, departmental rooms at the end adjacent to the main stairs, and faculty studies at the other.

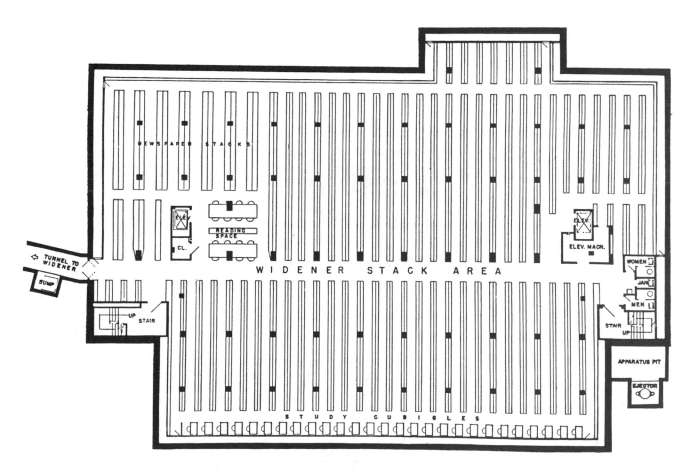

FIGURE 12.21 Harvard University, Lamont Library, storage stack for Widener. This stack is connected by a tunnel with the Widener building. The circulation pattern is simple, with a 51 ft (15.545) long range on one side and a 42 ft (12.802) range on the other side of a wide center aisle. Ranges with 3 ft 6 in. (1.067) wide aisles and with a reading area carved out of the stack. The alcove at the upper right and the shelving to the right of the machine room near the restrooms will be awkward to use in a natural sequential order. The double exterior walls are necessary to control ground water.

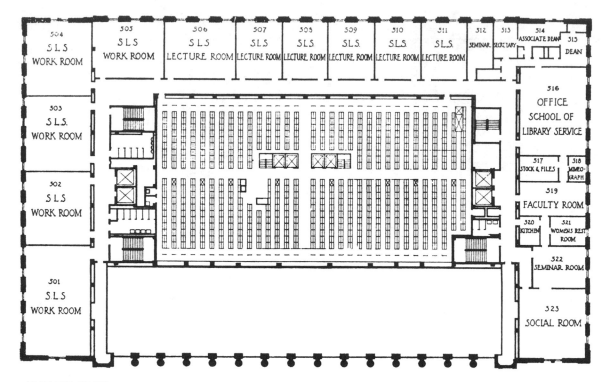

FIGURE 12.22 Columbia University, Butler Library, stack area. Shown is one of 14 levels which, though varying in size, are in the center of the building with rooms on each of the four sides. There is only one public entrance, that through the circulation area. This was one of the first modern stacks without ventilation slits between levels and with stairways and elevators closed off so as not to form a chimney effect.

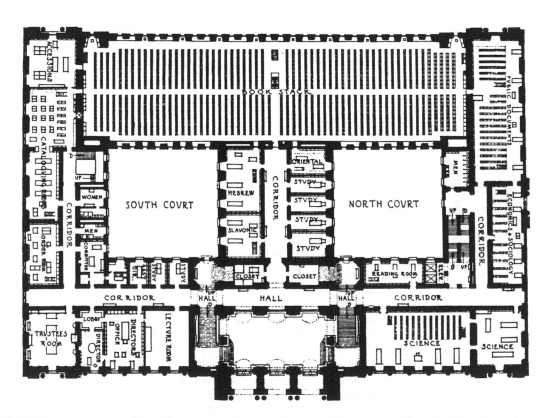

FIGURE 12.23 New York Public Library, stack area. The stack has seven identical levels under a monumental reading room and has an exceptionally clear traffic pattern for a very large area.

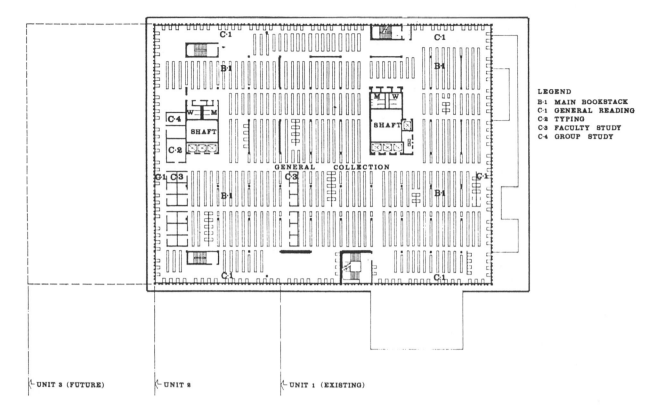

FIGURE 12.24 University of California at Los Angeles, Research Library. This floor plan is typical of the upper floors of the first two units of the Research Library. The heavy lines represent earthquake reinforcements, which can complicate shelving arrangements. The main stair is placed next to the main entrance to encourage use.

its defects. Each of them should be kept in mind, studied, and analyzed from the beginning. The traffic patterns in all their aspects should be diagrammed and tested in their relationship to other problems as the location of each area is considered. The simple and successful traffic patterns in the Olin Library at Cornell are noteworthy. Stephen A. McCarthy, the director of libraries, reported: "The continuous study of traffic patterns in the Olin Library moved the entrance from the middle of the north side of the building to the west side; it moved the elevators from the center toward the west end; and this in turn dictated the location of the graduate study rooms and the conference rooms at the west end. The disposition of many of the facilities in the building flows naturally from the traffic patterns."[4]

12.5 Influence of Specialized Needs of Equipment

Although the effect of equipment is of great importance to the design process, the design

[4] Personal communication to Keyes Metcalf for the first edition of this book.

team is urged to review the programming chapters (5, 6, 7, and 8) which cover in detail the issues of shelving, reader tables, acoustic control, and the like. It may also be useful at this point to scan Appendix B. This brief section is included here simply to emphasize the importance of a thorough understanding of equipment requirements, including floor loadings, space, lighting, temperature, and other requirements. The next section will discuss some aspects of layouts and the more detailed concerns of interior design. Equipment needs for power and signal service and wire management are covered in Section 13.1.

Two policy decisions are discussed here, however, as they may affect the layouts. Shall the furnishings and fixtures be stock or custom-built? Should they be contemporary or traditional in style?

Stock or Custom-Built. A small library can rarely afford to consider the purchase of anything except stock furniture, lighting fixtures, or other building components. To have them specially designed and built to order would be too expensive in all but exceptional cases. This situation may well be different for a very large building. If the number of chairs to be purchased runs into four figures, it may well be that a special design can be afforded. In many cases the custom-made chairs can be less expensive than those from a standard library-equipment house with its necessarily large overhead for selling and service. The danger arises from the fact that specially designed furniture does not always stand the test of time and is less likely to be well designed structurally.

A compromise between stock and custom-built furniture was used in connection with the selection of the chairs for the Lamont building at Harvard. The time was 1947, soon after the war, when furniture stocks were depleted and the types of chairs available were limited. However, some forty samples were found. The architect and the librarian, with advice from many others, selected the three that seemed closest to what they wanted. They then called in the manufacturers and asked whether they would make certain changes in the design and what the cost would be. One of the three was chosen. The manufacturer made the alterations requested after a number of different samples were submitted. The chairs have been satisfactory in every respect except for the finish. (The finishes available at that time were not as good as they are today.) Only one chair in 1100 broke in the first dozen years, despite the use and the abuse that are inevitable in a busy undergraduate library. But this procedure could not have been carried out without the aid of an architect who was interested and knowledgeable and a manufacturer who was ready to make use of its wide experience and also to work closely with the institution. Given these conditions, custom-built furniture may be a money saver; but a risk is involved.

Another potential advantage the planner may realize from custom furniture is the possibility of unique or special configurations. Carrels, for example, might be designed to fit the space or the special needs of the library. This is especially useful where audio or microform carrels are to be provided, as improvements over a stock item may be able to be realized. Circulation counters also can be stock or custom made; the difference may be little in cost, but a great deal in terms of meeting the program specifics or the aesthetic coherency of the furniture in the space.

Any one of the standard library-equipment houses has the knowledge and experience to produce first-class library furniture, and its better lines will generally fulfill the requirements, at least for community and many four-year colleges. Competition is keen enough to keep prices within reason. The manufacturer's special knowledge of library problems can also be used to good effect, particularly if a library consultant is not on the planning team. A library in a city where library equipment and furniture are manufactured can sometimes obtain considerable discounts from regular prices. A cabinetmaking firm, if controlled by persons belonging to the same religious group that sponsors the institution seeking equipment, may make special discounts. Much can be said for the use of furniture from manufacturers other than those who specialize in library equipment, as the furniture, especially the lounge chairs, may have aesthetic advantages. But make sure that it is sturdy and will stand the wear and tear of library use. The local situation may well affect the choice made.

Light fixtures are items for which a custom design may be considered. As with the example of chairs, a fixture for a carrel of special design may be excessively expensive in small quantities; however, the price may be worthwhile in larger quantities. In the Cecil H. Green Library at Stanford, a custom light fixture was designed for the over two hundred faculty studies and dissertation rooms. The goal was to provide excellent, glare-free light and an exceedingly energy-efficient fixture. In a later project, when only four fixtures were needed, the manufacturer could not reasonably produce such a small quantity. However, a single sculptural light fixture was created at considerable expense but for unusual aesthetic reasons.

Custom versus stock is a decision that might be applied to other elements as well, including carpet, signs, book returns, book trucks, tables for reading folios, and even shelving. Each case must be considered in the context of what is to be achieved and how much it will cost.

Contemporary or Traditional. The question of contemporary or traditional design is another perplexing one. Simple lines, good proportions, and carefully selected, properly cured, and well-finished wood or other materials of similar quality are the primary essentials; unfortunately they are likely to be expensive and may be difficult to obtain. Keep these four points in mind:

1. The functional aspects in the broad meaning of the term must be satisfactory. Sturdiness, comfort, appearance, and a reasonable cost are all possible with both traditional and contemporary furniture. They should come first.

2. Furniture should not be so extreme in its design that it will be dated, so that in the year 2000 it will be referred to, perhaps contemptuously, as "obviously 1980s." Only in a special area or room, one which is meant to be a "period piece" in terms of design, would an extreme design be suitable if it fits the character of the space. A reception area outside the administrative offices could be an instance.

3. The design of furniture should "fit" the building. This seemingly evasive statement is a way of conveying a subtle issue of taste. Furniture should usually be of the same style as the building, contemporary or one of the classic period styles. Yet a tasteful blend can be harmonious, and a contrasting accent can be very effective in carefully chosen locations. The Alvar Aalto tables and chairs in two rooms of Harvard's Lamont Library are liked by many though not all. A Gothic or Renaissance piece in a contemporary rarebook reading room may be found tasteful. An Italianate cabinet or Spanish chest can provide an item of interest. Such accents can add a richness and an interesting variation. However, furniture which is obviously left over from a tired building will look like a "hand-me-down," or army surplus and will not "fit" the building even if it may work functionally.

4. There is the economic aspect of quality, upkeep, and finishes, which are closely related. Quality is not good if upkeep is high or if frequent refinishing is necessary. The cost should have a definite relationship to quality and should generally be considered in connection with the expected length of useful life. On certain occasions consideration might properly be given to an inexpensive contemporary model with the idea of replacing it after a few years and before it is completely outdated.

In addition to fulfilling the functions assigned to it, furniture and equipment should be attractive, sturdy, and comfortable or practical. Sturdiness depends to a large extent on design and materials used. Good engineering involves a practical knowledge of factory procedures and also ingenuity. The problems of vandalism, discussed in Section 13.3, must also be considered. A study chair and table and other pieces of furniture and equipment can be said almost to pay for themselves in a relatively few years if no repairs are required. It is sometimes said, "the quality is built in." If that is indeed the case, the more expensive furnishings may well be the more economical.

12.6 The Schematic Phase of Interior Design

In the ideal design process the interior design effort will parallel that of the architectural design. All too often the interior design is left to the librarian or a purchasing agent. In any significant project it is recommended that the services of an interior designer should be part of the design effort and that involvement should begin during schematics. Assuming such is the case, the schematic phase of interior design will involve the preparation of layouts and a preliminary presentation of types of materials, including fabrics and carpets, colors, and other features.

Layouts carefully prepared during the architectural schematic phase are essential for testing the adequacy of the program and the space arrangements presented by the architect. If an interior designer is not used, this testing must be done by the librarian, building projects manager, or consultant. Tentative layouts are also essential for the librarian, trustees, university administrators, donors, and others for visualizing the nature of the space and the scale of the project. A plan of a single rectangular room without furniture could be an immense barn or a small closet to the individual who is not familiar with the use of scale, unless furniture or other elements are placed upon the drawing to which the viewer can relate. Figures 12.25 through 12.32 are intended to help the librarian visualize the kind of space needed for people in libraries.

As with the architectural design, the design process for the interiors should require numerous meetings with the designer and library representative and perhaps the institution's project manager. A tour of nearby libraries and review of the program are useful to start meaningful discussion. In some cases, particularly where an existing building is being remodeled for library purposes, the entire design effort may be under the guidance of an interior designer rather than an architect. In a few cases the architect will design a building with large empty spaces, leaving the interior arrangements and assignment of space entirely up to the interior designer; however, this approach is not recommended unless the architect and the interior designer are working closely together in the same design phase at the same time. Without such coordination, problems are certain to result.

Concerns about module and bay size, traffic routes, the relationships of major functions, durability of surfaces, flexibility for future change, a philosophy of what the library should be like, and many other aspects of the building program will be just as important for the interior designer as they are for the architect. However, the ability to change the interior design, particularly furniture layouts, will remain somewhat easier for a longer period of time during the design process than is the case with major architectural elements. The schematic phase of interior design is thus more of a testing of the space arrangements than it is a final arrangement of furniture patterns. Once the configuration of the structure and major components is established, it should only be changed with great care. However, furniture can, to a larger degree, be moved around even after the building is occupied. What then is the importance of the testing? Basically, the testing is to determine answers to the following, so any inadequacy can be addressed during the next design phase:

1. Is the amount of space provided sufficient for the number of elements that are to be placed in it? This is essentially a test of the program statement.
2. Is the configuration of the space suitable? Can the elements within the space be arranged in a logical order? This should take into consideration not only the shape of the space, but also other features such as doors, stairs, windows, skylights, lighting, etc.
3. Are there important conditions that must relate to the interior design? These would include the need for power outlets, communication systems, special lighting and other details that are closely related to the layout but that may be reflected in the architectural design.
4. Are there architectural qualities that will influence the interior design? These might include materials, colors, style, and other aspects for which the design of the interior arrangements should serve to complement the architecture.

These questions will be discussed in order in the following paragraphs.

1. *Is the architectural space adequate?* For any programmed function or area, there should, of course, be a tabulation of requirements, including the number and type of furniture, acoustical concerns, special lighting requirements, and other specific needs that will, at least in part, be reflected in the interior design. One of the first steps then is to prepare drawings, using the architectural design as a background and showing each of the significant furniture elements, including shelving, chairs, desks, side tables, floor lamps, lockers, carrels, typing stands, service counters, stools, and anything else that occupies floor space. Using the program as a basis, the interior designer or other responsible member of the design team will create a first draft or design, plotting out major functions with circulation

 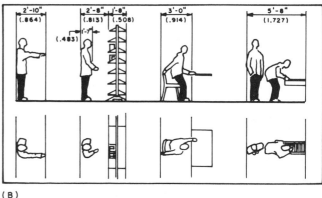

(A)   (B)

FIGURE 12.25 Human dimension. Note that the seated figure in A requires additional space to get into the seated position as shown in B. These dimensions are suitable for planning purposes, but it should be remembered that there will be exceptions.

FIGURE 12.26 Human dimensions in stack aisles. The kneeling position, second from left, would be difficult for many users. It is more likely that the reader would squat in alignment with the shelves in a minimum width aisle rather than facing the shelves. This illustration is based upon a range that is 21 in. (0.533) from front to front, which suggests 10½ in. (0.267) nominal depth shelves.

routes, space for book truck parking, or a queue waiting at a service point, and, of course, the specified furnishings together with adequate space for the user.

The interior design process is similar to that of the architectural effort, only on a smaller scale. Individual units within a major function will be grouped together and organized with consideration given to the concepts of communication, materials flow, privacy, and outlook. While the architect may provide a single large area for technical processing, the interior designer will divide up the space, perhaps only in terms of furniture groupings, into the smaller elements of binding preparation, finishing, gift and exchange, acquisitions, cataloging, serials processing, and perhaps an area for the supporting bibliographic tools. While at this stage it is not critical that all the functions within a space are properly arranged, it will be the beginning of the study of those crucial aspects of

the design detail that will make the facility function smoothly. It may also illustrate that the configurations of the space could be improved by altering the architectural envelope, which should still be possible at this stage of the design.

2. *Is the configuration of the space suitable?* The interior designer may well be influential in the decisions about the shape of a given space and its proportions and lines. In general, most rooms should be rectangular, usually not square, and the height of rooms should properly be related to the other dimensions. In connection with shape, it should be noted that round or triangular or, for that matter, octagonal rooms are wasteful of space, as furniture and equipment—this includes accommodations for readers, services to readers, and shelving—do not fit into them economically. In spite of the unfortunate experiences at the British Museum, the Library of Congress, the Brotherton Library at

FIGURE 12.27 Human dimensions in larger aisles. Again, this figure is based upon an unusual shelf dimension. These aisle widths are best suited for access by the handicapped and for heavy use. One common standard suggests 3 ft 6 in. (1.067) aisles for handicapped access. In some cases the width of the aisle in the far right illustration would be excessive, although having a continuous row of reading positions as suggested may substitute for an index table. At an index table, stools may be better than chairs.

the University of Leeds, the State Library in Melbourne, Australia, and many others, each generation of architects again tries out areas that are not rectangular, and the interior designer must deal with the problems or assets that result.

In earlier discussions of supervision and control, relationships of major functions, and communications and vertical transportation, noise has several times been mentioned. Noise and other distractions are not incidental matters; they are fundamental problems in the planning of traffic and circulation patterns which are part of the interior design. Sound-absorbing materials can do much to minimize noise, but, whenever possible, prevention is better than absorption. And some degree of background sound is essential. Visual distractions constitute a closely related and equally important subject. Window glare, garish color, and heavy traffic in one's field of vision can produce unwanted distractions.

It should be conceded that certain fortunate individuals find noise and motion no problem; those who have grown up amidst large families or have worked from an early age in open offices may be nearly immune to visual and auditory distractions. Many undergraduates, however, even those who prefer to study with the radio on, are not immune; and undergraduates, as well as more advanced students, may deserve consideration in this respect. The professor can usually find a secluded corner at home even if there is no private study in the library. The graduate student in many institutions is now provided with a reasonably quiet and secluded cubicle or carrel. But for the less advanced student, the only alternative to a library reading room may be the dormitory, where one's roommate may operate on a different timetable and gregarious friends may be plentiful. The reading room is likely to be crowded with contemporaries, and table space avail-

FIGURE 12.28 Human dimensions in very large aisles. These aisles are clearly intended for very heavy use. The figure at the far right assumes a file cabinet that is 17½ in. (0.445) deep, shallower than most. A typical card catalog cabinet, for example, is about 20 in. (0.508) deep if the drawer handles are included.

able there may be no more than 30 in. wide by 18 in. (762 mm × 457 mm) deep, which is not enough for spreading out books or, indeed, for opening more than one if space for taking notes is also required.

Fully as serious as any of the handicaps that have been suggested is the fact that the reading room or area may be in almost constant turmoil; it may settle down twenty minutes after a class period begins, only to be disrupted again ten minutes before the period ends as students begin to leave. Afternoons and evenings may be disturbed by more continual though less concentrated coming and going. In many ways contemporary undergraduates may be worse off than their predecessors; the great monumental reading rooms of earlier days tended to engulf the reader in the constant mix of sounds, just as a large stadium filled with a cheering crowd may leave the athletes oblivious of everything but their immediate surroundings. The

newer, more intimate reading areas are too often still surrounded by shelves that attract steady traffic. Entrance to the room is often through a single passageway in the center of the long side or, worse still, at one end; few readers can enter or leave without going past many tables at which others are attempting to study.

The foregoing account of the undergraduate's woes may be enough to indicate why the following basic principles need to be emphasized:

Noise and confusion should be kept out of reading areas insofar as possible. Circulation and reference desks should be elsewhere, with books, walls, distance, or acoustic materials— perhaps more than one of these barriers—to separate them from readers. The public catalogs and, to a lesser extent, shelves holding reference collections are also areas of relatively heavy traffic. Use of

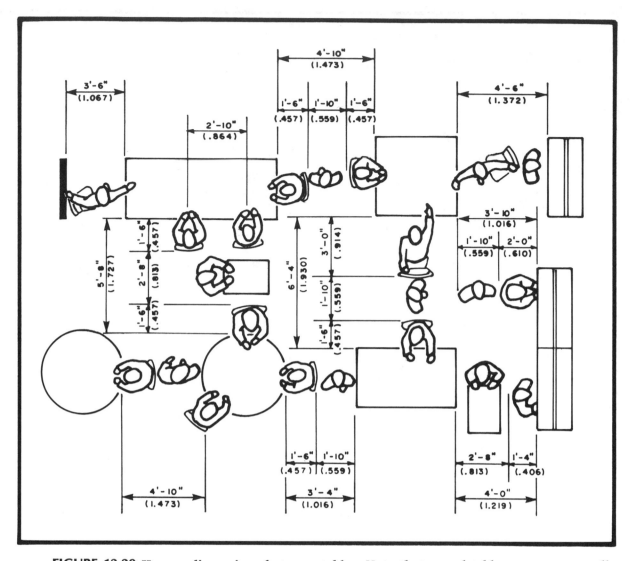

FIGURE 12.29 Human dimensions between tables. Note that round tables are not normally recommended for research purposes, but they may be desired in a staff room or in an area for light reading.

current periodicals involves a good deal of movement. If periodicals or reference books must be in the reading area, used also for general reading, they should at least be placed at one side or one end, with adequate acoustic insulation that can be provided by walls, acoustic floors and ceilings, and books.

Access to reading areas should be provided through as many well-distributed entrances as possible. If students can usually find a seat near the point at which they enter the room, they can be expected to leave the same way, and both visual and auditory disturbance can be kept to a minimum.

Individual seating accommodations are highly desirable. They will be most satisfactory if a barrier at the back of each individual table

can be built up to a height of 52 to 54 in. (1.320 to 1.371), which is enough to prevent the reader from seeing the head of the person in the opposite carrel. In a seat of this kind, one should be able to turn slightly away from the rest of the room and obtain visual privacy if desired.

Table surfaces should be large enough to permit the student to spread out the materials. Space on an individual table goes further than space on a large shared table; a surface measuring 22 × 33 in. (558 mm × 838 mm) is as useful on an individual table as a segment measuring 24 × 36 in. (610 mm × 914 mm) on a table that must be shared.

A plan designed to avoid disturbing readers should not make a maze of the library. Devious and complicated traffic lanes will discourage use

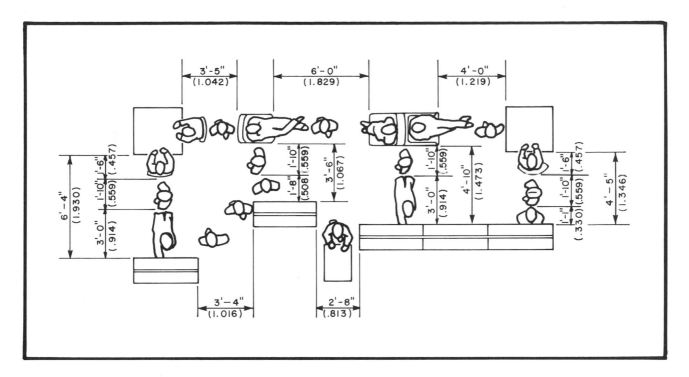

FIGURE 12.30 Human dimensions between lounge chairs, tables, and shelving.

of the building and cause frustration and wasted time. Some librarians would not agree with this point, but the fact is that the more difficult it is to find an empty seat, the more noise will be created.

Traffic patterns in bookstacks also vitally affect the welfare of readers. The tendency is to locate a larger and larger percentage of total reading accommodations in the stacks. It is important to keep heavily used traffic arteries away from open carrels.

Noise and other distractions should be kept in mind when planning traffic lanes throughout the building. Stairs in the vicinity of reading areas should be well sealed off. Elevator lobbies should be separated from reading areas.

Background sound from the ventilation system or from another "white sound" source is essential. While this goes beyond the scope of normal interior design, it is a crucial factor. Even with excellent acoustic materials provided on all of the surfaces, minor sounds such as the turning of pages become a distraction when there is no background sound. Everything can be heard clearly if there is nothing to mask it.

These are obvious principles, yet most libraries have disregarded one or more of them. Good traffic patterns, plus adequate lighting and ventilation, are essential if the library is to be a satisfactory place for work or study. For the most part, these are factors which can be greatly influenced by the interior designer at this stage of the project.

The flow of the classification sequence for the collections is another important area influenced by interior design. In this case there is little argument that simplicity is an asset. The librarians should think through the arrangement of the collections, including the obvious but often overlooked sequence of call numbers from the end of one range to its continuation in another. These should flow without great gaps of space. Where there are parallel blocks of ranges, the sequential line will likely double back on itself. However, where the blocks of ranges are interrupted or displaced by building elements, there can be considerable distance between the end of the call number sequence in one shelving area and the resumption of that sequence in the next. This problem is often aggravated in a tower library where a natural sequence is broken up by a separation of vertical as well as horizontal distance. Furthermore, it is virtually impossible to break the collections up into discrete packages, each with its properly proportioned amount of growth space so that

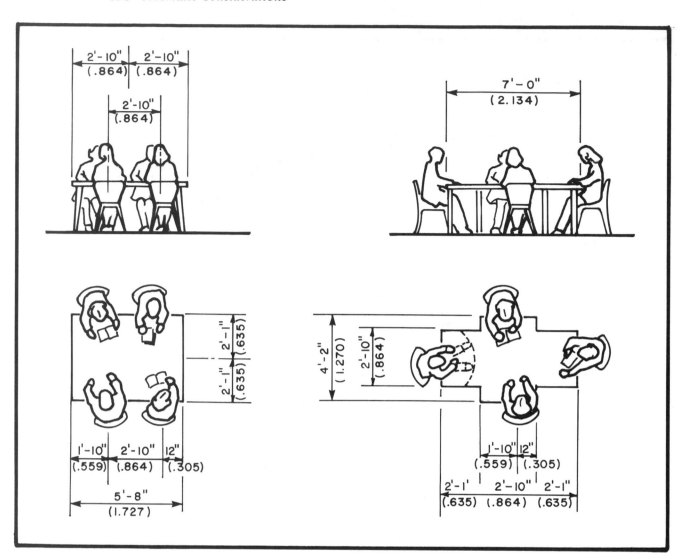

FIGURE 12.31 Human dimensions at tables. The unusual-shaped table at the right is more to illustrate minimum dimensions than to suggest an ideal table. The suggested width is not sufficient for the student doing serious research, although it is more likely that four students would sit at the table to the right because of the greater separation.

all of the stack areas run out of space at the same time.

In the staff areas, internal circulation, lighting, outlook, air flow, and other aspects must be considered in terms of architectural space. Noise here can also be a problem. The provision of an exterior book return in the circulation department staff area, for example, will produce noise which may suggest that staff positions should be located some distance away or that the return should be in a separate room. The acoustics in the technical processing areas will be important too; thus it is necessary to decide whether to place in separate rooms the computer printer, typists, photocopy machine, and conference accom-

modations, and to decide on their configuration during this schematic phase. Furthermore, the relationship of technical services to other functions such as the catalog, reference collections, or even rest rooms may influence the thinking about the shape of the space.

3. *What facility features are influenced by the interior design?* As the layouts are developed and approved, such items as the location and swing of doors, the need for electrical outlets and their exact location, and many other facility features will obviously require refinement. Since much of this effort can most conveniently be done during the design development phase, it is certainly one of the

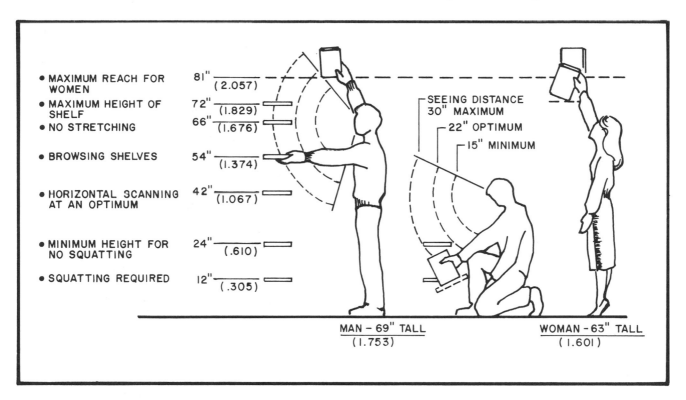

FIGURE 12.32 Human dimensions at shelving.

reasons for an early start on the interior designs. The following list represents the type of questions to be considered:

a. Is there to be wall-mounted shelving that will require special structure? A common structure for walls involves sheet metal studs and framing. Where the walls may support shelving, the spacing of the studs and the gauge of the metal may be affected, or a special horizontal member may be added to carry the shelving brackets. Plaster or gypsum board alone is not a good material to which to fasten shelves.

b. Are carrels to be provided with task lighting and/or future computer terminals? If so, the required access to power and signal sources can be achieved in a number of ways. The three key approaches involve bringing power and signal to the point needed either from the ceiling, through a system of walls, or through the floor. Future needs for flexibility are a major consideration as well.

c. Are there spaces such as faculty studies or enclosed carrels where the small amount of space requires a built-in work surface in order to achieve a furniture arrangement that fits and is most effective? If this is the case, there may be components of the interiors that should be included in the architectural design

documents and thus constructed by the general contractor. This may be true of service point counters and desks as well; but where this is done, it may be wise for the custom or built-in counter units to be modular and of similar construction to standard units manufactured by library supply houses to ensure flexibility for future change. Care must be taken to ensure that movable equipment fits the custom or built-in features. For example, if a two-drawer file unit is required to fit under a work surface, the clear height must anticipate the installation of carpet. The measurements made by the contractor will be from the concrete slab, not the top of the carpet.

d. Are there to be low partitions or office landscape systems that may affect the circulation of air? If this is the case, the mechanical engineers should be informed.

e. Is there to be a special wall where a portrait or a major donor plaque is to be placed? If there is, such things as fire pull boxes, hose cabinets, or clocks should be avoided. It can be quite a surprise at the time of occupancy to discover that a special wall has been usurped by safety or security devices.

f. Is there the possibility of a concentration of loads that may require special structural considerations? This type of problem will be most common in the conversion of an office space to library functions; it can be a problem if the interior layouts suggest compact storage on an upper floor.

g. Is the delivery route sufficiently wide to receive the furniture being planned? Some conference tables and oversized carrels are quite large. Without double doors it may be necessary to assemble the furniture in the space. To avoid this expense, the delivery routes to each major area should be considered.

This list is by no means a complete tabulation of the influences of the interior design on the arrangements of the physical facility. Much of the thinking on these issues will occur as the design process progresses, but they should not be overlooked.

4. *Should interior design reflect architectural features?* Any good interior designer will try to make the interiors and the architecture work well together so that each will complement the other. This effort will influence the designer's palette of form, light, scale, texture, and color. Clearly, successful interior design will require close communication between the interior designer and the architect.

While it is not the intention of this volume to influence the aesthetic design, it is recommended that the librarian be supportive of the designer's recommendations in this area, provided they work in functional and management terms and provided they fall within reasonable economic constraints.

The need for architect and interior designer to work especially closely is most acute if the building is to include a wall, door, stained glass windows, furniture, or other features from a grand private home which are to be incorporated, for example, into the rare-book quarters. The schematic design phase is the time when such reuse must be fixed as to exact dimensions of wall and ceiling; and the lighting requirements must be understood as the solutions may affect the architectural treatment. The seventeenth-century Sir Walter Raleigh rooms and the Early Carolina Rooms with mid-eighteenth century house paneling are examples, fitted within the Wilson Library of the University of North Carolina.

12.7 The Review Process

The schematic design phase is perhaps the most exhaustively reviewed phase of any project, as it is basically the only phase where the drawings represent the program in a graphic form to which nearly every reviewer can relate. Furthermore, it is a crucial phase for review in that it represents the larger and extremely important aspects of the relationships of major elements and the general feeling of the proposed building as a whole. It is not uncommon for faculty, students, staff, administration, donors, and trustees to all participate in some degree. The following two issues are of interest in the schematic review process:

1. *How are the plans reviewed, and by whom?* There are three common approaches, and it would not be unusual for each to be used on a major project.

The first is simply to display the drawings in an exhibit area and ask for comments. This might be supplemented by articles in the student newspaper, a staff bulletin, and a quarterly publication prepared for the friends of the library. While this technique is useful in terms of a broad exposure to the institutional community, there usually will be very little if any useful input to the design team. It serves as a form of community education, is good public relations, and should not be discouraged, yet it will do little to improve the product.

The second review technique involves making group presentations. The groups may be a faculty library committee, perhaps with student representation; a student group, perhaps made up of students who have, in response to a questionnaire, expressed interest in the design of the library; a special committee of faculty, staff, and students who review all facility projects for the institution; a donor or perhaps a group of potential donors or friends of the library; the trustees; and the library staff. The presentations may be made by the library administrator who is the library representative in the design team. For special groups, such as the trustees, the presentation may include or be made by the architect, but this type of presentation should be limited because of the time involved. A refined bubble diagram or other visual depiction may help in the understanding of spatial relationships. The building mass and scale may be conveyed by a small working model. The institutional architect or planner may make the presentation to the trustees, and a representative of the development or fundraising office may make presentations to donors. The project architect may be particularly interested in a presentation to a student group as it would represent the ultimate library user.

Presentations to all but very large groups will result in some interesting comments. Each group will have special interests. Students, for example, will be especially concerned about where the nearest snack facility is or the location of bike parking. Certain staff will wonder about safety conditions, the staff lounge, or the location of the showers. Other staff will have a keen interest in where they will sit, how far they must go to service desks, and what is the working environment. Potential donors will be interested in how prominent "their" space will be. Faculty will be concerned about adequate research space near the books and, perhaps, how they may obtain a computer terminal in their study. The trustees will be especially interested in the budget, the general aspects of the design, such as exterior facade and roof, and how the proposed facility fits into the campus. Operations and maintenance personnel will look at access, energy efficiency, and whether or not the facility meets the institutional standards. All of the comments should be responded to where possible, if not during the actual presentation, then in a follow-up.

The third technique is for individuals carefully to review the plans by themselves or as part of a small group. This should be done by most members of the design team, at least key department heads, the chief librarian, the institutional project manager, and those who are concerned about special aspects of security, safety, access, operations, and maintenance. This process may well include a library consultant. In this process the comments should be written and forwarded to the institution's project manager. Then a review meeting with the architect may be used to discuss each of the comments. For a major project such a review meeting may be broken up into the various interest groups. Otherwise, there will be considerable discussion of aspects that hold little interest for a large segment of those in the meeting. It would not be uncommon for such a session to last half a day.

2. *What kinds of things should one look for?* While each interest group will be looking at different aspects of the project, this paragraph will be indicative by listing some questions that the librarian or the library representative should raise.

Does the schematic presentation meet the operational intent of the program? Is there sufficient capacity for the collections, readers, staff, etc.? Is flexibility for future change adequately provided?

Are the major elements in proper relation to each other? Where compromise has been made, is it reasonable?

Imagine yourself walking through the building as a staff member, then as a student, a faculty member, and a first-time visitor. Is the sequence required to find a book logical? What is the sequence of processing new book materials? of a book being returned to shelving?

Are the fixed structural, mechanical, communication, and circulation elements situated properly? Are the stairs easily found? Is there sufficient flexibility to allow for internal reallocations of space? Is future expansion provided for? How will staff cope with routines and emergencies at all hours of day and evening, and on weekends?

Do the seating arrangements meet the philosophy of the library? Are the carrels large enough? Is there sufficient visual privacy? What will create noise, and is noise going to be a problem? Where are the lockers, phone, typing areas, group study rooms, and the like? Are the lounge chairs grouped so as to encourage or discourage conversation? Similar questions can be applied to staff areas.

Are there areas where the layout can be improved to save space? Has space saving been taken too far to the detriment of the function or flexibility of the library?

Are the books protected from direct sunlight? water? other elements? How is the outside book return dealt with?

How will deliveries be made, not only of books, but of furniture and equipment? How will the handicapped enter the library? Where will they park? How do you keep bikes away from the main entrance?

Will there be serious maintenance problems created by the scheme? Is a high ceiling or an unusual stairwell justified if it will result in frequent extra costs to change lights? Is there sufficient attention at this stage to energy concerns? How will the outside of exterior windows be cleaned, and will birds roosting on flat window ledges create a problem?

Is the overall design agreeable? Are there places to sit outside, and is this desirable;

Is the interior system of corridors clear? Are there areas for smoking? Does a suitable location exist for bulletin boards? Can a book-detection system be installed? Is there space for adding more computer terminals at the catalog or circulation points? If the system for dealing with course reserves is changed, how could it be done?

Are there elements that were left out of the program that clearly will need to be added at this point? When one sees the rough plans, a significant aspect may emerge that could have been forgotten in the program and in discussions.

Will the budget estimates require phasing of the project? Will it be likely that additive alternates will be required? Are there elements counted twice in the budget or left out altogether?

One could go on and on. Clearly, the review process is a time-consuming activity, but errors and problems caught here will be much more easily dealt with than those discovered later. Even though an excellent and detailed program may have been prepared, there will be problems to work out.

13

Design Development

There is a close relationship between the material in this chapter and that in the chapters on programming and schematic design. Readers having a role in the design development and contract documents phases should be familiar with the earlier phases of the project, and if they have not been involved from the beginning, a review should be undertaken.

13.1 The Scope of the Design Development Phase

The schematic phase, as stated in Chapter 12, is the process of analyzing the major factors of the site, program, and budget and of developing a conceptual approach to the building project. Once approved by the institution, the project designer moves into design development, or what is sometimes called the preliminary phase, which is a period of refinement and development of the schematic plans. The purpose of the design development phase is to establish the final relationships, sizes, scope, and appearance of the project, including major dimensions, materials, and finishes.

The exact services to be performed by the architect and consulting engineers will have been spelled out in their contract for services. Typically, the services would include the preparation of drawings, including plans, sections, elevations, typical construction details, and perhaps one or more three-dimensional sketches. These may be accompanied with one or several study models, final architectural and structural materials selection, and equipment layouts. The structural system together with its basic dimensions will be established, as will the approximate sizes and capacities of the mechanical and electrical equipment.

The aspects of energy conservation, lighting criteria, requirements for communications systems and acoustics, floor loading capacity, and any other major element affecting the design of the facility should be determined during the design development phase. While criteria for these aspects should be established as part of the program, it is during design development that the adopted concepts are tested, their influence on other elements analyzed, and more detailed budget information prepared. This is the time when final decisions should be made on major design criteria; a later decision will likely add significantly to the design cost.

Involvement of a number of people with diverse backgrounds will be required during the design development phase. Besides the architect, structural engineer, mechanical engineer, electrical engineer, cost consultant, library representative, and the institution's facility project manager, this is the time for detailed involvement, if wanted, of an energy consultant, value engineer, code consultant, interior designer, library consultant, and others who may be influential in shaping the final product. As in the schematic phase, numerous meetings should occur, but their emphasis will typically be more technical than those in the earlier phase. Even so, it is important for the library representative to continue to be involved, as many proposals and considerations can affect the operation of the library. Concerns typically found to be part of this phase of the design are discussed in the sections that follow.

It would be wrong to conclude from the above that a set of concepts is adopted in schematic work and that only refinements are made later. Perhaps half of the schematics first presented by architects will be rejected in some degree before and, once in awhile, even during the preliminary or design development phase. For examples, fenestration, energy economy, roof profile, entrance, and connection to an existing structure have each in different projects caused disagreement which led to repeated concepts being developed—sometimes over many months—before a consensus was reached in favor of one treatment.

13.2 Refine Schematics

As already suggested, a number of topics will be of importance during the design development phase. A list of topics, which is not intended to be exhaustive, might include:

1. Concepts of mechanical systems
2. Concepts of lighting and sun control
3. Fixed elements: bearing walls, columns, stairs, shafts, etc.
4. Structural system
5. Fire and other hazards
6. Outline specifications
7. Maintaining flexibility.

This section discusses these issues in the order presented here.

Concepts of Mechanical Systems. Mechanical systems normally include the design aspects of heating, ventilating, and air conditioning. In addition to these elements, plumbing, fire supression systems, elevators, and other mechanical devices are sometimes included, and thus these elements are briefly discussed in this section from the mechanical point of view.

Each of the basic mechanical issues—heating, ventilating, and air conditioning—presents complicated and highly technical engineering problems. They are dealt with in detail in the American Society of Heating, Refrigerating, and Air-Conditioning Engineers' *ASHRAE Handbook: 1981 Fundamentals* (New York, 1981). See also the *ASHRAE Handbook: 1982 Applications* (Atlanta, 1982) Chapter 3, Part IV, which deals with libraries and museums. A competent mechanical engineer, working closely with the architect, should design the systems and select the equipment. Tables and formulas for use are readily available. This section is not for engineers, but for administrative authorities of the institution, the building-planning committees, the business manager, and the librarian. It will attempt to present the problems which the architects and engineers must solve and also to indicate the types of installation from which the institution can select. Simplified comments on desirable requirements and costs will be given, with only enough detail to explain and outline the various facets of the problem and make it possible to guide the architect in regard to the library's requirements. The basic direction should be part of the basic program; however, the exact final requirements should be reached no later than the design development phase of the project.

In some parts of the world, climatic conditions make heating of any kind unnecessary; and in other parts the need for heat is so slight that it is uneconomical to provide a central heating system, and it is customary to get along with local units of one kind or another. In other areas the cost of central heating has in the past been large enough to make it impossible to consider. As a result, various emergency devices have been used, going all the way from electric heaters to kerosene stoves. Many scholars who have worked in older libraries in Europe have experienced the lack of adequate heating.

High temperature and humidity can be combatted by a design which takes advantage of cooling breezes and may keep the humidity from rising and mold from developing. Most academic and research libraries in India, where construction costs are low, are planned on this basis, with the floor area used for readers and books being much larger than would be required in the United States. Natural ventilation is a basic requirement, since the apparatus for artificial cooling is more expensive than in the United States and often, because of governmental regulations, cannot be considered. In an industrially underdeveloped country where cooling apparatus has to be imported, it costs more than in the United States and Western Europe and very much more in relation to other construction costs.

In libraries in the United States, with the possible exception of Hawaii, the need for heating of some kind is taken for granted. The same is true for most Western European countries and many other parts of the world, although in the tropics, where the outside temperature rarely falls much below 60 degrees F (15.6 degrees C), the problem can be ignored without any great consequent discomfort.

Heating is expensive to install, operate, and keep up, and the lack of it does not harm books. The paper in books stored in unheated or poorly heated rooms is in better condition than that in books in many American libraries where the custom for many years was to overheat. However, with increasing concern for energy and the preservation of library materials, overheating is becoming somewhat less of a problem. In general, provided that humidity is controlled, the lower the temperature, the longer the books will last. However, it would be difficult to imagine a library kept at 40 degrees F (4.4 degrees C) for the sake of paper preservation, with readers and staff wrapped up in overcoats and perhaps only their faces and a few fingers exposed. If cold bookstacks are found to be desirable, book-storage arrangements may have to be replanned and books and readers housed in separate quarters; this solution seems doubtful at present except in closed stacks such as is often the case for rare-book libraries and in the great libraries of Europe. In one example, the University of Toronto Robarts Library aimed at 60 degrees F (15.6 degrees C) for the two basement floors which were built double-strength for compact shelving. The University of Chicago Regenstein Library was planned with stacks cooler than normal and with all but a few tables in separate warmer areas. Original technical specifications for Regenstein called for equipment which, during normal library service hours, could maintain a mean of 68 degrees F (20 degrees C) year-round in stack areas and a mean of 72 degrees F (22.2 degrees C) year-round in reading areas. Equipment installed is designed to maintain these temperatures and has done so in previous years. However, under the university's austere energy conservation program of the 1980s, no attempt was made to maintain differential temperatures in Regenstein stack and reading areas, and mean service hour temperatures are roughly 68 degrees F (20 degrees C) winter time and 72–74 degrees F (22.2–23.4 degrees C) summer time building-wide.

A warehouse-type book-storage facility might require heat only for the control of humidity. If a library is to be heated, how and how much? Many Americans believe that comfort requires a temperature in cold weather of not less than 70 degrees F (21 degrees C), although most of them and a considerably larger percentage of persons in other English-speaking countries would be content with 65 degrees F (18 degrees C) in a draft-free room. On the other hand, there has been a tendency on the part of Americans engaged in sedentary pursuits to prefer 72 to 75 degrees F (22 to 24 degrees C) or even more on a cold winter day; and this practice is still followed in some facilities, even though energy cost and preservation concern suggest lower temperatures. It is generally agreed that there is no exact ideal temperature for comfort or productivity. It is also widely accepted that so long as the temperature remains in the comfort zone, productivity will not be affected. The range of the comfort zone will vary with the customs of clothing, the degree of acclimatization of the individual to the prevalent atmospheric conditions, the radiant temperatures of surrounding surfaces, the relative humidity, the velocity of air movement, the color of surroundings, and the health, age, and weight of the individual. It is almost certain that at any given temperature, individuals can be found who would not be happy. It also appears clear that most people are relatively comfortable in a library with the temperature maintained between 68 and 72 degrees F (20 and 22 degrees C), and many people can be comfortable within a range of 65 and 78 degrees F (18 and 26 degrees C), although the factors of acclimatization, customs, and air flow will be more important at the extremes. It is interesting to note that, provided the temperature is not high enough to induce perspiration, the factor of relative humidity plays a fairly minor role in the comfort level.

The atmospheric conditions for human comfort and book preservation conditions can be broken down into seven topics: heating, cooling, humidifying, dehumidifying, filtering, insulating, and ventilating.

Heating. In parts of the world where the average temperature day and night may be below 55 or 60 degrees F (13 or 16 degrees C) for weeks at a time, central heating is certainly indicated and can generally be found. A library in such a climate should be heated, whether the heat is derived from warm or hot air, through registers or by radiators of one kind or another, or by radiant heat. It should be provided along the outside walls, particularly near the windows and doors, to prevent drafts that can easily make the space uncomfortable and too often uninhabitable by a reader. Methods of providing the heat as well as the fuel to be used—gas, oil, coal, wood, electricity or solar energy—will vary according to locality.

Heating arrangements should not interfere with library activities and usable space. These facilities may occupy floor space and reduce the area available for other purposes. The problems will vary considerably. Vertical heating ducts take the most floor area and radiant heat the least. Horizontal ducts use cubage, sometimes on a large scale. It must be realized that the space used by the heating plant and the total cost of installation and operation will vary also. Each aspect is important, and unless the librarian and the officers of the institution understand the problem and insist on a satisfactory and reasonably economical solution, the results can be unfortunate.

Two other heating problems frequently cause difficulties. First, there is undesirable variation in temperature from one part of the building to another—for instance, one side of a reading room or the north side of the building as a whole. A good installation can avoid variations by the use of thermostats, proper insulation, and adequate zoning of ducts and piping. Thermostats, except those in private offices, should be designed so that they cannot be adjusted by anyone other than an authorized member of the staff.

Second, there is difficulty in reducing the quantity of heat provided on a warm day or in increasing it on a cold one. To do so requires monitoring instruments, a signal system, and flow-activation control mechanisms. The person responsible for the design should know the possibilities and costs involved, should understand what different heating methods will do, and should know their flexibility under different conditions in providing the desired temperature. These are technical areas, and the librarian need not perform an in-depth review of the mechanical design. Rather, the librarian should reach a general level of confidence in and understanding of the mechanical system in consultation with the design engineer so that there is reasonable expectation that the design issues have been properly addressed.

As to general design criteria, one should make sure that rooms are provided with reasonably uniform temperature and that they are not 60 degrees F (16 degrees C) beside the windows with a strong draft, while 70 to 75 degrees F (21 to 24 degrees C) elsewhere; that they do not have cold floors; that the heating does not provide a blast that is unpleasant to feel and noisy to hear unless it is the intention of the design to provide white sound by this means. Make sure that the mechanical engineers and architects have considered the heat loss through floors, walls, windows, unheated attics; that each room is a unit that has been figured separately; and that the pressure coming from heated air in a duct installation is sufficient to prevent cold air infiltrating through windows and door cracks.

The heating-plant capacity should be equal to its task in severe weather; that is, the heat load it provides for should be capable of equaling the heat loss through conduction, radiation, and infiltration. Careful calculation of the heat load is required because if the plant is too small and pushed beyond capacity, results will be unsatisfactory, but if it is too large, the installation cost will be unnecessarily high. Normally a heating system is designed to meet a specific theoretical "low" temperature, and when this "low" is exceeded, the designed room temperature will drop. In Boston, for instance, the design is quite generally for 0 degrees F (-18 degrees C). In Nashville, Tennessee, it is for plus 3 degrees F (-16 degrees C).

Heating is ordinarily by one or more of three methods or combinations of them:

1. Warm air, with heat supplied by bringing in air above room temperature to a degree sufficient to counteract the heat losses. Warm-air systems today generally have fans to propel the air, instead of depending on gravity. Air is ordinarily discharged at a temperature of 90 to 100 degrees F or, with certain types of installation, up to 135 degrees F (32 to 38 or up to 57 degrees C), because at lower temperatures the room will feel drafty as the air comes into a cooler space. It should be so arranged as to blow a curtain of warm air across cold or exposed walls and windows. A certain amount of fresh outside air is included, and the controls may vary the percentage during different hours of night and day. The velocity of the air is important. If too low, the ducts must be very large and there is risk of stratification within the space, resulting in a sense of stagnation or a lack of air movement. If too high, the system will be noisy and the rooms drafty. As has already been indicated, the mechanical engineers will use detailed formulas which involve all the pertinent factors. With proper system design and thermostatic controls, it is not difficult to provide a satisfactory range of temperature.

2. Hot water or steam, with the heat coming to the rooms through pipes and radiators or convectors. Hot water is ordinarily pushed along by a circulation pump, just as warm air is pushed by an air fan. Gravity systems have been used for both in the past, and may even have limited uses today. The pump in hot-water systems is to provide greater flexibility in design and to speed up response to changed requirements. The forced circulation makes possible smaller pipes and more sensitive control. Expansion tanks are a necessary adjunct, as well as properly located vents. The librarian and the officers of the institution should remember that these take space for housing, as does the other mechanical equipment. Enough area must be provided for this functional necessity, which all too frequently is crowded into too small a space for efficient operation by the seemingly more demanding needs of the library. Always remember that a properly planned and organized mechanical plant requires space for operation, maintenance, and possible later replacement of units by new ones which may differ in some dimensions.

3. Panel or radiant heating consisting of warm coils in the floor, ceiling, or walls, provided with warm air, warm water, or electric-resistant heating elements. Radiant systems require different formulas for figuring the amount of heat required.

In this connection the amount of heat—British Thermal Units, or BTUs as they are called—required to keep the temperature at the desired level can be determined by standard formulas. The formulas are based not only on the number of cubic feet of space to be heated but also on the heat loss and gain resulting from three sources:

The number of persons occupying the space. People produce heat, the amount depending on whether they are active or sedentary.

The heat provided by the lighting equipment. In the past this was a significant source of heat, amounting to enough to warm almost the entire building. With lower light levels and reduced general lighting resulting from steps to conserve energy, heat from light sources today will be less than in the past. Even so, the heat coming from lighting and people should not be left out of consideration when selecting equipment for cooling.

The heat loss or gain through floors, walls, doors, windows, skylights, and ceilings. In a library this comes chiefly from outside walls and windows, from the roof to some extent if there is no attic, and more and more often from the floors.

Cold coming through the floors results primarily from a cold unheated basement or from an overhang, resulting from a floor cantilevered out over the great outdoors, as in the University of Chicago Law Library. In these cases, unless heat is provided in the floor, or unless at least proper insulation is applied to the underside of the slab, the area around the periphery of the building may become almost uninhabitable in severe weather. The amount of the heat gained or lost through the ceiling will depend partly on the type of roof insulation, particularly in the ceiling of the top floor of the building. But the great problem is the outside walls. There the heat loss or gain depends on the construction of the walls, the insulation used, and the amount of window space, together with the kind of windows and the kind of glass used.

Some will remember the metal frame casement windows in older libraries, such as the New York Public Library Central Building at 42nd Street and Fifth Avenue, where the cold air has tended to come in around the frames because they are not quite tight. Metal sash loses heat more readily than wood sash through the frame itself. Casement windows present a problem, particularly those with poor-fitting metal sashes. Weather stripping can be useful in solving the problem. Leaky windows present a condensation problem also.

Fixed sash is often used today in air-conditioned buildings and largely eliminates the leakage problem as well as a security problem. With fixed windows the operation of the building is at the mercy of the air-conditioning system; if the unit breaks down in hot summer weather, the building can become unusable, with no relief available from open windows. At some extra cost fixed windows can have key-controlled opening panels for such emergencies and for exterior window washing. If the system relied upon is prone to break down, and particularly if a good repair mechanic is not always available—something which is not unusual in rural areas and sometimes even in large cities—the use of fixed windows may be questionable or consideration of an alternative backup system may be warranted. Still, the improved security of fixed sash has a very important benefit for research libraries.

Buildings with their walls made up largely of single-thickness glass lose more heat than those with masonry walls. Glass is made today that, it is claimed, will reduce heat loss from the cold, or heat gain from the sun for that matter, but it is rarely if ever completely satisfactory. Double- and triple-pane glass provides an air space between the layers. Quiet air is perhaps the best of all insulation materials, and double- or triple-pane glass reduces condensation of water on windows if the room is humidified in cold weather.

The architectural program should indicate the temperature to be maintained in the building as a whole and in the different parts if there is to be a variation within it. The institution's representatives should keep in mind the effect of different types of walls on the cost of heating and should certainly talk the problem over with the architect before plans are approved, in order to avoid misunderstanding. If the building is to be humidified, the walls should have a vapor barrier.

The possibility and desirability of installing heating pipes to melt snow on sidewalks at the entrance or on roofs and gutters should be kept in mind in planning heat installation. Roof pipes circulating hot water must be planned with care so that freezing temperatures will not burst the pipe if the system is inactive.

Cooling or Air Conditioning. Cooling is only a part of air conditioning, but the latter term is too often used loosely as though it were in itself all that there is to air conditioning. Cooling consists of reducing or removing unwanted heat by supplying cool air. An excess of heat, at times when a building is not heated artificially, results from heat transmitted to the space through its shell, directly or indirectly, from radiation from the sun, from the heat generated in the library from lights, people, electrical and gas appliances, and from outside air brought in for ventilation purposes. Artificial lighting, especially that with high intensity, complicates matters considerably, varying with the type of the light source. Incandescent lights use more current to produce the same amount of light than fluorescent and therefore generate much more heat for the same lighting intensity, perhaps 2½ times as much. Photocopy machines, computer terminals, electric typewriters, and other electrically powered equipment add their own heat as well.

The total heat load—that is, the load imposed by transmitted plus internally generated heat—must be determined to decide on the size of the cooling plant required. The temperature to be obtained by the cooling must be agreed upon. A larger plant will, for example, be required to provide for 60 degrees F (16 degrees C) than that required for 75 degrees F (24 degrees C). Again, formulas are available for use by the engineers. A total cooling load is divided into two parts—sensible heat, which shows on a dry-bulb thermometer and comes from the sources listed in the preceding paragraph, and the latent load, which is the cooling required to remove unwanted moisture from the air-conditioned space.

For comfort, cooling a room to 80 degrees F (27 degrees C) dry-bulb and 50 percent relative humidity is under some circumstances acceptable. If the outside temperature is 95 degrees F (35 degrees C), to cool to 70 degrees F (21 degrees C) would be unduly expensive and actually would provide too great a contrast for comfort, although this may be a desired level of cooling for the preservation of the books. Some quite satisfactory installations are made with a capacity to keep the temperature no more than 10 degrees F (5 degrees C) lower than it is outside. If persons are to remain in a room for long during periods of hot weather, a lower temperature may be more desirable than it would be if they are coming and going at short intervals. As was indicated earlier, the architects and engineers must be told the desired temperature to be maintained.

It is suggested, at least for comfort, that in hot weather there never be more than 15 degrees F (8 degrees C) difference between inside and outside temperature in the shade and that 72 degrees F (22 degrees C) be considered satisfactory until outside temperature gets above 82 degrees F (22 degrees C). When the temperature goes above 82 degrees outside, the inside temperature can reasonably go up at least 2 degrees for each 3 degree increase outside. It is suggested that from 72 to 75 degrees F (22 to 24 degrees C) for inside temperature might be planned for, and in very hot weather that it be permitted to rise higher simply because the installation will not accomplish anything more. Of course, where book preservation is the major concern, other criteria must be used.

Specifications will vary among countries and institutions depending on local circumstances. In Great Britain the norms have been determined by the government, and its grants for a university library building cover the cost needed to achieve the following: The conditions for open-access stacks and areas designed for human occupancy should have a steady controlled temperature range of 18.5

degrees C (65 degrees F) in winter to 21 degrees C (70 degrees F) in summer, and a relative humidity range of 50 to 60 percent, never to exceed 65 percent RH. It is expected that close control of temperature will not be necessary, and that from time to time, when the external climate is extreme, a substantial drift (of say 5–6 degrees F) can be tolerated over a period of time. When a university library holds a special collection of rare books, an air-conditioning system providing more precise conditions can be provided.

As already noted, it may be found that lower temperatures are desirable for book storage. These temperatures are not too difficult to maintain in many places if the stacks are in well-insulated locations, such as below-surface basements, where the ground temperature is between 45 and 60 degrees F (7 and 16 degrees C) the year around, as it is in most of the United States.

Humidification and Dehumidification. The third and fourth factors are humidification and dehumidification. Many persons have failed to understand or to realize that heating systems in places where there is severe winter weather, which may lower the outside temperature to as much as 20 to 30 degrees F below zero (−29 to −34 degrees C), will reduce the relative humidity in a room heated to 70 degrees F (21 degrees C) or more to a point where it is no more than 10 percent. What are the results? Most persons will become accustomed to it; the skin and the mucous membranes dry out and may feel unpleasant, and respiratory ailments may tend to increase.

Alas, bindings and paper under these conditions dry out also. Old pigskin bindings, after having survived for hundreds of years undamaged in English manor houses without central heat, warp in a short time under American library conditions, so that the cover leather binding has actually pulled off the boards. Dryness does tend to make poor-quality paper more brittle, and heat tends to cause a more rapid chemical deterioration, which is even greater with high humidity. The larger the amount of acid in the paper, the more rapid this action. Almost all newspapers dating back to the beginning of the wood-pulp era in the 1870s have a short life at best, and in a well-heated library that life will be greatly reduced, often to less than twenty-five years if the use is more than negligible.

The useful life span of printed and manuscript material might well be doubled if the relative humidity in the rooms where they are stored is kept to between 40 and 50 percent year around and if the temperatures are maintained at the lowest reasonable level. Fortunately, in the winter this is not too difficult, although it may be expensive to accomplish satisfactorily. With warm-air heating installations, moisture can be sprayed into the air as it enters the heating system. Five problems must be met, however.

1. The moisture must be controlled, because it may rust out the ducts as it settles on metal surfaces.

2. The water must be filtered; otherwise, when it evaporates it may leave a residue of solids which settles in the form of dust on books and elsewhere. Dust is a serious enemy to books, not only because of the dirt but also because, however fine it may be, it is an abrasive.

3. In severe winter weather, when air with a relative humidity that is satisfactory strikes the cold surface of a glass window or any other cold substance, the moisture tends to condense and will run down the window or the wall with possibly serious results.

4. The introduction of moisture, which may be by a steam jet, presents certain risks, particularly if a valve is stuck or a control device fails. Where there is water, it seems to always find its way to the books eventually. Means of early detection of such an event together with a fail-safe shut-off system and perhaps a remote alarm are suggested.

5. In spaces containing a small volume of air, such as display cases, the control of humidity is a particularly difficult problem, especially when one wishes to add humidity. Careful analysis of the problem will be required to avoid dramatic shifts in the humidity where a small area requires minute additions of moisture to maintain the desired level. It should be constantly monitored.

The authors have had some unpleasant experiences in trying to humidify rooms that were constructed years ago with no thought of later winter humidification. Double-pane glass—Thermopane, for instance—will prevent condensation, but it is, of course, expensive, particularly in our modern "glass-box" buildings. Satisfactory insulation of walls and inclusion of a vapor barrier will help solve the problem if there is not too much glass. But the five traps noted above which may waylay the unwary should be kept in mind.

If severe winter weather is of short duration, the condensation problem can sometimes be avoided without double glass by permitting the percentage of relative humidity to drop for a few hours. The 5 to 7 percent of their weight in moisture that is usually held in the books and bindings will help temporarily, but the period must not be prolonged more than perhaps 48 hours at the most or damage will result.

Winter humidification can be produced by adding moisture to the air brought into the building in connection with its heating. A rapid drop in outside temperature, however, will bring condensation on walls and particularly windows and the ductwork. Since all building materials are porous, condensation of moisture in the walls may freeze in severe weather conditions; and the expansion that comes from freezing may then cause structural cracks and severe damage in concrete or cinder blocks. As previously mentioned, a vapor barrier is required.

For display cases that must have a separate carefully controlled environment, one technique is to design a sealed case with no internal heat source and to provide space for a tray of silica gel or other material to control the humidity within the case. Such an approach assumes that the ambient room temperature is satisfactory for the materials being displayed. Air conditioning, especially humidity control, is a particularly difficult problem in display cases although it has been done with mixed success. Part of the problem is that most of the components of an air-conditioning system are designed to handle large volumes of air. Because of this, dramatic changes in the temperature and humidity within the case often result. Steam as a source of humidity in an air-conditioned display case is probably not a good choice unless a means of throttling the steam to very small levels can be found. A carefully designed evaporation system is likely to be a safer solution, although the maintenance problems typically will be greater.

Commercial quality controls for humidity can be used both for the controlling mechanism and for an alarm system. They generally are accurate to a tolerance of plus or minus 5 percent or less, but they tend to drift. In an installation requiring careful control, the use of commercial controls may require a maintenance adjustment and perhaps cleaning on a monthly basis. Industrial controls are generally more accurate, and maintenance should be reduced to perhaps an annual adjustment and cleaning, but industrial quality controls are significantly more expensive than commercial quality controls. When an alarm system is employed, it is suggested that it be separate from the control system except for a shut-off feature. Further, if commercial controls are used in the general system, the alarm system should be of industrial or equal quality.

Dehumidification is in most ways and in many locations as serious a problem as humidification. This is particularly true in coastal areas in climates where there are prolonged hot and humid spells. Where the normal summer temperature stands in the 80s (27–32 degrees C) with long periods of high humidity, mold spores, which are always present, begin to grow. This even happens frequently in New England and through the Northern and Central states, particularly if wet basements result from rains and floods during a humid hot spell.

It is difficult and expensive to remove moisture from the air. Four methods are used:

1. Condensing machinery in connection with the ventilation installation. This is expensive to install and to maintain and, like most apparatus with moving parts, can be expected to wear out in due course. Twenty years might be considered a normal satisfactory lifetime for most installations.

2. Chemical moisture absorbers. With these the air is passed through or over moisture-absorbing chemicals, such as silica gel. The capacity of this technique is fairly limited, although it is well suited for properly designed display cases. Removal of the water from the chemical will require a routine maintenance process. One simple procedure is to bake the absorbent to drive the water out. To be effective in a display case, the case must be sealed air tight.

3. Local portable unit dehumidifiers. These are sometimes installed in damp basements. They may resemble in shape the old-fashioned oil heaters. No expensive ducts are required, but the moisture they remove must either be carried out of the building by hand at comparatively short intervals during very humid weather or the unit must be provided with a drain connection that will result in the condensed water running outside.

4. A fourth method sometimes used is to exhaust the hot humid air with fans during the hours when the outside air is cooler than that inside but not too humid. The library is kept closed up in the daytime, with window shades lowered to prevent overheating from radiation from the sun, and then late at night, when the outside temperature is at its lowest point, an exhaust fan is set in motion, and the previous day's hot air is removed and replaced by the cool night air. Unfortunately, in very humid weather, it sometimes happens that the night air brought in is very close to the dewpoint and, if the daytime temperature does not go up, condensation inside may result and mold spores may grow. If a humidistat is placed in the intake and adjusted to stop the change in air when the relative humidity outside is too high, this difficulty can be largely obviated.

Filtering. All ventilation installations should, if possible, include filtering units. Removal of dust, pollen, and other air-borne particles results in a healthier atmosphere and lower maintenance costs for cleaning. It also prevents cooling and heating coils and ducts from becoming blocked, and, perhaps of even greater importance, prevents damage to books. Evidence that air passing through a library can be dirty is available in a good look at a used filter or at the accumulations of dust and dirt near air intakes. Filters may be of either a throwaway or a cleanable type, and they are manufactured to block particles of a certain size. A dual or even triple mechanical filtration, each successive filter of a greater efficiency rating, can improve the effectiveness. In earlier days air was passed through a water spray to remove the dust, and oil filters were sometimes used. As noted in Chapter 5, such systems may be desirable today, particularly for removing air-borne acids. However, there has been concern expressed in regard to volatile solvents which may be produced by an oil filtration process.

One of the factors of great importance in filtering is the removal of industrial chemical pollution from the air, which, particularly in our large cities, tends to include a considerable amount of sulfur dioxide. This, combined with the chemical residues left in a large proportion of modern paper, hastens the deterioration of the paper and, in fact, gradually permits it to burn up with the distressing results which we have all seen in an extreme form in late nineteenth- and twentieth-century newspapers. A wash or bath filter is the best way to eliminate sulfur dioxide and other noxious gases that are harmful to paper. These are expensive filters and may only be justified in special-collection areas of research libraries.

The location of the air intake is important. If it is close to the ground, it may take into the air-supply system the chemical and exhaust pollutions which unfortunately abound in urban areas.

Insulation. Both heating and cooling are provided to limit the inside environmental temperature changes. This maintenance of a desirable inside condition is greatly aided by insulation. Good insulation greatly decreases the demands on the heating and cooling systems, as has been suggested above. More money can be put into heating and cooling to make insulation unnecessary, or the reverse emphasis can be chosen. Engineers need to calculate the comparative costs to attain the specified design conditions. As one example, the Davis Library built in 1983 at the University of North Carolina, Chapel Hill, was determined to require insulation with an "R" value of 7.04 because the design goal of 10 was only in part met by an inside surface providing 0.61; a 3-in. average tapered roof-deck fill giving 0.84; a 5-in. structural concrete deck, 0.41; vapor barrier worth 0.15; a built-up roof with slag providing 0.78; and an outside factor of 0.17. While roofs are of prime concern, other exterior faces are important, especially the south and west exposures. The inert nature of insulation makes it an excellent investment for the long term, and it deserves more attention for the economy of the life cycle of a library building.

Ventilation. Heating, cooling, humidification, dehumidification, and filtering by themselves will not provide completely satisfactory atmospheric conditions. Ventilation must come with them. It requires a change of air rapid enough to counteract odors and pollution of any kind. Building codes and local rules govern minimum standards. In most places with limited occupancy, ventilation is provided for through the heating system in cold weather, or through leakage of air or open windows in hot weather, or by "gravity" circulation caused by the weight difference of hot and cold air. A slight positive pressure should be maintained so that leakage is cleaned air going out, not polluted air coming in. A ventilation system may be called a dilution process, by which odor or heat removed is equal to that generated on the premises. It is particularly useful in windowless or below-grade areas, where, without a change in air, a stale or musty odor may result. It is very important in photocopy alcoves or rooms, critical for audio-equipment areas and projection booths, and essential for computers if air conditioning is not provided.

The amount of fresh air that should be brought in will depend on the total cubic volume of the area and the amount of heat, moisture, and odor generated in it, which in turn will be largely affected by the number of persons occupying the premises and their activities. The amount of fresh air in terms of cubic volume per person required in a theater where the occupants are sitting quietly may be no more than 10 percent as much as is desirable in a gymnasium. Many ventilation systems are unsatisfactory primarily because they do not provide adequate changes of air. The code requires a minimum of 5 cubic feet of fresh air per minute (CFM) for each occupant, but it does not specify the number of air changes per hour. With 10 percent outside air used as a standard for recirculating systems, the amount of fresh air usually exceeds 5 CFM per person. The ventilation norm in the United States is 12 air changes per hour in toilets and 3 to 10 elsewhere, depending on the extent of smoking. The British norm is 10 in toilets and 6 elsewhere.

HVAC Summary. Air-conditioning and ventilation systems in libraries today are generally part of what are known as central-heating systems that cover the building as a whole. Indeed, in many academic institutions a single system may serve the whole institution. To be satisfactory, even with a perfect installation, there must be local thermostats or controls. The demands on the system will vary with the number of occupants, the direction of the wind, the amount of sunshine. No installation without local controls can be completely satisfactory, though local controls, of course, add to the cost.

In some buildings the whole system is based on local units, one for each room or section of the building, and makes use of room or unit conditioners, which are fairly common in single rooms in private houses, apartments, and offices. The Grinnell College Library has used this method. The use of local units to this extent is generally frowned on by mechanical engineers and maintenance personnel. Decentralized maintenance arrangements present complications, and the provision of satisfactory "comfort" cooling or heating within a reasonable degree of engineering standards is lost. On the other hand, there is less likelihood of the building becoming completely uninhabitable because of mechanical breakdown.

Air conditioning requires not only machinery, electric current, and the availability of an expert mechanic, but also an adequate water supply. If an adequate water supply is not available at a reasonable cost from local governmental or private agencies or perhaps from a well driven for the purpose, a cooling tower or, in small installations, an evaporative condenser will help. Note that there may be local restrictions against "waste water" used in air-conditioning systems and that wells have been known to run dry.

Whether or not a new library should provide for full air conditioning (that is, heating, cooling, humidification, dehumidification, and filtering, as well as a satisfactory change of air) will depend on local conditions and funds available. The decision may be difficult to make because the costs involved are considerable. Furthermore, a sizable and valuable space is required for the mechanical equipment and ducts, and cubage and floor area are the basic costs in a new building. Space for the mechanical room and perhaps for a water tower can, however, sometimes be found in an unused basement area or on the roof of an adjacent building, thereby saving valuable floor area in the new structure. Space was found in Widener at Harvard for the mechanical equipment and cooling towers for Houghton and Lamont libraries. Complete air conditioning is unnecessary in many institutions. If an institution is located in a section of the country where the number of days with the temperature rising above 85 degrees (29 degrees C) is limited, exhaust fans for use at night in all but very humid weather may solve the problem with reasonable satisfaction. The deciding factor may not be the comfort of the readers and the staff but the value of the collections. If so, a solution may possibly be found by segregating the rare and irreplaceable books and manuscripts and providing humidification and dehumidification for them but not for the building as a whole.

Two generations ago comparatively few libraries were air conditioned; indeed, satisfactory air conditioning had not been developed. Theoretically, the Widener Library, built in 1915, was air conditioned, but the system was so expensive and the results were so unsatisfactory that within a few months after the opening of the building it was given up and never used again. In the winter of 1941–42, when the Houghton Rare Book Library at Harvard was put into use, it had a complete air-conditioning installation which was very satisfactory until twenty years later, when the refrigerant condensing apparatus wore out and it became difficult to maintain the desired relative humidity. This condensing-equipment installation has been replaced. The air conditioning in the Lamont Undergraduate Library is not quite as elaborate as that in Houghton, but it has proved to be satisfactory, in spite of occasional lapses. As is commonly the case, it took some months to get the air conditioning properly adjusted when the building was first opened.

The inexperienced librarian expects to walk into a newly completed building and to be able to have the air-conditioning system operate in accordance with the design criteria set up for the architects and engineers. Unfortunately, all air-conditioning systems are fairly complicated and require a "shake-down cruise" of at least one year and often more during which (1) the controls, air flow, fan speed, valves, etc., are adjusted for accurate operation and maximum results, and (2) the best method of operation is learned by the personnel who are responsible, a method which often is quite different from those with which they have previously been acquainted.

Most new libraries throughout the country are now using air conditioning. In some cases, in order to save funds, unsatisfactory installations have been made. In others the air-conditioning ducts have been installed with the hope that the mechanisms involved would be acquired at a later time. Unfortunately when this has been done, the ducts have not always been adequate in size, and when the air conditioning system has been finally installed, its distribution has proved to be inadequate. Complete air conditioning is not recommended for all new library buildings. Undoubtedly there are libraries where, because of climatic conditions, comparatively small summer use, or lack of funds to provide for other equally or more important requirements, air conditioning is not essential. But it might not be an exaggeration to say that in a majority of cases in the United States, a new library without an air-conditioning system is obsolete at the time its doors are opened. This is certainly the case where research collections are involved.

From time to time the question of air conditioning an old library building comes up. Often it is feasible, though the installation tends to be more expensive than in a new building because holes for the ducts must be opened up in walls and floors; it may be difficult to conceal the ducts satisfactorily, and too often the results have not been up to standard. An example of a good installation of this kind is at the Newberry Library in Chicago. Sometimes it is possible and less expensive in an old building to provide local air conditioning for parts of the structure or to use small high-velocity ducts with sound absorbers, as was done at the Chinese-Japanese Library of Harvard. Top-floor rooms, where the attic can be used for the apparatus, or first-floor rooms adjacent to basements, where there is space unusable for other purposes, are possibilities. Window air conditioners are another, but they do not add to the attractiveness of a facade and are not satisfactory in other ways. Freestanding unit air conditioners are a possibility, but they will require a means of removing the heat, which requires either a water source or an exterior cooling device.

When considering the air-conditioning and ventilation problem, there are at least five alternatives, as follows:

1. Heating only. This is not recommended in most libraries.
2. Minimum recommended installation. Heating and ventilating with air filtration and controls which allow the use of nighttime air for cooling.
3. Comfort installation. Heating, ventilation, air filtration, good insulation, and cooling. This is recommended if the library is open to the public during long, hot, and humid periods or has a modest concern for the preservation of the books.
4. Conditioned installation. Heating, ventilation, air filtration, good insulation, cooling, and humidity control. This is the minimum recommended for situations noted in 3 if the collections have rare and irreplaceable books and manuscripts.
5. The ideal installation. Heating, ventilation, air filtration, cooling, and humidity control, all within certain specified narrow limits in order to maintain ideal conditions of temperature and humidity the

year around, regardless of outside conditions. Excellent insulation. This is recommended for all research libraries with valuable collections.

Of course, the cost of installation and operation increases with each step. If a library adopts the minimum procedure, it may be desirable to size the ductwork and equipment space so that the comfort and conditioning installations can be added in the future without undue cost. Filtering is desirable in any system that brings outside air into the library and is necessary in any area with considerable air pollution.

If air cooling for the building as a whole is not possible because of the cost and if use of the library during the unpleasantly hot months is limited, it may be desirable to install local room units in working areas and possibly in one reading area.

One word of warning about air conditioning. Because of the multitude of variables, it is less than an exact science. Some would even claim it is an art. Any installation should be designed by a reliable and competent architect and engineer.

The cost of heating, ventilation, and air conditioning depends primarily on the availability and the cost of three factors: (1) the heating agent, generally coal, oil or gas, solar energy, or exhaust steam from an electric generating plant; (2) the cooling agent, generally water; and (3) electric current to provide the power required. These costs vary considerably in different parts of the United States and in other countries and even from year to year in the same place. Many institutional heating plants today are so designed that a shift from coal to gas or oil can be made fairly readily and inexpensively.

There is a tremendous variation in water costs. Occasionally enough water at a desirable temperature can be provided by a well on the premises, yet an institution must be wary of well water for wells are notoriously unreliable. Often water costs are high enough so that a water-cooling tower will pay for itself; it may be required by law. It is desirable and economical to recirculate the water used for condensing the refrigerant.

The cost of electric current varies also. In figuring costs, the intensity of artificial light and the heat gain and loss resulting from too much natural light or poor insulation in walls and roofs may be a large factor. On the other hand, satisfactory physical conditions are bound to promote the use of the library and are well worth paying for.

Air conditioning creates acoustic problems. A satisfactory solution may require the use of an acoustic engineer. These problems may arise from:

1. Compressors or transformers immediately above, below, or beside a reading or workroom area.
2. Fan and motor noise, transmitted as vibrations felt through the structure and walls or heard through ductwork.
3. Air movement at too rapid a pace through supply or exhaust ductwork.
4. Cooling-tower fans, a noise usually more disturbing outside than inside the building and a serious matter when the building is near dormitories or residences, particularly at night when the noise seems to be amplified by the quiet prevailing elsewhere. This problem has been too often neglected. It is emphasized that problems are created by vibration if equipment is not adequately isolated from the structure.

In connection with the sections on lighting, heating, and ventilating, the possibility of the use of central power plants for the services required by a library should be mentioned. Central electric-generating plants are common, with service either available at a price from commercial companies or operated by the institution. Central steam generators and chilled water plants are generally available in larger institutions. The use of a centrally controlled electrical panel for heating and ventilation may also be indicated in a large operation in order to reduce personnel overhead in buildings unoccupied at night, on Sundays, and on holidays.

It is important for the institution to know whether the capacity of existing utilities is sufficient. An engineering study may be essential to determine this, even for major remodeling if heavier requirements are involved in support of audio-visual or computer installations and for air conditioning. A major addition or entirely new structure often requires enlarged utilities for electrical power generation and distribution, steam and chilled-water generation and distribution, sanitary and storm sewer systems, and perhaps even telecommunications. Libraries with precise environmental conditions are very demanding of utilities.

Finally, it is suggested that before the institution signs off on the design development phase for the mechanical system, the programming sections, particularly those in Chapter 5 dealing with the control of the environment, should be reviewed. Decisions made at this phase should be considered as fairly fixed; changes later will be costly.

To indicate how an environmental concept involves various mechanical systems, the 1986 Harvard Depository in Southborough, Massachusetts, is described. The Depository is protected by security guards and provided with smoke, heat, and intrusion alarms. The detection system is connected to the local fire department through a direct, dedicated telephone line. A pre-action sprinkler system was installed in the administrative area and the garage used for night storage of the electronic lift, areas separated from the stack by fire walls. The storage building itself meets fire code regulations without requiring a sprinkler system. Air quality is aided by the building's vapor barrier insulation. The interior environment is controlled for harmful particles, oxides of nitrogen, ozone, sulphur dioxide, and formaldehyde by carbon filters, and the quality of internal air improved constantly by the facility's heating and cooling process. The facility is constructed of materials that do not emit gases, and the closed stack also protects air quality. To control against infestation, HDI will fumigate when necessary before shelving materials. Materials are also protected by a sophisticated air filtration and rotation system. This environmental control system is designed to limit the rate of change in both temperature and humidity levels, rather than to maintain a single level of temperature and humidity.

The design criteria for temperature in HDI is to ± 3 degrees daily variation; for humidity, to ± 3 percent daily variation. The Depository's operating plan allows for gradual changes in temperature and humidity as the seasons change, with the rate of change strictly limited to 9 degrees F (5 degrees C) and 5 percent relative humidity per month. The maximum summer and minimum winter temperatures will be 70 and 50 degrees; and maximum summer and minimum winter relative humidity indexes, 60 and 40 percent. To maintain climate control standards, there is unobstructed air rotation space around each thirty-foot stack and between the stacks and the outer walls. Each aisle is served individually by multiple intakes (set low) and supply ducts (set high), and, as a further protection against the formation of microclimates, temperature and humidity sensors identify any stratification between the top and bottom of the stack. Air in the stack rotates a maximum of six times per hour.

Concepts of Lighting and Sun Control. Lighting is perhaps the most important and, at the same time, the most controversial aspect of library design. It is both an art and a science. Some aspects of lighting are easily specified and measured; others may be easy to describe, but measurement is difficult if not impossible. There is a considerable array of products available, each with a carefully planned sales pitch which often can serve to confuse and confound the library planner.

For a library to function at all, it must have light that works; and the librarian should therefore be keenly interested. What are the factors? One must consider reflective glare, direct glare, contrast, reflective qualities, the nature of the task, flicker, hum (from ballasts), aesthetics, scale, shape, intensity, energy consumption, life expectancy, the ease of cleaning, the distribution or diffusion of the light, color, and cost of replacement. To add to the complexity, the designer has natural light as well as incandescent, fluorescent, and high-intensity discharge light sources. Furthermore, the design of lighting fixtures is almost limitless.

This section will discuss a number of the aspects that should be considered during the decision process. The critical factors to be considered, not necessarily in their order of importance, include the type of light source, glare, contrast, intensity, aesthetics, flexibility, and cost. These factors will be discussed in the order listed. Together, these elements determine the quality of the light.

Light Sources. Until about 1900 the sun was the chief source of light in most libraries, and the need for making full use of sunlight was a more important consideration in library architecture than almost any other single factor. The Furness Library at the University of Pennsylvania is an interesting example of a library designed for the maximum use of natural light. However, natural light does present a number of problems.

Even what is considered good north light on a bright winter's day may prove to be a source of discomfort if fresh snow is on the ground, unless the windows are protected from the snow glare. South light with a low winter sun can be very troublesome in northern latitudes. Western windows, late in the day, make shielding of some kind essential in all parts of the world. In spite of wide overhangs and glare-protecting glass, expensive drapes or screening of one kind or another are desirable, and all of them have to be maintained and may have to be replaced oftener than has been generally anticipated. In spite of the architects' endeavors to utilize these corrective measures, complications continue to arise.

Perhaps the greatest concern about natural light in libraries is the damage it does to library materials if they are exposed to direct sunlight day in and day out. Of course, the sunlight can be filtered, and devices can be used to remove all direct sunlight. But the best control is to avoid natural light altogether in the collections area of the building.

Today most libraries have windows—some claim that many of them have too many windows. Nevertheless, in the United States, and to a lesser extent elsewhere, there is comparatively little dependence on natural light. Artificial illumination might be said to be required during approximately one-half of the hours that the average library is open for public use, and it is used, in fact, during a very much larger percentage of that period. However, concern for energy conservation suggests that even the use of artificial illumination needs to be controlled. In large areas of the building, the lighting may be turned off except when it is needed, provided the capability to do this is built into the design. Aside from the practical issues of natural versus artificial illumination, natural light is said by many to be important for psychological reasons. Yet in many libraries large areas used for reading, as well as for book storage, have no natural light today, and few people complain.

The Brigham Young University Library in Provo, Utah, in 1962 had two large underground floors with some 45,000 sq ft (4181 m²) each, seating for 1000, and no windows, but it was so well arranged and lighted that the reader soon forgot that windows were lacking. A major addition was completed in 1977 which also has two windowless underground floors so well lit that readers do not feel closed in or shut off. The Louisiana State University Library in Baton Rouge has a windowless lower floor with 66,000 sq ft (6130 m²) of floor space and accommodations for many readers.

Large window areas also have the serious disadvantage of permitting cold to enter in the winter and heat in the summer. Natural light, particularly if the sun shines directly into the room, almost inevitably brings unpleasant glare and shadows in its train. Yet it can be very pleasant. Natural light, as has been said, may be "for readers, not for reading," but its use is more successful if controlled. Windows, the problems they present, and methods to protect them are discussed later in this chapter.

Electric lamps today come in three main types: high-intensity discharge (HID), incandescent, and fluorescent. Because of their color, low pressure sodium and some mercury vapor light sources are not common in libraries. However, color corrected mercury and metal halide lamps are found in kiosk "up" light fixtures as well as in occasional "down" light fixtures in rooms with very high ceilings. High-pressure sodium fixtures may be found in a few institutions. HID lamps provide greater intensity than incandescent bulbs using an equal amount of current. They are slow in reaching their full intensity after being switched on, but the length of the delay has now been reduced, and there is a prospect of their increased use in the years ahead, often in combination with one of the other types of lamps. The fixture for mercury and other HID lamps may have a lens that is very important to maintain as it serves the function of an ultraviolet filter. Without this lens, there is risk of a health hazard due to potential excessive UV radiation. The HID bulb itself has a protective outer shell, yet in some cases, if this shell is broken, the lamp will continue to function while producing excessive amounts of UV radiation.

Metal-halide (HID) and quartz (incandescent) light sources are very intense; their use is typically for accent lighting or indirect or long range (high ceiling) lights. It should be realized that a fair amount of radiant heat is generated by this type of fixture, which can lead to some discomfort if it shines on people. This type of light source is not very suitable for general reading.

Incandescent tungsten bulbs and fluorescent tubes are by far the most common source of light in libraries. It is commonly recognized that incandescent bulbs produce an excellent quality of light. They are relatively expensive in terms of replacement and energy costs, but for special effects or circumstances, these should not be concerns. For general illumination, however, these costs are significant. An incandescent bulb, or any other high-intensity bulb, concentrates the source of light into a small space, which makes it easier to remove dust and dirt but creates more filament brightness; this must be shielded to prevent glare. One should realize, however, that any unshielded light source, however much it is dispersed, should be avoided because it causes discomfort if one looks directly at it or if it reflects off the task into the reader's eye.

For many years it was felt that the fluorescent tube was a poor second choice in many areas of the library. However, with its many advantages and improvements over the years, the pendulum has swung in favor of fluorescent, in spite of the slight flickering and ballast noise that are still common faults. It should be added that all of the HID lights require a ballast which often will produce a hum. Careful design and the selection of the correct ballast can reduce the hum. At a considerable increase in installation costs, modern remote ballasts can completely eliminate the humming, and the practice of using two parallel fluorescent tubes in each fixture or two tubes end to end on the same ballast will largely overcome the stroboscopic effect; the use of indirect or shielded lighting will also help, as will the replacement of the tubes before they fully burn out. Some authorities still believe that a few persons for some physiological reason are allergic to fluorescent lighting, and in a large library it may be desirable to provide for their use a limited number of seating accommodations with incandescent bulbs. It is a question whether the readers prefer it to the fluorescent lighting elsewhere in the building. They may simply prefer the earlier lighting pattern because it is less visually distracting and gives the feel of a home rather than a factory.

Some experts have suggested that something about the quality of fluorescent light makes it desirable to use a higher intensity than is used with incandescent, but that the glare can be overcome by adding a small amount of incandescent light to the fluorescent installation. This theory has not been generally accepted. There have been attempts to improve the color effects by going back to incandescent or to a combination of the two. While incandescent bulbs have by nature a warm color, and fluorescent and mercury tubes are visually cold, both mercury and fluorescent tubes are obtainable "color-corrected" to various degrees of warmth and can be further corrected by the use of colored reflectors. Where high-pressure sodium light is used, it is sometimes combined with metal halide lamps for color correction. Examples of this combination may be found in large department stores.

Fluorescent lamps project light satisfactorily at right angles to the tubes, but their reduced efficiency beyond the ends of the tubes makes it difficult, when using direct lighting, to light shelves or individual tables along a wall at right angles to them without the installation of additional tubes parallel to the wall and fairly close to it. If the fixtures installed provide primarily indirect light, this problem may be solved, provided the fixtures are not too far from the wall. Although light from unprotected fluorescent tubes will fade bindings, special sleeves are available that will provide the required protection to a large extent, but this form of protection will not reduce glare. A better solution is to control the unwanted light spectrum with a lens designed to filter ultraviolet light such as UFII or III Plexiglas. The Verd-a-ray Fadex light tube is a third solution. Fluorescent lamps can provide a good overall illumination with great flexibility, and, with a carefully selected fixture, they may make it easier than it is with incandescent bulbs to shift furniture and bookstacks around without relocating lighting fixtures.

One can choose from a number of fluorescent tubes having a variety of diameters, and each is effective for specific applications. There are many types of them: rapid-start, instant-start, jumbo, slimline, HO (high output), VHO (very high output), Watt Mizer, Fadex, circular, and square. Many of these and other varieties are or have been available in a wide variety of colors. By using a "lower light output ballast," 8 ft long (2.438) tubes using only 40 watts of current can be provided, thereby distributing the light obtained over a larger area than is the case with a 4 ft (1.219) tube using the same wattage. These tubes are used in the bookstacks, as well as in the reading areas, in Lamont. Both the tubes and the ballasts are involved in the HO and VHO installations.

The advantages of fluorescent lamps can be summed up as follows: They use less than one-half of the current required by incandescent lights to obtain the same intensity and result in less than one-half of the heat, a very important consideration if high-intensity lighting and air conditioning are to be used. Fluorescent tubes have a long life, up to ten times that of incandescent lamps, particularly if not turned on and off frequently. They give greater flexibility. They have the disadvantages of higher installation and tube-replacement costs, and fixture cleaning may take more time.

If lights are required for a large percentage of the hours during which the library is open, fluorescent light is cheaper, if the long view is taken, particularly if the cost of current is high. It should be remembered in this connection that many modern libraries rely almost altogether on artificial light because of the depth of the rooms from the outside walls combined with comparatively low ceilings and often with small window areas. Lights in reading areas are commonly left on during full opening hours in the United States, in spite of efforts of thrifty administrators to prevent it.

Glare. There are two general types of glare that concern the designer—direct and reflected glare. Both represent serious problems requiring attention. Direct glare results from the presence of areas of high brightness that can be seen in the periphery of one's vision. Direct glare can be produced by the brightness of a luminous ceiling, exposure to a window, or a brightly illuminated wall or other surface. Indirect glare results from the reflection of light off the surface of the task. Of all the qualities that can be discussed for light, the control of glare is probably the most important.

Glare can be controlled by locating the light fixture so that the reflection of light off the task is away from the reader's eyes and so that the brightness of the light source itself is not within the range of the reader's peripheral vision. This is most easily done where the task location is relatively fixed or when the reader can adjust the light source or reading position to avoid glare. A second alternative is to identify a fixture for general illumination which has qualities of low glare. Several possibilities with varying degrees of success exist.

Indirect light results in improved quality but reduced intensity derived from the same wattage. The amount of reduction depends on the distance the light must travel from the source to the task, the reflecting surfaces of the fixtures and ceilings and walls, and also the amount of dirt and dust on the fixtures and elsewhere. Even if the intensity is reduced, the quality may be so improved as to provide a higher degree of visual efficiency.

No individual fixtures are universally satisfactory, as most "systems" are more suitable for a specific lighting requirement rather than general illumination throughout. The lighting requirements for the lobby, circulation desk, display area, general reading areas, rest rooms, studies, and closets are all different; each may suggest a different approach or a certain degree of compromise. In reading rooms fluorescent lamps with troffers and reflectors are sometimes recessed into the ceiling, with acoustic tiles or plaster filling the space between the fixtures. The distance between the troffers depends on the intensity desired, on whether the tubes are single or multiple, and on their wattage. The fixtures and tubes do not need to be in rows. Different patterns can be used, but one must be careful to avoid what might be called a disorderly appearance, which too often causes distraction.

In the early 1960s, H. Richard Blackwell determined that a lens designed to polarize the light in the vertical axis would significantly reduce the problem of reflected glare for general illumination. He was able to demonstrate also that as the distribution of the light sources increased (again, for general illumination), the ability to read the task improved until the ultimate configuration of a fully luminous ceiling with polarizing lenses was reached. Several libraries installed polarized light fixtures, including the Meyer Memorial Library at Stanford, and it is generally accepted that this type of light is an improvement over other lens systems. However, the light source is still fairly bright, and, therefore, some glare from fixtures does occur some distance away in front of the reader.

Another fixture that has been popular recently is constructed of a specially anodized aluminum in the form of a parabolic reflector or series of reflectors. The key advantage of this system is that the light is cut off at an angle that dramatically limits direct glare. However, if one looks up into the fixture, the fluorescent tube is fully visible, which means that reflective glare can be a problem. This type of fixture is particularly well suited for

range aisle lighting or lighting where the location of the fixture in relation to the task can be determined to minimize reflected glare. However, the fixture probably is not ideal for general illumination.

A combination of the key principles of the two systems just described probably would produce the best possible general illumination, that is, a fixture which produces well-diffused light (even if not polarized) while cutting off the light at an angle (about 45 degrees) to eliminate direct glare. A quick test of a lighting fixture is to place a mirror in the position of the task. Then, if from a normal reading position you can see a bare tube or a very bright light source in the mirror, you will probably be looking at a fixture that produces enough reflected glare to be a problem.

Well-done indirect light is similar in quality to a luminous ceiling, and probably superior to separate fixtures with common translucent lenses. With the advent of improved HID light sources, the kiosk light fixture has been available as an excellent source of indirect light. However, this fixture consumes floor space; and in order to avoid excessive brightness, the ceiling must be fairly high, about 11 ft (3.353) being ideal. This type of lighting is attractive in part because of the efficiency of the HID light source, but the replacement of a HID bulb is not particularly cheap.

With indirect lighting, ceiling reflection is important. In small rooms the value of wall reflection should not be forgotten, and in larger ones the same holds for floor coverings. Other things being equal, light colors give better reflection, but glossy surfaces should be avoided.

One more comment about glare. It is important to avoid it anywhere both in its reflected and in its direct form, particularly in places where older persons are reading. The deleterious effects of glare increase considerably in middle life and later as a result of a physiological sclerosis of the lens.

Contrast. Eyestrain is reduced if the surroundings provide comparatively little contrast with pages of the book that is being read. It is recommended that tabletops be fairly light in color, floors not too dark, and the walls, ceilings, and woodwork on the light side. Then when the eye wanders from book to tabletop or to the floor or walls, the pupil of the eye does not have to shift in size, an adaptation which may cause temporary discomfort. A glossy-white table, used with direct lighting, tends to produce an excessive brightness in relation to the other surroundings. Glossy surfaces and finishes result in glare and should be avoided. In spite of what has been said, some architects and librarians feel that, even if dark surfaces in the reading room are less comfortable for the eyes and more light must be provided, they make the whole room so much more attractive that they should be used. A room without any color tone contrast can itself be tiring on eyes and aesthetically may seem to lack "character." Ralph Galbraith Hopkinson's *Architectural Physics: Lighting* contains objective studies of lighting problems. A chapter entitled "For the Future" lists some principles of good lighting, which follow:

1. We see better the more light we have, up to a point, but this light must be free from glare.
2. We see better if the main visual task is distinguished from its surroundings by being brighter, or more contrasting, or more colorful, or all three. It is therefore important to identify the main focal points and build up the lighting from their requirements.
3. We see better if the things we have to look at are seen in an unobtrusive and unconfusing setting, neither so bright nor so colorful that it attracts the attention away, nor so dark that work appears excessively bright with the result that the eyes are riveted on to the visual task. Good lighting therefore provides a moderate and comfortable level of general lighting, with preferential lighting on the work. This can be called "focal lighting."
4. The surroundings should be moderately bright, and this should be achieved by combination of lighting and decoration.
5. No source of light should be a source of glare discomfort. Excessively bright areas should never be visible. Windows should be provided with curtains, blinds or louvres, to be brought into use when the sky is very bright.
6. Plenty of light should reach the ceiling, in order to dispel any feeling of gloom, and to reduce glare.
7. Sources of light should be chosen to ensure that the color rendering which they give is satisfactory for the situation in which they will be found.
8. Care should be taken to eliminate any discomfort from flickering light sources.
9. A dull uniformity should at all costs be avoided. Small brilliant points of light can give sparkle to a scene without causing glare.
10. The lighting of a building should be considered always in relation to its design and in particular to the scheme of decoration to be installed. On no account should lighting be considered to be merely a matter of windows or fittings. The whole environment enters into a good lighting installation.[1]

Intensity. The topic of intensity was briefly treated in Section 5.3. Intensity is always a controversial subject, and it directly relates to several of the other lighting issues, especially glare, contrast, and the nature of the task being performed. This problem is confounded by the fact that intensity is relatively easy to measure while the other factors are not. Because of this, there has been an historic tendency to specify the exact intensity desired while little was said about anything else. In the last twenty-five years the fallacy of this approach has been well documented; the fact that quality is more important than quantity is generally accepted.

Ophthalmological research specialists recommend levels well below those proposed by the engineers and fixture manufacturers. Dr. David G. Cogan, chief of neuro-ophthalmology, National Eye Institute, Bethesda, Maryland, has clearly voiced his view: "The beliefs that relatively intense illumination is necessary for visual efficiency and that weak illumination induces organic disease of the eyes are probably the most widely held misconceptions pertaining to ophthalmology."[2] Dr. Cogan goes on to say that the recommendations of this science have come as a considerable surprise to those familiar with the human ability to adapt to dark and to those who are acquainted with previous reports that 10 footcandles (107.6 lx) were adequate for ordinary purposes and that not more than 20 footcandles (215.2 lx) were required for exceptionally fine work. He also says that intensities greater than 20 footcandles (215.2 lx) have no practical significance.

The Ferree and Rand research team, working in the field of physiological optics, found that if light is well distributed in the field of vision and there are no extremes of surface brightness, the eye can adjust to a wide range of intensity.

[1] Ralph Galbraith Hopkinson, *Architectural Physics: Lighting* (London: HMSO, 1963), p. 125.
[2] Quoted by Mr. Metcalf in the first edition, 1965.

It may be well to note in this connection that H. Richard Blackwell, whose 1958 studies on the effect of the quantity of illumination were so extensively quoted by the advocates of high intensity, clarified his position in a series of articles in which he insists that quality which is largely based on contrast is more important than intensity. In a contribution entitled "Lighting the Library—Standards for Illumination" he says:

> The light intensity we require depends drastically upon the task we are to perform.... The data certainly suggest that more light is needed for many tasks than for well-printed books.... Illumination quality, as measured by the task contrast a lighting system provides, is much more important than illumination quantity.... With the best quality light, considerably lower footcandles can be used.... Thus we can say categorically that the best lighting installation can provide the visibility criterion with less than one fourth of the light level required with the worst lighting installation.[3]

Under these circumstances what does a library planner do? One possibility is the course that was followed in the Lamont Library. Lighting there was installed to provide from 20 to 25 footcandles (215 lx–270 lx) maintained, but it is wired so that, with comparatively little expense for alterations, the intensity can be doubled. There seems to have been no need for a subsequent increase. In this connection it should be borne in mind that fluorescent lamps have gradually increased in light efficiency since then, and, as a consequence, the intensities available in Lamont have increased 25 percent rather than decreased, as they might be expected to do in some installations. Newer style ballasts could maintain the intensity at between 30 and 40 footcandles (322 lx and 430 lx) and simultaneously reduce by about 50 percent the electrical consumption.

Because desirable lighting levels are relative, when they are raised in one building in an institution, the levels in other buildings which had previously seemed satisfactory will begin to appear inadequate, and there may be a tendency to push up levels in one area or another.

In any consideration of intensity of light, it should again be noted that it is "maintained" light—the intensity provided when the light source has had some months of use—that is the concern.

The authors venture to suggest that:

1. It should always be remembered that high-intensity light of poor quality is less desirable than low-intensity light of good quality.

2. Every effort within reason should be made to improve the quality of visual atmosphere. The comfort of the readers and the aesthetic results are of first importance.

3. For persons with normal or close to normal vision, an intensity of 50 footcandles (540 lx) on the reading surface should be satisfactory for all but the most exacting reading tasks in a library.

4. Twenty-five to 30 footcandles (270 lx–322 lx) should be sufficient in most library reading areas so long as 50 (540 lx) are readily available in some areas and 75 (800 lx) in a very few places for those who have impaired or defective vision or who are using difficult-to-read manuscripts or other material. Fifty footcandles might be provided in large sections of the processing rooms where staff members are working long hours, frequently with difficult material, and in a small percentage, perhaps 25, of the public reading areas. It is suggested that these reading areas should not be too readily accessible or viewed from the rest of the building, as the higher intensity, when seen, will reduce pupil size, and one's own table with lower intensity will tend to appear as though it has inadequate light.

Different persons prefer different types of seating accommodations, different temperatures, and also different light intensities. In a large library it should be possible to provide what each one prefers, instead of making everything uniform, representing a compromise with mediocre results.

5. Light intensities in lobbies, corridors, smoking and lounge areas, stairwells, and toilets can be kept down to between 10 and 20 footcandles (107.6 lx and 215.2 lx), which is entirely adequate, except for concentrated reading and study. Then, when the reading and work areas are entered, they will seem bright.

The wiring throughout the building should be of a gauge heavy enough so that future changes made in fixtures in order to improve the quality, which may necessitate the use of higher-wattage light sources, will be possible without expensive rewiring.

---

[3] Reprinted in *Reader on the Library Building*, ed. by Hal B. Schell (Englewood, Colo.: Microcard Editions Books, 1975), pp. 215–20.

Aesthetics. The problems of aesthetics in lighting are fully as difficult as the selection of the light source, fixture, and arrangement. If we were willing to disregard aesthetics and accept a factory or grocery store atmosphere, satisfactory lighting from a strictly functional point of view is probably possible at lower cost. Fortunately, almost no institutions are satisfied with this.

In a library it may be desirable to provide a lighting environment in which the light sources are so unobtrusive that any fixture arrangement is aesthetically and visually satisfactory. The alternative is to carefully and specifically design the lighting environment including the exact location of each lighting fixture in relation to the anticipated task. This of course, does not maintain flexibility for furniture placement. Another point is that apparent brightness is relative, depending on one's position. A room seen through an open door from the outside on a bright day seems dark. If the room is entered and the eyes are given a little time to adjust, everything looks brighter. The eye has the ability to adapt itself to the conditions to which it is subjected.

The importance of the relation between the intensity in different locations in the same building is great. At the Air Force Academy near Colorado Springs, some of the rooms used by the processing staff have no windows. While theoretically the rooms are adequately lighted, the staff is unhappy because they enter their quarters from parts of the building where the Colorado sunlight coming through the glass outside walls has intensified the light far beyond any normal artificial illumination.

A brightly lighted supermarket has been found to attract customers. The same may hold true for the lobby of an academic library in an urban institution with brightly lighted stores on all sides. On the other hand, some may argue that the real reason for bright lights in stores is to create high turnover, a factor that is contrary to the goals of the academic or research library. Furthermore, the same amount of brightness is not necessarily useful or desirable in an academic library. An occasional room with greater or less brightness than the rest of the building can be visually interesting, if the areas are carefully selected—for example, exhibit quarters with case lighting but subdued ambient room lighting or a brightly lit below-grade periodical reading area.

Although the functional and quality aspects are generally considered first, the total aesthetic effects of lighting are important. They should relate to the architect's basic concept for the building and thus their design and specification generally are considered to be part of the architect's scope of work. This responsibility may be delegated to an electrical or illuminating engineer or to an interior designer selected by the architect or the institution.

Flexibility. Complete flexibility in lighting, as is the case in other areas, is expensive. It would require the best reasonable system of general illumination throughout the library, the exception being only those areas which will not change, such as rest rooms, closets, lobbies, and perhaps some offices. In most libraries this approach will require that all of the lights will be on during all hours of operation, although there could be zones where by separate circuits the lighting level might be controlled in perhaps two or three steps. While this form of lighting may be appropriate for a heavily used undergraduate library with limited separate shelving areas, it makes little sense today in any library where there are discrete shelving and reading areas, particularly in view of concerns for energy consumption.

In most cases, therefore, the best lighting for each major area of the library should be selected, which will mean that there will be either additional cost or compromise when the distribution of the functional areas changes. Sufficient capacity should be provided, perhaps only with conduit and junction boxes, so that the function of any area can be changed reasonably. In this regard, open reading areas probably are more likely to change than stack areas. The concept of providing a fairly low level of ambient lighting combined with task lighting in reading areas satisfies both energy conservation and the need for flexibility. If the lighting is properly done, the problems of glare and contrast can be minimized, and the psychological "feel" of the space enhanced. Individual range aisle switching is not flexible, but the potential energy savings may outweigh the advantages of flexibility by a considerable margin. At Stanford there have been several cases where it paid to install retrospectively separate switching for range aisles. If this can be justified economically, then certainly it warrants serious consideration at the time of construction. Clearly factors of aesthetics, function, long range planning, and cost must be considered before adopting a program of complete flexibility.

Cost. Lighting expenditures fall into three groups.

1. Installation costs, which include wiring, switches, fixtures, lamps, and the construction costs of the structure that derive from lighting and also those required to dispose of the heat generated by lighting. This last may be very considerable and should not be forgotten if high-intensity light is to be used.

2. The cost of maintenance and upkeep, which includes the repair and cleaning of the fixtures, and the replacement of lamps. Careful planning will help lessen the expense.

3. The cost of electric current, which depends primarily, after the installation has been made, on cost of current per kilowatt-hour (kWh) and the number of hours in a year that the lights are on, as well as the intensity provided, the efficiency of the lights, the type of fixtures used, and the ceiling heights. Current costs vary a great deal from place to place, but large users generally pay a lower rate. For many institutions a figure of about 10 cents per kWh will include the cost of current, plus the maintenance and repair of the installation and lamp replacement. The figures used in the following paragraphs are based on that rate; they are included for illustrative purposes only. Local experience should be relied on in reaching any final decision.

Costs should not be overemphasized, but disagreement over the desirable quality and intensity complicates the problem. Too often librarians and other administrative officers have given little thought to lighting costs because these have not been included in the library budget but have been paid directly by the institution. In the early 1960s Mr. Metcalf talked with a librarian in a fine new library with attractive lighting, giving unusually high intensity even for that time—over 100 footcandles (1100 lx)—and asked what the lighting bill came to. The reply was, "We don't know yet, but it has been suggested that it would come to some $400 a month." A little figuring—multiplying the wattage used in each bay by the number of bays, the hours of opening a week, and the cost per kWh of current used—indicated that $4,000 a month would be closer to the mark. Whether or not this amount would be serious expense for the university, which was endowed, is another matter; but because the building was almost a glass box, this intensity might be said to be

necessary or at least desirable, in order to avoid too great a contrast with the excessive natural light available through the glass walls.

In 1982 the median of large university libraries had a collection of 1,870,000 volumes and an average student body of 18,000. Such a library, if it occupies a single facility, would probably require at least 300,000 sq ft (27,870 m²) of floor space without making provision for future growth. Illuminating engineers report that 1½ watts of light per sq ft of floor space should provide 25 footcandles in a typical installation today. With energy-efficient light fixtures in an office setting, light levels in excess of 50 footcandles are possible with 1½ watts per sq ft. With task lighting and individual range aisle switching, the actual energy use will be a great deal less. Based on 1½ watts per sq ft, the 300,000 sq ft (27,870 m²) in the median university library would use 450,000 watts, or 450 kWh, in order to obtain uniform lighting throughout the building, and this, at 10 cents a kWh would cost 45 dollars an hour. If the average university library is open for public use 4,000 hours a year, this would mean $180,000 a year for lighting, excluding after-hour cleaning time. This cost estimate can be reduced, however, to perhaps $150,000 because hallways, which can appropriately have a lower intensity, and processing quarters, which are used for shorter hours, more than cancel out the cleaning time. Stack-lighting intensities are generally less but require nearly as much wattage per square foot, and in most libraries with open-access stacks, lights are kept on all day long. If the library uses 100 footcandles (which is the level frequently recommended) with an inefficient system, and if the above calculation is correct, lighting will cost $300,000 a year. If, on the other hand, half of the lighting is turned off at any given time, the savings would, of course, equal $150,000 a year, or more if the designed light levels are higher. Using present value formulas, at 10 percent interest, a savings of $150,000 for 5 years is equal to a current value of nearly $570,000, which may well justify a lighting design with local switching capability. These figures are presented simply to give some indication of the amount of money involved.

Conclusions. The questions that administrative officers must answer is whether it is more important to spend the money for better quality, greater control, or increased intensity of light, or for something else—books and service, for instance. What is reasonable? The authors suggest the following:

1. Whatever the cost, the lighting should be of a quality that will attract, not discourage use, and that will not be tiring to the reader.

2. Institutions should always watch for opportunities to improve the physical conditions provided for their students and staff, just as they should seek to improve the quality of the education that they provide. They should not be content with the present on the basis that what was good enough for the preceding generation is good enough for the generations to come.

3. There seems to be no evidence that, in earlier years when lower light intensities were customary, there was more defective vision than at present or that reading speed and comprehension were less than they are now.

4. The importance of the quality of the light and, in particular, the efficiency of the illuminant and fixture should be kept in mind. A low-efficiency fixture may require double the wattage to attain a specified light intensity but, at the same time, may improve the quality of the light made available.

Talk the problem over with the architect and the illuminating engineer, and make sure that everyone involved understands the situation and the financial implications. With these points in mind, it is suggested, as noted in the section on intensity, that a new library be wired so that at least 50 footcandles of light intensity on reading surfaces can be made available anywhere without complete rewiring, that it be provided in at least a few public rooms and in one-half of the staff work areas, and that in the rest of the building where reading is carried on, including the bookstack, from 25 to 30 footcandles (270 lx–322 lx) be installed. It should be noted that the bookstack intensity refers to reading surfaces 30 in. (762 mm) above the floor and not to the backs of the books on lower shelves. The high-intensity reading areas should include those for manuscripts, archives, and rare books and the space set aside for use by persons with defective vision. It should be noted that very small "egg-crate" fixtures and those with polarizing lenses can reduce intensity by perhaps 50 percent, but they may improve quality and give better aesthetic effects.

It is evident that, if as much as 100-footcandle illumination is used, the heat generated, even with fluorescent tubes, will become so great as to place additional loads on air-conditioning equipment or to make buildings almost impossibly hot in summer months if air conditioning is not available. The costs involved here are difficult to predict but will be considerable.

Several other comments are pertinent. First, if higher intensity light sources are deemed desirable, ways and means should be worked out so that during the winter the buildings can be heated as far as possible with the heat resulting from the lighting. This plan does not, however, relieve the overheating during the summer.

Second, if high-intensity lighting has been installed, particularly with tubes in pairs, it is possible to arrange light switches so that the right-hand tubes can be used one week and the left-hand ones the next (or some similar arrangement). This practice is in vogue in the Lamont Library main-entrance lobby. There the use of one-half of the tubes at a time practically doubles their life, a matter of some importance because, regrettably, a scaffolding is required when they are changed. There is the added advantage that when the reader goes from the entrance lobby to the reading areas, higher intensity is found, but still only 25 to 30 footcandles (270 lx–322 lx), and it seems to be satisfactory. Some codes will require switching of this nature as an energy-conservation technique.

Third, good reflecting surfaces can help, such as light ceiling, walls, and floors, particularly in bookstacks where lower shelves are a problem. Avoid glare, and do not neglect the importance of the aesthetic effect of light. Note that skylights can help with aesthetics; yet they may permit glare directly or reflected from the sun, may provide too great a contrast of intensity, and can cause problems when it comes to illuminating reading areas beneath the skylight for use after sunset.

Fourth, if the lights are to be left on all day in the reading areas and throughout the bookstacks, the wiring and switches can be greatly simplified and installation costs reduced. Switches should be controlled by the staff and should be inaccessible to readers where general illumination requires that all the lights should be on. Ideally, the switches should be centrally located to simplify the opening and closing process. However, local switching is recommended in most cases, perhaps with a low voltage master control, as discussed in Chapter 5.

In all significant projects the librarian should insist on seeing either an example or a mock-up of the general or typical lighting fixtures with the fixtures specified installed at the same point in relation to the task and provided with the same light source and similar surfaces as proposed for the building project. Only in this way can one be convinced that all the factors come together: intensity, lack of direct and reflective glare, ease of servicing, color, appearance, hum, flickering, etc., that contribute to the total lighting system. While it is not the intent to critique the aesthetic quality of the mock-up for the proposed lighting system, what is proposed must work well in the library environment.

There will be fixtures for which a mock-up is simply not practical. For example, a few display cases or a portrait may require special lighting techniques. (Display cases present a special problem for proper lighting to avoid reflective glare and heat buildup within the case.) Or, there may be an unusual architectural feature that calls for a unique fixture. In these cases the librarian can only ask for answers to the questions of glare, heat, intensity, service ability, cost, and the like which will be of concern.

Fixed Elements. During the design development phase, it is important that the final decision be made on shear walls, duct and elevator shafts, stairs, rest rooms, mechanical rooms, and telephone closets. The planning for functional relationships and flexibility will certainly have an influence, as will the size and configuration of the building scheme. Local codes often will require certain considerations for stairs and their location in regard to providing emergency egress. No building should be planned without checking the applicable codes and regulations, and it is urged that the designers consult with the code authorities during the design phases. Several points are listed here to consider in making the final decision on fixed elements.

1. Do the fixed elements work within the module? Structural or bearing walls, for example, can take the place of a range of shelving and have relatively little effect.

2. Looking toward the future, is it possible to anticipate a potential for a changed circulation pattern? What if one area of the library shrinks and another increases in size? How might a future addition affect the proposed arrangements? By moving the core or a structural wall one bay away, is there greater flexibility for future change? Is the orientation of the major elements correct?

3. Should other provisions be made for the future? Should a retaining or perimeter wall have knock-out panels or other features to allow for future expansion? Should openings be provided in structural walls, which can be relatively thick and difficult if not impossible to alter in the future? Openings for corridor passage, conveyors, as well as ducts and conduits should be considered.

4. Will the corridor and aisle circulation system resulting from the location of the fixed elements be clear and easy to use? Will it permit a reasonable arrangement for the stacks? Are there clues (needed especially in a large building) that will lead the reader back to the main stair, or will an abundance of signs be required?

5. Are the routes to other major library elements made as simple as possible?

6. Is the width of the stair adequate for the anticipated traffic (see Section 12.4)? Will the elevator accommodate the furniture and equipment, or is it planned that this material will be moved by the stairs? Has handicapped access been provided for?

7. Will the provision of utilities or mechanical services conflict with other aspects of the library? Remember that elevators and machine rooms make noise and that plumbing eventually will leak. A reading area next to the elevator machine room will be a problem, as will rest rooms located over a rare-book stack.

8. How is exit security handled? Are internal doors with alarms in the right places?

Walls. Interior walls may present other problems. Efforts have been made in recent years in many libraries to avoid wet walls—those that cannot be removed without breaking them up. In their place it is possible to use bookshelving or dry walls, which in nontechnical terms are simply movable partitions, often of steel. It should be understood that there is a range of flexibility in the nature of walls. On the one hand, shear walls cannot be moved. At the other extreme are office panel systems which are essentially furniture; their movement and reuse is a fairly simple matter. In between are masonry walls and stud partitions typically faced with gypsum or plaster wallboards. These can be moved, but surfaces will require patching, and mechanical, electrical, and lighting systems may be affected. Shelving as a partition or divider can often be satisfactory and, if free-standing, it is more flexible than anything except the low office panel partition, but it may create acoustical problems as noise is carried over from one area to another. Metal and glass partitions, as well as folding partitions, are also too often unsatisfactory acoustically. They must be fitted tightly to floor and ceiling with no gaps through which noise can penetrate. Movable steel partitions for offices and faculty studies are often considerably more expensive than wet walls. However, if moving is necessary as often as twice in ten years, it will probably be less expensive to provide steel partitions than to demolish and re-erect wet walls.

Dry partitions of Transite or of plaster or gypsum board with metal studs are being used extensively in all types of structures and can well be considered for library interior walls, as they are comparable in price to unplastered cinder or concrete block walls. Keep in mind the method by which shelving might be installed. Plaster or gypsum board is not strong enough to support shelving fully loaded with books; proper anchorage must be provided within the wall. Cinder and concrete block walls, particularly for inside walls, have been used much more in recent years than earlier. They may present a difficult problem when used for outside walls because of cracking, and waterproofing and insulation may be necessary if they are exposed to the elements. Another block used today is pumice. It is often left unpainted, as in the Harvard Divinity School Library, because of its pleasant natural color. No doubt in other parts of the world other types of block are available.

Windows. Windows represent another form of fixed element that should be settled in the design development phase. Windows are of many varieties. They may have wood or metal frames, be double hung or casement or have other arrangements for opening; they may be of different shapes and sizes and may be made of large or small panes of clear, opaque, or colored glass, to say nothing of glass blocks. The window pattern can take innumerable forms, and the resulting facade is of first importance aesthetically. The librarian should give particular attention to the affect of windows on library functions. Where windows exist, no shelving can later be located. On the other hand, windows provide light and

they can provide ventilation; and human reactions are aroused by their presence or absence since the exterior view can provide physiological visual relief, can enable one to judge the weather or degree of darkness, and may reveal the beauty of a tree or other vista.

Other things being equal, the closer the windows are placed to the ceiling, the higher the intensity of light admitted. But if the windows are above the eye level, nothing can be seen out of them, except possibly sky, tall trees, other buildings, or another part of the same building. There is some truth in the objection that any window through which you can see anything may be a distraction and will interfere with reading; on this basis one can advocate a completely windowless library. Many people today spend much of their working lives in windowless areas. On the other hand, comparatively few people are ready to recommend that a library be completely windowless, particularly in its reading areas and especially in areas occupied by the staff.

Halls, corridors, and stairwells do not need to rely on outside light and probably should be provided with at least low-intensity artificial lighting during all the hours the library is open. In all other areas, even if they are well supplied with windows, artificial light is required in most libraries today for approximately half of the hours of opening. Library users, at least in the United States, seldom depend on only natural light, and reading areas are artificially lighted throughout the day even when this interior source is functionally superfluous. If natural light is not depended upon, it is possible to plan a building with large sections far away from natural light. It should also be remembered that books are harmed by direct sunlight because high-intensity and ultraviolet rays fade bindings and hasten paper deterioration.

One of the important decisions in connection with windows concerns the percentage of the outside wall which should be of glass. In some states there are regulations for schools and some other public buildings specifying at least 20 percent glass, but these regulations are falling more and more into disuse with the improvements in artificial lighting and ventilation. For at least 25 years the "all-glass box" style of building has been a popular design solution. This can present physiological, psychological, and also functional problems. If any area in a library has an all-glass facade, it will be practically impossible to store books near the outside walls without harming them, unless, of course, the glass is completely covered up and protected. If the windows go down to the floor, there are several concerns: the possibility of a leak or flood from outside, the need to protect the glass from book trucks, a hesitancy by women with short skirts to sit by them as there is no modesty screening, and greater expense, since codes usually require tempered glass when glass is below 18 in. (457 mm) from the floor. If the windows are on the west or south, much of the space, if it is not shaded in some way, will be practically unusable for reading during parts of bright days because of unpleasant intensity, unless suitable protection of some kind is available. Ignoring the sun's effect on heating and ventilation problems, which can be an asset in a system utilizing solar heat, it is easy to overdo the use of glass as far as reading is concerned because of the resulting glare. On the other hand, it would be a shame in many locations to prevent the users of a library from looking out on a handsome lawn, trees, and distant hills. Mr. Metcalf remembered some years ago recommending large windows in every bay on one side of the Bennington College Library where a fine mountain view was available, and Pietro Belluschi saying, "This view will be appreciated more if there isn't too much glass."

Windows can also be protected from the outside in a number of ways:

1. With large, vertical metal fins a foot or so (say, 305 mm) wide which can be adjusted by a crank operated from inside the building or by automatic equipment that turns them with the sun. Because they are outdoors and have movable parts, they tend to get out of order and to become noisy in a high wind. It is suggested that persons who have had experience with them be consulted before they are adopted.

2. With screens of one kind or another parallel to the walls and windows, and placed a few feet away from them. Screens have been used for hundreds of years in India and were introduced on a large scale about 25 years ago in the United States by Edward Stone, Marcel Breuer, and other architects. They may be of metal or concrete, or they may be of hollow tiles of various depths, shapes, and sizes, through which comes comparatively little direct sunlight except for a few minutes

a few days in the year. They can be decorative and pleasing aesthetically. They are not inexpensive, and they may present a serious cleaning problem and become a nesting place for birds.

3. With a horizontal projecting shelf reaching out from the building at the level of the floor above. Such shelves may extend out 10 or 12 ft (3.048 or 3.658) or even more, and on the south and west sides, where the sun may be a particularly difficult problem, they will almost completely shut out the direct sunlight. This concept, utilizing cantilevered floors, is an important part of the system of sun control in the Cecil H. Green Library at Stanford. The lower western sun in late afternoon may be troublesome, but on lower floors at least, trees and shrubs should prevent any difficulty. If the shelves project too far, they shut out a good deal of light and may make the use of artificial light necessary throughout the day except during bright sunlight periods. There may be a temptation to use these projections as porches for strolling, or as outdoor reading areas, but such use involves various hazards; readers inside may be distracted and books may be passed from porches to the ground without proper authorization. On the whole, because of the limited number of days during the academic year when the weather and the sun make them satisfactory for use, outdoor reading areas in most of the temperate zones are seldom worth what they cost. This evaluation may change where summer schools become common, and outdoor reading areas may prove very useful in the tropics and in the parts of the temperate zones nearby.

The difficulty with screening from the outside is that any extra cost for the treatment, added to that of the glass itself, tends to be greater per unit of area than a good masonry or concrete wall. This certainly can be the case if the cost of inside sun control is added, as is discussed in Section 14.3. Windows may also let in so much light that they make higher intensities of artificial light desirable. They can, however, contribute considerably to the aesthetic design of the building. Covering large window areas with a few folds of cloth—light-colored glass-fiber curtains, for instance—is functional in preventing glare and also has aesthetic advantages both day and night, but especially at night for the reader, when curtains cover the hard, unpleasant, reflective surface of the glass; they also might be said to humanize the space enclosed. Lighting the area outside to a low intensity will also help create that effect.

Windows, particularly very large windows, make it more difficult to heat and cool the building properly. Single-pane glass does not keep out the cold or the heat as well as a masonry wall, particularly if the latter is satisfactorily insulated. Closely related to this objection are several other facts. If the building has winter humidification, water will condense and run down the windows when the outside temperature falls below the freezing point. If windows are sealed shut and the air conditioning breaks down, a serious situation develops; yet, unless the windows are locked or sealed shut, someone sooner or later will open them, and the effectiveness of the air conditioning will be ruined along with the control of security for the collections. On the other hand, it might be added that with air conditioning in an area where the electricity is likely to break down and where repair personnel are difficult to reach, it may be unwise to seal the windows. In a large city where such mishaps are less likely and where competent mechanics may be readily available, windows can be sealed without fear of serious consequences. A limited number of them should be openable by a key so that one can use them to get out on to a porch roof or elsewhere outside the building. It must be remembered that sealed windows must be cleaned from the outside, which will present a problem on upper floors unless some means of access is provided. Double-glazed windows are nearly always sealed and, as already indicated, they are practically necessary if the humidity in the winter is to be kept up above the middle thirties when the outside temperature falls below the freezing mark. With increased concern about energy, the benefit of double-glazed windows is far more attractive and their use is becoming more common.

There is one other point about windows as a fixed element. If seating can be adjacent to a window, even a small one, it is attractive, although this arrangement is not necessary for an open carrel. A small closed carrel, without a window, will rarely be popular. The same holds true even for a larger faculty study. Any room with much less than 60 sq ft (5.57 m²) that is completely closed and has no windows will be objectionable to many persons. Glass in the door or next to the door through which the occupant can look down a stack aisle or into an area with outside light will help, as will a high window near the ceiling. The use of bright colors will also be helpful. With even a small window, 40 to 50 sq ft (3.72 m² to 4.65 m²) may be adequate for a completely closed room. If the area is completely open, except for a front and back partition high enough so that the top of the head of the person in front cannot be seen, a carrel 3 ft (0.914) wide and 4 ft (1.220) on centers may be entirely satisfactory without windows. (In a research library, larger carrels are recommended.) It is worth repeating here that with the use of color and with seating arranged so that the reader does not face blank walls on two or three sides, most persons will very soon forget about the lack of windows. This has been proved in many recently built university libraries.

Doors. Still another element that should have fixed location during this phase of the design process, doors serve to bar or permit entrance and exit to a building and to secure interior spaces. They are also useful for acoustic purposes and to prevent the spread of fire. Each of these functions should be kept in mind, as well as the cost of doors, their psychological effect, and their effect on architectural harmony and ornamentation. They may slide horizontally or vertically, fold or revolve, but note that revolving doors should not be the only passage since wheelchairs cannot pass through them. If doors are hinged, it must be remembered that they can swing a full 180 degrees only when the hinge is on the side of the opening where the full swing is expected and where there is wall space available. Door closers may also be a hindrance. If the door is hinged so that it can go in both directions, it can with difficulty be made tight enough to avoid drafts and the transfer of sounds to the other side.

It is important to place each door with traffic patterns definitely in mind. Figure 13.1 shows how the door at the main entrance of the Widener bookstack, until a change was made, led everyone directly past the stack reading areas when it would have been possible to have the entrance adjacent to the main aisle that is 30 ft (9.144) away from the carrels. Figure 13.2 shows a door placed improperly and seriously complicating the use of a small area.

Double, or french, doors, one opening to the right and the other to the left, with no upright between, are unfortunate, particularly if there is much traffic and if the doors

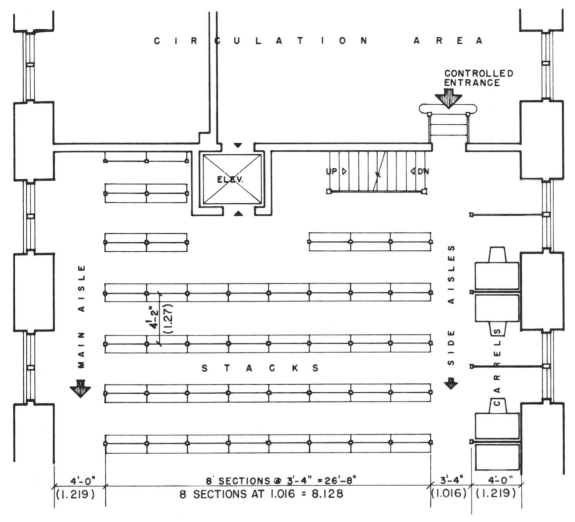

FIGURE 13.1 Main entrance to Widener Library stack area. The entrance leads directly to a secondary aisle which passes carrels. If it had been placed at the upper left of the drawing, it would have saved 60 ft (18.188) of walking for most users and made the carrel area quieter and less restless. In 1963 it was in fact moved to the mid point (between elevator and stairs) thereby retaining an office on the left and accommodating circulation staff functions to the right.

are heavy, because a person coming from the outside and pulling the right-hand door tends to swing in front of the left-hand door, and if a person is coming out at the same time accidents can happen. Where there are pairs of doors at a busy entrance, both should be hinged on either the right or the left. (See fig. 13.3.) Securing single doors is easier as well, as normal panic hardware on double doors where there is no astragal can be opened from the outside in a few seconds with a simple tool. The provision of an astragal with double doors is always a problem, though it can be arranged for the panels to close in the required order with a door coordinator. Yet coordinators seldom work well,

and they are noisy. However, the route for delivery of large furniture should not be forgotten. It may require some double or oversized doors, perhaps with one leaf fixed.

Ellison doors, which are hinged some 6 in. (152 mm) from the side of the door, may be useful for doorways 4 ft (1.220) wide or more, as they are easier to open. They may be dangerous when used by children; they are more expensive and are not desirable for narrow openings.

Frequently, doors in a library should have a glass panel at eye height, large enough to enable both tall persons and those in wheelchairs to see through it in order to prevent

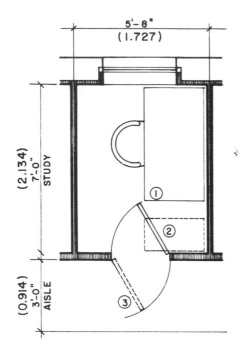

DOOR SWING

1. OBSTRUCTED BY FURNITURE
2. DISPLACES FURNITURE
3. OBSTRUCTS AISLE

FIGURE 13.2 Poorly placed door. This door interferes seriously with the use of the room. If the door had been placed farther to the left and hinged on the left, it could swing inward without difficulty. See also figure 4.6 for door swing problems.

accidents, as well as to make supervision possible, even if supervision is not ordinarily required. Eye level for an adult in a wheelchair ranges from 3 ft 7 in. to 4 ft 3 in. (1.090 to 1.295).

Folding doors are sometimes used to divide areas temporarily, for instance, to make a small classroom into two seminar rooms or to break up the staff lounge so that part of it can be used for other purposes. These doors may be wide enough so that they become partitions, in fact if not in name. They may be collapsible or of the hinged type. The chief problem in connection with them is that they are seldom sufficiently soundproof. The door itself may have all the required attributes, but the sliding mechanism at both top and bottom has gaps through which the sound is carried. If this is a serious matter, two folding doors parallel to each other can be installed with an air space in between. The great virtue of the folding door is the flexible division of space which it provides and the fact that it is

easier to operate and install than is a sliding door panel.

Roll-down doors may be desirable to secure a service point or wide entrance during certain hours of operation or, if solid, to provide a fire separation. These doors can be of open mesh construction or of visually solid construction similar to a roll-top desk. Their operation tends to be noisy, thus their use is only suitable for infrequent closure.

While the exact location and swing of a door can be refined at later stages of the design, such changes serve to frustrate the architect who will no doubt be under pressure to complete a complex set of contract documents. Later changes are not welcome. There are several things to look for in terms of door location and configuration.

1. Can a person on crutches or in a wheelchair open the door, enter the space, and close the door? Most common widths of wheelchairs are 2 ft to 2 ft 2 in. (610 mm to 660 mm). Aside from the width requirement for wheelchairs, the way the door swings may be critical. The ability to enter the building by pushing the door will help those with an armload of books. Devices to assist door opening and automatic openers should be considered.

2. Will the door stand open during part of its use? If this is expected, it should be able to swing out of the way of traffic and avoid blocking access to files, shelves, or other equipment. In an office or faculty study, it is often best to locate the door at least 12 in. (305 mm) from an adjacent and perpendicular wall so that shelving can be installed on the perpendicular wall. Some buildings will require fire separation, using doors which are normally open. These doors may be held open by a fusable link or a magnetic device controlled by the fire alarm system. The use of fusable link in this case is generally not recommended, as the heat required to activate the door will place the protected part of the building at risk. On the other hand, magnetic hold-open devices are fairly expensive. It is a fairly simple matter to design doors that are normally open so that they are contained in a pocket and thus have the appearance of a continuation of the wall surface. This concept is of course somewhat compromised if the door must also have panic hardware.

3. Are some doors needed for future flexibility? One technique for providing this kind of flexibility is to construct within the wall a door frame which can easily be activated at

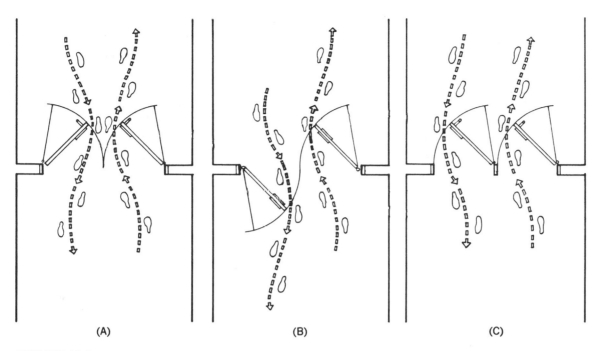

FIGURE 13.3 Double-door problems. (A) Doors opening one way only with danger of collision when used from opposite directions at the same time. Not recommended. (B) Doors opening both ways used from opposite directions at the same time present less danger of collision, but if they are outside doors with uneven air pressure, they may be difficult to keep closed when not in use. Possible. (C) Doors opening in one way only, but each hinged on left-hand upright. No danger of collisions. Recommended. Note that only B allows traffic in both directions to push any door open if one's hands are full.

a future date. If it is a metal frame, one must consider the hinge and latch locations for future need.

4. Will provision of a door affect air circulation? In small enclosed carrels it may be appropriate to install a louver or to undercut the door an inch or two (25 mm to 50 mm). (Remember the allowance for carpet.) However, this space will remove any acoustical quality that may be desired of the door.

5. Will the door require other special features such as a door closer, panic hardware, acoustic insulation or weather stripping, an alarm, or special locking devices? While this level of detail is not critical at this stage, it is well to be thinking of it, especially in any case that may require conduit for an alarm or electrically actuated lock.

Plumbing. A fixed element frequently regarded as part of the mechanical system, plumbing will be treated here as it relates to the location of the rest rooms, which in turn relate to the core elements.

The problems of plumbing are many and specialized. To solve the mechanical ones, it is usual to employ a sanitary or mechanical engineer to be responsible for the layout, the operations, and the code requirements of the installation. However, a number of questions ought to come to the attention of the planning team before they are answered. They are concerned mainly with the problems of (1) location, (2) noise, and (3) maintenance.

1. *Location.* Toilet facilities should be located in the library so that they are adjacent and convenient to the main traffic arteries and also so that both the visual and audible disturbances attendant upon their use will be isolated from the reading areas. The practical requirements of plumbing must also be kept in mind. Plumbing code regulations have not yet been standardized and vary considerably from place to place, but all of them require each fixture to be equipped with a "soil" and a "vent," the first a pipe which leads down to the basement and the sewer, the second a pipe which leads up to the roof and the atmosphere. Fixtures may be arranged in batteries, either horizontally or vertically, and their respective soils and vents may be combined. Naturally the more this combined piping principle is applied, the less expensive is the installation. Thus the grouping of toilets and other plumbing facilities

adjacent to one another in plan and above one another in section is economical and desirable.

Sometimes the bottom floors of a library are below the level of the sewer to which the plumbing fixtures are to connect. In this case fixtures on these levels should be reduced to a minimum, as they will have to be drained through an ejector which will pump their sewage up to the sewer above. A large installation of this sort is expensive to install, occupies space, and must be maintained. Its use should be avoided wherever practicable.

The piping connections, the toilet stalls, the fixtures, and the steel or marble and tile finishes generally used in connection with fixtures all combine to make these elements almost as permanent as stair and elevator wells. They are expensive to change and difficult, though not impossible, to move. For these reasons, toilets are often grouped with the stairs and elevators and vent shafts in such a manner that they interfere as little as possible with the flexibility of the spaces for readers and books, which form the bulk of the library.

The number of toilet fixtures required in any library varies with the number of reader accommodations provided. Often this number is regulated by law. It may be affected by the proximity or remoteness of the dormitory or other similar facilities. The number of seats provided in the library is, except under unusual circumstances, in excess of the number of readers present at any time. For this reason it is acceptable and usual library practice to provide at least one plumbing fixture for each 35 seating accommodations, in anticipation that this fixture normally can be expected to serve 25 readers. In tabulating fixtures in proportion to reader seats, urinals and water closets but not lavatories are counted. The total number of fixtures required should then be distributed in one or more toilet rooms for each sex so that they are as convenient as practicable to the readers. Sometimes separate facilities are provided for both staff and building help.

The arrangement of fixtures within the toilet room is important, for both appearance and privacy. An open space immediately inside the entrance to the lavatory area makes a better impression, and the use of screens beside the urinals, as well as stalls around the water closets, contributes to privacy. It is always desirable to enter large toilet rooms through vestibules, or to arrange the entry such that the sight line from the access point to the toilet room is blocked. The rooms themselves should allow space for anticipated traffic.

In all toilet rooms in a library, it is wise to install shelves for holding books and other papers while the facility is used. This is not only a convenience for readers but also a protection for the library materials. Each toilet stall should have a shelf large enough to hold at least an octavo book or a binder and, if a fold-down type, able to stay down if holding only a few papers. Similarly, in the vicinity of the lavatories, a shelf should be provided. There are many details about toilets, lavatories, urinals, and drinking fountains which concern persons with impaired eyesight or hearing, and those confined to wheelchairs. Consult published accessibility standards; for examples, see the Bibliography, section 3m.

Other plumbing fixtures are required, such as janitors' and work sinks, wash basins in work areas, kitchenettes, and drinking fountains. All of these, except the last, should be inaccessible to the public. Drinking fountains present a hazard if they are located in the vicinity of bookshelves. They should be isolated so that no water damage to books, except those carried by the users, can be expected. These other plumbing fixtures should also be grouped with the toilets if the maximum economy of installation is to be realized.

2. *Noise.* The problem most frequently neglected in connection with plumbing fixtures is the noise resulting from their use. This consideration is important in a modern library if the toilet facility is adjacent to reader and book storage areas. Unfortunately, the most efficient and easily maintained fixtures seem to be the noisiest. When this is coupled with the fact that the hard, washable finishes used in toilet rooms are anything but sound absorbing, the noise of a flushed water closet can easily penetrate beyond the walls of the toilet, unless special precautions are taken.

Be sure that the sanitary engineer has selected the quietest fixtures consistent with ease of maintenance and efficiency of operation. This statement applies to water closets and also to urinals and lavatories.

Do not accede to a ventilation requirement for an air supply through the doorways to the facility. This is an economical solution, but it leaves openings through which the sounds can escape into adjacent areas. It is better to soundproof the doors by weatherstripping and provide a self-contained ventilation system. In any case, all openings through the toilet-room walls should be protected with sound-absorbing boxes, and the walls themselves should be built to provide a reasonable amount of sound isolation.

The incidence of sound within the toilet room can be reduced by the use of an acoustical ceiling. It will soften the sounds within the room itself and, at the same time, will reduce the volume of sound that may be transmitted to the adjacent spaces through the walls and doors.

3. *Maintenance.* The best-quality plumbing fixtures and accessories are the most economical in the end, because the cost of their maintenance will be considerably reduced. In any public facility the abuse given to both fixtures and accessories is considerable and must be offset by a first-class installation of the best and strongest available.

Fixtures that are mounted off the floor will make cleaning easier. Modern water closets are made for wall mounting, as are lavatories and urinals. When these are combined with ceiling and wall-mounted stall divisions, the floor of a modern toilet room can be kept free of obstruction for the cleaning process. When fixtures are wall-mounted, the fastenings must be strong enough to resist the pressures imposed by a person's leaning his or her entire weight on the front edge. This caution is particularly true of lavatories. Usually they are installed with large metal brackets embedded in the wall and floor. These brackets, called chair carriers, receive and resist pressures imposed on the fixtures.

Often a floor drain is installed in the toilet room in order to help the cleaning up or hosing-out process. It is recommended. If one is installed, mopping or hosing must be done regularly; otherwise the trap, or the water seal that prevents the escape of sewer gases through the fixture, will dry out.

The floors and walls of a toilet room should be of hard solid materials easily cleaned and waterproof. Marble, tile, and terrazzo are usually used. The setting of these materials on the floor generally requires a "bed," and the structural floor must be recessed in order to accommodate it and a waterproof membrane; otherwise the floor of the toilet room would be higher than the surrounding areas.

This recessing adds to the cost of construction, as it interferes with the rapidity of execution desired during the rough construction period. Today, fortunately, adhesives are made which can successfully fasten tile to a concrete floor without the use of a bed, but there may be some risk of leakage in the event of a spill.

The type of plumbing that has been discussed above is termed "sanitary." The soil piping from the fixtures leads to a sanitary sewer and a disposal plant. Frequently, plumbing must be installed also to drain off the "storm" water both from the roofs and the grounds around the building. Since the introduction of storm water into the sanitary sewer is likely to overtax the disposal facilities and piping, the storm-water piping is generally connected to a storm sewer with independent and less elaborate methods of dispersal. Interior cold water pipes and roof or storm-water conductors should be insulated where they run horizontally through the building. Otherwise the cold water in the pipes will cause condensation, which is often mistaken for a leak.

Finally, it should be remembered that eventually nearly any pipe will leak. Leaking will require access for repair or replacement, but, more important, it may place the books at risk. In many ways the worst kind of water damage in a library results from a slow leak that goes undetected for an extended period. By the time it is discovered, the damage results in the total loss of the affected materials. The routing of plumbing can often be arranged to avoid crossing bookstacks, which, of course, will reduce the risk of water damage.

Structural Systems Fixed. The basic structural system of any building is made up of a combination of materials. Wood framing, for example, can be lightweight, as is common in residential construction, or heavy, as might be found in a warehouse. Steel can be exposed or encased, it can take the form of a truss or a beam, and it can be welded, bolted, or riveted. Concrete can be precast, cast in place, reinforced, prestressed, etc. To the librarian all of these options may result in considerable confusion about what his or her role might be in selecting a structural system. There are two roles, both of which should be followed. One is to ask questions to assure oneself about soundness, cost, quality, and appearance. The second is to learn enough to be understanding of the structural engineering and the required space and shapes of the structure as it affects the architectural plan.

Foundations. If a good solid foundation base is not available, should the building be floated on a concrete slab, or should it rest on caissons or piles? Should the foundation go down to solid rock, or is there sand, clay, or gravel which will provide a satisfactory base without going so deep? How deep below the surface will it be safe and economical to go for the lowest floor level of the building? Have arrangements been made for trial borings or test pits? One or the other is almost always desirable well before this stage is reached. The cost will generally be a separately budgeted item for which the institution is responsible. The answers to these questions are the engineer's province. The structural engineer can properly suggest alternatives and their financial and other implications. Some institutions retain a soil-mechanics consultant to work with the structural engineer.

The depth of the lowest level will, of course, be influenced by the soil and the slope of the ground and by the institution's desire or willingness to have one or more basements without any windows or with windows on only one, two, or three sides. A properly insulated basement with or without windows may often provide floor area that is even cheaper than space above ground to construct, maintain, and operate because walls can be less expensive, and heating and cooling may be simplified. However, underground space may not be very attractive to potential donors. Toronto's Robarts Library, built in 1973, is an instance of building height being dictated in part by the soil. Bedrock was down 70 ft (21.336), beneath sand filled with water to within 20 ft (6.096) of the surface. The building sits on heavily reinforced concrete 7 ft (2.134) thick, and the lowest level is only 12 in. (305 mm) above high water level.

Framing. Should the building framing be of wood, steel, steel protected by concrete, reinforced concrete, or precast or prestressed concrete? Should the floors be flat concrete slabs or of beam construction? Should the walls be of the bearing type? Wood is often the cheapest framing material, but since it may be a fire hazard, it is seldom used except in a very small library. Steel, unless covered with concrete, succumbs readily to

fire. Reinforced concrete brings with it fire resistance. Steel covered with concrete may be more expensive than reinforced concrete, but it is fire resistant. It may make smaller columns possible and may be therefore not only desirable but necessary if columns are to be kept to no more than the width of the stack ranges in order not to interfere with stack aisles. If precast concrete is used, care must be taken to make sure that joints are tight. Exterior walls must not leak around the windows or anywhere else. They should be well insulated. They have much to do with obtaining a satisfactory aesthetic effect, and care in the selection of brick or stone or other wall materials is required.

It may be well to obtain cost estimates for several different types of framing. Even if there is an expert on the planning team, decisions on these matters should certainly be left to the architect and structural engineers. If bearing walls are used, remember that they may limit flexibility for future stack and furniture layouts and for openings required later on when an extension is added to the building.

Ceilings and Roofs. Whether the roof is flat or sloping or gabled may be of importance to the institution if it is trying to provide architectural unity on its campus. Whether it is covered with slate or some other roofing material should certainly be considered from the point of view of maintenance, fire protection, and aesthetics. Remember that if a flat roof is recommended, it may afford no visually obscured place for the elevator penthouse and for ventilation apparatus that might cost less and be more efficient if it were placed there. There have been libraries constructed in which elevators do not reach to the two upper stack levels so as to prevent a penthouse showing on the roof. One can easily understand the inconvenience that results. A flat roof, particularly if the building is low and large, may present aesthetic problems.

The aesthetic aspects may be understandable, but this is a place where function is of first importance. Remember that climatic conditions must be considered in connection with roof design. A leaky roof cannot be tolerated. If skylights are used, don't forget their weakness in this respect, and see that special precautions are used. Plastic domes may be preferred, as they are generally easier to keep tight. Valleys resulting from gables or irregular construction can be a special hazard, as are gutters in an area with heavy snow and frequent freezing and melting. Roof insulation may be important to prevent overheating of the top floor and thereby adding to the ventilation problem.

Desirable ceiling qualities resemble those for roofs in most ways. Heat and cold and noise must not penetrate unduly from floor to floor. Well-designed ceilings should have satisfactory acoustic properties. Areas where quiet is a functional requirement should be specified in the program, but the design development phase is a good time to review this kind of requirement. Where acoustic isolation is required, the walls should fully enclose the space even above a suspended acoustic ceiling. This is all too frequently overlooked, and sound then carries between offices or other rooms where people want privacy. The decision whether or not ceilings should be furred and hung affects the decor and will determine whether there is hidden space for horizontal mechanical air distribution below the floor construction. (Ducts and pipes can be and often are exposed, as was attractively done in the library of Washington University in St. Louis.) Today most libraries are lighted from ceiling fixtures, either from those flush with the ceiling or hung from it. Consideration should be given to the possible difficulties in changing lighting sources—bulbs and tubes —when they are in or near the ceilings. Radiant heating is sometimes successfully placed in the ceiling.

The planning team should study the architect's proposals for walls, ceilings, and roofs. The architect should initiate them, but should be informed of the institution's previous experience and its wishes.

It is suggested that the library should have three concerns:

1. The structural system should be fire resistant. This pretty much rules out light timber and exposed steel construction, although with proper fire protection, these systems might be considered in certain circumstances. Indeed, there could easily be a requirement to renovate an existing structure for library use that is not of fire-resistant construction. If this is the case, special attention to fire protection will be required. The advice of the architect or a fire protection consultant would be of particular use in this matter.

2. The structural system should be flexible. On this subject the librarian should have a special interest in the module, the size of columns, the floor loading capacity, and the ability to alter internal arrangements, including nonstructural partitions and utilities, especially power and signal, as the need may require. In this regard, load-bearing walls may be a problem as would a floor system that would not permit the future drilling of a hole for conduit or plumbing. Beyond this, most structural systems can be designed for reasonable flexibility.

3. Cost is the final area of concern. The construction cost estimator is the best source of information for making a decision on cost. At any given time, the cost advantage of one system over another can change, but at some point in the design process, this decision must be made. The time to decide is during the design development phase in order to avoid significant duplication of design effort.

The fact that different structural systems imply different aesthetics should not be forgotten. A pressurized air bag structure, for example, may simply not be appropriate for the site although factors of cost may argue for its use in some cases. Questions of maintenance and long-term durability with such a system must be answered, as well. A system of truss or space frame construction, which is appropriate for very large, open spaces, may make little sense in a library. A space frame structure certainly will look different than a cast-in-place concrete structure, and appearance may be a significant factor. The best advice is to listen to your consultants, ask questions, and contribute to the decision as may be appropriate from the point of view of the function of the library.

Buildings are still known to collapse because of faulty construction, faulty engineering techniques, materials, or sometimes earthquakes, unprecedented floods, and hurricanes. In most areas building codes are in force to minimize such hazards. They should, of course, be observed. It should also be noted that building codes may be out of date and require what are obviously unnecessary precautions and expense. This problem may be outside the province of the librarian, but certainly the administration of the institution should be in a position to speak up and try to obtain suitable changes.

Fire and Other Hazards. Consideration of the design requirements in response to fire and other hazards will be part of each of the design phases, and Chapter 5 contains some discussion about treating these risks in the program. Even though this section is under the design development phase, much of the detailing of systems and devices will actually occur during the working drawing or construction documents phase of the design. However, the preparation of the budget estimate at the completion of the design development phase must include a sufficient budget increment to ensure that the response to fire and other hazards can be adequate. Therefore, some preliminary design thinking is required. It may show up in many cases as part of the outline specifications rather than on the drawings.

This section will deal with hazards of various kinds. Proper attention to them and to their causes during the planning process can reduce their occurrence and may avoid them altogether. They may be grouped as follows: (1) fire, (2) water, (3) acts of nature, (4) insects and mold, (5) theft, vandalism, and mutilation, and (6) injury to physically limited persons.

These headings overlap to some extent. Water damage, for instance, may, and frequently does, result indirectly from fire and from external storm conditions. Earthquakes, which here come under the heading "acts of nature," can bring destructive fires and floods in their train. Insect infestation and mold may stem from humid conditions which, in turn, are the result of dampness. A general cautionary point can be made: consider every conceivable threat to the library. Internal design factors that may endanger the collections or personnel can come from steam pipes, electrical transformers, pressured waterlines, toilet drains, etc. External design conditions which are potentially dangerous can derive from surface water drains, exterior doors, large trees near glass in the building, and other vulnerable circumstances. A good example of precautionary action: librarians at the University of Chicago required that several high-pressure steam lines be routed all the way around the Regenstein bookstacks in a service corridor, rather than, at less cost, straight across the ceiling of the stack; and electrical transformers for the building were placed in a vault, below grade, structurally separated from the building, but directly accessible from the shipping dock and truck driveway.

Fire Hazards. This is covered in much greater detail in a volume entitled *Managing the Library Fire Risk,* by John Morris,[4] a volume which should be examined with care by one or more members of any library building planning team. Fire hazards in a library stem in almost all cases from one of four sources:

1. The heating plant, where there may be defective or overheated chimneys or equipment, hot ashes and coals, or escaping gas.

2. Wiring used for lighting, heating, electrical devices, and appliances.

3. Careless housekeeping and smoking habits and use of matches, the storage of combustibles near heaters, and spontaneous combustion.

4. What might be called outside intervention, such as lightning, earthquakes, arson or fire originating elsewhere, or fires resulting from the use of welding and cutting torches by maintenance and other workers.

Each of these sources has been responsible for a considerable number of library fires, and the danger is likely to continue. The third and fourth sources might be said to fall outside the scope of this volume, except as good construction can prevent the spread of fire, if careless housekeeping or smoking habits have started it, and should also tend to lessen the risks from lightning or earthquakes by providing a structure and equipment which will minimize the hazards.

Since approximately one-fourth of library fires have their source in defects in the heating plant, it is evident that all parts of the heating installation that could become overheated to the point where fire might result should be designed and installed so as to prevent the possibility of fire. The same holds true for the electrical services. The engineers designing them should pay proper attention to the related building codes, which have been prepared to reduce risks and hazards of all kinds. The workers who install the heating plants should, of course, be competent also, and their work should be checked by experienced and knowledgeable inspectors. In the United States, the national codes of both the Electrical and the Heating, Ventilating, and Air Conditioning Societies should be used as a minimum standard.

But with the best of care, even if the construction itself is satisfactory, accidents may happen, although the better the quality of construction, the less chance there will be of

[4] John Morris, *Managing the Library Fire Risk,* 2nd ed. (Berkeley: Univ. of California, 1979).

fire starting. There are five major types of construction. They are listed below in order of cost, from the cheapest to the most expensive. The fire risks decrease as the more expensive types are used.

1. Wood-frame construction, in which the structural members are wood.

2. Ordinary construction, in which the supporting walls are masonry, the floors are wooden joists, the interior finish too often conceals space in which fire can spread, and there is little protection for the stair shafts. This was a common type of construction in older libraries. It can be used, however, with protection for the stair shafts by isolating them with masonry walls and self-closing fire doors. The wooden floor and roof joists can be, and often are, protected with fireproof plaster or gypsum board, and the concealed spaces can be fire-stopped. (Fire-stopped means that enclosed spaces are broken up, or made into small compartments, so that fire cannot easily spread inside the wall or under the floor.) If these three steps are taken, the risks are greatly diminished. If they are not, this construction is little better than the wood-frame type. Consequently, construction of this kind is of three grades: (a) where no attempt to protect from fire is made; (b) partially fire-protected with fireproof floors but with a roof with wooden rafters; and (c) fire-protected.

3. Noncombustible construction of steel or steel and masonry with exposed structural members. Exposed structural members do not necessarily mean exposed to view, but exposed to fire, that is, not protected from contact with a fire if it should start.

4. Mill construction, which is sometimes called "slow-burning," or heavy timber construction, with thick brick or masonry walls, floors of 3 or 4 in. (76 mm or 102 mm) planks, or 8 to 12 in. (203 mm to 305 mm) posts and girders of wood, and no concealed places behind interior finish. This construction is desirable for many buildings and is used especially in factories and warehouses.

To the layperson, the exposed steel and masonry construction might seem safer and more fire-resistant than the wooden mill type. But remember that steel exposed to fire will quickly buckle and collapse. Mill construction uses structural members of wood at least 3 in. (76 mm) in thickness. When they are exposed to fire, they will, of course, burn, but, because of size, they will burn so slowly that they will remain intact through a serious blaze, usually until the fire can be controlled.

5. Fire-resistant construction, more commonly called fireproof construction. It is usually of reinforced concrete or steel and masonry with steel structural members encased in concrete or other fire-resistant material. This type is recommended for academic and research libraries whenever possible.

The removal or lessening of hazards will not stop fires altogether. The question of fire detection, alarm, and extinguishing must be considered.

Insurance companies and code authorities usually insist that the solution of the problem in libraries is the installation of a sprinkler system. An examination of the Morris volume referred to above shows that there are various types of sprinklers available which should be considered. Historically, there has been a firmly held belief among librarians (including Mr. Metcalf in the first edition of this volume) that the risk of water damage exceeds the risk of fire in a properly constructed and maintained facility. However, if one considers that only the sprinkler heads affected by the fire are activated and the modern techniques of restoring water-damaged materials, then it can be argued that the risk of fire in a building without a sprinkler system is greater than the risk of loss from water. The Morris volume is quite enlightening in this regard.

Fire risk with or without sprinklers can be reduced if the eight following conditions prevail.

1. A building of fire-resistant or fireproof construction in a location with good public fire protection.

2. Division of the building into fire areas by the use of fire walls and fire doors. These areas may be as large as 15,000 sq ft (1400 m²) and in some cases even more. Fire codes may specify the size allowed, in order to limit the spread of fire to a predetermined area. The smaller the area, the smaller the spread of fire. This problem may have to be taken up with the fire authorities or the insurance companies. Many large areas without fire walls have been built and approved in recent years.

3. Elimination of vertical draft conditions and prevention of propagation of fire upward by means of horizontal barriers, such as fire-resistant continuous floors, enclosure of stairways and elevator shafts, and "fire-stopping" vertical mechanical shafts.

4. A minimum use of easily combustible materials in interior finish and furnishings,

through which fire spreads rapidly and poisonous gases may be generated.

5. The installation of a good detection and alarm system, regularly inspected and maintained in good working order.

6. Installation of protective devices, such as automatic closing of fire doors, or the use of self-closing fire doors, cutoff of air circulation ducts, and first-aid and fire-fighting equipment kept in good working order.

A poorly designed configuration of automatic fire doors may lead to disaster by leaving personnel on the wrong side. The self-closing doors may not be quite so satisfactory in preventing the spread of fire, but they can be opened from either side and might be said to be more considerate of human life if not of property. Some experts in the field suggest that fire walls and fire doors are old-fashioned and out of date, going back to 1890 building codes and insurance company standards, adopted when construction methods resulted in much greater hazards than are involved in good contemporary buildings. But always remember that, unless modern construction is used, special protection, such as a sprinkler system, should be installed, and that, even with modern construction, areas containing materials or use conducive to the incidence of fire should be isolated and sprinklers should be used.

7. Careful supervision of library operations, including good housekeeping practices and also control of smoking.

8. An effective system of periodic inspection of the entire premises for unsafe fire conditions, such as defective electrical wiring, or deficiencies in the air-conditioning or heating system.

While the authors currently recommend the use of sprinklers in most libraries, it should be added that the following kinds of building construction call for sprinkler protection:

1. Library buildings of wooden frame construction or located close to or beside such a building.
2. Libraries in areas not protected by an organized fire department or more than five miles from the nearest fire department station. In the few cases that fall in this category, the use of walls to prevent the spread of flames and smoke damage might be considered in addition to sprinklers.
3. Library buildings with highly combustible interior finishes and equipment.

These hazards should not be permitted, and if finishes or equipment of this kind have been installed, they should be replaced.

4. Libraries located in basements or other building areas to which access for effective fire fighting is difficult.
5. Library buildings of combustible construction in areas subject to high incidence of arson.
6. Those rooms or areas in libraries presenting greater than ordinary hazards, such as storage and work areas, carpenter shops, paint shops, printing and binding shops, garages, and so forth. Egress routes, while they may not present additional risk of fire, will provide greater safety for the building occupants if they are sprinklered. This is particularly true in buildings with transoms over the doors or with panels of glass along corridor walls.

It is well to consider the advantages of sprinkler systems. These include proved capability on a 24-hour basis to detect, control, and, in many cases, extinguish fires before they have caused extensive damage. In addition, sprinkler systems may discharge less water in extinguishing a fire than might otherwise be used. Because the particular sprinkler heads that open are immediately above the fire, they discharge water only into the actual combustion zone. The 15 to 20 gallons (57 to 76 liters) of water per minute normally discharged from a single sprinkler head can often do a far more effective extinguishing job than 250 gallons (946 liters) per minute discharged in a hit-and-miss manner from fire hoses.

Disadvantages include the chance of a broken pipe with water under pressure, a head accidentally or maliciously hit to weaken the keeper or knock off the plug, a "cold flow" in which part of the fusible keeper actually creeps (generally taking 18 years), a defective head which shows up without warning, or the installation of a head rated at too low a temperature for the particular location under extreme conditions. A glass bulb sprinkler head can be specified to avoid all possibility of "cold flow."

Sprinkler systems are not generally required in space occupied by offices, even though there may be furniture of wood, combustible floor coverings, and wooden wall paneling, as well as much paper in the open or stored in steel or wooden files. The fire hazard in ordinary offices is considered to be low. It would appear that sprinklers should not be required in those areas of libraries with comparable fire risks. However, if the building is to be fully protected, and if offices may be converted to other purposes, these areas must have sprinklers as well.

If a sprinkler system is not to be used, other types of fire detection and arrangements for fire extinguishing should be considered. These are described in detail in Chapter 5, as well as the Morris book, and only methods of fire extinguishing with portable equipment will be discussed here. To be useful, fire extinguishers should meet four fundamental requirements:

1. They must be located properly; at least one not more than 100 ft (30.480) from any person; one for every 2500 sq ft (232.25 m²) in most library areas, according to the hazards in that particular area; and at least one on each floor and one at the approach to each exit.
2. They must be in good mechanical condition, which means inspection at least annually by a competent person.
3. All staff members should be acquainted with their location and the way to use them.
4. Extinguishers must be appropriate for library use and not too large for use by staff members. ABC or Halon type extinguishers are recommended, as they can be used on any kind of fire.

The problem of fire extinguishers is complicated by the fact that there are different classes of fire—wood and paper, inflammable liquids, and those with the hazard of electrical shock. The various types of extinguishers include soda acid, water under high pressure, dry chemicals, Halon, and carbon dioxide. The soda-acid type is very effective with wood and paper fires, but it may damage the books. High-pressure water is easily controlled and generally preferred to soda acid. Carbon dioxide is useful for small fires and often recommended, but it is extremely dangerous to persons if used in large quantities. It is recommended especially for compartmentalized rare-book collections as being less damaging to books. Water under pressure under complete control, to avoid unnecessary water damage, should be considered. New types of dry chemicals, especially in the recently introduced Halon extinguisher, may prove satisfactory. Always remember that re-ignition, after a fire is apparently suppressed, is a serious danger.

Special problems and their possible solution should be considered. Danger may come from interior finishes and from open spaces with vertical drafts. Hazardous areas should be segregated and protected with sprinklers or possibly with fire walls. These may include garage areas for library vehicles; storage for gasoline-powered lawn mowers and for flammable fuels, lubricants, and paints; shipping and receiving areas; miscellaneous storage areas for recent gifts; binderies; carpenter, electrical, and print shops; heating plant; and a kitchen or kitchenette. The risk of fire in connection with burning grease in a kitchenette should be kept in mind, and a different type of extinguisher considered (an ABC or CO_2 or Halon; not water).

There is danger that air-circulating ducts can permit the spread of fire, as well as smoke. Dampers with fusible links should be required at points at which the ducts pass through fire walls and floors. These ducts should have shutoff valves that will close automatically when smoke appears, or, if they must be closed manually, the valves should be readily accessible. Where the fire damping system is automatic, the function of the dampers should not be compromised by the fire itself. The dampers must be accessible for inspection and resetting, a detail that is all too often overlooked. However, dampers are not a safe substitute for fan cutoff devices because they do not operate rapidly enough. Fan motors should be connected to a fire-detection system. The shutdown action is then immediate and automatic. The use of a smoke-detection device in the air-circulation system will help. Thermostats are sometimes installed in the circulating ducts to shut off the motors, but this is not recommended because damage can occur before the ducts are hot enough to actuate the thermostats.

Whether or not automatic protection is provided, there should always be a conveniently located station from which the circulating system may be manually shut down by the librarian or members of the staff. Many libraries lack such manual trip stations. Others have all such controls located in the building utility areas where they are readily accessible only to the maintenance personnel.

Smoke spreading throughout a building makes evacuation of personnel more difficult. Smoke also makes it difficult to determine the exact location of the fire itself. Air-circulating systems should therefore be capable of being shut down quickly in an emergency.

Electrical services should have ample capacity for the addition of new circuits and other safety factors. When fluorescent lighting is used, each ballast should be individually fused. Protection against circuit overloading should be provided by circuit breakers as opposed to simple fuses. Special emergency circuits supplied directly from the electrical service entrance points should be used for fire detection, alarm purposes, exit lights, and emergency lighting. If it appears, as is very often the case, that additional lighting is needed for exits, emergency power arrangements supplied by batteries or a standby generator might be considered.

While one mezzanine stack tier produces no special hazards, a series of one above another, often used in the last century, does. In spite of fire safety precautions, too many new libraries are being constructed with open stairways running between more than two floors, often for purely aesthetic rather than functional reasons. From the standpoint of safety, proper enclosures provide safer methods of exit and also prevent the open spaces from serving as flues for fire, smoke, and toxic gases.

A building planned with few or no windows means that emergency access in case of fire may be a matter of special significance. If the design of a new building calls for large open areas without fire walls, the overall fire safety measures taken must compensate for the increase in the single fire risk thus presented. Noncombustible acoustical materials should always be used.

Fire-risk consultants are sometimes recommended, but the institution must be careful not to choose one who is primarily a sales representative for some special piece of equipment. The right person will be hard to find. To some candidates, a remote possibility becomes an immediate hazard, and neither the laws of probability nor the value, or lack of it, of the material protected has any place in their analysis. Some large institutions that are self-insured and are particularly anxious to avoid losses, employ fire-prevention experts who may well give sounder advice than those with a different motivation.

Consider the possibility of special protection—a vault, for instance—for archival computer tapes or a microfilm copy of a catalog as replacement backup. A vault may also be considered for the extremely rare materials, for both security and fire safety.

Finally, always keep in mind the desirability of constant inspection to make sure that good housekeeping is observed. This is a matter of fundamental importance.

Water Hazards. Many librarians are much more worried, and properly so, about damage from water than from fire. As already noted, one source of this damage could be from sprinklers. Other obvious and common sources are floods from heavy rains or melting snow, water from broken pipes, faulty drains, inadequate waterproofing, spills, and leaky roofs. If there are drains under or in the basement floor, they should be arranged so that they can be cut off in case of floods when the water level rises to a point where water could back up through them into the building. Backwater valves should always be installed.

Broken or defective water, steam, and drain pipes present special problems in libraries because of the possibility of water damage to books. In planning a new library, the architect should locate water pipes so that in case of failure they can be reached easily and also so that books will not be exposed to damage. Several rare-book libraries have a protective apron under all water pipes, which will collect water from a leak, carry it to a safe place, and set off an alarm. The Newberry Library stack addition is even safer in that it has no water pipes within the stack spaces.

Rooftop mechanical rooms should have a waterproof floor with drains and provision for future vertical penetration through protected shafts, with waterproof curbs.

In addition to attention given to the location of pipes and waterproofing, water alarms may be considered. A sump pump should have a high-water alarm that is remotely annunciated to ensure a proper response. Simple detectors designed to sound an alarm if there is water on the floor can be specified as well. Furthermore, a humidity alarm, which activates a shutoff valve for the steam source in the building, can reduce the risk of a steam leak.

Acts of Nature. These include primarily lightning, earthquakes, and wind. Modern library buildings have rarely been struck by lightning, and unless the building construction creates a higher than average susceptibility, this should not present a problem today.

Earthquakes are another matter. Local building codes in regions where earthquakes are prevalent have introduced design and construction requirements which greatly reduce the probability of damage from earthquakes. If your library is in an earthquake zone, be sure that proper precautions for extra strength are used, following the provisions in the appropriate building codes. These sometimes present a functional problem, as they frequently result in solid structural walls in places where a main traffic artery would be placed under normal conditions, and special care in planning circulation patterns must be taken to avoid complications, which were discussed earlier. The design and attachment of shelving and major furniture, equipment, or art elements should have special attention.

Wind damage should not be a problem with a properly designed structure, though if the panes of glass are too large and the wind is very strong, glass breakage and its results may be serious. Wind damage is an especially important concern in hurricane or tornado areas or other locales subject occasionally to very high winds. Hurricane-force winds will drive water through even well-designed window casings. The continuing tendency toward the construction of "glass boxes" causes concern, particularly if the glass used is too thin and set too tight. In this connection, it should be noted that operable vertical fins that are used for sun protection required by too much glass tend to become noisy in a high wind and, after exposure to weather, may become immovable. Their design should be carefully considered. Furthermore, libraries within a mile of sea coasts or tidal bays may need to guard against wave action on the elevated sea level which can result from severe storms, when the surge may range from 5 ft (1.524) in small storms to as much as 25 ft (7.620) in the most powerful hurricanes.

Insects and Other Animal Life. Damage from insects, bookworms, silverfish, cockroaches, etc., has not been a significant problem in American libraries in recent years, but it has been very serious in tropical countries. Most insects dislike light. General cleanliness and good housekeeping do not please them. Ventilation and temperature control within the limits of human comfort do not satisfy them.

In spite of this, various precautions should be taken. Termites in northern parts of the United States, and more frequently in the South, have tended during recent years to be a problem in any wooden structure or in any part of a building where wood comes in direct or fairly close contact with the earth. They have done considerable damage in some libraries, eating out floor framing so that equipment and furniture drop to the floor below. Some major libraries, in which books are acquired from tropical countries, and others where modern construction is not in vogue, may have trouble with bookworms of one type or another. If a library acquires books on a large scale from all over the world, a small fumigation chamber for the treatment of book shipments would be desirable. The advent of the blast freezing technique of killing infestations shows great promise and may well become the best choice of fumigation systems, as it avoids the use of toxic chemicals. Where the use of toxic chemicals is not regarded as a problem, a vacuum chamber designed for the use of ethylene oxide has had wide acceptance. Provision of a room with negative air pressure and exhaust to the outside, together with reasonably air-tight construction, may serve as a staging area for infested materials. It should be remembered that bookworms and other insects may be very fond of leather, wood, parchment, and glue, as well as paper, and that great damage may result from their depredations.

If food is to be served in the library, the greatest care must be taken to provide for proper housekeeping, as cockroaches and mice tend to appear wherever there are food operations. This is the greatest objection to the installation of snack bars and food-dispensing operations in a library. It is a major objection. The best advice is do not have food service in a library.

Mold will develop whenever and wherever high humidity is present at the same time as high temperature. The mold spores seem to be ever present, waiting for suitable conditions to arise. Air conditioning with humidity control will solve the problem, but without it mold may grow almost anywhere in the temperate zone and still more prevalently in the tropics. If humidity control is not possible, keep the air moving and avoid dead air pockets in basements and elsewhere, particularly during sultry summer days and after heavy rains when basements may have taken in some water.

One final aspect. Just like some bell towers, some libraries have problems with bats. Bats especially like to live under Spanish tile roofs, and, on occasion, they have moved into the library building. As for the buildings, the best protection is a tightly sealed or fully screened outer envelope. Once inside the building, a bat is especially hard to capture, and it can be a real health hazard. Tiles, on the other hand, can be "bat proofed" by simply stuffing the open ends with a wad of fiberglass. If it is expected that bats may be a problem, and a tile roof is selected, the open ends should be sealed in this way. Any other openings to the outside should be screened with a mesh fine enough to keep a small mouse out. A coarse form of hardware cloth may not be fine enough in all cases. The openings should not exceed ¼ in. (6.4 mm).

Theft, Vandalism, and Mutilation. These are of interest in connection with library design chiefly because they can be reduced but not completely avoided by proper exit controls, supervision, and design. The latter is especially important, as will be explained.

Libraries in colleges and universities have had their share of vandalism over past centuries and there is every reason to expect that it will continue in the future. Although it will seldom include the mass "trashing" of windows which many American universities experienced in the late 1960s, there will be constant actions resulting in graffiti on walls, "ripping off" signs, and a wide variety of other activities which create undesirable conditions.

However, academic and research libraries do not get the worst of it. The design team for the library can learn from the experiences of schools and other types of institutions. The building design and its details, both exterior and interior, must minimize the opportunities for vandalism. The design development phase of planning is not the only time to consider these matters, but it is perhaps the principal time during the design process. The schematic phase will be of importance in terms of general placement on the site and configuration of the building. The design development phase should be when the great majority of conditions which could encourage vandalism can be averted by refinement of the plans. There has been a constant trend throughout this century toward a philosophy of openness, of access to collections. Yet, even if the librarian has not had bad experiences

in recent years, in the course of the building's existence, instances of maliciousness can be expected which might have been averted through a modest change in the design. At the same time one must not create an impression of siege conditions; the librarian does not want to design a structure which operates like a prison.

One other preliminary comment. There will be a wide variety of experiences in terms of the damage to structures in different parts of the world. A college in a rural setting in the State of Maine will not have the problems of a large commuter college located in a rather tough neighborhood of an inner city. Libraries in countries such as Great Britain and France may not have the extensive damage and, particularly, serious crime that exists in the United States. One would expect even less in academic libraries located in Japan, Sweden, or Switzerland. Furthermore, branch libraries will have nowhere near the degree of vandalism that exists in a large general library building. Yet no library is immune from some of the more innocuous outlets for human emotions.

It is well to understand what prompts these actions, to the extent that is possible, and then to see what approaches can be taken to ameliorate the results. There are eight conditions that may be separated as a convenient way of understanding the damage to buildings: (1) Wear and tear. For example, poor-quality carpet will, with heavy use, look shabby, soiled, and damaged and perhaps will be hazardous within a few years. (2) Accidental. A door where the restraining bar or bumper stop has come loose may slam into a wall and break the plaster or glass in the door. (3) Vindictive. Hostility may be directed against a library staff member or teacher because of a grudge. (4) Maliciousness. Rough play may be the result of sheer devilry. (5) Ideological. An attempt to dramatize a cause by a major public expression written on a building or fence or wall. (6) Acquisitive. Petty theft is the removal of building or street names. The more serious acquisitive vandal may rationalize theft for financial reasons, which can include the theft of material or equipment with the intention of resale. (7) Boredom. Where there is no constructive outlet for energy, the imagination may find opportunities. (8) Frustration. The reaction to impersonal conditions, the callous indifference of an institution, or the pressures of growing up and perhaps living for the first time away from home and under an increased academic pressure can lead some people to feel "boxed-in" and make them want to lash out at something, to vent their feelings of inability to deal with the situation.

To some psychologists, geneticists, sociologists and anthropologists, the more extreme of the above activities are due to a deep vein of violence or aggression in humans. Some would claim that excessive permissiveness engenders such antisocial behavior. Others accept it as all part of growing up and accommodating to society. When secondary schools have a huge problem with vandalism, one can expect that college-age people will not suddenly mature and adjust to a larger and more challenging social situation. Throughout history rebelliousness has been taken out on buildings and property. Feeling powerless, or perhaps dehumanized by a very impersonal physical environment, some individuals will take it upon themselves to alter that environment and create their own personal statement. Yet the contrast between New York City subway cars and the Moscow subway can serve to remind us that conditions can vary greatly from time to time and from place to place.

Preventing all vandalism is impossible. However, one can minimize it by dealing with some of its causes. It is not enough to say that all academic institutions should have enrollments of no more than 500 or that there should be no libraries other than small departmental branches, even though both would result in much less vandalism. Indeed, one does not design an academic building to deal with the rare individual who is intent on destruction. Even the security conditions in the most distinguished private research libraries are vulnerable, as the removal of the Gutenberg Bible from the especially secure Widener Memorial Room at Harvard reminds us.

There are five fundamental approaches to dealing with this condition. First, rules, and penalties for breaking them, can be established. Second, education of the clientele—to inform them of the cost of damage to property and the effect it has on their education or on their tuition payments or tax dollars. Third, flattery, which can take the form of greatly improving the quality of the furnishings with the result that people ordinarily live up to the implied expectations. Fourth, "target-hardening," i.e., making space and its

furnishings indestructable. This is a regrettable but often necessary treatment, frequently in secondary schools and occasionally in institutions of higher education. And fifth, diversion, by which is meant the elimination of obvious opportunities for damaging actions. The last three of these approaches should be carefully considered and choices made in the design of the library and its interiors. The key to successful design responses to vandalism is in the thoughtful planning of space, finishes, furnishings, and their details.

It seems to be part of the natural development of young people to explore and manipulate their environment. These actions rather naturally result in their testing their strength on buildings, dismantling things, throwing objects. While much damage may stem from a relatively opportunistic and casual form of behavior, if breakage or markings are not rather quickly repaired, the damage will spread like an epidemic. With respect to graffiti, it is wise to attempt to control where it appears rather than futilely trying to eliminate it completely.

Before indicating some of the particular actions that can be taken in regard to architecture, landscaping, and furniture, it is well to point out the desirability of reviewing plans by attempting to guess what library users may do or try. In this fashion it is useful to walk mentally through each room in the plans, walk around the building, and try each reading space or common area and, in particular, to consider the details. Will shoes mark the stair risers? Is there a column where one turns the corner such that a painted surface will be quickly soiled? Will the seams in upholstered chairs come at a place where it is easy to unconsciously pick at them or poke at them with a pencil?

Still, there will be limits. If an exceedingly heavy person stands on a lower shelf to reach a top shelf, a steel shelf is likely to bend. If several people yank on a handrail simultaneously as a game, it may well pull out of the wall. Consequently, the evaluation of areas should deal with the more common opportunities and not with the rare or unique case, since protecting against all such abuse would mean an uncomfortable, cold, hard, and unfriendly library and is certain to push the cost of the building up considerably. Remember that some modest changes in architectural programs can markedly reduce damage and vandalism. Libraries should be able with careful planning to channel activities into the most acceptable locations. For an example, bicycle and foot paths through landscaping and lawns are the result of faulty landscape design by not recognizing the human tendency to take the shortest route between two points, just as conditions within the library may seem to invite actions which result in damage or destruction.

As a general design approach, some principles can be applied. First, select the design and quality of materials so that the natural effects of age and wear do not provide an opportunity for idle abuse. Second, repair damage promptly to minimize any enjoyment by the perpetrator and to eliminate the visible reminder to others of what can be done. Third, utilize small modules or units so that the effect of damage is minimized and the cost of repair is reduced. Fourth, alter designs where an area might seem to have its aesthetic value improved by marking, such as a long and prominently located smooth wall. Fifth, lessen the rewarding feedback to the vandal. Sixth, provide visual or physical diversions to steer the individual away from potentially damaging activities.

A sample of actions that can be taken in the landscape, architectural, or interior design will suggest some applications of the above principles. Elsewhere in this volume other suggestions have been provided in order that buildings stand up well in use. These suggestions in part derive from a 1974 survey conducted by the National Association of School Security Directors.

1. *Site selection.* A building is more vulnerable if it is located by a main through highway or if it is adjacent to a playing field or public grade school. A building may have more damage if it is on the periphery of the campus site, if it is immediately adjacent to or in the center of campus student demonstrations, and if it is on a site to which many off-campus persons are attracted.

2. *Exterior surrounds.* Parking for bicycles and motor vehicles should be visible from the building windows and from major adjacent paths. Facilitate foot and bicycle traffic around the building, including police patrols, but do not have the paths within arms length of the building itself. Lights around the exterior can be argued pro and con, but it is generally felt that the grounds but not the building should be illuminated.

While lights will, during evening hours, serve as a deterrent, break-resistant lenses are desirable and the luminaire itself should be a minimum of 14 ft (4.267) high. The lights may be on a time clock in order to turn off at, for example, midnight or 1:00 A.M. Light poles must be of substantial material and set back at least a foot (305 mm) from the curb of any road. Bolts used to secure poles should be tack-welded. Light fixtures on buildings should preferably be recessed flush with the walls, especially if they are not very high. Trash receptacles should be sufficient in number and be quite heavy, while at the same time being easy to empty. Flat, light-colored surfaces at ground level may be protected from graffiti by placing them behind landscaping, using a heavily textured or dark surface. Consider using glass instead of a convenient writing wall.

3. *Landscaping.* Paths must provide logical access and direct routes and yet should generally keep people away from the sides of the building. Grade changes can help keep pedestrians and cyclists on walkways. Keep grounds free of rocks and loose bricks or pavers. Anchor tables and benches unless they are exceedingly heavy. Keep plants quite low and well away from any basement or ground level windows. Thorny plants are not a good protection since grounds keepers will be loathe to collect litter blown into them.

4. *Building shell.* Minimize niches, recesses, courtyards, and other hiding places created by the exterior configuration. Avoid ornate, nonfunctional building materials and protuberances, such as brackets, low overhangs, grills—anything that can be climbed on or swung from. Furthermore, be attentive to this point regarding special signs on buildings. For a sign in front of a building, a flower bed planted around the sign will sometimes protect it since the flowers seem to convey the idea that somebody cares. There should be no mail slots in the exterior, if at all possible. An exterior book return that delivers books inside the building may be a special problem. Where there is concern about vandalism here, the return should be contained within an enclosed room, and a fire suppression system should be required. An alternative is the freestanding book return, which creates other problems, including the risk of damage from rain. This is an area that may require special care. Above all, provide a cheerful and humanistic environment rather than one that

could seem repressive, impersonal, cold, and uncomfortable.

5. *Windows.* Most windows should be of moderate-sized panes and of standard sizes. Avoid any exterior transom and be wary of skylights and roof hatches. Any window facing an alley or service area may need break-resistant glazing. Laminated glass, acrylic, or polycarbonate glazing must be properly installed, perhaps using pop rivets and reverse installation (from the inside so that putty is not on the outside). Note that tempered glass is fairly easy to break unless it is also laminated.

6. *Doors.* Use heavyweight hardware. Leave no hinge pins exposed and removable on doors to any secure area. Consider door pivots rather than hinges. Always use a center column or an astragal for double doors unless panic hardware is not required and dead bolts can be used. In any room with free exterior access, such as rest rooms, never have an inside locked door leading into the rest of the building. Have a doorbell at the service entrance. Use interchangeable core key locking systems with multilevel master keys.

7. *Utilities.* Hide or recess and protect the location of utilities. Avoid utility tunnels connecting into any high-security area such as the rare-book stack. Provide a drain slot in any book return chute to reduce damage from flammable material being poured in and ignited, and a floor drain in case water is dumped in; or use a book return with a "snuffing-out device." Use flame retardant paint in vulnerable areas. To curb vandalism, interior roof drains or use of scuppers are preferable to downspouts. But be aware that the former can leak. Exterior drinking fountains and display fountains should be easily cleared of debris. Tamper-proof electric hand dryers might be considered if paper towels lead to littering.

8. *Interiors.* Elevator cars should have the operating panel provided with tamper-proof fasteners so that buttons cannot be creatively rewired. Car walls should be of a hard surface or perhaps carpeted. (Plastic laminate will chip at the edges. Woven metal mesh can be clogged with crayon unless the texture is in low relief and not mesh. Stainless steel is quite durable but, once defaced, cannot be retouched. Baked enamel can be scratched.) Have the ceiling of the car taller than can be reached by a reasonably tall individual. Solid-metal nonprotruding buttons will avoid the

breakage of plastic protruding ones. Study carrel surfaces should be hard and washable, such as plastic laminate. Do not provide soft ceilings below 8 ft (2.438) in study areas, and 10 ft (3.048) in corridors and rest rooms. Use washable epoxy paint in vulnerable areas. Recessed soap dispensers and shelves are desirable, but do not recess trash and paper receptacles as they jam once bent. Base supports for all rest room facilities should be provided, yet with access for persons in wheelchairs. Use the most minimal grouting in enameled tile walls in rest rooms. Reinforced doors are needed wherever audio-visual or business equipment is to be stored, and consider having no explanatory sign of the contents of such rooms. Use plastic lenses for all wall clocks, consider porcelainized chalkboards in seminar rooms and in after-hour study rooms. Consider walls where murals may discourage marking.

9. *Security.* Any intrusion detection system should be zoned to allow for partial building use. Where codes permit, fire alarm pull boxes might be placed in the rooms that are occupied rather than in hallways, and consider providing a ten-second delay on alarms to allow false ones to be verified by closed-circuit television and cancelled in order to reduce the results of pranks. Consider where a dish mirror might be useful, or closed circuit television. Use surface-mounted alarm system contacts or, even better, use hidden, recessed magnetic switches on doors and operable windows. Thought may also be given to magnetic coded card-entry systems which can record who, when, and where a room was entered and left, and which will control the door opening by authorization.

One should be particularly careful of the vulnerability of the mail room or staff entrance. There are likely to be more major security lapses here than elsewhere in the building. Cash management is another particularly vulnerable aspect of library procedures. An inset floor money safe with a slot for after-hour deposits may be useful in certain locations that collect cash in the late afternoon or evenings. Although it is regrettable, experience in commercial, as well as not-for-profit, organizations shows that something like two-thirds of all thefts are by staff. This is a matter which the librarians will need to think through carefully so that the building does not become like a bank in its operation, and yet does not provide opportunities which can serve to foster such actions.

From the above, it can be seen that details make a great deal of difference. There are frequently new materials and new ideas that the planners must be alert to and use when they seem advantageous. Library problems with fabric covered chairs, for example, have been considerably reduced by the use of Naugahyde, although a durable fabric may be more desirable for comfort and aesthetics.

It is hoped that damage to library buildings and destruction of property can be reduced. Human nature being what it is, however, it is well to design a library with a good deal of protection built in. There may come a time when a building superintendent, a concierge, or a live-in guard may be needed after service hours. Yet, this arrangement would hardly suffice for buildings that are open as much as a hundred hours a week. It is the obligation of the librarian and architect, as well as interior designer, to make the library a useful structure and one that will stand up under wear and occasional abuse.

Very valuable books should ordinarily be kept under lock and key, although unique material and volumes with the greatest value can be difficult to sell at their true value, particularly if they have concealed library ownership marks. The best method to prevent theft of irreplaceable materials is to place them on closed-access shelves. If the materials must be stored in a reading area open to the public, they should be protected by locked doors on the bookcases. These books should be made available only on signature from known, reliable persons, and the call slips should be kept in a safe place until the books have been returned and been examined to show that they have not been damaged. For less important books which are kept on open shelves, the best protection is examination of the holdings of all readers as they leave the building.

The question of book mutilation is a much more serious one, as there is no way to prevent it when students and others have free access to bookstacks and cannot always be supervised. There is little that can be done in library planning to minimize this problem. From time to time (fortunately, comparatively rarely) college students have been known to destroy books just for the sake of being destructive. The most difficult problem is mutilation, when a student cuts out a page so that its use can be more convenient or when phrases of special interest are highlighted or underlined for later reference. The latter has sometimes been encouraged unwittingly by professors who have forgotten that, if they suggest that students do it with their own books, students are likely to do it with library books. Book mutilation can be reduced if convenient photocopy machines are available for copying at a reasonable cost.

Injury to Handicapped Persons. It is necessary to take into account the special problems of those persons who are limited by being confined to wheelchairs, who require crutches, who are blind or have other sight impairment, who have hearing disabilities, who have faulty coordination due to brain, spinal, or other nerve injury, or who, because of age, have reduced mobility, flexibility, coordination, and perceptiveness.

Special consideration to problems of such persons should be given in planning a building. Help for these individuals should start from the outside, perhaps beginning with a parking area so designed that it will not be too difficult for a person on crutches or in a wheelchair to leave the car. Curbs must have appropriately placed ramps at least 3 ft (0.914) wide. The bottom of any sign projecting over a path must be at least 7 ft 6 in. (2.285) high. There should be no nearby trees that drop nuts or large seedpods or have limbs which break under ice or snow loads. Walks to the library should be at least 4 ft (1.219) wide, should not have a grade greater than 5 percent, and should not be interrupted by steps. At least one building main entrance should be reached without going up steps, and a ramp should be available if necessary. The ramp should have a slope not greater than a 1 ft (610 mm) rise in 12 ft (3.658), or approximately 8 percent. Where site conditions make 8 percent impossible, 10 percent is allowed over a single 7 ft 6 in. (2.286) length or 12 percent over a single 4 ft (1.219) length. On at least one side, and preferably on both sides, a ramp should have handrails 32 in. (813 mm) in height and extending 1 ft (305 mm) beyond the top and the bottom. The ends of the handrail should not become a hazard; they will not if they terminate on the side of a wall; curved rather than sharp ends will help. The rail diameter should be between 1¼ in. and 1½ in. (31.7 mm and 38.1 mm) and permit continuous sliding of the hand. Ramps should have a level platform before a door is reached. Any long ramp must have a 3 ft (914 mm) landing after each 30 or 40 ft (9.144 or 12.192) segment, depending on the total length. Where bicycle parking is a problem, special emphasis will be required to provide ample bicycle and mo-ped parking in order to avoid blocking the access route for the handicapped and others.

Doors should have a clear opening of not less than 32 in. (812 mm). The door itself will have to be 34 in. (863 mm) wide. This dimension applies to both exterior and interior doors. Use of automatic doors should be considered, at least for the main entrance. Doors with two leaves should be avoided, unless each provides a 32 in. (812 mm) clear opening. This amount is required for wheelchairs, as well as for persons using crutches. Typical length for occupied wheelchairs ranges from 4 ft to 4 ft 6 in. (1.219 to 1.372), and an average diameter of 5 ft 3 in. (1.600) is required to turn around. Motorized chairs for quadraplegics require more area, so generous spacing is needed.

For the sake of occupants of wheelchairs, there should be an elevator if the building has more than one level, with a door of at least 32 in. (812 mm) in the clear so that a wheelchair can enter it. Stairs should have handrails 32 in. (812 mm) above the tread at the face of the riser. Stairs with overhanging or square nosings should be avoided, as they present a hazard for persons with restriction in knee, ankle, or hip movements. Main stairs should have risers that do not exceed 7 in. (178 mm) unless an elevator is available, and tread size will be determined by formula. (Codes usually allow risers to be a maximum of 7½ in. (190.5 mm) high for general usage.)

Slippery floors are dangerous and should be avoided throughout the library. There should be a common level throughout each floor of a building. A step up or down going from a corridor to a toilet room, for instance, should be avoided, as should door sills or thresholds. Carpet laid on floor, stairs, and ramps should have a tight weave, low pile, and firm underlayment. No underlayment and uncut pile is preferable.

Every library should provide at least a few chairs with arms, as some persons can get up from a chair only by using the arms for support.

Other facilities that should be observed in order to make them accessible to the physically limited include drinking fountains and a public telephone with a shelf low enough so that a person in a wheelchair can roll up to it and reach the dial. Thresholds should be avoided even at the main entrance. Easily approached elevators and electrical switches of all kinds are also of importance. Regarding signs, consider that red-green is the most common color blind deficiency. Raised letters are needed for tactile sign reading at a standard height between 4 ft 6 in. and 5 ft (1.372 and 1.524). Hazards such as low-hanging signs and ceiling lights must be avoided; a minimum height of 6 ft 6 in. to 7 ft (1.980 to 2.134) from the floor is recommended for interiors. Some recent codes require the use of fire alarm horns that include a flashing light.

Detailed specifications can be found in documentation from the American National Standards Institute, located at 1430 Broadway, New York, New York 10018. These specifications or those promulgated by the Architectural and Transportation Barriers Compliance Board (ATBCB) may govern the design when federal money is involved. The ATBCB's "Minimum Guidelines and Requirements for Accessible Design" was published in the *Federal Register* of January 27, 1982. Other codes or standards may apply. In California, for example, the *California Administrative Code, Title 24* outlines the requirements for accessible facilities. A number of other states have similar codes or guides, e.g., Illinois, North Carolina, and the New York State University Construction Fund. If any of these standards or codes has been adopted by the local governing authorities, then care must be taken to ensure compliance. Guidance can also be obtained from, among others, the American Foundation for the Blind in New York, the Disabled Living Foundation in London, and Research Office of the Syracuse University School of Architecture.

Outline Specifications. At the completion of the design development phase, the specifications will not yet be fully developed. The general and special conditions, for example, will typically be omitted, and the specifications for each of the building trades will consist of a general description of the design intent. It is unlikely that specific products will be selected, although it is possible in a few cases. A more detailed description of the complete specifications will be found in Chapter 14.

While there is no fixed rule regarding the contents of the outline specifications, the following might be considered reasonable:

1. A project statement giving a general architectural description of the building.
2. An area analysis with the figures developed showing the gross and net floor area for each floor, together with the area assigned to mechanical functions, walls, circulation, and other features that contribute to the nonassignable space.
3. A program area analysis showing the area assigned to each program element, together with the excess or shortage in relation to the written program. Where the new facility is an addition, the analysis might include the breakdown of space assigned in the new and existing structures.
4. A structural statement describing the soil conditions and the proposed materials and technique. The codes which apply to the design may also be cited. The structural system will cover the footings, columns, bearing walls, and the floor and roof systems.
5. A mechanical statement giving a general description of the proposed system.
6. A general description of the electrical systems and any special computer accommodation.
7. A series of sections covering each of the building trades including a statement of the materials that are to be used, the finish, the scope of work within the trade, and in some cases the method of installation. In the outline specifications these descriptions will be fairly general, except perhaps when the institution requires a particular product for maintenance or operational purposes.

The librarian should pay special attention to those aspects that may adversely affect the operation of the library. Those would include shelving and special equipment, alarm systems, lighting, hardware, and perhaps the mechanical, general electrical, elevator, flooring, and painting sections. Others may be important, as well. One should review the requirements for samples, mock-ups, operational information (which may be covered later in the general or special conditions), and the operational aspects (quality, durability, flexibility, etc.) to ensure that the "owner" will receive what is wanted. It is important at this phase to ensure that there is sufficient information to generate a sound budget estimate, which often is essential before approval can be given to proceed to the next phase.

While the building program should have stated the most important requirements, the conditions affecting mechanical systems, lighting, plumbing, safety, and security must now be specified. The end result is dependent on following through on these points.

The Newberry Library in Chicago can be used as a good example of involvement. First of all, the library's conservation officer was an early and most important member of the planning team. He had great and consequential influence on the specifications for the building, with the important backing of the library so the conservation needs would be foremost. The basic design of the 1982 Bookstack Building was itself a result of this planning approach. Besides being off limits to readers, the building is windowless, of double-shell construction, and has no vertical penetrations between floors, no cooling tower on the top of the building and no mechanical equipment within the structure. Treatment of air, humidity, and access security is stringent. Special sheathing is provided to waterproof the basement level. The exterior double-shell wall is composed first of a layer of brick, then 1½ in. (38 mm) of air (an insulation layer), then an 8 in. (203 mm) concrete-block wall, another air cavity, and finally plaster board as the interior wall surface. The air-cleaning system uses three high efficiency filters to remove atmospheric particles and gaseous impurities. Environmental constraints are 60 degrees, plus or minus 5 degrees F (15.5 C plus or minus 2.8 degrees C), and 50 percent, plus or minus 3 percent, relative humidity diurnally and 50 percent, plus or minus 6 percent, seasonally. (The master microfilm copies are, however, controlled at 35 percent relative humidity.) All air mixing and humidity adjustments are done outside the Bookstack Building, in a structure linking the original building and the addition, before being fed horizontally by duct to each floor for distribution. Regarding access security, there is motion detection in some areas. Each staff member has a magnetic card which enables entrance to controlled parts of the building and into areas within the stack, and any use of the card makes a record of that person's entrance and departure. The fire protection system includes ionization smoke detectors and rate-of-rise temperature detectors, plus a Halon fire-extinguishing system in the vault which has walls with a four-hour rating. Physical intrusion, smoke, fire and environmental conditions are monitored through local reading devices, the results of which are fed through a field processing panel to a central computer. In addition to a printout record, the computer terminal provides precise display of current conditions in color keyed to the plan of mechanical features and security points and the sensing of those local conditions. Staff attend the monitoring station within the building on a 24-hour basis.

It is interesting to note that the Newberry Library had to obtain a variance from local building codes to permit the library to be designed so that stack aisle and emergency lighting could be switched off whenever there was no staff person on that particular stack floor. It also required a variance in order that the single emergency stair turret, which was required by code, could have a 30-second time delay on the exit door before it could be opened, so designed to alert staff that a person is in the stairwell, so closed circuit television could make a record and display at the central staff monitoring locations, and staff could take protective action. However, a variance was not allowed for a single security-card–activated pair of doors into each stack level; the county insisted on extra vestibule doors which automatically close when magnetic holds release upon sensing a fire—a requirement that added to the cost of the structure.

Computer Installations. Specifications must be quite rigorous and cover many aspects. Special building requirements for a mini- or larger computer may be needed for area security, electrical power including a backup source, insulation from electromagnetic interference, fire suppression, floor loading capacity, space for air-conditioning equipment and connections if the building as a whole does not meet required specifications, and lighting sectionally controlled and completely independent of computer power. Power requirements should be met with a voltage range controlled to not over 8 percent or below 8 percent. There must be a power line analyzer, lightning protection, and all lines in metallic conduit. Carpeting should be of a nonstatic type. Space must be sufficient for all doors on all equipment to be wide

open at the same time. Other specifications will be provided by the manufacturer, and a computer consultant is advisable on any sizable installation. Section 13.4 under The Catalog and Computer Terminals provides other comments applicable for any computer installation.

It is perhaps worth noting how difficult it is to judge what the computer requirements may be ten years away. Some university general library buildings included a computer room in the design. The University of Minnesota Wilson Library is an instance, yet it is not used for that purpose and is not expected later to be. Other buildings had no such designed space and were able to install small mainframe computers with no great difficulty. Many have minicomputers with no problem of accommodation. Distributed processing and use of mini- and microcomputers have changed the picture from that of a decade ago.

The University of Toronto Robarts Library, which was programmed in the mid-1960s and occupied in 1972–73, is a building which one of its planners has said "was planned for the computer age [but] considering the way things have gone, it might almost just as well not have been." Even so, in the 1960s, Toronto rejected use of very large cable ducts in every floor slab, which would have added 10 percent to the total construction cost. Instead it chose ordinary modular three-cell ductwork in floors in the reading rooms, workrooms, and a few other areas, and assumed that extra future cabling would be carried in troughs at ceiling level. By 1982 no need of such expedients had arisen. The Green Library addition at Stanford, seven years later than Robarts, used only vertical power and signal chases and a main artery trough (cable tray) run above the suspended ceiling. Extra power capacity was provided.

It may be worth noting that power requirements vary greatly. Color monitors and letter-quality printers use about three times as much energy as monochrome monitors and dot-matrix printers. Hard-disc storage generally uses more than floppy disc. Maximum electricity wattage required by devices will vary greatly; as typical examples, today some word processors may draw 420–540, terminals with keyboard and display from 60 to 300, CRT monitors from 40 to 120, printers from 100 to 310, and microcomputers, 65–400. Libraries may have three to four times as many devices 15 years from now, though the average wattage per device may decrease. It is for responsible institutional officers to assure the capacity to adapt to changing technology and yet not to overplan, which can with hindsight prove to be a waste of funds.

Maintaining Flexibility. Much attention has already been given to the topic of flexibility; little more needs to be said here except to underscore the importance of clear thinking and analysis of and reasonable solutions to library needs. Decisions will be made during the design development phase which will largely establish the nature of flexibility in the final product. By the time this phase is completed, the librarian and institution should feel that these decisions are correct, as they should not be changed at a later date except as they may apply to the development of project details. The needs of flexibility must be kept in mind during all of the design process including change orders during construction.

13.3 Testing the Budget

With the completion of the design development drawings and outline specifications, a budget estimate should be prepared. The process of budget estimates and budget control was discussed in Chapter 9. If the design team has done its work well, there should be no surprises resulting from the budget estimate but, unfortunately, this is often not the case. It seems to be the rule rather than the exception that each time there is a cost estimate, the projected cost increases. This occurs as a result of an increased understanding of the design as well as problems of site, material supply, or other factors that may come to light as the design progresses. It also results from what may be considered program improvements which are often related to the learning experience of the design exercise, or they may be related to newly developed technologies in library operations, energy control, maintenance process, and the like. On a large project several years may have passed between the first writing of the program and the completion of the design development phase, and things do change.

When the design team learns that its project no longer fits within the budget, the first reaction may be to obtain a confirming estimate. While another estimate may be lower, it should be remembered that any estimate can be off by as much as 10 percent; and, even though the estimator may not agree, this is probably a reasonable range, especially at this phase. Assuming that the design team has confidence in the abilities of the estimator, and assuming that there is sufficient breakdown (see the discussion of the cost model in Chapter 9) so that obvious errors or misunderstandings can be identified, one might reasonably question the merit of expending additional project money for a confirming estimate. It is probably better to take the bull by the horns and deal with the problem.

The choices are simple to identify but usually difficult to enact. For the design team the most pleasant solution would be to increase the budget. To do this, a fair amount of homework must be completed. There must be a clear understanding of why the budget estimate has increased. And, there must be sound justification for the need that leads to the increase. It is in this circumstance where, under certain political pressures, a confirming estimate may be warranted. The homework should include an analysis of the alternatives. Answers to questions such as those below should be in mind:

Can special alternative sources of funding be obtained? Are there different funding sources that might deal with energy conservation, providing handicapped access, code problems in existing facilities, providing landscaping outside the building, and the like?

Can the project be phased over a decade or so? Can deduct alternates be identified?

Can the project scope be reduced?

Can the quality be reduced? Care will be required here!

Are there construction techniques that could reduce the cost without adversely influencing the project? In an era of high inflation, the fast-track construction system has been claimed to reduce costs, but there are risks, and the end of design development is a late date to start a fast-track program. (The concept of fast-track is discussed in Chapter 15.)

Is there another part of the budget that can be reduced? Here, the only budget item that should be reduced, assuming the original budget was properly done, is the design contingency. This is justified because more is known about the project at this phase than when the budget was originally formulated.

If any of the above is possible with negligible effect on the project, it can then usually be assumed that additional funding is out of the question. If the above does not close the gap, some hard decisions will be required. The best advice that can be given is that the librarian should have a clear view of the priorities, to ensure that the facility will work well for future generations. In general, the authors tend to prefer add or deduct alternates over a reduction of the quality, reasonable flexibility, or the general arrangements established to this point.

It should be recognized that the design of alternates or significant changes in the project scope will affect the architect's fee. This knowledge should be clear at the start of any analysis resulting from budgetary problems. In Great Britain, where architects and quantity surveyors are expected to estimate building costs accurately, a bid (or tender) in excess of the agreed expenditure limit is modified by compensating savings determined by the design team and prepared by the architect at no cost to the institution.

13.4 Design Development of Interiors

The schematic phase of design is intended to test the assumptions made about space assignment and to aid both the designer and the owner in the analysis of the space arrangements. In the design development phase greater attention is paid to the dimensions of the furniture and equipment and its layout. Concerns about vandalism were discussed in Section 13.2, and concerns about details, durability, and color will be covered in Chapter 14. This section will discuss a number of issues in terms of layouts, mock-ups, and space utilization which should be at the heart of the design development phase of interiors.

Equipment layouts cannot be completed until there has been agreement upon the large-scale spatial relationships and the quantitative requirements for seating accommodations, volumes to be stored, and other space uses. Aesthetics and physical comfort are important. Equipment layouts should look good. A satisfactory layout must be based on properly designed, comfortable furniture of the right size for the task at hand, so arranged that it is easily accessible and provides the

desired work space without undue interference from or to others.

This section will deal with general principles for satisfactory layouts for seating accommodations, shelving, and card catalog cases and computer terminal catalog access. These involve most of the basic problems which must be met. As far as space utilization is concerned, the design of seating accommodations chiefly involves aisle space and working-surface areas. Shelving involves, as far as storage capacity is concerned, height and cubage in addition to floor area and the requirements for adjacent aisle space. Card catalog case arrangements involve problems similar to those for shelving, but the capacity for cards per a unit of floor space may vary even more than that for books, as cases may have trays in rows up to 15 or more in height, and the use of the aisle space tends to be much more concentrated than that for shelving or seating. An automated catalog using computer terminals will involve conditions similar to those found in seating at carrels, but a use pattern different from card catalogs can be anticipated.

The designer, with the program submitted by the institution as a guide, will in due course prepare schematic drawings or preliminary sketch plans which will be shown to the library's representatives. The first ones will probably do little more than indicate spatial relationships. Later, the floor areas of the different functions will be included, but in rough terms. Later still, proposed equipment layouts should be shown. These can sometimes be arranged by drawing in the equipment with the sizes that have been agreed upon. It can be done to advantage by using templates of paper, cardboard, or metal drawn to scale. These have the advantage of making it possible without erasure to shift the templates and find the most suitable arrangements. Making the drawing on grid paper, with each square, for instance, representing one foot or one quarter of a meter, may ease the task. If grid paper is not used, it is particularly desirable to have a large-scale drawing, so that it will be easier to move the templates around. A scale of 1 in. to 4 ft (or 1:50 in the metric system) is suggested, unless a very large area is to be covered. Special boards fitted up with magnets which hold a metal template in place are sometimes used. Many laypersons find it difficult to picture from a drawing just what the finished results will look like and to decide whether a 3 ft (914 mm) aisle between tables, for instance, is adequate, whether a 3 × 5-ft or a 4 × 6-ft (0.914 × 1.524 or 1.219 × 1.829) reading-room table is preferable for four persons, or whether a shelf 7 in. (178 mm) deep will give space enough for books. The architect, or interior designer, who is more experienced and adept with tasks of this kind, may be able to give satisfactory answers to questions, but in some cases a visual demonstration is desirable.

One method is to go to a library where tables, shelving, catalog cases, computer terminals, and other equipment of different sizes can be seen in their proper setting. A demonstration with furniture is useful in a library with rooms approximately the size planned in the new building. An experienced library consultant can suggest libraries to visit. In almost any large city or metropolitan area, it is possible to find examples of arrangements that would be useful.

If new types of equipment or methods of construction are to be used, there may be occasions when a mock-up on a larger or smaller scale will be advisable. When Princeton's Firestone Library was being planned, soon after the Second World War, the architects arranged for the construction of a four-bay mock-up. In two of the bays sample bookstacks of various types were installed. The other two were used for the layout of other accommodations. A false adjustable ceiling that could be cranked up and down was installed to test out ceiling heights. Sample lighting and other equipment was made available. Those interested had an almost ideal visual demonstration of problems for which solutions were desired. While this is an example of a fairly ambitious mock-up, smaller scale mock-ups using existing space and proposed lighting and furnishings can be useful. It must be remembered that the window areas and the intensity of the light coming from the outside at different times of day have an effect on the desired and required intensity of the light within the building as well as on its quality.

When Lamont was under construction and plans were made for a larger number of open carrels than had ever been used before in a library, sample carrels with tables of different sizes, with and without shelves, with backs of different heights, and with other variations were built and carefully studied.

Appendix B of this volume gives tables listing sizes of furniture of various types, aisle widths, the resulting capacity for books and readers, and other items of interest. If these tables are used in combination with library visits and suitable drawings, the results should be satisfactory. It should always be remembered that in furniture layouts, as in other things, circumstances alter cases. The interior design scheme may help to make a room look larger and more spacious, just as it may make it look more crowded and congested.

Satisfactory layouts may be products of an exact science, but often they are achieved only by reasoned judgment mixed with trial and error. The following ten general principles are suggested:

1. The optimum size of the proposed equipment should be agreed upon. Should a table for four be 3 × 5 ft, or would 4 × 6 ft (0.914 × 1.524 or 1.219 × 1.829) be more satisfactory, although it takes more space?
2. Aisles consume more space than equipment, and every aisle, to be economical in space utilization, should be used on both sides.
3. An aisle that has chairs backing into it should be wider than one without seating used even more heavily as a main traffic artery.
4. Visual and auditory distractions should be minimized, and design conditions should be studied with care.
5. Main traffic arteries in a straight line are preferable, unless they are at least 100 ft (30.480) or more long. If they have to turn corners and pass obstructions that are above eye level in height, a hemmed-in feeling and confusion may result.
6. A great reading room with row after row of tables parallel to each other gives an unpleasantly regimented effect, which shelving or screens 6 ft (1.829) high or more placed at intervals may help to eliminate.
7. A long row of open carrels along a wall on one or more sides of a room with table backs 4 ft 6 in. (1.372) high will not be nearly so monotonous as an equally long row of carrels placed between two ranges in a bookstack. In a long row of carrels or tables, a break used for lounge chairs or other seating arrangements may relieve the monotony. (See fig. 13.4.)

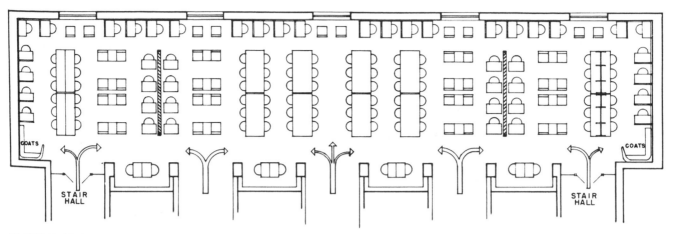

FIGURE 13.4 A variety of seating accommodations used in a large reading area. Students do not all want the same kind of accommodations. The use of a variety relieves monotony. There are too many large tables here, but comfortable semi-lounge chairs diminish the rigidity. Slanting-top tables, partitions on long tables, individual tables separated by screens, double carrels facing each other in shallow alcoves, all help. Note also the five entrances that reduce distances to be traveled to reach the seats, and the coatracks in two corners in sight of many readers. This plan is adapted from the Lamont reading room. See also figures 7.2 and 7.8.

8. Wall shelves in a large reading area are seldom desirable from the space assignment point of view, as they require wide aisles in front of them. Shelving can be placed more economically on ranges with shelving on both sides, as the aisle then receives full use.

9. Shelves along a reading room wall have the additional disadvantage of increasing the distances involved in using the collections and of creating visual and auditory distraction. Reference and other heavily used materials should be concentrated as far as possible, with accommodations for readers who will be using them adjacent on one or all sides.

10. A wall on one side and, to a greater extent, walls on both sides of an aisle or corridor make it seem narrower. A 3 ft (914 mm) corridor with walls on both sides reaching above eye level appears very narrow. A 3 ft (914 mm) corridor with an open carrel on one side and the ends of book ranges on the other will seem quite adequate visually and, when two persons pass in it, one of them can, if necessary, slip into the stack aisle or the space in front of an unoccupied carrel table while the other goes by. A room seems open with no obstructions above table height, that is, 30 in. (762 mm), plus or minus. Partitions 4 ft 6 in. (1.372) in height on

three sides of carrels do not take much away from a feeling of openness for a person who is standing; and one sitting and studying is generally not interested in openness and enjoys being partially shut off from neighbors so long as light and ventilation are good, and one can look out in at least one direction. Most persons will feel that floor cases in a reading room up to 5 ft 6 in. (1.676) high, which permit five shelves of books, will give a surprisingly open feeling compared to going down a 4 or 4½ ft. (1.219 or 1.372) wide aisle at right angles to the ranges, particularly if the ceiling is 8 ft (2.438) high or more.

One final general comment. The use of curved walls or those with angles that are not 90 degrees should always be questioned, especially in small buildings, as good space utilization will be difficult and never completely successful. Curved bay windows in their proper place can be attractive aesthetically, but they are expensive to construct, and furniture and equipment are seldom designed to fit them. Radial stacks planned on the basis that they permit better supervision may be useful under some conditions, but floor area varying from 10 percent up is lost, and some congestion inevitably results when ranges approach each other near the center where traffic is heaviest; it is invariably difficult to

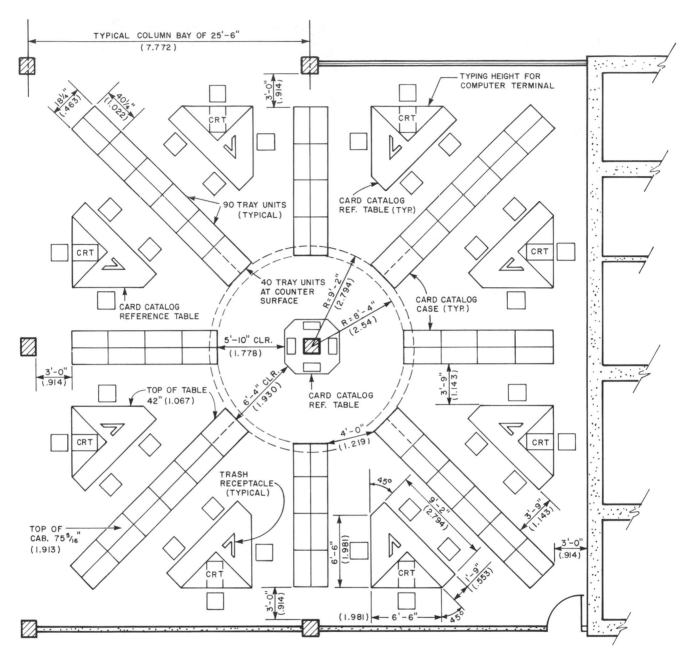

FIGURE 13.5 Stanford University, Cecil H. Green Library. Card catalog with counters designed for consultation of card trays and for computer terminals supporting the automated catalog. Note that each card case section nearest the center in each diagonal row is counter height for tray consultation and for traffic visibility near the center. This configuration of cases uses little more floor space than traditional arrangements (housing about 3,000 cards to each sq ft, or 32,000 per m²), and it considerably shortens the distance traveled by a person checking references that are not in alphabetical sequence. (See figure 13.25 for comparison.)

use the periphery to advantage. See, however, the radial catalog which can be satisfactory and take no more space than a more regular layout (fig. 13.5). If radial stacks are used in very large areas, somewhat better space utilization becomes possible, but most readers will find it difficult to keep properly oriented and will often have to come back to the center and take extra steps before going to another section. Circular arrangements for shelving and seating have been tried again and again in the past (e.g., Leeds, Manchester, and Northwestern), and as far as the authors have been able to learn have never proved to be completely satisfactory.

Seating Accommodations. As an aid in planning layouts, suggestions are presented for arrangements for seating accommmodations in reading areas and bookstacks. They are based on the theoretical discussion of seating arrangements in Chapter 7. Remember that academic and research (not public) libraries are under consideration and that the sizes and arrangements suggested are for academic and research use.

Besides the typical arrangements, a suitable proportion of reading accommodations must handle specialized tasks and must be adapted for needs of the physically handicapped and the left-handed. The latter, for example, applies to typing returns, tablet arms, and microtext reading arrangements. The working surface should be at a typing height of about 24 to 27 in. (610 mm to 685 mm) for computer terminals and microform readers, except for those carrels high enough to clear the arms of a wheelchair, which are typically 30 in. (762 mm). It is also important to avoid obstructions under the carrel or table which could be hit by the wheelchair arms or the knees of the seated reader. (Note: Do not use counters for typing, since a second typist will create surface jiggle and increase sound reverberation for the other. Stand-alone desks, carrels, or stands are best.) While the higher typing height represents the generally accepted standard, the lower height of 24 to 25 in. (610 mm to 635 mm) may be more ideally suited to the requirements of machines that involve long sessions in fairly rigid posture.

1. Single open carrels with the long axis of the tabletops at right angles to a wall. These may be in reading areas, in bookstacks with walls on one side and a subsidiary cross aisle on the other, or at the end of stack ranges beyond the aisle, or they may take the place of the last stack section in a range. Unless they are quite heavy, single carrels should preferably be fastened to the wall or floor in some way to stay in position. (See figs. 13.6–13.9.)

The suggested minimum size for the table tops, without bookshelf or shelves above, is 22 × 36 in. (558 mm × 914 mm); medium size 24 × 42 in. (610 mm × 1066 mm); generous 24 × 48 in. (610 mm × 1219 mm). Shelves are rarely recommended for undergraduate work or for carrels in the reference area. If they are used, 5 in. (127 mm) should be added to the depth of the tabletop. A preferable size is 27 × 42 in. (685 mm × 1066 mm). For a carrel for a graduate student writing a dissertation, a tabletop 27 × up to 48 in. (685 mm × 1219 mm) may be useful. Anything larger might be called extravagant, except where special equipment or large volumes will be used (e.g., art and music libraries and archival and manuscript reading rooms). For microform readers a carrel up to 60 in. (1524 mm) wide and 36 in. (914 mm) deep may not be too large.

If the table in the bookstack installations can be placed in a line with the stack ranges, the reader is in a better position to look out for visual relief. If the stack ranges are only 4 ft (1.219) on centers and the tables are to have the same spacing, a table that is more than 22 in. (558 mm) deep will leave the student less than 26 in. (660 mm) to get in and out of a seat. An armchair then becomes questionable, and the table leg under the corner where one enters should preferably be set back at least 6 in. (152 mm). Stack ranges 4 ft 6 in. (1.372) on centers will be possible on the same terms for a 27 in. (685 mm) deep table, with a shelf provided above. Ranges 4 ft 3 in. (1.295) on centers with a 23 in. (584 mm) table give 28 in. (711 mm) behind the table, minus the thickness of the back of the table. The carrels, of course, do not have to match the stack ranges in spacing, and for graduate carrels it may be desirable to provide greater distances on centers in spite of the resulting irregularity. Here the question of windows and the facade should be considered.

Single carrels similar to those just described (see fig. 13.7(B)), but with shelves to one side, are sometimes used. If space between carrel centers is at a premium, these may be useful. If the shelving faces the aisle, it can at the same time provide additional privacy. (See fig. 13.7(C).)

2. Single closed carrels along a bookstack wall and opening into a subsidiary stack aisle. These are sometimes called study cubicles or dissertation rooms. They are quite similar to the open carrels described above, but with partitions and a door. Unless considerably larger, they may be difficult to ventilate and to light and tend to cause claustrophobia. Partitions to the ceiling are not recommended for undergraduates; but, as security for the scholar's papers is a prime rationale for this type of carrel, the walls should be high enough to prevent unauthorized access. If the area, including the adjacent aisle, is at least as much as 5 ft × 6 ft 8 in. (1.524 × 2.032), it can be used for graduate students if there is glass in the door. Light from an

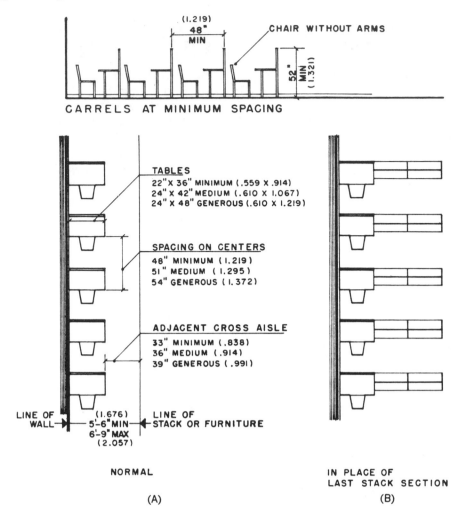

NORMAL

(A)

IN PLACE OF
LAST STACK SECTION

(B)

FIGURE 13.6 Carrels at right angles to a wall. (A) Suggests sizes and spacing and shows elevations. (B) Carrel in place of last stack section next to a wall. The working surface of the carrel should be in line with the stack range instead of the aisle, in order to make it easier to get into the chair. In other words, the 6 in. (0.152 mm) recess at the front support, as shown in the elevation, together with armless chairs are required to make these dimensions work. More generous spacing will allow armchairs and a carrel without the recessed front support. Handicapped access would be difficult with all but the most generous dimensions.

outside window will help. An enclosed area of approximately 6 ft × 6 ft (1.829 × 1.829) provides adequate space for a generous work surface, perhaps a section of shelving and a two-drawer letter file which many graduate students would welcome. With proper design, a person in a wheelchair could easily use the space. Figure 13.8 shows a closed carrel with a door.

3. Single carrels in place of a stack section at the end of a book range. (See fig. 13.6(B).) As far as space use is concerned, this is the most economical way to provide a seating accommodation, and it gives a great deal of se-

clusion, which many readers want. It presents four problems, however:

a. The space from front to back is limited to the distance between range centers, which in some cases is minimal.

b. Unless the tabletop is specially designed to occupy the full depth of the double-faced range, as shown in Figure 13.6(B), it may be difficult to get into the chair because the tabletop will jut out into the aisle.

c. Some readers, particularly if there is no adjacent outside window, will feel too shut in for comfort.

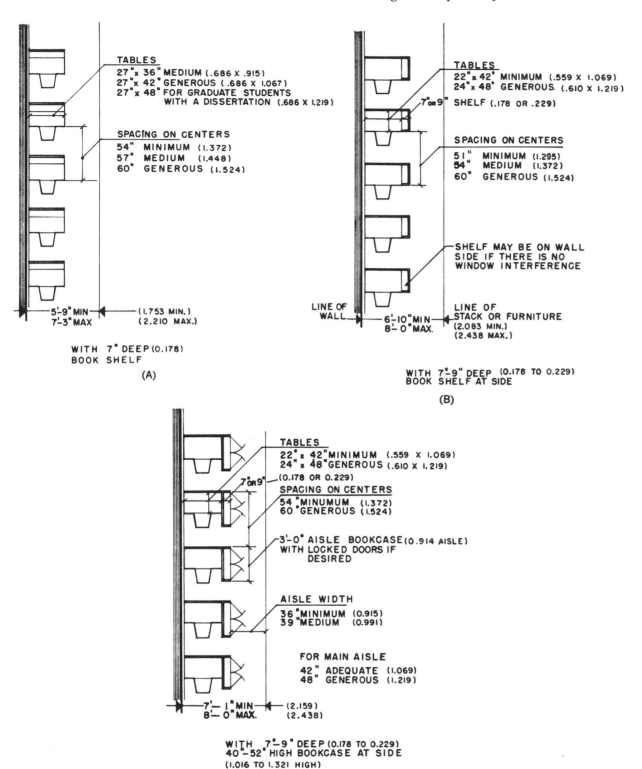

FIGURE 13.7 Carrels with shelves. (A) Shelf in front of reader. The table should be 5 in. (0.127 mm) deeper than one without a shelf, and adequate spacing between carrels may be difficult to arrange where it is desired to align the carrels with stack ranges. (B) Shelf at one side instead of in front. (It can be at either side.) This arrangement requires more width but less depth. (C) Shelf at one side facing the aisle. This arrangement can provide more shelf capacity and greater privacy; it also demands greater total width.

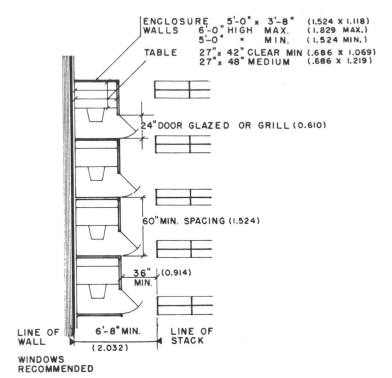

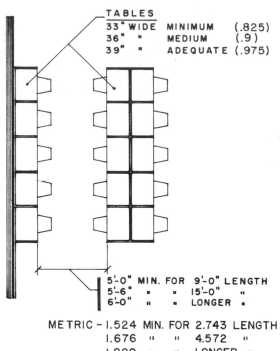

FIGURE 13.8 Closed carrel with door and shelf. If there is no window, wider spacing is desirable to prevent claustrophobia. Ventilation and lighting will present problems.

FIGURE 13.10 Reading-room table with divided partitions. Not very satisfactory if table seats more than four and reader is hemmed in on both sides. If light is hung from the partition, it tends to cause an unpleasant glare. If partitions between readers sitting side by side are extended on both sides to provide more privacy, they become too confining.

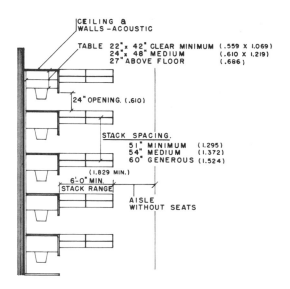

FIGURE 13.9 Partly open typing carrel in place of last stack section with acoustically treated walls and ceiling. Adjacent books also help to muffle sound. Absence of other seating close at hand makes doors unnecessary.

d. Since the seat is at the end of a blind aisle, the length of the range should not be more than half that of a range with cross aisles at both ends. Many codes will limit the length to 20 ft (6.096) as the maximum for a dead-end aisle.

If acoustic walls are installed on all sides except at the stack aisle, such a carrel will be satisfactory for typing and no door will be required. (See fig. 13.9.) The tabletop for typing should be at least 3 ft 6 in. (1.067) wide by at least 20 in. (508 mm) deep and 27 in. (685 mm) above the floor, instead of a standard 29 to 30 in. (736 mm to 762 mm). A work surface with adjustable height would be better. If used in this way as a typing carrel, with no door provided, the insertion of Celotex or other similar material between the front and back of the adjacent double-faced ranges will help acoustically, and the books themselves have good acoustical properties. However, this addition will reduce the flexibility for shelving the occasional oversized volume.

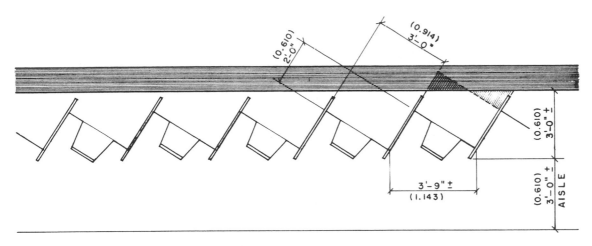

FIGURE 13.11 A dog-leg carrel, though disliked by many, is a compromise for one facing a wall. The partition on one side is extended enough to provide seclusion; the carrel is open on the other.

4. Single seats facing a reading room or stack wall or a high partition down the center of a regular reading room table. These are sometimes provided with a high partition at the sides, projecting 6 in. (152 mm) beyond the tabletop into the aisle, to cut one off from the neighbors. There is no place to look out when leaning back in the chair, except directly at the neighbor to the right or left. These have been used in long rows at Bryn Mawr College, M.I.T., Cornell University, the library on the undergraduate campus at the University of Tokyo, and elsewhere. They are not recommended, except in an open area in groups of four, where the reader can look out in at least one direction, because few students enjoy facing a blank wall, unless they can look out at least a few feet on one side without seeing a neighbor close at hand. (See fig. 13.10.)

The Notre Dame University Library has single carrels in a sawtooth, or what is known as a dog-leg arrangement, shown in Figure 13.11, which is popular in Sweden and elsewhere. This arrangement is preferable to those directly facing a wall, as the reader can look out on one side and still is protected from the neighbors. It requires no additional space.

5. Double carrels in rows in a reading room separated by partitions which are at least 52 in. (1.320) in height in the front and on one side of the working area. Working-surface sizes proposed for 1 above are adequate. Partitions in front can be held down to 3 to 10 in. (75 mm to 254 mm) above the tabletop, because a full view of one's neighbor all the

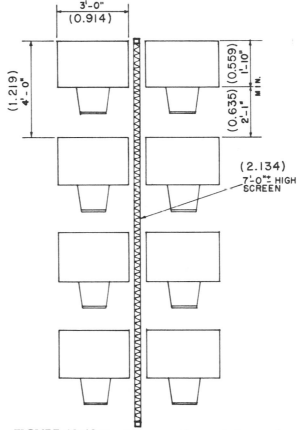

FIGURE 13.12 Double row of carrels in reading area separated by a screen. Carrels can be used with or without backs.

time is less distracting than a head bobbing up and down occasionally; but 52 in. (1.320) above the floor is preferable (fig. 7.5). In some places two rows of individual tables separated by a screen (as in fig. 13.12) may be useful.

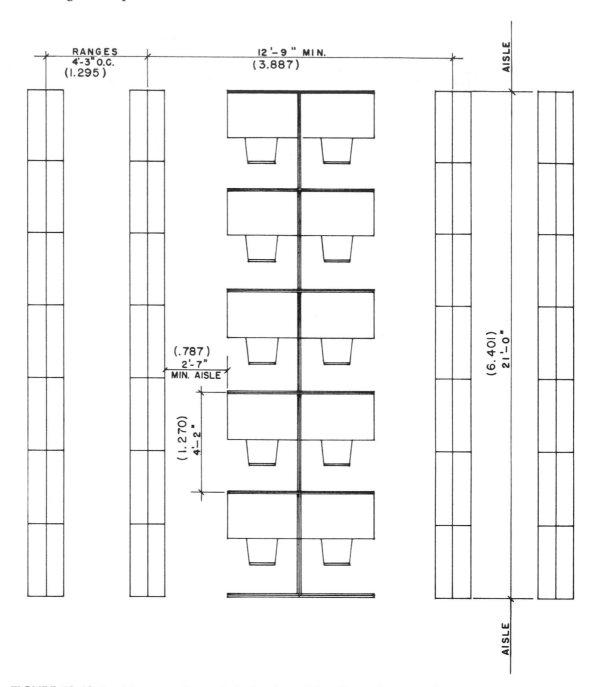

RANGES
4'-3" O.C.
(1.295)

12'-9" MIN.
(3.887)

AISLE

(.787)
2'-7"
MIN. AISLE

(1.270)
4'-2"

(6.401)
21'-0"

AISLE

FIGURE 13.13 Double row of carrels in bookstack in place of two stack ranges.

6. Double carrels in rows in place of two stack ranges. A carrel size of 33 × 22 in. (838 mm × 558 mm) can be used in place of two stack ranges, when ranges are 4 ft 3 in. (1.295) on centers, leaving an aisle of about 31 in. (787 mm) if 12 in. (304 mm) base shelves are used. A size of 36 × 22 in. (914 mm × 558 mm) can be used comfortably with ranges 4 ft 6 in. (1.372) on centers. By placing one or both end pairs at right angles to the others, the carrel range and the stack range length can be made to match with tabletops and dis-

tances between centers of standard size. (See fig. 13.13 and 13.14.)

7. Double carrels at right angles to a wall (as at Douglass College at Rutgers, the Uris Undergraduate Library at Cornell, and Brandeis), with partitions on two sides and with two readers facing in opposite directions or the same way. The partitions should be at least 52 in. (1.321) above the floor to prevent visual distraction. Tabletops of the same sizes as in 1 above are recommended. A distance of 4½ ft (1.372) on centers represents a min-

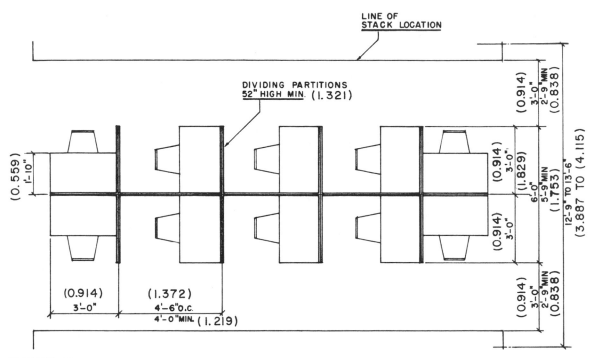

FIGURE 13.14 Double row of carrels in bookstack in place of two stack ranges, with end pairs turned at right angles to provide adjustment to length of ranges.

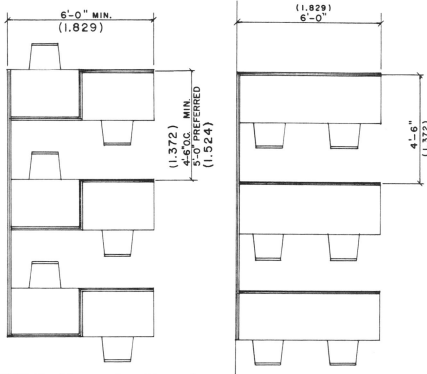

FIGURE 13.15 Double carrels with readers facing in different directions. Used at Douglass College at Rutgers and Uris Undergraduate Library at Cornell. This arrangement is quite possible, but arrangements shown in figure 13.17 are recommended.

FIGURE 13.16 Double carrels facing in the same direction. This arrangement is an adaptation of that used at Brandeis. It encourages conversation and thus is not generally recommended.

imum, with 5 ft (1.524) on centers preferred. This arrangement is possible but not recommended, because the readers are sitting side by side even when facing in opposite directions. (See figs. 13.15 and 13.16.) The arrangements described in the next three paragraphs are preferred.

8. Double-staggered carrels with the adjacent tabletops overlapping by one-half their depth, the same sizes as in 1 above, placed along walls, with 4½ ft (1.372) minimum on centers and 5 ft (1.524) preferred. Placing pairs of them on each side of a screen or low partition is quite possible, if the back of the inside carrel is kept low. (See figs. 13.17 and 13.18.)

9. Triple-staggered carrels in a reading area, preferably 5 ft (1.524) on centers with tabletops of the sizes proposed for others. If the center carrel in each group of three is thought to be too confined, the partition at the back of the table can be left out altogether or, preferably, held down in height to

from 3 to 10 in. (75 mm to 254 mm) above the tabletop to give some privacy. One set can be separated from another set of three by an aisle at least 3 ft (914 mm) wide; preferably one 3½ ft to 4 ft (1.067 to 1.219) wide should be used. A series of them, or of double-staggered carrels as proposed in the preceding paragraph, on each side of a partition might be considered in some cases, if a very large seating capacity is required with a small collection of books. It might be set up in a city university in a large study hall in order to increase capacity or be used in place of three stack ranges. (See fig. 13.18.)

10. "Pinwheel" groups of four carrels, preferably in a reading alcove. If the alcove is 12 × 12 ft (3.658 × 3.658) in the clear, tabletops 22 × 36 in. (558 mm × 914 mm) are recommended, with partitions at least 52 in. (1.320) in height, which extend 6 in. (152 mm) beyond the end of each table. Shelves are ordinarily not recommended in these cases, particularly if the tabletop is less than

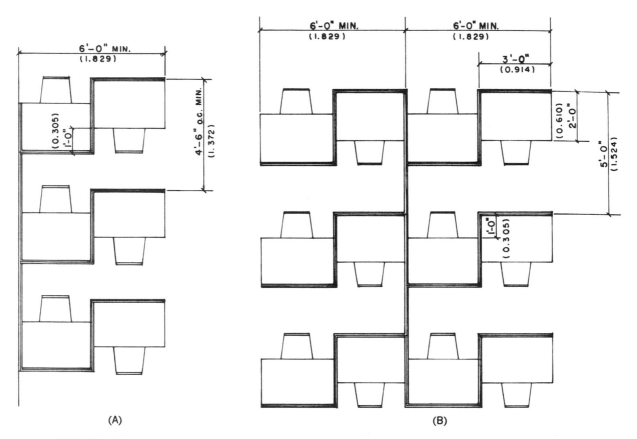

(A) (B)

FIGURE 13.17 Double-staggered carrels. (A) Double-staggered carrel adjacent to a wall. The carrel by the wall will be helped by a window. Partitions should be 52 in. (1.321) high or higher (Recommended). (B) Double-staggered carrels on each side of a screen or partition. A space saver, but recommended only when necessary to provide required seating capacity. The backs of the inside carrels should be no more than 40 in. (1.016) high.

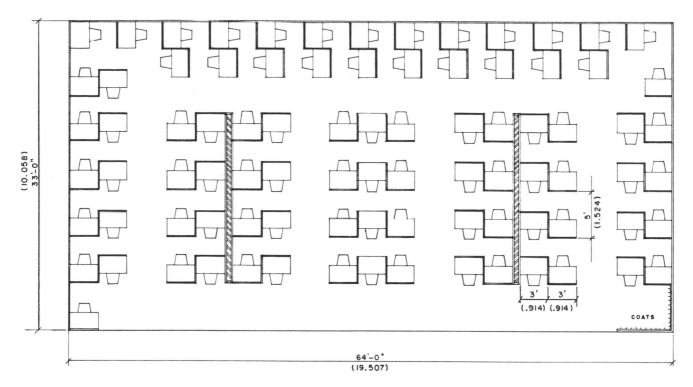

10.058 X 19.507 STUDY HALL (196.631)
33'x 64' STUDY HALL (2112 SQ FT)
88 SEATS

FIGURE 13.18 Triple-staggered carrels. This arrangement can be used in a large reading area in conjunction with double-staggered or other arrangements, or in place of three stack ranges which are 4 ft (1.219) on centers. If the top of the back of the center carrel is held to no more than 40 in. (1.016), the occupant will feel less hemmed in.

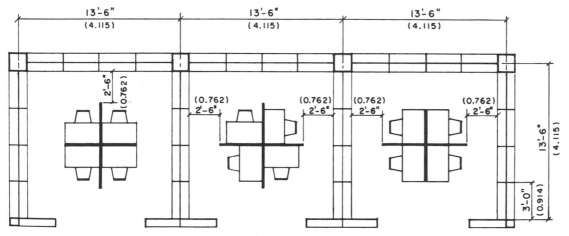

FIGURE 13.19 Carrels in alcoves. The pinwheel arrangement is suitable if alcove is at least 12 × 12 ft (3.658 × 3.658) inside measurement. Table for four with partitions is possible in a 12 × 9 ft (3.658 × 7.743) alcove. Not recommended for heavily used collections.

27 in. (685 mm) deep. Carrels with shelves or with a larger work surface will require somewhat more space.

This arrangement fits perfectly in a 27 ft (8.230) column spacing with two alcoves to a bay. If the module size is 25 ft 6 in. (7.772), the space in each alcove will be reduced a total of 9 in. (228 mm), and one of the shelf sections will be only 27 in. (685 mm). It can be used for shorter shelves or set up as wall

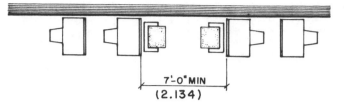

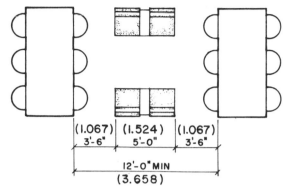

FIGURE 13.20 Lounge chairs replacing carrels along a wall or between tables for six in a reading area to relieve monotony. Conversation may be encouraged by this arrangement. Footrests are recommended.

space for a bulletin board or for a picture or other decoration.

If ventilation is adequate, alcoves can be partially closed in on the fourth side by a single or double-faced book section, which may help to use the space to advantage and make possible the best utilization of the available bay size. The main aisle between double rows of alcoves can be as narrow as 4½ ft (1.372). (See figs. 12.10(C) and 13.19.)

These pinwheel groups have been successful in large reading areas, but they tend to give an impression of disorderliness when not in an alcove. However, this impression may not be altogether bad, depending on one's philosophy, as it reduces the feeling of regimentation.

11. Carrels in alcoves with tables for four installed with 52 in. (1.321) high partitions in each direction. These alcoves may be as little as 9 ft (2.742) deep and 11 ft 3 in. to 12 ft (3.430 to 3.658) wide in the clear. With a 25 ft 6 in. (7.772) bay and 4 ft 6 in. (1.372) main aisle, an unusually large capacity is possible. (See figs. 12.10 (A and B) and 13.19.) With a 27 ft (8.230) bay, the space utilization is still good, and the main aisle can be wid-

ened to 6 ft (1.829), or the size of the carrels can be increased. The question of shelving books in alcoves such as these should be considered as, if frequent access is required, their use will be an annoyance for the readers.

12. Individual lounge chairs to break the monotony of a long row of carrels or tables, as shown in Figure 13.20.

13. Pairs or trios of lounge or semi-lounge chairs in units with low tables, which are at least 1 ft (305 mm) wide, preferably 1½ to 2 ft (457 mm to 610 mm), and of seat height, between each pair. These can be purchased in units and may be preferable to single chairs, which are more likely to be pushed out of position. They can be used in place of two single carrels if they take less than 9 ft (2.743) in length or in pairs or trios between rows of carrels or tables in a large reading area. However, as a single unit, some flexibility is lost. In reading areas lounge chairs should be arranged so as to discourage casual conversation.

Many of these arrangements for individual seating accommodations in lounge chairs or in carrels can be placed in between rows of standard library tables in a large reading area. They can also be placed, preferably in bay-size groups interspersed with carrels, in a large bookstack. (See figs. 13.20 and 13.21.) Small groups, sometimes called oases, such as are used at Princeton, may not be so desirable because they tend to complicate shelving arrangements and to become noisy, although many librarians like this arrangement. (See fig. 13.22.) The larger groups can be made quite attractive by changes in the lighting and floor covering; these breaks in the monotony of a very large stack are often a relief.

Bookstack Arrangements. The following eight principles should be kept in mind in connection with bookstack layouts.

1. Traffic patterns should be kept as simple as possible, particularly if open access is provided, so that the uninitiated or infrequent user can easily find the material wanted.

2. If there is more than one main aisle in a stack, finding books becomes more of a problem unless the aisle pattern is easy to perceive.

3. Blind corners or pockets, which result from stairwells and elevators, should be avoided if possible. If for any reason they seem necessary, it is suggested that they be used for purposes other than housing parts of the

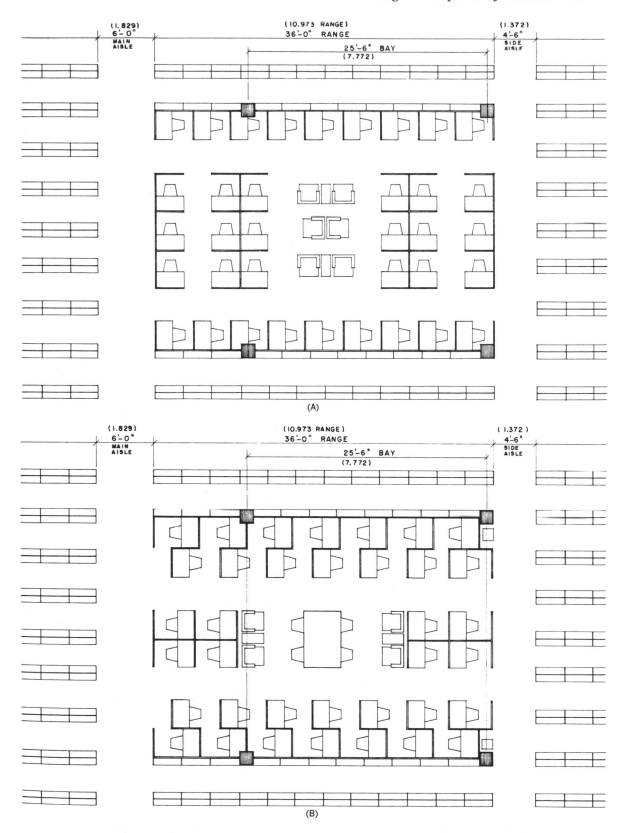

FIGURE 13.21 Large "oases" in bookstacks. These are large enough to provide variety in seating, and special lighting can help to overcome the monotony of a large bookstack. Less than 25 sq ft (2.323 m²) per person is required in these layouts. A special carrel will be required where it is notched around a column. If desired, either oasis shown can be reduced to one full bay in size without causing complications. For a research library this arrangement provides very restricted work space for the individual reader.

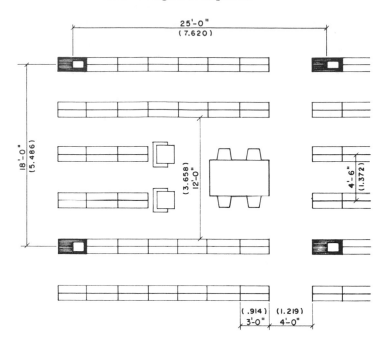

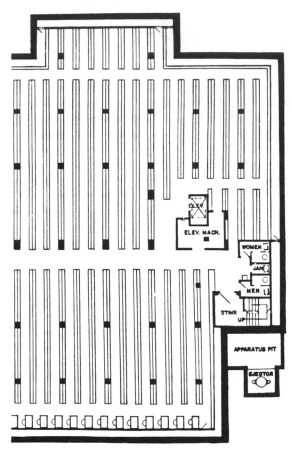

FIGURE 13.22 Small oasis in bookstacks. This tends to disrupt shelving arrangements. If done as suggested here, it may promote undesirable sociability. Such oases may become noisy unless occupied completely by individual seating with readers well protected from one another.

FIGURE 13.23 Blind corners and pockets in bookstack. The shelving above the long secondary cross circle at top and that to the right of the elevator can represent pockets unsuitable for the main collection, which should be arranged in a simple and logical sequence. These pockets are often unavoidable.

main collection, where there should be a simple and logical sequence of classes. (See fig. 13.23.)

4. Review the flow of the book classification sequence to eliminate complexities. Ideally, there will be no leaps from one part of a floor to another in following the classification flow. Simplicity in layout is desirable.

5. As in reading areas, every aisle should be useful to the space on both sides of it. This can sometimes be accomplished by placing carrels, studies, small conference rooms, or other rooms, such as seminars, on one side of an aisle, with book ranges on the other. (See fig. 12.20.) Book ranges can run to a wall with no cross aisle beyond it, or to a carrel at the wall end in place of the last section or sections of stacks, as shown in Figure 13.6(B). It should be repeated that a blind aisle between stack ranges should not be more than one-half the length agreed upon as the maximum suitable for a range with aisles at each end and, where the building code applies, no longer than the length of a dead-end corridor.

6. A bookstack arrangement which is a simple rectangle with no more than one center

and two side aisles is desirable, other things being equal, but it is not always practicable, particularly in a very large stack area. If more aisles are required, be sure to keep the traffic pattern as simple as possible. (See fig. 12.23.)

7. All stacks should have prominently displayed on each level in at least one place, and preferably in more than one, a chart showing the arrangements of the books on the shelves. The chart should always be oriented so that the reader will see it with the top of the chart in the direction that one faces. Too often this orientation has been neglected, with confusing results.

8. Stairs and elevators should be enclosed, to reduce fire risks. There should be adequate lobby space by any elevator door so that passengers (staff or public, including wheelchair users) and book trucks can get in and out without difficulty, and the same is

even more necessary for the stairs if they have doors that open into stack aisles. This area attracts graffiti, thus the selection of surface treatment is important. Three types of stack stairs are shown with dimensions in Figure 6.17.

The total stack capacity depends primarily on the number of stack sections, single or double-faced, that are installed in the area available. If the problems stemming from column sizes and column spacing are left out of consideration, capacity will be based on: (a) the width and number of main and subsidiary cross aisles, (b) the length of ranges, and (c) range spacing on centers, which in turn must be affected by stack aisle widths and shelf depths. This economy of stack layout was discussed in detail in Chapter 6.

The Catalog and Computer Terminals. Section 8.6 deals with the arrangement for the card catalog from the program point of view. This section will discuss briefly the requirements of the automated catalog and other machine-related equipment and the space requirements of the card catalog.

Computer terminals need not be centrally located as is the case with a manual charging system, a card catalog, or a reference collection in book format. However, a certain amount of skill is required to use any but the most straightforward system. Because of this problem of learning the inquiry process, it may be appropriate to locate a few terminals near a staffed information desk so that user assistance can be readily provided. For bibliographic access, if a main library is planning to have, for example, a dozen public terminals, perhaps four would be placed in juxtaposition to the card catalog and near an information desk; three might be located in the reference department near the main service point; three or four might be spread out in the major stack or reading areas; and one or two might be located in the periodicals reading area. Peer assistance is facilitated by some clustering. This distribution is, of course, a matter for local decision since many factors can bear on the distribution pattern.

At a service point where the online catalog is provided by terminal access, most of the terminals should be on a counter where they can be used by a standing person. The counter should be some 3 in. (76 mm) below normal counter height in order that the keyboard can be at a convenient elbow level for most people. A few terminals should be provided

at tables with seats, for those who prefer not to stand or need to do extensive searching, and in this case the table service should be at 25 in. (635 mm). At least one of these positions should be at a height where 27 in. (686 mm) arms of a wheelchair can fit easily under the table. The proportion of terminals at stand-up and sitting positions is also a matter for local consideration. Depending upon the nature of the database and extent of access to the system and the need to limit the amount of time or complexity of searches that can be entered, a library may wish to encourage brief use in order to minimize queuing and to keep costs down. Brief use is encouraged by terminals for use while standing. It may be desirable to arrange terminal positions so they could be raised or lowered if custom changes and as experience dictates. For example, keyboards mounted flush in the counter could become the preferred style, served by a higher counter.

While there is no exact formula for the appropriate number of terminals for a given user population, bibliographic access in a small college library might require one terminal for each 200 to 400 students without much queuing. For the central research library serving a very large user population, perhaps the number can be reduced to one per 500 to 1000 students. If most students have personal computers which can access the local area network, fewer public terminals will be needed in the library. The appropriate number for a particular library is influenced by a number of factors:

1. How decentralized is the library system, and how many service points are provided per building? Centralization will require fewer terminals without undue queuing.

2. How extensive are the data files available on the terminal? Use will be more limited if only the last five years of monograph holdings are accessible; use will be more extensive if full retrospective holdings and if journal indexing and abstracting are available.

3. How is user time constrained? If one can log on for a limited number of minutes, or if one has to use a debit card as an allotment of institutional funds, there are incentives to use the terminal wisely and quickly.

4. How easy is the computer system to use? If basic instruction is offline, or if online prompts are clear and simple, the terminal time is reduced.

5. Is an online public catalog linked to a circulation system? The convenience of such

an arrangement will likely increase its use by library clientele.

The best guide is the local experience with online catalogs. As with the provision of such other equipment as microtext readers, tape players, or calculators, the number provided can be equal to or a bit short of the anticipated demand, depending on available funds and educational goals. The demand may well grow rapidly and then level off. Only time, enrollment, data accessibility, and financial aspects will shape the actual future. Until use levels become more fully known, it is probably best to provide for the electrical capacity and space, and then build up terminal numbers as observation of use suggests and funds permit.

The numbers and distribution of terminals designed to support a videodisc system or other systems providing complete text may be somewhat different. A system intended to supplement the reference collection, for example, would likely require that most of the terminals should be in the reference area at the start. As the system grows in use and in capacity, it may, for example, in time replace the bulk of the reference collection in book format. When this occurs, it could make sense to distribute most of the terminals in appropriate subject reading areas of the library, though the cost and vulnerability to damage or misuse of the machines, difficulty of system use, and need for servicing might argue for centralization at first. As the proportion of reference work shifts from the book to the terminal, the number of terminals should increase, depending on factors similar to the above five for online terminals. For example, when it is anticipated that 50 percent of reference information will be accessed by a terminal, and the program provides for 30 seats in the reference area and a peak of ten users at one time, then it is likely that five reference terminals would be about the right number.

It is obvious that library staff use reference books as heavily as do other library users. Thus videotext terminals will need to be at the reference desk as well as terminals for accessing library catalogs and indexing-abstracting services. Desk or counter configuration may today need to accommodate two terminals as a minimum. Printers for hard copy will be attached, or integral to the CRT (cathode ray tube) and keyboard set, or wired to a nearby location. There may be a patron CRT monitor so there can be staff discussion with the patron about the search strategy that

staff is pursuing. Such an arrangement so that both parties can watch the search is preferable to a "lazy Susan" turntable for the CRT, since wire twisting can result if the turntable can turn through the full circle. Simultaneous viewing of one CRT is possible if the screen is placed at the end of a counter so the patron can watch over the shoulder of the searcher.

Even though the above argues for a somewhat larger service desk or counter than historically has been the case, one should remember that a staff member can do only so much at the desk and the library can afford only a limited staff. Thus, the planner should accommodate access terminals in the service configuration but must not let the image of future technological use lead to an excessive provision of equipment space.

Similar judgment may be applied to the use of terminals for access to journals, government documents, manuscripts, and other areas of the collection as this technology develops. However, economy may develop in time from the potential capacity of a single terminal to serve several functions and, perhaps, because access to the desired material may be quicker through simplified search strategies. Experience in this area is still very limited.

Terminals that are used in association with printed texts or taking notes will require a work surface that is somewhat larger than a standard carrel. While the work process will vary, a work surface of 30 by 60 in. (762 mm × 1524 mm) is not excessive for many installations. It also would be desirable to provide a degree of privacy for at least a few of these machines in order that there would be no embarrassment for those users who are inept, as they are learning to use the system or fumbling with a type of search they have not become familiar with. Furthermore, it would reduce embarrassment if individuals search a subject such as "birth control" about which they might feel some unease.

There should be space on one or both sides of the terminal so that the user can place books, papers, notebooks, purse, etc., and in order that the library could mount a briefing flip-chart or post simple instructions for entry into the catalog search process. There should be space for a printer if that facility is to be provided and is not part of the CRT display instrument itself. For each of these terminals a telephone line and two heavy-duty electrical outlets may be required; four are recommended as a minimum so that one might be available for test equipment. In most cases, some degree of wire management is also useful. The IBM guide listed in the Bibliography (section 3c) is useful on wiring arrangements.

Staff access terminals should not be forgotten for collection development, processing, and other functions. Where staff or patrons are expected to sit at a terminal for many hours, there should be special concern for comfort. Unlike reading a book, using a terminal often requires a relatively fixed posture over long periods of time which, in turn, suggests that superior seating and other features should be considered. Until the day when each staff member has a terminal, the height of the chair for a shared work station must be adjustable, and the work surface should perhaps initially be placed somewhat lower than the standard typing height of 27 in. (685 mm). A height of 24 to 25 in. (610 mm to 635 mm) has been suggested. The problems of glare have already been mentioned. Some staff will benefit from a footrest, and the back as well as the seat of a chair for a shared work station should be easily adjustable.

Terminals and most printers still make noise, though much less than a decade ago. Where there is a concern about noise, printers should be isolated acoustically or provided with plastic covers to muffle the sound. The best acoustic isolation includes providing partitions that fully enclose the space, running from the floor to the underside of the floor above. The treatment of ductwork may require attention, and the door may require insulation. The development of laser and ink jet printers should eliminate the problem for printers, although the clicking of most keyboards and the sound aspects of working at a terminal will remain as problems.

Screen reflective glare can be a problem, as it is with television sets and microform readers. If the screen is nearly vertical, the source of glare for the terminal will be quite different than it is for books. The image of a bright window behind the reader will be reflected in the screen, thereby making its use unpleasant if not impossible. The dimming of lights is generally not required for computer terminals, although an exception might be in an area of excessive illumination. Bright-light sources that fall within peripheral vision will be a problem even more than they are for reading a book. Because of the

angle of the screen, the terminal user can be very sensitive to this kind of problem. Terminals with adjustable screens ameliorate this problem.

Computer rooms go beyond the scope of this volume, except to note that, should one be part of the library program, expert advice must be obtained. Concerns about security, access, power, fire protection, mechanical systems, radio frequency disturbance, floor loadings, and the like should be addressed. This facility is not usually part of the library, though one might argue that information management is common to both the library and the computer facility and, therefore, they should be combined. As libraries become more automated and as more of civilization's record is stored in computers, this argument would seem to make some sense. However, to date, the activities of the computer center and the library are significantly different; and the linkage between the two functions can easily be made electronically. This relationship is clearly a matter for local determination, with its effect on the library building then to be studied.

As is the case with the computer terminal, one of the key aspects to consider with the card catalog is the nature of its use, a use which will diminish as online, microfiche, or other forms are increasingly adopted. The use of the card catalog will depend not only on the size of the student body and the faculty, but also on the ease with which the library's clientele can use the books directly from the shelves, avoiding to some extent the use of the catalog. In an open-access undergraduate library, where the number of students is large and the collection is limited, the catalog is used comparatively little. On the other hand, if stack access is forbidden or severely limited, the use of the catalog will be greatly increased. If use of the catalog is to be very heavy in relation to its size, the problem is to prevent the readers from getting in each other's way, and it may be well to spread the trays out in a ribbon arrangement with cases housing only a few trays in a vertical row and taking a great deal more floor space than would otherwise be required.

A discussion of catalog cabinet height, width, and depth is contained in Chapter 8. This section will discuss certain other details of the catalog cabinet and its arrangement.

How should the cases be arranged? If they are not backed up against a wall, which tends

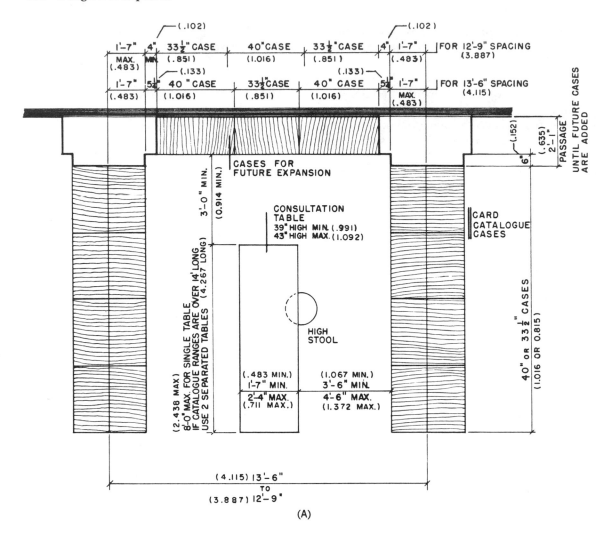

(A)

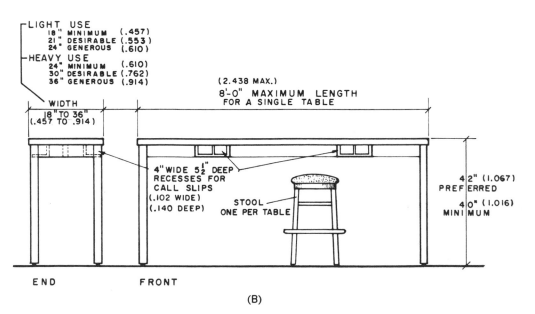

(B)

FIGURE 13.24 Consultation table adjacent to catalog cases. (A) If the table is placed between parallel rows of cases with aisles of suitable width, it will prevent obstruction and not require the trays to be carried uncomfortably long distances. (B) An end and front elevation of a consultation table, indicating possible widths and heights and accessories.

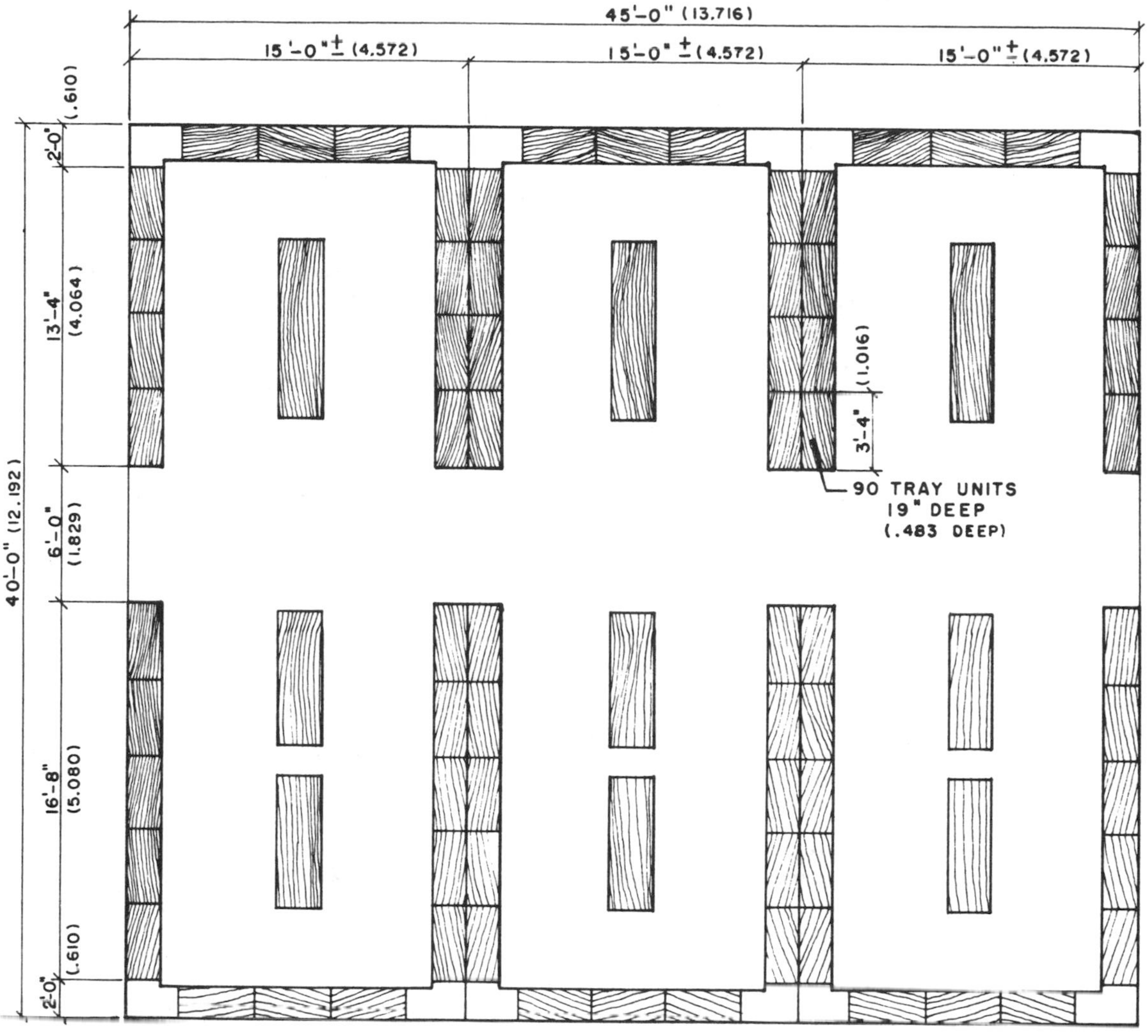

FIGURE 13.25 Catalog arrangement proposed for very large library with limited space available. This shows what can be done by placing cases on the third side of each bay and using units 15 trays high and 19 in. (0.483) deep, thereby housing 4000 cards to each square foot (43,000 per m²).

to limit flexibility, they are generally placed in double-faced rows parallel to each other, at suitable distances apart, so spaced that it is possible to go around either end of each row to reach the next one. (Provision of a consultation table, as noted in Chapter 8, can encourage users to move away from the cabinet while searching through a single drawer. Such a move will in turn ease access to the catalog drawers.) As catalogs become larger, it may be desirable and perhaps necessary to fill in one of the ends, making an alcove closed on three sides. (See fig. 13.24.) This may add to the capacity of the area by as much as 50 percent, but it must be remembered that, if corners are tight together, there is danger of bruised knuckles when a tray from the row next to the corner is pulled out. A 4 to 6 in.

(102 mm to 152 mm) break, preferably covered with a filler, is desirable on each side of the corner. A double row of alcoves with a corridor in between, perhaps 6 ft (1.829) wide, as shown in Figure 13.25, may give the largest possible capacity in a given area.

The Princeton University Library arrangement, shown in Figure 13.26 is another possibility, but it requires a reader either to carry the drawer a considerable distance or to use it at the catalog to the inconvenience of others and with possible damage to the cards if there are no sliding shelves.

Suggested layouts for four libraries, each representing a different situation as far as size and use are concerned, are shown in Figures 13.25 through 13.29. See also Figure 13.5 for accommodation of an automated catalog.

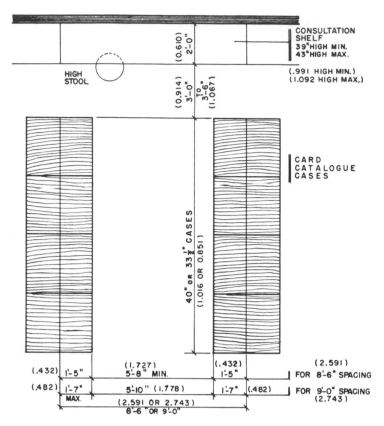

FIGURE 13.26 Consultation table along a wall at right angles to catalog cases. With this arrangement, cases can be placed closer together but trays must be carried considerably farther, and there will be a tendency to try to consult cards without removing trays. Congestion and damage to cards may result.

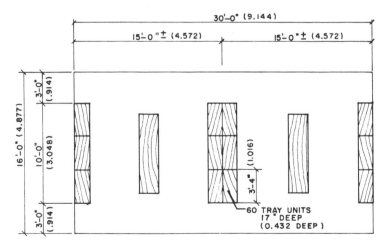

FIGURE 13.27 Catalog for a small library, with 3 ft (0.914) aisles at the end of each row of standard cases 6 trays wide and 10 high. This scheme houses 1500 cards in a square foot (16,000 m²) and is adequate spacing for a library with 300 seats.

The next problem deals with the use of reference "bread boards," or sliding shelves, which are often inserted halfway up in the case so that the reader standing at the catalog can conveniently use the trays from above or below without moving to an adjacent consultation table. Obstruction by users is a great inconvenience with a busy catalog (see fig. 13.30), and it is suggested that, in general, sliding shelves should not be installed in an academic installation. You may be sure that, if they are, they will be used. If no sliding shelf is provided, consultation tables should be installed close by. A discussion of consultation tables may be found in Chapter 8.

The final aspect to be considered is the actual construction of the catalog cabinets. At one time library designers in the United States were attracted to cases manufactured in Europe because of their superior appearance. However, this selection may lead to problems. For example, the United Nations Library in New York installed cases built in Sweden which would have been a success but for the fact that the clear height of the space in each tray, while high enough for 3 × 5 in. (76 mm × 127 mm) cards, was not high enough for standard guide cards, and these were bent over and soon broken. The librarian should also be careful about selecting a cabinet based on appearance alone. The construction of a good-looking cabinet can be just as good or, as in a few cases, it can be inferior. One newly designed cabinet had slanted drawer fronts, making it possible to withdraw them and return them to their places without the use of the customary handles, and this provided space for larger label holders, which are always welcome. But the slanted front was larger than necessary, and each tray required over 5 in. (127 mm), instead of a 4 to 4½ in. (102 mm to 115 mm) of vertical height, so that a 10-tray high case was higher than a 12-tray standard one. These design problems can be corrected.

With card catalogs problems can come from content labels that are too small and handles that are skimpy. The larger the label that can be used, the easier it will be to make it legible. Label holders that provide space for a tray number help to keep the trays from being misplaced, and sometimes special symbols or colors are used for the same purpose. The best type of handle is the almost closed ring-type into which a finger can be inserted, making it more difficult to drop a tray. Libraries

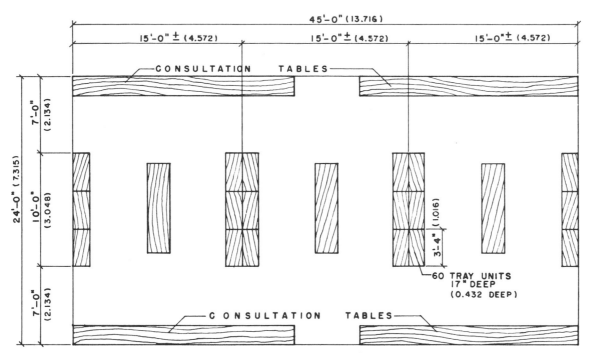

FIGURE 13.28 Catalog room for a small university library with 1000 seats. A larger proportion of the area is required for consultation tables and only 1000 cards per sq ft (11,000 per m²) of floor space is provided.

are advised to consider all the possibilities in connection with catalog tray hardware and to consult with manufacturers about the advantages and disadvantages of different types.

In many parts of the world, steel cases, which cost considerably less than well-made ones of wood, have come into use because of their lower price. They have two serious handicaps. They are noisy, and the gauge of steel used is light enough so that the drawers tend to become bent and difficult to use if wear and tear is heavy. It is only fair to add, however, that a very large number of substandard cases of wood, which stick in damp weather and pull apart at the poorly fabricated joints, have been acquired in this and other countries. Cases should not be bought from an inexperienced or unreliable manufacturer just because they are cheaper.

If cases with new designs are considered, it is suggested that specifications be used that will avoid the problems mentioned above. The construction of catalog cases is probably the most difficult cabinet work that can be found in a library. The wood used must be kiln-dried to prevent later disastrous shrinking and warping, and the joints must be carefully fitted. The trays receive severe strain as they are used. Only the best-quality materials are satisfactory. Samples of trays and hard-

ware should be required for approval with the understanding that they will be loaded with cards and perhaps "accidently" dropped. The mechanism of the rods and follower blocks should be tried; they don't always work well, and some are noisy. The design of the handle and label holder should be considered along with the ease of replacement, refinishing, or repair of potentially damaged parts. *Library Technology Reports* on catalog cabinets should be reviewed, and the experience of other libraries should be considered in making a final decision. As this is expensive equipment that will no doubt be in use for many years, it should be the best reasonable product that the library can afford, assuming that there will continue to be a card catalog or card shelflist which, of course, will not always be the situation.

Other interior design issues will be discussed in Chapter 14.

13.5 The Review Process

Although a series of formal steps can be followed in reviewing schematic designs and design development plans, the most creative work is usually done through solitary efforts at innovation or in the discussions and exchange of ideas when members of the plan-

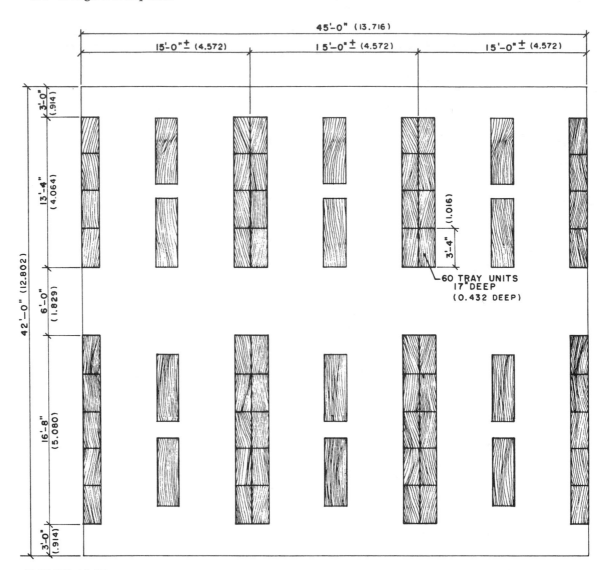

FIGURE 13.29 Catalog room for a typical large university library. Provision is made for 1500 cards per sq ft (16,000 per m²) of floor area with adequate space at tables for readers consulting them.

ning team interact with each other. It is in response to those questions and probing challenges, which sometimes back the architect or librarian figuratively to the wall, that a previously held concept is dropped, a new thought emerges, a variation is proposed, and an improvement in the design solution begins to take shape.

Some of these sessions can be difficult and some topics may be discussed for weeks or months. As an example, the Newberry Library in Chicago worked with a superior architect and had good internal planning specialists and good help from consultants. There were three major areas of contention between the architects and the client with respect to the ten-story bookstack facility which

was occupied in early 1982. The architect wanted to have windows at least in the four corners of this bookstack building, and it was after considerable debate that the library succeeded in eliminating all windows for reasons of security to the collections. A second point was the question of structural floors. The architect wished to have a poured floor for every second level and to have tiered stacks for the two levels resting on each structural floor. Here again, the discussion of functional advantages and costs was finally resolved to the satisfaction of the library staff when they were able to prove that the cost of the alternative designs was a toss-up and that there was improved flexibility and protection against fire and water if each floor was a poured structure. A third issue was the location of the addition on the site. This was a hotly debated matter, with the architect wanting it to be centered at the rear of the original building, itself a very symmetrical structure. The library administration was able after months of debate to locate the addition at the extreme west end of the site on the basis that it leaves far better space on the block for a still later addition, more useful space for delivery and parking in the interim, a more economical construction whenever another addition is built, and an appearance of the addition on the site that many regarded was equal to if not superior to the plan that had it centered on the back of the original building.

From the preceding example, it can be seen that for the librarian who has been directly involved in the design effort, the review process at the end of the design development phase should be fairly straightforward, assuming the major arguments have earlier been settled. The program requirements for specific space allocations and arrangements should have been essentially completed during the schematic review. Except where there have been major changes, which of course can happen, this type of review should not be necessary. Even so, the outline specifications often will contain a space analysis which may warrant review.

The library representative should also be fairly current with the development of the plans in detail. Because of this closeness to the project, it may be useful to involve fresh personnel in the review process. The design development phase will be the last time that it will be fairly easy to involve a larger representation of the staff and others in a fairly thorough review, as the construction documents are fairly difficult for the novice to read and understand, and their bulk generally limits easy distribution.

The design development review process may be similar to the schematic review process except that by this stage, major changes of space configuration cannot generally be tolerated. The reviewer must understand that the aspects warranting careful attention are those aspects of greater detail including perhaps the following:

Is adequate access provided for those who are physically handicapped?

Are the doors wide enough to move in major equipment? May extreme narrowness and

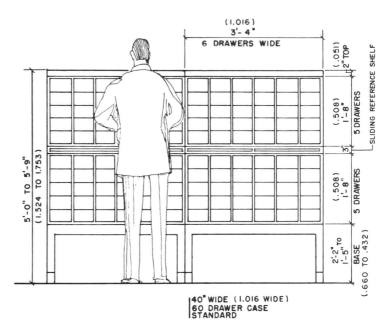

FIGURE 13.30 Catalog cases with sliding reference shelves. These are not recommended in a busy academic library because the user obstructs the use of many trays by others. Consultation tables should almost always be substituted; and if use is moderate, the table might be located in between these two cases.

height of entrance doors cause warping and other maintenance problems?

Is the arrangement of the collections workable?

Are the spaces dimensioned adequately to permit reasonable furniture and equipment layouts?

Has reasonable flexibility been provided?

Is the anticipated degree of security sufficient?

Is the system of artificial lighting suitable, and will sun control be adequate?

Are you comfortable with the mechanical systems? Is there reason to include a service tunnel instead of placing lines in the soil?

In those areas where maintenance and durability of products or surfaces can be identified, are they adequate?

Have the operational requirements been provided for? annunciator panels? book returns? public address systems? acoustic control? requirements of automation?

Are there sufficient janitorial facilities? public telephones? lockers? photocopying locations?

Is the proposed use of built-in equipment (as opposed to freestanding furniture) appropriate? Will a great amount of custom furniture be required? Is this a problem?

Are the doors properly located? Can shelving be installed conveniently on the adjacent wall?

Are any full-scale mock-ups needed to test an interior space, or is a small-scale model needed for exterior review?

Clearly, this list could be vastly expanded. Other similar questions may be found at the end of Chapter 12 dealing with the schematic review.

There are three techniques that may be used in the schematic review process:

1. A general display and widely distributed description of the project
2. Presentations of the project to appropriate groups
3. Detailed review by individuals and small groups.

For the design development phase, the latter two techniques are most appropriate, as the documents will have become more detailed and are less suitable for general display, except perhaps the floor plans. Donors, trustees, friends of the library, and others will be less interested in a detailed review at this phase except to be advised of any significant changes that may have occurred since the schematics. However, the people concerned with energy, maintenance, access, safety, and the like will take a greater interest as the building systems are designed in greater detail. Of course, the librarian should undertake a thorough review.

Where there are special technical consultants, including perhaps experts in energy, lighting, security, cost control, or other areas, it is during the design development stage that their advice may be crucial. While later reviews can also be beneficial as the more detailed design and specifications evolve, the direction will be set by the end of design development, and the testing of this direction at a later stage by the use of consultants will serve little beneficial purpose. Clearly, the special consultants must be part of the design development review process.

Part of the review process will include a testing of the budget. This aspect was discussed in Chapter 9 and Section 13.3 above. Should there be budget problems, this is the time to identify possible reductions or, even more appropriate at this phase, possibly add or deduct alternatives. In sorting out the budget, the project manager should remember to keep in mind the architect's fee which may change with alternatives or other aspects which add to the design effort.

The last aspect of the review will be the sign-off, which may involve a considerable number of people on a large project. Technically, the next design phase should not be started until the sign-off is complete; but when there is concern about the schedule and there is a high degree of confidence in the design, it may be appropriate to have the architect continue to work on the project even though there is some risk. On a large project the review process can take up to a month to complete, and with inflation the loss of a month can result in a substantial expense. However, when there are serious budget problems or other difficult issues requiring resolution, it is not appropriate to continue work until the sign-off is complete.

14

Construction Documents

14.1 The Scope of Construction Documents

Chapter 13 stated that the design development phase was that portion of the design effort dedicated to the refinement and development of the schematic plans. The end of design development establishes the final scope and appearance of the project, including relationships and sizes of the spaces, dimensions, architectural materials, and finishes. The construction document phase, sometimes called the working drawings, or contract documents, phase, will involve the exhaustive development of plans, elevations, sections, details, schedules, and specifications that will give sufficient description to the project so that a contractor can proceed to construction. It should be realized that the design process is not yet complete even at the end of the construction documents phase; there will be field orders, change orders, and clarifications, during the course of construction, as discussed in the next chapter.

The architect's scope is spelled out in the contract for design services. The work will include project administration and the coordination between the architectural work and the efforts of the other professions including the structural, mechanical, and electrical engineers, the landscape architect, and the interior designer. The architect's scope of work should also include the representation of the owner in presentations that may be required by various governmental agencies. The preparation of an environmental impact report, the application for a variance, or simply the process of plan approval by the code authorities or architectural review boards are part of the process of dealing with agencies.

The architect may be required to assist the owner in the preparation of bid documents, special conditions to be made part of the specifications, research on special materials or techniques, and the compilation of a project manual. Presentations of the project to the various interest groups also may involve the architect. The owner will be responsible for continued assistance in establishing design criteria and providing data, as necessary, in the review process, including the reporting of comments resulting from the various reviews.

Finally, the architect will be responsible for the preparation of the documents, including those of the associated consultants. These will include, typically at the 90 percent complete stage, an analysis of the anticipated construction cost, including the identification of factors leading to change in this budget estimate from earlier estimates.

The product of this work, which is by far the largest single segment of the architect's effort, will consist of sheets of drawings divided by their content (plans, sections, elevations, details, structural plans, etc.) and a book containing the written specifications. To the uninitiated these are often difficult to read and understand, since the drawings are diagrams drawn to scale, the writing is technical, and both are replete with conventions and abbreviations—a language understood by both architect and contractor but hard for the layperson to translate. Only a brief explanation of these documents can be attempted here in the hope of doing little more than acquaint the reader with their appearance and purpose. No library planning team should be considered complete if it does not include at least one member representing the institution who has had previous experience with and understanding of contract documents.

A more detailed discussion of the contract and legal documents themselves will be found in Chapter 15.

14.2 The Development of Working Drawing Details

As has been pointed out elsewhere in this volume, the clarity of the plans and specifications may have a considerable effect on bids. If the bidders cannot be absolutely sure of just what is expected of them, they may quite properly add a contingency figure to their estimates in preparing bids or make their own interpretation of the details, which is generally inadvisable. This lack of precision results in extras, and the final budget cost may be 5 percent or more higher than it would have been with better prepared working drawings and specifications.

Although the construction documents or working drawings tend to be very technical in nature, there are issues that may arise during this phase that must include the library representative in the process of resolution. Many of the problems dealt with in this section are even more technical than those considered in the preceding ones, and they will be discussed in even more superficial fashion. For these more technical issues the authors will attempt only to list the problems, define a few terms with which the librarian should be acquainted, and state some of the requirements that the building should meet to be functionally satisfactory. Lighting and ventilating have been discussed in Chapter 13 and elsewhere.

It is emphasized that most of the issues dealt with in this chapter should have been resolved well before review of the final, or even some of the preliminary, plans and documents. The essential nature of nearly all of these matters should be fixed before this phase. Yet the final review and refinements must come now if they are ever to be done. Change orders should be used only as a means of correcting matters which could not be known before the job was let.

Construction problems that must be given a final decision during the preparation of working drawings include: building materials of all kinds; details of windows of all kinds; exterior and interior walls and doors; plumbing, including rest room details; hardware; floor and ceiling coverings; design of built-ins; specifics of telephone, computer telecommunication, and power outlet locations; and lighting controls.

The librarian must leave the very technical problems to the specialists, although there should be a general understanding of the problems and the solutions which are selected. A competent architect will understand the problems, although the expert advice of the consulting engineers may be required for resolving various details.

1. Hardware. The selection of the hardware to be used in a library is important enough to require the attention of both the librarian and the building maintenance department, as well as that of the architect. The better the quality, the lower the maintenance and replacement needs in the future. The importance of quality in hardware cannot be overstressed. Too many recent library buildings have exterior doors which bang, scrape the floor, or do not close properly.

Door hardware that contains moving parts, such as a latch, if it is installed where it will be continuously turned and operated by the general public, will require considerable upkeep no matter how good the quality. Thus it is advisable to have most, if not all, of the heavily used doors operate on the "push-and-pull" principle and confine the use of latches and similar hardware to the staff areas of the library.

Push-and-pull doors require mechanical closing devices. These may be installed at the top of the door, incorporated in the hinges of the door itself, or recessed in the floor. (See fig. 14.1.) The third method results in the best appearance but needs considerable maintenance and is more expensive than either of the other two. The self-closing device located at the top of the door has generally proved to be the most satisfactory method from the overall point of view. In addition, modern hardware designers have considerably improved its appearance and, with only a small sacrifice in durability and some increase in cost, have produced devices that may be concealed either within the door or in the frame above. In this use of self-closing devices, care must be taken to avoid designing a gate or door that is too heavy for the closing device to handle, particularly where the gate swings both ways. In a double swinging configuration, the closing device must also center the gate, and if the mass of the gate is too great, it will typically stand ajar.

Self-closing doors are usually required for public safety at the entrances to stairs and other fire-protected shafts and spaces. They are necessary, in any case, on outside and vestibule entries if the air pressure, temperature, or humidity conditions within the library are to be maintained at levels different from those outside. (See fig. 14.1 (C and D).)

Sometimes, because of pressure difference, if outside doors are large and heavy, they become difficult to open; then automatic open-

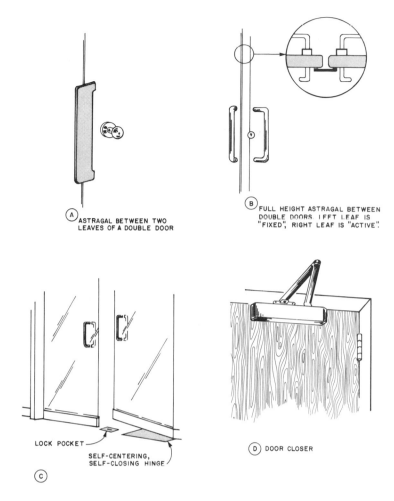

FIGURE 14.1 Door hardware.

ing devices by means of "magic carpets" or "electric eyes" are useful, but they are expensive to install and require continuous maintenance. "Assist" hardware is also available to provide much of the effort for opening the door once a person has pushed against the device, and the cost of maintenance is less than automatic opening devices. There is also a mechanical device already referred to, called the Ellison hinge, which decreases the area of the door that one pulls open without decreasing the usable width of the opening. It is considerably more expensive than the normal hardware. Its action is peculiar and feels strange to the user until one becomes accustomed to it. Although helpful on wide doors, it definitely seems to interfere with comfortable passage through a narrow door and may be dangerous when used by children.

Double doors should be avoided or at least seriously questioned, especially if they need to be locked. It is usually better to install two single doors side by side, rather than a double door, because there will be a slight gap between double doors. This gap leaks the controlled filtered air from inside, which can be an energy waste. It may create a draft, a discomfort for staff stationed nearby. It could permit rain or snow to get in under severe conditions. Furthermore, it destroys afterhour security if persons can insert a wire hook between the doors and pull down on an exit panic bar. An astragal (fig. 14.1 (A and B)) covers that gap but has its own problems, the most difficult being the coordination of the doors so that they always fully close after use. Various hardware designs are intended to solve this problem, but they often are less than satisfactory. Use of an astragal also tends to be noisy, and if it bangs, the door probably will be standing ajar.

If turning knobs and latches are used, it is wise, from a maintenance point of view, to have the hardware devices incorporated into a large escutcheon plate rather than individually mounted in or on the door. This placement strengthens the entire assembly and enables it to take more abuse from the users. Where handicapped access is a concern, knobs should be avoided. In their place lever-actuated latches may be used.

Locks are most important hardware items, and most large institutions have standardized the locking system they use in all their buildings. This standardization frequently restricts the choice of hardware and limits the price advantage of competitive bidding for the supply. This need no longer be so, because of the invention of removable "keyway" devices which enable any type of keying to be inserted easily into any lock. In the end, the decision on this matter of locks should be determined by the policy of the institution rather than by the librarian, the architect, or the planning team.

The method of keying, on the other hand, is in the province of the librarian who should determine which areas are to be locked and who should have keys for them. From this determination a system of master and submaster keys will be developed to suit the needs of the library. (See fig. 14.2.) A locksmith can, without too much difficulty, change the keying of any particular lock after it has been installed. This change is made even more rapidly and easily if the removable key-way device referred to above is installed. However, changing the keying after the fact is not without cost. In a large library there can be several hundred locks which should be keyed properly when they are installed. To avoid distribution of keys to the contractor, a special construction insert can be provided which will allow the use of a construction master key. Once the building is ready for activation, it is a simple matter to remove the insert, which voids the construction master key and activates the building keying system.

The locking of exit doors is usually a special problem, as public safety requires that in any emergency these doors should be capable of being opened from the inside without the use of a key. This requirement introduces two difficulties.

First, if the exit door is in an unsupervised area, it may be used by a reader to leave the library without passing a control point. This defect can be largely overcome by installing on the door a mechanical or electric alarm, which goes off if the door is opened, and perhaps also by requiring glass or other breakable material to be broken to open the door. In many cases it will be necessary to annunciate the door alarm remotely to ensure that the lock is reactivated.

Second, if the operation of the exit door is push-and-pull and it is to be locked from outside use, some method of releasing the lock from the inside must be installed. The device usually employed is a panic bar or handle, which releases the locking mechanism when pushed. However, the public safety laws frequently allow the use of small knob turns on the locking device if no considerable number of people will be in the building when it is locked.

2. Floors and Floor Coverings. The base for library floors may be of concrete, terrazzo, marble, ceramic tile, brick or wood; glass has sometimes been used in bookstacks, although it is not recommended, and steel decking is common in tiered stacks. Concrete is often left uncovered in little-used basements or even in bookstack areas, but it should be sealed to prevent dust from becoming troublesome. Terrazzo is often used in entrance lobbies and toilet rooms, but it may be slippery and dangerous when wet. Marble floors are expensive, and any but very hard marble, particularly if used on stairs and in heavily traveled areas, will wear down; marble stairs may eventually become dangerous.

Ceramic tile is long-wearing and can be considered in heavily used corridors where noise is not a problem. Brick pavers can be used in place of tile. They are less likely to be slippery when wet, and they wear well.

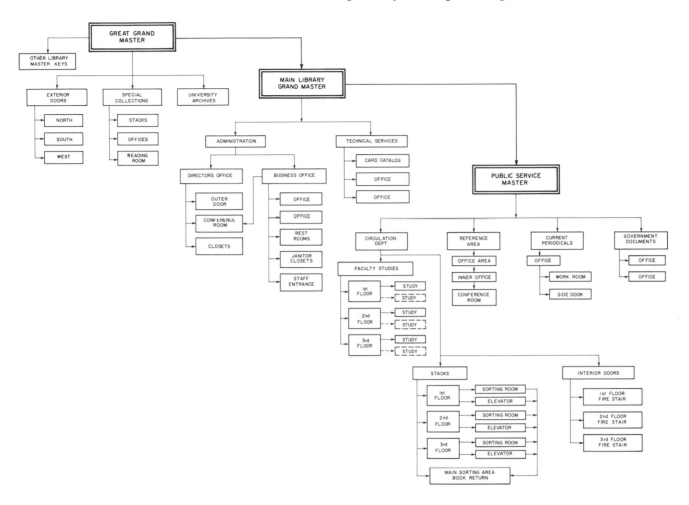

FIGURE 14.2 Key tree. In preparing a key tree, the assignment of space and the means of access must be fully understood. In this example some spaces, such as the studies and reference area conference room, are at the seventh level in the key hierarchy, which implies reduced security. Those areas that require greater security, such as the university archives and special collections, are at a much higher level. In this diagram each rectangle represents a unique key which will also open any door described by a subsequent rectangle. Each subsequent rectangle in the tree (following the lines and arrows) is a lower level in the key system structure.

The janitorial staff will claim that they are difficult to keep clean, and if book truck traffic is required, it will be especially noisy, due to the joints in the brick pattern. Wooden floors, particularly of hard wood, can be handsome and long-wearing, but they require considerable care to keep them in good condition. They have the advantage of permitting refinishing. Soft wood floors do not wear so long but can be suitable in certain areas. Glass floors, used in bookstack areas originally with the idea of letting light through from the floor below to light the bottom shelves, are little used now. They tend to produce static electricity in cold, dry winter weather, and in time they lose strength and can be broken by a sharp blow, with disastrous results. Steel decks in a tiered stack with limited use may simply

be painted. Where noise is a concern, the deck should be carpeted. Heavy traffic will require at least a layer of resilient flooring to protect the steel.

Most concrete library floors today, except those mentioned above, have a covering of one kind or another. These coverings are often tiles, generally 9 or 12 in. square, or even 12 by 24 in. (Metric dimensions are similar.) They may come in different patterns. Many of them are available in sheet form. These tiles include rubber, linoleum, cork, asphalt, and vinyls of various kinds, and carpet, which is discussed later. Each has its advantages and disadvantages. Cork, for instance, has high sound absorption and resilience, qualities which make it suitable for libraries, but it is difficult to maintain. The wear and the maintenance costs can be reduced by coating the tiles with a penetrating sealer and wax or some other recommended coating, such as varnish or lacquer. However, where there is heavy traffic, the protective sealer will soon wear, and the cork will deteriorate. Cork should not be used for on- or below-grade concrete floors which have not been adequately waterproofed. It is particularly important to have it laid on a dry, level, rigid, and clean subfloor. The quality of cork available in the American market has fallen off in recent years. Cork can still be found in some of the older libraries that has not had particularly good care and is in good condition after fifty years, but much of the cork that has been installed since the Second World War has not lasted. Some institutions have found that Spanish cork is more satisfactory and long wearing than the cork tile manufactured in this country.

Rubber floor coverings in general have good resistance to wear and residual indentation, and they are resilient and make a comfortable floor. They are generally not satisfactory on concrete floors in direct contact with the ground, unless the concrete slab has been waterproofed.

Linoleum, either in tile or sheet form, is less expensive than rubber tile. It has been on the market for many years and has had a good record. Its resistance to wear is satisfactory. It should not be installed on floors in direct contact with the ground. Heavy battleship linoleum has in the past made a particularly satisfactory library floor, but it is difficult or impossible today to find a good quality linoleum without importing it. The color selection is limited.

Vinyl floor coverings are the most commonly used material other than carpet. They tend to be less expensive than cork, rubber, and linoleum. Their surface is generally somewhat harder and, as a result, noisier, although the noise can be reduced by the use of a felt base. Vinyl asbestos has some advantages over regular vinyl. Vinyl tile floors do reflect glare as do other forms of tile, and they tend to project an "institutional look," which may or may not be desired.

Asphalt tile is one of the least expensive of floor coverings. It is one of the few types that can be satisfactorily installed on a below-grade concrete floor subjected to appreciable moisture from the ground, but it is not as resistant to wear and indentation as the other floors. In heavily used areas it will not last many years, but it has often been found satisfactory in restricted stack areas. It is considerably noisier than most of the other coverings.

An advantage of the last four types of floor covering, and of carpet tile, is the ability to cover a floor trench system when that is the means of bringing electric and telecommunication cables to work stations. Lift-out floor panels are standard in major computer facilities. They are expensive in other locations, generally costing three times as much as installing the power system in the plenum above the acoustic tile ceiling.

3. Carpets. Within the past thirty years carpets, which had been used in libraries previously only in exclusive areas and perhaps in the librarian's office or the board room, have been installed on a large scale in a constantly growing number of libraries throughout the United States and elsewhere. The areas chosen for carpeting have varied considerably. In some libraries it has been installed in reading rooms only; in others, throughout the building, except perhaps in little-used bookstacks. Some libraries have used it in the entrance lobby, on the basis that it was a first-class shoe cleaner and reduced maintenance requirements throughout the rest of the building; others have left it out of the lobby because it would wear out so quickly there.

The basic problems to be decided in connection with carpet might be said to be six in number:

1. What type and quality of carpeting should be purchased? The generally agreed-upon conclusion is that a carpet of first-class quality is justified because it will wear so much longer. There may be some dispute about which type is the best in this respect. In general a dense, closely packed pile will keep its looks and texture. Tightly twisted yarns can be expected to wear better than loosely twisted ones. A looped pile usually stands up better than a cut pile.

Carpet is available in roll or tile form, the tiles being approximately 20 to 24 in. (0.508 to 0.610) square. Carpet tile has several advantages, the most important of which is that it permits easy access to underfloor electrical or signal ductwork. A recent product which works well with carpet tile is a system of flat wiring which permits considerable flexibility for electrical and signal services without the normal requirement for conduit. A grid of flat wiring can be placed directly on concrete floor, glued or taped in place, and then covered by carpet tiles.

Some manufacturers of carpet tile claim that the tile does not need to be glued down; however, it is recommended that a release adhesive should be used on certain selected rows of tiles to control their movement. The authors feel that while the development of carpet tile is very promising, they do not yet have enough experience with the product to recommend its use enthusiastically. A good quality of carpet tile is somewhat more expensive (about 25 to 30 percent more) than a good grade of normal carpet. At least one carpet tile manufacturer makes a carpet with animal fibers (horse hair?) which, it is claimed, results in a very durable product. If a single tile is damaged, it can be easily replaced. But do not expect the color to match exactly after the passage of time.

Any carpet that becomes heavily soiled will tend to mat and will be difficult to clean. Wool has always made a fine carpet, having natural resiliency and ability to recover from crushing, but good nylons and acrylics do well in this respect also. The way the carpet is made is as important as the type of fiber used. However, nylon with static control is perhaps the most practical commercial grade of carpet.

Durability of colors is also a matter of importance. Expect fading, which may make it difficult to patch or match the carpet at a later time. Some shades, blue for example, tend to fade more rapidly than others. Some have superior qualities in concealing soiling. Light colors quite naturally show soil most, and combinations of color least.

2. How does the original cost of installation compare with that of other possible floor coverings? It does not pay to order any but high-quality carpet, and the cost of any quality carpet is without doubt greater than that of the most expensive cork, rubber, or vinyl tile or sheet covering that might be used as an alternative. A life-cycle cost analysis can be done to guide a decision. The resultant preferred material will vary depending on building area use, aesthetics desired, possible changes in use, maintenance frequency, ability to make patches or small replacements, as well as initial installed cost.

3. How do the wearing qualities compare with other possible coverings? Although the best modern carpet has first-class wearing qualities, the carpet manufacturers do not claim that it will wear as long as the best quality vinyl, rubber, and cork tile.

The Meyer Memorial Library at Stanford which opened in 1966 was provided with a combination of vinyl asbestos flooring and excellent quality wool carpet. Over the years more carpet was added for acoustic control; very little of the vinyl asbestos flooring remains exposed. The added carpet is all nylon, and the color does not quite match. In 1983, the carpet was still serviceable, but it looked tired. On the other hand, the vinyl asbestos tile, even where there is considerable traffic, still looked quite good after more than fifteen years. In both cases the levels of maintenance are less than would be recommended by the manufacturer, which is probably a more serious detriment to carpet than to tile.

4. What about the upkeep? This question of maintenance is a debatable feature. The carpet manufacturers claim that vacuum cleaning at frequent intervals will cost considerably less than the cleaning, buffing, and waxing which is advisable for other coverings, and that this factor will more than make up for the extra cost of the original installation and also for the cost of replacement if it is found that the carpet will not wear as long as another covering that might have been selected. This claim is based on the experience of hotels and to some extent upon schools that have used carpet. The decision on this point may well turn to the question of the level of maintenance that the institution is accustomed to provide for its floor coverings. A first-class hotel vacuum-cleans its carpets every day, but how often do other floor coverings anywhere in a college or university, including the library, receive anything more than a quick sweeping with a brush-broom? How often are floors buffed and waxed, a procedure which is time-consuming and expensive? Many libraries economize on maintenance, and many buff floors infrequently and wax them perhaps once or twice a year if they are the type that need waxing. Check with your maintenance department on this point before making your decision. Be sure you are comparing like with like.

5. Does carpet have other advantages in addition to a possible saving in maintenance cost? Here there can be no question. Carpets have superior acoustical properties, good enough so that costs for other acoustical installations may be reduced. In some places acoustical tile in the ceilings will be unnecessary with carpets on the floor. Sometimes, where there is a special acoustical problem, carpets will save money. In recent years, with low ceilings and intensive space utilization,

libraries have too often presented very unsatisfactory acoustic conditions. Carpets are pleasant to stand on, as well as quiet to walk on. They can also be used on vertical surfaces, such as the walls of an elevator or the front of a service counter, for both acoustical purposes and durability. There is no other floor covering, not even the best quality of rubber tile or cork, which will be as comfortable as a good carpet for a library attendant to stand on for hours at a time.

A less definite but not to be forgotten advantage of carpets is the effect on the behavior of the users of the library. In schools it has been found that children seem almost automatically to behave better with carpets. Rooms are quieter; the whole aspect and atmosphere changes; and all are more likely to conduct themselves as they should. If carpeting becomes the norm instead of occurring in a minority of public places, it will be hard to say how long the improved social behavior in carpeted libraries can be expected to last.

Another aesthetic virtue of carpet over other floor coverings is that it is available in a broad range of colors, textures, and patterns. Even custom colors are reasonable for any large installation, and the pattern of colors can be arranged so that those areas likely to receive the greatest wear can be replaced without need for an exact color match.

6. What about patching or repairing when the covering is damaged? One of the problems with the maintenance of all floors comes from the danger of scorching from cigarettes, from staining through careless use of ink, and so on. The carpet manufacturers insist that while a live cigarette may damage a carpet just as it will other floor coverings, or tabletops for that matter, it is possible to cut out a small section and patch it just as easily or more easily than with tile, and certainly more easily than with sheet material of one kind or another. Gum and ink stains, if gotten at promptly, can be cleaned or patched. The advantage of carpet tile in terms of patching has already been noted.

If you decide to install carpets in your library, you have four decisions to make in selecting them. What color do you want? What texture and pattern? What quality will you choose? How much are you prepared to pay? The first two are treated in Section 14.3 under Color. A few other points should be reviewed:

The padding or underlay on which the carpet is placed should not be neglected. A good base will lengthen the life of the carpet and improve its acoustical qualities, but it will also make travel somewhat more difficult for the handicapped and for book trucks. It is recommended that for most of the library, the carpet should be a direct glue-down installation without a pad. Where a pad is desired, a fairly dense pad with minimal "cush" should be selected. The book truck problem can be reduced by providing larger wheels on the trucks to reduce rolling resistance, but pads under the carpet are still a problem.

Be sure to realize that, if you use carpet in areas with very heavy traffic such as stairs and main traffic arteries, it should be the best quality, to prevent too rapid wear. An alternative is to devise a pattern or system so that carpet in the heavy-wear areas can easily be replaced without disturbing the aesthetics. Carpet seam location should also be checked since this can become a problem if it is right in a heavy traffic lane, wherever people will frequently turn or chairs will be moved.

In earthquake country some engineers recommend against putting carpet under shelving because of the reduced bearing rigidity or soft footing that results. Also, bolts that would normally be stressed in shear under earthquake loading become cantilevers structurally with a carpet spacer between the solid floor and the shelving unit, and cantilever forces may be more difficult to resist than shear forces.

Finally the obvious: do not forget that, in a remodeling project in which carpet is added, the doors will need to be undercut unless there was carpet there before.

4. Durable Surfaces. While carpet can provide an excellent and durable surface, thought should also be given to the durability of other surfaces. Walls in high traffic areas may be constructed with a vinyl surface rather than painted. While vinyl is very durable, it is often more difficult to repair than a painted surface. Elevator lobbies and main corridors may be candidates for vinyl wall coverings. Exposed corners of plaster or gypsum board walls may be protected with angle iron or a sheet metal bumper. See Section 13.2 for a treatment of vandalism and mutilation.

Concrete, while it is very durable, tends to absorb stains, particularly on columns where there is a lot of traffic or at the base where floor cleaning operations tend to add their own patina over time. Baseboards may be considered. Light woods, particularly for such items as a stair rail, will be difficult to keep looking clean. Counter tops should be made of a durable material, such as high-pressure plastic laminate, granite, or marble. Other materials may be equally good, but a wood surface tends to look bad in a fairly short period of time. Wood trim is somewhat less of a problem, but it too will require maintenance from time to time.

Ceilings are not normally thought of as problem areas from the standpoint of durability. However, where a concealed spline acoustic ceiling is specified, it eventually will be damaged due to the problems of access to the hidden space above. An exposed grid for an acoustic ceiling is recommended for suspended ceilings where long-term durability is desired.

The selection of colors is important in terms of the durability of surfaces. Light colors in general show dirt rapidly, but they are better for reflecting light. Dark colors, particularly on horizontal surfaces, tend to show dust. Something between light and dark is probably the best in most cases, but aesthetic concerns may override this logic. In areas of frequent soiling, a glossy finish will facilitate periodic washing. The designer should be sensitive to the maintenance problems in the library.

5. Public Address and White Sound Systems. Although public address systems were discussed in Chapter 5, a few points warrant stressing. Not all libraries will need such a system, and some librarians will be opposed to it, based upon an expectation of being pressured to page individual users, and thus creating a distraction for other readers. This problem can be controlled by library policy, and in a large library, the public address system is very useful in informing the reader of the closing of the library or, in the case of an emergency evacuation or practice drill, giving instructions to readers. The equipment is probably best located near the main circulation desk. The installation should be designed to avoid interference from other sources of electronic "noise," including separation of speaker lines from phone lines. Where conduit is required, separate conduit should be provided for the public address system. Consideration must be given to whether each study room and all faculty studies are to be covered, whether all staff areas should be included, and how it will actually serve in emergencies.

White sound may be desired in some cases, and the speakers of the public address system may serve this function. However, to do so would tend to reduce the flexibility needed to tailor a white sound system to the specific requirements of each space. Because of this, it is likely that the designer of a white sound system will recommend a totally separate system, with which the authors would agree. This approach also serves the important need to disguise the source of the white sound.

The matter of the distribution of the public address system and white sound system may differ as well. The public address system should be heard throughout the stacks and in most enclosed spaces, although it is unlikely that an individual faculty study would have a loudspeaker. Instead, a loudspeaker might be found in the corridor serving a bank of faculty studies. White sound, on the other hand, is intended for the open reading areas. It is not necessary in the general stacks or corridors except as it may be required to avoid its obvious application in the reading area; there should not be an abrupt change in the acoustic environment that draws attention to the white sound system. Of course, this problem becomes more difficult as the volume of the white sound system is increased. Music libraries should not have white sound in listening areas, and selected zones of the system must be easy to turn off in any area, such as an exhibition hall where a public talk and reception may occasionally be held. Noted earlier is the point that the authors feel that many white sound systems are too loud and that, with a reduction in volume, they would still represent an acoustic improvement while being far less obtrusive.

6. Built-ins. The decision about what is to be included as a built-in should have been made long before the working drawing phase is started. During this phase, however, the librarian will have the opportunity to be involved in the detail design, much of which has been discussed in earlier sections.

Components. Does the unit have the appropriate drawers, adjustable shelves, footrest, cabinets, and the like? Drawers obviously might include pencil drawers, box drawers for minor supplies, cash drawers, file drawers, card file drawers, and sliding shelves. Shelves might include some extra deep shelving for a few heavily used atlases at a reference desk, or books on hold or being returned at a circulation desk. Computer terminals, typewriters, and cash registers are likely to be situated on lower work surfaces, and they all may require some handy supplies.

Dimensions. The dimensions have been discussed elsewhere, but this is the time to review them. Counter height ranges from 36 to 41 in. (0.914 to 1.041). The authors prefer a higher counter for most library transactions, although the lower counter will be necessary where ideal conditions are desired for the handicapped. Typing and computer terminal heights should be adjustable or, if fixed, probably somewhat lower than what is normally accepted as standard. The standard typing height is 27 in. (0.686); a height of 25 in. (0.635) will probably be found to be more comfortable for more people. Built-in typing surfaces are not recommended for any typing area other than major service points because of the problems of noise transmission, though this is not a problem with computer terminals. Where there is a coat closet, is provision made for the handicapped? Check the rest rooms, lockers, public phones, and other facilities in this regard. Finally, check that the dimensions of lockers, built-in trash receptacles, book returns, and the like will provide the desired capacity.

Flexibility. The concept of flexibility, once it is decided to have a built-in unit, applies principally to service counters. The unit can be constructed on a module which provides the capacity to remove an individual unit and have it altered or to rearrange the units in a new counter configuration. This kind of flexibility will require unit construction where each part could be structurally freestanding, rather than a construction which shares vertical support from one unit to the next. There will be some increase in cost, but the modest added expense may be acceptable when consideration is given to the problems of future change. The top surface should be modular as well, which can be done with minimal inconvenience from seams in the surface. This, too, will add slightly to the expense, but it is recommended. For example, computer charging machines may be added later, necessitating the lowering of the counter, or machines may be removed and made self-service for the reader, perhaps resulting in the raising of the lower segment. Flexibility also involves wire management. This can easily be designed into the built-in unit in the form of an easily accessible chase running from unit to unit. At some point, access from this wire chase to the building power and signal system will be required. Do not forget to keep power and signal separated, or unwanted "noise" will be evident in the signal lines.

Hardware. In publicly accessible built-in equipment, the key concern about hardware is its vandal resistance. Exposed screws, for example, will be removed over time, and attractive attachments removed. At the service point, drawers, expected to be fairly heavy when loaded, might be provided with track-type glides. The doors on a cabinet can be sliders or swing open. The latter are preferred except where the door will get in the way due to limited space arrangements. Thought should be given to locks not only on the drawers and cabinets but also on major features, such as a roll-down screen at a service point that may be closed during part of the day. Often, this type of lock should be included as part of the building keying system, but it is overlooked because it is not on a door schedule.

Although they generally are not built in, the locks provided (or hasps without locks) at the lockers will need review. Are the lockers located where they must be routinely inspected? Will they be assigned? Are combination (recommended) or key-type locks desired? Can the combinations be changed? Is there need for a master key? The construction of lockers is another point. Are they located where noise will be a problem? (Most steel lockers are noisy.) Should one be able to see into the locker? Should the locker be large enough to house a portable typewriter or briefcase?

Special Details. Are there display panels, devices for holding graphics, or bins for handouts? Is there a niche for charge cards or scratch paper at a built-in consultation counter? Is there to be an annunciation panel designed as part of a service desk? Is there space under the counter or work surface for a trash basket, stool, chair, book truck, or other equipment that should be out of the way except when used? How are the phones dealt with? Is there a special place for the phone or a phone jack? Is there a panic button, and if so, is it located where it will not accidentally be activated? Is the front surface of the counter durable enough or set back sufficiently from the top to avoid damage from belt buckles or purses? Is there a toe space? Is there any part of the design that will catch fingers or clothing?

These, and many other questions should go through the mind of anyone involved in the design and review of built-ins. While the construction drawing phase is the best time to incorporate this type of thinking, there should be one other chance for input, that is during construction when the shop drawings are submitted. The librarian is advised, however, not to count on the shop drawings for this type of review for two reasons. First, because of the fact that time costs money, the review process during construction is always under pressure from the contractor. As a result, it is difficult for the library representative to be involved in the review process. Generally, the librarian will not see the shop drawings at all unless a special effort is made to do so.

The second reason not to put off a detailed review of the built-ins is that any change of scope—such as adding locks, making fixed shelves adjustable, or adding a cable chase—will result in an extra cost from the contractor which will not be competitively bid. Late changes will add to the cost; they should be avoided except where they are obviously necessary. The intent of the shop drawings is really to check the more detailed aspects of construction and materials technique. The design concepts should have already been well established in the construction drawings. Review of the shop drawings is important, however, to ensure that none of the concepts are compromised or lost because of misinterpretation, omission, or conflict of construction technique.

Conclusion. There are many aspects of the construction documents or working drawings phase which will require detailed involvement. Aspects discussed elsewhere in this volume, including lighting controls, clocks, specifications, arrangement of the stacks, graphics, systems of security, and computer terminal locations, will receive careful attention during this phase. The effort, when it is about 90 percent complete, will be tested one final time with a cost estimate, which is discussed in Chapter 9 and elsewhere for the other phases. With careful attention to the financial aspects of the decision and a little luck, there should be no problems. Section 14.4 discusses alternatives, some of which may be necessary where there are budgetary problems.

14.3 Construction Documents for Interiors

Depending upon the nature of the design contract for interior design services, the construction documents phase for interiors may or may not be separate from the architectural design. Where the architect also provides interior design services, much of the interior work, especially built-ins, will probably be designed by the architect's interior design staff. Where there is a separate interior designer contracted by the institution, the construction documents for interior design may not include the built-ins. They may, however, deal with signage (discussed in Chapter 16), carpet (found earlier in this chapter), and furniture. Clearly, the interior designer should also be involved with interior materials, color, and finish decisions, as well as the details of the built-ins, though these aspects will be treated in the architectural rather than the interiors construction documents.

This section will briefly discuss the construction document design process for interiors as well as aspects of color and furnishings. They clearly are and must be closely related to the architectural work.

1. The Process. Furniture, equipment, built-ins, colors, finishes, and other aspects one views while using the library are an intergal part of the library design. If the results are to be satisfactory aesthetically, they must be sympathetic and complementary to the architecture of the building. This does not mean that the same person must be responsible for all aspects of the design. Nor does it mean that in a modern building all of the furniture or other features must be modern as well. It is, for example, possible to design a more traditional rare-book room in a new and modern facility. It is equally possible to translate those positive aspects of more traditional design into a more modern design solution. The direction one takes in the rare-book room or, for that matter, in any part of the interior design, depends a great deal upon the philosophy of the designer and the institution. Any good architect or interior designer, working together or under separate contracts, can bring about the desired results.

Because most users and staff will be more aware of the building interior than any other aspect, the interior design has a strong effect on how the building is perceived. Since much of the interior design must follow the architectural, this design process will usually continue well after the construction phase has started. Movable furniture, of course, does not need to be ordered until perhaps nine months before the activation is anticipated, although a year might be a prudent when there are quantities of custom-designed furniture. Likewise, the carpet does not need to be selected until late in the project. When it is to be installed as part of the general construction contract, only the type of carpet needs to be specified, with the color to be selected later. Or, an "allowance" can be provided for the carpet, which fixes the dollar amount contained in the contract for carpet. An allowance may also be used for major built-in elements when it is desired that the furnishings and built-ins should be closely coordinated and the furniture remains to be specified as the architectural construction documents are completed.

Ideally, the interior design would be completed at the same time as the rest of the design phase, but this is in fact seldom the case. The colors for equipment, paint, vinyl wall coverings, and the like are often specified "color as selected by the architect," and samples are often required before the final decision is made. It seems that, even under the best of circumstances, the interior design process usually will overlap the construction phase.

Nevertheless, there should be much concern if the interior design process is not well along by the mid-point of the architectural construction document phase, if not earlier. This is because so much of the interior design effort will relate to the exact locations of the power outlets, door swings, lighting, signal ducts, and the like. Where carrels will be provided with task lights or computer terminal capability, their arrangement will be greatly affected by the arrangement of the required supporting utilities. Conversely, the exact location of the supporting services should only be established after the precise arrangement for the furniture has been determined. Adjustments in outlet locations can be made after the construction contract is signed, but this is not the ideal way to fine-tune the design. An allowance for outlets can also be provided, yet the decisions about location must be made early in the project, certainly before conduits are poured in concrete. It is best to have much of this work settled before construction starts.

As already stated, much of the interior design will be contained in the documentation prepared as the architectural contract documents. There may well be, however, separate contract documents for furnishings, carpet, and graphics, as each of these elements may be supplied and installed under a separate purchase contract. Of course, when the interior designer is working for the institution rather than the architect, the interior design contract documents will be separate as well. The actual documents will be similar to the architectural documents, in that there will be plans showing furniture, carpet, or other arrangements together with plans, elevations, sections, details, and specifications for the custom furniture. Furniture that is only slightly altered or selected directly from the manufacturer's stock will be treated in a schedule with cross-reference by furniture type and individual building areas or space. This schedule will indicate special features, such as the type of upholstery for a given chair or the configuration of a desk. The drawings will indicate where each item is to be placed. These documents will enable the institution to readily place orders and ultimately locate the furniture during the activation phase of the project.

2. Color. Color is but one of the several elements that the designer must work with. In addition to color, there is texture, scale, rhythm, symmetry, form, and light. It is color, however, that seems to generate the greatest controversy, and it is color that most dramatically is identified as an element one likes or dislikes.

The reaction to color seems to be constantly changing, and different societies have different ideas about color. In the United States the favored color scheme seems to change every decade or so. This is certainly evident in clothing, and it is apparent in our facilities, as well. At the turn of the century, a decor of pastel shades together with light-colored inlaid and enameled woods was the popular treatment. The teen years featured mustards, yellows, blues, and violets. By the 1920s silver, black, and white rooms were fashionable, although probably not in libraries. Glitter and white satin, as well as overstuffed furniture, came in the 1930s. The colors of the 1940s, affected by the war and the difficulty to obtain dyes, tended to be subdued—greens and tans. The 1950s was the juke-box gaudy decade; hot pink was popular. Indeed, Stanford still had one branch library in 1970 that sported a pink color, or perhaps it was called salmon. The 1960s was the electric era with brilliant primaries—red, blue, green. The 1970s tended to be somewhat more subdued, leaning toward the earthen tones.

What will the future bring? The bright colors seem to be fading to pastels or darkened by adding gray or black. Primary colors are no longer popular. We may be in an era in libraries in which the colors of book bindings are about right, perhaps with a little toning down. Oak is today's popular wood, although other woods are certainly being used. The solid oak furniture from the 1920s is generally felt to be attractive again. The use of "natural" materials, popular for some time, continues to have merit. Brick, for example, has been nearly timeless, as has bronze, marble, and other materials that have their own color. Lavender, purple, and plum are popular today (and all three tend to fade badly!), while yellow, orange, and turquoise, unless severely toned down, are not so popular. Gray may replace beige as the most common "neutral" color other than off-white.

What can one learn from this? First, it is very difficult to create something today that will not look dated in ten years. Second, natural materials are usually safe. Third, everything else is going to change. It is well to recognize that while bright colors may be an attraction at first, they often become overstimulating and even repulsive over time. On the other hand, dull colors may not be so attractive, but they are less likely to be repulsive. Too much color is probably just as wrong for the typical library as too little color. The eye needs elements to delight and stimulate, but they must not be overwhelming. Variety may be an important concept here. Finally, a fine quality job may well transcend the changing fads, and so the superior design treatment is judged over time to become classic.

It is the authors' philosophy that, provided there are no glaring diversions from common sense, this is an area best left to the design consultants. The library representative should be concerned, however, about maintenance, the effect of light on the colors or the colors on the quality of light, fading, and the like.

The interior designer will prepare a color and texture board for review and approval by the institution. It will include actual samples of the building materials, shelving color, upholstery fabrics, paint chips, hardware finish, carpet, wood finish, etc. When looking at the color samples, it is very important to be in a lighting situation similar to that anticipated in the proposed new library. Colors selected when viewed under one light source may simply look terrible in another light.

Where the colored surface is intended to reflect light, one should know that there are considerable differences in the amount of light reflected by different colors. For this reason lighter colors should be considered where the light levels will be low.

Texture will also play a role in terms of how color is perceived. The texture of a surface will reflect light in different ways depending upon the angle of observation. Carpet, for example, will look quite different when observed at 90 degrees or 30 degrees, a fact that is often overlooked when samples are viewed. It is best to have a large enough sample so that it can be placed for observation in a position similar to the planned configuration. Remember that surrounding colors will affect the color sample, as well. A small paint chip will always look different when applied to a wall, especially if it is a strong color. On a large surface it will tend to become more intense.

Carpet color is an important decision. While a very light carpet will show soil from dirt or mud that is tracked in and will show stains from any spilled coffee, colored soft drinks, and red wine, a very dark monochromatic carpet will show such items as paper fragments, paper clips, and even staples. Heavy matting of light monochromatic carpet will be particularly evident where people turn (examples are doorways, corridor angles, by a drinking fountain, stair landings, and in front of a service desk or counter). Still, a coarse or grainy mix of colors can be unattractive when viewed close at hand. A "salt and pepper" pattern may indeed make wear, soiling, and dropped material relatively unseen, yet it is often unappealing. Bands of colors can be even less suitable due to the dizzying or confusing impression. Viewing large installations is the best way to avoid error.

Clearly, there are many tricks and pitfalls to selecting colors and textures. For this and other reasons, interior design is best left to a professional expert. Good results are seldom obtained from a democratic process, as each individual will have different ideas and tastes. The best advice is to be careful about distracting colors, avoid high gloss surfaces, and shun the most recent fad. Super graphics, for example, unless done very well, will become old fast. For safety reasons, be certain to change floor color, both indoors and out, to call attention to short differences in levels, such as one to three steps. Consider that if an error may occur, it is probably better to err toward the subtle than toward the bold. This is especially the case since most library use is quiet and in solitary intellectual activity. However, this should not discourage the use of bold color where it is appropriate. Libraries without color tend to be uncomfortably drab. Finally, consider applying the concept of variety. Different reading areas, floors, or wings of the building can readily have different color treatments which will provide relief for the individual who dislikes a particular color. Variety can also be used as an aid for orientation which may be of importance in a large library. Since people differ in their tastes, it is well to provide some degree of variety, though not so much nor in such a distribution that the interior lacks coherence.

3. Furnishings. Much has already been discussed in regard to furnishings. Carpet was treated earlier in this chapter. Signs are covered in Chapter 16. Details of most library furniture are covered in the chapters on programming. This section, because of the importance of the topic, will discuss window treatment and book trucks, and review the more critical concerns about furnishings.

Window Treatment. While the architect generally is responsible for inside shielding of exterior windows, interior design will be affected. Consideration must be given to direct and indirect sun control as well as to visual privacy and aesthetics for interior windows.

Of course, sunlight can be prevented from interfering with readers or damaging books by covering the glass on the inside or out. On the inside old-fashioned window shades, which shut out the light almost totally, are possible. If they are made so that they can be drawn down from the top and up from the bottom, they can take care of the light under different conditions at different times of day, but, of course, constant adjustment is necessary.

Both horizontal and vertical venetian blinds are also possibilities. The horizontal ones have been used for many years. Their cords tend to wear out, and they may present a cleaning problem. But if they are used carefully, if they are not so large as to be difficult to manipulate, and if the outside air that comes in is filtered, they will last a great many years with little cleaning or repair. Vertical blinds are in some ways more effective, but they present the same problems, and in addition, if the room is high and the blinds are long, they tend to get out of order quickly.

Drapes of various materials are also used extensively. They can be very decorative. The Georgia Institute of Technology had a tremendous quantity of specially designed, made-to-order draperies which add a great deal to the decor of the library. Unfortunately, because the bright Georgia sunlight fades them rapidly and because it is expensive to replace them, the librarian, who had been enthusiastic about them, later issued a warning about their use. At the Massachusetts Institute of Technology, where the large windows on the south wall of the reading rooms look out over a very handsome view of the Charles River and the Boston skyline beyond, the draperies have presented similar difficulties. They burn out rapidly and, in addition, are so large and heavy that they are difficult to move. At the Air Force Academy a tremendous expanse of glass has been covered by draperies so extensive in size that it has been found necessary to operate them with motors, and if the motors break down while the drapes are drawn, they cannot be opened, or, if open, they cannot be drawn, and a good part of the reading area becomes uninhabitable.

There are a number of coatings that can be applied to windows to reduce heat gain. A polyester plastic sheeting coated on one side with microscopic metal particles and fixed with an adhesive to the inside of the window will reflect up to 80 to 85 percent of solar energy and make it impossible for the glass to become hot enough to produce excessive radiation. It is recommended for use in overheated rooms designed with huge expanses of glass. In some installations the glass has become hot enough to break. Clearly, some analysis is required before jumping to this solution. Glass can also be produced with various tints to filter and reduce the effect of the sun. This technique, combined with double glazing, can provide an excellent solution to most of the heat problems, although it is not without cost.

Book Trucks. Book trucks, which in other parts of the English-speaking world are called book trolleys, are essential in a library of any size. They are expensive pieces of equipment, whether they are custom-made or purchased from a library-equipment firm. The wheels are the most expensive and one of the most critical parts. They must be so arranged that the trucks can easily be swung around corners within a short radius, because stack aisles where they are used are frequently narrow.

The trucks can be made with only three wheels, two at one end and one at the other, but this configuration is likely to be unstable unless the trucks are very low slung.

Four-wheel trucks can have two wheels at one end and two at the other with one or both pairs on pivots (fig. 14.3). Unless the wheels are widely spaced, perhaps even projecting beyond the sides, the truck may be none too stable. Four pivot wheels may help to make trucks easier to turn in tight quarters, but when one swings in one direction and the other in a different one, they are inclined to be balky. A truck with two fixed wheels is easier for one person to steer, especially in a straight line. Four-wheel trucks are sometimes built with two wheels in the center and one at each end, the end ones being on pivots and, for the sake of stability, well out toward the end or even beyond it. This configuration allows the truck to negotiate tight corners while maintaining an ease of control for straight travel, but it can be quite unstable where there are floor level changes, such as at a ramp or upon entering an elevator.

The six-wheeled truck is similar in concept except that each end has two pivot wheels. The center pair of wheels may project slightly lower than the others so that by bearing down at the rear end of the truck and pushing it, the front wheels are freed from the floor and it is easy to turn. Trucks of this kind at the New York Public Library Reference Department were built 4 ft (1.219) long and wide enough for two deep rows of books on each of three shelves, providing for 24 lineal ft (7.315) in a full load, or more than will go on a standard single-faced stack section when it is completely filled. However, this truck would be an exceedingly heavy unit if fully loaded, and it may be difficult to push, particularly on a carpeted floor.

Be sure that the wheels, whether pivot or stationary, are first-class quality so that they will not bind. If possible, they should be made with ball bearings, should not have to be oiled, and should not squeak. The larger the wheels are in diameter, the more easily they will push, but unless carefully designed, the large wheels raise the center of gravity and affect stabililty. Even so, larger wheels are generally recommended, particularly where carpet is used. They should be made with a hard rubber or plastic rolling surface to minimize rolling resistance while assuring a reasonably quiet ride. For a book truck carrying a 200 lb. (90 kg)

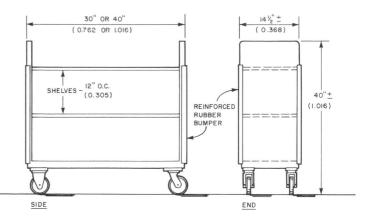

FIGURE 14.3 Book truck. Length depends on aisle widths and type of use. Width of 14 in. (0.356) is the minimum desirable to make possible shelving on each side. Width of 18 in. (0.457) is safer but may present difficulty in narrow aisles. Note rubber bumpers on corners.

load, a 5 in. (127 mm) wheel with a 1 to 1½ in. (25 to 38 mm) tread width should be selected. For larger trucks carrying a 400 to 500 lb. (181 to 227 kg) load, a 6 in. (152 mm) wheel with a tread width of 1½ in. (38 mm) is significantly better.

The body of the truck may be metal or wood. Trucks have been designed as a frame to accept standard library shelves. The critical aspect of the upper construction is the strength of the joints. As the book truck is pushed about the library, considerable lateral force is transferred through the frame of the truck to the wheels. If there is any weakness in the joints, they will eventually fail.

New trucks should not be acquired without bearing in mind the "bottlenecks" that they must go through in the building being planned, that is, the narrow aisles and sharp corners. Even where there is ample space, there is always danger of a book truck body bumping stacks and books if they protrude. The corner uprights and perhaps the sides of the book truck shelves should be fitted with bumper strips of leather, soft plastic, or rubber. An end-loading book truck, as illustrated in Figure 14.4, may be desirable in stacks with narrow aisles.

Watch for the distance between shelves when selecting trucks, so that books will seldom have to be turned down on their spines, which weakens their bindings. A distance of 12 in. (305 mm) on centers is suitable, providing for books 11 in. (280 mm) high. The truck shelves should ordinarily be wide enough so that two rows of good-sized books

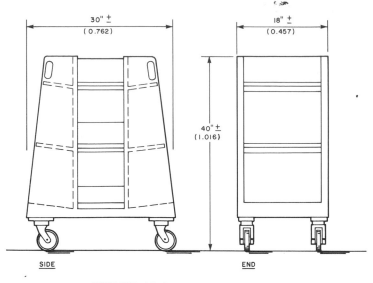

FIGURE 14.4 End-loading book truck for narrow aisles.

can be carried on each shelf without danger of their falling off, although a wide truck in a narrow aisle may make it impossible for a person to pass or for a staff member to withdraw books for shelving. A compromise may be that the book truck will need to stay out of the narrow range aisle, which often is not a serious problem except during major shifts or in areas of high use where the aisles should be wider. A truck shelf width of at least 14 in. (.0356) is advisable, and 16 in. or even 18 in. (0.406 or 0.457) is better if aisles are wide. Trucks come all the way from 22 in. (0.559) long to the 48 in. (1.219) mentioned earlier. They are generally from 39 to 45 in. (0.991 to 1.143) in overall height.

If materials are to be moved long distances, the provision of heavy rubber cords, commonly used to strap packages on a bicycle rack, are helpful to keep books from falling off. The means of hooking these cords onto the book truck should be considered, as projecting screw eyes can be somewhat of a hazard. No doubt a clever designer could solve this problem, but one idea may be to inset the screw eye or to place the eye on the end instead of the side.

The programmer might wish to specify special book trucks adapted for use as mobile lockers which can replace a need for standard lockers and provide greater flexibility for the student to maintain secured materials near a favored seating position. This has been done at the University of California at Los Angeles with good effect. The sides have been enclosed with transparent panels, with one side fitted with hinges and a lock.

Perhaps the most important aspect of book trucks at the programming stage is to ensure that adequate floor area is provided where quantities of trucks are to be stored. Areas where this may need to be considered include circulation discharge areas, sort rooms, technical processing areas, and perhaps the receiving room.

One final warning that will not be popular with many librarians: most catalogers, one might say most librarians, find book trucks altogether too convenient storage places and will tend to use them by their desks in place of bookcases. Because of the cost of their wheels, they are too expensive for use in this way; the moral is to provide sufficient bookcases for staff purposes.

Furnishings Concerns. As a form of review, it is urged that the following issues be considered as furniture is being selected.

1. Tables, carrels
   a. Ensure that where more than one seated position is provided at a single unit, it does not wiggle when one user is writing.
   b. Avoid fasteners that attract tampering. They should either be out of view or designed so that a simple tool cannot remove them.
   c. The work surface should not be glossy, exceedingly dark, or very light due to problems of glare.
   d. Where task lighting is to be provided, have a mock-up prepared to check for glare.
   e. Provide for the future installation of terminals or other similar equipment where appropriate. Check on wire management.
   f. Consider the process of refinishing which may be needed at a later date. A wood trim that is slightly below the main work surface will be easier to sand and refinish without damage to the main surface than one that is exactly flush. Review the process for removing fabric or acoustic panels for refinishing or replacement.
   g. Avoid bold colors on any back panel facing the reader.
   h. A desk of standard typing height of 25 in. (635 mm) is probably better for more people than the normally accepted 27 in. (686 mm). The best solution is a typing surface with adjustable height.
   i. Avoid built-in typing surfaces unless noise transmission is not a problem.

k. Provide some work surfaces high enough for wheelchair access, that is, 29 in. (737 mm) clear from the floor to the underside of the work surface. Five percent of the seating in this configuration is probably more than enough. Do not forget a typing position for a handicapped person in a wheelchair.

l. Select furniture that is adaptable for changed configurations. In this regard, individual units are superior to ganged units which cannot be taken apart.

m. Where a unit is superior for a right-handed person, such as space for note taking at a microtext reading station, provide a number (6–10 percent) for those who are left-handed.

2. Chairs

a. Avoid detail elements that can be picked at.

b. Consider using a densely woven fabric rather than vinyl; the library patron will favor it.

c. Review the process of reupholstery or refinishing.

d. Consider sled-base chairs for standard reader chairs in carpeted areas. Adjustable office chairs with wheels are probably even better, but their cost may limit their selection to faculty studies and staff areas.

e. Where lounge chairs are planned, provide a footrest. Consider a carpet-covered box large enough so two to six persons can use it as a footrest, as is used at Dartmouth College.

f. Provide a mix of armless and arm chairs. No more than 85 to 90 percent of the reader chairs should have arms if the preference of some people for armless chairs is to be satisfied.

g. Where high stools are provided at a counter, ensure that there is a footrest.

h. Above all else, select a reader chair that will withstand tipping, heavy use, and abuse. Durability will save considerable headaches in the future. On the other hand, many like a chair that will tip, thus providing a variety to the sitting position which can be a comfortable change.

3. Special equipment

a. Select a wastebasket that will not burn.

b. Do not forget pencil sharpeners, dictionary stands, tackboards, chalk-boards, projection equipment, etc. See Appendix C.

c. An atlas case with pullout shelves on roller mountings is superior to one with fixed shelves.

d. Do not forget sun control. It may involve drapes, window shades, and vertical or horizontal blinds. Be careful to select a product that will hold up under heavy use.

e. Consider clear plastic carrel dividers in some locations, such as used in the language laboratory at Osaka Gakuin University Library.

f. Review the sections in this volume on card catalogs, carpet, service points, shelving, mail room equipment, etc., when these are part of the interior design.

14.4 Establish the Alternatives and NIC Items

This section deals with one of the key means of budget control: the provision of construction alternatives that can be selected once the bid is received, and the removal of certain project elements from the construction contract so that decisions can be made at a later date or so that more economical methods of providing the product may be achieved. The NIC (Not In Contract) items are representative of the latter approach. While this topic has been discussed elsewhere in this volume, most notably in Chapter 9, it is of particular importance to the final stages of the design process when a financial problem is expected.

It should be stressed that the process of budget control should have been part of the design process right from the start. Major decisions about the project scope should have been made well before the final plans are nearing completion, and major construction alternatives such as an additional floor, basement, or an added wing should already be part of the plans. But one needs to know what can be done at this stage if it is likely that the project exceeds the funding available.

The *first* obvious option is to put the project on the shelf and seek additional funding. This is never a very happy solution, although it may be the only practical approach when the funding gap is exceptionally large. There are two contradictory problems involved. On the one hand, one may argue that with the cost of inflation, the funding possibilities may never catch up. This was the case at Stanford for the proposed new main library when the design was completed in early 1970. By 1974 it was clear that there was no realistic expectation that the project could ever be funded; thus it was started over from scratch. On the other hand, once construction is started on a building, many would argue that a gift or grant is much more difficult to obtain as the potential donor perceives that other, unrealized projects may currently have a higher urgency. Of course, this is not always the case, though it is a real concern. In the case of Stanford, a fine new facility was ultimately realized, although it is considerably smaller than the original plan. Examples abound of institutions that have pressed ahead under equally difficult circumstances. The authors cannot recommend the appropriate action, as each institution and project will have its own unique set of financial constraints. Thus, this is a matter for local discussion. One would hope, however, that with careful budget control and reasonable estimating procedures, this type of decision will not be faced.

The *second* option is to identify aspects of the project that could be removed without serious effect on the operational or academic program. As already stressed, major elements of this nature should have been identified at the end of the design development phase, if not earlier. At the end of the construction document phase, alternatives should be limited to those aspects that will not involve more than minor revisions to the documents. In selecting possible alternatives to add or deduct, great care must be exercised to avoid seriously affecting other aspects of the project.

The following list of possible alternatives should be viewed with considerable caution. None of them may be appropriate for a given institution. They are presented only as an illustration of the kind of elements that the design team should consider when there is a budget problem. Consideration may usefully be given to elements that can be removed totally and still allow the project to proceed. These might include, for example, some specialized mechanical devices such as an electronic book-detection system, a trash compactor or incinerator, an elaborate annunciator panel, a first-rate book-return system, or perhaps even an elevator. Other possibilities might include a fume hood, a fumigation chamber, a special display area, or a fountain. Shelving and perhaps other equipment and finishes might be reduced or

eliminated from an entire floor. The installation of a movable-shelving system might be put off to a future date.

Many of these possibilities will result in other costs. The removal of the book-detection system may add staff cost to the process of exit control. Loss of the fumigation chamber may require contracting for the services of an outside vendor for the treatment of infested materials (which may be beneficial). The loss of an elevator, unless other elevators remain, could have a significant effect on staff costs. On the other hand, all of the elements suggested can be added at a later date as funding permits. The increase in cost to add them later will probably exceed the cost of inflation, as it is always more costly to alter or add elements to an existing facility than to include them in the first place. This is due to problems of quantity, access, and working with an existing structure which requires extra coordination to ensure that everything fits. The advantage of making such elements alternatives in the contract documents is that a clear picture of their cost can be obtained, and a rational decision reached. It is suggested, however, that the number of alternatives be limited to perhaps no more than four to six items, as a lengthy list will likely result in other bidding problems. (One eastern state university library in 1985 went to bid with twenty-one alternates, including four for special cabinetwork, one for storm sash, two for HVAC, two for plumbing, six for electrical work, and one for a refrigeration room.)

A *third* area that warrants review is restrictive specifications. Demanding that a particular brand be used for virtually any aspect of the project removes the possibility of competitive bidding and usually increases the cost for that element. Aspects that may be in this category include shelving, hardware, mechanical systems and controls, and perhaps even unique or unusual architectural materials or finishes. When this is the approach taken, it is important to develop a carefully worded performance specification so that those features that are truly required are included. An alternative is to pre-qualify several vendors so that at least limited competition is assured. Stanford recently rejected a sole source bid for library shelving for a particular project. The result, after opening the bidding process up to competition, was a low bid at less than half the original bid. This is not meant to imply that the original vendor was being dishonest, but rather that an error in interpretation by the sole source bidder may later have been identified since the competitive bidding process requires a sharp pencil. Clearly, there must be a very sound basis for electing to specify any product as a sole source item.

The *fourth* possibility for dealing with budget problems involves quality. Here the authors are reluctant to urge cost cutting as, in the long run, the institution will almost always end up spending more. Still, the budget may require a review of the quality levels established in the project. Are there materials that could be substituted to achieve the same effect? Is a fancy hardwood specified for a ceiling treatment where a less expensive material might suffice? Might the amount of vinyl wall covering be reduced and replaced with paint? Other areas where quality might be reviewed include light fixtures, hardware, mechanical controls, surface treatments, carpet, furnishings, and the like. None of these is easily upgraded later, and all of them will have long-term effect on the utility of the facility. Of all the cost-cutting possibilities, this is generally the least satisfactory, although the review is warranted.

The *fifth* possibility to achieve a balanced budget is to identify elements that can be provided in less expensive ways. Often, for example, there are features in the contract documents which could be installed by other than the general contractor with a savings of the general contractor's contingency, profit, and overhead. These elements might include shelving, carpet, certain built-in equipment, drapes or blinds, chalkboards, tackboards, lockers, clocks, intrusion alarm systems, and the like. These elements then become NIC items. They are shown on the drawings for the general contractor's information, but they are installed under separate contract.

It is difficult to identify the exact savings that result from this technique, and it adds some element of risk that there will be budget problems later in the project. Further, where coordination of several trades may be involved, as is the case where light switches are incorporated in the shelving or the shelving supports the light fixtures, it may not be prudent to make the product an NIC item. Other than the issue of coordination, though, it is probably reasonable for the institution to assume the risk of cost rise, the problems of contracting, and the issues of coordination for products such as those listed above rather than include them as part of the general contract. While the savings may be modest, they probably are real.

Another similar area is the identification of aspects of the project that can be managed "in house" by the library or institutional staff. The move into the new facility is a good example, when student labor and staff supervision can probably save as much as 50 percent of the cost that a professional moving company might charge. The installation of furniture, signage, and such items as pencil sharpeners and tackboards can easily be done in house at considerable savings. These elements are part of the activation process which is dealt with in detail in Chapter 16.

14.5 The Review Process

The review of construction documents will differ in several respects from the review of earlier phases. First, it is a time when detailed review by the institution's engineers and maintenance personnel will ensure that the institution's facility design standards are met. The operations and maintenance people will be particularly interested in the access provided for mechanical equipment or other systems for maintenance procedures. They will want to learn and understand the mechanical system and its controls. The insurance and fire protection representatives will wish to review in detail the fire protection systems, where the control valves are, how the alarms are interphased with the campus system, and the like. The affirmative action officer may wish to review the contractual requirements for encouraging the use of minorities as subcontractors and as staff of the general contractor. An administrator responsible for handicapped access will have special interest in the elevator controls, the height of public phones, the features of the rest rooms, aisle and door widths, and a number of other details. In essence, the review of the contract documents is the only time when many of the concerns of the institution can really be checked.

The second unique aspect of the contract document phase is that, because of the number of documents, the only practical way to undertake a review in any depth is on an individual basis. It will do little good to present the working drawings to a group. Unless you have been involved in the design process or are familiar with reading contract documents, little will be gained by reviewing the entire set. As a courtesy, it may well be useful to offer the opportunity to review the documents to a fairly wide audience, but it is suggested that for any project of significant size, this general review should occur at a specified office rather than circulating sets to a large number of people. The exception to this recommendation is, of course, those administrators who have specific need to review aspects in the area of their responsibility. Furthermore, each member of the design team should have a chance to pore over the documents.

Third, the contract document review phase is the period in which various governmental agencies must conclude their approvals. These may include the fire marshal's office, the government building inspector's office, and perhaps an architectural review board (although it may wish to see drawings resembling schematics rather than working drawings), the health authorities, and perhaps others. The government plan-checking process is necessary before a permit will be issued, and on a large project, this process can take a month or more. In order to avoid a delay in the start of construction, it is reasonable to have the government plan checking start at the 90 percent complete stage, along with the institution's review. Any changes that occur as a result of the review process can easily be passed on to the government agency, and the plan-check process can thereby be accelerated. Once the review is complete, any final corrections or changes will be made on the documents, and the project will be ready to go out to bid.

What should the librarians or library representative look for? Nearly all of the concerns of the library should have been incorporated into the documents long before this stage is reached, although there may well be numerous details that have been discussed but never seen on the drawings or in the specifications. These are the key elements to check. It is also well to read everything, and when something is not clear or seems out of order, ask a question. Remember, too, that these drawings are not yet 100 percent complete; there will be some minor things missing. But if you are concerned about a detail or what is missing, ask about it. It certainly does not hurt to be thorough; it will be too late if an error or omission is not caught now.

What are the kinds of things that the librarian may wish to review? The following tabulation lists examples. Others have been mentioned earlier in this chapter and in previous chapters. The key to any review is to keep an open mind and think about what you see. This is always more easily said than done. Have your library building consultant also look over the plans. Often a fresh eye with similar interest and concern can turn up unseen issues to great benefit. The examples of what to look for:

1. Landscape drawings
    a. Check the grading plan. Make sure the exterior surfaces slope away from doors. Look for area drains. Does it look like there are enough? Where would ground water collect? Can snow be plowed wherever necessary?
    b. Do retaining walls have drainage apertures?
    c. Review the planting. Are there trees that will block windows? Are there deciduous trees whose leaves will clog drains? Will shrubs block egress from an emergency exit?
    d. Have a look at the arrangements for exterior lighting, especially at stairs. Will there be dark areas which seem dangerous? It may be difficult to replace the bulbs in the neat little light fixtures that are concealed in the steps—if they can be replaced at all. Will low light fixtures present a problem of glare? Are the light fixtures relatively vandal resistant?
    e. Watch for elements that provide natural bike racks, especially near the main entry. Can bicycles be sheltered in the rain?
    f. Have a look at the arrangements for an exterior book return. Is it well lighted? easily accessible?
    g. Is exterior seating appropriate or desired? Will people sit on walls? Will they take shortcuts and cross garden beds?
    h. Have trash containers and ash urns been included? Are they conveniently located? Where will the wind blow debris?
    i. How is the main trash removal from the building handled? Is there a dumpster that needs landscape treatment?
    j. Are there plantings that will create a security problem because they offer hiding places?

Others as well as library representatives will be interested in the switching for the light fixtures, the irrigation system, access for fire trucks, paving details, lawn-edging details, plants and how they are placed, preparation of the soil for planting, and many other aspects.

2. Architectural drawings. Most of this volume has been devoted to the design problems in libraries. The following is only a representative listing.

   a. Review the requirements of handicapped access.

   b. Security issues may warrant review. Which doors are locked, and how? Where are alarm devices? How will alarms be responded to?

   c. Are walls appropriately designed to receive wall-mounted shelving?

   d. How will the outside windows be cleaned? Do sills offer bird roosting sites?

   e. Are the details for the built-ins appropriate?

   f. Are the items that are "not in contract" properly labeled?

   g. Will one be able to move large carrels, tables, or other equipment where needed?

   h. If phasing is part of the project, is it clearly detailed?

   i. Is there provision in the drawings for dust control in an existing building?

   j. Check the details. Are display cases with internal lights well ventilated? How are they locked? Is built-in shelving adjustable?

   k. Is the roof access secured? How will roof utility areas be serviced?

   l. Do you understand the roofing system? Is it acceptable quality? What about the flashing and rain gutters?

   m. Check for thresholds. If they are not absolutely required, they should be avoided.

   n. Where acoustic control is a problem, do the walls extend through the suspended ceiling to the underside of the floor above?

   o. Is the ceiling an exposed grid or a concealed spline? or plaster or gypsum board? or other material? Will access for maintenance be a problem?

   p. Are entry mats included in the design? Will they creep? How easily can they be replaced? Has drainage been provided below mats where climate requires?

   q. Are the paper towel dispensers in the washrooms separate from the sinks so paper bits will not fall in the drain? Are adequate shelves provided in the washrooms? Is the floor waterproof? Has moisture-resistant gypsum board been specified?

   r. Is there enough room where the photocopy machine is to be placed to open all equipment doors to service the machine?

   s. If carpet is part of the contract documents, review the seaming plan in conjunction with furniture layouts. Are the seams located to minimize wear?

   t. Review the provisions for sun control. Where will drapes collect if pulled open?

   u. Are the doors undercut as necessary for ventilation and carpet installation?

   v. Do the dimensions for the height of built-in work surfaces take into account the thickness of the carpet? This may be critical where file cabinets or other standard units must relate to the built-in unit. Do the built-in work surfaces have sufficient underside bracing?

   w. Are there adequate coat racks?

   x. Is floor-to-ceiling glass protected from book truck traffic?

3. Structural drawings

   a. Have the columns or other structural elements changed size? Is head room impaired at any point?

   b. Is the ground-level structure over an underground area sufficient to support a fire truck?

   c. Has reasonable provision for future expansion been made?

   d. Are there any obvious structural surprises, such as a flared base or capital of a column?

4. Mechanical drawings

   a. Try to gain an understanding of how the mechanical system works and how it is controlled.

   b. Review access to duct shafts and mechanical equipment rooms. Are they secure? Will access require an altered furniture arrangement? Will service personnel be required to carry all of their tools, ladders, cleaning materials, spare parts, and the like through the library to gain access to the equipment? Will this weaken book security?

   c. Have the acoustical concerns been reasonably attended to? Which pieces of building equipment or operations are most likely to create disturbing noises?

d. Is the building divided into zones to allow shutting down the systems to those areas that close earlier than the major part of the library?

e. Look at the elevator cab design. Is there sufficient space for the floor indicator graphics? Are the surfaces durable?

f. Is the sump pump on stand-by emergency power? What about exhaust fans?

g. Is the floor of the mechanical room (if it is on the roof) waterproof and sloped, in order to drain? How will future pipes or changes be added without compromising the waterproof membrane?

h. Are there mechanical devices—such as reheat coils, duct vane actuator motors, and humidifiers—above the ceiling of the library that will require servicing from time to time? Is a hatch needed? Is any form of steam or water protection reasonable or appropriate?

i. Are all of the fire dampers accessible?

j. What kind of filters are shown?

k. Are there street-level air intakes that might invite a stink bomb?

l. Do the air delivery registers seem adequate or are there dead pockets? Check the bookstacks for any such apparent pockets. Will there be drafts where students or staff sit?

5. Plumbing drawings

a. Try to follow the routes of pipes to see where water hazards may occur. Keep in mind that these drawings are somewhat diagrammatic, but if water hazards are a concern, they can be dealt with by requiring specific routing.

b. Check the location of sprinkler main controls.

c. See if higher heat-range sprinkler heads are to be provided any place near a heat source. This includes under skylights!

d. In a tunnel connection, are there utilities that should be encased in a protective pipe? Are there any pipes or ducts where heads can be bumped?

e. Ensure that the mechanical rooms, rest rooms, and janitor closets have floor drains. Where are sewer clean-outs, and can they be kept outside of bookstack areas?

f. Have a look at the capacity of the sump pumps. What happens if one fails?

g. Review the drinking fountains, both in terms of their fixture design and their location. These can occasionally be a surprise, particularly for handicapped access.

h. Have a look at the plumbing under the washroom sinks. It seems a shame to install highly polished chrome pipes and then to cover them with sponge rubber to protect the knees of a person in a wheelchair.

6. Electrical drawings

a. Review the arrangement of light fixtures, particularly in relation to the furniture layouts.

b. Check the switching arrangements. If this aspect is not clear, ask about it. Are any light switches or thermostats on columns where they project and could be broken or hurt someone passing by?

c. If there are light fixtures shown that you are not familiar with, ask for a photocopy of the manufacturer's catalog description.

d. How will bulbs in difficult-to-reach light fixtures be replaced? Are there any fixtures where heat buildup will result in short life of the lamp?

e. Check power outlet locations. Ensure that, even in the stacks, outlets are provided for maintenance purposes.

f. Where the outlet is to be above the work surface, review the height shown.

g. Does each work station have sufficient outlets? Four are recommended.

h. Look at the indicated phone locations. Is there sufficient flexibility for alternative furniture arrangements?

i. Look at the arrangements for flexibility, including floor duct systems, cable trays in the ceiling, core voids in the floor, empty conduit runs, and the like. Do they work with possible furniture arrangements? Are they appropriate? Do the horizontal runs tie into vertical shafts? Is it clear that there will be sufficient capacity for both future flexibility and the installation of those aspects that are not part of the general contract such as phones, computer terminals, intrusion alarm system? If this is not clear, ask questions.

j. Are the floor outlets coordinated with the furniture arrangements? Are they flush or monument type, and will any of the latter be hazardous?

k. Can different areas of the building have the lights turned off while other areas remain open and active?

l. Is there a master clock system? If so, review the location of clocks. Staff areas should not be overlooked.

m. Is there a signal distribution closet on each floor? How will computer terminals in other public and staff areas be added in the future?

n. Does the products-of-combustion detection system reasonably cover the building?

o. How is emergency lighting dealt with? Will such lighting enable one to see exit lanes from every room in the building?

p. Are conduits shown for the security system? How about the electronic book detection system? Is there a conduit to each exterior door for the alarm system? Is the exterior book return protected in any way against malicious behavior?

q. What is the distribution of the white sound system, if provided? Is there indication of individual area control?

r. If low-voltage switching is provided, is there any special provision for providing access to the solenoid switches?

When they are hidden above the ceiling, they can be hard to find.

7. Specifications

a. Look at the general and special conditions. Is there reasonable protection for ongoing operations? Are noise and dust adequately dealt with?

b. You may wish to review a number of sections, but be sure to read the section on library shelving. Are the book supports correct? Are range indicators or finders indicated? Are the numbers of shelves per section and their dimensions correct? Is it clear that the dimensions are nominal or actual? Is the base closed or open? Is fastening of the shelving to the structure specified? All shelving details must be reviewed in these specifications.

c. Review the hardware schedule with the architectural plans. This is an area where errors can be easily made.

d. Have a look at the fixture schedules, such as for lavatories and lighting. Are some unfamiliar? If so, ask for manufacturer's information. For example, can a person with arthritic hands operate water faucet knobs?

Clearly, this list could go on and on. There is no substitute for simply spending a substantial block of time with the plans. As has been noted before, it is less expensive to make corrections at this stage than later. The time spent will be worthwhile.

15

Bidding, Legal, Business Concerns and Construction

This chapter deals with the bidding and construction phase of the project, which, on a small project, may span a period of only six to eight weeks but may require two years or more for a large project. It is a time of considerable satisfaction for the design team as the project finally takes form.

During the course of bidding and construction, there will be a continuing need for involvement by the library representative and others as there will frequently be a need for decisions and actions which may affect library operations. However, the intensity of involvement will generally be reduced until it is time to start planning for activation, although it is not uncommon for some design activity, particularly the interior design, to overlap the construction period.

15.1 The Management Team

In dealing with contractors, the architect is almost always the representative of the owner or institution. Technically, all approvals, directions, clarifications—virtually all communications—are to go through the architect to the general contractor, who then is responsible for passing information on to the various subcontractors. The only exceptions are when the project is very small or when a special arrangement is made, as might be the case in the renovation of an occupied building when close coordination is required with the occupants. In these cases, discussions about scheduling, for example, may occur through the institution's project manager or through a representative of the library. The architect, though, will still have primary responsibility for the project.

From the start of the bid period, because of the changed role of the architect, there will usually be other changes as well. Some institutions, for example, have an office specializing in construction. Even where the institutional project manager retains primary responsibility for the project, the key role for the institution may be assigned to a construction manager. In many cases, the construction manager will be assisted by one or several construction inspectors who are responsible for ensuring that the execution of the construction effort meets the full intent of the contract documents. Depending upon the circumstances, the architect may provide the detailed inspection services which would, of course, be reflected in the architect's contract and fees.

Once the contract is signed, the contractor takes on full responsibility for the construction site, including liability for injury or damages. Visits to the site must be arranged with the contractor's approval although there are usually a few named individuals, such as the architect, inspectors, project manager, and construction manager, who are granted free access by the construction contract document.

Besides inspections by representatives of the owner and the architect, there will be inspections by others. For example, there may be a soils engineer hired by the contractor, owner, or architect (depending on the contractual specifications) during the period of excavation. A materials-testing laboratory often will inspect the concrete placement and take samples for testing. During the course of construction, the code authorities will be involved in routine inspections. These on-site reviews will involve principally the building inspection, but occasionally they may include specialists in fire protection, elevators, health, and others.

The architect's consulting engineers will visit the site, although less frequently, to undertake an inspection. They include the structural, mechanical, electrical, and perhaps acoustical engineers as well as the landscape architect and other specialized consultants. Of course, it can be expected that the librarian will, from time to time, inspect the project.

The reports from all of these inspections should eventually be sent to the architect, who is responsible for coordinating any corrective action. The governmental inspectors will generally deal directly with the contractor, as it is the contractor who holds the building permit. The institutional representatives should, of course, report problems observed during an inspection through the project manager to the architect. The architect's consultants will deal directly with the architect.

As already suggested, most projects of any size will have a full-time inspector, or a clerk of works, representing the institution, whose duties are to see that the construction matches the working drawings and specifications, to keep track of the innumerable details, and to call the contractor's and architect's attention to discrepancies. The architect, as part of the contract, must supervise construction along the same lines. The differences between the supervision provided by the architect and the clerk of works are two:

1. The clerk's supervision is continuous and the architect's periodic, generally no more than once a week, unless at critical times and on a very large enterprise.

2. The architect can interpret and direct procedures and initiate required changes in structure or design, while the clerk's duty is to see that the requirements of the contract drawings and specifications are fulfilled by the contractor and crew.

Too often careless workers may seriously lower standards. Too often a contractor may hope to save money and increase profit by skimping on the concrete mix or finishings of all kinds, or by providing slightly inferior quality material which could escape detection if not watched. It is to be hoped that a reliable and honest contractor has the assignment and can be trusted; but particularly in government jobs, where the "lowest responsible bidder" must be assigned the contract, if the bid has been figured too closely and there is danger of financial loss, very careful supervision must be provided. It is very difficult to prove that a bidder able to be bonded by an insurance company is irresponsible; not all insurance companies have as high standards for contractors' qualifications as might be desired. A first-class clerk of works representing the institution and the architect is, therefore, of great value. The clerk of works must, of course, be acceptable to both the institution and the architect and can be employed by either but is not part of the usual architectural services.

From the preceding, it can be seen that technically, at least, the lines of communication are fairly rigid. It suggests that the librarian should not have direct contact with the contractor, except in response to a request through the architect, as confusion will result if the builder and foreman have more than one source of information and direction. If there are two sources, conflicting directions inevitably result. The librarian should, of course, be interested and also watchful, but all dealings must be through the architect, or, if this has been agreed upon, through the institution's or architect's representative at the construction site.

Any library questions or afterthoughts should be directed only through the owner's planner or inspector to the architect. In practice, some of these questions will come up properly in the job review meetings and may be answered and acted upon at once, yet it is necessary to remember the correct channels and who has what legal authority. When job meetings become touchy or heated, it is especially necessary to remember what legal role each plays. The library representative usually has the least authority during construction.

15.2 The Bid Package

A typical bid package for a large project will include an invitation to bid, instructions for bidders, the proposal, the agreement, general conditions, supplementary general conditions, the drawings, the technical specifications, and any addendum or clarification issued before the bid date. Most of this material is very technical in nature, and it is not the intent of this volume to go into great detail. However, for the information of those who may be interested, a brief description of the most important elements is presented here. For small projects, parts of the bid package are abbreviated or combined so as to reduce the volume.

Invitation to Bid. The invitation to bid solicits contractors to bid on the project. While each project may have a different format, it is not unusual for the invitation to include a brief description of the project, an outline of the nature of the bid, the time and place for the bid opening, and perhaps a statement reserving the right to reject bids. Other important aspects may be pointed out in the invitation, such as a requirement for a corporate surety bond for payment and performance to be provided by the successful bidder, or the requirement that the bid must be accompanied by a bid bond.

Legal Documents and Bidding. Normally, written specifications are accompanied by a preface or introduction which describes in detail (a) the "general conditions," or the legal contract terms under which the construc-

tion of the building is undertaken; (b) "supplementary general conditions" which serve to alter and amplify the "general conditions"; and (c) the "instructions to bidders," or the methods which will be used to arrive at and ensure the performance of these contract terms.

Since the first part of this preface, "general conditions," is basically a legal document, standard forms are available which incorporate into them the past experience of actual court or arbitration proceedings in connection with construction contracts. In the United States standard contract forms of the general conditions for the construction of buildings are prepared and distributed by the American Institute of Architects and are regularly revised in order to incorporate or recognize the most up-to-date procedures. The architectural organizations of other countries have similar forms. Public authorities and governments responsible for directing a large amount of construction frequently have prepared their own standard form of general conditions. Sometimes a lawyer may be engaged to draw up one for an individual project.

The general conditions define the rights, duties, and responsibilities in the mutual undertaking of the institution, the architect, the contractor, and subcontractors, and they determine or direct ownership, protection, inspection, changes, claims, termination, payments, insurance, bonds, liens, and other general procedures.

Most frequently the standard form is used for the general conditions, and its terms or procedures are adjusted to the local custom and law by means of the "supplementary general conditions." This supplement describes the modifications and additions to the standard form that may be desired or required on the particular project for which it is written. It is tailored to the specific project, to local conditions, and, perhaps, as the result of recent litigation, to the experience of the architect or institution.

The third part of the preface, "instructions to bidders," as its title implies, instructs all prospective contractors who are planning to bid or present proposals to the institution for constructing the building, on the methods they must follow and the obligations they must assume in their submission. These instructions are often accompanied by forms which are prescribed for the contractor's use (a) in submitting the proposal, or tender, (b) in providing for any required bonds or guarantees, and (c) in signing an agreement with the institution.

The instructions to bidders should document for the contractor the intentions of the institution and the architect relative to the scope of the work, the bidding procedures, and the method of contract award.

The "scope of the work" presents a general description of the work to be done by the contractor, the premises upon which this work is to be constructed, and the contract documents in which it is specifically defined. It should point out any difficulties the contractor might be expected to encounter during the conduct of the job because of the requirements and operations of the library or any other department of the institution. If it is planned to have the general contractor work with other contractors engaged by the institution under separate contracts or if the contractor will operate in the same building jointly with the library, the full implications of required cooperation and coordination should be expressed.

"Bidding procedures" need to be defined so that the bidder may know the proper channels to follow in order to obtain bidding documents, to request and receive interpretations and clarifications of them, and to submit the bid in proper form.

Bids may be received in several forms, the most common of which is the "lump sum." This term is used to indicate a proposal on the part of the contractor agreeing to provide all labor and materials required for completion of the project as specified and drawn for a stated sum of money. On occasion the contractor may be requested to submit only an estimate of the construction cost and the amount of the proposed fee for conducting and directing the building operation. Sometimes, in this instance, the contractor is expected to guarantee that the final construction cost will not exceed the total amount of his estimated cost. Various types of contractual possibilities are discussed in Section 15.3.

The bidder is frequently required to state alternate prices, which may be added to or deducted from the base price, either lump sum or estimated cost, for increasing the scope of the work or for omitting or changing some part of the specified scope or quality.

Plans. There should be an architectural plan showing each floor level of the building. It will illustrate this floor diagrammatically as if the roof or floor above had been removed, exposing the shape and size of all rooms and spaces and the location of all the doors, windows, columns, walls, stairs, elevators, and vertical shafts for distribution of mechanical services. In addition, all fixtures and furnishings built into or attached to the building, such as washroom fixtures and bookstacks, will be shown. The locations of loose furniture may also be indicated, as these will help materially to clarify the objectives of the plan. Such locations are usually indicated with dotted lines or on a separate plan, as movable equipment is rarely the responsibility of the building contractor, who uses the drawing in estimating and constructing the library. Dotted lines contrasting with the solid lines of the main parts of the plan indicate that the object or space so presented is not part of the work expected from the contractor. They are frequently marked with the initials NIC (Not In Contract).

The dimensions must be given on the plans in feet and inches, or meters, and drawn to scale. In other words, the plans must be exact and proportionately reduced from the actual "full" size desired in the completed building so that any desired dimension can be determined by measuring it on the drawing and multiplying that measurement by the amount of reduction employed. Architects and engineers use rulers that have this multiplication factor incorporated in their markings and which can then be read directly in feet and inches or meters. These rulers are called architect's, or engineer's, scales, and the act of using them is "scaling." The scale, or the amount of proportional reduction used, should clearly be stated on each plan. In the United States the term *architectural scale* is usually given to one expressing a foot by 1/16, 1/8, 1/4, 3/8, 1/2, 3/4, or 1 in.; the term *engineer's scale*, to one expressing a foot by 1/200, 1/100, 1/50, 1/40, 1/20, or 1/10 in. The usual architectural scales employed on plans are 1/16 in. = 1 ft or 1/8 in. = 1 ft or 1/4 in. = 1 ft. If a more detailed plan explanation is required, larger scales (3/8 in., 1/2 in., 3/4 in., and 1 in. to 1 ft) are used, but these are more frequently employed for sections. Metric scales, on the other hand, are referred to as 1:20, 1:25, 1:50, 1:75, 1:125 where 1 mm equals 20 mm (1:20), 1 mm equals 25 mm (1:25), or 1000 mm equals 50 meters (1:50), and so on. Since a scale of 1/4 in. = 1 ft represents a scale of about one fiftieth of full size, it would roughly be equal to a scale where 20 mm equals 1 meter or

1:50. Likewise, 1/8 in. scale would be similar to 1:100, and 1/2 in. scale is close to 1:25. It is interesting to note that the proportionate scales of the drawings between the two systems of measurement are very close to the same, being off by 4 percent.

In addition to the floors, plans of the roof and the plot are needed. These are sometimes combined on one drawing and usually use an engineer's scale, particularly if the building is a large one. However, architectural scales of 1/16 in., 1/32 in., or even 1/64 in. are sometimes employed. These would be equivalent to 1:200, 1:400, or 1:800 in metric terms. The roof plan is required to show the pitch, or direction of slope, the method of drainage on the roofs, and the location, housing, and size of mechanical services which project above the roof levels. Usually, safety regulations require door access or window access from the building to all flat roofs, a provision which is also an aid to maintenance and which should be shown on the roof plan.

If a great deal of mechanical equipment is on the roof, rather than within the building, a roof plan at an architectural scale may be required in order to illustrate properly the sizes and locations. The increasing importance and amount of mechanical work in modern buildings has led to such an extensive use of the roof for elevator equipment, fans, cooling towers, and related ductwork and piping that there is a tendency to enclose all of it on a separate floor or roofhouse of its own or to contain it within a barrier or fence built on the roof to screen the usually untidy appearance of this heterogeneous assembly of mechanical equipment. Radio and television antennae and even microwave dish receivers may be included. These problems are generally less acute in libraries than in laboratories or similar buildings requiring a high concentration of mechanical equipment, but they are present, particularly if the library is air conditioned.

The plot plan illustrates the location of the building relative to adjacent structures and the ground. It shows the source and direction of all services which must be brought into the building from outside and locates all walks, roads, parking areas, and planting beds and grass required as part of the completed building. If the site has existing trees, planting beds, walks, roads, or buildings, the plan should show them so that they may be properly protected during construction or removed as part of the contract. Frequently,

the land made available for the use of the contractor during the construction period must be restricted and protected so that the operations of both the institution and the contractors may be conducted without undue interference with each other. The limitation of the areas assigned to and to be protected by the contractor should be shown on the plot plan. In determining their size the architect must remember that space is required not only for storing and receiving equipment and building materials, but also for construction shanties, worker's facilities, and parking. Difficult access to the site will increase the building costs and the hardships placed on the contractor, and will be reflected in the construction cost.

The plot plan shows the relationship of the building to the ground by elevations or grades which indicate the number of feet, or meters, any particular spot is above sea level or some other predetermined point which will remain undisturbed during construction. These grades are based upon a survey of the site, usually made by a professional surveyor. The main floor of the building should be given a grade, and the elevations of the new grounds and walks should be indicated either by spot grades or by grade lines, which represent the cut that would result if all the ground above any particular elevation were removed.

In the United States grade elevations are usually indicated in feet and tenths or hundredths of a foot (261.25'), rather than in feet and inches (261' 3"), just as plot plans are usually in engineers' rather than architects' scales.

Elevations. The plans of the architect are supplemented by the elevations. Whereas the plan is a horizontal graphic representation of the library to a scale, the elevation is its vertical representation to a scale. Like that of the building plans, this scale is almost always an architectural one. The elevations show the building heights and the location in the vertical planes of the doors, windows, and columns or supports on the various facades, and the materials from which they and the walls are built. Thus it also illustrates the appearance of the building. Since it is a graphic representation, there is no attempt at perspective, and the most distant facade is drawn to the same scale as the closest. For each elevation a "picture" plane is chosen, usually parallel to the facade which is represented, and nothing is illustrated on that elevation which is not reached by a line drawn perpendicular to that chosen plane. Thus a rectangular building can be fully illustrated by four direct elevations, one taken parallel to each of its four sides. The elevation of one of these sides shows no part of any other.

This would not be true of another building shape with five sides or with odd angles; at least one of its facades would be shown foreshortened on one of the picture planes parallel to the other sides, since it can be reached by lines drawn perpendicular to that plane. A circular, or curved, shape results in a gradual increase in this foreshortening in proportion as the curve recedes away from the picture plane.

The foreshortened part of an elevation always shows the actual scale of the vertical dimensions, but the horizontal scale is reduced in accordance with the degree at which the plan slopes away from the picture plane.

An elevation is drawn to give information necessary in the construction of a building. The locations of floors, roofs, and other objects hidden by the facade that is being illustrated are shown by dotted lines. The design of features, such as windows and doors, can be drawn carefully once and repeated elsewhere only in outline. The indication of materials is stylized and usually confined to one end of the elevation.

It can be seen, as a result, that an elevation drawing frequently gives a very inadequate idea of the aesthetic appearance of the building. Such drawings are often used, however, as the basis for an elevation "rendering," which represents in different colors or values the materials and openings of the building and which often ranks among the most interesting and artistic products from an architect's office. These, of course, are usually products of an earlier design phase.

To the layperson, however, the stylization required in an elevation and its lack of perspective make this type of rendering somewhat difficult to visualize. As a result, during schematics many architects furnish their clients with rendered perspective drawings or models, both of which illustrate the aesthetic appearance of the building with more realism and are generally better understood.

Sections. To illustrate a building completely, the plans and elevations are supplemented by one or more "sections." A section is a vertical cut through a chosen part of the building and exposes the elevations and vertical relationships of the spaces through which the building is cut. It shows ceiling heights, construction methods, stair details, and interior design, and furnishes an excellent visual picture of the spatial relationships in the building, which can only be deduced from the plans and elevations.

Illustrative sections are usually drawn to the architectural scale used for the plans or elevations. However, one of the most frequent uses of sections is to detail specific objects or features in the building, in which case they are drawn to a much larger architectural scale, usually ¾ in. or 3 in. (which would be 1:16 or 1:4 in metric scale), but sometimes as large as one-half or actual full size. Detail sections of this nature may be cut either vertically or horizontally and are used to explain the construction details and shapes of walls, windows, toilets, stairs, and any other architectural feature which needs such careful illustration in order to ensure that the required soundness and appearance will be incorporated into the building.

A plan, elevation, or section is said to be "reflected" when the surfaces it illustrates are behind or above, rather than before or below the chosen plane or cut being used on the particular drawing in question. A reflected ceiling plan is a common example.

Since plans, elevations, sections, and details for a building are drawings to a scale, a desired size or dimension can be ascertained from the drawings by the use of a rule or scale. In addition, important dimensions which cannot be left subject to the small inaccuracies attendant upon scaling are written on these drawings. Notes explaining the construction or specifying the finish or materials that are being illustrated supplement the drafted information. The extent of the written dimensions and the items noted are indicated with arrows or dots at the end of light connecting lines.

Schedules. Drawings can no longer contain sufficient information to enable a contractor to estimate and build a satisfactory building. They must be supplemented with written directions. Most of these are incorporated into schedules, which may either be included on the drawings or bound in the specifications. Such schedules are usually keyed by symbols, numbers, or letters to those parts of the drawings to which they apply.

Schedules are most frequently used in the following ways:

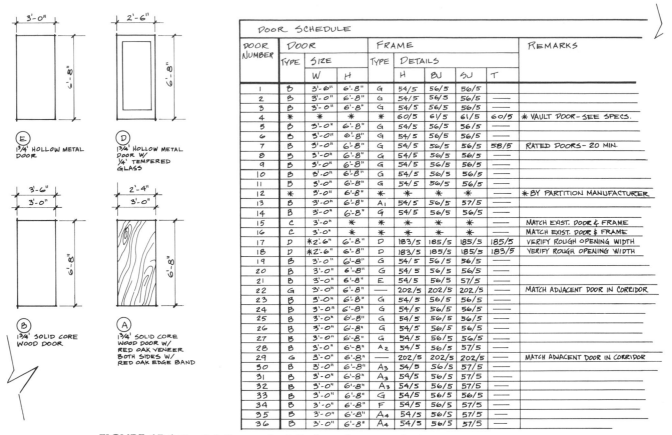

DOOR NUMBER	DOOR			FRAME					REMARKS
	TYPE	SIZE		TYPE	DETAILS				
		W	H		H	BJ	SJ	T	
1	B	3'-6"	6'-8"	G	54/5	56/5	56/5	—	
2	B	3'-0"	6'-8"	G	54/5	56/5	56/5	—	
3	B	3'-0"	6'-8"	G	54/5	56/5	56/5	—	
4	*	*	*	*	60/5	61/5	61/5	60/5	* VAULT DOOR–SEE SPECS.
5	B	3'-0"	6'-8"	G	54/5	56/5	56/5	—	
6	B	3'-0"	6'-8"	G	54/5	56/5	56/5	—	
7	B	3'-0"	6'-8"	G	54/5	56/5	56/5	58/5	RATED DOORS– 20 MIN.
8	B	3'-0"	6'-8"	G	54/5	56/5	56/5	—	
9	B	3'-0"	6'-8"	G	54/5	56/5	56/5	—	
10	B	3'-0"	6'-8"	G	54/5	56/5	56/5	—	
11	B	3'-0"	6'-8"	G	54/5	56/5	56/5	—	
12	*	3'-0"	6'-8"	*	*	*	*	—	* BY PARTITION MANUFACTURER
13	B	3'-0"	6'-8"	A1	54/5	56/5	57/5	—	
14	B	3'-0"	6'-8"	G	54/5	56/5	56/5	—	
15	C	3'-0"	*	*	*	*	*	—	MATCH EXIST. DOOR & FRAME
16	C	3'-0"	*	*	*	*	*	—	MATCH EXIST. DOOR & FRAME
17	D	*2'-6"	6'-8"	D	183/5	185/5	185/5	185/5	VERIFY ROUGH OPENING WIDTH
18	D	*2'-6"	6'-8"	D	183/5	185/5	185/5	183/5	VERIFY ROUGH OPENING WIDTH
19	B	3'-0"	6'-8"	G	54/5	56/5	56/5	—	
20	B	3'-0"	6'-8"	G	54/5	56/5	56/5	—	
21	B	3'-0"	6'-8"	E	54/5	56/5	57/5	—	
22	G	3'-0"	6'-8"	—	202/5	202/5	202/5	—	MATCH ADJACENT DOOR IN CORRIDOR
23	B	3'-0"	6'-8"	G	54/5	56/5	56/5	—	
24	B	3'-0"	6'-8"	G	54/5	56/5	56/5	—	
25	B	3'-0"	6'-8"	G	54/5	56/5	56/5	—	
26	B	3'-0"	6'-8"	G	54/5	56/5	56/5	—	
27	B	3'-0"	6'-8"	G	54/5	56/5	56/5	—	
28	B	3'-0"	6'-8"	A2	54/5	56/5	57/5	—	
29	G	3'-0"	6'-8"	—	202/5	202/5	202/5	—	MATCH ADJACENT DOOR IN CORRIDOR
30	B	3'-0"	6'-8"	A3	54/5	56/5	57/5	—	
31	B	3'-0"	6'-8"	A3	54/5	56/5	57/5	—	
32	B	3'-0"	6'-8"	A3	54/5	56/5	57/5	—	
33	B	3'-0"	6'-8"	G	54/5	56/5	56/5	—	
34	B	3'-0"	6'-8"	F	54/5	56/5	57/5	—	
35	B	3'-0"	6'-8"	A4	54/5	56/5	57/5	—	
36	B	3'-0"	6'-8"	A4	54/5	56/5	57/5	—	

FIGURE 15.1 Partial door schedule for a large project

1. *Room or finish schedules.* These schedules tabulate the materials which will form the finished surfaces of the walls, floors, ceilings, base, and dado, and verbally point out any special feature which may be required in a particular room. In order to key a room or finish schedule to the plans, each room is given a name, area designation, or number on both the plan and schedule. The finish schedule then tabulates the finishes after each space designation.

2. *Door schedules.* The doors or openings inside the building may be of different widths, heights, design, and material. (See fig. 15.1.) They may be solid or may contain glass panels. They may be flush wood or paneled metal. They may be hung in wood frames or metal bucks, which in turn may have sidelights or transoms. Ventilation requirements may call for the use of louvers in the doors or for leaving a specified amount of clear space between the bottom and the floor. Sound or temperature insulation may require soundproofing or weatherstripping.

The individual requirements for doors may be, and usually are, many and varied. As a result, each door or opening in the building is given a symbol which refers directly to the schedule, where the size and other characteristics can immediately be determined. This schedule is usually accompanied by scale elevations showing the main type of door designs which are being described.

3. *Hardware schedules, painting schedules, furniture schedules, and stack schedules.* These schedules relate to or supplement the finish and door schedules. Supplementary schedules such as these are often compiled during, rather than before the construction of the building, but they should be completed in time to have the materials and work based on them ready for installation and performance without delaying the progress of the job.

4. *Mechanical schedules.* Schedules for the finished materials required for the mechanical trades are important items in the appearance of the building. Electrical, plumbing, and heating fixtures have a functional purpose, and also a conspicuous and extensive aesthetic effect. Their location and use are generally keyed into the mechanical plans by schedules, and an adequate understanding of the completed library cannot be reached without carefully consulting these schedules.

5. *Engineering schedules.* The structural engineering also needs to be supplemented by schedules which indicate to the builder the size and strength of columns, beams, and floor slabs. If they are of steel, the size and weight must be given; if of concrete, the dimensions, the amount of reinforcing, and the strength of the mix is tabulated.

6. *Fixture schedules.* The electrical engineer will supply information sufficient to identify each light fixture in a schedule. (See fig. 15.2.) It is often surprising how many different light fixtures there will be in a new building.

Specifications. The drawings and the schedules explain and illustrate the size,

shape, finish, and relationship of all the spaces, walls, and materials contained in the building. They do not specify the quality of the materials or the level of the workmanship. These are described and enumerated in a written specification which accompanies and complements the drawings. In their modern form in the United States, specifications group under the various trades or suppliers all the work in the building which each will perform or furnish. The required quality is carefully explained and the expected performance of all materials is specified. The method of workmanship is described and procedures explained. The control of materials and work-

LIGHTING FIXTURE SCHEDULE

TYPE	DESCRIPTION

A	Recessed fluorescent fixture with oneway deep cell parabolic louver containing one F35T12 lamp and one single lamp ballast. See spec. Section 16500/2.03C for additional requirements.
	    Columbia #4551G-43-141-SU/A
	    Lightolier #CD1791R-1

AA	Same description as fixture Type A except fixture contains a two lamp ballast.
	    Columbia #4551G-43-141-SU/AA
	    Lightolier #CD1791R-1

AB	Same description as fixture Type A except the fixture does not contain a ballast, i.e., the lamp in this fixture is served from the two lamp ballast located in fixture Type AA.

B	Same description as fixture Type A except fixture contains two F35T12 lamps and one two lamp ballast.
	    Columbia #4551G-43-142-SU/B
	    Lightolier #CD1791R1-3

C	Recessed two lamp fluorescent fixture with one-way deep cell, parabolic louver assembly of semi-specular anodized aluminum sheet secured to housing with concealed latches. Die-formed steel housing with louvered or slotted back for plenum air return through the fixture, "quick connect" plate to permit wiring without opening fixture wire way, and perimeter slots with adjustable blade dampers for return air capability directly into the plenum. Provide snap-on shrouds for installation of fixtures in concealed spline ceiling in continuous rows as shown. Perimeter air slot finished in matte black; trim frame matte white baked-on enamel. Two F35T12 lamps.
	    Columbia #451G-43-142-HE-S
	    Lightolier #68574-HE-MOD

D	Surface mounted 4'-0" fluorescent fixture with extruded prismatic acrylic wrap-around diffuser and injection molded end caps. Two F35T12 lamps per fixture. Fixture rated for installation on low density ceilings.
	    Lightolier #10321-LD
	    Sylvania #ND-2404-LD

EA	Ceiling recessed mounted "edge-lit" exit sign with 277 volt ballast for F8T6 fluorescent lamps. Housing and trim shall be diecast aluminum. 6" high x 3/4" stroke engraved green letters on white background. Provide two F8T6 lamps (2 circuit) per housing. Ceiling trim plate to be painted matte white. Provide directional arrows as shown on drawings.
	    Prescolite #ER7 Series
	    McPhilben #45AR-6-F Series

FIGURE 15.2 Lighting fixture schedule. This is one of 9 pages of the fixture schedule for a large project in which some 57 different fixtures are described. In this case, they are part of the specifications.

manship explained in a carefully written specification can aid materially in accomplishing a satisfactory result both aesthetically and functionally.

Often the desired result or quality can best be attained by specifying one particular material or manufacturer. It may well be decided that the granite or limestone from a predetermined quarry is necessary for the proper appearance of the building, or that a particular stack or elevator manufacturer can best satisfy the functional requirements of the library. If so, only that material or, if legal, the particular manufacturer should be specified. In buildings for private institutions, this can be done directly by name or carried in the contract documents as an "allowance" of the amount of money determined as necessary for its purchase or installation. The specification may name a firm producing the required quality and add "or equal," thereby allowing others to bid but placing on them the requirement for proof of equivalency in every respect. If, however, other materials or manufacturers are considered as equals, the specifications will also name them. For public institutions or those projects funded by government agencies, the general requirement is that at least three manufacturers or suppliers be named, and the naming of only one is not allowed, except under unusual circumstances. If allowances are permitted in public work, the work covered by such a budget line must also be let competitively.

Specifications often describe in detail the material or manufactured items desired and allow any supplier or manufacturer who is able to satisfy the specifications to furnish the required items. It is common to treat metal bookshelving in this fashion. Several pages may be devoted to important details from bookends to cantilevered shelf brackets and from the quality of paint finish to the acceptable forms of interior cross bracing. If one or more names "or equal" are specified, the architect is responsible for deciding if a particular product is actually equal, although the owner often is a key part of this decision.

Specifications of shelving may need to be very detailed. The Harvard Depository, for example, required paint on the 6 ft (1.829) deep shelving to be non-acidic. The 18 in. (450 mm) long book trays, stored at right angles to the shelving, were specified to meet tests of strength, durability, ease of assembly, and potential acidity. Trays were sealed with a coating which gives a pH of 9.90, resists abrasion, and prevents absorption of acid, other gases, and moisture. Should the sealant wear away, each run of the paper composing the trays was tested to ensure non-acidity; paper pH was held between 7.2 and 8.5 and the pH of the glues between 10 and 10.5.

The sectional division into trades and suppliers most frequently used in specifications today is as follows: general requirements; site work; excavation and grading; concrete work; masonry; waterproofing; roofing; structural steel; miscellaneous metal work; doors, windows, and frames; carpentry; lathing and plastering; tile work; flooring; painting; glass and glazing; and the "mechanical trades,"i.e., plumbing; heating, ventilating, and air conditioning; and electrical work.

The last three sectional divisions of the specifications listed immediately above, the "mechanical trades," cover work which has become more important in recent years. For instance, in 1900, in a good many library buildings which are still in use today, the cost of the work assigned to the mechanical trades was no more than 15 percent of the total construction cost of the job. Today, it is rarely less than 35 percent and, if the library is air conditioned, may run as high as 45 percent.

As the importance of the mechanical trades in building construction has increased, so has the complexity of the installations. Electrical and pneumatic controls, computers, transformers, motors, fans, pumps, switchboards, valves, and contactors, to name the more usual devices hidden from view in panels, closets, and mechanical rooms, multiply with every added mechanical comfort; space is required to house them, and new building laws or regulations must be satisfied in order to ensure that any possible faulty operation will not create a hazard to the occupants or contents of the building. Just as the structural engineer prepares structural drawings and specifications and assures the architect that the strength of the floors, walls, and columns will be adequate to support the loads expected to be imposed on them by the building, its contents, and its occupants, the architect also engages mechanical engineers who are responsible for assuring the proper installation and operation of the mechanical systems. To accomplish this, these engineers prepare special plans devoted entirely to illustrating the work of the mechanical trades, write their sections of the specifications, and compile any schedules pertaining to these specifications and drawings.

The architect may employ one engineer to prepare the drawings and specifications for all the mechanical work or one or more separate specialists in the engineering work required for each of the three trades, that is, a heating, ventilating and air-conditioning engineer, an electrical and lighting engineer, and a sanitary and plumbing engineer.

These engineers are responsible to the architect for the preparation of drawings illustrating the installation and operation of the work assigned to their respective trades. These installations will occupy space and affect the appearance of the building, and their operation will be accompanied by a certain amount of noise and will affect the comfort of the occupants. In order to ensure that the satisfactory operation of the mechanical plant will not adversely affect either the aesthetics or the function of the library, the engineering drawings and specifications prepared to illustrate the mechanical trades must be coordinated with the architectural drawings and specifications prepared to illustrate the space relationships, sizes, finishes, and structure.

This coordination among the mechanical trades, the structure, the architecture, and the furnishings is difficult at best and can be only accomplished if the drawings ensure space enough in plan and elevation for the equipment, ductwork, and piping, and if they assign proper locations in the library areas for the visible parts of the installations. Every detail must be consonant with comfort and aesthetics and must not allow the work of one trade to conflict with that of another. In addition to this coordination on the drawings, the specifications require coordination on the job between trades; they state which trade will have precedence in the choice of the space available; and they indicate that the mechanical drawings are, of necessity, largely diagrammatic, so that the actual job installation must be made to fit precisely into the space assigned to it on the drawing or available for it on the job.

Addenda, Shop, and Detail Drawings. The architect has three other written instruments which are employed during the bidding and construction periods to ensure the completeness and proper interpretation of the working drawings and specifications.

The first of these is the addendum, which is a written amplification of the contract documents distributed after they have been issued to the bidders just before the bids have been received. It is the result of a careful review of the drawings and specifications by the architect, engineers, and the institution, a review which is often conducted during the bidding period and which should correct any discrepancies, conflicts, errors, omissions, or misunderstandings which may have crept into these documents during their preparation. Since addenda are prepared and issued before the award of a contract, they become part of the contract documents and are just as binding on the building contractor as the basic drawings and specifications.

The second and third of these instruments are produced during the construction period. The architect, during this period, may issue explanatory detail drawings, sometimes called "clarifications," which will enlarge and clarify sections of the original drawings so that the parts in question may be manufactured and installed in exact accordance with the functional and aesthetic requirements.

Much the same objective is also attained by shop drawings. The difference between a shop drawing and a detail drawing is that, whereas the latter is produced by the architect and permitted by the specifications, the former is required by the specifications and produced by the contractor and approved by the architect. Both are valuable tools, and both may make as important a contribution to the success of the work as do the supervision of construction and the written directives of the architect.

Details can be very important to review. For example, a seaming diagram may be required for carpet installations, at least for critical traffic areas, to guard against maintenance problems at seams which could appear much earlier than should be expected given normal wear.

15.3 The Type of Contract

The librarian should be aware of the fact that there are a number of different ways that a contract can be established. The decision as to how the contract will be set up may be made quite early in the project, but certainly no later than the end of the contract document phase. Most of the discussion in the preceding section assumed that the contract was based upon a competitive bid. Other contract methods include construction management (sometimes called CM), turnkey, design-build, fast track, negotiated based on cost plus overhead, negotiated as a lump sum, or a combination. Each of these will be discussed briefly.

Competitive Bid. This is probably the most common form of establishing a contract in the United States. For obvious reasons, it should assure the best possible price, provided the contract documents are clear and complete and provided reputable contractors bid the job. There are risks and consequent steps that can be taken to reduce those risks, though these go beyond the scope of this volume. Where there are unusual problems of working in an existing occupied building, and if the project is to be competitively bid, great care must be taken to ensure a smooth operation. In the case of the occupied building, probably some form of a negotiated contract is the safest, but unfortunately, this is not always possible. It should be noted that competitive bids are the norm for projects in publicly-financed institutions and are often required by governmental regulation. The lowest qualified bid must ordinarily be taken, for equipment as well as for construction and landscaping. Such a policy which requires contracting with the low bidder under competition is regarded as a protection against political pressures, thus reducing the chances of deals and kickbacks.

Construction Management. One technique of cost control is to hire a construction manager early in the design process to work with the design team to achieve the best product for the least cost. The construction manager in this case is usually a contractor who provides "value engineering." In the pure construction management project, the construction manager will provide cost estimates through the design process with a guarantee that the project can be constructed for the estimated price. At the completion of design, assuming that everyone finds the estimated cost within reason, the construction manager takes over as the general contractor as agreed upon by the last estimate. The weakness is that it is nearly impossible to know if the price is realistic. The advantage, of course, is that the general contractor is very much part of the project from virtually the beginning, which can be very beneficial.

A construction management contract can easily be segmented so that at the end of the contract documents phase, should the institution wish, the arrangement can be terminated and the project put out for competitive bid. But if this is likely, the construction manager should know from the start. It should be noted that there are fees involved for the construction management process.

Turnkey. A turnkey project is one in which the architect and/or construction manager is handed the program, schedule, and budget (or request for proposal) at the beginning, and it is agreed that the project will be produced within the schedule and budget for a fixed price. This technique is particularly well suited for a tight schedule. It is not very responsive to the evolution of the design in response to a changing environment, as the review process may be very limited. It has been used in academic institutions, and it has merit under certain circumstances. However, the authors would be reluctant to recommend this technique in most cases. An exception might be a warehouse storage facility, though even then the program must be exceptionally thorough if the product is to meet fully the needs of the institution.

Design-Build. A variation of the turnkey project is the design-build concept which may take several forms; the following outline suggests the general procedure. First, a very complete program is developed, including the detailing of basic design and planning requirements. The building module, size, and shape; the size and location of wall openings, stairs, rooms, and other building and site elements; the design criteria for the structural, electrical, and mechanical systems including the testing requirements; and the bottom line budget figure are established with considerable care. The detail necessary in the program phase is such that a person well established in architectural construction must be involved, and unless this expertise is available in house, there will be fees to be added to the established budget figure.

The second step takes the form of a competition. Again, the program must spell out the exact details. One project allows the prequalified participants three weeks to review the program (in this case referred to as a request for proposal, or RFP), after which eight weeks are provided for the development of the participant's proposal. All drawings and other documentation are to be carefully prepared to hide the identity of the participant during the judging process. The process, for example, involves specifying exactly the paper to be used for the drawings, as well as the use of a separate auditing firm who receives the documentation and assigns numbers to each item. The judging process is also detailed. It may involve a system of quality points which are assigned to the proposal. The winning entry is thus the one with the lowest price per quality point. Any entry that exceeds the basic budget is rejected.

In the example referred to, the winner receives the contract, and the five runners-up receive a stipend of $5000 each. This cost, as well as the cost of administration for the competition, must also be added to the base budget to determine the total project cost.

The third phase establishes a firm contract for the preparation of the construction documents and the construction itself for a fixed fee. The construction may be either conventional or fast track, as discussed below. Alternatives are not allowed, and change orders are strictly the responsibility of the contractor.

As with the turnkey process, the evolution of the design in concert with the librarian and evolving library needs is limited. It is an interesting concept that warrants consideration, but it may not be ideal for exceedingly complex projects. As with any approach, there are risks.

Fast Track. The fast-track approach to a project breaks the project up into several sequential projects such as site preparation and mass excavation, footings and foundations, the structural shell, the exterior envelope and interior partitions, and interior finishes and equipment. The concept holds that while construction is under way on one phase, the design work can continue on the next phase, resulting in an accelerated schedule and presumably cost savings, especially in an era of high inflation. There are substantial risks with the fast-track method, and it probably should only be considered for a fairly straightforward project which might have extended over one or more years. Among the risks are changing code requirements, a lack of firm commitment to a final budgeted cost for much of the project, and the risk that a design change at a later date will render earlier work obsolete. Except under special circumstances of exceptional urgency, the authors are reluctant to recommend the fast-track method.

Negotiated Contract. Just as the name implies, a negotiated contract exists when a single contractor is asked to submit a proposal for a project. Design contracts are, in effect, negotiated contracts. They can be based on cost plus overhead, with perhaps an agreed-upon maximum, or they can be a fixed-price contract, often called a lump-sum contract. Contractors welcome negotiated contracts as the risk of losing money is almost zero. By the same token, negotiated contracts usually will cost more, although this is difficult to prove unless there is also a competitive bid. However, it is unlikely that a contractor will provide a proposal for a negotiated contract when there is also going to be a competitive bid. One or the other technique must be chosen.

The major advantage of the negotiated contract is that there is greater flexibility to work with the contractor in refining schedules, construction techniques, or even design details during the course of the project. The negotiated contract is especially suitable in difficult renovation work when the scheduling may be very complex or where there is a great deal of unknown work in an existing structure. Most publicly funded institutions can only use a negotiated contract under very unusual conditions; and on most large projects it is probably not an appropriate approach even in very remote or difficult locations.

Combination. For a given circumstance a combination of the above techniques may be used. For example, a negotiated contract with a construction manager may be formulated to oversee the work, but the subcontractors may be required to submit competitive bids with final acceptance by the institution. Or the excavation might be contracted as a negotiated bid, and the balance of the work as a competitive bid. The concept of the fast track method might involve the prepurchase by the institution of major items, such as the structural steel or the mechanical equipment, which is then assigned to the contractor once construction starts.

Nearly all of the techniques have good and bad points; the final decision will be in the hands of the institution's business offices, with the advice of the architect and perhaps the institution's project or construction experts. For the librarian the area of greatest concern will likely be in renovation projects in an occupied facility where the ongoing operational needs of the library must be accommodated. The nature of the contract will dramatically affect the specifications and drawings in this case, as the more competitive the bid, the more carefully one must describe the requirements of the project to ensure expected results. Another way of looking at this is to expect that with greater competition, more change orders will be required as surprises are found and room for negotiation is limited.

In most cases, but not all, the type of bid received determines the method of contract award. Thus a lump-sum bid usually results in a lump-sum contract, an estimated cost-plus-fee bid in a cost-plus-fee contract, and a guaranteed-maximum estimate in a guaranteed-maximum-cost contract. Public authorities are usually required to let all building contracts on a lump-sum basis. The advantages of this type of contract are several. In theory, the cost of construction can be budgeted at a specific amount, and all risks of actual costs greater than those estimated are assumed by the contractor. However, the fact is that there will be change orders, which are discussed later. On the open and highly competitive construction market, lower bids are apt to be realized than by any other method. Of particular importance to the public authorities is the fact that such bidding eliminates the possibility of favoritism if the award is made to the lowest responsible bidder. Frequently, on private work, the bidders are limited to an invited or previously approved group of contractors whose former work has been satisfactory to the institution and the architect. In this case, also, the award is usually made to the lowest bidder. The institution, however, in both public and private work, retains the right to reject any and all bids, if it is in its or the public's interest legally to do so.

The lowest bid does not always provide the best building. If time of completion is a factor, if the quality of construction desired is unusually high, if the project requires an extraordinary approach to the design and methods of erection, or if the proper determination of the full scope of the work by means of drawings and specifications is difficult, the fee type of contract is frequently used.

A fee contract is usually negotiated directly with a chosen contractor of predetermined competence and ability, but the selection is sometimes the result of competitive bidding between two or more. The final choice between them can be based either on the fee requested, the amount of the estimated cost,

the time required for completion, or any combination of the three. This type of contract has every advantage except that of predetermined minimal cost. Because of the careful selection of bidders, the choice of a contractor may be made and construction begun before the drawings and specifications are fully finished. Thus months may be cut from the schedule for completion of construction. The contractor is one selected on the basis of ability rather than of minimal cost, and the institution and architect have much greater control over construction procedures and purchases. The advice, experience, and cooperation of the contractor are made available during the determination of building procedures and costs rather than afterwards.

In any case, when the plans and specifications have been prepared, the bids have been received, and the contract has been let, a new member of the planning team has been chosen. The contractor enters the picture, and actual construction begins. Obviously, the contractor is essential to the success of the project, perhaps at this stage the most important member of the team, for upon the contractor's shoulders rests the responsibility to construct what has earlier been only a concept drawn from the minds of architects, librarians, and engineers and set down in diagrams and words on paper.

15.4 The Review Process

This section will discuss the review process and, to some extent, the planning process that occurs following bidding and during construction.

Once the bids are opened, the bid is good for a fixed period of time as specified in the contract documents. Sixty days is typical. During this period, the successful contractor is selected and a period of review and/or negotiation takes place. The bid review rarely will involve the librarian although the librarian may have some interest in assuring that certain aspects are carefully considered.

In a competitive bid, if the bids are all within 10 percent of each other, there is reasonable assurance that a good bid has been received. A "good" bid means that bidders did a thorough job, did material "take offs" carefully, and prepared estimates with a minimum of padding over their necessary margin of profit. A set of bids which range much more than 10 percent may indicate a booming construction business climate which is not favorable to the institution, or that the drawings and specifications have omissions or ambiguities which the contractor covers by bidding higher than would otherwise have been necessary, or that the institution's reputation suggests extra meetings or time delays which can push up costs to the contractor. Where there is one exceptionally low bid, there is always the possibility of an error on the part of the contractor. Unless there are human errors or other problems, such as an incomplete bid, the lowest bidder should be awarded the contract provided the bid is within the established budget. In this instance, the review process will likely be limited to checking that all of the bid requirements have been met and that the contractor's firm is financially sound.

Should the limitations of the budget or a low bid suggest a change in the project scope, there will follow a period of negotiation. In contracts which involve public funds, it is generally required, and in all competitive bidding it is wise, to limit any change in contract scope after receipt of bids to a small percentage of the total proposed construction cost, generally 5 percent. Thus a proposed construction bid of $1,000,000 can be legally and properly negotiated up to $1,050,000 or down to $950,000, by changing the scope of the work after consultation with the contractor.

If, however, the desired change in proposed construction cost is greater than 5 percent, some amount of competitive rebidding is generally advisable from the point of view of the institution and is more considerate of the bidders. This rebidding may be confined to the three or four lowest original general contract bidders, and even to certain subcontract bidders, such as those for heating and ventilating, electrical, or plumbing work, if the increase or decrease in the scope of work is to be confined to one or more of these trades.

The use of additive or deductive alternates is another common way of dealing with this problem. The advantage of alternates is that each is quoted or bid before the fact, which should result in better prices.

The problem becomes a bit more difficult if the low bidder is substantially below the next lowest bidder. Here, the concern is that an error has been made or there was a misinterpretation of the contract documents. The owner may wish to review the bid with the low bidder and perhaps the second lowest bidder to try to understand the reason for the discrepancy. The review process may follow the format of the cost model as discussed in Chapter 9. If an error is found in the low bid, it should be rejected, or the bidder should be allowed to withdraw, and the next lowest bid taken. Negotiations with the low competitive bidder to compensate for an error would normally be regarded as unethical. Furthermore, entering a contract with a contractor who has made a known mistake will result in later problems; to do so is not good business practice.

With a negotiated contract the review process is limited to a comparison of the contractor's quote with earlier estimates prepared by the architect or a separate cost estimator. The comparison might be along the lines of the cost model approach. The negotiation might include altering the requirements of the contract to keep the cost within the budget, or identifying errors or misunderstandings and taking corrective action. Here, negotiation in regard to an error is completely ethical as there is no competition involved.

A second area of review and perhaps negotiation is for a change in proposed subcontractors who are, for one reason or another, more acceptable to the institution or the architect. In any case, a list of the principal subcontractors which the general contractor proposes to use should be reviewed and agreed upon. Sometimes a change in subcontractors may be negotiated without change in the proposed cost, but more frequently a small increase is required in order to effect such changes.

In public bidding for states and cities in the United States, the principal subcontractors may be required by law to submit "filed" bids, that is, bids the amounts of which are public knowledge, or even to submit the separate bids directly to the awarding authorities.

In private work in the United States, the general contractors are sometimes required to name the principal subcontractors and their respective costs in the bid proposal, but separate bids are rarely taken on any subcontract. If closer control of the subcontractor selection is desired, the "allowance" method is usually employed.

In work requiring funds from the United States federal government, the naming of subcontractors or the filing of their bids is usually omitted and sometimes forbidden under present construction procedures. The omission of this requirement from the bidding rules generally results in a lower total construction bid.

When the subcontractors' bids are filed, or recorded, a change from one subcontractor to another may be made by adding or, rarely, deducting the recorded difference in bids to or from the total proposed cost. Under most public bidding laws the contractor is not restricted in the choice of subbidders, but the institution is required to accept the lowest responsible subbidder. In private institutional work no such restriction exists, and a discreet review of the subcontractors who will be employed on the work may be an advantageous procedure.

A third type of review that may occur before signing the contract takes the form of an interview with the contractor and the proposed construction superintendent. Such an interview would be outlined in the bid package, including a description of the nature of the concerns to be addressed in the interview. While the interview process probably is not a very effective means of assuring a certain quality level, it does serve to introduce the key players and to express particular concerns about the project. Of course, this can also occur at the construction kick-off meeting discussed later.

After these negotiations, if required, have been completed, or even during the negotiation period, general contractors may be willing to commence construction upon receipt of a "letter of intent." Such a letter, sent to the contractor by an authorized officer of the institution or by the architect, states the conditions under which it is the intent to award the contract. Work may then be commenced, pending the preparation, approval, and signing of the formal contractual documents, and pending the receipt of the building permit which is usually obtained by the contractor.

Once the contract is signed, there may be a construction kick-off meeting, including members of the design team, the contractor, perhaps several major subcontractors, and others, such as the institution's risk manager, fire marshal, and construction manager. This meeting has three purposes. First, it serves as an introduction of each of the key officers for the project. Second, it offers a forum for questions such as, where do you want the excavated dirt? Or, how are parking permits obtained for the construction crew? Or, is there any preference about where the job

shack is to be placed? Third, it is an opportunity for various persons to underscore special concerns. For example, the fire marshal may be concerned about maintaining emergency access to nearby buildings. The architect may have a concern about the finish quality of exposed concrete. The project manager may have concerns about the employment of minority personnel. The librarians may have special concerns about water, dust, noise, and power outages.

During the course of construction, the routinely scheduled site meetings will provide a major vehicle for review. The librarian or library representative should be a member of the site meeting group. While much of the discussion will not involve the librarian, there will be issues and discussions the results of which can affect the future operations of the library. The architect will keep and distribute minutes of the site meetings. It is helpful if the minutes indicate the status of each issue, and who is responsible for action. An unresolved issue should reappear in each set of minutes until resolved in order to avoid forgetting or losing an issue that may need attention.

Where there are change orders or field orders (discussed in Section 15.6) that deal with finishes, fixtures, or details affecting the utility or operation of the facility, the project manager should ensure that the library representative has a chance to review the issue. This assurance often will be given orally in the site meeting, but it may involve reviewing the documentation prepared by the architect. A similar opportunity to review the documents should occur with the shop drawings; yet the librarian will need to be watchful, for the shop drawings all too often are approved without the librarian's involvement. Most of the shop drawings will be of little interest to the librarian, but those dealing with built-ins, special equipment, or shelving are very important. The librarian should insist upon being involved in the review of those shop drawings of special interest.

Finally, there will be the inspections in which the librarian will no doubt be involved from time to time. During a tour of the project, it is quite reasonable to ask questions, however, one must not tell the contractor what to do! Should there be a problem, one should take it up with the inspector or project manager.

15.5 Special Concerns

During a task which will occupy many people on highly skilled and unskilled jobs over many months, with constantly changing conditions and many hazardous situations, the library staff will need to be alert to a few matters.

Construction Zone. This area is specified in the contract documents. The owner or client may specify another area for the parking of cars, although construction workers will not walk very far, and they usually arrive well before the library staff in the morning. Routes for hauling heavy loads may be approved to keep from interfering unduly with other activities, to minimize hazards to students walking or bicycling, or to protect a secondary campus road with inadequate roadbed which cannot handle very heavy vehicles. The designated contractor's yard is off limits to all others without special permission, and there are legal liability reasons to be scrupulous in observing the limits. Job review meetings will usually be held in the general contractor's office on the site. However, visits to the project, usually with hard hats, must be approved by the clerk of works and, until the very last stages, are usually escorted due to the many hazards which can exist. Arrangements for workers to pass through or work in a connecting building outside the construction zone can become and should be a matter of agreement at a job review meeting. These intrusions, however, are difficult to control; library staff can expect some surprises no matter how much planning and discussion have occurred.

Schedule. The contract may deal with the question of when the finished building will be turned over to the institution and made available for installing the movable furniture and equipment that is not included in the basic contract. This may be handled in one of four ways, as follows:

1. The contract may make no mention of time—a procedure that is not recommended.
2. It may state an estimated time for completion (usually based on calendar days).
3. It may state an agreed-upon time for completion.
4. It may state an agreed-upon time for completion with penalty and benefit payments if time is delayed or bettered.

If either 3 or 4 is to be used, it should be included in the bid form or the negotiations; 4 is rarely used in institutional work, since its chief application is to commercial business which can make or lose money through early or late completion dates. In other words, it may be argued that an actual monetary loss must be demonstrated before a contractor will be required to pay a penalty. However, this does not prevent the inclusion of a penalty clause in the contract with a predetermined fee to be charged for each day (specified as a working or calendar day) that beneficial occupancy is delayed. One should realize, though, that this penalty is very rarely applied. The contractor has other incentives, including the final payment, to ensure that the project is completed in a timely manner.

While an agreed-upon completion date is a little more forceful than an estimated date, it is impossible to enforce if the agreement is not met, and means little more than an estimated date. Either the estimated or agreed-upon construction period is quite common in institutional work, but both generally represent optimistic estimates on the part of the contractor, and the inevitable and usually excusable delays sometimes postpone completion quite seriously.

The following factors may affect the building construction and, therefore, the completion date.

1. The start of construction may be delayed. There are a variety of possible causes.
   a. The contract documents may be delayed because the architect fails to complete the task on schedule. The firm may have been delayed by the institution's constantly holding up decisions on vital points, by a shortage of help, or by the inability to get the details from the engineers who are doing the mechanical services or other planning. Any of these, in turn, could hold up approval by a governmental authority and delay issuance of the building permit.
   b. The time when the plans and specifications are ready may not be propitious for taking bids. An economic boom with great building activity may result in bids 10 percent higher than if they could have been taken earlier, and perhaps a delay may result in lower bids.
   c. Plans and specifications may be ready for the taking of bids during a strike. An increase in wages may result in higher prices, and contractors are cautious about making close bids. Fre-

quently there is an anticipated and sometimes a previously agreed-upon wage-rate increase which affects bidding, as the bidders are well aware that the increase is due to come. It does not necessarily have to be accompanied by a strike. A strike itself is no more likely to affect bidding than the anticipation of one. A strike during construction will delay completion but may not materially affect the cost to the institution, unless the contract contains some form of negotiated cost-plus-fee agreements.

    d. Weather conditions may be unfavorable. In many areas a late spring, for instance, may delay the start of work for two or three weeks. Frozen ground, a late heavy snow, an early beginning of the rainy period, and so on are all possible delaying factors.

2. Local labor conditions may affect the completion. Labor may not be available at the required time. Strikes, for instance, may interfere, or a building boom in a nearby city may attract labor away from the job. The contractor is anxious to carry on the work at a pace that will provide the largest possible profit. The construction company does not want to have to import labor from outside the area at extra cost. On the other hand, the longer it has to keep its team in operation, the lower the profit tends to be.

3. The nature of change orders can have a major effect. A poor foreman may be unable to get the work properly coordinated, and considerable delay in finishing the task may result, or the contractor may become engrossed in more profitable work elsewhere and not push the library project. The effectiveness of the owner's or architect's job inspector is another factor; if omissions and poor workmanship are reported week by week, there should be less corrective action on the punch list at the end, and mop-up tasks can be done far more expeditiously.

4. Soil, weather, and supply of materials or heavy equipment may slow down construction. Faulty or unfortunate test borings that have failed to discover ledge rock, pockets of quicksand or peat, or other soil conditions affecting the foundation can cause considerable delays. Unexpected wet spells or a very severe winter may also bring about loss of progress before the roof is on and the exterior walls closed in. If much of the material for use within the structure is brought in from a distance, there is always a possibility of delay, first at the point where it is fabricated and second in transportation to the site.

It can be seen from the above that "there is many a slip 'twixt the cup and the lip." At any rate, the time schedule should be given careful consideration, and the contractor should be requested to notify the institution as promptly as possible if any delay is anticipated in the completion date so that the institution can alter its plans. These may be of very great importance to accommodate to a new semester, to meet a schedule for the old building to be used for other purposes, or to receive furniture deliveries and plan book collection moves which require careful scheduling, hiring of special crews, or other preparations. The simple matter of scheduling a dedication can become a major issue if the schedule is not clear.

The contractor is usually required to prepare a project schedule showing the time frame for each of the major segments of work. This schedule may be a critical path chart, a bar chart, or some other technique (see fig. 15.3), though the method used is not of prime importance. What is important is that the schedule should be maintained and updated. As delays occur or are anticipated, for whatever reason, they should be noted on the schedule. This sounds very reasonable and simple, but in fact it is a problem to achieve. The job superintendent, who is the key manager of the construction effort, is likely to be so wrapped up in day-to-day activities that scheduling anything more than a week in advance is unlikely. Typically, where a master schedule is required, it is prepared on a computer by a scheduling specialist who is only vaguely familiar with the plans, who probably knows nothing about the site conditions, and who may know very little about the mode of operation of a particular contractor. Without information from the manager in the field, this schedule has little value. To be useful, it must be maintained on a weekly basis. This activity should thus be a basic requirement to be undertaken as part of the site meeting process.

One final point about the schedule. The schedule logistics for the dedication were mentioned above. Because the dedication usually involves a number of busy people, it may need to be scheduled as much as a year in advance. Because of the uncertainties of construction, the prudent planner should allow ample time between the anticipated com-

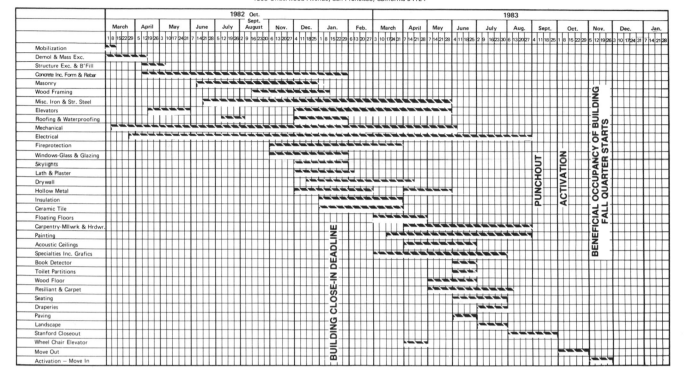

BRAUN MUSIC CENTER
LELAND STANFORD JR. UNIVERSITY
Progress Schedule
Engstrum & Nourse-Stolte
1303 Underwood Avenue, San Francisco, California 94124

DATE: 3/31/82
REV: 11/15/82

FIGURE 15.3 Construction schedule. The schedule was prepared early in the construction phase of the project: activation actually occurred in late 1983 and early 1984, with the dedication in March 1984. The schedule reflects construction of a complex building with substantial attention to acoustics. The building is approximately 55,000 sq ft (5,100 m²) gross, of which the library represents nearly 45 percent of the space.

pletion of construction and the dedication date. On a major project six months may not be too much, and, even with this much time, there will likely be a rush to make the final preparations for the dedication.

Security and Hazards. With dozens of workers temporarily working on the library job, the chance for accidents is great. Heavy equipment is less the cause than the more mundane: just taking chances, cutting corners, or being careless or tired. The result can be an injured back, a cut, occasionally a broken bone or a fire or flood. Furthermore, theft of materials or tools can be a temptation. Thus safety rules and security are major concerns of contractors and of the institution.

The authorized construction zone is a principal worry. Yet from the institution's point of view, properties next to the project and traffic routes can be the chief concern. Utility trenches need proper barriers and flashing lights for nighttime warning. People on cam-

pus are so familiar with their customary routes that a small temporary digging may cause an accident. On most campuses bicycles are ridden on seemingly random routes, sometimes at high speed, and major accidents, even deaths have occurred. Motorbike riders sometimes act as if they have the right of way even when in pedestrian malls. So construction barriers and signs must be prominent and properly located to assure reasonable safety when construction is under way.

The institution has the right to expect reasonable cleanliness near and on the construction site. Lengths of lumber should not be left around. Broken glass, loose nails, flammable material, and other hazards need to be disposed of promptly. It is sad that nearly every major library construction has its accidents. If one worked with the college inspector who fell over a low barrier in a dark attic, dropped ten feet and lay unconscious for an hour, or if one remembers the old construction trade rule of thumb "for each million dollars, one life," one has reason to require good safety precautions.

In any work on a building addition, the security of the original building is made far more vulnerable. Temporary holes in walls, temporary walls, extra keys being distributed, and many strangers in and around the premises—these and similar lapses in security can result in loss. It is not the casual or professional book theft, but people who have little regard for higher education or libraries who may find appealing an electric typewriter, an upholstered chair, or a large bolt of carpeting. During construction projects, opportunities do present themselves to the unethical.

Temporary Heat. In cold climates construction in the winter months is complicated by the need to provide temporary heat, in order to prevent the freezing of building materials that initially contain moisture, such as concrete, mortar, plaster, adhesives, and paint, to dry out the building so that moisture damage to the finished materials may be avoided, and to eliminate the danger of "freeze-ups" in the mechanical and plumbing installations.

Temporary heat may be provided in many ways. In the open, concrete is usually poured only at above freezing temperatures, and it is then protected with straw covering until it has dried out, or "cured." Otherwise, this work is done under tarpaulins or similar tent coverings and kept above freezing by space heaters. Another technique is to use electric insulating blankets, although it is expensive. A concrete mix that more rapidly reaches its working strength will help reduce the expense. Antifreeze "admixtures" have been used in the concrete mix, but at the present time most engineers object to their use because of the effect they may have on the ultimate strength and durability of the mix. In any case, the new concrete must not be allowed to freeze until it has reached its design strength.

When the building's structural frame is in position, it may be completely or partially covered with a temporary skin of tarpaulins or plastic, often transparent, and the enclosed portions heated with space heaters. If the exterior walls are complete, only the window and door areas need this temporary protection in order to enclose the building.

The types of space heaters employed for temporary heat vary, depending upon whether gas, coal, oil, or electricity is used. The most commonly used types in very cold climates are charcoal braziers and oil-fired unit heaters, which are frequently equipped with electrically operated blowers.

When the heating system for the building has been installed and all window and door openings have been either permanently or temporarily closed against the weather, the contractor is frequently allowed to use the heating system for supplying temporary heat, provided always that no permanent damage to the system is allowed to result. Where this is permitted, the owner should insist on new filters before acceptance of the building.

In institutions which are equipped with central heating plants, the steam may be either sold to the contractor or provided free of charge if the quality of weather protection and the amount of heating requirements can be controlled.

In any case, all construction contracts for buildings in climates susceptible to subfreezing temperatures during the construction period should contain specified requirements for temporary heat, generally entirely at the expense of the contractor, who is responsible for closing in the construction and for maintaining and providing the labor, equipment, and fuel necessary to keep the closed-in space at several degrees above freezing temperatures. When the installation of finished woodwork, flooring, or painting is in progress, the required minimum temperature should be raised to simulate that of an occupied space (or about 60 to 65 degrees F, 16 to 18 degrees C).

Payments. Payments to the general contractor on account and to all subcontractors are usually made monthly and cover the cost of all labor and materials incorporated in the construction and all materials on the site at the time the application for the payment is made, less any retention that may be specified in the contract. This application is itemized and prepared about ten days before each monthly payment is due. It is submitted to the architect for approval and may be required to be supported by receipts or vouchers for material, labor, or subcontractor payments.

If a clerk of works or resident engineer is employed on the job, that person's approval of the contractor's application for payment is generally made a prerequisite to final approval by the architect. When the application for payment is approved, the architect issues to the institution a certificate for payment to the contractor for such amount of the application as the architect decides is properly due at the time. The requisition should then be honored by the institution.

Payments to the contractor may be withheld by direction of the architect if defective work is not remedied or if the contractor fails to make proper payments to subcontractors for material and labor, or for other actions detrimental to the interests of the institution, but payment must be made once these grounds for withholding it are removed. Payments made to the contractor by the institution do not indicate the terms of the contract.

After final payment the contractor legally commits the construction company to remedy any defects due to faulty materials or workmanship which appear within a period of one year after the date of occupancy by the owner or the date of substantial completion of the building. Before final payment the contractor should supply the owner with evidence and affidavits that all its obligations have been paid for material and labor entailed as a result of the contract.

In order to ensure such payments and to facilitate completion of the work if the contractor should default before it is completed, it is usually the custom for the institution to retain 10 percent of the funds applied for by the contractor during the progress of the work. This retained percentage is insurance that the contractor will fulfill financial obligations before the retention is paid. If the contractor fails to do so, the institution may then pay these obligations directly with the retained percentage.

Frequently, on large buildings which require a large sum of money and a long construction period, this 10 percent retainage becomes quite considerable by the time the building is well along, and the continued withholding by the institution creates a financial hardship on the contractor. For this reason, either through prior arrangement or in consideration of this hardship, the institution frequently rewards the contractor for acceptable execution of the contract by reducing the retained percentage in proportion to the amount of work remaining to be done.

Before final payment the architect, the institution, and the contractor should jointly prepare a check, or "punch," list which itemizes all the known defects, deficiencies, and omissions which remain to be corrected or completed on the job before the contractual obligations can be considered to have been fulfilled. The library representative should be very much involved in the compilation of this list.

Renovation Conditions. Construction problems are a modest concern for the librarian of a new separate building and yet they are often a headache during a renovation project. This kind of project was treated in detail in Section 10.4, and it should be read for its applicability to construction of new structures, additions, and renovations.

Phasing can be a special need and yet a complex problem in renovation. On the one hand, the general contractor will wish to bring in one trade to do all its work for the whole renovation project. On the other hand, the library probably will need to occupy and operate parts of certain floors while renovation goes on in other areas. These often are not compatible goals. To save money, the institution needs to make it as convenient for the contractor as is reasonable, preferably clearing one major section entirely and then relocating staff and collections to release the rest to the contractor at a later date.

In renovating the Stanford Green Library old wing, it was worked out so that library units and collections had only one move, except for the Government Documents Library which had to camp out for several months on a different floor and the staff room which was given up for several months. Even so, the contractor caused substantial disruptions in technical services while plumbers, electricians, and sheet metal trades worked next to the ceiling, having to move scaffolding in and around and occasionally over staff desks.

Probably few library staff can say that they enjoyed the renovation while it progressed. Most would probably liken it to a battle zone. Yet it behooves management to work out a reasonable accommodation for the contractor, and the staff can well suffer a bit—as will the contractor in other terms—for the staff can look forward to improved conditions once the job is done.

Phasing should be worked out in writing by the librarian and planner, sometimes with the architect's guidance, and then negotiated with the contractor. Some give and take is necessary, especially by the library staff since tough requirements will only drag out the work, cost more, result in frayed tempers, and perhaps produce some examples of inferior workmanship. It is suggested that for a renovation the contractor should be required to maintain a rolling schedule which anticipates the specific activities for two weeks and which is updated at each weekly meeting. This type of schedule will be of great help in the coordination of power shutdowns and the required interruptions of the other utilities. Access, noise, and delivery problems may be anticipated as well so that the progress of the project may be as smooth as possible.

15.6 Change Orders

The institution and its planning team will find, if they did not realize it in advance, that their tasks have not been completed when the building contract is signed, the time schedules set, and the construction begun. Every project will have problems. Even with the greatest of attention to detail in the contract documents, there will be errors, omissions, conflicts, and surprises during the construction period. These problems can be reduced with a carefully prepared set of documents; nevertheless, they are never all eliminated except on the smallest of projects. Many decisions will have to be faced as the building work proceeds.

Change orders reverse earlier decisions or take care of previous omissions on the part of the planning team, the architect, and possibly the engineers involved. Change orders may also, and frequently do, reinstate items or work previously omitted in the interest of economy, particularly if a more favorable bid was received than had been expected or additional funds are made available. Use of the change order must be quite limited as will be seen below.

Usually, minor conflicts or other problems will be resolved on the spot by the contractor, perhaps with the approval of the inspector. However, if there is a cost or time delay involved, the solution to the problem must go through formal channels. There may be a requirement for clarification drawings from the architect, followed by the submission of a quote from the contractor. If solution to the problem is urgent and it is clear that its cost will be minor (say, no more than $2000 to $5000), a field order may be written to authorize the change in work. At a later date the field orders will be incorporated into a change order, which alters the basic contract. A field order may be issued by the project inspector to keep the work moving, but a change order always comes from the architect. It will include the current contract price and schedule, the added or deducted sum resulting from the change order, any added or deducted construction time, and signatures of the architect, owner, and contractor.

The representatives of the institution must remember that change orders have to be given sufficient lead time. While the height of an electrical outlet can in most cases be easily changed before installation, a change in door swing, as another example, may mean that door, frame, and lockset that were ordered long before must now be changed and perhaps at extra cost.

Also, while the change order process is a means of correcting design flaws or accommodating a changing program, it should be remembered that the work authorized by a change order is not competitively bid and that the process of arriving at an approved change order is expensive for all parties. Because of these factors, the change orders should only be used when absolutely necessary. The librarian should be particularly aware of this point, as the temptation is to request minor changes as new and better ideas come to mind. This temptation must be suppressed except where a change of great importance is identified. Most change orders should be limited to the changes that are required because of the conditions of the site and of errors and omissions in the drawings, not changes in the program.

The contractor can, of course, take advantage of change orders to increase unduly the contract cost. The librarian's view tends to be that this increase is unwarranted, but in the contractor's defense, it should be pointed out that the construction company would generally prefer that no changes be made during the progress of the work. Any change, no matter how small, may upset schedules and procedures to some extent and will cost the contractor money, just because it is a change. That is why contractors do not allow full value for work omitted and charge more than normal rates for work added.

There are, it must be admitted, legally minded contractors who comb the specifications and drawings for omissions and discrepancies on which extra charges can be based, although in general the contractor is eager for the sake of reputation, if nothing else, to present a complete and acceptable job to the institution. The institution will almost always enjoy the services of a satisfactory contractor if it has a free hand in the selection of bidders.

If change orders add to the cost of the building and to the sum that must be made available, a problem arises unless there is a contingency line item in the original budget, part of which was left over after the contract was signed. There should always be a sum for contingencies in the budget, both before and after the signing of the contract or contracts. This figure can vary from as much as 12½ percent at preliminary stages of the planning to as little as 2½ percent after the contract is awarded. The usual figure is 10 percent at the design development stage, 7½ percent after quantity survey estimates, and perhaps 5 percent after the award of the contract. The economic climate at the time of planning may properly affect the percentages; in periods of inflation they may need to be made greater than at other times.

To have a good margin is always desirable because the winning bid may be higher than was expected, and also because of the possibility of the need for change orders. Even though the librarian has been cautioned against their use, it is generally cheaper and more suitable to place change orders if it is evident that they are desirable than to wait and make alterations after construction is finished.

One important precaution if trouble is to be avoided: the AIA (American Institute of Architects) general conditions of the contract includes an agreement on procedures to be followed in any changes made in the working drawings and specifications. This agreement, or any similar agreement found in the supplementary general conditions, must be followed.

Change Order Example. Presented below is an example of change orders that one may expect on any major project. At first glance, it may appear as though most of the items will be of special interest to the librarian, and in some respects, this may be the case. By this stage of the project, however, most of the changes should be little more than technical adjustments requiring little response from the librarian. Still, it is well that a library representative be aware of the construction progress, including change orders, to ensure against surprises or mistakes resulting from a lack of understanding by the contractor and others of the special needs of the library. The typical change order covers the results of several bulletins or field orders. In this case, it is the change order that formally adjusts the project cost and schedule.

C.O.1. Deletes two feet of construction fence, where is was decided that a six foot high fence would suffice in place of the eight foot fence spec-

ified. Also, the add alternate (completion of the third floor) is accepted as part of the construction contract.

C.O.2. Adds caissons and other footings due to unexpected soil conditions.

C.O.3. Allows payment of a unit cost for footings as established in the original bid package; makes changes in the basement electrical layout and service desk reflecting late design changes; adds electrical room door labels as required by the county inspector; approves substitution of materials from those specified for the electrical feeder, door hold devices and pipe hanger supports in order to reduce cost and expedite the project.

C.O.4. Adds fountain machine room rough-in in response to expectation that a donor has been identified who will pay for the fountain (which is not currently in the project). The work accepted here will save re-doing landscape work at a later date.

C.O.5. Alters the central stair hand rail in response to a design error (the rail, as designed, was too large for a normal person to grip); approves the interior transparent woodwork finish following submittal of a number of samples; changes an operable window to a fixed window to improve security in the mail room; and authorizes payment of the expense for soils testing as an added contractual element.

C.O.6. Details changes of the first floor layouts because a major wall was constructed one foot off of its designed location. (It was decided more was to be gained through minor adjustment than by requiring the contractor to rip out the wall and start over.) Adds panic hardware at several doors that was missed in the specifications, and approves a change in the exterior lighting in response to recent changes in the campus lighting plan.

C.O.7. Provides for a change in the faculty study shelving, including the shelves and the wall framing required to support the shelves, in response to continued development of detailed furniture layouts; makes changes in the elevator shaft resulting from a conflict in the drawings.

C.O.8. Removes ceiling light fixtures in the reading areas where it was decided to use task lighting with kiosk type light fixtures for ambient lighting; and establishes the exact method of fastening and supporting the Spanish tile roofing (which was not clearly specified).

C.O.9. Alters the chalk boards, tack boards, and several door swings in response to furniture layouts; makes a number of miscellaneous mechanical changes; and provides for a contract for balancing the mechanical systems.

C.O.10. Revises the fascias, soffits, wall framing and related insulation to resolve a problem discovered by the contractor; adds flashing and reglets in an area where water problems are anticipated; and establishes elevator finishes not previously specified. Deletes a portion of the site work because of an adjacent construction project which recently started. Provides for testing of the shot-in fasteners for the suspended ceiling.

C.O.11. Makes changes in the gutters, drains, and ceiling layouts including related duct and lighting work to resolve conflicts which have developed; alters furred space in the exterior walls because original space was not large enough for pipe joints and other fixtures; establishes the locker keying; and alters a retaining wall due to new grade levels as determined by the adjacent project.

C.O.12. Adds book lockers in the library shelving and deletes range finders and card holders (which are added to the separate graphics contract). Adds a ventilation fan for the sound system, and modifies the air diffusers in the lobby, as a design improvement.

C.O.13. Provides for miscellaneous electrical revisions in response to the furniture layouts; adds risers for door stops where the doors were undercut for ventilation; relocates sprinkler pipe and outlets where the old and new buildings join; and authorizes painting of the diffusers specified in the previous change order.

C.O.14. Adds filler at window wall blind pockets and paint at the exposed wall ends behind glass at certain faculty studies; revises exterior doors because of structural problems; provides for testing of the roof gutters; and adds a time extension of 42 days because of a lengthy rainy season.

C.O.15. Revises light fixtures as required to accommodate ceiling conditions; provides identification plates for the exterior stand pipes to replace those previously supplied, but lost by the owner; adds hardwood base (omitted on one wall in the original drawings); and relocates a floor outlet reflecting continued work on the furnishings.

C.O.16. Details in legal terms the various aspects of a dispute between the owner and contractor, including points of agreement in regard to payment and completion schedules.

C.O.17. Alters the cabinets in the photocopy areas to allow for a larger machine; provides tamper-proof thermostat covers and mounting for humidity gauges; and adds door hardware, and phone and power outlets discovered to be needed as the planning for activation progresses.

C.O.18. Outlines miscellaneous mechanical and electrical revisions resulting largely from a walk-through by the campus physical plant personnel; adds a catch basin where there is concern about excessive run-off; adds a few door astragals; provides for repainting factory finishes on electrical raceway to match other architectural metal on the project; adds hooks for the hanging of a large art work that is to be given to the library; and adds heavy duty casters on a mobile sorting unit to replace the original casters that simply were too weak; provides for the removal and re-installation of the floor mounted door stops, following the carpet installation by others; alters the book return slide/conveyor where the designed slide does not work; and deletes the graphic allowance, following a decision to contract separately for the graphics.

C.O.19. Makes cost adjustments for "allowance" items; alters the final grading to reflect new conditions; and revises the entrance-exit gate control devices, to achieve wider workable gates.

It can be seen from this example that the need for change orders comes from a number of sources including:

Continuing work on furniture layouts

Changes in the library operational program which are judged to be of an essential nature

Discovered surprises, or unknown conditions previously hidden

Contractual matters dealing with testing, allowances, approval of alternatives, and disputes

Conflicts, errors, and omissions in the drawings and specifications

Outside forces such as weather problems, strikes, and changes in the availability of materials and projects

Continued review during the construction process by numerous personnel who may, for a variety of reasons (such as code, campus standards, or operational necessity) require that changes be made.

15.7 Inspections

It has already been noted that during the construction effort, there should be numerous inspections by highly qualified individuals. Most of these people know what to look for or observe. All too frequently these individuals focus on code requirements, safety conditions, or trade specifics, such as concrete pouring. Those checks are necessary; however, they may well ignore or pay scant attention to critical library operational conditions. In particular, branch libraries and college libraries may have this problem. Librarians are urged to make inspections at least weekly when work commences on electrical switches and convenience outlets, door frames, and windows and throughout the work on interior finishes and built-ins.

What might the librarian look for on the occasional tour? That is not an easy question. To help answer it, the following list of things that might concern a librarian may suggest some general directions.

While the floors are exposed, are there large and deep puddles after a rain? Will these irregularities cause problems with the adjustment of the shelving, typically limited to about ½ in. or 12 mm? Adjustments even this large will leave gaps above many carpets.

As the concrete forms are being placed, note whether the outlets look right. In walls the height of the outlet may be important. Don't forget clock and signal outlets.

Watch for sandblasting, as windows in existing buildings should be closed while it is going on.

In a renovation, watch for fire hazards including smoking and especially welding. Any welding operation in an existing building should require two people, one with an appropriate fire extinguisher. The welding process should be completed or stopped at least an hour before people leave the site, to guard against the possible latent effects of a hot spot.

Where there is an addition, watch for possible water intrusion into the existing facility as the walls are opened up.

Review with the inspector the importance of accurate dimensions, particularly where shelving must be placed between columns. As the architect's representative is likely to be new to the project, details such as this may be forgotten.

Be aware of potential damage to waterproof membranes. Where waterproofing is applied to a basement wall, is it protected during the backfill operation? As the rest room floors, roofs, or other areas with waterproofing are being constructed, are they being subjected to loads that may cause damage?

Review all door, gate, and window swings. Do they work freely? Will they interfere with planned shelving or movable furniture?

As the built-ins are completed, check that the drawers and doors do not bind, that the locks work as intended, and that there are no sharp edges. Where future access may be required for power and signal, check for a removable access panel or other means of access.

During the installation of a complex electronic system, ask the inspector to ensure that adequate wiring diagrams are in hand or being prepared.

As the carpet is being installed, have the inspector watch the seaming patterns to ensure that they match those shown on the plans.

As the job nears completion, try everything. Each detail in the drawing, schedules, and specifications should be checked if it has aesthetic or functional importance. Look for chipped paint, scratched finishes, missing items, binding doors, locks that stick, etc., etc.

During the course of construction, be aware that this kind of inspection may not be welcomed by the contractor or others. Requests to visit must be made, ordinarily through channels, and permission received. Tact will be required in asking for an explanation or pointing out a condition that appears to differ from drawings or specifications. The owner has a right to inspect and should exercise it. For instance, Swarthmore College librarians found deviations from specifications which could be, and were, corrected during construction: unsuitable doors on offices and seminar rooms, incorrect operable windows, and shelving that would intrude into space planned for microform readers and printers. The point must be clear that you, as the ultimate client, must be able to properly use the facility for many years after the contractor leaves. Corrective work is always easier to achieve while the contractor is still on the job.

15.8 Wrap-up

During the construction the librarian should be alert to possible changes in the field conditions, should review certain shop drawings, should critique mock-ups, and must be prepared to step in when new decisions are required. Meanwhile, construction wrap-up will be approaching. This entails preparing for beneficial occupancy (moving in before the final acceptance), and, ultimately, acceptance of the building. The final inspections will result in a list of items requiring correction. There will sometimes be a need to start moving into a portion of the building before the entire project is accepted. Once the library starts to occupy a space, it is in essence accepted, and the warranty clock is started. If the mechanical systems must be operational to allow occupancy, then they too are in essence turned over to the institution. From that point on, problems newly identified become more difficult to resolve because there is always the question of who is legally responsible. If damage to a surface has not been previously identified, it is probable that the contractor will not freely correct the problem once the space is occupied.

Before the building is finally and legally accepted, the representative of the institution should have in hand the signed-off building permits, a set of as-built drawings showing the actual constructed conditions, operations manuals outlining maintenance routines, approval from the architect for final payment, documentation relieving the institution of any responsibility for mechanic's liens or other obligations of the contractor, and a report on the balancing of the temperature and ventilation or air-conditioning systems. There may be other contractual requirements as well, such as a final cleaning, training for the institution's operations and maintenance staff, and a one-year maintenance agreement for the landscaping. These details can stretch out for some period of time, and the contractor will likely be upset about not receiving the final payment. But, eventually, the building will fully belong to the institution.

One final point that was mentioned earlier in this volume. The contracts may require a meeting of the design team and the contractor one year after occupancy. The intent of this meeting is to promote a process of education for all involved. Philosophically, this is a nice idea, but in reality it probably has very limited value. While it is not the intent of the authors to discourage such a meeting, we wonder if it is worth the time of a number of busy people, though it is something to consider.

16

Activation

Although any librarian would realize that it takes many months if not some years to plan a library before construction starts, one may not realize that library staff will be even more busy during the final months of construction. The work will in lesser degree continue for one or a number of years beyond occupancy of the new facility. The activities covered in this chapter will vary markedly in the time required and the number of individuals who are involved; yet they can be surprisingly time consuming for any new building, a sizable addition, a major branch, as well as substantially converted or rebuilt space.

A highly experienced building consultant has described activation as follows:

Then comes the moving process and the dedication. By this time the librarians will be in such a state of shock and euphoria that all mistakes will be rationalized and everyone will be happy. For the next two years the library staff will budget a sizeable share of their time to showing visitors through the building, much to the annoyance of students who are trying to study, but there will come a day when the visitors go elsewhere and the mistakes have been corrected, the faculty will have settled into their studies and everyone will be happy and proud of the new library.[1]

This conclusion may be whimsy. The real decisions and tasks involved before, during, and after activation are nonetheless considerable. The building occupancy and initial period of use can be a sore trial for the staff and a matter of grave disappointment to faculty and students if those final steps of occupying and operating a building are not as carefully managed as were the earlier stages in the planning process. Preparation for occupancy should therefore start a year or two in advance. A time schedule, perhaps using

[1] Ralph E. Ellsworth, *Planning the College and University Library Building: A Book for Campus Planners and Architects*, 2nd ed. (Boulder, Colo.: Pruett Pr., 1968), p. 121.

the PERT (program evaluation and review technique) or critical path planning method, can help assure a timely and comprehensive staff effort.

Although the activation process does not involve expense comparable to that required for construction, it is still a good test of the librarian's service to the community. Indeed, the reputation of the library staff will for a while rest just as much on the success of the activation as it will in the long run on the basic suitability of the building structure itself.

16.1 Preparing for Occupancy

The purchase of movable equipment should be a very early concern. Whether the furnishings have been designed by the architectural firm or an interior design consultant, or selected by the library and the institution without outside assistance, it may well take a great many months or well over a year for some furniture to be selected, purchased, delivered, and, if necessary, assembled for installation. In cases where specialized furniture needs to be custom designed—for example, to accommodate audio-visual or computer needs or special requirements for use of nonbook materials—it may require a year or more to have designs drawn to scale, bids requested and evaluated, contracts signed, and fabrication completed.

Perhaps during programming, and certainly not later than the design development effort, decisions will have been made about which items are outside the scope of the architect, the interior designer, and the general contractor. Those items such as built-in furnishings, stack shelving, and items tied in with the electrical or mechanical systems will commonly have been in the basic contract. But furnishings which are stock items, are not built-ins, are not tied in with electrical or mechanical systems, and are not required to be installed before some task of the general contractor will commonly be purchased by the institution separately from the construction contract. This arrangement enables the institution to make decisions at a much later time and to save the management or overhead costs when that responsibility is assigned to the contractor. In such an arrangement, the purchasing office of the institution should advise on the necessary lead time; and the library staff must do everything possible to assure that the list of needs is complete, the specifications are accurate, the budget covers all essential priority items, and the purchase orders are placed according to required lead time so that all material will be delivered at or very soon before the time when the contractor plans to finish the building and turn it over to the institution. Close effective work between library staff and the institution's purchasing department is of paramount importance.

This book does not provide exhaustive treatment of furniture selection; however, the necessity of obtaining functional compatibility and reasonable aesthetic harmony between the furnishings and the building is an obvious goal. This criterion applies to re-used and refurbished furniture as well as to new items. If early delivery is anticipated, arrangements will need to be made for equipment to be stored on campus or in a commercial building unless the manufacturer is able to hold it until it is actually needed in the new building. It may be possible for the manufacturers of equipment and furniture and for the carpet installer to hold the items for a few weeks. If the manufacturer is a considerable distance away, it may be desirable to have all materials critical to the initial operation of the library shipped for local holding in order to minimize delivery problems when the building is ready for furnishing.

There are a number of business aspects and logistical problems in obtaining the movable furniture and equipment, some deriving from the fact that one can almost never be certain that the contractor will be able to complete the building on the stipulated date. The date for actual turnover of the building for occupancy may not be known until a very few weeks before that time is reached. Further, there may well be negotiation between the contractor and the institution about whether part or all of the building should be turned over at one time, whether it should be turned over before all of the punch-list items are completed or before landscaping is finished. It should therefore be evident that one or two years lead time for the movable equipment is not too much for large quantities and especially for non-stock items, such as oversized catalog consultation tables, a portfolio display case, custom exhibition cases, or a special-shaped conference table.

In the year or more before occupancy, the library staff need to understand the detailed layout of the new facility and its service philosophy, develop the collection deployment, and learn security and safety arrangements. Few will be familiar enough with architectural drawings to be able to fully grasp directional problems, the best routes from place to place, what can and cannot be seen, what acoustic problems may turn up, and the general ambience of the new space and what it may mean to their own unit. It is well during the final stages of construction for small groups of the staff to be taken through the building by the project manager, with authorization from the contractor. Early in the project hard hats will be required for those going on a tour, but late in the project they may not be necessary, though normal caution is required since hazardous objects may be lying on the floor or stairs and other areas may be unfinished. These tours for selected staff should help their understanding of functional arrangements and enable them to moderate criticism, improve understanding of how the whole structure will work, inform their staff of the new possibilities, contribute to the revision of existing regulations and practices of their unit or the preparation of new procedures and regulations, as well as help staff morale by letting them in on an exciting preview. Such tours may be offered occasionally for the faculty library committee or senior officers of the institution. The staff who were responsible for fundraising, the dean of instruction, and indeed the president may welcome a tour late in the construction phase. This gesture helps those individuals see the results of their support. It may help with further fundraising if there are still financial needs for the building or for furnishings; and certainly it would enable academic officers and the faculty to talk with their colleagues so that there is a general understanding of any change in habits that may be required and the role the library may play in the teaching and research program of the institution.

Revised and additional rules and regulations are frequently required in a new facility. The building may have included new functions and specialized quarters, each of which requires explaining to the community and clarifying for those on the library staff who will operate or manage them. Thus there may be revised staff manuals to be drafted and reviewed with staff, and printed guides or brochures which explain altered services.

These take time to produce. There may be new audio-visual or computer facilities, different book-checking arrangements at building exits, new book-return accommodations, arrangements for use of typewriters or personal computers, new service areas or combined service desks, altered arrangements for required course readings or for current periodical issues, new photographic services, and other such features. Preliminary draft documents should be prepared while construction proceeds, though published versions should only be distributed after staff is assured of final building and equipment details and room numbers. Frequently such regulations or documents need at least slight revision within months of occupancy, and so interim versions may be prudent. Occupancy of a new or extensively remodeled building is, after all, the most convenient time to make changes which previous physical conditions inhibited.

Embarrassing moments and difficulties may be avoided if the librarian determines which are new conditions and services and assigns to appropriate staff the preparation of operating and contingency plans and the drafting of the required documents. This responsibility should even involve such matters as handling cash for fines for overdue or lost books, deposits for audio headsets, checking tags for personal typewriters brought within the building, issuing keys or combination locks, arranging building closing routines and daily staff entrance before the building opens for service. These are examples of things that warrant attention.

Another key step preparatory to occupancy is budgeting for additional staff positions, if any are necessary to the operation of the facility. This may require requesting increases a year or two in advance of occupancy and opening of the new facility. It may mean starting even further in advance if the opening of the facility is rather late in a fiscal year, the institution has a biennial budget, or the institution's budget cycle requires twelve months or more for justification, negotiation, and approval. It may be desirable to add temporary staff several years earlier if a new book collection is being formed and needs to be purchased and cataloged. A small cadre may need to be hired and trained two or three months in advance in order to understand a major new building and help with final plans for moving in and opening the facility. The demands on a new facility may increase only slightly for a modest building expansion but may double or even triple if the facility is a new one and constitutes a very significant improvement in quality and size from the previous quarters. The number of books circulated, the number of students and faculty who remain to study in the library, the number of reference questions, the use of specialized facilities and services, and merely the traffic within the building and in and out of the exits may be strikingly greater than was the case previously.

The probable growth in use should be estimated and built into budget planning for the first years of the building. Depending on estimates of anticipated activity, additional staff may be needed to handle a 25 or 50 percent increase in use over the first year of occupancy, and the number may need to rise to accommodate perhaps a 100 percent increase in the next few years over use previous to occupancy. The judgment of increased use and its pattern of growth over two or three years are matters that each institution will have to judge for itself. The institution should recognize that this increased use is certain to come in any facility which is much improved and that the dimension of it cannot be exactly predetermined. Thus some allowance in the number of staff in the first year or two is often justified, and, in any event, some budgetary flexibility is prudent to accommodate changes within the first year. To spoil the effect of a fine new library building on the academic program of the institution because the staff is inadequate in size or quality or both would be exceedingly unfortunate.

Examples of increased use in a comparable new facility in another institution may help academic budget officers realize the prospects. They no doubt hoped that the academic program would benefit when they supported the library addition or new building; and, although increased budgets may cause them problems, their predisposition for an improved institution should result in a sympathetic response to library staffing requirements in the facility. Typically, a major new facility will seem to bring unforeseen additional use; student use that was nowhere evident seems to materialize almost overnight. There may be a particularly heavy use from the very start, as was the case in the Lamont Library at Harvard, and reduction in use of an older nearby library may be negligible or

at least quite temporary. A major undergraduate library building and a nearby major research library, one brand new and the other old, may both grow in use quite steadily from the very beginning. When the new library at Louisiana State University in Baton Rouge was occupied, the use of the library by students more than doubled immediately. At Cornell just after occupancy of the Uris Undergraduate Library, there was an attendance some 50 percent larger than when it was the Central Library of the University, while the Olin Research Library was used by approximately the same number as formerly used the old building; so the net increase in use was over 150 percent. The University of Michigan found that the major addition to its main library resulted in growth that went up some 20 to 30 percent the first year and a similar amount the second year. Stanford's large addition to its main library resulted in a similar growth pattern, though of much greater degree, while use of the nearby undergraduate library dipped during the first two or three months and thereafter returned to its former level. Given similar experiences in a large number of buildings erected in recent decades, one should anticipate that this growth will occur, find parallel situations if possible in order to provide a basis for planning, and budget to support those conditions.

Tours of the building four to six months before occupancy will help key staff understand in three-dimensional space what they were trying to understand from architectural drawings. As examples, it may become evident that sunlight conditions are not what the staff expected, the need for directional signs is different from that anticipated, a visual discord may become apparent, or the usefulness of an art object may be evident in the building itself whereas its desirability was not seen when reviewing plans. A number of these insights may take months to clarify, have policies approved, or have brochures printed before opening day.

In the last month or so before occupancy, other tours will be helpful. Certain library staff need to review the building to plan the move of furniture and book collections. There needs to be an understanding by selected library staff about alarm systems, emergency exits, telephone outlets, valves, electrical outlets, switches, or circuit breakers. Representatives of the fire and police departments as well as the grounds and building operations staff need to review the building from their perspective even though they have had plans in hand; and these operational personnel must have explained to them the academic program intent of the building, its security provisions and library reasons for their existence, and the importance of the performance criteria for environmental systems and critical electrical systems. There will also need to be agreement on the schedule for caretaking or janitorial service in the building, covering such matters as the issuance of master keys or access to areas with special security, the frequency of emptying paper receptacles in the rest rooms, vacuuming of carpeted areas, dusting empty shelves in the stacks, and the hours when vacuuming or other noisy operations should take place in order not unduly to disturb readers.

At the end of the construction period, the university or college should be given as-built architectural plans, which show the precise route taken by wiring conduit, ducts, and pipes that was not detailed in the architect's working drawings. Instruction manuals for mechanical, electrical, and security systems need to be given to institutional authorities. The door locks will probably have had key blanks inserted to enable the construction crew to open all doors during their work in the building, and those key blanks need to be pulled at the time that the institution takes control of the building. A keying pattern must be designed, based on a hierarchical diagram tree which can be quite complicated for a large building. (See fig. 14.2.) The library staff will need to decide who needs key access to each room, where magnetic card access is to be provided, what group of unique locks shall be controlled by one master key, which grand or great-grand masters can save some staff carrying many keys, and what limits are desired on exterior and high- security door access. The issuance of keys to library staff is generally planned some months in advance; cutting the number of keys required of each type may take many weeks. Keys then need to be signed for and issued and a key control system set up. The activation of this system is a matter of important timing in order that the construction crews who had free access to the building do not have unintended access once expensive and specialized equipment is moved in. All too often there have been instances of large rolls of carpeting, furniture, soft chairs, or electrical equipment being sto-

len during the activation period or immediately after the institution takes responsibility for the building. The security at this stage is a matter of great importance.

Security is, of course, complicated if the institution takes partial occupancy of the building. Such occupancy may be required in order to have sufficient time to move the book collections in. Conversely, the collections may not be able to be moved if the contractor is still working on the bookstack installation while other parts of the building may need to be occupied. The final clean-up is an obligation of the contractor. However, the institution may choose to conduct an additional clean-up with its own staff, or the clean-up may be covered by part of the budgeted activation funds that allows cleaning to be performed by a commercial firm. This clean-up is not merely the normal cleaning of brick pavers, tile floors, carpeting, and windows; it should also include most, if not all, vertical surfaces where dust will have accumulated. The amount of dust created during construction is great; and the cleaner the facility can be, particularly if it is an air-conditioned building with an excellent filtration system, the better for the book-collection and people spaces when the building is occupied and the mechanical equipment is in use.

During the last week or two before the institution takes responsibility for the building, security systems may be installed and tested. Alternatively, the institution may have a separate contract with a security firm and wish to have that work completely apart from the contractor's responsibility. In such an arrangement, which is rather more common, the alarm-system electrical runs would be pulled in advance but the alarm devices and monitors would be installed immediately after the contractor has turned over the building. If library security staff are needed, they should be hired, and, in any event, appropriate staff must be given necessary training on use of the system before the institution takes over the building.

Installing telephones is another task which may require several weeks, particularly where phone instruments are rearranged in a building which received a major addition. Indeed, in the planning of the building, there may have been provision for what seemed to be the ultimate number of instruments; library managers will need to determine a few months in advance which outlets will be activated, how many lines will be provided, what type of instruments, and that the budget support is available.

16.2 Signs

Large buildings require posted room numbers, name signs, directional guides, public directories, and other graphics to assist users in finding their way in the building. These are sometimes supplemented by printed leaflets, flyers, and other handouts which provide more detailed explanation of library services or resources. From at least medieval times there have been shelf guides to book collections, ranges of sections, and individual sections; and one can find examples in Duke Humfrey's Library at Oxford University. Today in any college or university library, there must perforce be a considerable effort to facilitate self-service by the clientele. There simply are not enough staff available during all service hours to provide basic direction to several hundred or even ten thousand people who may use the library building in a single day, and such use of staff would, of course, not be cost effective. Furthermore, it is well known that many students and faculty are hesitant to ask for help in using the library even when an information or reference desk is obviously placed and staffed to provide assistance. The psychology of this reticence may stem from a subconscious belief that in an institution of higher education one should know how to use something as basic as a library if one has qualified to matriculate in such an institution.

Be that as it may, a good proportion of library users will seldom ask or will ask only as a matter of last resort. A large academic or research library is not simple in function or layout even for those who are constant users. A library may have a dozen reading areas and may have huge book collections shelved in various rooms or areas or stacks. Each room or area of the library serves a different subject matter, type of material, or segment of the clientele. Any information desk personnel can handle only a limited number of questions, even if every patron were willing to ask and were willing to wait a few seconds or a minute to ask for help. The library can be relatively complex, especially in a very large institution or when there are individuals from on or off campus who are occasional users and should be guided

in finding their own way to the appropriate library service or area.

Thus signs in an academic library are a matter of considerable importance. These graphics will certainly include the name on the building, its hours of opening, the location of each major library service, a list of library officers who may be frequently sought by visitors, and particular reading rooms and bookshelf areas. However, not all information which the institution wishes to convey to clientele need be displayed on signs. If that were done, the library would look like the worst main street—garish with the profusion of signs visually clashing! In fact, if there are too many signs in view, the mind tends to ignore them all. Contrast the effectiveness of signs in the best hotels with that of those in the hard-sell drug stores. Whenever there needs to be considerable explanation that may occupy a paragraph or a couple of pages, it is better to have inexpensively printed flyers or other handouts available. Examples might be a description of what materials are and are not represented in the card catalog, the range of specialized facilities and services to help handicapped or physically limited individuals, or perhaps the location and current hours of service in all the branch libraries throughout a university campus.

In the design of a set of graphics, there are some principles that may be suggested for all academic libraries. In designing signs, put yourself in the position of an occasional library user and think of the sequence of questions that arise when one wishes to use the library without staff assistance. Try to have enough signs or guides to answer each of the most frequently asked questions (or have available leaflets or flyers to serve that purpose) but not so many that they present a clutter. The library must try to achieve an effective array though modest in number. Most signs should be kept to a very few words, perhaps five or six at the most for large signs indicating functional areas or services. Signs of more moderate size may have somewhat more information, for example, a building floor directory, list of key staff offices, and perhaps an indexed campus map. Remember that only a few signs need to be read from quite a distance, for which super graphics are occasionally used; other signs can be much more modest in size if they need only be read when one is within four or five paces. The former instance may include identification of a loan desk or photocopy service, while the latter type may include room numbers or the subject section locations within the current periodical display. Certain signs should be in braille for tactile reading, for example, floor levels and room numbers and names. Meaning must be unambiguous. Signs are usually not a place to try humor or to use a specialized local meaning which is campus jargon or an "in joke." In some cases bilingual signs would be appropriate, and with increasing frequency, use of international standard symbols can be helpful and much briefer than text signs, though commonly symbols and words would be used in combination. Use of color coding can be appropriate, but it should be used only if the meaning is absolutely clear or can quickly be learned. Tracking a particularly difficult route from one functional area to another, and one which is used with frequency, may be aided by a line on the floor or a tile or a carpet color stripe which leads between the two locations.

Signs should be tasteful. They should appear to be compatible with the architecture and decor. This requirement need not lessen their prominence at all. Signs of all sizes can be of one design, or of only two or three designs which bear a family resemblance. This characteristic can be particularly useful in graphics for a building addition, to relate the old and new portions. Some people prefer a classic typeface, such a Centaur or Bodoni, while others may prefer a sans serif face; some like subtle understatement, while others prefer boldness and striking color. But remember that large graphics are a type of architectural treatment just as much as windows, lights, walls, and floor. They can help to create an environment and, unless developed in the context of the architectural palette, may seem discordant.

The minimum effective size of lettering is a function of the distance and angle from which it must be read, the lighting on the sign, the general visual field against which it will be read, the height and width of the letter strokes, and the degree of contrast between the letters and the background colors of the sign. One must consider effectiveness at night and when the space is rather full of people. Mock-ups are highly desirable, even when the design is by an expert architect, interior designer, or graphics designer.

Changeability may be a final principle. It is particularly important that most signs be

rather easily and inexpensively changed, since over time library functions shift in location, individual library departments are renamed, senior staff depart, and popular terminology changes. Library staff must handle such changes within the operating budget. Signs should nevertheless be tamper resistant and even theft resistant. Surprising as it may seem, the imaginative student seems to find it a challenge to add one or a few characters to make an entirely different meaning out of words in a sign. Student minds working the way they do, the theft of signs as souvenirs extends even to small signs that identify study rooms or carrels specified for the handicapped. As in other aspects of the library building, making signs relatively impervious to mistreatment may be nearly as essential in an academic institution as it would seem to be on the streets.

The selection of signs, text, and location requires care and may consume months. To return to the first principle, one can follow a sequence moving from the general to the specific for the clientele expected to come to the building. Thus in a highly specialized branch library one need not have a campus map mounted in the lobby, perhaps not even floor plans for that branch, but one would treat its basic functions and shelf areas. In the main research library of a university and perhaps for many a college library, a campus map as well as the library building floor plans may save many questions. Indeed, in a very complicated building there may need to be a building cross-section. A few libraries have used such elaborate devices as pushbutton illuminated directories. Signs can be placed and words chosen to help smooth over what may have been architectural weaknesses, such as not being able to see the principal circulation desk from a reference desk. Decisions will have to be made about whether the sign needs to be legible from fifty feet or more, whether the sign should be on translucent material if hung from the ceiling, whether it should be high enough for visibility amidst a crowd of people or kept low enough so that persons using bifocals will not have a problem with smaller letters.

In numbering rooms, one needs to consider whether to put the number and the name of the room on, beside, or over the door. If the door has a large glass panel, one should probably not put more than one or two rather small words on the glass since any appreciable blocking of view or distraction of those walking toward the door may result in somebody inadvertently being hit as the door swings open. (An advantage of wording or decorations on non-swinging glass doors or floor-length windows is the safety of seeing the glass. This is provided by the Shakespearean quotations on some windows at the Sedgwick Library, University of British Columbia.) Putting the sign beside the door best serves the purpose for those doors that may occasionally be propped open. Placing the designation over the door may work if the architect has left room over the frame, though it may be too high and thus the designation may be more easily overlooked than if it were at eye level. Compromises occasionally need to be made for specific conditions.

Another detail: consideration may be given to putting bold words on top of catalog cases to indicate the content of each linear segment of card catalog trays when a catalog has three or four thousand trays. Similar treatment can help location of major subjects or types of reference materials, such as to indicate the sections for dictionaries, encyclopedias, atlases, phone books, etc., or in other situations for history, literature, and religion.

This section has not been intended to answer questions, for each building is unique. Those responsible for the library management must, however, adopt a coherent plan. The detailing of the exact text of each sign may be delegated to a small staff committee, or each administrative unit may suggest needs in its area. However, one individual responsible for coordinating the public services of the library or of the project should do a precise review of the text for every single sign. This review should include testing on a few individuals, perhaps some student employees as well as the designer. Of course, local codes will usually dictate signs for location of fire extinguishers and emergency exit routes, even the color and size of the characters in such signs. Where codes do not determine specific signs, internationally recognized symbols can be usefully employed as noted earlier. One final word of advice: when in doubt about the necessity for a sign, do not install it, and if in doubt about the wording or location, try a temporary sign.

The time needed for designing, manufacturing, and mounting needs consideration. The time requirement will in part depend on the choice of design, a matter which can be handled in various ways. If a standard campus design exists, no time is expended on design. Otherwise, the choice is between commercially available standard signs, a special design, and quite often, a combination of these two. The options in choosing the designer are reliance on the architect if the task is in the contracted scope of services, on an interior designer, on an institutional service, or on the library graphics staff if such exists. Regardless of the chosen route, it is advisable to arrange for some guidance from those responsible both for the architectural design and for selection of the interior finishes and furnishings. This may well be another case of an institution getting what it pays for; little investment of funds will result in only a modest achievement.

Signs may be prepared rather quickly if they are all bought from a library supply house or produced within the library or by a printing or graphics service of the institution. Months of advance notice, however, may be required for large or nonstandard orders to be sure that the local supplier can fill the entire order from local stock or get timely delivery, or that the in-house production unit has time available or can hire additional staff and obtain equipment needed to produce the signs. Specially designed signs may require as many as four or five months when new designs and a custom product is wanted, or when there is a large directory to be silkscreened and framed, or when special coloring or illumination is needed. Thus for a large and relatively complex building, the graphics program design, fabrication, and mounting could well be initiated with final text in hand six to twelve months before occupancy.

Since signs will seldom be part of the general contract, they ordinarily cannot be installed until the building has been turned over to the institution, and so the building may be opened with few, or at least not all, of the permanent signs in place. Temporary signs will bridge the gap. The priority for putting up signs can be designated so that the in-house studio or commercial firm produces first those that are most important for initial use and for appearance at the dedication ceremony. Certainly the clientele should be understanding if there are some typed or handwritten signs which serve as temporary room numbers. Indeed, the classes of books to be housed in a particular range of the stacks are often not final until the deployment of books in the stack has been completed and any unanticipated crowded sections have been spread out. So temporary signs do not become permanent, a deadline for completing permanent installation should be established.

The permanent installation may be done by the library's own crew, although commercial custom products will usually be installed by the manufacturer as part of the contract. Installation will involve drilling where signs are mounted on concrete walls, and hangers will be used for those to be suspended from a ceiling. During installation it is desirable for one individual in the library who is fully familiar with the graphics program to be present much of the time since there may have been generalized placement instructions (such as 48 in. off the floor, just to the right of the door, etc.) but the exact location will need to take into account special field conditions. A permanent sign may be very difficult to move an inch or more without leaving a visible mark, and so precision in installation is important.

Estimating and budgeting for the cost of signs is referred to in Chapter 9. It usually is part of an activation allowance. Occasionally it may be left to be covered in the contingency for the project, though this is inadvisable. The cost estimate will vary greatly, depending on whether it is an in-house product or a standard commercial or specialized commercial design. Typical of the last is, of course, the name on the building, though that may be the one sign that the architect and the contractor have responsibility for. Signs which are generally done in-house are the range indicators for shelving of book materials and the labels for card catalog trays. Between these extremes there are many options and the price will vary accordingly. Generally one cannot estimate cost on a square foot or meter basis as one can so many other costs. Rather it is a combination of three factors: the number of rooms and the range of service in the library which must be given signs, the complexity of the building which demands more or less, and the quality of the product. Signs for a large university main library building could easily cost as much as $15,000 to $20,000—without a pushbutton illuminated directory!

Illustrations in publications cited in the Bibliography indicate the wide range of possibilities and thus help the institution answer some of the questions raised.

16.3 Room Numbering

Earlier in this volume it was pointed out that, given no other direction, the architect will establish a floor, room, and area numbering or lettering system in the design process, at the latest during design development. Ideally, this system and the one used in the completed building will be the same, thus saving confusion and repeated effort as the building is activated and the graphics system completed. For example, an early room or area numbering system that is agreed to be final can provide accuracy in fundraising descriptions of a certain room, panel boards for security and safety alert systems, drafts of staff operating manuals, and furniture move plans. Numbering is, however, treated here because the graphics art design and installation may be part of the general signage task, although numbers for floors, in elevators, and of major areas are sometimes part of the architectural design and basic construction. Like so many other efforts, this choice of system often appears to be a simple task, while it can actually be quite complex.

An institutional policy in regard to room numbers may dictate a system and rule out certain configurations. Otherwise, while any particular building may have features that suggest special considerations, ten principles should be considered.

1. Similar numbers should, if possible, occur in the same location on each floor. For example, one would expect to find 212A directly above 112A. Clearly, this only works for those spaces that are repeated on each floor, but even if the general number group is repeated on each floor, it will be an aid to orientation.

2. There should be provision for adding spaces or dividing spaces. This is usually done by reserving numbers for such contingencies or by adding an alpha character.

3. Given a room number, one should find that the logical pattern of the numbering scheme should aid in finding the room. Finding the room, however, can be a problem in a large library, for unlike a hotel or large office building, it has large areas with unstructured corridors. One technique is some form of a matrix, but be careful to avoid too many tricks that may require careful learning of the system.

4. Try to keep the system simple. Four-digit numbers are preferable to five-digit numbers. In a large building this may mean

that a perfect solution covering every possibility is not reasonable. The "perfect" solution can simply be too complex.

5. Ideally, the system can be expanded to any future building addition. This may be uncertain if the addition could go on two or more sides, yet it may be worth a try.

6. If range or range aisles can fit within the numbering system, it would be advantageous, provided it does not add undue complexity. Carrel numbers probably would stretch the system beyond reasonable limits, though the carrels might be lettered, such as l30G being the seventh in area 30 on the first floor.

7. Some may suggest that indication of the room function within the numbering system would be advantageous. However, it is doubtful that this would aid the user (or fire department) in finding a space; the authors do not recommend functional orientation. Separate numbering systems for carrels, ranges, lockers, and the like (such as C100, R821, and L47) may be entirely appropriate.

8. Some directionality is an advantage. As one proceeds across the floor, the numbers should change in a logical sequence, such as front to back, left to right, or another natural sequence. This demand probably rules out a spiral; and it should, in most cases, rule out using odd numbers for one side of the building and even numbers for the other unless the building is organized on a long central corridor.

9. In branch libraries, if the prevalent building scheme does not suffice, the library may have one number in building terms and be subnumbered independently within the library area (such as L1-12 for the twelve library areas or zones and offices).

10. Above all, the numbering system should be easily explained to the user. Building directories should be designed to illustrate the logic of the numbering system and should, if possible, be oriented consistently as the user would view them at the head of main stairs, beside elevator doors, or in a lobby location.

Having outlined the principles of a numbering system, what is the next step? The first digit should be easy, as it will almost invariably represent the floor, with "1" being the entry level, "0" being a lower level (or, where there are multiple basements, "A, B, C. . ."), and 2, 3, 4 . . . being the upper floors. In the rare case of a library exceeding ten floors, two digits may be required for the floor level.

The next two digits should indicate fairly closely where on a given floor the room is located. The logical sequence mentioned above enters at this point. Libraries typically have major vertical movement cores centralized in the building; and the question no doubt will be, where should the sequence start? One quickly discovers that starting in the center leads to a complex and difficult system to learn. It is probably best to start at one side or to develop a simple matrix, such that the central stair is actually located in the center of the numbering system. Except for a very simple layout, clockwise numbering probably will be a problem just as a spiral numbering system is.

The final digit (preferably only one) will identify exactly the space. It is this digit that should also provide for future divisions of the space. A large room may be identified by the first three digits, while smaller rooms opening off of it are identified by the fourth character, a letter or number. In this case a clockwise pattern is appropriate.

Numbering-lettering schemes are a great expense to change. Thus it is well to test the proposed scheme on a sampling of faculty, staff, and students. Checking large or comparable buildings in the area can show problems to be avoided. Figure 16.1 suggests three distinct approaches for numbering, each responding to the nature of the building itself.

16.4 Moving In

The actual physical move is a chore. To make the process as easy and smooth as possible, the task should be worked out in detail in advance in order to save time and confusion while the move is taking place. This section does not provide guidance for detailed planning and execution. Nevertheless, some questions needing resolution and a few techniques are suggested, with extensive information provided in the Bibliography. The logistical problems of a move can be quite complex. Will the physical plant be ready when the move is scheduled to take place? Will the approach walks and driveway to the building be completed? Will the equipment and the furniture have arrived and been installed? Will the light, heat, and the elevators be operational so that the building is habitable? What is to be done about library service during the move; will it continue or be shut down for a few days or even a few weeks? Can course reserves be provided at another temporary location? Will the move be made at a time of year when the service load is low? How will it proceed if there is rain or snow? How can rapid relocation of computer terminals be accomplished? How should fragile materials be protected? What responsibility do staff have for moving or preparing their own desk area materials? Is there money and help available for preparation for moving and the shift itself? What extra help must be employed?

The equipment to be used in connection with moving must be ready and available. There is, of course, a basic difference whether one uses a commercial firm or does it completely in-house. If it is necessary to minimize the time taken by the move and if there is a suitable budget, using an experienced commercial firm may be much the wisest course, especially if the library is a large one some distance from its predecessor. If a move is the distance of a city block or farther, quite clearly trucks are going to be needed. Commercial movers or professional movers within the institution are essential, of course, for particularly heavy equipment and, generally, for office furniture. They not only have special equipment but are trained to move such items efficiently and safely. The location of each piece of equipment that is to be moved must be determined. This includes office equipment, files, pictures, the card catalog, pamphlet files, current periodicals, and so forth. Do not overlook the special types of materials that are not included in the main collection, such as the rare books, manuscripts, anything that goes into a vault if one has been provided, the duplicates that have not been disposed of, the uncataloged materials and those in process, the unbound periodicals, and office collections.

Moving the book collection is quite a different matter. Although Harvard used an excellent commercial firm for a great many moves, even of short distances, it is more common to use library staff and student help for relatively short moves. In this case the library must have book trucks and boxes or containers. The containers in which the books are to be packed may have to be designed and constructed, which may take time, or they may be rented. Regardless of whether the move is to a new wing, into remodeled space, or to a distant building, ways and means must be decided for moving the material in the least expensive and most expeditious manner. Keep in mind that safety of the people

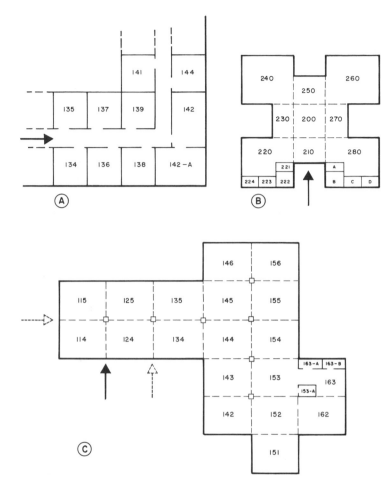

FIGURE 16.1 Room numbering. A number of schemes are possible. Use of odd-even is most suitable for a linear progression of spaces, such as found in an office building (A). (Note that 142-A is so numbered because it opens off 142; if it had a door directly off the corridor, it would be 140.) A clockwise numbering system (B) may be suitable for a symmetrical building where the numbered zones contain rooms of the particular numerical sequence. If there are more than 10 rooms in any zone, then an alpha character may designate the specific room. In very large buildings, both the odd-even and rotational schemes will be difficult. The best arrangement may be a very simple matrix where the numbered zones become larger as one progresses across the building in two directions (C). Ideally, the numbers would increase starting from the entrance. The temptation to add the concept of odd-even in the deployment of number zones in a large building should be avoided, as simplicity seems to serve the lost patron better than sophistication.

involved and the material is very important. The well-planned move that is carried out successfully can be one of the most satisfying experiences that a librarian will ever have, but an ill-planned one can be a catastrophe and is to be avoided at all costs.

The largest task is the decision on the location of each book in the new quarters; the more precise the decision, the better. This means that measurements of books in each class must be made so there are no unfortunate surprises during the move and that, so far as possible, material has to be moved only once. This plan may be complicated by the need to reintegrate stored parts of the collections. If a second move is necessary, it should not be more than a few feet, so books will not again have to go on to book trucks or into boxes. It is necessary for each range and section in the new space to be numbered (e.g., 127C4 for shelf 4 in section C of range 127) and labeled in some way so that it is easy to find, with a card attached to it, perhaps with temporary tape, showing just what classification block is to be placed in each section and with a duplicate of that card placed with the specific material in the old library.

Decisions are needed on whether to shelve in strict classification sequence, or whether, for example, political science should be next to history and on the largest stack floor or near the government document library. Stack floors may or may not be uniform in size, while the spaces taken by classification segments never are the same size. Should the same subject in two classification schemes, e.g., Dewey and L.C., be shelved on the same floor? Should a subject classification be started on one floor if it would have to be concluded on another, or are there small collections that could fit the remaining floor space and thus keep all of any one classification on one floor? Would certain collections be a greater loss than others if they were shelved in a basement with some vulnerability to water damage, and are certain collections in need of the best environment for book preservation? Should classifications with heaviest use be placed near the stack entrance to minimize traffic? Can one plan the deployment to reach the largest possible number of years without having to shift the collections, until each shelf or at least each range reaches absolute capacity at about the same time? As for details, decisions will have to be made about how full the shelves are to be, how much space is to be left in each section or on each shelf, and whether top and bottom shelves are initially to be left vacant. A piece of tape on the front edge of each shelf to be used can indicate when the shelf is full to working capacity.

The fullness of shelves may properly differ from one part of the collections to another. Volumes in classifications no longer used may be shelved nearly to capacity, accounting only for books in circulation. A journal run would fill shelves except for space at the end for future growth; and the space left for the desired number of years before stack capacity is reached can be reckoned by the current annual space required. The plan may recognize that some parts of the collection are more dynamic in growth than others, and some may deliberately be of very limited growth. In large collections it is well to precisely allocate a block of sections or ranges to a segment of the classification, and certain classifications to a floor, for otherwise seemingly careful measurement on each shelf can accumulate errors and the deployment in one area may come up with books to fill a few sections too many or many sections may be needlessly left empty.

The method of the shifting itself must be determined. Questions such as the following need to be thought out. Should it be done by hand, by hand cart, by an endless chain of students or others passing the books from one to another, or by book trucks? If the last method is selected, can the trucks be pushed out of one building and into the other without difficulty? Should dollies be used with boxes piled on them, or will a motor truck or pallet lift be required? How do you get from one floor to another in the old and in the new building? A critical constraint: the speed of moving may depend on the number of elevators available in both wings or the two buildings. If elevators are inadequate, it may help to arrange shifts so that books going to a level where an elevator will not be needed can be moved concurrently with those that require an elevator. Will a temporary book chute or a ramp be useful to carry books from the older building to the ground floor or outside? Will it be worthwhile with a very large collection to install a temporary endless-belt conveyor? Are the books to be cleaned and fumigated at the time of moving before going into the new location?

Different methods used for book moves are explained in references given in the Bibliography. Two points are obvious. There must be detailed planning, and there must be a staff member in charge who is good at coordinating and getting people to work smoothly and rapidly. A major challenge is to keep everyone busy and yet not too busy. It may well be that one person can effectively plan the job and do the measuring and labeling, but that a person of different talents should be in charge of the actual shift. Yet in such a case, teamwork by the two persons and immediate access by the latter to the former during the move is very important. Responsible staff should be at each end of the move, with hand radios or ready access to phones, to coordinate the rate of flow, particularly if books from different areas are being moved simultaneously. Each team needs good instruction as to the process, sequence of the move, attention to book order, and the proper way of lifting loaded boxes (with bent knees and straight back) to guard against injuries.

If the books are to be moved in boxes, should boxes be of a size requiring one or two persons to move a full box? If the latter, books can be placed in single or in double rows; boxes may be 36 in. (914 mm) long with a single row, or 18 in. (457 mm) square for double rows. They may be of plastic, heavy cardboard, wood, or papier-mâché. They should be deep enough so that for books that are less than 11¼ in. (286 mm) high, the boxes can be stacked one on top of another. If books are placed loose on ordinary library book trucks, there is always danger of their falling off. Books are safer if there are no avoidable hazards in connection with the move.

Boxes can be stored on book trucks if the book trucks are of the right dimensions, but dollies that are up to 2 ft (610 mm) wide and a little over 3 ft (914 mm) long may be more suitable. If dollies are used, they should have ends that rise far enough so that the boxes cannot fall off; the ends can also be used for pushing and pulling. Dollies should be narrow enough so that they can go down a stack aisle and long enough to hold a 36 in. (914 mm) box or two 18 in. (457 mm) boxes. The boxes can be placed on the dolly and filled from the shelves; the individual books will not be handled again until they reach their destination. The boxes can be three deep on the dolly at the time it is moved, the second and top ones being put in place before they are filled, but they must, of course, be unloaded and shelved in the same sequence. During slack times members of the team can shelf read to certify the book sequence, re-

moving the working capacity tape once the shelf order is correct.

If the books are to be shifted with dolly trucks and transported in motor trucks, a satisfactory loading dock must be available, as it is impossible to push a loaded dolly truck from the ground up a ramp into a motor truck. The use of a fork or pallet lift can be efficient. These comments are perhaps enough to indicate the problems; and a study of the literature on the subject may indicate the best solution for a particular library.

The costs for a move will, of course, vary greatly and must be budgeted, as described in Chapter 9. Cost estimates need to be obtained and will depend heavily on the amount of commercial moving utilized, the employment of students, number and capacity of elevators, as well as the efficiency with which the smoothness of the move was planned. No examples of moving costs are given since they go out of date rapidly and each move is a unique set of conditions. However, it can be stated that direct costs can be kept down if students and other hourly employees of the library move all of the books. Cost can also be kept down if the move can be done over many weeks and therefore have the best equipment, the most efficient use of vertical transportation, trained supervisors and an experienced crew, and a minimum of overtime and premium payments. In most cases, this means scheduling the move for as early as possible in the summer vacation. Even this arrangement may not give a sufficient margin.

The librarian in one large university, planning to move into a new building during the Christmas holidays, realized in time that the building would not be ready and relaxed the pressure on the contractor, with the result that the building was barely completed in time to move in at the end of the next summer. Some librarians have absolutely refused to attempt a major move during the regular academic school year, yet Cornell managed successfully to complete its shift in midwinter, just in time for the second semester, in spite of the severe upstate New York weather. The move was made possible because a tunnel connected the old building with the new. Comparatively few libraries will enjoy such an advantage. The major part of the move of the 75,000 volumes from Widener to the Lamont Undergraduate Library took place in four hours on a Sunday morning during the Christmas holidays with the aid of forty staff members who volunteered to help, working with four elevators in the old building, using the tunnel connecting the buildings and two elevators in the new one. This move, which brought five loaded book trucks every three minutes to Lamont, is a good example of careful planning worked out in the greatest detail.

Unexpected delays that make postponement of moving necessary often come from delays in arrival of equipment, rather than from slowness of construction. The trouble may stem from the supplier, but in too many cases it results from delay on the part of the institution in selecting and ordering the equipment. Many librarians, and even too many business managers, fail to realize that an order for anything but stock furniture takes time to design, to produce, and to ship and, in the case of bookstacks, to install. Even stock furniture is often out of stock, particularly if ordered in large quantities, and it may have to be fabricated after it is ordered. It is of the utmost importance to order furniture, equipment, and stack units in time for delivery when needed.

16.5 Settling In and the Shakedown Period

From the first day of moving in until the end of the warranty period of the contract, there is likely to be a certain turmoil. This will be a period for the surfacing of certain unanticipated problems, cleaning, punch-list residuals, final equipment adjustments, and perhaps a constant difficulty with balancing the ventilation or air-conditioning system.

A sense of humor during this period will be beneficial as will persistence in following through on the myriad issues that may arise. Staff adjustment may be very rapid in some cases and difficult in others. Staff may find that the acoustic conditions, direct sunlight, or ventilation drafts may be disturbing. Unfamiliarity with the new quarters may be unsettling to those who very much enjoyed their niches in the previous quarters. All of these complaints need to be listened to sympathetically. The staff should be encouraged to raise questions so that those responsible for the building can analyze the nature and cause of the condition, consider whether it needs immediate correction, whether it is something that can be postponed or should be treated

as part of a normal operating budget process, or that nothing need be done because the problem arises from a certain resistance to change. It also is desirable to require staff to live with the new quarters for a few months in order to see whether the problem is persistent and major or whether it is merely the experienced difference between the old and the new. For example, some staff may feel much more claustrophobic in the new quarters or, conversely, may feel they are now living in a goldfish bowl. Perhaps the staff can be led to realize in advance that working conditions will be different, that the ambience of the new quarters will be different by design, and that change should be expected and time allowed for people to try out and accommodate to the new circumstances.

Similarly, students and faculty may be very complimentary of the new quarters but also may be vociferous in their complaints about something they feel was overlooked and which is to them very disturbing. It is wise to listen sympathetically to each complaint, sorting out those which seem to be personal idiosyncrasies and those which are indicative of some fundamental problem. Problems are certain to exist—some minor, some inconsequential, and a few major. Some of these may have been on the contractor's punchlist, and it may be many months before each of those items is analyzed, diagnosed, and corrected or a solution negotiated. Some typical examples can suggest the range of conditions: incorrect wiring of switching, a blocked ventilation duct, carpet seams that gape, a door scraping the floor, settling which results in sticking doors, key problems in lock tumblers which are still new, humming in a faulty ballast, a door which was not hung correctly, or hardware not heavy enough to withstand the amount of use already evident, and problems with audio facilities that may be difficult to trace. The institutional representatives and the contractor need to continue to work on the punch-list residuals; and the architect and the representative of the institution will need to consult on unanticipated conditions, determine which are covered by the bid documents, which were planning oversights, and which are of such urgency that they must be corrected whether funded or not.

"It would be foolish to expect that any library could be planned, designed, and built without mistakes having been made or problems having occurred."[2] This statement by planners of the McLaughlin Library of the University of Guelph is representative of how almost any librarian or other member of the planning team would feel after going though the process on any large library building. The University of Guelph Library is an exceptional building, but in the published report of its creation, a handful of problems are enumerated.[3] Furnishings: the custom designs were not adequately tested and the librarians were not insistent enough in some of their specifications; service counters and card catalog trays have been particular problems. Basement space: this was more chopped up by walls than they now wish and some areas were not sized properly for the operations, such as for binding preparation or storing bulk collections before processing. Doors: access to certain rooms was too narrow to admit the equipment that was to be used. Coat rooms: except for occasional large groups of visitors, the public coat areas in the upper and lower lobbies are seldom used nor do the students use individual coat rods throughout the stacks, but instead use the back of their chairs or the corner of carrel tops. Closing bell: an alarm for emergencies or fires was included, yet a means of alerting users to closing was overlooked. Staff facilities: more attractive space could have been provided, perhaps at the top of thc building; a democratic decision to allow individual tea and coffee making has proved time consuming and untidy in comparison to vending machines; staff lockers have been somewhat of a problem and coat hooks should have been installed in the women's washrooms. Access by the handicapped: the entrance doors are too heavy for a person confined to a wheelchair to handle alone (the severe climate requires fast-acting heavy-duty door closers). Sun control: the use of exterior horizontal and vertical sun fins and louvers on the second and third floors are effective except for a few weeks a year when at certain times of the day the sun is not screened by these exterior devices. Glass in doors: faculty studies have no glass panels. Not having them has been an inconvenience for staff who need to determine if they are occupied. Floor covering: the only major area of the library that was not carpeted was technical services where

vinyl tile was used; maintenance problems have resulted and the noise level is high; carpeting should have been provided. Furthermore, there were found to be too many service points to staff. An architectural consultant felt the original design, with each upper floor the same size, was not sympathetic to its site. So the fourth (top) floor was redesigned into three smaller floors, extending it to six—with a bad loss of important library service objectives thereby.

Thus, even in an exceedingly successful building, there will be a variety of matters which would have been done otherwise if one had full hindsight while the planning process still allowed time. Other examples are provided on pages 3–19 in the proceedings of the 1965 Library Buildings Institute. One need not fret over this result. Every building has some problems, but none is so difficult that during the shakedown period practical solutions cannot be found without excessive expense or effort.

This period of settling in and adjustment will go on for much of a year in a large building (and perhaps for some weeks in a branch library). Most of the problems will surface and be resolved in the first four to six months, although some may be tenacious. Problems such as the ventilation system in Stanford's Meyer Memorial Library persisted from 1966 until 1979, when a completely rebuilt ventilation system had to be installed after years of complaints and persistent problems, and acoustical conditions until 1982, when acoustical isolation of the three upper floors was achieved. Relations with an institution's plant operations department will be particularly important during this shakedown period, most particularly for the HVAC and security alarm systems. One can expect relatively few electrical problems and fewer plumbing problems. Drainage, however, should be specially watched because of the horrendous damage that can come from faulty plumbing or inadequate drains. Drain problems can become apparent during the first heavy rains or the first spring thaw, creating peak conditions which should have been accommodated by the engineering design.

Cleaning up is another task of the shakedown period. If the contractor did a good job of cleaning before turning over the building, the institution is fortunate indeed. The contractors usually do a "broom clean" job. Although a commercial cleaning firm may have

[2] Stephen Langmead and Margaret Beckman, *New Library Design* (Toronto: Wiley, 1970), p. 84.
[3] Ibid., pp. 84–85.

done a thorough job, there is a good likelihood that some areas remain which need extra cleaning. A particular question to resolve is whether to clean the book collection before moving the books from old quarters, which may not have been air conditioned, into new quarters, bringing much of the dirt with the books. Clearly, it is best to clean or at least hand-vacuum before the books are moved or as the move is started. Time may not permit this, however, and in such an eventuality the cleaning of books in the new facility may be an important part of the shakedown. Cleaning books could be combined with the final specific shelf placement for the collections in their new quarters, that is, the individual adjustment of shelves so as to accommodate quarto or folio volumes if they were temporarily shelved flat or on their spines during the rush of moving.

A sometimes neglected point should not be forgotten. Before opening day it is desirable to give the staff a few days or a full week to settle in the new surroundings. This gives them time to reshelve their operational materials, get their desks back in operating condition, handle the exact placement of files, handouts, supplies, and review the new or revised regulations and procedures which are to be followed. This also could include time for selected spot-checking of book sequencing to assure that the new classification deployment was executed accurately.

It is suggested that on opening day and during the weeks or few months immediately following, operations will be smoothest and a favorable impression made on the clientele if a public service staff somewhat larger than normal can be on duty. A special temporary information desk might be located in the lobby if the regular reference or information desks are close to the entrance. It will also help if a short fact sheet about the building and small floor plans are available to hand out to students and visitors. There will be a demand for tours, and, therefore, the library staff may save time by offering a guided tour at regular intervals, perhaps each hour on the hour during the first week, tapering off to once a day after the first month. Tours may or may not be needed in new branch library facilities. Tours for institutional staff and neighboring librarians may also be in demand and can in fact be offered as part of the dedication events. All library staff should recognize that the building was provided for the students and faculty, and if the library staff take pains to assure that it is seen in that light and that the staff are not overly concerned with their own working amenities, the relations between the staff and users can ride the crest of this exciting event.

16.6 Dedication

Recognition of those who have contributed funds for a library building is an important and sensitive matter. Without support from governmental sources, an institution is completely dependent on individuals, foundations, and a combination of fundraising efforts to finance a library building. Even if financing is entirely governmental, as was the case for the California Northern Regional Library Facility, it is still desirable to thank publicly those who were instrumental in obtaining funds and approvals and were otherwise important to the project. The fundraising will occasionally be completed before the building is under construction. In most cases, however, an institution is motivated to start construction when a majority of funds has been pledged because construction price increases warrant a gamble on the ability to put the final financing in place. Of course, this complicates the dedication because the final list of contributors will not be known. In part for this reason, the dedication may take place some months after the library is open for use.

Ceremonies in connection with the start and completion of a library building are invariably helpful in donor relations, and the decisions about what to have and when need consideration by several institutional officers. An event may be desirable as a way of publicly thanking donors who wish to have their name associated with a building that will be visible and long-lasting, it may be a way of publicizing the institution's needs and therefore encouraging other gifts, and finally it may be an occasion to bring attention to the academic achievements of the institution and thus contribute toward its long-term reputation and encourage support from the neighboring community, governmental circles, alumni, and friends. It is customary to have a ceremony of some kind at the groundbreaking or early during the construction. This may be completely informal or may be accompanied by speeches. It may come when the excavation starts. There may be a cornerstone laying, with the insertion in the cornerstone of documents appropriate to the occasion and dealing with the institution's history and the donor's relationship to it. The stone may be placed with the aid of a senior representative of the institution as well as the donor. The groundbreaking ceremony can provide festivities, which everyone enjoys from time to time.

Long before the new building is completed, moved into, and opened to the public, it is to be hoped that the institution and the librarian will have been making plans for a dedication or other ceremony to celebrate the completion. The cost of such programs can range from a small sum to tens of thousands of dollars, the larger sums covered perhaps by a special gift if they are not budgeted into the building project itself. This dedication can take place just before or during the occupancy, as happened at the National Library of Medicine and the Library of Congress Madison Memorial Building, but it is generally preferable to schedule it after the library is in full operation, so that those interested can observe the resultant use of, and activity in, the new building. Each institution must decide for itself what it hopes to accomplish by this ceremony.

The planning for such ceremonies takes a good deal of time and may involve library staff, faculty, the administration of the institution, and perhaps trustees. The donor may also be involved if there is one major contributor. Where more than one or two sources of gift funds are involved, it is wise for the institution to start at least six months in advance of the event to determine the means for recognizing donations, settle on the design of plaques, obtain approval from the donor to make public the name, and approve the exact form in which the name will appear. It may require even longer advance scheduling if a major political figure or other celebrity is to participate. The institution will have to decide whether every individual is listed regardless of the size of the gift or whether the recognition will include only those who contributed above a certain amount. In each institution there can, of course, be a variety of ways of handling this, and it may be possible to list every individual "including several who requested anonymity" in a printed booklet that can be handed out as a keepsake at the dedication. The formal plaque may list only those who contributed above one thousand or five thousand

dollars, with the text also reading "Supporting gifts were made by many other individuals." If there is to be a formal portrait of the principal donor, it will also need to be budgeted; and if a painting is to be done, it may need to be started as much as a year before the dedication so that it can be completed and approved by the donor, framed, shipped, installed, and lighted appropriately.

An example of the text contained on a plaque is shown in Figure 16.2. Figures 16.3–16.6 illustrate parts of brochures and programs issued on the occasion of groundbreaking and dedication ceremonies.

An important decision is the extent to which individual spaces are to be labeled with signs or whether a single plaque in the lobby or by the main entrance will suffice. In some institutions it has been thought desirable to "sell" individual rooms, offices, study carrels—one can go to almost any length. The small brass plaques on chairs and other items of furniture and equipment are still occasionally offered. In deciding such matters, the institution administration will need to consider its style of fundraising and donor recognition, whether the fundraising requirements must call upon donations of small amounts as well as medium- and large-sized gifts, what the long-term consequences are if a precedent is set with labeling parts of the building for smaller gifts, and how such signs or plaques affect the aesthetic aspects of the building.

The program itself may include general cultural or social programs such as a dance or a musical concert, a major address on a subject of broad importance to the institution, a benediction or an offering of prayer and thanks, some formality thanking the donors, and officially turning the library building over to the board of trustees. It may also give recognition to the design concepts as presented by the library administration and interpreted by the architect and interior designer. The dedication ceremony generally is a reasonably brief program though it may be accompanied by one or several luncheons or dinners for donors and a variety of other events that may extend over two or three days. Credit should be given where credit is due; generous appreciation and gratitude for all participants, including the contractor, is a welcome part of such a happy occasion, although it is a matter for local decision, and a great deal of variety occurs in such events.

On behalf of the Stanford University community in this and
generations to come, we gratefully acknowledge
the gifts of those who made possible the construction of this library building and
the renewal of the adjoining structure of 1919. Together, they are dedicated as the

CECIL H. GREEN LIBRARY

on this 11th day of April, 1980.

Gifts were made by

Ida M. and Cecil H. Green
The James Irvine Foundation
The Kresge Foundation

Martha and Royal Robert Bush
W. B. Carnochan
Betsy B. and William A. Clebsch
Jean and Dewey Donnell

Frances K. and Charles D. Field
Charlotte J. and Richard E. Guggenhime
Gulf Oil Foundation
Elise and Walter A. Haas
Constance W. and Edde K. Hays
William R. and Flora L. Hewlett
Margaret and George D. Jagels
Lucile W. and Daniel E. Koshland
Florence Thompson Kress
Roger and Elly Lewis

Louis R. Lurie Foundation
Mrs. Eugene McDermott and Mary McDermott
The Eugene McDermott Foundation
The Charles E. Merrill Trust
PACCAR Foundation
Gaye and James C. Pigott
Alan J. and Marie Louise Schwabacher Rosenberg
Dorcas Hardison Thille
Doreen and Calvin K. Townsend
Ann Pigott Wyckoff

*Gifts were made by many others. The generosity of all those whose
philanthropy has provided this library is deeply appreciated.*

Peter S. Bing Peter S. Bing
President of the Board of Trustees

R. W. Lyman Richard W. Lyman
President of the University

David C. Weber David C. Weber
Director of University Libraries

Michael H. Jameson Michael H. Jameson
Chairman of the Academic Council Committee on Libraries

Design of the 1980 addition to the CECIL H. GREEN LIBRARY
and of the renewed west wing was the work of
Hellmuth, Obata & Kassabaum, Inc., architects.
Marquis Associates, interior designers, and Intrinsics, Inc., graphics.
In addition, we gratefully recognize the contributions of faculty,
consultants, contractors, advisors, and members of the Stanford University staff.

FIGURE 16.2 Donor recognition. Note the varying emphasis in the presentation of the text in the donor graphic that is placed in the lobby of the Cecil H. Green Library at Stanford. The text of this donor graphic also appears in a handout that was made available at the dedication of the building.

In the case of a major renovation, a dedication or celebration is also common, and in the case of opening new branch library quarters, there usually will be at least a reception for members and friends of the department. Depending on the need for donor recognition, there may be reason to have an elaborate event.

The occasion of the dedication of a major library building could be used to focus attention on the place of the library in the institution's educational program and its support of teaching and research, as well as noting the expected effect of the new building on the institutional ability to serve students and faculty. This may be a time to conduct a major symposium presenting recognized authorities speaking on some problems of in-

terest to libraries all over the country. This sort of program may be beneficial to the institution and its staff and to the library world in general. Such an occasion is generally accompanied by a luncheon, reception, or perhaps a banquet to which the distinguished guests are invited.

With the improved facilities now available, the demands made upon the library for service and materials will take a leap forward; and to have to reduce hours of service, as has been known to happen for financial reasons, would be a serious blow to the prestige of the library and the institution. In too many instances the use of funds to construct the library has left the institution unable to provide full services for the long hours desired by the students, to fund staff for the refer-

Groundbreaking Ceremony
Saturday, April 16, 1983
11:00 a.m.

Presiding
Susan Brynteson
Director of Libraries

Welcome
Dr. E. A. Trabant
President

Remarks
The Honorable Pierre S. du Pont IV
Governor

Mr. J. Bruce Bredin
Chairman, Board of Trustees

The Honorable Richard S. Cordrey
President Pro-Tempore, Delaware Senate

The Honorable Robert F. Gilligan
Majority Leader, Delaware House of Representatives

Dr. Samuel Lenher
Chairman, 150th Anniversary Advisory Committee

Mr. Gordon Pfeiffer
President, University of Delaware Library Associates

Address
Dr. Carol E. Hoffecker
Richards Professor of History, University of Delaware
and President, University Faculty Senate
"The First State and Its University, A Tradition of Partnership"

Groundbreaking

Luncheon

FIGURE 16.3 Groundbreaking ceremony program, University of Delaware.

Program

CONCERT	University Band *William H. Hill, Conducting*
INVOCATION	Rev. Bert Johnson *Lutheran Campus Pastor*
GREETINGS AND INTRODUCTION OF SPECIAL GUESTS	G. Homer Durham *President of the University*
REMARKS	Governor Samuel P. Goddard
REMARKS	Senator Carl Hayden
"PAGEANTRY" — WASHBURN	University Band
ADDRESS	Norman H. Strouse

FIGURE 16.4 Dedication convocation program for Charles Trumbull Hayden Library, Arizona State University, November 22, 1966.

ence desk in the evening, or even to pay for light and heat during certain hours. If problems of this kind have arisen or are likely to arise, the symposium is a chance to publicize the needs and perhaps to bring in the funds required.

Successful dedications require, in addition to a good program, much additional planning. Who is to be invited? What plans should be made for the housing and transportation of out-of-town guests? Who will pay for each local expense? Will there need to be attendants assigned to accompany distinguished donors and other visitors who may have physical problems getting around on campus? Must special parking be arranged, or a shuttle vehicle provided? Are name tags needed? Do chairs have to be rented? Will a lectern be needed? Will library staff provide guided tours of the building before or after the dedication to the friends whose interest and support is essential? Will there need to be flowers, music, photographs, a news story issued, and perhaps an awning or tent if rain is possible or if speakers and dignitaries may be in the hot sun for some time? Then there are invitations, perhaps a map to find the parking and dedication site, programs, a keepsake, and

THOMAS COOPER LIBRARY DEDICATION

Wednesday, December 8, 1976

11:00 a.m.

PROGRAM

Presiding .... Dr. William H. Patterson
President of the University

Invocation .... Dr. Lauren Brubaker
University Chaplin

Speaking for the Construction Project

For the architects .... Louis M. Wolff
Lyles, Bissett, Carlisle & Wolff

For the builder .... Archie S. Dargan
Dargan Construction Company

For the University Administration .... Harold Brunton
Vice President for Operations

Acceptance

On behalf of the Board of Trustees .... T. Eston Marchant
Chairman

On behalf of the Faculty and Students .... Dr. Keith E. Davis
Provost

On behalf of the Library Staff .... Kenneth E. Toombs
Director of Libraries

Music .... USC Student Brass Ensemble

Introduction of Speaker .... President Patterson

Address .... Jack Dalton
"The Cornerstone"

Benediction .... Dr. Brubaker

FIGURE 16.5 Dedication program for Thomas Cooper Library, University of South Carolina, Columbia.

Program	
Dedication of the **JOHN T. WAHLQUIST LIBRARY**	
October 15, 1982 2 p.m.	
Processional	**University Trumpet Ensemble**
Welcome	**William Dusel** *Executive Vice President Emeritus*
Greetings	**Maureen Pastine** *Library Director* **Tony Anderson** *Associated Student Body President*
Introduction of Guests	**Gail Fullerton** *President*
Keynote speaker	**Charles Burdick** *University Archivist and Professor of History*
Vocal solo	**Gus Lease**
Remembrances of John T. Wahlquist	**Arthur K. Lund** **Halsey C. Burke** **William Sweeney**
Remarks	**John T. Wahlquist** *President Emeritus*
Dedication	**Gail Fullerton** *President*
Reception and Tours	**John T. Wahlquist Library**

FIGURE 16.6 Dedication program for John T. Wahlquist Library, San Jose State University.

Dedication reception:	
food	$1,600
wine (donated)	n.c.*
Luncheon for major donors:	
catering	1,200
bus	155
invitations and placecards	75
Major speaker:	
honorarium and travel	900
dinner party evening before	120
dinner party after ceremony	145
lodging	140
Plant services:	
audience chairs, speakers platform, and sound amplification	665
grounds clean-up	245
Music before dedication and during reception	n.c.*
Invitations and program:	
stamps	225
program design	270
program production	860
invitation production	635
ad in student paper	100
flowers	65
	$7,400

*no cost

FIGURE 16.7 Example of major expenses for a library building dedication.

thank-you notes to be written after the ceremony to those who contributed significantly and generously. The institution may have a manual giving guidance on the multitude of details which such ceremonies involve. Though relative costs can vary greatly, the example shown in Figure 16.7 suggests some of the major extra expenditures of a dedication.

While each institution administration must decide for itself what is appropriate to its traditions and its style, and although it is possible to skip such ceremonies, it is an occasion to celebrate and take public recognition of the importance of such an event.

16.7 After the Warranty Period

If the warranty runs the customary twelve months after the contractor turned the building over to the institution, there is a need to solve during that period various adjustments and residual problems. After this period is over, it would, however, not be surprising for some significant problems to remain. The Meyer Memorial Library problems referred to in Section 16.4 are a case in point. Some physical problems in a building may be very difficult and expensive to solve; their resolution leads one back to some fundamental considerations in the need for building alterations, which are dealt with in Chapters 2, 3,

and 4. Thus in some cases, the next building project cycle may start as soon as the building is completed. Yet it would be imprudent to press the case right after dedication of the new space!

An especially serious matter is planning to maintain the new or renovated space in reasonable condition. Accounting data serve to suggest that a college or university place in escrow at least 1 percent of the replacement value of its physical plant each year to be used later for maintenance. In fact, the Syracuse University vice president for facilities administration has recommended that colleges and universities set aside 1.5 to 3 percent of the total replacement value of their buildings and equipment for renewal and replacements.[4] Exceedingly few institutions do this. As a result, it is well known that academic institutions have a formidable backlog of building maintenance problems, the result sometimes of decades of neglect. In 1973 repair or replacement was judged necessary in 20 percent of campus buildings and utilities. Each institution must face this problem, and it is merely pointed out because it is shortsighted to pour money into emergency patches when

[4] Harvey H. Kaiser, *Crumbling Academe* (Washington, D.C.: Association of Governing Boards of Universities and Colleges, 1984), p. 33, 35–37.

a regular, sound building-maintenance plan would in the long run be a more economical approach.

It may be useful after the building has been occupied and had time to become settled for the head librarian to lead a serious review of the project and its end result with the responsible librarians, architects, building representatives of the institution, and perhaps one or more consultants. What might have been done better the next time, and thus what lessons may be learned and should be recorded to help those dealing with future projects? At least a few universities do this for major projects. An historical record of the entire building project will help those who wish to learn from the project in the near term and those who work on institutional history. Finally, there is the obligation of those involved in a major project to respond to requests for sharing the experience with others who may be faced with a similar challenge, just as those involved with the present one may have benefited from others.

APPENDIX A

Program Examples

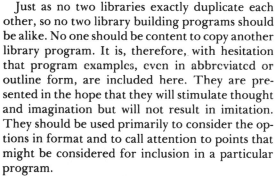

Just as no two libraries exactly duplicate each other, so no two library building programs should be alike. No one should be content to copy another library program. It is, therefore, with hesitation that program examples, even in abbreviated or outline form, are included here. They are presented in the hope that they will stimulate thought and imagination but will not result in imitation. They should be used primarily to consider the options in format and to call attention to points that might be considered for inclusion in a particular program.

To be most helpful to the architect, the program moves from the conceptual and general to the small components and specific details. This appendix starts with three examples. First is the outline of the program for the Tufts University Library, Medford, Massachusetts, prepared by the librarian, Joseph Komidar.

Foreword by the President Explaining the Educational Philosophy of the University and the Purpose of the Library.

- I. Librarian's Statement
- II. General Objectives and Requirements
- III. Pattern of Library Service
- IV. Outline of Space Needs
- V. Size and Space Needs of the Library Collections
- VI. Accommodations for Readers and Description of Spaces
  - A. Vestibules and Entrance Lobbies
  - B. Exits and Supervision
  - C. Main Desk
  - D. Public Catalog
  - E. Reference Collection
  - F. Bibliography Collection
  - G. Periodical Collection
  - H. Reserve Book Room
  - I. Documents Collection
  - J. Map Collection
  - K. General and Special Collections
  - L. Crane Reading Room
  - M. Exhibits
  - N. Browsing Room
  - O. Group Study Rooms
  - P. Typing Rooms
  - Q. Audio-Visual Area
  - R. Microtext Reading Area
  - S. Curriculum Laboratory
  - T. Faculty Studies
  - U. Facilities for Smoking
  - V. Toilet Facilities
  - W. Coat Rooms
  - X. Table Sizes
  - Y. Chairs
- VII. Staff Accommodations
  - A. Administration and Department Heads
  - B. Book Selection and Processing
    1. Acquisitions
    2. Cataloging
    3. Mechanical Preparations
    4. Bindery Preparations
  - C. Supply Closet
  - D. Receiving and Shipping Room
  - E. Storage Room for Equipment
  - F. Library Staff Room
  - G. Facilities for Janitor and Maids

527

VIII. Space Relationships and Traffic Flow
    A. Readers
        1. Reading and Borrowing
        2. Reference
    B. Service Staff
  IX. Architectural Program
    A. Site Planning Conditions
    B. Conditions for the Building Design
        1. Space Requirements
            a. General Distribution by Major Space Categories
                (1) Space for Reading Material
                (2) Seating in Library for Readers
                (3) Work Space for Staff
                (4) Architectural Space
            b. Detailed Allocation of Areas in Library
                (1) Reference Material
                (2) Periodical Indexes
                (3) Bibliographies
                (4) Crane Collection
                (5) Browsing Area
                (6) Reserve Room
                (7) Current Periodicals
                (8) General Collections
                (9) Documents
                (10) Special Collections
                (11) Maps
                (12) Microtext Area
                (13) Audio-Visual Area
                (14) Typing Rooms
                (15) Group Study Rooms
                (16) Extra Seat Allowance throughout Public Spaces
                (17) Main Desk
                (18) Public Catalog
                (19) Preparations Room
                (20) Administration Office
                (21) Other Staff Accommodations
                (22) Seminar Spaces
                (23) Curriculum Laboratory Alcove
                (24) Local Government Collection
                (25) Faculty Studies
                (26) Smoking Area
                (27) Architectural Space
        2. Construction Requirements
        3. Story Heights and Column Spacing
        4. Mechanical Installations
        5. Expansion

Susan A. Schultz, librarian of the Asbury Theological Seminary in Wilmore, Kentucky, prepared a twelve-page program for a library building, and then ingeniously placed the requirements for the five basic physical elements in tabular outline form on one sheet, which is shown as figure A.1.

The third example is the 1975 program scope for the Cecil H. Green Library at Stanford University.

TABLE OF CONTENTS

Introduction
Program History
Academic Plan or Function of the Main Library
Location and Site
Architectural Compatibility
General Building Configuration and Access
Functional Relationships
General Criteria for Heat, Light, etc.
Memorial Names
Architect's Scope of Work
Procedures and References during Design and Construction
Synopsis of Space Requirements
Summary of Space Requirements
Detail of Space Requirements
  1. Administrative Services
      Financial Office Group
      Personnel Office
      Mail and Supply Service
      Photocopy
  2. Book Selection
  3. Acquisition
      Fumigation Area
  4. Cataloging
  5. Government Documents
      Public Services
  6. Circulation
      Stacks and Readers
      Student Seating
      Microtext-Newspaper
  7. General Reference
      Map Service
      Theatre Collection
      Interlibrary Collection Services
  8. Special Collections
      Exhibit Area
      Robinson Room
  9. University Archives
 10. Card Catalog and National Bibliographies

Program Divisions A library program can be divided into five parts as follows:

1. Information about the institution and its objectives
2. General requirements of the library
3. Basic needs and area requirements
4. Spatial relationships
5. Information about particular building areas.

The above arrangement will be followed here. The examples used show some overlap between the different groups. Also, the last two sections may be reversed, the relationships giving the overview and the much longer requirements giving the detailed picture.

Information about an Institution and Its Objectives. Quotations abbreviated from the program prepared for the University of California at Santa Cruz, a new campus of the University of California. (This is from the program for the first stage of a large library. It was planned to be adequate for seven years after its completion.) The author is Donald T. Clark.

THE LIBRARY AND THE UNIVERSITY IT WILL SERVE

The following features will have a direct bearing on shaping the library organization and building.

1. During this period the student body will be almost exclusively made up of undergraduates, and the first unit should be designed primarily for undergraduate use.

ASBURY SEMINARY LIBRARY PROGRAM

BASIC ELEMENT	SPACE NO.	FUNCTION	LOCATION-RELATIONSHIP	SPACE QUANTITIES (PRESENT / 15 YRS / 30 YRS)	EQUIPMENT-FURNITURE	REMARKS-QUESTIONS	FLOOR PREFERENCE (GND / MAIN / UPPER)	SPACE REQUIREMENTS
I READER SERVICE	I-1	READING & STUDY	CLOSE TO STACKS-SMALL AREAS	170-200 READERS	TABLES, DESKS, CHAIRS	MAKE LATITUDE FOR STUDY AND CLIMATE ANALYSIS	X? / X / X	200 to 20-35 SF/PERSON = 4,000 to 7,000 SF
	I-2	RESERVE BOOK READING		INCLUDED IN ABOVE	USE READING ROOM ABOVE	WHAT IS CLOSED RESERVE?		
	I-3	RESEARCH	OFF STACK AREA	AS MANY AS POSSIBLE	CARRELS, CHAIRS	WHAT PERCENT OF READERS	X / X	
	I-4	BROWSING	NEAR PERIODICALS, VIEW BOOKS	20±	LOUNGE CHAIRS, STAND-UP DESKS		X / X	20 x 35=700 = 2 BAYS
	I-5	STUDY HALL	NEAR ENTRY-OUTSIDE DESK CONTROL	20-30	TABLES, CHAIRS, DESKS, TABLES	WHAT SIZE	X	30x35=1050 = 2-3 BAYS
II HOUSING MATERIALS	II-1	GENERAL BOOKS	FREE STANDING STACKS ADJACENT TO GENERAL READING AREA	42,000 / 91,000 / 136,000	120 components / 364 / 544	5 VOLS/LIN. FT	X / X	
	II-2	REFERENCE BOOKS	NEAR AND COUNTER SHELVING	4,000 / 6,000 / 8,000	+800 FT / 1200 FT. / 1600 FT.	9-10" COUNTER HT. SHELVES	X / X	
	II-3	BIBLIOGRAPHY	BETWEEN SERVICE CENTER AND STAFF WORK AREA	285 / 425 / 600	SHELVING FOR LG. CATALOG ETC. COUNTER FOR CBI VOLS.		X / X	
	II-4	PERIODICALS BND	SHELVES LIKE REF. BOOKS & ADJ. BINDING STACKS	1,500 / 3,000 / 5,000	+300 FT / 600 FT / 1000 FT		/ X	
	II-5	UNBOUND & TIED	ROOM LOCKABLE BUT ACCESSIBLE	380 TITLES 500 TITLES	1500 LF 3000 LF 5800 LF		X	
	II-6	CURRENT	IN MAIN READING AREA NEAR CIRCULATION DESK	234 LF	SPECIAL SHELVING W/SLANTED SHELF & STORAGE FOR CURRENT VOLUMES		X / X	
	II-7	NEWSPAPERS-CURRENT			NEWSPAPER SHELVING		X / X	NEAR CARD CAT. & BIBLIO. RM.
	II-8	PAMPHLETS	IN SERVICE AREA		2 LEGAL / 5-8 LEGAL FILES		X / X	
	II-9	MICRO-PRINTS, FILMS	STORE NEAR SERVICE AREA	600	SPECIAL CASES		X / X	
	II-10	AUDIO VISUAL	STORE IN SERVICE AREA	2000 SLIDES, TAPES FOR RECORDER	SPECIAL CABINETS			
	II-11	PICTURES MOUNTED	STORE IN SERVICE NEAR PAM. FILE		2 or 3 JUMBO FILE		X	
	II-12	RELIGIOUS EDUCATION CURRICULUM LAB	SECOND FLOOR		DESK, TABLES, CHAIRS, FILES			
III SERVICE AREA	III-1	CIRCULATION	NEAR ENTRANCE-VIEW OF STAFF WORK AREA AND READING		CIRCULATION DESK, SWIVEL CHAIRS, 2-3 TRUCKS	ARRANGED SO NORMAL NOISE DOES NOT DISTURB READERS-ELEC. PLUGS	X	
	III-2	BOOK LIFT	NEAR CIRCULATION DESK-ADJACENT TO RECORDING AND					
	III-3	WORK AREA	ACCESS TO PUBLIC & STAFF FOR CIRCULATION AND REFERENCE		TYPING DESK-EXEC. DESK-REFERENCE CABINET-STANDING HEIGHT			
	III-4	CARD CATALOGUE						
	III-5	EXHIBIT & DISPLAY	MAIN ENTRANCE		BUILT-IN AND MOVABLE		X	
	III-6	BULLETIN BOARDS	MAIN ENTRANCE AND ELSEWHERE					
	III-7	EXIT CONTROL	STAFF AREA			PLANNED SO CHECKER COULD CONTROL	X	
IV STAFF WORK AREA	IV-1	LIBRARIAN	QUITE ACCESSIBLE TO PUBLIC		EXECUTIVE DESK, SWIVEL CHAIR, 2-3 POSTURE CHAIRS, CABINET, BOOK SHELVES		X	
	IV-2	SECRETARY	& STAFF THRU SECRETARY SUITE FOR 3 PERSONS WITH CONN. OFFICE SERVING LIBRARIAN AND ASSISTANT LIBRARIAN		TYPEWRITER DESK, SWIVEL CHAIR, 4 FILE CASES, TABLE, PIGEON HOLE FOR NOTICES	WRAPPING CENTER FOR SMALL PARCELS	X	
		ACQUISITIONS PUBLIC SERVICE						
		CONFERENCE ROOM TABLE & 6 CHAIRS	ADJOINING LIBRARIANS OFFICE-ALSO FOR PREVIEWING SLIDES, FILM ETC.				X	
	IV-2	ACQUISITIONS SERVICE ASSIST. LIBRARIAN	EASY ACCESS TO BIBLIOGRAPHY ROOM CAT. DEPT. AND CIRC. AREA		EXEC. DESK, SWIVEL CHAIR, BOOK SHELVES AND 2 FILE CASES		X	
	IV-3	RECEIVE & SHIPPING	GROUND FLOOR ½ LOAD DOCK		WORK TABLE, SHELVES		X	
	IV-4	PROCESSING LIB. MAT.	SPACE BEHIND CIRC. DESK	OFFICE, SEMI-PRIVATE	EXECUTIVE DESK, SWIVEL CHAIR, LOUNGE CHAIR, TRUCK,		X	
		CATALOGUER			TYPE. SHELVES, DESK, BOOKSHELVES		X	
		LIBRARY ASSISTANT-TYPIST	NEXT TO CATALOGUER TYPIST		CHK. PAD, KARDEX, WORK TABLE FOR PASTING, SINK		X	
		BOOK PREPARATION	NEAR TO CATALOGUER "MESSY" WORK LOCATE OUT OF SITE		BOOK SHELVES, MENDING COUNTER		X	
	IV-5	PHOTO COPYING	ACCESS TO SECRETARIES AND CIRCULATION STAFF		THERMO-FAX MACHINERY		X	
V SPECIAL SERVICES	V-1	ARCHIVES	STORE ASBURY'S HISTORICAL RECORDS	REMOTE AREA OR SEPARATE	TABLE, STOR. PLACE FOR SUPPLIES SHELVING-MAY BE BEHIND		X	
	V-2	AUDIO-VISUAL	LANGUAGE STUDY-PREACHING-MUSIC	15 to 20 PERSONS	CONSOLE, BOOTHS, STAGING, TABLETS		X	
	V-3	BUILDING OPERATION AND MAINTENANCE	JANITOR'S OFFICE		JANITOR'S CLOSETS		X	
	V-4	COAT ROOM OR RACKS					X	
	V-5	CONFERENCE ROOMS	STUDENT GROUP STUDY CONFERENCES	REMOTE LOCATION 2 ROOMS SEATING 6	TABLES AND CHAIRS		X / X	
	V-6	FACULTY STUDIES	RESEARCH	REMOTE=ACCESS WITH HISTORY A.V.			X / X	
	V-7	HERITAGE ROOM	NEAR MAIN ENTRANCE	EXHIBIT WOMEN'S OF HISTORY ATS				
	V-8	LIBRARY LECTURES	GROUND FLOOR	ACCESS WITH LIBRARY			X	
	V-9	MUSIC LISTENING	FOR MUSIC CLASSES	ADJ. TO A.V. LEARNING CENTER	IND. LIST. IN A.V. CENTER		X	
	V-10	REST ROOMS					X	
	V-11	STAFF LOUNGE AND WOMENS REST ROOM	STAFF MEETINGS ACCESS FROM LECTURE ROOM	TO SEAT 12-15	LOUNGE FURNITURE		X	
	V-12	STORAGE	GIFT BOOKS RECEIVE SHIP &		WORK TABLE, BOOK SHELVE LOCKERS, FOR STORE 1 TYPEWRITER,		X	
	V-13	TYPING ROOM	REMOTE		TABLES, DESKS, CHAIRS		X	

FIGURE A.1 Asbury Seminary Library program.

2. During the initial stages there will be emphasis on liberal arts education, with most students majoring in arts and sciences. What laboratories are to the natural and physical sciences, libraries are to the liberal arts.

3. Within the liberal arts the heaviest emphasis will be upon the social sciences and the humanities.

4. A very high percentage of students will be living on campus. This will mean that more than the average number of study spaces should be provided.

5. Much will be done to foster an exciting intellectual climate and with it there will be an emphasis upon independent study.

6. New methods of instruction, study, and communication will be encouraged, and the latest developments in communication and programmed learning will have a prominent part in teaching.

7. The library will be a service agency for many non-book types of material—maps, manuscripts, microfilm, film strips, tape recordings, pictures, and so forth, and many mechanical devices will be used to further study activities. Flexibility should be present to provide for inevitable changes that will come with improvements in library technology.

8. In this period the dominant academic unit will be the residential college in which will be combined many educational and curricular student and faculty activities. Each college will have libraries and reading rooms with collections of some ten thousand volumes, but the technical processing of books for the residential college libraries will be done within the university library. Since certain typical study hall activities will be provided by the colleges, more attention can be given to individual study stations in the university library.

9. Santa Cruz is part of the University of California, which means that the resources of other campuses will be available through interlibrary loans and travel. The library will emphasize the collection of bibliographical material, so as to make known the holdings of other institutions. The building should be so designed as to take advantage of newer developments for doing this. We do not know what they are, but we can probably count on greater use of machines.

10. The demands for a new emerging university will differ considerably from those of an older, well-established campus. Space factors derived from the experience of older institutions should not be blindly applied but should be used with recognition of the rapid growth potential. For example, because of the desired rapid buildup in the collection of books, a larger than normal acquisition staff will be needed.

11. The nature of the university will be changing from year to year, from a beginning as a liberal arts college to a full-grown university. Flexibility in building design and in equipment is an essential. There should be a minimum of built-in objects. The library must be so located that it may expand, and the building program should be thought of in units or stages.

Quotations here and later are abbreviated from the program requirements for the library of the University of Wisconsin–Milwaukee, by Mark M. Gormley.

The objectives of the library are based on the objectives of the University itself. They are:

1. To make available the books, periodicals, governmental publications, and other library materials necessary for conducting a successful university program. This program includes the teaching of undergraduate and graduate courses and research and service programs.

2. To train a competent library staff to service and interpret the library's collections.

3. To provide the physical facilities and equipment that will assist in the use of these library materials.

4. To assist and cooperate with faculty members in their varied instructional and research programs.

5. To instruct students in the efficient and effective use of library materials.

6. To encourage students to develop the habit of self-education.

7. To offer a program of library service that not only will meet but will exceed the requirements and standards of the various professional associations and accrediting agencies.

8. To integrate the library program with local, regional, national, and international library resources.

The basic purpose of a university library is quite simple. It must provide the records of civilization and assist students and faculty to retrieve and interpret them. While this purpose can be expressed simply, neither the function of the library nor its design is a simple problem.

The success of the library will depend upon a clear conception of the true function of this specific library and an architectural solution that will insure efficient operation, provide great flexibility of space, be direct, logical, and easily understood in its arrangement, and provide an environment that is friendly, intimate, warm and pleasant. This library is not to be a static, cold monument; it must be a live, vital place, constantly growing and changing as needs dictate.

The design must be basically a solution of the interior functions. The exterior should reflect the feeling and quality of the interior. Windows are necessary only for relief for the occupants, and should be used cautiously and sparingly. Exterior materials should be chosen in relation to other buildings, either constructed or to be constructed on the campus.

The library should have a special quality that is distinct from classroom buildings and clearly establishes it as the academic heart of the campus.

A library is composed of books and other media for the storage and retrieval of information. Properly planned it is the catalyst in the creation of ideas. Our library is to be a research-oriented library in which undergraduates can be served most efficiently.

Avoid segregating readers too much according to academic level by having certain facilities for undergraduates in one area, and the provision of other areas for more advanced student readers. All materials are to be available to all university personnel. It is only by exposing eager students to a wealth of material that we can develop latent potential in the people that we are pledged to develop intellectually. A library is a place in which the discovery of ideas becomes exciting.

For the faculty the library is a potent teaching instrument. Books beyond the prescribed text of a particular course are the usual rather than the incidental tools of contemporary education. The professor must have access to the materials for research which strengthen him and through him the students whose intellectual background he is developing.

The library is to be one large central building that will house library facilities for all the disciplines on the campus. There will be no organized departmental or satellite libraries in other buildings.

Quotations excerpted from the program of the Gerald R. Ford Presidential Library at the University of Michigan describe its clientele.

No one will have reason to enter the stacks except the staff, and the arrangement of the research room must allow ready access to the stacks by the staff while precluding it for the researchers. All materials used by the researcher will generally be brought to him in the research room by a staff member.

Visits to the research room may vary as widely as from 500 upwards of 2000 per year. The 150 to 700 individuals who will make these visits fall generally into the following classes:

(1) High school and undergraduate students 24%
(2) Graduate students doing research on dissertations 21%
(3) Faculty members doing research on books and articles 25%
(4) Journalists/free-lance writers 12%
(5) Government researchers/writers 4%
(6) Other/unidentified 14%

The users of the research room are not casual browsers or the idly curious, but serious scholars focusing on the President and his administration. The high school and undergraduate students are usually advanced placement individuals and are often brought as a class for specialized research topics. Researchers usually make advance written application for permission to use the materials, and their application must show that they are engaged in research for which the Library has unique holdings.

The average length of stay at a Presidential library for a particular researcher is four days, however, it is not uncommon to have researchers spend several months, and biographers may spend upwards of a year. More than two-thirds of the researchers will come from distances greater than 50 miles, and will need to find inexpensive lodgings in the vicinity. Approximately 60 percent of these will arrive by car, with the rest coming to the Library on foot or by public transportation. Because the academic profession is attractive to physically handicapped persons, a higher than average percentage of the researchers will be incapacitated in some way, and the facilities must be planned to accommodate such persons.

Normal Activities of Researchers

In the majority of cases, the researcher will have written or telephoned the Library in advance of arriving, and the staff will be aware of the general nature of his project. When a researcher first comes to the Library, he will be oriented on the nature of the holdings as they relate to his topic and the rules and procedures to be followed. Ideally, this orientation should take place in a room adjacent to the research room. This room should be comfortably furnished to put the researcher at ease and allow the staff member to communicate with him on an informal basis. Researchers may often need to consult further with staff during their visit, and if this room is located adjacent to the research room, it will

enable longer conversations to take place without disturbing others in the research room. Since eating, drinking, and smoking are not allowed in the research room, this area can also serve as a place for the researcher to relax during his stay in the Library. National Archives regulations for research rooms prohibit briefcases, pocketbooks, and other large packages which could be used to conceal documents. Therefore, an area near the research room should contain 20 to 24 lockers where researchers may deposit their belongings while in the research room. It would also be convenient to have facilities here for hats, coats, and umbrellas.

Once in the research room, the researcher will need to consult several of the finding aids which will enable him to locate the materials he wishes to see. Finding aids may be in printed form, card catalogue, or computerized. Space for the card catalogue should be provided in an area convenient to the working area of the staff member on duty in the research room. Space for the computer terminal should also be close to the staff member; printed finding aids may be shelved along the wall. Bookcase space (preferably with built-in shelving) should also be provided in the research room for approximately 150 linear feet of standard reference works for researcher use.

In most cases, the researcher coming to the Library will have used most printed materials pertinent to his subject before he arrives. This is not always the case, but persons coming from a distance to do research usually prefer, for financial reasons, to make their stay as short as possible. Therefore, they tend to concentrate during their visit on use of the unique archival resources of the Library, and the research room should be planned with this function in mind.

General Requirements of the Library. Selections adapted from the Lafayette College Library building program by Clyde Haselden.

The library at Lafayette College is a central element in the educational program of the College. It should provide a workshop equivalent to the laboratory for students in courses in the humane and social studies. It should supplement the course work of all students and perhaps especially those in the sciences and engineering through facilities and programs that attract and stimulate the individual to broad self-education. Though it cannot in a full sense be a research library, it should have sufficient research facilities and resources to allow the faculty, particularly in the humanities and in the social studies, to develop as scholars in their fields. The aim of the library program in its various functions must be to cultivate the capacity to enjoy all forms of recorded human experience and achievement and the capacity to use these resources with sound judgment in independent effort that may continue after graduation from college.

To fulfill this function, the new library building must be able to take care of the following broadly defined functions:

1. Supplement the educational program of the college by acquiring, cataloguing and shelving in one central location the necessary books, periodicals and other library materials.
2. Increase knowledge of the basic reference sources by guidance in the use of library facilities.

3. Cultivate interest in and appreciation of books and their value by assistance in the development of the reading habit.

4. Encourage individual and group study by providing carrels, faculty studies and seminars as well as quiet, attractive and comfortable reading areas.

General Characteristics

1. Utility should take precedence over architectural style in planning an effective interior arrangement. While ornamentation and monumentality are to be avoided, an attractive and pleasant interior is essential.

Flexible space relationships are necessary to provide for the rearrangement of units to meet future needs. The building should be planned for library work with emphasis on efficient and economical service.

Expansion of the building—horizontal or vertical—should be decided now in relation to site, cost, efficiency of operation, and general appearance. [etc.]

The University of Wisconsin–Milwaukee program includes these statements.

Concept of flexibility. The basic premise of the plan relationships must be based on growth and change. This will require modular layout for walls, lighting, air conditioning, book stacks, and so forth, to permit an easy interchange between book stacks and seating. Reading areas are to be interspersed with the book stacks to create smaller quieter areas and a better environment for study. Ease of creating new areas by moving stacks and seating furniture is essential.

This is to be an open-stack design. Books will be shelved on free-standing stacks 7 ft 6 in. high.

Entrance. There is to be a single point of entrance and a separate single point of exit past a control point. This will permit the use of an open-stack system and greater freedom in the location of books and seating areas. Exits required for fire regulations should be equipped with signal devices. A weather vestibule is required.

Floor loading. The floors must be designed for 150 pounds per square foot live load to permit location of book stacks in any location.

Air Conditioning. The entire facility must be air conditioned. Filters of high capacity should be used to filter dust and smoke.

Acoustics. Control of sound is all too often neglected in libraries, and the use of acoustical floor, wall, and ceiling materials must be studied. If solution becomes a serious problem, the services of a competent acoustic consultant must be sought.

Lighting. Fluorescent lighting should be used throughout with serious consideration given to locating the ballasts in a remote area. A good light level shall be maintained in the reading areas with higher intensity in the technical processes area and over the card catalogue.

Furniture and equipment should be harmonious with the building and contemporary in design. Contrasts are desirable. A variety of reader facilities are to be provided, such as individual carrels, group study tables, and occasional chairs.

Toilets. There shall be no public toilets on the first floor. A staff men's toilet should be provided near the director's office. A staff women's toilet and rest area should be provided in a convenient location. Adequate public toilets should be provided in secondary areas.

Elevators. It has been the general policy of the University that a student can walk three flights, plus the basement. Elevators are intended to serve the library services, faculty use, and paraplegic patrons.

The University of Southern California Hancock Library used an interesting method of presenting the objectives in selecting an air-conditioning system.

Library Area: Third Floor Level, Rare Book Storage Area

Description of Use: Access is limited to staff. Doors will be kept closed and locked at all times. No work or study areas are included in this space. There are no windows.

Issue*	Must	Want	Wt.**
System will aid in smoke control		X	2
Humidity Control 50% plus or minus 5% *annual* deviation evaporative system with industrial quality electronic controls	X		
Liquid leakage hazards not installed in area		X	
Temperature closely controlled in range of 60–65 degrees		X	
Ability to remove NO, SO, and Ozone		X	
Equipment and fan noise reduced to a minimum		X	7
Minimum particulate air filtration MIL STD 282 DOP efficiency greater than 60%	X		
Flexible to accept interior partition changes		X	5
No perimeter wall penetrations required		X	1
Appearance of units and ductwork comply with aesthetics of room design and decor		X	8
Time to repair reduced to minimum		X	3
Maintenance and repair activity undisturbing to library operations		X	6
Equipment located and designed for easy regular maintenance tasks		X	4

*The financial issues of initial cost, annual owning cost and operating cost have not been addressed in this listing.

**Weighting of importance to end-user (library) is indicated by a scale of 1–10, where 1 means most important.

Selections from the program for a large university library deal with expansion and style.

General Statement

Because building additions will be needed in the future, the architect should visualize a complete structure at least twice as large as will be required to meet the space requirements given below. The design of the initial structure should be sufficiently independent as not to seem abbreviated or awaiting completion. At the same time it must be part of a harmoniously conceived future completed structure. The architect shall submit elevations and perspective drawing of the completed as well as of the initial structure. The site [which has been selected] provides room for additions to the west and south, and the architect shall specify adjacent to the initial structure the approximate areas which should be reserved for future additions.

The architect should be under no obligation to reproduce the architectural style of other buildings on the campus. On the contrary, a new departure should be most appropriate. The site itself encourages independence in this respect. The sort of monumentality which interferes with the comfortable and efficient use of the library should be avoided. The library building ought by its appearance to invite the passerby to enter, and not intimidate by cold impersonality. As the heart of the University, the library will combine genuine functionalism with aesthetic imagination and avoid every sort of aesthetic falsity, pretentiousness, or slovenliness. If the University is to make full use of the opportunity, the new structure will add to the campus a significant example of the best work of modern American architecture.

Two portions from the University of Chicago Regenstein Library program, the primary author being Herman H. Fussler.

Flexibility

It is not a contradiction to assert that the success of a large, research library building will be critically related to an accurate analysis of functions and a skillful translation of these into efficiently planned and related space and equipment, while at the same time one asserts, with equal conviction, that changes in library functions and requirements are absolutely inevitable, and the library must be able to adapt to them over a long period of time.

The new library building reflects the dual nature of this problem; i.e., it must be well planned to perform its tasks as these are now understood, and it must have very great capability for easy and economical change in space use and relationships in the future. The building must achieve these objectives at reasonable cost.

"Total" flexibility is in some ways a chimera and, in a building of this size, such complete flexibility in the use of space may be prohibitive in cost and, in terms of probable functions, not absolutely essential. However, a very substantial degree of flexibility is a firm requirement, and can, we believe, be provided at reasonable costs.

Apart from basic design features, e.g., floor loads, ventilation, lighting, module size, etc., long range flexibility will be critically related to: (1) the way in which the bookstack space is distributed in relation to other facilities; (2) a design that will easily permit a variety of functions in substantial areas of the building—and especially in those areas that, initially, are located between reader or staff areas and the bookstack; (3) the use of movable partitions, furniture, and equipment; (4) a well chosen module size; (5) the efficient location and grouping of fixed elements, e.g., stairways, elevators, toilets, air ducts, etc.; (6) adequate ducts for the later installation of a variety of communication circuits; (7) basic equipment capability and design, e.g., the book conveyor, pneumatic tube system, etc.; and (8) floor structures adequate for bookstack loads in all or most parts of the building.

This matter of flexibility, at reasonable cost, is stressed for these reasons:

(1) Some important aspects of the proposed building are relatively new and untried. It is believed that these plans are sound, but a more conventional pattern of relationships must be readily possible if they are not.

(2) Patterns of book relationships and reader needs are constantly changing in a university. Libraries have always found it difficult to adapt to these changing needs; the new building must not only minimize these difficulties, but provide easy and economical responses to changing requirements.

(3) The new library is deliberately being planned as an experimental laboratory for the investigation of better channels for the flow of information. It must be possible to rearrange some elements of the library to facilitate this work.

(4) There will be unpredictable changes in the number of students, intensity of library use, and the growth of segments of the collections.

Building Control

The architect should recognize that three interrelated control systems are involved in the structure. This may seem unduly complex, but there presently appears to be no easy alternative.

(1) All persons upon leaving the building will be asked to present books and briefcases at the building exit for inspection to determine that the books have been properly charged to an authorized borrower. The physical arrangements for this check are important and should be discussed with the owner early in the planning.

Note: It is planned that anyone may presently enter the building, and proceed at will to any of the specialized reading areas. It is not impossible that in the future, the University might find it necessary to limit those persons using the specialized reading rooms—or even the library building—to University students, faculty, and staff, except by special permission.

(2) Only authorized persons will be permitted into the bookstack. They will need to show University-issued identification cards in order to enter the stack, and will be asked to leave coats, books and briefcases at the stack entrance (usually these will be left in lockers, carrels, reading rooms, etc.).

(3) The Library must secure as promptly as possible as complete a record as possible of books taken from reading rooms or the bookstacks. This record is essential to good library service to readers.

It is assumed that a very high proportion of the charging operations from the bookstack will take place at the specialized subject facility stack entrances, but the load on the central Circulation Desk is also likely to be substantial. It would in some instances be an economy in the reader's time and staff time to be able to combine the general circulation desk book control responsibility with the building exit control, but we anticipate that the probable traffic loads, and physical relationships will make this impossible.

An example of a treatment of information technology is from the University of North Carolina at Chapel Hill, Davis Library program, prepared by Gordon Rutherford, University Planning Officer.

Computers and Library Technology

Modern libraries, like other modern institutions, are making increasing use of automated systems and are likely to become increasingly reliant on computers and related data processing equipment in connection with their research, technical and administrative support functions. The Library is presently using computer systems in four functional areas: (1) bibliographic searching, (2) cataloging, (3) interlibrary loan, and (4) circulation. The Library does not have its own computer installation to service these systems. Terminals are used for bibliographic searching which connect with Lockheed Corporation computers in California. Video terminals are used for cataloging and interlibrary loan which connect with computers in the Ohio College Library Center in Columbus, Ohio. In connection with the circulation system, keypunch and other data input equipment are installed in the Library, but processing operations are performed by the University's Administrative Data Processing installation.

It is contemplated that the number of terminals and other data input equipment will increase as these operations expand in volume and scope. For example, there is only one terminal presently employed in the BA/SS Reference Department for bibliographic searching. As search workloads increase that Department may need more terminals; furthermore, computerized searching also will be expanded to the other reference departments. The OCLC system will be utilized more extensively both for automated cataloging and interlibrary loan operations. In addition, this system probably will be used eventually in connection with acquisitions operations. The circulation system may be refined and expanded to provide more statistical information for management in connection with loan policies, storage requirements, and user patterns and trends. In addition, it can be anticipated that other library functions and services will be automated. Major potentials for automation include library book accounting and order procedures, and the development and maintenance of an on-line catalog to replace the conventional card catalog.

In all of these areas, a substantial increase in the number of computer terminals can be expected, and to a lesser extent, an increase in keypunch and other data input equipment requirements. For example, an on-line catalog may require upwards of 30 terminals in the main catalog area alone, with other terminals scattered throughout other parts of the library. There may eventually be over fifty terminals throughout the building.

Space projections in applicable functional areas in the Program generally have taken this into account, although exact numbers are not always specified. Of significance in planning the building, however, is that this equipment will require a certain amount of isolation and sound-proofing, and conduits sufficient to provide the wiring necessary to meet power requirements. It is *not* contemplated that the Library will need a large, main-frame computer installation. The current trend is away from this need in Libraries with the growth of large commercial data processing services and library network centers. However it may be advisable eventually to install a mini-computer in the Library. A definite need cannot be determined at this time. The minicomputer would perform message routing and other processing functions auxiliary to those performed at the major DP centers, and would serve to expedite service. If such equipment becomes a reality, it probably would be housed in Wilson Library. With respect to the terminal and other equipment cited above, this equipment will need to be located within the respective areas of functional responsibility. There would be no "central" terminal room, for example. Circulation system equipment must be housed in the Circulation Department, although it may be advisable to isolate keypunch operations from the rest of the work staff because of noise factors.

In summary, the impact of technological changes on building requirements are as follows:

Collection:
: (1) little over-all change in physical nature, collection will remain preponderantly print materials (books and journals);
(2) some increase in the proportion of non-print materials, mostly microforms;
(3) continued expansion of total housing;

Staff:
: (1) total number of employees will increase;
(2) skills and equipment required for certain jobs may change dramatically, requiring retraining, especially in certain reference and technical services areas;
(3) space needed per employee will remain essentially at current levels.

Library Services:
: (1) space needed for the public catalog will remain stable; the card catalog may shrink but space will be needed for terminal access, use of printed catalog supplements, or microform readers if catalog supplements are on microfilm or microfiche;
(2) more machine-oriented operations in public service and technical services departments requiring ample power outlets, special access and security, and sufficient work space;
(3) additional desk-top or table space needed for microform readers;
(4) special rooms (carrels) required for viewing and listening to non-book materials (i.e., records, tapes, video cassettes, TV, etc.).

Library Users: (1) special space (such as semiprivate cubicles) will be required at key reference areas for patrons to confer with staff skilled in the use of computerized searching, abstracting, and indexing techniques, who will act as interfaces between user needs and the use of the technology;

(2) special "wet" carrels will be needed equipped for patrons to use earphones and A-V equipment, with appropriate equipment security and soundproofing;

(3) areas scattered throughout building where patrons and staff can access machine-readable catalogs;

(4) people will continue to require comfortable, quiet and attractive work and study space not affected by the new technologies.

In conclusion, it is predicted that changes in technology over the next twenty years will not significantly alter the *total amount* of the various types of space required in the new building, but advancing technologies will change significantly in certain areas the manner in which the space is used. It will be important that the design of the building allow for great flexibility in order to convert to the use of the new technologies with a minimum of disruption to occupied space, without the necessity of major building alterations, and at minimal expense. Necessary interior walls and partitions should be moveable, access to electrical and phone connections should be numerous and certain areas should be easily convertible to the storage and use of non-book materials.

Basic Needs and Area Requirements. An example from an eastern liberal arts college.

SPACE REQUIREMENTS

Seating—public		*Seating—staff*	
Lobby	4	Circulation desk	3
General reading room	150	Circulation office	2
Bibliography area	3	Reference librarian's	
Microfilm room	5	desk and office	3
Browsing room	20	Librarians's office	10
Rare book room	4	Secretary's office	3
Reading areas, upper		Order department	2
floors	180	Cataloguing	
Periodicals reading		department	5
area, basement	70	Receiving room	2
Faculty studies	10	Listening room	1
Conference rooms	48	Periodicals workroom	
Typing booths	8	and reading area	3
Listening room and		Janitor's workshop	1
booths	20	Staff lounge	10
	522		45

Book Storage Capacity
(Excluding temporary shelving in staff offices and workrooms)

Reference collection	10,000
Bibliography	1,000
Browsing	4,000
Rare books and special collections	7,000
Basement stack	80,000
Stacks on upper floors	200,000
	302,000

SPACE REQUIREMENTS BY FLOOR

The figures below represent no more than an experimental worksheet and are far from exact. Estimates of the size of most facilities are rough approximations in round numbers. Some are incompetent guesses, such as the area in the basement for mechanical equipment and the auditorium. The latter, of course, may be in a separate wing or excluded altogether. No allowance is made for mechanical equipment on the roof, and none is made for the loss of space on each floor due to partitions, columns, and corridors other than stack aisles. There is therefore a considerable margin of error in the totals, probably on the under side.

Basement		*Main floor*	
	sq ft.		sq ft.
Stacks	5,400	Vestibule	360
Periodicals display		Lobby	2,200
and reading area	2,100	Circulation desk, etc.	600
Maps	250	Circulation office	200
Faculty studies	100	General reading room	
Conference rooms	430	and reference	
Receiving and		collection	5,200
shipping	500	Bibliography	
Periodicals workroom	450	collection	150
Janitor's workroom	200	Browsing room	1,200
Storage	350	Librarian's and	
Stairwells, elevator	400	secretary's offices	600
Mechanical		Reference librarian	300
equipment	1,000	Microfilm room	500
Auditorium	2,200	Order and cataloguing	
Toilets	200	departments	1,300
	13,580	Stairwells, elevator	400
			13,010

Second floor		*Third floor*	
Stack	7,700	Stack	7,700
Reading area	2,700	Reading area	2,700
Rare book room	900	Conference rooms	430
Conference rooms	430	Faculty studies	200
Faculty studies	200	Stairwells, elevators	400
Staff lounge	500	Listening room	1,200
Stairwells, elevator	400	Unassigned	430
Toilets	200		13,060
	13,030		

Excerpts from the program of a residential suburban college and one for an urban university are in Tables A.1 and A.2.

The 1963 program summary of the University of Chicago Regenstein Library is given in Table A.3.

Spatial Relationships. Spatial relationships can be presented in various ways in the program prepared for the architect: in writing in the main text; in tabular form; or in diagrams. The library as a whole can be covered in one section of the text, in one column of a table, in one diagram, or scattered through the program in the sections dealing with specific floor levels, or areas of the building. Paragraphs below provide examples of different methods.

Figure A.1, mentioned earlier, summarizes in the column headed "Location-Relationship" the

TABLE A.1. SUMMARY OF REQUIREMENTS

1. Public areas	Volumes	Seats	Area
a. General stack area	233,500		15,600 S.F.
b. General reading area		410	10,250
c. Reference & bibliography	6,000	20	1,000
d. Night study area		60	1,400
e. Public catalog			500
f. Periodicals & newspapers		15	400
g. Browsing & new books	1,000	20	600
h. Seminar rooms (4)		40	750
i. Typing rooms (4)		20	400
j. Leverton collection & "Treasure" room	7,500	15	700
Subtotal public areas	248,000	600	32,075 S.F.

2. Staff areas	Volumes	Staff (min-max)	Area
a. Circulation desk & closed reserve	2,000	1–3	400 S.F.
b. Office (shared w/i, c)		1–2	150
c. Technical processing area (1 room)		3–6	900
d. Director and secretary		2–2	400
e. Librarian		1–1	200
f. Mail sorting magazine rec. gift storage	2,000*	1	500
g. Staff lounge locker & toilets			250
h. Vault & fireproof storage			200
i. Mail drop			50
Subtotal staff areas	2,000	8–15	3,050 S.F.

3. Service areas	Staff	Area
a. Mechanical room		1,000 S.F.
b. Superintendent's office	1	150
c. Janitors' closets (1 per floor)	1	100
d. Elevator 3 floors		125
e. Toilet rooms (M & W on each floor)		600
Subtotal service areas	2	1,975 S.F.

4. Summary of areas	Volumes	Seats	Area
a. Public areas	248,000	600	32,075 S.F.
b. Staff areas	2,000	8–15†	3,050
c. Service areas		2†	1,975
d. Subtotal			37,100
e. Circulation (7½% of d)			2,700
f. Wall thicknesses, ducts, columns, etc. (10% of d + e)			4,000
Grand total			43,800 S.F.

*Not considered in 250,000 total
†Staff or service personnel

TABLE A.2. SUMMARY OF FACILITIES

	Seats for readers	Books	Staff	Sq ft
Lobby				
Circulation dept.			12	1,300
Browsing alcove	10	1,000		500
Card catalog				2,300
Bibliography collection	15	4,200		1,100
Reference room	50	8,000	4	3,050
Periodical room	60		6	3,300
Technical services area			29	3,420
Reserve book & study area	225	14,500	2	8,200
Stacks				
General stacks		865,000		72,000
General study areas	300			9,000
Carrels	250			4,000
Seminar rooms	130			3,900
Conference & smoking rooms	90			2,700
Faculty studies	75			7,500
Typing rooms	15			450
Special collections area	15	8,000	1	1,400
Audio-visual area	99		2	3,050
Administrative offices			5	1,200
Receiving & shipping room			1	700
Library staff room			45	1,450
Book repair room			1	500
Check room				250
Stock & supply room				150
Equipment storage room				300

proposed spatial relationships in the Asbury Theological Seminary Library.

Figures A.2 to A.4, selected from the Santa Cruz program, indicate desired relationships for each library area as the first line Location under the heading "Architectural Requirements."

Figure A.5, from the University of Chicago Regenstein Library program, provides major and secondary traffic relationships among functions.

Figure A.6 is from the architect's 1975 program analysis report for the Western Illinois University Library, prepared to demonstrate the understanding of the program requirements.

Figure A.7 is a drawing from the program for the Francis A. Countway Library of Medicine of the Harvard Medical School and the Boston Medical Library, and is used to illustrate "accessibility priorities," which do not explain what should be next to what, but only what should be more accessible than something else.

Figures A.8 to A.10 show diagrammatic sketches for spatial relationships in the program for a new building for Lake Forest College, with a sketch for each floor level.

SPACE DESCRIPTION
SANTA CRUZ CAMPUS

SPACE NUMBER ....3...
........1.... Like spaces

PROJECT.......University.Library,..Unit.1...
DEPARTMENT ....

USE OF SPACE
................GENERAL.OFFICE..
................Reception.area;..secretaries,..mail,..clerk-typist....................
....

AREA AND OCCUPANCY
Assignable area each space in square feet: ....375...
Classroom or Seminar — number of seats: ....
Teaching Laboratory — number of student stations: ....
Teaching Laboratory — number of lockers per station: ....
Other spaces — normal number of occupants:...............3.+.visitors*..............................

ARCHITECTURAL REQUIREMENTS
Location: ....Adjacent.to.offices.of.the.University.Librarian.and.......
...Assistant.University.Librarian;.in.a.location.easily.accessible.to...
Dim general.public,.faculty,.staff.and.students..................................
Special floor loading: ....
Special acoustical: ....
Other: ....
....

MECHANICAL AND ELECTRICAL REQUIREMENTS
Sink with utilities: ....
Lab utilities: ....
Special environmental conditions: ....
Special electric services: ....Outlets.at.each.desk.for.office.machines............
Special exhaust: ....
Other: ....Telephone.outlet;..conduit.for.teletype.cable.......
....

COMMENTS
................*Space.for.people.waiting.to.see.Librarian.or.Assistant........
......Librarian....Space.for.personnel.and.financial.records,..storage.of....
forms, supplies, sorting mail.

EQUIPMENT — FIXED AND MOVABLE

Quantity	Description
3	typist desks, 60x30
3	typist chairs
2	tables, 60x30
2	storage cabinets, 36x78x24
3	side chairs
1	lounge chair
1	couch
6	5-drawer files, 2 with locks
2	wastebaskets
1	wastebasket, large
1	caddy file
1	bookcase
1	TWX teletype unit

Prepared by ___ D. T. Clark ___ Date ___ May 1963 ___ DDP-4
UCSC, 3/63

FIGURE A.2 University of California at Santa Cruz Library program. General office.

SPACE DESCRIPTION
SANTA CRUZ CAMPUS

SPACE NUMBER ....15..
........1..... Like spaces

PROJECT........University.Library,.Unit.1..
DEPARTMENT ....

USE OF SPACE
.............TECHNICAL.PROCESSES:..ACQUISITIONS.....................................
....
....

AREA AND OCCUPANCY
Assignable area each space in square feet: ....1350...........................
Classroom or Seminar — number of seats: ....
Teaching Laboratory — number of student stations: ....
Teaching Laboratory — number of lockers per station: ....
Other spaces — normal number of occupants:............9.............................

ARCHITECTURAL REQUIREMENTS
Location: ....Contiguous.with.Cataloging,.or.both.may.be.in.one.area;.
....should.be.adjacent.to.Receiving,.Shipping.and.Bindery.Prep....Direct.
Dim.access.to.public.catalog,..No.through.traffic.................................
Special floor loading: ....
Special acoustical: ....
Other: ....One.micro.film.and.one.micro.card.reader.to.be.shared.with
....Catalog.Department..

MECHANICAL AND ELECTRICAL REQUIREMENTS
Sink with utilities: ....
Lab utilities: ....
Special environmental conditions: ....
Special electric services: ....Wiring.for.eventual.IBM.equipment.(keytronic.sorter)
Special exhaust: ....
Other: ....Electric.outlets.at.each.desk.for.electric.type-
....writers,.adding.machines,.etc...Telephone.outlets.............................

COMMENTS
.............Single-face..bookstacks.against.walls,..remainder.of.shelving in
......corner.near.entrance.to.room...

EQUIPMENT — FIXED AND MOVABLE

Quantity	Description		
5	desks, 60x30	1	supply cabinet, 36x90x24
4	desks, typist	1	microfilm reader
5	swivel arm chairs	1	microcard reader
4	typist chairs	9	wastebaskets
3	side chairs	1	wardrobe cabinet
1	typewriter table		
1	custom built reference book desk and shelves (for Publishers catalogs, CBI, etc.)		
1	adding machine		
6	book trucks		
1	5-drawer file, legal		
3	5-drawer files		
1	15-drawer catalog unit		
4	Kardex units		
12	bookcases, 36x90x10		
1	Thermofax or Verifax		

Prepared by ____D. T. Clark____ Date ____May 1963____ DDP-4
UCSC, 3/63

FIGURE A.3 University of California at Santa Cruz Library program. Technical processes: acquisition.

SPACE DESCRIPTION
SANTA CRUZ CAMPUS

SPACE NUMBER ....19..
.... Like spaces

PROJECT............ University Library, Unit 1
DEPARTMENT ....

USE OF SPACE
.... RECEIVING AND SHIPPING ROOM
..Receiving and shipping room for all materials coming to or leaving the
..Library; temporary storage space for acquisitions; work area for minor
repairs to library equipment.

AREA AND OCCUPANCY
   Assignable area each space in square feet: 565
   Classroom or Seminar — number of seats: ....
   Teaching Laboratory — number of student stations: ....
   Teaching Laboratory — number of lockers per station: 1
   Other spaces — normal number of occupants: 1

ARCHITECTURAL REQUIREMENTS
   Location: .... Contiguous with the Technical Processes Area; must be
.adjacent to and on same level as loading platform............................
   Dimensions: ....
   Special floor loading: ....
   Special acoustical: .... Sound control of noisy operations........................
   Other: ....
   ....

MECHANICAL AND ELECTRICAL REQUIREMENTS
   Sink with utilities: .... Sink with drainboard........................
   Lab utilities: ....
   Special environmental conditions: ....
   Special electric services: ....
   Special exhaust: ....
   Other: ....
   ....

COMMENTS
.... Space for storing 8 bindery boxes (3'x 1') in 2 piles of 4........
.... Space for parking book trucks and moving book trucks around........
.... Doors wide enough to take furniture and equipment.

EQUIPMENT — FIXED AND MOVABLE

Quantity	Description		
1	storage cabinet, 36x78x24	1	5-drawer file
1	gravity-feed conveyor to	1	large paper cutter
	receiving desk, Technical	1	small paper cutter
	Processes area	1	wastebasket, extra large
1	postal scales	1	wastebasket
1	gummed paper dispenser		
1	postal meter		
1	custom-built work table		
1	workbench		
1	small tool cabinet		
8	bookcases, 36x90x10		
3	book trucks		
1	hand truck		
1	dolly		
1	desk, 60x30		
1	stool		
2	typist chairs		

Prepared by _____ D. T. Clark _____ Date _____ May 1963 _____ DDP-4
UCSC, 3/63

FIGURE A.4 University of California at Santa Cruz Library program. **Receiving and shipping room.**

TABLE A. 3. TABLE OF CONTENTS AND SUMMARY OF SPACE REQUIREMENTS

	Seats	Sq. ft.	Reference
Introduction	—	—	p. 1-4
General Public Services			
General Circulation	—	3,180	A-1
Reference, Bibliography, & Interlibrary Loan	100	5,658	A-2
Reserved Book Facility	250	11,349	A-3
Microtext Reading	35	2,612	A-4
Smoking & Conversation Lounges	—	3,350	A-5
Checking & Locker Facilities	—	800	A-6
Public Catalog	—	3,050	A-7
The General Bookstack	109[a]	167,725	A-8
Specialized Public Services			
Business, Economics, Geography Facility	340	12,310	B-1
Education-Psychology Facility	297	10,584	B-2A
Curriculum Laboratory & Children's Books	47	2,757	B-2B
Social Sciences Facility	323	13,603	B-3
Graduate Library School Facility	72	8,945	B-4
Theology Facility	180	6,690	B-5
Humanities-History Facility	306	11,162	B-6A
Modern Poetry & Recordings Facility	36	1,994	B-6B
Department of Special Collections	67	14,698	B-7
Asian Center	100	17,757	B-8
Faculty Studies	(250)	13,500	B-9
Map Library	(14)	(4,768)	B-10
Technical, Administrative, and Other Services			
Serial Records Department	—	2,411	C-1
Cataloging Department	—	5,446	C-2
Acquisitions Department	—	3,005	C-3
Gifts Department	—	914	C-4
Binding & Labeling Department	—	2,017	C-5
Storage Processing & Custodian Units	—	560	C-6
Preparations Division: Staff Lockers-Toilets	—	350	C-7
Preparations Division: Supply Area	—	100	C-8
Preparations Division: Bibliographical Center	—	1,835	C-9
Staff Room	—	2,380	C-10
Printing & Shipping Department & Loading Dock	—	2,251	C-11
Library Supplies & Storage	—	1,343	C-12
Computer Facility	—	5,000	C-13
Administrative Offices	—	1,756	C-14
Department of Photographic Reproduction	—	4,170	C-15
TOTALS	2,262[b]	345,262	

a) 10 seats in general collections and 99 distributed among other subjects

b) Excludes lounge seats, etc., but includes all seminar seats (236)

	Reference
Other Information	
Seminar Facilities	D-1
Exhibit Facilities	D-2
Telephones & Related Circuits	D-3
Lighting	D-4
Expansion	D-5
Flexibility	D-6
Carrels	D-7
Site, General Design, & Building Entrances	D-8
Air Treatment	D-9
Building Control	D-10

Summary	
Seats, including seminars, but excluding lounges	2,262
Allocated space, square feet	345,262
Estimated minimum gross space, sq.ft. @ 122%	421,220
GLS offices & classrooms, @ 122%	−8,195
Library purposes, including computer space	413,025 sq.ft.

Figure A.11 is a diagrammatic sketch taken from the program for the University of North Carolina Davis Library, indicating spatial primary and secondary relationships.

Figure A.12 is also from the architect's 1975 program analysis report for the Western Illinois University Library, with this comment:

The following diagrams demonstrate the various program relationships called for in the University program report. The main difference between the first two drawings is the position of the main control point near the entry. Diagram 1 shows, as suggested in the program report, that it is possible for certain functions to be located outside the Control Area. After discussion with the staff, it was determined that the only spaces that could be outside Control were the Administrative Suite, the Public Lounge, and the main large Conference Room. If this diagram is followed, upon entering the building into the lobby, it would be possible to go directly to the Administrative Suite, the Public Lounge, or Conference Room without passing through Control. All other building spaces that the public has access to would be entered by first passing through Control. Program Relationship Diagram 2 [not illustrated] suggests that, because there are so few areas that can work outside Control, it might be feasible to place all building program areas inside the Control Area, meaning that the public entering the building would first go through Control before proceeding to any other area. Both Program Relationship Diagrams 1 and 2 not only show the relationships of the various functions outlined in the program, but also show the relative size of each space as they relate to each other.

Information about Particular Building Areas. The questions proposed in Chapter 5 and following should be answered, giving the requirements for the number of readers, and the types of seating accommodations that should be provided in each public room, the number of volumes and other material that should be housed, and the spatial and other requirements for the staff. This is one of the more difficult parts of the program to prepare. It requires a great deal of detailed work. No attempt will be made here to provide examples which will answer all the questions, but the following will give some indication as to what might well be done.

a. Printed forms can be prepared, see Figures A.2 to A.4 for examples used by the University of California, Santa Cruz. Similar sheets may be required for every room in the building.

b. Statements might be prepared, as in these selected from the program of a large university library.

Reference Service Desk

1. Suggested Size: 400 square feet
2. Use: Desk/counters where patrons may ask for reference help in locating and using library materials.
3. Maximum occupancy at one time: 3 librarians
4. Relation to other areas or rooms: Ground floor. Between public card catalog and reference reading. Near index reference.
5. Special requirements: Vertical files and low shelving. Direct phone from stack levels.

Reference Indexes

1. Suggested Size: 1200 square feet
2. Use: Consultation of periodical indexes, British Museum and Library of Congress catalogs
3. Maximum occupancy at one time: 40 (30 seated)
4. Relation to other areas or rooms: Ground floor. Between public card catalog and reference reading, behind or near reference service.
5. Special requirements: 6 specially constructed index reference tables (60 × 20). 16 sections of 3′ wall shelving, 7′ high.

Bibliography Room

1. Suggested size: 2,500 square feet
2. Use: Consultation of trade and national bibliographies by library staff and others.
3. Maximum occupancy at one time: 25
4. Relation to other areas or rooms: between cataloguing work area and book order area, but so placed that faculty may enter the room without being obliged to walk through those rooms.
5. Special requirements: Consultation tables for large volumes, standing height counters and shelving (30 3′ sections).

Other examples are here provided, showing variety of format and specificity of detail:

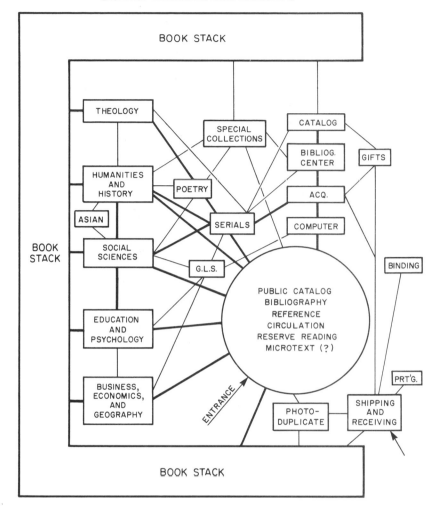

FIGURE A.5 University of Chicago Regenstein Library program. A partial view of library internal relationships.

A circulation department description for the University of Chicago Regenstein Library.

Collection shelving for the University of Chicago John Crerar Science Library.

Administrative offices for the University of Texas Perry-Casteñada Library.

Audiovisual quarters for the Gerald R. Ford Presidential Library.

Copy shop for the University of Oklahoma Bizzell Library.

Interlibrary lending, photoduplication, and microform quarters for the University of Chicago Crerar Library.

Learning resource center for the Brigham Young University Harold B. Lee Library.

Map library for the University of Chicago Regenstein Library.

Microform reading room for the University of North Carolina Davis Library.

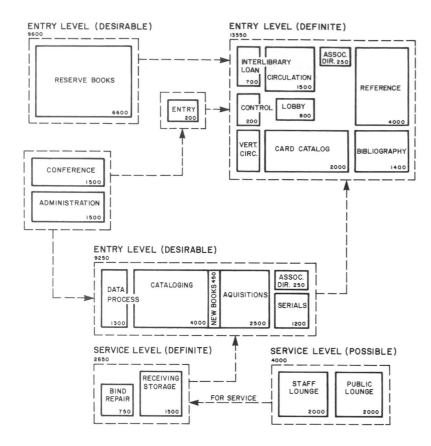

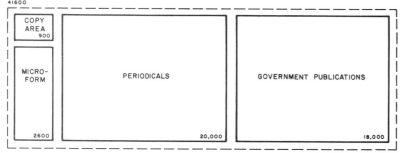

KEY SPATIAL RELATIONSHIPS

FIGURE A.6 Western Illinois University Library. Architect's program analysis report.

Seminar facilities for the University of Chicago Regenstein Library.

Special collections vault for the Gerald R. Ford Library.

GENERAL CIRCULATION
(UNIVERSITY OF CHICAGO–REGENSTEIN)

Purpose: This department is responsible for the delivery of books to readers, returning books to the bookstack, and for the records of all books (with the probable exception of reserve) charged to readers. It will be responsible for inspection or other controls at building or stack exits, and it is likely to be a focal point for general information inquiries on the main library floor.

Major Elements and Space Requirements

	Sq. ft.
Circulation desk, approx. 35 ft. long with at least six service positions	210
Bins for master, quarter, faculty charges	150
Book slipping and sorting work area	500
Office—glass-enclosed	100
Work space for clerical staff, 9 positions	900
Book truck parking space	50
Book lift and pneumatic tube stations	170
Staff locker space (30 @ 2 sq. ft., including stack staff)	60
Staff consoles (2 @ 30 sq. ft.)	60
Circulation lobby and waiting space	700 est.
New book display and consultation space (8 sections of shelving and six seats in lobby area, preferably near stack entrance)	230
Stack entrance control desk	50
Building exit control desks	(architect)
TOTAL	3,180

Suggested Location and Relationships

Should be on first floor with direct access to bookstack, bookstack service elevators, stack stairways, and book lift conveyor system. The circulation desk must be near the Public Card Catalog and the Reference-Bibliography Collection. It should be conspicuous from main building entrance. The possibility of combining the circulation desk with one of the building exit controls should be considered, though the traffic load is likely to make such a combination undesirable. The pneumatic tube stations should be in, or immediately adjacent to the desk.

A very close relationship between the circulation work space, the reserve book work space, and the general stack "master" paging station is desired. To achieve this relationship, if reserve is not on the first floor, it may be possible to place the circulation sorting and work areas, and pneumatic tube stations on the floor immediately below the circulation desk. Special communication and book delivery devices would be required between this work center and the desk itself. Access, direct or remote, to the computer will be essential.

Arrangement

The effective relationship of the elements in this area is highly critical and requires very careful study. Schematic layouts will be available.

Total charges on a daily basis are expected to be between 1,000 and 2,000 items. At any one time, space to handle the records for 100,000 outstanding charges is essential, and this space must be expansible to handle records for 150,000 charges. Up to 3,000 books may be returned per day in peak load periods. Additional system load data are available.

The book delivery system in the building should be sufficiently flexible to permit a reader to request and receive a book located anywhere in the bookstack, at the Circulation desk, or at the desk of any of the specialized subject facilities.

A well-designed system of booklifts or a book conveyor (the merits and deficiencies of each to be discussed) and a pneumatic tube system (capable of handling IBM cards— $3\frac{1}{4} \times 7\frac{3}{8}$—without bending), and other means of effective internal communication for messages and books between subject areas, the circulation desk, and the bookstack are essential.

Unless a book conveyor has unusual characteristics, it is believed that the return of books to the bookstack may best be accomplished by means of booktrucks and bookstack elevator.

Books may be charged mechanically or manually at remote locations with rapid transmission of the information to the central records file. The existing circulation system is expected to become more highly mechanized at the time of, or before, the move to the new building, and that system, in turn, is expected to be changed for one based upon a computer record of transactions. For these reasons, substantial flexibility is required in the installation.

Special Equipment and Other Requirements

Pneumatic tubes for charge records and call slips, connected to all major departments of the Library. Book conveyor or book lifts connecting to the bookstack and other major service areas. Provision for circuits to computer consoles. Conduits or electrical chases for other electrical communication equipment. Space for the later installation of book carrying pneumatic tubes (Lamson 5″ × 13″ system) to the proposed Science Library should be provided. A system is planned that will permit the fast delivery of books from either building to the other.

A call board over the delivery desk will probably be required. There should be at least one exterior, lockable book return slot near the main entrance to the library with space for the return of books when the building is closed.

TABLE A.4 SHELVING FOR THE CATALOGED COLLECTIONS (UNIVERSITY OF CHICAGO–CRERAR)

	1	2	3	4	5	6
	Area	Number of Volumes	Volumes Per Sfs	Number of Sfs	Square Ft /Sfs	Square Footage Total
Area A: Outside Controlled Area		0				0
Area B: Principal Service Floor						
(a) Reference		37,400	100	374	10	3,740
(b) Reserve		3,000	125	24	7.75	186
(c) Current Serials 6,000 titles		6,000	27	222	10	2,200
(d) Microforms				10	10	100
Area C: Biological and Medical Area						
(e) Conventional		300,000	115	2,607	7.75	20,000
Area D: General and Physical Science Area						
(f) Conventional		420,000	115	3,652	7.75	28,000
Area E: Compact Shelving						
(g) Compact		530,000	175	3,028	5	15,140
Area F: No Designated Location		0				0
TOTALS:		1,296,400		9,917		69,366

Compact Storage: Detail for Area E (above)

A. *Function*
   To provide compact storage for both Crerar unique holdings and Chicago science holdings with imprint dates prior to 1960.
B. *Space Requirements*
   Seating...0
   Shelving for an estimated 530,000
      volumes @ approx. 35 vols/sq ft............ 15,140
   Other Public Furnishings and Equipment........... 0
   Staff Work Area.................................... 0

   TOTAL SPACE REQUIREMENT 15,140
C. *Notes*
   The estimate for the numbers of volumes to be shelved in this area takes two figures from the table in Section IX: Collections:

Biological and Medical volumes before
   1960 (Column 4, Line (e)):   200,696
General and Physical Science volumes
   before 1960 (Column 4, Line (h)): 302,437
                          TOTAL 503,133

In order to allow for sampling and other errors which may have influenced the calculation of Table [A.4], calculate square footage based upon a maximum capacity of 530,000 volumes. See "Three Estimates for Compact Storage Requirements in the New Science Library, Using Cut-Off Dates of 1940, 1950, and 1960," for a full commentary on the calculation of the 530,000 figure.

The compact storage area is presumed to be a no-growth collection.

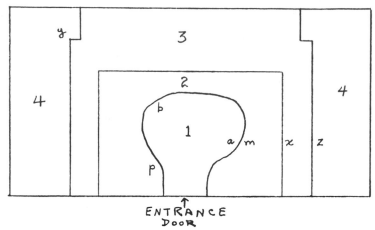

ENTRANCE DOOR

Accessibility Priorities are shown by the numerals 1, 2, 3, and 4. The entrance door gives immediate access to Priority 1 areas. All the areas in Priority 1 are necessarily near each other, e.g., area a and area b. This is not true in the case of Priority 4, e.g., areas y and z. Proximity is possible across Priority lines, e.g., areas a and m, or even areas a and x. Thus, it is possible to have a Priority 4 area like Cataloging staff at z reasonably close to a Priority 1 area like the Public Catalog at a. The diagram shows everything on a single horizontal plane. Possibilities for achieving efficient space relationships are increased by bringing areas into vertical proximity by a wise use of stairs and elevators.

FIGURE A.7 Accessibility priorities for the Francis A. Countway Library of Medicine, Harvard University Medical School, and the Boston Medical Library.

ADMINISTRATIVE OFFICES AND OTHER REQUIREMENTS (UNIVERSITY OF TEXAS)

1. *Administrative offices.*—An area on the main or an alternate floor will house the chief librarian and his supporting staff for administration. Space in this same area will be utilized for the secretarial staff, the clerical staff, the accounting staff, as a reception area, for a conference room and for other purposes.

Library administrative office, estimated in square feet: Total (see Schematic M) 4,032.

Schematics

This section is intended to further demonstrate the relationship of one major library area to other areas and to record estimates of the square feet to be assigned to each. These estimates are based upon policies used generally for determining space allocations, the present utilization of space for these functions and staff knowledge of the operations that will be assigned to each area.

Space for accommodating readers, for the storage of library materials and for the staff to conduct library services are of concern. Major allocations are subject to subdivision for efficient library operation, with some overlapping of reader and staff use of many areas.

In preparing space estimates *Higher Education Facilities Planning and Management Manual Four, Academic Support Facilities,* hereafter referred to as *Manual Four,* has been relied upon. Published in 1971, it records modern space requirements based upon practice and current trends. (Reference: *Higher Education Facilities Planning and Management Manuals, Manual Four, Academic Support Facilities, Planning and Systems Division,* Western Interstate Commission for Higher Education in Cooperation with the American Association of Collegiate Registrars and Admissions Officers, [U.S. Office of Education Contract Number OEG 0-9-150167-4534, May 1971.]

Schematic M: Administrative Office

This grouping of offices is planned to house the University Librarian, the Associate University Librarian and assistants assigned to heading the major divisions of the library including technical processes, public services, systems and management, business and personnel, and branch library supervision.

The supporting administrative staff requiring space assignments include the executive assistant, secretarial staff, receptionist and clerical assistants. Library bookkeepers are assigned space in this unit in order to conserve space in the main floor assignment to acquisitions.

A conference room large enough to handle meetings of department heads is desirable. For thirty people at 20 square feet per person, about 600 square feet will be required for the conference room. [See Fig. A.13.]

AUDIOVISUAL QUARTERS (GERALD R. FORD LIBRARY)

Audiovisual. The library will have 300,000 to one million photographic negatives, almost two-thirds of which will be color. These present significant storage and preservation problems. A separate low temperature storage area of 750 sq. ft. (large enough to accommodate still picture negatives, motion picture negatives, and microfilm negatives) should be designed into the building equipped with adjustable steel shelving for the storage of these negatives. Provisions should be made to control temperature at 28 degrees F (plus or minus two degrees) and relative humidity at 50 percent (plus or minus five percent).

A storage area of approximately 2000 square feet for photographic prints, audio tapes, video tapes, and motion picture film must also be provided near the audiovisual work area. This area should be equipped with adjustable steel shelving sufficient to accommodate 1000 linear feet of materials and ten five-drawer legal-sized filing cabinets. Two large steel roller drawers (of the type commonly used for map storage) should be provided for oversize items. Both these areas should be near the photographic laboratory.

Audiovisual Laboratory. The photographic laboratory will require from 1,500 to 2,000 square feet of floor space. It should be on the lowest floor of the building, adjacent to rooms used for storage of supplies, machinery rooms, etc. Special attention should be given to material used on the floor of this area so that it will be warmer and more comfortable than a basement floor usually is. In addition to standard photographic laboratory features, such as a room for supplies and a dark room, a photographic laboratory should include or have closely available to it an empty area that can be used for taking photographs of large museum objects. This room can also be used for overnight storage of photographs or manuscripts being copied by the staff and should be under security protection.

COPY SHOP (UNIVERSITY OF OKLAHOMA)

Number Required: 1
Purpose and Function:
The Copy Shop serves Library users by providing copies of materials on Xerox copiers and microform printers. It may also do large copy jobs for the Libraries' Administration. Other types of printing will also be done in this area.

Normal Occupancy: 3
   Visitors: 1
   Visitors (Customers):   6
Spatial and Functional Relationship to Other Areas:
   The Copy Shop should be easily available to Library
   users, and be fairly near Current Periodicals and/or
   Reserve and Microforms.
Services:
   1. Telephone
   2. 12 grounded outlets
   3. 120V and 220V circuits
Special Requirements:
   1. Security for supplies, cash receipts, and the em-
      ployees responsible
   2. Humidity controls
   3. Buzzer under counter which buzzes at the OU Cam-
      pus Police offices
Equipment:
   1. 4 Xerox copiers
   2. 8 microform reader/printers
   3. 6 sections of wall-hung shelving
   4. 2 3′ × 8′ tables
   5. 2 side chairs
   6. 2 single-pedestal desks
   7. 3 posture chairs
   8. 2 supply cabinets, 2′ × 3′

            Total Area Required: 1,090 s.f.

INTER-LIBRARY LENDING, PHOTODUPLICATION, AND
            MICROFORM QUARTERS
      (UNIVERSITY OF CHICAGO–CRERAR)

A.   *Function:* Inter-Library Loan and photoduplication

   To provide a location for the processing and administration of requests and to provide a centralized photocopy service for library users, employing higher performance equipment than will be available with the coin-
operated machines located elsewhere in the building, as
well as an in-house facility for making photocopies requested for inter-library loan.

B.   *Space Requirements*

   Seating   0

   Shelving (see below)   0
   Other Public Furnishings and Equipment
      2 1-place table-and-chair sets @ 15 30
      2 Seats for waiting patrons @ 7   14
                                             44

   Staff Work Area
      Inter-Library Lending
         1 Office (Chief)   150
        10 Work Areas (Professional
            and Clerical) @ 125   1,250
         1 Bookkeeping machine   24
         8 Work files @ 32   256
         1 Public counter with cash register 9
         1 OCLC Terminal   25
         1 TWX machine   25
         2 LDMS Terminals @ 25   50
         8 Booktrucks @ 4   32
         4 Standard sfs @ 8   32
                                           1,853

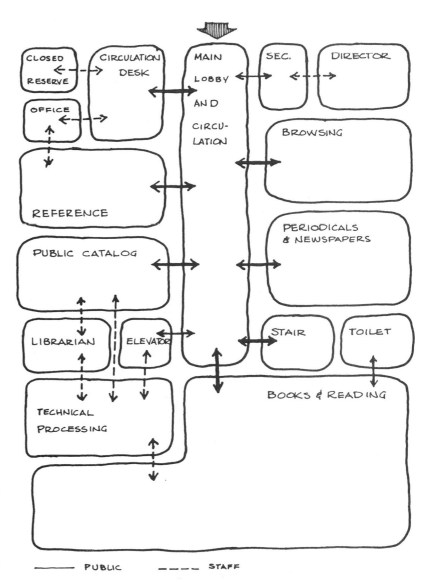

**FIGURE A.8 Lake Forest College Library. Spa-
tial relationships for ground-floor requirements shown in diagrammatic form.**

   Photoduplication Department
      1 Microprinter   32
      2 Micro-readers @ 16   32
      3 Xerographic copiers @ 10   30
      1 Step-and-repeat microfiche
         camera   40
      1 Microfiche-to-Microfiche copier 10
     10 Supply cabinets @ 16   160
     19 Standard sfs @ 8   152
                                          456
      Total Space requirements   2,353

A.   *Function:* Microforms
   To provide area user stations for microfilm and microfiche readers and reader/printers, facilities for listening
to audiotapes and viewing videotapes, shelving and study
space for related indexes and other bibliographic materials, and user-accessible storage for selected titles in
microform; and to provide in the staff area space for
storing and servicing the microform and audiovisual collections and equipment.

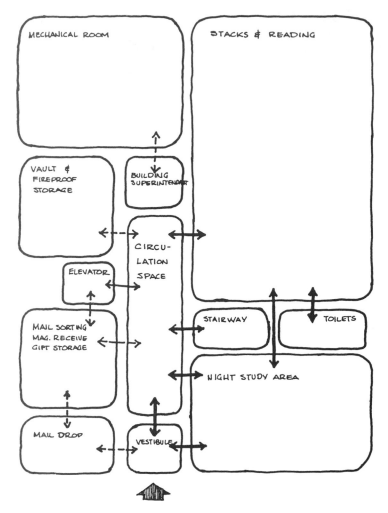

FIGURE A.9 Lake Forest College Library. Spatial relationships for main-floor requirements. (See Fig. A.8 for ground floor and Fig. A.10 for second floor.)

B. *Space Requirements*

Seating

8 Seats at 4-place tables @ 35	280	
2 Seats at 1-place tables @ 35	70	
10 User stations for microform readers @ 40	400	
1 User station for videotapes @ 40	40	
1 User station for audio materials @ 40	40	
		830

Shelving

10 Low (3') sfs for indexes and bibliographies @ 10	100	

Other Public Furnishings and Equipment

4 Microfiche readers	
1 Microfiche reader/printer	Space
4 Microfilm readers	provided
1 Microfilm reader/printer	in Seating
1 Videotape player	above
1 Audio machine	

0

2 810-linear inch capacity microfiche cabinets @ 9	18	
2 880-35 mm roll capacity microfilm cabinets @ 9	18	
		36

Staff Work Area

2 Work areas @ 125	250	
15 Assorted cabinets for film or fiche @ 9	135	
		385
Total space requirement		1,351

C. *Notes*

It would be desirable to locate this area close enough to the general reference staff so that they can provide assistance in its use over the same number of hours as they offer reference service.

It would be desirable to locate this area adjacent to a general reading area into which the microform department might expand as required over time.

LEARNING RESOURCE CENTER
(BRIGHAM YOUNG UNIVERSITY)

Facility (function) 69: Electronic Control Area

Number Required:	1
Floor Area:	4,075 sq. ft.
Floor Material:	Carpet
Wall Material:	Painted lava block or movable partitions
Ceiling Material:	Acoustic tile or other sound absorbent material
Ceiling Height:	9 ft. minimum
Recommended Location:	West end, second level of Addition

Justification or Use of Facility:
Electronic head-end equipment only for audio distribution will be located in this area. (CCTV originates in another facility on Campus.) Carrel study may also be located in this area.

Furniture and Equipment to be Furnished by Owner:
Electronic Instructional Media head-end equipment, for audio only.

Special Requirements:
Windows required, interior
Air conditioning capacity for extra heat from electronic equipment
Space under raised floor to be pressurized for cooling of electronic equipment
Access to campus utility tunnel and campus distribution system for telephone, audio, television, and computer
Electrical ground, details available
Electronic equipment shall be installed on raised computer room type flooring. This raised floor shall be approximately 8" above the Library floor level, not recessed into the floor. Raised floor shall be installed as needed.
Not all of the 4,075 square feet will be used for electronic functions when the building is first occupied. A partial partition shall separate that portion so that the remainder can be used for Learning Resources study. Alarm system to prevent theft of electronic equipment.

Utilities Required: Electrical, 120V, single-phase

MAP LIBRARY
(UNIVERSITY OF CHICAGO–REGENSTEIN)

A. *Purpose:* The Map Library will house and service the Library's collections of maps and aerial photographs and a substantial portion of its atlases. The special nature of this material requires special equipment and makes self-service by users undesirable or impossible. Reading and staff work space will therefore have to be provided adjacent to the map storage areas.

B. *Major Elements and Space Requirements*

	Sq.ft.
175 map cases (4' × 3' plus ½ of 4' aisle) @ 20	3500
16 single-face sections shelving 12" deep for atlases and gazetteers, @ 9	144
6 folio atlas cases (3' × 2') for large atlases, @ 12	72
Reading room	
12 seats, @ 40	480
2 light tables, @ 36	72
1 staff work and sorting room	400
1 office for curator	100
	4,768*

*Special Note: It is recognized that there may not be sufficient space for this collection in the building. A review of whether to try to include it or not shall be made by the owner early in the planning process. The space has *not* been included in space summary figures.

C. *Suggested Location:* Natural relationship will be with Economics, Business, and Geography insofar as users are concerned. However, the Map Library should not displace the book stack space immediately adjacent to this reader facility.

D. *Arrangements:* The work area, which will inevitably present a cluttered appearance, should be separated from the public areas by partially solid or obscured partitions. It should be so located, or the doorways should be so disposed, that the Map Library's users will not be led into the work area. The partitions need not extend to the ceiling. Layout must allow for a cabinet (4' × 3' × 5' in height) for the temporary storage of maps being processed, for a supply cabinet 4' × 2' × 6' in height, and for 2 long work tables at least 4' deep.

MICROFORM READING ROOM
(UNIVERSITY OF NORTH CAROLINA)

Purpose

To house, service, and provide reader stations for the bulk of the library's microform collections.

Suggested Location and Relationships

A location vertically adjacent to the two Reference Departments, with maximum ease of user access, is highly desirable.

Arrangement

Public Service Desk (400 net sq. ft.) should be immediately visible upon entering room. This Desk will house attendants, reader-printers and duplicators, a card catalog and guides, and it will be noisy. Arrangement should be such that, either by location or sound-conditioning, Reader Stations (carrels) are protected from noise as much as possible.

Microform storage (4,000 net sq. ft.) will be a mix of open shelving, 140 microfilm cabinets, and other forms, with specifications to be provided. Storage space may be in two stages: (1) approximately 20% should be immediately and horizontally adjacent to the Public Service

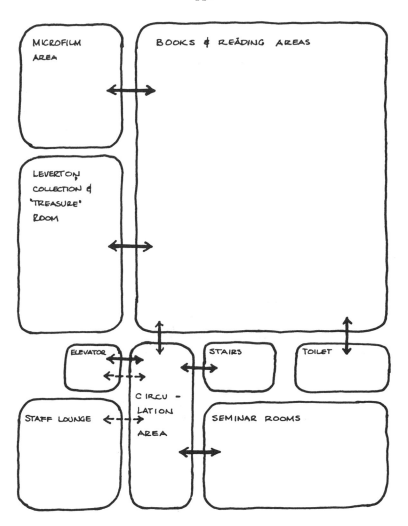

FIGURE A.10 **Lake Forest College Library. Spatial relationships for second-floor requirements.**

Desk; (2) 80% can be at a greater distance, horizontally or vertically, provided there is direct access from the Public Service Desk. This 80% could be part of the Book Stacks, provided that humidity requirements can be met and that it is enclosed, or secured from the Book Stacks proper.

Special Equipment and Other Requirements

Subdued overhead lighting in Reader Station area; principal light source will be from carrels themselves.

110V outlets for each Reader Station.

In Microform Storage areas, a humidity level of 45–55% must be maintained.

Reader Stations

1. The five closed carrels (200 net sq. ft.) should each have a LMM Superior Library Microfilm Reader (Model AB) or equivalent. Dimensions of this unit as follows: Height: 60 in. (152cm), Depth: 30 in. (76cm), Width: 48 in. (122cm), Weight: 195 lb. (88Kg).

In addition each carrel should be equipped with a chair, a small table or workbench, and individually controlled indirect light source. The occupant of the carrel should be able to control the direction and intensity of his light, (i.e., some sort of light on a flexible shaft, such as a gooseneck, with a rheostat control for intensity).

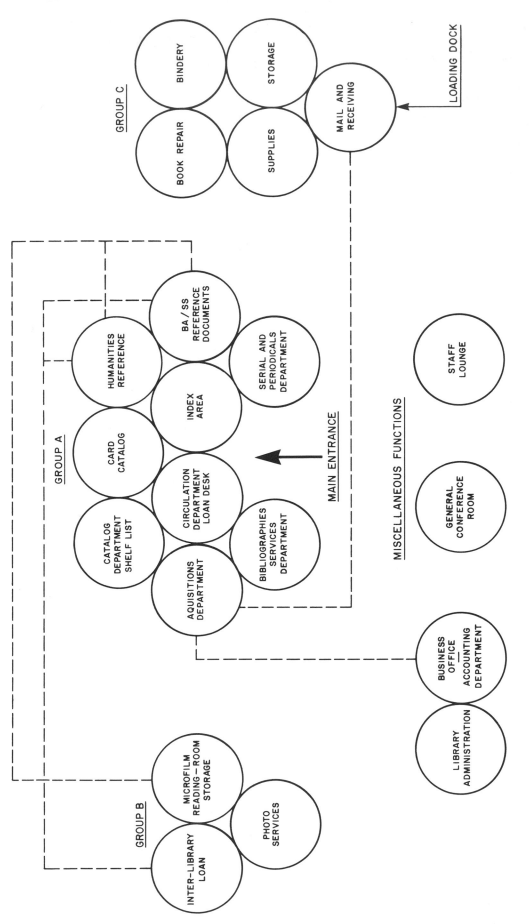

FIGURE A.11 University of North Carolina Davis Library. Spatial primary and secondary functional relationships.

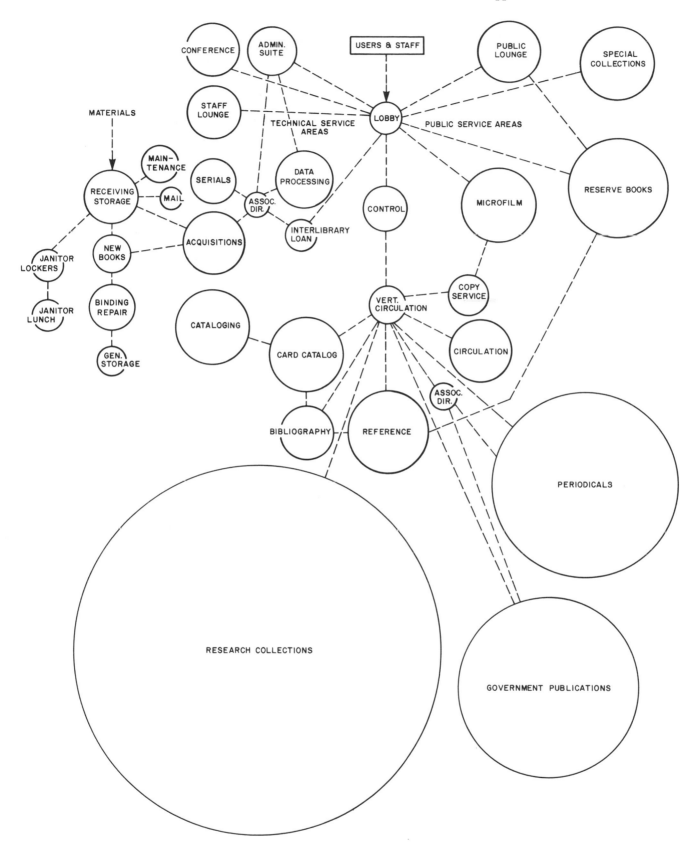

PROGRAM RELATIONSHIP DIAGRAM 1

FIGURE A.12 Western Illinois University Library. Program relationship diagram 1 from architect's program analysis report.

SCHEMATIC M
ADMINISTRATIVE OFFICES

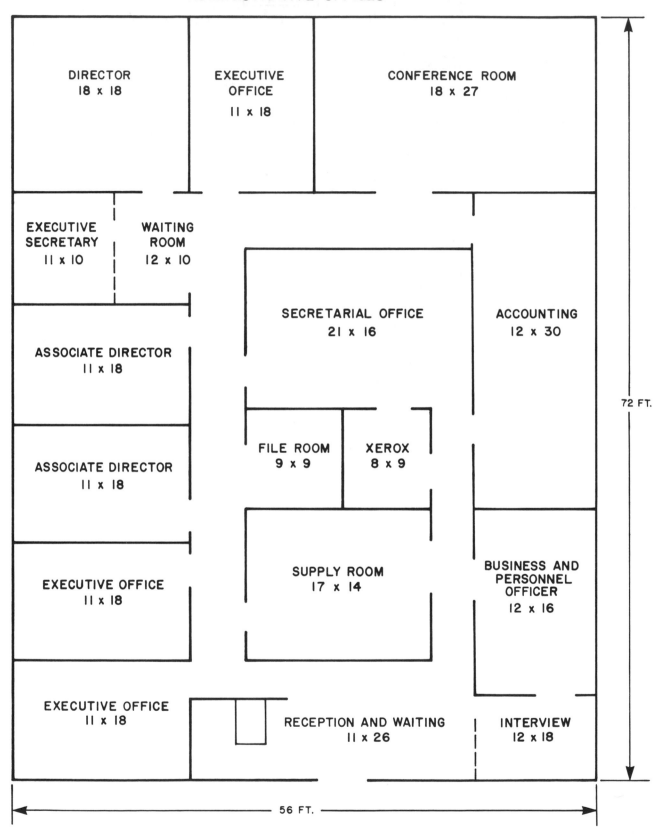

FIGURE A.13 University of Texas, Perry-Castañeda Library. Administrative office, schematic M.

One of the five carrels should be easily convertible into a station for reading microfiche, although most of the concentrated lengthy uses of microfilm will involve *roll* microfilm.

2. The forty open carrels (1,000 net sq.ft.) should be divided as follows: roll film readers (LMM model AB as in 1. above), 15; Microfiche readers, 20; and micro-opaque readers, 5.

a. The 15 stations for roll film readers should be designed to accommodate the same machine as described in 1. above except that stations will not be enclosed and table or workbench will not be necessary. These units rest on the floor and will not need a table to hold them.

b. The twenty microfiche stations would be equipped with tabletop readers such as the Realist Vantage L with dimensions as follows: Height: 17 in., Depth: 9 inches, Width: 13 in., Weight: 26 lbs.

These machines can be lined up along a large table, two or three machines per table, with adequate chairs accompanying. Each station should have individually controlled lighting, (reading lamps as in 1. above).

c. The five micro-opaque readers should be tabletop units also. A design such as the Readex Universal Micro-Viewer, Model 5, would be used. Its dimensions are as follows: Height: 23 in., Depth: 20 in., Width: 11 in., Weight: 24 lbs.

Other specifications for opaque readers should be similar to those for microfiche.

The room, as a whole, should be lighted with indirect, subdued lighting. Each station should have some control over its individual lighting conditions. THIS IS IMPORTANT! User resistance to microforms, according to latest studies, has been minimized by offering personalized lighting.

SEMINAR FACILITIES
(UNIVERSITY OF CHICAGO)

As a part of the facilities in most of the specialized subject areas, one or more "standard" seminar rooms are indicated. Unless indicated otherwise, these are intended to be multi-purpose facilities:

They are to be used for special course seminars requiring library materials in connection with the actual teaching process that cannot, for various reasons, be handled satisfactorily in reserve.

During hours in which such space is not engaged for seminars, it should be available for small groups of students who wish to work together.

Since the size of the groups will vary, it is proposed that seminars seat readers in units of 8, divided by folding partitions.

The space should be convertible to other uses, and the external partitions for the seminar should be prefabricated and movable.

The doors should have large clear glass lights.

Each room should have a pull-down (non-mechanized) projection screen, ample electrical outlets, a blackboard, and some wall fixtures to which bracket shelving may be attached.

Unless indicated otherwise, the seminars should open either into the regular reading areas or into the control areas of the specialized subject facilities.

Some 10–12 sections of shelving, the exact number to depend upon the general layout, are to be located in the reading room adjacent to the seminar.

A sketched arrangement is available.

SPECIAL COLLECTIONS VAULT
(GERALD R. FORD LIBRARY)

In all Presidential libraries there are restrictions on the use of some of the manuscript and microform holdings. These restrictions (for purposes of this discussion) are of three types: (1) those imposed by law or Executive Order for the protection of national security; (2) those imposed by the donor to avoid unwarranted invasion of personal privacy; and (3) those imposed by the archival staff to avoid loss or destruction of rare and valuable items. Each of these requires separate handling facilities, and items of one category cannot be intermingled with items from another category.

Federal laws and various agency requirements prescribe standards for the vault necessary for storage of national security classified materials. Specifications for construction of such a vault are available from the National Archives and Records Service. This vault area should be about 1,500 square feet, with adjustable steel shelving sufficient to hold 1,500 linear feet of material. The balance of the area will be used for locking file cabinets and processing tables. This vault should have a "day door" and adequate ventilation, as staff will frequently need to work in this area.

The area used for storage of donor restricted material and rare/valuable material should be separated by a semi-movable partition. The quantity of donor restricted material will be initially high, but will decline over the years as the need to keep this material closed decreases. Conversely, the material which will be placed in the rare/valuable category will increase over the years as more time is allocated to processing and preserving the documents. This area should have the same floorspace as the security classified vault (1,500 square feet), but should be entirely devoted to adjustable steel shelving.

APPENDIX B

Formulas and Tables

The data and tabulations given here are at best only approximations and may be altered by local conditions; they are not arrived at by exact scientific calculation. Seven groups are treated here:

  I. Column spacing
 II. Ceiling heights and floor areas
III. Reader accommodations
 IV. Bookstack capacity (excluding problems that are affected by column spacing)
  V. Card catalog capacity
 VI. Computer terminals
VII. Government and other standards and planning guides. These are from the State of Oregon, Association of College and Research Libraries, Western Interstate Commission for Higher Education, the Province of Quebec, and the University Grants Committee of Great Britain

I. Column Spacing

A. *Stack areas.* No one size is perfect for column sizes or column spacing.

Other things being equal, the larger the bay size, the better, so long as it does not unduly increase construction costs, floor-to-floor heights, or column sizes.

Column spacing—that is, the distance between column centers—is generally more important in concentrated stack areas than in combined stack and reading areas, because in the latter suitable adjustments are easier to make.

Clear space between columns—this is *not* the space between column centers—in a column range should preferably be a multiple of the shelving unit (typically 3 ft or 900 mm) plus an additional 4 in. (0.102) to allow for irregularities in the column sizes and for the end uprights in the range. Note that some shelving types require a "growth" factor, that is, the center-to-center spacing required for each section is slightly more than the nominal section width.

Range spacing and range lengths have a greater effect on book capacity than the distance between columns in a column range. The reduction of space between range centers by 1 in. (25.4 mm) increases book capacity by approximately 2 percent. The reduction of space used for cross aisles at right angles to the ranges is also of importance.

If practicable, columns should be no greater than 14 in. (0.356) in the direction of a range, and the dimension in the other direction should be kept down to 18 in. (0.457). If over 14 in. (0.356) in the direction of the range is necessary, the column might almost as well be 32 in. (0.813) in that direction. It could then occupy the space of a full stack section and perhaps enclose a heating duct. If a column is wider than the range, it will jut into the stack aisle. Irregular length stack sections are inconvenient, unduly expensive, and can often be replaced to advantage by a lectern or consultation table.

Tables B.1A and B.1B deal with standard layouts in commonly used module sizes.

TABLE B.1A. SQUARE MODULES WITH THE COLUMN SPACING A MULTIPLE OF THE SHELVING UNIT (PLUS HALF A SHELVING UNIT FOR THE COLUMN ITSELF)[a]

Bay Size	Sections Between Columns Standard 3 ft.	Sections Between Columns Standard 900 mm.	Ranges to a Bay	Range Spacing on Centers
19'6" × 19'6"	6		5	3'10"
	6		4	4'10 1/2"
	6		3	6'6"
5.7 m × 5.7 m		6	5	1.154
		6	4	1.442
		6	3	1.923
22'6" × 22'6"	7		6	3'9"
	7		5	4'6"
	7		4	5'7 1/2"
6.8 m × 6.8 m		7	6	1.133
		7	5	1.360
		7	4	1.700
25'6" × 25'6"	8		7	3'7 5/7"
	8		6	4'3"
	8		5	5'1 1/5"
	8		4	6'4 1/2"
7.7 m × 7.7 m		8	7	1.100
		8	6	1.283
		8	5	1.540
		8	4	1.925
28'6" × 28'6"	9		8	3'6 3/4"
	9		7	4'0 6/7"
	9		6	4'9"
	9		5	5'8 2/5"
8.6 m × 8.6 m		9	8	1.075
		9	7	1.229
		9	6	1.433
		9	5	1.720

a) Column size should not be wider than the depth of the range; 14 × 4 in. up to 14 × 18 in. or, for the metric, 350 × 350 mm up to 350 × 450 mm.

TABLE B.1B. SQUARE MODULES WITH COLUMN SPACING A MULTIPLE OF STANDARD SECTION[a]

Bay Size	Sections Between Columns Standard 3 ft.	Sections Between Columns Standard 900 mm.	Ranges to a Bay	Range Spacing on Centers
18' × 18'	5		5	3'7 1/5"
	5		4	4'6"
	5		3	6'
5.4 m × 5.4 m		5	5	1.080
		5	4	1.350
		5	3	1.800
21' × 21'	6		6	3'6"
	6		5	4'2 2/5"
	6		4	5'3"
6.3 m × 6.3 m		6	6	1.050
		6	5	1.260
		6	4	1.575
24' × 24'	7		7	3'5 1/7"
	7		6	4'
	7		5	4'9 3/5"
	7		4	6'
7.2 m × 7.2 m		7	7	1.029
		7	6	1.200
		7	5	1.440
		7	4	1.800
27' × 27'	8		8	3'4 1/2"
	8		7	3'10 2/7"
	8		6	4'6"
	8		5	5'4 4/5"
	8		4	6'9"
8.1 m × 8.1 m		8	8	1.012
		8	7	1.157
		8	6	1.350
		8	5	1.620
		8	4	2.025

a) Columns should not be wider than the depth of the range. 18 × 32 in. or, for the metric, 450 × 800 mm is suggested.

The following comments may be useful in connection with Tables B.1A and B.1B:

1. Spacing of 3 ft 9 in. (1.143) or less should be used for closed-access storage only where handicapped access is not required, with ranges not more than 30 ft (9.144) long and not more than 18 in. (0.457) deep.

2. Spacing 3 ft 9 in. to 4 ft 1 in. (1.143 to 1.245) can be used to advantage for large, little-used, limited-access stacks, with ranges up to 30 ft (9.144) long. Closed-access ranges up to 60 ft (18.288) long have been used successfully with 18 in. (0.457) or less deep, 4 ft or 4 ft 1 in. (1.219 to 1.245) on centers. Where conformance with wheelchair access codes is required, wider spacing will be necessary.

3. Spacing 4 ft 2 in. to 4 ft 6 in. (1.270 to 1.372) can be used for open-access stacks, preferably held to 18 in. (0.457) in depth, with the range length based on the amount of use. With 18 in. (0.457) deep shelving units and 4 ft 6 in. (1.372) spacing, most (but not all) handicapped accessibility codes will be satisfied.

4. Spacing 4 ft 6 in. to 5 ft (1.372 to 1.524) is generous even for heavily used, open-access undergraduate stacks if ranges are five sections long and 4 ft 6 in. (1.372) on centers, and in some cases up to ten sections long if 5 ft (1.524) on centers. In most cases, handicapped accessibility requirements can be met within this spacing category.

5. Spacing 5 ft to 5 ft 10 in. (1.524 to 1.778) is unnecessarily generous for any regular stack shelving and is often adequate for periodical display cases and for heavily used reference collections.

6. Spacing 6 ft (1.829) or greater is adequate for newspaper shelving and generous for periodical display cases.

Square bays are more flexible than those that form a long rectangle and are generally somewhat cheaper if the ceiling height is limited. But if the latter are used, the number of suitable sizes can be greatly increased. Table B.2 shows possibilities

TABLE B.2. LONG RECTANGULAR MODULES, 22 FT 6 IN. IN ONE DIRECTION[a]

Bay Size	Ranges to a Bay	Range Spacing on Centers
22′6″ × 18′	4	4′6″
22′6″ × 20′	5	4′
22′6″ × 20′10″	5	4′2″
22′6″ × 21′8″	5	4′4″
22′6″ × 24′	6	4′
22′6″ × 25′	6	4′2″
22′6″ × 26′	6	4′4″
22′6″ × 27′	6	4′6″

a) A bay of this size will give seven sections 3 ft long between 14-in. columns in the direction of the column range. The column sizes suggested in Table B.1A are suitable here.

with 22 ft 6 in. in one direction and different spacing in the other direction.

Similar tables can be prepared for a multitude of dimensions, including metric dimensions.

If section lengths are changed from 3 ft to some other size, such as 3 ft 1 in., 3 ft 2 in., 3 ft 3 in., 3 ft 4 in., 3 ft 5 in., or 3 ft 6 in., or, in countries using the metric system, from .90 to .95, 1.00, or 1.05 m, tables comparable to Tables B.1A, B.1B, and B.2 above should be prepared with those lengths as a base. In Table B.1B, note that the bay size is a multiple of the sections between the columns *plus* one section.

Always keep in mind the probable cost advantages available if standard sizes are used. Remember that columns so large that they interfere with aisles are seldom necessary.

B. *Seating accommodations.* Column spacing is of less importance in connection with seating accommodations than with shelving. Tables B.3 and B.4 show the maximum number of carrels available on one side of standard-size bays and the number of studies available in such bays, assuming the use of minimum-size reading accommodations. Some would argue that by providing more space, greater utilization will be realized. Provision for wheelchairs will also have its effect. The authors urge care in using this data.

Any small room will seem less confining if it has a window, and since window wall space is generally at a premium, a room can well have one of its short sides on the window wall.

II. Ceiling Heights and Floor Areas. Minimum and maximum ceiling heights and floor areas involve basic functional and aesthetic problems. Suggestions from the functional point of view are proposed as an aid in reaching decisions.

A. *Ceiling heights.* Ceiling heights greater than functionally necessary may be desirable aesthetically but involve increased cost, unused cubage, and larger areas to allow the stairs to reach a higher level. Ceiling heights have desirable functional minimums also and, if reduced beyond these minimums, may be unpleasant to the users, may se-

TABLE B.3. CARRELS[a]

Bay Size	Open[b]	Double- or Triple-Staggered[c]	Small Closed[d]	Large Closed[e]
18′ (5.5 m)	4	4	4	3
19½′ (5.9 m)	4	4	4	3
21′ (6.4 m)	5	4	4	4
22½′ (6.9 m)	5	5	5	4
24′ (7.3 m)	6	5	5	4
25½′ (7.8 m)	6	5	5	5
27′ (8.2 m)	6	6	6	5

a) A carrel, as used here, is an area in which a reader is cut off from any neighbor who is closer than 3 ft (0.914) on either side or front and back and one side. The minimum desirable width of an adequate carrel working surface is 2 ft 9 in. (0.838), which is as useful as 3 ft (0.914) for each person at a table with two or more persons sitting side by side. Minimum depth suggested is 20 in. (0.508).

b) Distance between centers should be not less than 4 ft 3 in. (1.295), unless the front table leg is set back 4 to 6 in. (102 to 152 mm) and armless chairs are used, in which case the distance on centers can be reduced to 4 ft (1.219). Any distance over 4 ft 6 in. (1.372) is unnecessarily generous. A clear space of 27 in. (0.686) or more between working surface and partition at the rear is recommended. A shelf above the table interferes with overhead lighting and makes a deeper table desirable.

c) Distance between centers should seldom be less than 4 ft 6 in. (1.372); 5 ft (1.524) is preferred; anything greater is unnecessarily generous. With triple-staggered carrels, the back of the center one should be held down to no more than 10 in. (0.254) above the tabletop if it is believed the person in the middle would feel boxed in.

d) Distance between centers should be not less than 4 ft 6 in. (1.372); and 5 ft (1.524) is preferred. Watch out for ventilation. A window is psychologically desirable. Closed carrels are not recommended for undergraduates or any student not actually engaged in writing a dissertation. Glass in the door or grilles can be provided for supervision.

e) A room less than 6 ft (1.829) long at right angles to the desk will permit shelves above the desk or a bookcase behind the occupant, but preferably not both. One less than 6 ft (1.829) parallel to the desk will not permit a 4-ft (1.219) long desk, and a second chair, and may make it necessary to open the door outward.

riously affect book capacity and flexibility, and may needlessly complicate lighting and ventilation. Table B.5 suggests functional minimums and maximums.

B. *Floor areas.* Both the number of floors in a library and the area of each floor may be important functionally and aesthetically. Decisions in regard to floors may be influenced by the site surroundings, the slope of the ground, and the value of the property. It is obvious, however, that a skyscraper with only 5,000 sq ft (465 m²) on each floor would be undesirable, and that a 250,000 sq ft (23,225 m²) area on one floor would involve unnecessary and undesirable horizontal traffic.

Table B.6 makes suggestions (which at best are only approximations) as to the percentage of the

TABLE B.4. FACULTY STUDIES AND SMALL MULTIPURPOSE ROOMS

Bay Size	Small Faculty Study[a]	Small Conference Room or Generous Faculty Study[b]
18′ (5.5 m)	3	2
19½′ (5.9 m)	3	2
21′ (6.4 m)	3	2
22½′ (6.9 m)	3	2
24′ (7.3 m)	4	3
25½′ (7.8 m)	4	3
27′ (8.2 m)	4	3

a) A room of this size can house a large desk, shelving, a filing case, and permit a door to open in except for those studies provided for handicapped persons, where additional space will be required. It is suggested that a "generous" faculty study be provided for this purpose.

b) This will provide for conference rooms for four, an adequate small staff office, or a generous faculty study. It should be at least 8 ft (2.4 m) in the clear in one direction and have a total area of over 70 sq ft (6.5 m²).

gross floor area of a library building which functionally should be on the entrance or central-services level in a typical academic library.

III. Accommodations for Readers. Seating accommodations for readers and the service to readers are the largest space consumers in most libraries. The required areas depend on:

A. The number of accommodations provided

B. The types of accommodations and the percentage of each

C. The dimensions of the working surfaces for each type of accommodation

D. The average floor area required for each type of accommodation

E. Additional space required for service to readers.

A. *Formulas for percentage of students for whom seating accommodations are required.* The formula used should depend on:

1. The quality of the student body and the faculty. The higher the quality, the greater the library use.

2. The library facilities provided. The more satisfactory the seating accommodations and the services provided, the greater the use.

3. The quality of the collections. Superior collections increase use.

4. The curriculum. In general, students in the humanities and social sciences use the library more than do those in the pure and applied sciences.

5. The emphasis placed on textbook instruction, which tends to reduce library use, and the emphasis placed by the faculty on the library and on nontextbook reading.

6. The percentage of graduate students and the fields in which they work.

7. Whether the student body is resident or commuting, and, if the former, whether the dormi-

TABLE B.5. CLEAR CEILING HEIGHTS

Area	Suggested Minimum[a]	Suggested Functional Maximum[b]
Bookstack[c]	7′6″ (2.286)	8′6″ (2.590)
Stacks with lights at right angle to ranges[d]	8′4″ (2.540)	8′9″ (2.667)
Stacks with lights on range tops functioning by ceiling reflection	9′0″ (2.743)	9′6″ (2.896)
Reading areas under 100 sq ft (9.29 m²)	7′6″ (2.286)	8′6″ (2.590)
Individual seating in large areas	8′4″ (2.540)	9′6″ (2.896)
Large reading rooms over 100 ft long (30.5 m) broken by screens or bookcases	9′6″ (2.896)	10′6″ (3.200)
Entrance or main level with over 20,000 sq ft (1860 m²)	9′6″ (2.896)	10′6″ (3.200)
Floor with mezzanine[e]	15′6″ (4.724)	18′6″ (5.639)

a) Heights lower than specified have been used successfully on occasion, but ceiling lights should be recessed and good ventilation assured. Financial savings will be comparatively small. Note that the local codes may affect the minimum height; many codes require sprinklers to be at least 18 in. (0.457) above combustible materials, which suggests a minimum height of 9 ft (2.743) where there is standard shelving. The code authorities should be consulted prior to settling upon a minimum height.

b) Greater heights may be useful aesthetically and provide added flexibility by making areas available for a wider range of purposes.

c) 7 ft 6 in. (2.286) is the lowest height which permits an adequate protective base (equivalent of a kickplate) and seven shelves 12 in. (0.305) on centers (standard for most academic libraries) with suitable clearance at the top. The top shelf will be 6 ft 4 in. (1.930) above the floor, the greatest height that can be reached without difficulty by a person 5 ft (1.524) tall. Space above 7 ft 6 in. is not useful for storage of open-access collections and will be confusing if used for other shelving.

d) This height used with fluorescent tubes, at right angles to the ranges, permits stack ranges to be shifted closer together or farther apart without rewiring, and is high enough so that heat from the tubes will not damage the books on the top shelf. If the fixtures are flush or nearly flush with the ceiling, the clear height can be reduced a few inches.

e) Mezzanines provide inexpensive space if they occupy at least 50 percent of the floor area (building codes may prohibit them unless the mezzanine is partitioned off and made a separate unit), and if the overall height of the two resulting levels is not much more than 6 ft (1.829) greater than would be provided if there were no mezzanine.

tories provide suitable study facilities. Heaviest library use in most residential institutions is in the evening; in commuter institutions, during the daytime hours.

8. Whether the location is rural, suburban, or urban. Large population centers tend to decrease

TABLE B.6. SUGGESTED FORMULAS FOR PERCENTAGE OF GROSS FLOOR AREA FUNCTIONALLY DESIRABLE ON THE CENTRAL-SERVICES LEVEL[a]

Gross Building Area in sq ft (m²)	Size of Collections in Volumes (given in 1,000s)	Minimum percentages of Gross Area on Central-Services Level
Under 20,000 (1860)	Under 100	40–50
20,000–45,000 (1860–4180)	100–250	33⅓–40
40,000–80,000 (3720–7430)	250–500	25–33⅓
75,000–150,000 (6970–13,940)	500–1,000	20–30
135,000+ (12,540+)	1,000+	16⅔–25

a) Central services as used here include the main control point, circulation and reference services, reference and bibliographical collections, the public catalog, and acquisition and catalog departments. Note that automation may facilitate location of technical processing departments on a level other than that accommodating central services.

These computations are approximations only, but smaller figures than those in the last column will often necessitate shifting part of the central services to other levels and, incidentally, may add considerably to staff payrolls.

evening use because of housing/transportation factors and other available activities and attractions.

9. The departmental library arrangements which may make available other reading facilities and reduce the use of the central library.

10. The institution's policy in regard to use by persons other than those connected with it.

Table B.7 suggests formulas for percentage of students for whom seating is suggested.

B. *Suggestions for types of seating accommodations and the percentage of each type.*

1. Undergraduate Student Accommodations

a. Tables for four or more. Not more than 20 percent. Should be largely restricted to those in reserved-book and reference rooms.

b. Lounge chairs. Not more than 15 percent. Should in general be restricted to lounge areas, smoking rooms, current-periodical rooms, or used to break up unpleasantly long rows of other types of accommodations. In many libraries 8 to 10 percent of seating of this kind is adequate.

c. Individual accommodations. Up to 85 percent. In most cases these should provide for working surfaces cut off from immediately adjacent neighbors, by aisles or partitions on one, two, or three sides. The partitions should be high enough—52 in. (1.321)—so that heads do not bob up or down above them and cause visual distraction. These accommodations may include:

(1) Tables for one. These can be quite satisfactory along a wall or screen if the readers

TABLE B.7. FORMULAS FOR PERCENTAGE OF STUDENTS FOR WHOM SEATING ACCOMMODATIONS ARE SUGGESTED

Type of Institution	Percentage
Graduate-level professional school library	50–100
Arts and humanities research branch	50–80
Superior residential coeducational liberal arts college in rural area or small town	50-60
Superior residential liberal arts college for men or women in rural area or small town	45–50
Superior residential liberal arts college in a small city	40–45
Graduate-level science research branch	35–50
Superior residential university	35–40
Typical residential university	25–30
Typical commuting university	10–20

all face in the same direction. When placed in a reading area, they are not recommended.

(2) Tables for two with partitions down the center. For limited use only.

(3) Tables for four or more with partitions in both directions. A great improvement over a table for four without partitions.

(4) Pinwheel arrangement for four. Satisfactory, but requires more space than 3 above.

(5) Double carrels with readers facing in different directions. Not as satisfactory as 6 below.

(6) Double-staggered carrels.

(7) Pairs of double-staggered carrels on both sides of a screen.

(8) Triple-staggered carrels in place of three stack ranges or in a large reading area.

(9) Rows of single carrels at right angles to a wall in bookstack or reading area.

(10) Single carrels in place of last stack section at the end of a blind stack aisle.

(11) Typing carrels similar to 10 above, but with special acoustic protection.

(12) Rows of double carrels in a reading area or in place of two stack ranges.

Closed carrels are rarely recommended for undergraduates. Shelves in carrels tend to encourage undesirable monopolization. A shelf outside the carrel with an open or locked cupboard provides for books and papers to be reserved and makes possible longer hours of carrel use.

2. Graduate Student Accommodations

a. At tables for multiple seating. Not recommended for general seating, although some tables are desirable for those who feel a need to spread out or who are using very large volumes, maps, or newspapers.

b. Open carrels of any of the types proposed in 1 above. Graduate carrels may have shelves over the working surface, but this will require deeper table tops because of lighting problems, unless the shelves are installed at one side.

c. Closed carrels. See C and D below for working surface dimensions and requirements. Closed carrels require special care for satisfactory lighting and ventilation. Unless larger than necessary to provide adequate working surfaces, claustrophobia tends to result. A window for each carrel or an attractive grill on at least one side will help.

3. Faculty Accommodations. If possible, closed studies should be provided for faculty members engaged in research projects which require the use of library materials. They should generally not be used as offices. See C and D below for working surface dimensions and floor area requirements.

C. *Dimensions of working surface for each type of seating accommodation.* Table B.8 gives suggested minimum and adequate dimensions. No attempt is made to propose maximum or generous sizes.

D. *Average floor area required for different types of accommodation.* The floor area requirements suggested in Table B.9 are at best approximations, but they may be helpful in preliminary stages of planning.

E. *Additional space required for service to readers.* Space for direct access to seating accommodations is dealt with in Table B.9 and elsewhere.

Additional space required includes:

Assignable Areas

The public catalog

Space around the bibliographical and reference and current-periodical collections, which is required because of heavy use

Public areas outside service desks

Special accommodations for microfilm reproductions, maps, manuscripts, archives, and other collections not shelved in the main stack area. These may include audio-visual areas of various types.

Staff working quarters

Nonassignable Areas

Entrances, vestibules, and lobbies

Corridors

Areas used primarily as traffic arteries

Stairwells and elevator shafts

Toilets

Mechanical and electrical equipment space

Walls and columns

It is suggested that not less than 25 sq ft (2.32 m²) per reader in assignable or nonassignable areas will be required for the services in these groups, and that unless the special accommodations mentioned above are held to a reasonable minimum and careful planning is provided throughout, the 25 sq ft may have to be increased to 35 sq ft. In many cases the space required for reader accommodations will appropriately be 35 sq ft (3.25 m²) or even larger, and it is urged that the area needed for accommodations should be calculated exclusive of the nonassignable area that is generally applied as a factor to the total program requirements based upon the anticipated efficiency of the building. Note also that the requirements for providing handicapped access and the growing use of special equipment such as computers, video equipment, and microform readers may argue for more than the minimum space.

TABLE B.8. SUGGESTED WORKING SURFACE AREA FOR EACH PERSON[a]

Type of Accommodation	Minimum Size	Adequate Size
Table for multiple seating for reserved-book use	33″ × 21″ (0.838 × 0.533)	36″ × 24″ (0.914 × 0.610)
Individual table or open carrel for undergraduate	33″ × 20″ (0.838 × 0.508)[b]	36″ × 22″ (0.914 × 0.559)
Open carrel for graduate student without bookshelf over it	36″ × 24″ (0.914 × 0.610)[c]	42″ × 24″ (1.067 × 0.610)
Carrel, open or closed, for graduate student writing dissertation, with a bookshelf	36″ × 27″ (0.914 × 0.686)[d]	48″ × 30″ (1.219 × 0.762)
Faculty study	48″ × 30″ (1.219 × 0.762)	60″ × 30″ (1.524 × 0.762) if shelving is over it

a) Note that while surface dimensions are given, the critical issue is the amount of work area. While some surface configurations may be inefficient, a rectangle is not the only suitable shape. In general, an undergraduate may need 6 to 8 sq ft (0.557 to 0.743 m²) of surface, depending on the task and the size of materials, a graduate student 7 to 10 sq ft (0.650 to 0.929 m²), and a professor or graduate student working on a thesis or dissertation 9 to 12 sq ft (0.836 to 1.115 m²). Those in fields such as chemistry, engineering, and mathematics will need less surface space; those in earth sciences, systematic biology, art history, music, and most other humanities and some social sciences will need the more generous provision.

b) A space of 33 × 20 in. (0.838 × 0.508) goes farther in an individual accommodation than at a large table because others do not intrude on the space. Remember that this is a *minimum* size.

c) Shelves are frequently not recommended over open carrels because they make it easier for an unauthorized student to monopolize a carrel.

d) A shelf over a carrel table requires additional depth because it interferes with lighting. A closed carrel should preferably have a window, glass in the door, and more space around the table than an open one, or claustrophobia may result.

For these and other reasons discussed in the text, the authors recommend using 30 to 35 sq ft (2.79 to 3.25 m²) for typical seating, and larger figures for selected facilities in research libraries such as microtext reading rooms.

To determine the space required for the nonassignable areas, it is suggested that an efficiency of 67 percent be assumed for small libraries, with up to an efficiency of 75 percent for large libraries. One may then divide the total assignable space for all functions by the assumed percentage to establish the total required gross area. The difference between the net assignable and the gross area is, of course, the anticipated nonassignable area.

IV. Bookstack Capacity. Bookstack capacity is based on: (A) the number of volumes shelved in a standard stack section, and (B) the floor area requirements for a standard stack section, as follows.

A. *The number of volumes shelved in a standard stack section.* The number of volumes that can be shelved in a standard stack section depends on: (1) book heights and the number of shelves per section; (2) book thickness; (3) the decision in regard to what is considered a section usefully full of books.

1. Book heights and shelves per section. Stack sections in academic libraries in the United States are considered standard if they are 7 ft 6 in. (2.286) high and 3 ft (0.914) wide. Sections of this height make possible seven shelves 12 in. (0.305) on centers over a 4 in. (0.102) base. This spacing is adequate for books which are 11 in. (0.279) tall or less, which, as shown in Table B.10, include 90 percent of the books in a typical collection.

It is suggested that most of the remaining 10 percent will be concentrated in a comparatively few subjects, that 70 percent of this 10 percent will be between 11 and 13 in. (0.279 to 0.330) tall, and that six shelves 14 in. (0.356) on centers will provide for them.

2. Book thickness and the number of volumes that can be shelved satisfactorily on each linear unit of shelving. No two libraries are alike in this regard. The average thickness will depend on (a) the definition of a volume; (b) binding policy, particularly for pamphlets, serials, and periodicals; (c) the collection under consideration. A commonly used formula for thickness of books is shown in Table B.11.

3. The decision on when a section is full. In Table B.11 a suggested number of volumes per single-faced section is proposed. It is evident that if books are shelved by subject, it is unwise to fill the shelves completely, and any estimate must be an approximation. For many libraries 125 volumes per stack section is considered safe, although Robert Henderson's "cubook" formula proposes only 100 volumes per section.

Shelving 125 volumes to a single-faced section, as suggested by Wheeler and Githens, is a practice often used, but it is safer and preferable to estimate the number of standard sections the collection now fills completely and then add 50 percent to that number to determine the present requirements for comfortable shelving arrangements. This would make the shelves two-thirds full on the average and would leave 1 ft (0.305) of unused space available on each shelf. If collections are growing each year by 5 percent of the collection at the end of the previous year, it will take between five and six years for the shelves to become six-sevenths full, and to leave an average of 5 in. (0.127) vacant on each shelf. By the time this occurs, the annual

TABLE B.9. APPROXIMATE FLOOR AREA REQUIREMENTS FOR DIFFERENT TYPES OF SEATING ACCOMMODATIONS[a]

Type of Accommodations	Requirements in Sq Ft (m²)		
	Minimum	Adequate	Generous
Small lounge chair[b]	20 (1.86)	25 (2.32)	30 (2.79)
Large lounge chair[c]	25 (2.32)	30 (2.79)	35 (3.25)
Individual table[d]	25 (2.32)	30 (2.79)	35 (3.25)
Tables for four[e]	22½ (2.09)	25 (2.32)	27½ (2.56)
Tables for more than four[f]	20 (1.86)	22½ (2.09)	25 (2.32)
Individual carrels[g]	20 (1.86)	22½ (2.09)	25 (2.32)
Double carrels[h]	22½ (2.09)	25 (2.32)	27½ (2.56)
Double-staggered carrels[i]	22½ (2.09)	25 (2.32)	27½ (2.56)
Triple-staggered carrels[j]	22½ (2.09)	25 (2.32)	27½ (2.56)
Double row of carrels with partitions between, placed in a reading room or in place of two stack ranges[k]	22½ (2.09)	25 (2.32)	27½ (2.56)

a) The figures used here include: (1) area of working surface if any; (2) area occupied by chair; (3) area used for direct access to the accommodations; and (4) reasonable share of all the assignable space used for main aisles in the room under consideration.

b) These chairs, if in pairs, should be separated by a small table to prevent congestion and to hold books not in use.

c) Large lounge chairs are expensive, space-consuming, and an aid to slumber, but they are highly regarded by students. They may or may not be appropriate.

d) Individual tables are space-consuming, are generally disorderly in appearance because unless anchored they are easily moved, and result in a feeling of commotion if there is traffic on all sides. Not recommended except along a wall or screen.

e) Tables for four are the largest ones recommended, unless pressure for additional capacity is great.

f) Tables for more than four are space-savers, but few readers like to sit with someone on each side. Readers will avoid using them as far as possible.

g) Individual carrels are economical in use of space if placed at right angles to a wall, adjacent to an aisle that must be provided under any circumstances. They reduce visual distraction if partitions 52 in. (1.320) or more in height are provided on at least two of the four sides.

h) Double carrels are useful, but the staggered ones described below are preferred.

i) Double-staggered carrels are as economical of space as tables for four and reduce visual distraction.

j) Triple-staggered carrels are as economical of space as tables for six or more and reduce visual distraction.

k) Double rows of carrels are economical in space use and reduce visual distraction.

TABLE B.10. BOOK HEIGHTS[a]

8″ (0.203) or less	25%	12″ (0.305)	94%
9″ (0.229) or less	54	13″ (0.330)	97
10″ (0.254) or less	79	Over 13″ (0.330)	3
11″ (0.279) or less	90		

a) Adapted from Rider's *Compact Storage*, p. 45, which was based to a considerable extent on research done by Van Hoesen and Kilpatrick on the height of books in academic libraries.

TABLE B.11. VOLUMES PER SHELF FOR BOOKS IN DIFFERENT SUBJECTS[a]

Subject	Volumes per Standard Shelf	Volumes per Single-faced Section
Circulating (nonfiction)	24	168
Fiction	24	168
Economics	24	168
General literature	21	147
History	21	147
Reference	18	108
Art (not including large folios)	21	126
Technical and scientific	18	126
Medical	15	105
Public documents	15	105
Bound periodicals	15	105
Law	15	105

a) This table, or a variation of it based upon the same data, is in common use by stack manufacturers. It was used by Wheeler and Githens, who suggest that 125 volumes per single-faced section be considered practical average working capacity. The figures here represent full capacity, although as a general guideline, they should be considered as conservative. Actual measurements often suggest that greater quantities are possible, and thus an analysis of the existing collection as outlined elsewhere is recommended.

cost of labor for the constant moving of books that will be necessary, plus the damage done to bindings by the moving, leaving out of consideration the resulting inconvenience, may well be greater than the interest on the capital sum required to provide for additional shelving.

Table B.12 shows the period required for a collection that now occupies two-thirds of available space to reach six-sevenths or between 85 and 86 percent of absolute capacity at different rates of growth.

Table B.13 shows the period required for a collection that now occupies one-half of the available shelving to grow to the point where it occupies six-sevenths of the shelving, with the growth at various percentage rates. In both tables the rates are figured with the annual increase estimated at a given percentage of the previous year's total and by a percentage of the total at the time the estimate is made, that is, arithmetically instead of geometrically.

B. *Floor area requirements for a standard stack section.* The floor area requirements for a standard

TABLE B.12. YEARS REQUIRED FOR A COLLECTION TO INCREASE FROM TWO-THIRDS TO SIX-SEVENTHS OF FULL CAPACITY

Rate of Growth	Years					
	3⅓%	4%	5%	6%	8%	10%
Geometric increase[a]	7+	6+	5+	4+	3+	2+
Arithmetic increase[b]	8+	7+	6−	5−	4−	3−

a) A geometric increase represents an increase of a given percentage each year of the total number of volumes at the end of the previous year.

b) An arithmetic increase represents an increase each year of a given percentage of the total number of volumes at the time used as a base and so does not become larger year by year.

TABLE B.13. YEARS REQUIRED FOR A COLLECTION TO INCREASE FROM 50 TO 85 PERCENT OF FULL CAPACITY

Rate of Growth	Years					
	3⅓%	4%	5%	6%	8%	10%
Geometric increase	16+	13+	11+	9+	7+	5−
Arithmetic increase	27+	18−	14+	12−	9−	7+

stack section depend primarily on: (1) range spacing; (2) range lengths; (3) the number of cross aisles and their widths; (4) cross aisle area charged against adjacent reader accommodations; (5) nonassignable space.

1. Range spacing. Range spacing should be based on column spacing, which was discussed at the beginning of this appendix; on shelf depths, which are discussed in *a* below; and on stack-aisle widths, dealt with in *2* below.

a. Shelf depths. Depths as used here are based on double-faced bracket shelving with 2 in. (51 mm) between the back of the shelf on one side of the range and the back of the shelf on the other side. Shelf depths specified by stack manufacturers are 1 in. (25 mm) greater than the actual depth, that is, a 7-in. (0.178) "actual" shelf is called an 8 in. (0.203) nominal shelf, because 8 in. (0.203) is available if half the 2 in. (51 mm) noted above is assigned to the shelves on each side of a double-faced shelf section. Table B.14 shows depths of books. If these figures are correct (they represent the average in research and academic libraries), a shelf with 8 in. (0.203) actual depth, together with the space available between shelves on the two sides of a double-faced section, will provide for practically any book that does not have to be segregated because of its height, and 8 in. (0.203) actual-depth shelves (they are designated by the manufacturers as 9 in. (0.229) shelves) are recommended in place of the 7 or 9 in. (0.178 or 0.229) actual-depth shelves which are commonly used. In many libraries a 7 in. (0.178) actual-depth shelf is suitable for a large part of the collections, although deeper shelving is normally preferable. Where diagonal or other bracing occurs in the space between the backs of the shelves, a shelf 1 in. (25 mm) deeper than discussed above is recommended.

TABLE B.14. PERCENTAGE OF BOOKS IN AN ACADEMIC COLLECTION BELOW DIFFERENT DEPTHS MEASURED FROM THE BACK OF THE SPINE TO THE FORE-EDGE OF THE COVERS[a]

5″ (0.127) or less	25%	9″ (0.229) or less	94%
6″ (0.152) or less	54	10″ (0.254) or less	97[b]
7″ (0.178) or less	79	Over 10″ (0.254)	3
8″ (0.203) or less	90		

a) Adapted from Rider's *Compact Book Storage*, p. 45.

b) An 8 in. actual-depth shelf (*i.e.*, a 9 in. (0.203/0.229) nominal-depth shelf) will house a 10 in. (0.254) deep book without difficulty, unless there is another deep book immediately behind it. Most books over 10 in. (0.254) deep will be more than 11 in. (0.279) tall and should be segregated on special shelving which is more than 9 in. (0.229) in nominal depth.

2. Stack-aisle widths and stack-range lengths. Stack-aisle widths should be based on the amount of use by individuals, by the need to provide for handicapped access, and by trucks and the length of the range before a cross aisle is reached. Other things being equal, the longer the range, the wider the aisle should be because of increased frequency of the need for one to pass another person or a truck and to have to back out of a very narrow aisle. While 1 in. (25 mm) makes little difference, 2 or 3 in. (51 or 76 mm) does. Table B.15 suggests desirable stack-aisle widths in conjunction with stack-range lengths under different types and amounts of use.

Do not forget that stack-aisle widths must be based, indirectly at least, on the column spacing dealt with at the beginning of this appendix, and are affected as well by the shelf depths discussed in *1.a* above, if columns are not to obstruct the aisles. The distance between column centers should be an exact multiple of the distance between the center of parallel stack ranges within the stack bay, which in turn is determined by the sum of the depth of a double-faced range and the width of a stack aisle.

3. Widths for main and subsidiary cross-stack aisles. Cross-aisle widths should be based on amount of use and are inevitably affected by the column spacing. Column spacing often makes it difficult to provide any cross-aisle widths except the width of a standard section or a multiple of this width. If standard shelving width is altered or if columns equal to one-half a standard section, less about 4 in. (0.102) for stack uprights and error, are used and the column range is filled out with a lectern, 4 ft 6 in. (1.372) aisles can be made available.

Table B.16 suggests desirable cross-aisle widths under different types and amounts of use.

4. Cross-aisle area charged against adjacent reader accommodations. The effect on floor area requirements per stack section and volume capacity per net unit of stack area, resulting from the provision of reader accommodations in the form of stack carrels should be considered. The assign-

TABLE B.15. SUGGESTED STACK-AISLE WIDTHS AND STACK-RANGE LENGTHS[a]

Typical Use of Stack	Aisle Width[b]		Range Lengths (Sections)[c]	
	Min.	Max.	Min.	Max.
Closed-access storage stack	24″ (0.610)	30″ (0.762)	10	20
Limited-access, little-used stack for over 1,000,000 volumes	26″ (0.660)	31″ (0.787)	10	16
Heavily used open-access stack for over 1,000,000 volumes	31″ (0.787)	36″ (0.914)	8	12
Very heavily used open-access stack with less than 1,000,000 volumes	33″ (0.838)	40″ (1.016)	5	10
Newspaper stack with 18″ (0.457) deep shelves	36″ (0.914)	45″ (1.143)	5	10
Reference and current-periodical room stacks	36″ (0.914)	60″ (1.524)	4	8
Current-periodical display stacks	42″ (1.067)	60″ (1.524)	4	7

a) These are suggestions only and not to be considered definite recommendations. Circumstances alter cases.

b) Stack-aisle widths of 24 in. (0.610) should be considered an absolute minimum and are rarely justifiable. Anything under 26 in. (0.660) is difficult with a book truck, even when the use is light. The minimum width proposed should generally be used only with the minimum range lengths suggested. For handicapped access local codes may require an aisle width of 36 in. (0.914), 42 in. (1.067) or, in rare cases, more.

c) Stack-range lengths are often determined by available space, rather than by their suitability. The maximum lengths shown in the table should generally be used only with the maximum aisle widths suggested. The "standard" section of 3 ft (0.914) is used here as the unit of measure.

ment of one-half of the adjacent cross-aisle area to reader space when carrels are on one side of the cross aisle and bookstack ranges are on the other, may increase rather than decrease book capacity per unit of net stack area, and, in addition, provide desirable and economical seating accommodations adjacent to the books. See Table B.17.

If closed carrels open from a subsidiary aisle, they will make it seem narrower.

It is evident that a large number of variables are involved in bookstack capacity. Table B.17 is based on the floor area required for a single-faced standard section in stack layouts, with different range spacing, range lengths, and cross-aisle widths, as well as stack carrels. A similar chart may easily be prepared for other units using proportional ratios. For example, with range spacing of 1.5 m and generous cross aisles, the area required is 1.5 × 836 divided by 1.524 = .823 m².

Table B.18 shows stack capacity per unit of floor area if 100, 125, 150, or 160 volumes per standard

TABLE B.16. SUGGESTED CROSS-AISLE WIDTHS[a]

Typical Use of Stack	Main Aisle		Subsidiary Cross-aisle[b]	
	Min.	Max.	Min.	Max.
Closed-access storage	3′ (0.914)	4′6″ (1.372)	2′6″ (0.762)	3′6″ (1.067)
Limited-access stack	3′ (0.914)	4′6″ (1.372)	3′ (0.914)	3′6″ (1.067)
Heavily used open-access stack	4′ (1.219)	5′ (1.524)	3′ (0.914)	4′ (1.219)
Heavily used open-access stack for large collection and ranges 30′ (9.144) long	4′6″ (1.372)	6′ (1.829)	3′3″ (0.991)	4′6″ (1.372)

a) These are suggestions only and not to be considered definite recommendations. Circumstances alter cases. In determining minimum or maximum widths, keep in mind the length and width of the book trucks used, the need for handicapped access, and the amount of use. Minimum-width stack aisles should not be accompanied by minimum cross aisles. From the widths shown in the table, up to 4 in. (0.102) may have to be subtracted to provide for adjacent stack uprights and irregularities in column sizes.

b) If open carrels adjoin a subsidiary aisle, they will make it seem wider, but traffic will tend to be disturbing to the carrel occupants.

TABLE B.17. FLOOR AREA REQUIRED FOR ONE SINGLE-FACED STANDARD SECTION

Range Spacing	Square Feet (Square Meters) with Minimum Cross Aisles[a]	Square Feet (Square Meters) with Generous Cross Aisles[b]	Square Feet (Square Meters) with Adequate Cross Aisles Combined with Carrels[c]
5′6″ (1.676)	9.075 (.843)	9.90 (.920)	9.281 (.862)
5′0″ (1.524)	8.25 (.766)	9.00 (.836)	8.4375 (.784)
4′6″ (1.372)	7.425 (.690)	8.10 (.753)	7.60 (.706)
4′3″ (1.295)	7.0125 (.651)	7.65 (.711)	7.225 (.671)
4′0″ (1.219)	6.60 (.613)	7.20 (.669)	6.75 (.627)

a) Based on a 5-section blind-aisle range on each side of a 3 ft (0.914) center aisle.

b) Based on two 3 ft (0.914) side aisles and a 6 ft center aisle separated by 10 section ranges.

c) Based on 3 ft (0.914) side aisles between carrels and 10 section ranges, the latter separated by a 4 ft 6 in. (1.372) center aisle. One-half of the side aisles are charged against the carrels, but even on 5 ft (1.524) centers the carrels occupy only 22½ sq ft (2.090 m²), and the floor area for a section is low.

stack section is used in connection with 7, 8⅓, 9, or 10 sq ft and .65, .75, .85, or .95 m² occupied by each section.

5. Nonassignable space. Nonassignable space includes, as far as its effect on book capacity is con-

TABLE B.18. VOLUME CAPACITY PER 1,000 SQUARE FEET AND 100 SQUARE METERS OF STACK AREA WITH DIFFERENT NUMBER OF SQUARE FEET AND SQUARE METERS AND DIFFERENT NUMBER OF VOLUMES PER SECTION

Sq Ft per Section[b]	Number of Sections in 1,000 Sq Ft	Volumes per 1,000 Sq Ft with Different Number of Volumes per Section[a]			
		100[g]	125[h]	150[i]	160[j]
10[c]	100	10,000	12,500	15,000	16,000
9[d]	111	11,100	13,875	16,650	17,760
8⅓[e]	120	12,000	15,000	18,000	19,200
7[f]	143	14,300	17,875	21,450	22,880

m² Per Section	Number of Sections in 100 m²	Volumes per 100 m² with Different Number of Volumes per Section			
		100	125	150	160
.95	105	10,500	13,125	15,750	16,800
.85	118	11,800	14,750	17,700	18,880
.75	133	13,300	16,625	19,950	21,280
.65	153	15,300	19,125	22,950	24,480

a) Volumes per section has been covered in detail in IV.A of this appendix.

b) Examination of Table B.17 should help in determining area to allow for a single-faced section. This matter has been covered in IV.B of this appendix.

c) 10 sq ft (.93 m²) per section is the "cubook" formula proposed by R. W. Henderson. Where handicapped access is required, this is a satisfactory figure for a large collection with open access.

d) See Table B.17 for an example.

e) The authors suggest that this is a satisfactory and safe figure to use for a large collection accessible to graduate students and a limited number of undergraduates, but with limited handicapped access.

f) Adequate for a very large collection with limited access.

g) 100 volumes per section is the "cubook" formula.

h) The authors suggest that this is a safe figure for comfortable working capacity in an average library. See IV.A of this appendix for a full discussion.

i) The number of 150 volumes per section is too often proposed by architects and librarians. While it is a possible figure, it approaches full capacity and should be used only in cases where additional space is immediately available when capacity is reached. The time to consider what comes next will have passed.

j) The number of 160 volumes per section should not be considered for most academic libraries, unless the collection has an unusually high percentage of abnormally thin volumes, e.g., individually bound pamphlets or Oriental collections with the traditionally slim Chinese fascicle or ts's (satsu in Japanese).

cerned, the floor space occupied by columns, mechanical services, and vertical transportation of all kinds. We mention it here simply to call attention to it. In a carefully designed stack for 25,000 volumes or more on one level, nonassignable space should not amount to more than 10 percent of the gross stack area, and considerably less with a larger installation. However, it is recommended that, in most cases, nonassignable space should be calculated for the total facility using the complete program as a basis, in which case a figure of 25 to 33 percent of the gross area is reasonable.

V. Card Catalog Capacity. In planning a card catalog room, estimates quite similar to those used for book stack capacity must be made. They should include:

A. The capacity for each card catalog unit used

B. The floor space required to file 1,000 cards comfortably

C. The allocation for computer terminals, microfiche readers, or other ancillary catalog devices, and perhaps explanatory displays and other guides to accessing the collections. Terminals are treated in section VI. Other of these space needs, such as displays, should be locally determined and cannot be recommended here.

A. *The capacity of each card catalog unit.* The capacity of each card catalog unit depends on: (1) the number of trays it contains; (2) the depth of each tray and the usable depth in inches or millimeters of cards that can be filed in it without undesirable and uneconomical congestion; (3) the thickness of the card stock, that is, the number of cards that will occupy 1 in. or 25 mm of filing space.

1. The number of trays in a card cabinet. This depends on the number of trays in each direction, that is, vertically and horizontally. Cabinets are made in a great many different sizes, but, for large installations, 6 trays wide and 10 to 12 trays high are considered standard, giving 60 or 72 to a unit.

A cabinet with 14 or even 16 trays high is possible, with a fairly low base so that the top one will be within reach. This will give 84 or 96 trays to a unit.

Cabinets five trays wide of different heights are also available, but may be more expensive per tray unless purchased in large quantities. They have the advantage of fitting into a standard stack unit of 3 ft or 900 mm.

2. The depth of the trays. Trays can be purchased in almost any depth, but an outside dimension of just over 15, 17, and 19 in. (0.380, 0.430, and 0.480) might be considered standard. A tray under 15 in. (0.380) is uneconomical in floor space used if the catalog is large. Those over 19 in. are so heavy when full as to make their use a doubtful blessing. It is urged that one standard length should be selected for any catalog, for mixed lengths will result in the shorter drawers being dropped.

3. The thickness of cards and the number that will occupy 1 inch (25 mm) of filing space. Experience indicates that 100 average cards to 1 in. (25 mm) of filing space is a safe figure to use today. Cards tend to thicken somewhat as they get older. Cards used earlier in the century were considerably thicker than those used today.

Table B.19 shows the capacity for cabinets six trays wide with different heights and different tray

TABLE B.19. CARD CAPACITY FOR STANDARD CARD CABINETS SIX TRAYS WIDE[a]

Number of Trays High	Tray Length		
	15″ (0.381)[b]	17″ (0.432)[c]	19″ (0.483)[d]
10	51,000	60,000	69,000
12	61,200	72,000	82,800
14	71,400	84,000	96,600
16	81,600	96,000	110,400

a) Cabinets six trays wide occupy approximately 40 in. (1.016) in width. Five-tray–wide cabinets occupy approximately 33⅓ in. (0.851) in width and can be placed in a standard 3 ft (0.914) wide stack section. They will probably cost more per tray, but they may fit into the available space to advantage, sometimes combined with the wider units.

b) A 15-in. tray is estimated to provide 12 in. (0.381/0.305) of net filing space, which, if filled to 71 percent capacity, will house comfortably approximately 850 cards which average 1/100 in. (.254 mm) in thickness.

c) A 17-in. tray is estimated to provide 14 in. (0.432/0.356) of net filing space, which, if filled to 72 percent of capacity, will house comfortably approximately 1000 cards which average 1/100 in. (.254 mm) in thickness.

d) A 19-in. tray is estimated to provide 16 in. (0.483/0.406) of net filing space, which, if filled to 73 percent of capacity, will house comfortably approximately 1150 cards which average 1/100 in. (.254 mm) in thickness. These trays may be uncomfortably heavy when filled to capacity.

depths, based on 100 cards to 1 in., with the net available filing space filled to a comfortable working capacity. The term "tray depth" refers to the overall depth of the cabinet in which the trays are housed. From this figure, 3 in. (76 mm) should be subtracted to obtain the gross filing space available, and comfortable working capacity can be estimated at between 70 and 75 percent of the gross filing space, with a somewhat larger percentage usable with the longer trays.

The capacities noted can be increased by at least 10 percent before they become completely unmanageable, but it is strongly recommended that the lower figure be used in estimating comfortable working capacity.

B. *Floor space required to file 1000 cards comfortably.* The space requirements depend on:

1. The depth of the trays is a somewhat variable factor, as already noted

2. The height of the cabinets

3. The space between cabinets set aside for consultation tables and for those who use the catalog. This should depend on the intensity of use at the time of peak loads. A small catalog with heavy use requires much more floor area for 1000 cards than does a large one with light use.

4. The space assigned to main and secondary aisles used to approach the cards.

Figures 13.25 to 13.29 show different arrangements based primarily on the intensity of use and secondarily on the size of the catalog, which ranges from 1000 to 4000 cards per sq ft of floor space for the whole area.

Every library building program should indicate the number of cards that should be housed and any available information about the amount of use at the time of peak loads.

VI. Computer Terminals. Computer terminals will vary from simple keyboards with a display screen to units that require additional space for a small computer, a printer, documentation, and space for notes or copy.

For work stations that will be fitted with a terminal, it is suggested that an additional 20 sq ft (1.86 m²) be provided. Public terminals for the card catalog area or for charging out books should each be provided 25 sq ft (2.32 m²). Terminal stations provided for composing a dissertation should be provided with at least 35 sq ft, preferably 50 sq ft (3.25 to 4.65 m²).

The number of terminals to be provided will vary dramatically depending upon the academic program of the institution and the intent to shift to automated processes in the working environment. One rule of thumb that may be used for public terminals is that one should plan on at least one catalog terminal for each 1000 patrons who use the facility daily. One circulation terminal should be provided for each 10,000 weekly circulations. Caution is urged here as experience is still fairly limited. It is probably better to err on the high side in terms of allocating available space, and to add terminals slowly until queueing is no longer a problem.

Other data and design guidance is provided in Section 13.4 under Design Development of Interiors.

VII. Government and Other Standards and Planning Guides. It is possible, and in some cases necessary, to base space-assignment figures on standards promulgated by governmental authorities supervising the institutions concerned. These standards can be helpful but, like all formulas and tables, they should be used with caution because as has been emphasized throughout this volume, situations differ and circumstances alter cases. Do not put yourself into a strait jacket. With this word of warning, standards for five different groups are noted.

A. *Oregon State System of Higher Education.* Chapter 3.12 in *Planning and Procedures Handbook for Campus and Building Development* (1980), which deals with library space standards, includes the following recommendations.

1. Reader space should be provided for 15 percent of the full-time-equivalent (FTE) undergraduate students, and 25 percent of the FTE graduate students. Reader space is based upon 25 sq ft (2.32 m²) for undergraduates and 30 sq ft (2.79 m²) for graduate students.

2. Some space may be added for an allocation to faculty use depending upon the academic field. For example, 15 sq ft (1.39 m²) is added for each FTE faculty member in fields such as business, economics, philosophy, and the social sciences, while 3 sq ft (0.28 m²) is added for faculty in architecture, communications, music, the physical sciences, engineering, etc.

3. The space for books is broken down and shown in Table B.20.

The space allowances shown in Table B.21, which have been developed by measuring collections and the space required for storing, handling and using nonbook materials, will be used in projecting their space needs.

4. For library staff and administration, space equal to 25 percent of the space required for the collections and readers is provided.

B. *Standards for College Libraries.* Adopted by the Association of College and Research Libraries in

TABLE B.20. VOLUMES PER UNIT AREA

	Health, Science & Law		All Others	
	Per Sq Ft	Per m²	Per Sq Ft	Per m²
100,000 volumes	9	97	10	108
Next 100,000 volumes	10	108	12	129
Next 800,000 volumes	12	129	14	151
Next 1,000,000 volumes	15	161	16	172

TABLE B.21. FORMULA FOR NONBOOK MATERIALS

Item	Items per Sq Ft (m²) of Floor Space Suggested Standard	Space to Be Allotted in Minimum Units of Sq Ft (m²)
Microcards	6,000 (64,580)	10 (0.93)
Microprints	1,400 (15,070)	10 (0.93)
Microfiche 4″ × 6″	2,500 (26,910)	10 (0.93)
Microfiche 3″ × 5″	6,000 (64,580)	10 (0.93)
Microfilm reels	60 (645)	10 (0.93)
Filmstrips	200 (2,150)	10 (0.93)
Slides	700 (7,530)	12 (1.11)
Transparencies	500 (5,380)	10 (0.93)
Motion picture reels	12 (130)	12 (1.11)
Video tape reels	3 (32)	10 (0.93)
Computer tape reels	9 (97)	10 (0.93)
Tape reels	30 (320)	10 (0.93)
Phonograph discs	75 (810)	10 (0.93)
Picture files	500 (5,380)	10 (0.93)
Maps	50 (540)	30 (2.79)
Pamphlets	150 (1,610)	10 (0.93)
Test files	150 (1,610)	10 (0.93)
Multimedia kits	9 (97)	10 (0.93)
Government documents	50 (540)	10 (0.93)
Unbound periodicals	15 (160) bibliographical units	10 (0.93)
Archives } Manuscripts }	Space requirements for collection will be submitted by institutional librarian.	

1986. They may be found in the March 1986 issue of *C&RL News*.

STANDARD 6: FACILITIES

6 The library building shall provide secure and adequate housing for its collections, and ample well-planned space for users and staff and for the provision of services and programs.

Commentary

Successful library service presupposes an adequate library building. Although the type of building will depend upon the character and purposes of the institution, it should in all cases be functional, providing secure facilities for accommodating the library's resources, sufficient space for their administration and maintenance, and comfortable reading and study areas for users. A new library building should represent a coordinated planning effort involving the library director and staff, the college administration, and the architect, with the director responsible for the preparation of the building program.

The needs of handicapped persons should receive special attention and should be provided for in compliance with the Architectural Barriers Act of 1968 (Public Law 90-480) and the Rehabilitation Act of 1973, Section 504 (Public Law 93-516) and their amendments.

Particular consideration must be be given to any present or future requirements for equipment associated with automated systems or other applications of library technology. Among these might be provision for new wiring, cabling, special climate control and maximum flexibility in the use of space. Consideration should also be given to load-bearing requirements for compact shelving and the housing of mixed formats including microforms.

6.1 The size of the library building shall be determined by a formula (see Formula C [Figure B.1]) which takes into account the enrollment of the college, the extent and nature of its collections, and the size of its staff.

6.2 In designing or managing a library building, the functionality of floor plan and the use of space shall be the paramount concern.

Commentary

The quality of a building is measured by such characteristics as the utility and comfort of its study and office areas, the design and durability of its furniture and equipment, the functional interrelationships of its service and work areas, and the ease and economy with which it can be operated and used.

6.3 Except in certain circumstances, the college library's collections and services shall be administered within a single structure.

Commentary

Decentralized library facilities in a college have some virtues, and they present some difficulties. Primary among their virtues is their convenience to the office or laboratories of some members of the teaching faculty. Primary among their weaknesses is the resulting fragmentation of the unity of knowledge, the relative isolation of a branch library from most users, potential problems of staffing and security, and the cost of maintaining certain duplicative services or functions. When decentralized library facilities are being considered, these costs and benefits must be carefully compared. In general, experience has shown that decentralized library facilities

The size of the college library building shall be calculated on the basis of a formula which takes into consideration the size of the student body, the size of the staff and its space requirements, and the number of volumes in the collections. To the result of this calculation must be added such space as may be required to house and service nonprint materials and microforms, to provide bibliographic instruction to groups, and to accommodate equipment and services associated with various forms of library technology.

a. *Space for users.* The seating requirement for the library of a college where less than 50 percent of the FTE enrollment resides on campus shall be one for each five students. That for the library of a typical residential college shall be one for each four FTE students. Each study station shall be assumed to require 25 to 35 square feet of floor space, depending upon its function.

b. *Space for books.* The space allocated for books shall be adequate to accommodate a convenient and orderly distribution of the collection according to the classification system(s) in use, and should include space for growth. Gross space requirements may be estimated according to the following formula.

	Square Feet / Volume
For the first 150,000 volumes	0.10
For the next 150,000 volumes	0.09
For the next 300,000 volumes	0.08
For holdings above 600,000 volumes	0.07

c. *Space for staff.* Space required for staff offices, service and work areas, catalogs, files, and equipment, shall be approximately one-eighth of the sume of the space needed for books and users as calculated under a) and b) above.

This formula indicates the net assignable area required by a library if it is to fulfill its mission with maximum effectiveness. "Net assignable area" is the sum of all areas (measured in square feet) on all floors of a building, assignable to, or useful for, library functions or purposes. (For an explanation of this definition see *The Measurement and Comparison of Physical Facilities for Libraries,* American Library Association, 1970.)

Libraries which provide 90 to 100% of the net assignable area called for by the formula shall be graded A in terms of space; 75–80% shall be graded B; 60–74% shall be graded C; and 50–59% shall be graded D.

Figure B.1 Formula C

may not be in the best academic or economic interest of a college.

C. *Higher Education Facilities Planning and Management Manuals.* The Planning and Management Systems Division, Western Interstate Commission for Higher Education and the American Association of Collegiate Registrars and Admissions Officers published a seven-part series of manuals in 1971. Manual 4, on academic support facilities, covers libraries. It presents a very well thought-out statement of planning guidelines or standards, from which the following is extracted.

1. DENSITY OF STACK UTILIZATION BY TYPE OF MATERIAL

Type of Material	Items per Stack Unit	Sq ft per Stack Unit	m² per Stack Unit
Bound volumes	125	8.7	.808
Documents and pamphlets	1,000	8.7	.808
Microfilm reels	400	8.7	.808
Microfilm cards	10,000	8.7	.808
Newspaper titles unbound	7	8.7	.808
Newspaper-bound vols.	9	8.7	.808
Periodical titles—unbound	15	15.0	1.394
Periodical titles—boxed	30	8.7	.808
Recordings	500	8.7	.808
Reference volumes	75	15.0	1.394
Maps	1,000	42.0	3.902
Slides	5,000	17.0	1.579

2. PROPORTIONS OF PROJECTED USER POPULATIONS TO BE PROVIDED WITH READER STATIONS

Type of User	Percent Provided Seating
Lower division	20
Upper division	
Humanities	30
Social sciences	30
Life sciences	20
Physical sciences	20
Business	30
Education	30
Graduate	
Humanities	40
Social sciences	40
Life sciences	25
Physical sciences	25
Business	30
Education	30
Faculty	25
Public users	3

3. ASSIGNABLE AREA PER READER STATION

Type of Station	Sq ft	m²
Open tables	25	2.323
Small carrels	30	2.787
Research carrels	40	3.716
Microform & A-V	40	3.716
Typing	30	2.787
Lounge	30	2.787
Small group	25	2.323
Faculty studies	50	4.645

D. *The Generation of Space According to the Provincial Norms.* A Canadian example, published in 1978, comes from the Office of Institutional Research, Concordia University, Montreal.

1. It is usual for the library to accommodate 25 percent of the university's student population.

2. Twenty-five sq ft (2.32 m²) is adequate per seat.

3. On average, 15 volumes could be stored in each sq ft of stack area (or 161 volumes per m²).

4. An average of 75 volumes per FTE student would satisfy the institution's students and faculty. (The authors urge extreme caution in using a figure such as this!)

4. AREA TO BE PROVIDED STAFF

Type of Staff	Sq ft Per Person	m² Per Person
Administration		
Director	240	22.297
Associate director	160	14.864
Assistant director	120	11.148
Director of systems	120	11.148
Secretary	100	9.290
Acquisitions		
Head	150	13.935
Area specialists	120	11.148
Clerical	100	9.290
Cataloging		
Head	150	13.935
Catalogers	120	11.148
Clerical	100	9.290
Reference		
Reference librarians	120	11.148
Clerical	100	9.290
Circulation		
Head	150	13.935
Circulation librarian	120	11.148
Clerical	100	9.290
Reserve		
Librarian	120	11.148
Clerical	100	9.290
Interlibrary Loan		
Librarian	120	11.148
Clerical	100	9.290
Binding and Mending		
Technician	250	23.226
Clerical	250	23.226
Photocopy		
Technician	250	23.226
Clerical	100	9.290
Shipping and Receiving		
Clerical	300	27.871
Office Support		
Conference room	25	2.323
Staff room	25	2.323

5. Sufficient staff space for the library would be available on the basis of 1.25 sq ft (0.116 m²) per FTE student. (Again, the authors urge caution!)

6. Equipment associated with the library can be based upon 0.75 sq ft (0.070 m²) per FTE student. (Once again, caution!)

This text is not a standard, but rather a planning guide. It is interesting in that the entire space program is related to the student enrollment, a measure that says little about striving for excellence. The figures probably were never intended for use in planning a library for an institution with a significant graduate population offering doctoral degrees. It is also interesting to note the following guidelines used by Concordia University in planning its new library facility.

1. Shelving is based upon a 5 percent simple growth rate for 20 years, or double the currently occupied shelving. The space required is based upon ranges 1.5 m on center (59 in.), 1.25 m cross aisles (49 in.), and 10 double-faced section ranges of 9 m each (29 ft 6 in.), which works out to .769 m² (8.27 sq ft) per section. (Canadian and some European libraries can have problems if metric is used for planning a building to accommodate standard stacks of U.S. manufacturers.)

2. Seating is based upon full-time equivalent(FTE) enrollment for undergraduates and actual student count for graduate students, with the following percentage of the population assigned.

Undergraduates
Lower Division (All)	20%
Upper Division	
Humanities, Social Sciences (including Fine Arts)	30%
Life Sciences	20%
Physical Sciences (including Engineering)	30%
Commerce	35%
Education	35%

Graduate Students—Masters Program
Humanities (including Fine Arts)	45%
Social Sciences	40%
Life Sciences	25%
Physical Sciences (including Engineering)	25%
Commerce	35%
Education	35%
Graduate Students—Doctoral	100%

A reduction factor of .67 is applied to the Masters program seating to account for general purpose seating.

The area assigned for seating breaks down as follows:

	sq m	sq ft
Individual open carrels	2.325	25.0
Tables for four (per table)	10.25	110.3
Lounge chairs	2.5	26.9
Graduate/faculty closed carrels	4.0	43.1
Microform, A-V, or typing carrels	3.0	32.3
Catalog consultation stations	2.0	21.5
Seats in seminar rooms	2.0	21.5
Catalog card cabinets (including standing room)	2.0	21.5

3. For staff areas the Concordia standards provide office space as follows:

Division head, department head, staff officer	18 m²	(194 sq ft)
Librarian or other professional	10 m²	(108 sq ft)
Senior assistants	6 m²	(65 sq ft)

In addition, for each office area, there is to be a small conference room for four people of 10.25 m² (110 sq ft). It should also be noted that these space assignments do not include the space required for special equipment beyond that found in a fairly standard office.

E. *Capital Provision for University Libraries: Report of a Working Party.* In Great Britain the University Grants Committee (UGC) has established library norms or standards relating to the funding of new facilities, which were published in 1976. While they appear to be somewhat more restrictive than the other standards outlined, it should be remembered that they were established to identify the most worthy projects needing funding rather than to propose an ideal library program. Even so, the proposed allocations are no doubt influential in Great Britain.

The key emphasis of the UGC report is the creation of a system of "self-renewing" libraries limited in size. It is assumed that beyond the standard of 3.8 (12½ ft) of shelving, or 0.68 m² (7.32 sq ft) per FTE student, materials will be removed for various forms of storage at nearly the same rate as incoming materials. Most of the materials are assumed to be on open-access shelves; thus, using their rule of thumb of 5.83 m² per 1000 volumes (or nearly 16 volumes per sq ft), the formula works out to about 117 volumes per FTE student. By comparison, the statistics of the 101 universities reported in the *1981–82 ARL Statistics* (Washington, D.C.: Association of Research Libraries, 1982) indicate an average of over 460 volumes per FTE student. Numerous factors can be considered in this comparison; it should not be taken as an absolute. The point is made simply to illustrate the restrictive nature of the UGC standards.

The following represents the UGC norms for library accommodation expressed as a feasible working scale:

1. Reader places are based upon 1:5 (20 percent) for arts students and 1:7 (14.3 percent) for science students. Where postgraduate research students are not provided space in other buildings, their needs may be added to the library requirements. The total area is determined using 2.39 m² (25.7 sq ft) per reader station.

2. Materials space requirements based upon working capacity are determined by the following assumptions:

	m² Per 1000 Items	Items Per Sq Ft
Open access books	4.65	20
Closed access (fixed) books	4.03	23
Closed access (rolling) books	2.07	45
Open access bound journals	9.35	10
Closed access (fixed) bound journals	8.06	11.5
Closed access (rolling) bound journals	4.13	22.5
Typical mix	5.83	16
Periodicals—¼ display, ¾ storage	25.13	3.7

These figures include the necessary factor to establish working capacity based upon 85 percent of absolute capacity.

3. The administration and all other support functions can be provided in space equal to 18 percent of the sum determined in 1 and 2 above excluding any reader space added for postgraduate students.

4. Reasonable provision for growth over a 10-year period will be taken into account.

From the preceding five examples, as well as others discussed in this volume, it is clear that a considerable range of guidelines and standards may be found; and any given guideline must be used with care, for the circumstance of the local situation should be the controlling factor.

APPENDIX C

A List of Equipment That Might Be Overlooked

You will [forget] if you don't make a memorandum of it.

The Queen in *Alice in Wonderland.*

This list supplements the sixteen chapters of the text. No attempt is made here to include equipment for audio-visual work, computer installations, conservation laboratories, graphics studios, manuscripts and archives, microform readers, music, photographic installations, and print rooms. It is suggested that librarians discuss with faculty and students the needs for these and other types of equipment and consult specialists in the various fields about their selection and spatial and physical requirements.

Ashtrays and smoking urns: One or the other or both are needed wherever smoking is permitted. Should be deep enough so that a flip of a page will not scatter ashes. If too small or attractive, they will tend to disappear. Urns, if used at building entrances, should be attractive, probably partially filled with sand to prevent conflagrations, tall enough to be reached with ease, and heavy enough to discourage their removal. Trash receptacles should be next to urns so the one will not be used for the other purpose.

Bells, buzzers, public address systems, and gongs: Some simple methods are desirable for calling the attention of readers to closing time and emergencies, and of staff when they are needed at a ser-

vice desk. Differentiation between the two is required, and those for staff members should not involve sharp sounds. Portable staff paging beepers are sometimes ideal. Mobile two-way communication systems for late-night building patrols (e.g., 10–12 PFMF) can be extremely useful. Telephone bells should be muted. (Do not forget that the use of telephones by staff in public areas can be extremely disturbing unless the instrument is properly placed and protected.) Visual calling systems or annunciator panels can sometimes be useful.

Bicycle racks or stands: Should provide ability to chain both wheels to the rack. Preferably should be sheltered from rain and where some degree of oversight is provided to minimize vandalism.

Bookends: Not only needed in stacks but also in staff areas and faculty studies.

Book rests: Needed in rare-book rooms to hold large books safely and at a convenient angle for reading.

Book trucks: Useful in a variety of staff locations, wherever there is frequent movement of volumes, manuscript boxes, and other library materials. Number and types of book trucks needed are usually underestimated.

Building directory: Should be available in the entrance lobby in all but very small libraries where almost the entire building is visible from the entrance. Should be easily changeable but quite tamperproof; a locking glass cover can serve the purpose.

Bulletin boards or tackboards: If suitably placed, can be useful as dispensers of information. If well designed, can be attractive. Cork or other soft surface can be easily used with thumbtacks. Needed in each staff work area. A glass cover in a frame that is locked will prevent unauthorized use in public areas. Good lighting is a necessity.

Cash box or cash register: Useful where cash and checks are handled with regard to overdue fines, library privileges, computer search and copying charges.

Chalkboards or blackboards: Can be very useful in small or large conference and bibliographic instruction rooms for readers or for staff. Smooth, light-colored boards for chemical markers are sometimes used. Flip chart stands are also useful.

Clocks: Should be in all but the smallest offices, workrooms, and reading areas, so placed as to be in sight of as large a percentage of the occupants as possible in order to reduce disturbing traffic that would result if they could be seen only from certain areas. In a large library a master clock system is often justified since even a ten-minute power outage would otherwise mean manually resetting every clock in the building.

Coatrooms and coatracks: Supervised coatrooms are little used in academic libraries, as rapid change in readers makes them impractical. Unsupervised rooms are hazardous, particularly in large urban institutions, and are seldom used except in independent research libraries, archives, and rare-book and manuscript quarters. Coat hooks scattered around the building within sight of the reader or staffed position are generally preferable. Coat hooks on carrel partitions or at individual work stations help to solve the problem. The hook should be large enough for a hat and perhaps an umbrella. Climatic conditions should affect the decision in regard to their use.

Computer terminals or personal computers: These are probably going to replace the typewriter in most working environments. Probably the most important aspects are adjustable, glare-free installations with adequate outlets and "clean" power as well as access to signal systems.

Corners: Particularly plaster- or wood-covered columns or corners in exposed places should be protected by impact-resistant materials such as steel angles, vinyl tile, buckram, or high projecting bases.

Cutoffs for water, light, and power: Should be easily accessible to library and maintenance staff but made inaccessible to the public by the use of cupboards and locks, if they are located in a public room. It is advantageous in a multistory library to have the electrical controls for all public areas throughout the building located at or close to the main circulation desk.

Desk and table legs: Can be protected by brass or other types of shoes or base material.

Dictionary stands: The floor or table stands can be used in various places, including secretarial quarters, where an unabridged dictionary or other large volume is frequently consulted.

Directional signs and door labels: Should be attractively designed, carefully placed, and easy to read and to change. Frequently overlooked is the sign at the entrance to the building to indicate hours of opening, and since these hours change frequently, flexibility is essential.

Display racks: Holding library guides, brochures, or flyers, racks can be wall-mounted, floor, or counter stands to accommodate various sizes of printed matter.

Dolly: Very useful for moving crates, book boxes, binding shipments, stock of photocopy paper, and even some furniture.

Doormats: Are one good way to reduce maintenance costs if they are selected and serviced to meet local conditions. Cocoa mats sunk in the floor are effective, but should be small enough so that cleaning will not shrink them so much as to result in dangerous cracks. Rubber mats with corrugations are sometimes useful. Some libraries use carpeting or carpet tile on the basis that in spite of cost it will pay for itself in lower cleaning expenditures. Also used are carpet insets in removable nonskid rubber mats with beveled edges, so that they rest on top of the finished floor. In climates subject to snow and slush, a grating close to the main entrance doors, through which the snow and slush can fall from the feet, has been found to reduce the maintenance considerably and improve the appearance of the adjacent interior flooring.

Door saddles and sills: Should not be used where book trucks will pass. It is well to avoid them under interior doors in any case. They serve a useful purpose, however, on exterior doors, by providing a weather stop which helps to eliminate the penetration of water and drafts into the building.

Drapes, shades, and curtains: Often needed for sun control, minimizing heat loss and gain, or aesthetic purposes. Their relation to furniture is important so as to reduce damage as they are opened or closed, raised or lowered. See also *Venetian blinds.*

Drinking fountains: Should be placed where spilled water will not damage books or result in dangerously slippery floors. An exterior fountain may be prone to vandalism, even if it is in an open area some distance from the building; yet it can be much appreciated by joggers, other campus persons, and visitors.

Electric fans: Suitable wiring outlets should be provided for them if the building is not air conditioned. Wall-hung fans save floor space.

Electric outlets: Floor, base, and wall plugs will never be cheaper than in the original wiring installation and may be useful for electric fans and typewriters; electric erasers; reading, dictating, and copying machines; vacuum cleaners; buffers; for use with turntables, table and floor lamps, telephones, electronic and computer equipment, carrel installations, and so forth. Note that some computer equipment may require "clean" power.

Emergency lights: Required for public buildings by many building codes for use in public and staff areas, and should generally be made available even if not required. They are often battery-powered, and placed so as to make it easy to reach exits in the case of an emergency.

Emergency power: As a backup power supply for elevators, sump pumps, alarm systems, emergency lights, any stand-alone computer, and other critical equipment, it may require a generator, especially if it is to provide for the operation of motors. Otherwise, it can be provided by batteries.

Exhibit cases: Provide a place for enough of them, but do not have too many. They should be attractive and well designed, protected from theft and vandalism, and appropriately lighted. Some entrance lobbies are suitable for them, as are wide corridors. Separate rooms are expensive in their use of space and may require expensive supervision. Exhibit support requires a variety of formed plastic book stands or cradles of several types and sizes.

Exit signs: Check their location with building and fire codes.

Fire extinguishers: Provide enough of them in carefully considered locations. Select them with the risks in mind. The Halon type is generally preferable to others in libraries.

Fire hoses: May be required by building codes and insurance contracts. If they are installed, they should be accessible but placed so as to reduce danger of misuse.

Fireplaces: Rarely desirable in an academic library, in spite of being attractive.

Floor drains: Should be provided in any place prone to water hazards, including rest rooms and mechanical rooms. If these drains occur above occupied library space, the floor should be waterproof.

Floor lamps: Can be very attractive in a browsing room, but tend to be expensive and difficult to keep in repair; they may be tempting to thieves.

Floor-plan charts: Are a necessity on each level of a large building. It is important to orient them so that the user is facing the same direction that is shown at the top of the plan. The architect is equipped to prepare them and will be glad to render this service. They should be produced so that they can accommodate changes inexpensively.

Fly screens: If windows are to be opened and flying insects, birds, or bats are a local nuisance, be sure that screens are provided. If in doubt, at least provide suitable construction for later installation.

Footstools: Placed by lounge furniture, will save chairs from being pulled up to serve as footrests. They provide variety in seating options, save wear on other chairs, and for some locations can appropriately be designed of a size to accommodate two or more users.

Garages: Seldom required in an academic library, except one located in an urban setting. A campus transportation pool may offer garaging for needed library vehicles.

Globes: If a large one is on hand or anticipated, a suitable space with adequate square footage should be planned for it. Consider whether electric power may be needed, as well as the best lighting arrangement.

Heating coils: Used during rainy and snowy periods under sidewalk or entrance plaza, coils will lower maintenance costs and reduce the formation of ice.

High stools and high swivel chairs: High stools that can be pushed out of the way under card catalog consultation tables will be appreciated by the reader. High swivel chairs with suitable footrests for use by staff members serving the public may prevent backaches and tired feet. They bring the eyes of a staff member more or less on the level with the reader's, a matter of considerable importance and convenience to both, particularly short staff members.

Incinerators: Rarely desirable in a library. Decision in regard to their use may depend on the institution's policy on waste disposal. They represent a prospective fire hazard, and, if used too promptly, may result in inadvertent loss of irreplaceable material. All precautions for fire protection should be adopted if they are installed. A compactor or a heavy duty shredder may be useful.

Light table: Useful for tracing of maps or other drawings. Must be near large work table and have electrical outlet nearby.

Lockers: Should be available for staff members. For this use, they are generally full size, at least 5 ft to 6 ft (1.524 to 1.829) high. In areas of moderate climate, smaller lockers are suitable, and those may only be necessary for staff who do not have an office or lockable drawer at a desk. If installed for readers, adjacent to open carrels, they can be much smaller, designed to allow space to store books, notes, and a typewriter. The noise they produce may suggest that they should be removed from the carrels.

Mail counter (sorting counter): Be sure to provide one in the shipping room, acquisition department, serials department, and in other places where large amounts of material must be sorted. A suitable number of large pigeonholes should be available close at hand for categorizing, routing, or task assignment.

Mending equipment: A properly equipped book mending room, generally adjacent to the processing areas, is desirable, whether or not the library has a bindery. This may include a board cutter, gang punch, wire stitcher, glue pot, label pasting machine, standing press, and map edger.

Mirrors: Can be used to facilitate supervision of critical areas, though seldom used for this purpose in academic libraries. See also *Television, closed circuit.*

Outdoor and roof reading areas: Can be useful and very pleasant, particularly in mild climates, if satisfactorily located in relation to sun and wind. However they may present a serious collection control problem. Dust, dirt, and rain complicate matters.

Outside lighting: Desirable at entrances, loading docks, and corners. Can be used for decorative as well as functional purposes, such as illumination of paths, bicycle parking, book return depository, building name, and hours of service.

Pallet lift: A device very useful for lifting and moving a platform on which books, boxes, or cartons can be stacked.

Pencil sharpeners: Will be a convenience to readers and staff if easily seen and placed where they will not obstruct traffic or cause a disturbance. They should be permanently installed to avoid theft.

Photocopy machines: Require wide distribution in a large library and each machine must be given adequate space to service it. Photocopy machines may be supplemented by computer-driven printers. Both will require significant supplies. Acoustic control and air-return problems require careful consideration of environment.

Pictures: Art work, such as framed prints, photographs, or posters, can make a lot of difference in the aesthetics of staff quarters and public spaces. Again, security must be a consideration.

Print shop: Some academic institutions will have installations elsewhere on the campus, but a place in a large library where students can learn typesetting and the principles of book design can be useful and appropriate.

Radiators: If they are installed behind bookcases, be sure proper insulation is provided to protect books. They can also cause discomfort, and even danger, to adjacent readers, particularly if steam heat is used.

Receptions or entertainment support: Unless renting supplies is preferred, useful dishes will include punch bowls, ladles, trays, glasses, tea and coffee servers, etc.

Repair, book: See *Mending equipment.*

Return-book slot: Be sure that a book placed in such a slot cannot be retrieved by an unauthorized person, even if one or two hundred books preceded it, and that it will not drop so far as to damage it or one that preceded it. Also make sure that appropriate fire and vandalism protection has been considered. If in an outside wall, the slot should be protected from the weather and small animals, and should drop the book in a convenient location inside the building. Can be used inside a building on top of or in the front of a desk. Conservation experts will often question the wisdom of a book return, especially those that penetrate the exterior wall.

Side chairs: Useful by certain desks, such as those of a secretary and a supervisor, where a visitor may wish to sit and converse for a minute or two.

Signs: Exterior lettering identifying the building is important, but should generally be confined to a few words. Labels at public-service desks with names and sometimes titles may save time and confusion for readers and staff. See also *Directional signs.*

Skylights: Unless well designed, tend to develop leaks. Can be heat producers, but an annual coat of whitewash will help. Sometimes older skylights are replaced with squares of fluorescent lights in fixtures that do not alter the character of the room. Ultraviolet filtration will probably be required.

Staff lunchroom: A system for making coffee and tea, a microwave oven, refrigerator, sink, and cupboards can be made available in one area. Ample trash receptacles are necessary. Be very careful to avoid encouraging mice and vermin.

Staff quiet room: Considered essential for a staff of as few as six. Should be equipped with a cot. Hot and cold water and a medicine chest should be available close at hand. This room can be used for the public in emergency cases. Some codes will specify the exact requirements.

Stools: Better than chairs when needed at reference counters, index and abstract tables, and similar items needing short use. See also *High stools.*

Sump pump: Be sure one is provided in the basement if there is danger of flooding. Complete protection can be obtained only with a duplex installation, so that maintenance repair or a breakdown will not temporarily complicate matters. Even then, it is sometimes desirable to have an adjacent overflow area, for use during flash floods, which can receive any water temporarily in excess of that which can be handled by the pump.

Supply closets: Do not forget the need for a number of small closets, cupboards, or cabinets in administrative and departmental offices and at least one large one for bulky library and building-maintenance supplies kept under lock and key. If computer supplies are also needed, this space will increase proportionately.

Table lamps: Tend to result in glare and restrict reader's comfort unless they are adjustable. Too often subject to vandalism in an academic library, and yet, some form of the table lamp may help give a warm feeling to the environment and is quite common as a "task" light in energy-efficient design.

Telephones (public): Are desirable and will be used heavily in most libraries. Place them just off main traffic arteries for ease of locating and yet where some confidentiality of the conversation is possible and the talking involved will not disturb readers. Should be available for handicapped persons.

Television, closed circuit: Can be used to facilitate supervision of critical areas.

Toilet-room equipment: Hooks for coats and purses, mirrors, paper towels and receptacles or drying equipment, sanitary napkin and tampon dispensers, and soap holders or soap dispensers. Also remember shelves on which to lay parcels, books, or papers in toilet stalls as well as beside the hand-drying location.

Tools: Many simple repairs can be handled promptly and economically with some basic hand tools.

Trash chutes: May be desirable in or adjacent to janitor's closets on each floor, but guard against fire hazards.

Trash containers: Useful at building entrances for small bits of paper, wrappers, etc. See also comments under *Ashtrays and smoking urns.*

Umbrella racks: If coatracks are scattered around the building, umbrella racks may be likewise, but they involve water problems. See other comments under *Coatrooms and coatracks.*

Unit air-conditioners: If building as a whole is not air conditioned, units can be useful in offices and perhaps workrooms or shelving areas for materials especially sensitive to extreme heat.

Vacuum cleaners: Both portable and building-wide equipment should be considered. Installation costs and the presence of satisfactory air filtering may be factors in the decisions reached.

Vaults and safes: Are expensive and must be adequately ventilated to prevent mold, but can be very useful on occasion. In many cases, a screened enclosure in the regular bookstack will be sufficient, particularly if a small safe for cash and other valuables is available.

Vending machines: May have a place just outside the library or in a public lounge area, yet one must remember that food attracts vermin, and wrappers too often do not find their way into trash containers provided for the purpose. They also should be considered for staff lounges and lunchrooms. In all cases, distance from bookshelves and closeness to the vender delivery access are desirable. A hard floor surface to facilitate frequent cleaning is necessary.

Venetian blinds: Horizontal and vertical blinds are available, each with certain advantages. The larger horizontal and most vertical ones can be more prone to present maintenance problems. Cleaning is difficult.

Vertical filing cabinets: Provide suitable space for them in offices and at reference desks, for instance. Select them carefully from the different types (wood or steel) and sizes that are available on the market. Filing cases standing so that they face each other should be at least 3 ft 6 in. (1.067) apart to provide for easy access, even when used by only one person at a time. Lateral files can be used where the front to front space is limited, but even here 3 ft 6 in. clear is a comfortable minimum.

Washbasins: Are desirable in workrooms where several staff members are on duty to help with cleanliness and prevent the loss of time and supervision involved in going to a toilet room.

Wastebaskets: An adequate number will reduce maintenance costs, and all should be fireproof. If too light, they will be misplaced. If too attractive, they will disappear. If too heavy and too hard with sharp corners, they will be a hazard. Do not forget large ones for paper towels in toilet rooms, for wrappings in the shipping room and wherever book materials are received and opened, for trash in food locations, and by copying machines.

APPENDIX D

Environmental Conditions for Book Preservation

Since books are fragile and most are chemically unstable, the conditions of shelving, using, and exhibiting are of critical importance to their survival. The same can be said for other paper and other materials whether printed, archival, or manuscript records.

Given the singular importance of the library environment for their longevity, two guidelines are presented, the first from the Association of Research Libraries and the second from the Research Libraries Group.

INTRODUCTION TO ENVIRONMENTAL ISSUES*

The environment has a direct and continuing effect on the physical condition of all objects, influencing the rate of natural processes and often introducing elements that alter the nature and direction of those processes. This is true whether the objects be living—plants or animals—or inanimate—stones, buildings, automobiles, books. The degree to which inanimate objects are susceptible to environmental pressures depends upon their physical and chemical structure. Some materials are very stable through a broad range of environmental conditions, while others can tolerate little change in their surroundings without themselves undergoing change.

In the range from granite to snow balls, most library materials lie in a middle zone, relatively stable but re-

*From the *Preservation Planning Manual* (Washington, D.C.: Association of Research Libraries, 1982), p. 40-42.

quiring protection from extremes, relatively sturdy but requiring some physical support. Buildings and bookstacks afford a large measure of protection and support, but their effectiveness in prolonging the life of their contents depends on the extent to which they control several factors: temperature, relative humidity, light, air quality, and bacterial and higher life forms. Planning for new library buildings, and for the improvement of existing facilities, requires a basic knowledge of the role these factors play in the survival of library materials.

Detailed information about the effects of the environment on library materials will be found in the *Preservation Planning Program Resource Notebook*. Although different materials have slightly different requirements for optimal storage, the following conditions should be the goal for average collections containing a variety of materials:

TEMPERATURE should be kept at 65 degrees plus or minus 5 degrees [18 ± 3°C] year-round. in collections subject to regular use.

Storage collections should be maintained at lower temperatures, which will slow the rate of deterioration, if materials will not undergo frequent temperature fluctuations as might occur if they are often withdrawn for use (surfaces of cold materials brought into a warm room may be subject to condensation). As a rough rule of thumb, chemical reactions—which generally mean deterioration in library materials—double with each increase of ten degrees Celsius. Even more importantly, temperature has a direct effect on relative humidity: changes in temperature cause moisture to move in and out of hygroscopic (moisture-absorbing) ma-

572

RELATIVE HUMIDITY should be maintained at 50 percent plus or minus 5 percent all year round for most collections.

Excessive variations in either direction, and fluctuations of more than a few percentage points in a single twenty-four hour period, should be avoided. Collections which include vellum should be maintained at 60–65 percent. Film-based materials (microforms, films, slides) are best stored at 35 percent plus or minus 5 percent, but only if they are not likely to be moved frequently into areas of higher humidity. Master microform collections should always be kept at the lower level.

LIGHT sources should provide 30 to 50 foot-candles (300-500 lux), and a maximum of 75 microwatts lumen (a measure of ultraviolet radiation).

Both visible and invisible light have cumulative damaging effects, providing energy which promotes chemical reactions within materials, some of which become self-perpetuating even after the original energy source is withdrawn. Most buildings, especially modern buildings, are lit at levels well above those required for comfortable reading and personal safety. Control of light is particularly important in stack areas, to prevent fading and cracking of covers and the edges of text blocks; and it is crucial in exhibit areas, where ancient treasures may be quickly ruined if not adequately protected.

AIR in enclosed storage areas should be filtered to achieve at least 90 percent efficiency on the "ASHRAE Dust Spot Test." (ASHRAE is the American Society of Heating, Refrigerating and Air Conditioning Engineers.)

Sulfur compounds and other gaseous substances should be removed through adsorption systems. (Electrostatic precipitators should never be used, since they generate damaging ozone.) Dirt and airborne chemical pollutants contribute to a wide variety of deteriorative processes.

SUPPORT STRUCTURES (e.g., shelves, cabinets, book trucks) should be designed for maximum protection of the materials stored or moved on/in them.

To provide such protection, structures should be of a size appropriate to the materials; there should be enough of them to prevent over-crowding; they should be maintained to prevent the development of rust, splinters or sharp edges; and they should be conveniently located so that they will in fact be used. As a general rule, book "drops" are antithetical to preservation. If they cannot be eliminated altogether, they should be (1) designed or modified to minimize the distance materials fall and to protect items inside from being damaged when more are deposited; (2) emptied frequently; and (3) locked when the library is open.

REGULAR CLEANING SCHEDULES should be established to eliminate sources of food and shelter for bacteria, insects, and vermin.

These are counsels of perfection that few institutions can meet in their entirety. But the difficulties they present are not justification for giving up the effort, any more than the cost of a roof and furnace justify leaving the building open to rain and snow.

Environmental Characteristics of Library Facilities

Every enclosed space presents a unique set of environmental factors, but a number of common characteristics are present in most libraries:

Rooms are often large, but interior space is divided by furniture, partitions, cabinets and shelves into many small units. Air circulation is therefore uneven, which creates numerous mini-environments with potentially different conditions in the same room. Large collections are commonly divided among several rooms, on different floors, often in separate buildings, each one presenting a new set of conditions.

Patterns in a central stack will be unlike those in a combined storage/reading area. Conditions in closed cases or cabinets may be quite different from those of the air surrounding them. Materials stored against an outside wall may experience much greater fluctuations than those stored only a few feet away from the wall.

Many older buildings have high ceilings in reading areas, but very low ceilings in stack cores; each create special problems for environmental control, compounded by the fact that few older buildings are equipped with modern climate control systems.

Newer buildings generally have climate control systems, but often have non-openable windows; when the system fails, as it inevitably does, temperature and relative humidity may fluctuate drastically. Modern buildings often incorporate vast window-walls in their design, increasing the potential for damage from ultraviolet light and contributing to heat and humidity problems.

Very humid seasons or climates bring special problems of mold and insect attack, while arid regions and the low humidity of heated buildings produce dessication and embrittlement. The physical mass of a large collection, and the hygroscopic nature of most record materials affect the efficiency of control systems: as materials absorb and give off moisture to remain in equilibrium with the surrounding temperature and humidity, they tend to buffer the climate at their own expense, promoting falsely reassuring humidity readings.

Most libraries must rely on persons outside the library staff—university or local government employees—for the maintenance of library facilities, and even for acquiring basic information about those facilities, such as how to turn down the heat or shut off water in a leaking pipe.

Awareness and understanding of all these characteristics is essential for an effective review of existing conditions, and for planning to improve the library's physical environment.

ENVIRONMENTAL CONTROL FOR LIBRARY COLLECTIONS*

Control of the environment is critical and perhaps the major element affecting the longevity of library materials. It is the single most important element in any preservation program, especially in a research library that has the responsibility for preserving items used infrequently.

Since a disproportionate number of library preservation problems, from floods to security breaches, are the result of basic defects in library physical plants, it is especially important that conservators, whether staff or consultants, sit on any library committee planning new facilities or the renovation of existing library structures. It would be helpful, moreover, for conservators to be

*From the *RLG Preservation Manual* (Stanford, Calif.: the Research Libraries Group, 1983) p. 59-61.

pecially important that conservators, whether staff or consultants, sit on any library committee planning new facilities or the renovation of existing library structures. It would be helpful, moreover, for conservators to be given the opportunity to meet with design architects prior to the inception of architectural drawings and specifications for new structures or those to be renovated and to review all drawings and specifications prior to construction.

Generally accepted storage conditions for most library materials are roughly as follows . . . .

1. Temperature: 65 degrees F, plus or minus 5 degrees [18 ± 3°C].

Lower temperatures are better for library materials but uncomfortable for humans and may not be energy-efficient. (Books that are very cold, such as those transported in cold periods, should be warmed slowly before locating them in humid areas to avoid condensation.) The speed of chemical reaction depends in large part on temperature, *on the average* doubling with each 10 degrees C rise (conversely halving with each 10 degrees C drop) in temperature. The actual rate varies considerably in different kinds of materials undergoing different reactions. Typically, for library materials, the rate of deterioration resulting from degradation reactions may double, or even triple, with every 10 degree C (approximately 18 degrees F) increase, most paper deteriorating at a higher rate.

2. Relative humidity: 45 percent, plus or minus 5 percent.

Relative humidity (RH) indicates the amount of moisture in the air at a given temperature at a particular instant; raising the temperature will lower the RH, while lowering the temperature will raise the RH. Mold is likely to grow at 60–65 percent RH or higher.

3. Environmental control systems: It is highly desirable that libraries have an environmental control system to control both temperature and humidity. Air conditioning systems generally control only the temperature. The most efficient environmental control systems will include filters to screen out particulate matter. In those areas of high pollution, these systems will include a catalytic absorbance surface (or some other mechanism) that will remove major pollutants such as oxides of nitrogen and sulfur dioxide. A regular schedule of maintenance for the filter system will be an integral aspect of any efficient environmental control system. Electrostatic precipitators

that produce ozone should not be used. Air pollutants can cause serious damage to library materials. Particulate pollution can result in abrasion, and chemical pollution may cause destructive interaction with the component structure of library materials.

4. Air movement: Sufficient air movement is also important for all collections. The free movement and regular replacement of air can reduce pockets of high relative humidities and decrease the likelihood of mold and insect infestation. Good air movement is especially important where environmental control systems are lacking or inadequate. If air ducts are cleaned regularly or their filters changed often, dust or soot build-up will be avoided.

5. Protection from light: Light can fade and weaken library materials, especially the high-energy short wavelengths of light in the ultraviolet (UV) and blue end of the spectrum. Sunlight is the greatest source of UV radiation. Many of the fluorescent lights give off large amounts of UV radiation, whereas incandescent lights give off low quantities of UV radiation. The mid-range of UV radiation (440 millimicrons) and lower indicate dangerous levels of UV radiation. It is important to exclude rigorously UV radiation of 400 millimicrons and lower through the use of filters or other means. At higher wavelengths, intensities should be maintained at the minimum level required for visual discrimination.

6. Protection from fire: Fire detection and alarm systems are essential in providing a structural environment aimed at protecting library materials from disaster. Careful evaluation of fire extinguishing systems is required. The best sprinkler systems are of the "pre-action system" design that contains no pressure unless activated by smoke. Halon, a gaseous suppressant, does not damage library materials, but is expensive for large areas. Carbon dioxide also poses little threat to library materials but is extremely dangerous to humans. Periodic fire and electrical code inspections are routine for the responsible administrator.

7. Protection from water: To protect the library from water damage, it is important to inspect regularly and maintain roof areas and their drainage systems, internal and external. Thorough and periodic inspection of plumbing, sanitary drains, and heat or steam piping is essential. Installation of a water-alert system is advisable, particularly in basement areas or in areas without internal drainage.

Glossary

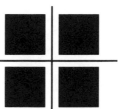

No attempt has been made to make this a complete glossary of library or building construction terms. It includes only those that are used in the volume, those that have not been defined in detail in the text, and that might not be understood by members of the groups for whom it was written. As an effort has been made to avoid technical jargon and most abstract terms, the list is shorter than might have been expected.

Absolute capacity: The theoretical maximum number of volumes that can fit on shelves, in contrast to *working capacity, q.v.*

Academic program: The institution's design of courses of instruction with requirements of distribution, departmental concentration, and credits for degree qualification.

Access flooring: A raised structural floor composed of modular lift-out floor panels (commonly two feet square), suspended on pedestals, with positive electrical grounding, leaving an underfloor plenum space for ducts, conduits, cables, etc. The floor panels can be surfaced with plastic laminate, vinyl asbestos, or carpeting.

Accession number: A serial or other number designed strictly as an inventory control over library materials acquired and to be added to the useful collections.

Accordian door or partition: A set of hinged panels, folding compactly as an accordion when not in use, moved on ceiling and/or floor tracks to form a solid barrier. See *Movable partition.*

Acoustic material: Porous material for treating interior room surfaces so as to absorb sound, reduce its reverberation, and thus minimize undesirable qualities of the sound.

Acquisitions department: The technical services unit reponsible for purchasing, claiming, invoice approval, and account management for all book materials being added to the collections. May include gift receiving, exchange programs, and approval arrangements.

Activation: The steps required to bring a completed physical structure to operational functioning. It includes such aspects as checking out the HVAC system, activating the intrusion system, installing necessary signs, placing furniture in final location, installing phones, and moving staff and collections.

Actual dimension: In shelving, the measured dimensions of the shelf as opposed to *nominal dimension, q.v.* Applies as well to structural elements, bricks, doors, etc., where the actual dimension is somewhat less (typically) than the nominal dimension.

Add alternate: See *Bid alternate.*

Addendum (contract): A written amplification of the contract documents after they have been issued to the bidders but before the bids have been received.

Adders: Bookstack range components which have only one column or end section since they attach to a full "starter" unit.

Air conditioning: The artificial control of humidity, temperature, purity, and motion of air within buildings. In libraries the objective may be to secure either human comfort or the proper environment for the preservation of library materials. Sometimes called "climatization."

Aisle: A passageway between furniture or equipment; for instance, between ranges of shelving in a bookstack, between rows of reading accommodations (chairs or chairs and tables), or between tables and shelving in a reading area. As used in this volume, an aisle at right angles to stack ranges is called a cross aisle. A main cross aisle is the main street of a bookstack and generally will have book ranges on both sides and will be wider than a subsidiary or secondary cross aisle, which may have ranges on one side and carrels or faculty studies on the other. An aisle between two parallel ranges is called a range or stack aisle.

Alcove: An area enclosed on three sides by walls, partitions, or bookcases, or a combination of these, normally large enough to accommodate a table and from one to four readers.

Allowance: A sum budgeted, identified in the contract documents, and made part of a larger contract on the basis of an estimated range of final cost rather than by contractual bid. Thus, a sum may be held by the general contractor for carpeting, and the final cost set by bidding or negotiation within the maximum set by the allowance.

Ambient light: See *Light sources—Ambient.*

Ambient sound: The constant general background sound produced by air currents, rain, electrical ballasts, white sound systems, etc. This background is in contrast to brief higher-volume sounds such as footsteps, coughs, voiced sounds, music, bird and animal sounds, thunder, door and intermittent machine sounds, etc.

Annunciator: A device giving an audible or visual signal.

Annunciator panel: A display board with signals, usually lights and sound, which indicate a change in condition in an exact location or area. It commonly informs staff of a smoke or fire condition, a security break or incursion, a water sump condition, or humidity variation beyond engineered limits. Also a numeric panel used to notify a patron upon the completion of a transaction. Such a panel is frequently used where books are paged from a closed stack.

Arcade: A roofed passageway, often with free-standing columns or pillars on at least one side.

Architectural space: See *Nonassignable space.*

Arrears: A backlog of work, frequently used with reference to any materials waiting for cataloging. A "working arrearage" is the material housed in or adjacent to work quarters which is needed to keep all catalogers efficiently busy with materials in their fields of subject and linguistic expertise. It is distinct from an excess to the working arrearage which becomes operationally inefficient and may need to be remotely housed.

Artifacts: Research libraries always have some collections other than media and book materials. These may include coins, stamps, busts, student memorabilia, or selected institutional realia such as a ground-breaking shovel.

As builts: The working drawings with contractors' refinements, giving precise location of wire runs, ducts, etc., so as, for example, to enable maintenance workers years later to know exactly where to find intermediate portions of a cable or other utility run.

Assignable space: See *Net space.*

Astragal: A flange fixed to one of a pair of doors to cover the gap and provide a tighter fitting against passage of air, smoke, water, etc.

Audio-visual materials: Aids to teaching "through ear and eye," *e.g.,* phonograph discs, cassettes, tape recordings, films, and filmstrips. Plastic models, show panels, etc., are also included, and the various mechanical devices for programmed instruction are sometimes referred to by the term. These are often referred to collectively as media.

Auxiliary collection: See *Storage libraries.*

Backfill: The compacted earth fill beside a foundation wall, added to replace soil excavation which was necessary for the construction.

Balancing: The adjustment of HVAC air outlets and control systems so as to provide uniform or specified air flow, temperature, and humidity among various zones or rooms in a building.

Ballast: An electrical device to provide increased voltage for fluorescent tubes and HID (high-intensity discharge) light sources.

Bar chart: A graph of parallel broad lines indicating the length of time, quantity, or personnel for a specific task.

Base board: A wood, plastic, or other hard strip or finish piece to cover the joint between wall and floor and protect the lower wall surface from damage as from shoes, chair legs, mops, vacuum cleaners, etc. Sometimes called a "skirting."

Bay: See *Module.*

Beneficial occupancy: A legal term referring to the use of the facility before final acceptance. The warranty period on those portions of the facility in use by the owner begins with the date of beneficial occupancy.

Berm: The shoulder of a road or a narrow earth ledge at top of an embankment. In landscape or site design, refers to the building up of dirt to form a mound. "Berming down" is sometimes used to refer to a slope of the site down to a lower level of the building.

Bib table: See *Index table.*

Bibliographic tool: A volume, or its equivalent in other formats, listing or indexing publications. Includes (1) a *catalog, q.v.,* which lists publications actually held in one or several library collections, (2) a bibliography, which lists publications within the defined scope, regardless of whether they are all in a particular library, and (3) an index, which analyzes the contents within one or more publications.

Bid alternate: An amount to be added to or deducted from the base bid if the owner chooses to add or delete the work covered by the alternate.

Bid bond: A legal financial obligation serving to guarantee the contractor's seriousness in submitting a construction bid.

Bid package: The set of documents issued to contractors invited to bid on construction. Includes working drawings, material and performance specifications, general conditions, the bid form, and other related instructions.

Black Friday: The extra paid day off acknowledged in labor contracts in the United States which occurs on alternate Fridays in many of the construction trades.

BM: The common reference to the British Museum, the library of which is now the British Library. One of its divisions is the *BLLD,* the British Library Lending Division, located at Boston Spa in Yorkshire.

Boiler plate: The standard legal and procedural requirements which can be added without substantial change to the specifications as part of the bid package.

Book detection system: The equipment for electronically determining if library books are going out an exit. All processes require a "target" of magnetized material or electronic circuitry affixed in the volume. Some systems alter the sensitivity of the target when the book is charged out and discharged. Other systems do not alter the sensitivity, thus requiring the volume to be handed to staff for inspection of charging and thereby bypassing the sensing equipment so as to prevent the turnstiles from locking or an alarm from sounding.

Book return: An arrangement to receive materials being returned. Among various options, this may include a slide or chute onto a counter, a slot in a service desk leading to a depressible-floor bin on wheels, or a stand-alone covered box similar to an outdoor postal box.

Book-return shelf: One or more shelves on which materials returning from circulation are held for charge records to be canceled or, thereafter, for sorting preparatory to returning the materials to their proper location. Also, shelves distributed throughout the stacks, typically of a contrasting color, where patrons are encouraged to place books they have removed from the shelves.

Book sizes: Technically derives from the number of folds of standard sizes of book papers. One fold giving four pages is "folio." Two folds giving eight pages is "quarto." Three folds giving sixteen pages is "octavo." A folio book typically measures 12–19 in. (300–480 mm) in height. A quarto book typically measures 10–12 in. (250–300 mm) in height. An octavo book typically measures 8–10 in. (200–250 mm) in height. A duodecimo book typically measures 7–8 in. (180–200 mm) in height. An elephant folio book typically measures over 20 in. (over 500 mm) in height.

Book truck: A small cart consisting of a set of shelves on wheels used for transporting books within the library. Called a "book trolley" in many countries.

Boring report: The soils test report resulting from analysis of the soil core removed from a drilled hole in the ground.

Bracing: See *Hat channel, Spreader, Strut bracing, Sway bracing,* and *Unitizing.*

Bracket shelving: Also known as cantilevered shelving. Developed very early in this century, it is formed of structural columns with holes or slots on the vertical face. Shelves are supported at the two ends by brackets which in turn hook into the holes or slots. The brackets hold the shelf from above and form bookends, though a movable bookend is commonly added to support the righthand-most volume when the shelf is not full. Where the bracket supports the shelf from below, it is frequently called "flush-bracket," or newspaper shelving.

Bread board: A card catalog adjunct which can be pulled out at counter height so as to hold a catalog tray for inspection, similar in operation to the sliding board in some kitchens on which bread is sliced. A similar pullout shelf is frequently found in a desk.

Breezeway: That part of a building which constitutes a roofed ground-level opening, usually a passageway, through which the outside air currents can move.

Brief: Used as a noun to refer to a building *program, q.v.*

Brittle books: Volumes with paper which has so deteriorated in strength that pages break when folded.

Broadside: An unfolded sheet printed on only one side.

Browsing collection: Popular fiction and nonfiction works of current interest which may be shelved in a prominent location to encourage cultural and recreational reading.

Bubble diagram: A set of library units or functions, each enclosed in a rough circle sized to simulate the floor area required and laid on paper so as to depict the physical two-dimensional relation of the elements.

Building code: The civil regulations governing the construction and alterations of buildings in a given locality, setting forth requirements and restrictions as to the use, safety, size, and type of building in certain zones and areas.

Built-in: Those furnishings which are attached to or an integral part of the building and thus included in the construction contract.

Caisson: A watertight metal or concrete compartment open at the bottom, used for the construction of foundation piers, particularly when the subsoil conditions require these piers to be extended below the ground water level.

Call number: The set of symbols identifying a particular item in a library collection, indicating its location and used to request that a specific physical item be brought from the stack, shelves, or other storage location.

Canopy top: Slightly projecting roof-like cover over sections of shelving.

Cantilever: A beam or slab projecting beyond the vertical column or wall construction so that it is supported on one end or side only and is capable of carrying weight throughout its projection. The cantilever structure can also be oriented vertically, as is the case of shelving that is bolted to the floor.

Carrel: A small partitioned desk or one-person alcove with writing surface at which the reader may be permitted to retain books. Open carrels often consist of desks with visual barriers formed by open bookshelves or low partitions.

Closed carrels have doors and often soundproof semipermanent walls and are also called study or dissertation rooms. See also *Wet carrel.*

Case shelving: A type of shelving which is open only in front. It may or may not have doors: solid, glazed, or wire grilled.

Case work: Cabinets of custom fabrication, often attached to the building and therefore part of the general construction contract.

Casement windows: Window units hinged vertically so that they open outwards or inwards. They can be operated either manually or by means of a mechanical crank attachment.

Catalog: A list of materials held in a particular collection or library. Library catalogs exist in the form of (1) book catalogs, (2) computer-accessed catalogs on terminals, (3) microfiche catalogs often produced by computers, and (4) card catalogs. The catalog most often found in American libraries is the dictionary catalog on cards. See also *Official catalog.*

Catalog department: The administrative unit of a library where books are cataloged and classified. See also *Technical services.*

Catalog tray: A drawer in which cards or slips are filed, several drawers being enclosed in a cabinet.

Caulking: Pliable material used to make a joint watertight or airtight.

Centers, or on centers: The distance between the centers of two pieces of similar equipment or construction placed parallel to each other. Generally used in connection with stack ranges, carrels in a reading area, tables in a reading room, desks in a workroom, parallel rows of catalog cases for the library's catalog, or with columns or windows.

Chair rail: A hard horizontal molding affixed to the wall at a height to protect that surface from chair backs.

Chamfer: A bevel or rounding of sharp furniture or architectural edges to make its use more comfortable or to provide a transition between two surfaces, for example, the 45-degree edge of a concrete beam.

Change order: A refinement during construction approved by the owner and issued by the project architect to the contractor so as to alter some particular condition or specification in the contract documents.

Charge cards: The slip used to record the borrowing of a particular item. Also termed a circulation card or, if it is maintained in the item, a book card.

Chute: A term used to refer to a slide or tube used for a *book return, q.v.,* trash receptacle, or mail-handling system.

Circulation department: Service department for loan transactions, often also responsible for the supervision of the book stacks. See also *Readers' services.*

Circulation space: The floor area required for traffic within a building. Typically this includes lobbies, corridors, main and side aisles, stack range aisles, passageways, stairs, ramps and halls, but not the space in which a reading chair may be adjusted and not space for people to move about amidst furniture if the square footage assigned for the furniture or for the operation as a whole includes space for people to move (*e.g.,* the floor area immediately behind a counter).

Classification: The numerical or alpha-numerical notation by which library materials may be given an ordered subject arrangement on the shelving and which accommodates additions in their logical place within the scheme.

Clean-out: Used as a noun to denote the access to plumbing systems which enable a rather easy reaming or flushing of segments which may become clogged.

Clean power: An electrical circuit dedicated to computer usage where the simultaneous use of other equipment which could produce interference, if serviced by the same circuit, is avoided.

Climatization: See *Air conditioning.*

Closed-access stacks or closed stacks: Stacks to which only members of the library staff normally are admitted.

Closed-circuit television: A type of television in which the signal is not broadcast as in ordinary television but is transmitted by cable or wire to one or more receivers. Existing telephone lines have been used in experimental installations. Possible applications of closed-circuit television in libraries include transmission of educational programs to auditoriums and classrooms and transmission of documents—pages of books or manuscripts—and of bibliographical information from a central service point to distant monitoring stations. It can also be used as an aid to supervision.

Code: See *Building code.*

Code authority: The governmental offices given legal responsibility for the administration of the governing codes and ordinances as they affect the building and its occupants during its lifetime. Besides safety, the codes and ordinances may apply to access, zoning requirements, energy usage, and other aspects established by law.

Coffered ceiling: A ceiling with a pattern of indentations created from form work in the case of concrete construction or from a system of beams in other construction. Portions of a coffered ceiling may serve no structural purpose and may be purely decorative and formed in plaster or acoustic material, although the concept is based on a structural solution to spanning a space with minimal materials.

Collateral reading: Suggested or recommended reading designated by the teaching faculty to supplement required reading. See also *Reserve books.*

COM upholstery: "Customer's own material." Refers to furniture for which the upholstery fabric is provided separately.

Commercial shelving: Inexpensive metal shelving, also known as industrial shelving, which is supported by uprights at each corner of the shelving unit or section. Adjustable with the use of nuts and bolts or clips.

Commons: See *Staff commons.*

Compact storage: A bookstack, usually for lesser-used materials, which has much greater capacity than is usual, either by taller sections and exceptionally narrow aisles or by one form of *movable shelving, q.v.*

Compartment: Sometimes used to refer to two sections of shelving back-to-back.

Conduit: The pipe or tube through which is pulled electrical wire or cable.

Confirming estimate: A second estimate prepared by a separate estimating firm used to verify the estimate prepared by the architect.

Conservation department: The total quarters required for the workshop, laboratory, or studio in which preservation treatment is given to selected library materials. It includes needed office space, but may or may not include ancillary areas for exhibits, instruction, microfilming, film processing, etc.

Construction documents: See *Contract documents.*

Construction zone: The precise area specified in the bid package which can be fenced in and is legally under control of the contractor during the entire period of construction. It may or may not include parking for crews. It will include area for field offices, materials stockpiling, portable toilets, trash or waste collection, and vehicle access from one or more paved roads as necessary.

Consultation counter: A table or similar surface at which one stands in the card catalog area if a particular tray is to be taken from the cabinet for use. It is sometimes provided with built-in receptacles for charge cards, scratch slips for notes, and catalog explanatory handouts. A stool may be provided for extended use.

Contingency figure: A safety factor included in cost estimates, schedules, or design criteria to cover any anticipated inflation or unanticipated demands and to provide for expenses which may occur at a later date, the amount of which is unknown at the time of estimating.

Contour: The outline of a figure or form, or a line drawn to join points of similar elevation on a site or landscape plan.

Contract documents: The agreement, general conditions, special conditions, addenda, change orders, etc., including the set of working drawings. See also *Working drawings.*

Contractor, general: The firm which has the general construction contract with the institution, which may or may not include mechanical, electrical, and other work according to the construction documents. See also *Subcontractor.*

Conveyor: Occasionally used in libraries for continuous horizontal or vertical movement of sizable numbers of books.

Core voids: Holes through a floor slab made by placing tubes in the formwork on a predetermined module before pouring the concrete. Core voids may be useful at a future date in providing flexibility for signal and power installation from the ceiling area of the floor below.

Cost model: A financial formula or format applicable to estimating construction cost which facilitates the process of comparative analysis both with other projects and earlier estimates on the same project.

Counter height: The working surface distance from the finished floor level, so as to provide a height which is convenient for persons who are standing. The convenient height (typically from 39 to 42 in. or 990 to 1066 mm for transaction counters and 36 in. or 914 mm for sorting) will vary, depending on function and the typical elbow height of the persons for whom it is designed.

Course reserves: Books segregated for short-term circulation. In some countries called "short loan collection."

Crawl space: A subfloor volume, usually found under the ground floor and with unfinished floor, which has headroom so low as to force ducking or crawling to move therein.

Critical path method: Developed in 1956, CPM uses a graphic flow chart of multiple interdependent tasks to show the shortest time possible to complete construction and occupy a building. By determining which operations are most demanding of time, including off-site fabrication and procurement of materials, and which are prerequisite to one or several subsequent operations, the minimum total elapsed time is demonstrated. See also *Milestone chart.*

Cross aisle: The bookstack aisle which passes through the midst of the stack, perpendicular to the range aisles which are the narrow passageway between two ranges. See also *Aisle.*

CRT: An acronym for cathode ray tube, also called a video display, which creates textual images on a fluorescent screen. With a keyboard, used in many library operations, such as searching catalogs and indexes and creating and revising records as part of processing materials.

Crunch point: A term sometimes used to indicate the year in which the library expects its book collection to reach the shelving *working capacity, q.v.*

Cubage: The volume of space as defined by the building envelope or outer shell. Net cubage applies to the volume of space between walls and below the visible ceiling. Gross cubage usually applies to the total space occupied by a building.

Cubicle: See *Carrel.*

Cubook: A term devised by Robert Henderson of the New York Public Library for a book of average size. He estimated that 100 cubooks could be housed in a standard single-faced stack section 3 ft wide and 7 ft 6 in. high (0.914 × 1.186 m).

Curtain wall: A nonload-bearing thin exterior wall system which envelops a structure, located between and often in front of the main peripheral structural members of steel or reinforced concrete.

Dado: See *Wainscot.*

Dead load: The weight of all fixed items in a building. It includes the structure, lighting, partitions, and permanently fixed elements such as equipment in a penthouse. It contrasts with *live load, q.v.*

Deck: Area occupied by one level of a bookstack, referred to in this volume as a stack level.

Dedicated circuit: An electrical circuit used for a specific purpose either due to the power requirements of the equipment being serviced or in order to provide *clean power, q.v.*

Deduct alternate: See *Bid alternate.*

Depository library: A library legally designated to receive government publications without charge.

Design development plans: Drawings developed in much greater detail following the schematic plans. Also known as preliminary plans. These drawings show not only structural building elements but also location and space requirements for everything to be contained in the building. Together with outline specifications, design development plans serve as the basis for preliminary cost estimates.

Desk height: Similar to *counter height, q.v.;* however, determined for seating with one's feet on the floor and knees bent at right angles (typically 29 to 30 in. or 736 to 762 mm).

Detail drawings: Produced by the architect to explain, enlarge, and clarify sections of the construction documents.

Detection system: See *Book detection system.*

Development office: The fundraising office.

Dictionary stand: A slightly sloping support large enough to hold an unabridged dictionary. It usually has a front lip to prevent the volume from falling, and it may rest so as to hold the book at counter height above a table or counter, or stand on its own legs or pedestal.

Directory: A public listing of offices, departments, special rooms, officials, and specialists. It is often prominently mounted in the building lobby or by the elevator. There may also be local directories on individual floors. See also *Signs.*

Display shelves: See *Sloping shelves.*

Dissertation room: A one- or two-person enclosed study with locking door, providing private, secure space in which an advanced student may work and leave personal notes, papers, books, typewriter, and other materials.

Divisional plan: See *Subject-divisional plan.*

Donor graphic: The one or several plaques, wall lettering, or other signage acknowledging those who helped finance the building.

Double-acting (door): A door with the leaf able to swing both inwards and outwards, rather than being prevented from swinging in one direction by the frame or jamb.

Double-faced section: Two single-faced stack sections back-to-back, generally attached to the same upright. Also called a "compartment."

Double-hung (window): A two-paneled window in which one panel slides up and the other down. To work well, the window panels are counterbalanced with a system of pulleys and weights hidden in the window frame.

Downspout: A roof drainpipe, usually attached to the exterior wall, carrying rain water from gutters under the edge of a roof to a lower level or to the ground.

Draw-out shelves: A type of compact shelving in which the shelf height is fixed and each shelf is actually a drawer, enabling full occupancy of space behind the front visible volumes.

Drop: The same as a *book return, q.v.*

Dry bulb temperature: The temperature determined by any accurate thermometer without the influence of evaporating water. A combination of the dry bulb and wet bulb temperatures is used to determine the relative humidity using a psychrometric chart.

Dry wall construction: The use of plywood or gypsum board (also called plasterboard, sheetrock, or wallboard) for the construction of walls or, in some cases, ceilings. It excludes any wet process such as plaster, masonry, or concrete, whether or not it is structural.

Duct: The pipe or other tubular passage through which air is carried.

Duct shaft: The vertical building void between floors which constitutes a clear route for ducts or conduits and can facilitate their servicing as required.

Dummy: A block of wood or other material used to replace a book in its normal shelf location, usually in its proper classified location. The block has the book identification with note indicating its actual location. Commonly used for folio volumes when the catalog and stack directory do not alert one to a special location for oversized materials.

Dumpster: A very large metal trash receptacle for outdoor lifting and dumping by refuse trucks. A proprietary term.

Duplex outlet: A standard electrical receptacle with the capacity to receive two plugs. Can also be doubled into a fourplex or double duplex outlet.

Economizer cycle: A mode of operation for the HVAC system where the air being returned from the building is compared with outside air, and the air source that requires the least energy to condition is selected. Where humidity is a factor, fairly sophisticated control devices are required.

Efficiency (energy): The extent to which a building is designed to operate on comparatively low levels of energy through the use of various technologies including insulation, solar devices, special controls, and other devices.

Efficiency (space): A factor derived by dividing the net assignable area by the gross area of the building; commonly used for comparative purposes and as a measure of the planning effectiveness.

Egress route: The legal exit required for emergency such as fire, smoke, or earthquake.

Elephant folio: See *Book sizes.*

Elevation (drawing): A vertical representation of a building, interior and/or exterior, drawn to a scale.

Elevator: A platform for the mechanical vertical transportation of passengers, books, or freight, from one level of a building to the others. When used for passengers, the platform should be completely enclosed by walls and roof. Called a "lift" in many countries. See also *Two-to-one roping.*

Ellison doors: Trade name for heavy balanced swing doors with pivots placed about 6 in. from the side frame at top and bottom. Doors swing both in and out at the same time because part of the swinging action goes in the reverse direction. They use less space than ordinary doors with hinges directly on the side frame. Their use is especially applicable to wide outside doors where wind problems exist and for interior parts of the building where the suction between air-conditioned and nonair- conditioned rooms makes the operation of usual door hardware difficult.

Emergency exit: A legal exit designed exclusively for egress during fire or other emergency conditions.

Emergency lighting and power: An auxiliary system powered by backup generators and/or by batteries so as to provide minimally adequate light for exiting and power for emergency horns or other systems.

End panel: The finished vertical surface of steel or wood at the end of a section or range of bookshelves. For steel shelving formed of structural columns and cantilevered shelves, these panels are nonstructural. In case type or slotted shelving, they are structural.

ENR Index: A monthly record of average building construction prices published in the *Engineering News Record* and used to establish cost trends.

Ephemera: Library collections of clippings, pamphlets, offprints, programs, and other such slight and fugitive material.

Fabric of architecture: The palette of materials, colors, textures, and shapes which is charactcristic of an architcctural stylc or is chosen for a particular building. Also called "architectural character."

Facsimile: (1) A reproduction of a manuscript or printed document made by lithographic or photographic processes; not a reprint. (2) Transmission of photographic images of documents by a patented telegraphic process. See also *Closed-circuit television* and *TelAutograph.*

False floor: See *Access flooring.*

Fast track: The process of bidding successive portions of a building construction project so that work can start before the full set of bid documents is finished. The bidding may be in two or more stages. The intent is to speed the date of completion and to save some cost of price rises during construction.

Fenestration: The window systems, including fixed and operable sashes and integral screening if any.

Fiche: A transparent sheetfilm containing reproductions of a number of pages greatly reduced in size. They are one form of *microreproduction, q.v.*

Field order: A temporary document requiring an immediate change or plan of work during construction, issued by the project architect and to be followed up by a formal *change order, q.v.*

File tub: A bin holding circulation charge cards for all outstanding loans. It is usually at table or counter height and has legs and wheels for rolling around the work area.

Fire damper: An adjustable plate or louver in ventilation ducts which automatically closes to prevent smoke or fire passage when a fire alarm is activated.

Fire tower: A vertical emergency egress stair which is separately vented so that smoke and heat from within the building cannot contaminate the exit route. It may be at the exterior wall where it can be vented to the atmosphere.

Flashing: A material (copper, galvanized steel, lead, aluminum, stainless steel, titanium alloy, zinc, or impregnated fabric) used as a protective covering to prevent water penetration into the building at joints between horizontal and vertical building surfaces such as roofs, floors, and walls, at the head of sills or exterior wall openings, and on all sides of roof openings for gables, dormers, skylights, domes, pipes, drains, etc.

Fluorescent light: See *Light sources.*

Flush-bracket shelving: See *Bracket shelving.*

Flushing the building: The staff process of checking all public parts of the library to be sure everyone has left at closing time.

Folio: The size of a volume formed by folding a sheet once. See also *Book sizes.*

Follower block: The adjustable support for cards to the rear of a card catalog tray or file drawer.

Footcandle: Unit of illumination equal to one lumen per square foot, which is the amount provided by a light source of one candle at a distance of one foot; equals 10.76 lux (lx). Full sunlight with the sun at the zenith is of the order of 10,000 footcandles on a horizontal surface. This term is often replaced by the use of "lumen per square foot."

Footing: See *Foundations.*

Footing drain: A system of perforated pipe which is installed at the perimeter of the building foundations designed to remove ground water before it leaks into a basement or underground space. A footing drain may connect to the storm sewer or to a sump pump, which, in turn, is connected to the storm sewer.

Footprint of building: The outside configuration of a building at grade level, usually determined as it relates to finished grading but ignoring berms, swales, dry moats, and similar sculpturing for drainage, light, air, or aesthetic purposes.

Fore-edge: The edge of a book, opposite the binding edge or spine, *i.e.,* the front edge.

Foundations: The supporting members of a building or structure at the ground or its underpinning if it is supported by columns; the footings at the bottom of each column or pier are its foundations. The type of foundation required for a building depends on its structural system and on the ground and climate. In soft soils piles may have to be driven down 100 ft (30.480) or more. On rocks little more than dowels may be necessary to anchor the building. If a building has no basement but is erected directly on a concrete slab, that is the foundation. If a building has bearing walls supporting the roof, the foundations are the lowest divisions of these walls.

Freestanding stacks: Library stacks whose principal support is the floor of the story they occupy. Stack manufacturers do not regard a stack as freestanding unless its bases are so broad that they do not require strut bracing running from one range to another or other methods to provide stabilization, such as fastening to the floor. See *Multitier stack.*

French drain: A drain that is simply a trench in the ground, often filled with gravel so as to absorb more water.

Front matter: Similar to *boiler plate, q.v.,* dealing with the general aspects of a program or specification.

Fugitive material: See *Ephemera.*

Fumigation chamber: A small enclosed area which can temporarily house book materials on racks or trucks or shelves, can be sealed, perhaps evacuated of air, and filled with gas to kill insects or their larvae.

Furring (walls, ceilings): The application of a layer of thin wood or metal to provide a level surface to receive the final surface, such as for lathing, plastering, etc., or to make an air space.

General contractor: See *Contractor, general.*

Glare: Light reflectance or imbalance of brightness which is sufficiently severe so as to impair reading. It is a particular problem when external light, such as from a window, is visible on a CRT screen or when overhead or table lighting bounces into the reader's eyes from the table surface.

Government documents: Publications issued by governmental agencies, departments, offices, etc. The term usually is not inclusive of those issued by quasi-governmental organizations, such as a joint exercise of power agreement, nor of reports issued as part of a research or study contract for work performed by a nongovernmental agency. Also known as public documents.

Grade: The elevation above sea level. A sloping grade has an incline or pitch described as so many degrees, or as, for example, rising one foot over a horizontal distance of five feet. To grade a site would be to shape the topography of the site to meet the design criteria.

Graphics: See *Signs.*

Gross space: The total area enclosed by a building, expressed in terms of cubic footage or square footage of floor area, including walls. Gross space generally includes rooftop machine rooms, projections, and mechanical spaces and also one-half of all spaces not enclosed with walls but provided with a roof and a floor. To the floor-to-floor heights used in computing cubic footage, 1½ ft (450 mm) is generally added below the lowest floor to allow for foundations.

Group study room: An enclosed room designed primarily to enable a small number of people to talk as they study or work on a project together.

Grout: The thin mortar filling spaces usually between masonry components.

Growth factor: A factor in commercial shelving to allow space for the shelf supports.

Growth rate: The annual percentage rate at which the collections expand.

Growth space: The difference between the space needed for current occupancy and capacity. As the term is applied to the book collections, it is usually the difference between current occupancy and *working capacity, q.v.*

Gusset plate: A structural element to assure strength in bookstack shelving and structural building components where they join.

Handicapped access: The route by which persons who are physically limited can come and go within the building and its approach. It may include ramps, door-opening devices, and other means of facilitating access by those who have sight, mobility, or dexterity limitations.

Hard hat: The protective helmet worn on construction sites to guard against falling objects or areas of low head clearance.

Hat channel: A bent steel form resembling the shape of a hat in section, often used as overhead bracing to connect a bank of ranges for structural rigidity. Two hat channels fastened together have been used as the structural column in steel shelving, although the C shape is now more common. See also *Strut bracing.*

Humidistat: A control device that measures humidity and adjusts the mechanical system in response to change in humidity.

HVAC: An abbreviation, frequently used in engineering documents, for the heating, ventilating, and air-conditioning system for a building.

Hygrometer: An instrument to display the humidity of a room. A recording hygrometer will provide a 24-hour or one-week graphic record of humidity conditions throughout that period.

Hygro-thermograph: A device to record the humidity and temperature in a room. Commonly used to monitor bookstack conditions, especially those where rarities are housed, thereby providing a means to check that the HVAC system is performing as it was engineered to do.

Incandescent light: See *Light sources.*

Index: See *Bibliographic tool.*

Index table: A large table with sufficient width to shelve indexes and other frequently used reference works down the middle, sometimes on a second or third tier of shelves, and still have room in front to open and use one or more volumes. Sometimes called a "bib table," short for bibliography table.

Industrial shelving: See *Commercial shelving.*

Insulation: The materials used for reducing the passage of sound, heat, or cold from outside to inside a building and, at times, from one part of a building to adjacent space.

Intercom system: A telephone system providing direct communcation between stations on the same premises. Local systems may be independent of or associated with the nationwide telephone network. The equipment often has such features as provision for conference calling, hands-free talking, and switching executive phones to public-address systems.

Intrusion alarm system: A system to protect the building or rooms therein against unauthorized entry by giving an immediate alert to staff when the security has been breached. The local devices are wired to an *annunciator panel, q.v.,* and may be linked to a campus security office, which is monitored at all hours.

Isometric drawing: A form of three-dimensional projection in which each plane is drawn in true dimension and at an oblique angle view for clarity of presentation.

Kickplate: A protective reinforcement at the bottom of a door.

Kiosk lighting: Columns in the middle of rooms, providing ambient light by indirect diffusion from a hidden light source.

Knee space: The area needed beneath counters and desks for adequate leg space.

Lally columns: Columns made of a cylindrical steel-pipe shell filled with concrete. Special types have additional reinforcement consisting of steel bars. "Lally" is a registered proprietary term of 1897.

Lambert: A unit of brightness equal to one lumen per square centimeter.

Landscape offices: Semiprivate office space, created by arranging relatively low partitions in a large open space. The partitions may vary from just overhead height for a seated person to overhead height for a standing person. They may be acoustically treated; somewhat easily movable; provided with electricity, communications, and task lighting; and mated with desk and shelves or other office accessories.

Lateral file: Cabinet drawers which pull out from the long side rather than from the more common narrow side. In this arrangement, the file folders usually can be viewed by looking sideways instead of head on. The lateral file has the advantage in some locations of extending less than half as far into the passageway.

Lateral force: Horizontal pressures commonly produced by collisions, earthquakes, winds, etc.

Layout: The plan for distribution of furniture, utilities, and equipment in a building.

LC: The frequently used abbreviation for the U.S. Library of Congress.

Legal file: A correspondence cabinet with drawers of a size to house documents used in procedures of law; the document size is 8½ × 13 to 16 in. (215 × 330 to 406 mm), as opposed to that for a *letter file, q.v.*

Letter file: A correspondence cabinet with drawers of a size to house common documents, memoranda, and other papers to a maximum size of 8½ × 11 in. (215 × 280 mm).

Lift: In American library usage, the term often denotes the book elevator, not the passenger elevator as referred to in many other countries. Lifts are operated by electric motors or by hand. In construction, a lift is the procedure for the placement of concrete, particularly in a wall or other vertical element.

Light sources:

Ambient light is the general area lighting provided by direct and indirect sunlight and by reflected or direct general artificial light. This latter artificial light excludes *task lighting,* which is directed solely for one individual's benefit.

Fluorescent light is generated by an electrical-discharge lamp in which the radiant energy from the discharge is transferred by suitable materials (usually phosphors) into wavelengths giving high luminosity.

High-intensity discharge is a new source of energy-efficient light. HID includes low- and high-pressure sodium and mercury vapor lights. All HID fixtures require some form of transformer or ballast. In the HID lamp the transmission of current through a gas produces the light.

Incandescent light is produced by a light bulb in which a metallic substance glows at white heat. Common bulbs are the tungsten lamp and the quartz halogen lamp.

Polarized lighting is produced by a lens which controls the emission direction so as to reduce visibility of the light source within normal sight lines when one is reading.

Task lighting is local lighting produced by a device, sometimes adjustable, and concentrated on the desk surface or other specific task location.

Lintel: The horizontal structural beam at the top of a door or window.

Live load: Any weight within a building which is not fixed, such as that potentially shifting due to the movement of people, books, materials, equipment, and vehicles. It contrasts with *dead load, q.v.*

Load bearing: Used in reference to a wall which is specifically engineered to withstand all reasonable anticipated weights of all parts of the building that rest thereon.

Lobby: A hall or foyer at or near the building entrance.

Locked stack: That part of the public bookstack which is walled or caged off to house materials needing extra security.

Lumen: The flux of light.

Lump sum: A single, fixed price payment, as opposed to cost plus or time and materials.

Lux: The International System unit of illumination which is equal to one lumen per square meter.

Mail room: Quarters used for processing packages and other mail for internal and external delivery. Also called receiving room, shipping room, and sometimes functionally broadened to include supply stock and issuance, building security, caretaking or janitorial service, and the superintendent function.

Main library: A building which is the administrative center of a system, where the principal collections are housed, and various business services and technical processing procedures are located.

Master clock system: A group of clocks in a building or area of campus, where one clock can be reset and all the "slave" clocks conform.

Master plan: The general scheme under which a particular project will be developed, or the full scheme for long-term development of a building. It thus involves going beyond the immediate phase of construction.

Mercury vapor lamps: Tubular lamps in which mercury vapor is made luminous by the passage of an electric current.

Mezzanine: A level of a building extending over only a part of the area available to it and leaving the remainder with additional height.

Microform reader: A machine for enlarging a microtext for reading at or about its original size. If it can also produce a copy of that enlargement, it is termed a reader-printer.

Microreproductions: Microphotographic copies of printed or manuscript matter. The principal forms are microfilm on reels, microfiche (sheet microfilm), microcards (opaque paper positives), and microprint (paper opaques which are duplicated in large editions by a photomechanical process). Also known as *microforms.*

Microtext: The graphic texts and illustrations contained on microreproductions.

Milestone chart: A planning and scheduling table which plots time targets for completion of particular tasks, trades, or phases of construction. In a more elaborate form it has been developed into a detailed work-flow schema called PERT (program evaluation and review technique) which is milestone or event-oriented. See also *Critical path method.*

Mock carrel: A semipartitioned segment of a table for several persons which gives the semblance of an individual carrel.

Mock-up: A full-sized replica or dummy of a part of a building or a particular piece of furniture or equipment, often made of a substitute material, such as wood or plaster.

Modem: A device which modulates and demodulates signals to be transmitted over data communications facilities, and is thus the telecommunications link for a computer terminal.

Modesty panel: The skirt of a carrel, counter, desk, or table which hides from view the legs of one sitting behind it.

Modular construction: A system of building construction in which the floor area is divided into equal units defined by structural columns at the corners, instead of by load-bearing walls. This system makes it possible to provide or to extend areas for the different departments as desired. A modular library is one constructed on this principle.

Module: One of the square, rectangular, or triangular units of space into which a modular construction is divided; one or more modules form a *bay,* or the space between four columns.

Monograph: A book or separate volume or volumes of text constituting a substantial treatise on a particular subject, as distinct from *serial, q.v.*

Morgue: A reference file of clippings.

Movable partition: A room divider which can be folded, collapsed, accordioned, or drawn so as to turn two separately usable spaces into one.

Movable shelving: A form of compact shelving that is denser than any other method permitting direct shelf access.

Mullion: The vertical frame (structural or nonstructural) member between adjacent windows.

Multitier stack: A type of multistory stack construction which was by far the most popular type before the Second World War and is still found in many large research libraries. The stack consists of vertically and horizontally interconnected sections and ranges of shelving, stacked one on top of another, which are self-supporting and support the total weight of the books stored. Its installation makes it unnecessary to have load-bearing upper floors in the building itself. The same columns which accept the shelves also support the thin stack floors. Multitier stacks ensure maximum capacity, but the stack area lacks flexibility.

Negotiated bid: A means of reaching a contract with one construction firm where the cost and terms of construction are developed as the result of conferring and responding, one to the other until agreement is reached.

Net space: The part of the gross space left after deducting the nonassignable space or balance area; the assigned or programmed space. Often called "assignable space" or "usable area."

Newspaper rack: An open bin or frame for holding several issues of a newspaper, each one held firmly at its left margin by a rigid "stick" from which the issue is suspended in the bin.

NIC: An acronym for "not in contract"; used on drawings to indicate those items that are excluded from the job under contract.

Noise, electrical: The interference that can be heard in electrically transmitted sounds which comes about when power and signal lines are not adequately separated or insulated one from the other.

Nominal dimension: Typically, a dimension based upon measurement from the center line between two units or, in the case of lumber dimensions, the accepted center line of the saw required to cut the wood to size. For standard library shelving, the nominal width is the dimension from the center of one shelf upright to the center of the next, while the nominal depth is measured from the center of a double-faced section to the front face of the shelf. For bricks, the nominal dimension is from the center of the grout line. For pipe, the inside diameter is the nominal diameter.

Nonassignable space: Floor area that is not available for direct library purposes. It normally includes space required for stairwells, rest rooms, mechanical equipment, janitors closets, etc.

Non-losable book support: A type of book support with a sufficiently thick bulk so that it cannot inadvertently "knife" the pages of a book shelved next to it.

Nose: The stair-tread front edge. Also referred to as "nosing."

Oasis: A group reading area in the midst of a bank of shelving.

Occupancy permit: A formal approval of the completed construction project by the appropriate governmental agencies, including the fire marshal and the building inspection department, authorizing the occupancy of the building. In some cases the final signatures on the building permit are equivalent to the occupancy permit.

Octavo: The size of an average book, typically 8–10 in. (200–250 mm) in height. See also *Book sizes.*

Official catalog: A catalog maintained for the use of the library staff. The entries in this catalog often include details for the guidance of catalogers, such as added entry tracings and entry authority information.

On centers: See *Centers.*

Open-access stack: Bookstack to which readers are admitted.

Optical disk: A very high-density flat medium containing visual matter to be viewed on a laser-reading display screen.

Order department: See *Acquisitions department.*

OSHA: Abbreviation for Occupational Safety and Health Administration, an agency of the U.S. Department of Labor, which since 1970 has authority for setting minimum building conditions affecting health and safety for staff. In many states this function has been shifted to a state agency such as Cal OSHA in California.

Outlet: See *Duplex outlet.*

Oversized book: A volume too large to be shelved in its normal classified location, where it may be represented by a *dummy, q.v.*

Paging system: An electronic radio device, sometimes called a "beeper," used to summon a staff member. It is distinct from the PA, or *public address system, q.v.,* which directs a generally audible message to a particular part of a building.

Palette of the designer: The set of materials selected for a particular project by the interior designer and the architect. It consists of physical surfaces (metal, wood, glass, cloth, plastic) as well as colors, textures or finishes, and shapes. May be called the *fabric of architecture, q.v.*

Pam box: An abbreviated reference to a pamphlet box, usually an open-backed box of cardboard which stands on shelves like a volume and houses up to a handful of pamphlets.

Panic alarm: An alarm, usually silent, that may be activated at a service desk in the event of a threat. Annunciation of the panic alarm at a central location may summon the police or a staff member, who may quietly go to the scene to assess the situation.

Panic hardware: Door-opening devices that release the catch when one pushes against a waist-high horizontal bar. A door alarm may be made part of the panic hardware or provided as a separate unit for security purposes.

Parapet: A low wall around the edge of a roof serving as a guard for those working on the roof and sometimes as a visual refinement to improve the roof line as seen from the ground.

Parging (walls): The lining of the layers in outer walls with mortar or plaster to give a smooth surface for greater insulation and to reduce fire risks and water penetration.

Performance bond: A legal financial obligation serving to guarantee a contractor's execution of the contract.

Periodicals: See *Serials.*

Permit: The legal document issued by a county or other local authority to authorize construction of new structure or renovation.

Perspective: The drawing which depicts a three-dimensional view of the landscape, building, or interior arrangement so as to convey the relative scale and visual relationships of objects as they would actually appear to a person standing at a particular vantage point. The lines from near to far converge to one, two, or, rarely, three distant vanishing points.

Phonograph disc: A sound recording on a thin, flat circular plate.

Pitch: See *Grade.*

Plans: Drawings cutting horizontally through the building so as to show walls, doors, windows and other arrangements of a floor. See also *Design development plans* and *Schematic plans.*

Plant room: A term for mechanical equipment space, which may include areas for electrical, telephone, and security equipment. Also referred to as mechanical room.

Plenum: The contained space between hung ceiling and underside of the floor above which serves as an air passage. It is, in effect, a large duct space.

Pneumatic controls: Machine or instrument control and adjustment devices which are activated by air pressure. The HVAC system is frequently controlled by a pneumatic system.

Pneumatic tubes: The pipe or conduit system used for the transportation of books or of call slips. Cartridges containing books or call slips are propelled by air pressure or by vacuum.

Pointing: The cement or mortar grout which fills and finishes the joints of brickwork.

Polarized lighting: See *Light sources.*

Portal: The entrance to the building or stack area through which library users are directed. A portal monitor is a staff member who supervises and may control entry by screening unauthorized visitors.

Portfolio: A case for holding the loose pages or signatures of an unbound book or other material. The case has the semblance of a book, often a very large book, and is tied or otherwise held closed when not in use. The term is improperly used in libraries to refer to any extremely large volume, bound or unbound, which must be shelved horizontally; "elephant folio" is the proper term for these volumes. See *Book sizes.*

Precast: A concrete building component which is formed off-site or within the construction zone and then moved into place.

Prefabricated: Wooden, metal, or other small (transportable) building components assembled off-site by carpenters, sheet-metal workers, or other trades. A prefabricated building is manufactured in a factory and assembled on the site.

Preliminary plans: See *Design development plans.*

Preservation: Treatment to prolong the life of book materials, including actions of the *conservation department, q.v.*

Press: See *Range.*

Privileges desk: The counter or office where library staff may inquire of visitors regarding their authorization to use library services if they are not members of the faculty, staff, or student body. This desk may be called by such other names as visitors access, registration, or information, and the function may be handled at the reference or circulation desks or librarian's office.

Products-of-combustion system: A fire and smoke detection device with wiring to an *annunciator panel, q.v.,* which activates an alarm if smoke (or sometimes dust) is present. Other similar devices detect a rapid increase in heat (rate-of-heat-rise), but they are not as effective in detecting a fire.

Program: The academic courses of instruction; also the academic plan for curriculum development; and in this book primarily the comprehensive document describing and detailing the library building and its space requirements, its philosophy of service, functional areas and relationships, and spatial content and details as needed to communicate to the architects the desires of the owner-user. In the latter sense, called a "brief" in some countries.

Public address system: A wired pattern of loudspeakers over which staff can make announcements to one or various parts of a building, such as for an emergency or to forewarn of the closing time. It is distinct from an *intercom system* or a *paging system, q.v.*

Public documents: See *Government documents.*

Public services: See *Readers' services.*

Pull box: The fire-alarm box which can be activated in case of fire, smoke, or other emergencies in order to evacuate the building and notify the fire department.

Punch list: The final inspection list prepared by the construction inspector or architect of work not meeting the construction documents specifications and which is to be completed or corrected by the contractor. Called a "schedule of defects" in some countries.

Q-deck: A pattern of electrical signal ducts laid in a concrete floor slab to facilitate changing outlet locations as need shifts. A registered proprietary term of 1946.

Quarto: A volume larger than the average, typically 10–12 in. (250–300 mm) in height. See *Book sizes.*

Raised-floor system: See *Access flooring.*

Range (shelving): A row of sections of bookcases, single- or double-faced, with uprights or shelf supports common to both sides. Called a "press" in British usage. See also *Aisles* and *Centers.*

Range indicator: The label at the end of a range of shelving which gives the outer limits of the classification numbers for volumes shelved therein.

Readers' services: The departments of a library which deal with the public directly, such as the *Circulation department,* the *Reference department,* the interlibrary loan office. Photographic reproduction service is often included in this group. See also *Technical services.*

Ready reference collection: Those few books used so heavily by the reference staff or needing the security of desk location that they are shelved at or right behind the service counter or desk and are not directly accessible to readers except upon a specific request.

Reference department: The department of a library which helps the reader use the library's resources and provides assistance in the search for information. The department usually supervises and maintains the collection of reference books which are not for circulation but for consultation in the library only.

Register: A grill through which air is delivered or removed from the space.

Reheat coils: A device used to increase the temperature of the air to the desired level for a specific area or room. A room thermostat would control the reheat coil where this system is used.

Rendering: Any drawing that is illustrated in detail, usually with shadows, texture, plants, people, and other details suitable for presentation. Typically, the term applies to the perspective illustration which is used to convey the merits of the design.

Reserved books: Books for assigned or collateral reading removed from their regular positions in the stacks and placed on open reserve shelves or closed reserve shelves. If the latter, they are available only by signing a call slip. They are sometimes withdrawn from the shelves by a stack attendant and given to the reader over a counter and sometimes selected from restricted shelves by the reader who then gives a signed call slip to the attendant before leaving the restricted area.

Retention: The practice of withholding a predetermined percentage of the payment owed to any consultant or contractor until final approvals are obtained.

RFP: Refers to a "request for proposal," a form of business invitation for a vendor, consultant, or manufacturer to submit a specific performance proposal in response to a written specification of need.

Riser: The upright piece of a stair step, from tread to tread. See also *Tread.* Also refers to the vertical run of a duct or pipe system.

Roller shelves: Deep shelves fitted with many small rollers constituting support for the horizontal shelving of very large volumes.

Sash: The wooden or metal framework in which panes of glass are set for installation in windows or doors. A double-hung window has upper and lower sashes; a casement window has a sash that opens on hinges fastened to the upright side of the frame. Fixed sash windows do not open.

Scale: A standard basis for measurement. In the United States the most common scales for architects and engineers are the customary (imperial) and metric respectively. The term "drawing to scale" means that all parts are drawn to the same precise reduced proportion of full size.

Schedule of defects: Used to refer to a *punch list, q.v.*

Schematic plans: Drawings for proposed floor layouts. They are developed for review and approval before the preliminary or design development plans. Sometimes several sets must be prepared before one is accepted.

Scupper: The opening in a parapet to allow water to run out when downspouts are clogged and thus to prevent roof failure.

Section (architectural): A drawing illustrating the graphic picture resulting from a theoretical cutting along a predetermined line, with a view through the building or a portion of it. The expressive French term for this type of drawing is *coupe.*

Section (shelving): The compartment of a single set of shelves between uprights, usually, in the United States, 3 ft wide and 7 ft 6 in. high (0.914×2.286). A double-faced section is two sets back-to-back. A section is called a "tier" in British usage.

Security system: See *Book detection system* and *Intrusion alarm system.*

Seismic force: See *Lateral force.*

Seismic load: A horizontal load on the structure equal to a fraction of the vertical loading as established by code. This load is typically resisted through a heavy, rigid structural system and/or shear walls combined with floor membranes and other structural elements.

Seminar room: A small classroom for a course with library-intensive requirements. Such a room sometimes houses a core collection in a particular field for the convenience of advanced students and their teachers.

Sense of place: The architectural and design treatment which provides discussion areas, work stations, lounges, benches, and other places where people work, rest, or linger and may feel comfortable, "at home," and invited. As is sometimes stated, one may have a proprietary feeling of "turf," even as animals may stake out a domain which is theirs. At the work station, the term often applies to the ability of the staff members to make arrangements suitable to their liking so that a sense of security or comfort is obtained.

Sequence of the collection: See *Shelving sequence.*

Serials: Publications which are periodically issued in parts more or less regularly and are intended to continue indefinitely. These include magazines, journals, proceedings, transactions, weeklies, monthlies, annuals, newspapers, and the like. Weekly and monthly journals and magazines are termed *periodicals.* Serials contrast with *monograph, q.v.* Serials acquisition work may be the responsibility of an individual within the technical services department.

Service point: A staffed location where the clientele of the library can receive information, guidance, book service, photocopying, or other staff service.

Shear walls: Structural bearing walls of sufficient size and nature to withstand special lateral forces such as earthquake tremors.

Shelflist: A file describing all volumes in the exact sequence as on the shelf, so as to constitute the basis for an inventory.

Shelving: See *Bracket shelving, Case shelving, Commercial shelving, Movable shelving,* as well as *Stack.*

Shelving by size: A method of sorting large collections of books into a few groups of about the same height so as to increase the volume capacity of the shelves.

Shelving sequence: The logical flow of arranged items from one section of shelving to the next, one range to another, and one floor to another. It is usually determined by the classification of books which are deployed by class numbers on shelves in a ribbon pattern which is intended to facilitate location of any one item.

Shop drawings: Drawings which are prepared by the manufacturers or the suppliers of special building equipment and are provided to the contractor for use in preparing its installation. They illustrate in detail the size, operation, and features of the special equipment and should be approved by the architect before fabrication and installation.

Short loan collection: Materials consisting of required or recommended reading for courses of instruction, separately shelved, and available only for short-term circulation, e.g., a few hours or overnight.

Signal duct: The tubular passage for signal (computer, telephone, television, etc.) wires. See also *Conduit, Duct,* and *Q-deck.*

Sign-off: The formal process by which representatives of various responsible offices provide their signature approval. Sign-offs by the library and various institutional offices may be required for each phase of the design process as well as at the completion of construction.

Signs: The set of symbols or other visual messages visible from a distance which assist the user of a building to understand locations of functions and services, emergency directions, explanations of activities, donor recognition, and other matters of general necessity or aesthetic purpose.

Site: The assigned land area for a building, including such open spaces around the structure to accommodate any required setbacks.

Sling psychrometer: An instrument used to determine the relative humidity based upon the difference of the wet and dry bulb temperature.

Sloip: An acronym formed from the words "space left over in planning," an architectural studio term for unintentional extra spaces.

Sloping shelves: Shelves with a backward tilting bed used to facilitate reading book titles and call numbers on low shelves. Infrequently used because books tend to move back and thus out of sight on the shelf and because the shelves are not useful in other locations. The current issue of a journal is often placed flat on a very different type of sloping shelf (either fixed or designed to lift up and disclose back issues), and this type is commonly called "display shelves."

Slotted shelving (divider type): A type of shelving in which both the shelf and its turned up back have a pattern of slots which serve to support dividers; used in place of pamphlet boxes.

Soffit: The underside of an arch, stair, beam, or cornice; commonly refers to the underside of a projecting roof overhang.

Solenoid switches: A system of electrical switching using low voltage such that the line power or high voltage is switched remotely. Advantages are that the low-voltage control wires do not need to be in conduit and multiple switching points can easily be established.

Sort room: An area in or near the bookstacks where staff can pre-arrange materials being returned to the shelving, thus simplifying the reshelving process.

Special collections department: The department caring for and serving the rare books, manuscripts, and other materials requiring special security and specialized services. Sometimes called "limited access," "reserve," or "treasure" collection.

Special conditions: That section of a bid document which explains any unusual condition which must be met by the contractor.

Specifications: Written documents in which an architect enumerates and describes the quality of the materials to be used and the level of the workmanship required.

Spine: The sewn or binding edge of a book; the back.

Spreader: A large beam running between bookstack range columns to provide lateral stability, in lieu of "unitizing" or sway bracing.

Sprinkler system (fire): A network of pipes and overhead sprinklers designed to suppress a fire. The system is activated at individual sprinkler heads by the melting of a fusable link at a predetermined temperature.

Stack (book): Space for the storage of books. See also *Compact storage, Free-standing stack, Movable shelving,* and *Multitier stack.*

Stack access: The point at which library users may or may not be checked for authorized entry to the bookshelves. Also called the "stack portal," "control point," or "stack entrance."

Stack directory: The public index of deployment for all materials housed in the bookstack.

Stack uprights: Columns which act as bookstack shelf supports and divide the stacks into sections or compartments. In a *multitier* stack, they carry the load on the levels above.

Staff commons: The lunchroom or lounge for employees of the library.

Stall: See *Carrel.*

Standard conditions: That section of a bid document which explains conditions which must be met by the contractor in any work for that institution, such as affirmative action employment requirements for all trades, including subcontractors.

Standards: The building trade conditions which have been adopted by the national association or local chapter and which are mandated for the construction job by brief reference in the bid document. Also refers to requirements which may be placed upon the design or construction of a project but not necessarily established by code. Most professional agencies develop and distribute standards for all kinds of issues, including preservation requirements, handicapped access, energy control, etc.

Starters: The complete basic unit of a bookstack range. Its columns or ends commonly have slots on the outside as well as inside so that one or more *adder* units may be attached to form a range of shelving.

Storage libraries: Three distinct types of storage arrangements for less frequently used books have developed among libraries in the United States: (1) local storage of auxiliary or secondary-access collections in buildings or parts of buildings owned by the parent institution; (2) cooperative storage in warehouse-type buildings owned jointly by several libraries, each of which retains ownership of the materials it is storing; (3) cooperative-storage libraries, into which books are released from the individual contributing libraries and become jointly owned property.

Stroboscopic effect: The flickering created by light periodically interrupted.

Strut bracing: The horizontal overhead beam connecting a bank of ranges and formed of metal bars or *hat channels, q.v.*

Stubbed out: The provision of utility lines to the point of service, with the final fixtures not installed. Similar to roughed in. By this construction arrangement at a particular building spot, the possibility exists for adding utility service in the future, for example for water, drainage, power, or signal.

Stud: The vertical wooden or metal column which frames a wall and serves to support the wallboard, gypsum board, paneling, or other wall material. A common studwall is formed on "2-by-4s" spaced 16 in. on center (400 mm) although 12 in. and 24 in. (305 mm and 600 mm) spacing are occasionally used.

Study: A fully enclosed private space for reading and research. The word is used to convey more generous and usually more acoustically isolated accommodation than enclosed *carrels* or *dissertation rooms.*

Subcontractor: Specialty firm (sometimes merely referred to as "sub") that has contracted with the general contractor for part of the construction job.

Subject-divisional plan: Organization adopted by some U.S. academic libraries whereby resources and services are subdivided according to subject content of the collection. Subject-trained librarians are responsible for the technical and readers' services in typical areas, such as humanities and social sciences, physical sciences, life sciences, etc. Under the full subject-divisional plan no centralized functional departments exist in the library. There are several variants of the plan; often it includes readers' services only, while the technical services are operated in a centralized fashion and there is a single public catalog.

Subject reading area: A portion of the building seating which specifically relates to a subject in the adjacent book collection or which is designated for use by scholars in a specific subject.

Suggestion box: A receptacle for receiving comments, action requests, book purchase recommendations, and complaints. Provides a visible encouragement to advising staff and offers an anonymous method if one so chooses.

Sump pump: An automatic pump to evacuate water from a low point in or under a building.

Support staff: The nonprofessional staff of a library. Sometimes called the "classified staff," it includes staff members with clerical, technical, and other skills, as well as those in unskilled positions.

Surge space: Extra space available for temporary demands. Such space may be needed during periods of renovation to house a library unit temporarily. It is also useful in accommodating momentary cataloging *arrears, q.v.*

Suspended ceiling: A nonstructural hung ceiling, usually a system, providing a finished appearance and covering ducts and pipes which may run above it. It may or may not have special acoustical properties, and may or may not integrate lighting fixtures and HVAC registers.

Swale: A shallow gully formed beside an inclined road or walk to control water runoff. In landscape design, a swale is roughly the opposite of a *berm, q.v.*

Sway bracing: The lengthwise stabilization of a section or range by use of heavy crossrods forming an X. Sway bracing ordinarily must occur every four to six sections in a long range.

Take-off: The process of tabulating a detailed listing of each of the components in a building so as to create a meaningful cost estimate. The take-off is usually broken down into categories that involve unique trades or vendors.

Task lighting: See *Light sources.*

Technical reports: Published research results, produced by laboratories in limited quantities and generally serving as timely reports of progress or as final reports under a contract requirement. They may in some instances be superseded by more formal journal publication.

Technical services: The materials processing departments of a library responsible for the planning and development of resources as well as their maintenance and bibliographic control, *e.g.,* acquisitions, cataloging and classification, periodicals and other serials, conservation, binding and preparing the book for the shelf (labeling, etc.). Photographic reproduction is sometimes included in technical services. See also *Readers' services.*

TelAutograph: A facsimile telegraph for reproducing handwriting. The motions of the transmitting pencil are reproduced by a receiving pen controlled by electromagnetic impulses. A registered proprietary term.

Tempered air: A ventilation system in which the air is moderated by heat but the warmed air is not intended to heat the space.

Tender: A term used in some countries for the legal contract covering construction projects.

Terminal: An electronic device which, when connected to a computer, enables one to read or manipulate the data. Also called a *CRT, q.v.,* if it includes a screen display.

Terminal reheat: See *Reheat coil.*

Terrazzo: A hard flooring material made of marble or other stone chips set in mortar and then ground and polished.

Texture: The surface roughness and degree of shadow which can give a substance the appearance of being fibrous, grainy, patterned, or woven.

Thermopane: An insulating double- or triple-glazed pane for windows or doors. A registered proprietary term of 1931. Another trade name is *Twindow,* a registered proprietary term of 1946.

Thermostat: An instrument to control the temperature of a room. It may or may not be tied in with the HVAC controls for automatic adjustment to regain the specified condition, although it is intended to be. When display of only the temperature is required, a thermometer is the appropriate device.

Threshold: A doorsill, providing a slightly raised floor beneath the closed door to reduce drafts and water intrusion, provide a surface level with adjacent carpeting, and minimize some vandalism and security risks.

Tier: See *Multitier stack* and *Section (shelving).* See also *Section (shelving)* for British usage.

Transfer case: A cardboard box typically used to house a large quantity of manuscripts.

Tread (stair): The upper, horizontal surface of a step or stairway.

Trolley: See *Book truck.*

Truck: See *Book truck.*

Turn key: A contractual arrangement whereby one firm provides all services including design and construction. The buyer must only "turn the key" to have a dependable, fully operational installation.

Twindow: See *Thermopane.*

Two-to-one roping (elevators): A method for governing cab rate of movement. Electric traction elevators have either 2:1 or 1:1 roping. With 2:1 machines the cab speed is only half the rope speed, whereas with 1:1 machines the cab speed is the same as the rope speed.

Two-way radio: Radio communication carried on between two or more localities with portable equipment which permits receiving and transmitting of messages.

Typing height: The distance from the finished floor to the typewriter base surface which is convenient for typing if one is seated. This is typically 25 to 27 in. (0.635 to 0.686).

Typing return: The wing on a desk which provides a special typewriter location at proper height for a person who otherwise must use the desk surface.

Ultraviolet light: Light in wavelengths from about 4000 to about 40 angstroms, a natural part of fluorescent lighting and daylight which causes accelerated chemical deterioration in book paper and cloth bindings unless specifically filtered out.

Undercut: The gap at the base of a door to permit it to clear carpeting when swung open or to allow some air passage for HVAC purposes.

Union catalog: The list of holdings of a group of libraries rather than of just one. The term is applied to the central catalog of a university library if it offers branch and independent library materials in a unified list.

Unitizing: The welding of corners in case or commercial shelving to provide stability. This technique can sometimes be used in addition to or in lieu of sway bracing, spreaders, or top horizontal hat-channel bracing.

Vapor barrier: A thin sheet, usually of metallic foil and sheet plastic impenetrable by moisture, or liquid that hardens into a similarly impenetrable sheathing. Vapor barriers are designed to prevent passage of moisture through the structure (walls, floors, roofs) and to avoid condensation within.

Vestibule: A small enclosed antechamber or outer lobby at a building entrance, designed to control air drafts, help contain the climate inside the building, and provide protection against energy losses.

Videodisc: A very high-density flat disk storing information, frequently entertainment material, to be viewed on a laser-reading instrument with a low-resolution display screen.

Visqueen: A heavy-gauge plastic sheeting used for dust control and vapor barriers in construction projects. A registered proprietary name of 1946.

Wainscot: The lower part of an interior wall faced with wood or colored differently from the upper part. Also known as *dado.*

Warehouse library: See *Storage libraries.*

Weeding: The practice of withdrawing books from the collection, either by discarding superfluous copies or transferring infrequently used books to storage or to other libraries.

Wet carrel: A carrel with electronic devices to enable use of film, video, or other media.

White sound: The acoustic background deliberately created and controlled to mask disturbing sounds. Also called "pink sound" or, as Mr. Metcalf would say, "acoustic perfume."

Will calls: Books which have been located and are being briefly held for patrons who requested them.

Wing: The ell on a building, often used to refer to an addition to the original structure.

Wire management: The design of various components of the facility, especially furnishings, so that devices requiring power and/or signal wires can be easily accommodated without an array of unsightly and confusing wires. Wire management involves care in the placement of conduits as well as cable trays, chases, outlets, and other devices needed to manage the wires in a safe and neat way.

Working capacity: The percentage of the total theoretical shelf capacity which can be occupied before the interfiling of new acquisitions in the classification causes such crowding on some shelves that books are damaged by careless users and shifts are rather frequently required by staff to interpolate new items.

Working drawings: The set of drawings which is part of the detailed contract documents used for the preparation of bids and for the erection of the building; they show site, architectural, structural, mechanical, electrical, landscape, and other types of information to illustrate construction details.

Selective Annotated Bibliography

This bibliography is a selection of the books and articles published through 1985 which have been useful in the preparation of this volume and which may be useful to its readers for further study of particular aspects of planning. It is more extensive in specific coverage of library building planning over the past twenty-five years. Only a few publications are included under Special Topics. For example, there are many highly detailed texts, handbooks, manuals, and technical reports on each aspect and trade in the construction industry, and only a few of the more general or more useful to librarians are here included.

It is not intended to be a list of the "best" literature on the subject, since quality was not the only criterion for selection; accessibility, language, and country of origin were also taken into account. All of the items are in English, and most have an American frame of reference, since the authors assume that readers of the volume, whatever their nationality, will want and expect to get an American approach to the subject.

A long list of building programs would have been included except for the fact that these programs are published in limited editions for local use and are not generally available. The ALA Headquarters Library has many programs and building folders (containing data, drawings, and photos) which may be borrowed and will provide a list of those for colleges and universities. Other programs are quoted in Appendix A and should be useful to the person writing a program or outlining its main

sections, but readers are warned of the dangers of copying blindly the program of another institution.

The best approach to current material is through *Library Literature* (New York: H. W. Wilson Co.), published bimonthly with annual cumulations. The *Proceedings* of the Building Institutes deal with buildings that are just being planned or under construction, and are useful as case studies.

The items in the bibliography are arranged in alphabetical order under the following headings:

1. General Works
   a. Bibliographies
   b. Building institutes
   c. Other general works
   d. State planning guides
2. Special Subject Libraries
   a. General works
   b. Specific subjects and types of materials
3. Special Topics
   a. Acoustics
   b. Architects
   c. Automation and electronic developments
   d. Bookstacks
   e. Climate
   f. Construction
   g. Consultants
   h. Contracts
   i. Fire protection
   j. Floor coverings
   k. Furniture and equipment

l. Signs

m. Handicapped readers

n. Heating, ventilating, and air conditioning

o. Interior design

p. Lighting

q. Moving

r. Programs

s. Remodeling

t. Security

u. Site selection

v. Study facilities

A reference is cited only once under the heading that best describes the item as a whole. It should be noted that many of the references cited under General Works contain much valuable material that could be listed under the various subheadings of Special Topics. Significant lists of bibliographic citations are found in many references and are there indicated.

1. General Works

a. Bibliographies

American Library Association, Buildings for College and University Libraries Committee. *Planning College and University Library Buildings: A Select Bibliography.* Chicago: Library Administration and Management Assn., 1981. 13p.

Council for Advancement and Support of Education (CASE). *CASE RESOURCES.* Washington, D.C.: The Council, 1982.

A publications list including the following on fundraising:

> *Alumni Fund Ideas,* ed. by Virginia L. Carter. 1979. 48p.
>
> *The Art of Asking: A Volunteer's Guide to Asking for the Major Gift,* by W. Noel Johnston. 1982. 2p.
>
> *The Big Gift,* comp. by the editors of *CASE Currents.* 1982. 56p.
>
> *The Capital Campaign,* by the editors of *CASE Currents.* 1979. 64p.
>
> *Corporate Support,* by the editors of *CASE Currents.* 1981. 56p.
>
> *How to Write for Development,* by Henry Gayley. 1981. 50p.
>
> *An Introduction to Annuity, Charitable Remainder Trust, and Bequest Programs,* by William Dunseth. 1982. 37p.
>
> *Planned Giving Ideas,* ed. by Virginia L. Carter and Catherine S. Garigan. 1979. 30p.
>
> *Trustees in Fund Raising,* by the editors of *CASE Currents.* 1981. 40p.
>
> *Understanding and Increasing Foundation Support,* ed. by J. David Ross. 1981. 94p.

Cowgill, Clinton H., and George E. Pettengill. "The Library Building," *AIA Building Type Reference Guide* (BTRG 3-3), reprinted from May and June 1959 issues of *Journal of the AIA.* 32p.

Useful for its extensive bibliography, which was compiled by Mr. Pettingill, librarian of the American Institute of Architects.

Schutze, Gertrude. "Annotated Bibliography," in Chester M. Lewis, ed., *Special Libraries: How to Plan and Equip Them,* pp. 92-102. SLA Monograph no. 2. New York: Special Library Assn., 1963.

An extensive and useful annotated bibliography.

b. Building Institutes and Conferences

The First Library Building Plans Institute, sponsored by the ACRL Building Committee. *Proceedings of the Meetings at Ohio State University, Columbus, Ohio, April 25 and 26, 1952.* ACRL Monographs, no. 4. Chicago: ALA, 1952. 81p.

The plans of seven libraries are presented and discussed; floor plans are included. This series of institutes has followed the precedent established by the Cooperative Committee on Library Building Plans. The purpose of the institutes was to provide a clearinghouse for the exchange of ideas on the planning of new library buildings and to make it possible for preliminary plans of libraries of colleges and universities to be critically reviewed. Subsequent institutes devoted to building plans or equipment were held in 1953, 1954, January 1955, and July 1955, 1959, and from 1961 to 1966. The institute papers and building critiques with plans were published by ACRL or ALA.

Libraries for Research and Industry: Planning and Equipment, ed. by Margaret P. Hilligan. SLA Monograph no. 1. New York: Special Libraries Assn., 1955. 58p.

Based on a program on library planning and equipment that the Science-Technology Division presented at the forty-fourth annual meeting of the Special Libraries Association at Cincinnati, Ohio, May 16–21, 1954, with the hope "that it would be helpful to those working on plans for a new library, as well as for others who were remodeling or faced with having to make every square inch of area count."

Library Interior Layout and Design, ed. by Rolf Fuhlrott and Michael Dewe. IFLA Publications, no. 24. New York: Saur, 1982. 145p., illus.

The twelve papers constitute the proceedings of the fourth IFLA Building Seminar, held in Denmark in June 1980. Of special note are papers on security, fire protection, energy saving, HVAC, graphic design, and lighting.

c. General Works

Bareither, Harlan D., and Jerry L. Schillinger. *University Space Planning; Translating the Educational Program of a University into Physical Facility Requirements.* Urbana: University of Illinois, 1968. 153p.

A detailed description of the systematic administrative process for space planning at the University of Illinois. Index.

Bleton, Jean. "The Construction of University Libraries: How to Plan and Revise a Project." *UNESCO Bulletin for Libraries* 17: 307–15, 345 (November-December 1963).

A summary article based on the author's considerable experience in planning new university libraries in postwar France.

Brawne, Michael. *Libraries: Architecture and Equipment.* New York: Praeger, 1970. 187p., photographs, with floor plans and sections.

Interior and exterior photographs of European and American libraries, a good number of them academic, with explanatory text.

Cohen, Aaron, and Elaine Cohen. *Designing and Space Planning for Libraries: A Behavioral Guide.* New York: Bowker, 1979. 250p., illus., bibl.

Treats planning of new or remodeled libraries, including layout of space, furniture and equipment, energy use, lighting, decoration, acoustics, and moving.

Dober, Richard P. *Campus Planning.* New York: Reinhold, 1963. 314p.

A superior broad view of how campuses develop, this heavily illustrated volume provides extensive comment on plans and buildings of dozens of colleges and universities in North America. It also treats types of buildings functionally and aesthetically, and indicates in detail the procedures that have to be covered in preparing campus plans. Index.

Ellsworth, Ralph E. *Academic Library Buildings; A Guide to Architectural Issues and Solutions.* Boulder: Colorado Associated University Press, 1973. 530p.

A very helpful picture book, classified and indexed, of exteriors and interior details of dozens of libraries from coast to coast, including several in Europe. Also 27 floor plans and accompanying comments by the author.

Ellsworth, Ralph E. *Planning the College and University Library Building, A Book for Campus Planners and Architects,* 2d ed. Boulder, Colo.: Pruett Press, 1968. 145p.

A concise, practical outline of the problems involved in most aspects of planning procedures, especially the early stages, and a more detailed discussion of the basic elements of a library structure. Numerous diagrams and floor plans illustrate the various points that must be considered in planning, such as stack arrangement, audio-visual layout, central exit-control points, and the subject divisional library.

Environmental Evaluations. Ann Arbor: School Environments Research Publication no. 2. Ann Arbor: University of Michigan, 1965. 186p.

Human need for and reaction to architectural space are covered in six chapters by faculty experts on physical space; heat, light, and sound as part of environments; and the social setting. Considerable list of relevant published literature.

Galvin, Hoyt R., and Martin Van Buren. *The Small Public Library.* Paris: UNESCO, 1959. 133p.

Contains useful material and points of view for those concerned with planning academic libraries.

Gelfand, Morris A. *University Libraries for Developing Countries.* Paris: UNESCO, 1968. 157p.

Chapter 11 is a concise treatment of planning and equipping the library building.

Higher Education Facilities Planning and Management Manuals. 7 vols. Technical Report no. 17. Boulder, Colo.: Western Interstate Commission for Higher Education, 1971. Bibl.

This national effort presents in seven pamphlets detailed discussion of program planning, evaluation of existing facilities, analysis techniques, and facilities planning and management methodologies. The series was primarily prepared for community colleges and four-year institutions, both public and private, yet it was expected to be useful in larger institutions. Volume 4 treats libraries extensively with some data on audio-visual facilities, museums, and data processing and computing facilities. Volume 7 provides a glossary and bibliography.

Langmead, Stephen, and Margaret Beckman. *New Library Design; Guide Lines to Planning Academic Library Buildings.* Toronto: Wiley, 1970. 117p.

An exemplary comprehensive treatment of the rationale and process of designing the McLaughlin Library, University of Guelph. Included are plans, photographs, tables, bibliography, and a detailed decision chart.

Library Buildings for Library Service; Papers Presented before the Library Institute at the University of Chicago, August 5–10, 1946, ed. by Herman H. Fussler. Chicago: ALA, 1947, 216p.

Contains a dozen papers by leading librarians and architects on various aspects of library planning, including historic development of library buildings, functions, role of the architect, lighting, air treatment, building design, etc.; an important and still very useful collection of papers, but should be supplemented by more recent material.

Lodewycks, K. A.: *Essentials of Library Planning.* Melbourne: 1961. 136p. Processed.

Based on the author's research and experience in planning the Baillieu Library at the University of Melbourne. Not a finished text on library planning, but one volume containing a wealth of detail and information which is not readily available elsewhere; will be of value to anyone planning a large library.

Lyle, Guy R. *The Administration of the College Library.* 4th ed. New York: Wilson, 1974. 320p.

Chapter 16 on library building and equipment covers the basic elements of planning a building and includes material on the planning team, programming, and space requirements for various functions.

Lytte, R. J. *American Metric Construction Handbook.* Farmington, Mich.: Structures Publishing Co., 1976. 304p.

Considerable information on conversion to metric and its application in different trades.

Mason, Ellsworth. "Lighting and Mechanical Progress in Universities." *Library Trends* 18: 245–61 (October 1969).

Practical advice on lighting, electrical power requirements, ventilating systems, acoustics, elevators and escalators, book conveyor systems, communication systems, and security systems.

Mason, Ellsworth. *Mason on Library Buildings.* Metuchen, N.J., and London: Scarecrow, 1980. 333p.

A compilation of Mason's trenchant comments on planning, writing the building program, lighting, air-handling systems, and interior design. Includes on pp. 263–321 a detailed illustrative model program. Gives extensive critiques of three general libraries, an undergraduate library, a rare book library, and a medical library, with floor plans and exterior and interior photographs—Brown, Dalhousie, and Toronto, Sedgewick Undergraduate at British Columbia, Beinecke at Yale, and Countway Library of Medicine at Harvard. Well indexed.

Metcalf, Keyes D., and Ralph Ellsworth. *Planning the Academic Library: Metcalf and Ellsworth at York,* ed. by Harry Faulkner Brown. Newcastle upon Tyne: Oriel Press, 1971. 97p.
One or the other author expounds on planning, user needs, modules and dimensions, the program, some areas in academic libraries, mechanical equipment, traffic patterns, and furnishings.

Panero, Julius, and Martin Zelnik. *Human Dimension and Interior Space; A Source Book of Design Reference Standards.* New York: Whitney Library of Design, 1979. 320p., illus., index.
A reference work of anthropometric data in both inches and centimeters, based primarily on measurements at the Universities of Paris, Newcastle, and Michigan and three studies by or for the U.S. government. Includes chapters on seating, individual spaces, offices, and elderly and physically disabled people.

Planners and Planning; A Report from the Community College Planning Center on Community College Facilities. [N.Y., 1966]. 64p., illus.
A good general guide to more demanding ways of planning and building facilities.

Planning the University Library Building, ed. by John E. Burchard, Charles W. David, and Julian P. Boyd. Princeton, N.J.: Princeton University Press, 1949; reprinted, Chicago: ALA, 1953. 145p.
A useful work for anyone seriously interested in planning a university library building; it covers most of the problems which are likely to arise in preparing the program and discusses the advantages and disadvantages of the various attacks which have been made on these problems; largely based on discussions of the Cooperative Committee on Library Building Plans from 1944 to 1949.

Ranganathan, S. R. "University Library Building." *Annals of Library Science* 5: 22–32 (March 1958).
A concise summary from an Indian point of view of the basic principles of good library design; prescribes standards for area per reader, volumes per square meter in stack rooms, and specifications for furniture and fittings.

Reader on the Library Building, ed. by Hal B. Schell. Englewood, Colo.: Microcard Editions Books, 1975. 359p., illus.
Useful reprints of 42 classic articles published from 1933 to 1970 covering various aspects of planning, including staff spaces, lighting, furnishings, and equipment. Most illustrations in the original articles were not reprinted here.

Rogers, Rutherford D., and David C. Weber. "Building Planning." In *University Library Administration,* pp. 325–57. New York: Wilson, 1971.
A concise treatment of the subject, with a useful chart of "preferred area relationships." Appendix XIII presents detailed indexed floor plans for the Washington University Library and the Olin Library of Cornell University.

Running Out of Space—What Are the Alternatives? ed. by Gloria Novak. Chicago: ALA, 1978. 160p.
Fifteen papers presented at the 1975 ALA preconference of the Buildings for Colleges and University Libraries Committee. Covers book storage, microforms, renovation of existing space, and funding.

Thompson, Anthony. *Library Buildings of Britain and Europe.* London: Butterworth, 1963. 326p., illus., bibl.
A useful reference work; Part I summarizes the problems of creating a library building; part II traces in outline the history of library buildings and gives detailed analyses of a large number of buildings erected since 1930. Examples are mostly from Britain, with some from Europe and elsewhere; includes photographs and plans on uniform scales; numerous bibliographical references at the ends of chapters and accompanying descriptions of particular buildings.

Thompson, Godfrey. "Libraries." In *VNR Metric Handbook of Architectural Standards,* comp. by Patricia Tutt and David Adler, pp. 293–99. New York: Van Nostrand Reinhold, 1979. 504p., illus., index.
First published in 1969 at the time of the British change to the metric system.

Thompson, Godfrey. *Planning and Design of Library Buildings.* 2d ed. London: Architectural Press; New York: Nichols, 1977. 189p., charts, drawings, photographs, index, extensive bibl.
A basic authoritative comprehensive text on planning libraries of all types. It is particularly useful on space standards, equipment and furnishings, and the planning process and schedule of decisions.

Toffler, Alvin. "Libraries." In *Bricks and Mortarboards: A Report on College Planning and Building,* pp. 69–98. New York: Educational Facilities Laboratories, [1964].
A stimulating and forward-looking view of academic libraries.

University Grants Committee. *Capital Provision for University Libraries; Report of a Working Party.* London: HMSO, 1976. 42p.
Professor Richard Atkinson and committee here recommend the principle of a "self-renewing library of limited growth." Page 26 presents UGC norms for library accommodation; page 16 recommends the new basis for determining appropriate size.

University Library Buildings, ed. by David C. Weber. v.18, no. 2 (Oct. 1969) of *Library Trends.* References, 11 plans, index.
Eleven papers on design and specialized planning issues.

University Planning and Design: A Symposium. ed. by Michael Brawne. Architectural Association Paper no. 3. London: Lund Humphries, 1967. 126p.

Papers from a seminar held in 1964 to discuss architectural and academic concepts of the physical environment of a dozen "new universities" in England. Includes four papers on general aspects of British university planning, covering the period since October 1963 when the report on "Higher Education" under the chairmanship of Lord Robbins was published. Tables, illustrations of campus plans, and a useful bibliography. No index.

Wheeler, Joseph L., and Alfred Morton Githens. *The American Public Library Building.* New York: Scribner's, 1941. 484p.

A comprehensive treatise in six parts and 42 chapters; profusely illustrated with photographs, drawings, plans, tables, and charts. While it deals primarily with public libraries, much of the material is also pertinent to academic libraries. It is still one of the most useful books on the subject, but it should be supplemented by more recent material.

Wild, Friedemann. *Libraries for Schools and Universities.* New York: Van Nostrand Reinhold, 1972. 136p., plans.

Every page has plans, usually with bookstack and furnishings included. Covers 17 university, 3 college, 9 special subject, 6 city, and 3 state or national libraries; of these, 17 are in Germany and 10 in the United States.

d. State Planning Guides

State manuals and planning studies exist in most states to deal with facility planning in state-supported institutions. A few examples are cited which have been prepared by or for state agencies:

Arkansas: "Space Inventory and Utilization Manual for the Comprehensive Facilities Planning Study," 1967.

California: "Higher Education Facilities Planning Guide," 1970. Sections II.4, III.3, and Appendix B.

California: "The University of California Libraries—A Plan for Development," 1977.

Colorado: "Guideline Procedures and Criteria for Campus Development and Capital Outlay Planning," 1974–82.

Illinois: "Accessibility Standards Illustrated [from] the Capital Development Board," 1978.

Michigan: "Provisional Procedures for Reporting, Evaluating, and Projecting the Physical Facilities Requirements of the Community Colleges in Michigan," 1970.

New York: "Guidelines for Assessing the Adequacy of Academic Libraries," 1976.

New York: "Space Projection Criteria for Capital and Long Range Facilities Planning Purposes," 1970.

Oregon: "Planning and Procedures Handbook for Campus and Building Development," Chapter 8.12: Space Standards—Library, 1980.

Tennessee: "Procedures for Projecting Physical Space Requirements for Tennessee Higher Education," 1969.

Texas: "Facilities Inventory Manual," 1971.

Wisconsin: "Procedures for Physical Facilities and Utilization Studies," 1967.

2. Special Subject Libraries

a. General Works

Anthony, L. J. "Library Planning," in *Handbook of Special Librarianship and Information Work.* Chapter 8, pp. 309–64. 3d ed. London: ASLIB, 1967.

An excellent treatment of planning for special libraries, university branch libraries, and very small libraries.

Planning the Special Library, ed. by Ellis Mount. SLA Monograph, no. 4. New York: Special Libraries Assn., 1972. 122p.

Brief treatment of many aspects of planning and equipping the special library. Includes a 21-page "Checklist with Guidelines for Library Planning" by J. S. Rockwell and J. E. Flegal. See also "Planning Facilities for Sci-Tech Libraries," ed. by Ellis Mount, v.3, no.4 (Summer 1983) of *Science & Technology Libraries.*

Special Libraries: How to Plan and Equip Them, ed. by Chester M. Lewis. SLA Monograph, no. 2. New York: Special Libraries Assn. 1963. 117p., illus.

A collection of 14 papers on planning and equipping special libraries, and descriptions of ten recently completed installations with floor plans and illustrations. An extensive annotated bibliography and a directory of manufacturers and suppliers are appended.

Walsh, Robert R. "Branch Library Planning in Universities." *Library Trends,* 18: 210–22 (October 1969).

Good coverage of the types of problems faced in universities.

b. Specific Subjects and Types of Materials

A great many individual special libraries have been described, especially in the *Library Journal* and *Special Libraries.* The following are some of the most useful or extensive.

Art:

Humphry, James, III. "The New Thomas J. Watson Library at the Metropolitan Museum of Art," *Special Libraries,* 56:393–99 (July–August 1965).

Audio:

Hancock, Alan. *Planning for Educational Mass Media.* London and New York: Longman, 1977, 383p.

Chapters 12 and 17 provide illustrated production and servicing of television, radio, and audiovisual materials, including details for seating arrangements.

Harrison, Helen P. *Film Library Techniques: Principles of Administration.* New York: Hastings House, 1973. 277p., bibl., index.
Chapters 6 and 11 treat storage layout planning, and space needs and relationships.

Irvine, Betty Jo. *Slide Libraries: A Guide for Academic Institutions, Museums, and Special Collections.* 2d ed., Littleton, Colo.: Libraries Unlimited, 1979. 321p., illus., bibl., index.
Chapters 6 and 7 provide treatment on storage systems, environmental controls, and planning layouts of physical facilities.

Rensselaer Polytechnic Institute. Center for Architectural Research. *Educational Facilities with New Media.* Washington, D.C., National Education Assn., 1966. [232p.], illus.
Includes policy guidance, principles and criteria for facility design, and a technical guide including treatment of lighting, acoustics, climate, furniture, and equipment.

Law:

Mersky, Roy M. "A Decade of Academic Law Library Construction." *Library Journal,* 104:2519–24 (December 1, 1979).

Schwartz, Mortimer. "Building Planning for a New Library." *Law Library Journal* 81:73–87 (May 1968).
Emphasizing law libraries, this general article covers shelving, measures to minimize book theft, heating, air conditioning, lighting, listening facilities, floor covering, staff area, planning for automation, storage areas, reader areas, and other.

Maps:

Bahn, Catherine. "Map Libraries: Space and Equipment," in *Special Libraries Association Geography and Map Division Bulletin* 46:3–17 (December 1961). Reprinted in *Map Librarianship: Readings,* comp. by Roman Drazniowski, pp. 364–84. Metuchen, N.J., and London: Scarecrow Press, 1975.

Hill, J. Douglas. "Map and Atlas Cases." *Library Trends* 13:481–87 (April 1965).
Practical advice on dimensions and alternative methods of storage.

LeGear, C. E. *Maps: Their Care, Repair and Preservation in Libraries.* Rev. ed. Washington, D.C.: Library of Congress, 1956, 75p.
Includes discussion of map storage equipment, drawer dimensions, capacities, and room layouts.

Medicine:

Fry, Alderson. "Library Planning, Furniture, and Equipment." In *Handbook of Medical Library Practice,* 3d ed., ed. by Gertrude L. Annan and Jacqueline W. Felter, pp.284–330. Chicago: Medical Library Assn., 1970.
Thorough article covering the whole range of library planning from beginning the plan and writing specifications to moving, expanding, and remodeling.

Hitt, Samuel. "Space Planning for Health Science Libraries." In *Handbook of Medical Library Practice,* 4th ed., v.3, ch.10. Chicago: Medical Library Assn., publication expected in 1987.

Microtexts:

American National Standards Institute.
See current standards, e.g., "Practice for Storage of Processed Safety Photographic Film," ANSI PH1.43-19 (1983), and "Requirements for Photographic Filing Enclosures for Storing Processed Photographic Films, Plates, and Paper," ANSI PH1.53-19 (1982).

Boss, Richard W., with Deborah Raikes. *Developing Microform Reading Facilities.* Westport, Conn., Microform Review, 1982. 198p. illus., bibl., glossary, index.
Chapters 3 and 5 give specific detailed advice on aspects of space design, layouts, storage areas and equipment.

Weber, David C. "Design for a Microtext Reading Room." *Unesco Bulletin for Libraries* 20:303–8 (November–December 1966).
Covers questions of decentralization of collections and equipment, floor location in a large library, spatial relations and standards within the facility, lighting, HVAC, and acoustics.

Music:

Fling, Robert Michael. *Shelving Capacity in the Music Library.* MLA Technical Reports, no.7. Philadelphia: Music Library Assn., 1981. 36p., illus.

Freitag, Wolfgang. "On Planning a Music Library." *Fontes artis musicae* 11:35–49 (1961). Reprinted in *Reader in Music Librarianship,* by Carol June Bradley, pp. 283–94. Washington, D.C.: Microcard Editions Books, 1973.

Pickett, A. G., and M. M. Lemcoe. *Preservation and Storage of Sound Recordings.* Washington, D.C.: Library of Congress, 1959. 74p.
While most of this report deals with the chemical and mechanical properties of discs and tape, Chapters 2.B, "Handling and Storage," 2.G, "Predicting Shelf Life," and 3.E, "Summary of Conclusions and Recommendations for Storage of Phonograph Discs," are more directly concerned with architectural problems, selections of shelving, air conditioning, etc.

Wallace, Mary. "Time-Space and the Music Library." *Music Library Association Notes* 27:12–18 (1970).
An excellent treatment of the special concerns of shelving and other equipment needs to accommodate scores, records, and tapes.

Science and Technology:

Graham, Ronald A., A. E. Lee, and R. L. Meyer. "The Creation of a New Technical Information Center for a Diversified Chemical Corporation." *Journal of Chemical Documentation* 8:60–66 (May 1968).

Mount, Ellis. "Library Facilities and Equipment." In *University Science and Engineering Libraries; Their Operation, Collections and Facilities,* Chapter 9, pp. 108–20. Contributions in Librarianship and Information Science, 15. Westport, Conn.: Greenwood, 1975.

Palmer, R. Ronald, and William Maxwell Rice. *Modern Physics Buildings.* New York: Reinhold, 1961. 324p.

A comprehensive guide for college and university administrators, architects, and members of physics departments; the chapter on libraries contains a useful checklist and other information, but the book is cited here as an example of what has been done in another field.

Strauss, Lucille, Irene M. Streiby, and Alberta L. Brown. "Physical Layout and Equipment." In *Scientific and Technical Libraries: Their Organization and Administration,* Chapter 4, pp. 55–89. Library Science and Documentation, no.4. New York: Interscience, 1964.

Special Collections:

Archer, H. Richard. "Display and Exhibit Cases." *Library Trends,* 13:474–80 (April 1965).

Practical advice helpful in the design of display and exhibit cases.

Byrd, Cecil K. "Quarters for Special Collections and University Libraries." *Library Trends* 18:223–34 (Oct. 1969).

Undergraduate:

Kuhn, Warren B. "Undergraduate Libraries in a University." *Library Trends* 18:188–209 (October 1969).

3. Special Topics

a. Acoustics

National Research Council, Building Research Institute. *Noise Control in Buildings.* Washington, D.C.: National Research Council, 1959. 136p.

Analyzes the noise-control problems arising in all types of buildings because of the increased use of lighter weight construction for exterior walls, interior partitions, and floors; noise problems created by mechanical equipment are also discussed; recommendations for noise control and a complete model specification for the control of noise from mechanical equipment provide practical guidance for the building designer.

Noise and Vibration Control, ed. by Leo L. Beranek. New York: McGraw-Hill, 1971. 650p.

Includes technical chapters on sound in small spaces and large rooms, isolation of vibrations, and criteria for noise and vibration in buildings.

Parkin, Peter H., H. R. Humphreys, and J. R. Cowell. *Acoustics, Noise and Buildings.* 4th ed. London: Faber & Faber, 1979. 297p., index.

A more technical book and especially helpful for audio facilities is *Acoustic Design and Noise Control,* by Michael Rettinger (New York: Chemical Publishing Co., 1973).

b. Architects

American Institute of Architects: Besides the three works cited below, the AIA publishes *Architectural Graphic Standards* (now in 7th ed.), *Current Techniques in Architectural Practice, Energy Planning for Buildings,* as well as pamphlets and flyers on specific topics such as adaptive reuse of old buildings, contractor's qualifications, instructions to bidders, owner-architect agreement, public art in architecture, and use of solar energy.

Architect's Handbook of Professional Practice. 3 vols. Washington, D.C.: AIA, 1983. Loose-leaf.

Contains 20 chapters in individual brochure form, plus 38 AIA Documents in a binder. Chapter I is a circular of information on the *AIA Handbook* and a catalog of publications and documents; other chapters deal with selection of an architect, owner-architect agreements, consultants, contracts, etc. The institutes of some other countries publish similar material.

"Building Together." *Library Association Record* 65:440–52 (December 1963).

Two papers, one by an architect (D. W. Dickenson) and the other by a librarian (E. M. Broome), discussing the teamwork that is necessary for a successful library building.

Compensation Guidelines for Architectural and Engineering Services: A Management Guide to Cost-Based Compensation. 2d ed., rev. Washington, D.C.: AIA, 1980. 37p. plus a complete sample set of AIA forms recommended for use with the Guidelines.

Handbook of Architectural Design Competitions. 2d ed. Washington, D.C.: AIA, 1982.

Detailed information regarding the running of a design competition.

Lewis, Myron, and Mark Nelson. "How to Work with an Architect." *Wilson Library Bulletin* 57:44–46 (September 1982).

Good treatment, and especially useful with respect to branch libraries.

McAdams, Nancy R. "Selecting an Architect for the Library." *Texas Library Journal,* 41, no.2:38–43 (Summer 1965).

This is useful to all librarians for the information it gives about the architectural profession, selection of an architectural firm including determining factors and the selection procedure, the architect's professional services, and payment for architectural services.

"Standard Regulations for International Competitions in Architecture and Town Planning," *RIBA Kalendar,* pp. 30–31. London, 1962–63.

These regulations were the subject of a recommendation to the member states adopted during the ninth session of the General Conference of UNESCO, New Delhi, 1956.

c. Automation and Electronic Developments

Educational Facilities Laboratory. *The Impact of Technology on the Library Building.* New York: Educational Facilities Laboratory, 1967. 20p.

Describes how computers, microforms, and new communications technology are being used in libraries and the effect of these developments on layout, space allocations, HVAC, electric capacity, lighting, seating, card catalogs, and shelving.

IBM Corporation. *A Building Planning Guide for Communication Wiring.* Research Triangle Park, N.C.: IBM Corp., 1982. 88p., illus., glossary, index.

A manual to help plan space for data and voice communication wiring systems in a new or existing building. Covers wiring from work areas to wiring closets and from closet to closet; also types of raceways for cable distribution, riser systems, grounding and lightning protection, and security for cable and equipment. Does not address specific product of any company nor does it treat computer room wiring and power.

Rohlf, Robert H. "Building-Planning Implications of Automation," in *Library Automation; A State of the Art Review*, pp. 33–36. Chicago: ALA, 1969.

Covers the concept of changes in library services, some specific physical requirements for fully automated systems, and cost implications.

Rupp, Bruce. *Human Factors of Workstations with Visual Displays.* 3d ed. San Jose, Calif.: International Business Machines Corp., 1984. 64p., graphs, bibl.

Latter sections briefly treat the configuration of workstations, including seated work position, work surfaces, and display location, as well as environmental considerations of lighting and acoustic noise.

d. Bookstacks:

Boll, John J. *To Grow or Not to Grow? A Review of Alternatives to New Academic Library Buildings.* LJ Special Report, no.15. New York: Bowker, 1980. 32p., illus., references, index.

Includes considerable review of various book storage alternatives.

Ellsworth, Ralph E. *The Economics of Book Storage in College and University Libraries.* Metuchen, N.J.: Association of Research Libraries and Scarecrow Press, 1969. 135p., illus., bibl.

Provides description of various systems, comparison of space economics, and details of calculating comparative cost.

Harrar, Helen Joanne. "Cooperative Storage Warehouses." *College and Research Libraries* 25:37–43 (January 1964).

Analysis of the economics of three types of cooperative facilities.

Muller, Robert H.: "Evaluation of Compact Book Storage Systems," in *The Third Library Building Plans Institute . . . Proceedings*, ACRL Monographs, no. 11, pp. 77–93. Chicago: ACRL, 1954.

An analysis of various systems including Remington Rand, Ames, Hamilton, and Art Metal; contains illustrations, plans, and tables; an abridged version of this study was published in *College and Research Libraries* 15:300–8 (July 1954). with the title "Compact Storage Equipment; Where to Use It and Where Not."

Poole, Frazer, G. "Selection and Evaluation of Library Bookstacks." *Library Trends* 13:411–32 (April 1965).

Extensive comparison of steel case and bracket shelving with description of performance tests for structure and for finishes.

Rider, Fremont. *Compact Book Storage.* New York: Hadham Press, 1949. 90p.

Discusses the need for, and various methods of, storing books compactly, including conventional shelves.

Schunk, Russell J. "Stack Problems and Care." *Library Trends*, 4:283–90 (January 1956).

Summarizes the main requirements of a stack system and describes typical equipment; discusses stack administration, types of stacks, control of access in closed and open stacks, control of atmospheric conditions, cleaning, efficient service, lighting.

Snead and Co. *Library Planning, Bookstacks and Shelving.* Jersey City, N.J.: Snead and Co., 1915. 271p.

Contains much material of historical value as well as numerous plans and photographs of major libraries in the United States.

Van Buren, Martin. "What to Look for When Buying Shelving." *Library Journal* 90:1614–17 (April 1, 1965).

e. Climate

Aronin, Jeffrey Ellis. *Climate and Architecture.* New York: Reinhold, 1953. 304p., illus., bibl., index.

Extensive treatment of design conditions affected by sun, temperature, wind, precipitation, lightning, and humidity.

Banks, Paul. "Environmental Standards for Books and Manuscripts." *Library Journal*, 99:339–43 (February 1, 1974).

Recommends book storage area temperature be set at 60 degrees F., plus or minus 5 degrees, and gives recommendations on humidity, air cleanliness, ventilation, light. Provides extensive comments on exhibition quarters; shelving and book supports; book trucks; storage of microfilm; and systems for protection, detection, and continual monitoring of the design conditions.

Canadian Conservation Institute, National Museums of Canada. *Technical Bulletins.* Ottawa, 1975–80.

To date, four useful studies have been issued.

No. 1: "Relative Humidity: Its Importance, Measurement and Control in Museums," 1975.

No. 3: "Recommended Environmental Monitors for Museums, Archives and Art Galleries," 1978.

No. 5: "Environmental Norms for Canadian Museums, Art Galleries and Archives," 1979.

No. 7: "Fluorescent Lamps," 1980.

These have been reprinted in the Association of Research Libraries *Preservation Planning Program Resource Notebook*, comp. by Pamela W. Darling. Washington, D.C.: ARL, 1982.

Fry, Maxwell, and Jane Drew. *Tropical Architecture in the Dry and Humid Zones.* New York: Reinhold, 1964. 264p., illus., index.

Practical guidance with extensive appendices on such aspects as sun path data; water supply; building materials; thermal movements in buildings; special glass; building costs; plant material; and protection against earthquakes, fungus, hurricanes, lightning, and termites.

Plumbe, Wilfred J. *The Preservation of Books in Tropical and Subtropical Countries*. Kuala Lumpur: Oxford University Press, 1964. 72p., illus., bibl.
Contains practical advice on anti-termite measures, dust storms, and wood preservation.

f. Construction

Building Maintenance and Preservation: A Guide for Design and Management, ed. by Edward D. Mills. London: Butterworths, 1980. 203p., illus., index.
Contains chapters on design, materials, structure, economics, safety, security and management of interiors and exteriors.

The McGraw-Hill Construction Business Handbook: A Practical Guide to Accounting, Credit, Finance, Insurance, and Law for the Construction Industry, ed. by Robert F. Cushman. New York: McGraw-Hill, 1978. Various paging, index.
Includes treatment of contracts, OSHA compliance, bid errors, changes and extras, time extensions, compensation for delay, liability, bonds, and handling of disputes.

g. Consultants

Ellsworth, Ralph E. "Consultants for College and University Library Building Planning." *College and Research Libraries*, 21:263–68 (July 1960).
Describes the duties of the consultant, the most important of which is to help the institution prepare a written program; he then tells in detail how to proceed with the program. A model outline of a successful program written by Ellsworth Mason for Colorado College is reprinted here.

Haas, Warren J. "Role of the Building Consultant." *College and Research Libraries* 30:365–68 (July 1969).
Comments on the consultant's specific roles during five stages of building development: the initial program, program development, early design, final design, and working drawings and specifications.

h. Contracts:

Marke, Julius J.: "Construction and Maintenance." *Library Trends* 6:459–68 (April 1958).
Shows how the laws of contract apply to the relationship between librarian, "owner," and architect; detailed discussion of the owner-architect contract, the difference between a private institution negotiating with a contractor and a government agency entering into such a relationship; fees and legal forms are mentioned and illustrated by actual case references; fully documented in 36 footnotes.

i. Fire Protection

Morris, John: *The Library Disaster Preparedness Handbook*. Chicago: ALA, 1986. 128p., illus., bibl.

A practical guide to protection from natural and human enemies of buildings and collections as well as of staff and patrons.

Morris, John: *Managing the Library Fire Risk*. 2nd ed. Berkeley, Univ. of California, 1975. 147p., illus., bibl.
A practical guide prepared as a project of the Office of Risk and Management and Safety, University of California.

Protecting the Library and Its Resources: A Guide to Physical Protection and Insurance. Report on a study conducted by Gage-Babcock & Associates, Inc. Library Technology Project Publications, no. 7. Chicago: ALA, 1963. 322p.
The first section of the book, dealing primarily with fire and to a lesser degree with other types of physical losses and their prevention, is required reading for library planners. Fire-defense measures and equipment—including the pros and cons of sprinkler systems—in existing buildings and in relation to the planning of new buildings are discussed in considerable detail.

j. Floor Coverings

Armstrong Technical Data, 1964–65. Lancaster, Pa.: Armstrong Cork Company, Floor Division, 1964. 56p.
Particularly useful for the comparative data on the physical characteristics and cost of various types of resilient floors.

Berkeley, Bernard. *Floors: Selection and Maintenance*. LTP Publications, no. 13. Chicago: ALA, 1969. 316p.
Five chapters detailing properties of the major categories of floors and floor coverings: resilient, carpeting, masonry, wood, and formed-in-place. Two chapters on selection criteria and maintenance practices and equipment.

Berkeley, Bernard, and Cyril S. Kimball. "The Selection and Maintenance of Commercial Carpet." *Cornell Hotel and Restaurant Administration Quarterly* 3:47–78 (February 1963).
Useful for anyone contemplating the use of carpeting in a library; contains illustrations, tables, references, and a glossary.

k. Furniture and Equipment

Library Technology Project. *Publications* 1–19. Chicago: ALA, 1961–75.
This series covers a variety of equipment assessments and guides, including bookstacks, circulation systems, photocopying, and record players. Two, which are devoted to fire protection (1963) and floors (1969), are of special relevance and are separately listed here.

Salmon, Eugene N. "Resources in Library Technology." *Library Journal* 89:1495–502 (April 1, 1964).
An essay on the sources of information available to assist in the solution of technical problems; includes a list of associations and organizations and a selected bibliography.

Van Buren, Martin. "Design of Library Furniture." *Library Trends* 13:388–95 (April 1965).

Provides principles of library furniture design and records University of Arkansas 1959 data on preferred dimensions for chairs used for reading and writing. Other helpful articles in this issue treat construction and selection of furniture in specific library areas; see especially those by Stephen D. Pryce and Donald D. Powell.

Van Buren, Martin. "A Guide to the Preparation of Furniture Specifications and Bidding Documents." *Library Journal* 91:5845–50 (December 1, 1966).
Advice on advertising for bids, general conditions to bidders, construction specifications, the schedule of equipment, tabulation and evaluation of bids, and other aspects.

l. Signs

Ballinger, Louise Bowen, and R. A. Ballinger. *Sign, Symbol and Form,* New York: Van Nostrand Reinhold, 1972. 191p., illus.
Examples of a great variety of signs in Europe and North America.

Crosby, Fletcher Forbes. *A Sign Systems Manual.* New York: Praeger, 1970. 76p., illus.
Examples of interior and exterior graphics with a great deal of practical design information.

Mallery, Mary S., and Ralph E. DeVore. *A Sign System for Libraries.* Chicago: ALA, 1982. 33p., illus.
Details of signs in the Western Maryland Public Libraries.

Sign Systems for Libraries; Solving the Wayfinding Problem, comp. and ed. by Dorothy Pollet and Peter C. Haskell. New York: Bowker, 1979. 271p., illus., index.
Chapters cover the theory of signage, architectural techniques for wayfinding, sign language and materials and methods, coordinating graphics and architecture, and particular solutions for special and university and research libraries. Appended are "Technical and Psychological Considerations for Sign Systems in Libraries" and an extensive annotated bibliography on visual guidance systems.

Spencer, Herbert, and Linda Reynolds. *Directional Signing and Labelling in Libraries and Museums: A Review of Current Theory and Practice.* London: Royal College of Art, 1977. 117p., illus.
Covers theoretical and practical guidelines for directional signing, notices, and instructions in public spaces. Based on examining signs in 27 libraries and 18 museums, interviews with designers of such systems and psychologists, and a literature survey.

m. Handicapped Readers

Dalton, Phyllis I. *Library Service to the Deaf and Hearing Impaired.* Phoenix: Onyx Press, 1985. 371p.
Chapter 16 on "environmental setting for the service" briefly treats acoustics, elevators, lighting, meeting rooms, office design, safety, signs, work quarters, and the cost and implementation of accommodations.

Goldsmith, Selwyn. *Designing for the Disabled.* 2d ed. London: Royal Institute of British Architects, 1967. 207p., illus., index.
Detailed recommendations, generally in both metric and customary scales, for building elements and finishes and specific parts of public buildings.

Jones, Michael A. *Accessibility Standards Illustrated.* Springfield, Ill.: Capital Development Board, 1978. 217p., illus., index.
A superior guide to interior and exterior provisions which are suitable for those with auditory, visual or ambulatory handicaps.

Milner, Margaret. *Adapting Historic Campus Structures for Accessibility.* Washington, D.C.: GPO, for the Association of Physical Plant Administrators of Universities and Colleges, 1981. 90p., illus., bibl., index.
Recommendations and six design studies for overcoming architectural barriers to handicapped persons in older buildings. Supplements *Creating an Accessible Campus* published by APPA in 1978.

n. Heating, Ventilating, and Air-Conditioning

Butti, Ken, and John Perlin. *A Golden Thread: 2500 Years of Solar Architecture and Technology.* New York: Van Nostrand Reinhold, 1980. 289p. illus., index.
A history with a minimum of engineering data.

Grad, I., and A. Greenberg. "Air Conditioning for Books and People." *Architectural Record,* 121:231–34 (June 1957).
A good summary article with useful explanation of desirable background sound.

Griffin, Charles W. *Energy Conservation in Buildings: Techniques for Economical Design.* Washington, D.C.: Construction Specifications Institute, 1974. 183p.
A good comprehensive guide to techniques.

Kut, David, and Gerard Hare. *Applied Solar Energy; A Guide to the Design, Installation and Maintenance of Heating and Hot Water Services.* London: Architectural Press, 1979. 149p.
Excellent concise treatment of a rapidly changing field.

Stein, Richard G. *Architecture and Energy.* New York: Anchor Press, 1977. 322p., illus., index.
An excellent introduction to design for the economy of energy use.

Total Energy. New York: Educational Facilities Laboratories, 1967. Technical Report, no.2. 53p. illus.
Describes on-site power generation providing heat in winter and cooling in summer as well as continuous light and power. Deals with both initial and long-range operating costs of mechanical and electrical systems.

o. Interior Design

Cohen, Elaine, and Aaron Cohen. *Automation, Space Management, and Productivity; A Guide for Libraries.* New York: Bowker, 1981. 221p., illus., bibl., index.
Information on office and public staff furniture and space arrangements to accommodate machine

use. Also useful chapters on acoustics and energy consumption.

"Color and the Use of Color by the Illuminating Engineer." *Illuminating Engineering* 57:764–76 (December 1962).
Illustrated guide to color selection covering hue, value, chroma, color selection, color schemes, dominant colors, color character, and other topics.

Draper, James, and James Brooks. *Interior Design for Libraries*. Chicago: ALA, 1979. 152p., glossary, index.
A step-by-step guide to the fundamentals of redesigning and decorating.

Faulkner, Waldron. *Architecture and Color*. New York: Wiley, 1972. 146p., illus., glossary.
A fundamental treatment of color and color of or on materials as used in buildings.

Friedmann, Arnold, John F. Pile, and Forrest Wilson. *Interior Design; An Introduction to Architectural Interiors*. New York: American Elsevier, 1970. 303p., illus.
A basic text which covers a wide range from "the nature of good design" to "an introduction to interior construction." Also includes a chapter on professional practice of designers, both small and large offices, as well as practice which is independent or part of architectural offices.

Fussler, Herman H. *Photographic Reproduction for Libraries; A Study of Administrative Problems*. Chicago: University of Chicago Press, 1942.
The arrangement and construction of a laboratory is detailed and illustrated, pp.107–27.

Mason, Ellsworth. "A Well-Wrought Interior Design." *Library Journal* 92:743–47 (February 15, 1967).
A variety of practical advice on the interior design process as well as specifics on chairs and tables.

Nikas, Mary: "Function First in Library Design." *Contract: The Business Magazine of Commercial Furnishing and Interior Architecture* 9:74–83 (November 1968).
How to achieve good design in the library, features to avoid, planning for automation and expansion, traffic flow, furnishings, and use of art work.

Pierce, William S. *Furnishing the Library Interior*. Books in Library and Information Science, no.29. New York: Dekker, 1980. 288p., illus., index.
Good coverage of furnishings in particular library areas, the selection and evaluation of furniture and equipment, and business pointers. Sample specifications are included, pp. 253–74.

p. Lighting

Berens, Conrad, and C. L. Crouch. "Is Fluorescent Lighting Injurious to the Eyes?" *American Journal of Ophthalmology*, 45:47–54 (April 1958).
The thesis of the article is that when fluorescent tubes are installed and maintained with proper shielding so that they are not glaring, they have no harmful effects on the eyes or skin of healthy individuals. Contains a good bibliography.

Blackwell, H. R. "Development and Use of a Quantitative Method for Specification of Interior Illumination Levels on the Basis of Performance Data." *Illuminating Engineering* 54:317–53 (June 1959).
The IES recommendations for lighting levels in libraries are based on the author's studies, which show that 30 footcandles are needed for printed materials and 70 footcandles for reading involving the taking of penciled notes. Should be supplemented by his series "Vision Engineering" in *Lighting*, 1963–64. (See below.)

Blackwell, H. R. "Vision Engineering." *Lighting* 79–83 (July 1963–March 1967).
An important monthly series of 45 articles in which the author, one of the leading authorities on the subject, develops methods for evaluating all aspects of lighting quality and quantity, and their effects upon the ease of seeing, visual comfort, and aesthetic pleasantness, in terms too technical for the layman. A summary appeared in vol. 83, no. 3 (March 1967).

Carmichael, Leonard, and Walter F. Dearborn. *Reading and Visual Fatigue*. Boston, Houghton Mifflin, 1947. 443p.
The most comprehensive study of the subject currently available; includes a bibliography of more than 400 items.

Great Britain, Department of the Environment. Welsh Office. *Sunlight and Daylight; Planning Criteria and Design of Buildings*. London: HMSO, 1971. 49p., illus., index.
Sets out criteria and methods for designing in order to let in daylight when buildings are close together.

Hopkinson, R. G. *Lighting: Architectural Physics*. London: Department of Scientific and Industrial Research, Building Research Station, 1963. 360p.
A textbook for architectural students based on principles which give first consideration to the needs of the individual in the context of environment; an outstanding work for architects and librarians seriously interested in the problems of lighting; contains an extensive bibliography.

Lam, William M. C. *Perception and Lighting as Form-givers for Architecture*. New York: McGraw-Hill, 1977. 310p., illus., bibl., glossary, index.
Clear and comprehensive treatment of visual perception, lighting, ceiling systems, and other aspects of designing the luminous environment. Pages 97–99 provide 22 rules of thumb for good design.

Larson, Leslie. *Lighting and Its Design*. New York: Whitney Library of Design, 1964. 228p.
A designer with an architectural background analyzes and questions the illuminating engineering approach to lighting, and prefers the points of view of aesthetics and design, the ophthalmologist, the psychologist, and the psychiatrist. The sections on lighting and vision; recommended levels of illumination; on fluorescent, incandescent, and mercury vapors compared; and on luminous surfaces, pp. 15-35, are of special interest to li-

brarians, and challenge high-intensity recommendations.

Metcalf, Keyes D. *Library Lighting.* Washington, D.C.: Assn. of Research Libraries, 1970. 99p. Short bibliography.

This extensive treatment details lighting problems, provides advice from distinguished professionals (architects, illuminating engineers, interior designers, ophthalmologists, university financial and physical plant officers, and scholars), and makes specific recommendations.

Phillips, Derek. *Lighting in Architectural Design.* New York: McGraw-Hill, 1964. 310p.

Bridges the gap between architects and illuminating engineers.

q. Moving

Kurkul, Donna Lee. "The Planning, Implementation, and Movement of an Academic Library Collection." *College and Research Libraries* 44:220–34 (July 1983).

Gives methodology, including planning formulas, for the series of book moves from 1975 to 1982 which were necessitated by the additions to and renovation of the Smith College Neilson Library.

Kurth, William H., and W. Ray Grim. *Moving a Library.* New York: Scarecrow, 1966. 220p.

Details of moving large or small libraries, including administrative aspects, the actual moving operation, the chronology of events of the master move plan, and excerpts from moving contracts of the National Library of Medicine and UCLA.

Spyers-Duran, Peter. *Moving Library Materials.* Milwaukee: Library Associates of University of Wisconsin-Milwaukee, 1964. 51p.

Deals in detail with moving problems in public and academic libraries; includes illustrations and bibliography.

r. Programs

Macdonald, Angus Snead. "Building Design for Library Management." *Library Trends* 2:463–69 (January 1954).

Outlines the program that should be established by library management to serve as a guide to the architect; such factors as planning of areas, equipment, and aesthetic features are discussed.

Park, Leland M. "The Whys and Hows of Writing a Building Program." *Library Scene* 5:2–5 (September 1976).

Practical concise statement on writing a college building program.

Reece, E.J. "Library Building Programs: How to Draft Them." *College and Research Libraries* 13:198–211 (July 1952).

Stresses the importance of a program and consultation and teamwork between architect and librarian; the program should be "the simplest possible statement of the problem, as definite as it can be in all matters dealing with the purpose, function and conditioning of the building, and as free as possible in all matters dealing with plan arrange-

ments and design." A good treatment of the subject.

s. Remodeling

Bryan, James E. "Remodeling of Library Buildings." *ALA Bulletin* 43:77–81 (February 1949).

How to make remodeling studies; the article, although written for public library situations, contains a "check list for remodeling" which can be used in any library.

Falkner, Ann. *Without Our Past? A Handbook for the Preservation of Canada's Architectural Heritage.* Toronto: Toronto University Press, 1977. 242p., illus., bibl.

Excellent report on how one country created preservation policy, inventories, evaluates and selects, re-uses, and enhances older structures.

Haynes, Robert E. *Historic Preservation Bibliography.* 2d rev. ed. Heritage Conservation and Recreation Service Publ. no. 8. Washington, D.C.: U.S. Department of the Interior, 1979. 28p.

Includes federal publications of standards and technical information about methods for preserving and maintaining historic properties.

t. Security

Bahr, Alice Harrison. *Book Theft and Library Security Systems, 1981–82.* White Plains, N.Y.: Knowledge Industry Publications, 1981. 156p., illus., bibl.

Electromechanical exit control arrangements are detailed.

Grealy, Joseph I. *School Crime and Violence: Problems and Solutions.* Fort Lauderdale, Fla.: Peters, 1979. 358p.

Chapter 4 provides useful discussion of safety and security of facilities and equipment. Pages 315–39 enumerate architectural and planning features for lessening the results of vandalism, a compilation made by Frank G. Irwin at the University of Tennessee.

Handbook of Building Security Planning and Design. ed. by Peter E. Hopf. New York: McGraw-Hill, 1979. 31 chapters individually paged.

Aimed at the design professions, this detailed illustrated guide provides good chapters on earthquake, hurricane, tornado, and flood protection, as well as on security components including camera surveillance, doors, electronic security, fire detection, glass, lighting, locks, safes and vaults, and sprinkler systems.

Irwin, F. Gordon. "Planning Vandalism Resistant Educational Facilities." *Journal of Research and Development in Education,* 11:42–52 (Winter 1978).

Provides an overview of 1959–76 literature on school vandalism, and summarizes the results of a study recommending 363 building features to protect against or to survive vandalism. It is based on contributions of 134 members of the National Association of School Security Directors.

Newman, Oscar. *Design Guidelines for Creating Defensible Space.* Prepared for the National Institute of Law Enforcement and Criminal Justice of the U.S. Department of Justice. Washington, D.C.: GPO, 1976. 213p.

Prepared for architects and planners, this handbook describes and illustrates architectural design concepts that foster a more proprietary attitude by individuals toward their buildings and neighborhoods.

Wise, James. "A Gentle Deterrent to Vandalism." *Psychology Today*, 16:31–38 (October 1981).

A good way of thinking about what causes damage to buildings and property.

Zeisel, John. *Stopping School Property Damage: Design and Administrative Guidelines to Reduce School Vandalism*. Rosslyn, Va.: American Assn. of School Administrators, 1976. 106p., illus. (ERIC no. ED136447).

This study from the Harvard University Graduate School of Design presents design responses to the problems of accidental damage, wear and tear, and illegal but nonmalicious property damage, both interior and exterior. Included are an extensive "accountability checklist" and an annotated bibliography.

u. Site Selection

Bacon, Edmund N. *Design of Cities*. New York: Viking, 1967. 296p.

A clear, delightful, and superbly illustrated explanation of design philosophies and decisions which in the past and today influence the urban environment. No index.

Lynch, Kevin. *Site Planning*. 2d ed. Cambridge: MIT Press, 1971. 384p., illus., index.

Thorough treatment of building placement—the art, its principles, and general comments on its technicalities. Little specifically on academic institutions, but an excellent presentation on the full range of issues which affect site planning.

Turner, Paul Venable. *Campus; An American Planning Tradition*. Cambridge and London: MIT Press, 1984. 337p., illus., plans, index.

An excellent history from Colonial times to the present, providing stylistic and conceptual treatment of college and university campus development.

v. Study Facilities

Community College Planning Center on Student Study Facilities. *A Study on Studying; A Report*. Stanford, Calif.: Stanford University School of Education School Planning Laboratory, 1965. 56p., illus.

Graphic presentation of 1964 study habit preferences of over 600 students in six community colleges.

Cook, James J. "Increased Seating in the Undergraduate Library: A Study in Effective Space Utilization," in *Case Studies in Systems Analysis in a University Library*, pp. 142–70, edited by Barton R. Buckhalter. New York: Scarecrow, 1968.

This University of Michigan library, opened in 1958, was changed in 1965 to reflect a study of student furniture preference. Shelving was reoriented. Tables present and plans show the arrangements before and after.

Deasy, C.M. *Design for Human Affairs*. New York: Wiley, 1974. 183p., illus., bibl.

A clear, concise statement of social and psychological factors which condition people's use of physical surroundings, and how behavioral scientists can contribute helpfully to building design.

Hall, Edward T. *The Hidden Dimension*. New York: Doubleday, 1966. 201p., illus.

An anthropologist treats the use of space—personal distance, social distance, and public distance—and highlights cultural differences in use of space.

The Neglected Majority: Facilities for Commuting Students. New York: Educational Facilities Laboratories, 1977. 76p.

A useful report on needs of those living off campus.

Sommer, Robert. *Personal Space: The Behavioral Basis of Design*. Englewood Cliffs, N.J., Prentice-Hall, 1969. 177p.

A classic sociological treatment of people's spatial behavior.

Spatial Representation and Behavior Across the Life Span: Theory and Application, ed. by Lynn S. Liben, Arthur H. Patterson, and Nora Newcombe. New York: Academic Press, 1981. 404p.

Psychologists treat how space is used by persons of different ages and sexes.

Student Reactions to Study Facilities, with Implications for Architects and College Administrators, a report to the Presidents of Amherst College, Mount Holyoke College, Smith College, and The University of Massachusetts, prepared under the auspices of The Committee for New College, by Stuart M. Stoke and others. Amherst, Mass.: 1960. 60p.

The Committee's study confirms what has been common knowledge among librarians—that students prefer intimate or individual study facilities and that the traditional vaulted reading room is obsolete.

Zeisel, John. *Sociology and Architectural Design*. Social Science Frontiers series. New York: Russell Sage Foundation, 1975. 57p., bibl.

A perspective for cooperation between architects and sociologists in improving design for human space.

Index of Figures and Tables

611

Index

Keyes D. Metcalf achieved international recognition during his six-decade career as a library administrator at the New York Public Library and the Harvard University Libraries, and as a consultant to more than 600 library building projects on six continents. The first edition of his landmark work was published in 1965. Metcalf died in 1983.

Philip D. Leighton is Building Projects Manager of the Stanford University Libraries, and was previously Facilities Project Manager at Stanford. He holds a master's degree in architecture.

David C. Weber is Director of the Stanford University Libraries and a past president of two ALA divisions, Association of College and Research Libraries and Resources and Technical Services Division. He is the co-author of *University Library Administration* (H. W. Wilson, 1970) and has published articles in numerous journals.